ORGANIZATIONAL BEHAVIOR
Improving Performance and Commitment in the Workplace

Fifth Edition

JASON A. COLQUITT
University of Georgia

JEFFERY A. LEPINE
Arizona State University

MICHAEL J. WESSON
Texas A&M University

McGraw Hill Education

ORGANIZATIONAL BEHAVIOR: IMPROVING PERFORMANCE AND COMMITMENT IN THE WORKPLACE, FIFTH EDITION

Published by McGraw-Hill Education, 2 Penn Plaza, New York, NY 10121. Copyright © 2017 by McGraw-Hill Education. All rights reserved. Printed in the United States of America. Previous editions © 2015, 2013, 2011, and 2009. No part of this publication may be reproduced or distributed in any form or by any means, or stored in a database or retrieval system, without the prior written consent of McGraw-Hill Education, including, but not limited to, in any network or other electronic storage or transmission, or broadcast for distance learning.

Some ancillaries, including electronic and print components, may not be available to customers outside the United States.

This book is printed on acid-free paper.

1 2 3 4 5 6 7 8 9 0 DOR/DOR 1 0 9 8 7 6

ISBN 978-1-259-54509-2
MHID 1-259-54509-1

Senior Vice President, Products & Markets: *Kurt L. Strand*
Vice President, General Manager, Products & Markets: *Michael Ryan*
Vice President, Content Design & Delivery: *Kimberly Meriwether David*
Managing Director: *Susan Gouijnstook*
Director: *Michael Ablassmeir*
Director, Product Development: *Meghan Campbell*
Lead Product Developer: *Kelly Delso*
Product Developer: *Kelly I. Pekelder*
Marketing Manager : *Elizabeth Trepkowski*

Director, Content Design & Delivery: *Terri Schiesl*
Program Manager: *Mary Conzachi*
Content Project Managers: *Christine A. Vaughan; Keri Johnson*
Buyer: *Jennifer Pickel*
Design: *Srdjan Savanovic*
Content Licensing Specialists: *Ann Marie Jannette; Shannon Manderscheid*
Cover Image: © *Paramount Pictures/Photofest*
Typeface: *10/12 STIX MathJax*
Compositor: *SPi Global*
Printer: *R. R. Donnelley*

All credits appearing on page or at the end of the book are considered to be an extension of the copyright page.

Library of Congress Cataloging-in-Publication Data

Names: Colquitt, Jason, author. | LePine, Jeffery A., author. | Wesson, Michael J.
Title: Organizational behavior : improving performance and commitment in the workplace / Jason A. Colquitt, University of Georgia, Jeffery A. LePine, Arizona State University, Michael J. Wesson, Texas A&M University.
Description: Fifth Edition. | New York : McGraw-Hill Education, [2016] | Revised edition of the authors' Organizational behavior, 2015. | Includes index.
Identifiers: LCCN 2015045777 | ISBN 9781259545092 (alk. paper)
Subjects: LCSH: Organizational behavior. | Personnel management. | Strategic planning. | Consumer satisfaction. | Job satisfaction.
Classification: LCC HD58.7 .C6255 2016 | DDC 658.3—dc23
LC record available at http://lccn.loc.gov/2015045777

The Internet addresses listed in the text were accurate at the time of publication. The inclusion of a website does not indicate an endorsement by the authors or McGraw-Hill Education, and McGraw-Hill Education does not guarantee the accuracy of the information presented at these sites.

Dedication

To Catherine, Cameron, Riley, and Connor, and also to Mom, Dad, Alan, and Shawn. The most wonderful family I could imagine, two times over.

-J.A.C.

To Marcie, Izzy, and Eli, who support me and fill my life with meaning and joy. And to my parents and siblings, Susan, Karen and David, who somehow put up with me in my youth.

-J.A.L.

To Liesl and Dylan: Their support in all I do is incomparable. They are my life and I love them both. To my parents: They provide a foundation that never wavers.

-M.J.W.

About the Authors

JASON A. COLQUITT

Jason A. Colquitt is the William H. Willson Distinguished Chair in the Department of Management at the University of Georgia's Terry College of Business. He received his PhD from Michigan State University's Eli Broad Graduate School of Management and earned his BS in psychology from Indiana University. He has taught organizational behavior and human resource management at the undergraduate, masters, and executive levels and has also taught research methods at the doctoral level. He has received awards for teaching excellence at the undergraduate, masters, and executive levels.

Jason's research interests include organizational justice, trust, team effectiveness, and personality influences on task and learning performance. He has published more than 30 articles on these and other topics in *Academy of Management Journal, Academy of Management Review, Journal of Applied Psychology, Organizational Behavior and Human Decision Processes,* and *Personnel Psychology.* He recently served as editor-in-chief for *Academy of Management Journal* and has served on a number of editorial boards, including *Academy of Management Journal, Journal of Applied Psychology, Organizational Behavior and Human Decision Processes, Personnel Psychology, Journal of Management,* and *International Journal of Conflict Management.* He is a recipient of the Society for Industrial and Organizational Psychology's Distinguished Early Career Contributions Award and the Cummings Scholar Award for early to mid-career achievement, sponsored by the Organizational Behavior division of the Academy of Management. He was also elected to be a representative-at-large for the Organizational Behavior division.

Jason enjoys spending time with his wife, Catherine, and three sons, Cameron, Riley, and Connor. His hobbies include playing basketball, playing the trumpet, watching movies, and rooting on (in no particular order) the Pacers, Colts, Cubs, Spartans, Gators, Hoosiers, and Bulldogs.

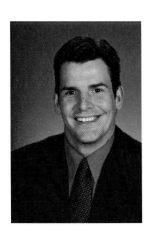

JEFFERY A. LEPINE

Jeffery A. LePine is the PetSmart Chair in Leadership in the Department of Management at Arizona State University's W.P. Carey School of Business. He received his PhD in organizational behavior from the Eli Broad Graduate School of Management at Michigan State University. He also earned an MS in management from Florida State University and a BS in finance from the University of Connecticut. He has taught organizational behavior, human resource management, and management of groups and teams at undergraduate and graduate levels. He has also delivered courses to doctoral students in research methods, meta-analysis, and scale development. He received the Outstanding Doctoral Professor Award from the W.P. Carey school of Business for his teaching and mentoring of doctoral students and his work as PhD program director.

Jeff's research interests include team functioning and effectiveness, individual and team adaptation, citizenship behavior, voice, employee engagement, and occupational stress. He has published more than 30 articles on these and other topics in *Academy of Management Journal, Academy of Management Review, Journal of Applied Psychology, Organizational Behavior and Human Decision Processes,* and *Personnel Psychology.* He has served as associate editor of *Academy of Management Review* and *Journal of Applied Psychology.*

He has also served on the editorial boards of *Academy of Management Journal, Academy of Management Review, Journal of Applied Psychology, Organizational Behavior and Human Decision Processes, Personnel Psychology, Journal of Management, Journal of Organizational Behavior,* and *Journal of Occupational and Organizational Psychology.* He is a recipient of the Society for Industrial and Organizational Psychology's Distinguished Early Career Contributions Award and the Cummings Scholar Award for early to mid-career achievement, sponsored by the Organizational Behavior division of the Academy of Management. He was also elected to the Executive Committee of the Human Resource Division of the Academy of Management. Prior to earning his PhD, Jeff was an officer in the U.S. Air Force.

Jeff spends most of his free time with his wife, Marcie, daughter, Izzy, and son, Eli. He enjoys being manager of Eli's soccer team, playing guitar, mountain biking in the desert, and working on his growing collection of classic Pontiac muscle cars.

MICHAEL J. WESSON

Michael J. Wesson is an associate professor in the Management Department at Texas A&M University's Mays Business School. He received his PhD from Michigan State University's Eli Broad Graduate School of Management. He also holds an MS in human resource management from Texas A&M University and a BBA from Baylor University. He has taught organizational behavior and human resource management–based classes at all levels but currently spends most of his time teaching Mays MBAs, EMBAs, and executive development at Texas A&M. He was awarded Texas A&M's Montague Center for Teaching Excellence Award.

Michael's research interests include organizational justice, leadership, organizational entry (employee recruitment, selection, and socialization), person–organization fit, and compensation and benefits. His articles have been published in journals such as *Journal of Applied Psychology, Personnel Psychology, Academy of Management Review,* and *Organizational Behavior and Human Decision Processes.* He currently serves on the editorial board of the *Journal of Applied Psychology* and is an ad hoc reviewer for many others. He is active in the Academy of Management and the Society for Industrial and Organizational Psychology. Prior to returning to school, Michael worked as a human resources manager for a *Fortune* 500 firm. He has served as a consultant to the automotive supplier, health care, oil and gas, and technology industries in areas dealing with recruiting, selection, onboarding, compensation, and turnover.

Michael spends most of his time trying to keep up with his wife, Liesl, and son, Dylan. He is a self-admitted food and wine snob, home theater aficionado, and college sports addict. (Gig 'em Aggies!)

Preface

Why did we decide to write this textbook? Well, for starters, organizational behavior (OB) remains a fascinating topic that everyone can relate to (because everyone either has worked or is going to work in the future). What makes people effective at their job? What makes them want to stay with their employer? What makes work enjoyable? Those are all fundamental questions that organizational behavior research can help answer. However, our desire to write this book also grew out of our own experiences (and frustrations) teaching OB courses using other textbooks. We found that students would end the semester with a common set of questions that we felt we could answer if given the chance to write our own book. With that in mind, *Organizational Behavior: Improving Performance and Commitment in the Workplace* was written to answer the following questions.

DOES ANY OF THIS STUFF REALLY MATTER?

Organizational behavior might be the most relevant class any student ever takes, but that doesn't always shine through in OB texts. The introductory section of our book contains two chapters not included in other books: *Job Performance* and *Organizational Commitment*. Being good at one's job and wanting to stay with one's employer are obviously critical concerns for employees and managers alike. After describing these topics in detail, every remaining chapter in the book links that chapter's content to performance and commitment. Students can then better appreciate the practical relevance of organizational behavior concepts.

IF THAT THEORY DOESN'T WORK, THEN WHY IS IT IN THE BOOK?

In putting together this book, we were guided by the question, "What would OB texts look like if all of them were first written now, rather than decades ago?" We found that many of the organizational behavior texts on the market include outdated (and indeed, scientifically disproven!) models or theories, presenting them sometimes as fact or possibly for the sake of completeness or historical context. Our students were always frustrated by the fact that they had to read about, learn, and potentially be tested on material that we knew to be wrong. Although historical context can be important at times, we believe that focusing on so-called evidence-based management is paramount in today's fast-paced classes. Thus, this textbook includes new and emerging topics that others leave out and excludes flawed and outdated topics that some other books leave in.

HOW DOES ALL THIS STUFF FIT TOGETHER?

Organizational behavior is a diverse and multidisciplinary field, and it's not always easy to see how all its topics fit together. Our book deals with this issue in two ways. First, all of the chapters in our book are organized around an integrative model that opens each chapter (see the back of the book). That model provides students with a road map of the course, showing them where they've been and where they're going. Second, our chapters are tightly focused around specific topics and aren't "grab bag–ish" in nature. Our hope is that students (and instructors) won't ever come across a topic and think, "Why is this topic being discussed in this chapter?"

DOES THIS STUFF HAVE TO BE SO DRY?

Research on motivation to learn shows that students learn more when they have an intrinsic interest in the topic, but many OB texts do little to stimulate that interest. Put simply, we wanted to create a book that students enjoy reading. To do that, we used a more informal, conversational style when writing the book. We also tried to use company examples that students will be familiar with and find compelling. Finally, we included insert boxes, self-assessments, and exercises that students should find engaging (and sometimes even entertaining!).

NEW AND IMPROVED COVERAGE

- *Chapter 1: What Is OB?*—This chapter now opens with a wraparound case on Google. The case describes how Google bases its human resource decisions on data rather than opinion, including decisions about hiring and organizational change initiatives. The case also describes Project Oxygen, an internal study conducted by Google to study whether "managers matter." The study showed how employees with better managers thrived more than employees with worse managers, and the project also revealed behaviors that better managers shared. The chapter also introduces a new key term—analytics—to capture the use of data in decision making.

- *Chapter 2: Job Performance*—This chapter features a new wraparound case on JPMorgan Chase, which overviews how employee effectiveness depends on a variety of different behaviors and, given costly legal and regulatory problems, how employee behaviors that contribute to the company in a negative way are now emphasized. The case describes steps JPMorgan Chase has taken to manage the costly negative aspects of employee job performance. Most notably, the company is using a computer algorithm to try to catch rule breakers before they actually break a rule. Our OB at the Bookstore feature has been changed to *A World Gone Social.* This bestselling book overviews implications of social media to managers and emphasizes how social media may encourage employees to engage in behaviors that contribute to the company in ways that are both positive and negative.

- *Chapter 3: Organizational Commitment*—Goldman Sachs serves as the wraparound case in this edition, spotlighting the things the company does to keep its employees loyal, even given their grueling workweeks. The case also describes how Goldman's role in the events leading up to the Great Recession might affect employee's commitment levels. Our OB on Screen feature has changed to *Chef,* a film that spotlights a talented chef who is no longer committed to the restaurant he works for. The OB at the Bookstore selection is now *Widgets,* a book that lays out "the new rules" for keeping employees committed in the contemporary workplace. The chapter also introduces a new key term—volunteering—in describing how a company's charitable efforts can breed loyalty.

- *Chapter 4: Job Satisfaction*—This chapter's wraparound case now highlights Twitter, the company that's changed much of how information is shared and absorbed. Twitter employees derive satisfaction from the impact of their product and the collaborative culture forged by top management. The case also focuses on Twitter's efforts to give back to the low-income neighborhood where their new headquarters resides, asking the degree to which satisfaction can depend on a company's outreach—not just its products. The OB at the Bookstore selection is now *Are You Fully Charged?,* which examines three drivers of mental sharpness and physical health. One of those is meaningfulness—the sense that one's job activities make a difference for others. The OB on Screen feature examines the distinction between job satisfaction and life satisfaction. *Her* depicts an employee who, by all accounts, is good at his job and enjoys it. Something is still missing, however, illustrating that happiness depends on more than just one's job.

- *Chapter 5: Stress*—The Internal Revenue Service (IRS) is now featured in the wraparound case for this chapter. The chapter opening provides a snapshot of the organization and what it's like to work there. In particular, the opening builds to convey the fact that jobs at this particular government agency are quite stressful. The case provides details regarding several factors that are causing stress among IRS employees and the challenges faced by managers to control the situation. The OB on Screen now features the movie *Gravity,* which provides insight into the stressful demands experienced in a life threatening situation. The bestselling book *Essentialism* is now our OB at the Bookstore feature. The authors of this book describe how doing less not only results in less stress, but also higher effectiveness. This attractive message is complemented by good advice for putting this strategy into practice. Finally, the chapter also includes reference to new research findings, including an updated list of the most and least stressful jobs.

- *Chapter 6: Motivation*—This chapter now opens with a wraparound case on Deloitte, the "Big Four" accounting and professional services firm. The case describes the changes made in Deloitte's performance evaluation process, which has significant effects on employee engagement. The OB on Screen feature focuses on psychological empowerment using *Big Hero 6,* where Hiro Hamata decides to pursue a path of purpose after being inspired by his older brother and a robotics professor. The OB at the Bookstore focuses on *Hundred Percenters,* a take on motivation that argues for HARD goals: goals that are Heartfelt, Animated, Required, and Difficult.

- *Chapter 7: Trust, Justice, and Ethics*—Uber serves as the wraparound case for the revised chapter. As the app-based taxi cab alternative has grown in scope and profile, it has grappled with a number of ethical controversies. Those include its pricing, its handling of location data, and its drivers attempting to actively hinder the performance of rival companies. *Whiplash* is the OB on Screen selection for the chapter, with the focus being on a professor who embodies abusive supervision by using profanity and derogatory remarks in an attempt to motivate the drummer in his prestigious jazz band. The OB at the Bookstore selection is now *The Road to Character,* which describes how the priorities of contemporary society have eaten away at certain virtues that fall under the integrity umbrella.

- *Chapter 8: Learning and Decision Making*—UPS serves as the wraparound case in this edition, highlighting the company's unique training facility and the "340 methods" drivers must learn to do their job effectively. The case describes how UPS is now trying to automate the process by which UPS drivers deliver packages and the decision-making quandary that creates for their employees. The OB on Screen feature now focuses on *Interstellar,* highlighting how difficult it is to make a rational decision in the midst of a very emotional situation. The chapter also includes a number of research updates as well as several new company examples.

- *Chapter 9: Personality and Cultural Values*—This chapter's wraparound case is now Chipotle. The case describes the 13 traits that the fast-growing burrito chain prioritizes when hiring employees and promoting managers. Chipotle prioritizes those traits over experience, given that time spent with other fast-food companies is as likely to be a hindrance as a help. *Boyhood* represents the OB on Screen selection, with the film following Mason Evans Jr. from his childhood to his first day in college. The film allows you to see how Mason's personality develops over the course of his life, providing a forum for discussing the nature and nurture issues that shape personality.

- *Chapter 10: Ability*—New material in this chapter focuses on abilities that are thought to enhance creativity and innovation, which complement the wraparound case on IDEO, an award-winning global design firm that emphasizes emotional intelligence in its people practices. *The Innovators* is now our OB at the Bookstore feature. This book describes how the most important innovations of the digital age were largely a function of collaboration and, following from this, abilities that help people work effectively with others. This provides a great counterpoint to the idea that innovations are a function of the genius of individuals. The new movie for our OB on Screen feature is *Lucy.* This movie provides a provocative description of the relationship between cognitive ability and emotional intelligence. We also now include a caveat in our discussion of how scores on cognitive ability tests may be used by organizations in hiring.

- *Chapter 11: Teams: Characteristics and Diversity*—Deutsch Lufthansa AG serves as the new wraparound case for this chapter. The chapter opens with a discussion of the nature of the flight crews on which the success of Deutsch Lufthansa's passenger airline business depends. The case focuses on the crash of Germanwing's Flight 9525. Although attributed to the troubled co-pilot who intentionally crashed the plane, the case explores the incident in terms of flight crew characteristics. The OB on Screen now discusses the movie *Avengers: Age of Ultron,* which provides excellent examples of task, goal and outcome interdependence. *The Hard Hat* is now featured in our OB at the Bookstore feature. This book provides a powerful example of an outstanding team player; an individual who engaged in all the right team role behaviors.

- *Chapter 12: Teams: Processes and Communication*—This chapter includes an updated opening that describes how NASA astronauts work together in crews to accomplish missions. The case describes a planned mission to Mars and some of the unique challenges relating to team processes that the astronaut crew will likely face. The OB on Screen feature now centers on *The SpongeBob Movie: Sponge Out of Water,* a lighthearted example of nature and benefits of effective teamwork. Our OB at the Bookstore feature has been changed to *Making Conflict Work,* which overviews how conflict can be managed so that it enhances team effectiveness. We also include updated research findings related to many of the chapter's concepts.

- *Chapter 13: Leadership: Power and Negotiation*—This chapter features a new wraparound case on Theranos's CEO Elizabeth Holmes—a leader who is consistently mentioned as one of the most powerful women in business and certainly one of the richest. Her rise to power is detailed through the use of expertise and a passion for the company she created. The case highlights the issues that come with her severe desire to keep Theranos technology a secret and what that means for her leadership. It also details what most people would describe as an "extreme" dedication. The chapter has been updated with new research, tie-ins with other chapters, as well as a number of new leadership examples including Ginni Rommety's (IBM) ability to develop consensus and the Uber leadership team's new approach to conflict resolution. The new OB on Screen feature uses *Foxcatcher* to illustrate forms of power and what happens when a leader has lots of some (organizational) and none of the others (personal).

- *Chapter 14: Leadership: Styles and Behaviors*—The chapter begins with a new wraparound case featuring the controversial Elon Musk and SpaceX. The opener and the case highlight Musk's ability to be a transformative leader and the passion he creates among those around him. It also highlights how his vision comes along with an extremely hands-on leadership style and the issues that creates. *A new OB at the Bookstore feature highlights Herminia Ibarra's *Act Like a Leader, Think Like a Leader,* which is a book not afraid to push back on things. Ibarra's take is that all of the "inward" leadership development movement is overrated and we should start with behaviors. The chapter includes a number of new research findings as well as updated company examples, including organizations such as Iron Mountain and Google's Project OXYGEN.

- *Chapter 15: Organizational Structure*—Zappos is the focus of this chapter's new wraparound case that highlights the company's reorganization into "Holocracy," which is essentially a no-job-title, self-management type of structure. While that sounds cool at first, it creates a lot of problems. Fourteen percent of Zappos' workforce took off when the CEO offered buyouts to those who felt they didn't fit with the new structure. The problems with getting new hires adjusted to the culture is also raised. A number of new company examples such as McDonald's, Campbell Soup, and updated detail on the company split at HP have been added. A new OB on Screen features *The Imitation Game, which* illustrates trying to get a good idea around an organization's chain of command and centralized decision making structure.

- *Chapter 16: Organizational Culture*—This chapter has a new wraparound case that focuses on General Motors and the tough task that CEO Mary Barra has in front of her. GM is the epitome of a negative and impossible to change culture. It should frame culture differently than most students tend to think about it (which is mostly positive). The chapter has been updated with new research and has a slew of new company examples, including Patagonia, Clif Bar, and others. The OB at the Bookstore feature now highlights *Work Rules!,* a new book by Google's head of People Operations on how Google creates its culture. The chapter also introduces a new key term—sustainability culture—in describing how many companies are following their values and mission both inside and outside the organization.

Acknowledgments

An enormous number of persons played a role in helping us put this textbook together. Truth be told, we had no idea that we would have to rely on and put our success in the hands of so many different people! Each of them had unique and useful contributions to make toward the publication of this book, and they deserve and thus receive our sincere gratitude.

We thank Michael Ablassmeir, our executive editor, for his suggestions and guidance on the third, fourth and fifth editions, and John Weimeister for filling that same role with earlier editions. We are thankful to both for allowing us to write the book that we wanted to write. Thanks also go out to Kelly Pekelder, our product developer, for keeping us on track and being such a pleasure to work with during this revision. We also owe much gratitude to our marketing manager, Casey Keske. We also would like to thank Christine Vaughan, Srdjan Savanovic, Carrie Burger, and Keri Johnson at McGraw-Hill, as they are the masterminds of much of how the book actually looks as it sits in students' hands; their work and effort were spectacular. A special thanks also goes out to Jessica Rodell (University of Georgia) and Megan Endres (Eastern Michigan University) for their assistance with our CONNECT content.

We would also like to thank our students at the undergraduate, masters, and executive levels who were taught with this book for their constructive feedback toward making it more effective in the classroom. Thanks also to our PhD students for allowing us to take time out from research projects to focus on this book.

Finally, we thank our families, who gave up substantial amounts of time with us and put up with the stress that necessarily comes at times during an endeavor such as this.

Jason Colquitt

Jeff LePine

Michael Wesson

Text Features: OB Insert Boxes

OB ON SCREEN

This feature uses memorable scenes from recent films to bring OB concepts to life. Films like *Interstellar*, *Gravity*, *Her*, *Big Hero 6*, *Whiplash*, and *Boyhood* offer rich, vivid examples that grab the attention of students.

© *Paramount Pictures/Photofest*

*"**Very comprehensive.** Well laid-out. **Interesting.** Good mix of theoretical material and practical insights."*

OB AT THE BOOKSTORE

This feature links the content in each chapter to a mainstream, popular business book. Books like *Essentialism*, *The Road to Character*, and *Quiet* represent the gateway to OB for many students. This feature helps them put those books in a larger context.

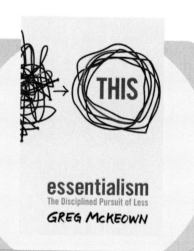

Photo of cover: © Roberts Publishing Services

OB ASSESSMENTS

This feature helps students see where they stand on key OB concepts in each chapter. Students gain insights into their personality, their emotional intelligence, their style of leadership, and their ability to cope with stress, which can help them understand their reactions to the working world.

© Royalty-Free/Corbis RF

"The material presented in this chapter is well balanced. Again, the tables, charts, and figures help to organize the material for students."

OB INTERNATIONALLY

Changes in technology, communications, and economic forces have made business more global and international than ever. This feature spotlights the impact of globalization on the organizational behavior concepts described in this book. It describes cross-cultural differences in OB theories, how to apply them in international corporations, and how to use OB to manage cultural diversity in the workplace.

© Namas Bhojani/AP Images

Supplement Features

PowerPoint® Presentation Slides

Prepared by Jason Colquitt, the PowerPoint presentation slides are designed to help instructors deliver course content in a way that maintains students' engagement and attention. The slides include a Notes section where Jason speaks to the instructor, offering specific tips for using the slides (and the book). The Notes also provide bridges to many of the resources in the Instructor's Manual, including innovative teaching tips and suggestions for using OB on Screen. Finally, the PowerPoints also include bonus OB Assessments for instructors who want additional assessments for their teaching.

Instructor's Manual

Prepared by Jason Colquitt, this manual was developed to help you get the most out of the text in your own teaching. It contains an outline of the chapters, innovative teaching tips to use with your students, and notes and answers for the end-of-chapter materials. It also provides a guide for the assessments in the book, and suggestions for using the OB on Screen feature. The manual also contains additional cases, exercises, and OB on Screen selections from earlier editions of the book, giving you extra content to use in your teaching.

Tegrity Campus: Lectures 24/7

 Tegrity Campus is a service that makes class time available 24/7 by automatically capturing every lecture in a searchable format for students to review when they study and complete assignments. With a simple one-click start-and-stop process, you capture all computer screens and corresponding audio. Students can replay any part of any class with easy-to-use browser-based viewing on a PC or Mac.

Educators know that the more students can see, hear, and experience class resources, the better they learn. In fact, studies prove it. With patented Tegrity "search anything" technology, students instantly recall key class moments for replay online, or on iPods and mobile devices. Instructors can help turn all their students' study time into learning moments immediately supported by their lecture. To learn more about Tegrity, watch a 2-minute Flash demo at **http://tegritycampus.mhhe.com**.

AACSB Tagging

 McGraw-Hill Education is a proud corporate member of AACSB International. Understanding the importance and value of AACSB accreditation, this text recognizes the curricula guidelines detailed in the AACSB standards for business accreditation by connecting selected questions in the test bank to the six general knowledge and skill guidelines in the AACSB standards.

The statements contained in this text are provided only as a guide for the users of this textbook. The AACSB leaves content coverage and assessment within the purview of individual schools, the mission of the school, and the faculty. While *Organizational Behavior* and the teaching package make no claim of any specific AACSB qualification or evaluation, we have within *Organizational Behavior* labeled selected questions according to the six general knowledge and skills areas.

Blackboard Partnership

McGraw-Hill and Blackboard have teamed up to simplify your life. Now you and your students can access Connect and Create right from within your Blackboard course—all with one single sign-on. The grade books are seamless, so when a student completes an integrated Connect assignment, the grade for that assignment automatically (and instantly) feeds your Blackboard grade center. Learn more at www.domorenow.com.

McGraw-Hill Campus

McGraw-Hill Campus is a new one-stop teaching and learning experience available to users of any learning management system. This institutional service allows faculty and students to enjoy single sign-on (SSO) access to all McGraw-Hill materials, including the award-winning McGraw-Hill Connect platform, from directly within the institution's website. With McGraw-Hill Campus, faculty receive instant access to teaching materials (e.g., e-textbooks, test banks, PowerPoint slides, learning objects, etc.), allowing them to browse, search, and use any instructor ancillary content in our vast library at no additional cost to instructor or students. In addition, students enjoy SSO access to a variety of free content and subscription-based products (e.g., McGraw-Hill Connect). With McGraw-Hill Campus enabled, faculty and students will never need to create another account to access McGraw-Hill products and services. Learn more at www.mhcampus.com.

Create

Craft your teaching resources to match the way you teach! With McGraw-Hill Create, www.mcgrawhillcreate.com, you can easily rearrange chapters, combine material from other content sources, and quickly upload content you have written, like your course syllabus or teaching notes. Find the content you need in Create by searching through thousands of leading McGraw-Hill textbooks. Arrange your book to fit your teaching style. Create even allows you to personalize your book's appearance by selecting the cover and adding your name, school, and course information. Order a Create book and you'll receive a complimentary print review copy in three to five business days or a complimentary electronic review copy (eComp) via e-mail in about one hour. Go to www.mcgrawhillcreate.com today and register. Experience how McGraw-Hill Create empowers you to teach *your* students *your* way.

McGraw-Hill Customer Experience Group Contact Information

At McGraw-Hill, we understand that getting the most from new technology can be challenging. That's why our services don't stop after you purchase our products. You can e-mail our Product Specialists 24 hours a day to get product training online. Or you can search our knowledge bank of Frequently Asked Questions on our support website. For Customer Support, call **800-331-5094,** or visit www.mhhe.com/support. One of our Technical Support Analysts will be able to assist you in a timely fashion.

McGraw-Hill Connect®
Learn Without Limits

Connect is a teaching and learning platform that is proven to deliver better results for students and instructors.

Connect empowers students by continually adapting to deliver precisely what they need, when they need it, and how they need it, so your class time is more engaging and effective.

Course outcomes improve with Connect.

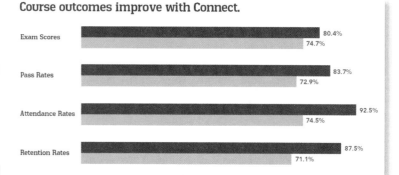

	With Connect	Without Connect
Exam Scores	80.4%	74.7%
Pass Rates	83.7%	72.9%
Attendance Rates	92.5%	74.5%
Retention Rates	87.5%	71.1%

88% of instructors who use **Connect** require it; instructor satisfaction **increases** by 38% when **Connect** is required.

Using **Connect** improves passing rates by **10.8%** and retention by **16.4%**.

Analytics

Connect Insight®

Connect Insight is Connect's new one-of-a-kind visual analytics dashboard—now available for both instructors and students—that provides at-a-glance information regarding student performance, which is immediately actionable. By presenting assignment, assessment, and topical performance results together with a time metric that is easily visible for aggregate or individual results, Connect Insight gives the user the ability to take a just-in-time approach to teaching and learning, which was never before available. Connect Insight presents data that empowers students and helps instructors improve class performance in a way that is efficient and effective.

Connect helps students achieve better grades

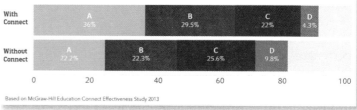

	A	B	C	D
With Connect	36%	29.5%	22%	4.3%
Without Connect	22.2%	22.3%	25.6%	9.8%

Based on McGraw-Hill Education Connect Effectiveness Study 2013

Students can view their results for any **Connect** course.

Mobile

Connect's new, intuitive mobile interface gives students and instructors flexible and convenient, anytime–anywhere access to all components of the Connect platform.

Adaptive

THE FIRST AND ONLY **ADAPTIVE READING EXPERIENCE** DESIGNED TO TRANSFORM THE WAY STUDENTS READ

More students earn **A's** and **B's** when they use McGraw-Hill Education **Adaptive** products.

SmartBook®

Proven to help students improve grades and study more efficiently, SmartBook contains the same content within the print book, but actively tailors that content to the needs of the individual. SmartBook's adaptive technology provides precise, personalized instruction on what the student should do next, guiding the student to master and remember key concepts, targeting gaps in knowledge and offering customized feedback, driving the student toward comprehension and retention of the subject matter. Available on smartphones and tablets, SmartBook puts learning at the student's fingertips—anywhere, anytime.

Over **4 billion questions** have been answered, making McGraw-Hill Education products more intelligent, reliable, and precise.

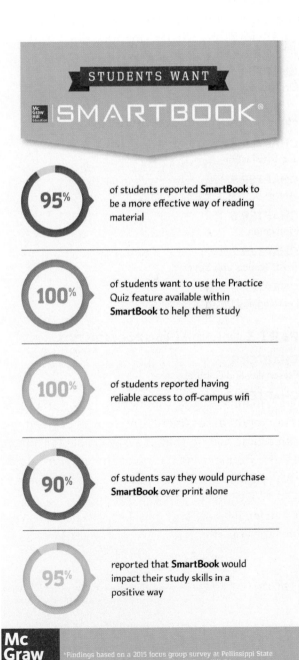

STUDENTS WANT

McGraw Hill Education SMARTBOOK®

95% of students reported **SmartBook** to be a more effective way of reading material

100% of students want to use the Practice Quiz feature available within **SmartBook** to help them study

100% of students reported having reliable access to off-campus wifi

90% of students say they would purchase **SmartBook** over print alone

95% reported that **SmartBook** would impact their study skills in a positive way

Mc Graw Hill Education

Brief Contents

PART 1 INTRODUCTION TO ORGANIZATIONAL BEHAVIOR 3

CHAPTER 1 4
What Is Organizational Behavior?

CHAPTER 2 30
Job Performance

CHAPTER 3 62
Organizational Commitment

PART 2 INDIVIDUAL MECHANISMS 93

CHAPTER 4 94
Job Satisfaction

CHAPTER 5 126
Stress

CHAPTER 6 162
Motivation

CHAPTER 7 196
Trust, Justice, and Ethics

CHAPTER 8 234
Learning and Decision Making

PART 3 INDIVIDUAL CHARACTERISTICS 265

CHAPTER 9 266
Personality and Cultural Values

CHAPTER 10 306
Ability

PART 4 GROUP MECHANISMS 337

CHAPTER 11 338
Teams: Characteristics and Diversity

CHAPTER 12 374
Teams: Processes and Communication

CHAPTER 13 410
Leadership: Power and Negotiation

CHAPTER 14 442
Leadership: Styles and Behaviors

PART 5 ORGANIZATIONAL MECHANISMS 479

CHAPTER 15 480
Organizational Structure

CHAPTER 16 508
Organizational Culture

INTEGRATIVE CASES 540

GLOSSARY/SUBJECT INDEX 549

NAME INDEX 569

COMPANY INDEX 583

Table of Contents

PART 1 INTRODUCTION TO ORGANIZATIONAL

BEHAVIOR 3

CHAPTER 1 4

What Is Organizational Behavior?

  What Is Organizational Behavior? 6

    Organizational Behavior Defined 6

    An Integrative Model of OB 7

  Does Organizational Behavior Matter? 10

    Building a Conceptual Argument 10

    Research Evidence 13

    So What's So Hard? 15

  How Do We "Know" What We Know About Organizational
    Behavior? 16

  Summary: Moving Forward in This Book 21

TAKEAWAYS 24

KEY TERMS 24

DISCUSSION QUESTIONS 24

CASE 25

EXERCISE 26

ENDNOTES 27

CHAPTER 2 30

Job Performance

  Job Performance 32

  What Does It Mean to Be a "Good Performer"? 34

    Task Performance 34

    Citizenship Behavior 38

    Counterproductive Behavior 41

    Summary: What Does It Mean to Be a "Good Performer"? 46

  Trends Affecting Performance 47

    Knowledge Work 47

    Service Work 47

  Application: Performance Management 48

    Management by Objectives 48

    Behaviorally Anchored Rating Scales 49

    360-Degree Feedback 49

    Forced Ranking 50

    Social Networking Systems 51

TAKEAWAYS 52

KEY TERMS 53

DISCUSSION QUESTIONS 53

CASE 54

EXERCISE 55

ENDNOTES 56

CHAPTER 3 62

Organizational Commitment

  Organizational Commitment 64

  What Does It Mean to Be "Committed"? 65

    Types of Commitment 65

    Withdrawal Behavior 72

    Summary: What Does It Mean to Be "Committed"? 77

  Trends That Affect Commitment 77

    Diversity of the Workforce 79

    The Changing Employee–Employer Relationship 79

  Application: Commitment Initiatives 81

TAKEAWAYS 84

KEY TERMS 84

DISCUSSION QUESTIONS 85

CASE 85

EXERCISE 86

ENDNOTES 87

PART 2 INDIVIDUAL MECHANISMS 93

CHAPTER 4 94

Job Satisfaction

  Job Satisfaction 96

  Why Are Some Employees More Satisfied Than Others? 97

    Value Fulfillment 98

    Satisfaction with the Work Itself 100

    Mood and Emotions 106

    *Summary: Why Are Some Employees More Satisfied Than
     Others?* 111

  How Important Is Job Satisfaction? 111

    Life Satisfaction 114

  Application: Tracking Satisfaction 117

TAKEAWAYS 118

KEY TERMS 119

DISCUSSION QUESTIONS 119

CASE 119

EXERCISE 120

ENDNOTES 121

CHAPTER 5 126
Stress

Stress 128

Why Are Some Employees More "Stressed" Than Others? 129

Types of Stressors 130

How Do People Cope with Stressors? 135

The Experience of Strain 137

Accounting for Individuals in the Stress Process 139

Summary: Why Are Some Employees More "Stressed" Than Others? 142

How Important Is Stress? 142

Application: Stress Management 145

Assessment 145

Reducing Stressors 145

Providing Resources 147

Reducing Strains 149

TAKEAWAYS 150

KEY TERMS 151

DISCUSSION QUESTIONS 151

CASE 152

EXERCISE 153

ENDNOTES 154

CHAPTER 6 162
Motivation

Motivation 164

Why Are Some Employees More Motivated Than Others? 165

Expectancy Theory 166

Goal Setting Theory 171

Equity Theory 175

Psychological Empowerment 180

Summary: Why Are Some Employees More Motivated Than Others? 182

How Important Is Motivation? 182

Application: Compensation Systems 185

TAKEAWAYS 188

KEY TERMS 188

DISCUSSION QUESTIONS 189

CASE 189

EXERCISE 190

ENDNOTES 191

CHAPTER 7 196
Trust, Justice, and Ethics

Trust, Justice, and Ethics 198

Why Are Some Authorities More Trusted Than Others? 199

Trust 200

Justice 205

Ethics 212

Summary: Why Are Some Authorities More Trusted Than Others? 219

How Important Is Trust? 220

Application: Social Responsibility 221

TAKEAWAYS 222

KEY TERMS 223

DISCUSSION QUESTIONS 223

CASE 223

EXERCISE 224

ENDNOTES 226

CHAPTER 8 234
Learning and Decision Making

Learning and Decision Making 236

Why Do Some Employees Learn to Make Decisions Better Than Others? 236

Types of Knowledge 237

Methods of Learning 238

Methods of Decision Making 244

Decision-Making Problems 246

Summary: Why Do Some Employees Learn to Make Decisions Better Than Others? 254

How Important Is Learning? 255

Application: Training 256

TAKEAWAYS 257

KEY TERMS 257

DISCUSSION QUESTIONS 258

CASE 258

EXERCISE 259

ENDNOTES 260

PART 3 INDIVIDUAL CHARACTERISTICS 265

CHAPTER 9 266
Personality and Cultural Values

Personality and Cultural Values 268

How Can We Describe What Employees Are Like? 269

The Big Five Taxonomy 269

Other Taxonomies of Personality 281

Cultural Values 283

*Summary: How Can We Describe What Employees
Are Like?* 286

How Important Are Personality and Cultural Values? 287

Application: Personality Tests 289

TAKEAWAYS 293

KEY TERMS 293

DISCUSSION QUESTIONS 294

CASE 294

EXERCISE 295

ENDNOTES 296

CHAPTER 10 306
Ability

Ability 308

What Does It Mean for an Employee to Be "Able"? 309

Cognitive Ability 309

Emotional Ability 314

Physical Ability 319

*Summary: What Does It Mean for an Employee to
Be "Able"?* 323

How Important Is Ability? 324

Application: Selecting High Cognitive Ability Employees 325

TAKEAWAYS 328

KEY TERMS 329

DISCUSSION QUESTIONS 329

CASE 329

EXERCISE 330

ENDNOTES 331

PART 4 GROUP MECHANISMS 337

CHAPTER 11 338
Teams: Characteristics and Diversity

Team Characteristics and Diversity 340

What Characteristics Can Be Used to Describe Teams? 341

Team Types 342

Variations within Team Types 344

Team Interdependence 346

Team Composition 351

*Summary: What Characteristics Can Be Used to Describe
Teams?* 359

How Important Are Team Characteristics? 360

Application: Team Compensation 361

TAKEAWAYS 362

KEY TERMS 362

DISCUSSION QUESTIONS 363

CASE 363

EXERCISE 364

ENDNOTES 366

CHAPTER 12 374
Teams: Processes and Communication

Team Processes and Communication 376

Why Are Some Teams More Than the Sum of Their Parts? 377

Taskwork Processes 379

Teamwork Processes 383

Communication 385

Team States 389

*Summary: Why Are Some Teams More Than the Sum
of Their Parts?* 392

How Important Are Team Processes? 392

Application: Training Teams 395

Transportable Teamwork Competencies 395

Cross-Training 395

Team Process Training 397

Team Building 397

TAKEAWAYS 398

KEY TERMS 398

DISCUSSION QUESTIONS 399

CASE 399

EXERCISE 400

ENDNOTES 403

CHAPTER 13 410
Leadership: Power and Negotiation

Leadership: Power and Negotiation 412

Why Are Some Leaders More Powerful Than Others? 413

Acquiring Power 413

Using Influence 418

Power and Influence in Action 421

Negotiations 427

*Summary: Why Are Some Leaders More Powerful
Than Others?* 429

How Important Are Power and Influence? 431

Application: Alternative Dispute Resolution 432

TAKEAWAYS 433

KEY TERMS 433

DISCUSSION QUESTIONS 434

CASE 434

EXERCISE 435

ENDNOTES 436

CHAPTER 14 442
Leadership: Styles and Behaviors

Leadership: Styles and Behaviors 444

Why Are Some Leaders More Effective Than Others? 446

Leader Decision-Making Styles 447

Day-to-Day Leadership Behaviors 451

Transformational Leadership Behaviors 456

Summary: Why Are Some Leaders More Effective Than Others? 462

How Important Is Leadership? 464

Application: Leadership Training 466

TAKEAWAYS 467

KEY TERMS 468

DISCUSSION QUESTIONS 468

CASE 469

EXERCISE 470

ENDNOTES 471

PART 5 ORGANIZATIONAL MECHANISMS 479

CHAPTER 15 480
Organizational Structure

Organizational Structure 482

Why Do Some Organizations Have Different Structures Than Others? 483

Elements of Organizational Structure 483

Organizational Design 490

Common Organizational Forms 492

Summary: Why Do Some Organizations Have Different Structures Than Others? 498

How Important Is Structure? 498

Application: Restructuring 500

TAKEAWAYS 501

KEY TERMS 502

DISCUSSION QUESTIONS 502

CASE 502

EXERCISE 503

ENDNOTES 504

CHAPTER 16 508
Organizational Culture

Organizational Culture 510

Why Do Some Organizations Have Different Cultures Than Others? 511

Culture Components 511

General Culture Types 515

Specific Culture Types 515

Culture Strength 518

Maintaining an Organizational Culture 521

Changing an Organizational Culture 523

Summary: Why Do Some Organizations Have Different Cultures Than Others? 527

How Important Is Organizational Culture? 527

Application: Managing Socialization 530

TAKEAWAYS 531

KEY TERMS 532

DISCUSSION QUESTIONS 532

CASE 533

EXERCISE 534

ENDNOTES 534

INTEGRATIVE CASES 540

GLOSSARY/SUBJECT INDEX 549

NAME INDEX 569

COMPANY INDEX 583

ORGANIZATIONAL BEHAVIOR
Improving Performance and Commitment in the Workplace

INTRODUCTION TO ORGANIZATIONAL BEHAVIOR

CHAPTER 1
What Is Organizational Behavior?

CHAPTER 2
Job Performance

CHAPTER 3
Organizational Commitment

What Is Organizational Behavior?

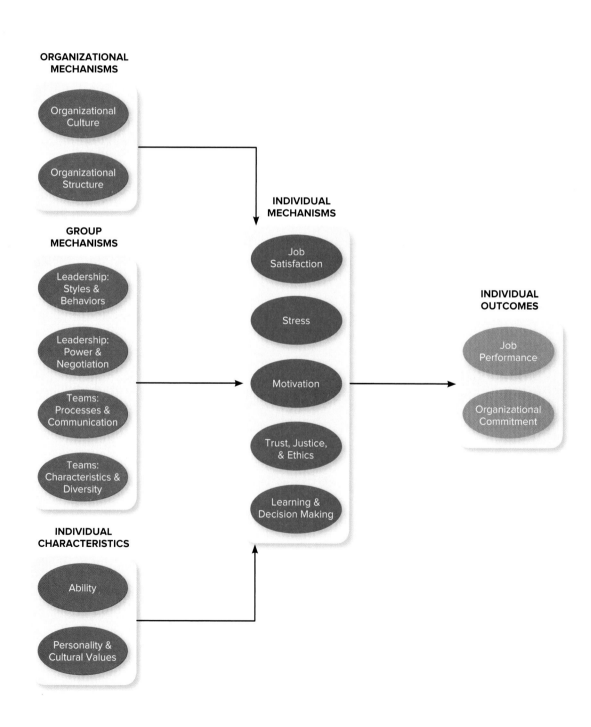

© Simon Dawson/Bloomberg/Getty Images

✓ LEARNING GOALS

After reading this chapter, you should be able to answer the following questions:

1.1 What is the definition of "organizational behavior" (OB)?

1.2 What are the two primary outcomes in studies of OB?

1.3 What factors affect the two primary OB outcomes?

1.4 Why might firms that are good at OB tend to be more profitable?

1.5 What is the role of theory in the scientific method?

1.6 How are correlations interpreted?

GOOGLE

Google is a company built on data. Its search engine uses data on how often sites are visited to rank-order the results of search queries. Its ads use data on client bids and landing page relevance to decide where to place ads on a page. More targeted ads also use data on previous browsing sessions to prioritize ads relevant to one's interests, hobbies, and habits. All of these data uses are key to Google's business and explain, in part, how it has grown into an organization with 60,000 employees working in 40 countries.

But Google is a company built on data in another, more literal, sense. Google's People Operations group bases its human resource decisions on data, rather than opinion. Hiring decisions are based on structured measures of ability, personality, and cultural fit rather than the gut instincts of specific managers. The process of evaluating and rewarding people has evolved based on careful study of what works and what doesn't. Change initiatives are based on results from Googlegeist, the company's annual attitude survey. And those initiatives are tested using carefully designed experiments before they're rolled out more broadly. Google's People Analytics team even has an internal think tank—the People and Innovation Lab (PiLab)—staffed in part by employees with PhDs in organizational behavior, industrial/organizational psychology, sociology, and economics.

Laszlo Bock, Google's senior vice president of People Operations, summarizes the company's philosophy: "Relying on data—indeed, expecting every conversation to be rooted in data—upends the traditional role of managers. It transforms them from being providers of intuition to facilitators in a search for truth . . . One of the core principles of Google has always been 'Don't politick. Use data.'" Bock notes that this embracing of the technical side of human resources has allowed a company built by engineers to trust in the importance of management. It seems that many of those data-based conversations have worked out, as Google has maintained its standing as one of *Fortune's* 100 Best Companies to Work For, earning the top spot in the most recent rankings. Google's employees point to the corporate culture and the exceptional perks, of course. But they also point to the people. As one veteran of the company explained, "The best perk of working at Google is working at Google . . . We are surrounded by smart, driven people who provide the best environment for learning I've ever experienced."

WHAT IS ORGANIZATIONAL BEHAVIOR?

Before we describe what the field of organizational behavior studies, take a moment to ponder this question: Who was the single *worst* coworker you've ever had? Picture fellow students who collaborated with you on class projects; colleagues from part-time or summer jobs; or peers, subordinates, or supervisors working in your current organization. What did this coworker do that earned him or her "worst coworker" status? Was it some of the behaviors shown in the right column of Table 1-1 (or perhaps all of them)? Now take a moment to consider the single *best* coworker you've ever had. Again, what did this coworker do to earn "best coworker" status— some or most of the behaviors shown in the left column of Table 1-1?

If you found yourself working alongside the two people profiled in the table, two questions would be foremost on your mind: "*Why* does the worst coworker act that way?" and "*Why* does the best coworker act that way?" Once you understand why the two coworkers act so differently, you might be able to figure out ways to interact with the worst coworker more effectively (thereby making your working life a bit more pleasant). If you happen to be a manager, you might formulate plans for how to improve attitudes and behaviors in the unit. Such plans could include how to screen applicants, train and socialize new organizational members, manage evaluations and rewards for performance, and deal with conflicts that arise between and among employees. Without understanding why employees act the way they do, it's extremely hard to find a way to change their attitudes and behaviors at work.

1.1

What is the definition of "organizational behavior" (OB)?

ORGANIZATIONAL BEHAVIOR DEFINED

Organizational behavior (OB) is a field of study devoted to understanding, explaining, and ultimately improving the attitudes and behaviors of individuals and groups in organizations. Scholars in management departments of universities and scientists in business organizations conduct

TABLE 1-1	The Best of Coworkers, the Worst of Coworkers
THE BEST	**THE WORST**
Have you ever had a coworker who usually acted this way?	*Have you ever had a coworker who usually acted this way?*
Got the job done, without having to be managed or reminded	Did not got the job done, even with a great deal of hand-holding
Adapted when something needed to be changed or done differently	Was resistant to any and every form of change, even when changes were beneficial
Was always a "good sport," even when bad things happened at work	Whined and complained, no matter what was happening
Attended optional meetings or functions to support colleagues	Optional meetings? Was too lazy to make it to some required meetings and functions!
Helped new coworkers or people who seemed to need a hand	Made fun of new coworkers or people who seemed to need a hand
Felt an attachment and obligation to the employer for the long haul	Seemed to always be looking for something else, even if it wasn't better
Was first to arrive, last to leave	Was first to leave for lunch, last to return

The Million-Dollar Question:
Why do these two employees act so differently?

research on OB. The findings from those research studies are then applied by managers or consultants to see whether they help meet "real-world" challenges. OB can be contrasted with two other courses commonly offered in management departments: human resource management and strategic management. **Human resource management** takes the theories and principles studied in OB and explores the "nuts-and-bolts" applications of those principles in organizations. An OB study might explore the relationship between learning and job performance, whereas a human resource management study might examine the best ways to structure training programs to promote employee learning. **Strategic management** focuses on the product choices and industry characteristics that affect an organization's profitability. A strategic management study might examine the relationship between firm diversification (when a firm expands into a new product segment) and firm profitability.

The theories and concepts found in OB are actually drawn from a wide variety of disciplines. For example, research on job performance and individual characteristics draws primarily from studies in industrial and organizational psychology. Research on satisfaction, emotions, and team processes draws heavily from social psychology. Sociology research is vital to research on team characteristics and organizational structure, and anthropology research helps inform the study of organizational culture. Finally, models from economics are used to understand motivation, learning, and decision making. This diversity brings a unique quality to the study of OB, as most students will be able to find a particular topic that's intrinsically interesting and thought provoking to them.

AN INTEGRATIVE MODEL OF OB

Because of the diversity in its topics and disciplinary roots, it is common for students in an organizational behavior class to wonder, "How does all this stuff fit together?" How does what gets covered in Chapter 3 relate to what gets covered in Chapter 13? To clarify such issues, this

| FIGURE 1-1 | Integrative Model of Organizational Behavior |

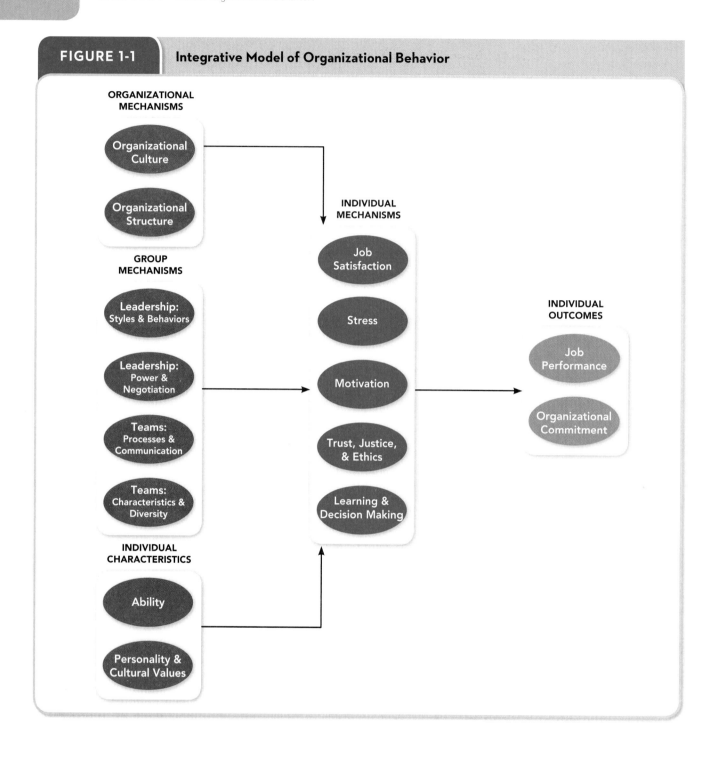

textbook is structured around an integrative model of OB, shown in Figure 1-1, that's designed to provide a roadmap for the field of organizational behavior. The model shows how the topics in the next 15 chapters—represented by the 15 ovals in the model—all fit together. We should stress that there are other potential ways of combining the 15 topics, and Figure 1-1 likely oversimplifies the connections among the topics. Still, we believe the model provides a helpful guide as you move through this course. Figure 1-1 includes five different kinds of topics.

INDIVIDUAL OUTCOMES The right-most portion of the model contains the two primary outcomes of interest to organizational behavior researchers (and employees and managers in

1.2

What are the two primary outcomes in studies of OB?

organizations): *job performance* and *organizational commitment.* Most employees have two primary goals for their working lives: to perform their jobs well and to remain a member of an organization that they respect. Likewise, most managers have two primary goals for their employees: to maximize their job performance and to ensure that they stay with the firm for a significant length of time. As described in Chapter 2, there are several specific behaviors that, when taken together, constitute good job performance. Similarly, as described in Chapter 3, there are a number of beliefs, attitudes, and emotions that cause an employee to remain committed to an employer.

This book starts by covering job performance and organizational commitment so that you can better understand the two primary organizational behavior goals. Our hope is that by using performance and commitment as starting points, we can highlight the practical importance of OB topics. After all, what could be more important than having employees who perform well and want to stay with the company? This structure also enables us to conclude the other chapters in the book with sections that describe the relationships between each chapter's topic and performance and commitment. For example, the chapter on motivation concludes by describing the relationships between motivation and performance and motivation and commitment. In this way, you'll learn which of the topics in the model are most useful for understanding your own attitudes and behaviors.

INDIVIDUAL MECHANISMS Our integrative model also illustrates a number of individual mechanisms that directly affect job performance and organizational commitment. These include *job satisfaction,* which captures what employees feel when thinking about their jobs and doing their day-to-day work (Chapter 4). Another individual mechanism is *stress,* which reflects employees' psychological responses to job demands that tax or exceed their capacities (Chapter 5). The model also includes *motivation,* which captures the energetic forces that drive employees' work effort (Chapter 6). *Trust, justice, and ethics* reflect the degree to which employees feel that their company does business with fairness, honesty, and integrity (Chapter 7). The final individual mechanism shown in the model is *learning and decision making,* which deals with how employees gain job knowledge and how they use that knowledge to make accurate judgments on the job (Chapter 8).

1.3

What factors affect the two primary OB outcomes?

INDIVIDUAL CHARACTERISTICS Of course, if satisfaction, stress, motivation, and so forth are key drivers of job performance and organizational commitment, it becomes important to understand what factors improve those individual mechanisms. Two such factors reflect the characteristics of individual employees. *Personality and cultural values* reflect the various traits and tendencies that describe how people act, with commonly studied traits including extraversion, conscientiousness, and collectivism. As described in Chapter 9, personality and cultural values affect the way people behave at work, the kinds of tasks they're interested in, and how they react to events that happen on the job. The model also examines *ability,* which describes the cognitive abilities (verbal, quantitative, etc.), emotional skills (other awareness, emotion regulation, etc.), and physical abilities (strength, endurance, etc.) that employees bring to a job. As described in Chapter 10, ability influences the kinds of tasks an employee is good at (and not so good at).

GROUP MECHANISMS Our integrative model also acknowledges that employees don't work alone. Instead, they typically work in one or more work teams led by some formal (or sometimes informal) leader. Like the individual characteristics, these group mechanisms shape satisfaction, stress, motivation, trust, and learning. Chapter 11 covers *team characteristics and diversity*—describing how teams are formed, staffed, and composed, and how team members come to rely on one another as they do their work. Chapter 12 then covers *team processes and communication*—how teams behave, including their coordination, conflict, and cohesion. The next two chapters focus on the leaders of those teams. We first describe how individuals become leaders in the first place, covering *leader power and negotiation* to summarize how individuals attain authority over others (Chapter 13). We then describe how leaders behave in their leadership roles, as *leader styles and behaviors* capture the specific actions that leaders take to influence others at work (Chapter 14).

ORGANIZATIONAL MECHANISMS Finally, our integrative model acknowledges that the teams described in the prior section are grouped into larger organizations that themselves affect satisfaction, stress, motivation, and so forth. For example, every company has an *organizational structure* that dictates how the units within the firm link to (and communicate with) other units (Chapter 15). Sometimes structures are centralized around a decision-making authority, whereas other times, structures are decentralized, affording each unit some autonomy. Every company also has an *organizational culture* that captures "the way things are" in the organization—shared knowledge about the values and beliefs that shape employee attitudes and behaviors (Chapter 16).

SUMMARY Each of the chapters in this textbook will open with a depiction of this integrative model, with the subject of each chapter highlighted. We hope that this opening will serve as a roadmap for the course—showing you where you are, where you've been, and where you're going. We also hope that the model will give you a feel for the "big picture" of OB—showing you how all the OB topics are connected.

DOES ORGANIZATIONAL BEHAVIOR MATTER?

Having described exactly what OB is, it's time to discuss another fundamental question: Does it really matter? Is there any value in taking a class on this subject, other than fulfilling some requirement of your program? (You might guess that we're biased in our answers to these questions, given that we wrote a book on the subject!) Few would disagree that organizations need to know principles of accounting and finance to be successful; it would be impossible to conduct business without such knowledge. Similarly, few would disagree that organizations need to know principles of marketing, as consumers need to know about the firm's products and what makes those products unique or noteworthy.

However, people sometimes wonder whether a firm's ability to manage OB has any bearing on its bottom-line profitability. After all, if a firm has a good-enough product, won't people buy it regardless of how happy, motivated, or committed its workforce is? Perhaps for a time, but effective OB can help keep a product good over the long term. This same argument can be made in reverse: If a firm has a bad-enough product, isn't it true that people won't buy it, regardless of how happy, motivated, or committed its workforce is? Again, perhaps for a time, but the effective management of OB can help make a product get better, incrementally, over the long term.

Consider this pop quiz about the automotive industry: Which automaker finished behind only Lexus and Porsche in a recent study of initial quality by J.D. Power and Associates?[1] Toyota? Nope. Honda? Uh-uh. The answer is Hyundai (yes, Hyundai). The automaker has come a long way in the decade since comedian Jay Leno likened a Hyundai to a bobsled ("It has no room, you have to push it to get going, and it only goes downhill!").[2] More recent models—including those built in a manufacturing plant in Montgomery, Alabama—are regarded as good looking and well made, with *Consumer Reports* tabbing the Hyundai Elantra SE as the best small sedan in a recent set of rankings.[3] Says one investor, "Hyundai is a brand that is on the verge of being aspirational. People are saying they are proud to own it, not just to settle for it."[4] That turnaround can be credited to the company's increased emphasis on quality. Work teams devoted to quality have been expanded eightfold, and almost all employees are enrolled in special training programs devoted to quality issues.[5] Hyundai represents a case in which OB principles are being applied across cultures. Our **OB Internationally** feature spotlights such international and cross-cultural applications of OB topics in each chapter.

BUILDING A CONCEPTUAL ARGUMENT

Of course, we shouldn't just accept it on faith that OB matters, nor should we merely look for specific companies that appear to support the premise. What we need instead is a conceptual argument that captures why OB might affect the bottom-line profitability of an organization.

OB INTERNATIONALLY

Changes in technology, communications, and economic forces have made business more global and international than ever. To use Thomas Friedman's line, "The world is flat." The playing field has been leveled between the United States and the rest of the world. This feature spotlights the impact of globalization on the organizational behavior concepts described in this book and covers a variety of topics.

Cross-Cultural Differences. Research in cross-cultural organizational behavior has illustrated that national cultures affect many of the relationships in our integrative model. Put differently, there is little that we know about OB that is "universal" or "culture free."

International Corporations. An increasing number of organizations are international in scope, with both foreign and domestic operations. Applying organizational behavior concepts in these firms represents a special challenge—should policies and practices be consistent across locations or tailored to meet the needs of the culture?

Expatriation. Working as an expatriate—an employee who lives outside his or her native country—can be particularly challenging. What factors influence expatriates' job performance and organizational commitment levels?

Managing Diversity. More and more work groups are composed of members of different cultural backgrounds. What are the special challenges involved in leading and working in such groups?

Sources: T.L. Friedman. *The World Is Flat.* New York: Farrar, Straus and Giroux, 2002; H. Aguinis and C.A. Henl. "The Search for Universals in Cross-Cultural Organizational Behavior." In *Organizational Behavior: The State of the Science*, ed. J. Greenberg, Mahwah, NJ: Erlbaum, 2003, pp. 373–411.

One such argument is based on the **resource-based view** of organizations. This perspective describes what exactly makes resources valuable—that is, what makes them capable of creating long-term profits for the firm.[6] A firm's resources include financial (revenue, equity, etc.) and physical (buildings, machines, technology) resources, but they also include resources related to organizational behavior, such as the knowledge, ability, and wisdom of the workforce, as well as the image, culture, and goodwill of the organization.

The resource-based view suggests that the value of resources depends on several factors, shown in Figure 1-2. For example, a resource is more valuable when it is *rare*. Diamonds, oil, Babe Ruth baseball cards, and Action Comics #1 (the debut of Superman) are all expensive precisely because they are rare. Good people are also rare—witness the adage "good people are hard to find." Ask yourself what percentage of the people you've worked with have been talented, motivated, satisfied, and good team players. In many organizations, cities, or job markets, such employees are the exception rather than the rule. If good people really are rare, then the effective management of OB should prove to be a valuable resource.

© Dave Martin/AP Images

Hyundai's emphasis on work teams and training has increased the quality of its cars, like these models built in its Montgomery, Alabama, plant.

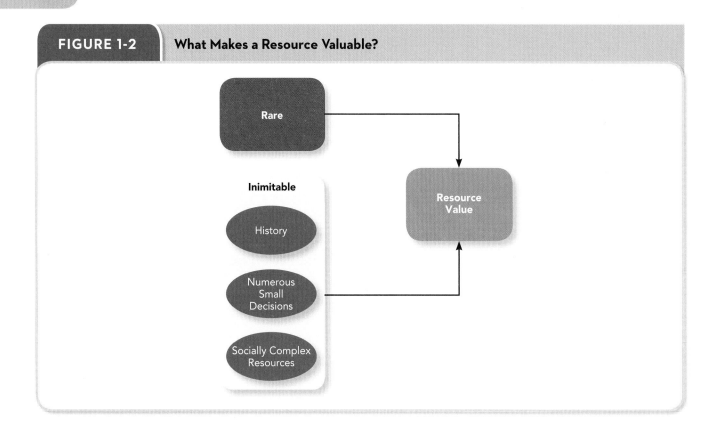

FIGURE 1-2   **What Makes a Resource Valuable?**

The resource-based view also suggests that a resource is more valuable when it is **inimitable,** meaning that it cannot be imitated. Many of the firm's resources can be imitated, if competitors have enough money. For example, a new form of technology can help a firm gain an advantage for a short time, but competing firms can switch to the same technology. Manufacturing practices can be copied, equipment and tools can be approximated, and marketing strategies can be mimicked. Good people, in contrast, are much more difficult to imitate. As shown in Figure 1-2, there are three reasons people are inimitable.

HISTORY People create a **history**—a collective pool of experience, wisdom, and knowledge that benefits the organization. History cannot be bought. Consider an example from the consumer electronics retailing industry where Microsoft, taking a cue from Apple, launched its first retail store in Scottsdale, Arizona, in 2009.[7] The company hopes that the stores will give it a chance

Microsoft opened its first retail stores in 2009, including this one in Mission Viejo, California. The look and feel of Microsoft's stores is very similar to Apple's retail outlets.

© Joshua Lott/Reuters/Corbis

to showcase its computer and mobile phone operating systems, along with its hardware and gaming products. Microsoft faces an uphill climb in the retail space, however, because Apple has an eight-year head start after opening its first store in 2001, in McLean, Virginia.[8] Microsoft's position on the "retail learning curve" is therefore quite different, suggesting that it will grapple with many of the same issues that Apple resolved years ago.

NUMEROUS SMALL DECISIONS The concept of **numerous small decisions** captures the idea that people make many small decisions day in and day out, week in and week out. "So what?" you might say, "Why worry about small decisions?" To answer that question, ask yourself what the biggest decisions are when launching a new line of retail stores. The location of them maybe, or perhaps their look and feel? It turns out that Microsoft placed their stores near Apple's, and mimicked much of their open, "Zen" sensibility. Said one patron, "It appears that the Microsoft Store in Mission Viejo is dressed up as the Apple Store for Halloween."[9] Big decisions can be copied; they are visible to competitors and observable by industry experts. In contrast, the "behind the scenes" decisions at the Apple Store are more invisible to Microsoft, especially the decisions that involve the hiring and management of employees. Apple seems to understand the inimitable advantage that such decisions can create. A recent article in *Workforce Management* included features on the top human resources executives for 20 of the most admired companies in America.[10] Interestingly, the entry for Apple's executive was cryptic, noting only that the company "keeps its human resources executive shrouded in secrecy and refuses to respond to any questions about HR's contribution to the company's most admired status."

SOCIALLY COMPLEX RESOURCES People also create **socially complex resources,** like culture, teamwork, trust, and reputation. These resources are termed "socially complex" because it's not always clear how they came to develop, though it is clear which organizations do (and do not) possess them. One advantage that Apple has over Microsoft in the retail wars is the unusual amount of interest and enthusiasm created by products like the iPad, iPhone, iPod, and MacBook Air. Those products have an "it factor" that brings customers into the store, and Apple itself sits atop *Fortune*'s list of 50 most admired companies in the world.[11] Competitors like Microsoft can't just acquire "coolness" or "admiration"—they are complex resources that evolve in ways that are both murky and mysterious.

RESEARCH EVIDENCE

Thus, we can build a conceptual argument for why OB might affect an organization's profitability: Good people are both rare and inimitable and, therefore, create a resource that is valuable for creating competitive advantage. Conceptual arguments are helpful, of course, but it would be even better if there were hard data to back them up. Fortunately, it turns out that there is a great deal of research evidence supporting the importance of OB for company performance. Several research studies have been conducted on the topic, each employing a somewhat different approach.

1.4

Why might firms that are good at OB tend to be more profitable?

One study began by surveying executives from 968 publicly held firms with 100 or more employees.[12] The survey assessed so-called high performance work practices—OB policies that are widely agreed to be beneficial to firm performance. The survey included 13 questions asking about a combination of hiring, information sharing, training, performance management, and incentive practices, and each question asked what proportion of the company's workforce was involved in the practice. Table 1-2 provides some of the questions used to assess the high-performance work practices (and also shows which chapter of the textbook describes each particular practice in more detail). The study also gathered the following information for each firm: average annual rate of turnover, productivity level (defined as sales per employee), market value of the firm, and corporate profitability. The results revealed that a one-unit increase in the proportion of the workforce involved in the practices was associated with an approximately 7 percent decrease in turnover, $27,000 more in sales per employee, $18,000 more in market value, and $3,800 more in profits. Put simply, better OB practices were associated with better firm performance.

Although there is no doubting the importance of turnover, productivity, market value, and profitability, another study examined an outcome that's even more fundamental: firm survival.[13] The study focused on 136 nonfinancial companies that made initial public offerings (IPOs) in 1988. Firms that undergo an IPO typically have shorter histories and need an infusion of cash to grow or introduce some new technology. Rather than conducting a survey, the authors of this study examined the prospectus filed by each firm (the Securities and Exchange Commission requires that prospectuses contain honest information, and firms can

TABLE 1-2	Survey Questions Designed to Assess High-Performance Work Practices

SURVEY QUESTION ABOUT OB PRACTICE	COVERED IN CHAPTER
What is the proportion of the workforce whose jobs have been subjected to a formal job analysis?	2
What is the proportion of the workforce who are administered attitude surveys on a regular basis?	4
What is the proportion of the workforce who have access to company incentive plans, profit-sharing plans, and/or gain-sharing plans?	6
What is the average number of hours of training received by a typical employee over the last 12 months?	8, 10
What is the proportion of the workforce who have access to a formal grievance procedure and/or complaint resolution system?	7
What proportion of the workforce are administered an employment test prior to hiring?	9, 10
What is the proportion of the workforce whose performance appraisals are used to determine compensation?	6

Source: From M.A. Huselid. "The Impact of Human Resource Management Practices on Turnover, Productivity, and Corporate Financial Performance." *Academy of Management Journal,* Vol. 38, pp. 635–72. Copyright © 1995. Reproduced with permission of Academy of Management via Copyright Clearance Center.

be liable for any inaccuracies that might mislead investors). The authors coded each prospectus for information that might suggest OB issues were valued. Examples of valuing OB issues included describing employees as a source of competitive advantage in strategy and mission statements, emphasizing training and continuing education, having a human resources management executive, and emphasizing full-time rather than temporary or contract employees. By 1993, 81 of the 136 firms included in the study had survived (60 percent). The key question is whether the value placed on OB predicted which did (and did not) survive. The results revealed that firms that valued OB had a 19 percent higher survival rate than firms that did not value OB.

A third study focused on *Fortune*'s "100 Best Companies to Work For" list, which has appeared annually since 1998.[14] Table 1-3 provides some highlights from the 2015 version of the list. If the 100 firms on the list really do have good OB practices, and if good OB practices really do influence firm profitability, then it follows that the 100 firms should be more profitable. To explore this premise, the study went back to the original 1998 list and found a "matching firm" for those companies that were included.[15] The matching firm consisted of the most similar company with respect to industry and size in that particular year, with the added requirement that the company had not appeared on the "100 Best" list. This process essentially created two groups of companies that differ only in terms of their inclusion in the "100 Best." The study then compared the profitability of those two groups of companies. The results revealed that the "100 Best" firms were more profitable than their peers. Indeed, the cumulative investment return for a portfolio based on the 1998 "100 Best" companies would have doubled the return for the broader market.

TABLE 1-3	The "100 Best Companies to Work For" in 2015	
1. Google	50. Goldman Sachs	81. Publix
2. Boston Consulting	51. American Express	82. Bright Horizons
3. ACUITY	53. Marriott	83. TDIndustries
4. SAS	54. QuickTrip	85. Mars
5. Robert W. Baird	55. Whole Foods	86. Zappos
7. Wegman's	63. KPMG	88. Cheesecake Factory
9. Genentech	70. Cisco	90. Adobe
24. Twitter	73. Mayo Clinic	91. Capital One
27. Container Store	74. PWC	93. Nordstrom
32. St. Jude	78. Hyatt	95. Nationwide
47. Four Seasons	79. Ernst & Young	97. Deloitte
49. Aflac	80. General Mills	98. Accenture

Source: From M. Moskowitz and R. Levering. "The 100 Best Companies to Work For." *Fortune,* March 15, 2015.

SO WHAT'S SO HARD?

Clearly this research evidence seems to support the conceptual argument that good people constitute a valuable resource for companies. Good OB does seem to matter in terms of company profitability. You may wonder then, "What's so hard?" Why doesn't every company prioritize the effective management of OB, devoting as much attention to it as they do accounting, finance, marketing, technology, physical assets, and so on? Some companies do a bad job when it comes to managing their people. Why is that?

One reason is that there is no "magic bullet" OB practice—one thing that, in and of itself, can increase profitability. Instead, the effective management of OB requires a belief that several different practices are important, along with a long-term commitment to improving those practices. This premise can be summarized with what might be called the **Rule of One-Eighth**:

One must bear in mind that one-half of organizations won't believe the connection between how they manage their people and the profits they earn. One-half of those who do see the connection will do what many organizations have done—try to make a single change to solve their problems, not realizing that the effective management of people requires a more comprehensive and systematic approach. Of the firms that make comprehensive changes, probably only about one-half will persist with their practices long enough to actually derive economic benefits. Because one-half times one-half times one-half equals one-eighth, at best 12 percent of organizations will actually do what is required to build profits by putting people first.[16]

The integrative model of OB used to structure this book was designed with this Rule of One-Eighth in mind. Figure 1-1 suggests that high job performance depends not just on employee motivation but also on fostering high levels of satisfaction, effectively managing stress, creating a trusting climate, and committing to employee learning. Failing to do any one of those things could hinder the effectiveness of the other concepts in the model. Of course, that systemic nature reveals another reality of organizational behavior: It's often difficult to "fix" companies that struggle with OB issues. Such companies often struggle in a number of different areas and on a number of different levels. For more discussion about why firms struggle to manage their people, see our **OB at the Bookstore** feature, which appears in each chapter to showcase a well-known business book that discusses OB concepts.

OB AT THE BOOKSTORE

This feature spotlights bestselling business books that complement the content of each chapter. Drawing a bridge from our chapters to these books lets you see how the titles at the bookstore complement the concepts in our integrative model of OB.

THE ADVANTAGE
by Patrick Lencioni (San Francisco: Jossey-Bass, 2012).

Photo of cover: © Roberts Publishing Services

As I sat there at the conference listening to one presentation after another highlighting the remarkable and unorthodox activities that have made this organization so healthy, I leaned over and quietly asked the CEO a semirhetorical question: "Why in the world don't your competitors do any of this?"

After a few seconds, he whispered, almost sadly, "You know, I honestly believe they think it's beneath them."

And there it was.

With those words, Lencioni explains why so many organizations wind up doing a poor job of managing OB. Lencioni uses the term "healthy" to describe an organization with high morale, low turnover, minimal politics, and high productivity. In other words, "health" has to do with the management of people, unlike "smarts," which Lencioni describes as organizations having effective strategy, marketing, finance, and technology.

Lencioni argues that organizational health is a key part of maintaining a competitive advantage, for two reasons. First, it's rarer than organizational smarts. As Lencioni notes when reflecting on his consulting experience, "In twenty years of consulting to clients in virtually every industry, I have yet to meet a group of leaders who made me think, *Wow, these people just don't know enough about their business to succeed.*" In contrast, he notes that plenty of organizations clearly lacked health, in part because managers were so dismissive of its importance. Second, organizational health has a "multiplier effect" on smarts, allowing companies to "tap into" their knowledge, experience, and expertise to a greater extent than their competitors.

So how can organizations become healthier? Lencioni argues that they need to have a cohesive and stable leadership team that is focused on building trust and commitment while holding employees accountable for their performance. Put differently, being healthy requires mastering a number of different concepts in our integrative model of OB.

HOW DO WE "KNOW" WHAT WE KNOW ABOUT ORGANIZATIONAL BEHAVIOR?

Now that we've described what OB is and why it's an important topic of study, we now turn to how we "know" what we know about the topic. In other words, where does the knowledge in this textbook come from? To answer this question, we must first explore how people "know" about anything. Philosophers have argued that there are several different ways of knowing things:[17]

- **Method of experience:** People hold firmly to some belief because it is consistent with their own experience and observations.
- **Method of intuition:** People hold firmly to some belief because it "just stands to reason"—it seems obvious or self-evident.

- **Method of authority:** People hold firmly to some belief because some respected official, agency, or source has said it is so.
- **Method of science:** People accept some belief because scientific studies have tended to replicate that result using a series of samples, settings, and methods.

Consider the following prediction: Providing social recognition, in the form of public displays of praise and appreciation for good behaviors, will increase the performance and commitment of work units. Perhaps you feel that you "know" this claim to be true because you yourself have always responded well to praise and recognition. Or perhaps you feel that you "know" it to be true because it seems like common sense—who wouldn't work harder after a few public pats on the back? Maybe you feel that you "know" it to be true because a respected boss from your past always extolled the virtue of public praise and recognition.

However, the methods of experience, intuition, and authority also might have led you to the opposite belief—that providing social recognition has no impact on the performance and commitment of work units. It may be that public praise has always made you uncomfortable or embarrassed, to the point that you've tried to hide especially effective behaviors to avoid being singled out by your boss. Or it may seem logical that social recognition will be viewed as "cheap talk," with employees longing for financial incentives rather than verbal compliments. Or perhaps the best boss you ever worked for never offered a single piece of social recognition in her life, yet her employees always worked their hardest on her behalf. From a scientist's point of view, it doesn't really matter what a person's experience, intuition, or authority suggests; the prediction must be tested with data. In other words, scientists don't simply assume that their beliefs are accurate; they acknowledge that their beliefs must be tested scientifically.

Scientific studies are based on the scientific method, originated by Sir Francis Bacon in the 1600s and adapted in Figure 1-3.[18] The scientific method begins with **theory,** defined as a collection of assertions—both verbal and symbolic—that specify how and why variables are related, as well as the conditions in which they should (and should not) be related.[19] More simply, a theory tells a story and supplies the familiar who, what, where, when, and why elements found in any newspaper or magazine article.[20] Theories are often summarized with theory diagrams, the "boxes and arrows" that graphically depict relationships between variables. Our integrative model of OB in Figure 1-1 represents one such diagram, and there will be many more to come in the remaining chapters of this textbook.

A scientist could build a theory explaining why social recognition might influence the performance and commitment of work units. From what sources would that theory be built? Well, because social scientists "are what they study," one source of theory building is introspection.

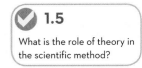

1.5

What is the role of theory in the scientific method?

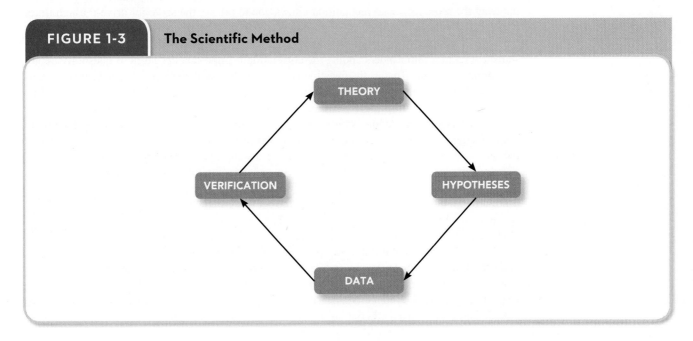

| FIGURE 1-3 | The Scientific Method |

However, theories may also be built from interviews with employees or from observations where scientists take notes, keep diaries, and pore over company documents to find all the elements of a theory story.[21] Alternatively, theories may be built from research reviews, which examine findings of previous studies to look for general patterns or themes.[22]

Although many theories are interesting, logical, or thought provoking, many also wind up being completely wrong. After all, scientific theories once predicted that the earth was flat and the sun revolved around it. Closer to home, OB theories once argued that money was not an effective motivator and that the best way to structure jobs was to make them as simple and mundane as possible.[23] Theories must therefore be tested to verify that their predictions are accurate. As shown in Figure 1-3, the scientific method requires that theories be used to inspire **hypotheses.** Hypotheses are written predictions that specify relationships between variables. For example, a theory of social recognition could be used to inspire this hypothesis: "Social recognition behaviors on the part of managers will be positively related to the job performance and organizational commitment of their units." This hypothesis states, in black and white, the expected relationship between social recognition and unit performance.

Assume a family member owned a chain of 21 fast-food restaurants and allowed you to test this hypothesis using the restaurants. Specifically, you decided to train the managers in a subset of the restaurants about how to use social recognition as a tool to reinforce behaviors. Meanwhile, you left another subset of restaurants unchanged to represent a control group. You then tracked the total number of social recognition behaviors exhibited by managers over the next nine months by observing the managers at specific time intervals. You measured job performance by tracking drive-through times for the next nine months and used those times to reflect the minutes it takes for a customer to approach the restaurant, order food, pay, and leave. You also measured the commitment of the work unit by tracking employee retention rates over the next nine months.

1.6

How are correlations interpreted?

So how can you tell whether your hypothesis was supported? You could analyze the data by examining the **correlation** between social recognition behaviors and drive-through times, as well as the correlation between social recognition behaviors and employee turnover. A correlation, abbreviated r, describes the statistical relationship between two variables. Correlations can be positive or negative and range from 0 (no statistical relationship) to 1 (a perfect statistical relationship). Picture a spreadsheet with two columns of numbers. One column contains the total numbers of social recognition behaviors for all 21 restaurants; the other contains the average drive-through times for those same 21 restaurants. The best way to get a feel for the correlation is to look at a scatterplot—a graph made from those two columns of numbers. Figure 1-4 presents three scatterplots, each depicting different-sized correlations. The strength of the correlation can be inferred from the "compactness" of its scatterplot. Panel (a) shows a perfect 1.0 correlation; knowing the score for social recognition allows you to predict the score for drive-through times perfectly. Panel (b) shows a correlation of .50, so the trend in the data is less obvious than in Panel (a) but still easy to see with the naked eye. Finally, Panel (c) shows a correlation of .00—no statistical relationship. Understanding the correlation is important because OB questions are not "yes or no" in nature. That is, the question is not "*Does* social recognition lead to higher job performance?" but rather "*How often* does social recognition lead to higher job performance?" The correlation provides a number that expresses an answer to the "how often" question.

So what is the correlation between social recognition and job performance (and between social recognition and organizational commitment)? It turns out that a study very similar to the one described was actually conducted, using a sample of 21 Burger King restaurants with 525 total employees.[24] The correlation between social recognition and job performance was .28. The restaurants that received training in social recognition averaged 44 seconds of drive-through time nine months later versus 62 seconds for the control group locations. The correlation between social recognition and retention rates was .20. The restaurants that received training in social recognition had a 16 percent better retention rate than the control group locations nine months later. The study also instituted a financial "pay-for-performance" system in a subset of the locations and found that the social recognition effects were just as strong as the financial effects.

Of course, you might wonder whether correlations of .28 or .20 are impressive or unimpressive. To understand those numbers, let's consider some context for them. Table 1-4 provides some notable correlations from other areas of science. If the correlation between height and weight is

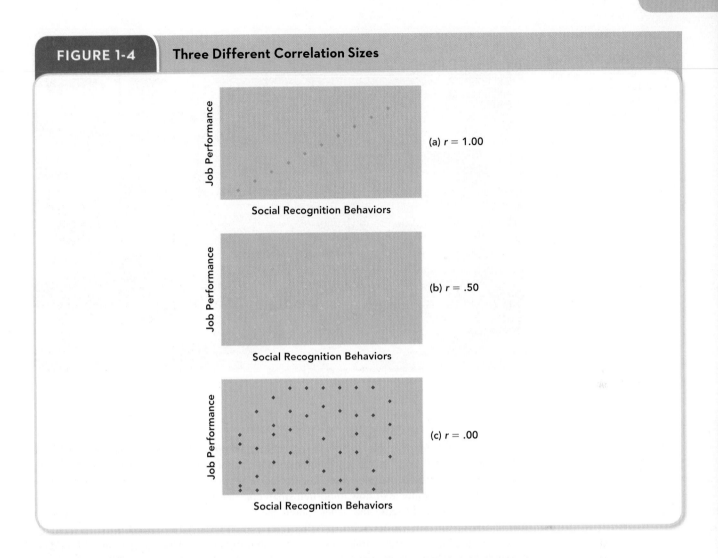

FIGURE 1-4 **Three Different Correlation Sizes**

(a) $r = 1.00$

(b) $r = .50$

(c) $r = .00$

TABLE 1-4 **Some Notable Correlations**

CORRELATION BETWEEN . . .	r	SAMPLE SIZE
Height and weight	.44	16,948
Ibuprofen and pain reduction	.14	8,488
Antihistamines and reduced sneezing	.11	1,023
Smoking and lung cancer within 25 years	.08	3,956
Coronary bypass surgery and 5-year survival	.08	2,649

Source: From Robert Hogan. "In Defense of Personality Measurement: New Wine for Old Whiners." *Human Performance,* Vol. 18, 2005, pp. 331–41.

only .44, then a correlation of .28 between social recognition and job performance doesn't sound too bad! In fact, a correlation of .50 is considered "strong" in organizational behavior research, given the sheer number of things that can affect how employees feel and act.[25] A .30 correlation is considered "moderate," and many studies discussed in this book will have results in this range.

A study of Burger King restaurants revealed a correlation between social recognition—praise and appreciation by managers—and employees' performance and commitment. Such studies contribute to the growing body of organizational behavior knowledge.

© *Wilfredo Lee/AP Images*

Finally, a .10 correlation is considered "weak" in organizational behavior research. It should be noted, however, that even "weak" correlations can be important if they predict costly behaviors such as theft or ethical violations. The .08 correlation between smoking and lung cancer within 25 years is a good example of how important small correlations can be.

Does this one study settle the debate about the value of social recognition for job performance and organizational commitment? Not really, for a variety of reasons. First, it included only 21 restaurants with 525 employees—maybe the results would have turned out differently if the study had included more locations. Second, it focused only on restaurant employees—maybe there's something unique about such employees that makes them particularly responsive to social recognition. Third, it may be that the trained locations differed from the control locations on something *other than* social recognition, and it was that "something" that was responsible for the performance differences. You may have heard the phrase, "correlation does not imply causation." It turns out that making **causal inferences**—establishing that one variable really does cause another—requires establishing three things.[26] First, that the two variables are correlated. Second, that the presumed cause precedes the presumed effect in time. Third, that no alternative explanation exists for the correlation. The third criterion is often fulfilled in experiments, where researchers have more control over the setting in which the study occurs.

The important point is that little can be learned from a single study. The best way to test a theory is to conduct many studies, each of which is as different as possible from the ones that preceded it.[27] So if you really wanted to study the effects of social recognition, you would conduct several studies using different kinds of samples, different kinds of measures, and both experimental and nonexperimental methods. After completing all of those studies, you could look back on the results and create some sort of average correlation across all of the studies. This process is what a technique called **meta-analysis** does. It takes all of the correlations found in studies of a particular relationship and calculates a weighted average (such that correlations based on studies with large samples are weighted more than correlations based on studies with small samples). It turns out that a meta-analysis has been conducted on the effects of social recognition and job performance. That analysis revealed an average correlation of .21 across studies conducted in 96 different organizations in the service industry.[28] That meta-analysis offers more compelling support for the potential benefits of social recognition than the methods of experience, intuition, or authority could have provided.

Indeed, meta-analyses can form the foundation for **evidence-based management**—a perspective that argues that scientific findings should form the foundation for management education, much as they do for medical education.[29] Proponents of evidence-based management argue that human resources should be transformed into a sort of R&D department for managing people.[30] Notes one advocate, "In R&D, you go into the laboratory, you experiment and you keep up with the research that others do . . . . Can you imagine walking into the R&D lab at a pharmaceutical company, asking the chief chemist about an important new study and having him respond that they don't keep up with the literature on chemistry?" Verizon Business, the Basking Ridge, New Jersey–based unit of Verizon Communications, is one example of a company that is moving toward evidence-based management. The company notes that the dollars spent on human resources issues demand more than an intuition-based justification for new plans. More informed decisions come from running systematic experiments in smaller units of an organization, making greater use of internal data, hiring PhDs with relevant expertise, and pursuing collaborations with academics. Such practices form the foundation for the use of **analytics** as a tool for management, with analytics defined as the use of data (rather than just opinion) to guide decision making.[31] For a look at how analytics is used in the world of sports, see our **OB on Screen** feature, which appears in each chapter and uses well-known movies to demonstrate OB concepts.

SUMMARY: MOVING FORWARD IN THIS BOOK

The chapters that follow will begin working through the integrative model of OB in Figure 1-1, beginning with the individual outcomes and continuing with the individual, group, and organizational mechanisms that lead to those outcomes. Each chapter begins by spotlighting a company that historically has done a good job of managing a given topic or is currently struggling with a topic. Theories relevant to that topic will be highlighted and discussed. The concepts in those theories will be demonstrated in the **OB on Screen** features to show how OB phenomena have "come to life" in film. The **OB at the Bookstore** feature will then point you to bestsellers that discuss similar concepts. In addition, the **OB Internationally** feature will describe how those concepts operate differently in different cultures and nations.

Each chapter ends with three sections. The first section provides a summarizing theory diagram that explains why some employees exhibit higher levels of a given concept than others. For example, the summarizing theory diagram for Chapter 4 will explain why some employees are more satisfied with their jobs than others. As we noted in the opening of this chapter, knowledge about *why* is critical to any employee who is trying to make sense of his or her working life or any manager who is trying to make his or her unit more effective. How often have you spent time trying to explain your own attitudes and behaviors to yourself? If you consider yourself to be an introspective person, you've probably thought about such questions quite a bit. Our **OB Assessments** feature will help you find out how reflective you really are. This feature also appears in each chapter of the textbook and allows you to gain valuable knowledge about your own personality, abilities, job attitudes, and leadership styles.

The next concluding section will describe the results of meta-analyses that summarize the relationships between that chapter's topic and both job performance and organizational commitment. Over time, you'll gain a feel for which of the topics in Figure 1-1 have strong, moderate, or weak relationships with these outcomes. This knowledge will help you recognize how everything in OB fits together and what the most valuable tools are for improving performance and commitment in the workplace. As you will discover, some of the topics in OB have a greater impact on how well employees perform their jobs, whereas others have a greater impact on how long employees remain with their organizations. Finally, the third concluding section will describe how the content of that chapter can be applied, at a specific level, in an

OB ON SCREEN

This feature is designed to illustrate OB concepts in action on the silver screen. Once you've learned about OB topics, you'll see them playing out all around you, especially in movies.

MONEYBALL

You don't put a team together with a computer, Billy. . . . Baseball isn't just numbers; it's not science. If it was, then anybody could do what we're doing. But they can't because they don't know what we know. They don't have our experience and they don't have our intuition.

With those words, Grady Fuson (Ken Medlock) tries to show Billy Beane (Brad Pitt) the error of his ways in *Moneyball* (Dir. Bennett Miller, Columbia Pictures, 2011). Billy is the general manager of the Oakland Athletics (A's). After losing to the New York Yankees in the playoffs, Billy's been forced to trim a payroll that is already a third of what the Yankees pay. To the angst of his head scout Grady, Billy turns to Pete Brand, aka "Google boy," a recent hire with a degree in economics from Yale. Pete is well versed in "sabermetrics"—the scientific search for objective baseball knowledge begun by Bill James, with a nod to the Society for American Baseball Research (SABR).

© Columbia Pictures/Photofest

The film, based on the Michael Lewis bestseller,[32] shows how science can complement experience and intuition. For example, Pete's advanced analytics showed that "on-base percentage"—a statistic dependent not just on hits but also on walks—was a more valid indicator of a player's value than the home runs emphasized by traditional scouts. Ironically, the success of *Moneyball* caused a number of baseball teams to hire "sabermetricians," erasing some of the advantages that Billy's approach had given Oakland.[33] Indeed, the use of advanced analytics has taken hold in other professional sports, most notably the National Basketball Association.[34] Hopefully evidence-based management will allow organizational managers to do what sports managers are doing—test their theories of success with data.

actual organization. For example, the motivation chapter concludes with a section describing how compensation practices can be used to maximize employee effort. If you're currently working, we hope that these concluding sections will help you see how the concepts you're reading about can be used to improve your own organizations. Even if you're not working, these application sections will give you a glimpse into how you will experience OB concepts once you begin your working life.

OB ASSESSMENTS

This feature is designed to illustrate how OB concepts actually get measured in practice. In many cases, these OB assessments will provide you with potentially valuable insights into your own attitudes, skills, and personality. The OB assessments that you'll see in each chapter consist of multiple survey items. Two concepts are critical when evaluating how good the OB assessments are: *reliability* and *validity*. Reliability is defined as the degree to which the survey items are free from random error. If survey items are reliable, then similar items will yield similar answers. Validity is defined as the degree to which the survey items seem to assess what they are meant to assess. If survey items are valid, then experts on the subject will agree that the items seem appropriate.

INTROSPECTION

How introspective are you? This assessment is designed to measure introspection—sometimes termed "private self-consciousness"—which is the tendency to direct attention inward to better understand your attitudes and behaviors. Answer each question using the response scale provided. Then subtract your answers to the boldfaced questions from 4, with the difference being your new answers for those questions. For example, if your original answer for question 5 was "3," your new answer is 1 (4 − 3). Then sum your answers for the 10 questions. (Instructors: Assessments on scientific interests and methods of knowing can be found in the PowerPoints in the Connect Library's Instructor Resources and in the Connect assignments for this chapter).

0	1	2	3	4
EXTREMELY UNCHARACTERISTIC OF ME	SOMEWHAT UNCHARACTERISTIC OF ME	NEUTRAL	SOMEWHAT CHARACTERISTIC OF ME	EXTREMELY CHARACTERISTIC OF ME

1. I'm always trying to figure myself out. _____

2. Generally, I'm not very aware of myself. _____

3. I reflect about myself a lot. _____

4. I'm often the subject of my own daydreams. _____

5. I never scrutinize myself. _____

6. I'm generally attentive to my inner feelings. _____

7. I'm constantly examining my motives. _____

8. I sometimes have the feeling that I'm off somewhere watching myself. _____

9. I'm alert to changes in my mood. _____

10. I'm aware of the way my mind works when I work through a problem. _____

SCORING AND INTERPRETATION

If your scores sum up to 26 or above, you do a lot of introspection and are highly self-aware. You may find that many of the theories discussed in this textbook will help you better understand your attitudes and feelings about working life.

Source: From A. Fenigstein, M.F. Scheier, and A.H. Buss, "Public and Private Self-Consciousness: Assessment and Theory," *Journal of Consulting and Clinical Psychology,* Vol. 43, August 1975, pp. 522–27. Copyright © 1975 by the American Psychological Association. Adapted with permission. No further reproduction or distribution is permitted without written permission from the American Psychological Association.

TAKEAWAYS

1.1 Organizational behavior is a field of study devoted to understanding and explaining the attitudes and behaviors of individuals and groups in organizations. More simply, it focuses on *why* individuals and groups in organizations act the way they do.

1.2 The two primary outcomes in organizational behavior are job performance and organizational commitment.

1.3 A number of factors affect performance and commitment, including individual mechanisms (job satisfaction; stress; motivation; trust, justice, and ethics; learning and decision making), individual characteristics (personality and cultural values; ability), group mechanisms (team characteristics and diversity; team processes and communication; leader power and negotiation; leader styles and behaviors), and organizational mechanisms (organizational structure; organizational culture).

1.4 The effective management of organizational behavior can help a company become more profitable because good people are a valuable resource. Not only are good people rare, but they are also hard to imitate. They create a history that cannot be bought or copied, they make numerous small decisions that cannot be observed by competitors, and they create socially complex resources such as culture, teamwork, trust, and reputation.

1.5 A theory is a collection of assertions, both verbal and symbolic, that specifies how and why variables are related, as well as the conditions in which they should (and should not) be related. Theories about organizational behavior are built from a combination of interviews, observation, research reviews, and reflection. Theories form the beginning point for the scientific method and inspire hypotheses that can be tested with data.

1.6 A correlation is a statistic that expresses the strength of a relationship between two variables (ranging from 0 to ± 1). In OB research, a .50 correlation is considered "strong," a .30 correlation is considered "moderate," and a .10 correlation is considered "weak."

KEY TERMS

- Organizational behavior (OB)   *p. 6*
- Human resource management   *p. 7*
- Strategic management   *p. 7*
- Resource-based view   *p. 11*
- Inimitable   *p. 12*
- History   *p. 12*
- Numerous small decisions   *p. 13*
- Socially complex resources   *p. 13*
- Rule of One-Eighth   *p. 15*
- Method of experience   *p. 16*
- Method of intuition   *p. 16*
- Method of authority   *p. 17*
- Method of science   *p. 17*
- Theory   *p. 17*
- Hypotheses   *p. 18*
- Correlation   *p. 18*
- Causal inference   *p. 20*
- Meta-analysis   *p. 20*
- Evidence-based management   *p. 21*
- Analytics   *p. 21*

DISCUSSION QUESTIONS

1.1 Assuming you possessed the right technical skills, would a job at Google be appealing to you? What would be the most important positives associated with the position, in your view? What would be the most important negatives?

1.2   Think again about the worst coworker you've ever had—the one who did some of the things listed in Table 1-1. Think about what that coworker's boss did (or didn't do) to try to improve his or her behavior. What did the boss do well or poorly? What would you have done differently, and which organizational behavior topics would have been most relevant?

1.3   Which of the individual mechanisms in Figure 1-1 (job satisfaction; stress; motivation; trust, justice, and ethics; learning and decision making) seems to drive your performance and commitment the most? Do you think you're unique in that regard, or do you think most people would answer that way?

1.4   Create a list of the most successful companies that you can think of. What do these companies have that others don't? Are the things that those companies possess rare and inimitable (see Figure 1-2)? What makes those things difficult to copy?

1.5   Think of something that you "know" to be true based on the method of experience, the method of intuition, or the method of authority. Could you test your knowledge using the method of science? How would you do it?

CASE: GOOGLE

Assume you were working in People Operations for a company that didn't always see the value in managerial roles—to the point where it once experimented with getting rid of them! Let's further assume that this company did see the value in data—in numbers that could be used to test arguments. What would you do? At Google, they launched a study to prove that management mattered. It was called Project Oxygen, so named because good managers could be "breaths of fresh air" that are crucial to a company's survival. It was launched by the PiLab within Google's People Analytics team. As the study began, one of the lab's members noted, "We knew the team had to be careful. Google has high standards of proof, even for what, at other places, might be considered obvious truths. Simple correlations weren't going to be enough."

How did Project Oxygen go about the task of proving that managers mattered? One approach they took was separating managers into high- and low-scoring groups. They used two tools to do so: the performance evaluation ratings of the managers by their bosses and data from the Googlegeist employee attitude survey. Once the high- and low-scoring groups were created, the team compared them on several important variables of interest. The results showed that employees working for high-scoring managers had more job satisfaction, lower turnover rates, and better job performance than employees working for low-scoring managers. Indeed, those differences remained apparent even when statistically controlling for the seniority, rank, and performance of the employees. One lab member summarized, "It turned out that the smallest incremental increases in manager quality were quite powerful. Good managers *do* matter."

Prasad Setty, Google's vice president of People Analytics, argues that the use of analytics must move from description to analysis and insight to prediction. So, with the knowledge in hand that managers mattered at Google, what was the next step for Project Oxygen and the PiLab team? Using that awareness to nurture better managers at Google, the team conducted "double-blind" interviews with the high- and low-scoring managers, meaning that the interviewers were not aware of which group the managers were in and the managers were not aware of the focus of the study. The carefully constructed interview scripts were meant to uncover a set of behaviors that united the best managers in the company. The study resulted in the so-called "Oxygen 8" behaviors of great managers: empowering, coaching, expressing a vision, showing concern for well-being, being results-oriented, focusing on career development, being an effective communicator, and possessing key technical skills. Soon the tools used to evaluate leaders were reorganized around the Oxygen 8, with training seminars devised to help improve performance on them. The team also organized panel discussions with high-scoring managers from all functional groups. As one member explained, "We realized that engineers don't necessarily want to hear about management from people in HR. But they are willing to listen to engineering managers whom they respect."

1.1   If you set out to prove that "managers matter" in a company, how would you do it? What data would you want to gather, and what would you look for in those data?

1.2   What do you think of the Oxygen 8 behaviors? Does it surprise you that those eight were the most vital in an organization like Google? Which would you view as most important and why?

1.3   Consider the skepticism that some engineers seem to feel about management at Google. How common do you think that attitude is in today's organizations? What can be done to combat such attitudes?

Sources: L. Bock, *Work Rules! Insights from Inside Google that Will Transform How You Live and Lead,* New York: Twelve, 2015; J. Colvin, "Personal Bests," *Fortune,* March 3, 2015; D.A. Garvin, "How Google Sold Its Engineers on Management," *Harvard Business Review,* December, 2013; D.A. Garvin, "Google's Project Oxygen: Do Managers Matter?" *Harvard Business School Case* 9-313-110, October 15, 2013; M. Moskowitz and R. Levering, "The 100 Best Companies," *Fortune,* March 15, 2015.

EXERCISE: IS OB COMMON SENSE?

The purpose of this exercise is to take some of the topics covered in this textbook and examine whether improving them is "just common sense." This exercise uses groups, so your instructor will either assign you to a group or ask you to create your own. The exercise has the following steps:

1.1   Consider the theory diagram shown below. It explains why two "independent variables" (the quality of a movie's script and the fame of its stars) affect a "dependent variable" (how much the movie makes at the box office).

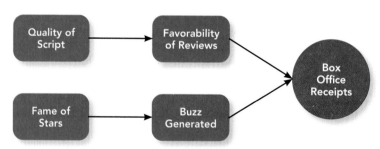

1.2   Now build your own theory diagram about organizational behavior. In your groups, choose one of the following four topics to use as your dependent variable:

- *Job satisfaction:* The pleasurable emotions felt when performing job tasks.
- *Strain:* The headaches, fatigue, or burnout resulting from workplace stress.
- *Motivation:* The intensity and persistence of job-related effort.
- *Trust in supervisor:* The willingness to allow a supervisor to have significant influence over key job issues.

Using a transparency, laptop, whiteboard, or chalkboard, build a theory diagram that summarizes the factors that affect your chosen dependent variable. To be as comprehensive as possible, try to include at least four independent variables. Keep your books closed! You should build your diagrams using only your own experience and intuition.

1.3   Each group should present its theory diagram to the class. Do the predicted relationships make sense? Should anything be dropped? Should anything be added?

1.4   Now compare the theory diagram you created with the diagrams in the textbook (Figure 4-7 for Job Satisfaction, Figure 5-3 for Strain, Figure 6-7 for Motivation, and Figure 7-7 for Trust in Supervisor). How does your diagram compare to the textbook's diagrams? (Search the bold-faced key terms for any jargon that you don't understand.) Did you leave out some important independent variables or suggest some variables that have not been supported by the academic research summarized in the chapters? If so, it shows that OB is more than just common sense.

ENDNOTES

1.1   Kiley, D. "Hyundai Still Gets No Respect." *BusinessWeek,* May 21, 2007, pp. 68–70.

1.2   Ihlwan, M., and C. Dawson. "Building a 'Camry Fighter': Can Hyundai Transform Itself into One of the World's Top Auto Makers?" *BusinessWeek,* September 6, 2004, http://www.businessweek.com/magazine/content/04_36/b3898072.htm.

1.3   ConsumerReports.org. "Top Picks," (n.d.), http://www.consumerreports.org/cro/cars/new-cars/cr-recommended/top-picks/overview/top-picks-ov.htm.

1.4   Taylor, A. III. "Hyundai Smokes the Competition." *Fortune,* January 18, 2010, pp. 62–71.

1.5   Taylor. "Hyundai Smokes the Competition." Ihlwan, M.; L. Armstrong; and M. Eldam. "Kissing Clunkers Goodbye." *BusinessWeek,* May 17, 2004, http://www.businessweek.com/magazine/content/04_20/b3883054.htm.

1.6   Barney, J.B. "Looking Inside for Competitive Advantage." In *Strategic Human Resource Management,* ed. R.S. Schuler and S.E. Jackson. Malden, MA: Blackwell, 1999, pp. 128–41.

1.7   McIntyre, D.A. "Microsoft Launches Retail Stores to Save Windows." *Time,* February 13, 2009, http://www.time.com/time/business/article/0,8599,1879368,00.html.

1.8   Edwards, C. "Commentary: Sorry, Steve: Here's Why Apple Stores Won't Work." *BusinessWeek,* May 21, 2001, http://www.businessweek.com/magazine/content/01_21/b3733059.htm.

1.9   Frommer, D. "Microsoft's New Retail Stores Look Just Like Apple Stores." *Business Insider,* November 1, 2009, http://www.businessinsider.com/microsofts-new-retail-stores-look-just-like-apple-stores-2009-11.

1.10   Hansen, F. "Admirable Qualities." *Workforce Management,* June 23, 2008, pp. 25–32.

1.11   Tkaczyk, C. "The World's Most Admired Companies." *Fortune,* March 1, 2015.

1.12   Huselid, M.A. "The Impact of Human Resource Management Practice on Turnover, Productivity, and Corporate Financial Performance." *Academy of Management Journal* 38 (1995), pp. 635–72.

1.13   Welbourne, T.M., and A.O. Andrews. "Predicting the Performance of Initial Public Offerings: Should Human Resource Management Be in the Equation?" *Academy of Management Journal* 39 (1996), pp. 891–919.

1.14   Levering, R., and M. Moskowitz. "And the Winners Are" *Fortune,* February 2, 2009, pp. 67–78.

1.15   Fulmer, I.S.; B. Gerhart; and K.S. Scott. "Are the 100 Best Better? An Empirical Investigation of the Relationship Between Being a 'Great Place to Work' and Firm

Performance." *Personnel Psychology* 56 (2003), pp. 965–93.

1.16 Pfeffer, J., and J.F. Veiga. "Putting People First for Organizational Success." *Academy of Management Executive* 13 (1999), pp. 37–48.

1.17 Kerlinger, F.N., and H.B. Lee. *Foundations of Behavioral Research.* Fort Worth, TX: Harcourt, 2000.

1.18 Bacon, F.; M. Silverthorne; and L. Jardine. *The New Organon.* Cambridge: Cambridge University Press, 2000.

1.19 Campbell, J.P. "The Role of Theory in Industrial and Organizational Psychology." In *Handbook of Industrial and Organizational Psychology,* Vol. 1, edited by, M.D. Dunnette and L.M. Hough. Palo Alto, CA: Consulting Psychologists Press, 1990, pp. 39–74.

1.20 Whetten, D.A. "What Constitutes a Theoretical Contribution?" *Academy of Management Review* 14 (1989), pp. 490–95.

1.21 Locke, K. "The Grounded Theory Approach to Qualitative Research." In *Measuring and Analyzing Behavior in Organizations,* ed. F. Drasgow and N. Schmitt. San Francisco, CA: Jossey-Bass, 2002, pp. 17–43.

1.22 Locke, E.A., and G.P. Latham. "What Should We Do About Motivation Theory? Six Recommendations for the Twenty-First Century." *Academy of Management Review* 29 (2004), 388–403.

1.23 Herzberg, F.; B. Mausner; and B.B. Snyderman. *The Motivation to Work.* New York: John Wiley, 1959; Taylor, F. W. *The Principles of Scientific Management.* New York: Harper & Row, 1911.

1.24 Peterson, S.J., and F. Luthans. "The Impact of Financial and Nonfinancial Incentives on Business-Unit Outcomes over Time." *Journal of Applied Psychology* 91 (2006), pp. 156–65.

1.25 Cohen, J.; P. Cohen; S.G. West; and L.S. Aiken. *Applied Multiple Regression/Correlation Analysis for the Behavioral Sciences.* Mahwah, NJ: Erlbaum, 2003.

1.26 Shadish, W.R.; T.D. Cook; and D.T. Campbell. *Experimental and Quasi-Experimental Designs for Generalized Causal Inference.* Boston, MA: Houghton Mifflin, 2002.

1.27 Ibid.

1.28 Stajkovic, A.D., and F. Luthans. "A Meta-Analysis of the Effects of Organizational Behavior Modification on Task Performance,

1975–1995." *Academy of Management Journal* 40 (1997), pp. 1122–49.

1.29 Rousseau, D.M.; J. Manning; and D. Denyer. "Evidence in Management and Organizational Science: Assembling the Field's Full Eight of Scientific Knowledge Through Syntheses." *Academy of Management Annals* 2 (2008), pp. 475–515; Briner, R.B.; D. Denyer; and D.M. Rousseau. "Evidence-Based Management: Concept Cleanup Time?" *Academy of Management Perspectives* 23 (2009), pp. 19–32.

1.30 Hansen, F. "Merit-Pay Payoff?" *Workforce Management,* November 3, 2008, pp. 33–39.

1.31 Davenport, T.H. "Analytics 3.0." Harvard Business Review, December, 2013.

1.32 Lewis, M. *Moneyball.* New York: Norton, 2003.

1.33 Fox, J. "The Moneyball Myth." *Bloomberg Businessweek,* October 20, 2011, pp. 110–11.

1.34 Schwartz, J. "Net Loss." *Slate,* February 28, 2013, http:// www.slate.com/ articles/sports/ sports_nut/2013/02/ nba_stats_gurus_ can_t_work_together_ anymore_that_s_a_ problem.html.

chapter 2

Job Performance

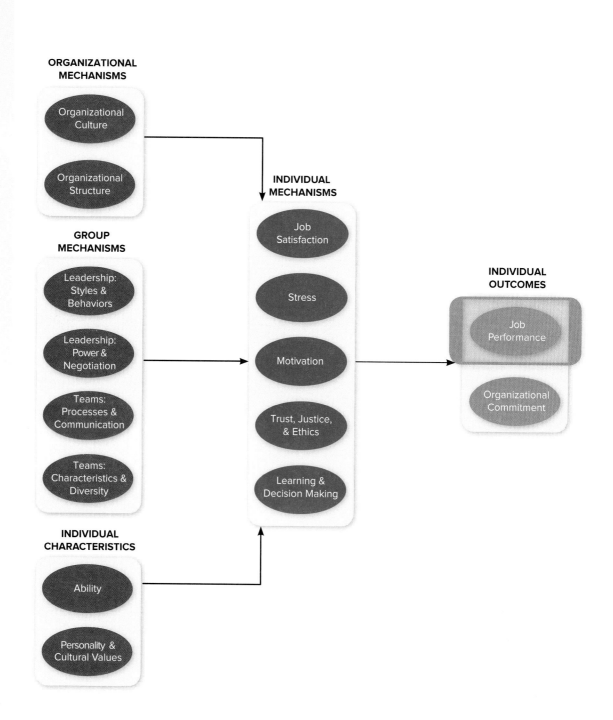

ORGANIZATIONAL MECHANISMS

- Organizational Culture
- Organizational Structure

GROUP MECHANISMS

- Leadership: Styles & Behaviors
- Leadership: Power & Negotiation
- Teams: Processes & Communication
- Teams: Characteristics & Diversity

INDIVIDUAL CHARACTERISTICS

- Ability
- Personality & Cultural Values

INDIVIDUAL MECHANISMS

- Job Satisfaction
- Stress
- Motivation
- Trust, Justice, & Ethics
- Learning & Decision Making

INDIVIDUAL OUTCOMES

- Job Performance
- Organizational Commitment

© John Moore/Getty Images

☑ LEARNING GOALS

After reading this chapter, you should be able to answer the following questions:

2.1 What is job performance?

2.2 What is task performance?

2.3 How do organizations identify the behaviors that underlie task performance?

2.4 What is citizenship behavior?

2.5 What is counterproductive behavior?

2.6 What workplace trends are affecting job performance in today's organizations?

2.7 How can organizations use job performance information to manage employee performance?

JPMORGAN CHASE

JPMorgan Chase is one of the oldest financial institutions in the United States. Its roots go back to the late 1700s when Arron Burr and Alexander Hamilton established a company to supply fresh water to the inhabitants of Lower Manhattan. Burr inserted creative language in the company's charter, allowing him to use the company's excess capital to start a commercial bank in 1799. This bank, called The Bank of the Manhattan Co., was the only competitor to a bank Alexander Hamilton founded 15 years earlier. If you're a history buff you may already know that the two became antagonistic, and that, in addition to serving as Thomas Jefferson's vice president for one term, Burr also killed Hamilton in a duel in 1804.

Over the next 200 years, hundreds of mergers resulted in today's JPMorgan Chase. Most relevant to the company's namesake was the merger of The Bank of the Manhattan Co. and Chase National Bank in 1955, and then the merger of this company—called The Chase Manhattan Group—and J.P. Morgan and Co. in 2000. Today, with assets of $2.6 trillion and operations in 60 countries, the company's 240,000 employees must perform their jobs effectively to serve customers in investment banking, consumer financial services, small business and commercial banks, financial transaction processing, asset management, and private equity.

So what does effective job performance mean for employees of JPMorgan Chase? Obviously the answer depends a great deal on the specific job in question. Whereas the job performance of an investment banker may depend on the amount of money a client company makes on an initial public offering, the job performance of a customer service representative may depend on whether concerns of customers are resolved quickly. There are also general aspects of job performance that are determined by the company's business practices. Across jobs at JPMorgan Chase, employees need to be cooperative and have a customer focus, an entrepreneurial spirit and discipline. Finally, the company has recently had costly legal and regulatory problems and has responded to these challenges, in part, by emphasizing ways in which employees contribute negatively to the company. Accordingly, effective job performance at JPMorgan Chase means that employees must not only perform their core job duties well and engage in activities that support the company's way of doing business, but they must also refrain from engaging in behaviors that violate company policies and regulations.

JOB PERFORMANCE

We begin our journey through the integrative model of organizational behavior with job performance. Why begin with job performance? Because understanding one's own performance is a critical concern for any employee, and understanding the performance of employees in one's unit is a critical concern for any manager. Consider for a moment the job performance of your university's basketball coach. If you were the university's athletic director, you might gauge the coach's performance by paying attention to various behaviors. How much time does the coach spend on the road during recruiting season? How effective are the coach's practices? Are the offensive and defensive schemes well designed, and are the plays called during games appropriate? You might also consider some other behaviors that fall outside the strict domain of basketball. Does the coach run a clean program? Do players graduate on time? Does the coach represent the university well during interviews with the media and when in public?

Of course, as your university's athletic director, you might be tempted to ask a simpler question: Is the coach a winner? After all, fans and boosters may not care how good the coach is at the previously listed behaviors if the team fails to win conference championships or make it deep into the NCAA tournament. Moreover, the coach's performance in terms of wins and losses has important implications for the university because it affects ticket sales, licensing fees, and booster donations. Still, is every unsuccessful season the coach's fault? What if the coach develops a well-conceived game plan but the players repeatedly make mistakes at key times in the game? What if the team experiences a rash of injuries or inherits a schedule that turns out to be much tougher than originally thought? What if a few games during the season are decided by fluke baskets or by bad calls by the referees?

This example illustrates one dilemma when examining job performance. Is performance a set of behaviors that a person does (or does not) perform, or is performance the end result of those behaviors? You might be tempted to believe it's more appropriate to define performance in terms of results rather than behaviors. This is because results seem more "objective" and are more connected to the central concern of managers—"the bottom line." For example, the job performance of salespeople is often measured by the amount of sales revenue generated by each person over some time span (e.g., a month, a quarter, a year). For the most part, this logic makes perfect sense: Salespeople are hired by organizations to generate sales, and so those who meet or exceed sales goals are worth more to the organization and should be considered high performers. It's very easy to appreciate how the sales revenue from each salesperson might be added up and used as an indicator of a business's financial performance.

However, as sensible as this logic seems, using results to indicate job performance creates potential problems. First, employees contribute to their organization in ways that go beyond bottom-line results, and so evaluating an employee's performance based on results alone might give you an inaccurate picture of which employees are worth more to the organization. Second, there is evidence that managers' focus on bottom line results can create a bottom line mentality among employees, which in turn, results in social undermining—sabotaging coworkers' reputations or trying to make them look bad.[1] Similarly, as our opening example illustrates, the quest to enhance the bottom line of JPMorgan Chase may have led employees to violate policies and regulations, which in turn, cost the company billions of dollars. Third, results are often influenced by factors that are beyond the employees' control—product quality, competition, equipment, technology, budget constraints, coworkers, and supervisors, just to name a few. Fourth, even if these uncontrollable factors are less relevant in a given situation, there's another problem with a results-based view of job performance: results don't tell you how to reverse a "bad year." That is, performance feedback based on results doesn't provide people with the information they need to improve their behavior. Walgreens, for example, uses knowledge of job performance behaviors to create comprehensive training and development programs so that employees can be effective at various jobs they may have throughout their careers with the company.[2] In sum, given that the field of OB aims to understand, predict, and improve behavior, we refer to job performance as behavior. We use the term "results" or "job performance results" to describe the important outcomes that are associated with those behaviors.

So what types of employee behaviors constitute job performance? To understand this question, consider that **job performance** is formally defined as the value of the set of employee behaviors that contribute, either positively or negatively, to organizational goal accomplishment.[3] This definition of job performance includes behaviors that are within the control of employees, but it places a boundary on which behaviors are (and are not) relevant to job performance. For example, consider the behavior of a server in a restaurant that prides itself on world-class customer service. Texting a friend during a work break would not usually be relevant (in either a positive or negative sense) to the accomplishment of organizational goals. That behavior is therefore not relevant to the server's job performance. However, texting in the middle of taking a customer's order would be relevant (in a negative sense) to organizational goal accomplishment. That behavior, therefore, is relevant to the server's job performance.

2.1

What is job performance?

© *Mike Carlson/Getty Images*

Geno Auriemma has led the University of Connecticut women's basketball team to ten national championships, five perfect seasons, and 100 percent graduation rate for all four-year players. He's been the Naismith College Coach of the Year six times since taking over the team in 1985. If the Huskies suffered through a couple losing seasons, would Coach Auriemma be considered a low performer?

WHAT DOES IT MEAN TO BE A "GOOD PERFORMER"?

Our definition of job performance raises a number of important questions. Specifically, you might be wondering which employee behaviors fall under the umbrella heading of "job performance." In other words, what exactly do you have to *do* to be a "good performer"? We could probably spend an entire chapter just listing various behaviors that are relevant to job performance. However, those behaviors generally fit into three broad categories.[4] Two categories are *task performance* and *citizenship behavior*, both of which contribute positively to the organization. The third category is *counterproductive behavior*, which contributes negatively to the organization. The sections that follow describe these broad categories of job performance in greater detail.

TASK PERFORMANCE

Task performance includes employee behaviors that are directly involved in the transformation of organizational resources into the goods or services that the organization produces.[5] If you read a description of a job in an employment ad online, that description will focus on task performance behaviors—the tasks, duties, and responsibilities that are a core part of the job. Put differently, task performance is the set of explicit obligations that an employee must fulfill to receive compensation and continued employment. For a flight attendant, task performance includes announcing and demonstrating safety and emergency procedures and distributing food and beverages to passengers. For a firefighter, task performance includes searching burning buildings to locate fire victims and operating equipment to put out fires. For an accountant, task performance involves preparing, examining, and analyzing accounting records for accuracy and completeness. Finally, for an advertising executive, task performance includes developing advertising campaigns and preparing and delivering presentations to clients.[6]

2.2

What is task performance?

Although the specific activities that constitute task performance differ widely from one job to another, task performance also can be understood in terms of more general categories. One way of categorizing task performance is to consider the extent to which the context of the job is routine, changing, or requires a novel or unique solution. **Routine task performance** involves well-known responses to demands that occur in a normal, routine, or otherwise predictable way. In these cases, employees tend to behave in more or less habitual or programmed ways that vary little from one instance to another.[7] As an example of a routine task activity, you may recall watching an expressionless flight attendant robotically demonstrate how to insert the seatbelt tongue into the seatbelt buckle before your flight takes off. Seatbelts haven't really changed since … oh … 1920, so the instructions to passengers tend to be conveyed the same way, over and over again.

In contrast, **adaptive task performance,** or more commonly "adaptability," involves employee responses to task demands that are novel, unusual, or, at the very least, unpredictable.[8] For example, on August 2, 2005, Air France Flight 358, carrying 297 passengers and 12 crew members from Paris, France, to Toronto, Canada, skidded off the runway while landing and plunged into a ravine. Amid smoke and flames, the flight attendants quickly responded to the emergency and assisted three-quarters of the 297 passengers safely off the plane within 52 seconds, before the emergency response team arrived. One minute later, the remaining passengers and 12 crew members were out safely.[9] From this example, you can see that flight attendants' task performance shifted from activities such as providing safety demonstrations and handing out beverages to performing emergency procedures to save passengers' lives. Although flight attendants receive training so they can handle emergency situations such as this one, executing these behaviors effectively in the context of an actual emergency differs fundamentally from anything experienced previously.

Adaptive behaviors are becoming increasingly important as globalization, technological advances, and knowledge-based work increase the pace of change in the workplace.[10] In fact, adaptive task performance has become crucial in today's global economy where companies have been faced with the challenge of becoming more productive with fewer employees on staff. For example, Sheboygan Falls, Wisconsin–based Johnsonville Sausage feels that adaptability is important for employees at all levels of the organization and has invested significant resources in training to ensure that employees develop competency in this aspect of job performance.[11] As another example, at the German chemical and pharmaceutical company Bayer, the hiring of plant directors involves the search for candidates who not only possess a wide range of skills and abilities so that they can adapt to various job demands, but in addition, competence in helping others adapt to changes that occur in the workplace.[12] Table 2-1 provides a number of examples of adaptability that are relevant to many jobs in today's economy.[13]

Finally, **creative task performance** is the degree to which individuals develop ideas or physical outcomes that are both novel and useful.[14] The necessity of including both novelty and usefulness in the definition of creativity can be illustrated with the following example of what effective performance for a swimsuit designer involves. Consider first the case of a swimsuit designer who suggests in a meeting that next season's line of swimsuits should be made entirely out of chrome-plated steel. Although this idea might be very novel, for many reasons it's not likely to be very useful. Indeed, someone who offered an idea like this would likely be considered silly rather than creative. Another swimsuit designer suggests in the meeting that swimsuits for next season should be made out of materials that are attractive and comfortable. Although

TABLE 2-1	**Behaviors Involved in Adaptability**
BEHAVIORS	**SPECIFIC EXAMPLES**
Handling emergencies or crisis situations	Quickly analyzing options for dealing with danger or crises and their implications; making split-second decisions based on clear and focused thinking
Handling work stress	Remaining composed and cool when faced with difficult circumstances or a highly demanding workload or schedule; acting as a calming and settling influence to whom others can look for guidance
Solving problems creatively	Turning problems upside-down and inside-out to find fresh new approaches; integrating seemingly unrelated information and developing creative solutions
Dealing with uncertain and unpredictable work situations	Readily and easily changing gears in response to unpredictable or unexpected events and circumstances; effectively adjusting plans, goals, actions, or priorities to deal with changing situations
Learning work tasks, technologies, and work situations	Quickly and proficiently learning new methods or how to perform previously unlearned tasks; anticipating change in the work demands and searching for and participating in assignments or training to prepare for these changes
Demonstrating interpersonal adaptability	Being flexible and open-minded when dealing with others; listening to and considering others' viewpoints and opinions and altering one's own opinion when it's appropriate to do so
Demonstrating cultural adaptability	Willingly adjusting behavior or appearance as necessary to comply with or show respect for others' values and customs; understanding the implications of one's actions and adjusting one's approach to maintain positive relationships with other groups, organizations, or cultures

Source: E.E. Pulakos, S. Arad, M.A. Donovan, and K.E. Plamondon, "Adaptability in the Workplace: Development of a Taxonomy of Adaptive Performance," *Journal of Applied Psychology* 85 (2000), pp. 612–24. Copyright © 2004 by the American Psychological Association. Adapted with permission. No further reproduction or distribution is permitted without permission from the American Psychological Association.

under some circumstances such an idea might be useful, the idea is not novel because attractiveness and comfort are generally accepted design elements for swimsuits. Someone who offered an idea like this might be appreciated for offering input, but no one would consider this individual's performance to be particularly creative. Finally, a third designer for this swimsuit manufacturer suggests that perhaps a two-piece design would be preferred for women, rather than a more traditional one-piece design. Although such an idea would not be considered creative today, it certainly was in 1946 when, in separate but nearly simultaneous efforts, Jacques Heim and Louis Reard introduced the bikini.[15]

Although you might be tempted to believe that creative task performance is only relevant to jobs such as artist and inventor, its emphasis has been increasing across a wide variety of jobs. Indeed, more than half the total wages and salary in the United States are paid to employees who need to be creative as part of their jobs, and as a consequence, some have argued that we are at the "dawn of the creative age."[16] This increase in the value of creative performance can be explained by the rapid technological change and intense competition that mark today's business landscape.[17] In this context, employee creativity is necessary to spark the types of innovations that enable organizations to stay ahead of their competition. Creative ideas do not always get implemented, thus it is important to recognize creative performance behaviors, as well as the creative outcomes that result from those behaviors.[18]

Now that we've given you a general understanding of task performance behaviors, you might be wondering how organizations identify the sets of behaviors that represent "task performance" for different jobs. Many organizations identify task performance behaviors by conducting a **job analysis**. Although there are many different ways to conduct a job analysis, most boil down to three steps. First, a list of the activities involved in a job is generated. This list generally results from data from several sources, including observations, surveys, and interviews of employees. Second, each activity on this list is rated by "subject matter experts," according to things like the importance and frequency of the activity. Subject matter experts generally have experience performing the job or managing the job and therefore are in a position to judge the importance of specific activities to the organization. Third, the activities that are rated highly in terms of their importance and frequency are retained and used to define task performance. Those retained behaviors then find their way into training programs as learning objectives and into performance evaluation systems as measures to evaluate task performance.

As an example, to determine training objectives for production workers, Toyota uses a highly detailed job analysis process to identify important tasks as well as the behaviors necessary to effectively complete those tasks.[19] The core job tasks involved in the job of a bumper-molding operator, for example, include "routine core tasks," "machine tending," and "quality," and each of these tasks further consists of several more detailed steps. For example, routine core tasks include de-molding, trimming, spray-molding, and sanding. Each of these tasks can be broken down further into more detailed steps, and in turn, the specific behaviors involved in each step become the focus of the training. For example, to de-mold the left side of the bumper, the worker must "use left thumb to push along edge of bumper," "place pressure in the crease of thumb," "push toward left side away from mold," and "grasp top edge when bumper is released." Although this level of detail might seem like an awful lot of analysis for what one might imagine to be a relatively straightforward job, Toyota competes on the basis of quality and cost, and its success in selling millions of Priuses, Camrys, Tacomas, and Highlanders each year has been attributed to its ability to train production workers to follow the standardized and efficient procedures.[20]

2.3

How do organizations identify the behaviors that underlie task performance?

Toyota production workers assemble vehicles using a highly standardized and efficient set of tasks.

© Eric Gay/AP Images

Men's Wearhouse, the Houston-based retailer, provides another good example of an organization that uses task performance information to manage its employees.[21] The company first gathers information about the employee's on-the-job behaviors. For example, the job of wardrobe consultant involves greeting, interviewing and measuring customers properly, ensuring proper alteration revenue is collected, and treating customers in a warm and caring manner. After the information is gathered, senior managers provide feedback and coaching to the employee about which types of behaviors he or she needs to change to improve. The feedback is framed as constructive criticism meant to improve an employee's behavior. Put yourself in the place of a Men's Wearhouse wardrobe consultant for a moment. Wouldn't you rather have your performance evaluated on the basis of behaviors such as these rather than some overall index of sales? After all, those behaviors are completely within your control, and the feedback you receive from your boss will be more informative than the simple directive to "sell more suits next year than you did this year."

If organizations find it impractical to use job analysis to identify the set of behaviors needed to define task performance, they can turn to a database the government has created to help with that important activity. The **Occupational Information Network** (or **O*NET**) is an online database that includes, among other things, the characteristics of most jobs in terms of tasks, behaviors, and the required knowledge, skills, and abilities (http://www.onetonline.org). Figure 2-1 shows the O*NET output for a flight attendant's position, including many of the tasks discussed previously in this chapter. Of course, O*NET represents only a first step in figuring out the important tasks for a given job. Many organizations ask their employees to perform tasks that their competitors do not, so their workforce performs in a unique and valuable way. O*NET cannot capture those sorts of unique task requirements that separate the most effective organizations from their competitors.

For example, the authors of a book titled *Nuts* identify "fun" as one of the dominant values of Southwest Airlines.[22] Southwest believes that people are willing to work more productively and creatively in an environment that includes humor and laughter. Consistent with this belief, flight

FIGURE 2-1	O*NET Results for Flight Attendants

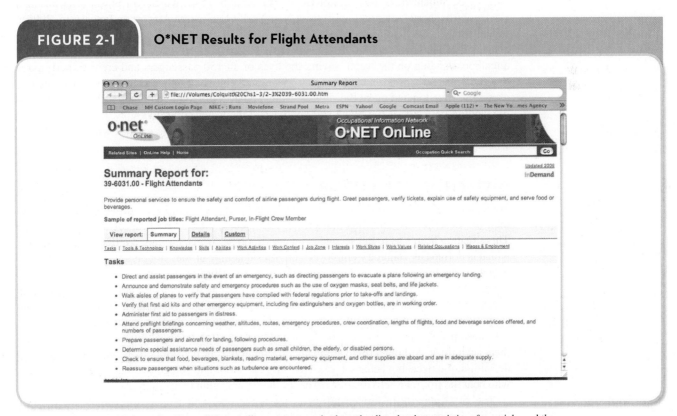

O*NET, or Occupational Information Network, is an online government database that lists the characteristics of most jobs and the knowledge required for each. This sample is for the job of flight attendant.

The pilot of Flight 1549 displayed exceptional performance and saved the lives of his passengers and crew.

© Steven Day/AP Images

attendant task performance at Southwest includes not only generic flight attendant activities, such as those identified by O*NET, but also activities that reflect a sense of humor and playfulness. Effective flight attendants at Southwest tell jokes over the intercom such as, "We'll be dimming the lights in the cabin . . . pushing the light-bulb button will turn your reading light on. However, pushing the flight attendant button will not turn your flight attendant on."[23] As another example, Nisshinbo Automotive, a part of the Japanese company Nisshinbo Holdings, was faced with the challenge of increasing productivity with fewer workers. They developed a system where they not only evaluated and compensated employees for behaviors reflected in their job descriptions, but also in behaviors that supported the company's mission defined more broadly.[24] In summary, though O*NET may be a good place to start, the task information from the database should be supplemented with information regarding behaviors that support the organization's values and strategy.

Before concluding our section on task performance, it's important to note that task performance behaviors are not simply performed or not performed. Although poor performers often fail to complete required behaviors, it's just as true that the star performers often exceed all expectations for those behaviors.[25] In fact, you can probably think of examples of employees who have engaged in task performance that's truly extraordinary. As an example, consider the case of Chesley B. Sullenberger, the pilot of US Airways Flight 1549, which lost power after hitting a flock of birds shortly after taking off from New York's LaGuardia Airport on January 15, 2009.[26] Sullenberger calmly discussed the problem with air traffic control and decided that the only course of action was to land in the Hudson River. Three minutes after the bird strike, he executed a textbook landing on the water, saving the lives of all 150 passengers and crew. Experts agree that Sullenberger's performance that day was remarkable. Not only did Sullenberger accurately assess the situation and make the right decision about where to ditch the aircraft, he also piloted the landing perfectly. If the plane had approached the water going too slow, it would have lost lift and crashed into the water nose first; if the plane had been going too fast when it touched, it would have flipped, cart-wheeled, and disintegrated.[27]

CITIZENSHIP BEHAVIOR

Sometimes employees go the extra mile by actually engaging in behaviors that are not within their job description—and thus that do not fall under the broad heading of task performance. This situation brings us to the second category of job performance, called **citizenship behavior**, which is defined as voluntary employee activities that may or may not be rewarded but that contribute to the organization by improving the overall quality of the setting in which work takes place.[28] Have you ever had a coworker or fellow student who was especially willing to help someone who was struggling? Who typically attended optional meetings or social functions to support his or her colleagues? Who maintained a good attitude, even in trying times? We tend to call those people "good citizens" or "good soldiers."[29] High levels of citizenship behavior earn them such titles. Although there are many different types of behaviors that might seem to fit the definition of citizenship behavior, research suggests two main categories that differ according to who benefits from the activity: coworkers or the organization (see Figure 2-2).[30]

The first category of citizenship behavior is the one with which you're most likely to be familiar: **interpersonal citizenship behavior**. Such behaviors benefit coworkers and colleagues and involve assisting, supporting, and developing other organizational members in a way that

2.4

What is citizenship behavior?

FIGURE 2-2 | Types of Citizenship Behaviors

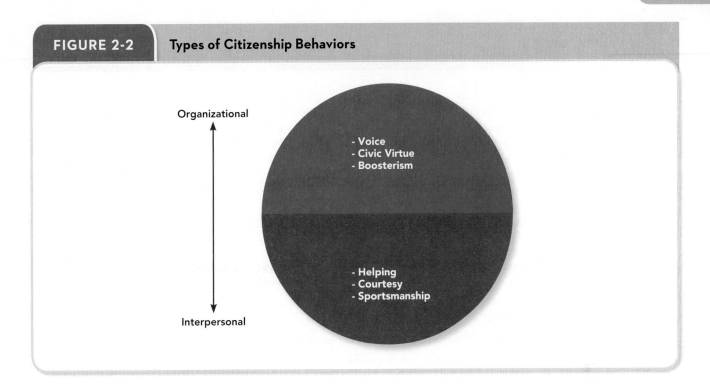

goes beyond normal job expectations.[31] For example, **helping** involves assisting coworkers who have heavy workloads, aiding them with personal matters, and showing new employees the ropes when they first arrive on the job. Do you consider yourself a helpful person? Check the **OB Assessments** feature to see how helpful you really are. **Courtesy** refers to keeping coworkers informed about matters that are relevant to them. Some employees have a tendency to keep relevant facts and events secret. Good citizens do the opposite; they keep others in the loop because they never know what information might be useful to someone else. **Sportsmanship** involves maintaining a good attitude with coworkers, even when they've done something annoying or when the unit is going through tough times. Whining and complaining are contagious; good citizens avoid being the squeaky wheel who frequently makes mountains out of molehills.

Although interpersonal citizenship behavior is important in many different job contexts, it may be even more important when employees work in small groups or teams. A team with members who tend to be helpful, respectful, and courteous is also likely to have a positive team atmosphere in which members trust one another. This type of situation is essential to foster the willingness of team members to work toward a common team goal rather than goals that may be more self-serving.[32] In fact, if you think about the behaviors that commonly fall under the "teamwork" heading, you'll probably agree that most are examples of interpersonal citizenship behavior (see Chapter 12 on team processes and communication for more discussion of such issues).[33]

The second category of citizenship behavior is **organizational citizenship behavior**. These behaviors benefit the larger organization by supporting and defending the company, working to improve its operations, and being especially loyal to it.[34] For example, **voice** involves speaking up and offering constructive suggestions for change.[35] Good citizens react to bad rules or policies by constructively trying to change them as opposed to passively complaining about them (see Chapter 3 on organizational commitment for more discussion of such issues).[36] **Civic virtue** refers to participating in the company's operations at a deeper-than-normal level by attending voluntary meetings and functions, reading and keeping up with organizational announcements, and keeping abreast of business news that affects the company. **Boosterism** means representing the organization in a positive way when out in public, away from the office, and away from work. Think of friends you've had who worked for a restaurant. Did they always say good things about the restaurant when talking to you and keep any "kitchen horror stories" to themselves? If so, they were being good citizens by engaging in high levels of boosterism.

OB ASSESSMENTS

HELPING

How helpful are you? This assessment is designed to measure helping, an interpersonal form of citizenship behavior. Think of the people you work with most frequently, either at school or at work. The questions below refer to these people as your "work group." Answer each question using the scale below, then sum up your answers. (Instructors: Assessments on sportsmanship, boosterism, political deviance, and trait creativity can be found in the PowerPoints in the Connect Library's Instructor Resources and in the Connect assignments for this chapter).

1 STRONGLY DISAGREE	2 MODERATELY DISAGREE	3 SLIGHTLY DISAGREE	4 NEITHER DISAGREE NOR AGREE	5 SLIGHTLY AGREE	6 MODERATELY AGREE	7 STRONGLY AGREE

1. I volunteer to do things for my work group. _____

2. I help orient new members of my work group. _____

3. I attend functions that help my work group. _____

4. I assist others in my group with their work for the benefit of the group. _____

5. I get involved to benefit my work group. _____

6. I help others in this group learn about the work. _____

7. I help others in this group with their work responsibilities. _____

SCORING AND INTERPRETATION

If your scores sum up to 40 or higher, you perform a high level of helping behavior, which means you frequently engage in citizenship behaviors directed at your colleagues. This is good, as long as it doesn't distract you from fulfilling your own job duties and responsibilities. If your scores sum up to less than 40, you perform a low level of helping behaviors. You might consider paying more attention to whether your colleagues need assistance while working on their task duties.

Source: L.V. Van Dyne and J.A. LePine, "Helping and Voice Extra-Role Behaviors: Evidence of Construct and Predictive Validity," *Academy of Management Journal* 41 (1998), pp. 108–19.

Three important points should be emphasized about citizenship behaviors. First, as you've probably realized, citizenship behaviors are relevant in virtually any job, regardless of the particular nature of its tasks,[37] and research suggests that these behaviors can boost organizational effectiveness.[38] As examples, research conducted in a paper mill found that the quantity and quality of crew output was higher in crews that included more workers who engaged in citizenship behavior.[39] Research in 30 restaurants also showed that higher levels of citizenship behavior promoted higher revenue, better operating efficiency, higher customer satisfaction, higher performance quality, less food waste, and fewer customer complaints.[40] Thus, it seems clear that citizenship behaviors have a significant influence on the bottom line.

Second, because citizenship behaviors are relatively discretionary and influenced by the specific situation the employee is working in, they can vary significantly over time.[41] In other words, an employee who engages in citizenship behavior during one point in time might not engage in citizenship behavior at other points in time. As an example, it's likely that you've had a very positive experience working with another student or colleague on a project and were willing to invest a great deal of extra effort in order to be helpful. At some point, however, the person with whom you were working may have done something that made you feel much less positive about the collaboration and, as a consequence, you decided to withhold your extra help so that you could focus your energies elsewhere.

Third, from an employee's perspective, it may be tempting to discount the importance of citizenship behaviors—to just focus on your own job tasks and leave aside any "extra" stuff. After all, citizenship behaviors appear to be voluntary and optional, whereas task performance requirements are not. However, discounting citizenship behaviors is a bad idea because supervisors don't always view such actions as optional. In fact, research on computer salespeople, insurance agents, petrochemical salespeople, pharmaceutical sales managers, office furniture makers, sewing machine operators, U.S. Air Force mechanics, and first-tour U.S. Army soldiers has shown that citizenship behaviors relate strongly to supervisor evaluations of job performance, even when differences in task performance are also considered.[42] As we discuss in our **OB Internationally** feature, the tendency of supervisors to consider citizenship behaviors in evaluating overall job performance appears to hold even across countries with vastly different cultures.[43] Of course, this issue has a lot of relevance to you, given that in most organizations, supervisors' evaluations of employee job performance play significant roles in determining employee pay and promotions. Indeed, employee citizenship behavior has been found to influence the salary and promotion recommendations people receive, over and above their task performance.[44] Put simply, it pays to be a good citizen.

COUNTERPRODUCTIVE BEHAVIOR

Now we move from the "good soldiers" to the "bad apples." Whereas task performance and citizenship behavior refer to employee activities that help the organization achieve its goals and objectives, other activities in which employees engage do just the opposite. This third broad category of job performance is **counterproductive behavior**, defined as employee behaviors that intentionally hinder organizational goal accomplishment. The word "intentionally" is a key aspect of this definition; these are things that employees mean to do, not things they accidentally do. Although there are many different kinds of counterproductive behaviors, research suggests that—like task performance and citizenship behavior—they can be grouped into more specific categories (see Figure 2-3).[45]

Property deviance refers to behaviors that harm the organization's assets and possessions. For example, **sabotage** represents the purposeful destruction of physical equipment, organizational processes, or company products. Do you know what a laser disc is? Probably not—and the reason you don't is because of sabotage. A company called DiscoVision (a subsidiary of MCA) manufactured laser discs in the late 1970s, with popular movie titles like *Smokey and the Bandit* and *Jaws* retailing for $15.95. Although this price is approximately the same as a new movie on a Blu-ray disc today, it was far less than the $50–$100 needed to buy videocassettes (which were of inferior quality) at the time. Unfortunately, laser discs had to be manufactured in clean rooms because specs of dust or debris could cause the image on the television to freeze, repeat, skip, or drop out. When MCA merged with IBM in 1979, the morale of the employees fell, and counterproductive behaviors began to occur. Employees sabotaged the devices that measured the cleanliness of the rooms. They also began eating in the rooms—even popping potato chip bags to send food particles into the air. This sabotage eventually created a 90 percent disc failure rate that completely alienated customers. As a result, despite its much lower production costs and higher-quality picture, the laser disc disappeared, and the organizations that supported the technology suffered incredible losses.[46]

Even if you've never heard of the laser disc, you've certainly eaten in a restaurant. The cost of counterproductive behaviors in the restaurant industry is estimated to be 2–3 percent of revenues per year, but what may be more disturbing is the nature of those counterproductive behaviors.[47] Thirty-one percent of employees who responded to a survey knowingly served improperly prepared food, 13 percent intentionally sabotaged the work of other employees, and 12 percent admitted to intentionally contaminating food they prepared or served to a customer (yuck!). At

2.5

What is counterproductive behavior?

OB INTERNATIONALLY

As we've already explained, citizenship behavior tends to be viewed as relatively voluntary because it's not often explicitly outlined in job descriptions or directly rewarded. However, people in organizations vary in their beliefs regarding the degree to which citizenship behavior is truly voluntary, and these differences have important implications. As an example, consider a situation in which an employee engages in citizenship behaviors because of his or her belief that the behaviors are part of the job. However, this employee works for a supervisor who believes that citizenship behaviors are unnecessary. Assuming that the supervisor would not consider the citizenship behaviors on a performance evaluation, the employee would likely react negatively because he or she has not been recognized for putting effort into activities that help other members of the organization.

So what types of factors cause differences in beliefs regarding whether or not citizenship behavior is discretionary? One factor that would appear to be important is national culture. It is widely believed that the culture in countries like the United States, Canada, and the Netherlands encourages behaviors that support competition and individual achievement, whereas the culture in countries like China, Colombia, and Portugal encourages behaviors that promote cooperation and group interests over self-interests. On the basis of these cultural differences, it seems logical to expect that people from the former set of countries would consider citizenship behavior relatively unimportant compared with people from the latter set of countries. In reality, however, the findings from one recent study comparing Canadian and Chinese managers found that this cultural stereotype was simply not true. Managers in both countries not only took citizenship behavior into account when evaluating overall job performance, but the weight they gave to citizenship behavior in their overall evaluation of employees was the same. One explanation for this result is that the realities of running effective business organizations in a global economy have a significantly stronger impact on managerial practices than do cultural norms. It is important to note that the results of this study do not mean that we can ignore culture when trying to understand employee job performance. In fact, there are reasons to believe that cultural differences are important to consider when designing and implementing systems to manage employee performance.

Sources: F.F.T. Chiang and T.A. Birtch, "Appraising Performance across Borders: An Empirical Examination of the Purposes and Practices of Performance Appraisal in a Multi-Country Context." *Journal of Management Studies* 47 (2010), pp. 1365–92; G. Hofstede, *Cultures and Organizations: Software of the Mind.* New York: McGraw-Hill, 1991; E. W. Morrison, "Role Definitions and Organizational Citizenship Behavior: The Importance of the Employee's Perspective." *Academy of Management Journal* 37 (1994), pp. 1543–67. M. Rotundo, and J.L. Xie, "Understanding the Domain of Counterproductive Work Behavior in China." *International Journal of Human Resource Management* 86 (2008), pp. 856–77.

a minimum, such sabotage of the restaurant's product can lead to a bad meal and a customer's promise to never return to that establishment. Of course, such behaviors can also lead to food poisoning, health code violations, and a damaging lawsuit. Employees who sabotage customers may do so, under certain circumstances, as a response to perceived mistreatment by customers. It's important to note, however, that retaliation in this manner is not justified, so it's still considered a form of counterproductive behavior.[48]

Theft represents another form of property deviance and can be just as expensive as sabotage (if not more). Research has shown that up to three-quarters of all employees have engaged in counterproductive behaviors such as theft, and the cost of these behaviors is staggering.[49] For example, one study estimated that 47 percent of store inventory shrinkage was due to employee theft and that this type of theft costs organizations approximately $14.6 billion per year.[50] Maybe

FIGURE 2-3 | Types of Counterproductive Behaviors

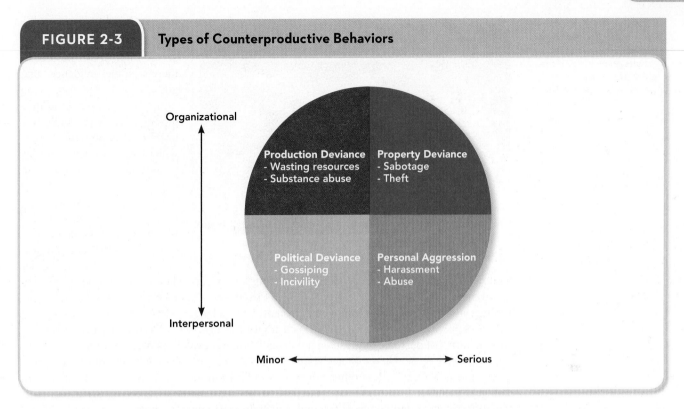

Source: Adapted from S.L. Robinson and R.J. Bennett, "A Typology of Deviant Workplace Behaviors: A Multidimensional Scaling Study," *Academy of Management Journal* 38 (1995), pp. 555–72.

you've had friends who worked at a restaurant or bar and been lucky enough to get discounted (or even free) food and drinks whenever you wanted. Clearly that circumstance is productive for you, but it's quite counterproductive from the perspective of the organization.

Production deviance is also directed against the organization but focuses specifically on reducing the efficiency of work output. **Wasting resources,** when employees use too many materials or too much time to do too little work, is the most common form of production deviance. Manufacturing employees who use too much wood or metal are wasting resources as are restaurant employees who use too many ingredients when preparing the food. Workers who work too slowly or take too many breaks are also wasting resources because "time is money" (see Chapter 3 on organizational commitment for more discussion of such issues). **Substance abuse** represents another form of production deviance. If employees abuse drugs or alcohol while on the job or shortly before coming to work, then the efficiency of their production will be compromised because their work will be done more slowly and less accurately.

In contrast to property and production deviance, **political deviance** refers to behaviors that intentionally disadvantage other individuals rather than the larger organization. **Gossiping**—casual conversations about other people in which the facts are not confirmed as true—is one form of political deviance. Everyone has experienced gossip at some point in time and knows the emotions people feel when they discover that other people have been talking about them. Such behaviors undermine the morale of both friendship groups and work groups. **Incivility** represents communication that's rude, impolite, discourteous, and lacking in good manners.[51] The erosion of manners seems like a society-wide phenomenon, and the workplace is no exception. Taken one by one, these political forms of counterproductive behavior may not seem particularly serious to most organizations. However, in the aggregate, acts of political deviance can create an organizational climate characterized by distrust and unhealthy competitiveness. Beyond the productivity losses that result from a lack of cooperation among employees,

Counterproductive behavior by employees can be destructive to the organization's goals. In some settings, such as a restaurant, it can even be a problem for customers.

© Frank Wartenberg/Picture Press/Getty Images

organizations with this type of climate likely cannot retain good employees. Moreover, there's some evidence that gossip and incivility can "spiral"—meaning that they gradually get worse and worse until some tipping point, after which more serious forms of interpersonal actions can occur.[52]

Those more serious interpersonal actions may involve **personal aggression,** defined as hostile verbal and physical actions directed toward other employees. **Harassment** falls under this heading and occurs when employees are subjected to unwanted physical contact or verbal remarks from a colleague. **Abuse** also falls under this heading; it occurs when an employee is assaulted or endangered in such a way that physical and psychological injuries may occur. You might be surprised to know that even the most extreme forms of personal aggression are actually quite prevalent in organizations. For example, on average in the United States about one employee each week is murdered by a current or previous coworker.[53] As another example, about 54 million Americans are bullied at work each year.[54] Bullying involves psychological harassment and abuse directed toward an individual or group of individuals.[55] Examples of bullying include humiliation, social isolation, and systematic maltreatment, all of which results in the target of these behaviors feeling helpless.[56] It might surprise you to learn that the source of the bullying is often a boss. We don't believe that bosses are inherently evil, but some undoubtedly lose sight of the line between being tough and being a bully, and that what matters isn't the intent of the behavior, but rather the perception of the person to whom the behavior is targeted.[57] Acts of personal aggression can also be quite costly to organizations. For example, Mitsubishi Motor Manufacturing of America settled a class action sexual harassment lawsuit for $34 million after women at a plant in Normal, Illinois, complained of widespread and routine groping, fondling, lewd jokes, lewd behavior, and pornographic graffiti.[58]

Four points should be noted about counterproductive behavior. First, there's evidence that people who engage in one form of counterproductive behavior also engage in others.[59] In other words, such behaviors tend to represent a pattern of behavior rather than isolated incidents. Second, like citizenship behavior, counterproductive behavior is relevant to any job. It doesn't matter what the job entails; there are going to be things to steal, resources to waste, and people to be uncivil toward. Third, counterproductive behavior may be contagious. For example, researchers have found evidence that abusive behavior on the part of supervisors may result in organizational deviance of subordinates and vise versa.[60] Fourth, it's often surprising which employees engage in counterproductive behavior. You might be tempted to guess that poor performers would be the ones who engage in high levels of counterproductive behavior, and that highly effective task performers do not engage in counterproductive behavior. In fact, however, there's only a weak negative correlation between task performance and counterproductive behavior,[61] and if you think about it for a moment, you can probably come up with a few examples of people who are very effective in their jobs but who also engage in high levels of counterproductive behavior. Sometimes the best task performers are the ones who can best get away with counterproductive actions, because they're less likely to be suspected or blamed. Moreover, counterproductive behaviors might even be tolerated for a while where the individual is able to effectively accomplish very challenging tasks. Our **OB on Screen** feature illustrates an example of this apparent contradiction in behavior.

OB ON SCREEN

FLIGHT

The FAA and the NTSB took 10 pilots, placed them in simulators, re-created the events that led to this plane falling out of the sky. Do you know how many of them were able to safely land the planes? Not one. Every pilot crashed the aircraft, killed everybody on board. You were the only one who could do it!

With those words, South Jet Air attorney Hugh Lang (Don Cheadle) tells Captain Whip Whitaker (Denzel Washington) that his performance as a pilot is extraordinary in the movie *Flight* (Dir. Robert Zemeckis, Paramount Pictures, 2012). On a trip from Orlando to Atlanta, the aircraft Whip was flying malfunctioned, and to get the plane out of an uncontrollable dive, Whip managed to invert it and fly it this way, eventually rolling it upright just before crash-landing in a field. Normally, a pilot who performs such a feat, and who saves the lives of most of his passengers and crew, would be considered a hero. But there's a hitch. You see, Whip not only consumed copious amounts of alcohol and drugs before flying, but he actually mixed himself a strong cocktail *while* flying. Although Whip had nothing to do with the equipment malfunction, and in spite of his heroics, responsibility for the crash and for the six deaths that resulted would likely rest with him and his employer if investigators found out about his condition.

© Paramount Pictures/Photofest

The movie centers on a dichotomy in Whip's job performance. On the one hand, he's remarkably competent in the activities involved in flying a jet. In fact, to the extent that the equipment malfunction was totally unforeseen and required altogether new responses to cope with the situation, Whip is particularly strong in the adaptive performance aspect of task performance. On the other hand, substance abuse is considered to be a form of counterproductive behavior. This contrast in positive and negative job performance behaviors should serve as a reminder that it's a mistake to presume that employees are effective or ineffective in their jobs based on how well they do in one aspect of job performance, however visible this aspect of job performance may be.

SUMMARY: WHAT DOES IT MEAN TO BE A "GOOD PERFORMER"?

So what does it mean to be a "good performer"? As shown in Figure 2-4, being a good performer means a lot of different things. It means employees are good at the particular job tasks that fall within their job description, whether those tasks are routine or require adaptability or

---

FIGURE 2-4   What Does It Mean to Be a "Good Performer"?

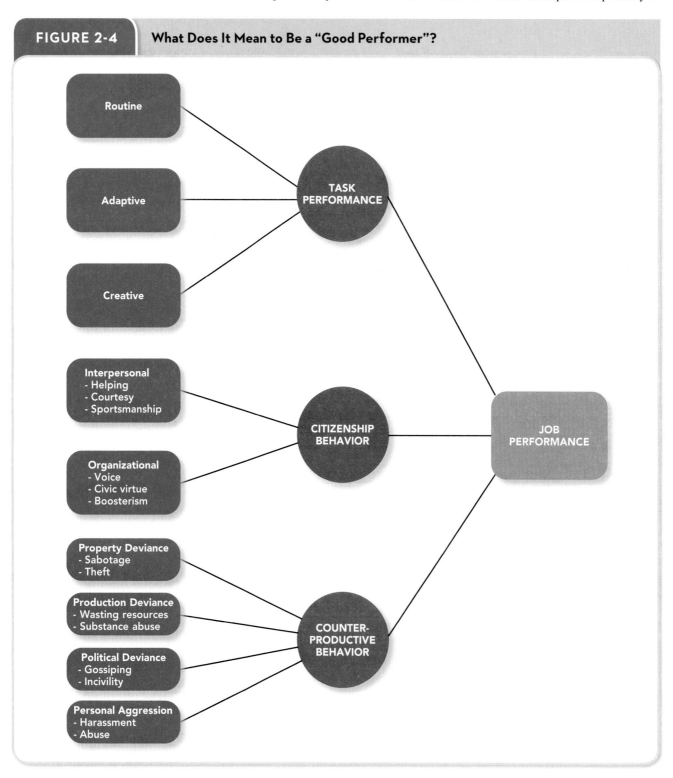

creativity. But it also means that employees engage in citizenship behaviors directed at both coworkers and the larger organization. It also means that employees refrain from engaging in the counterproductive behaviors that can badly damage the climate of an organization. The goal for any manager is, therefore, to have employees who fulfill all three pieces of this good performer description.

As you move forward in this book, you'll notice that almost every chapter includes a description of how that chapter's topic relates to job performance. For example, Chapter 4 on job satisfaction will describe how employees' feelings about their jobs affect their job performance. You'll find that some chapter topics seem more strongly correlated with task performance, whereas other topics are more strongly correlated with citizenship behavior or counterproductive behavior. Such differences will help you understand exactly how and why a given topic, be it satisfaction, stress, motivation, or something else, influences job performance. By the end of the book, you'll have developed a good sense of the most powerful drivers of job performance.

TRENDS AFFECTING PERFORMANCE

Now that we've described exactly what job performance is, it's time to describe some of the trends that affect job performance in the contemporary workplace. Put simply, the kinds of jobs employees do are changing, as is the way workers get organized within companies. These trends put pressure on some elements of job performance while altering the form and function of others.

KNOWLEDGE WORK

Historically speaking, research on organizational behavior has focused on the physical aspects of job performance. This focus was understandable, given that the U.S. economy was industrial in nature and the productivity of the employees who labored in plants and factories was of great concern. However, by the early 1990s, the majority of new jobs required employees to engage in cognitive work, applying theoretical and analytical knowledge acquired through formal education and continuous learning.[62] Today, statistics from the U.S. Department of Labor confirm that this type of work, also called **knowledge work,** is becoming more prevalent than jobs involving physical activity.[63]

 2.6

What workplace trends are affecting job performance in today's organizations?

In addition to being more cognitive, knowledge work tends to be more fluid and dynamic in nature. Facts, data, and information are always changing. Moreover, as time goes by, it becomes easier to access more and more of these facts and data, using Google on an iPhone for example. In addition, the tools used to do knowledge work change quickly, with software, databases, and computer systems updated more frequently than ever. As those tools become more powerful, the expectations for completing knowledge work become more ambitious. After all, shouldn't reports and presentations be more comprehensive and finished more quickly when every book used to create them is available online 24/7 rather than at some library? In fact, as many have recently noted, expectations regarding knowledge work can become overwhelming for employees, and as a consequence, new and innovative ways of performing this type of work may be necessary.[64]

SERVICE WORK

One of the largest and fastest growing sectors in the economy is not in industries that produce goods but rather in industries that provide services. **Service work,** or work that provides nontangible goods to customers through direct electronic, verbal, or physical interaction, accounts for approximately 55 percent of the economic activity in the United States,[65] and

Amazon CEO Jeff Bezos stresses the importance of customer service.

© *Marcus A. Donner/AP Images*

about 20 percent of the new jobs created are service jobs, trailing only professional services in terms of growth.[66] Retail salespersons, customer service representatives, and food service workers represent the bulk of that service job growth. By comparison, maintenance, repair, construction, and production jobs are projected to account for only 4–7 percent of new jobs over the next several years.

The increase in service jobs has a number of implications for job performance. For example, the costs of bad task performance are more immediate and more obvious. When customer service representatives do their job duties poorly, the customer is right there to notice. That failure can't be hidden behind the scenes or corrected by other employees chipping in before it's too late. In addition, service work contexts place a greater premium on high levels of citizenship behavior and low levels of counterproductive behavior. If service employees refuse to help one another or maintain good sportsmanship, or if they gossip and insult one another, those negative emotions get transmitted to the customer during the service encounter. Maintaining a positive work environment therefore becomes even more vital.

In fact, some very notable organizations compete successfully by placing special emphasis on the performance of people who do service work. Amazon, for example, believes that the best way to ensure that customers keep using its website to purchase merchandise is to ensure customers are satisfied with their experience, especially when a transaction goes wrong, such as if merchandise arrives broken or an order doesn't ship because the product is back ordered.[67] Amazon customer service employees receive a great deal of training so that they can provide timely and consistent responses to customers who have questions or problems. In fact, customer service is so important to Amazon that each and every employee, including CEO Jeff Bezos, spends two days a year answering customer service calls.[68] Apparently all this training has paid off: Amazon now ranks number one in customer service quality, scoring above companies such as The Ritz-Carlton and Lexus, which are famous for providing world-class customer service.[69]

APPLICATION: PERFORMANCE MANAGEMENT

2.7

How can organizations use job performance information to manage employee performance?

Now that we've described what job performance is, along with some of the workplace trends that affect it, it's time to discuss how organizations use job performance information. Good companies understand the linkage between employee job performance and organizational performance, and as a consequence they invest resources collecting information about employee performance so that it can be managed in a way that helps the organization achieve its mission. In this section, we describe general ways in which job performance information is used to manage employee performance. We spotlight four of the most representative practices: management by objectives, behaviorally anchored rating scales, 360-degree feedback, and forced ranking. We'll also discuss how social networking software is being used for performance management purposes in organizations.

MANAGEMENT BY OBJECTIVES

Management by objectives (MBO) is a management philosophy that bases an employee's evaluations on whether the employee achieves specific performance goals.[70] How does MBO work? Typically, an employee meets with his or her manager to develop a set of mutually agreed-upon objectives that are measurable and specific (see Chapter 6 on motivation for more discussion of such issues). In addition, the employee and the manager agree on the time period for achieving those objectives and the methods used to do so. An example of a performance objective for a line manager in a factory might be something like, "Reducing production waste by 35 percent within three months by developing and implementing new production procedures." Employee performance then can be gauged by referring to the degree to which the employee achieves results that are consistent with the objectives. If the line manager cuts production waste by 37 percent within three months, the manager's performance would be deemed effective, whereas if the manager only cuts production waste by 2 percent, his or her performance would be deemed ineffective. MBO is best suited for managing the performance of employees who work in contexts in which objective measures of performance can be quantified.

BEHAVIORALLY ANCHORED RATING SCALES

You might have noticed that MBO emphasizes the results of job performance as much as it does the performance behaviors themselves. In contrast, **behaviorally anchored rating scales (BARS)** measure performance by directly assessing job performance behaviors. The BARS approach uses "critical incidents"—short descriptions of effective and ineffective behaviors—to create a measure that can be used to evaluate employee performance. As an example of a BARS approach, consider the measure of task performance shown in Table 2-2, which focuses on the "planning, organizing, and scheduling" dimension of task performance for a manager.[71] The rater reads the behaviors on the far left column of the measure and matches actual observations of the behavior of the manager being rated to the corresponding level on the measure by placing a check in the blank.[72]

Typically, supervisors rate several performance dimensions using BARS and score an employee's overall job performance by taking the average value across all the dimensions. Because the critical incidents convey the precise kinds of behaviors that are effective and ineffective, feedback from BARS can help an employee develop and improve over time. That is, employees can develop an appreciation of the types of behaviors that would make them effective. Such information provides a nice complement to MBO, which is less capable of providing specific feedback about why an objective might have been missed.

360-DEGREE FEEDBACK

The **360-degree feedback** approach involves collecting performance information not just from the supervisor but from anyone else who might have firsthand knowledge about the employee's performance behaviors. These other sources of performance information typically include the employee's subordinates, peers, and customers. With the exception of the supervisor's ratings, the ratings are combined so that the raters can remain anonymous to the employee. Most 360-degree feedback systems also ask the employee to provide ratings of his or her own performance. The hope is that this 360-degree perspective will provide a more balanced and comprehensive examination of performance. By explicitly comparing self-provided ratings with the ratings obtained from others, employees can develop a better sense of how their performance may be deficient in the eyes of others and exactly where they need to focus their energies to improve.

Although the information from a 360-degree feedback system can be used to evaluate employees for administrative purposes such as raises or promotions, there are problems with that sort of application. First, because ratings vary across sources, there is the question of which source is most "correct." Even if multiple sources are taken into account in generating an overall performance score, it's often unclear how the information from the various sources should be weighted. Second, raters may give biased evaluations if they believe that the information will be used for compensation, as opposed to just skill development. Peers in particular may be unwilling to provide negative information if they believe it will harm the person being rated.

TABLE 2-2		BARS Example for "Planning, Organizing, and Scheduling"
RATING	**RATING**	**BEHAVIORAL ANCHORS**
[7]	Excellent	• Develops a comprehensive project plan, documents it well, obtains required approval, and distributes the plan to all concerned.
[6]	Very Good	• Plans, communicates, and observes milestones; states week by week where the project stands relative to plans. Maintains up-to-date charts of project accomplishment and backlogs and uses these to optimize any schedule modifications required. • Experiences occasional minor operational problems but communicates effectively.
[5]	Good	• Lays out all the parts of a job and schedules each part to beat schedule; will allow for slack. • Satisfies customer's time constraints; time and cost overruns occur infrequently.
[4]	Average	• Makes a list of due dates and revises them as the project progresses, usually adding unforeseen events; investigates frequent customer complaints. • May have a sound plan but does not keep track of milestones; does not report slippages in schedule or other problems as they occur.
[3]	Below Average	• Plans are poorly defined; unrealistic time schedules are common. • Cannot plan more than a day or two ahead; has no concept of a realistic project due date.
[2]	Very Poor	• Has no plan or schedule of work segments to be performed. • Does little or no planning for project assignments.
[1]	Unacceptable	• Seldom, if ever, completes project because of lack of planning and does not seem to care. • Fails consistently due to lack of planning and does not inquire about how to improve.

Source: D.G. Shaw, C.E. Schneier, and R.W. Beatty, "Managing Performance with a Behaviorally Based Appraisal System," in *Applying Psychology in Business: The Handbook for Managers and Human Resource Professionals,* ed. J.W. Jones, B.D. Steffy, and D.W. Bray (Lexington, MA: Lexington Books, 2001), pp. 314–25.

As a result, 360-degree feedback is best suited to improving or developing employee talent, especially if the feedback is accompanied by coaching about how to improve the areas identified as points of concern.

FORCED RANKING

One of the most notable strategies that Jack Welch, *Fortune*'s Manager of the 20th Century,[73] used to build a great workforce at General Electric involved evaluations that make clear distinctions among employees in terms of their job performance. Although Welch considered several systems that could differentiate employees, the most effective relied on the "vitality curve," depicted in Figure 2-5, which forces managers to rank all of their people into one of three categories: the top 20 percent (A players), the vital middle 70 percent (B players), or the bottom 10 percent (C players). The A players are thought to possess "the four Es of GE leadership: very high *energy* levels, the ability to *energize* others around common goals, the *edge* to make tough yes-and-no decisions, and finally the ability to consistently *execute* and deliver on their promises."[74] The

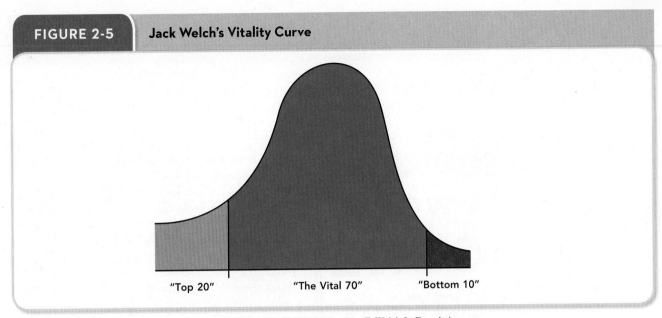

FIGURE 2-5 | **Jack Welch's Vitality Curve**

"Top 20"   "The Vital 70"   "Bottom 10"

Source: From *Jack* by Jack Welch with John A. Byrne. Copyright © 2001 by the John F. Welch Jr. Foundation.

B players are developed. According to Welch, B players are the backbone of the company but lack the passion of As. The C players are those who cannot get the job done and are let go. The system was taken so seriously at GE that managers who couldn't differentiate their people tended to find themselves in the C category.[75]

Today, approximately 20 percent of *Fortune* 500 companies use some variant of Welch's **forced ranking** system, which is popularly known as "rank and yank" or the "dead man's curve."[76] However, there are some important controversies to consider. For example, some believe the system is inherently unfair because it forces managers to give bad evaluations to employees who may be good performers, just to reach a preestablished percentage. As another example, employees may become hypercompetitive with one another to avoid finding themselves in a lower category. This type of competitiveness is the opposite of what may be needed in today's team-based organizations.

SOCIAL NETWORKING SYSTEMS

Most of you reading this book are familiar with social networking services such as Facebook and Twitter. Well, this technology has recently been applied in organizational contexts to develop and evaluate employee job performance.[77] As an example, Accenture uses a Facebook-styled program called "Performance Multiplier," which requires that employees post and update weekly and quarterly goals. Managers then monitor the information and provide feedback.[78] As another example, a Toronto-based software company called Rypple uses a Twitter-like program to enable employees to post questions about their own performance so that other employees can give them anonymous feedback.[79] Although the effectiveness of social networking applications for performance evaluation and employee development purposes has not been studied scientifically, there are some advantages that make us believe that they will grow in popularity. For example, these types of systems provide performance information that is much more timely, relative to traditional practices that measure performance quarterly or even yearly. Although it might be unpleasant to learn from your peers that a presentation you gave was boring, it's much better than giving 50 boring presentations over the course of the year and then getting the news from your boss. For an interesting discussion of other implications of social media to employee job performance, see our **OB at the Bookstore** feature.

AT THE BOOKSTORE

A WORLD GONE SOCIAL
by Ted Coiné and Mark Babbitt (New York: Amacom, 2014).

Welcome to the social age.

Photo of cover: © Roberts Publishing Services

With those words, authors Coiné and Babbitt explain that companies today exist in a world that's much more social, collaborative and open than in the "industrial age" of the past, and that accordingly, companies must adapt their practices to survive. In particular, the authors suggest that organizational leaders and employees need to change the way they think and behave in order to leverage social media and avoid its traps. The book covers a wide array of topics that are relevant to management, but of special interest are the implications of social media to employee job performance.

Most generally, the authors describe how social media creates new opportunities for employees to contribute positively to the organization. For example, Chapter 4 discusses how recruiting new employees can be more effective when existing employees use social media to champion a job opportunity, the organization, or its brands. As the authors note, "Who else would you want talking to a potential team member about joining your company instead of the competition than the person who has drunk the most company Kool-Aid and shows it every day on social networking sites?" Of course, social media creates opportunities for employees to make negative contributions to the organization as well. The authors provide several examples of how a single complaint posted on social media by an employee can become amplified by others who casually weigh in on the matter. The problem here is obvious. Potential employees and customers could view this information and interpret it as an objective real time resource to make employment or purchase decisions.

In sum, although social media creates opportunities for new forms of citizenship performance, it also creates opportunities for counterproductive performance as well. The challenge for managers is to identify implications of social media to job performance, and to incorporate this knowledge into organizational practices and policies. As we alluded to above, for example, the first step might be to identify specific types of social media related activities that contribute positively and negatively to the organization. These activities could then be reflected in changes to hiring, training and development, and performance feedback systems.

TAKEAWAYS

2.1   Job performance is the set of employee behaviors that contribute to organizational goal accomplishment. Job performance has three dimensions: task performance, citizenship behavior, and counterproductive behavior.

2.2   Task performance includes employee behaviors that are directly involved in the transformation of organizational resources into the goods or services that the organization produces.

Examples of task performance include routine task performance, adaptive task performance, and creative task performance.

2.3 Organizations gather information about relevant task behaviors using job analysis and O*NET.

2.4 Citizenship behaviors are voluntary employee activities that may or may not be rewarded but that contribute to the organization by improving the overall quality of the setting in which work takes place. Examples of citizenship behavior include helping, courtesy, sportsmanship, voice, civic virtue, and boosterism.

2.5 Counterproductive behaviors are employee behaviors that intentionally hinder organizational goal accomplishment. Examples of counterproductive behavior include sabotage, theft, wasting resources, substance abuse, gossiping, incivility, harassment, and abuse.

2.6 A number of trends have affected job performance in today's organizations. These trends include the rise of knowledge work and the increase in service jobs.

2.7 MBO, BARS, 360-degree feedback, and forced ranking practices are four ways that organizations can use job performance information to manage employee performance.

KEY TERMS

- Job performance — p. 33
- Task performance — p. 34
- Routine task performance — p. 34
- Adaptive task performance — p. 34
- Creative task performance — p. 35
- Job analysis — p. 36
- Occupational Information Network (O*NET) — p. 37
- Citizenship behavior — p. 38
- Interpersonal citizenship behavior — p. 38
- Helping — p. 39
- Courtesy — p. 39
- Sportsmanship — p. 39
- Organizational citizenship behavior — p. 39
- Voice — p. 39
- Civic virtue — p. 39
- Boosterism — p. 39
- Counterproductive behavior — p. 41
- Property deviance — p. 41
- Sabotage — p. 41
- Theft — p. 42
- Production deviance — p. 43
- Wasting resources — p. 43
- Substance abuse — p. 43
- Political deviance — p. 43
- Gossiping — p. 43
- Incivility — p. 43
- Personal aggression — p. 44
- Harassment — p. 44
- Abuse — p. 44
- Knowledge work — p. 47
- Service work — p. 47
- Management by objectives (MBO) — p. 48
- Behaviorally anchored rating scales (BARS) — p. 49
- 360-degree feedback — p. 49
- Forced ranking — p. 51

DISCUSSION QUESTIONS

2.1 Describe your "job" as a student in terms of the job performance dimensions discussed in this chapter. What would be the benefit of approaching student performance from a behavior perspective rather than from an outcome (grades) perspective? What would the downsides of this approach be? How would grading policies in your classes have to change to accommodate a behavior approach to student performance?

2.2 Describe the job that you currently hold or hope to hold after graduation. Now look up that job in the O*NET database. Does the profile of the job fit your expectations? Are any task behaviors missing from O*NET's profile?

2.3 Describe a job in which citizenship behaviors would be especially critical to an organization's functioning, and one in which citizenship behaviors would be less critical. What is it about a job that makes citizenship more important?

2.4 Figure 2-3 classifies production deviance and political deviance as more minor in nature than property deviance and personal aggression. When might those "minor" types of counterproductive behavior prove especially costly?

2.5 Consider how you would react to 360-degree feedback. If you were the one receiving the feedback, whose views would you value most: your manager's or your peer's? If you were asked to assess a peer, would you want your opinion to affect that peer's raises or promotions?

CASE: JPMORGAN CHASE

JPMorgan Chase and its predecessor institutions have long had a significant impact on the lives of Americans and others throughout the world. For example, the company took on the responsibility for financing large-scale risky large projects such as the Erie Canal, the Panama Canal, and the railroad expansion that opened the door to commerce and economic development throughout the United States. The company has also been at the forefront of important innovations such as credit cards, automatic teller machines, and online banking. In fact, it's not too far of a stretch to suggest that both creativity and the willingness to take bold risks for high returns have been hallmarks of effective employees at JPMorgan Chase, and this has been true throughout its long history. Less we not forget that the genesis of the company rests with the creative language inserted into the charter of a fledgling water company by one of its principals so that excess capital could be invested in opportunities to make money in a risky environment.

Unfortunately, bold and creative behavior of employees at JPMorgan Chase has not always resulted in positive consequences. In fact, the company has recently paid tens of billions of dollars in fines, settlements, and legal fees due to highly questionable employee behavior. As an example, the company paid $13 billion in a settlement for allegedly selling fraudulent mortgage backed securities to Fannie Mae and Freddie Mac in the years leading up to the financial crisis of 2008. Other highly publicized probes into the company include its involvement in Bernie Madoff's Ponzi scheme, rigging of currency and energy markets, and the London Whale incident in which a team of employees gambled on complex financial derivatives that resulted in more than $6 billion in trading loses.

As a response to these incidents, which obviously hurt the company's reputation and bottom line, company executives have taken a number of major steps. For example, CEO Jamie Dimon published a document that acknowledges the company's role in these incidents and outlines expectations of employees with regard to compliance with legal and ethical standards. The company also set up phone and e-mail lines so employees can anonymously report compliance concerns and related bad behavior. Perhaps the most notable initiative has been the use of a computer algorithm, originally developed for counterterrorism, that monitors and analyzes a large set of employee behaviors to try to catch employees before they actually do anything that results in a costly problem. Employees who miss a compliance class, violate minor rules regarding personal trading, exceed risk limits, or use certain words in e-mails may be flagged as being likely to violate a regulation or policy. Although JPMorgan Chase has not described all the information considered by the system, or what will be done to employees who are identified as likely rule breakers, it hopes that surveillance of employees will help the company police itself better and build a culture where employees understand that bad behavior will not be tolerated.

2.1 Which dimensions of job performance do you think JPMorgan Chase emphasized prior to the financial crisis and the costly legal problems that followed? In what ways did this emphasis contribute to both the company's success and its problems?

2.2 Which dimensions of job performance do you think JPMorgan Chase is emphasizing now? In what ways will this shift in emphasis help the company? Might there be reasons to believe the shift in emphasis will hurt the company?

2.3 Which specific dimension of job performance is the company trying to manage with the computer algorithm? How might there be unintended job-performance related consequences of using this system? Explain how the company could manage some of the potential downsides of the system?

Sources: JPMorgan Chase & Co. "How We Do Business," 2014, http://files.shareholder.com/downloads/ONE/0x0x 799950/14aa6d4f-f90d-4a23-96a6-53e5cc199f43/How_We_Do_Business.pdf; JPMorgan Chase & Co. "The History of JPMorgan Chase & Co.," 2008, http://www.jpmorganchase.com/corporate/About-JPMC/document/shorthistory.pdf; and S. Hugh "JPMorgan Tests an Algorithm to Identify Potential Rule Breakers Before they Stray." *Bloomberg Businessweek*, April 13–15, 2015, pp. 34–35.

EXERCISE: PERFORMANCE OF A SERVER

The purpose of this exercise is to explore what job performance means for a server in a restaurant. This exercise uses groups of participants, so your instructor will either assign you to a group or ask you to create your own group. The exercise has the following steps:

2.1 Conduct a job analysis for a restaurant server. Begin by drawing a circle like the one below. Use that circle to summarize the major job dimensions of a restaurant server. For example, one job dimension might be "Taking Orders." Divide the circle up with four additional job dimensions. Now get more specific by listing two behaviors per job dimension. For example, two behaviors within the "Taking Orders" dimension might be "Describing the Menu" and "Making Recommendations." At the end of step 1, you should have a list of eight specific behaviors that summarize the tasks involved in being a restaurant server. Write your group's behaviors down on the board or on a transparency, leaving some space for some additional behaviors down the line.

2.2 Take a look at the resulting list. Did you come up with any behaviors that would be described as "citizenship behaviors"? If you didn't include any in your list, does that mean that citizenship behavior isn't important in a restaurant setting? If your group includes someone who has worked as a server, ask him or her to describe the importance of citizenship behavior. Come up with two especially important citizenship behaviors and add those to your list.

2.3 Take another look at your list. Did you come up with any behaviors that would be described as "counterproductive behaviors"? If you didn't include any, does that mean that counterproductive behavior isn't an important concern in a restaurant setting? If your group includes someone who has worked as a server, ask him or her to describe the potential costs of counterproductive behavior. Come up with two costly counterproductive behaviors and add (the avoidance of) them to your list.

2.4 Class discussion (whether in groups or as a class) should center on how a restaurant owner or manager might use the resulting list to evaluate the performance of restaurant servers. How could this list be used to assess server performance? Would such an approach be valuable? Why or why not?

ENDNOTES

2.1 Duffy, M.K.; K.L. Scott; J.D. Shaw; B.J. Tepper; and K. Aquino. "A Social Context Model of Envy and Social Undermining." *Academy of Management Journal* 55 (2012), pp. 643–66; and Greenbaum, R.L.; M.B. Mawritz; and G. Eissa. "Bottom-Line Mentality as an Antecedent of Social Undermining and the Moderating Roles of Core Self-Evalutions and Conscientiousness." *Journal of Applied Psychology* 97 (2012), pp. 343–59.

2.2 Shawel, T. "Homegrown Career Development." *HR Magazine*, April 2011, pp. 36–38.

2.3 Campbell, J.P. "Modeling the Performance Prediction Problem in Industrial and Organizational Psychology." In *Handbook of Industrial and Organizational Psychology*, Vol. 1, 2nd ed., ed. M.D. Dunnette and L.M. Hough. Palo Alto, CA: Consulting Psychologists Press,

1990, pp. 687–732; and Motowidlo, S.J.; W.C. Borman; and M.J. Schmit. "A Theory of Individual Differences in Task and Contextual Performance." *Human Performance* 10 (1997), pp. 71–83.

2.4 Borman, W.C., and S.J. Motowidlo. "Expanding the Criterion Domain to Include Elements of Contextual Performance." In *Personnel Selection in Organizations*, ed. N. Schmitt and W.C. Borman. San Francisco: Jossey-Bass, 1993, pp. 71–98.

2.5 Ibid.

2.6 Occupational Information Network (O*NET) OnLine (n.d.), http://online.onetcenter.org/.

2.7 Weiss, H.M., and D.R. Ilgen. "Routinized Behavior in Organizations." *Journal of Behavioral Economics* 24 (1985), pp. 57–67.

2.8 LePine, J.A.; J.A. Colquitt; and A. Erez. "Adaptability to Changing Task

Contexts: Effects of General Cognitive Ability, Conscientiousness, and Openness to Experience." *Personnel Psychology* 53 (2000), pp. 563–93.

2.9 CBC News. "Plane Fire at Pearson Airport: Flight 358." Indepth Website, August 8, 2005, http://www.cbc.ca/news/background/plane_fire/.

2.10 Ilgen, D.R., and E.D. Pulakos. "Employee Performance in Today's Organizations." In *The Changing Nature of Work Performance: Implications for Staffing, Motivation, and Development*, ed. D.R. Ilgen and E.D. Pulakos. San Francisco: Jossey-Bass, 1999, pp. 1–20.

2.11 Haneberg, L. "Training for Agility: Building the Skills Employees Need to Zig and Zag." *Training and Development*, September 2011, pp. 51–56.

2.12 Associated Press. "Unemployed Find Old Jobs Now Require More Skills."

Gainesville Sun, October 11, 2010, p. 7A.

2.13 Pulakos, E.D.; S. Arad; M.A. Donovan; and K.E. Plamondon. "Adaptability in the Workplace: Development of a Taxonomy of Adaptive Performance." *Journal of Applied Psychology* 85 (2000), pp. 612–24.

2.14 Amabile, T.M. "How to Kill Creativity." *Harvard Business Review* 76 (1998), pp. 76–88.

2.15 "Bikini Trivia: History of the Bikini" (n.d.), http://www. everythingbikini.com/ bikini-history.html.

2.16 Florida, R. "America's Looming Creativity Crisis." *Harvard Business Review* 82 (2004), pp. 122–36.

2.17 Grant, A.M., and J.W. Berry. "The Necessity of Others Is the Mother of Invention: Intrinsic and Prosocial Motivations, Perspective Taking, and Creativity." *Academy of Management Journal* 54 (2011), pp. 73–96; and George, J.M. "Creativity in Organizations." *Academy of Management Annals*, Vol. 1, ed. J.P. Walsh and A.P. Brief. New York: Erlbaum, 2007, pp. 439–77.

2.18 Baer, M. "Putting Creativity to Work: The Implementation of Creative Ideas in Organizations." *Academy of Management Journal* 55 (2012), pp. 1102–19.

2.19 Liker, J.K., and D. P. Meier. *Toyota Talent: Developing Your People the Toyota Way*. New York: McGraw-Hill, 2007.

2.20 Ibid.

2.21 O'Reilly III, C.A., and J. Pfeffer. *Hidden Value: How Great Companies Achieve Extraordinary Results with Ordinary People*. Boston: Harvard Business School Press, 2000.

2.22 Freidberg, K., and J. Freidberg. *Nuts! Southwest Airlines' Crazy Recipe for Business and Personal Success*. Austin, TX: Bard Press, 1996.

2.23 Kaplan, M.D.G. "What Are You, a Comedian?" *USA Weekend.com*, July 13, 2003, http://www .usaweekend.com/03_ issues/030713/030713 southwest.html.

2.24 Krell, E. "All for Incentives, Incentives for All." *HR Magazine*, January 2011, pp. 35–38.

2.25 Ibid.

2.26 McFadden, R.D. "Pilot Is Hailed after Jetliner's Icy Plunge." *NYTimes. com*, January 16, 2009, http://www.nytimes. com/2009/01/16/ nyregion/16crash. html?_r=1&hp.

2.27 Newman, R. "How Sullenberger Really Saved US Airways Flight 1549." *USNews. com*, April 13,

2009, http://www. usnews.com/blogs/ flowchart/2009/2/3/ how-sullenberger-really-saved-us-airways-flight-1549.html.

2.28 Borman and Motowidlo, "Expanding the Criterion Domain."

2.29 Organ, D.W. *Organizational Citizenship Behavior: The Good Soldier Syndrome*. Lexington, MA: Lexington Books, 1988.

2.30 Coleman, V.I., and W.C. Borman. "Investigating the Underlying Structure of the Citizenship Performance Domain." *Human Resource Management Review* 10 (2000), pp. 25–44.

2.31 Ibid.

2.32 MacMillan, P. *The Performance Factor: Unlocking the Secrets of Teamwork*. Nashville, TN: Broadman & Holman, 2001.

2.33 LePine, J.A.; R.F. Piccolo; C.L. Jackson; J.E. Mathieu; and J.R. Saul. "A Meta-Analysis of Teamwork Process: Towards a Better Understanding of the Dimensional Structure and Relationships with Team Effectiveness Criteria." *Personnel Psychology* 61 (2008), pp. 273–307.

2.34 Coleman and Borman, "Investigating the Underlying Structure."

2.35 Coleman, V.I., and W.C. Borman. "Investigating the Underlying Structure of the

Citizenship Performance Domain." *Human Resource Management Review* 10 (2000), pp. 25–44.

2.36   Burris, E.R. "The Risks and Rewards of Speaking Up: Managerial Responses to Employee Voice." *Academy of Management Journal* 55 (2012), pp. 851–75; Liu, W.; S. Tangirala; W. Lam; Z. Chen; R.T. Jia; and X. Huang. "How and When Peers' Positive Mood Influence Employees' Voice." *Journal of Applied Psychology* 100 (2015), pp. 976–89; and Van Dyne, L., and J.A. LePine. "Helping and Voice Extra-Role Behavior: Evidence of Construct and Predictive Validity." *Academy of Management Journal* 41 (1998), pp. 108–19.

2.37   Motowidlo, S.J. "Some Basic Issues Related to Contextual Performance and Organizational Citizenship Behavior in Human Resource Management." *Human Resource Management Review* 10 (2000), pp. 115–26.

2.38   Podsakoff, N.P; S.W. Whiting; P.M. Podsakoff; and B.D. Blume. "Individual- and Organizational-Level Consequences of Organizational Citizenship Behaviors: A Meta-Analysis." *Journal of Applied Psychology* 94 (2009), pp. 122–41;

and Podsakoff, P.M.; S.B. MacKenzie; J.B. Paine; and D.G. Bachrach. "Organizational Citizenship Behaviors: A Critical Review of the Theoretical and Empirical Literature and Suggestions for Future Research." *Journal of Management* 26 (2000), pp. 513–63.

2.39   Podsakoff, P.M.; M. Ahearne; and S.B. MacKenzie. "Organizational Citizenship Behavior and the Quantity and Quality of Work Group Performance." *Journal of Applied Psychology* 82 (1997), pp. 262–70.

2.40   Walz, S.M., and B.P. Neihoff. "Organizational Citizenship Behaviors and Their Effect on Organizational Effectiveness in Limited-Menu Restaurants." In *Academy of Management Best Papers Proceedings*, ed. J.B. Keys and L.N. Dosier. Statesboro, GA: College of Business Administration at Georgia Southern University, 1996, pp. 307–11.

2.41   Dalal, R.S.; H. Lam; H.M. Weiss; E.R. Welch; and C.L. Hulin. "A Within-Person Approach to Work Behavior and Performance: Concurrent and Lagged Citizenship-Counterproductivity Associations, and Dynamic Relationships with Affect and Overall Job Performance."

Academy of Management Journal 52 (2009), pp. 1051–66.

2.42   Allen, T.D., and M.C. Rush. "The Effects of Organizational Citizenship Behavior on Performance Judgments: A Field Study and a Laboratory Experiment." *Journal of Applied Psychology* 83 (1998), pp. 247–60; Avila, R.A.; E.F. Fern; and O.K. Mann. "Unraveling Criteria for Assessing the Performance of Sales People: A Causal Analysis." *Journal of Personal Selling and Sales Management* 8 (1988), pp. 45–54; Lowery, C.M., and T.J. Krilowicz. "Relationships among Nontask Behaviors, Rated Performance, and Objective Performance Measures." *Psychological Reports* 74 (1994), pp. 571–78; MacKenzie, S.B.; P.M. Podsakoff; and R. Fetter. "Organizational Citizenship Behavior and Objective Productivity as Determinants of Managerial Evaluations of Salespersons' Performance." *Organizational Behavior and Human Decision Processes* 50 (1991), pp. 123–50; MacKenzie, S.B.; P.M. Podsakoff; and R. Fetter. "The Impact of Organizational Citizenship Behavior on Evaluation of Sales Performance." *Journal of Marketing* 57 (1993), pp. 70–80; MacKenzie, S.B.; P.M. Podsakoff; and J.B.

Paine. "Effects of Organizational Citizenship Behaviors and Productivity on Evaluation of Performance at Different Hierarchical Levels in Sales Organizations." *Journal of the Academy of Marketing Science* 27 (1999), pp. 396–410; Motowidlo, S.J., and J.R. Van Scotter. "Evidence That Task Performance Should Be Distinguished from Contextual Performance." *Journal of Applied Psychology* 79 (1994), pp. 475–80; Podsakoff, P.M., and S.B. MacKenzie. "Organizational Citizenship Behaviors and Sales Unit Effectiveness." *Journal of Marketing Research* 3 (February 1994), pp. 351–63; and Van Scotter, J.R., and S.J. Motowidlo. "Interpersonal Facilitation and Job Dedication as Separate Facets of Contextual Performance." *Journal of Applied Psychology* 81 (1996), pp. 525–31.

2.43 Rotundo, M., and P.R. Sackett. "The Relative Importance of Task, Citizenship, and Counterproductive Performance to Global Ratings of Job Performance: A Policy Capturing Approach." *Journal of Applied Psychology* 87 (2002), pp. 66–80.

2.44 Allen and Rush, "The Effects of Organizational Citizenship Behavior on Performance Judgments"; Kiker, D.S., and S.J. Motowidlo. "Main

and Interaction Effects of Task and Contextual Performance on Supervisory Reward Decisions." *Journal of Applied Psychology* 84 (1999), pp. 602–9; and Park, O.S., and H.P Sims Jr. "Beyond Cognition in Leadership: Prosocial Behavior and Affect in Managerial Judgment." Working Paper, Seoul National University and Pennsylvania State University, 1989.

2.45 Robinson, S.L., and R.J. Bennett. "A Typology of Deviant Workplace Behaviors: A Multidimensional Scaling Study." *Academy of Management Journal* 38 (1995), pp. 555–72.

2.46 Cellitti, D.R. "MCA DiscoVision: The Record That Plays Pictures," June 25, 2002, http://www.oz.net/blam/DiscoVision/RecordPlaysPictures.htm.

2.47 Hollweg, L. "Inside the Four Walls of the Restaurant: The Reality and Risk of Counter-Productive Behaviors," 2003, http://www.batrushollweg.com/files/Website.Inside_the_Four?_Walls_of_the_Restaurant1.Reprint_9.pdf.

2.48 Wang, M.; H. Liao; Y. Zhan; and J. Shi. "Daily Customer Mistreatment and Employee Sabotage Against Customers: Examining Emotion and Resource Perspectives." *Academy of Management Journal* 54 (2011), p. 31.

2.49 Harper, D. "Spotlight Abuse—Save Profits." *Industrial Distribution* 79 (1990), pp. 47–51.

2.50 Hollinger, R.C., and L. Langton. *2004 National Retail Security Survey*. Gainesville: University of Florida, Security Research Project, Department of Criminology, Law and Society, 2005.

2.51 Andersson, L.M., and C.M. Pearson. "Tit for Tat? The Spiraling Effect of Incivility in the Workplace." *Academy of Management Review* 24 (1999), pp. 452–71.

2.52 Ibid.

2.53 Armour, S. "Managers Not Prepared for Workplace Violence." *USA Today*, July 19, 2004, http://www.usatoday.com/money/workplace/2004-07-15-workplace-violence2_x.htm.

2.54 Daniel, T.A. "Tough Boss or Workplace Bully?" *HR Magazine*, June 2009, pp. 83–86.

2.55 Baillien, E.; N. De Cuyper; and H. De Witte. "Job Autonomy and Workload as Antecedents of Workplace Bullying: A Two-Wave Test of Karasek's Job Demand Control Model for Targets and Perpetrators." *Journal of Occupational and Organizational Psychology* 84 (2010), pp. 191–208.

2.56 Cowie, H.; P. Naylor; I. Rivers; P.K. Smith; and

B. Pereira. "Measuring Workplace Bullying." *Aggression and Violent Behavior* 7 (2002), pp. 35–51; Baillien et al. "Job Autonomy and Workload as Antecedents of Workplace Bullying" and Einarsen, S.S.; B. Matthisen; and L.J. Hauge. "Bullying and Harassment at Work. In *The Oxford Handbook of Personnel Psychology*, ed. S. Cartwright and C.L. Cooper. London: Sage, 2009, pp. 464–95.

2.57 Ibid.

2.58 PBS. "Isolated Incidents?" *Online Newshour*, April 26, 1996, http://www.pbs.org/newshour/bb/-business/april96/mitsubishi_4-26.html.

2.59 Sackett, P.R. "The Structure of Counterproductive Work Behaviors: Dimensionality and Performance with Facets of Job Performance." *International Journal of Selection and Assessment* 10 (2002), pp. 5–11.

2.60 Lian, H.; D.L. Ferris; R. Morrison; and D.J. Brown. "Blame it on the Supervisor or the Subordinate? Reciprocal Relations Between Abusive Supervision and Organizational Deviance". Journal of Applied Psychology 99 (2014), pp. 651–664.

2.61 Sackett, P.R., and C.J. DeVore. "Counterproductive Behaviors at Work." In *Handbook of Industrial, Work, and Organizational Psychology*, Vol. 1, ed. N. Anderson; D.S. Ones; H.K. Sinangil; and C. Viswesvaran. Thousand Oaks, CA: Sage, 2001, pp. 145–51.

2.62 Drucker, P.F. "The Age of Social Transformation." *The Atlantic Monthly* 274 (1994), pp. 53–80.

2.63 U.S. Department of Labor, Bureau of Labor Statistics. "Tomorrow's Jobs" (n.d.), http://stats.bls.gov/oco/oco2003.htm.

2.64 Allen, D. *Getting Things Done*. New York: Penguin Books, 2001.

2.65 U.S. Census Bureau. "Welcome to the Service Annual Survey," March 30, 2009, http://www.census.gov/econ/www/servmenu.html.

2.66 Hecker, D. "Occupational Employment Projections to 2012." *Monthly Labor Review* 127 (2004), pp. 80–105, http://www.proquest.com.

2.67 Green, H. "How Amazon Aims to Keep You Clicking." *BusinessWeek*, March 2, 2009, pp. 34–40.

2.68 Ibid.

2.69 McGregor, J. "Behind the List." *BusinessWeek*, March 2, 2009, p. 32.

2.70 Drucker, P.F. *The Practice of Management*. New York: Harper and Brothers, 1954.

2.71 Shaw, D.G.; C.E. Schneier; and R.W. Beatty. "Managing Performance with a Behaviourally Based Appraisal System." In *Applying Psychology in Business: The Handbook for Managers and Human Resource Professionals*, ed. J.W Jones; B.D. Steffy; and D.W. Bray. Lexington, MA: Lexington Books, 2001, pp. 314–25.

2.72 Pulakos, E.D. "Behavioral Performance Measures." In *Applying Psychology in Business: The Handbook for Managers and Human Resource Professionals*, ed. J.W. Jones; B.D. Steffy; and D.W. Bray. Lexington, MA: Lexington Books, 2001, pp. 307–13.

2.73 "*Fortune* Selects Henry Ford Businessman of the Century," November 1, 1999, http://www.timewarner.com/corp/print/0,20858,667526,00l.html.

2.74 Welch, J.F. Jr. *Jack: Straight from the Gut*. New York: Warner Books, 2001, p. 158.

2.75 Ibid.

2.76 Johnson, G. "Forced Ranking: The Good, the Bad, and the Alternative." *Training Magazine*, May 2004, pp. 24–34.

2.77 McGregor, J. "Job Review in 140 Keystrokes: Social Networking-Style Systems Lighten up the Dreaded Performance Evaluation." *BusinessWeek*, March 29, 2009, p. 58.

2.78 Ibid.

2.79 Ibid.

Organizational Commitment

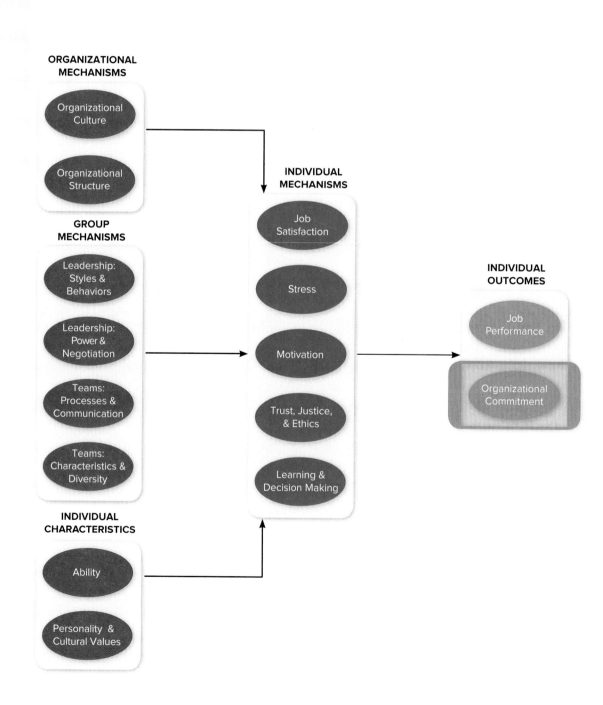

©Bloomberg/Getty Images

LEARNING GOALS

After reading this chapter, you should be able to answer the following questions:

3.1 What is organizational commitment? What is withdrawal behavior? How are the two connected?

3.2 What are the three types of organizational commitment, and how do they differ?

3.3 What are the four primary responses to negative events at work?

3.4 What are some examples of psychological withdrawal? Of physical withdrawal? How do the different forms of withdrawal relate to each other?

3.5 What workplace trends are affecting organizational commitment in today's organizations?

3.6 How can organizations foster a sense of commitment among employees?

GOLDMAN SACHS

How long would you want to work for this company? Its headquarters is a 43-story glass tower on the Hudson River in New York, complete with a huge fitness center offering 70 classes per week. Its cafeteria includes rotating selections from some of Manhattan's top restaurants, along with the typical fare. Plus, it offers a compressed work week, job sharing, and the ability to work from home (indeed, 30% of its employees do so on any given day). Is that sounding pretty good? Well, you should also know that the workweeks will be 70–80 hours, which is par for the course in the industry. And you might not want to have an "off day" because you'll be working alongside the best and brightest—others who've survived a grueling hiring process with up to 30 interviewers and an "acceptance rate" lower than Harvard's.

The company, of course, is Goldman Sachs, the 144-year old investment bank with more than 13,000 employees worldwide. The trick for Goldman is to retain its talent, even in the face of demanding workweeks and even given the marketability of its overachievers. How does it do that? Well, for one, Goldman provides good economic reasons for employees to stay. The average compensation across its employees is $380,000, with Goldman prioritizing pay more than most competitors. And that's leaving aside the perks that—in addition to the preceding listing—include a high-profile speaker series and a champion dragon-boating team. Of course, you may need that salary to pay for one of the perks, as the cafeteria pricing is based on demand. Eat during the noon rush and it'll be a bit pricier! What would you expect from an investment bank?

But the reasons to stay at Goldman transcend economics. There's a collaborative culture within the company that encourages bonds among employees. There are more than 80 "affinity networks" that help them connect with people of similar interests, background, and circumstances. Employees also collaborate on important volunteering projects run by nonprofits. "The culture of collaboration is not just a myth," explains one Goldman employee. What's more, the same hiring process that results in talented people results in people you'd want to work alongside. Explains CEO Lloyd Blankfein, "You don't have to be the smartest person, but it's probably the highest combination of smart and interesting and interested-in-the-world kind of people."

ORGANIZATIONAL COMMITMENT

Organizational commitment sits side-by-side with job performance in our integrative model of organizational behavior, reflecting one of the starting points for our journey through the concepts covered in this course. Why begin with a discussion of organizational commitment? Because it's not enough to have talented employees who perform their jobs well. You also need to be able to hang on to those employees for long periods of time so that the organization can benefit from their efforts. Put yourself in the shoes of a business owner. Let's say you spent a great deal of time recruiting a graduate from the local university, selling her on your business, and making sure that she was as qualified as you initially believed her to be. Now assume that, once hired, you took a personal interest in that employee, showing her the ropes and acting as mentor and instructor. Then, just as the company was set to improve as a result of that employee's presence, she leaves to go to work for a competitor. As an employer, can you think of many things more depressing than that scenario?

Unfortunately, that scenario is not far-fetched. The U.S. Bureau of Labor Statistics estimates that the average American will have 10.8 jobs between the ages of 18 and 42.[1] That projection is based in part on an overall turnover (or "attrition") rate of around 16 percent across all industries. Such statistics are nerve-wracking to employers because turnover can be quite expensive. Estimates suggest that turnover costs between 90 percent and 200 percent of an employee's annual salary.[2] Why so expensive? Those estimates include various costs, including the administrative costs involved in the separation, recruitment expenses, screening costs, and training and orientation expenses for the new hire. They also include "hidden costs" due to decreased morale, lost organizational knowledge, and lost productivity.

 3.1

What is organizational commitment? What is withdrawal behavior? How are the two connected?

Organizational commitment is defined as the desire on the part of an employee to remain a member of the organization.[3] Organizational commitment influences whether an employee stays a member of the organization (is retained) or leaves to pursue another job (turns over).

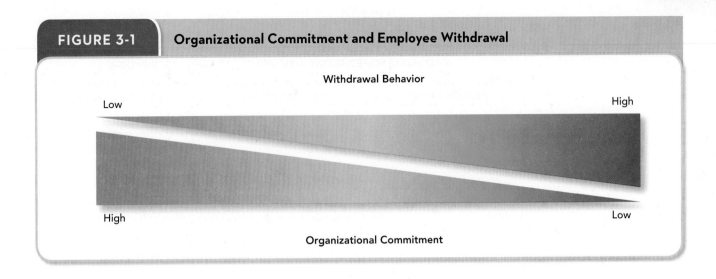

FIGURE 3-1 | **Organizational Commitment and Employee Withdrawal**

Withdrawal Behavior

Low — High

High — Low

Organizational Commitment

Our attention in this chapter is focused primarily on reducing voluntary turnover by keeping the employees whom the organization wants to keep, though we will touch on involuntary turnover in a discussion of layoffs and downsizing. Employees who are not committed to their organizations engage in **withdrawal behavior,** defined as a set of actions that employees perform to avoid the work situation—behaviors that may eventually culminate in quitting the organization.[4] The relationship between commitment and withdrawal is illustrated in Figure 3-1. Some employees may exhibit much more commitment than withdrawal, finding themselves on the green end of the continuum. Other employees exhibit much more withdrawal than commitment, finding themselves on the red end of the continuum. The sections that follow review both commitment and withdrawal in more detail.

WHAT DOES IT MEAN TO BE "COMMITTED"?

One key to understanding organizational commitment is to understand where it comes from. In other words, what creates a desire to remain a member of an organization? To explore this question, consider the following scenario: You've been working full-time for your employer for around five years. The company gave you your start in the business, and you've enjoyed your time there. Your salary is competitive enough that you were able to purchase a home in a good school system, which is important because you have one young child and another on the way. Now assume that a competing firm contacted you while you were attending a conference and offered you a similar position in its company. What kinds of things might you think about? If you created a list to organize your thoughts, what might that list look like?

TYPES OF COMMITMENT

One potential list is shown in Table 3-1. The left-hand column reflects some emotional reasons for staying with the current organization, including feelings about friendships, the atmosphere or culture of the company, and a sense of enjoyment when completing job duties. These sorts of emotional reasons create **affective commitment,** defined as a desire to remain a member of an organization due to an emotional attachment to, and involvement with, that organization.[5] Put simply, you stay because you *want* to. The middle column reflects some cost-based reasons for staying, including issues of salary, benefits, and promotions, as well as concerns about uprooting a family. These sorts of reasons create **continuance commitment,** defined as a desire to remain a member of an organization because of an awareness of the costs associated with leaving it.[6] In other words, you stay because you *need* to. The right-hand column reflects some obligation-based reasons for staying with the current organization, including a sense that a debt is owed

3.2

What are the three types of organizational commitment, and how do they differ?

TABLE 3-1	The Three Types of Organizational Commitment	
WHAT MAKES SOMEONE STAY WITH HIS/HER CURRENT ORGANIZATION?		
AFFECTIVE COMMITMENT (EMOTION-BASED)	**CONTINUANCE COMMITMENT (COST-BASED)**	**NORMATIVE COMMITMENT (OBLIGATION-BASED)**
Some of my best friends work in my office . . . I'd miss them if I left.	I'm due for a promotion soon . . . will I advance as quickly at the new company?	My boss has invested so much time in me, mentoring me, training me, showing me the ropes.
I really like the atmosphere at my current job . . . it's fun and relaxed.	My salary and benefits get us a nice house in our town . . . the cost of living is higher in this new area.	My organization gave me my start . . . they hired me when others thought I wasn't qualified.
My current job duties are very rewarding . . . I enjoy coming to work each morning.	The school system is good here, my spouse has a good job . . . we've really put down roots where we are.	My employer has helped me out of a jam on a number of occasions . . . how could I leave now?
Staying because you **want** to.	Staying because you **need** to.	Staying because you **ought** to.

Committed employees often have strong positive feelings about one particular aspect of their job, such as their colleagues, their manager, or the particular work they do.

© *Liquid Library/Jupiter Images RF*

to a boss, a colleague, or the larger company. These sorts of reasons create **normative commitment,** defined as a desire to remain a member of an organization due to a feeling of obligation.[7] In this case, you stay because you *ought* to.

As shown in Figure 3-2, the three types of organizational commitment combine to create an overall sense of psychological attachment to the company. Of course, different people may weigh the three types differently. Some employees may be very rational and cautious by nature, focusing primarily on continuance commitment when evaluating their overall desire to stay. Other employees may be more emotional and intuitive by nature, going more on "feel" than a calculated assessment of costs and benefits. The importance of the three commitment types also may vary over the course of a career. For example, you might prioritize affective reasons early in your work life before shifting your attention to continuance reasons as you start a family or become more established in a community. Regardless of how the three types are prioritized, however, they offer an important insight into *why* someone might be committed and what an organization can do to make employees feel more committed.

Figure 3-2 also shows that organizational commitment depends on more than just "the organization." That is, people aren't always committed to companies; they're also committed to the top management that leads the firm at a given time, the department in which they work, the manager who directly supervises them, or the specific team or coworkers with whom they work most closely.[8] We use the term **focus of commitment** to refer to the various people, places, and things that can inspire a desire to remain a member of an organization. For example, you might choose

FIGURE 3-2	Drivers of Overall Organizational Commitment

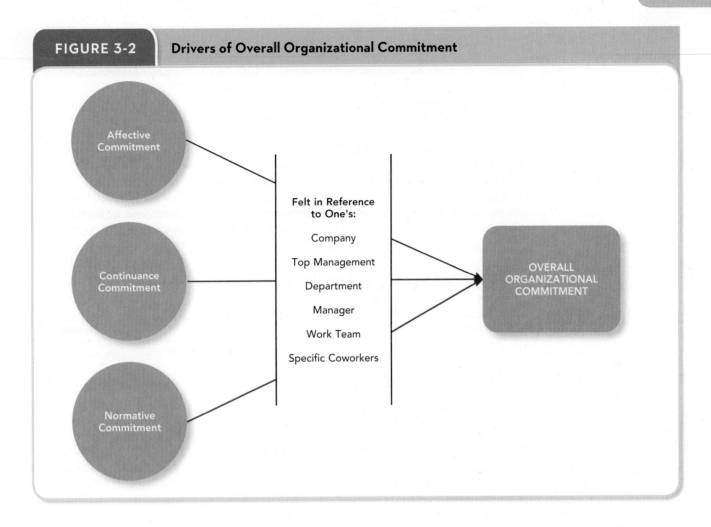

to stay with your current employer because you're emotionally attached to your work team, worry about the costs associated with losing your company's salary and benefits package, and feel a sense of obligation to your current manager. If so, your desire to remain cuts across multiple types of commitment (affective, continuance, and normative) and multiple foci (or focuses) of commitment (work team, company, manager). Now that you're familiar with the drivers of commitment in a general sense, let's go into more depth about each type.

AFFECTIVE COMMITMENT One way to understand the differences among the three types of commitment is to ask yourself what you would feel if you left the organization. Consider the reasons listed in the left-hand column of Table 3-1. What would you feel if, even after taking all those reasons into account, you decided to leave your organization to join another one? Answer: You'd feel a sense of *sadness*. Employees who feel a sense of affective commitment identify with the organization, accept that organization's goals and values, and are more willing to exert extra effort on behalf of the organization.[9] By identifying with the organization, they come to view organizational membership as important to their sense of self.[10] Is affective commitment something that you feel for your current employer or have felt for a past employer? Check the **OB Assessments** feature to find out.

It's safe to say that if managers could choose which type of commitment they'd like to instill in their employees, they'd choose affective commitment. Moreover, when a manager looks at an employee and says "She's committed" or "He's loyal," that manager usually is referring to a behavioral expression of affective commitment.[11] For example, employees who are affectively committed to their employer tend to engage in more interpersonal and organizational citizenship behaviors, such as helping, sportsmanship, and boosterism. One meta-analysis of 22 studies with

OB ASSESSMENTS

AFFECTIVE COMMITMENT

How emotionally attached are you to your employer? This assessment is designed to measure affective commitment—the feeling that you *want* to stay with your current organization. Think about your current job or the last job that you held (even if it was a part-time or summer job). Answer each question using the response scale provided. Then subtract your answers to the bold-faced questions from 6, with the difference being your new answers for those questions. For example, if your original answer for question 3 was "4," your new answer is "2" (6 − 4). Then sum your answers for the six questions. (Instructors: Assessments on continuance commitment, normative commitment, and embeddedness can be found in the PowerPoints in the Connect Library's Instructor Resources and in the Connect assignments for this chapter).

1 STRONGLY DISAGREE	2 DISAGREE	3 NEUTRAL	4 AGREE	5 STRONGLY AGREE

1. I would be very happy to spend the rest of my career in this organization. _____

2. I really feel as if this organization's problems are my own. _____

3. **I do not feel like "part of the family" at my organization.** _____

4. **I do not feel "emotionally attached" to this organization.** _____

5. This organization has a great deal of personal meaning for me. _____

6. **I do not feel a strong sense of belonging to my organization.** _____

SCORING AND INTERPRETATION

If your scores sum up to 20 or above, you feel a strong sense of affective commitment to your current or past employer, which means that you feel an emotional attachment to the company or the people within it. This means that you would leave voluntarily. If your scores sum up to less than 20, you have a weaker sense of affective commitment to your current or past employer. This result is especially likely if you responded to the questions in reference to a part-time or summer job, as there might not have been enough time to develop an emotional bond.

Source: From N.J. Allen and J.P. Meyer, "The Measurement and Antecedents of Affective, Continuance, and Normative Commitment to the Organization," *Journal of Occupational Psychology* 63 (1990), pp. 1–18.

more than 6,000 participants revealed a moderately strong correlation between affective commitment and citizenship behavior.[12] (Recall that a meta-analysis averages together results from multiple studies investigating the same relationship.) Such results suggest that emotionally committed employees express that commitment by "going the extra mile" whenever they can.

Because affective commitment reflects an emotional bond to the organization, it's only natural that the emotional bonds among coworkers influence it.[13] We can, therefore, gain a better understanding of affective commitment if we take a closer look at the bonds that tie employees together. Assume you were given a sheet with the names of all the employees in your department or members of your class. Then assume you were asked to rate the frequency with which you communicated with each of those people, as well as the emotional depth of those communications. Those ratings could be used to create a "social network" diagram that summarizes the bonds among employees. Figure 3-3 provides a sample of such a diagram. The lines connecting the 10 members of the work unit represent the communication bonds that tie each of them

FIGURE 3-3 A Social Network Diagram

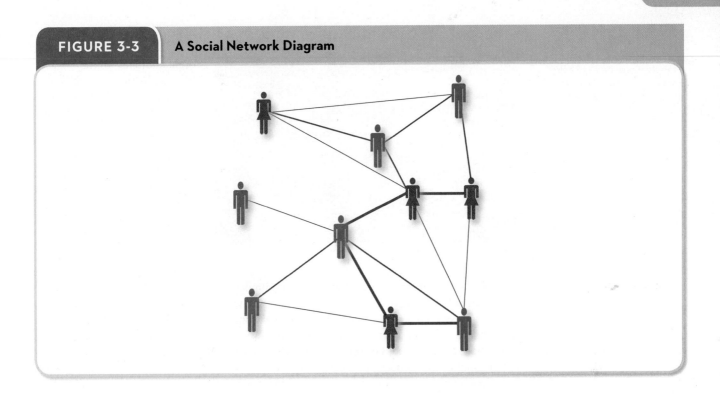

together, with thicker lines representing more frequent communication with more emotional depth. The diagram illustrates that some employees are "nodes," with several direct connections to other employees, whereas others remain at the fringe of the network.

The **erosion model** suggests that employees with fewer bonds will be most likely to quit the organization.[14] If you look at Figure 3-3, who's most at risk for turning over? That's right—the employee who has only one bond with someone else (and a relatively weak bond at that). From an affective commitment perspective, that employee is likely to feel less emotional attachment to work colleagues, which makes it easier to decide to leave the organization. Social network diagrams can also help us understand another explanation for turnover. The **social influence model** suggests that employees who have direct linkages with "leavers" will themselves become more likely to leave.[15] In this way, reductions in affective commitment become contagious, spreading like a disease across the work unit. Think about the damage that would be caused if the central figure in the network (the one who has linkages to five other people) became unhappy with the organization

More and more companies are beginning to understand the value in helping employees connect. SAS, the Cary, North Carolina–based software company, provides a number of perks that bring employees together.[16] Those include a billiard hall; intramural tennis, baseball, and volleyball; pool and fitness facilities; and even a hair salon. Sabre Holdings, the Southlake, Texas–based owner of Travelocity, created an internal social network system called Sabre Town.[17] More company-focused than Facebook, Sabre Town includes profiles of employee skills, experience, and customer contacts, along with groups built around common personal interests. One such group is Mom2Mom, which allows employees to connect and converse about day care centers, pediatricians, and work–family balance issues.

CONTINUANCE COMMITMENT Now consider the reasons for staying listed in the middle column of Table 3-1. What would you feel if, even after taking all those reasons into account, you decided to leave your organization to join another one? Answer: You'd feel a sense of *anxiety*. Continuance commitment exists when there's a profit associated with staying and a cost associated with leaving,[18] with high continuance commitment making it difficult to change organizations because of the steep penalties associated with the switch.[19] One factor that increases continuance commitment is the total amount of investment (in terms of time, effort, energy, etc.) employees

SAS, the Cary, North Carolina-based software company, offers a number of recreational perks to help employees stay connected to one another.

© *Charley Kurz/laif/Redux*

have made in mastering their work roles or fulfilling their organizational duties.[20] Picture a scenario in which you've worked extremely hard for a number of years to finally master the "ins and outs" of working at a particular organization, and now you're beginning to enjoy the fruits of that labor in terms of financial rewards and better work assignments. That effort might be wasted if you moved to another organization (and had to start over on the learning curve).

Another factor that increases continuance commitment is a lack of employment alternatives.[21] If an employee has nowhere else to go, the need to stay will be higher. Employment alternatives themselves depend on several factors, including economic conditions, the unemployment rate, and the marketability of a person's skills and abilities.[22] Of course, no one likes to feel "stuck" in a situation, so it may not be surprising that the behavioral benefits associated with affective commitment don't really occur with continuance commitment. There's no statistical relationship between continuance commitment and citizenship behavior, for example, or any other aspects of job performance.[23] Continuance commitment, therefore, tends to create more of a passive form of loyalty.

It's important to note that some of the reasons in the middle column of Table 3-1 center on personal or family issues. Continuance commitment focuses on personal and family issues more than the other two commitment types, because employees often need to stay for both work and nonwork reasons. One concept that demonstrates the work and nonwork forces that can bind us to our current employer is **embeddedness,** which summarizes employees' links to their organization and community, their sense of fit with their organization and community, and what they would have to sacrifice for a job change.[24] As demonstrated in Table 3-2, embeddedness strengthens continuance commitment by providing more reasons employees need to stay in their current positions

TABLE 3-2	Embeddedness and Continuance Commitment	
	"Embedded" People Feel:	
FACET	**FOR THE ORGANIZATION:**	**FOR THE COMMUNITY:**
Links	• I've worked here for such a long time. • I'm serving on so many teams and committees.	• Several close friends and family live nearby. • My family's roots are in this community.
Fit	• My job utilizes my skills and talents well. • I like the authority and responsibility I have at this company.	• The weather where I live is suitable for me. • I think of the community where I live as home.
Sacrifice	• The retirement benefits provided by the organization are excellent. • I would sacrifice a lot if I left this job.	• People respect me a lot in my community. • Leaving this community would be very hard.

Source: Adapted from T.R. Mitchell, B.C. Holtom, T.W. Lee, C.J. Sablynski, and M. Erez, "Why People Stay: Using Job Embeddedness to Predict Voluntary Turnover," *Academy of Management Journal* 44 (2001), pp. 1102–21.

(and more sources of anxiety if they were to leave).[25] Research suggests that embeddedness helps employees weather negative events that occur,[26] and that it matters across cultures.[27]

Think about your current situation. If you're a college student who is working part-time, you likely don't feel very embedded. Your links to your job are probably only short term, and you may feel that the job is more routine than you'd like from a fit perspective. You probably also wouldn't feel you were sacrificing much if you left the job. From a community perspective, you may be going to school in a different city or state than where you grew up, again resulting in few links, low perceived fit, or a lack of felt sacrifice. However, if you're a full-time employee who is relatively established in your job and community, you may feel quite embedded in your current situation.[28]

Alcon Labs seems to understand the value of continuance commitment. The Fort Worth, Texas–based leader in eye care products enjoys a voluntary turnover rate of less than 2 percent.[29] One likely reason for that low rate is the benefits package Alcon offers its employees. For example, Alcon offers a 401(k) retirement plan in which it matches 240 percent of what employees contribute, up to a total of 5 percent of total compensation. So, for example, if an employee invests $500 toward retirement in a given month, Alcon contributes $1,200. That policy more than doubles the most generous rates of other companies, allowing employees to build a comfortable "nest egg" for retirement more quickly. Clearly, employees would feel a bit anxious about giving up that benefit if a competitor came calling.

NORMATIVE COMMITMENT Now consider the reasons for staying listed in the right-hand column of Table 3-1. What would you feel if, even after taking all those reasons into account, you decided to leave your organization to join another one? Answer: You'd feel a sense of *guilt*. Normative commitment exists when there is a sense that staying is the "right" or "moral" thing to do.[30] The sense that people *should* stay with their current employers may result from personal work philosophies or more general codes of right and wrong developed over the course of their lives. They may also be dictated by early experiences within the company, if employees are socialized to believe that long-term loyalty is the norm rather than the exception.[31]

Aside from personal work philosophies or organizational socialization, there seem to be two ways to build a sense of obligation-based commitment among employees. One way is to create a feeling that employees are in the organization's debt—that they owe something to the organization. For example, an organization may spend a great deal of money training and developing an employee. In recognition of that investment, the employee may feel obligated to "repay" the organization with several more years of loyal service.[32] Think about how you'd feel if your employer paid your tuition, allowing you to further your education, while also providing you with training and developmental job assignments that increased your skills. Wouldn't you feel a bit guilty if you took the first job opportunity that came your way?

Another possible way to build an obligation-based sense of commitment is by becoming a particularly charitable organization. For example, many companies encourage employees to engage in **volunteering**—the giving of time or skills during a planned activity for a nonprofit or charitable group.[33] Such companies may encourage volunteering on employees' own personal time, or may create "corporate volunteering" programs where employees can give time or skills during the workday. Are such efforts a distraction for employees that interferes with their jobs? Quite the contrary, as research suggests that employees who volunteer are actually more engaged in their work than employees who don't. Moreover, employees who volunteer are given "credit" for those activities by their colleagues.[34] For the organization, charitable activities can provide good public relations, potentially generating goodwill for its products and services and helping attract new recruits.[35] They can also help existing employees feel better about the organization, creating a deeper sense of normative commitment. Those benefits may be particularly relevant with younger employees, as evidence indicates that recent generations are somewhat more charitably minded than previous ones. In support of that view, a growing number of MBA graduates are joining socially conscious online networks, such as Netimpact.org (see Chapter 7 on trust, justice, and ethics for more discussion of such issues).[36]

Comcast recognizes the value of normative commitment. For around a decade, the Philadelphia–based media company has organized Comcast Cares Day.[37] Originally, the day consisted of

50 employees working at a local charity event. One recent year, 60,500 employees, their family members, and volunteers worked with local and national nonprofits on a variety of activities, from planting gardens to cleaning up riverbanks. The head of Comcast's community involvement program contends that Comcast Cares Day was not created to help attract and maintain employees. Still, she admits that it's been a positive unintended consequence, especially for younger employees.

WITHDRAWAL BEHAVIOR

As noted earlier, one study suggested that 60 percent of employees plan to look for another job once the economy improves.[38] Organizational commitment is, therefore, a vital concern, given that organizations will need to be fully staffed when business picks back up and industries become even more competitive. Indeed, organizational commitment is at its most important when employees are at their most needed. To paraphrase the old saying, "When the going gets tough, the organization doesn't want you to get going." In tough times, organizations need their employees to demonstrate loyalty, not "get going" right out the door. Of course, it's those same tough times that put an employee's loyalty and allegiance to the test.

Consider the following scenario: You've been working at your company for three years and served on a key product development team for the past several months. Unfortunately, the team has been struggling of late. In an effort to enhance the team's performance, the organization has added a new member to the group. This member has a solid history of product development but is, by all accounts, a horrible person to work with. You can easily see the employee's talent but find yourself hating every moment spent in the employee's presence. This situation is particularly distressing because the team won't finish its work for another nine months, at the earliest. What would you do in this situation?

3.3

What are the four primary responses to negative events at work?

Research on reactions to negative work events suggests that you might respond in one of four general ways.[39] First, you might attempt to remove yourself from the situation, either by being absent from work more frequently or by voluntarily leaving the organization. This removal is termed **exit,** defined as an active, destructive response by which an individual either ends or restricts organizational membership.[40] Second, you might attempt to change the circumstances by meeting with the new team member to attempt to work out the situation. This action is termed **voice,** defined as an active, constructive response in which individuals attempt to improve the situation (see Chapter 2 on job performance for more discussion of such issues).[41] Third, you might just "grin and bear it," maintaining your effort level despite your unhappiness. This response is termed **loyalty,** defined as a passive, constructive response that maintains public support for the situation while the individual privately hopes for improvement.[42] Fourth, you might just go through the motions, allowing your performance to deteriorate slowly as you mentally "check out." This reaction is termed **neglect,** defined as a passive, destructive response in which interest and effort in the job declines.[43] Sometimes neglect can be even more costly than exit because it's not as readily noticed. Employees may neglect their duties for months (or even years) before their bosses catch on to their poor behaviors.

Taken together, the exit–voice–loyalty–neglect framework captures most of the possible responses to a negative work event. Where does organizational commitment fit in? Organizational commitment should decrease the likelihood that an individual will respond to a negative work event with exit or neglect (the two destructive responses). At the same time, organizational commitment should increase the likelihood that the negative work event will prompt voice or loyalty (the two constructive responses). Consistent with that logic, research indeed suggests that organizational commitment increases the likelihood of voice and loyalty while decreasing the likelihood of exit and neglect.[44] To see two of the exit–voice–loyalty–neglect options in action, see our **OB on Screen** feature.

If we consider employees' task performance levels together with their organizational commitment levels, we can gain an even clearer picture of how people might respond to negative work events. Consider Table 3-3, which depicts combinations of high and low levels of organizational commitment and task performance. **Stars** possess high commitment and high performance and are held up as role models for other employees. Stars likely respond to negative events with voice because they have the desire to improve the status quo and the credibility needed to inspire change.[45]

CHEF

Well why don't you cook the menu without a chef and we see how it goes tonight?

With those words, Chef Carl Casper (Jon Favreau) quits his job in *Chef* (Dir. Jon Favreau, Aldamisa Entertainment, 2014). Carl is just a few days removed from receiving a scathing review from Ramsey Michel (Oliver Platt), the most respected food critic in Los Angeles. And now he's taken to Twitter, challenging Michel to give him a second try, this time with an all new menu. As Carl explains to the hostess, Molly (Scarlett Johansson), "We're not pushing specials today—the whole menu is special." When Molly sees the excitement in Carl's eyes, he goes on, "I'm excited. I'm finally happy . . . I'm happy, OK? Am I allowed to be happy, at work?"

© Open Road Films (II)/Photofest

Unfortunately for Carl, the restaurant's owner—Riva (Dustin Hoffman)—doesn't want that special menu. Instead, he wants the unusually large crowd to experience the kind of entrées they can expect week in and week out. Riva walks back into the kitchen to protest, noting, "So now suddenly you're gonna be an artist. Well, be an artist on your own time." Carl argues that the crowd is there to see him face off against the critic and to eat his food. Corrects Riva, "It's my food because it's my restaurant. I pay for the glasses, I pay for the napkins, I pay for the spoons . . . "

Given an ultimatum, Carl chooses to walk out of the kitchen, and out of Riva's employ. He was deeply committed to his craft—to being a chef. Put differently, he had high *occupational commitment.* But he was no longer committed to Riva. Moreover, given his talent, Carl assumed he had other options—other restaurants that would hire him. Thus, his exit. The same was not true for Carl's sous-chef, Tony. Carl assumes Tony will follow him out of the kitchen and on to whatever comes next. But Tony is less established in his career—he needs to remain loyal for reasons that Carl doesn't. Where does Carl go next? Here's a hint: His next kitchen is smaller.

It's pretty easy to spot the stars in a given unit, and you can probably think about your current or past job experiences and identify the employees who would fit that description. **Citizens** possess high commitment and low task performance but perform many of the voluntary "extra-role" activities that are needed to make the organization function smoothly.[46] Citizens are likely to respond to negative events with loyalty because they may lack the credibility needed to inspire change but do possess the desire to remain a member of the organization. You can spot citizens

TABLE 3-3	Four Types of Employees	

		Task Performance	
		HIGH	**LOW**
Organizational	**HIGH**	Stars	Citizens
Commitment	**LOW**	Lone wolves	Apathetics

Source: Adapted from R.W. Griffeth, S. Gaertner, and J.K. Sager, "Taxonomic Model of Withdrawal Behaviors: The Adaptive Response Model," *Human Resource Management Review* 9 (1999), pp. 577–90.

by looking for the people who do the little things—showing around new employees, picking up birthday cakes, ordering new supplies when needed, and so forth.

Lone wolves possess low levels of organizational commitment but high levels of task performance and are motivated to achieve work goals for themselves, not necessarily for their company.[47] They are likely to respond to negative events with exit. Although their performance would give them the credibility needed to inspire change, their lack of attachment prevents them from using that credibility constructively. Instead, they rely on their performance levels to make them marketable to their next employer. To spot lone wolves, look for the talented employees who never seem to want to get involved in important decisions about the future of the company. Finally, **apathetics** possess low levels of both organizational commitment and task performance and merely exert the minimum level of effort needed to keep their jobs.[48] Apathetics should respond to negative events with neglect because they lack the performance needed to be marketable and the commitment needed to engage in acts of citizenship.

It's clear from this discussion that exit and neglect represent the flip side of organizational commitment: withdrawal behavior. How common is withdrawal behavior within organizations? Quite common, it turns out. One study clocked employees' on-the-job behaviors over a two-year period and found that only about 51 percent of their time was actually spent working! The other 49 percent was lost to late starts, early departures, long coffee breaks, personal matters, and other forms of withdrawal.[49] As a manager, wouldn't you like to feel like there was more than a coin-flip's chance that your employees were actually working during the course of a given day?

As shown in Figure 3-4, withdrawal comes in two forms: psychological (or neglect) and physical (or exit). **Psychological withdrawal** consists of actions that provide a mental escape from the work environment.[50] Some business articles refer to psychological withdrawal as "warm-chair attrition," meaning that employees have essentially been lost even though their chairs remain occupied.[51] This withdrawal form comes in a number of shapes and sizes.[52] The least serious is *daydreaming,* when employees appear to be working but are actually distracted by random thoughts or concerns. *Socializing* refers to the verbal chatting about nonwork topics that goes on in cubicles and offices or at the mailbox or vending machines. *Looking busy* indicates an intentional desire on the part of employees to look like they're working, even when not performing work tasks. Sometimes, employees decide to reorganize their desks or go for a stroll around the building, even though they have nowhere to go. (Those who are very good at managing impressions do such things very briskly and with a focused look on their faces!) When employees engage in *moonlighting,* they use work time and resources to complete something other than their job duties, such as assignments for another job.

Perhaps the most widespread form of psychological withdrawal among white-collar employees is *cyberloafing*—using Internet, e-mail, and instant messaging access for their personal enjoyment rather than work duties.[53] Some estimates suggest that typical cubicle dwellers stop what they're doing about once every three minutes to send e-mail, check Facebook or Twitter, surf over to YouTube, and so forth.[54] Such distractions consume as much as 28 percent of employees' workdays and cost some $650 billion a year in lost productivity. Sports fans seem particularly vulnerable. Estimates suggest that Fantasy Football league transactions consume as much as $1.5 billion in productivity during a typical season.[55] The spring isn't much better, as

3.4

What are some examples of psychological withdrawal? Of physical withdrawal? How do the different forms of withdrawal relate to each other?

FIGURE 3-4	Psychological and Physical Withdrawal

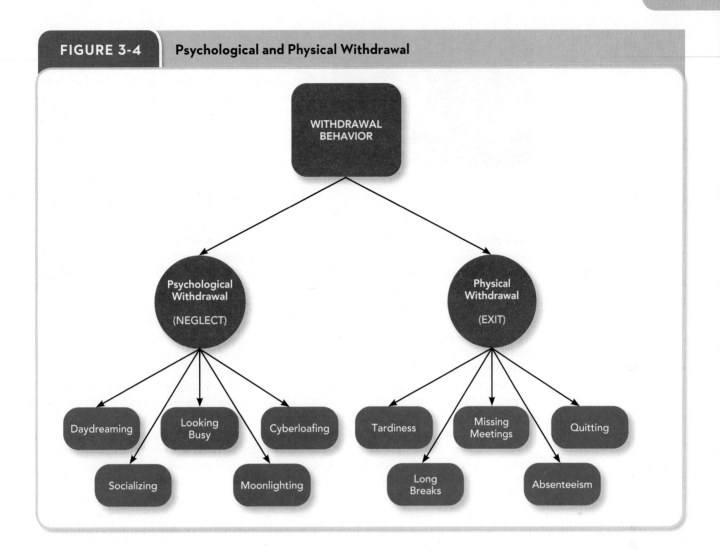

estimates suggest that employers lose $1.2 billion as employees watch NCAA tournament games online.[56] Some employees view cyberloafing as a way of "balancing the scales" when it comes to personal versus work time. For example, one participant in a cyberloafing study noted, "It is alright for me to use the Internet for personal reasons at work. After all, I do work overtime without receiving extra pay from my employer."[57] Although such views may seem quite reasonable, other employees view cyberloafing as a means to retaliate for negative work events. One participant in the same study noted, "My boss is not the appreciative kind; I take what I can whenever I can. Surfing the net is my way of hitting back."

Physical withdrawal consists of actions that provide a physical escape, whether short term or long term, from the work environment.[58] Physical withdrawal also comes in a number of shapes and sizes. *Tardiness* reflects the tendency to arrive at work late (or leave work early).[59] Of course, tardiness can sometimes be unavoidable, as when employees have car trouble or must fight through bad weather, but it often represents a calculated desire to spend less time at work.[60] *Long breaks* involve longer-than-normal lunches, soda breaks, coffee breaks, and so forth that provide a physical escape from work. Sometimes, long breaks stretch into *missing meetings,* which means employees neglect important work functions while away from the office. As a manager, you'd like to be sure that employees who leave for lunch are actually going to come back, but sometimes that's not a safe bet!

Absenteeism occurs when employees miss an entire day of work.[61] Of course, people stay home from work for a variety of reasons, including illness and family emergencies. There's also a rhythm to absenteeism. For example, employees are more likely to be absent on Mondays or

In an effort to curb absenteeism, some companies have turned to private investigators to try to catch "sick" employees who are playing hooky.

© Brand X Pictures/Jupiterimages RF

Fridays. Moreover, streaks of good attendance create a sort of pressure to be absent, as personal responsibilities build until a day at home becomes irresistible.[62] That type of absence can sometimes be functional because people may return to work with their "batteries recharged."[63] Group and departmental norms also affect absenteeism by signaling whether an employee can get away with missing a day here or there without being noticed.[64]

One survey suggests that 57 percent of U.S. employees take sick days when they're not actually sick, a trend that has some companies going to extreme measures.[65] IKEA, the Sweden-based furniture maker, recently made headlines for spying on its French employees for various reasons—including checking on their sick leave use.[66] In the United States, private investigation firms charge around $75 per hour to send investigators in search of employees who may be playing hooky. Rick Raymond, an investigator in Florida, once followed a supposedly sick employee to Universal Studios.[67] The employee rode three roller coasters that take automatic pictures at the sharpest turns. Raymond bought all three, which conveniently included time and date stamps. When the employee later claimed that the photos weren't her, Raymond responded by playing back video of her volunteering at an animal show in the park! The news isn't all bad for would-be work-skippers. Some of the same firms that track employees provide training on how to elude the boss's surveillance attempts.

Finally, the most serious form of physical withdrawal is *quitting*—voluntarily leaving the organization. As with the other forms of withdrawal, employees can choose to "turn over" for a variety of reasons. The most frequent reasons include leaving for more money or a better career opportunity; dissatisfaction with supervision, working conditions, or working schedule; family factors; and health.[68] Note that many of those reasons reflect avoidable turnover, meaning that the organization could have done something to keep the employee, perhaps by offering more money, more frequent promotions, or a better work situation. Family factors and health, in contrast, usually reflect unavoidable turnover that doesn't necessarily signal a lack of commitment on the part of employees.

Regardless of their reasons, some employees choose to quit after engaging in a very thorough, careful, and reasoned analysis. Typically some sort of "shock," whether it be a critical job change, a negative work experience, or an unsolicited job offer, jars employees enough that it triggers the thought of quitting in them.[69] Once the idea of quitting has occurred to them, employees begin searching for other places to work, compare those alternatives to their current job, and—if the comparisons seem favorable—quit.[70] This process may take days, weeks, or even months as employees grapple with the decision. In other cases, though, a shock may result in an impulsive, knee-jerk decision to quit, with little or no thought given to alternative jobs (or how those jobs compare to the current one).[71] Of course, sometimes a shock never occurs. Instead, an employee decides to quit as a result of a slow but steady decrease in happiness until a "straw breaks the camel's back" and voluntary turnover results.

Figure 3-4 shows 10 different behaviors that employees can perform to psychologically or physically escape from a negative work environment. A key question remains though: "How do all those behaviors relate to one another?" Consider the following testimonials from uncommitted (and admittedly fictional) employees:

- "I can't stand my job, so I do what I can to get by. Sometimes I'm absent, sometimes I socialize, sometimes I come in late. There's no real rhyme or reason to it; I just do whatever seems practical at the time."
- "I can't handle being around my boss. I hate to miss work, so I do what's needed to avoid being absent. I figure if I socialize a bit and spend some time surfing the web, I don't need to ever be absent. But if I couldn't do those things, I'd definitely have to stay home . . . a lot."
- "I just don't have any respect for my employer anymore. In the beginning, I'd daydream a bit during work or socialize with my colleagues. As time went on, I began coming in late or taking a long lunch. Lately I've been staying home altogether, and I'm starting to think I should just quit my job and go somewhere else."

Each of these statements sounds like something that an uncommitted employee might say. However, each statement makes a different prediction about the relationships among the withdrawal behaviors in Figure 3-4. The first statement summarizes the **independent forms model** of withdrawal, which argues that the various withdrawal behaviors are uncorrelated with one another, occur for different reasons, and fulfill different needs on the part of employees.[72] From this perspective, knowing that an employee cyberloafs tells you nothing about whether that employee is likely to be absent. The second statement summarizes the **compensatory forms model** of withdrawal, which argues that the various withdrawal behaviors negatively correlate with one another—that doing one means you're less likely to do another. The idea is that any form of withdrawal can compensate for, or neutralize, a sense of dissatisfaction, which makes the other forms unnecessary. From this perspective, knowing that an employee cyberloafs tells you that the same employee probably isn't going to be absent. The third statement summarizes the **progression model** of withdrawal, which argues that the various withdrawal behaviors are positively correlated: The tendency to daydream or socialize leads to the tendency to come in late or take long breaks, which leads to the tendency to be absent or quit. From this perspective, knowing that an employee cyberloafs tells you that the same employee is probably going to be absent in the near future.

Which of the three models seems most logical to you? Although all three make some sense, the progression model has received the most scientific support.[73] Studies tend to show that the withdrawal behaviors in Figure 3-4 are positively correlated with one another.[74] Moreover, if you view the behaviors as a causal sequence moving from left (daydreaming) to right (quitting), the behaviors that are closest to each other in the sequence tend to be more highly correlated.[75] For example, quitting is more closely related to absenteeism than to tardiness, because absenteeism is right next to it in the withdrawal progression. These results illustrate that withdrawal behaviors may begin with very minor actions but eventually can escalate to more serious actions that may harm the organization.

SUMMARY: WHAT DOES IT MEAN TO BE "COMMITTED"?

So what does it mean to be a "committed" employee? As shown in Figure 3-5, it means a lot of different things. It means that employees have a strong desire to remain a member of the organization, maybe because they want to stay, need to stay, or feel they ought to stay. Regardless of the reasons for their attachment though, retaining these employees means stopping the progression of withdrawal that begins with psychological forms and then escalates to behavioral forms. Note that the negative sign (–) in Figure 3-5 illustrates that high levels of overall organizational commitment reduce the frequency of psychological and physical withdrawal. Note also that psychological withdrawal goes on to affect physical withdrawal, which represents the progressive nature of such behaviors.

As you move forward in this book, you'll notice that every chapter includes a description of how that chapter's topic relates to organizational commitment. For example, Chapter 4 on job satisfaction describes how employees' satisfaction levels influence their organizational commitment. Chapter 7 on trust, justice, and ethics explains how employees' trust in management influences their organizational commitment. Sometimes you'll notice that a given chapter's topic relates more strongly to organizational commitment than to job performance. Other times, however, the topic may relate similarly to commitment and performance, or even relate more strongly to performance. Regardless, such differences will help you see exactly why the various topics in this book are so important to managers.

TRENDS THAT AFFECT COMMITMENT

Now that we've described exactly what organizational commitment represents, it's time to describe some of the trends that affect it in the contemporary workplace. Put simply, the composition of the workforce is changing, as is the traditional relationship between employees and employers. These trends put pressure on some types of commitment and alter the kinds of withdrawal seen in the workplace.

FIGURE 3-5   What Does It Mean to Be "Committed"?

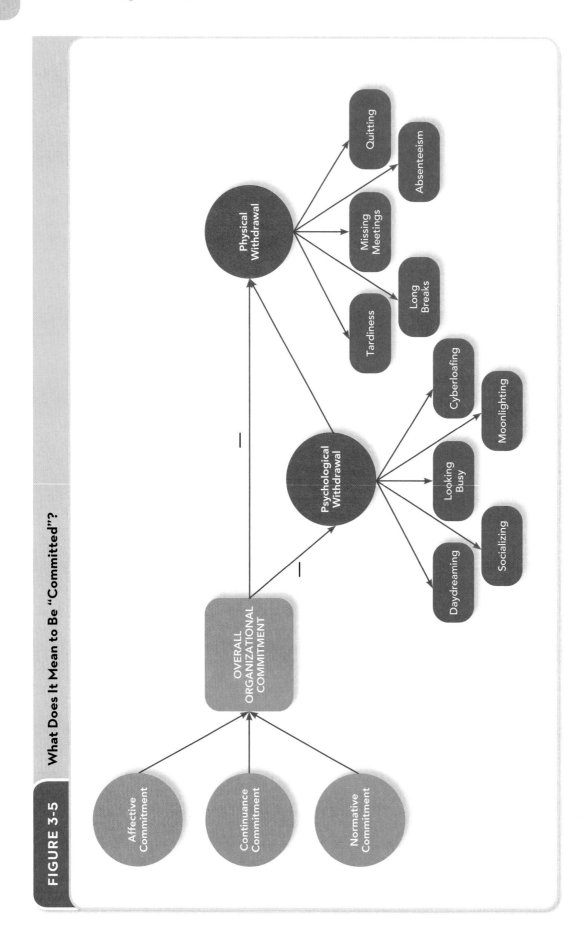

DIVERSITY OF THE WORKFORCE

 3.5

What workplace trends are affecting organizational commitment in today's organizations?

One of the most visible trends affecting the workplace is the increased diversity of the U.S. labor force. Demographically speaking, the percentage of the workforce that is white is expected to drop to around 65 percent by 2016.[76] Meanwhile, the percentage of minorities in the workforce is expected to rise to the following levels: African Americans (12 percent), Hispanics (15 percent), and Asians (6 percent). Thus, by 2016, minority groups will make up one-third of the workforce. Meanwhile, women have virtually matched men in terms of workforce percentages, with 53 percent of jobs filled by men and 47 percent by women. These statistics show that the "white, male-dominated" workforce is becoming a thing of the past.

The workforce is becoming diverse in other ways as well. The percentage of members of the workforce who are 60 years or older is expected to grow to 10 percent in 2016.[77] As the 78 million Baby Boomers near retirement, they're expected to remain in the workforce significantly longer than previous generations.[78] Research suggests that remaining a member of the workforce is actually beneficial to older people's health, keeping them more mentally and physically fit. Moreover, medical advances are helping older employees stay vital longer, just as the physical labor component of most jobs keeps shrinking. The Baby Boomers are also one of the most educated generations, and research suggests that their continued participation in the workforce could add $3 trillion a year to the country's economic output. That, combined with the uncertainty surrounding Social Security and stock market–based retirement plans, makes staying in the workforce a logical call.

As the economy continues to become more global, U.S. businesses face another important form of diversity: More and more employees are foreign-born. Although stereotypes view immigrants as staffing blue-collar or service jobs, many of the most educated employees come from abroad. Consider that half of the PhDs working in the United States are foreign-born, as are 45 percent of the physicists, computer scientists, and mathematicians.[79] At the same time, more and more American employees are working as expatriates who staff offices in foreign countries for long periods of time. Serving as an expatriate can be a very stressful assignment for employees as they adjust to a new country, a new style of working, and increased distance from family and friends. See our **OB Internationally** feature for more discussion of organizational commitment in multinational corporations.

These forms of diversity make it more challenging to retain valued employees. Consider the social network diagram in Figure 3-3. As work groups become more diverse with respect to race, gender, age, and national origin, there's a danger that minorities or older employees will find themselves on the fringe of such networks, which potentially reduces their affective commitment. At the same time, foreign-born employees are likely to feel less embedded in their current jobs and perceive fewer links to their community and less fit with their geographic area. This feeling may reduce their sense of continuance commitment. Recent trends suggest that the most educated and skilled immigrants are leaving the U.S. workforce at a rate of about 1,000 a day, particularly when their home country's economy begins to boom.[80]

THE CHANGING EMPLOYEE-EMPLOYER RELATIONSHIP

A few generations ago, many employees assumed that they would work for a single organization for their entire career. The assumption was that they would exchange a lifetime of loyalty and good work for a lifetime of job security. That perception changed in the 1980s and 1990s as downsizing became a more common part of working life. In 1992, downsizing statistics peaked as 3.4 million jobs were lost, and annual job losses have remained that high ever since.[81] Downsizing represents a form of involuntary turnover, when employees are forced to leave the organization regardless of their previous levels of commitment. The increase in downsizing has gone hand-in-hand with increases in temporary workers and outsourcing, fundamentally altering the way employees view their relationships with their employers.

Companies usually downsize to cut costs, particularly during a recession or economic downturn. Does downsizing work? Does it make the company more profitable? One study suggests that the answer is "not usually." This study examined 3,628 companies between 1980 and 1994,

OB INTERNATIONALLY

Fostering organizational commitment can be more complex in multinational corporations, for two primary reasons. First, multinational corporations provide two distinct foci of commitment: Employees can be committed to the local subsidiary in which they work, or they can be committed to the global organization. Research on commitment in multinational corporations suggests that employees draw a distinction between those two foci when judging their commitment. Specifically, employees distinguish between the prestige of their local subsidiary and the reputation of the larger organization. They also distinguish between the support provided by their local supervisor and the support provided by the global organization's top management. Such results reveal that it's possible to be committed to the local office but not the overall organization, or vice versa.

Second, multinational corporations require many employees to serve as expatriates for significant periods of time. Research suggests that the organizational commitment of expatriates depends, in part, on how well they adjust to their foreign assignments. Research further suggests that expatriates' adjustment comes in three distinct forms:

- *Work adjustment.* The degree of comfort with specific job responsibilities and performance expectations.
- *Cultural adjustment.* The degree of comfort with the general living conditions, climate, cost of living, transportation, and housing offered by the host culture.
- *Interaction adjustment.* The degree of comfort when socializing and interacting with members of the host culture.

A study of American multinational corporations in the transportation, service, manufacturing, chemical, and pharmaceutical industries showed that all three forms of adjustment relate significantly to affective commitment. If expatriates cannot feel comfortable in their assignment, it's difficult for them to develop an emotional bond to their organization. Instead, they're likely to withdraw from the assignment, both psychologically and physically.

What factors contribute to an expatriate's adjustment levels? It turns out that work adjustment depends on many of the same things that drive domestic employees' job satisfaction and motivation. Cultural and interaction adjustment, in contrast, are very dependent on spousal and family comfort. If an expatriate's spouse or children are unhappy in their new environment, it becomes very difficult for the expatriate to remain committed. Fortunately, research suggests that cultural and interaction adjustment can increase with time, as experiences in the host nation gradually increase expatriates' sense of comfort and, ultimately, their commitment to the work assignment.

Source: J.S. Black, M. Mendenhall, and G. Oddou, "Toward a Comprehensive Model of International Adjustment: An Integration of Multiple Theoretical Perspectives," *Academy of Management Review* 16 (1991), pp. 291–317; R. Hechanova, T.A. Beehr, and N.D. Christiansen, "Antecedents and Consequences of Employees' Adjustment to Overseas Assignment: A Meta-Analytic Review," *Applied Psychology: An International Review* 52 (2003), pp. 213–36; C. Reade, "Antecedents of Organizational Identification in Multinational Corporations: Fostering Psychological Attachment to the Local Subsidiary and the Global Organization," *International Journal of Human Resource Management* 12 (2001), pp. 1269–91; M. A. Shaffer, and D.A. Harrison, "Expatriates' Psychological Withdrawal from International Assignments: Work, Nonwork, and Family Influences," *Personnel Psychology* 51 (1998), pp. 87–118.

of which 59 percent downsized 5 percent or more of their workforce at least once and 33 percent fired 15 percent or more of their workforce at least once.[82] The most important result was that downsizing actually harmed company profitability and stock price. In fact, it typically took firms two years to return to the performance levels that prompted the downsizing in the first place. The exception to this rule was companies that downsized in the context of some larger change in assets (e.g., the sale of a line of business, a merger, an acquisition). However, such firms were relatively rare; only one-eighth of the downsizers were involved in some sort of asset change at the time the layoffs occurred.

Why doesn't downsizing tend to work? One reason revolves around the organizational commitment levels of the so-called survivors. The employees who remain in the organization after a downsizing are often stricken with "survivor syndrome," characterized by anger, depression, fear, distrust, and guilt.[83] One study found that downsizing survivors actually experienced more work-related stress than did the downsizing victims who went on to find new employment.[84] Survivor syndrome tends to reduce organizational commitment levels at the worst possible time, as downsizing survivors are often asked to work extra hard to compensate for their lost colleagues. Indeed, a study of 3,500 Boeing employees revealed some particularly stark examples of survivor syndrome.[85] Specifically, the study showed that employees who survived a 33 percent downsizing had depression scores that were nearly twice as high as those who left. They were also more likely to binge drink and experience chronic sleeping and health problems.

The change in employee–employer relationships brought about by a generation of downsizing makes it more challenging to retain valued employees. The most obvious challenge is finding a way to maintain affective commitment. The negative emotions aroused by survivor syndrome likely reduce emotional attachment to the organization. Moreover, if the downsizing has caused the loss of key figures in employees' social networks, then their desire to stay will be harmed. However, a second challenge is to find some way to maintain normative commitment. The sense that people *should* stay with their employer may have been eroded by downsizing, with personal work philosophies now focusing on maximizing marketability for the next opportunity that comes along. Even if employees felt obligated to remain at a firm in the past, seeing colleagues get dismissed in a downsizing effort could change that belief rather quickly.

One way of quantifying the change in employee–employer relationships is to assess how employees view those relationships psychologically. Research suggests that employees tend to view their employment relationships in quasi-contractual terms. Specifically, **psychological contracts** reflect employees' beliefs about what they owe the organization and what the organization owes them.[86] These contracts are shaped by the recruitment and socialization activities that employees experience, which often convey promises and expectations that shape beliefs about reciprocal obligations. Some employees develop **transactional contracts** that are based on a narrow set of specific monetary obligations (e.g., the employee owes attendance and protection of proprietary information; the organization owes pay and advancement opportunities).[87] Other employees develop **relational contracts** that are based on a broader set of open-ended and subjective obligations (e.g., the employee owes loyalty and the willingness to go above and beyond; the organization owes job security, development, and support).[88] Seeing one's coworkers downsized can constitute a "breach" of an employee's psychological contract, and research suggests that psychological contract breach leads to psychological and physical withdrawal.[89] However, trends such as downsizing, use of temporary workers, and outsourcing may also cause employees to define their contracts in more transactional (as opposed to relational) terms.

APPLICATION: COMMITMENT INITIATIVES

Now that you've gained a good understanding of organizational commitment, as well as some of the workforce trends that affect it, we close with a discussion of strategies and initiatives that can be used to maximize commitment. What exactly can companies do to increase loyalty? At a general level, they can be supportive. **Perceived organizational support** reflects the degree to which employees believe that the organization values their contributions and cares about their well-being.[90] Organizations can do a number of things to be supportive, including providing adequate rewards, protecting job security, improving work conditions, and minimizing the impact of politics.[91] In a sense, such support represents the organization's commitment to its employees. A meta-analysis of 42 research studies with almost 12,000 participants revealed that perceptions of support are strongly related to organizational commitment.[92] That same review showed that perceptions of support are associated with lower levels of psychological and physical withdrawal. For more wisdom on fostering commitment, see our **OB at the Bookstore** feature.

3.6

How can organizations foster a sense of commitment among employees?

OB AT THE BOOKSTORE

WIDGETS
by Rodd Wagner (New York: McGraw Hill, 2015).

YOUR PEOPLE ARE NOT YOUR GREATEST ASSET. They're not yours, and they're not assets . . . You don't own your people. Many of them don't trust you. Some don't like you. Too many won't stick it out with you. And the ones you need most have the credentials to walk out fastest if you treat them poorly.

Photo of cover: © Roberts Publishing Services

With those words, Rodd Wagner summarizes the importance (and challenge) that surrounds organizational commitment in today's workplace. Commitment is important, but many companies do a really bad job fostering it. Wagner and his research team conducted interviews and surveys at hundreds of companies to pursue two goals: (1) to get a sense of where most employees fall on the commitment spectrum and (2) to identify "new rules" for increasing loyalty.

Their results on the first goal suggest that 19 percent of employees are "demoralized"—feeling that their employer treats them like "widgets." Another 23 percent are "frustrated"—with moments of positivity surrounded by the sense that the company is poorly run. Another 29 percent are "encouraged"—neither invigorated to give their best nor upset enough to leave. That leaves only 30 percent in the "energized" camp—feeling like employers do a great job of treating them like human beings, not "assets."

What should companies do to help more employees find their way into that 30 percent? What are the so-called "new rules" for fostering commitment? Wagner discusses 12 rules. Although some are more relevant to other topics in our integrative model of OB, many are directly relevant to the three types of commitment. For example, Rule #1, "Get Inside Their Heads," is relevant to affective commitment. It urges managers to truly understand their employees—what they want from their work and how managers can help give it to them. As another example, Rule #3, "Make Money a Non-Issue," affects continuance commitment. Pay employees fairly so that concerns about pay don't short-circuit loyalty.

Are you curious whether your current or previous employer is following these rules, and whether you're "energized," "demoralized," or somewhere in between? If so, just Google "New Rules Index" to find out!

Beyond being supportive, organizations can engage in specific practices that target the three forms of commitment. For example, organizations could foster affective commitment by increasing the bonds that link employees together. Ben & Jerry's holds monthly "joy events" during which all production stops for a few hours to be replaced by Cajun-themed parties, table tennis contests, and employee appreciation celebrations.[93] Monsanto, the St. Louis, Missouri–based provider of agricultural products, groups staffers into "people teams" charged with designing employee-bonding activities like "snowshoe softball."[94] Such tight bonding among employees may explain why Monsanto's voluntary turnover rate is only 3 percent. Companies like PepsiCo and Procter & Gamble pay particular attention to mentoring and team-building programs for female and minority employees to create a sense of solidarity among employees who might otherwise remain on the fringe of social networks.[95]

From a continuance commitment perspective, the priority should be to create a salary and benefits package that creates a financial need to stay. One study compared the impact of a variety of human resource management practices on voluntary turnover and found that two of the most significant predictors were average pay level and quality of the benefits package.[96] Of course, one factor that goes hand-in-hand with salaries and benefits is advancement/promotion because salaries cannot remain competitive if employees get stuck in neutral when climbing the career ladder.[97] Perhaps that's why companies that are well known for their commitment to promotion-from-within policies, like A.G. Edwards and the Principal Financial Group, also enjoy especially low voluntary turnover rates.[98] Paying attention to career paths is especially important for star employees and foreign-born employees, both of whom have many options for employment elsewhere.[99]

From a normative commitment perspective, the employer can provide various training and development opportunities for employees, which means investing in them to create the sense that they owe further service to the organization. As the nature of the employee–employer relationship has changed, opportunities for development have overtaken secure employment on the list of employee priorities.[100] IBM is one company with a reputation for prioritizing development. Its "workforce management initiative" keeps a database of 33,000 résumés to develop a snapshot of employee skills.[101] IBM uses that snapshot to plan its future training and development activities, with $400 million of the company's $750 million training budget devoted to giving employees the skills they may need in the future. If employees find developmental activities beneficial and rewarding, they may be tempted to repay those efforts with additional years of service.

A final practical suggestion centers on what to do if withdrawal begins to occur. Managers are usually tempted to look the other way when employees engage in minor forms of withdrawal. After all, sometimes such behaviors simply represent a break in an otherwise busy day. However, the progression model of withdrawal shows that even minor forms of psychological withdrawal often escalate, eventually to the point of absenteeism and turnover. The implication is, therefore, to stop the progression in its early stages by trying to root out the source of the reduced commitment. Many of the most effective companies make great efforts to investigate the causes of low commitment, whether at the psychological withdrawal stage or during exit interviews. As one senior oil executive acknowledged, the loss of a talented employee warrants the same sort of investigation as a technical malfunction that causes significant downtime on an oil rig.[102]

© Lou Dematteis/Reuters/Corbis

Ben & Jerry's, founded by Ben Cohen and Jerry Greenfield, goes to great lengths to encourage employees to hang out together and have fun during their workweek. Such bonding activities lower turnover and encourage valued employees to remain.

TAKEAWAYS

3.1 Organizational commitment is the desire on the part of an employee to remain a member of the organization. Withdrawal behavior is a set of actions that employees perform to avoid the work situation. Commitment and withdrawal are negatively related to each other—the more committed employees are, the less likely they are to engage in withdrawal.

3.2 There are three types of organizational commitment. Affective commitment occurs when employees *want* to stay and is influenced by the emotional bonds between employees. Continuance commitment occurs when employees *need* to stay and is influenced by salary and benefits and the degree to which they are embedded in the community. Normative commitment occurs when employees feel that they *ought* to stay and is influenced by an organization investing in its employees or engaging in charitable efforts.

3.3 Employees can respond to negative work events in four ways: exit, voice, loyalty, and neglect. Exit is a form of physical withdrawal in which the employee either ends or restricts organizational membership. Voice is an active and constructive response by which employees attempt to improve the situation. Loyalty is passive and constructive; employees remain supportive while hoping the situation improves on its own. Neglect is a form of psychological withdrawal in which interest and effort in the job decrease.

3.4 Examples of psychological withdrawal include daydreaming, socializing, looking busy, moonlighting, and cyberloafing. Examples of physical withdrawal include tardiness, long breaks, missing meetings, absenteeism, and quitting. Consistent with the progression model, withdrawal behaviors tend to start with minor psychological forms before escalating to more major physical varieties.

3.5 The increased diversity of the workforce can reduce commitment if employees feel lower levels of affective commitment or become less embedded in their current jobs. The employee–employer relationship, which has changed due to decades of downsizing, can reduce affective and normative commitment, making it more of a challenge to retain talented employees.

3.6 Organizations can foster commitment among employees by fostering perceived organizational support, which reflects the degree to which the organization cares about employees' well-being. Commitment can also be fostered by specific initiatives directed at the three commitment types.

KEY TERMS

- Organizational commitment   *p. 64*
- Withdrawal behavior   *p. 65*
- Affective commitment   *p. 65*
- Continuance commitment   *p. 65*
- Normative commitment   *p. 66*
- Focus of commitment   *p. 66*
- Erosion model   *p. 69*
- Social influence model   *p. 69*
- Embeddedness   *p. 70*
- Volunteering   *p. 71*
- Exit   *p. 72*
- Voice   *p. 72*
- Loyalty   *p. 72*
- Neglect   *p. 72*
- Stars   *p. 72*
- Citizens   *p. 73*
- Lone wolves   *p. 74*
- Apathetics   *p. 74*
- Psychological withdrawal   *p. 74*
- Physical withdrawal   *p. 75*
- Independent forms model   *p. 77*
- Compensatory forms model   *p. 77*
- Progression model   *p. 77*
- Psychological contracts   *p. 81*
- Transactional contracts   *p. 81*
- Relational contracts   *p. 81*
- Perceived organizational
  support   *p. 81*

DISCUSSION QUESTIONS

3.1 Which type of organizational commitment (affective, continuance, or normative) do you think is most important to the majority of employees? Which do you think is most important to you?

3.2 Describe other ways that organizations can improve affective, continuance, and normative commitment, other than the strategies suggested in this chapter. How expensive are those strategies?

3.3 Consider times when you've reacted to a negative event with exit, voice, loyalty, or neglect. What was it about the situation that caused you to respond the way you did? Do you usually respond to negative events in the same way, or does your response vary across the four options?

3.4 Can organizations use a combination of monitoring and punishment procedures to reduce psychological and physical withdrawal? How might such programs work from a practical perspective? Do you think they would be effective?

3.5 Can you think of reasons the increased diversity of the workforce might actually increase organizational commitment? Why? Which of the three types of commitment might explain that sort of result?

3.6 Studies suggest that decades of downsizing have lowered organizational commitment levels. Can you think of a way that an organization can conduct layoffs without harming the commitment of the survivors? How?

CASE: GOLDMAN SACHS

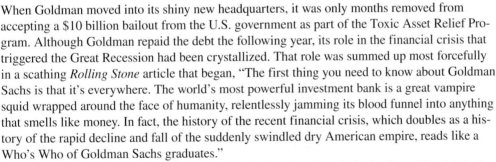

When Goldman moved into its shiny new headquarters, it was only months removed from accepting a $10 billion bailout from the U.S. government as part of the Toxic Asset Relief Program. Although Goldman repaid the debt the following year, its role in the financial crisis that triggered the Great Recession had been crystallized. That role was summed up most forcefully in a scathing *Rolling Stone* article that began, "The first thing you need to know about Goldman Sachs is that it's everywhere. The world's most powerful investment bank is a great vampire squid wrapped around the face of humanity, relentlessly jamming its blood funnel into anything that smells like money. In fact, the history of the recent financial crisis, which doubles as a history of the rapid decline and fall of the suddenly swindled dry American empire, reads like a Who's Who of Goldman Sachs graduates."

Regardless of how valid the criticisms of Goldman were, its role in the financial crisis had an impact on its reputation—in the eyes of both the public and its employees. Indeed, applications for open positions declined in the years following the bailout. After all, few graduating students aspire to work for a "great vampire squid." Still, Goldman seems to have weathered the storm. Those inside Goldman point to its collaborative culture as a steeling force that helped it weather the crisis. Says John Rogers, an executive vice president, "I will always believe that the culture was one of the most important factors in getting us through the crisis." CEO Lloyd Blankfein agrees, noting, "I think of the culture as the operating system . . . Our culture is what allowed us to reprogram ourselves . . . The operating system was intact."

Goldman has also gotten more aggressive in image advertising—marketing that focuses on the company's brand itself, rather than specific products and services. It launched a national branding campaign around the slogan "Progress is everyone's business." It also created more of a presence on Twitter, LinkedIn, and YouTube. Rogers describes the efforts like this: "There was a conversation that was taking place about Goldman Sachs, and we had the option to either be a part of it or not be a part of it. We had seen the effect of not being a part of it."

3.1   If you were working in a company that struggled through a crisis like Goldman's, how exactly would that experience harm your organizational commitment? Would the impact be felt most intensely with affective, continuance, or normative commitment?

3.2   Are there ways in which such a crisis could strengthen your organizational commitment? Which form (or forms) would be strengthened?

3.3   How sensitive do you think you are to corporate image, whether when applying for jobs or staying with an employer? Do you think image advertising is capable of helping with these sorts of issues? Why or why not?

Sources: A. Vandermey, "Yes, Goldman Sachs Really Is a Great Place to Work," *Fortune,* February 3, 2014; M. Taibbi, "The Great American Bubble Machine," *Rolling Stone,* April 5, 2010.

EXERCISE: REACTING TO NEGATIVE EVENTS

The purpose of this exercise is to explore how individuals react to three all-too-common scenarios that represent negative workplace events. This exercise uses groups, so your instructor will either assign you to a group or ask you to create your own group. The exercise has the following steps:

3.1   Individually read the following three scenarios: the annoying boss, the boring job, and pay and seniority. For each scenario, write down two specific behaviors in which you would likely engage in response to that scenario. Write down what you would actually do, as opposed to what you wish you would do. For example, you may wish that you would march into your boss's office and demand a change, but if you would actually do nothing, write down "nothing."

Annoying Boss	You've been working at your current company for about a year. Over time, your boss has become more and more annoying to you. It's not that your boss is a bad person, or even necessarily a bad boss. It's more a personality conflict—the way your boss talks, the way your boss manages every little thing, even the facial expressions your boss uses. The more time passes, the more you just can't stand to be around your boss.	Two likely behaviors:
Boring Job	You've been working at your current company for about a year. You've come to realize that your job is pretty boring. It's the first real job you've ever had, and at first it was nice to have some money and something to do every day. But the "new job" excitement has worn off, and things are actually quite monotonous. Same thing every day. It's to the point that you check your watch every hour, and Wednesdays feel like they should be Fridays.	Two likely behaviors:
Pay and Seniority	You've been working at your current company for about a year. The consensus is that you're doing a great job—you've gotten excellent performance evaluations and have emerged as a leader on many projects. As you've achieved this high status, however, you've come to feel that you're underpaid. Your company's pay procedures emphasize seniority much more than job performance. As a result, you look at other members of your project teams and see poor performers making much more than you, just because they've been with the company longer.	Two likely behaviors:

3.2 In groups, compare and contrast your likely responses to the three scenarios. Come to a consensus on the two most likely responses for the group as a whole. Elect one group member to write the two likely responses to each of the three scenarios on the board or on a transparency.

3.3 Class discussion (whether in groups or as a class) should center on where the likely responses fit into the exit–voice–loyalty–neglect framework. What personal and situational factors would lead someone to one category of responses over another? Are there any responses that do not fit into the exit–voice–loyalty–neglect framework?

ENDNOTES

3.1 Shepherd, L. "Focusing Knowledge Retention on Millennials." *Workforce Management,* August 2010, p. 6.

3.2 Allen, D.G.; P.C. Bryant; and J.M. Vardaman. "Retaining Talent: Replacing Misconceptions with Evidence-Based Strategies." *Academy of Management Perspectives* 24 (2010), pp. 48–64.

3.3 Meyer, J.P., and N.J. Allen. *Commitment in the Workplace.* Thousand Oaks, CA: Sage, 1997; and Mowday, R.T.; R.M. Steers; and L.W. Porter. "The Measurement of Organizational Commitment." *Journal of Vocational Behavior* 14 (1979), pp. 224–47.

3.4 Hulin, C.L. "Adaptation, Persistence, and Commitment in Organizations." In *Handbook of Industrial and Organizational Psychology,* Vol. 2, ed. M.D. Dunnette and L.M. Hough. Palo Alto, CA: Consulting Psychologists Press, 1991, pp. 445–506.

3.5 Allen, N.J., and J.P. Meyer. "The Measurement and Antecedents of Affective, Continuance and Normative Commitment to the Organization." *Journal of Occupational Psychology* 63 (1990), pp. 1–18; Meyer, J.P., and N.J. Allen. "A Three-Component Conceptualization of Organizational Commitment." *Human Resource Management Review* 1 (1991), pp. 61–89; and Meyer and Allen, *Commitment in the Workplace.*

3.6 Ibid.

3.7 Ibid.

3.8 Meyer and Allen, *Commitment in the Workplace.*

3.9 Mowday et al., "The Measurement of Organizational Commitment."

3.10 Ashforth, B.E.; S.H. Harrison; and K.G. Corley. "Identification in Organizations: An Examination of Four Fundamental Questions." *Journal of Management* 34 (2008), pp. 325–74.

3.11 Ibid.

3.12 Meyer, J.P.; D.J. Stanley; L. Herscovitch; and L. Topolnytsky. "Affective, Continuance, and Normative Commitment to the Organization: A Meta-Analysis of Antecedents, Correlates, and Consequences." *Journal of Vocational Behavior* 61 (2002), pp. 20–52.

3.13 Mathieu, J.E., and D.M. Zajac. "A Review and Meta-Analysis of the Antecedents, Correlates, and Consequences of Organizational Commitment." *Psychological Bulletin* 108 (1990), pp. 171–94.

3.14 Johns, G. "The Psychology of Lateness, Absenteeism, and Turnover." In *Handbook of Industrial, Work, and Organizational Psychology,* ed. N. Anderson; D.S. Ones; H.K. Sinangil; and C. Viswesvaran. Thousand Oaks, CA: Sage, 2001, pp. 232–52.

3.15 Ibid.

3.16   Flint, J. "Analyze This." *Bloomberg Businessweek,* February 21–27, 2011, pp. 82–83.

3.17   Ladika, S. "Socially Evolved." *Workforce Management,* September 2010, pp. 18–22.

3.18   Kanter, R.M. "Commitment and Social Organization: A Study of Commitment Mechanisms in Utopian Communities." *American Sociological Review* 33 (1968), pp. 499–517.

3.19   Stebbins, R.A. *Commitment to Deviance: The Nonprofessional Criminal in the Community.* Westport, CT: Greenwood Press, 1970.

3.20   Becker, H.S. "Notes on the Concept of Commitment." *American Journal of Sociology* 66 (1960), pp. 32–42.

3.21   Rusbult, C.E., and D. Farrell. "A Longitudinal Test of the Investment Model: The Impact of Job Satisfaction, Job Commitment, and Turnover of Variations in Rewards, Costs, Alternatives, and Investments." *Journal of Applied Psychology* 68 (1983), pp. 429–38.

3.22   Meyer and Allen, *Commitment in the Workplace.*

3.23   Meyer et al., "Affective, Continuance, and Normative Commitment."

3.24   Mitchell, T.R.; B.C. Holtom; T.W. Lee; C.J. Sablynski; and M. Erez. "Why People Stay: Using Job Embeddedness to Predict Voluntary Turnover." *Academy of Management Journal* 44 (2001), pp. 1102–21.

3.25   Felps, W.; T.R. Mitchell; D.R. Hekman; T.W. Lee; B.C. Holtom; and W.S. Harman. "Turnover Contagion: How Coworkers' Job Embeddedness and Job Search Behaviors Influence Quitting." *Academy of Management Journal* 52 (2009), pp. 545–61; and Hom, P.W.; A.S. Tsui; J.B. Wu; T.W. Lee; A.Y. Zhang; P.P. Fu; and L. Li. "Explaining Employment Relationships with Social Exchange and Job Embeddedness." *Journal of Applied Psychology* 94 (2009), pp. 277–97.

3.26   Burton, J.P.; B.C. Holtom; C.J. Sablynski; T.R. Mitchell; and T.W. Lee. "The Buffering Effects of Job Embeddedness on Negative Shocks." *Journal of Vocational Behavior* 76 (2010), pp. 42–51.

3.27   Ramesh, A., and M.J. Gelfand. "Will They Stay or Will They Go? The Role of Job Embeddedness in Predicting Turnover in Individualistic and Collectivistic Cultures." *Journal of Applied Psychology* 95 (2010), pp. 807–23.

3.28   Ng, T.W.H., and D.C. Feldman. "Organizational Embeddedness and Occupational Embeddedness across Career Stages." *Journal of Vocational Behavior* 70 (2007), pp. 336–51.

3.29   Levering, R., and M. Moskowitz. "The 100 Best Companies to Work For." *Fortune,* January 24, 2005, pp. 64–94.

3.30   Allen and Meyer, "The Measurement and Antecedents of Affective, Continuance and Normative Commitment to the Organization"; Meyer and Allen, "A Three-Component Conceptualization"; and Meyer and Allen, *Commitment in the Workplace.*

3.31   Wiener, Y. "Commitment in Organizations: A Normative View." *Academy of Management Review* 7 (1982), pp. 418–28.

3.32   Meyer and Allen, "A Three-Component Conceptualization."

3.33   Rodell, J.B. "Finding Meaning through Volunteering: Why Do Employees Volunteer and What Does It Mean for Their Jobs?" *Academy of Management Journal* 56 (2013), pp. 1274–94.

3.34   Rodell, J.B., and J.W. Lynch. "Perceptions of Employee Volunteering: Is It "Credited" or "Stigmatized" by Colleagues? *Academy of Management Journal* (in press).

3.35 Grow, B. "The Debate over Doing Good." *BusinessWeek,* August 15, 2005, pp. 76–78.

3.36 Ibid.

3.37 Rafter, M.V. "Appealing to Workers' Civic Side." *Workforce Management,* August 2010, p. 3.

3.38 Frauenheim, E. "The Manager Question." *Workforce Management,* April 2010, pp. 19–24.

3.39 Hirschman, A.O. *Exit, Voice, and Loyalty: Responses to Decline in Firms, Organizations, and States.* Cambridge, MA: Harvard University Press, 1970; and Farrell, D. "Exit, Voice, Loyalty, and Neglect as Responses to Job Dissatisfaction: A Multidimensional Scaling Study." *Academy of Management Journal* 26 (1983), pp. 596–607.

3.40 Hirschman, *Exit, Voice, and Loyalty;* Farrell, "Exit, Voice, Loyalty, and Neglect"; and Rusbult, C.E.; D. Farrell; C. Rogers; and A.G. Mainous III. "Impact of Exchange Variables on Exit, Voice, Loyalty, and Neglect: An Integrating Model of Responses to Declining Job Satisfaction." *Academy of Management Journal* 31 (1988), pp. 599–627.

3.41 Ibid.

3.42 Ibid.

3.43 Farrell, "Exit, Voice, Loyalty, and Neglect"; and Rusbult et al., "Impact of Exchange Variables."

3.44 Withey, M.J., and W.H. Cooper. "Predicting Exit, Voice, Loyalty, and Neglect." *Administrative Science Quarterly* 34 (1989), pp. 521–39; and Burris, E.R.; J.R. Detert; and D.S. Chiaburu. "Quitting Before Leaving: The Mediating Effects of Psychological Attachment and Detachment on Voice." *Journal of Applied Psychology* 93 (2008), pp. 912–22.

3.45 Griffeth, R.W.; S. Gaertner; and J.K. Sager. "Taxonomic Model of Withdrawal Behaviors: The Adaptive Response Model." *Human Resource Management Review* 9 (1999), pp. 577–90.

3.46 Ibid.

3.47 Ibid.

3.48 Ibid.

3.49 Cherrington, D. *The Work Ethic.* New York: AMACOM, 1980.

3.50 Hulin, C.L.; M. Roznowski; and D. Hachiya. "Alternative Opportunities and Withdrawal Decisions: Empirical and Theoretical Discrepancies and an Integration." *Psychological Bulletin* 97 (1985), pp. 233–50.

3.51 Fisher, A. "Turning Clock-Watchers into Stars." *Fortune,* March 22, 2004, p. 60.

3.52 Hulin et al., "Alternative Opportunities and Withdrawal Decisions."

3.53 Lim, V.K.G. "The IT Way of Loafing on the Job: Cyberloafing, Neutralizing, and Organizational Justice." *Journal of Organizational Behavior* 23 (2002), pp. 675–94.

3.54 Jackson, M. "May We Have Your Attention, Please?" *BusinessWeek,* June 23, 2008, p. 55.

3.55 Spitznagel, E. "Any Given Monday." *Bloomberg Businessweek,* September 13–19, 2010, pp. 81–83.

3.56 Gerdes, L. "Nothin' But Net." *BusinessWeek,* March 26, 2007, p. 16.

3.57 Lim, "The IT Way of Loafing on the Job."

3.58 Hulin et al., "Alternative Opportunities and Withdrawal Decisions."

3.59 Koslowsky, M.; A. Sagie; M. Krausz; and A.D. Singer. "Correlates of Employee Lateness: Some Theoretical Considerations." *Journal of Applied Psychology* 82 (1997), pp. 79–88.

3.60 Blau, G. "Developing and Testing a Taxonomy of Lateness Behavior." *Journal of Applied Psychology* 79 (1994), pp. 959–70.

3.61 Muchinsky, P.M. "Employee Absenteeism: A Review of the Literature." *Journal of Vocational Behavior* 10 (1977), pp. 316–40; and Harrison, D.A. "Time for Absenteeism: A 20-Year Review of Origins, Offshoots, and Outcomes." *Journal of Management* 24 (1998), pp. 305–50.

3.62   Fichman, M. "Motivational Consequences of Absence and Attendance: Proportional Hazard Estimation of a Dynamic Motivation Model." *Journal of Applied Psychology* 73 (1988), pp. 119–34.

3.63   Martocchio, J.J., and D.I. Jimeno. "Employee Absenteeism as an Affective Event." *Human Resource Management Review* 13 (2003), pp. 227–41.

3.64   Nicholson, N., and G. Johns. "The Absence Climate and the Psychological Contract: Who's in Control of Absence?" *Academy of Management Review* 10 (1985), pp. 397–407.

3.65   Spitznagel, E. "The Sick-Day Bounty Hunters." *Bloomberg Businessweek,* December 6–12, 2010, pp. 93–95.

3.66   Lucas, S. "The Shock and Awe of IKEA's Employee Spying Program." *Inc.,* December, 2013.

3.67   Ibid.

3.68   Campion, M.A. "Meaning and Measurement of Turnover: Comparison of Alternative Measures and Recommendations for Research." *Journal of Applied Psychology* 76 (1991), pp. 199–212.

3.69   Lee, T.W., and T.R. Mitchell. "An Alternative Approach: The Unfolding Model of Voluntary Employee Turnover." *Academy of Management Review* 19 (1994), pp. 51–89; Lee, T.W., and T.R. Mitchell. "An Unfolding Model of Voluntary Employee Turnover." *Academy of Management Journal* 39 (1996), pp. 5–36; Lee, T.W.; T.R. Mitchell; B.C. Holtom; L.S. McDaniel; and J.W. Hill. "The Unfolding Model of Voluntary Turnover: A Replication and Extension." *Academy of Management Journal* 42 (1999), pp. 450–62; and Lee, T.H.; B. Gerhart; I. Weller; and C.O. Trevor. "Understanding Voluntary Turnover: Path-Specific Job Satisfaction Effects and the Importance of Unsolicited Job Offers." *Academy of Management Journal* 51 (2008), pp. 651–71.

3.70   Mobley, W. "Intermediate Linkages in the Relationship Between Job Satisfaction and Employee Turnover." *Journal of Applied Psychology* 62 (1977), pp. 237–40; and Hom, P.W.; R. Griffeth; and C.L. Sellaro. "The Validity of Mobley's (1977) Model of Employee Turnover." *Organizational Behavior and Human Performance* 34 (1984), pp. 141–74.

3.71   Lee and Mitchell, "An Alternative Approach"; Lee and Mitchell, "An Unfolding Model of Voluntary Employee Turnover"; Lee and Mitchell, "The Unfolding Model of Voluntary Turnover"; and Porter, L.W., and R.M. Steers. "Organizational, Work, and Personal Factors in Employee Turnover and Absenteeism." *Psychological Bulletin* 80 (1973), pp. 151–76.

3.72   Johns, "The Psychology of Lateness, Absenteeism, and Turnover."

3.73   Rosse, J.G. "Relations among Lateness, Absence, and Turnover: Is There a Progression of Withdrawal?" *Human Relations* 41 (1988), pp. 517–31.

3.74   Mitra, A.; G.D. Jenkins Jr.; and N. Gupta. "A Meta-Analytic Review of the Relationship Between Absence and Turnover." *Journal of Applied Psychology* 77 (1992), p. 879–89; Koslowsky et al., "Correlates of Employee Lateness"; and Griffeth, R.W.; P.W. Hom; and S. Gaertner. "A Meta-Analysis of Antecedents and Correlates of Employee Turnover: Update, Moderator Tests, and Research Implications for the Next Millennium." *Journal of Management* 26 (2000), pp. 463–88.

3.75   Koslowsky et al., "Correlates of Employee Lateness."

3.76 U.S. Bureau of Labor Statistics, 2005, http://www.wnjpin.net/OneStopCareerCenter/LaborMarketInformation/lmi03/uslfproj.htm (accessed October 26, 2005).

3.77 Ibid.

3.78 Coy, P. "Old. Smart. Productive." *BusinessWeek,* June 27, 2005, pp. 78–86.

3.79 Fisher, A. "Holding on to Global Talent." *BusinessWeek,* October 31, 2005, p. 202.

3.80 Fisher, "Holding on to Global Talent."

3.81 Morris, J.R.; W.F. Cascio; and C.E. Young. "Downsizing after All These Years: Questions and Answers about Who Did It, How Many Did It, and Who Benefited from It." *Organizational Dynamics* 27 (1999), pp. 78–87.

3.82 Ibid.

3.83 Devine, K.; T. Reay; L. Stainton; and R. Collins-Nakai. "Downsizing Outcomes: Better a Victim Than a Survivor?" *Human Resource Management* 42 (2003), pp. 109–24.

3.84 Ibid.

3.85 Conlin, M. "When the Laid-Off Are Better Off." *BusinessWeek,* November 2, 2009, p. 65.

3.86 Rousseau, D.M. "Psychological and Implied Contracts in Organizations." *Employee Responsibilities and Rights Journal* 2 (1989), pp. 121–39.

3.87 Rousseau, D.M. "New Hire Perceptions of Their Own and Their Employer's Obligations: A Study of Psychological Contracts." *Journal of Organizational Behavior* 11 (1990), pp. 389–400; Robinson, S.L.; M.S. Kraatz; and D.M. Rousseau. "Changing Obligations and the Psychological Contract: A Longitudinal Study." *Academy of Management Journal* 37 (1994), pp. 137–52; and Robinson, S.L., and E.W. Morrison. "Psychological Contracts and OCB: The Effect of Unfulfilled Obligations on Civic Virtue Behavior." *Journal of Organizational Behavior* 16 (1995), pp. 289–98.

3.88 Ibid.

3.89 Robinson, S.L. "Violating the Psychological Contract: Not the Exception but the Norm." *Journal of Organizational Behavior* 15 (1994), pp. 245–59; Robinson, S.L. "Trust and Breach of the Psychological Contract." *Administrative Science Quarterly* 41 (1996), pp. 574–99; Zhao, H.; S.J. Wayne; B.C. Glibkowski; and J. Bravo. "The Impact of Psychological Contract Breach on Work-Related Outcomes: A Meta-Analysis." *Personnel Psychology* 60 (2007), pp. 647–80; and Bal, P.M.; A.H. De Lange; P.G.W. Jansen; and M.E.G. Van der Velde. "Psychological Contract Breach and Job Attitudes: A Meta-Analysis of Age as a Moderator." *Journal of Vocational Behavior* 72 (2008), pp. 143–58.

3.90 Eisenberger, R.; R. Huntington; S. Hutchison; and D. Sowa. "Perceived Organizational Support." *Journal of Applied Psychology* 71 (1986), pp. 500–507.

3.91 Rhoades, L., and R. Eisenberger. "Perceived Organizational Support." *Journal of Applied Psychology* 87 (2002), pp. 698–714; and Allen, D.G.; L.M. Shore; and R.W. Griffeth. "The Role of Perceived Organizational Support and Supportive Human Resources Practices in the Turnover Process." *Journal of Management* 29 (2003), pp. 99–118.

3.92 Rhoades and Eisenberger, "Perceived Organizational Support."

3.93 Dessler, G. "How to Earn Your Employees' Commitment." *Academy of Management Executive* 13 (1999), pp. 58–67.

3.94 Levering and Moskowitz, "In Good Company."

3.95 Fisher, A. "How You Can Do Better on Diversity." *Business-Week,* November 15, 2005, p. 60; and Fisher, "Holding on to Global Talent."

3.96 Shaw, J.D.; J.E. Delery; G.D. Jenkins Jr.; and N. Gupta. "An Organization-Level Analysis of Voluntary and Involuntary Turnover." *Academy of Management Journal* 41 (1998), pp. 511–25.

3.97 Dessler, "How to Earn Your Employees' Commitment."

3.98 Levering and Moskowitz, "In Good Company."

3.99 Fisher, "Holding on to Global Talent"; and Fisher, A. "How to Keep your Stars from Leaving."

BusinessWeek, July 26, 2005, p. 44.

3.100 Cappelli, P. "Managing without Commitment." *Organizational Dynamics* 28 (2000), pp. 11–24.

3.101 Byrnes, N. "Star Search." *BusinessWeek,* October 10, 2005, pp. 68–78.

3.102 Ibid.

PART 2

INDIVIDUAL MECHANISMS

CHAPTER 4
Job Satisfaction

CHAPTER 5
Stress

CHAPTER 6
Motivation

CHAPTER 7
Trust, Justice, and Ethics

CHAPTER 8
Learning and Decision Making

Job Satisfaction

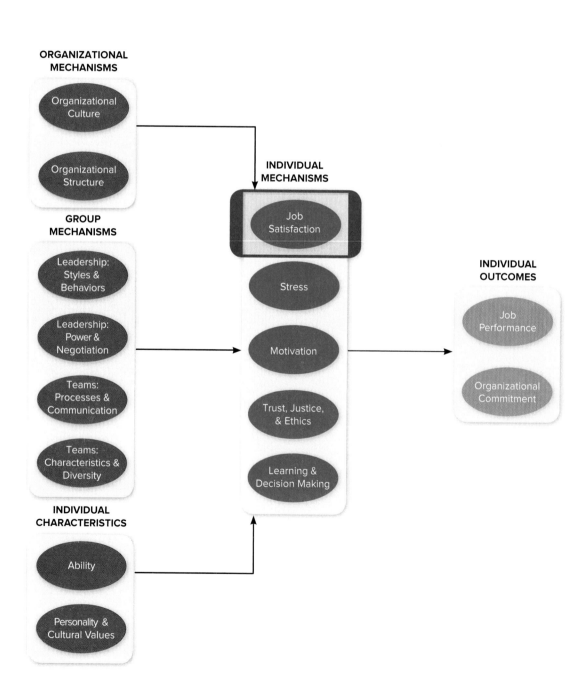

ORGANIZATIONAL MECHANISMS

Organizational Culture

Organizational Structure

GROUP MECHANISMS

Leadership: Styles & Behaviors

Leadership: Power & Negotiation

Teams: Processes & Communication

Teams: Characteristics & Diversity

INDIVIDUAL CHARACTERISTICS

Ability

Personality & Cultural Values

INDIVIDUAL MECHANISMS

Job Satisfaction

Stress

Motivation

Trust, Justice, & Ethics

Learning & Decision Making

INDIVIDUAL OUTCOMES

Job Performance

Organizational Commitment

© Noah Berger/Reuters/Corbis

✅ LEARNING GOALS

After reading this chapter, you should be able to answer the following questions:

4.1 What is job satisfaction?

4.2 What are values, and how do they affect job satisfaction?

4.3 What specific facets do employees consider when evaluating their job satisfaction?

4.4 Which job characteristics can create a sense of satisfaction with the work itself?

4.5 How is job satisfaction affected by day-to-day events?

4.6 What are mood and emotions, and what specific forms do they take?

4.7 How does job satisfaction affect job performance and organizational commitment? How does it affect life satisfaction?

4.8 What steps can organizations take to assess and manage job satisfaction?

TWITTER

Think about a job that you've had, that you currently have, or that you're on track for having in the future. How often will you see the result of your work being used by other people, day in and day out? At Twitter, that answer is "very often." Explains former CEO Dick Costolo, "When you work at Twitter, you get an opportunity to work at a company and on a platform that is visibly changing the world every day." Executives makes sure that Twitter employees maintain a sense of the significance of their technology. Twice a month, at so-called tea times, employees gather in a spacious open room where important and popular tweets are illustrated. Executives also discuss important company milestones, relevant business numbers, and anything else the crowd wants to ask about.

A sense of "being in it together" is an important part of the culture at Twitter. New hires are greeted with shout-outs from the company's internal tweeting system, Birdhouse. And executives want to know what employees have to say, new hires included. As Costolo describes, "As you grow as a company, the view from the top becomes more and more distorted." So employees are encouraged to view their bosses as peers and colleagues—to ask sharp questions and offer pointed suggestions. Such suggestions may prove vital at a company with slowing user growth and flat stock market performance, even as revenues and earnings improve. There may need to be a "next thing" for Twitter, and the best ideas for that next thing probably reside within the rank-and-file.

If so, Twitter gives its employees plenty of places to talk about their ideas. The top of their headquarters—called the Twitterloin because of its location at the edge of San Francisco's Tenderloin neighborhood—contains a 16,500-square-foot rooftop deck with outdoor couches and synthetic grass. Several floors down sits the Lodge—two log cabins purchased on Craigslist that create an indoor hang-out space for employees. And, of course, like many Silicon Valley firms, Twitter offers free food, along with free yoga and improv classes. Given the significance of their product, the openness of their culture, and the nature of those perks, it's no wonder that Twitter receives 230 applications for each open position—more than even Google.

JOB SATISFACTION

This chapter takes us to a new portion of our integrative model of organizational behavior. Job satisfaction is one of several individual mechanisms that directly affects job performance and organizational commitment. If employees are very satisfied with their jobs and experience positive emotions while working, they may perform their jobs better and choose to remain with the company for a longer period of time. Think about the worst job that you've held in your life, even if it was just a summer job or a short-term work assignment. What did you feel during the course of the day? How did those feelings influence the way you behaved, in terms of your time spent on task and citizenship behaviors rather than counterproductive or withdrawal behaviors?

4.1

What is job performance?

Job satisfaction is a pleasurable emotional state resulting from the appraisal of one's job or job experiences.[1] In other words, it represents how you *feel* about your job and what you *think* about your job. Employees with high job satisfaction experience positive feelings when they think about their duties or take part in task activities. Employees with low job satisfaction experience negative feelings when they think about their duties or take part in their task activities. Unfortunately, workplace surveys suggest that satisfied employees are becoming more and more rare. For example, one recent survey showed that just 45 percent of Americans were satisfied with their jobs, down from 61 percent two decades ago.[2] What explains the drop? The same survey revealed declines in the percentage of employees who find their work interesting (51 percent), who are satisfied with their boss (51 percent), and who like their coworkers (57 percent). Reversing such trends requires a deeper understanding of exactly what drives job satisfaction levels.

WHY ARE SOME EMPLOYEES MORE SATISFIED THAN OTHERS?

So what explains why some employees are more satisfied than others? At a general level, employees are satisfied when their job provides the things that they value. **Values** are those things that people consciously or subconsciously want to seek or attain.[3] Think about this question for a few moments: What do you want to attain from your job, that is, what things do you want your job to give you? A good wage? A sense of achievement? Colleagues who are fun to be around? If you had to make a list of the things you value with respect to your job, most or all of them would likely be shown in Table 4-1. This table summarizes the content of popular surveys of work values, broken down into more general categories.[4] Many of those values deal with the things that your work can give you, such as good pay or the chance for frequent promotions. Other values pertain to the context that surrounds your work, including whether you have a good boss or good coworkers. Still other values deal with the work itself, like whether your job tasks provide you with freedom or a sense of achievement.

4.2

What are values, and how do they affect job satisfaction?

TABLE 4-1	Commonly Assessed Work Values

CATEGORIES	SPECIFIC VALUES
Pay	• High salary • Secure salary
Promotions	• Frequent promotions • Promotions based on ability
Supervision	• Good supervisory relations • Praise for good work
Coworkers	• Enjoyable coworkers • Responsible coworkers
Work Itself	• Utilization of ability • Freedom and independence • Intellectual stimulation • Creative expression • Sense of achievement
Altruism	• Helping others • Moral causes
Status	• Prestige • Power over others • Fame
Environment	• Comfort • Safety

Key Question:
Which of these things are most important to you?

Sources: Adapted from R.V. Dawis, "Vocational Interests, Values, and Preferences," in *Handbook of Industrial and Organizational Psychology,* Vol. 2, Ed. M.D. Dunnette and L.M. Hough (Palo Alto, CA: Consulting Psychologists Press, 1991), pp. 834–71; and D.M. Cable and J.R. Edwards, "Complementary and Supplementary Fit: A Theoretical and Empirical Investigation," *Journal of Applied Psychology* 89 (2004), pp. 822–34.

Consider the list of values in Table 4-1. Which would make your "top five" in terms of importance right now, at this stage of your life? Maybe you have a part-time job during college and you value enjoyable coworkers or a comfortable work environment above everything else. Or maybe you're getting established in your career and starting a family, which makes a high salary and frequent promotions especially critical. Or perhaps you're at a point in your career that you feel a need to help others or find an outlet for your creative expression. (In our case, we value fame, which is what led us to write this textbook. We're still waiting for Fallon's call—or at least Kimmel's). Regardless of your "top five," you can see that different people value different things and that your values may change during the course of your working life.

VALUE FULFILLMENT

Values play a key role in explaining job satisfaction. **Value-percept theory** argues that job satisfaction depends on whether you *perceive* that your job supplies the things that you *value*.[5] This theory can be summarized with the following equation:

$$\text{Dissatisfaction} = (V_{want} - V_{have}) \times (V_{importance})$$

In this equation, V_{want} reflects how much of a value an employee wants, V_{have} indicates how much of that value the job supplies, and $V_{importance}$ reflects how important the value is to the employee. Big differences between wants and haves create a sense of dissatisfaction, especially when the value in question is important. Note that the difference between V_{want} and V_{have} gets multiplied by importance, so existing discrepancies get magnified for important values and minimized for trivial values. As an example, say that you were evaluating your pay satisfaction. You want to be earning around $70,000 a year but are currently earning $50,000 a year, so there's a $20,000 discrepancy. Does that mean you feel a great deal of pay dissatisfaction? Only if pay is one of the most important values to you from Table 4-1. If pay isn't that important, you probably don't feel much dissatisfaction.

Value-percept theory also suggests that people evaluate job satisfaction according to specific "facets" of the job.[6] After all, a "job" isn't one thing—it's a collection of tasks, relationships, and rewards.[7] The most common facets that employees consider in judging their job satisfaction appear in Figure 4-1. The figure includes the "want vs. have" calculations that drive satisfaction with pay, promotions, supervision, coworkers, and the work itself. The figure also shows how satisfaction with those five facets adds together to create "overall job satisfaction." Figure 4-1 shows that employees might be satisfied for all kinds of reasons. One person may be satisfied because she's in a high-paying job and working for a good boss. Another person may be satisfied because he has good coworkers and enjoyable work tasks. You may have noticed that a few of the values in Table 4-1, such as working for moral causes and gaining fame and prestige, are not represented in Figure 4-1. Those values are missing because they're not as relevant in all jobs, unlike pay, promotions, and so forth.

The first facet in Figure 4-1, **pay satisfaction,** refers to employees' feelings about their pay, including whether it's as much as they deserve, secure, and adequate for both normal expenses and luxury items.[8] Similar to the other facets, pay satisfaction is based on a comparison of the pay that employees want and the pay they receive.[9] Although more money is almost always better, most employees base their desired pay on a careful examination of their job duties and the pay given to comparable colleagues.[10] As a result, even nonmillionaires can be quite satisfied with their pay (thankfully for most of us!). Take the employees at NuStar Energy, the San Antonio–based asphalt refiner and operator of oil pipelines storage.[11] The company pays more than the industry average, with merit pay and equity grants for nonexecutives. And either everyone gets a bonus or no one does. Those sorts of pay policies make it more bearable to stand next to hot asphalt in a flame-retardant suit, hard hat, shatterproof glasses, and steel-toed boots!

The next facet in Figure 4-1, **promotion satisfaction,** refers to employees' feelings about the company's promotion policies and their execution, including whether promotions are frequent, fair, and based on ability.[12] Unlike pay, some employees may not want frequent promotions

4.3

What specific facets do employees consider when evaluating their job satisfaction?

FIGURE 4-1   The Value-Percept Theory of Job Satisfaction

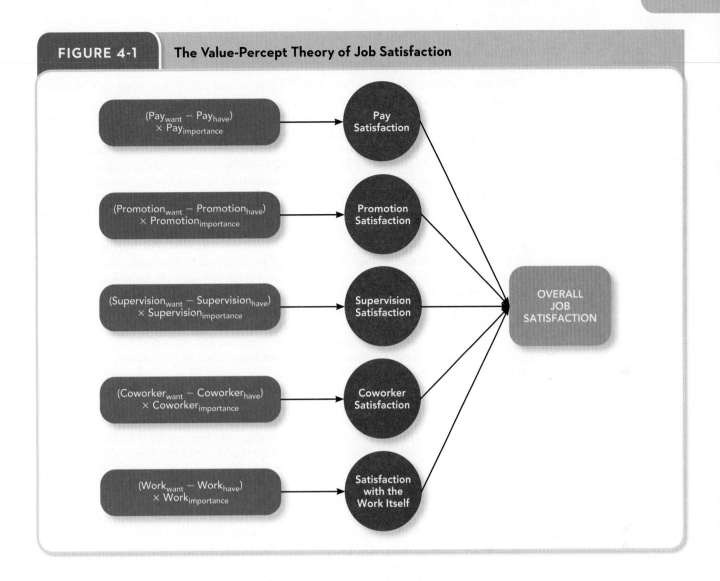

because promotions bring more responsibility and increased work hours.[13] However, many employees value promotions because they provide opportunities for more personal growth, a better wage, and more prestige. Nordstrom, the Seattle-based high-end retailer, does a good job fostering promotion satisfaction on the part of its employees. New sales clerks are often promoted within a year, with potential leaders put on the fast track with a six-month training program.[14] Indeed, five of the nine members of Nordstrom's executive committee started off on the sales floor. "Leadership is grounded in experience," notes one executive. "We want to make sure people get enough experiences to grow their career."

Supervision satisfaction reflects employees' feelings about their boss, including whether the boss is competent, polite, and a good communicator (rather than lazy, annoying, and too distant).[15] Most employees ask two questions about their supervisors: (1) "Can they help me attain the things that I value?" and (2) "Are they generally likable?"[16] The first question depends on whether supervisors provide rewards for good performance, help employees obtain necessary resources, and protect employees from unnecessary distractions. The second question depends on whether supervisors have good personalities, as well as values and beliefs similar to the employees' philosophies. General Mills, the Minneapolis–based manufacturer of food products, works hard to foster a sense of supervision satisfaction. The company stresses leadership development courses at its General Mills Institute and rotates employees across jobs to broaden the experiences they bring to leadership roles.[17] One manager describes the company's culture this way, "I've noticed a manager three roles ago is still putting in good words for me, and still checking up on me. It's something that's common at General Mills, and something I've started to do as well."

Coworker satisfaction refers to employees' feelings about their fellow employees, including whether coworkers are smart, responsible, helpful, fun, and interesting as opposed to lazy, gossipy, unpleasant, and boring.[18] Employees ask the same kinds of questions about their coworkers that they do about their supervisors: (1) "Can they help me do my job?" and (2) "Do I enjoy being around them?" The first question is critical because most of us rely, to some extent, on our coworkers when performing job tasks. The second question also is important because we spend just as much time with coworkers as we do with members of our own family. Coworkers who are pleasant and fun can make the workweek go much faster, whereas coworkers who are disrespectful and annoying can make even one day seem like an eternity. Perkins COIE, the Seattle–based law firm that represents Starbucks, Google, Microsoft, and Intel, fosters coworker satisfaction in an unusual—and downright sneaky—way. The firm encourages the creation of "happiness committees," small groups within each department that perform random acts of kindness, like leaving gifts at an employee's work station.[19] The twist? The rosters of the happiness committees are kept secret from the rank-and-file.

The last facet in Figure 4-1, **satisfaction with the work itself,** reflects employees' feelings about their actual work tasks, including whether those tasks are challenging, interesting, respected, and make use of key skills rather than being dull, repetitive, and uncomfortable.[20] Whereas the previous four facets described the outcomes that result from work (pay, promotions) and the people who surround work (supervisors, coworkers), this facet focuses on what employees actually *do*. After all, even the best boss or most interesting coworkers can't compensate for 40 or 50 hours of complete boredom each week! How can employers instill a sense of satisfaction with the work itself? One way is to emphasize the most challenging and interesting parts of the job. At Dream-Works Animation, the Glendale, California–based producer of *Shrek* and *Kung Fu Panda,* employees are encouraged to attend "Life's a Pitch" workshops that allow them to hone their presentation skills.[21] The company also helps employees flex their creative muscles by offering free drawing, sculpting, and improv classes. The CEO, Jeffrey Katzenberg, notes, "Our philosophy is that if you love your work, and you love coming to work, then the work will be exceptional."

In summary, value-percept theory suggests that employees will be satisfied when they perceive that their job offers the pay, promotions, supervision, coworkers, and work tasks that they value. Of course, this theory begs the question: Which of those ingredients is most important? In other words, which of the five facets in Figure 4-1 has the strongest influence on overall job satisfaction? Several research studies have examined these issues and come up with the results shown in Figure 4-2. The figure depicts the correlation between each of the five satisfaction facets and an overall index of job satisfaction. (Recall that correlations of .10, .30, and .50 indicate weak, moderate, and strong relationships, respectively.)

Figure 4-2 suggests that satisfaction with the work itself is the single strongest driver of overall job satisfaction.[22] Supervision and coworker satisfaction are also strong drivers, and promotion and pay satisfaction have moderately strong effects. Why is satisfaction with the work itself so critical? Well, consider that a typical workweek contains around 2,400 minutes. How much of that time is spent thinking about how much money you make? 10 minutes? Maybe 20? The same is true for promotions—we may want them, but we don't necessarily spend hours a day thinking about them. We do spend a significant chunk of that time with other people though. Between lunches, meetings, hallway chats, and other conversations, we might easily spend 600 minutes a week with supervisors and coworkers. That leaves almost 1,800 minutes for just us and our work. As a result, it's hard to be satisfied with your job if you don't like what you actually do.

SATISFACTION WITH THE WORK ITSELF

Given how critical enjoyable work tasks are to overall job satisfaction, it's worth spending more time describing the kinds of tasks that most people find enjoyable. Researchers began focusing on this question in the 1950s and 1960s, partly in reaction to practices based in the "scientific

| FIGURE 4-2 | Correlations between Satisfaction Facets and Overall Job Satisfaction |

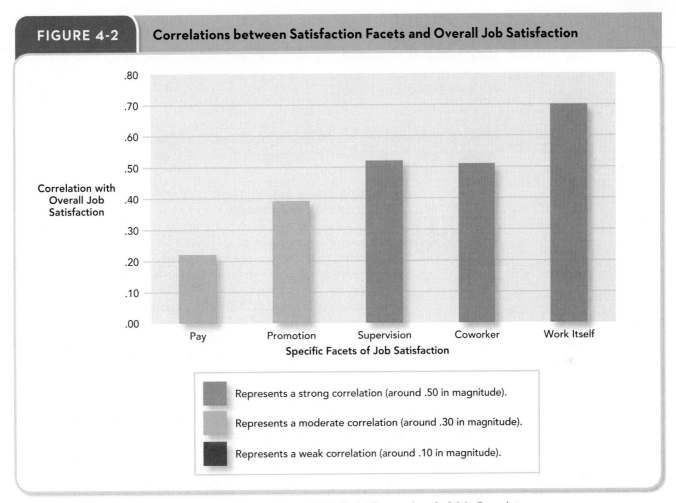

Represents a strong correlation (around .50 in magnitude).

Represents a moderate correlation (around .30 in magnitude).

Represents a weak correlation (around .10 in magnitude).

Sources: G.H. Ironson, P.C. Smith, M.T. Brannick, W.M. Gibson, and K.B. Paul, "Construction of a Job in General Scale: A Comparison of Global, Composite, and Specific Measures," *Journal of Applied Psychology* 74 (1989), pp. 193–200; and S.S. Russell, C. Spitzmuller, L.F. Lin, J.M. Stanton, P.C. Smith, and G.H. Ironson, "Shorter Can Also Be Better: The Abridged Job in General Scale," *Educational and Psychological Measurement* 64 (2004), pp. 878–93.

management" perspective. Scientific management focuses on increasing the efficiency of job tasks by making them more simplified and specialized and using time and motion studies to plan task movements and sequences carefully.[23] The hope was that such steps would increase worker

© Paul Sakuma/AP Images

Employees at DreamWorks Animation can express their creativity at work in a number of ways, including free drawing, sculpting, and improv classes, and courses on honing their pitching and presentation skills.

OB AT THE BOOKSTORE

ARE YOU FULLY CHARGED?

by Tom Rath (Arlington, VA: Missionday, 2015).

If you fail to do meaningful work that makes a difference today, the day is gone forever. You can try to make up for it tomorrow, but most likely you won't. Before you know it, several days will have gone by, then a few years.

ARE YOU
FULLY CHARGED?

THE 3 KEYS
TO ENERGIZING YOUR
WORK AND LIFE

TOM RATH

#1 NEW YORK TIMES BEST SELLING AUTHOR OF
STRENGTHSFINDER 2.0

Photo of cover: © Roberts Publishing Services

With those words, Tom Rath illustrates the importance of a daily perspective on meaningfulness. Rath notes that most people think of meaningfulness when reflecting on prior decades, asking "what have I accomplished in my work?" or "what has my life really meant?" It's less overwhelming—and more effective—to view meaningfulness as something that can be accomplished day in and day out. Indeed, Rath views doing so as one of three drivers of being "fully charged," a term that reflects sharpness of mind and strength of body. Rath's review of the scientific literature identifies three drivers of being fully charged. Besides meaningfulness, they include creating positive interactions and making choices that improve health.

In addition to his review of existing studies, Rath surveyed more than 10,000 people about the things that drive one's "charge." His results for meaningfulness showed that only 20% of people reported doing meaningful work the day before. Moreover, his research suggests that employees' odds of being intrinsically satisfied increase by 250 percent if they're one of those 20 percent. How, then, can people go about ensuring that their day includes some meaningful activities? Rath provides a number of tips. He suggests looking for "small wins" where you create a small positive change for someone else in your day. That focus on others is important because meaningfulness tends to come from an other-focus, not a self-focus. He also suggests keeping the beneficiaries of your work in the forefront of your mind. He uses the example of grocery store shelf stockers, noting that they're saving customers time and making it easier to share meals at home with their families. Finally, he suggests focusing on "initiating." We spend much of our day reacting to events. Instead, share a new idea, invest in another person's growth, or forge a new interpersonal connection.

---

productivity and reduce the breadth of skills required to complete a job, ultimately improving organizational profitability. Instead, the simplified and routine jobs tended to lower job satisfaction while increasing absenteeism and turnover.[24] Put simply: Boring jobs may be easier, but they're not necessarily better.

So what kinds of work tasks are especially satisfying? Research suggests that three "critical psychological states" make work satisfying. The first psychological state is believing in the **meaningfulness of work,** which reflects the degree to which work tasks are viewed as something that "counts" in the employee's system of philosophies and beliefs (see Chapter 6 on motivation for more discussion of such issues).[25] Trivial tasks tend to be less satisfying than tasks that make employees feel like they're aiding the organization or society in some meaningful way. For more on meaningfulness, see our **OB at the Bookstore** feature. The second

4.4

Which job characteristics can create a sense of satisfaction with the work itself?

psychological state is perceiving **responsibility for outcomes,** which captures the degree to which employees feel that they're key drivers of the quality of the unit's work.[26] Sometimes employees feel like their efforts don't really matter because work outcomes are dictated by effective procedures, efficient technologies, or more influential colleagues. Finally, the third psychological state is **knowledge of results,** which reflects the extent to which employees know how well (or how poorly) they're doing.[27] Many employees work in jobs in which they never find out about their mistakes or notice times when they did particularly well.

Think about times when you felt especially proud of a job well done. At that moment, you were probably experiencing all three psychological states. You were aware of the result (after all, some job had been done well). You felt you were somehow responsible for that result (otherwise, why would you feel proud?). Finally, you felt that the result of the work was somehow meaningful (otherwise, why would you have remembered it just now?). The next obvious question then becomes, "What kinds of tasks create these psychological states?" **Job characteristics theory,** which describes the central characteristics of intrinsically satisfying jobs, attempts to answer this question. As shown in Figure 4-3, job characteristics theory argues that five core job

---

FIGURE 4-3   Job Characteristics Theory

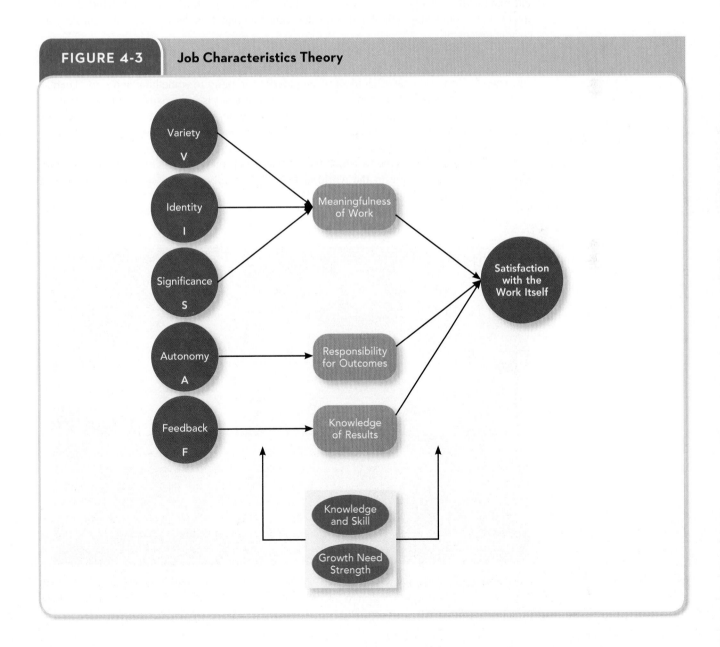

characteristics (variety, identity, significance, autonomy, and feedback, which you can remember with the acronym "VISAF") result in high levels of the three psychological states, making work tasks more satisfying.[28]

The first core job characteristic in Figure 4-3, **variety,** is the degree to which the job requires a number of different activities that involve a number of different skills and talents.[29] When variety is high, almost every workday is different in some way, and job holders rarely feel a sense of monotony or repetition.[30] Of course, we could picture jobs that have a variety of boring tasks, such as screwing different sized nuts onto different colored bolts, but such jobs do not involve a number of different skills and talents.[31]

Evidence indicates that our preference for variety is hardwired into our brains. Research in psychiatry and neuroscience shows that the brain releases a chemical called dopamine whenever a novel stimulus (a new painting, a new meal, a new work challenge) is experienced, and we tend to find this dopamine release quite pleasurable. Unfortunately, the amount of dopamine present in our brains declines over our life spans. One neuroscientist therefore suggests that the best way to protect our dopamine system is through novel, challenging experiences, writing, "The sense of satisfaction after you've successfully handled unexpected tasks or sought out unfamiliar, physically and emotionally demanding activities is your brain's signal that you're doing what nature designed you to do."[32] Something to think about the next time you plan to order the same old thing at your favorite restaurant!

The second core job characteristic in Figure 4-3, **identity,** is the degree to which the job requires completing a whole, identifiable, piece of work from beginning to end with a visible outcome.[33] When a job has high identity, employees can point to something and say, "There, I did that." The transformation from inputs to finished product is very visible, and the employee feels a distinct sense of beginning and closure.[34] Think about how you feel when you work for a while on some project but don't quite get it finished—does that lack of closure bug you? If so, identity is an important concern for you.

Significance is the degree to which the job has a substantial impact on the lives of other people, particularly people in the world at large.[35] Virtually any job can be important if it

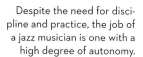

Despite the need for discipline and practice, the job of a jazz musician is one with a high degree of autonomy.

© Nick White/Digital Vision/Getty Images RF

helps put food on the table for a family, send kids to college, or make employees feel like they're doing their part for the working world. That said, significance as a core job characteristic captures something beyond that—the belief that this job *really matters.* When employees feel that their jobs are significant, they can see that others value what they do and they're aware that their job has a positive impact on the people around them.[36] There's the sense that, if their job was taken away, society would be the worse for it.

Autonomy is the degree to which the job provides freedom, independence, and discretion to the individual performing the work.[37] When your job provides autonomy, you view the outcomes of it as the product of your efforts rather than the result of careful instructions from your boss or a well-written manual of procedures.[38] Autonomy comes in multiple forms, including the freedom to control the timing, scheduling, and sequencing of work activities, as well as the procedures and methods used to complete work tasks.[39] To many of us, high levels of autonomy are the difference between "having a long leash" and being "micromanaged."

The last core job characteristic in Figure 4-3, **feedback,** is the degree to which carrying out the activities required by the job provides employees with clear information about how well they're performing.[40] A critical distinction must be noted: This core characteristic reflects feedback obtained *directly from the job* as opposed to feedback from coworkers or supervisors. Most employees receive formal performance appraisals from their bosses, but that feedback occurs once or maybe twice a year. When the job provides its own feedback, that feedback can be experienced almost every day.

The passages in this section illustrate the potential importance of each of the five core characteristics. But how important are the core characteristics to satisfaction with the work itself? Meta-analyses of around 200 different research studies employing around 90,000 total participants showed that the five core job characteristics are moderately to strongly related to work satisfaction.[41] However, those results don't mean that *every* employee wants more variety, more autonomy, and so forth. The bottom of Figure 4-3 includes two other variables: **knowledge and skill** and **growth need strength** (which captures whether employees have strong needs for personal accomplishment or developing themselves beyond where they currently are).[42] In the jargon of theory diagrams, these variables are called "moderators." Rather than directly affecting other variables in the diagram, moderators influence the strength of the relationships between variables. If employees lack the required knowledge and skill or lack a desire for growth and development, more variety and autonomy should *not* increase their satisfaction very much.[43] However, when employees are very talented and feel a strong need for growth, the core job characteristics become even more powerful. A graphical depiction of this moderator effect appears in Figure 4-4, where you can see that the relationship between the core job characteristics and satisfaction becomes stronger when growth need strength increases.

Given how critical the five core job characteristics are to job satisfaction, many organizations have employed job characteristics theory to help improve satisfaction among their employees. The first step in this process is assessing the current level of the characteristics to arrive at a "satisfaction potential score." See our **OB Assessments** feature for more about that step. The organization, together with job design consultants, then attempts to redesign aspects of the job to increase the core job characteristic levels. Often this step results in **job enrichment,** such that the duties and responsibilities associated with a job are expanded to provide more variety, identity, autonomy, and so forth. Research suggests that such enrichment efforts can indeed boost job satisfaction levels.[44] Moreover, enrichment efforts can heighten work accuracy and customer satisfaction, though training and labor costs tend to rise as a result of such changes.[45] However, employees needn't necessarily wait for enrichment efforts to improve levels of the core job characteristics. Many employees can engage in **job crafting,** where they shape, mold, and redefine their jobs in a proactive way.[46] For example, they might alter the boundaries of their jobs by switching certain tasks, they might change specific collaborative relationships, or they might reenvision how they view their work, relative to the broader context of the organization's mission.

4.5

How is job satisfaction affected by day-to-day events?

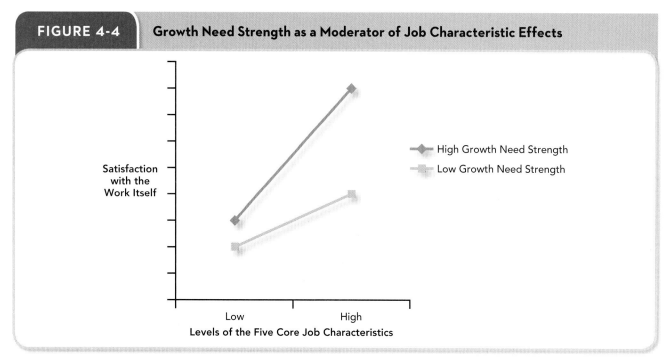

FIGURE 4-4   **Growth Need Strength as a Moderator of Job Characteristic Effects**

Source: Adapted from B.T. Loher, R.A. Noe, N.L. Moeller, and M.P. Fitzgerald, "A Meta-Analysis of the Relation of Job Characteristics to Job Satisfaction," *Journal of Applied Psychology* 70 (1985), pp. 280–89.

MOOD AND EMOTIONS

Let's say you're a satisfied employee, maybe because you get paid well and work for a good boss or because your work tasks provide you with variety and autonomy. Does this mean you'll definitely be satisfied at 11:00 a.m. next Tuesday? Or 2:30 p.m. the following Thursday? Obviously it doesn't. Each employee's satisfaction levels fluctuate over time, rising and falling like some sort of emotional stock market. This fluctuation might seem strange, given that people's pay, supervisors, coworkers, and work tasks don't change from one hour to the next. The key lies in remembering that job satisfaction reflects what you think and feel about your job. So part of it is rational, based on a careful appraisal of the job and the things it supplies. But another part of it is emotional, based on what you feel "in your gut" while you're at work or thinking about work. So satisfied employees feel good about their job *on average,* but things happen during the course of the day to make them feel better at some times (and worse at others).

Figure 4-5 illustrates the satisfaction levels for one employee during the course of a workday, from around 9:00 a.m. to 5:00 p.m. You can see that this employee did a number of different things during the day, from answering e-mails to eating lunch with friends to participating in a brainstorming meeting regarding a new project. You can also see that the employee came into the day feeling relatively satisfied, though satisfaction levels had several ebbs and flows during the next eight hours. What's responsible for those ebbs and flows in satisfaction levels? Two related concepts: mood and emotions.

4.6

What are mood and emotions, and what specific forms do they take?

What kind of mood are you in right now? Good? Bad? Somewhere in between? Why are you in that kind of mood? Do you really even know? (If it's a bad mood, we hope it has nothing to do with this book!) **Moods** are states of feeling that are often mild in intensity, last for an extended period of time, and are not explicitly directed at or caused by anything.[47] When people are in a good or bad mood, they don't always know who (or what) deserves the credit or blame; they just happen to be feeling that way for a stretch of their day. Of course, it would be oversimplifying things to call all moods either good or bad. Sometimes we're in a serene mood; sometimes we're in an enthusiastic mood. Both are "good" but obviously feel quite different. Similarly, sometimes we're in a bored mood; sometimes we're in a hostile mood. Both are "bad" but, again, feel quite different.

OB ASSESSMENTS

CORE JOB CHARACTERISTICS

How satisfying are your work tasks? This assessment is designed to measure the five core job characteristics. Think of your current job or the last job that you held (even if it was a part-time or summer job). Answer each question using the response scale provided. Then subtract your answers to the boldfaced question from 8, with the difference being your new answer for that question. For example, if your original answer for question 2 was "5," your new answer is "3" (8 – 5). Then use the formula to compute a satisfaction potential score (SPS). (Instructors: Assessments on growth need strength, emotional labor, flow, and positive emotionality can be found in the PowerPoints in the Connect Library's Instructor Resources and in the Connect assignments for this chapter).

1	2	3	4	5	6	7
VERY INACCURATE	MOSTLY INACCURATE	SLIGHTLY INACCURATE	UNCERTAIN	SLIGHTLY ACCURATE	MOSTLY ACCURATE	VERY ACCURATE

V1. The job requires me to use a number of complex or high-level skills. _____

V2. The job is quite simple and repetitive. _____

I1. The job is arranged so that I can do an entire piece of work from beginning to end. _____

I2. The job provides me the chance to completely finish the pieces of work I begin. _____

S1. This job is one where a lot of other people can be affected by how well the work gets done. _____

S2. The job itself is very significant and important in the broader scheme of things. _____

A1. The job gives me a chance to use my personal initiative and judgment in carrying out the work. _____

A2. The job gives me considerable opportunity for independence and freedom in how I do the work. _____

F1. Just doing the work required by the job provides many chances for me to figure out how well I am doing. _____

F2. After I finish a job, I know whether I performed well. _____

$$SPS = \left| \frac{V1+V2+I1+I2+S1+S2}{6} \right| \times \left| \frac{A1+A2}{2} \right| \times \left| \frac{F1+F2}{2} \right|$$

$$SPS = \left| \frac{}{6} \right| \times \left| \frac{}{2} \right| \times \left| \frac{}{2} \right|$$

$$SPS = \boxed{} \times \boxed{} \times \boxed{} = \boxed{}$$

SCORING AND INTERPRETATION

If your score is 150 or above, your work tasks tend to be satisfying and enjoyable. If your score is less than 150, you might benefit from trying to "craft" your job by taking on more challenging assignments and collaborations, or reenvisioning the way your job fits into the organization's mission.

Sources: J.R. Hackman and G.R. Oldham, *The Job Diagnostic Survey: An Instrument for the Diagnosis of Jobs and the Evaluation of Job Redesign Projects* (New Haven, CT: Yale University, 1974); and J.R. Idaszak and F. Drasgow, "A Revision of the Job Diagnostic Survey: Elimination of a Measurement Artifact," *Journal of Applied Psychology* 72 (1987), pp. 69–74.

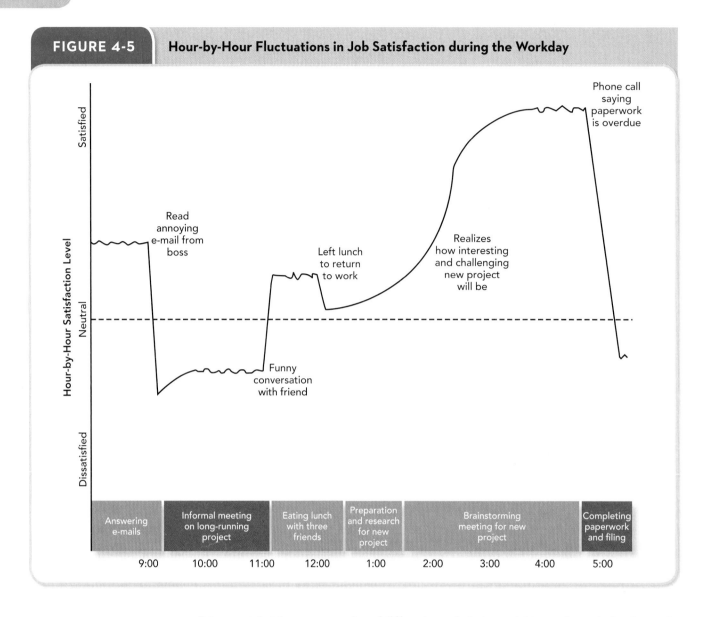

FIGURE 4-5 | **Hour-by-Hour Fluctuations in Job Satisfaction during the Workday**

It turns out that there are a number of different moods that we might experience during the workday. Figure 4-6 summarizes the different moods in which people sometimes find themselves. The figure illustrates that moods can be categorized in two ways: **pleasantness** and **activation.** First, the horizontal axis of the figure reflects whether you feel pleasant (in a "good mood") or unpleasant (in a "bad mood").[48] The figure uses green colors to illustrate pleasant moods and red colors to illustrate unpleasant moods. Second, the vertical axis of the figure reflects whether you feel activated and aroused or deactivated and unaroused.[49] The figure uses darker colors to convey higher levels of activation and lighter colors to convey lower levels. Note that some moods are neither good nor bad. For example, being surprised or astonished (high activation) and quiet or still (low activation) are neither pleasant nor unpleasant. As a result, those latter moods are left colorless in Figure 4-6.

Figure 4-6 illustrates that the most intense positive mood is characterized by feeling enthusiastic, excited, and elated. When employees feel this way, coworkers are likely to remark, "Wow, you're sure in a good mood!" In contrast, the most intense negative mood is characterized by feeling hostile, nervous, and annoyed. This kind of mood often triggers the question, "Wow, what's gotten you in such a bad mood?" If we return to our chart of hour-by-hour job satisfaction in Figure 4-5, what kind of mood do you think the employee was in while answering e-mails? Probably a happy, cheerful, and pleased mood. What kind of mood was the employee in during the informal meeting on the long-running project? Probably a grouchy, sad, and blue mood.

| FIGURE 4-6 | Different Kinds of Mood |

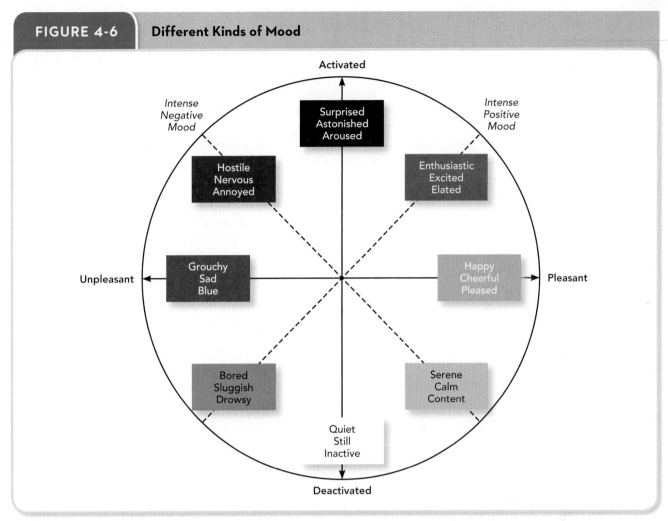

Sources: Adapted from D. Watson and A. Tellegen, "Toward a Consensual Structure of Mood," *Psychological Bulletin* 98 (1985), pp. 219–35; J.A. Russell, "A Circumplex Model of Affect," *Journal of Personality and Social Psychology* 39 (1980), pp. 1161–78; and R.J. Larsen and E. Diener, "Promises and Problems with the Circumplex Model of Emotion," in *Review of Personality and Social Psychology: Emotion,* Vol. 13, ed. M.S. Clark (Newbury Park, CA: Sage, 1992), pp. 25–59.

Finally, what kind of mood do you think the employee was in during the brainstorming meeting for the new project? Clearly, an enthusiastic, excited, and elated mood. This employee would report especially high levels of job satisfaction at this point in time.

Some organizations take creative steps to foster positive moods among their employees. For example, Quicken Loans, the Detroit–based online lender, provides Razor scooters to help team members go from place to place inside their headquarters.[50] Many of those places are adorned with scratch-and-sniff wallpaper and graffiti created by local artists. Or consider these offerings by Booz Allen Hamilton, the McLean, Virginia–based consulting firm. Employees can participate in ice cream socials, pet photo contests, and hula lessons.[51] Such perks may not rival the importance of pay, promotions, supervision, coworkers, and the work itself as far as job satisfaction is concerned, but they can help boost employees' moods during a particular workday.

Although novel and unusual perks can be valuable, the most intense forms of positive mood often come directly from work activities, like the brainstorming project in Figure 4-5. Research suggests that two conditions are critical to triggering intense positive mood. First, the activity in question has to be challenging. Second, the employee must possess the unique skills needed to meet that challenge. That high challenge–high skill combination can result in **flow**—a state in which employees feel a total immersion in the task at hand, sometimes losing track of how much time has passed.[52] People often describe flow as being "in the zone" and report heightened states of clarity, control, and concentration, along with a sense of enjoyment, interest, and loss of self-consciousness.[53] Although you may have experienced flow during leisure activities, such as playing sports or making music, research suggests that we experience flow more often in our working lives. Much of our leisure time is spent in passive recreation, such as watching TV or chatting with friends, that lacks the challenge needed to trigger flow states. Work tasks, in contrast, may supply the sorts of challenges that require concentration and immersion—particularly when those tasks contain high levels of variety, significance, autonomy, and so forth (see Chapter 6 on motivation for more discussion of such issues).

Returning to Figure 4-5, it's clear that specific events triggered variations in satisfaction levels. According to **affective events theory,** workplace events can generate affective reactions—reactions that then can go on to influence work attitudes and behaviors.[54] Workplace events include happenings, like an annoying e-mail from a boss or a funny conversation with a friend, that are relevant to an employee's general desires and concerns. These events can trigger **emotions,** which are states of feeling that are often intense, last for only a few minutes, and are clearly directed at (and caused by) someone or some circumstance. The difference between moods and emotions becomes clear in the way we describe them to others. We describe moods by saying, "I'm feeling grouchy," but we describe emotions by saying, "I'm feeling angry *at my boss.*"[55] According to affective events theory, these emotions can create the ebb and flow in satisfaction levels in Figure 4-5 and can also trigger spontaneous behaviors.[56] For example, positive emotions may trigger spontaneous instances of citizenship behavior, whereas negative emotions may trigger spontaneous instances of counterproductive behavior.

As with mood, it's possible to differentiate between specific examples of positive and negative emotions. Table 4-2 provides a summary of many of the most important.[57] **Positive emotions** include joy, pride, relief, hope, love, and compassion. **Negative emotions** include anger,

TABLE 4-2	Different Kinds of Emotions
POSITIVE EMOTIONS	**DESCRIPTION**
Joy	A feeling of great pleasure
Pride	Enhancement of identity by taking credit for achievement
Relief	A distressing condition has changed for the better
Hope	Fearing the worst but wanting better
Love	Desiring or participating in affection
Compassion	Being moved by another's situation
NEGATIVE EMOTIONS	
Anger	A demeaning offense against me and mine
Anxiety	Facing an uncertain or vague threat
Fear	Facing an immediate and concrete danger
Guilt	Having broken a moral code
Shame	Failing to live up to your ideal self
Sadness	Having experienced an irreversible loss
Envy	Wanting what someone else has
Disgust	Revulsion aroused by something offensive

Source: Adapted from R.S. Lazarus, *Emotion and Adaptation* (New York: Oxford University, 1991).

anxiety, fear, guilt, shame, sadness, envy, and disgust. What emotion do you think the employee experienced in Figure 4-5 when reading a disrespectful e-mail from the boss? Probably anger. What emotion do you think that same employee enjoyed during a funny conversation with a friend? Possibly joy, or maybe relief that lunch had arrived and a somewhat bad day was halfway over. Leaving lunch to return to work might have triggered either anxiety (because the bad day might resume) or sadness (because the fun time with friends had ended). Luckily, the employee's sense of joy at taking on a new project that was interesting and challenging was right around the corner. The day did end on a down note, however, as the phone call signaling overdue paperwork was likely met with some mix of anger, fear, guilt, or even disgust (no one likes paperwork!).

Of course, just because employees *feel* many of the emotions in Table 4-2 during the workday doesn't mean they're supposed to *show* those emotions. Some jobs demand that employees live up to the adage "never let 'em see you sweat." In particular, service jobs in which employees make direct contact with customers often require those employees to hide any anger, anxiety, sadness, or disgust that they may feel, suppressing the urge to spontaneously engage in some negative behavior. Such jobs are high in what's called **emotional labor,** or the need to manage emotions to complete job duties successfully.[58] Flight attendants are trained to "put on a happy face" in front of passengers, retail salespeople are trained to suppress any annoyance with customers, and restaurant servers are trained to act like they're having fun on their job even when they're not.

Is it a good idea to require emotional labor on the part of employees? Research on **emotional contagion** shows that one person can "catch" or "be infected by" the emotions of another person.[59] If a customer service representative is angry or sad, those negative emotions can be transferred to a customer (like a cold or disease). If that transfer occurs, it becomes less likely that customers will view the experience favorably and spend money, which potentially harms the bottom line. From this perspective, emotional labor seems like a vital part of good customer service. Unfortunately, other evidence suggests that emotional labor places great strain on employees and that their "bottled up" emotions may end up bubbling over, sometimes resulting in angry outbursts against customers or emotional exhaustion and burnout on the part of employees (see Chapter 5 on stress for more discussion of such issues).[60]

SUMMARY: WHY ARE SOME EMPLOYEES MORE SATISFIED THAN OTHERS?

So what explains why some employees are more satisfied than others? As we show in Figure 4-7, answering that question requires paying attention to the more rational appraisals people make about their job and the things it supplies for them, such as pay, promotions, supervision, coworkers, and the work itself. Satisfaction with the work itself, in turn, is affected by the five core job characteristics: variety, identity, significance, autonomy, and feedback. However, answering that question also requires paying attention to daily fluctuations in how people feel, in terms of their positive and negative moods and positive and negative emotions. In this way, a generally satisfied employee may act unhappy at a given moment, just as a generally dissatisfied employee may act happy at a given moment. Understanding those sorts of fluctuations can help managers separate long-term problems (boring tasks, incompetent coworkers) from more short-lived issues (a bad meeting, an annoying interaction).

HOW IMPORTANT IS JOB SATISFACTION?

Several factors influence an employee's job satisfaction, from pay to coworkers to job tasks to day-to-day moods and emotions. Of course, the most obvious remaining question is, "Does job satisfaction really matter?" More precisely, does job satisfaction have a significant impact on job performance and organizational commitment—the two primary outcomes in our integrative model of OB? Figure 4-8 summarizes the research evidence linking job satisfaction to job performance and organizational commitment. This same sort of figure will appear in each of the remaining chapters of this book, so that you can get a better feel for which of the concepts in our integrative model has the strongest impact on performance and commitment.

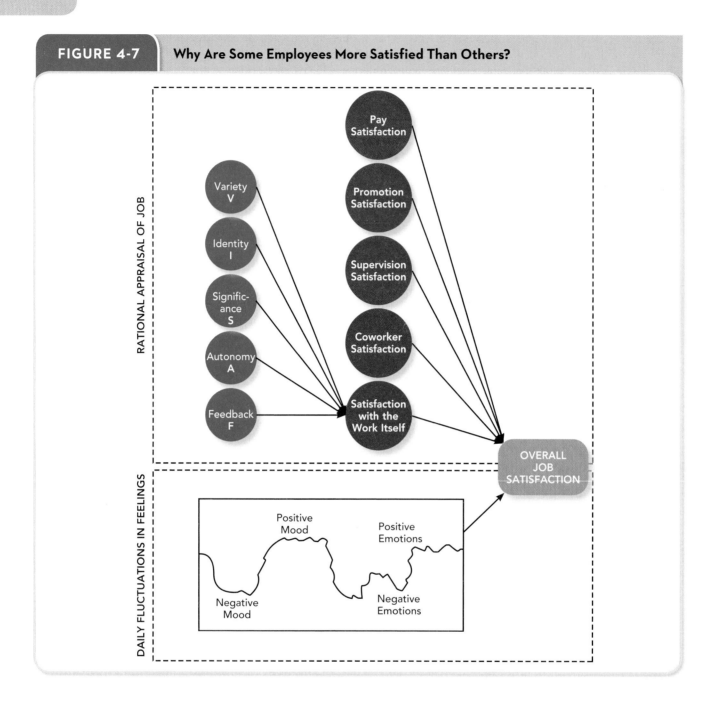

FIGURE 4-7   Why Are Some Employees More Satisfied Than Others?

4.7

How does job satisfaction affect job performance and organizational commitment? How does it affect life satisfaction?

Figure 4-8 reveals that job satisfaction does predict job performance. Why? One reason is that job satisfaction is moderately correlated with task performance. Satisfied employees do a better job of fulfilling the duties described in their job descriptions,[61] and evidence suggests that positive feelings foster creativity,[62] improve problem solving and decision making,[63] and enhance memory and recall of certain kinds of information.[64] Positive feelings also improve task persistence and attract more help and support from colleagues.[65] Apart from these sorts of findings, the benefits of job satisfaction for task performance might best be explained on an hour-by-hour basis. At any given moment, employees wage a war between paying attention to a given work task and attending to "off-task" things, such as stray thoughts, distractions, interruptions, and so forth. Positive feelings when working on job tasks can pull attention away from those distractions and channel people's attention to task accomplishment.[66] When such concentration occurs, an employee is more focused on work at a given point in time. Of course, the relationship between satisfaction and task performance can

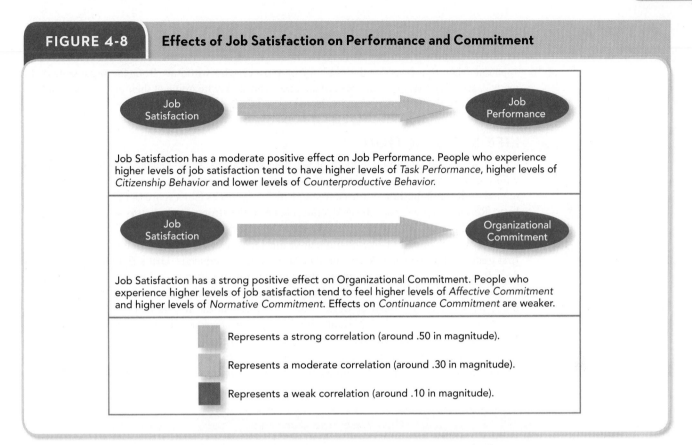

FIGURE 4-8 | **Effects of Job Satisfaction on Performance and Commitment**

Sources: A. Cooper-Hakim and C. Viswesvaran, "The Construct of Work Commitment: Testing an Integrative Framework," *Psychological Bulletin* 131 (2005), pp. 241–59; R.S. Dalal, "A Meta-Analysis of the Relationship between Organizational Citizenship Behavior and Counterproductive Work Behavior," *Journal of Applied Psychology* 90 (2005), pp. 1241–55; D.A. Harrison, D.A. Newman, and P.L. Roth, "How Important Are Job Attitudes? Meta-Analytic Comparisons of Integrative Behavioral Outcomes and Time Sequences," *Academy of Management Journal* 49 (2006), pp. 305–25; T.A. Judge, C.J. Thoreson, J.E. Bono, and G.K. Patton, "The Job Satisfaction–Job Performance Relationship: A Qualitative and Quantitative Review," *Psychological Bulletin* 127 (2001), pp. 376–407; J.A. LePine, A. Erez, and D.E. Johnson, "The Nature and Dimensionality of Organizational Citizenship Behavior: A Critical Review and Meta-Analysis," *Journal of Applied Psychology* 87 (2002), pp. 52–65; and J.P. Meyer, D.J. Stanley, L. Herscovitch, and L. Topolnytsky, "Affective, Continuance, and Normative Commitment to the Organization: A Meta-Analysis of Antecedents, Correlates, and Consequences," *Journal of Vocational Behavior* 61 (2002), pp. 20–52.

work in reverse to some extent, such that people tend to enjoy jobs that they can perform more successfully.[67] Meta-analyses tend to be less supportive of this causal direction, however.[68]

Job satisfaction also is correlated moderately with citizenship behavior. Satisfied employees engage in more frequent "extra mile" behaviors to help their coworkers and their organization.[69] Positive feelings increase their desire to interact with others and often result in spontaneous acts of helping and other instances of good citizenship.[70] In addition, job satisfaction has a moderate negative correlation with counterproductive behavior. Satisfied employees engage in fewer intentionally destructive actions that could harm their workplace.[71] Events that trigger negative emotions can prompt employees to "lash out" against the organization by engaging in rule breaking, theft, sabotage, or other retaliatory behaviors.[72] The more satisfied employees are, the less likely they'll feel those sorts of temptations.

Figure 4-8 also reveals that job satisfaction influences organizational commitment. Why? Job satisfaction is strongly correlated with affective commitment, so satisfied employees are more likely to want to stay with the organization.[73] After all, why would employees want to leave a place where they're happy? Another reason is that job satisfaction is strongly correlated with normative commitment. Satisfied employees are more likely to feel an obligation to remain with their firm[74] and a need to "repay" the organization for whatever it is that makes them so satisfied, whether good pay, interesting job tasks, or effective supervision. However, job satisfaction is uncorrelated with continuance commitment, because satisfaction does not create a cost-based need to remain with the organization. Taken together, these commitment effects become more apparent when you consider the kinds of employees who withdraw from the organization. In many cases, dissatisfied employees are the ones who sit daydreaming at their desks, come in late, are frequently absent, and eventually decide to quit their jobs.

LIFE SATISFACTION

Of course, job satisfaction is important for other reasons as well—reasons that have little to do with job performance or organizational commitment. For example, job satisfaction is strongly related to **life satisfaction,** or the degree to which employees feel a sense of happiness with their lives. Research shows that job satisfaction is one of the strongest predictors of life satisfaction. Put simply, people feel better about their lives when they feel better about their jobs.[75] This link makes sense when you realize how much of our identity is wrapped up in our jobs. What's the first question that people ask one another after being introduced? That's right—"What do you do?" If you feel bad about your answer to that question, it's hard to feel good about your life.

The connection between job satisfaction and life satisfaction also makes sense given how much of our lives are spent at work. Table 4-3 presents the results of one study that examines time spent on daily activities, along with reported levels of positive and negative feelings during the course of those activities.[76] The participants in the study spent most of their day at work. Unfortunately, that time resulted in the highest levels of negative feelings and the second-lowest levels of positive feelings (behind only commuting). Home and leisure activities

TABLE 4-3	How We Spend Our Days		
ACTIVITY	**AVERAGE HOURS PER DAY**	**POSITIVE FEELINGS**	**NEGATIVE FEELINGS**
Working	6.9	3.62	0.97
On the phone	2.5	3.92	0.85
Socializing	2.3	4.59	0.57
Eating	2.2	4.34	0.59
Relaxing	2.2	4.42	0.51
Watching TV	2.2	4.19	0.58
Computer/e-mail/Internet	1.9	3.81	0.80
Commuting	1.6	3.45	0.89
Housework	1.1	3.73	0.77
Interacting with kids	1.1	3.86	0.91
Napping	0.9	3.87	0.60
Praying/meditating	0.4	4.35	0.59
Exercising	0.2	4.31	0.50
Intimate relations	0.2	5.10	0.36

Notes: Positive and negative feelings measured using a scale of 0 (not at all) to 6 (very much).
Source: From D. Kahneman, A.B. Krueger, D.A. Schkade, N. Schwarz, and A.A. Stone, "A Survey Method for Characterizing Daily Life Experience: The Day Reconstruction Method," *Science* 306 (2004), pp. 1776–80. Reprinted with permission from AAAS.

OB ON SCREEN

HER

They're just letters. They're just other people's letters.

With those words, Theodore (Joaquin Phoenix) deflects a compliment about his work from his coworker Paul (Chris Pratt) in *Her* (Dir. Spike Jonze, Annapurna Pictures, 2013). Theodore is one of the more talented writers at Beautiful Handwritten Letters.com, an organization that does just that. Customers send in some photos and stray thoughts and Theodore writes a sincere, eloquent, and personalized letter. He then prints the letter on stationary before sending it on its way.

© Warner Bros./Photofest

Theodore is good at his job. He's a gifted writer, he's good at sensing the essence of a relationship, and he has a deep and sensitive soul. For example, when a client named Roger noted that he was in Prague on business and was missing Rachel, Theodore quickly crafted a letter that referred to Rachel's "sweet little cute crooked tooth." He'd noticed the tooth in a picture Roger had sent. And, because he'd been writing them letters for eight years, he knew their particular brand of humor and sentiment. It's that sort of skill that compels Paul to tell Theodore how much he enjoys his letters.

Theodore's struggle throughout the film is not his job—it's the other activities in Table 4-3 that reflect the other parts of life. He's going through a divorce and has withdrawn from some of his friendships. He even commutes home from the office to a playlist labeled "melancholy." Explains Theodore, "Sometimes I think I have felt everything I'm ever gonna feel. And from here on out, I'm not gonna feel anything new. Just lesser versions of what I've already felt." Put differently, he no longer feels the kinds of emotions he's writing about in those letters. All that begins to change when Theodore installs OS1, an artificially intelligent operating system who names herself Samantha. As Samantha moves from organizing e-mails and proofreading letters to engaging with Theodore on a more emotional level, his life gets fuller and more satisfying. But does that sort of relationship have any real future?

(e.g., socializing, relaxing, exercising, intimate relations) were deemed much more satisfying but took up a much smaller portion of the day. The implication is clear: If we want to feel better about our days, we need to find a way to be more satisfied with our jobs. For a look at job and life satisfaction in the (near?) future, see our **OB on Screen** feature.

OB INTERNATIONALLY

The "money can't buy happiness" adage can even be supported using nation-level data. For example, survey data in the United States, Britain, and Japan show that people are no happier today than they were 50 years ago, even though average incomes have more than doubled during that span.

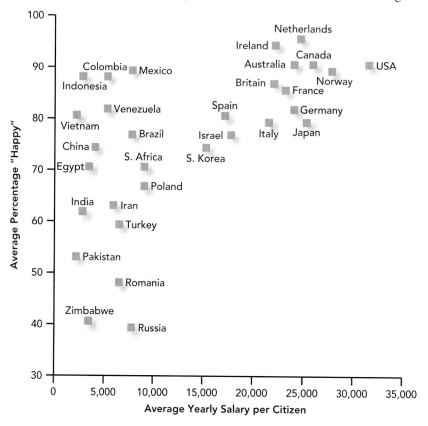

Comparing countries reveals that nations above the poverty line are indeed happier than nations below the poverty line. However, once that poverty threshold gets crossed, additional income is not associated with higher levels of life satisfaction. For example, the United States is the richest country on earth, but it trails nations like the Netherlands and Ireland in life satisfaction. Understanding differences in life satisfaction across nations is important to organizations for two reasons. First, such differences may influence how receptive a given nation is to the company's products. Second, such differences may affect the kinds of policies and practices an organization needs to use when employing individuals in that nation.

Source: R. Layard, qtd. in Diener, E., and E. Suh. "National Differences in Subjective Well-Being." In *Well-Being: The Foundations of Hedonic Psychology,* ed. D. Kahneman, E. Diener, and N. Schwarz. New York: Russell Sage Foundation, 1999, pp. 434–50.

Indeed, increases in job satisfaction have a stronger impact on life satisfaction than do increases in salary or income. It turns out that the adage "money can't buy happiness" is partially true. Research suggests that life satisfaction increases with one's salary up to a level of around $75,000 per year. After that, more money doesn't seem to bring more happiness.[77] Such findings may seem surprising, given that pay satisfaction is one facet of overall job satisfaction (see Figure 4-1). However, you might recall that pay satisfaction is a weaker driver of overall job satisfaction than other facets, such as the work itself, supervision, or coworkers (see Figure 4-2). For more on the relationship between money and happiness, see our **OB Internationally** feature.

APPLICATION: TRACKING SATISFACTION

Because job satisfaction seems to be a key driver of job performance, organizational commitment, and life satisfaction, it's important for managers to understand just how satisfied their employees are. Several methods assess the job satisfaction of rank-and-file employees, including focus groups, interviews, and attitude surveys. Of those three choices, attitude surveys are often the most accurate and most effective.[78] Attitude surveys can provide a "snapshot" of how satisfied the workforce is and, if repeated over time, reveal trends in satisfaction levels. They also can explore the effectiveness of major job changes by comparing attitude survey results before and after a change.

Although organizations are often tempted to design their own attitude surveys, there are benefits to using existing surveys that are already in wide use. One of the most widely administered job satisfaction surveys is the Job Descriptive Index (JDI). The JDI assesses all five satisfaction facets in Figure 4-1: pay satisfaction, promotion satisfaction, supervisor satisfaction, coworker satisfaction, and satisfaction with the work itself. The JDI also has been subjected to a great deal of research attention that, by and large, supports its accuracy.[79] Furthermore, the JDI includes a companion survey—the Job in General (JIG) scale—that assesses overall job satisfaction.[80] Excerpts from the JDI and JIG appear in Table 4-4.[81] One strength of the JDI is that the questions are written in a very simple and straightforward fashion so that they can be easily understood by most employees.

The developers of the JDI offer several suggestions regarding its administration.[82] For example, they recommend surveying as much of the company as possible because any unsurveyed employees might feel that their feelings are less important. They also recommend that surveys be anonymous so that employees can be as honest as possible without worrying about being punished for any critical comments about the organization. Therefore, companies must be careful in collecting demographic information on the surveys. Some demographic information is

4.8

What steps can organizations take to assess and manage job satisfaction?

TABLE 4-4	Excerpts from the Job Descriptive Index and the Job in General Scale

Think of the work you do at present. How well does each of the following words or phrases describe your work? In the blank beside each word or phrase below, write

<u>Y</u> for "Yes" if it describes your work
<u>N</u> for "No" if it does NOT describe it
<u>?</u> for "?" if you cannot decide

Pay Satisfaction[a]	**Coworker Satisfaction**[a]
_____ Well-paid	_____ Stimulating
_____ Bad	_____ Smart
_____ Barely live on income	_____ Unpleasant
Promotion Satisfaction[a]	**Satisfaction with Work Itself**[a]
_____ Regular promotions	_____ Fascinating
_____ Promotion on ability	_____ Pleasant
_____ Opportunities somewhat limited	_____ Can see my results
Supervision Satisfaction[a]	**OVERALL JOB SATISFACTION**[b]
_____ Knows job well	_____ Better than most
_____ Around when needed	_____ Worthwhile
_____ Doesn't supervise enough	_____ Worse than most

[a] The Job Descriptive Index, © Bowling Green State University (1975, 1985, 1997).
[b] The Job in General Scale, © Bowling Green State University (1982, 1985).
Source: W.K. Balzer, J.A. Kihn, P.C. Smith, J.L. Irwin, P.D. Bachiochi, C. Robie, E.F. Sinar, amp; L.F. Parra, 2000, "Users' Manual for the Job Descriptive Index (JDI; 1997 version) and the Job in General Scales." In J.N. Stanton amp; C.D. Crossley (ed.), *Electronic Resources for the JDI and JIG.* Bowling Green, OH, Bowling Green State University.

vital for comparing satisfaction levels across relevant groups, but too much information will make employees feel like they could be identified. Finally, the developers suggest that the survey should be administered by the firm's human resources group or an outside consulting agency. This structure will help employees feel that their anonymity is more protected.

Once JDI data have been collected, a number of interesting questions can be explored.[83] First, the data can indicate whether the organization is satisfied or dissatisfied by comparing average scores for each facet with the JDI's "neutral levels" for those facets (the "neutral levels" are available in the JDI manual). Second, it becomes possible to compare the organization's scores with national norms to provide some context for the firm's satisfaction levels. The JDI manual also provides national norms for all facets and breaks down those norms according to relevant demographic groups (e.g., managers vs. nonmanagers, new vs. senior employees, gender, education). Third, the JDI allows for within-organization comparisons to determine which departments have the highest satisfaction levels and which have the lowest.

The results of attitude survey efforts should then be fed back to employees so that they feel involved in the process. Of course, attitude surveys ideally should be a catalyst for some kind of improvement effort.[84] Surveys that never lead to any kind of on-the-job change eventually may be viewed as a waste of time. As a result, the organization should be prepared to react to the survey results with specific goals and action steps. For example, an organization with low pay satisfaction may react by conducting additional benchmarking to see whether compensation levels are trailing those of competitors. An organization with low promotion satisfaction might react by revising its system for assessing performance. Finally, an organization that struggles with satisfaction with the work itself could attempt to redesign key job tasks or, if that proves too costly, train supervisors in strategies for increasing the five core job characteristics on a more informal basis.

TAKEAWAYS

4.1 Job satisfaction is a pleasurable emotional state resulting from the appraisal of one's job or job experiences. It represents how you feel about your job and what you think about your job.

4.2 Values are things that people consciously or subconsciously want to seek or attain. According to value-percept theory, job satisfaction depends on whether you perceive that your job supplies those things that you value.

4.3 Employees consider a number of specific facets when evaluating their job satisfaction. These facets include pay satisfaction, promotion satisfaction, supervision satisfaction, coworker satisfaction, and satisfaction with the work itself.

4.4 Job characteristics theory suggests that five "core characteristics"—variety, identity, significance, autonomy, and feedback—combine to result in particularly high levels of satisfaction with the work itself.

4.5 Apart from the influence of supervision, coworkers, pay, and the work itself, job satisfaction levels fluctuate during the course of the day. Rises and falls in job satisfaction are triggered by positive and negative events that are experienced. Those events trigger changes in emotions that eventually give way to changes in mood.

4.6 Moods are states of feeling that are often mild in intensity, last for an extended period of time, and are not explicitly directed at anything. Intense positive moods include being enthusiastic, excited, and elated. Intense negative moods include being hostile, nervous, and annoyed. Emotions are states of feeling that are often intense, last only for a few minutes, and are clearly directed at someone or some circumstance. Positive emotions include joy, pride, relief, hope, love, and compassion. Negative emotions include anger, anxiety, fear, guilt, shame, sadness, envy, and disgust.

4.7 Job satisfaction has a moderate positive relationship with job performance and a strong positive relationship with organizational commitment. It also has a strong positive relationship with life satisfaction.

4.8 Organizations can assess and manage job satisfaction using attitude surveys such as the Job Descriptive Index (JDI), which assesses pay satisfaction, promotion satisfaction, supervision satisfaction, coworker satisfaction, and satisfaction with the work itself. It can be used to assess the levels of job satisfaction experienced by employees, and its specific facet scores can identify interventions that could be helpful.

KEY TERMS

- Job satisfaction — p. 96
- Values — p. 97
- Value-percept theory — p. 98
- Pay satisfaction — p. 98
- Promotion satisfaction — p. 98
- Supervision satisfaction — p. 99
- Coworker satisfaction — p. 100
- Satisfaction with the work itself — p. 100
- Meaningfulness of work — p. 102
- Responsibility for outcomes — p. 103
- Knowledge of results — p. 105
- Job characteristics theory — p. 103
- Variety — p. 103
- Identity — p. 104
- Significance — p. 104
- Autonomy — p. 105
- Feedback — p. 105
- Knowledge and skill — p. 105
- Growth need strength — p. 105
- Job enrichment — p. 105
- Job crafting — p. 105
- Moods — p. 106
- Pleasantness — p. 108
- Activation — p. 108
- Flow — p. 109
- Affective events theory — p. 110
- Emotions — p. 110
- Positive emotions — p. 110
- Negative emotions — p. 110
- Emotional labor — p. 111
- Emotional contagion — p. 111
- Life satisfaction — p. 114

DISCUSSION QUESTIONS

4.1 Which of the values in Table 4-1 do you think are the most important to employees in general? Are there times when the values in the last three categories (altruism, status, and environment) become more important than the values in the first five categories (pay, promotions, supervision, coworkers, and the work itself)?

4.2 What steps can organizations take to improve promotion satisfaction, supervision satisfaction, and coworker satisfaction?

4.3 Consider the five core job characteristics (variety, identity, significance, autonomy, and feedback). Do you think that any one of those characteristics is more important than the other four? Is it possible to have too much of some job characteristics?

4.4 We sometimes describe colleagues or friends as "moody." What do you think it means to be "moody" from the perspective of Figure 4-6?

4.5 Consider the list of positive and negative emotions in Table 4-2. Which of these emotions are most frequently experienced at work? What causes them?

CASE: TWITTER

Although its rooftop deck and interior log cabins are noteworthy, the neighborhood where Twitter's new headquarters resides is also worth discussing. It sits in South of Market, just at the edge of the Tenderloin—a neighborhood with decaying hotels, low income housing, a high homeless population, and a violent crime rate that's 35 times higher than elsewhere in San Francisco. The city offered Twitter a six-year suspension of its payroll tax to take over the Art Deco Building on Market Street, which was built in 1937. In return, the city hopes that Twitter's presence will lead to additional development and revitalization of the neighborhood. Indeed, the so-called Twitter tax break has led other tech firms to move to the area, including Uber and Square.

Twitter's decision to move to the edge of the Tenderloin has two obvious implications for employee job satisfaction. On the one hand, Twitter employees—most of whom prefer to live in San Francisco proper—are spared the bus ride to suburbs like Mountain View or Cupertino. On the other hand, having a safe and pleasant work environment is a key concern for most employees. But the decision has implications for job satisfaction that are not as obvious. For one, the neighborhood provides an opportunity for Twitter to "give back" charitably, philanthropically, and economically. Indeed, Twitter gave $367,000 to local nonprofits while also offering office space for fundraisers and events. It's also opening the Twitter NeighborNest, a learning center staffed by Twitter volunteers that will offer free computer, housing, and employment classes to anyone in the neighborhood—with child care included. The company also works with the Boys and Girls Club and with the San Francisco Food Bank.

Executives argue that the company's "neighborhood mission" is actually something that entices prospective recruits. Caroline Barlerin, head of community outreach and philanthropy for the company, argues, "If you want to attract the best talent, this is key . . . I wanted the employees here to feel that we are putting down roots in the community. In order to do that they have to be a part of that community." It's too soon to say what Twitter's efforts—and its presence—will do to the Tenderloin. Indeed, increased development and heightened property values may make it difficult for existing neighborhood residents to stay in the area. But, to the degree that Twitter employees view the outreach as another part of their jobs, the activities in the Tenderloin give them another piece of significance in their workweek.

4.1   How important is *where* one works, in comparison to *what* one is doing? How much does suburb vs. city seem to matter, and how critical does a sense of safety tend to be?

4.2   If you worked for Twitter in the Tenderloin, how involved would you want to be in its community outreach efforts? Why?

4.3   Volunteering has the potential to inject different kinds of job tasks to an employee's regular employment duties. When companies encourage volunteering, do you think volunteers wind up having higher job satisfaction or lower job satisfaction? Why, and what might it depend on?

Sources: R. Johnson, "Prostitution, Homelessness and Drugs Surround Twitter's New HQ," *Business Insider,* March 15, 2014; M. Lev-Ram, "Welcome to the Twitterloin," *Fortune,* March 15, 2015; A. Levy, "Tech's Quest to Revive San Francisco's Underbelly," *CNBC Technology,* April 28, 2015; M. Moskowitz and R. Levering. "The 100 Best Companies," *Fortune,* March 15, 2015; and N. Rapp, "Top of the Heap," *Fortune,* March 15, 2015.

EXERCISE: JOB SATISFACTION ACROSS JOBS

The purpose of this exercise is to examine satisfaction with the work itself across jobs. This exercise uses groups, so your instructor will either assign you to a group or ask you to create your own group. The exercise has the following steps:

4.1   Use the OB Assessments for Chapter 4 to calculate the Satisfaction Potential Score (SPS) for the following four jobs:

a.   A third-grade public school teacher.

b.   A standup comedian.

c.   A computer programmer whose job is to replace "15" with "2015" in thousands of lines of computer code.

d.   A president of the United States.

4.2   Which job has the highest SPS? Which core job characteristics best explain why some jobs have high scores and other jobs have low scores? Write down the scores for the four jobs in an Excel file on the classroom computer or on the board.

4.3   Class discussion (whether in groups or as a class) should center on two questions. First, is the job that scored the highest really the one that would be the most enjoyable on a day-in, day-out basis? Second, does that mean it would be the job that you would pick if you could snap your fingers and magically attain one of the jobs on the list? Why or why not? What other job satisfaction theory is relevant to this issue?

ENDNOTES

4.1   Locke, E.A. "The Nature and Causes of Job Satisfaction." In *Handbook of Industrial and Organizational Psychology,* ed. M. Dunnette. Chicago: Rand McNally, 1976, pp. 1297–1350.

4.2   "Americans' Job Satisfaction Falls to Record Low." Associated Press, January 5, 2010, http://www.msnbc. msn.com/id/34691428/ns/business-careers.

4.3   Locke, "The Nature and Causes of Job Satisfaction"; Rokeach, M. *The Nature of Human Values.* New York: Free Press, 1973; Schwartz, S.H. "Universals in the Content and Structure of Values: Theoretical Advances and Empirical Tests in 20 Countries." In *Advances in Experimental Social Psychology,* Vol. 25, ed. M. Zanna. New York: Academic Press, 1992, pp. 1–65; and Edwards, J.R., and D.M. Cable. "The Value of Value Congruence." *Journal of Applied Psychology* 94 (2009), pp. 654–77.

4.4   Dawis, R.V. "Vocational Interests, Values, and Preferences." In *Handbook of Industrial and Organizational Psychology,* Vol. 2, ed. M.D. Dunnette and L.M. Hough Palo Alto, CA: Consulting Psychologists Press, 1991, pp. 834–71; and Cable, D.M., and J.R. Edwards. "Complementary and Supplementary Fit: A Theoretical and Empirical Integration." *Journal of Applied Psychology* 89 (2004), pp. 822–34.

4.5   Locke, "The Nature and Causes of Job Satisfaction."

4.6   Judge, T.A., and A.H. Church. "Job Satisfaction: Research and Practice." In *Industrial and Organizational Psychology: Linking Theory with Practice,* ed. C.L. Cooper and E.A. Locke. Oxford, UK: Blackwell, 2000, pp. 166–98.

4.7   Locke, "The Nature and Causes of Job Satisfaction."

4.8   Smith, P.C.; L.M. Kendall; and C.L. Hulin. *The Measurement of Satisfaction in Work and Retirement.* Chicago: Rand McNally, 1969.

4.9   Lawler, E.E. *Pay and Organizational Effectiveness: A Psychological View.* New York: McGraw-Hill, 1971.

4.10   Locke, "The Nature and Causes of Job Satisfaction."

4.11   Moskowitz, M.; R. Levering; and C. Tkaczyk. "100 Best Companies to Work For." *Fortune,* February 7, 2011, pp. 91–101.

4.12   Smith et al., "The Measurement of Satisfaction."

4.13   Locke, "The Nature and Causes of Job Satisfaction."

4.14   Tkaczyk, C. "Nordstrom." *Fortune,* October 18, 2010, p. 37.

4.15   Smith et al., "The Measurement of Satisfaction."

4.16   Locke, "The Nature and Causes of Job Satisfaction."

4.17   Burchell, M., and J. Robin. *The Great Workplace: How to*

Build It, How to Keep It, and Why It Matters. San Francisco: Jossey-Bass, 2011.

4.18 Smith et al., "The Measurement of Satisfaction."

4.19 Burchell and Robin, *The Great Workplace.*

4.20 Smith et al., "The Measurement of Satisfaction."

4.21 Murphy, R. M. "Happy Campers." *Fortune,* April 25, 2011.

4.22 Ironson, G.H.; P.C. Smith; M.T. Brannick; W.M. Gibson; and K.B. Paul. "Construction of a Job in General Scale: A Comparison of Global, Composite, and Specific Measures." *Journal of Applied Psychology* 74 (1989), pp. 193–200; Russell, S.S.; C. Spitzmuller; L.F. Lin; J.M. Stanton; P.C. Smith; and G.H. Ironson. "Shorter Can Also Be Better: The Abridged Job in General Scale." *Educational and Psychological Measurement* 64 (2004), pp. 878–93; Bowling, N.A., and Hammond, G.D. "A Meta-Analytic Examination of the Construct Validity of the Michigan Organizational Assessment Questionnaire Job Satisfaction Subscale." *Journal of Vocational Behavior* 73 (2008), pp. 63–77; and Judge, T.A.; R.F. Piccolo; N.P. Podsakoff; J.C. Shaw; and B.L. Rich.

"The Relationship between Pay and Job Satisfaction: A Meta-Analysis." *Journal of Vocational Behavior* 77 (2010), pp. 157–67.

4.23 Taylor, F.W. *The Principles of Scientific Management.* New York: Wiley, 1911; and Gilbreth, F.B. *Motion Study: A Method for Increasing the Efficiency of the Workman.* New York: Van Nostrand, 1911.

4.24 Hackman, J.R., and E.E. Lawler III. "Employee Reactions to Job Characteristics." *Journal of Applied Psychology* 55 (1971), pp. 259–86.

4.25 Hackman, J.R., and G.R. Oldham. *Work Redesign.* Reading, MA: Addison-Wesley, 1980.

4.26 Ibid.

4.27 Ibid.

4.28 Hackman, J.R., and G.R. Oldham. "Motivation through the Design of Work: Test of a Theory." *Organizational Behavior and Human Decision Processes* 16 (1976), pp. 250–79.

4.29 Hackman and Oldham, *Work Redesign.*

4.30 Turner, A.N., and P.R. Lawrence. *Industrial Jobs and the Worker.* Boston: Harvard University Graduate School of Business Administration, 1965.

4.31 Hackman and Lawler, "Employee Reactions to Job Characteristics."

4.32 Berns, G. *Satisfaction: The Science of Finding True Fulfillment.* New York: Henry Holt, 2005, p. xiv.

4.33 Hackman and Oldham, *Work Redesign.*

4.34 Turner and Lawrence, *Industrial Jobs and the Worker.*

4.35 Hackman and Oldham, *Work Redesign.*

4.36 Grant, A.M. "The Significance of Task Significance: Job Performance Effects, Relational Mechanisms, and Boundary Conditions." *Journal of Applied Psychology* 93 (2008), pp. 108–24.

4.37 Hackman and Oldham, *Work Redesign.*

4.38 Turner and Lawrence, *Industrial Jobs and the Worker.*

4.39 Breaugh, J.A. "The Measurement of Work Autonomy." *Human Relations* 38 (1985), pp. 551–70.

4.40 Hackman and Oldham, *Work Redesign.*

4.41 Humphrey, S.E.; J.D. Nahrgang; and F.P. Morgeson. "Integrating Motivational, Social, and Contextual Work Design Features: A Meta-Analytic Summary and Theoretical Extension of the Work Design Literature." *Journal of Applied Psychology* 92 (2007), pp. 1332–56; and Fried, Y., and G.R. Ferris. "The Validity of the Job Characteristics Model: A Review and Meta-Analysis."

Personnel Psychology 40 (1987), pp. 287–322.

4.42 Hackman and Oldham, *Work Redesign.*

4.43 Loher, B.T.; R.A. Noe; N.L. Moeller; and M.P. Fitzgerald. "A Meta-Analysis of the Relation of Job Characteristics to Job Satisfaction." *Journal of Applied Psychology* 70 (1985), pp. 280–89.

4.44 Campion, M.A., and C.L. McClelland. "Interdisciplinary Examination of the Costs and Benefits of Enlarged Jobs: A Job Design Quasi-Experiment." *Journal of Applied Psychology* 76 (1991), pp. 186–98.

4.45 Ibid.

4.46 Wrzesniewski, A., and J.E. Dutton. "Crafting a Job: Revisioning Employees as Active Crafters of Their Work." *Academy of Management Review* 26 (2001), pp. 179–201; and Tims, M.; A.B. Bakker; and D. Derks. "Development and Validation of the Job Crafting Scale." *Journal of Vocational Behavior* 80 (2012), pp. 173–86.

4.47 Morris, W.N. *Mood: The Frame of Mind.* New York: Springer-Verlag, 1989.

4.48 Watson, D., and A. Tellegen. "Toward a Consensual Structure of Mood." *Psychological Bulletin* 98 (1985), pp. 219–35; Russell, J.A.

"A Circumplex Model of Affect." *Journal of Personality and Social Psychology* 39 (1980), pp. 1161–78; and Larsen, R.J., and E. Diener. "Promises and Problems with the Circumplex Model of Emotion." In *Review of Personality and Social Psychology: Emotion,* Vol. 13, ed. M.S. Clark. Newbury Park, CA: Sage, 1992, pp. 25–59.

4.49 Ibid.

4.50 Moskowitz et al., "100 Best Companies to Work For."

4.51 Ibid.

4.52 Csikszentmihalyi, M. *Finding Flow: The Psychology of Engagement with Everyday Life.* New York: Basic Books, 1997; Csikszentmihalyi, M. *Flow: The Psychology of Optimal Experience.* New York: Harper-Perennial, 1990; and Csikszentmihalyi, M. *Beyond Boredom and Anxiety.* San Francisco: Jossey-Bass, 1975.

4.53 Quinn, R.W. "Flow in Knowledge Work: High Performance Experience in the Design of National Security Technology." *Administrative Science Quarterly* 50 (2005), pp. 610–41; Jackson, S.A., and H.W. Marsh. "Development and Validation of a Scale to Measure Optimal Experience: The Flow State Scale." *Journal of Sport and*

Exercise Psychology 18 (1996), pp. 17–35; and Bakker, A.B. "The Work-Related Flow Inventory: Construction and Initial Validation of the WOLF." *Journal of Vocational Behavior* 72 (2008), pp. 400–14.

4.54 Weiss, H.M., and R. Cropanzano. "Affective Events Theory: A Theoretical Discussion of the Structure, Causes, and Consequences of Affective Experiences at Work." In *Research in Organizational Behavior,* Vol. 18, ed. B.M. Staw and L.L. Cummings. Greenwich, CT: JAI Press, 1996, pp. 1–74.

4.55 Weiss, H.M., and K.E. Kurek. "Dispositional Influences on Affective Experiences at Work." In *Personality and Work: Reconsidering the Role of Personality in Organizations,* ed. M.R. Barrick and A.M. Ryan. San Francisco: Jossey-Bass, 2003, pp. 121–49.

4.56 Weiss and Cropanzano, "Affective Events Theory."

4.57 Lazarus, R.S. *Emotion and Adaptation.* New York: Oxford University, 1991.

4.58 Hochschild, A.R. *The Managed Heart: Commercialization of Human Feeling.* Berkeley: University of California Press, 1983; and Rafaeli, A., and R.I. Sutton. "The Expression of Emotion in Organizational Life." *Research in Organizational Behavior* 11 (1989), pp. 1–42.

4.59 Hatfield, E.; J.T. Cacioppo; and R.L. Rapson. *Emotional Contagion.* New York: Cambridge University Press, 1994.

4.60 Ashkanasy, N.M.; C.E.J. Hartel; and C.S. Daus. "Diversity and Emotion: The New Frontiers in Organizational Behavior Research." *Journal of Management* 28 (2002), pp. 307–38.

4.61 Judge, T.A.; C.J. Thoreson; J.E. Bono; and G.K Patton. "The Job Satisfaction–Job Performance Relationship: A Qualitative and Quantitative Review." *Psychological Bulletin* 127 (2001), pp. 376–407.

4.62 Baas, M.; C.K.W. De Dreu; and B.A. Nijstad. "A Meta-Analysis of 25 Years of Mood—Creativity Research: Hedonic Tone, Activation, or Regulatory Focus." *Psychological Bulletin* 134 (2008), pp. 779–806; and Lyubomirsky, S.; L. King; and E. Diener. "The Benefits of Frequent Positive Affect: Does Happiness Lead to Success?" *Psychological Bulletin* 131 (2005), pp. 803–55.

4.63 Brief, A.P., and H.M. Weiss. "Organizational Behavior: Affect in the Workplace." *Annual Review of Psychology* 53 (2002), pp. 279–307.

4.64 Isen, A.M., and R.A. Baron. "Positive Affect as a Factor in Organizational Behavior." *Research in Organizational Behavior* 13 (1991), pp. 1–53.

4.65 Tsai, W.C.; C.C. Chen; and H.L. Liu. "Test of a Model Linking Employee Positive Moods and Task Performance." *Journal of Applied Psychology* 92 (2007), pp. 1570–83.

4.66 Beal, D.J.; H.M. Weiss; E. Barros; and S.M. MacDermid. "An Episodic Process Model of Affective Influences on Performance." *Journal of Applied Psychology* 90 (2005), pp. 1054–68; and Miner, A.G., and T.M. Glomb. "State Mood, Task Performance, and Behavior at Work: A Within-Persons Approach." *Organizational Behavior and Human Decision Processes* 112 (2010), pp. 43–57.

4.67 Locke, "The Nature and Causes of Job Satisfaction."

4.68 Riketta, M. "The Causal Relation between Job Attitudes and Job Performance: A Meta-Analysis of Panel Studies." *Journal of Applied Psychology* 93 (2008), pp. 472–81.

4.69 LePine, J.A.; A. Erez; and D.E. Johnson. "The Nature and Dimensionality of Organizational Citizenship Behavior: A Critical Review and Meta-Analysis." *Journal of Applied Psychology* 87 (2002), pp. 52–65.

4.70 Lyubomirsky et al., "The Benefits of Frequent Positive Affect"; and Dalal, R.S.; H. Lam; H.M. Weiss; E.R. Welch; and C.L. Hulin. "A Within-Person Approach to Work Behavior and Performance: Concurrent and Lagged Citizenship-Counterproductivity Associations, and Dynamic Relationships with Affect and Overall Job Performance." *Academy of Management Journal* 52 (2009), pp. 1051–66.

4.71 Dalal, R.S. "A Meta-Analysis of the Relationship between Organizational Citizenship Behavior and Counterproductive Work Behavior." *Journal of Applied Psychology* 90 (2005), pp. 1241–55.

4.72 Yang, J., and J.M. Diefendorff. "The Relations of Daily Counterproductive Workplace Behavior with Emotions, Situational Antecedents, and Personality Moderators: A Diary Study in Hong Kong." *Personnel Psychology* 62 (2009), pp. 259–95; and Dalal et al., "A Within-Person Approach to Work Behavior and Performance."

4.73 Cooper-Hakim, A., and C. Viswesvaran. "The Construct of Work

Commitment: Testing an Integrative Framework." *Psychological Bulletin* 131 (2005), pp. 241–59; Harrison, D.A.; D. Newman; and P.L. Roth. "How Important Are Job Attitudes? Meta-Analytic Comparisons of Integrative Behavioral Outcomes and Time Sequences." *Academy of Management Journal* 49 (2006), pp. 305–25; and Meyer, J.P.; D.J. Stanley; L. Herscovitch; and L. Topolnytsky. "Affective, Continuance, and Normative Commitment to the Organization: A Meta-Analysis of Antecedents, Correlates, and Consequences." *Journal of Vocational Behavior* 61 (2002), pp. 20–52.

4.74 Ibid.

4.75 Tait, M.; M.Y. Padgett; and T.T. Baldwin. "Job and Life Satisfaction: A Reexamination of the Strength of the Relationship and Gender Effects as a Function of the Date of the Study." *Journal of Applied Psychology* 74 (1989), pp. 502–507; Judge, T.A., S. Watanabe. "Another Look at the Job Satisfaction–Life Satisfaction Relationship." *Journal of*

Applied Psychology 78 (1993), pp. 939–48; and Erdogan, B.; T.N. Bauer; D.M. Truxillo; and L.R. Mansfield. "Whistle While You Work: A Review of the Life Satisfaction Literature." *Journal of Management* 38 (2012), pp. 1038–83.

4.76 Kahneman, D.; A.B. Krueger; D.A. Schkade; N. Schwarz; and A.A. Stone. "A Survey Method for Characterizing Daily Life Experience: The Day Reconstruction Method." *Science* 306 (2004), pp. 1776–80.

4.77 Kahneman, D., and A. Deaton. "High Income Improves Evaluation of Life but Not Emotional Well-Being." *Proceedings of the National Academy of Sciences* 107 (2010), pp. 16489–93.

4.78 Saari, L.M., and T.A. Judge. "Employee Attitudes and Job Satisfaction." *Human Resource Management* 43 (2004), pp. 395–407.

4.79 Kinicki, A.J.; F.M. McKee-Ryan; C.A. Schriesheim; and K.P. Carson. "Assessing the Construct Validity of the Job Descriptive Index: A Review and Meta-Analysis."

Journal of Applied Psychology 87 (2002), pp. 14–32; Hanisch, K.A. "The Job Descriptive Index Revisited: Questions about the Question Mark." *Journal of Applied Psychology* 77 (1992), pp. 377–82; and Jung, K.G.; A. Dalessio; and S.M. Johnson. "Stability of the Factor Structure of the Job Descriptive Index." *Academy of Management Journal* 29 (1986), pp. 609–16.

4.80 Ironson et al., "Construction"; and Russell et al., "Shorter Can Also Be Better."

4.81 Balzer, W.K.; J.A. Kihn; P.C. Smith; J.L. Irwin; P.D. Bachiochi; C. Robie; E.F. Sinar; and L.F. Parra. "Users' Manual for the Job Descriptive Index (JDI; 1997 version) and the Job in General Scales." In *Electronic Resources for the JDI and JIG*, ed. J.M. Stanton and C.D. Crossley. Bowling Green, OH: Bowling Green State University, 2000.

4.82 Ibid.

4.83 Ibid.

4.84 Saari and Judge, "Employee Attitudes."

chapter 5

Stress

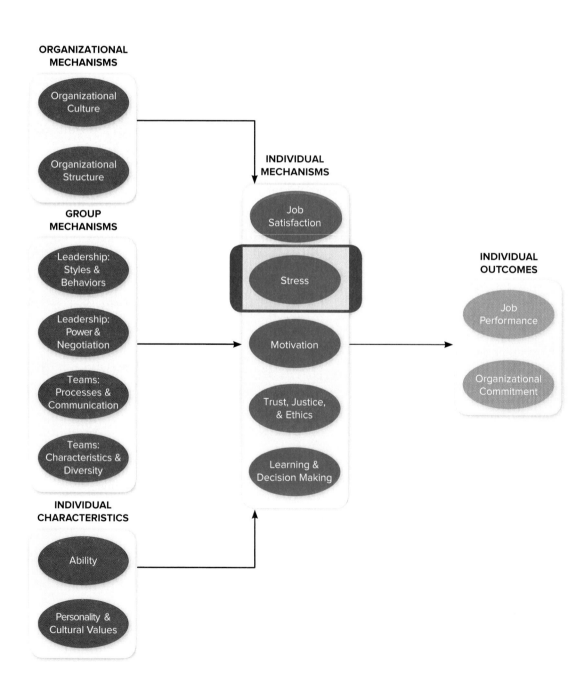

ORGANIZATIONAL MECHANISMS

Organizational Culture

Organizational Structure

GROUP MECHANISMS

Leadership: Styles & Behaviors

Leadership: Power & Negotiation

Teams: Processes & Communication

Teams: Characteristics & Diversity

INDIVIDUAL CHARACTERISTICS

Ability

Personality & Cultural Values

INDIVIDUAL MECHANISMS

Job Satisfaction

Stress

Motivation

Trust, Justice, & Ethics

Learning & Decision Making

INDIVIDUAL OUTCOMES

Job Performance

Organizational Commitment

© Justin Lane/epa/Corbis

✅ LEARNING GOALS

After reading this chapter, you should be able to answer the following questions:

5.1 What is stress, and how is it related to stressors and strains?

5.2 What are the four main types of stressors?

5.3 How do individuals cope with stress?

5.4 How does the Type A Behavior Pattern influence the stress process?

5.5 How does stress affect job performance and organizational commitment?

5.6 What steps can organizations take to manage employee stress?

INTERNAL REVENUE SERVICE

April 15th has special meaning to most working Americans, and not because it's a holiday or some other call for celebration. No, this is the day each year when our income taxes are due. Regardless of how you feel about this particular day, and about taxes in general, chances are you haven't thought a lot about the organization responsible for creating all those forms you have to fill out to calculate how much money you owe (or how much money is owed to you). In fact, the Internal Revenue Service, or IRS, has a long history that can be traced to back to 1862. President Lincoln and Congress enacted an income tax to pay for expenses of the Civil War, and at the same time, they created a government post called the Commissioner of Internal Revenue to administer the new tax.

Employment at the IRS was initially a function of appointments made by politicians and government officials. That is, the agency was run as a patronage system, so you had to know someone to get your job there (and keep it). However, in 1952 President Truman reorganized the agency to conform to a professional civil service system. This means that employees are hired on a competitive basis after filling out an application and taking employment tests, and once hired, they're promoted to jobs with more responsibility and higher pay on the basis of criteria such as performance and seniority. Civil service jobs have the reputation of being low stress due to high job security, responsibility for a narrow set of clear tasks driven by bureaucratic rules, and a lack of pressure to perform beyond the minimum. If you've thought about the job of an IRS employee, you probably envisioned someone sitting at a desk piled with tax returns, robotically checking entries on each line looking for errors and signs of fraud.

In actuality, IRS employees have jobs that are quite demanding. Consider the challenges of working with an increasingly complex tax code and constantly evolving technologies to serve a growing population of taxpayers, most of whom are not keen on filling out forms and handing over a significant portion of their paycheck each month. Couple this with the addition of new responsibilities associated with the Affordable Health Care Act, a tight federal budget, limited resources, and several highly publicized scandals, and you have a perfect recipe for unhealthy levels of employee stress.

STRESS

5.1

What is stress, and how is it related to stressors and strains?

Stress is an OB topic that's probably quite familiar to you. Even if you don't have a lot of work experience, consider how you feel toward the end of a semester when you have to cram for several final exams and finish a term paper and other projects. At the same time, you might have also been looking for a job or planning a trip with friends or family. Although some people might be able to deal with all of these demands without becoming too frazzled, most people would say this type of scenario causes them to feel "stressed out." This stressed out feeling might even be accompanied by headaches, stomach upsets, backaches, or sleeping difficulties. Although you might believe your stress will diminish once you graduate and settle down, high stress on the job is more prevalent than it's ever been before.[1] The federal government's National Institute for Occupational Safety and Health (NIOSH) summarized findings from several sources that indicated up to 40 percent of U.S. workers feel their jobs are "very stressful" or "extremely stressful."[2] Unfortunately, high stress is even more prevalent in the types of jobs that most of you are likely to have after you graduate. In fact, managers are approximately 21 percent more likely than the average worker to describe their jobs as stressful.[3] Moreover, as we described in the chapter opening, your level of stress may be even greater if you take a job in an organization, such as the IRS, where employees have to cope with change and uncertainty in a context of limited resources. Table 5-1 provides a list of jobs and their rank in terms of how stressful they are.

Stress is defined as a psychological response to demands that possess certain stakes for the person and that tax or exceed the person's capacity or resources.[4] The demands that cause people to experience stress are called **stressors.** The negative consequences that occur when demands tax or exceed a person's capacity or resources are called **strains.** These definitions illustrate that stress depends on both the nature of the demand and the person who confronts it. People differ in terms of how they perceive and evaluate stressors and the way they cope with them. As a result, different people may experience different levels of stress even when confronted with the exact same situation.

TABLE 5-1   Jobs Rated from Least Stressful (1) to Most Stressful (200)

LEAST STRESSFUL JOBS	STRESS LEVEL	MOST STRESSFUL JOBS	STRESS LEVEL
1. Tenured University Professor	5.03	143. Elementary School Teacher	27.37
2. Audiologist	6.33	148. Management Consultant	28.24
3. Medical Records Technician	7.48	150. Air Traffic Controller	28.58
4. Jeweler	8.10	154. Surgeon	28.90
8. Librarian	10.61	163. Construction Foreman	30.92
14. Software Engineer	12.13	166. Lumberjack	32.00
18. Computer Service Technician	12.64	172. Attorney	36.40
24. Occupational Therapist	13.14	175. Sales Representative	36.95
29. Chiropractor	13.55	179. Real Estate Agent	38.57
30. Actuary	14.09	180. Social Media Manager	38.60
35. Multimedia Artist	14.40	183. Stockbroker	39.97
39. Hair Stylist	14.59	185. Advertising Account Executive	43.24
40. Meteorologist	14.65	189. Taxi Driver	46.18
42. Loan Officer	14.73	191. Senior Corporate Executive	47.55
47. Biologist	15.10	194. Event Coordinator	49.73
50. Optician	15.57	195. Police Officer	50.81
53. Veterinarian	15.83	196. Airline Pilot	59.12
63. Chemist	17.00	198. Newspaper Reporter	69.67
74. Sustainability Manager	18.50	199. Firefighter	71.64
84. Accountant	19.85	200. Enlisted Military Personnel	74.83

Source: Adapted from L. Krantz and T. Lee. *The Jobs Rated Almanac,* 2015. (Lake Geneva, WI: iFocus Books, 2015). The stress level score is calculated by summing points in 10 categories: deadlines, working in the public eye, competitiveness, physical demands, environmental conditions, hazards, own life at risk, another's life at risk, public encounters, and employment change.

WHY ARE SOME EMPLOYEES MORE "STRESSED" THAN OTHERS?

To fully understand what it means to feel "stressed," it's helpful to consider the **transactional theory of stress.** This theory explains how stressors are perceived and appraised, as well as how people respond to those perceptions and appraisals.[5] When people first encounter stressors, the process of **primary appraisal** is triggered.[6] As shown in Figure 5-1, primary appraisal occurs as people evaluate the significance and the meaning of the stressor they're confronting. Here, people first consider whether a demand causes them to feel stressed, and if it does, they consider the implications of the stressor in terms of their personal goals and overall well-being.

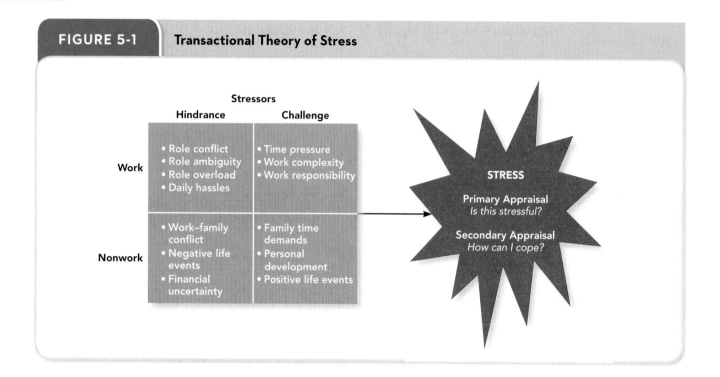

FIGURE 5-1   Transactional Theory of Stress

As an example of a primary appraisal, consider the job of a cashier at a well-run convenience store. In this store, cashiers engage in routine sales transactions with customers. Customers walk in the store and select merchandise, and the cashiers on duty ring up the sale and collect the money. Under normal day-to-day circumstances at this store, well-trained cashiers would not likely feel that these transactions are overly taxing or exceed their capacity, so those cashiers would not likely appraise these job demands as stressful. Job demands that tend not to be appraised as stressful are called **benign job demands.**

However, consider how convenience store cashiers would react in a different store in which the cash register and credit card machine break down often and without warning. The cashiers who work at this store would likely view their job as being more stressful. This is because they would have to diagnose and fix problems with equipment while dealing with customers who are growing more and more impatient. Furthermore, the cashiers in this store might appraise the stressful situation as one that unnecessarily prevents them from achieving their goal of being viewed as an effective employee in the eyes of the customers and the store manager.

Finally, consider a third convenience store in which the cashiers' workload is higher due to additional responsibilities that include receiving merchandise from vendors, taking physical inventory, and training new employees. In this store, the cashiers may appraise their jobs as stressful because of the higher workload and the need to balance different priorities. However, in contrast to the cashiers in the previous example, cashiers in this store might appraise these demands as providing an opportunity to learn and demonstrate the type of competence that often is rewarded with satisfying promotions and pay raises.

TYPES OF STRESSORS

5.2

What are the four main types of stressors?

In the previous two examples, the cashiers were confronted with demands that a primary appraisal would label as "stressful." However, the specific demands in the two examples have an important difference. Having to deal with equipment breakdowns or unhappy customers is not likely to be perceived by most employees as having implications that are personally beneficial; in fact, the opposite is likely to be true. These kinds of stressors are called **hindrance stressors,** or stressful demands that people tend to perceive as hindering their progress toward personal accomplishments or goal attainment.[7] Hindrance stressors most often trigger negative emotions such as anxiety and anger.[8]

In contrast, having to deal with additional responsibilities is likely to be perceived by most employees as having long-term benefits. These kinds of stressors are called **challenge stressors,** or stressful demands that people tend to perceive as opportunities for learning, growth, and achievement. Although challenge stressors can be exhausting, they often trigger positive emotions such as pride and enthusiasm. Figure 5-1 lists a number of hindrance and challenge stressors, some of which are experienced at work and some of which are experienced outside of work.[9]

WORK HINDRANCE STRESSORS The various roles we fill at work are the source of different types of work-related hindrance stressors.[10] One type of work-related hindrance stressor is **role conflict,** which refers to conflicting expectations that other people may have of us.[11] As an example of role conflict that occurs from incompatible demands within a single role that a person may hold, consider the job of a call center operator. People holding these jobs are expected to communicate with as many people as possible over a given time period. The expectation is that the call center operator will spend as little time as possible with the people on the other end of the line. At the same time, however, operators are also expected to be responsive to the questions and concerns raised by the people they talk with. Because effectiveness in this aspect of the job may require a great deal of time, call center operators are put in a position in which they simply cannot meet both types of expectations.

Role ambiguity refers to a lack of information about what needs to be done in a role, as well as unpredictability regarding the consequences of performance in that role.[12] Employees are sometimes asked to work on projects for which they're given very few instructions or guidelines about how things are supposed to be done. In these cases, employees may not know how much money they can spend on the project, how long it's supposed to take, or what exactly the finished product is supposed to look like. Role ambiguity is often experienced among new employees who haven't been around long enough to receive instructions from supervisors or observe and model the role behaviors of more senior colleagues. Students sometimes experience role ambiguity when professors remain vague about particular course requirements or how grading is going to be performed. In such cases, the class becomes stressful because it's not quite clear what it takes to get a good grade.

Role overload occurs when the number of demanding roles a person holds is so high that the person simply cannot perform some or all of the roles effectively.[13] Role overload as a source of stress is becoming very prevalent for employees in many different industries, and in fact, studies have shown that this source of stress is more prevalent than both role conflict and role ambiguity.[14] For example, the workload for executives and managers who work in investment banking, consulting, and law is so high that 80-hour workweeks are becoming the norm.[15] Although this trend may not be surprising to some of you, people holding these jobs also indicate that they would not be able to effectively complete most of the work that's required of them, even if they worked twice as many hours.

One final type of work-related hindrance stressor, **daily hassles,** refers to the relatively minor day-to-day demands that get in the way of accomplishing the things that we really want to accomplish.[16] Examples of hassles include having to deal with unnecessary paperwork, office equipment malfunctions, annoying interactions with abrasive coworkers, and useless communications. Although these examples of daily hassles may seem relatively minor, taken together, they can be extremely time consuming and stressful. Indeed, according to one survey, 40 percent of executives spend somewhere between a half-day and a full day each week on communications that are not useful or necessary.[17]

© Terry Vine/Blend Images LLC RF

Call center operators experience role conflict. On the one hand, they need to be polite and responsive to the people with whom they're speaking. On the other hand, they need to spend as little time as possible on each call.

WORK CHALLENGE STRESSORS One type of work-related challenge stressor is **time pressure**—a strong sense that the amount of time you have to do a task is just not quite enough.[18] Although most people appraise situations with high time pressure as rather stressful, they also tend to appraise these situations as more challenging than hindering. Time pressure demands tend to be viewed as something worth striving for because success in meeting such demands can be intrinsically satisfying. As an example of this positive effect of high time pressure, consider Michael Jones, an architect at a top New York firm. His job involves overseeing multiple projects with tight deadlines, and as a result, he has to work at a hectic pace. Although Jones readily acknowledges that his job is stressful, he also believes that the outcome of having all the stress is satisfying. Jones is able to see the product of his labor over the Manhattan skyline, which makes him feel like he's a part of something.[19]

Work complexity refers to the degree to which the requirements of the work—in terms of knowledge, skills, and abilities—tax or exceed the capabilities of the person who is responsible for performing the work.[20] As an example of work complexity, consider the nature of employee development practices that organizations use to train future executives and organizational leaders. In many cases, these practices involve giving people jobs that require skills and knowledge that the people do not yet possess. A successful marketing manager who is being groomed for an executive-level position may, for example, be asked to manage a poorly performing production facility with poor labor relations in a country halfway around the world. Although these types of developmental experiences tend to be quite stressful, managers report that being stretched beyond their capacity is well worth the associated discomfort.[21]

Work responsibility refers to the nature of the obligations that a person has toward others.[22] Generally speaking, the level of responsibility in a job is higher when the number, scope, and importance of the obligations in that job are higher. As an example, the level of work responsibility for an air traffic controller, who may be accountable for the lives of tens of thousands of people every day, is very high.[23] Controllers understand that if they make an error while directing an aircraft—for example, saying "turn left" instead of "turn right"—hundreds of people can die in an instant. Although controller errors that result in midair collisions and crashes are extremely rare, the possibility weighs heavily on the minds of controllers, especially after they lose "the picture" (controller jargon for the mental representation of an assigned airspace and all the aircraft within it) due to extreme workloads, a loss of concentration, or equipment malfunctions. As with people's reactions to time pressure and work complexity, people tend to evaluate demands associated with high responsibility as both stressful and potentially positive. For an interesting example of a job filled with challenge stressors, see our **OB on Screen** feature.

NONWORK HINDRANCE STRESSORS Although the majority of people in the United States spend more time at the office than anywhere else,[24] there are a number of stressful demands outside of work

The job of an air traffic controller is stressful because of the challenging demands. In particular, air traffic controllers know that during each shift they work, they'll be responsible for ensuring that thousands of people arrive at their destinations safely and on time.

© Monty Rakusen/Cultura/Getty Images RF

OB ON SCREEN

GRAVITY

Explorer's been hit. Explorer, do you read? Explorer, over, Explorer? Astronaut is off structure. Dr. Stone is off structure. Dr. Stone detach! You must detach!

With those words, Astronaut Matt Kowalski (George Clooney) provides a glimpse into the predicament that he and his crew face in the movie *Gravity* (Dir.: Alfonso Cuarón, Warner Bros., 2013). Kowalski and rookie astronaut Ryan Stone (Sandra Bullock) are on a spacewalk when an orbiting field of debris collides with their space shuttle, destroying it. The movie centers on the challenges that Kowalski and Stone face as they try to save themselves. For example, after navigating 60 miles in their spacesuits to the International Space Station, they find that it too has been damaged. They also discover that the parachute of the Soyuz module they were hoping to use for their trip back to Earth had deployed already. The two decided to use the Soyuz module to get to a Chinese space station where they hoped would be another return module, but disaster strikes again. The tether holding Kowalski and Stone rips apart and the two become separated, and Kowalski floats away to his demise. Fire then ignites on the space station and Stone has to do another spacewalk to physically separate the Soyuz just as the debris field makes its return.

© Warner Bros./Photofest

The demands that Kowalski and Stone face are obviously stressful. Having to deal with the disaster is atypical (even for astronauts), the stakes couldn't be higher, and both are uncertain they possess the ability and resources to pull through. The more interesting question is how the situation would likely be appraised. On the one hand, the situation has thwarted progress of the crew's original mission, and there are times when things appear hopeless. On the other hand, the situation has high levels of time pressure, complexity, and responsibility, and understandably, the astronauts are driven to deal with things in a very focused way. So does Stone cope with the stressful demands effectively and make it home? You'll have to watch the film to find out.

that have implications for managing behavior in organizations.[25] In essence, stressors experienced outside of work may have effects that "spill over" to affect the employee at work.[26] One example of nonwork hindrance stressors is **work–family conflict,** a special form of role conflict in which the demands of a work role hinder the fulfillment of the demands of a family role (or vice versa).[27] We most often think of cases in which work demands hinder effectiveness in the family context, termed "work to family conflict." For example, employees who have to deal with lots of hindrances at work may have trouble switching off their frustration after they get home, and as a consequence, they may become irritable and impatient with family and friends. However, work–family conflict can occur in the other direction as well. For example, "family to work conflict" would occur if a salesperson experiencing the stress of marital conflict comes to work harboring emotional pain and negative feelings, which makes it difficult to interact with customers effectively. Although there are many benefits to having an active and well-rounded life, it's important to recognize that both work to family conflict and family to work conflict tend to be higher for employees who are strongly embedded in their work organizations and their communities.[28]

Nonwork hindrance stressors also come in the form of **negative life events.**[29] Research has revealed that a number of life events are perceived as quite stressful, particularly when they result in significant changes to a person's life.[30] Table 5-2 provides a listing of some commonly experienced life events, along with a score that estimates how stressful each event is perceived to be. As the table reveals, many of the most stressful life events do not occur at work. Rather, they include family events such as the death of a spouse or close family member, a divorce or marital separation, a jail term, or a personal illness. These events would be classified as hindrance stressors because they hinder the ability to achieve life goals and are associated with negative emotions.

A third type of nonwork hindrance stressor is **financial uncertainty.** This type of stressor refers to conditions that create uncertainties with regard to the loss of livelihood, savings, or the ability to pay expenses. This type of stressor is highly relevant during recessions or economic downturns. When people have concerns about losing their jobs, homes, and life savings because of economic factors that are beyond their control, it's understandable why nearly half of the respondents to a recent survey indicated that stress was making it hard for them to do their jobs.[31]

NONWORK CHALLENGE STRESSORS Of course, the nonwork domain can be a source of challenge stressors as well.[32] **Family time demands** refer to the time that a person commits to participate in an array of family activities and responsibilities. Specific examples of family time demands include time spent involved in family pursuits such as traveling, attending social events and organized activities, hosting parties, and planning and making home improvements. Examples of **personal development** activities include participation in formal education programs, music lessons, sports-related training, hobby-related self-education, participation in local government, or volunteer work. Finally, Table 5-2 includes some **positive life events** that are sources of nonwork challenge stressors. For example, marriage, the addition of a new family member, and graduating from school are stressful in their own way. However, each is associated with more positive, rather than negative, emotions.

TABLE 5-2	Stressful Life Events		
LIFE EVENT	**STRESS SCORE**	**LIFE EVENT**	**STRESS SCORE**
Death of a spouse	100	Trouble with in-laws	29
Divorce	73	Outstanding achievement	28
Marital separation	65	Begin or end school	26
Jail term	63	Change in living conditions	25
Death of close family member	63	Trouble with boss	23
Personal illness	53	Change in work hours	20
Marriage	50	Change in residence	20
Fired at work	47	Change in schools	20
Marital reconciliation	45	Change in social activities	18
Retirement	45	Change in sleeping habits	16
Pregnancy	40	Change in family get-togethers	15
Gain of new family member	39	Change in eating habits	15
Death of close friend	37	Vacations	13
Change in occupation	36	The holiday season	12
Child leaving home	29	Minor violations of the law	11

Source: Adapted from T.H. Holmes and R.H. Rahe, "The Social Re-Adjustment Rating Scale," *Journal of Psychosomatic Research* 11 (1967), pp. 213–18.

HOW DO PEOPLE COPE WITH STRESSORS?

5.3

How do individuals cope with stress?

According to the transactional theory of stress, after people appraise a stressful demand, they ask themselves, "What *should* I do?" and "What *can* I do?" to deal with this situation. These questions, which refer to the **secondary appraisal** shown in Figure 5-1, center on the issue of how people cope with the various stressors they face.[33] **Coping** refers to the behaviors and thoughts that people use to manage both the stressful demands they face and the emotions associated with those stressful demands.[34] As Table 5-3 illustrates, coping can involve many different types of activities, and these activities can be grouped into four broad categories based on two dimensions.[35] The first dimension refers to the method of coping (behavioral versus cognitive), and the second dimension refers to the focus of coping (problem solving versus regulation of emotions).

The first part of our coping definition highlights the idea that methods of coping can be categorized on the basis of whether they involve behaviors or thoughts. **Behavioral coping** involves the set of physical activities that are used to deal with a stressful situation.[36] In one example of behavioral coping, a person who is confronted with a lot of time pressure at work might choose to cope by working faster. In another example, an employee who has several daily hassles might cope by avoiding work—coming in late, leaving early, or even staying home. As a final example, employees often cope with the stress of an international assignment by returning home from the assignment prematurely. As our **OB Internationally** feature illustrates, international assignments are becoming increasingly prevalent, and the costs of these early returns to organizations can be significant.

In contrast to behavioral coping, **cognitive coping** refers to the thoughts that are involved in trying to deal with a stressful situation.[37] For example, the person who is confronted with an increase in time pressure might cope by thinking about different ways of accomplishing the work more efficiently. As another example of cognitive coping, employees who are confronted with daily hassles might try to convince themselves that the hassles are not that bad after all, perhaps by dwelling on less annoying aspects of the daily events.

Whereas the first part of our coping definition refers to the method of coping, the second part refers to the focus of coping—that is, does the coping attempt to address the stressful demand or the emotions triggered by the demand?[38] **Problem-focused coping** refers to behaviors and cognitions intended to manage the stressful situation itself.[39] To understand problem-focused coping, consider how the people in the previous paragraphs coped with time pressure. In the first example, the person attempted to address the time pressure by working harder, whereas in the second example, the person thought about a strategy for accomplishing the work more efficiently. Although the specific coping methods differed, both of these people reacted to the time pressure similarly, in that they focused their effort on meeting the demand rather than trying to avoid it.

In contrast to problem-focused coping, **emotion-focused coping** refers to the various ways in which people manage their own emotional reactions to stressful demands.[40] The reactions to

TABLE 5-3	Examples of Coping Strategies	
	PROBLEM-FOCUSED	**EMOTION-FOCUSED**
Behavioral Methods	• Working harder • Seeking assistance • Acquiring additional resources	• Engaging in alternative activities • Seeking support • Venting anger
Cognitive Methods	• Strategizing • Self-motivating • Changing priorities	• Avoiding, distancing, and ignoring • Looking for the positive in the negative • Reappraising

Source: Adapted from J.C. Latack and S.J. Havlovic, "Coping with Job Stress: A Conceptual Evaluation Framework for Coping Measures," *Journal of Organizational Behavior* 13 (1992), pp. 479–508.

The number of expatriates, or employees who are sent abroad to work for their organization, has increased recently. In one survey, for example, 47 percent of the companies reported an increase in the number of expatriate assignments over the previous year, and 54 percent projected increases in these assignments in the following year. This survey also indicated that more than half of all employees sent abroad expected their assignment to last between one and three years. Unfortunately, a significant number of expatriate assignments do not succeed because the employee returns home earlier than planned. In fact, up to 40 percent of all American expatriates return home early, and it has been estimated that each early return costs the host organization approximately $100,000. Of course, a second way that international assignments fail is when the expatriate performs at an unsatisfactory level.

One key factor that influences the commitment and effectiveness of expatriates is how they handle the stress of being abroad. Expatriates who experience more stress as a result of cultural, interpersonal, or job factors tend to be less satisfied with their assignment, more likely to think about leaving their assignment early, and more likely to perform at subpar levels. One practice that could prove useful in managing expatriate stress is cross-cultural training, which focuses on helping people appreciate cultural differences and interacting more comfortably with the host-country nationals. Unfortunately, this type of training isn't offered as frequently as you might think. Surveys suggest that many U.S. companies offer no formal cross-cultural training at all. Even when training is offered, it tends to focus more on language skills than on cultural understanding and interaction skills. Given that the number of expatriate assignments is on the rise, organizations might be well served if they increased emphasis on training in these types of skills so that their expatriates are better able to cope with the stress from being abroad.

Sources: P. Bhaskar-Shrinivas, D.A. Harrison, M.A. Shaffer, and D.M. Luk, "Input-Based and Time-Based Models of International Adjustment: Meta-Analytic Evidence and Theoretical Extensions," *Academy of Management Journal* 48 (2005), pp. 257–81; J.S. Black, M. Mendenhall, and G Oddou, "Toward a Comprehensive Model of International Adjustment: An Integration of Multiple Theoretical Perspectives," *Academy of Management Review* 16 (1991), pp. 291-317; M.E. Mendenhall, T.M. Kulmann, G.K. Stahl, and J.S. Osland, "Employee Development and Expatriate Assignments," in *Blackwell Handbook of Cross-Cultural Management,* ed. M.J. Gannon and K.L. Newman (Malden, MA: Blackwell, 2002), pp. 155–84; and *Global Relocation Trends, 2005 Survey Report,* Woodridge, IL: GMAC Global Relocation Services, 2006, http://www.gmacglobalrelocation.com/insight_support/global_relocation.asp.

the daily hassles that we described previously illustrate two types of emotion-focused coping. In the first example, the employee used avoidance and distancing behaviors to reduce the emotional distress caused by the stressful situation. In the second example, the employee reappraised the demand to make it seem less stressful and threatening. Although people may be successful at changing the way different situations are construed to avoid feeling unpleasant emotions, the demand or problem that initially triggered the appraisal process remains.

Of course, the coping strategy that's ultimately used has important implications for how effectively people can meet or adapt to the different stressors that they face. In the work context, for example, a manager would most likely want subordinates to cope with the stress of a heavy workload by using a problem-focused strategy—working harder—rather than an emotion-focused strategy—leaving work several hours early to create distance from the stressor. Of course, there are some situations in which emotion-focused coping may be functional for the person. As an example, consider someone who repeatedly fails to make it through the auditions for the TV show *The Voice,* despite years of voice lessons and countless hours of practice. At some point, if he did not have the capability to cope emotionally—perhaps by lowering his aspirations—his self-esteem could be damaged, which could translate into reduced effectiveness in other roles that they fill.

How do people choose a particular coping strategy? One factor that influences this choice is the set of beliefs that people have about how well different coping strategies can address different demands. In essence, people are likely to choose the coping strategy they believe has the highest likelihood of meeting the demand they face. For example, successful students may come to understand that the likelihood of effectively coping with demanding final exams is higher if they study hard rather than trying to escape from the situation by going out until 3:00 a.m. The choice also depends on the degree to which people believe that they have what it takes to execute the coping strategy effectively. Returning to the previous example, if students have already failed the first two exams in the course, despite trying hard,

© Manchan/Getty Images RF

Although avoidance and distancing behaviors may reduce the emotional distress one feels, these strategies do not help manage the demand that's causing the stress.

they may come to believe that a problem-focused coping strategy won't work. In this situation, because students may feel helpless to address the demand directly, an emotion-focused coping strategy would be more likely.

Another critical factor that determines coping strategy choice is the degree to which people believe that a particular strategy gives them some degree of control over the stressor. If people believe that a demand can be addressed with a problem-focused coping strategy and have confidence that they can use that problem-focused strategy effectively, then they will feel some control over the situation and will likely use a problem-focused strategy. If people believe that a demand cannot be addressed with a problem-focused strategy or do not believe they can effectively execute that strategy, then they'll feel a lack of control over the situation and will tend to use an emotion-focused coping strategy.

So what determines how people develop a sense of control? It appears that one important factor is the nature of the stressful demand itself. In particular, people are likely to feel less control over a stressor when they appraise it as a hindrance rather than a challenge. Consider one of the life events in Table 5-2: "Trouble with boss." This event would most likely be appraised as a hindrance stressor because it serves to thwart goal achievement and triggers negative emotions. If you're like most people, you would want to change the behavior of your boss so that the trouble would stop and you could get on with your work. However, it's also likely that you would feel like you have little control over this situation because bosses are in a position of power, and complaining to your boss's boss might not be an option for you. The anxiety and hopelessness triggered by the situation would further erode any sense of control over the situation, likely leading to emotion-focused coping.[41]

THE EXPERIENCE OF STRAIN

Earlier in this chapter, we defined strain as the negative consequences associated with stress. But how exactly does stress cause strain? Consider the case of Naomi Henderson, the CEO of RIVA, a Rockville, Maryland–based market research firm. The job of CEO is quite demanding, and Henderson found herself working 120 hours a week to cope with the heavy workload. One night she woke up to go to the bathroom and found that she literally could not move—she was paralyzed. After she was rushed to the emergency room, the doctor told Henderson and her husband that her diagnosis was stress. The doctor recommended rest in bed for 14 hours a day for six weeks.[42] Although this example may seem extreme to you, the demands of many managerial and executive-level jobs are often excessive,[43] and the negative health consequences that result are fairly predictable. In fact, if you've ever been in a situation in which you've experienced heavy stress for more than a couple of days, you can probably appreciate the toll that stress can take on you. Although people react to stress differently, you may have felt unusually exhausted, irritable, and achy. What might be surprising to you is that the mechanism within your body that gives you the ability to function effectively in the face of stressful demands is the same mechanism that ends up causing you these problems. So what is this mechanism?

Essentially, the body has a set of responses that allow it to adapt and function effectively in the face of stressful demands, but if the stressful demands do not ramp down or the demands occur too frequently, the body's adaptive responses become toxic.[44] More specifically, when people are confronted with a stressor, their bodies secrete chemical compounds that increase their heart rate and blood pressure, as blood is redirected away from vital organs, such as the spleen, to the brain and skeletal muscles.[45] Unfortunately, if the chemicals in the blood remain elevated because of prolonged or repeated exposure to the stressor, the body begins to break down, and several negative consequences are set into motion. As shown in Figure 5-2, those negative consequences come in three varieties: physiological strains, psychological strains, and behavioral strains.[46]

Physiological strains that result from stressors occur in at least four systems of the human body. First, stressors can reduce the effectiveness of the body's immune system, which makes it more difficult for the body to ward off illness and infection. Have you ever noticed that you're more likely to catch a cold during or immediately after final exam week? Second, stressors can harm the body's cardiovascular system, cause the heart to race, increase blood pressure, and create coronary artery disease. Third, stressors can cause problems in the body's musculoskeletal system. Tension headaches, tight shoulders, and back pain have all been linked to a variety of stressors. Fourth, stressors cause gastrointestinal system problems. Symptoms of this type of strain include stomachaches, indigestion, diarrhea, and constipation.[47]

FIGURE 5-2   Examples of Strain

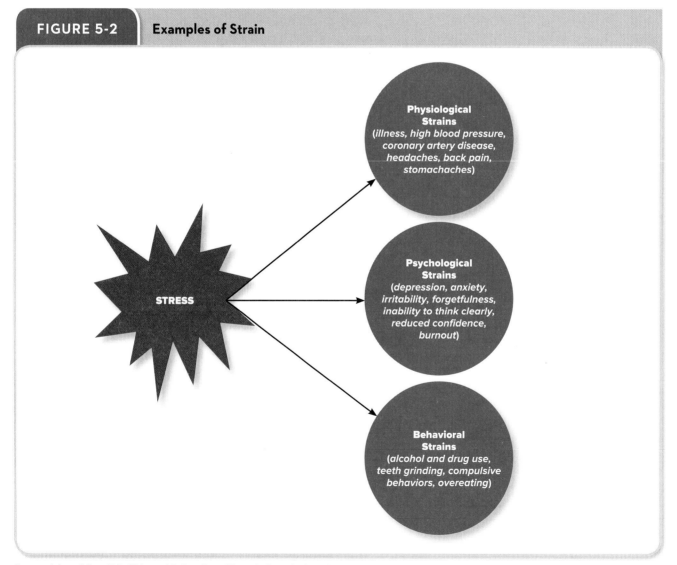

Source: Adapted from R.L. Kahn and P. Byosiere. "Stress in Organizations." Handbook of Industrial and Organizational Psychology, Vol. 4. M.D. Dunnette; J.M.R. Hourgh, and H.C. Triandis. Palo Alto, CA: Consulting Psychologists Press, 1992, pp. 517–650.

Although you might be tempted to dismiss the importance of physiological strains because the likelihood of serious illness and disease is low for people in their 20s and 30s, research shows that dismissal may be a mistake. For example, high-pressure work deadlines increase the chance of heart attack within the next 24 hours by a factor of six.[48] So even though your likelihood of suffering a heart attack may be low, who would want to increase their risk by 600 per-

© Newman Lowrance/AP Images

Having started more than 300 games straight, Brett Favre is well known among sports fans for his durability as an NFL quarterback. However, his durability did not mean that he was immune to the effects of stress. He retired from football three times in the span of three years, and burnout played an important role in these decisions.

cent? Furthermore, the negative physiological effects of stress persist over time and may not show up until far into the future. One study showed that eye problems, allergic complaints, and chronic diseases could be attributed to stress measured eight years earlier.[49]

Psychological strains that result from stressors include depression, anxiety, anger, hostility, reduced self-confidence, irritability, inability to think clearly, forgetfulness, lack of creativity, memory loss, and (not surprising, given the rest of this list) a loss of sense of humor.[50] You might be tempted to think of these problems as isolated incidents; however, they may reflect a more general psychological condition known as **burnout,** which can be defined as the emotional, mental, and physical exhaustion that results from having to cope with stressful demands on an ongoing basis.[51] There are many familiar examples of people who have experienced burnout, and the majority of them illustrate how burnout can lead to a decision to quit a job or even change careers. As an example, after playing for 17 seasons for the Green Bay Packers, Brett Favre decided to retire from professional football after leading his team to the NFC championship game in 2008.[52] Favre explained to reporters that he was just tired of all the stress.[53] The pressure of the challenge of winning compelled him to spend an ever-increasing amount of time preparing for the next game, and over time, this pressure built up and resulted in exhaustion and reduced commitment. Of course, Favre would un-retire to play for the New York Jets in 2008, only to re-retire after the season. Favre again un-retired in 2009 and joined the Minnesota Vikings. He re-retired, for the final time, after the 2010 season. Such changes of heart are not unusual after someone retires from an exciting job due to burnout. A break from stressors associated with the work not only gives the person a chance to rest and recharge, but it also provides a lot of free time to think about the excitement and challenge of performing again.

Finally, in addition to physiological and psychological strains, the stress process can result in *behavioral strains.* Behavioral strains are unhealthy behaviors such as grinding one's teeth at night, being overly critical and bossy, excessive smoking, compulsive gum chewing, overuse of alcohol, and compulsive eating.[54] Although it's unknown why exposure to stressors results in these specific behaviors, it's easy to see why these behaviors are undesirable both from personal and organizational standpoints.

ACCOUNTING FOR INDIVIDUALS IN THE STRESS PROCESS

So far in this chapter, we've discussed how the typical or average person reacts to different sorts of stressors. However, we've yet to discuss how people differ in terms of how they react to demands. One way that people differ in their reactions to stress depends on whether they exhibit the **Type A Behavior Pattern.** "Type A" people have a strong sense of time urgency and tend to be impatient, hard-driving, competitive, controlling, aggressive, and even hostile.[55] If you walk, talk, and eat at a quick pace, and if you find yourself constantly annoyed with people who do things too slowly, chances are that you're a Type A person. With that said, one way to tell for sure is to fill out the Type A questionnaire in our **OB Assessments** feature.

OB ASSESSMENTS

TYPE A BEHAVIOR PATTERN

Do you think that you're especially sensitive to stress? This assessment is designed to measure the extent to which you're a Type A person—someone who typically engages in hard-driving, competitive, and aggressive behavior. The items below refer to how you feel, think, and behave in different situations. Indicate your level of agreement with each item as honestly as possible using the response scale provided. (Instructors: Assessments on challenge stressors, hindrance stressors, and strain can be found in the PowerPoints in the Connect Library's Instructor Resources and in the Connect assignments for this chapter).

1 STRONGLY DISAGREE	2 DISAGREE	3 SLIGHTLY DISAGREE	4 NEUTRAL	5 SLIGHTLY AGREE	6 AGREE	7 STRONGLY AGREE

1. I hate to be late for appointments. _____
2. I'm a very competitive person. _____
3. I anticipate what others are going to say by nodding, and I sometimes interrupt and finish for them. _____
4. I'm always rushed. _____
5. I'm impatient when waiting. _____
6. I go "all out" when trying to accomplish something. _____
7. I multitask, and am always thinking about what I have to do next. _____
8. I'm expressive and often gesture when speaking. _____
9. I do most things, even eating and walking, in a hurry. _____
10. I'm a driven person—I work hard and I'm serious about accomplishing my goals. _____
11. I often express feelings like frustration, irritation, and anger. _____
12. I'm very ambitious. _____

SCORING AND INTERPRETATION

Sum your answers for the 12 items. If your scores sum up to 60 or above, you might be a Type A person, which means that you may perceive higher stress levels in your life and be more sensitive to that stress. If your scores sum up to 36 or below, chances are that you would be considered a Type B person. This means that you sense less stress in your life and are less sensitive to the stress that's experienced.

Source: "Items based on R.H. Friedman & R. H. Rosenman. "Association of Specific Overt Behavior Pattern with Blood and Cardiovascular Findings." Journal of the American Medical Association, 169 (1959), pp. 1286–1269.

5.4

How does the Type A Behavior Pattern influence the stress process?

In the context of this chapter, the Type A Behavior Pattern is important because it can influence stressors, stress, and strains. First, the Type A Behavior Pattern may have a direct influence on the level of stressors that a person confronts. To understand why this might be true, consider that Type A persons tend to be hard-driving and have a strong desire to achieve. Because the behaviors that reflect these tendencies are valued by the organization, Type A individuals receive "rewards" in the form of increases in the amount and level of work required. In addition, because Type A people tend to be aggressive and competitive, they may be more prone to interpersonal conflict. Most of you would agree that conflict with peers and coworkers is an important stressor.

Second, in addition to the effect on stressors, the Type A Behavior Pattern is important because it influences the stress process itself.[56] This effect of the Type A Behavior Pattern is easy to understand if you consider that hard-driving competitiveness makes people hypersensitive to demands that could potentially affect their progress toward their goal attainment. In essence, Type A individuals are simply more likely to appraise demands as being stressful rather than being benign.

Third, and perhaps most important, the Type A Behavior Pattern has been directly linked to coronary heart disease[57] and other physiological, psychological, and behavioral strains.[58] The size of the relationship between the Type A Behavior Pattern and these strains is not so strong as to suggest that if you're a Type A person, you should immediately call 911. However, the linkage is strong enough to suggest that the risk of these problems is significantly higher for people who typically engage in Type A behaviors.

Another individual factor that affects the way people manage stress is the degree of **social support** that they receive. Social support refers to the help that people receive when they're confronted with stressful demands, and there are at least two major types.[59] One type of social support is called **instrumental support,** which refers to the help people receive that can be used to address the stressful demand directly. For example, if a person is overloaded with work, a coworker could provide instrumental support by taking over some of the work or offering suggestions about how to do the work more efficiently. A second type of social support is called **emotional support.** This type of support refers to the help people receive in addressing the emotional distress that accompanies stressful demands. As an example, the supervisor of the individual who is overloaded with work might provide emotional support by showing interest in the employee's situation and appearing to be understanding and sympathetic. As alluded to in these examples, social support may come from coworkers as well as from supervisors. However, social support also may be provided by family members and friends outside the context of the stressful demand.[60]

Similar to the Type A Behavior Pattern, social support has the potential to influence the stress process in several different ways. However, most research on social support focuses on the ways that social support buffers the relationship between stressors and strains.[61] For example, a supervisor who engages in supportive behaviors may make the same level of stressful demands seem more fair and less threatening.[62] Subordinates of this supervisor, therefore, would tend to experience less strain than subordinates of another supervisor who does not engage in supportive behaviors. Moreover, high levels of social support provide a person with instrumental or emotional resources that are useful for coping with the stressor, which tends to reduce the harmful consequences of the stressor to that individual. With low levels of social support, the person does not have extra coping resources available, so the stressor tends to have effects that are more harmful. In essence, this perspective casts social support as a "moderator" of the relationship between stressors and strains (recall that moderators are variables that affect the strength of the relationship between two other variables). In this particular case, the relationship between stressors and strain tends to be weaker at higher levels of social support and stronger at lower levels of social support. Although not every research study has found support for the buffering effect of social support,[63] the majority of research evidence has been supportive.[64]

© Ingram Publishing RF

Social support from friends, coworkers, and family can be a big help in managing stress, even though it often occurs outside the stress-causing environment.

SUMMARY: WHY ARE SOME EMPLOYEES MORE "STRESSED" THAN OTHERS?

So what explains why some employees are more stressed than others? As shown in Figure 5-3, answering that question requires paying attention to the particular stressors the employee is experiencing, including hindrance and challenge stressors originating in both the work and nonwork domains. However, feeling stressed also depends on how those stressors are appraised and coped with, and the degree to which physiological, psychological, and behavioral strains are experienced. Finally, answering the question depends on whether the employee is Type A or Type B and whether the employee has a high or low amount of social support. Understanding all of these factors can help explain why some people can shoulder stressful circumstances for weeks at a time, whereas others seem to be "at the end of their rope" when faced with even relatively minor job demands.

| **FIGURE 5-3** | **Why Are Some Employees More "Stressed" Than Others?** |

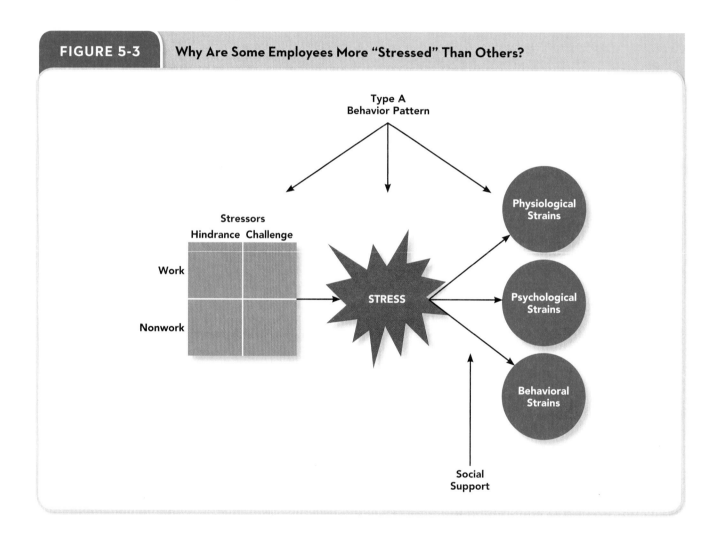

HOW IMPORTANT IS STRESS?

5.5

How does stress affect job performance and organizational commitment?

In the previous sections, we described how stressors and the stress process influence strains and, ultimately, people's health and well-being. Although these relationships are important to understand, you're probably more curious about the impact that stressors have on job performance and organizational commitment, the two outcomes in our integrative model of OB. Figure 5-4

FIGURE 5-4 — Effects of Hindrance Stressors on Performance and Commitment

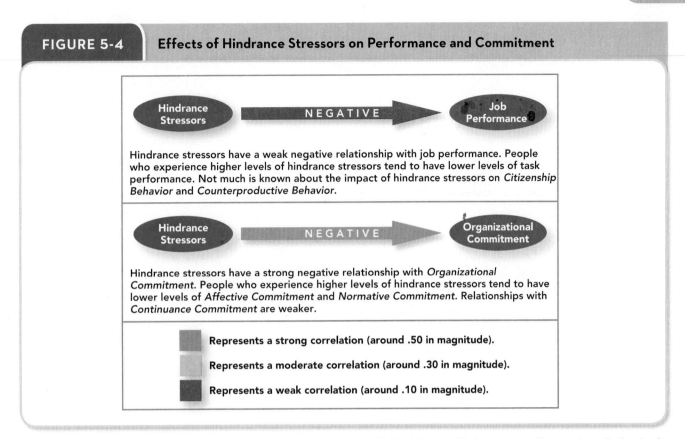

Sources: J.A. LePine, N.P. Podsakoff, and M.A. LePine, "A Meta-Analytic Test of the Challenge Stressor–Hindrance Stressor Framework: An Explanation for Inconsistent Relationships Among Stressors and Performance," *Academy of Management Journal* 48 (2005), pp. 764–75; and N.P. Podsakoff, J.A. LePine, and M.A. LePine, "Differential Challenge Stressor–Hindrance Stressor Relationships with Job Attitudes, Turnover Intentions, Turnover, and Withdrawal Behavior: A Meta-Analysis," *Journal of Applied Psychology* 92 (2007), pp. 438–54.

summarizes the research evidence linking hindrance stressors to performance and commitment, and Figure 5-5 summarizes the research evidence linking challenge stressors to performance and commitment. It is certainly true that there are important associations between nonwork stressors, strains, and other important outcomes.[65] However, we limit our discussion here to relationships with work stressors rather than nonwork stressors, because this is where researchers have focused the most attention.

Figure 5-4 reveals that hindrance stressors have a weak negative relationship with job performance.[66] A general explanation for this negative relationship is that hindrance stressors result in strains and negative emotions that reduce the overall level of physical, cognitive, and emotional energy that people could otherwise bring to their job duties.[67] The detrimental effect that strains have on job performance becomes quite easy to understand when you consider the nature of the individual strains that we mentioned in the previous section. Certainly, you would agree that physiological, psychological, and behavioral strains in the form of illnesses, exhaustion, and drunkenness would detract from employee effectiveness in almost any job context. Additionally, these strains may be associated with negative emotions and thoughts that trigger counterproductive work behavior.[68]

Figure 5-4 also reveals that hindrance stressors have a strong negative relationship with organizational commitment.[69] Why might this be? Well, hindrance stressors evoke strains, which are generally dissatisfying to people, and as we discussed in the previous chapter, satisfaction has a strong impact on the degree to which people feel committed to their organization.[70] People who work at jobs that they know are causing them to feel constantly sick and exhausted will likely be dissatisfied with their jobs and feel less desire to stay with the organization and more desire to consider alternatives.

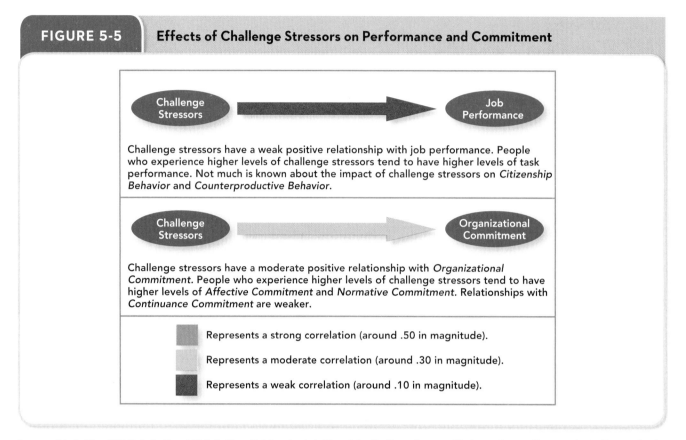

FIGURE 5-5   **Effects of Challenge Stressors on Performance and Commitment**

Sources: J.A. LePine, N.P. Podsakoff, and M.A. LePine, "A Meta-Analytic Test of the Challenge Stressor–Hindrance Stressor Framework: An Explanation for Inconsistent Relationships Among Stressors and Performance," *Academy of Management Journal* 48 (2005), pp. 764–75; and N.P. Podsakoff, J.A. LePine, and M.A. LePine, "Differential Challenge Stressor–Hindrance Stressor Relationships with Job Attitudes, Turnover Intentions, Turnover, and Withdrawal Behavior: A Meta-Analysis," *Journal of Applied Psychology* 92 (2007), pp. 438–54.

Turning now to challenge stressors, the story becomes somewhat different. As shown in Figure 5-5, challenge stressors have a weak relationship with job performance and a moderate relationship with organizational commitment. However, in contrast to the results for hindrance stressors, the relationships are positive rather than negative.[71] In other words, employees who experience higher levels of challenge stressors also tend to have higher levels of job performance and organizational commitment. These relationships stand in sharp contrast with the lower levels of job performance and organizational commitment that result when employees confront higher levels of hindrance stressors. So what explains this difference? Although challenge stressors result in strains, which detract from performance and commitment, they also tend to trigger the type of positive emotions and problem-focused coping strategies that are characteristic of employees who are highly engaged in their jobs.[72] The net benefits of these positive emotions, problem-focused coping strategies, and engagement outweigh the costs of the added strain, meaning that challenge stressors tend to be beneficial to employee performance and commitment when both the positives and negatives are considered.[73] These positive effects of challenge stressors have been demonstrated for executives,[74] employees in lower-level jobs,[75] and even students.[76] It's important to point out, however, that high levels of challenge stressors may have negative consequences that only become apparent over the long term. People whose jobs are filled with challenge stressors experience strains that can result in illness, but because they tend to be more satisfied, committed, and engaged with their jobs, they come to work anyway. This phenomenon, which is referred to as *presenteeism,* can result in prolonged illness, as well as the spread of illness, and ultimately a downward spiral of impaired performance and employee health.[77] In fact, it may surprise you to learn that the reductions in productivity that result from presenteeism are even larger than reductions in productivity that result from employee absenteeism.[78]

APPLICATION: STRESS MANAGEMENT

Previously, we described how employee stress results in strains that cost organizations in terms of reduced employee performance and commitment. However, there are other important costs to consider that relate to employee health. Most organizations provide some sort of health care benefits for their employees,[79] and all but the smallest organizations pay worker's compensation insurance, the rates for which are determined, in part, by the nature of the job and the organization's history of work-related injuries and illnesses. So what role does stress play in these costs?

Well, it turns out that these health-related costs are driven to a great extent by employee stress. Estimates are that between 60 and 90 percent of all doctor visits can be attributed to stress-related causes,[80] and the cost of providing health care to people who experience high levels of stress appears to be approximately 50 percent higher than for those who experience lower levels of stress.[81] Statistics from jobs in different industries indicate that the frequency of worker's compensation claims is dramatically higher when the level of stress on the job is high. As one example, the frequency of claims was more than 800 percent higher for a copy machine distributor when the level of stress at the job site was high.[82] So what do all these costs mean to you as a student of organizational behavior or as a manager?

For one thing, the relationship between stress and health care costs means that there may be huge dividends for organizations that learn how to manage their employees' stress more effectively. In fact, surveys indicate that the vast majority of companies in the United States provide benefits, in one form or another, that are intended to help employees cope with stressful demands and reduce the associated strains.[83] As an example of the lengths some companies go to manage their employees' stress and strains, Google provides access to massage, yoga, meditation, and even napping pods—reclining chairs with egg-shaped caps that fold down to cover the occupant's head and torso.[84] Next, we describe some more general approaches that organizations use to manage employee stress.

5.6

What steps can organizations take to manage employee stress?

ASSESSMENT

The first step in managing stress is to assess the level and sources of stress in the workplace. Although there are many ways to accomplish this type of evaluation, often referred to as a *stress audit,* managers can begin by asking themselves questions about the nature of the jobs in their organization to estimate whether high stress levels may be a problem.[85] The first category of questions might involve the degree to which the organization is going through changes that would likely increase uncertainty among employees. As an example, a merger between two companies might increase employees' uncertainty about their job security and possible career paths. As another example, employees in an organization that has transitioned to team-based work might be concerned about how their individual performance contributions will be recognized and rewarded. A second category of questions might center on the work itself. These questions typically focus on the level and types of stressors experienced by the employees. The third category of questions could involve the quality of relationships between not only employees but also employees and the organization. Here, an important question to consider is whether organizational politics play a large role in administrative decisions.

REDUCING STRESSORS

Once a stress audit reveals that stress may be a problem, the next step is to consider alternative courses of action. One general course of action involves managing stressors, which may be accomplished in one of two ways. First, organizations could try to eliminate or significantly reduce stressful demands. As an example, companies sometimes institute policies that try to limit the demands faced by their employees. Xonex Relocation, a relocation services company located in New Castle, Delaware, prohibits employees from working during lunch and eating at their desks, and they structured workflow so that employees don't leave the office in the evening with unfinished work hanging over their heads.[86] This practice is consistent with research showing that health care workers become much less likely to comply with rules regarding hand hygiene

The use of napping pods is just one example of how far companies go to help manage employee stress and strains.

© Lynn Johnson/National Geographic Image Collection/Alamy

(washing their hands before interacting with a new patient) as demands build up over the course of a long shift and that compliance rates with the same hand hygiene rules increase significantly when longer breaks are given between shifts.[87] As another example of this approach, 19 percent of organizations in one recent survey used *job sharing* to reduce role overload and work–family conflict.[88] Job sharing doesn't mean splitting one job into two but rather indicates that two people share the responsibilities of a single job, as if the two people were a single performing unit. The assumption underlying the practice is that "although businesses are becoming 24–7, people don't."[89] You might be tempted to believe that job sharing would be most appropriate in lower-level jobs, where responsibilities and tasks are limited in number and relatively easy to divide. In actuality, job sharing is being used even at the highest levels in organizations. At Boston–based Fleet Bank, for example, two women shared the position of vice president for global markets and foreign exchange for six years until their department was dissolved when Fleet was acquired by Bank of America. During this time, they had one desk, one chair, one computer, one telephone, one voicemail account, one set of goals, and one performance review. They each worked 20–25 hours a week and performed the role effectively and seamlessly.[90]

Another example of how companies reduce stressors is employee sabbaticals. A *sabbatical* gives employees the opportunity to take time off from work to engage in an alternative activity. Estimates indicate that approximately 11 percent of large companies offer paid sabbaticals, and almost one-third offer unpaid sabbaticals.[91] American Express, for example, allows employees who have 10 years' tenure to apply for a paid sabbatical of up to six months. These employees are encouraged to work for a nonprofit organization or school, but the institution cannot have religious or political affiliations.[92] PricewaterhouseCoopers also offers paid sabbaticals for up to six months for personal growth reasons or for work in social services; this program is available to employees with as little as two years' experience.[93] Relative to job sharing, sabbaticals allow for a cleaner break from the stressful routine for a fairly lengthy period of time, so for the period of the sabbatical, the employee's stress may be quite low. In fact, some companies are experimenting with discretionary vacations policies that allow employees to take time off whenever they feel they need it (and for however long they feel they need it).[94] However, because the level of stressors never changes in the job itself, the employee is likely to experience the same level of stress upon returning from the sabbatical or vacation. See our **OB at the Bookstore** feature for an additional perspective about ways to reduce the number and level of stressors in one's job.

AT THE BOOKSTORE

ESSENTIALISM
by Greg McKeown (New York: Crown Business, 2014).

. . . by investing in fewer things we have the satisfying experience of making significant progress in the things that matter most.

Photo of cover: © Roberts Publishing Services

With those words, author McKeown summarizes the main thesis of his book. That is, because practically everything we do is unimportant, it's possible to function at a higher level by doing less, not more. Although the idea that the majority of what we do is unimportant sounds like hyperbole—if not downright insulting—it's true that we can become overwhelmed with minutia. We say "yes" to requests to do more because we believe that doing so is a part of the job, to please others, and for political reasons. Over time, however, we end up being stretched to the limit—feeling like we couldn't be any busier and any less productive. According to McKeown, the key to changing this pattern is to learn how to filter through all the demands we have and to focus on those that are most vital. The book's chapters present a roadmap to put this philosophy of essentialism to work.

The first step is to develop an essentialist mindset. This involves a deep appreciation that not everything is important and that there is great power in the choices we make. The second step is to discern the essential from everything else. Here the key is to identify activities and outcomes that not only are vital to the job but also are personally meaningful. The third step is to eliminate unimportant demands. As you might imagine, this part of the book is very important for practical reasons. That is, the essentialist philosophy seems to fly in the face of the reality of the workplace in which our bosses and coworkers have expectations of us. McKeown explains how to set boundaries and say "no" gracefully so that these relationships are not damaged and we continue to receive help and support. In the end, it's important to note that McKeown's message isn't about doing less just for the sake of doing less. Rather, it's about making good choices regarding how we use our time and energy so we can maximize our potential for being effective.

PROVIDING RESOURCES

Although reducing stressors may reduce the overall level of stress that a person experiences, this approach is likely to be most beneficial when the focus of the effort is on hindrance stressors rather than challenge stressors.[95] Hindrance stressors such as role ambiguity, conflict, and overload not only cause strain, but also decrease commitment and job performance. In contrast, though challenge stressors such as time pressure and responsibility cause strain, they also tend to be motivating and satisfying, and as a consequence, they generally are positively related to commitment and performance.

So as a supplement to reducing stressors, organizations can provide resources that help employees cope with stressful demands.[96] One way that organizations provide resources to employees is through *training interventions* aimed at increasing job-related competencies and skills. Employees who possess more competencies and skills can handle more demands before they begin to appraise these demands as overly taxing or exceeding their capacity. Training that increases employee competencies and skills is also beneficial to the extent that it promotes a sense that the demands are more controllable, and as we discussed in a previous section, a sense of control promotes problem-focused coping strategies. As an example of the effectiveness of this type of practice, consider the results of a study that examined the benefits of a 20-hour training program in which employees developed skills in stress management, developing a supportive social network, conflict resolution, communication, and assertiveness. Seven months later, employees in 17 organizations who went through the training program felt they possessed more resources to cope with stress and had fewer symptoms of strain than employees who didn't go through the training program.[97]

A second way that organizations provide resources to employees so that they can cope more effectively is through *supportive practices* that help employees manage and balance the demands that exist in the different roles they have.[98] Although we only have room in this chapter to describe a few of these practices, Table 5-4 lists many examples, as well as the percentage of organizations that were found to use them in a survey of almost 400 organizations.[99]

The first supportive practice example is flextime, which was used by 56 percent of the organizations in the survey. Organizations that use flextime give employees some degree of latitude in terms of which hours they need to be present at the workplace. Flexible working hours give employees the ability to cope with demands away from work, so they don't have to worry about these demands while they're at work. As another example, 37 percent of the organizations in the survey allowed telecommuting on a part-time basis. By providing the opportunity to work at home or some other location with computer access, employees are put in a better position to cope with demands that might be impossible to cope with otherwise. Compressed workweeks, which is used by approximately one-third of all companies in the survey, allows full-time employees to work additional hours on some days and have shorter days or time off on others. As with flextime and telecommuting, compressed workweeks give employees the ability to manage both work and nonwork role demands. We should also note that practices such as flextime, telecommuting, and compressed workweeks not only facilitate stress management but also appear to have other benefits. At companies such as Xerox, Corning, and UPS, implementing these types of practices resulted in improvements in productivity, innovation, absenteeism, and turnover.[100] Moreover, although these practices have a range of benefits to employees who actually use them, there is also evidence that their availability alone may be beneficial with regard to enhancing employee job attitudes and commitment.[101]

TABLE 5-4	Supportive Practices Used by Organizations		
PRACTICE	% OF SMALL ORGANIZATIONS	% OF MEDIUM ORGANIZATIONS	% OF LARGE ORGANIZATIONS
Flextime	57	56	56
Part-time telecommuting	36	33	43
Compressed workweek	27	30	41
Bring child to work if needed	43	25	18
Full-time telecommuting	14	18	24
Lactation program	8	20	28
Onsite child care	1	3	13
Company-supported child care center	0	1	11

Source: From M.E. Burke, "2005 Benefits Survey Report," Society of Human Resource Management.

Despite their benefits, companies occasionally decide to end supportive practices during tough times or transitions when the value of employee interaction is amplified. As an example, newly appointed Yahoo CEO, Marissa Mayer, banned the practice of telecommuting to increase employee productivity and encourage richer face-to-face collaboration among employees.[102] Finally, it's important to note that managers sometimes attribute employees' use of these types of practices to low organizational commitment, and when this happens, employees are less likely to receive pay raises and promotions.[103]

REDUCING STRAINS

As an alternative to managing stressors, many organizations use practices that reduce strains.[104] One type of strain-reducing practice involves training in *relaxation techniques,* such as progressive muscle relaxation, meditation, and miscellaneous calming activities like taking walks, writing in a journal, and deep breathing.[105] Although these relaxation techniques differ, the basic idea is the same—they teach people how to counteract the effects of stressors by engaging in activities that slow the heart rate, breathing rate, and blood pressure.[106] As an example of a relatively simple relaxation technique, consider the recommendation of Herbert Benson, a physician and president of the Mind/Body Medical Institute in Boston. He suggests that people under stress should repeat a word, sound, prayer, phrase, or motion for 10–20 minutes once or twice a day and, during that time, try to completely ignore other thoughts that may come to mind.[107] As another example, recall the case of Naomi Henderson, the market research firm CEO who literally became paralyzed by all the stress in her job. Well, we're happy to say that Henderson got better, but she was able to do so only after being treated by a physician who helped her learn how to reduce her own strains by doing "mental aerobics." Those exercises involved taking breaks every hour to stretch and do deep breathing, taking short naps to replenish energy, and learning how to say no politely to unreasonable demands.[108] As a final example, BlueCross BlueShield of Tennessee has trained approximately one-fifth of its 4,500 employees in the use of biofeedback technology to reduce the stress associated with financial uncertainties stemming from the economic downturn.[109] The training uses a heart monitor and software to help people learn how to change their heart rhythms from an irregular pattern to a regular pattern by shifting from an anxious emotional state to a more positive one. Apparently, the training worked: A preliminary evaluation of the program revealed that those employees who received biofeedback training reported being less exhausted and anxious than they were before the training.

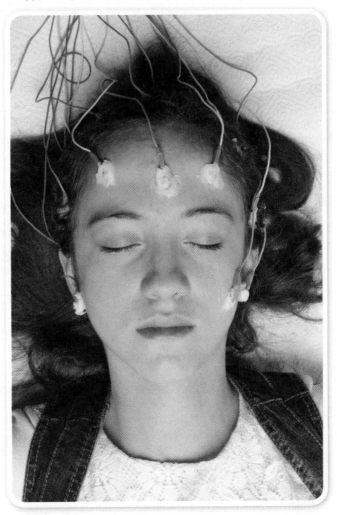

People can learn how to reduce strain using biofeedback technology.

© *minemero/iStock/Getty Images Plus/Getty Images RF*

A second general category of strain-reducing practices involves *cognitive–behavioral techniques*. In general, these techniques attempt to help people appraise and cope with stressors in a more rational manner.[110] To understand what these techniques involve, think of someone you know who not only exaggerates the level and importance of stressful demands but also predicts doom and disaster after quickly concluding that the demands simply cannot be met. If you know someone like this, you might recommend cognitive–behavioral training that involves "self-talk," a technique in which people learn to say things about stressful demands that reflect rationality and optimism. So, when confronted with a stressful demand, this person might be trained to say, "This demand isn't so tough; if I work hard I can accomplish it." Cognitive–behavioral training also typically involves instruction about tools that foster effective coping. So, in addition to the self-talk, the person might be trained on how to prioritize demands, manage time, communicate needs, and seek support.[111] As an example of this type of training, Austin, Texas–based Freescale Semiconductor Inc. trains its 6,000 employees how to be "resilient" to stressful situations, such as those that occur when employees have to interact with team members from other departments in the organization that do not share the same goals.[112] The training teaches employees strategies, such as planning for the stressful encounter and using social support, which give them the ability to use a problem-focused approach to coping with their stress.

A third category of strain-reducing practices involves *health and wellness programs*. For example, almost three-quarters of the organizations in one survey reported having *employee assistance programs* intended to help people with personal problems such as alcoholism and other addictions. More than 60 percent of organizations in this survey provided employees with wellness programs and resources. The nature of these programs and resources varies a great deal from organization to organization, but in general, they're comprehensive efforts that include health screening (blood pressure, cholesterol levels, pulmonary functioning) and health-related courses and information. Other examples of health and wellness programs intended to reduce strain include smoking cessation programs, onsite fitness centers or fitness center memberships, and weight loss and nutrition programs.[113] Today, health and wellness programs that encourage and support exercise are a growing trend. As an example, Humana, a *Fortune* 100 health care administration company, implemented a program that allows the 8,500 employees who work at their corporate headquarters in Louisville, Kentucky, to borrow bikes for free from kiosks located throughout the city.[114] As another example, consider how Grant Thornton, the Chicago–based tax, audit, and advisory firm, encourages exercise: It spent more than $200,000 helping 230 of its employees train and compete in a marathon. It also reimburses employees for participation in up to three races or walks per year, and it even set up running clubs in each of its 50 offices.[115] Investments in exercise make sense because the effects of strains, such as burnout and depression, can be reduced with physical activity. In particular, exercise can prevent a downward spiral where an employee feels burned out, and this feeds into depression, which increases burnout, and so on. But, how well do these efforts actually pay off?[116] L.L.Bean initiated a comprehensive wellness program for roughly 5,000 of its employees that included health assessments, health-coaching, and onsite fitness and nutrition programs, and found that the program had a positive return on investment after the first year and reduced health care costs by almost $400 per employee.[117]

TAKEAWAYS

5.1 Stress refers to the psychological response to demands when there's something at stake for the individual and coping with these demands would tax or exceed the individual's capacity or resources. Stressors are the demands that cause the stress response, and strains are the negative consequences of the stress response.

5.2 Stressors come in two general forms: challenge stressors, which are perceived as opportunities for growth and achievement, and hindrance stressors, which are perceived as hurdles to goal achievement. These two stressors can be found in both work and nonwork domains.

5.3 Coping with stress involves thoughts and behaviors that address one of two goals: addressing the stressful demand or decreasing the emotional discomfort associated with the demand.

5.4 Individual differences in the Type A Behavior Pattern affect how people experience stress in three ways. Type A people tend to experience more stressors, appraise more demands as stressful, and are prone to experiencing more strains.

5.5 The effects of stress depend on the type of stressor. Hindrance stressors have a weak negative relationship with job performance and a strong negative relationship with organizational commitment. In contrast, challenge stressors have a weak positive relationship with job performance and a moderate positive relationship with organizational commitment.

5.6 Because of the high costs associated with employee stress, organizations assess and manage stress using a number of different practices. In general, these practices focus on reducing or eliminating stressors, providing resources that employees can use to cope with stressors, or trying to reduce the strains.

KEY TERMS

- Stress   p. 128
- Stressors   p. 128
- Strains   p. 128
- Transactional theory of stress   p. 129
- Primary appraisal   p. 129
- Benign job demands   p. 130
- Hindrance stressors   p. 130
- Challenge stressors   p. 131
- Role conflict   p. 131
- Role ambiguity   p. 131
- Role overload   p. 131
- Daily hassles   p. 131
- Time pressure   p. 132
- Work complexity   p. 132
- Work responsibility   p. 132
- Work–family conflict   p. 133
- Negative life events   p. 134
- Financial uncertainty   p. 134
- Family time demands   p. 134
- Personal development   p. 134
- Positive life events   p. 134
- Secondary appraisal   p. 135
- Coping   p. 135
- Behavioral coping   p. 135
- Cognitive coping   p. 135
- Problem-focused coping   p. 135
- Emotion-focused coping   p. 135
- Burnout   p. 139
- Type A Behavior Pattern   p. 139
- Social support   p. 141
- Instrumental support   p. 141
- Emotional support   p. 141

DISCUSSION QUESTIONS

5.1 Prior to reading this chapter, how did you define stress? Did your definition of stress reflect stressors, the stress process, strains, or some combination?

5.2 Describe your dream job and then provide a list of the types of stressors that you would expect to be present. How much of your salary, if any at all, would you give up to eliminate the most important hindrance stressors? Why?

5.3 If you had several job offers after graduating, to what degree would the level of challenge stressors in the different jobs influence your choice of which job to take? Why?

5.4 How would you assess your ability to handle stress? Given the information provided in this chapter, what could you do to improve your effectiveness in this area?

5.5 If you managed people in an organization in which there were lots of hindrance stressors, what actions would you take to help ensure that your employees coped with the stressors using a problem-focused (as opposed to emotion-focused) strategy?

CASE: INTERNAL REVENUE SERVICE

Each year the IRS processes approximately 240 million tax returns and collects about $3 trillion. This is a huge amount of money, constituting more than 90 percent of all receipts to the United States. This fact is not lost to IRS employees, who find great satisfaction in knowing that their efforts help keep the country running. At the same time, however, being an IRS employee is difficult, in part, because the public doesn't appreciate the agency's mission. To most people, the IRS is responsible for the cost and hassle of filing and paying taxes, time-consuming audits, and seizures of homes and businesses. In fact, although IRS employees feel their jobs are personally meaningful, they are often unwilling to tell acquaintances who they work for.

There are several reasons why working at the IRS has been made even more difficult over the last several years. First, in an attempt to make the IRS more efficient, the agency was reorganized from a decentralized structure with 33 regions responsible for different functions (collections, customer service, audits, and criminal investigations) to a centralized structure with four national units that serve different customers (individuals, small businesses, large corporations, and nonprofits). This change reduced interaction among team members, and along with it, camaraderie and social support. Second, there have been significant budget cuts, and as a consequence, there are fewer employees and resources available to accomplish the work. Employees not only have to perform the responsibilities of multiple jobs, but they also have to spend their own money on basic supplies like pens, paper, and staples. Finally, a number of well-publicized scandals have worsened the public's perception of the agency. You may remember the well-publicized video of IRS executives dressed as Star Trek characters, the news clip of the IRS employees staying in lavish presidential suites at a conference, and the news story of employees being rehired by the agency after they were fired for not paying their taxes. Although these incidents were a function of a few bad apples, they reflected poorly on the agency and were demoralizing to employees.

To make matters worse, there are signs that the agency's effectiveness is declining. For example, only 40 percent of all people who call the IRS for help ever get through to someone, and in many cases, those who get through are simply told to refer to the IRS website or hire an accountant. The number of criminal investigations and audits is down sharply as well. Although this might sound like a good thing from a taxpayer's perspective, the system depends on voluntary compliance, and if enough people think it's worth the risk not to pay their taxes, a real crisis may unfold. All this is leading to pressure on the government to make significant changes to the IRS. Although the potential for change may provide a ray of hope for stressed-out employees, it also creates an air of uncertainty, which may be adding to their stress.

5.1 Identify the different types of stressors experienced by IRS employees. Describe how the different stressors are likely to influence employee well-being, commitment, and job performance. How might these consequences be linked to the decline in the agency's effectiveness?

5.2 How did the reorganization of the IRS influence employee stress? What changes could the organization make to address this unintended consequence of the reorganization?

5.3 What other steps could the IRS take to manage the stress of its employees? How might leaders help employees deal with uncertainty in the organization moving forward?

Sources: *Internal Revenue Service 2014 Data Book*, Publication 55B, March 2015, Washington DC; *IRS Historical Fact Book: A Chronology: 1646-1992*. Department of the Treasury, Internal Revenue Service, 1993, Publication 1694 (12-92) Catalog Number 15087N, Washington DC; D. Leonard and R. Rubin, "The Taxman Bemmeth." *Bloomberg Businessweek*, April 13–19, 2015, pp. 50–55; and L. Rein. "Declining IRS Workforce Leaves Calls Unanswered as Tax Day Approaches, Union Says." *The Washington Post*, April 6, 2015, http://www.washingtonpost.com/blogs/federal-eye/wp/2015/04/06/declining-force-of-irs-employees-leaves-calls-unanswered-as-tax-day-approaches-union-says/.

EXERCISE: MANAGING STRESS

The purpose of this exercise is to explore ways of managing stress to reduce strain. This exercise uses groups, so your instructor will either assign you to a group or ask you to create your own group. The exercise has the following steps:

5.1   One method of managing stress is finding a way to reduce the hindrance stressors encountered on the job. In your group, describe the hindrance stressors that you currently are experiencing. Each student should describe the two to three most important stressors using the accompanying chart. Other students should then offer strategies for reducing or alleviating the stressors.

HINDRANCE STRESSORS EXPERIENCED	STRATEGIES FOR MANAGING STRESSORS
Role conflict:	
Role ambiguity:	
Role overload:	
Daily hassles:	

5.2   Another method of managing stress is to improve work–life balance. The accompanying figure represents how "waking hours" are divided among five types of activities: school, work, personal relaxation, time with friends, and time with family. Draw two versions of your own circle: your waking hours as they currently are and your waking hours as you wish them to be. Other students should then offer strategies for making the necessary life changes.

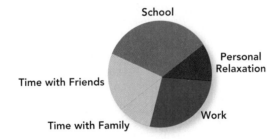

5.3   A third method of managing stress is improving *hardiness*—a sort of mental and physical health that can act as a buffer, preventing stress from resulting in strain. The following table lists a number of questions that can help diagnose your hardiness. Discuss your answers for each question; then, with the help of other students, brainstorm ways to increase that hardiness factor.

HARDINESS FACTOR	STRATEGIES FOR IMPROVING FACTOR
Relaxation: Do you spend enough time reading, listening to music, meditating, or pursuing your hobbies?	
Exercise: Do you spend enough time doing cardiovascular, strength, and flexibility sorts of exercises?	
Diet: Do you manage your diet adequately by eating healthily and avoiding foods high in fat?	

5.4 Class discussion (whether in groups or as a class) should center on two issues. First, many of the stress-managing factors, especially in steps 2 and 3, take up precious time. Does this make them an ineffective strategy for managing stress? Why or why not? Second, consider your Type A score in the OB Assessments for this chapter. If you are high on Type A, does that make these strategies more or less important?

Source: D. Marcic, J. Seltzer and P. Vail. *Organizational Behavior: Experiences and Cases.* Cincinnati, OH: South-Western, 2001.

ENDNOTES

5.1 Miller, J., and M. Miller. "Get a Life!" *Fortune,* November 28, 2005, pp. 109–24, www.proquest.com (March 27, 2007).

5.2 Sauter, S.; L. Murphy; M. Colligan; N. Swanson; J. Hurrell Jr.; F. Scharf Jr.; R. Sinclair; P. Grubb; L. Goldenhar; T. Alterman; J. Johnston; A. Hamilton; and J. Tisdale. *Stress at Work,* DHHS (NIOSH) Publication No. 99–101. Cincinnati, OH: U.S. Department of Health and Human Services, Public Health Service, Centers for Disease Control and Prevention, National Institute for Occupational Safety and Health, 1999.

5.3 Johnson, S.R., and L.D. Eldridge. *Employee-Related Stress on the Job: Sources, Consequences, and What's Next,* Technical Report #003. Rochester, NY: Genesee Survey Services, Inc., 2004.

5.4 Lazarus, R.S., and S. Folkman. *Stress, Appraisal, and Coping.* New York: Springer, 1984.

5.5 Ibid.

5.6 Ibid.

5.7 LePine, J.A.; M.A. LePine; and C.L. Jackson. "Challenge and Hindrance Stress: Relationships with Exhaustion, Motivation to Learn, and Learning Performance." *Journal of Applied Psychology* 89 (2004), pp. 883–91; LePine, J.A.; N.P. Podsakoff; and M.A. LePine. "A Meta-Analytic Test of the Challenge Stressor–Hindrance Stressor Framework: An Explanation for Inconsistent Relationships among Stressors and Performance." *Academy of Management Journal* 48 (2005), pp. 764–75; and Podsakoff, N.P.; J.A. LePine; and M.A. LePine. "Differential Challenge Stressor–Hindrance Stressor Relationships with Job Attitudes, Turnover Intentions, Turnover, and Withdrawal Behavior: A Meta-Analysis." *Journal of Applied Psychology* 92 (2007), pp. 438–54.

5.8 Rodell, J.B., and T.A. Judge. "Can 'Good' Stressors Spark 'Bad' Behaviors? The Mediating Role of Emotions in the Links of Challenge and Hindrance Stressors with Citizenship and Counterproductive Behaviors." *Journal of Applied Psychology* 94 (2009), pp. 1438–51.

5.9 LePine, J.A.; M.A. LePine; and J.R. Saul. "Relationships among Work and Non-Work Challenge and Hindrance Stressors and Non-Work and Work Criteria: A Theory of Cross-Domain Stressor Effects." In *Research in Occupational Stress and Well Being,* ed. P.L. Perrewé and D.C. Ganster. San Diego: JAI Press/Elsevier, 2006, pp. 35–72.

5.10 Kahn, R.; D. Wolfe; R. Quinn; J. Snoek; and R.A. Rosenthal. *Organizational Stress: Studies in Role Conflict and Ambiguity.* New York: Wiley, 1964; and

Pearce, J. "Bringing Some Clarity to Role Ambiguity Research." *Academy of Management Review* 6 (1981), pp. 665–74.

5.11 Kahn et al., *Organizational Stress;* Rizzo, J.R.; R.J. House; and S.I. Lirtzman. "Role Conflict and Ambiguity in Complex Organizations." *Administrative Science Quarterly* 15 (1970), pp. 150–63.

5.12 Ibid.

5.13 Kahn et al., *Organizational Stress.*

5.14 Narayanan, L.; S. Menon; and P. Spector. "Stress in the Workplace: A Comparison of Gender and Occupations." *Journal of Organizational Behavior* 20 (1999), pp. 63–74.

5.15 Miller and Miller, "Get a Life!"

5.16 Chamerlain, K., and S. Zika. "The Minor Events Approach to Stress: Support for the Use of Daily Hassles." *British Journal of Psychology* 18 (1990), pp. 469–81.

5.17 Mandel, M. "The Real Reasons You're Working So Hard . . . and What You Can Do about It." *BusinessWeek,* October 3, 2005, pp. 60–67, http://www.proquest.com (accessed March 27, 2007).

5.18 Kahn et al., *Organizational Stress.*

5.19 O'Connor, A. "Cracking under Pressure? It's Just the Opposite for Some; Sick of Work—Last of Three Articles: Thriving under Stress." *The New York Times,* Section A, Column 5, September 10, 2004, p. 1, http://www.proquest.com (accessed March 27, 2007).

5.20 Schaubroeck, J.; D.C. Ganster; and B.E. Kemmerer. "Job Complexity, 'Type A' Behavior, and Cardiovascular Disorder: A Prospective Study." *Academy of Management Journal* 37 (1994), pp. 426–39.

5.21 McCall, M.W.; M.M. Lombardo; and A.M. Morrison. *The Lessons of Experience: How Successful Executives Develop on the Job.* Lexington, MA: Lexington Books, 1988.

5.22 Edwards, J.R., and R.V. Harrison. "Job Demands and Worker Health: Three-Dimensional Reexamination of the Relationships between Person-Environment Fit and Strain." *Journal of Applied Psychology* 78 (1993), pp. 628–48; and French, J.R.P. Jr.; R.D. Caplan; and R.V. Harrison. *The Mechanisms of Job Stress and Strain.* New York: Wiley, 1982.

5.23 Abrahm, S. "From Wall Street to Control Tower." *The New York Times,* March 20, 2010, http://www.nytimes.com/2010/03/21/jobs/21preoccupations.html.

5.24 Neufeld, S. "Work-Related Stress: What You Need to Know" (n.d.), http://healthplace.healthology.com/focus_article.asp?f5mentalhealth&c5work_related_stress.

5.25 Hoobler, J.M.; S.J. Wayne; and G. Lemmon. "Bosses' Perceptions of Family–Work Conflict and Women's Promotability: Glass Ceiling Effects." *Academy of Management Journal* 52 (2009), pp. 939–57.

5.26 Crouter, A. "Spillover from Family to Work: The Neglected Side of the Work–Family Interface." *Human Relations* 37 (1984), pp. 425–42; and Rice, R.W.; M.R. Frone; and D.B. McFarlin. "Work and Nonwork Conflict and the Perceived Quality of Life." *Journal of Organizational Behavior* 13 (1992), pp. 155–68.

5.27 Dahm, P.C.; T.M. Glomb; C. Flaherty Manchester; and S. Leroy. "Work-Family Conflict and Self-Discrepant Time Allocation at Work." *Journal of Applied Psychology* 100 (2015), pp. 767–92; Netemeyer, R.G.; J.S. Boles; and R. McMurrian. "Development and Validation of Work–Family Conflict and Family–Work Conflict Scales." *Journal of Applied Psychology* 81 (1996), pp. 400–10; and

Shockley, K.M., and T.D. Allen. "Deciding Between Work and Family: An Episodic Approach." *Personnel Psychology* 68 (2015), pp. 283–318.

5.28 Ng, T.W.H., and D.C. Feldman. "The Effects of Organizational and Community Embeddedness on Work-to-Family and Family-to-Work Conflict." *Journal of Applied Psychology* 97 (2012), pp. 1233–51.

5.29 Cohen, S.; D.A. Tyrrell; and A.P. Smith. "Negative Life Events, Perceived Stress, Negative Affect, and Susceptibility to the Common Cold." *Journal of Personality and Social Psychology* 64 (1993), pp. 131–40.

5.30 Holmes, T.H., and R.H. Rahe. "The Social Readjustment Rating Scale." *Journal of Psychosomatic Research* 11 (1967), pp. 213–18; and U.S. Department of Health and Human Services, Office of the Surgeon General. "Mental Health: A Report of the Surgeon General" (n.d.), http://www.surgeongeneral.gov/library/mentalhealth/home.html.

5.31 Frauenheim, E., and J. Marquez. "Reducing the Fear Factor." *Workforce Management,* November 18, 2008, pp. 17–22.

5.32 LePine et al., "Relationships among Work and Non-Work Challenge and Hindrance Stressors and Non-Work and Work Criteria."

5.33 Lazarus and Folkman, *Stress, Appraisal, and Coping.*

5.34 Folkman, S.; R.S. Lazarus; C. Dunkel-Schetter; A. Delongis; and R.J. Gruen. "Dynamics of a Stressful Encounter: Cognitive Appraisal, Coping, and Encounter Outcomes." *Journal of Personality and Social Psychology* 50 (1986), pp. 992–1003.

5.35 Latack, J.C., and S.J. Havlovic. "Coping with Job Stress: A Conceptual Evaluation Framework for Coping Measures." *Journal of Organizational Behavior* 13 (1992), pp. 479–508.

5.36 Ibid.

5.37 Latack and Havlovic, "Coping with Job Stress."

5.38 Kahn et al., *Organizational Stress;* and Lazarus and Folkman, *Stress, Appraisal, and Coping.*

5.39 Latack and Havlovic, "Coping with Job Stress."

5.40 Ibid.

5.41 Lazarus, R.S. "Progress on a Cognitive–Motivational–Relational Theory of Emotion." *American Psychologist* 46 (1991), pp. 819–34.

5.42 Daniels, C. "The Last Taboo: It's Not Sex. It's Not Drinking. It's Stress—and It's Soaring." *Fortune,* October 28, 2002, pp. 136–44, www.proquest.com (accessed March 27, 2007).

5.43 Miller and Miller, "Get a Life!"

5.44 Selye, H. *The Stress of Life.* New York: McGraw-Hill, 1976.

5.45 Cannon, W.B. "Stresses and Strains of Homeostasis." *American Journal of Medical Science* 189 (1935), pp. 1–14; and Goldstein, D.L. *Stress, Catecholamines, & Cardiovascular Disease.* New York: Oxford University Press, 1995.

5.46 Kahn, R.L., and P. Byosiere. "Stress in Organizations." In *Handbook of Industrial and Organizational Psychology,* Vol. 4, ed. M.D. Dunette; J.M.R. Hough; and H.C. Triandis. Palo Alto, CA: Consulting Psychologists Press, 1992, pp. 517–650.

5.47 Defrank, R.S., and J.M. Ivancevich. "Stress on the Job: An Executive Update." *Academy of Management Executive* 12 (1998), pp. 55–66; and Haran, C. "Do You Know Your Early Warning Stress Signals?" 2005, http://abcnews.go.com/Health/Healthology/story?id=421825.

5.48 Stöppler, M.C. "High Pressure Work Deadlines Raise Heart

Attack Risk," http://stress.about.com/od/heartdissease/a/deadline.htm (accessed October 1, 2005).

5.49 Leitner, K., and M.G. Resch. "Do the Effects of Job Stressors on Health Persist over Time? A Longitudinal Study with Observational Stress Measures." *Journal of Occupational Health Psychology* 10 (2005), pp. 18–30.

5.50 Defrank and Ivancevich, "Stress on the Job"; and Haran, "*Do You Know?*"

5.51 Pines, A., and D. Kafry. "Occupational Tedium in the Social Services." *Social Work* 23 (1978), pp. 499–507.

5.52 ESPN.com. "Mentally Tired Favre Tells Packers His Playing Career Is Over," March 4, 2008, http://sports.espn.go.com/nfl/news/story?id=3276034.

5.53 Packers.com. "Brett Favre Retirement Press Conference Transcript—March 6," March 6, 2008, http://packers.com.

5.54 Defrank and Ivancevich, "Stress on the Job."

5.55 Friedman, M., and R.H. Rosenman. *Type A Behavior and Your Heart.* New York: Knopf, 1974.

5.56 Ganster, D.C. "Type A Behavior and Occupational Stress. Job Stress: From Theory to Suggestion." *Journal of Organizational Behavior Management* 8 (1987), pp. 61–84.

5.57 Friedman and Rosenman, *Type A Behavior;* and Yarnold, P.R., and F.B. Bryant. "A Note on Measurement Issues in Type A Research: Let's Not Throw Out the Baby with the Bath Water." *Journal of Personality Assessment* 52 (1988), pp. 410–19.

5.58 Abush, R., and E.J. Burkhead. "Job Stress in Midlife Working Women: Relationships among Personality Type, Job Characteristics, and Job Tension." *Journal of Counseling Psychology* 31 (1984), pp. 36–44; Dearborn, M.J., and J.E. Hastings. "Type A Personality as a Mediator of Stress and Strain in Employed Women." *Journal of Human Stress* 13 (1987), pp. 53–60; and Howard, J.H.; D.A. Cunningham; and P.A. Rechnitzer. "Role Ambiguity, Type A Behavior, and Job Satisfaction: Moderating Effects on Cardiovascular and Biochemical Responses Associated with Coronary Risk." *Journal of Applied Psychology* 71 (1986), pp. 95–101.

5.59 Cooper, C.L.; P.J. Dewe; and M.P. O'Driscoll. *Organizational Stress.* Thousand Oaks, CA: Sage 2001.

5.60 Fusilier, M.R.; D.C. Ganster; and B.T. Mayes. "Effects of Social Support, Role Stress, and Locus of Control on Health." *Journal of Management* 13 (1987), pp. 517–28.

5.61 Nahum-Shani, I., and P.A. Bamberger. "Explaining the Variable Effects of Social Support on Work-Based Stressor-Strain Relations: The Role of Perceived Pattern of Support Exchange." *Organizational Behavior and Human Decision Processes* 114 (2011), pp. 49–63.

5.62 Zhang, Y.; J.A. LePine; B. R. Buckman; and F. Wei. "It's Not Fair . . . Or Is It? The Role of Justice and Leadership in Explaining Work Stressor-Job Performance Relationships." *Academy of Management Journal* 57 (2014), pp. 675–97.

5.63 Jayaratne, S.; T. Tripodi; and W.A. Chess. "Perceptions of Emotional Support, Stress, and Strain by Male and Female Social Workers." *Social Work Research and Abstracts* 19 (1983), pp. 19–27; Kobasa, S. "Commitment and Coping in Stress among Lawyers." *Journal of Personality and Social Psychology* 42 (1982), pp. 707–17; and LaRocco, J.M., and A.P. Jones. "Co-Worker and Leader Support as Moderators of Stress–Strain Relationships in Work Situations." *Journal of Applied Psychology* 63 (1978), pp. 629–34.

5.64 Kahn and Byosiere, "Stress in Organizations."

5.65 Nohe, C.; L.L. Meier; K. Sonntag; and A. Michel. "The Chicken or the Egg? A Meta-Analysis of Panel Studies of the Relationship between Work-Family Conflict and Strain." *Journal of Applied Psychology* 100 (2015), pp. 522–36.

5.66 LePine et al., "A Meta-Analytic Test."

5.67 Cohen, S. "After Effects of Stress on Human Performance and Social Behavior: A Review of Research and Theory." *Psychological Bulletin* 88 (1980), pp. 82–108; and Crawford, E.R.; LePine, J.A.; and Rich, B.L. "Linking Job Demands and Resources to Employee Engagement and Burnout: A Theoretical Extension and Meta-Analytic Test." *Journal of Applied Psychology* 95 (2010), pp. 834–48.

5.68 Meier, L.L., and P.E. Spector. "Reciprocal Effects of Work Stressors and Counterproductive Work Behavior: A Five Wave Longitudinal Study." *Journal of Applied Psychology* 98 (2013), pp. 529–39.

5.69 Podsakoff et al., "Differential Challenge Stressor–Hindrance Stressor Relationships."

5.70 Bedeian, A.G., and A. Armenakis. "A Path-Analytic Study of the Consequences of Role Conflict and Ambiguity." *Academy of Management Journal* 24 (1981), pp. 417–24; and Schaubroeck, J.; J.L. Cotton; and K.R. Jennings. "Antecedents and Consequences of Role Stress: A Covariance Structure Analysis." *Journal of Organizational Behavior* 10 (1989), pp. 35–58.

5.71 LePine et al., "A Meta-Analytic Test"; and Podsakoff et al., "Differential Challenge Stressor–Hindrance Stressor Relationships."

5.72 Crawford, LePine, and Rich, "Linking Job Demands and Resources to Employee Engagement and Burnout."

5.73 Ibid.

5.74 Cavanaugh, M.A.; W.R. Boswell; M.V. Roehling; and J.W. Boudreau. "An Empirical Examination of Self-Reported Work Stress among U.S. Managers." *Journal of Applied Psychology* 85 (2000), pp. 65–74.

5.75 Boswell, W.R.; J.B. Olson-Buchanan; and M.A. LePine. "The Relationship between Work-Related Stress and Work Outcomes: The Role of Felt-Challenge and Psychological Strain." *Journal of Vocational Behavior* 64 (2004), pp. 165–81.

5.76 LePine et al., "Challenge and Hindrance Stress."

5.77 Myers, L. "Transforming Presenteeism into Productivity" *Workspan,* July 2009, pp. 40–43.

5.78 Miller, S. "Most Employees Underestimate Health Impact on Productivity." *HR Magazine,* June 2009, p. 20.

5.79 Burke, M.E. "2005 Benefits Survey Report." Alexandria, VA: Society of Human Resource Management Research Department, 2005.

5.80 Perkins, A. "Medical Costs: Saving Money by Reducing Stress." *Harvard Business Review* 72 (1994), p. 12.

5.81 Sauter, S.; L. Murphy; M. Colligan; N. Swanson; J. Hurrell Jr.; F. Scharf Jr.; R. Sinclair; P. Grubb; L. Goldenhar; T. Alterman; J. Johnston; A. Hamilton; and J. Tisdale. "Is Your Boss Making You Sick?" (n.d.), http://abcnews.go.com/GMA/Careers/story?id=1251346&gma=true.

5.82 Defrank and Ivancevich, "Stress on the Job."

5.83 Noyce, J. "Help Employees Manage Stress to Prevent Absenteeism, Errors." *Minneapolis–St. Paul Business Journal,* August 22, 2003, http://twincities.bizjournals.com/twincities/

stories/2003/08/25/
smallb2.html; and
Burke, "2005 Benefits
Survey Report."

5.84 Hoffman, J. "Napping Gets a Nod at the Workplace." *Bloomberg Businessweek,* August 26, 2010, http://www.business week.com/magazine/content/10_36/b4193084949626.htm; and Yarow, J. "Googlers Take Naps in Bizarre Contraption." *Business Insider SAI,* June 17, 2010, http://www.business insider.com/google-sleep-pods-2010-6.

5.85 Defrank and Ivancevich, "Stress on the Job"; and Cooper, C.L. "The Costs of Stress at Work." *The Safety & Health Practitioner* 19 (2001), pp. 24–26.

5.86 Rafter, M. V. "The Yawning of a New Era." *Workforce Management,* December 2010, pp. 3–4.

5.87 Hengchen, D.; K.L. Milkman; D. A. Hofmann; and B. R. Staats. "The Impact of Time at Work and Time off from Work on Rule Compliance: The Case of Hand Hygiene in Health Care." *Journal of Applied Psychology* 100 (2015), p. 846–62.

5.88 Burke, "2005 Benefits Survey Report."

5.89 Miller and Miller, "Get a Life!"

5.90 Ibid.; and Cunningham, C.R., and S.S. Murray. "Two

Executives, One Career." *Harvard Business Review* 83 (February 2005), pp. 125–31.

5.91 Sahadi, J. "The World's Best Perk." *CNNMoney.com,* June 13, 2006, http://money.cnn.com/2006/06/13/commentary/everyday/sahadi/index.htm.

5.92 Ibid.

5.93 Ibid.

5.94 Milligan. S. "Greetings from Unlimited Vacationland." *HR Magazine,* March (2015), p. 28–36.

5.95 LePine et al., "A Meta-Analytic Test"; and Podsakoff et al., "Differential Challenge Stressor–Hindrance Stress Relationships."

5.96 Hakanen, J.J.; M.C.W. Peeters; and R. Perhoniemi. "Enrichment Processes and Gain Spirals at Work and at Home: A 3-Year Cross-Lagged Panel Study." *Journal of Occupational and Organizational Psychology* 84 (2011), pp. 8–30; and Sonnentag, S., and M. Frese. "Stress in Organizations." In *Comprehensive Handbook of Psychology: Vol. 12, Industrial and Organizational Psychology,* ed. W.C. Borman; D.R. Ilgen, and R.J. Klimoski. New York: Wiley, 2003, pp. 453–91.

5.97 Vuori, J.; S. Toppinen-Tanner; and P. Mutanen. "Impacts of Resource-Building

Group Intervention on Career Management and Mental Health in Work Organizations: Randomized Controlled Field Trial." *Journal of Applied Psychology* 97 (2012), pp. 273–86.

5.98 Allen, T.D.; R.C. Johnson; K.M. Kiburz; and K.M. Shockley. "Work-Family Conflict and Flexible Work Arrangements: Deconstructing Flexibility. *Personnel Psychology* 66 (2013), pp. 345–76.

5.99 Burke, "2005 Benefits Survey Report."

5.100 Defrank and Ivancevich, "Stress on the Job"; and Austin, N.K. "Work–Life Paradox." *Incentive* 178 (2004), p. 18.

5.101 Butts, M.B.; W.J. Casper; and T.S. Yang. "How Important are Work-Family Support Policies? A Meta-Analytic Investigation of Their Effects on Employee Outcomes." *Journal of Applied Psychology* 98 (2013). pp. 1–25.

5.102 Goudreau, J. "Back to the Stone Age? New Yahoo CEO Marissa Mayer Bans Working from Home." *Forbes,* http://www.forbes.com/sites/jennagoudreau/2013/02/25/back-to-the-stone-age-new-yahoo-ceo-marissa-mayer-bans-working-from-home/ (accessed February 25, 2013).

5.103 Leslie, L.M.; C. Flaherty Manchester; T.Y. Park; and S.A. Mehng. "Flexible Work Practices: A Source of Career Premiums or Penalties?" *Academy of Management Journal* 55 (2012), pp. 1407–28.

5.104 Murphy, L.R. "Stress Management in Work Settings: A Critical Review of Health Effects." *American Journal of Health Promotion* 11 (1996), pp. 112–35.

5.105 Neufeld, *Work-Related Stress.*

5.106 Haran, *"Do You Know?"*

5.107 Ibid.

5.108 Daniels, "The Last Taboo."

5.109 Frauenheim and Marquez, "Reducing the Fear Factor."

5.110 Sonnentag and Frese, "Stress in Organizations."

5.111 Neufeld, *Work-Related Stress.*

5.112 Atkinson. W. "Turning Stress into Strength." *HR Magazine,* January 2011, pp. 49–52.

5.113 Ibid.; Burke, "2005 Benefits Survey Report."

5.114 Kvamme, N. "Humana's Freewheelin' Program Proves to Be Good for Business."

Workspan, August 2008, pp. 75–78.

5.115 Doheny, K. "Going the Extra Mile." *Workforce Management,* January 19, 2009, pp. 27–28.

5.116 Toker, S., and M. Biron. "Job Burnout and Depression: Unraveling Their Temporal Relationship and Considering the Role of Physical Activity." *Journal of Applied Psychology* 97 (2012), pp. 699–770.

5.117 Sohre, K. "What Are These Companies Doing about Health Care Management That You Aren't?" *Workspan,* March 2010, pp. 22–26.

chapter 6

Motivation

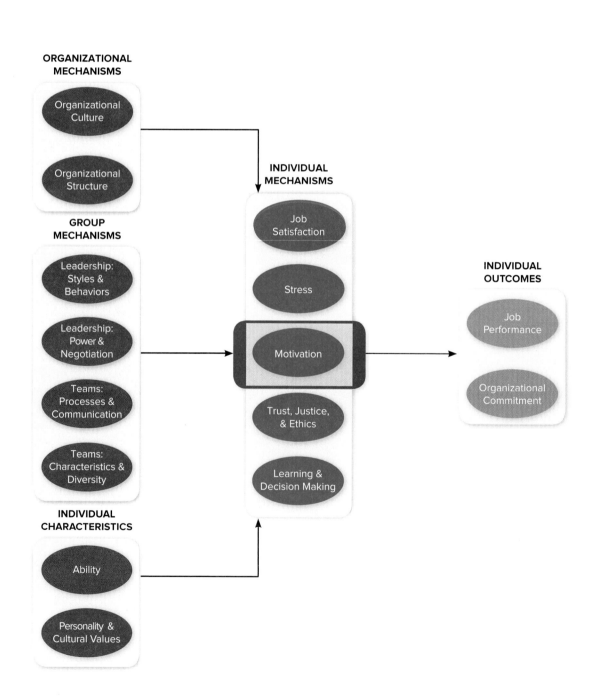

ORGANIZATIONAL MECHANISMS

Organizational Culture

Organizational Structure

GROUP MECHANISMS

Leadership: Styles & Behaviors

Leadership: Power & Negotiation

Teams: Processes & Communication

Teams: Characteristics & Diversity

INDIVIDUAL CHARACTERISTICS

Ability

Personality & Cultural Values

INDIVIDUAL MECHANISMS

Job Satisfaction

Stress

Motivation

Trust, Justice, & Ethics

Learning & Decision Making

INDIVIDUAL OUTCOMES

Job Performance

Organizational Commitment

© Simon Dawson/Bloomberg via Getty Images

After reading this chapter, you should be able to answer the following questions:

6.1 What is motivation?

6.2 What three beliefs help determine work effort, according to expectancy theory?

6.3 What two qualities make goals strong predictors of task performance, according to goal setting theory?

6.4 What does it mean to be equitably treated according to equity theory, and how do employees respond to inequity?

6.5 What is psychological empowerment, and what four beliefs determine empowerment levels?

6.6 How does motivation affect job performance and organizational commitment?

6.7 What steps can organizations take to increase employee motivation?

DELOITTE

onsider the following four statements. "Given what I know of this person's performance, I would always want him or her on my team." "This person is ready for promotion today." "Given what I know of this person's performance, and if it were my money, I would award this person the highest possible compensation increase and bonus." "This person is at risk of low performance." Those four statements are used as "performance snapshots" for employees at Deloitte, the New York–based professional services firm with more than 65,000 employees. Team leaders rate employees on those four statements (using a strongly disagree to strongly agree scale) at the end of each project. If projects stretch across several months, the ratings occur once a quarter. The snapshots are then used—in conjunction with factors such as project difficulty and citizenship behavior—to arrive at an annual compensation decision.

The snapshots are also meant to fuel regular check-ins, where leaders talk to their employees about recent work, job changes, and upcoming priorities. In this way, fostering motivation becomes a 12-month priority rather than a once-a-year chore. Explains Ashley Goodall, the director of leader development at Deloitte, "For us, these check-ins are not *in addition to* the work of a team leader; they *are* the work of a team leader . . . If you want people to talk about how to do their best work in the near future, they need to talk often."

Of course, motivation at Deloitte is fostered by more than just performance snapshots, conversations, and compensations. The company also understands that employees exert more effort when they're using their strengths—when they're doing tasks that they are competent at and confident about. That insight came from an internal study where Deloitte compared employees on its best teams to a representative comparison group of employees. The groups were compared on a number of survey items, with one item being an especially strong differentiator: "I have the chance to use my strengths every day." Now Deloitte uses self-assessments to identify strengths, so that employees can share them with their leaders and teams. Moreover, surveys suggest that 96 percent of Deloitte's employees view their jobs as providing great challenges within which to use those strengths. One employee noted, "It challenges me every day and continues to introduce me to new areas of taxation. This is what makes me excited when I walk into work every day."

MOTIVATION

6.1

What is motivation?

Few OB topics matter more to employees and managers than motivation. How many times have you wondered to yourself, "Why can't I get myself going today?" Or how many times have you looked at a friend or coworker and wondered, "Why are they working so slowly right now?" Both of these questions are asking about "motivation," which is a derivation of the Latin word for movement, *movere*.[1] Those Latin roots nicely capture the meaning of motivation, as motivated employees simply move faster and longer than unmotivated employees. More formally, **motivation** is defined as a set of energetic forces that originates both within and outside an employee, initiates work-related effort, and determines its direction, intensity, and persistence.[2] Motivation is a critical consideration because effective job performance often requires high levels of both ability and motivation (see Chapter 10 on ability for more discussion of such issues).[3]

The first part of our motivation definition illustrates that motivation is not one thing but rather a set of distinct forces. Some of those forces are internal to the employee, such as a sense of purpose or confidence, whereas others are external to the employee, such as the goals or incentives an employee is given. The next part of that definition illustrates that motivation determines a number of facets of an employee's work effort. These facets are summarized in Figure 6-1, which depicts a scenario in which your boss has given you an assignment to work on. Motivation determines *what* employees do at a given moment—the direction in which their effort is channeled. Every moment of the workday offers choices between task and citizenship sorts of actions or withdrawal and counterproductive sorts of actions. When it's 3:00 p.m. on a Thursday, do you keep working on the assignment your boss gave you, or do you check social networks or surf the web for a while? Once the direction of effort has been decided, motivation goes on to determine *how hard* an employee works—the intensity of effort—and *for how long*—the persistence of effort. We all have friends or coworkers who work extremely hard for . . . say . . . 5 minutes. We

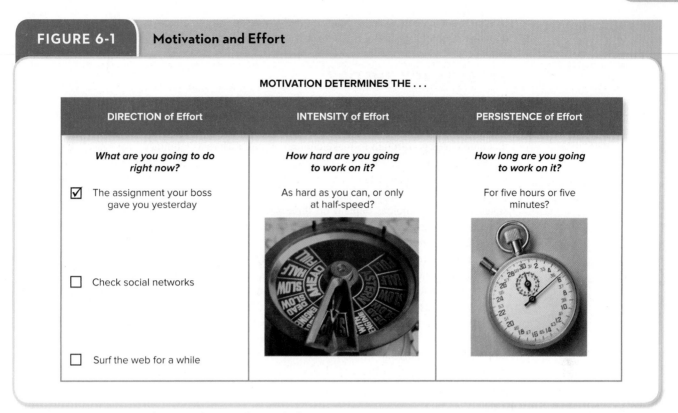

FIGURE 6-1   **Motivation and Effort**

MOTIVATION DETERMINES THE . . .

DIRECTION of Effort	INTENSITY of Effort	PERSISTENCE of Effort
What are you going to do right now?	*How hard are you going to work on it?*	*How long are you going to work on it?*
☑ The assignment your boss gave you yesterday	As hard as you can, or only at half-speed?	For five hours or five minutes?
☐ Check social networks		
☐ Surf the web for a while		

Photos: Left: © Royalty-Free/Corbis RF; Right: © Royalty-Free/Corbis RF

also have friends or coworkers who work extremely long hours but always seem to be functioning at half-speed. Neither of those groups of people would be described as extremely motivated.

As the opening example illustrates, organizations are always on the lookout for new and better ways to motivate their employees. These days, however, those discussions are more likely to focus on a concept called **engagement.** You can think of engagement as a contemporary synonym, more or less, for high levels of intensity and persistence in work effort. Employees who are "engaged" completely invest themselves and their energies into their jobs.[4] Outwardly, engaged employees devote a lot of energy to their jobs, striving as hard as they can to take initiative and get the job done.[5] Inwardly, engaged employees focus a great deal of attention and concentration on their work, sometimes becoming so absorbed, involved, and interested in their tasks that they lose track of time (see Chapter 4 on job satisfaction for more discussion of such issues).[6] Many companies attempt to measure engagement on their annual employee surveys, often by assessing factors that are believed to foster intense and persistent work effort.[7] One recent survey by Gallup suggests that only 30 percent of employees are engaged—a percentage that has held fairly steady for a decade.[8] Given those numbers, it's not surprising that a recent survey of human resources executives indicated an increased emphasis on improving engagement levels.[9] That emphasis is critical, as research suggests that low levels of engagement can be contagious, crossing over from one employee to another.[10]

WHY ARE SOME EMPLOYEES MORE MOTIVATED THAN OTHERS?

There are a number of theories and concepts that attempt to explain why some employees are more motivated (or engaged) than others. The sections that follow review those theories and concepts in some detail. Most of them are relevant to each of the effort facets described in Figure 6-1.

However, some of them are uniquely suited to explaining the direction of effort, whereas others do a better job of explaining the intensity and persistence of effort.

EXPECTANCY THEORY

6.2

What three beliefs help determine work effort, according to expectancy theory?

What makes you decide to direct your effort to work assignments rather than taking a break or wasting time? Or what makes you decide to be a "good citizen" by helping out a colleague or attending some optional company function? **Expectancy theory** describes the cognitive process that employees go through to make choices among different voluntary responses.[11] Drawing on earlier models from psychology, expectancy theory argues that employee behavior is directed toward pleasure and away from pain or, more generally, toward certain outcomes and away from others.[12] How do employees make the choices that take them in the "right direction"? The theory suggests that our choices depend on three specific beliefs that are based in our past learning and experience: expectancy, instrumentality, and valence. These three beliefs are summarized in Figure 6-2, and we review each of them in turn.

Expectancy represents the belief that exerting a high level of effort will result in the successful performance of some task. More technically, expectancy is a subjective probability, ranging from 0 (no chance!) to 1 (a mortal lock!) that a specific amount of effort will result in a specific level of performance (abbreviated E $\rightarrow$ P). Think of a task at which you're not particularly good, such as writing romantic poetry. You may not be very motivated to write romantic poetry because you don't believe that your effort, no matter how hard you try, will result in a poem that "moves" your significant other. As another example, you'll be more motivated to work on the assignment described in Figure 6-1 if you're confident that trying hard will allow you to complete it successfully.

FIGURE 6-2	Expectancy Theory

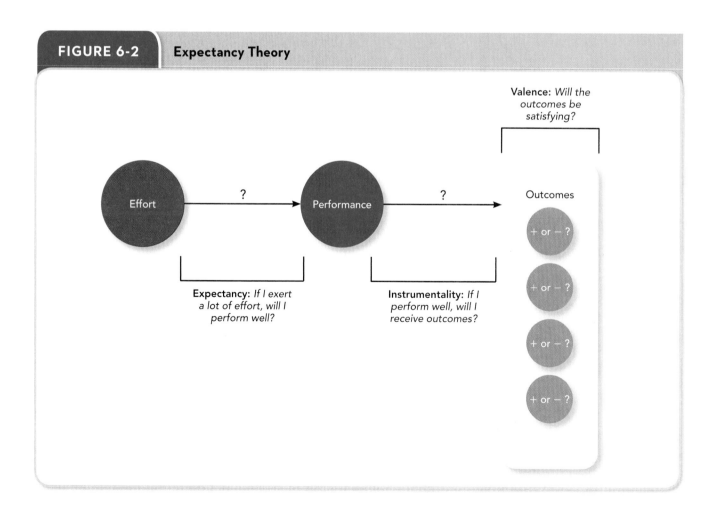

FIGURE 6-3 — Sources of Self-Efficacy

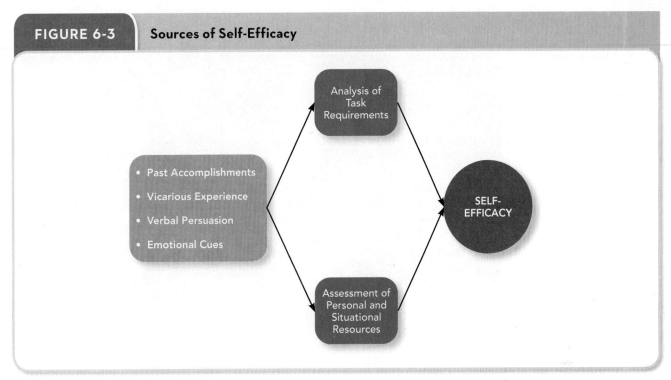

Sources: Adapted from A. Bandura, "Self-Efficacy: Toward a Unifying Theory of Behavioral Change," *Psychological Review* 84 (1977), pp. 191–215; and M.E. Gist and T.R. Mitchell, "Self-Efficacy: A Theoretical Analysis of Its Determinants and Malleability," *Academy of Management Review* 17 (1992), pp. 183–211.

What factors shape our expectancy for a particular task? One of the most critical factors is **self-efficacy,** defined as the belief that a person has the capabilities needed to execute the behaviors required for task success.[13] Think of self-efficacy as a kind of self-confidence or a task-specific version of self-esteem.[14] Employees who feel more "efficacious" (i.e., self-confident) for a particular task will tend to perceive higher levels of expectancy—and therefore be more likely to choose to exert high levels of effort. Why do some employees have higher self-efficacy for a given task than other employees? Figure 6-3 can help explain such differences.

When employees consider efficacy levels for a given task, they first consider their **past accomplishments**—the degree to which they have succeeded or failed in similar sorts of tasks in the past.[15] They also consider **vicarious experiences** by taking into account their observations and discussions with others who have performed such tasks.[16] Self-efficacy is also dictated by **verbal persuasion** because friends, coworkers, and leaders can persuade employees that they can "get the job done." Finally, efficacy is dictated by **emotional cues,** in that feelings of fear or anxiety can create doubts about task accomplishment, whereas pride and enthusiasm can bolster confidence levels.[17] Taken together, these efficacy sources shape analyses of how difficult the task requirements are and how adequate an employee's personal and situational resources will prove to be.[18] They also explain the content of most pregame speeches offered by coaches before the big game; such speeches commonly include references to past victories (past accomplishments), pep talks about how good the team can be (verbal persuasion), and cheers to rally the troops (emotional cues).

INSTRUMENTALITY **Instrumentality** represents the belief that successful performance will result in some outcome(s).[19] More technically, instrumentality is a set of subjective probabilities, each ranging from 0 (no chance!) to 1 (a mortal lock!) that successful performance will bring a set of outcomes (abbreviated P O). The term "instrumentality" makes sense when you consider the meaning of the adjective "instrumental." We say something is "instrumental" when it helps attain something else—for example, reading this chapter is instrumental for getting a good grade in an OB class (at least, we hope so!).[20] Unfortunately, evidence indicates that many employees

Pregame speeches, like this dramatization of Herb Brooks's in *Miracle,* are often geared around bolstering a team's self-efficacy. Said Brooks before the USA took on the Soviet Union in the 1980 Olympics, "Tonight, we skate with 'em. Tonight, we stay with 'em .... Tonight, we are the greatest hockey team in the world!"

© *Buena Vista Pictures/Photofest*

don't perceive high levels of instrumentality in their workplace. One survey of more than 10,000 employees revealed that only 35 percent viewed performance as the key driver of their pay.[21] By comparison, 60 percent viewed seniority as the key driver.

Although organizations often struggle to foster instrumentality in the best of times, linking performance to outcomes is even more difficult during an economic downturn. One human resources consulting firm estimated that 31 percent of organizations froze pay in 2009, with that estimate falling to 13 percent in 2010 and 2 percent in 2011.[22] 3M, the St. Paul, Minnesota–based maker of Post-it notes and Scotch tape, is one example of a firm that is only now unfreezing its pay. Executives at 3M indicated that pay increases would return after being frozen since 2009. Summarizes one human resources consultant, "There really is a mindset that you can only do that for so long."[23] As the economy improves, good performers will begin to expect rewards and may look elsewhere if their company does not provide them.

VALENCE **Valence** reflects the anticipated value of the outcomes associated with performance (abbreviated V).[24] Valences can be positive ("I would prefer *having* outcome X to not having it"), negative ("I would prefer *not having* outcome X to having it"), or zero ("I'm bored . . . are we still talking about outcome X?"). Salary increases, bonuses, and more informal rewards are typical examples of "positively valenced" outcomes, whereas disciplinary actions, demotions, and terminations are typical examples of "negatively valenced" outcomes.[25] In this way, employees are more motivated when successful performance helps them attain attractive outcomes, such as bonuses, while helping them avoid unattractive outcomes, such as disciplinary actions.

What exactly makes some outcomes more "positively valenced" than others? In general, outcomes are deemed more attractive when they help satisfy needs. **Needs** can be defined as cognitive groupings or clusters of outcomes that are viewed as having critical psychological or physiological consequences.[26] Although scholars once suggested that certain needs are "universal" across people,[27] it's likely that different people have different "need hierarchies" that they use to evaluate potential outcomes. Table 6-1 describes many of the needs that are commonly studied in OB.[28] The terms and labels assigned to those needs often vary, so the table includes our labels as well as alternative labels that might sometimes be encountered.

Table 6-2 lists some of the most commonly considered outcomes in studies of motivation. Outcomes that are deemed particularly attractive are likely to satisfy a number of different needs. For example, praise can signal that interpersonal bonds are strong (satisfying relatedness needs)

| TABLE 6-1 | Commonly Studied Needs in OB |

NEED LABEL	ALTERNATIVE LABELS	DESCRIPTION
Existence	Physiological, Safety	The need for the food, shelter, safety, and protection required for human existence.
Relatedness	Love, Belongingness	The need to create and maintain lasting, positive, interpersonal relationships.
Control	Autonomy, Responsibility	The need to be able to predict and control one's future.
Esteem	Self-Regard, Growth	The need to hold a high evaluation of oneself and to feel effective and respected by others.
Meaning	Self-Actualization	The need to perform tasks that one cares about and that appeal to one's ideals and sense of purpose.

Sources: Adapted from E.L. Deci and R.M Ryan, "The 'What' and 'Why' of Goal Pursuits: Human Needs and the Self-Determination of Behavior," *Psychological Inquiry* 11 (2000), pp. 227–68; R. Cropanzano, Z.S. Byrne, D.R. Bobocel, and D.R. Rupp, "Moral Virtues, Fairness Heuristics, Social Entities, and Other Denizens of Organizational Justice," *Journal of Vocational Behavior* 58 (2001), pp. 164–209; A.H. Maslow, "A Theory of Human Motivation," *Psychological Review* 50 (1943), pp. 370–96; and C.P. Alderfer, "An Empirical Test of a New Theory of Human Needs," *Organizational Behavior and Human Performance* 4 (1969), pp. 142–75.

while also signaling competence (satisfying esteem needs). Note also that some of the outcomes in Table 6-2, such as bonuses, promotions, and praise, result from other people acknowledging successful performance. These outcomes foster **extrinsic motivation**—motivation that is controlled by some contingency that depends on task performance.[29] Other outcomes in the table, such as enjoyment, interestingness, and personal expression, are self-generated, originating in the mere act of performing the task. These outcomes foster **intrinsic motivation**—motivation that is felt when task performance serves as its own reward.[30] Taken together, extrinsic and intrinsic motivation represent an employee's "total motivation" level.

You might wonder which of the outcomes in the table are most attractive to employees. That's a difficult question to answer, given that different employees emphasize different needs. However, two things are clear. First, the attractiveness of many rewards varies across cultures. One expert on cross-cultural recognition programs notes, "Different cultures have different motivators. In fact, giving a gift card could be extremely insulting because it could be saying that you are bribing them to do what they already do."[31] Good performance on a project in an American company might earn a trip to Las Vegas. However, trips to alcohol- and gambling-intensive areas are taboo in parts of Asia or the Middle East.[32] A better award in India would be tickets to a newly released movie or a moped for navigating in congested areas.[33]

Second, research suggests that employees underestimate how powerful a motivator pay is to them.[34] When employees rank the importance of extrinsic and intrinsic outcomes, they often put pay in fifth or sixth place. However, research studies show that financial incentives often have a stronger impact on motivation than other sorts of outcomes.[35] One reason is that money is relevant to many of the needs in Table 6-1. For example, money can help satisfy existence needs by helping employees buy food, afford a house, and save for retirement. However, money also conveys a sense of esteem because it signals that employees are competent and well regarded.[36] In fact, research suggests that people differ in how they view the **meaning of money**—the degree to which they view money as having symbolic, not just economic, value.[37] The symbolic value of money can be summarized in at least three dimensions: achievement

TABLE 6-2	Extrinsic and Intrinsic Outcomes

EXTRINSIC OUTCOMES	INTRINSIC OUTCOMES
Pay	Enjoyment
Bonuses	Interestingness
Promotions	Accomplishment
Benefits and perks	Knowledge gain
Spot awards	Skill development
Praise	Personal expression
Job security	(Lack of) Boredom
Support	(Lack of) Anxiety
Free time	(Lack of) Frustration
(Lack of) Disciplinary actions	
(Lack of) Demotions	
(Lack of) Terminations	

Sources: Adapted from E.E. Lawler III and J.L. Suttle, "Expectancy Theory and Job Behavior," *Organizational Behavior and Human Performance* 9 (1973), pp. 482–503; J. Galbraith and L.L. Cummings, "An Empirical Investigation of the Motivational Determinants of Task Performance: Interactive Effects between Instrumentality–Valence and Motivation–Ability," *Organizational Behavior and Human Performance* 2 (1967), pp. 237–57; E. McAuley, S. Wraith, and T.E. Duncan, "Self-Efficacy, Perceptions of Success, and Intrinsic Motivation for Exercise," *Journal of Applied Social Psychology* 21 (1991), pp. 139–55; and A.S. Waterman, S.J. Schwartz, E. Goldbacher, H. Green, C. Miller, and S. Philip, "Predicting the Subjective Experience of Intrinsic Motivation: The Roles of Self-Determination, the Balance of Challenges and Skills, and Self-Realization Values," *Personality and Social Psychology Bulletin* 29 (2003), pp. 1447–58.

(i.e., money symbolizes success), respect (i.e., money brings respect in one's community), and freedom (i.e., money provides opportunity).[38]

Who's more likely to view money from these more symbolic perspectives? Some research suggests that men are more likely to view money as representing achievement, respect, and freedom than are women.[39] Research also suggests that employees with higher salaries are more likely to view money in achievement-related terms.[40] Younger employees are less likely to view money in a positive light, relative to older employees.[41] Differences in education do not appear to affect the meaning of money, however.[42] How do you view the meaning of money? See our **OB Assessments** feature to find out.

MOTIVATIONAL FORCE According to expectancy theory, the direction of effort is dictated by three beliefs: expectancy (E → P), instrumentality (P → O), and valence (V). More specifically, the theory suggests that the total "motivational force" to perform a given action can be described using the following formula:[43]

$$\text{Motivational Force} = \boxed{E \rightarrow P} \times \boxed{\Sigma[(P \rightarrow O) \times V]}$$

The Σ symbol in the equation signifies that instrumentalities and valences are judged with various outcomes in mind, and motivation increases as successful performance is linked to more and more attractive outcomes. Note the significance of the multiplication signs in the formula: Motivational force equals zero if any one of the three beliefs is zero. In other words, it doesn't matter

OB ASSESSMENTS

THE MEANING OF MONEY

How do you view money—what meaning do you attach to it? This assessment will tell you where you stand on the three facets of the meaning of money—money as achievement, money as respect, and money as freedom. Answer each question using the response scale provided. Then follow the instructions to score yourself. (Instructors: Assessments on intrinsic motivation, self-efficacy, engagement, and equity sensitivity can be found in the PowerPoints in the Connect Library's Instructor Resources and in the Connect assignments for this chapter).

1 STRONGLY DISAGREE	2 DISAGREE	3 SLIGHTLY DISAGREE	4 NEUTRAL	5 SLIGHTLY AGREE	6 AGREE	7 STRONGLY AGREE

1. Having money means that I've achieved something. _____
2. Having money shows that I've succeeded. _____
3. Having money is a symbol of accomplishment. _____
4. Having money signifies that I've performed well. _____
5. Having money brings respect from others. _____
6. Having money can make others admire you. _____
7. Having money is worthy of others' esteem. _____
8. Having money can make you more well-regarded. _____
9. Having money brings more freedom. _____
10. Having money can create opportunities. _____
11. Having money provides more autonomy. _____
12. Having money brings independence. _____

SCORING AND INTERPRETATION

· Money as Achievement: Sum up items 1–4. _____
· Money as Respect: Sum up items 5–8. _____
· Money as Freedom: Sum up items 9–12. _____
· Money as Achievement: High = 13 or above. Low = 12 or below.
· Money as Respect: High = 15 or above. Low = 14 or below.
· Money as Freedom: High = 20 or above. Low = 19 or below.

If you scored high on all three dimensions, then you view money as having multiple, noneconomic meanings. This result means that money is likely to be a powerful motivator for you.

Source: Original items. See T.L. Tang, "The Meaning of Money Revisited," *Journal of Organizational Behavior* 13 (1992), pp. 197–202, for an alternative measure of these concepts.

how confident you are if performance doesn't result in any outcomes. Similarly, it doesn't matter how well performance is evaluated and rewarded if you don't believe you can perform well.

GOAL SETTING THEORY

So, returning to the choice shown in Figure 6-1, let's say that you feel confident you can perform well on the assignment your boss gave you and that you also believe successful performance will bring valued outcomes. Now that you've chosen to direct your effort to that assignment, two critical questions remain: How hard will you work, and for how long? To shed some more light on these questions, you stop by your boss's office and ask her, "So, when exactly do you need this done?" After thinking about it for a while, she concludes, "Just do your best." After returning to your desk, you realize that you're still not sure how much to focus on the assignment, or how long you should work on it before turning to something else.

Goal setting theory views goals as the primary drivers of the intensity and persistence of effort.[44] Goals are defined as the objective or aim of an action and typically refer to attaining a specific standard of proficiency, often within a specified time limit.[45] More specifically, the theory argues that assigning employees **specific and difficult goals** will result in higher levels of performance than assigning no goals, easy goals, or "do-your-best" goals.[46] Why are specific and difficult goals more effective than do-your-best ones? After all, doesn't "your best" imply the highest possible levels of effort? The reason is that few people know what their "best" is (and even fewer managers can tell whether employees are truly doing their "best"). Assigning specific and difficult goals gives people a number to shoot for—a "measuring stick" that can be used to tell them how hard they need to work and for how long. So if your boss had said, "Have the assignment on my desk by 10:30 a.m. on Tuesday, with no more than two mistakes," you would have known exactly how hard to work and for how long.

Of course, a key question then becomes, "What's a difficult goal?" Figure 6-4 illustrates the predicted relationship between goal difficulty and task performance. When goals are easy, there's no reason to work your hardest or your longest, so task effort is lower. As goals move from moderate to difficult, the intensity and persistence of effort become maximized. At some point, however, the limits of a person's ability get reached, and self-efficacy begins to diminish. Also at that point, goals move from difficult to impossible, and employees feel somewhat helpless when attempting to achieve them. In turn, effort and performance inevitably decline. So a difficult goal is one that stretches employees to perform at their maximum level while still staying within the boundaries of their ability.

The effects of specific and difficult goals on task performance have been tested in several hundred studies using many kinds of settings and tasks. A sampling of those settings and tasks is shown in Table 6-3.[47] Overall, around 90 percent of the goal setting studies support the beneficial effects of specific and difficult goals on task performance.[48] Although some of the settings and tasks shown in the table are unlikely to be major parts of your career (archery, handball, LEGO

6.3

What two qualities make goals strong predictors of task performance, according to goal setting theory?

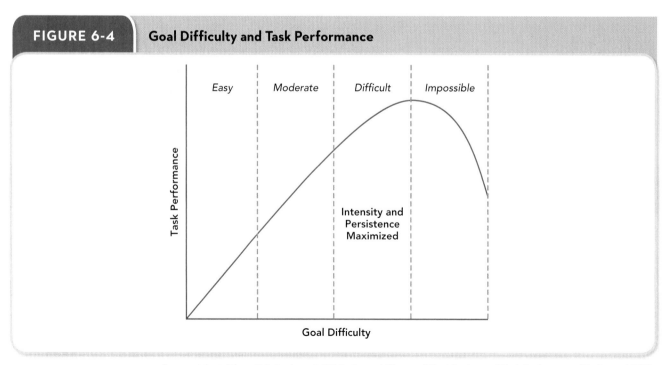

FIGURE 6-4   **Goal Difficulty and Task Performance**

Source: Adapted from E.A. Locke and G.P. Latham, *A Theory of Goal Setting and Task Performance* (Englewood Cliffs, NJ: Prentice Hall, 1990).

TABLE 6-3	Settings and Tasks Used in Goal Setting Research

SETTINGS AND TASKS

Air traffic control	Management training
Archery	Marine recruit performance
Arithmetic	Maze learning
Beverage consumption	Mining
Chess	Proofreading
Computer games	Production and manufacturing
Course work	Puzzles
Energy conservation	Safety behaviors
Exercise	Sales
Faculty research	Scientific and R&D work
Juggling	Sit-ups
LEGO construction	Studying
Logging	Weight lifting
Managing and supervision	Weight loss

Source: Adapted from E.A. Locke and G.P. Latham, *A Theory of Goal Setting and Task Performance* (Englewood Cliffs, NJ: Prentice Hall, 1990).

construction), others should be very relevant to the readers (and authors!) of this book (managing and supervision, studying, faculty research). Then again, who wouldn't want a career in LEGO construction?

Why exactly do specific and difficult goals have such positive effects? Figure 6-5 presents goal setting theory in more detail to understand that question better.[49] First, the assignment of a specific and difficult goal shapes people's own **self-set goals**—the internalized goals that people use to monitor their own task progress.[50] In the absence of an assigned goal, employees may not even consider what their own goals are, or they may self-set relatively easy goals that they're certain to meet. As a self-set goal becomes more difficult, the intensity of effort increases, and the persistence of effort gets extended. However, goals have another effect; they trigger the creation of **task strategies,** defined as learning plans and problem-solving approaches used to achieve successful performance.[51] In the absence of a goal, it's easy to rely on trial and error to figure out how best to do a task. Under the pressure of a measuring stick, however, it becomes more effective to plan out the next move. Put differently, goals can motivate employees to work both harder and smarter.

Figure 6-5 also includes three variables that specify when assigned goals will have stronger or weaker effects on task performance. In the jargon of theory diagrams, these variables are called "moderators." Rather than directly affecting other variables in the diagram, moderators affect the strength of the relationships between variables. One moderator is **feedback,** which consists of updates on employee progress toward goal attainment.[52] Imagine being challenged to beat a friend's score on a video game but having your own score hidden as you played. How would you know how hard to try? Another moderator is **task complexity,** which reflects how complicated the information and actions involved in a task are, as well as how much the task changes.[53] In

| FIGURE 6-5 | Goal Setting Theory |

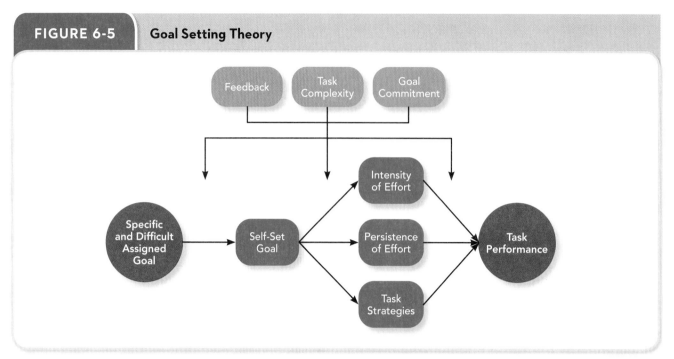

Sources: Adapted from E.A. Locke and G.P. Latham, *A Theory of Goal Setting and Task Performance* (Englewood Cliffs, NJ: Prentice Hall, 1990); E.A. Locke and G.P. Latham, "Building a Practically Useful Theory of Goal Setting and Task Motivation: A 35-Year Odyssey," *American Psychologist* 57 (2002), pp. 705–17; and G.P. Latham, "Motivate Employee Performance through Goal-Setting," in *Blackwell Handbook of Principles of Organizational Behavior*, ed. E.A. Locke (Malden, MA: Blackwell, 2000), pp. 107–19.

general, the effects of specific and difficult goals are almost twice as strong on simple tasks as on complex tasks, though the effects of goals remain beneficial even in complex cases.[54] Goal setting at Wyeth, the Madison, New Jersey–based pharmaceuticals company, illustrates the value of goals for complex tasks (after all, what's more complicated than chemistry?).[55] When Robert Ruffolo was appointed the new chief of R&D several years ago, he was concerned about the low number of new drug compounds being generated by Wyeth's labs. His solution? He gave scientists a goal of discovering 12 new drug compounds every year, up from the 4 compounds they were previously averaging, with bonuses contingent on reaching the goals. Wyeth's scientists have reached the goal every year since, and the goal was eventually upped to 15 compounds per year.

The final moderator shown in Figure 6-5 is **goal commitment,** defined as the degree to which a person accepts a goal and is determined to try to reach it.[56] When goal commitment is high, assigning specific and difficult goals will have significant benefits for task performance. However, when goal commitment is low, those effects become much weaker.[57] The importance of goal commitment raises the question of how best to foster commitment when assigning goals to employees. Table 6-4 summarizes some of the most powerful strategies for fostering goal commitment, which range from rewards to supervisory support to employee participation.[58]

Microsoft recently revised its use of goal setting principles in an effort to boost goal commitment and task performance.[59] The company had become concerned that employees viewed their goals as objectives they *hoped* to meet rather than objectives they were

As the chief of research and development at Wyeth, Inc., a pharmaceutical company, Robert Ruffolo offered company scientists a bonus for discovering 12 new drug compounds every year. They've done it every year and are now reaching for a new goal of 15.

© *Bloomberg/Getty Images*

TABLE 6-4	Strategies for Fostering Goal Commitment

STRATEGY	DESCRIPTION
Rewards	Tie goal achievement to the receipt of monetary or nonmonetary rewards.
Publicity	Publicize the goal to significant others and coworkers to create some social pressure to attain it.
Support	Provide supportive supervision to aid employees if they struggle to attain the goal.
Participation	Collaborate on setting the specific proficiency level and due date for a goal so that the employee feels a sense of ownership over the goal.
Resources	Provide the resources needed to attain the goal and remove any constraints that could hold back task efforts.

Sources: Adapted from J.R. Hollenbeck and H.J. Klein, "Goal Commitment and the Goal-Setting Process: Problems, Prospects, and Proposals for Future Research," *Journal of Applied Psychology* 72 (1987), pp. 212–20; H.J. Klein, M.J. Wesson, J.R. Hollenbeck, and B.J. Alge, "Goal Commitment and the Goal-Setting Process: Conceptual Clarification and Empirical Synthesis," *Journal of Applied Psychology* 84 (1999), pp. 885–96; E.A. Locke, G.P. Latham, and M. Erez, "The Determinants of Goal Commitment," *Academy of Management Review* 13 (1988), pp. 23–29; and G.P. Latham, "The Motivational Benefits of Goal-Setting," *Academy of Management Executive* 18 (2004), pp. 126–29.

committed to meeting. Moreover, approximately 25–40 percent of employees were working under goals that were either not specific enough or not measurable enough to offer feedback. To combat these trends, managers are now trained to identify five to seven **S.M.A.R.T. goals** for each employee and to link rewards directly to goal achievement. The S.M.A.R.T. acronym summarizes many beneficial goal characteristics, standing for **S**pecific, **M**easurable, **A**chievable, **R**esults-Based, and **T**ime-Sensitive. (Although that acronym is a useful reminder, note that it omits the all-important "Difficult" characteristic.) Managers and employees at Microsoft participate jointly in the goal setting process, and managers offer support by suggesting task strategies that employees can use to achieve the goals. In this way, managers and employees come to understand the "how" of achievement, not just the "what."[60] For insights into how goal setting operates across cultures, see our **OB Internationally** feature.

EQUITY THEORY

Returning to our running example in Figure 6-1, imagine that at this point, you've decided to work on the assignment your boss gave you, and you've been told that it's due by Tuesday at 10:30 a.m. and can't have more than two mistakes in it. That's a specific and difficult goal, so your browser hasn't been launched in a while, and you haven't even thought about checking Facebook. In short, you've been working very hard for a few hours, until the guy from across the hall pops his head in. You tell him what you're working on, and he nods sympathetically, saying, "Yeah, the boss gave me a similar assignment that sounds just as tough. I think she realized how tough it was though, because she said I could use the company's playoff tickets if I finish it on time." Playoff tickets? Playoff tickets?? Looks like it's time to check Facebook after all . . . .

Unlike the first two theories, **equity theory** acknowledges that motivation doesn't just depend on your own beliefs and circumstances but also on what happens to *other people*.[61] More specifically, equity theory suggests that employees create a "mental ledger" of the outcomes (or rewards) they get from their job duties.[62] What outcomes might be part of your mental ledger? That's completely up to you and depends on what you find valuable, though Table 6-5 provides a listing of some commonly considered outcomes. Equity theory further suggests that employees create a mental ledger of the inputs (or contributions and investments) they put into their job duties.[63] Again, the composition of your mental ledger is completely specific to you, but Table 6-5 provides a listing of some inputs that seem to matter to most employees.

OB INTERNATIONALLY

Research in cross-cultural OB suggests that there are some "universals" when it comes to motivation. For example, interesting work, pay, achievement, and growth are billed as motivating forces whose importance does not vary across cultures. Of course, some motivation principles do vary in their effectiveness across cultures, including some of the strategies for fostering goal commitment.

- **Types of goals.** Should goals be given on an individual or a groupwide basis? Employees in the United States usually prefer to be given individual goals. In contrast, employees in other countries, including China and Japan, prefer to receive team goals. This difference likely reflects the stronger emphasis on collective responsibility and cooperation in those cultures.
- **Rewards.** Rewards tend to increase goal commitment across cultures, but cultures vary in the types of rewards that they value. Employees in the United States prefer to have rewards allocated according to merit. In contrast, employees in other countries—including China, Japan, and Sweden—prefer that rewards be allocated equally across members of the work unit. Employees in India prefer a third allocation strategy—doling out rewards according to need. These cultural differences show that nations differ in how they prioritize individual achievement, collective solidarity, and the welfare of others.
- **Participation.** National culture also affects the importance of participation in setting goals. Research suggests that employees in the United States are likely to accept assigned goals because the culture emphasizes hierarchical authority. In contrast, employees in Israel, which lacks a cultural emphasis on hierarchy, do not respond as well to assigned goals. Instead, employees in Israel place a premium on participation in goal setting.
- **Feedback.** Culture also influences how individuals respond when they receive feedback regarding goal progress. As with participation, research suggests that employees in the United States are more likely to accept feedback because they are comfortable with hierarchical authority relationships and have a strong desire to reduce uncertainty. Other cultures, like England, place less value on reducing uncertainty, making feedback less critical to them.

Sources: H. Aguinis and C.A. Henle, "The Search for Universals in Cross-Cultural Organizational Behavior," in *Organizational Behavior: The State of the Science,* ed. J. Greenberg (Mahwah, NJ: Erlbaum, 2003), pp. 373–411; P.C. Earley and C.B Gibson, "Taking Stock in Our Progress on Individualism–Collectivism: 100 Years of Solidarity and Community," *Journal of Management* 24 (1998), pp. 265–304; M. Erez, "A Culture-Based Model of Work Motivation," in *New Perspectives on International Industrial/Organizational Psychology,* ed. P.C. Earley and M. Erez (San Francisco: New Lexington Press, 1997), pp. 193–242; M. Erez and P.C. Earley, "Comparative Analysis of Goal-Setting Strategies Across Cultures," *Journal of Applied Psychology* 72 (1987), pp. 658–65; and P.G. Audia and S. Tams, "Goal Setting, Performance Appraisal, and Feedback across Cultures," in *Blackwell Handbook of Cross-Cultural Management,* ed. M.J. Gannon and K.L. Newman (Malden, MA: Blackwell, 2002), pp. 142–54.

6.4

What does it mean to be equitably treated according to equity theory, and how do employees respond to inequity?

So what exactly do you do with these mental tallies of outcomes and inputs? Equity theory argues that you compare your ratio of outcomes and inputs to the ratio of some **comparison other**—some person who seems to provide an intuitive frame of reference for judging equity.[64] There are three general possibilities that can result from this "cognitive calculus," as shown in Figure 6-6. The first possibility is that the ratio of outcomes to inputs is balanced between you and your comparison other. In this case, you feel a sense of equity, and you're likely to maintain the intensity and persistence of your effort. This situation would have occurred if you had been offered playoff tickets, just like your colleague.

The second possibility is that your ratio of outcomes to inputs is less than your comparison other's ratio. According to equity theory, any imbalance in ratios triggers **equity distress**—an internal tension that can only be alleviated by restoring balance to the ratios.[65] In an underreward case, the equity distress likely takes the form of negative emotions such as anger or envy. One way to stop feeling those emotions is to try to restore the balance in some way, and Figure 6-6

TABLE 6-5 | **Some Outcomes and Inputs Considered by Equity Theory**

OUTCOMES	INPUTS
Pay	Effort
Seniority benefits	Performance
Fringe benefits	Skills and abilities
Status symbols	Education
Satisfying supervision	Experience
Workplace perks	Training
Intrinsic rewards	Seniority

Source: Adapted from J.S. Adams, "Inequity in Social Exchange," in *Advances in Experimental Social Psychology,* Vol. 2, ed. L. Berkowitz (New York: Academic Press, 1965), pp. 267–99.

FIGURE 6-6 | **Three Possible Outcomes of Equity Theory Comparisons**

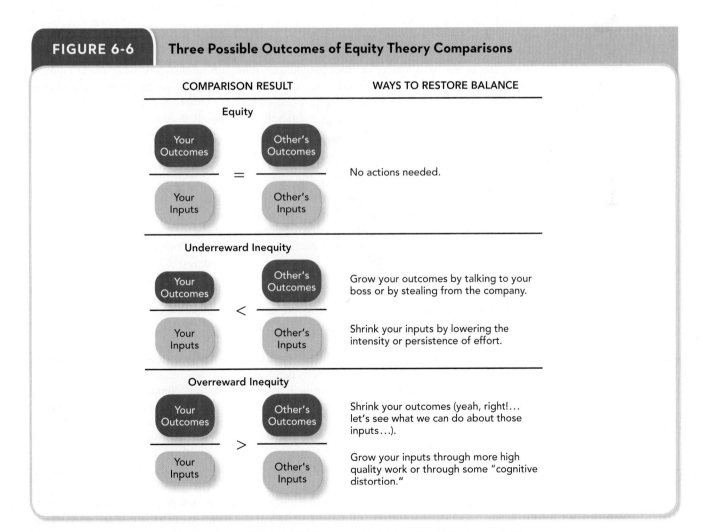

Source: Adapted from J.S. Adams, "Inequity in Social Exchange," in *Advances in Experimental Social Psychology,* Vol. 2, ed. L. Berkowitz (New York: Academic Press, 1965), pp. 267–99.

reveals two methods for doing so. You could be constructive and proactive by talking to your boss and explaining why you deserve better outcomes. Such actions would result in the growth of your outcomes, restoring balance to the ratio. Of course, anger often results in actions that are destructive rather than constructive, and research shows that feelings of underreward inequity are among the strongest predictors of counterproductive behaviors, such as employee theft (see Chapter 7 on trust, justice, and ethics for more on such issues).[66] More relevant to this chapter, another means of restoring balance is to shrink your inputs by lowering the intensity and persistence of effort. Remember, it's not the total outcomes or inputs that matter in equity theory—it's only the ratio.

The third possibility is that your ratio of outcomes to inputs is greater than your comparison other's ratio. Equity distress again gets experienced, and the tension likely creates negative emotions such as guilt or anxiety. Balance could be restored by shrinking your outcomes (taking less money, giving something back to the comparison other), but the theory acknowledges that such actions are unlikely in most cases.[67] Instead, the more likely solution is to increase your inputs in some way. You could increase the intensity and persistence of your task effort or decide to engage in more "extra mile" citizenship behaviors. At some point though, there may not be enough hours in the day to increase your inputs any further. An alternative (and less labor-intensive) means of increasing your inputs is to simply rethink them—to reexamine your mental ledger to see if you may have "undersold" your true contributions. On second thought, maybe your education or seniority is more critical than you realized, or maybe your skills and abilities are more vital to the organization. This **cognitive distortion** allows you to restore balance mentally, without altering your behavior in any way.

There is one other way of restoring balance, regardless of underreward or overreward circumstances, that's not depicted in Figure 6-6: Change your comparison other. After all, we compare our "lots in life" to a variety of other individuals. Table 6-6 summarizes the different kinds of comparison others that can be used.[68] Some of those comparisons are **internal comparisons,** meaning that they refer to someone in the same company.[69] Others are **external comparisons,** meaning that they refer to someone in a different company. If a given comparison results in high levels of anger and envy or high levels of guilt and anxiety, the frame of reference may be shifted. In fact, research suggests that employees don't just compare themselves to one other person; instead, they make multiple comparisons to a variety of different others.[70] Although it may be possible to create a sort of "overall equity" judgment, research shows that people draw distinctions between the various equity comparisons shown in the table. For example, one study showed that job equity was the most powerful driver of citizenship behaviors, whereas occupational equity was the most powerful driver of employee withdrawal.[71]

These mechanisms make it clear that judging equity is a very subjective process. Recent data from a Salary.com report highlight that very subjectivity. A survey of 1,500 employees revealed that 65 percent of the respondents planned to look for a new job in the next three months, with 57 percent doing so because they felt underpaid. However, Salary.com estimated that only 19 percent of those workers really were underpaid, taking into account their relevant inputs and the current market conditions. In fact, it was estimated that 17 percent were actually being overpaid by their companies! On the one hand, that subjectivity is likely to be frustrating to most managers in charge of compensation. On the other hand, it's important to realize that the intensity and persistence of employees' effort is driven by their own equity perceptions, not anyone else's.

Perhaps many employees feel they're underpaid because they compare their earnings with their CEOs'. Just consider the 2013 compensation for these CEOs: Larry Ellison of Oracle ($96 million), Les Moonves of CBS ($70 million), Ron Johnson (formerly) of JCPenney ($53 million), Michael Jeffries of Abercrombie & Fitch ($48 million), Bob Iger of Walt Disney ($40 million), and Mark Parker of Nike ($35 million).[72] Those figures include salary, bonuses, stock and option awards, nonequity incentive awards, pension plan contributions, and other forms of compensation.

Estimates suggest that CEO pay has fallen by 5–10 percent, which commonly occurs during economic downturns.[73] Even those diminished values, however, reflect a disconnect between what CEOs make and what the typical employee makes.[74] In 1980, the median compensation for CEOs was 33 times that of the average worker. Three decades later, that ratio is more than 100

| TABLE 6-6 | Judging Equity with Different Comparison Others |

COMPARISON TYPE	DESCRIPTION AND SAMPLE SURVEY ITEM
Job Equity	Compare with others doing the same job in the same organization. Sample survey item: *Compared with others doing the same job as me in my company with similar education, seniority, and effort, I earn about:*
Company equity	Compare with others in the same organization doing substantially different jobs. Sample survey item: *Compared with others in my company on other jobs doing work that is similar in responsibility, skill, effort, education, and working condition required, I earn about:*
Occupational equity	Compare with others doing essentially the same job in other organizations. Sample survey item: *Compared with others doing my job in other companies in the area with similar education, seniority, and effort, I earn about:*
Educational equity	Compare with others who have attained the same education level. Sample survey item: *Compared with people I know with similar education and responsibility as me, I earn about:*
Age equity	Compare with others of the same age. Sample survey item: *Compared with those of my age, I earn about:*

40% less	30% less	20% less	10% less	About the same	10% more	20% more	30% more	40% more

Source: R.W. Scholl, E.A. Cooper, and J.F. McKenna, "Referent Selection in Determining Equity Perceptions: Differential Effects on Behavioral and Attitudinal Outcomes," *Personnel Psychology* 40 (1987), pp. 113–24. Copyright © 1987, John Wiley & Sons. Reprinted with permission.

times the average worker's compensation (and 1,000 times for the companies mentioned in the prior paragraph). Why do boards of directors grant such large compensation packages to CEOs? Although there are many reasons, some have speculated that the pay packages represent status symbols, with many CEOs viewing themselves in celebrity terms, along the lines of professional athletes.[75] Alternatively, CEO pay packages may represent rewards for years of climbing the corporate ladder or insurance policies against the low job security for most CEOs.

Can such high pay totals ever be viewed as equitable in an equity theory sense? Well, CEOs likely have unusually high levels of many inputs, including effort, skills and abilities, education, experience, training, and seniority. CEOs may also use other CEOs as their comparison others—as opposed to rank-and-file employees—making them less likely to feel a sense of overreward inequity. Ultimately, however, the equity of their pay depends on how the company performs under them. Unfortunately, one analysis revealed a near-zero correlation between CEO pay and share-holder returns.[76]

Some organizations grapple with concerns about equity by emphasizing pay secrecy (though that doesn't help with CEO comparisons, given that the Securities and Exchange Commission demands the disclosure of CEO pay for all publicly traded companies). One survey indicated that 36 percent of companies explicitly discourage employees from discussing pay with their colleagues, and surveys also indicate that most employees approve of pay secrecy.[77] Is pay secrecy a good idea? Although it has not been the subject of much research, there appear to be pluses and minuses associated with pay secrecy. On the plus side, such policies may reduce conflict between employees while appealing to concerns about personal privacy. On the minus side, employees may respond to a lack of accurate information by guessing at equity levels, possibly perceiving more underpayment inequity than truly exists. In addition, the insistence on secrecy might cause employees to view the company with a sense of distrust (see Chapter 7 on trust, justice, and ethics for more on this issue).[78]

PSYCHOLOGICAL EMPOWERMENT

Now we return, for one last time, to our running example in Figure 6-1. When last we checked in, your motivation levels had suffered because you learned your coworker was offered the company's playoff tickets for successfully completing a similar assignment. As you browse the web in total "time-wasting mode," you begin thinking about all the reasons you hate working on this assignment. Even aside from the issue of goals and rewards, you keep coming back to this issue: You would never have taken on this project *by choice.* More specifically, the project itself doesn't seem very meaningful, and you doubt that it will have any real impact on the functioning of the organization.

Those sentiments signal a low level of **psychological empowerment,** which reflects an energy rooted in the belief that work tasks contribute to some larger purpose.[79] Psychological empowerment represents a form of intrinsic motivation, in that merely performing the work tasks serves as its own reward and supplies many of the intrinsic outcomes shown in Table 6-2. The concept of psychological empowerment has much in common with our discussion of "satisfaction with the work itself" in Chapter 4 on job satisfaction. That discussion illustrated that jobs with high levels of variety, significance, and autonomy can be intrinsically satisfying.[80] Models of psychological empowerment argue that a similar set of concepts can make work tasks intrinsically motivating. Four concepts are particularly important: meaningfulness, self-determination, competence, and impact. To see these concepts at play with advanced technology, see our **OB on Screen** feature.

Meaningfulness captures the value of a work goal or purpose, relative to a person's own ideals and passions.[81] When a task is relevant to a meaningful purpose, it becomes easier to concentrate on the task and get excited about it. You might even find yourself cutting other tasks short so you can devote more time to the meaningful one or thinking about the task outside of work hours.[82] In contrast, working on tasks that are not meaningful brings a sense of emptiness and detachment. As a result, you might need to mentally force yourself to keep working on the task. Managers can instill a sense of meaningfulness by articulating an exciting vision or purpose and fostering a noncynical climate in which employees are free to express idealism and passion without criticism.[83] For their part, employees can build their own sense of meaningfulness by identifying and clarifying their own passions. Employees who are fortunate enough to be extremely passionate about their work sometimes describe it as "a calling"—something they were born to do.[84]

Self-determination reflects a sense of choice in the initiation and continuation of work tasks. Employees with high levels of self-determination can choose what tasks to work on, how to structure those tasks, and how long to pursue those tasks. That sense of self-determination is a strong driver of intrinsic motivation, because it allows employees to pursue activities that they themselves find meaningful and interesting.[85] Managers can instill a sense of self-determination in their employees by delegating work tasks, rather than micromanaging them, and by trusting employees to come up with their own approach to certain tasks.[86] For their part, employees can gain more self-determination by earning the trust of their bosses and negotiating for the latitude that comes with that increased trust.

Competence captures a person's belief in his or her capability to perform work tasks successfully.[87] Competence is identical to the self-efficacy concept reviewed previously in this chapter; employees with a strong sense of competence (or self-efficacy) believe they can execute the particular behaviors needed to achieve success at work. Competence brings with it a sense of pride

6.5

What is psychological empowerment, and what four beliefs determine empowerment levels?

OB ON SCREEN

BIG HERO 6

Well, if you like things easy, then my program isn't for you. We push the boundaries of robotics here. My students go on to shape the future. Nice to meet you Hiro, good luck with the bot fights.

With those words, Professor Robert Callaghan (James Cromwell) challenges Hiro Hamada (Ryan Potter) in *Big Hero 6* (Dir. Don Hall and Chris Williams, Disney, 2014). Hiro is a genius-level 13-year-old who's currently on his way to a "bot fight," where the robot he built will compete against other people's robots. Hiro's older brother Tadashi (Daniel Henney) created an excuse to drop by his "nerd lab" at the San Fransokyo Institute of Technology's Ito Ishioka Robotics Lab. There Hiro got to see all the cool things that Tadashi's friends—Go Go, Wasabi, and Honey Lemon—are doing under Professor Callaghan's tutelage.

© Walt Disney Studios Motion Pictures/Photofest

None of those things are as cool as what Tadashi himself is working on. When Tadashi pulls a piece of duct tape off Hiro's arm, the "Ouch!" activates Baymax, a big puffy vinyl personal health care companion. "On a scale of 1 to 10, how would you rate your pain?" inquires Baymax, before scanning Hiro and giving him an antibacterial spray. With Baymax's calm and cuddly demeanor, his advanced scanning capabilities, and his medical knowledge, he could be a boon to older people who find their medical care becoming more and more complex. As Tadashi notes proudly, "THIS is what I've been working on . . . He's gonna help a lot of people."

Between Tadashi's work and Professor Callaghan's charge to help shape the future, Hiro sees the light. Even though he could make a lot of money by (illegally) betting on his bot in the bot fights, that wouldn't bring much purpose. It wouldn't have much meaningfulness. What he wants to do now is determine to go down a path where he can impact society. As this realization hits him, Hiro exclaims, "I HAVE to go here. If I don't go to this nerd school, I'm gonna lose my mind!"

and mastery that is itself intrinsically motivating. Managers can instill a sense of competence in their employees by providing opportunities for training and knowledge gain, expressing positive feedback, and providing challenges that are an appropriate match for employees' skill levels.[88] Employees can build their own competence by engaging in self-directed learning, seeking out feedback from their managers, and managing their own workloads.

Impact reflects the sense that a person's actions "make a difference"—that progress is being made toward fulfilling some important purpose.[89] Phrases such as "moving forward," "being on track," and "getting there" convey a sense of impact.[90] The polar opposite of impact is "learned helplessness"—the sense that it doesn't matter what a person does, nothing will make a difference. Here, phrases such as "stuck in a rut," "at a standstill," or "going nowhere" become more relevant. Managers can instill a sense of impact by celebrating milestones along the journey to

Young employees at MindTree, an information technology consulting firm, are given mentoring and personal attention to build a sense of empowerment.

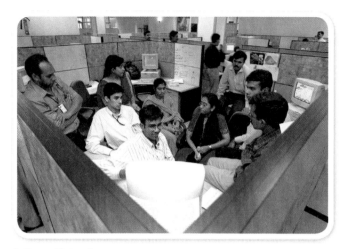

© *Namas Bhojani/AP Images*

task accomplishment, particularly for tasks that span a long time frame.[91] Employees can attain a deeper sense of impact by building the collaborative relationships needed to speed task progress and initiating their own celebrations of "small wins" along the way.

Studies of generational trends point to the increasing interest of psychological empowerment as a motivating force. For example, one survey of 3,332 teens worldwide revealed that 78 percent viewed personal fulfillment as a key motivator.[92] There is also a sense that younger employees enter the workplace with higher expectations for the importance of their roles, the autonomy they'll be given, and the progress they'll make in their organizational careers. That trend is especially apparent in India, where the younger generation is coming of age in a time of unprecedented job opportunities due to the tech-services boom. MindTree, an IT consulting firm headquartered in New Jersey and Bangalore, India, takes steps to prevent young employees from feeling "lost in a sea of people."[93] The company places new hires into "houses" with their own assembly space and work areas, providing opportunities for more personal attention and mentoring. Infosys, another IT consulting firm based in Bangalore, established a "Voice of Youth Council" that places a dozen under-30 employees on its executive management committee. The committee gives younger employees the chance to impact the company's operations. Bela Gupta, the council's youngest member at 24 years of age, describes the experience as "very empowering."

SUMMARY: WHY ARE SOME EMPLOYEES MORE MOTIVATED THAN OTHERS?

So what explains why some employees are more motivated than others? As shown in Figure 6-7, answering that question requires considering all the energetic forces that initiate work-related effort, including expectancy theory concepts (expectancy, instrumentality, valence), the existence (or absence) of specific and difficult goals, perceptions of equity, and feelings of psychological empowerment. Unmotivated employees may simply lack confidence due to a lack of expectancy or competence or the assignment of an unachievable goal. Alternatively, such employees may feel their performance is not properly rewarded due to a lack of instrumentality, a lack of valence, or feelings of inequity. Finally, it may be that their work simply isn't challenging or intrinsically rewarding due to the assignment of easy or abstract goals or the absence of meaningfulness, self-determination, and impact. For more on how these concepts combine to drive effort, see our **OB at the Bookstore** feature.

HOW IMPORTANT IS MOTIVATION?

Does motivation have a significant impact on the two primary outcomes in our integrative model of OB—does it correlate with job performance and organizational commitment? Answering that question is somewhat complicated, because motivation is not just one thing but rather a set of energetic forces. Figure 6-8 summarizes the research evidence linking motivation to job performance and organizational commitment. The figure expresses the likely combined impact of those energetic forces on the two outcomes in our OB model.

FIGURE 6-7 | Why Are Some Employees More Motivated Than Others?

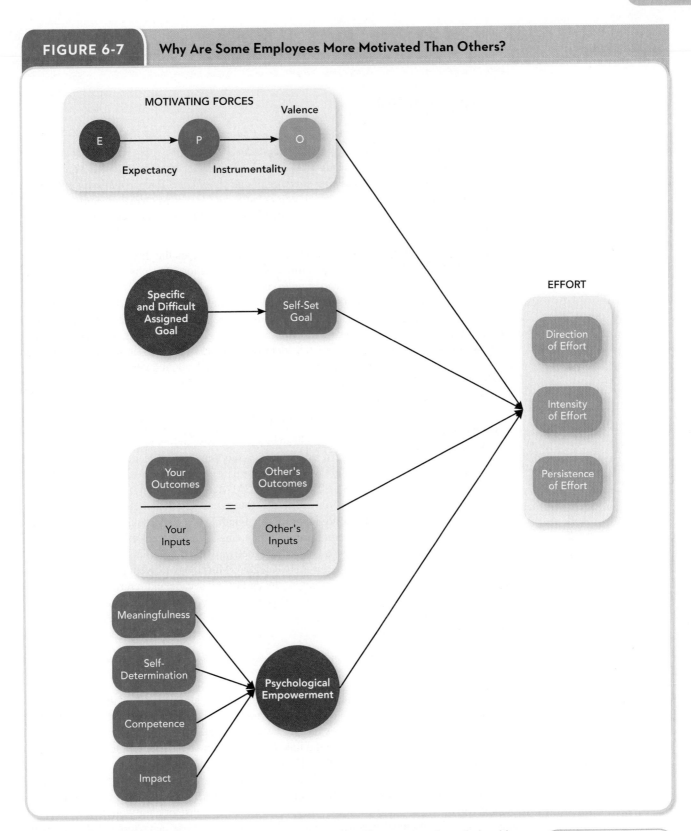

Turning first to job performance, literally thousands of studies support the relationships between the various motivating forces and task performance. The motivating force with the strongest performance effect is self-efficacy/competence, because people who feel a sense of internal self-confidence tend to outperform those who doubt their capabilities.[94] Difficult goals are the second most powerful motivating force; people who receive such goals outperform the

6.6

How does motivation affect job performance and organizational commitment?

OB AT THE BOOKSTORE

HUNDRED PERCENTERS
by Mark Murphy (New York: McGraw-Hill, 2014).

Behind the scenes of every truly great accomplishment is a challenging goal that tried and tested people's beliefs about what was possible. A goal that made people feel they were contributing to achieving something meaningful and significant. Your people want to know "Why is achieving this goal important and meaningful?"... if you leave them to figure it out all alone ... they'll eventually go looking for another organization that does help them find the sense of purpose they want.

Photo of cover: © Roberts Publishing Services

With those words, Murphy describes the importance of both goals and meaningfulness for motivation. Murphy describes the most motivated employees as "Hundred Percenters"—those who give all of their effort during their workdays. Unfortunately, Murphy's research suggests that only 35 percent of employees feel like their organization inspires them to give 100 percent. Why is that? Murphy's research identified 14 questions that comprise his Hundred Percenter Index, two of which talk about goals and meaningfulness:

- "My assigned individual goals for this year will help me grow and develop."
- "The work I do makes a difference in people's lives."

How should managers increase agreement with those two statements, in order to promote "hundred percenter" levels of effort? Murphy devotes the first part of his book to goal setting. However, instead of arguing for SMART goals, he argues for HARD ones. That acronym argues that goals should be Heartfelt (arousing an emotional attachment), Animated (vividly described and presented), Required (critical to one's work existence), and Difficult (testing limits and leaving comfort zones). In this way, Murphy elevates difficulty in the same way as goal setting theory, while also noting that goals can themselves bring purpose. As an example of a HARD goal, Murphy gives Kennedy's famous objective to land a man safely on the moon before the end of the decade and return him safely to the earth. As some support for the value of HARD goals, Murphy's research reveals 49 percent more engagement for employees who agreed with this statement: "I can vividly picture how great it will feel when I achieve my goals."

recipients of easy goals.[95] The motivational force created by high levels of valence, instrumentality, and expectancy is the next most powerful motivational variable for task performance.[96] Finally, perceptions of equity have a somewhat weaker effect on task performance.[97]

Less attention has been devoted to the linkages between motivation variables and citizenship and counterproductive behavior. With respect to the former, employees who engage in more work-related effort would seem more likely to perform "extra mile" sorts of actions because those actions themselves require extra effort. The best evidence in support of that claim comes from research on equity. Specifically, employees who feel a sense of equity on the job are more likely to engage in citizenship behaviors, particularly when those behaviors aid the organization.[98] The same employees are less likely to engage in counterproductive behaviors because such behaviors often serve as a retaliation against perceived inequities.[99]

As with citizenship behaviors, the relationship between motivation and organizational commitment seems straightforward. After all, the psychological and physical forms of withdrawal that characterize less committed employees are themselves evidence of low levels of motivation.

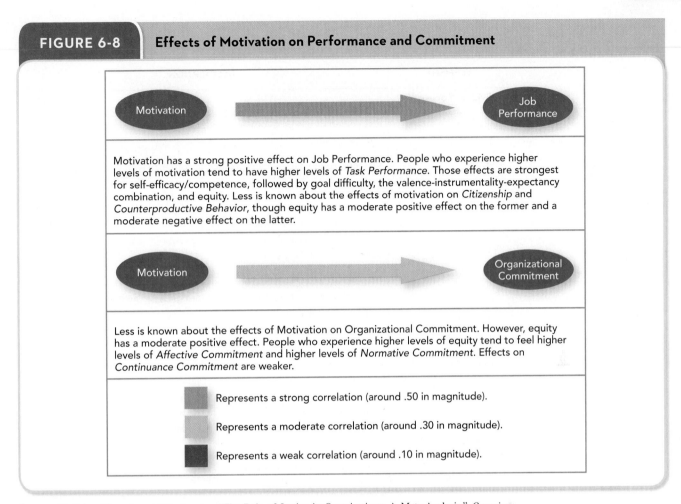

FIGURE 6-8 Effects of Motivation on Performance and Commitment

Motivation → Job Performance

Motivation has a strong positive effect on Job Performance. People who experience higher levels of motivation tend to have higher levels of *Task Performance*. Those effects are strongest for self-efficacy/competence, followed by goal difficulty, the valence-instrumentality-expectancy combination, and equity. Less is known about the effects of motivation on *Citizenship* and *Counterproductive Behavior*, though equity has a moderate positive effect on the former and a moderate negative effect on the latter.

Motivation → Organizational Commitment

Less is known about the effects of Motivation on Organizational Commitment. However, equity has a moderate positive effect. People who experience higher levels of equity tend to feel higher levels of *Affective Commitment* and higher levels of *Normative Commitment*. Effects on *Continuance Commitment* are weaker.

Represents a strong correlation (around .50 in magnitude).

Represents a moderate correlation (around .30 in magnitude).

Represents a weak correlation (around .10 in magnitude).

Sources: Y. Cohen-Charash and P.E. Spector, "The Role of Justice in Organizations: A Meta-Analysis," *Organizational Behavior and Human Decision Processes* 86 (2001), pp. 287–321; J.A. Colquitt, D.E. Conlon, M.J. Wesson, C.O.L.H. Porter, and K.Y. Ng, "Justice at the Millennium: A Meta-Analytic Review of 25 Years of Organizational Justice Research," *Journal of Applied Psychology* 86 (2001), pp. 425–45; J.P. Meyer, D.J. Stanley, L. Herscovitch, and L. Topolnytsky, "Affective, Continuance, and Normative Commitment to the Organization: A Meta-Analysis of Antecedents, Correlates, and Consequences," *Journal of Vocational Behavior* 61 (2002), pp. 20–52; A.D. Stajkovic and F. Luthans, "Self-Efficacy and Work-Related Performance: A Meta-Analysis," *Psychological Bulletin* 124 (1998), pp. 240–61; W. Van Eerde and H. Thierry, "Vroom's Expectancy Models and Work-Related Criteria: A Meta-Analysis," *Journal of Applied Psychology* 81 (1996), pp. 575–86; and R.E. Wood, A.J. Mento, and E.A. Locke, "Task Complexity as a Moderator of Goal Effects: A Meta-Analysis," *Journal of Applied Psychology* 72 (1987), pp. 416–25.

Clearly employees who are daydreaming, coming in late, and taking longer breaks are struggling to put forth consistently high levels of work effort. Research on equity and organizational commitment offers the clearest insights into the motivation—commitment relationship. Specifically, employees who feel a sense of equity are more emotionally attached to their firms and feel a stronger sense of obligation to remain.[100]

APPLICATION: COMPENSATION SYSTEMS

The most important area in which motivation concepts are applied in organizations is in the design of compensation systems. Table 6-7 provides an overview of many of the elements used in typical compensation systems. We use the term "element" in the table to acknowledge that most organizations use a combination of multiple elements to compensate their employees. Two points must be noted about Table 6-7. First, the descriptions of the elements are simplistic; the

TABLE 6-7	Compensation Plan Elements

ELEMENT	DESCRIPTION
Individual-Focused	
Piece-rate	A specified rate is paid for each unit produced, each unit sold, or each service provided.
Merit pay	An increase to base salary is made in accordance with performance evaluation ratings.
Lump-sum bonuses	A bonus is received for meeting individual goals but no change is made to base salary. The potential bonus represents "at risk" pay that must be re-earned each year. Base salary may be lower in cases in which potential bonuses may be large.
Recognition awards	Tangible awards (gift cards, merchandise, trips, special events, time off, plaques) or intangible awards (praise) are given on an impromptu basis to recognize achievement.
Unit-Focused	
Gainsharing	A bonus is received for meeting unit goals (department goals, plant goals, business unit goals) for criteria controllable by employees (labor costs, use of materials, quality). No change is made to base salary. The potential bonus represents "at risk" pay that must be re-earned each year. Base salary may be lower in cases in which potential bonuses may be large.
Organization-Focused	
Profit sharing	A bonus is received when the publicly reported earnings of a company exceed some minimum level, with the magnitude of the bonus contingent on the magnitude of the profits. No change is made to base salary. The potential bonus represents "at risk" pay that must be re-earned each year. Base salary may be lower in cases in which potential bonuses may be large.

reality is that each of the elements can be implemented and executed in a variety of ways.[101] Second, the elements are designed to do more than just motivate. For example, plans that put pay "at risk" rather than creating increases in base salary are geared toward control of labor costs. As another example, elements that stress individual achievement are believed to alter the composition of a workforce over time, with high achievers drawn to the organization while less motivated employees are selected out. Finally, plans that reward unit or organizational performance are designed to reinforce collaboration, information sharing, and monitoring among employees, regardless of their impact on motivation levels.

 6.7

What steps can organizations take to increase employee motivation?

One way of judging the motivational impact of compensation plan elements is to consider whether the elements provide difficult and specific goals for channeling work effort. Merit pay and profit sharing offer little in the way of difficult and specific goals because both essentially challenge employees to make next year as good (or better) than this year. In contrast, lump-sum bonuses and gain sharing provide a forum for assigning difficult and specific goals; the former does so at the individual level and the latter at the unit level. Partly for this reason, both types of plans have been credited with improvements in employee productivity.[102]

Another way of judging the motivational impact of the compensation plan elements is to consider the correspondence between individual performance levels and individual monetary outcomes. After all, that correspondence influences perceptions of both instrumentality and equity. Profit sharing, for example, is unlikely to have strong motivational consequences because an individual employee can do little to improve the profitability of the company, regardless of his or her job performance.[103] Instrumentality and equity are more achievable with gain sharing because the relevant unit is smaller and the relevant outcomes are more controllable. Still, the highest instrumentality and equity levels will typically be achieved through individual-focused compensation elements, such as piece-rate plans or merit pay plans.

Of the two individual-focused elements, merit pay is by far the more common, given that it is difficult to apply piece-rate plans outside of manufacturing, sales, and service contexts. Indeed, one review estimated that merit pay is used by around 90 percent of U.S. organizations.[104] Criticisms of merit pay typically focus on a smaller than expected differentiation in pay across employees. One survey reported that pay increases for top performers (5.6 percent on average) are only modestly greater than the pay increases for average performers (3.3 percent on average).[105] Such differences seem incapable of creating a perceived linkage between performance and outcomes (though merit reviews can also have indirect effects on pay by triggering promotions).[106]

A number of factors constrain instrumentality and equity in most applications of merit pay. As noted earlier, one such factor is budgetary constraints because many organizations freeze or limit pay increases during an economic downturn. Another factor is the accuracy of the actual performance evaluation. Think of all the times you've been evaluated by someone else, whether in school or in the workplace. How many times have you reacted by thinking, "Where did that rating come from?" or "I think I'm being evaluated on the wrong things!" Performance evaluation experts suggest that employees should be evaluated on behaviors that are controllable by the employees (see Chapter 2 on job performance for more discussion of such issues), observable by managers, and critical to the implementation of the firm's strategy.[107] The managers who conduct evaluations also need to be trained in how to conduct them, which typically involves gaining knowledge of the relevant behaviors ahead of time and being taught to keep records of employee behavior between evaluation sessions.[108]

Even if employees are evaluated on the right things by a boss who has a good handle on their performance, other factors can still undermine accuracy. Some managers might knowingly give inaccurate evaluations due to workplace politics or a desire to not "make waves." One survey showed that 70 percent of managers have trouble giving poor ratings to underachieving employees.[109] Unfortunately, such practices only serve to damage instrumentality and equity because they fail to separate star employees from struggling employees. To ensure that such separation occurs, Yahoo! instituted a "stacked ranking" system to determine compensation, in which managers rank all the employees within their unit from top to bottom.[110] Employees at the top end of those rankings then receive higher bonuses than employees at the bottom end. Although such practices raise concerns about employee morale and excessive competitiveness, research suggests that such forced distribution systems can boost the performance of a company's workforce, especially for the first few years after their implementation.[111]

Finally, another factor that can hinder the effectiveness of merit pay is its typical once-a-year schedule. How long a shelf life can the motivational benefits of a salary increase really have? One month? Two months? Six? Such concerns have led a number of organizations to supplement other compensation elements with more widespread use of recognition awards. For example, Symantec, the Mountain View, California–based software firm, uses something called an Applause Program.[112] It honors employees in real time with a combination of gift cards (worth up to $1,000) and electronic thank-you cards. Estimates suggest that around 65 percent of employees have been recognized with some form of "applause" since the program launched. The Everett Clinic, based in Everett, Washington, uses a number of different recognition awards, colorfully named HeroGrams, Caught in the Act cards, and Pat on the Back cards.[113] Explains Daniel Debow, the founder of Rypple, a performance management system that resembles Facebook in its look and feel, "We live in a real-time world . . . so it's crazy to think people wouldn't want real-time feedback."[114]

TAKEAWAYS

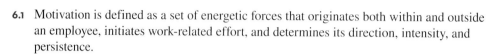

6.1 Motivation is defined as a set of energetic forces that originates both within and outside an employee, initiates work-related effort, and determines its direction, intensity, and persistence.

6.2 According to expectancy theory, effort is directed toward behaviors when effort is believed to result in performance (expectancy), performance is believed to result in outcomes (instrumentality), and those outcomes are anticipated to be valuable (valence).

6.3 According to goal setting theory, goals become strong drivers of motivation and performance when they are difficult and specific. Specific and difficult goals affect performance by increasing self-set goals and task strategies. Those effects occur more frequently when employees are given feedback, tasks are not too complex, and goal commitment is high.

6.4 According to equity theory, rewards are equitable when a person's ratio of outcomes to inputs matches those of some relevant comparison other. A sense of inequity triggers equity distress. Underreward inequity typically results in lower levels of motivation or higher levels of counterproductive behavior. Overreward inequity typically results in cognitive distortion, in which inputs are reevaluated in a more positive light.

6.5 Psychological empowerment reflects an energy rooted in the belief that tasks are contributing to some larger purpose. Psychological empowerment is fostered when work goals appeal to employees' passions (meaningfulness), employees have a sense of choice regarding work tasks (self-determination), employees feel capable of performing successfully (competence), and employees feel they are making progress toward fulfilling their purpose (impact).

6.6 Motivation has a strong positive relationship with job performance and a moderate positive relationship with organizational commitment. Of all the energetic forces subsumed by motivation, self-efficacy/competence has the strongest relationship with performance.

6.7 Organizations use compensation practices to increase motivation. Those practices may include individual-focused elements (piece-rate, merit pay, lump-sum bonuses, recognition awards), unit-focused elements (gain sharing), or organization-focused elements (profit sharing).

KEY TERMS

- Motivation   *p. 164*
- Engagement   *p. 165*
- Expectancy theory   *p. 166*
- Expectancy   *p. 166*
- Self-efficacy   *p. 167*
- Past accomplishments   *p. 167*
- Vicarious experiences   *p. 167*
- Verbal persuasion   *p. 167*
- Emotional cues   *p. 167*
- Instrumentality   *p. 167*
- Valence   *p. 168*
- Needs   *p. 168*
- Extrinsic motivation   *p. 169*
- Intrinsic motivation   *p. 169*
- Meaning of money   *p. 169*
- Goal setting theory   *p. 172*
- Specific and difficult goals   *p. 172*
- Self-set goals   *p. 173*
- Task strategies   *p. 173*
- Feedback   *p. 173*
- Task complexity   *p. 173*
- Goal commitment   *p. 174*
- S.M.A.R.T. goals   *p. 175*
- Equity theory   *p. 175*
- Comparison other   *p. 176*
- Equity distress   *p. 176*
- Cognitive distortion   *p. 178*
- Internal comparisons   *p. 178*
- External comparisons   *p. 178*
- Psychological empowerment   *p. 180*
- Meaningfulness   *p. 180*
- Self-determination   *p. 180*
- Competence   *p. 180*
- Impact   *p. 181*

DISCUSSION QUESTIONS

6.1 Which of the outcomes in Table 6-2 are most appealing to you? Are you more attracted to extrinsic outcomes or intrinsic outcomes? Do you think that your preferences will change as you get older?

6.2 Assume that you were working on a group project and that one of your teammates was nervous about speaking in front of the class during the presentation. Drawing on Figure 6-3, what exactly could you do to make your classmate feel more confident?

6.3 Consider the five strategies for fostering goal commitment (rewards, publicity, support, participation, and resources). Which of those strategies do you think is most effective? Can you picture any of them having potential drawbacks?

6.4 How do you tend to respond when you experience overreward and underreward inequity? Why do you respond that way rather than with some other combination in Figure 6-6?

6.5 Think about a job that you've held in which you felt very low levels of psychological empowerment. What could the organization have done to increase empowerment levels?

CASE: DELOITTE

The "performance snapshot" system developed by Deloitte—that revolved around the four statements mentioned earlier—was the result of a long process of retooling. The old system had many elements that are common in large firms. Specific objectives were set at the highest levels of the company at the beginning of each year and were "cascaded" down to lower levels. As projects were finished, employees were rated on the degree to which their performance met those objectives. Those ratings were then the subject of discussion at end-of-year "consensus meetings," where employees were given an overall performance score for the year. One of the voices in those consensus meetings was an employee-assigned "counselor" who represented the employee to encourage an accurate and unbiased accounting.

Unfortunately, 58 percent of the Deloitte executives surveyed felt like the system did not increase employee engagement levels. More specifically, the company felt that the old system came up short on some important dimensions. First, the specific objectives that were set at the beginning of the year sometimes became outdated and less pivotal as the year moved on, robbing the system of a certain agility. Moreover, the once-a-year conversation was too infrequent to give employees the feedback they needed, when they needed it. Most importantly, though, Deloitte estimated that it spent 2 million hours a year on the cascading objectives, project ratings, consensus meetings, and conversations about the scores and the system. As Ashley Goodall summarized, "We wondered if we could somehow shift our investment of time from talking to ourselves about ratings to talking to our people about their performance and careers—from a focus on the past to a focus on the future."

Deloitte also wanted "performance snapshot" statements that were more behavioral than descriptive. That is, the company wanted managers to rate what they themselves would actually do—in terms of choosing a person for their team or giving them the highest possible raise—rather than rating the skills, qualities, or characteristics of the person. Deloitte did a thorough review of scientific research on performance evaluations and felt that such behavioral statements could reduce what's called "idiosyncratic rater effects"—biases on the part of a boss that can inject noise into ratings. That sort of noise can rob systems of the instrumentality needed to foster high levels of engagement. As she reflects on Deloitte's system, Goodall is encouraged while pointing to one remaining question: transparency. On the one hand, knowing their performance snapshot numbers can trigger conversations between employees and their leaders, while also allowing progress to be tracked over time. On the other hand, being forced to share performance snapshots with employees could cause leaders to "sugarcoat" them. For now, Deloitte encourages employees to focus on the check-ins with their leader and their annual compensation decision. The snapshots remain "for leader eyes only."

6.1   What do you think of the four statements Deloitte is now using as performance snapshots: "Given what I know of this person's performance, I would always want him or her on my team." "This person is ready for promotion today." "Given what I know of this person's performance, and if it were my money, I would award this person the highest possible compensation increase and bonus." "This person is at risk of low performance." Are they sufficient? Would you want to add, remove, or change any?

6.2   The old system relied on more than just the opinions of team leaders, given the importance of objectives, consensus meetings, counselors, and so forth. If you were a Deloitte employee, would you feel comfortable with giving team leaders such a pivotal role in your evaluation (and compensation)?

6.3   What's your opinion on the transparency issue? Would the system function more or less effectively if all of the snapshot numbers were shared with employees? Why do you feel that way?

Sources: M. Buckingham and A. Goodall, "Reinventing Performance Management," *Harvard Business Review,* April, 2015; and Deloitte LLP, "What You Should Know," *Great Place to Work Institute,* http://reviews.greatplacetowork.com/deloitte-llp (accessed July 10, 2015).

EXERCISE: EXPLAINING PAY DIFFERENCES

The purpose of this exercise is to demonstrate how compensation can be used to influence motivation. This exercise uses groups, so your instructor will either assign you to a group or ask you to create your own group. The exercise has the following steps:

6.1   Read the following scenario:

Chris Clements and Pat Palmer are both computer programmers working for the same *Fortune* 500 company. One day they found out that Chris earns $60,820 per year, while Pat earns $72,890. Chris was surprised and said, "I can't think of any reason why we should be paid so differently." "I can think of at least 10 reasons," Pat responded. Can you, like Pat, think of at least 10 reasons that could cause this difference in salary between two people? These reasons can be legal or illegal, wise or unwise.

6.2   Going around the group from member to member, generate a list of 10 conceivable reasons why Pat may be earning more than Chris. Remember, the reasons can be legal or illegal, wise or unwise.

6.3   Consider whether the theories discussed in the chapter—expectancy theory, goal setting theory, equity theory, and psychological empowerment—are relevant to the list of reasons you've generated. Maybe one of the theories supports the wisdom of a given reason. For example, maybe Pat's job is more difficult than Chris's job. Equity theory would support the wisdom of that reason because job difficulty is a relevant input. Maybe one of the theories questions the wisdom of a given reason. For example, maybe Chris's boss believes that salary increases are a poor use of limited financial resources. Expectancy theory would question the wisdom of that reason because that philosophy harms instrumentality.

6.4   Elect a group member to write the group's 10 reasons on the board. Then indicate which theories are relevant to the various reasons by writing one or more of the following abbreviations next to a given reason: EX for expectancy theory, GS for goal setting theory, EQ for equity theory, and PE for psychological empowerment.

6.5   Class discussion (whether in groups or as a class) should center on which theories seem most relevant to the potential reasons for the pay differences between Chris and Pat. Are there some potential reasons that don't seem relevant to any of the four theories? Do those reasons tend to be legal or illegal, wise or unwise?

Source: Adapted from Renard, M.K. "It's All about the Money: Chris and Pat Compare Salaries." Journal of Management Education 32 (2008), pp. 248–61.

ENDNOTES

6.1 Steers, R.M.; R.T. Mowday; and D. Shapiro. "The Future of Work Motivation." *Academy of Management Review* 29 (2004), pp. 379–87; and Latham, G.P. *Work Motivation: History, Theory, Research, and Practice.* Thousand Oaks, CA: Sage, 2006.

6.2 Latham, G.P., and C.C. Pinder. "Work Motivation Theory and Research at the Dawn of the Twenty-First Century." *Annual Review of Psychology* 56 (2005), pp. 485–516.

6.3 Maier, N.R.F. *Psychology in Industry,* 2nd ed. Boston: Houghton Mifflin, 1955.

6.4 Kahn, W.A. "Psychological Conditions of Personal Engagement and Disengagement at Work." *Academy of Management Journal* 33 (1990), pp. 692–724.

6.5 Rich, B.L.; J.A. LePine; and E.R. Crawford. "Job Engagement: Antecedents and Effects on Job Performance." *Academy of Management Journal* 52 (2009), pp. 617–35; Schaufeli, W.B.; M. Salanova; V. Gonzalez-Roma; and A.B. Bakker. "The Measurement of Engagement and Burnout: A Two Sample Confirmatory Factor Analytic Approach." *Journal of Happiness Studies* 3 (2002), pp. 71–92; and Macy, W.H., and B. Schneider. "The Meaning of Employee Engagement." *Industrial and Organizational Psychology* 1 (2008), pp. 3–30.

6.6 Ibid.; and Rothbard, N.P. "Enriching or Depleting? The Dynamics of Engagement in Work and Family Roles." *Administrative Science Quarterly* 46 (2001), pp. 655–84.

6.7 Harter, J.K.; F.L. Schmidt; and T.H. Hayes. "Business-Unit-Level Relationship between Employee Satisfaction, Employee Engagement, and Business Outcomes: A Meta-Analysis." *Journal of Applied Psychology* 87 (2002), pp. 268–79.

6.8 O'Boyle, E., and J. Harter. "State of the American Workplace." Gallup, June 29, 2013, http://www.gallup.com/strategicconsulting/163007/state-american-workplace.aspx.

6.9 Woolley, S. "New Priorities for Employers." *Bloomberg Businessweek,* September 13–19, 2010, p. 54.

6.10 Bakker, A.B., and D. Xanthopoulou. "The Crossover of Daily Work Engagement: Test of an Actor-Partner Interdependence Model." *Journal of Applied Psychology* 94 (2009), pp. 1562–71.

6.11 Vroom, V.H. *Work and Motivation.* New York: Wiley, 1964.

6.12 Ibid.; see also Thorndike, E.L. "The Law of Effect." *American Journal of Psychology* 39 (1964), pp. 212–22; Hull, C.L. *Essentials of Behavior.* New Haven: Yale University Press, 1951; and Postman, L. "The History and Present Status of the Law of Effect." *Psychological Bulletin* 44 (1947), pp. 489–563.

6.13 Bandura, A. "Self-Efficacy: Toward a Unifying Theory of Behavioral Change." *Psychological Review* 84 (1977), pp. 191–215.

6.14 Brockner, J. *Self-Esteem at Work.* Lexington, MA: Lexington Books, 1988.

6.15 Bandura, "Self-Efficacy."

6.16 Ibid.

6.17 Ibid.

6.18 Gist, M.E., and T.R. Mitchell. "Self-Efficacy: A Theoretical Analysis of Its Determinants and Malleability." *Academy of Management Review* 17 (1992), pp. 183–211.

6.19 Vroom, *Work and Motivation.*

6.20 Pinder, C.C. *Work Motivation.* Glenview, IL: Scott, Foresman, 1984.

6.21 Stillings, J., and L. Snyder. "Up Front: The Stat." *BusinessWeek,* July 4, 2005, p. 12.

6.22 Henneman, T. "Cracks in the Ice." *Workforce Management,* November 2010, pp. 30–36.

6.23 Ibid.

6.24 Vroom, *Work and Motivation.*

6.25 Pinder, *Work Motivation.*

6.26 Landy, F.J., and W.S. Becker. "Motivation Theory Reconsidered." In *Research in Organizational Behavior,* Vol. 9, ed. B.M. Staw and L.L. Cummings. Greenwich, CT: JAI Press, 1987, pp. 1–38; and Naylor, J.C.; D.R. Pritchard; and D.R. Ilgen. *A Theory of Behavior in Organizations.* New York: Academic Press, 1980.

6.27 Maslow, A.H. "A Theory of Human Motivation." *Psychological Review* 50 (1943), pp. 370–96; and Alderfer, C.P. "An Empirical Test of a New Theory of Human Needs." *Organizational Behavior and Human Performance* 4 (1969), pp. 142–75.

6.28 Ibid.; see also Deci, E.L., and R.M. Ryan. "The 'What' and 'Why' of Goal Pursuits: Human Needs and the Self-Determination of Behavior." *Psychological Inquiry* 11 (2000), pp. 227–68; Cropanzano, R.; Z.S. Byrne; D.R. Bobocel; and D.R. Rupp. "Moral Virtues, Fairness Heuristics, Social Entities, and Other Denizens of Organizational Justice." *Journal of Vocational Behavior* 58 (2001), pp. 164–209; Williams, K.D. "Social Ostracism." In *Aversive Interpersonal Behaviors,* ed. R.M. Kowalski. New York: Plenum Press, 1997, pp. 133–70; and Thomas, K.W., and B.A. Velthouse. "Cognitive Elements of Empowerment: An 'Interpretive' Model of Intrinsic Task Motivation." *Academy of Management Review* 15 (1990), pp. 666–81.

6.29 Deci and Ryan, "The 'What' and 'Why'"; and Naylor et al., *A Theory of Behavior in Organizations.*

6.30 Ibid.

6.31 Huff, C. "Motivating the World." *Workforce Management,* September 24, 2007, pp. 25–31.

6.32 Speizer, I. "Incentives Catch on Overseas, but Value of Awards Can Too Easily Get Lost in Translation." *Workforce,* November 21, 2005, pp. 46–49.

6.33 Huff, "Motivating the World"; and Speizer, "Incentives Catch on Overseas."

6.34 Rynes, S.L.; B. Gerhart; and K.A. Minette. "The Importance of Pay in Employee Motivation: Discrepancies between What People Say and What They Do." *Human Resource Management* 43 (2004), pp. 381–94; and Rynes, S.L.; K.G. Brown; and A.E. Colbert. "Seven Common Misconceptions about Human Resource Practices: Research Findings versus Practitioner Beliefs." *Academy of Management Executive* 16 (2002), pp. 92–102.

6.35 Rynes et al., "The Importance of Pay."

6.36 Ibid.

6.37 Mitchell, T.R., and A.E. Mickel. "The Meaning of Money: An Individual Differences Perspective." *Academy of Management Review* 24 (1999), pp. 568–78.

6.38 Tang, T.L. "The Meaning of Money Revisited." *Journal of Organizational Behavior* 13 (1992), pp. 197–202; and Mickel, A.E., and L.A. Barron. "Getting 'More Bang for the Buck.'" *Journal of Management Inquiry* 17 (2008), pp. 329–38.

6.39 Tang, T.L. "The Development of a Short Money Ethic Scale: Attitudes toward Money and Pay Satisfaction Revisited." *Personality and Individual Differences* 19 (1995), pp. 809–16.

6.40 Tang, "The Meaning of Money Revisited."

6.41 Ibid.; and Tang, "The Development of a Short Money Ethic Scale."

6.42 Tang, "The Development of a Short Money Ethic Scale."

6.43 Vroom, *Work and Motivation;* and Lawler III, E.E., and J.L.

Suttle. "Expectancy Theory and Job Behavior." *Organizational Behavior and Human Performance* 9 (1973), pp. 482–503.

6.44 Locke, E.A. "Toward a Theory of Task Motivation and Incentives." *Organizational Behavior and Human Performance* 3 (1968), pp. 157–89.

6.45 Locke, E.A.; K.N. Shaw; L.M. Saari; and G.P. Latham. "Goal Setting and Task Performance: 1969–1980." *Psychological Bulletin* 90 (1981), pp. 125–52.

6.46 Locke, E.A., and G.P. Latham. *A Theory of Goal Setting and Task Performance.* Englewood Cliffs, NJ: Prentice Hall, 1990.

6.47 Ibid.

6.48 Ibid.

6.49 Ibid.; see also Locke, E.A., and G.P. Latham. "Building a Practically Useful Theory of Goal Setting and Task Motivation: A 35-Year Odyssey." *American Psychologist* 57 (2002), pp. 705–17; and Latham, G.P. "Motivate Employee Performance through Goal-Setting." In *Blackwell Handbook of Principles of Organizational Behavior,* ed. E.A. Locke. Malden, MA: Blackwell, 2000, pp. 107–19.

6.50 Locke and Latham, *A Theory of Goal Setting.*

6.51 Locke et al., "Goal Setting and Task Performance."

6.52 Ibid.; Locke and Latham, *A Theory of Goal Setting;* and Locke and Latham, "Building a Practically Useful Theory."

6.53 Wood, R.E.; A.J. Mento; and E.A. Locke. "Task Complexity as a Moderator of Goal Effects: A Meta-Analysis." *Journal of Applied Psychology* 72 (1987), pp. 416–25.

6.54 Ibid.

6.55 Barrett, A. "Cracking the Whip at Wyeth." *BusinessWeek,* February 6, 2006, pp. 70–71.

6.56 Hollenbeck, J.R., and H.J. Klein. "Goal Commitment and the Goal-Setting Process: Problems, Prospects, and Proposal for Future Research." *Journal of Applied Psychology* 72 (1987), pp. 212–20; see also Locke et al., "Goal Setting and Task Performance."

6.57 Klein, H.J.; M.J. Wesson; J.R. Hollenbeck; and B.J. Alge. "Goal Commitment and the Goal-Setting Process: Conceptual Clarification and Empirical Synthesis." *Journal of Applied Psychology* 84 (1999), pp. 885–96; and Donovan, J.J., and D.J. Radosevich. "The Moderating Role of Goal Commitment on the Goal Difficulty–Performance Relationship: A Meta-Analytic Review and Critical Reanalysis." *Journal of Applied Psychology* 83 (1998), pp. 308–15.

6.58 Hollenbeck and Klein, "Goal Commitment and the Goal-Setting Process"; Klein et al., "Goal Commitment"; Locke, E.A.; G.P Latham; and M. Erez. "The Determinants of Goal Commitment." *Academy of Management Review* 13 (1988), pp. 23–29; and Latham, G.P. "The Motivational Benefits of Goal-Setting." *Academy of Management Executive* 18 (2004), pp. 126–29.

6.59 Shaw, K.N. "Changing the Goal Setting Process at Microsoft." *Academy of Management Executive* 18 (2004), pp. 139–42.

6.60 Ibid.

6.61 Adams, J.S., and W.B. Rosenbaum. "The Relationship of Worker Productivity to Cognitive Dissonance about Wage Inequities." *Journal of Applied Psychology* 46 (1962), pp. 161–64.

6.62 Adams, J.S. "Inequity in Social Exchange." In *Advances in Experimental Social Psychology,* Vol. 2, ed. L. Berkowitz. New York: Academic Press, 1965, pp. 267–99; and Homans, G.C. *Social Behaviour: Its Elementary Forms.* London: Routledge & Kegan Paul, 1961.

6.63 Ibid.

6.64 Adams, "Inequality in Social Exchange."

6.65 Ibid.

6.66 Greenberg, J. "Employee Theft as a Reaction to Underpayment Inequity: The Hidden Cost of Paycuts." *Journal of Applied Psychology* 75 (1990), pp. 561–68; and Greenberg, J. "Stealing in the Name of Justice: Informational and Interpersonal Moderators of Theft Reactions to Underpayment Inequity." *Organizational Behavior and Human Decision Processes* 54 (1993), pp. 81–103.

6.67 Adams, "Inequality in Social Exchange."

6.68 Scholl, R.W.; E.A. Cooper; and J.F. McKenna. "Referent Selection in Determining Equity Perceptions: Differential Effects on Behavioral and Attitudinal Outcomes." *Personnel Psychology* 40 (1987), pp. 113–24.

6.69 Ibid.

6.70 Ibid.; see also Finn, R.H., and S.M. Lee. "Salary Equity: Its Determination, Analysis, and Correlates." *Journal of Applied Psychology* 56 (1972), pp. 283–92.

6.71 Scholl et al., "Referent Selection."

6.72 Smith, E.B., and P. Kuntz. "Some CEOs Are More Equal Than Others." *Bloomberg Businessweek,* May 2, 2013, pp. 70–73.

6.73 Silver-Greenberg, J., and A. Leondis. "How Much Is a CEO Worth?" *Bloomberg Businessweek,* May 10–16, 2010, pp. 70–71; and Silver-Greenberg, J.; T. Kalwarski; and A. Leondis. "CEO Pay Drops, But . . . Cash Is King." *Bloomberg Businessweek,* April 5, 2010, pp. 50–56.

6.74 Kirkland, R. "The Real CEO." *Fortune,* July 10, 2006, pp. 78–92; and Smith and Kuntz, "Some CEOs Are More Equal Than Others."

6.75 Sulkowicz, K. "CEO Pay: The Prestige, the Peril." *BusinessWeek,* November 20, 2006, p. 18.

6.76 Silver-Greenberg and Leondis, "How Much Is a CEO Worth?"

6.77 Colella, A.; R.L. Paetzold; A. Zardkoohi; and M. Wesson. "Exposing Pay Secrecy." *Academy of Management Review* 32 (2007), pp. 55–71.

6.78 Ibid.

6.79 Thomas, K.W., and B.A. Velthouse. "Cognitive Elements of Empowerment: An 'Interpretive' Model of Intrinsic Task Motivation." *Academy of Management Review* 15 (1990), pp. 666–81.

6.80 Hackman, J.R., and G.R. Oldham. *Work Redesign.* Reading, MA: Addison-Wesley, 1980.

6.81 Thomas and Velthouse, "Cognitive Elements of Empowerment"; Spreitzer, G.M. "Psychological Empowerment in the Workplace: Dimensions, Measurement, and Validation." *Academy of Management Journal* 38 (1995), pp. 1442–65; Deci, E.L., and R.M. Ryan. *Intrinsic Motivation and Self-Determination in Human Behavior.* New York: Plenum, 1985; and Hackman and Oldham, *Work Redesign.*

6.82 Thomas, K.W. *Intrinsic Motivation at Work: Building Energy and Commitment.* San Francisco: Berrett-Koehler, 2000.

6.83 Ibid.

6.84 Bunderson, J.S., and J.A. Thompson. "The Call of the Wild: Zookeepers, Callings, and the Double-Edged Sword of Deeply Meaningful Work." *Administrative Science Quarterly* 54 (2009), pp. 32–57; Duffy, R.D., and W.E. Sedlacek. "The Presence of and Search for a Calling: Connections to Career Development." *Journal of Vocational Behavior* 70 (2007), pp. 590–601; and Hagmaier, T., and A.E. Abele. "The Multidimensionality of Calling: Conceptualization, Measurement and a Bicultural Perspective." *Journal of Vocational Behavior* 81 (2012). pp. 39–51.

6.85 Thomas and Velthouse, "Cognitive Elements of Empowerment"; and Spreitzer, "Psychological Empowerment."

6.86 Thomas, *Intrinsic Motivation at Work.*

6.87 Thomas and Velthouse, "Cognitive Elements

of Empowerment"; and Spreitzer, "Psychological Empowerment."

6.88 Thomas, *Intrinsic Motivation at Work.*

6.89 Thomas and Velthouse, "Cognitive Elements of Empowerment."

6.90 Thomas, *Intrinsic Motivation at Work.*

6.91 Thomas, *Intrinsic Motivation at Work.*

6.92 Gerdes, L. "Get Ready for a Pickier Workforce." *BusinessWeek,* September 18, 2006, p. 82.

6.93 Hamm, S. "Young and Impatient in India." *BusinessWeek,* January 28, 2008, pp. 45–48.

6.94 Stajkovic, A.D., and F. Luthans. "Self-Efficacy and Work-Related Performance: A Meta-Analysis." *Psychological Bulletin* 124 (1998), pp. 240–61.

6.95 Wood et al., "Task Complexity as a Moderator."

6.96 Van Eerde, W., and H. Thierry. "Vroom's Expectancy Models and Work-Related Criteria: A Meta-Analysis." *Journal of Applied Psychology* 81 (1996), pp. 575–86.

6.97 Cohen-Charash, Y., and P.E. Spector. "The Role of Justice in Organizations: A Meta-Analysis." *Organizational Behavior and Human Decision Processes* 86 (2001), pp. 287–321; and Colquitt, J.A.; D.E. Conlon; M.J. Wesson; C.O.L.H. Porter; and K.Y. Ng. "Justice at the Millennium: A Meta-Analytic

Review of 25 Years of Organizational Justice Research." *Journal of Applied Psychology* 86 (2001), pp. 425–45.

6.98 Ibid.

6.99 Ibid.

6.100 Ibid.

6.101 Lawler III, E.E. *Rewarding Excellence: Pay Strategies for the New Economy.* San Francisco: Jossey-Bass, 2000; and Gerhart, B.; S.L. Rynes; and I.S. Fulmer. "Pay and Performance: Individuals, Groups, and Executives." *Academy of Management Annals,* 3 (2009), pp. 251–315.

6.102 Ibid.; see also Durham, C.C., and K.M. Bartol. "Pay for Performance." In *Handbook of Principles of Organizational Behavior,* ed. E.A. Locke. Malden, MA: Blackwell, 2000, pp. 150–65; and Gerhart, B.; H.B. Minkoff; and R.N. Olsen. "Employee Compensation: Theory, Practice, and Evidence." In *Handbook of Human Resource Management,* ed. G.R. Ferris, S.D. Rosen, and D.T. Barnum. Malden, MA: Blackwell, 1995, pp. 528–47.

6.103 Ibid.

6.104 Gerhart et al., "Pay and Performance"; and Cohen, K. "The Pulse of the Profession: 2006–2007 Budget Survey." *Workspan,* September 2006, pp. 23–26.

6.105 Hansen, F. "Merit-Pay Payoff?" *Workforce Management,* November 3, 2008, pp. 33–39.

6.106 Ibid.

6.107 Latham, G., and S. Latham. "Overlooking Theory and Research in Performance Appraisal at One's Peril: Much Done, More to Do." In *Industrial and Organizational Psychology: Linking Theory with Practice,* ed. C.L. Cooper and E.A. Locke. Oxford, UK: Blackwell, 2000, pp. 199–215.

6.108 Ibid.

6.109 Sulkowicz, K. "Straight Talk at Review Time." *BusinessWeek,* September 10, 2007, p. 16.

6.110 McGregor, J. "The Struggle to Measure Performance." *BusinessWeek,* January 9, 2006, pp. 26–28.

6.111 Scullen, S.E.; P.K. Bergey; and L. Aiman-Smith. "Forced Distribution Rating Systems and the Improvement of Workforce Potential: A Baseline Simulation." *Personnel Psychology* 58 (2005), pp. 1–32.

6.112 Shepherd, L. "Getting Personal." *Workforce Management,* September 2010, pp. 24–29.

6.113 Ibid.

6.114 Pyrillis, R. "The Reviews Are In." *Workforce Management,* May 2011, pp. 20–25.

chapter 7

Trust, Justice, and Ethics

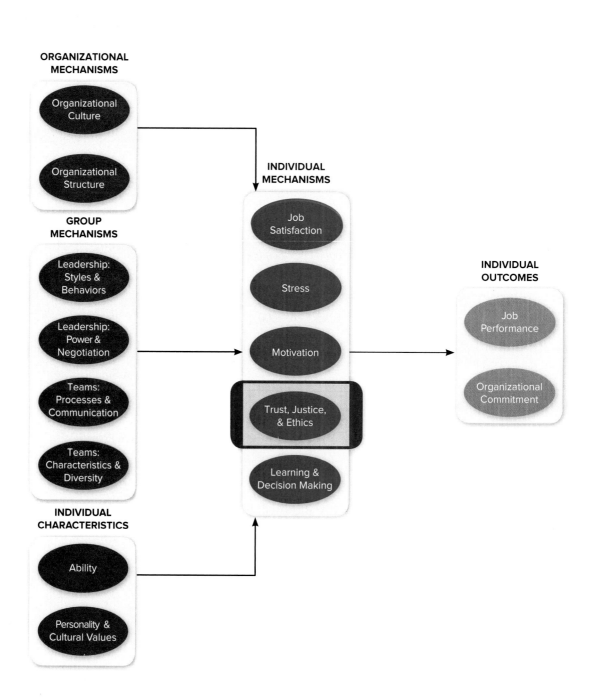

© Evelyn Hockstein/For The Washington Post via Getty Images

LEARNING GOALS

After reading this chapter, you should be able to answer the following questions:

7.1 What is trust, and how does it relate to justice and ethics?

7.2 In what three sources can trust be rooted?

7.3 What dimensions can be used to describe the trustworthiness of an authority?

7.4 What dimensions can be used to describe the fairness of an authority's decision making?

7.5 What is the four-component model of ethical decision making?

7.6 How does trust affect job performance and organizational commitment?

7.7 What steps can organizations take to become more trustworthy?

UBER

Picture this. You walk out of a restaurant, capping off a long day in the city you're visiting on business. The restaurant's on the edge of downtown, far from any hotels, including yours. You could have asked the maitre d' to call a cab, or you could call one yourself after some searching on your smartphone. You don't need to do either, however, because you've already launched Uber and set your pickup location. Your driver's car appears on a map, six minutes away, and you get his name and picture. Once he picks you up in his black Cadillac, he'll drop you at your hotel and—here's the best part—you'll just get out. No rummaging for cash, no change, no tip, and no receipt request. Uber simply charges your credit card through the app and e-mails you a receipt.

Uber grew out of a conversation between Travis Kalanick and Garrett Camp, with the idea being to create a time-share service for fancy cars. Camp worked on an iPhone app while Kalanick developed relationships with cabbies in San Francisco. As business took off, Kalanick became CEO, bringing his own unique style to managing the company. What is that style? Well, to understand that question, it helps to know that Kalanick likens himself to Winston Wolfe, the "fixer" from *Pulp Fiction* who

just "solves problems." Under Kalanick's playbook, Uber enters a new market experimentally, waiting to see how the bodies that regulate taxi and limousine services respond. If relevant rules are not enforced within 30 days, something Kalanick calls "regulatory ambiguity," Uber comes in more aggressively. Besides, Kalanick contends that Uber is essentially just a software company—not subject to the laws and regulations that city mayors want it to follow.

If Kalanick practices business by walking right up to ethical lines, Uber and its employees have occasionally crossed them. The company's been criticized for its "surge pricing," where prices get higher at peak times. Although Uber prices tend to be similar to cabs in general, surge pricing resulted in Jessica Seinfeld—the wife of Jerry—spending $415 to take her children to a nighttime event. The company was also criticized for insufficient background checks after a driver was charged with vehicular manslaughter 10 years after earning a citation for reckless driving. And what about Uber's employees? They've been criticized for contacting cars from competing services before canceling just before pickup—literally slowing down the competition.

TRUST, JUSTICE, AND ETHICS

One reason companies care about ethical issues is that a firm's reputation is one of its most prized possessions. An organization's **reputation** reflects the prominence of its brand in the minds of the public and the perceived quality of its goods and services.[1] Reputation is an intangible asset that can take a long time to build but, as Ben Franklin once noted, can be cracked as easily as glass or china.[2] That's especially the case today, when one bad experience with any company can be tweeted, shared on Facebook, posted on a blog, or videotaped and uploaded to YouTube. Although we typically think about a company's reputation in reference to potential consumers, it matters to employees as well. Recruitment experts maintain that top performers want to work at organizations with clean reputations, in part because they want to protect their own personal image. Indeed, one survey found that 78 percent of adults would rather work at a company with an excellent reputation and an average salary than at a company with a high salary and a poor reputation.[3] Who are some companies with excellent reputations? Table 7-1 provides the top 25 from *Fortune*'s list of "Most Admired Companies."

Reputations depend on many things, but one of the most important factors is trust. **Trust** is defined as the willingness to be vulnerable to a trustee based on positive expectations about the trustee's actions and intentions.[4] If a customer trusts the quality of a company's products or services, that customer is willing to accept the consequences of paying money to the company. If a potential recruit trusts the words of a company's management, that recruit is willing to accept the consequences of becoming a member of the organization. Both examples illustrate that trusting reflects a willingness to "put yourself out there," even though doing so could be met with disappointment. The examples also highlight the difference between "trust" and "risk." Actually making yourself vulnerable—by buying products or accepting a job—constitutes risk. Trust reflects the willingness to take that risk. Unfortunately, trust in many companies has declined sharply

TABLE 7-1	The World's Most Admired Companies
1. Apple	14. Nordstrom
2. Google	15. BMW
3. Berkshire Hathaway	16. Costco
4. Amazon.com	17. Procter & Gamble
5. Starbucks	18. Whole Foods
6. Walt Disney	19. Singapore Airlines
7. Southwest Airlines	20. Microsoft
8. American Express	21. 3M
9. General Electric	22. Wells Fargo
10. Coca-Cola	23. Goldman Sachs
11. Johnson & Johnson	24. Toyota
12. FedEx	25. IBM
13. Nike	

Source: From C. Tkaczyk, "The World's Most Admired Companies," *Fortune*, March 1, 2015. Copyright © 2015 Time Inc. Used under license.

due to corporate scandals and the economic downturn. Indeed, one recent survey revealed that only 44 percent of Americans say they trust business, down from 58 percent in the fall of 2007.[5] "Trust is what drives profit margin and share price," notes the CEO of one branding and marketing firm. "It is what consumers are looking for and what they share with one another."

This chapter focuses on trust in organizational authorities, a group that could include the CEO of an organization, its top management team, or supervisors and managers within the firm. These authorities "put a face on a company," giving employees and customers a means of judging a company's reputation. These authorities are also capable of having a significant influence on the performance and commitment of employees. As you'll see in the chapter, trust in these authorities depends on two related concepts. **Justice** reflects the perceived fairness of an authority's decision making.[6] When employees perceive high levels of justice, they believe that decision outcomes are fair and that decision-making processes are designed and implemented in a fair manner. Justice concepts can be used to explain why employees judge some authorities to be more trustworthy than others.[7] **Ethics** reflects the degree to which the behaviors of an authority are in accordance with generally accepted moral norms.[8] When employees perceive high levels of ethics, they believe that things are being done the way they "should be" or "ought to be" done. Ethics concepts can be used to explain why authorities decide to act in a trustworthy or untrustworthy manner.

7.1

What is trust, and how does it relate to justice and ethics?

WHY ARE SOME AUTHORITIES MORE TRUSTED THAN OTHERS?

Think about a particular boss or instructor—someone you've spent a significant amount of time around. Do you trust that person? Would you be willing to let that person have significant influence over your professional or educational future? For example, would you be willing to let that person serve as a reference for you or write you a letter of recommendation, even though you'd have no way of monitoring what he or she said about you? When you think about the level of trust you feel for that particular authority, what exactly makes you feel that way? This question speaks to the factors that drive trust—the factors that help inspire a willingness to be vulnerable.

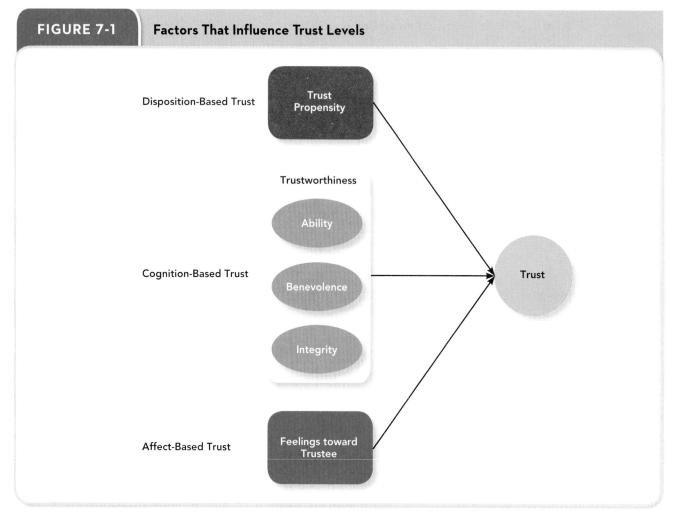

FIGURE 7-1   **Factors That Influence Trust Levels**

Sources: Adapted from R.C. Mayer, J.H. Davis, and F.D. Schoorman, "An Integrative Model of Organizational Trust," *Academy of Management Review* 20 (1995), pp. 709–34; and D.J. McAllister, "Affect- and Cognition-Based Trust as Foundations for Interpersonal Cooperation in Organizations," *Academy of Management Journal* 38 (1995), pp. 24–59.

TRUST

7.2

In what three sources can trust be rooted?

As shown in Figure 7-1, trust is rooted in three different kinds of factors. Sometimes trust is **disposition-based,** meaning that your personality traits include a general propensity to trust others. Sometimes trust is **cognition-based,** meaning that it's rooted in a rational assessment of the authority's trustworthiness.[9] Sometimes trust is **affect-based,** meaning that it depends on feelings toward the authority that go beyond any rational assessment.[10] The sections that follow describe each of these trust forms in more detail.

DISPOSITION-BASED TRUST   Disposition-based trust has less to do with a particular authority and more to do with the trustor. Some trustors are high in **trust propensity**—a general expectation that the words, promises, and statements of individuals and groups can be relied upon.[11] Some have argued that trust propensity represents a sort of "faith in human nature," in that trusting people view others in more favorable terms than do suspicious people.[12] The importance of trust propensity is most obvious in interactions with strangers, in which any acceptance of vulnerability would amount to "blind trust."[13] On the one hand, people who are high in trust propensity may be fooled into trusting others who are not worthy of it.[14] On the other hand, those who are low in trust propensity may be penalized by not trusting someone who is actually deserving of it. Both situations can be damaging; as one scholar noted, "We are doomed if we trust all and

OB ASSESSMENTS

TRUST PROPENSITY

Are you a trusting person or a suspicious person by nature? This assessment is designed to measure trust propensity—a dispositional willingness to trust other people. Answer each question using the response scale provided. Then subtract your answers to the boldfaced questions from 6, with the difference being your new answers for those questions. For example, if your original answer for question 4 was "4," your new answer is "2" (6 – 4). Then sum up your answers for the eight questions. (Instructors: Assessments on procedural justice, moral attentiveness, and moral identity can be found in the PowerPoints in the Connect Library's Instructor Resources and in the Connect assignments for this chapter).

1	2	3	4	5
STRONGLY DISAGREE	DISAGREE	NEUTRAL	AGREE	STRONGLY AGREE

1. **One should be very cautious with strangers.** _____

2. Most experts tell the truth about the limits of their knowledge. _____

3. Most people can be counted on to do what they say they will do. _____

4. **These days, you must be alert or someone is likely to take advantage of you.** _____

5. Most salespeople are honest in describing their products. _____

6. Most repair people will not overcharge people who are ignorant of their specialty. _____

7. Most people answer public opinion polls honestly. _____

8. Most adults are competent at their jobs. _____

SCORING AND INTERPRETATION

If your scores sum up to 21 or above, you tend to be trusting of other people, which means you're often willing to accept some vulnerability to others under conditions of risk. If your scores sum up to 20 or below, you tend to be suspicious of other people, which means you're rarely willing to accept such vulnerability.

Sources: R.C. Mayer and J.H. Davis, "The Effect of the Performance Appraisal System on Trust for Management: A Field Quasi-Experiment," *Journal of Applied Psychology* 84 (1999), pp. 123–36. Copyright © 1999 by the American Psychological Association. Adapted with permission. No further reproduction or distribution is permitted without written permission from the American Psychological Association. See also F.D. Schoorman, R.C. Mayer, C. Roger, and J.H. Davis. "Empowerment in Veterinary Clinics: The Role of Trust in Delegation." Presented in a Symposium on Trust at the 11th Annual Conference, Society for Industrial and Organizational Psychology (SIOP), April 1996, San Diego.

---

equally doomed if we trust none."[15] Where do you stack up on trust propensity? See our **OB Assessments** feature to find out.

Where does our trust propensity come from? As with all traits, trust propensity is a product of both nature and nurture (see Chapter 9 on personality and cultural values for more discussion of such issues). If our parents are dispositionally suspicious, we may either inherit that tendency genetically or model it as we watch them exhibit distrust in their day-to-day lives. Research also suggests that trust propensity is shaped by early childhood experiences.[16] In fact, trust propensity may be one of the first personality traits to develop because infants must immediately learn to trust their parents to meet their needs. The more our needs are met as children, the more trusting

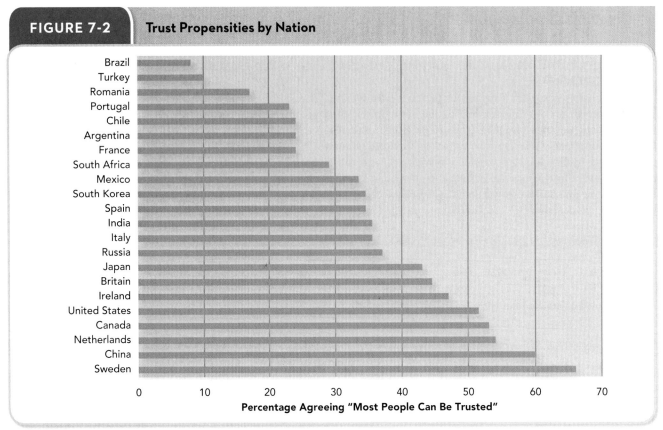

FIGURE 7-2	Trust Propensities by Nation

Source: Adapted from J.J. Johnson and J.B. Cullen, "Trust in Cross-Cultural Relationships," in *Blackwell Handbook of Cross-Cultural Management*, ed. M.J. Gannon and K.L. Newman (Malden, MA: Blackwell, 2002), pp. 335–60.

we become; the more we are disappointed as children, the less trusting we become. Our propensities continue to be shaped later in life as we gain experiences with friends, schools, churches, local government authorities, and other relevant groups.[17]

The nation in which we live also affects our trust propensity. Research by the World Values Study Group examines differences between nations on various attitudes and perceptions.

Children whose needs are generally met tend to grow into trusting adults.

© *Brand X Pictures/PunchStock RF*

The study group collects interview data from 45 different societies with a total sample size of more than 90,000 participants. One of the questions asked by the study group measures trust propensity. Specifically, participants are asked, "Generally speaking, would you say that most people can be trusted or that you can't be too careful in dealing with people?" Figure 7-2 shows the percentage of participants who answered "Most people can be trusted" for this question, as opposed to "Can't be too careful," for several of the nations included in the study. The results reveal that trust propensity levels are actually relatively high in the United States, especially in relation to countries in Europe and South America.

COGNITION-BASED TRUST Disposition-based trust guides us in cases when we don't yet have data about a particular authority. However, eventually we gain enough knowledge to gauge the authority's **trustworthiness,** defined as the characteristics or attributes of a trustee that inspire trust.[18] At that point, our trust begins to be based on cognitions we've developed about the authority, as opposed to our own personality or disposition. In this way, cognition-based trust is driven by the authority's "track record."[19] If that track record has shown the authority to be trustworthy, then vulnerability to the authority can be accepted. If that track record is spotty however, then trust may not be warranted. Research suggests that we gauge the track record of an authority along three dimensions: ability, benevolence, and integrity.[20]

The first dimension of trustworthiness is **ability,** defined as the skills, competencies, and areas of expertise that enable an authority to be successful in some specific area (see Chapter 10 on ability for more discussion of such issues).[21] Think about the decision-making process that you go through when choosing a doctor, lawyer, or mechanic. Clearly one of the first things you consider is ability because you're not going to trust them if they don't know a scalpel from a retractor, a tort from a writ, or a camshaft from a crankshaft. Of course, listing a specific area is a key component of the ability definition; you wouldn't trust a mechanic to perform surgery, nor would you trust a doctor to fix your car! The ability of business authorities may be considered on a number of levels. For example, managers may be judged according to their functional expertise in a particular vocation but also according to their leadership skills and their general business sense.

The second dimension of trustworthiness is **benevolence,** defined as the belief that the authority wants to do good for the trustor, apart from any selfish or profit-centered motives.[22] When authorities are perceived as benevolent, it means that they care for employees, are concerned about their well-being, and feel a sense of loyalty to them. The mentor–protégé relationship provides a good example of benevolence at work, in that the best mentors go out of their way to be helpful apart from concerns about financial rewards.[23] The management at Meijer, the Grand Rapids, Michigan–based supermarket chain, seems to understand the importance of benevolence.[24] Meijer recently added a five-day course on "positive organizational scholarship" to its leadership training program. The training stresses the importance of positive communication and a culture of kindness in the organization. The chain, which operates 180 stores with 60,000 employees, is attempting to compete with the likes of Walmart by maximizing the commitment of its workforce. David Beach, the vice president of workforce planning and development, noted, "We realized that we need our company to be a place where people want to work."[25]

The third dimension of trustworthiness is **integrity,** defined as the perception that the authority adheres to a set of values and principles that the trustor finds acceptable.[26] When authorities have integrity, they are of sound character—they have good intentions and strong moral discipline.[27] Integrity also conveys an alignment between words and deeds—a sense that authorities keep their promises, "walk the talk," and "do what they say they will do."[28] Unfortunately, one survey indicated that only around 20 percent of American workers view senior managers as acting in accordance with their words.[29] Domino's Pizza recently showed an unusual amount of integrity in its advertising and business operations. Despite the fact that its market share was holding steady, the company admitted that customers didn't think its pizza was all that great.[30] Domino's president vowed to put 40 percent more herbs in its sauce, use better cheese, and add a special glaze to its crust. The end result is a better-tasting pizza (in our humble opinion, anyway!), an increase in sales,[31] and the sense that Domino's management "tells it how it is."

Questions about integrity extend beyond senior management, however. For example, studies suggest that rank-and-file employees lie more frequently when communicating by e-mail because there are no "shifty eyes" or nervous ticks to give them away. Indeed, one study showed that people were more likely to lie via e-mail than when writing letters using pen and paper.[32] Why would those contexts differ, when neither is face-to-face? It may be that e-mail feels more fleeting than paper and that the ability to delete what you write—even if you ultimately don't—makes you choose words more casually. Regardless, the lies can begin even before employees are hired, as one survey of managers by CareerBuilder.com revealed that 49 percent had caught an applicant lying on a résumé.[33] Among the more colorful "exaggerations" were claims of membership in Mensa, listing a degree from a fictitious university, and pretending to be a Kennedy. For more discussions of integrity, see our **OB at the Bookstore** feature.

7.3

What dimensions can be used to describe the trustworthiness of an authority?

OB AT THE BOOKSTORE

THE ROAD TO CHARACTER
by David Brooks (New York: Random House, 2015).

Occasionally, even today, you come across certain people who seem to possess an impressive inner cohesion . . . They possess the self-effacing virtues of people who are inclined to be useful but don't need to prove anything to the world: humility, restraint, reticence, temperance, respect, and soft self-discipline . . . They perform acts of sacrificial service with the same modest everyday spirit they would display if they were just getting the groceries . . . These are the people we are looking for.

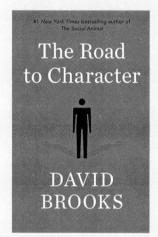

Photo of cover: © Roberts Publishing Services

With those words, Brooks highlights the kinds of people that the world could use a few more of. Although every generation has a tendency to view prior generations in more positive terms, Brooks does describe some aspects of contemporary society that hinder the development of character—a concept similar to the integrity dimension of trustworthiness. For example, our "always connected" state has eliminated moments of quiet reflection. It is those moments where we weigh our virtues against our vices—where we contemplate whether our flaws are less flawed today than yesterday. Now, we reach for the smartphone in those moments. As another example, society's emphasis on meritocracy and achievement has changed the traits that we collectively value. As children are raised to get into the right college, land the right job, and stay on the right career path, the lauded traits have moved from "generosity" to "tenacity," from "selflessness" to "grit." As still another example, parents and educators understandably tell children and students to "listen to their inner voice" as they navigate through life. Unfortunately, that inner focus weakens the salience of what Brooks calls the "moral ecology"—society's norms, assumptions, beliefs, and habits about right and wrong.

Brooks summarizes the effects of these trends in noting, "This cultural, technological, and meritocratic environment hasn't made us a race of depraved barbarians. But it has made us less morally articulate. Many of us have instincts about right and wrong, about how goodness and character are built, but everything is fuzzy." How can we become more articulate in our thinking about and discussing of character? Brooks's closing chapter provides some suggestions.

AFFECT-BASED TRUST Although ability, benevolence, and integrity provide three good reasons to trust an authority, the third form of trust isn't actually rooted in reason. Affect-based trust is more emotional than rational. With affect-based trust, we trust because we have feelings for the person in question; we really like them and have a fondness for them. Those feelings are what prompt us to accept vulnerability to another person. Put simply, we trust them because we like them. Some of that trust can even be chemical, as research shows that something as common as a hug can stimulate a hormone called oxytocin—sometimes called the "cuddle chemical"—that causes your brain to be more trusting.[34]

Affect-based trust acts as a supplement to the types of trust discussed previously.[35] Figure 7-3 describes how the various forms of trust can build on one another over time. In new relationships, trust depends solely on our own trust propensity. In most relationships, that propensity eventually gets supplemented by knowledge about ability, benevolence, or integrity, at which point cognition-based trust develops. In a select few of those relationships, an emotional bond develops, and our feelings for the trustee further increase our willingness to accept vulnerability. These relationships are characterized by a mutual investment of time and energy, a sense of deep attachment, and the realization that both parties would feel a sense of loss if the relationship were dissolved.[36]

© Press Association/AP Images

After admitting that the company needed to change its pizza recipe and ingredients, Domino's set out to get people to try the new and improved version.

SUMMARY Taken together, disposition-based trust, cognition-based trust, and affect-based trust provide three completely different sources of trust in a particular authority. In the case of disposition-based trust, our willingness to be vulnerable has little to do with the authority and more to do with our genes and our early life experiences. In the case of affect-based trust, our willingness to be vulnerable has little to do with a rational assessment of the authority's merits and more to do with our emotional fondness for the authority. Only in the case of cognition-based trust do we rationally evaluate the pluses and minuses of an authority, in terms of its ability, benevolence, and integrity. But how exactly do we gauge those trustworthiness forms? One way is to consider whether authorities adhere to rules of justice.

JUSTICE

It's often difficult to assess the ability, benevolence, and integrity of authorities accurately, particularly early in a working relationship. What employees need in such circumstances is some sort of observable behavioral evidence that an authority might be trustworthy. Justice provides that sort of behavioral evidence because authorities who treat employees more fairly are usually judged to be more trustworthy.[37] As shown in Table 7-2, employees can judge the fairness of an authority's decision making along four dimensions: distributive justice, procedural justice, interpersonal justice, and informational justice.

7.4

What dimensions can be used to describe the fairness of an authority's decision making?

DISTRIBUTIVE JUSTICE **Distributive justice** reflects the perceived fairness of decision-making outcomes.[38] Employees gauge distributive justice by asking whether decision outcomes—such as

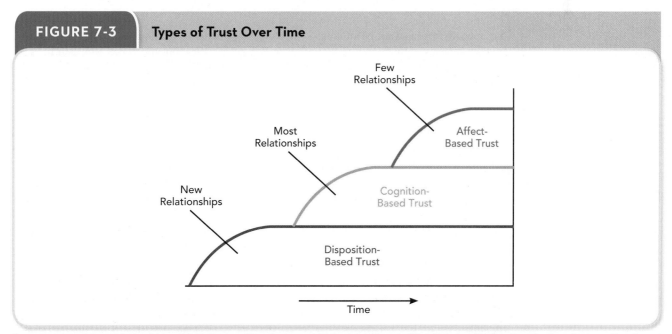

FIGURE 7-3 **Types of Trust Over Time**

Sources: Adapted from R.J. Lewicki and B.B. Bunker, "Developing and Maintaining Trust in Work Relationships," in *Trust in Organizations: Frontiers of Theory and Research,* ed. R.M. Kramer and T.R. Tyler (Thousand Oaks, CA: Sage, 1996), pp. 114–39; and R.C. Mayer, J.H. Davis, and F.D. Schoorman, "An Integrative Model of Organizational Trust," *Academy of Management Review* 20 (1995), pp. 709–34.

TABLE 7-2	The Four Dimensions of Justice

DISTRIBUTIVE JUSTICE RULES	DESCRIPTION
Equity vs. equality vs. need	Are rewards allocated according to the proper norm?
PROCEDURAL JUSTICE RULES	
Voice	Do employees get to provide input into procedures?
Correctability	Do procedures build in mechanisms for appeals?
Consistency	Are procedures consistent across people and time?
Bias suppression	Are procedures neutral and unbiased?
Representativeness	Do procedures consider the needs of all groups?
Accuracy	Are procedures based on accurate information?
INTERPERSONAL JUSTICE RULES	
Respect	Do authorities treat employees with sincerity?
Propriety	Do authorities refrain from improper remarks?
INFORMATIONAL JUSTICE RULES	
Justification	Do authorities explain procedures thoroughly?
Truthfulness	Are those explanations honest?

Sources: J.S. Adams, "Inequity in Social Exchange," in *Advances in Experimental Social Psychology,* Vol. 2, ed. L. Berkowitz (New York: Academic Press, 1965), pp. 267–99; R.J. Bies and J.F. Moag, "Interactional Justice: Communication Criteria of Fairness," in *Research on Negotiations in Organizations,* Vol. 1, ed. R.J. Lewicki, B.H. Sheppard, and M.H. Bazerman (Greenwich, CT: JAI Press, 1986), pp. 43–55; G.S. Leventhal, "The Distribution of Rewards and Resources in Groups and Organizations," in *Advances in Experimental Social Psychology,* Vol. 9, ed. L. Berkowitz and W. Walster (New York: Academic Press, 1976), pp. 91–131; G.S. Leventhal, "What Should Be Done with Equity Theory? New Approaches to the Study of Fairness in Social Relationships," in *Social Exchange: Advances in Theory and Research,* ed. K. Gergen, M. Greenberg, and R. Willis (New York: Plenum Press, 1980), pp. 27–55; and J. Thibaut and L. Walker, *Procedural Justice: A Psychological Analysis* (Hillsdale, NJ: Erlbaum, 1975).

pay, rewards, evaluations, promotions, and work assignments—are allocated using proper norms. In most business situations, the proper norm is equity, with more outcomes allocated to those who contribute more inputs (see Chapter 6 on motivation for more discussion of such issues). The equity norm is typically judged to be the fairest choice in situations in which the goal is to maximize the productivity of individual employees.[39]

However, other allocation norms become appropriate in situations in which other goals are critical. In team-based work, building harmony and solidarity in work groups can become just as important as individual productivity. In such cases, an equality norm may be judged fairer, such that all team members receive the same amount of relevant rewards.[40] The equality norm is typically used in student project groups, in which all group members receive exactly the same grade on a project, regardless of their individual productivity levels. In cases in which the welfare of a particular employee is the critical concern, a need norm may be judged fairer. For example, some organizations protect new employees from committee assignments and other extra activities, so that they can get their careers off to a productive start.

PROCEDURAL JUSTICE In addition to judging the fairness of a decision outcome, employees may consider the process that led to that outcome. **Procedural justice** reflects the perceived fairness of decision-making processes.[41] Procedural justice is fostered when authorities adhere to rules of fair process. One of those rules is voice, or giving employees a chance to express their opinions and views during the course of decision making.[42] A related rule is correctability, which provides employees with a chance to request an appeal when a procedure seems to have worked ineffectively. Research suggests that these rules improve employees' reactions to decisions,[43] largely because they give employees a sense of ownership over the decisions. Employees tend to value voice and appeals, even when they don't result in the desired outcome,[44] because they like to be heard. That is, the expression of opinions is a valued end, in and of itself, when employees believe that their opinions have been truly considered.

Aside from voice and correctability, procedural justice is fostered when authorities adhere to four rules that serve to create equal employment opportunity.[45] The consistency, bias suppression, representativeness, and accuracy rules help ensure that procedures are neutral and objective, as opposed to biased and discriminatory. These sorts of procedural rules are relevant in many areas of working life. As one example, the rules can be used to make hiring practices more fair by ensuring that interview questions are unbiased and asked in the same manner across applications. As another example, the rules can be used to make compensation practices fairer by ensuring that accurate measures of job performance are used to provide input for merit raises.

These sorts of procedural justice rules are critical because employment data suggest that gender and race continue to have significant influences on organizational decision making. Compensation data suggest that women earn 83 cents for every dollar earned by a man. Such differences are even greater in highly skilled jobs such as doctors (63 cents), lawyers (78 cents), financial analysts (69 cents), and CEOs (74 cents).[46] Some portion of the gender pay gap can be explained by the kinds of fields men and women are drawn to and the "caregiving tax" that some women pay by being more responsible for child care than male significant others. Even after accounting for such factors, however, estimates still suggest that women earn 91 cents for every dollar a man makes.[47] As a result, sex discrimination cases have risen dramatically in recent years, with each victory adding weight to existing concerns about justice. As one employment lawyer put it, "Employees already mistrust employers. So each time a case reveals a secret that was never told, employees think, 'Aha! They really are paying men more than women.' "[48]

Compensation data also suggest that African American men earn only 76 percent of what Caucasian men earn.[49] Education differences don't explain the gap because Caucasian high school dropouts are twice as likely to find jobs as African American dropouts. Such differences are likely due to procedural injustice in some form, with procedures functioning in an inconsistent, biased, and inaccurate manner across Caucasian and African American applicants. Indeed, one study of almost 9,000 personnel files in an information technology firm found that Caucasian men received bigger merit raises than minority and female employees, even when their performance evaluation ratings were identical.[50] The study's author noted, "The disparities are small but very real. And any difference is evidence of bias."

Consumer Reports serves as a good example of procedural justice in action. The magazine conducts the tests for its influential automotive ratings on its own 327-acre test site.[51] The ratings are performed by both experienced engineers and more typical drivers, while also taking into account surveys of the magazine's print and online subscribers. *Consumer Reports* helps ensure bias suppression by refusing to include advertisements in its magazine.[52] It also buys all its test cars anonymously from regular dealerships, as opposed to using the vehicles offered by automakers. It helps ensure accuracy by putting 5,000–6,000 miles on a car for as long as 10 months and taking the car through approximately 50 different tests. Indeed, to measure fuel efficiency, it installs a fuel meter directly on the gas line, rather than relying on the accuracy of the vehicle's own gauges. Finally, *Consumer Reports* helps ensure consistency by putting each vehicle through the exact same set of examinations. Although automakers have occasionally sued *Consumer Reports* to protest negative ratings, the magazine has never lost a case and has never paid a dime in settlements.

You might be wondering, "Does procedural justice really matter—don't people just care about the outcomes that they receive?" In the case of *Consumer Reports,* don't companies care just about the score their products receive, not how those scores are actually calculated? Research suggests that distributive justice and procedural justice combine to influence employee reactions, as shown in Figure 7-4.[53] It's true that when outcomes are good, people don't spend as much time worrying about how fair the process was, as illustrated by the green line in the figure, which shows that procedural justice has little impact on reactions when outcome favorability is high. However, when outcomes are bad, procedural justice becomes enormously important, as illustrated by the red line in the figure. Research shows that negative or unexpected events trigger

FIGURE 7-4   Combined Effects of Distributive and Procedural Justice

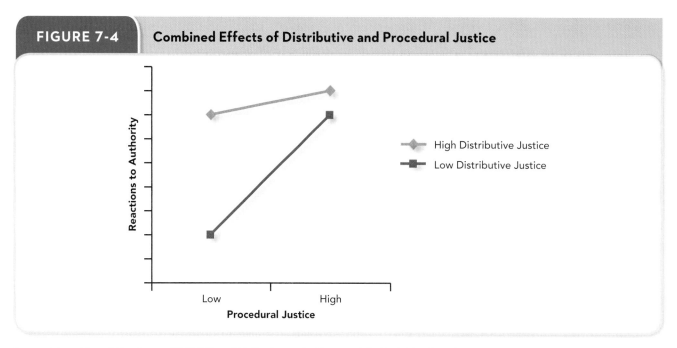

Source: Adapted from J. Brockner and B.M. Wiesenfeld, "An Integrative Framework for Explaining Reactions to Decisions: Interactive Effects of Outcomes and Procedures," *Psychological Bulletin* 120 (1996), pp. 189–208.

a thorough examination of process issues, making adherence to rules like consistency, bias suppression, and accuracy much more vital.[54]

In fact, research shows that procedural justice tends to be a stronger driver of reactions to authorities than distributive justice. For example, a meta-analysis of 183 studies showed that procedural justice was a stronger predictor of satisfaction with supervision, overall job satisfaction, and organizational commitment than distributive justice.[55] Why does the decision-making process sometimes matter more than the decision-making outcome? Likely because employees understand that outcomes come and go—some may be in your favor while others may be a bit disappointing. Procedures, however, are longer lasting and stay in place until the organization redesigns them or a new authority arrives to revise them.

INTERPERSONAL JUSTICE In addition to judging the fairness of decision outcomes and processes, employees might consider how authorities treat them as the procedures are implemented. **Interpersonal justice** reflects the perceived fairness of the treatment received by employees from authorities.[56] Interpersonal justice is fostered when authorities adhere to two particular rules. The respect rule pertains to whether authorities treat employees in a dignified and sincere manner, and the propriety rule reflects whether authorities refrain from making improper or offensive remarks. From this perspective, interpersonal *injustice* occurs when authorities are rude or disrespectful to employees, or when they refer to them with inappropriate labels.[57]

When taken to the extremes, interpersonally unjust actions create **abusive supervision,** defined as the sustained display of hostile verbal and nonverbal behaviors, excluding physical contact.[58] Our **OB on Screen** shows an example of one abusive supervisor. A national study suggests that approximately 15 percent of employees are victims of abusive behaviors, ranging from angry outbursts to public ridiculing to being used as scapegoats for negative events.[59] Estimates also indicate that such actions cost U.S. businesses around $24 billion annually due to absenteeism, health care costs, and lost productivity.[60] Employees who are abused by their supervisors report more anxiety, burnout, and strain, as well as less satisfaction with their lives in general.[61] They are also more likely to strike back at their supervisors with counterproductive behaviors—a response that may even spill over to their coworkers and the larger organization.[62]

Why are interpersonally unjust actions so damaging? One reason may be that people remember unfair acts more vividly than fair ones. A recent study asked 41 employees to complete a

WHIPLASH

You know Charlie Parker became "Bird" because Jones threw a cymbal at his head . . . see what I'm sayin'?

With those words, Professor Terence Fletcher (J. K. Simmons) hints at his teaching philosophy in *Whiplash* (Dir. Damien Chazelle, Bold Films, 2014). Fletcher is having a hallway conversation with Andrew Neiman (Miles Teller), a drummer who's about to get his first shot with the top jazz band at New York's Shaffer Conservatory. Once the conversation is over, Neiman mans the kit as the band plays *Whiplash,* a bit under-tempo to allow him to get comfortable. Unfortunately, Neiman doesn't get the tempo right, resulting in Fletcher throwing something at the 19-year old. "Why do you suppose I just hurled a chair at your head, Neiman?" asks Fletcher after Neiman peers back over his music stand. That question is followed by a painful inquiry about whether Neiman is a "rusher" or a "dragger."

© Sony Pictures Classics/Photofest

Fletcher believes the greats—like Charlie Parker—only became great because they were pushed. And his brand of pushing has all the hallmarks of abusive supervision, including profane, derogatory, and prejudicial remarks. Fletcher later wonders aloud what would have happened if a young Parker hadn't been pushed when he struggled with his saxophone. "So imagine if Jones had just said, 'Well, that's okay, Charlie . . . that was all right. Good job.' And then Charlie thinks to himself, '. . . I did do a pretty good job.' End of story. No Bird. That, to me, is an absolute tragedy . . . There are no two words in the English language more harmful than 'good job.' "

Although Fletcher's abuse does seem motivational in the short term, by making students practice harder and harder, many wind up leaving the band (and music altogether). Neiman himself struggles with keeping any balance in his life as he tries to cope with Fletcher's prodding. As the two look back on their time together, Neiman asks, "But is there a line? You know, maybe you go too far, and you discourage the next Charlie Parker from ever becoming Charlie Parker?" Answers Fletcher, "No, man, no. Because the next Charlie Parker would never be discouraged." Fortunately for them, many of Fletcher's students were.

survey on interactions with authorities and coworkers four times a day for two to three weeks.[63] Two kinds of interactions were coded—positive experiences and negative experiences—and participants also reported on their current mood (e.g., happy, pleased, sad, blue, unhappy). The results of the study showed that positive interactions were more common than negative interactions, but the effects of negative interactions on mood were five times stronger than the effects

When interpersonal injustice gets taken to the extreme, it can turn into abusive supervision. Estimates suggest that 15 percent of employees are victims of abusive behaviors at work.

© Dynamic Graphics/PictureQuest RF

of positive interactions. Such findings suggest that a violation of the respect and propriety rules looms much larger than adherence to those rules.[64]

For these reasons, some companies have taken advantage of a growing number of "civility training" programs offered by consulting firms.[65] One such program is CREW—Civility, Respect, and Engagement in the Workplace—that was developed for the Veterans Health Administration, the Washington, DC–based hospital arm of the Veterans Affairs Department. The program was administered to more than 900 workgroups over a six-month period, with the groups learning about the benefits of respectful communication and how to bring more civility to contentious situations, such as problem solving and dispute contexts. The director of organizational health for the VHA notes, "It's a simplistic formula. It's just: How do we want to treat each other?"[66] She notes that the benefits of the program have seemed to be "viral," with increased respect being contagious at the VHA.

INFORMATIONAL JUSTICE Finally, employees may consider the kind of information that authorities provide during the course of organizational decision making. **Informational justice** reflects the perceived fairness of the communications provided to employees from authorities.[67] Informational justice is fostered when authorities adhere to two particular rules. The justification rule mandates that authorities explain decision-making procedures and outcomes in a comprehensive and reasonable manner, and the truthfulness rule requires that those communications be honest and candid. Although it seems like common sense that organizations would explain decisions in a comprehensive and adequate manner, that's often not the case. For example, RadioShack, the Fort Worth, Texas–based home electronics retailer, was recently criticized for firing 400 employees via e-mail.[68] Employees at corporate headquarters received messages on a Tuesday morning saying: "The work force reduction notification is currently in progress. Unfortunately your position is one that has been eliminated." After receiving the 18-word message, employees had 30 minutes to make phone calls and say good-bye to fellow employees, before packing up their belongings in boxes and plastic bags.

These sorts of informational injustices are all too common, for a variety of reasons. One factor is that sharing bad news is the worst part of the job for most managers, leading them to distance themselves when it's time to play messenger.[69] A survey of 372 human resources professionals revealed that almost 75 percent felt stress, anxiety, and depression when they had to conduct layoffs during the economic downturn.[70] Another factor may be that managers worry about triggering a lawsuit if they comprehensively and honestly explain the reasons for a layoff, a poor evaluation, or a missed promotion. Ironically, that defense mechanism is typically counterproductive because research suggests that honest and adequate explanations are actually a powerful strategy for reducing retaliation responses against the organization.[71] In fact, low levels of informational justice can come back to haunt the organization if a wrongful termination claim is actually filed. How? Because the organization typically needs to provide performance evaluations for the terminated employee over the past few years, to show that the employee was fired for poor performance.[72] If managers refrained from offering candid and honest explanations on those evaluations, then the organization can't offer anything to justify the termination.

One study provides a particularly effective demonstration of the power of informational justice (and interpersonal justice). The study occurred in three plants of a midwestern manufacturing company that specialized in small mechanical parts for the aerospace and automotive industries.[73] The company had recently lost two of its largest contracts and was forced to cut wages by 15 percent in two of the three plants. The company was planning to offer a short, impersonal explanation for the pay cut to both of the affected plants. However, as part of a research study, the company was convinced to offer a longer, more sincere explanation at one of the plants. Theft levels were then tracked before, during, and after the 10-week pay cut using the company's standard accounting formulas for inventory "shrinkage."

The results of the study are shown in Figure 7-5. In the plant without the pay cut, no change in theft levels occurred over the 10-week period. In the plant with the short, impersonal explanation, theft rose dramatically during the pay cut, likely as a means of retaliating for perceived inequity, before falling to previous levels once the cut had passed. Importantly, in the plant with the long, sincere explanation, the rise in theft was much less significant during the pay cut, with theft levels again falling back to normal levels once the cut had ended. Clearly, the higher levels of informational and interpersonal justice were worth it from a cost-savings perspective. The difference in theft across the two plants is remarkable, given that the long, sincere explanation was only a few minutes longer than the short, impersonal explanation. What's a few extra minutes if it can save a few thousand dollars?

© Jb Reed/Bloomberg via Getty Images

RadioShack violated the norms of informational justice by laying off 400 employees in Fort Worth via a curt e-mail of 18 words.

SUMMARY Taken together, distributive, procedural, interpersonal, and informational justice can be used to describe how fairly employees are treated by authorities. When an authority adheres to the justice rules in Table 7-2, those actions provide behavioral data that the authority might be trustworthy. Indeed, studies show that all four justice forms have strong correlations with employee trust levels.[74] All else being equal, employees trust authorities who allocate outcomes

---

FIGURE 7-5   **The Effects of Justice on Theft During a Pay Cut**

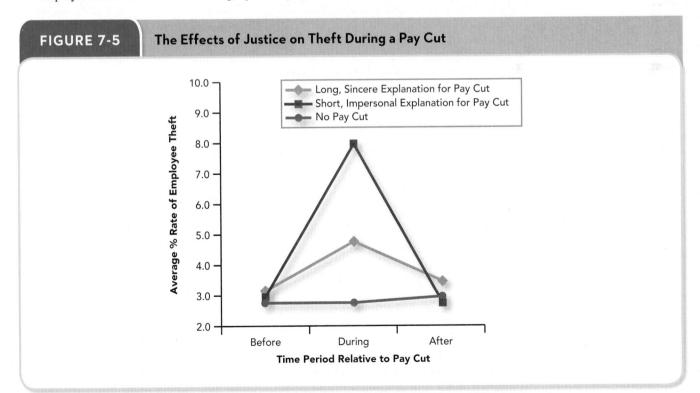

Source: Adapted from J. Greenberg, "Employee Theft as a Reaction to Underpayment Inequity: The Hidden Cost of Paycuts," *Journal of Applied Psychology* 75 (1990), pp. 561–68.

fairly; make decisions in a consistent, unbiased, and accurate way; and communicate decision-making details in a respectful, comprehensive, and honest manner. Which authorities are most likely to adhere to these sorts of rules? Research on ethics can provide some answers.

ETHICS

Research on ethics seeks to explain why people behave in a manner consistent with generally accepted norms of morality and why they sometimes violate those norms.[75] The study of business ethics has two primary threads to it. One thread is *prescriptive* in nature, with scholars in philosophy debating how people *ought* to act using various codes and principles.[76] The prescriptive model is the dominant lens in discussions of legal ethics, medical ethics, and much of economics. The second thread is *descriptive* in nature, with scholars relying on scientific studies to observe how people *tend* to act based on certain individual and situational characteristics. The descriptive model is the dominant lens in psychology. Although the differences between these two threads give the study of business ethics a certain complexity, the philosophical and empirical approaches can be integrated to develop a more complete understanding of ethical behavior.

Some studies of business ethics focus on unethical behavior—behavior that clearly violates accepted norms of morality.[77] Unethical behaviors in organizations can be directed at employees (e.g., discrimination, harassment, health and safety violations, ignoring labor laws), customers (e.g., invading privacy, violating contract terms, using false advertising, fabricating test results), financiers (e.g., falsifying financial information, misusing confidential information, trading securities based on inside information), or society as a whole (e.g., violating environmental regulations, exposing the public to safety risks, doing business with third parties who are themselves unethical).[78] How prevalent are such behaviors? Recent surveys suggest that 76 percent of employees have observed illegal or unethical conduct in their organizations within the past 12 months.[79] Those base rates may be even higher in some countries, as described in our **OB Internationally** feature.

Other studies focus on what might be termed "merely ethical" behavior—behavior that adheres to some minimally accepted standard of morality.[80] Merely ethical behaviors might include obeying labor laws and complying with formal rules and contracts. Still other studies focus on what could be called "especially ethical" behaviors—behaviors that exceed some minimally accepted standard of morality. Especially ethical behaviors might include charitable giving or **whistle-blowing,** which occurs when former or current employees expose illegal or immoral actions by their organization.[81] Whistle-blowing can be viewed as especially ethical because whistle-blowers risk potential retaliation by other members of the organization, especially when whistle-blowers lack status and power.[82] Ironically, the company often winds up benefitting from that risk taking, as whistle-blowing can bring significant improvements to the ethical culture in an organization over the long term.[83]

7.5

What is the four-component model of ethical decision making?

Why do some authorities behave unethically while others engage in ethical (or especially ethical) behaviors? One set of answers can be derived from research in social psychology. The **four-component model** of ethical decision making argues that ethical behaviors result from a multistage sequence beginning with moral awareness, continuing on to moral judgment, then to moral intent, and ultimately to ethical behavior.[84] Figure 7-6 presents an adaptation of this model. In addition to depicting the four components, the figure illustrates that unethical behavior can be triggered by characteristics of a person or the situation.[85] Put differently, and drawing on the adage "one bad apple can spoil the barrel," ethical behavior can be driven by both good versus bad apples and good versus bad barrels.[86] The sections that follow review the components of this model in more detail.

MORAL AWARENESS The first step needed to explain why an authority acts ethically is **moral awareness**, which occurs when an authority recognizes that a moral issue exists in a situation or that an ethical code or principle is relevant to the circumstance.[87] Ethical issues rarely come equipped with "red flags" that mark them as morally sensitive.[88] Sometimes authorities act unethically simply because they don't perceive that moral issues are relevant in a given situation, so the ethical merits of certain actions are never debated. For example, let's say you own a clothing retailer that specializes in fashion-forward styles at low prices. You know that Diane von Furstenberg's styles are hot this year, and your buying team just discovered a vendor that makes cheap knockoffs of those styles. Do you buy clothes from that vendor and hang them on your racks?

OB INTERNATIONALLY

If unethical actions are defined as behaviors that fall below minimum standards of morality, the key question becomes, "Whose standards of morality?" Research on business ethics across cultures reveals that different countries have different baseline levels of unethical actions. Transparency International is an organization that monitors unethical practices in countries around the world. Using data from businesspeople, risk analysts, investigative journalists, country experts, and public citizens, the organization rates countries on a scale of 1 (unethical) to 10 (ethical). Here are some of the scores from the 1999 version of the rankings:

SCORE	COUNTRY	SCORE	COUNTRY
10.0	Denmark	3.8	South Korea
9.8	Finland	3.6	Turkey
9.4	Sweden	3.4	China
9.2	Canada	3.4	Mexico
8.7	Australia	3.2	Thailand
8.6	Germany	3.0	Argentina
7.7	Hong Kong	2.9	Colombia
7.7	Ireland	2.9	India
7.5	United States	2.6	Ukraine
6.8	Israel	2.6	Venezuela
6.6	France	2.6	Vietnam
6.0	Japan	2.4	Russia
4.9	Greece	1.6	Nigeria
4.7	Italy	1.5	Cameroon

These rankings reveal the challenges involved for any multinational corporation that does business in areas at the top and bottom of the rankings. Should the company have the same ethical expectations for employees in all countries, regardless of ethical norms? For now, that seems to be the most common position. For example, the Coca-Cola Company's Code of Business Conduct "applies to all the Company's business worldwide and to all Company employees." The code is given to all employees and covers topics such as conflicts of interest, dealing with government officials, customer and supplier interactions, and political contributions. The code also describes the disciplinary actions associated with any violations of the code.

Source: D. C. Robertson, "Business Ethics Across Cultures," in *The Blackwell Handbook of Cross-Cultural Management,* ed. M.J. Gannon and K.L. Newman (Malden, MA: Blackwell, 2002), pp. 361–92.

Is there an ethical issue at play here? On the one hand, you might be tempted to say that imitation is the way that fashion trends spread—that the "gurus of style" expect their products to be copied. Besides, a skirt is a skirt, and knockoffs are part of the game in a lot of businesses. On the other hand, Diane von Furstenberg's styles are her intellectual property, and the people who work for her label put a great deal of time, effort, and talent into their clothes. It turns out this scenario has played out with Forever 21, the Los Angeles–based specialty retailer.[89] Beginning in 2004, more than 50 labels have sued Forever 21 for copying their clothes, including Diane

FIGURE 7-6   The Four-Component Model of Ethical Decision Making

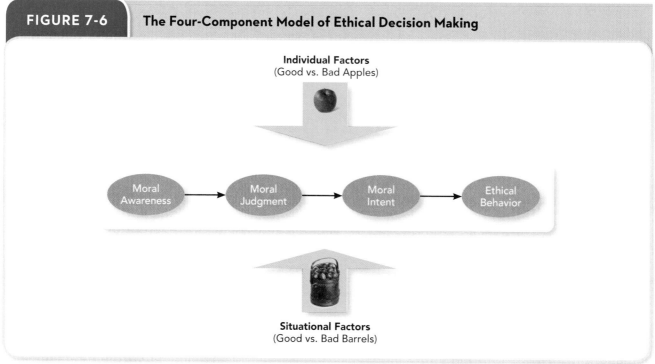

Individual Factors
(Good vs. Bad Apples)

Moral Awareness → Moral Judgment → Moral Intent → Ethical Behavior

Situational Factors
(Good vs. Bad Barrels)

Source: Adapted from J.R. Rest, *Moral Development: Advances in Research and Theory* (New York: Praeger, 1986).

von Furstenberg, Anna Sui, and Anthropologie. "Their design is swathed in mystery," notes one expert on copyright law. "But it probably looks a bit like a crime scene, with the chalk outline of the garments they're copying."[90] Such charges are difficult to prove because U.S. copyright law protects original prints and graphics, not actual designs. Forever 21 wound up settling those lawsuits, noting that the company ultimately has to trust the integrity of its clothing vendors. Indeed, one executive notes that she chooses from among 400 items a day, spending only about 90 seconds to review a piece.

Moral awareness depends in part on characteristics of the issue itself, as some issues have more built-in ethical salience than others. A concept called **moral intensity** captures the degree to which an issue has ethical urgency.[91] As described in Table 7-3, moral intensity is driven by two general concerns, both of which have more specific facets.[92] First and foremost, a particular issue is high in moral intensity if the potential for harm is perceived to be high. An act that could injure 1,000 people is more morally intense than an act that could injure 10 people, and an act that could result in death is more morally intense than an act that could result in illness.[93] Second, a particular issue is high in moral intensity if there is social pressure surrounding it. An act that violates a clear social norm is more morally intense than an act that seems similar to what everyone else is doing. In the case of Forever 21, moral intensity might seem low because selling cheap knockoffs benefits its customers, and interactions with customers are much more common and salient than interactions with designers.

Moral awareness also depends on the way authorities observe and perceive the events that happen around them. A concept called **moral attentiveness** captures the degree to which people chronically perceive and consider issues of morality during their experiences.[94] Research in cognitive psychology shows that people pay more attention to stimuli that are significant, vivid, and recognizable. Authorities who are morally attentive tend to view the world through a lens of morality, giving ethical issues a particular significance, vividness, and recognizability. That lens colors the way they identify and interpret information and also shapes the way they analyze and reflect on it. Morally attentive people are likely to report that they face several ethical dilemmas in a typical day, that many of the decisions they face have ethical consequences, that they regularly think about issues of morality, and that they enjoy pondering moral issues. In the case of Forever

TABLE 7-3	The Dimensions of Moral Intensity	
GENERAL DIMENSION	**SPECIFIC FACET**	**DESCRIPTION**
Potential for harm	Magnitude of consequences	How much harm would be done to other people?
	Probability of effect	How likely is it that the act will actually occur and that the assumed consequences will match predictions?
	Temporal immediacy	How much time will pass between the act and the onset of its consequences?
	Concentration of effect	Will the consequences be concentrated on a limited set of people, or will they be more far reaching?
Social pressure	Social consensus	How much agreement is there that the proposed act would be unethical?
	Proximity	How near (in a psychological or physical sense) is the authority to those who will be affected?

Sources: Adapted from T.M. Jones, "Ethical Decision Making by Individuals in Organizations: An Issue-Contingent Model," *Academy of Management Review* 16 (1991), pp. 366–95; and A. Singhapakdi, S.J. Vitell, and K.L. Kraft, "Moral Intensity and Ethical Decision-Making of Marketing Professionals," *Journal of Business Research* 36 (1996), pp. 245–55.

21, it may be that top management was not morally attentive enough to recognize that buying copies of more expensive designs represented an ethical issue. That premise may make some sense, given that Forever 21 has had other ethical struggles. It has settled multiple lawsuits with garment workers' groups alleging unfair business practices and wage violations. The company claims it didn't know about the conditions in its suppliers' factories, but lawyers maintain that the company squeezes suppliers so much on price that they are partially responsible for the violations.

Some business schools are taking an unusual approach to increasing moral awareness on the part of their students. New York University, the University of California at Berkeley, Purdue, and Penn State have invited convicted white-collar criminals to speak to students about their unethical actions, as well as the consequences of those actions.[95] For example, Walter Pavlo Jr. earns up to $2,500 a visit to detail the $6 million money-laundering scheme he perpetrated at MCI. The 40-year-old served two years in federal prison and is now divorced, unemployed, and living with his parents. Such testimonials can highlight the potential harm involved in unethical actions while also making students a bit more attentive to ethical issues. Although some professors consider the payment of convicted felons to be an ethical issue in its own right, part of what Pavlo earns goes to make restitution for his crimes. One professor at Penn State summarizes, "Here's a real person telling students what happened to his life. I don't think there's any substitute for that."[96]

MORAL JUDGMENT Some authorities may recognize that a moral issue exists in a given situation but then be unable to determine whether a given course of action is right or wrong. The second step needed to explain why an authority acts ethically is therefore **moral judgment,** which reflects the process people use to determine whether a particular course of action is ethical or unethical.[97] One of the most important factors influencing moral judgment is described in Kohlberg's theory of **cognitive moral development.**[98] This theory argues that as people age and mature, they move through various stages of moral development—each more mature and sophisticated than the prior one. All else equal, authorities who operate at more mature stages of moral development should demonstrate better moral judgment. You might wonder how the moral development of a person can be measured. One approach is to

Forever 21, a Los Angeles–based specialty retailer, has been sued by more than 50 labels for allegedly stealing their designs in order to sell significantly cheaper versions to its customers.

© Kervork Djansezian/AP Images

give people a series of ethical dilemmas like the one in Table 7-4, then ask questions to gain insights into their decision-making process.[99]

According to Kohlberg, people begin their moral development at the *preconventional* stage.[100] At this stage, right versus wrong is viewed in terms of the consequences of various actions for the individual. For example, children seek to avoid punishment for its own sake, regardless of any concern about moral order. Similarly, children obey adults for its own sake, regardless of the respect or wisdom shown by those adults. Over time, the desire to obtain pleasure and avoid pain expands to the formation of "you scratch my back, I'll scratch yours" sort of exchanges. Such relationships remain self-interested however, with little concern for loyalty, gratitude, or fairness. In the case of the ethical dilemma in Table 7-4, viewing question 1 as one of the most important issues would signal preconventional thinking.

As people mature, their moral judgment reaches the *conventional* stage.[101] At this stage, right versus wrong is referenced to the expectations of one's family and one's society. At first, people seek the approval of friends and family members, conforming to stereotypes about what's right. Question 2 in Table 7-4 reflects this sort of priority. Over time, people come to emphasize the laws, rules, and orders that govern society. Concepts such as doing one's duty and maintaining the social order come to be valued for their own sakes. Question 3 reflects this level of moral sophistication. Research suggests that most adults find themselves at the conventional stage.[102] That positioning is relevant to organizations because it shows that moral judgment can be influenced by organizational policies, practices, and norms.

The most sophisticated moral thinkers reach the *principled* (or postconventional) stage.[103] At this stage, right versus wrong is referenced to a set of defined, established moral principles. Research suggests that fewer than 20 percent of Americans reach this principled stage.[104] Philosophers have identified a number of **moral principles** that serve as prescriptive guides for making moral judgments, with some of the most influential shown in Table 7-5. Rather than viewing a given principle as the single, best lens for making decisions, it's better to view the principles as a prism for shedding light on a given situation from a number of different angles.[105] The consequentialist principles in Table 7-5 judge the morality of an action according to its goals, aims, or outcomes (these principles are sometimes termed "teleological," after the Greek word

TABLE 7-4	Ethical Dilemma Used to Assess Moral Development

Pat is responsible for providing expenditure estimates for his/her unit to the controller in his/her company who then determines the budget for all units in the company. Upper management has always emphasized the importance of providing timely and accurate financial estimates, and they have backed up this policy by disciplining managers for inaccurate or late estimates. Pat recently realized that the figures that he/she supplied contained a mistake. The mistake was that an expense was projected to be larger than it should have been. It will not affect the ability of the company to stay within the budget. However, the money could be used to cover other company expenditures. Up to this point, no one else has identified the mistake and it is unlikely that they will. Should Pat report the mistake?

On a scale from 1 = *No Importance* to 5 = *Great Importance*, rate how important each of the following questions are to your decision:

1. Could Pat receive a harsher punishment if the company finds the mistake without his/her help?
2. Whether Pat's subordinates and peers would lose faith in Pat if Pat is caught instead of reporting the mistake himself/herself.
3. Whether or not company policy ought to be respected by all employees.
4. Would reporting the mistake do any good for Pat or society?
5. What values Pat has set for himself/herself in his/her personal code of behavior?

Source: From Greg Loviscky, *Journal of Business Ethics,* "Assessing Managers' Ethical Decision-Making: An Objective Measure of Managerial Moral Judgment," Vol. 73. Copyright © 2007, Springer Netherlands. Reprinted with permission.

for "goal").[106] Question 4 in Table 7-4 reflects these sorts of concerns. The nonconsequentialist principles judge the morality of an action solely on its intrinsic desirability (these principles are sometimes termed "deontological," after the Greek word for "duty," or "formalist," due to their emphasis on formalized codes and standards). Viewing question 5 as one of the most important issues in the dilemma would signal nonconsequentialist thinking.

Returning to the Forever 21 example, a utilitarian analysis would focus on whether the "greatest happiness" was created by giving their customers access to cutting-edge designs at cheap prices, even if doing so harmed the profitability of the labels. An egoistic analysis would focus on whether buying "copycat" clothes from vendors boosted the short-term and long-term interests of the company. Is selling those clothes vital to the company's mission, or are the risks to the reputation and brand of the company severe enough that a change in course is warranted? Although the takeaways from those analyses may be debatable, the judgment of the three remaining principles seems clearer. From the perspective of the ethics of duties, society would clearly be harmed if all companies copied the intellectual property of their competitors, though some customers would likely endorse the company's practices. From an ethics of rights perspective, Forever 21's actions can be viewed as disrespecting the designers' rights to consent and expression (and justice, given that they were offered no compensation for the use of their intellectual property). Finally, an analysis using virtue ethics would suggest that Forever 21's actions lacked the virtue of honesty.

MORAL INTENT Assuming that an authority recognizes that a moral issue exists in a situation and possesses the cognitive moral development to choose the right course of action, one step remains: The authority has to *want* to act ethically. **Moral intent** reflects an authority's degree of commitment to the moral course of action.[107] The distinction between awareness or judgment on the one hand and intent on the other is important, because many unethical people know and understand that what they're doing is wrong—they just choose to do it anyway. Why? Sometimes situational factors encourage people to go against their moral convictions. For example, organizations may possess unethical cultures, where violations of moral codes become the rule rather than the exception (see Chapter 16 on organizational culture for more discussion of such issues).[108] As another

TABLE 7-5	Moral Principles Used in the Principled Stage	
TYPE OF PRINCIPLE	**SPECIFIC PRINCIPLE**	**DESCRIPTION (AND CONTRIBUTORS)**
Consequentialist	Utilitarianism	An act is morally right if it results in the greatest amount of good for the greatest number of people—sometimes termed the "greatest happiness principle" (Jeremy Bentham, John Stuart Mill).
	Egoism	An act is morally right if the decision maker freely decides to pursue either short-term or long-term interests. Markets are purported to limit the degree to which one egoist's interests harm the interests of another (Adam Smith).
Nonconsequentialist	Ethics of duties	An act is morally right if it fulfills the "categorical imperative"—an unambiguously explicit set of three crucial maxims: (a) the act should be performable by everyone with no harm to society; (b) the act should respect human dignity; (c) the act should be endorsable by others (Immanuel Kant).
	Ethics of rights	An act is morally right if it respects the natural rights of others, such as the right to life, liberty, justice, expression, association, consent, privacy, and education (John Locke, John Rawls).
	Virtue ethics	An act is morally right if it allows the decision maker to lead a "good life" by adhering to virtues like wisdom, honesty, courage, friendship, mercy, loyalty, modesty, and patience (Aristotle).

Source: Adapted from A. Crane and D. Matten, *Business Ethics* (New York: Oxford University Press, 2007).

example, economic pressures from assigned goals or specific incentives can encourage people to set aside their moral judgment, at least for a time.[109]

What explains the ability of some people to resist situational pressures and stay true to their moral judgment? One factor is **moral identity**—the degree to which a person self-identifies as a moral person.[110] Our self-concepts have a number of components to them: We may define ourselves by what we do, where we come from, what our family status is, or what cultural or ethnic groups we belong to. People with strong moral identities define themselves as compassionate, generous, honest, kind, fair, and hardworking. Their emotional well-being and sense of self is wrapped up in living up to those virtues. Moreover, the actions they take in their daily life—from the things they buy, to the hobbies they have, to the groups they join—are viewed as symbols of those virtues. Research suggests that people with strong moral identities volunteer more for charitable work and donate more to charity drives.[111] Research also suggests that moral identity "moderates" the effects of moral judgment on ethical behavior. Recall that in the language of theory diagrams, moderators affect the strength of the relationship between two variables. For example, one study shows that managers who emphasize specific ethics principles are less likely to engage in unethical behaviors (e.g., calling in sick to take a day off, ignoring others' unethical actions), but only when they define themselves as a moral person.[112] When morality is not an important piece of their identity, their moral principles have no relationship with their actual behavior.

SUMMARY Taken together, the stages of the four-component model can be used to explain why authorities act in an ethical or unethical manner. When authorities are morally aware, when they have sophisticated moral judgment, and when they possess strong moral intent, chances are their actions will tend to be ethical. By extension, those authorities should attend more to the rules of distributive, procedural, interpersonal, and informational justice, because treating employees fairly is itself an ethical act.[113] Those authorities should also be viewed as trustworthy, in that moral awareness, judgment, and intent should result in higher levels of both benevolence and integrity.

SUMMARY: WHY ARE SOME AUTHORITIES MORE TRUSTED THAN OTHERS?

So what explains why some authorities are more trusted than others? As shown in Figure 7-7, answering that question requires understanding the different sources in which trust can be rooted, including dispositions, cognitions, and affect. Disposition-based trust is rooted in an individual's trust propensity, whereas affect-based trust is rooted in a fondness for the authority.

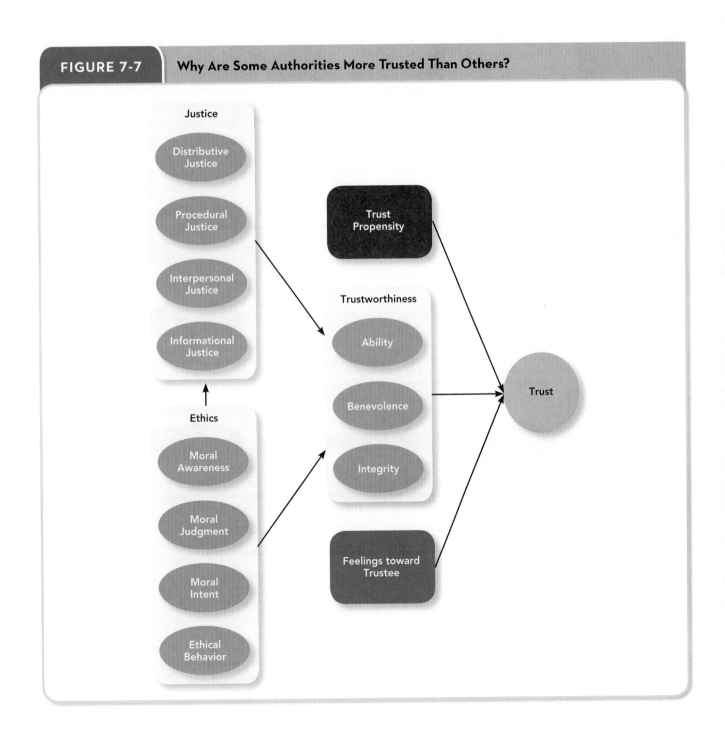

| FIGURE 7-7 | Why Are Some Authorities More Trusted Than Others? |

Cognition-based trust is driven by perceptions of trustworthiness, as employees attempt to assess the ability, benevolence, and integrity of authorities. Unfortunately, it's often difficult to gauge trustworthiness accurately, so employees instead look to more observable behaviors that can be used as indirect evidence of trustworthiness. Those behaviors may center on the justice of authorities, with employees considering the distributive, procedural, interpersonal, and informational justice they have experienced at work. The justice and general trustworthiness of authorities in turn can be explained by authorities' own moral awareness, moral judgment, and moral intent.

HOW IMPORTANT IS TRUST?

7.6

How does trust affect job performance and organizational commitment?

Does trust have a significant impact on the two primary outcomes in our integrative model of OB—does it correlate with job performance and organizational commitment? Figure 7-8 summarizes the research evidence linking trust to job performance and organizational commitment. The figure reveals that trust does affect job performance. Why? One reason is that trust is moderately correlated with task performance. A study of employees in eight plants of a tool manufacturing company sheds some light on why trust benefits task performance.[114] The study gave employees survey measures of their trust in two different authorities: their plant's manager and the company's top management team. Both trust measures were significant predictors of employees' **ability to focus,** which reflects the degree to which employees can devote their attention to work, as opposed to "covering their backside," "playing politics," and "keeping an eye on the boss." The ability to focus is clearly vital to task performance in many jobs, particularly when job duties become more complex.

FIGURE 7-8   **Effects of Trust on Performance and Commitment**

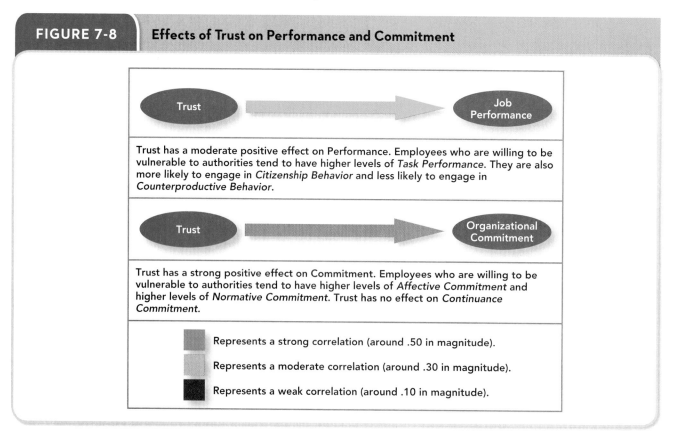

Sources: K.T. Dirks and D.L. Ferrin, "Trust in Leadership: Meta-Analytic Findings and Implications for Research and Practice," *Journal of Applied Psychology* 87 (2002), pp. 611–28; and J.A. Colquitt, B.A. Scott, and J.A. LePine, "Trust, Trustworthiness, and Trust Propensity: A Meta-Analytic Test of Their Unique Relationships with Risk Taking and Job Performance," *Journal of Applied Psychology* 92 (2007), pp. 909–27.

Trust also influences citizenship behavior and counterproductive behavior. Why? One reason is that the willingness to accept vulnerability changes the nature of the employee–employer relationship. Employees who don't trust their authorities have **economic exchange** relationships that are based on narrowly defined, quid pro quo obligations that are specified in advance and have an explicit repayment schedule.[115] Economic exchanges are impersonal and resemble contractual agreements, such that employees agree to fulfill the duties in their job description in exchange for financial compensation. As trust increases, **social exchange** relationships develop that are based on vaguely defined obligations that are open-ended and long term in their repayment schedule.[116] Social exchanges are characterized by mutual investment, such that employees agree to go above and beyond their duties in exchange for fair and proper treatment by authorities. In social exchange contexts, employees are willing to engage in beneficial behaviors because they trust that those efforts will eventually be rewarded (see Chapter 3 on organizational commitment for more discussion of such issues).

Figure 7-8 also reveals that trust affects organizational commitment. Why? One reason is that trusting an authority increases the likelihood that an emotional bond will develop,[117] particularly if that trust is rooted in positive feelings for the authority. Trusting an authority also makes it more likely that a sense of obligation will develop, because employees feel more confident that the authority deserves that obligation. When negative events occur, employees who trust the authority are willing to accept the vulnerability that comes with continued employment,[118] remaining confident in their belief that the situation will eventually improve.

APPLICATION: SOCIAL RESPONSIBILITY

Now that you understand the factors that drive trust in authorities and the importance of trust levels to performance and commitment, we turn our attention to a very practical question: "How can organizations become more trustworthy?" Certainly that's a big question with no single answer. However, one strategy is to focus the organization's attention on **corporate social responsibility,** a perspective that acknowledges that the responsibilities of a business encompass the economic, legal, ethical, and citizenship expectations of society.[119] This perspective maintains the belief that the foundation of any business is profitability, because organizations must fulfill their economic responsibilities to their employees and their shareholders. However, the social responsibility lens supplements that belief by arguing that the company's obligations do not end with profit maximization.

 7.7

What steps can organizations take to become more trustworthy?

The legal component of corporate social responsibility argues that the law represents society's codification of right and wrong and must therefore be followed.[120] Fulfilling this component speaks to the integrity of the organization and suggests that it has reached the conventional level of moral development. Further violations of intellectual property or labor laws on Forever 21's part would signal a breach of this component, so protecting its reputation will likely require an emphasis on the origins of vendor's designs and a monitoring of their factory conditions. Many organizations turn to compliance officers to police the legality of their operations. For example, Computer Associates International, a New York–based maker of computer security software, recently installed a new compliance officer.[121] As part of a series of reforms to avoid a trial over accounting fraud, the company gave its new officer, who was a former chief trial attorney for the U.S. Navy, unprecedented power. The officer has direct access to the CEO, can go over the CEO's head if need be, and has the authority to fire managers and employees who violate company guidelines.

The ethical component of corporate social responsibility argues that organizations have an obligation to do what is right, just, and fair and to avoid harm.[122] Fulfilling this component is relevant to the benevolence and integrity of the organization and suggests that it has reached the principled level of moral development.[123] Regardless of its legal implications, the way Forever 21 manages its relationships with its vendors speaks to the ethical makeup of its culture. What can organizations do to improve that ethical makeup? J.M. Smuckers, the Orrville, Ohio–based food and beverage maker, requires all of its 3,500 employees to attend training sessions on moral awareness and moral judgment. Employees go through programs every 3–5 years and sign a nine-page ethics statement annually. That statement, which the company treats as a living document, spells out the codes and principles that Smuckers employees can use to navigate moral dilemmas.

The citizenship component of corporate social responsibility argues that organizations should contribute resources to improve the quality of life in the communities in which they work.[124] Sometimes this component involves philanthropic efforts, in which donations of time or cash are given to charitable groups. At Home Depot, for example, 50,000 of its 325,000 employees donated a total of 2 million hours to community groups in a single year.[125] The citizenship component may also involve efforts geared toward environmental sustainability. On that front, a number of notable companies, from Nike to Walmart to General Electric, have focused on adopting "green" manufacturing processes.[126] Walmart has taken steps to reduce waste and inefficiency, an important goal given that the company is the nation's largest private user of electricity.[127] General Electric issues an annual "citizenship report" to highlight several aspects of its corporate social responsibility, from increases in volunteer hours to efforts to reduce air pollution.[128]

TAKEAWAYS

7.1   Trust is the willingness to be vulnerable to an authority based on positive expectations about the authority's actions and intentions. Justice reflects the perceived fairness of an authority's decision making and can be used to explain why employees judge some authorities as more trustworthy than others. Ethics reflects the degree to which the behaviors of an authority are in accordance with generally accepted moral norms and can be used to explain why authorities choose to act in a trustworthy manner.

7.2   Trust can be disposition-based, meaning that one's personality includes a general propensity to trust others. Trust can also be cognition-based, meaning that it's rooted in a rational assessment of the authority's trustworthiness. Finally, trust can be affect-based, meaning that it's rooted in feelings toward the authority that go beyond any rational assessment of trustworthiness.

7.3   Trustworthiness is judged along three dimensions. Ability reflects the skills, competencies, and areas of expertise that an authority possesses. Benevolence is the degree to which an authority wants to do good for the trustor, apart from any selfish or profit-centered motives. Integrity is the degree to which an authority adheres to a set of values and principles that the trustor finds acceptable.

7.4   The fairness of an authority's decision making can be judged along four dimensions. Distributive justice reflects the perceived fairness of decision-making outcomes. Procedural justice reflects the perceived fairness of decision-making processes. Interpersonal justice reflects the perceived fairness of the treatment received by employees from authorities. Informational justice reflects the perceived fairness of the communications provided to employees from authorities.

7.5   The four-component model of ethical decision making argues that ethical behavior depends on three concepts. Moral awareness reflects whether an authority recognizes that a moral issue exists in a situation. Moral judgment reflects whether the authority can accurately identify the "right" course of action. Moral intent reflects an authority's degree of commitment to the moral course of action.

7.6   Trust has a moderate positive relationship with job performance and a strong positive relationship with organizational commitment.

7.7   Organizations can become more trustworthy by emphasizing corporate social responsibility, a perspective that acknowledges that the responsibilities of a business encompass the economic, legal, ethical, and citizenship expectations of society.

KEY TERMS

- Reputation — *p. 198*
- Trust — *p. 198*
- Justice — *p. 199*
- Ethics — *p. 199*
- Disposition-based trust — *p. 200*
- Cognition-based trust — *p. 200*
- Affect-based trust — *p. 200*
- Trust propensity — *p. 200*
- Trustworthiness — *p. 202*
- Ability — *p. 203*
- Benevolence — *p. 203*
- Integrity — *p. 203*
- Distributive justice — *p. 205*
- Procedural justice — *p. 206*
- Interpersonal justice — *p. 208*
- Abusive supervision — *p. 208*
- Informational justice — *p. 210*
- Whistle-blowing — *p. 212*
- Four-component model — *p. 212*
- Moral awareness — *p. 212*
- Moral intensity — *p. 214*
- Moral attentiveness — *p. 214*
- Moral judgment — *p. 215*
- Cognitive moral development — *p. 215*
- Moral principles — *p. 216*
- Moral intent — *p. 217*
- Moral identity — *p. 218*
- Ability to focus — *p. 220*
- Economic exchange — *p. 221*
- Social exchange — *p. 221*
- Corporate social responsibility — *p. 221*

DISCUSSION QUESTIONS

7.1 Which would be more damaging in organizational life—being too trusting or not being trusting enough? Why do you feel that way?

7.2 Consider the three dimensions of trustworthiness (ability, benevolence, and integrity). Which of those dimensions would be most important when deciding whether to trust your boss? What about when deciding whether to trust a friend? If your two answers differ, why do they?

7.3 Putting yourself in the shoes of a manager, which of the four justice dimensions (distributive, procedural, interpersonal, informational) would you find most difficult to maximize? Which would be the easiest to maximize?

7.4 Which component of ethical decision making do you believe best explains student cheating: moral awareness, moral judgment, or moral intent? Why do you feel that way?

7.5 Assume you were applying for a job at a company known for its corporate social responsibility. How important would that be to you when deciding whether to accept a job offer?

CASE: UBER

It's common for a disruptive startup to find controversy. Uber, however, seems to have earned more than its share as its reach has broadened—opening up doors for competitors while hindering its reputation among its drivers and the business press. For example, Lyft—a ride-sharing service with its own app—seized on the surge pricing issue by branding itself as "your friend with a car." Kalanick himself outraged Uber's drivers by looking ahead to driverless car technology, suggesting, "Once we get rid of the dude in the car, Uber will be cheaper." Such reputational issues may not seem like much when Uber is dominating its market. Still, technologies can be copied and market share leads can eventually be lost. At that point, customers may choose the most trustworthy service and traditional cabbies might migrate to the company that values them the most.

One of Uber's most public missteps was directed at the business press—a group that can have a significant impact on the reputation of any company. At a dinner in New York attended by policy and media figures, Uber's senior vice president of business, Emil Michael, was reacting to some of the unflattering articles that had been written about the company. According to reports, he floated the idea of spending a million dollars to hire opposition researchers to look into the personal lives and families of business journalists. The remarks were chilling, of course, given that Uber has data on pickup and dropoff locations for its clients. Once the controversy hit, Michael clarified things with this statement: "The remarks attributed to me at a private dinner—borne out of frustration during an informal debate over what I feel is sensationalistic media coverage of the company I am proud to work for—do not reflect my actual views and have no relation to the company's views or approach. They were wrong no matter the circumstance and I regret them." Still, the comments and resulting fallout deepened concerns about what Uber can do with its cache of data on user habits and whereabouts.

There are signs that Uber has begun to attend more carefully to its reputation. For example, it recently launched a program that partners with General Motors, Toyota, and Ford that allows drivers to borrow money at better rates. Uber serves as a middleman of sorts between drivers who may have subpar credit and the car salespeople and lenders they are shopping with. This initiative is meant to get drivers on the streets in Uber-worthy vehicles sooner, while allowing drivers to turn a profit more quickly. Here's the interesting part: Uber takes no commission on these transactions when it easily could. Perhaps it feels that the goodwill the program generates with its drivers is worth more than the economic gain of such transactions.

7.1 In general, do you think potential customers are aware of the broader reputational issues faced by the companies who make their products and services? How sensitive are you to such issues?

7.2 How sensitive do you think employees are to the sometimes controversial statements that might be made by their CEOs? How important are CEO comments to an employee's own sense of the trustworthiness of the organization?

7.3 One of the ethical challenges faced by Uber—concerns about the privacy and use of the user data it collects—is shared by many tech firms. Is this the type of issue that will decrease in importance over time, with customers being desensitized to it? Or will it instead grow in importance?

Sources: J. Heimans and H. Timms, "Understanding 'New Power,'" *Harvard Business Review,* December, 2014; J. Hempel, "Hey, Taxi Company, You Talkin' to Me?" *Fortune,* October 7, 2013; A. Lashinsky, "Uber Banks on World Domination," *Fortune,* October 6, 2012; E. Porteus, "Invasion of the Taxi Snatchers," *Bloomberg Businessweek,* February 24–March 2, 2015; and B. Smith, "Uber Executives Suggest Digging Up Dirt on Journalists," *BuzzFeed,* November 17, 2014.

EXERCISE: UNETHICAL BEHAVIOR

The purpose of this exercise is to explore how authorities can prevent unethical behaviors on the part of their employees. This exercise uses groups, so your instructor will either assign you to a group or ask you to create your own group. The exercise has the following steps:

7.1 Read the following scenario:

Alex Grant recently graduated from college and is excited to be starting his first job as a store manager for The Grocery Cart, a large supermarket chain. The company has a very good management training program, and it is one of the fastest growing chains in the nation. If Alex does well managing his first store, there are a number of promising advancement opportunities in the company. After completing the store management training program,

Alex met with Regina Hill, his area supervisor. She informed Alex that he would be taking charge of a medium-volume store ($250,000 in sales/week) in an upper-class neighborhood. This store had been operating without a store manager for the past six months. The store had also not made a profit in any of the monthly financial reports for the last year.

Hill also shared the following information with Alex: Because the store has been without a store manager for the last six months, the assistant manager (Drew Smith) has been in charge. Drew is known for being highly competent and a solid performer. However, there have been complaints that he is frequently rude to employees and insults and ridicules them whenever they make mistakes. Turnover among sales clerks and cashiers at this store has been somewhat higher than in other stores in the area. The average pay of clerks and cashiers is $7.25/hour. The last two semiannual inventories at this store showed significant losses. There has been a large amount of theft from the store stockroom (an area where only employees are allowed). Given that the store has generally done well in sales (compared with others in the area) and that most expenses seem well under control, Hill believes that the profitability problem for this store is primarily due to theft. Therefore, she suggested that Alex's plans for the store should focus on this priority over any others.

7.2   As a manager, what steps should Alex take to reduce employee theft? Come up with a list of three ideas. Elect a group member to write the group's three ideas on the board or on a transparency.

7.3   Now read the following scenario:

When Alex arrived for his first day of work in his new store, he saw that Drew was in the process of terminating an employee (Rudy Johnson) who had been caught stealing. Alex immediately went to the break room of the store where the termination interview was being conducted to learn more about the situation. Drew informed Alex that Rudy had been a grocery clerk for the past six weeks and that he had apparently figured out how to tell if the alarms to the stockroom doors were off. Rudy would then open the back stockroom doors and stack cases of beer outside the store to pick up after his shift. After Drew caught Rudy doing this, Drew had a conversation with one of his friends who works as a restaurant manager down the street. Drew's friend noted that he had hired Rudy a few months ago and that he'd been caught stealing there too.

Turning to Rudy, Drew asked, "So, Rudy, what do you have to say for yourself?" Rudy quickly replied: "Look here, [expletive], you don't pay me enough to work here and put up with this garbage. In fact, you're always riding everyone like they're your personal servant or something. So I was trying to get some beer. I've seen you let stockers take home damaged merchandise a dozen times. So just because they cut open a box of cookies, which we all know they do on purpose, they get to take stuff home for free. For that matter, we've all seen you do the same thing! I've never seen you make a big deal about this stuff before. Why can't I get a few cases of beer? What's the big deal?"

7.4   Do these events give you any additional insights into how to decrease employee theft in this store? If so, elect a group member to write an additional one or two reasons in your spot on the board or on your transparency.

7.5   Class discussion (whether in groups or as a class) should center on whether the theft that's occurring at The Grocery Cart reveals a problem of moral awareness, moral judgment, or moral intent. In addition, does the theft point to a problem with "bad apples," a "bad barrel," or both?

Source: Adapted from E.C. Tomlinson, "Teaching the Interactionist Model of Ethics," Journal of Management Education 33 (2009), pp. 142–65.

ENDNOTES

7.1 Rindova, V.P.; I.O. Williamson; A.P. Petkova; and J.M. Sever. "Being Good or Being Known: An Empirical Examination of the Dimensions, Antecedents, and Consequences of Organizational Reputation." *Academy of Management Journal* 48 (2005), pp. 1033–49.

7.2 Frauenheim, E. "Does Reputation Matter?" *Workforce Management,* November 20, 2006, pp. 22–26.

7.3 Ibid.

7.4 Mayer, R.C.; J.H. Davis; and F.D. Schoorman. "An Integrative Model of Organizational Trust." *Academy of Management Review* 20 (1995), pp. 709–34; and Rousseau, D.M.; S.B. Sitkin; R.S. Burt; and C. Camerer. "Not So Different After All: A Cross-Discipline View of Trust." *Academy of Management Review* 23 (1998), pp. 393–404.

7.5 Kiley, D., and B. Helm. "The Great Trust Offensive." *BusinessWeek,* September 29, 2008, pp. 38–41.

7.6 Greenberg, J. "A Taxonomy of Organizational Justice Theories." *Academy of Management Review* 12 (1987), pp. 9–22.

7.7 Lind, E.A. "Fairness Heuristic Theory: Justice Judgments as Pivotal Cognitions in Organizational Relations." In *Advances in Organizational Justice,* ed. J. Greenberg and R. Cropanzano. Stanford, CA: Stanford University Press, 2001, pp. 56–88; Van den Bos, K. "Fairness Heuristic Theory: Assessing the Information to Which People Are Reacting Has a Pivotal Role in Understanding Organizational Justice." In *Theoretical and Cultural Perspectives on Organizational Justice,* ed. S. Gilliland, D. Steiner, and D. Skarlicki. Greenwich, CT: Information Age, 2001, pp. 63–84; and Van den Bos, K.; E.A. Lind; and H.A.M. Wilke. "The Psychology of Procedural and Distributive Justice Viewed from the Perspective of Fairness Heuristic Theory." In *Justice in the Workplace,* Vol. 2, ed. R. Cropanzano. Mahwah, NJ: Erlbaum, 2001, pp. 49–66.

7.8 Treviño, L.K.; G.R. Weaver; and S.J. Reynolds. "Behavioral Ethics in Organizations: A Review." *Journal of Management* 32 (2006), pp. 951–90.

7.9 McAllister, D.J. "Affect- and Cognition-Based Trust as Foundations for Interpersonal Cooperation in Organizations." *Academy of Management Journal* 38 (1995), pp. 24–59.

7.10 Ibid.

7.11 Mayer et al., "An Integrative Model"; Rotter, J.B. "A New Scale for the Measurement of Interpersonal Trust." *Journal of Personality* 35 (1967), pp. 651–65; Rotter, J.B. "Generalized Expectancies for Interpersonal Trust." *American Psychologist* 26 (1971), pp. 443–52; and Rotter, J.B. "Interpersonal Trust, Trustworthiness, and Gullibility." *American Psychologist* 35 (1980), pp. 1–7.

7.12 Rosenberg, M. "Misanthropy and Political Ideology." *American Sociological Review* 21 (1956), pp. 690–95; and Wrightsman Jr., L.S. "Measurement of Philosophies of Human Nature." *Psychological Reports* 14 (1964), pp. 743–51.

7.13 Mayer et al., "An Integrative Model."

7.14 Jones, W.H.; L.L. Couch; and S. Scott. "Trust and Betrayal: The Psychology of Getting Along and Getting Ahead." In *Handbook of Personality Psychology,* ed. R. Hogan, J.S. Johnson, and S.R. Briggs. San Diego, CA: Academic Press, 1997, pp. 465–82.

7.15 Stack, L.C. "Trust." In *Dimensionality of Personality,* ed. H. London and J.E. Exner Jr. New York: Wiley, 1978, pp. 561–99.

7.16 Webb, W.M., and P. Worchel. "Trust and Distrust." In *Psychology of Intergroup Relations,* ed. S. Worchel and W.G. Austin. Chicago: Nelson-Hall, 1986, pp. 213–28; and Erickson, E.H. *Childhood and Society,* 2nd ed. New York: Norton, 1963.

7.17 Stack, "Trust."

7.18 Mayer et al., "An Integrative Model."

7.19 McAllister, "Affect- and Cognition-Based Trust as Foundations for Interpersonal Cooperation in Organizations"; and Lewicki, R.J., and B.B. Bunker. "Developing and Maintaining Trust in Work Relationships." In *Trust in Organizations: Frontiers of Theory and Research,* ed. R.M. Kramer and T.R. Tyler. Thousand Oaks, CA: Sage, 1996, pp. 114–39.

7.20 Mayer et al., "An Integrative Model."

7.21 Ibid.; and Gabarro, J.J. "The Development of Trust, Influence, and Expectations." In *Interpersonal Behavior: Communication and Understanding in Relationships,* ed. G. Athos and J.J. Gabarro. Englewood Cliffs, NJ: Prentice Hall, 1978, pp. 290–303.

7.22 Mayer et al., "An Integrative Model."

7.23 Ibid.

7.24 Marquez, J. "Kindness Pays . . . Or Does It?" *Workforce Management,* June 25, 2007, pp. 41–49.

7.25 Ibid.

7.26 Mayer et al., "An Integrative Model."

7.27 Wright, T.A., and J. Goodstein. "Character Is Not 'Dead' in Management Research: A Review of Individual Character and Organizational-Level Virtue." *Journal of Management* 33 (2007), pp. 928–58; and Gabarro, "The Development of Trust, Influence, and Expectations."

7.28 Mayer et al., "An Integrative Model"; Simons, T. "Behavioral Integrity: The Perceived Alignment between Managers' Words and Deeds as a Research Focus." *Organization Science* 13 (2002), pp. 18–35; and Dineen, B.R.; R.J. Lewicki; and E.C. Tomlinson. "Supervisory Guidance and Behavioral Integrity: Relationships with Employee Citizenship and Deviant Behavior." *Journal of Applied Psychology* 91 (2006), pp. 622–35.

7.29 Dineen et al., "Supervisory Guidance"; and Bates, S. "Poll: Employees Skeptical about Management Actions." *HR Magazine,* June 2002, p. 12.

7.30 Lencioni, P. "The Power of Saying 'We Blew It.'" *Bloomberg Businessweek,* February 22, 2010, p. 84.

7.31 Penenberg, A.L. "Doctor Love." *Fast Company,* July/August 2010, pp. 78–83, 113.

7.32 Naquin, C. E.; T.R. Kurtzerg; and L.Y. Belkin. "The Finer Points of Lying Online: E-mail Versus Pen and Paper." *Journal of Applied Psychology* 95 (2010), pp. 387–94.

7.33 Stead, D. ". . . And I Invented Velcro." *BusinessWeek,* August 4, 2008, p. 15.

7.34 Penenberg, "Doctor Love."

7.35 McAllister, "Affect- and Cognition-Based Trust"; Lewicki and Bunker, "Developing and Maintaining Trust"; and Lewis, J.D., and A. Weigert. "Trust as a Social Reality." *Social Forces* 63 (1985), pp. 967–85.

7.36 McAllister, "Affect- and Cognition-Based Trust."

7.37 Lind, "Fairness Heuristic Theory: Assessing"; Van den Bos, "Fairness Heuristic Theory: Justice"; and Van den Bos et al., "The Psychology of Procedural and Distributive Justice."

7.38 Adams, J.S. "Inequity in Social Exchange." In *Advances in Experimental Social Psychology,* Vol. 2, ed. L. Berkowitz. New York: Academic Press, 1965, pp. 267–99; and Leventhal, G.S. "The Distribution of Rewards and Resources in Groups and Organizations." In *Advances in Experimental Social Psychology,* Vol. 9, ed. L. Berkowitz and W. Walster. New York: Academic Press, 1976, pp. 91–131.

7.39 Leventhal, "The Distribution of Rewards."

7.40 Ibid.

7.41 Leventhal, G.S. "What Should Be Done with Equity Theory? New Approaches to the Study of Fairness in Social Relationships." In *Social Exchange: Advances in Theory and Research,* ed. K. Gergen, M. Greenberg, and R. Willis. New York: Plenum Press, 1980, pp. 27–55; and Thibaut, J., and L. Walker. *Procedural Justice: A Psychological Analysis.* Hillsdale, NJ: Erlbaum, 1975.

7.42 Folger, R. "Distributive and Procedural Justice: Combined Impact of 'Voice' and Improvement on Experienced Inequity." *Journal of Personality and Social Psychology* 35 (1977), pp. 108–19.

7.43 Colquitt, J.A.; D.E. Conlon; M.J. Wesson; C.O.L.H. Porter; and K.Y. Ng. "Justice at the Millennium: A Meta-Analytic Review of 25 Years of Organizational Justice Research." *Journal of Applied Psychology* 86 (2001), pp. 425–45.

7.44 Tyler, T.R.; K.A. Rasinski; and N. Spodick. "Influence of Voice on Satisfaction with Leaders: Exploring the Meaning of Process Control." *Journal of Personality and Social Psychology* 48 (1985), pp. 72–81; Earley, P.C., and E.A. Lind. "Procedural Justice and Participation in Task Selection: The Role of Control in Mediating Justice Judgments." *Journal of Personality and Social Psychology* 52 (1987), pp. 1148–60; Lind, E.A.; R. Kanfer; and P.C. Earley. "Voice, Control, and Procedural Justice: Instrumental and Noninstrumental Concerns in Fairness Judgments." *Journal of Personality and Social Psychology* 59 (1990), pp. 952–59; and Korsgaard, M.A., and L. Roberson. "Procedural Justice in Performance Evaluation: The Role of Instrumental and Non-Instrumental Voice in Performance Appraisal Discussions." *Journal of Management* 21 (1995), pp. 657–69.

7.45 Leventhal, "What Should Be Done with Equity Theory?"

7.46 Kolhatkar, S. "Emasculation Nation." *Bloomberg Businessweek,* September 17–23, 2012, pp. 102–103.

7.47 Coy, P., and E. Dwoskin. "Shortchanged."

Bloomberg Businessweek, June 25–July 1, 2012, pp. 6–7.

7.48 Morris, "How Corporate America Is Betraying Women." *Fortune,* January 10, 2005, pp. 64–74.

7.49 Hansen, F. "Race and Gender Still Matter." *Workforce Management,* September 11, 2006, p. 12.

7.50 Castilla, E.J. "Gender, Race, and Meritocracy in Organizational Careers." *American Journal of Sociology* 113 (2008), pp. 1479–1526; and Hansen, F. "Merit-Pay Payoff?" *Workforce Management,* November 3, 2008, pp. 33–39.

7.51 Taylor, A., III "No Test Dummies." *Fortune,* June 11, 2007, pp. 49–52.

7.52 Leonard, D. "Who's Afraid of Steve Jobs?" *Bloomberg Businessweek,* July 26–August 1, 2010, pp. 58–63.

7.53 Brockner, J., and B.M. Wiesenfeld. "An Integrative Framework for Explaining Reactions to Decisions: Interactive Effects of Outcomes and Procedures." *Psychological Bulletin* 120 (1996), pp. 189–208.

7.54 Ibid.

7.55 Colquitt et al., "Justice at the Millennium"; and Cohen-Charash, Y., and P.E. Spector. "The Role of Justice in Organizations: A

Meta-Analysis." *Organizational Behavior and Human Decision Processes* 86 (2001), pp. 278–321.

7.56 Bies, R.J., and J.F. Moag. "Interactional Justice: Communication Criteria of Fairness." In *Research on Negotiations in Organizations,* Vol. 1, ed. R.J. Lewicki, B.H. Sheppard, and M.H. Bazerman. Greenwich, CT: JAI Press, 1986, pp. 43–55; and Greenberg, J. "The Social Side of Fairness: Interpersonal and Informational Classes of Organizational Justice." In *Justice in the Workplace: Approaching Fairness in Human Resource Management,* ed. R. Cropanzano. Hillsdale, NJ: Erlbaum, 1993, pp. 79–103.

7.57 Bies, R.J. "Interactional (In)justice: The Sacred and the Profane." In *Advances in Organizational Justice,* ed. J. Greenberg and R. Cropanzano. Stanford, CA: Stanford University Press, 2001, pp. 85–108.

7.58 Tepper, B.J. "Consequences of Abusive Supervision." *Academy of Management Journal* 43 (2000), pp. 178–90.

7.59 Schat, A.C.H.; M.R. Frone; and E.K. Kelloway. "Prevalence of Workplace Aggression in the U.S. Workforce: Findings from a National Study." In *Handbook of Workplace Violence,* ed. E.K. Kelloway, J. Barling,

and J.J. Hurrell. Thousand Oaks, CA: Sage, 2006, pp. 47–89.

7.60 Tepper, B.J.; M.K. Duffy; C.A. Henle; and L.S. Lambert. "Procedural Injustice, Victim Precipitation, and Abusive Supervision." *Personnel Psychology* 28 (2006), pp. 101–23.

7.61 Tepper, B.J. "Abusive Supervision in Work Organizations: Review, Synthesis, and Research Agenda." *Journal of Management* 33 (2007), pp. 261–89.

7.62 Mitchell, M.S., and M.L. Ambrose. "Abusive Supervision and Workplace Deviance and the Moderating Effects of Negative Reciprocity Beliefs." *Journal of Applied Psychology* 92 (2007), pp. 1159–68; Tepper, B.J.; C.A. Henle; L.S. Lambert; R.A. Giacalone; and M.K. Duffy. "Abusive Supervision and Subordinates' Organizational Deviance." *Journal of Applied Psychology* 93 (2008), pp. 721–32; and Tepper, B.J.; J.C. Carr; D.M. Breaux; S. Geider; C. Hu; and W. Hua. "Abusive Supervision, Intentions to Quit, and Employees' Workplace Deviance: A Power/Dependence Analysis." *Organizational Behavior and Human Decision Processes* 109 (2009), pp. 156–67.

7.63 Miner, A.G.; T.M. Glomb; and C. Hulin.

"Experience Sampling Mode and Its Correlates at Work." *Journal of Occupational and Organizational Psychology* 78 (2005), pp. 171–93.

7.64 Gilliland, S.W.; L. Benson; and D.H. Schepers. "A Rejection Threshold in Justice Evaluations: Effects on Judgment and Decision-Making." *Organizational Behavior and Human Decision Processes* 76 (1998), pp. 113–31.

7.65 Hauser, S.G. "The Degeneration." *Workforce Management,* January 2011, pp. 16–21.

7.66 Hauser, "The Degeneration."

7.67 Bies and Moag, "Interactional Justice"; and Greenberg, "The Social Side of Fairness."

7.68 "RadioShack Fires 400 Employees by Email" (n.d.), http://abcnews.go.com/Technology/wireStory?id52374917&CMPOTC-RSS-Feeds0312.

7.69 Folger, R., and D.P. Skarlicki. "Fairness as a Dependent Variable: Why Tough Times Can Lead to Bad Management." In *Justice in the Workplace: From Theory to Practice,* ed. R. Cropanzano. Mahwah, NJ: Erlbaum, 2001, pp. 97–118.

7.70 Marquez, J.; E. Frauenheim; and M. Schoeff Jr. "Harsh Reality." *Workforce Management,* June 22, 2009, pp. 18–23.

7.71 Shaw, J.C.; R.E. Wild; and J.A. Colquitt. "To Justify or Excuse?: A Meta-Analysis of the Effects of Explanations." *Journal of Applied Psychology* 88 (2003), pp. 444–58.

7.72 Orey, M. "Fear of Firing." *BusinessWeek,* April 23, 2007, pp. 52–62.

7.73 Greenberg, J. "Employee Theft as a Reaction to Underpayment Inequity: The Hidden Cost of Paycuts." *Journal of Applied Psychology* 75 (1990), pp. 561–68.

7.74 Colquitt et al., "Justice at the Millennium"; and Cohen-Charash and Spector, "The Role of Justice."

7.75 Treviño et al., "Behavioral Ethics"; and Tenbrunsel, A.E., and K. Smith-Crowe. "Ethical Decision Making: Where We've Been and Where We're Going." *Academy of Management Annals* 2 (2008), pp. 545–607.

7.76 Donaldson, T., and T.W. Dunfee. "Toward a Unified Conception of Business Ethics: Integrative Social Contracts Theory." *Academy of Management Review* 19 (1994), pp. 252–84.

7.77 Treviño et al., "Behavioral Ethics."

7.78 Kaptein, M. "Developing a Measure of Unethical Behavior in the Workplace: A Stakeholder Perspective." *Journal of Management* 34 (2008), pp. 978–1008.

7.79 Covey, S.M.R. *The Speed of Trust: The One Thing That Changes Everything.* New York: The Free Press, 2006.

7.80 Treviño et al., "Behavioral Ethics."

7.81 Near, J.P., and M.P. Miceli. "Organizational Dissidence: The Case of Whistle-Blowing." *Journal of Business Ethics* 4 (1985), pp. 1–16.

7.82 Rehg, M.T.; M.P. Miceli; J.P. Near; and J.R. Van Scotter. "Antecedents and Outcomes of Retaliation Against Whistleblowers: Gender Differences and Power Relationships." *Organization Science* 19 (2008), pp. 221–40.

7.83 Miceli, M.P.; J.P. Near; and T.M. Dworkin. "A Word to the Wise: How Managers and Policy-Makers Can Encourage Employees to Report Wrongdoing." *Journal of Business Ethics* 86 (2009), pp. 379–96.

7.84 Rest, J.R. *Moral Development: Advances in Research and Theory.* New York: Praeger, 2006.

7.85 Treviño, L.K. "Ethical Decision Making in Organizations: A Person-Situation Interactionist Model." *Academy of Management Review* 11 (1996), pp. 601–17;

and Kish-Gephart, J.J.; D.A. Harrison; and L.K. Treviño. "Bad Apples, Bad Cases, and Bad Barrels: Meta-Analytic Evidence about Sources of Unethical Decisions at Work." *Journal of Applied Psychology* 95 (2010), pp. 1–31.

7.86 Tomlinson, E.C. "Teaching the Interactionist Model of Ethics." *Journal of Management Education* 33 (2009), pp. 142–65; and Treviño, L.K., and M.E. Brown. "Managing to be Ethical: Debunking Five Business Ethics Myths." *Academy of Management Executive* 18 (2004), pp. 69–83.

7.87 Rest, *Moral Development.*

7.88 Butterfield, K.D.; L.K. Treviño; and G.R. Weaver. "Moral Awareness in Business Organizations: Influence of Issue-Related and Social Context Factors." *Human Relations* 53 (2000), pp. 981–1017.

7.89 Berfield, S. "Steal This Look." *Bloomberg Businessweek,* January 24–30, 2011, pp. 90–96.

7.90 Ibid.

7.91 Jones, T.M. "Ethical Decision Making by Individuals in Organizations: An Issue-Contingent Model." *Academy of Management Review* 16 (1991), pp. 366–95.

7.92 Singhapakdi, A.; S.J. Vitell; and K.L. Kraft. "Moral Intensity and Ethical Decision-Making of Marketing Professionals." *Journal of Business Research* 36 (1996), pp. 245–55.

7.93 Jones, "Ethical Decision Making by Individuals in Organizations."

7.94 Reynolds, S.J. "Moral Attentiveness: Who Pays Attention to the Moral Aspects of Life?" *Journal of Applied Psychology* 93 (2008), pp. 1027–41.

7.95 Porter, J. "Using Ex-Cons to Scare MBAs Straight." *Business-Week*, May 5, 2008, p. 58.

7.96 Ibid.

7.97 Rest, *Moral Development.*

7.98 Kohlberg, L. "Stage and Sequence: The Cognitive Developmental Approach to Socialization." In *Handbook of Socialization Theory*, ed. D.A. Goslin. Chicago: Rand McNally, 1969, pp. 347–480; and Kohlberg, L. "The Claim to Moral Adequacy of a Highest Stage of Moral Judgment." *Journal of Philosophy* 70 (1973), pp. 630–46.

7.99 Rest, J. *Manual for the Defining Issues Test.* Minneapolis, MN: Center for the Study of Ethical Development, 1986; and Loviscky, G.E.; L.K. Treviño; and R.R. Jacobs. "Assessing

Managers' Ethical Decision-Making: An Objective Measure of Managerial Moral Judgment." *Journal of Business Ethics* 73 (2007), pp. 263–85.

7.100 Kohlberg, "Stage and Sequence"; and Kohlberg, "The Claim to Moral Adequacy."

7.101 Ibid.

7.102 Treviño et al., "Behavioral Ethics"

7.103 Kohlberg, "Stage and Sequence"; and Kohlberg, "The Claim to Moral Adequacy."

7.104 Treviño et al., "Behavioral Ethics;" and Rest, J.; D. Narvaez; M.J. Bebeau; and S.J. Thoma. *Postconventional Moral Thinking: A Neo-Kohlbergian Approach.* Mahwah, NJ: Erlbaum, 1999.

7.105 Crane and Matten, *Business Ethics.* New York: Oxford University Press, 2007.

7.106 Ibid.

7.107 Rest, *Moral Development.*

7.108 Kaptein, M. "Developing and Testing a Measure for the Ethical Culture of Organizations: The Corporate Ethics Virtues Model." *Journal of Organizational Behavior* 29 (2008), pp. 923–47; Schminke, M.; M.L. Ambrose; and D.O. Neubaum. "The Effect of Leader Moral Development on Ethical Climate and Employee Attitudes."

Organizational Behavior and Human Decision Processes 97 (2005), pp. 135–51; and Treviño, "Ethical Decision Making in Organizations"

7.109 Schweitzer, M.E.; L. Ordòñez; and B. Douma. "Goal Setting as a Motivator of Unethical Behavior." *Academy of Management Journal* 47 (2004), pp. 422–32.

7.110 Aquino, K., and A. Reed II. "The Self-Importance of Moral Identity." *Journal of Personality and Social Psychology* 83 (2002), pp. 1423–40.

7.111 Ibid.

7.112 Reynolds, S.J., and T.L. Ceranic. "The Effects of Moral Judgment and Moral Identity on Moral Behavior: An Empirical Examination of the Moral Individual." *Journal of Applied Psychology* 92 (2007), pp. 1610–24.

7.113 Schminke, M.; M.L. Ambrose; and T.W. Noel. "The Effects of Ethical Frameworks on Perceptions of Organizational Justice." *Academy of Management Journal* 40 (1997), pp. 1190–1207; and Wendorf, C.A.; S. Alexander; and I.J. Firestone. "Social Justice and Moral Reasoning: An Empirical Integration of Two Paradigms in Psychological Research." *Social Justice Research* 15 (2002), pp. 19–39.

7.114 Mayer, R.C., and M.B. Gavin. "Trust in Management and Performance: Who Minds the Shop While the Employees Watch the Boss?" *Academy of Management Journal* 48 (2005), pp. 874–88.

7.115 Blau, P. *Exchange and Power in Social Life*. New York: Wiley, 1964; and Shore, L.M.; L.E. Tetrick; P. Lynch; and K. Barksdale. "Social and Economic Exchange: Construct Development and Validation." *Journal of Applied Social Psychology* 36 (2006), pp. 837–67.

7.116 Ibid.

7.117 Dirks, K.T., and D.L. Ferrin. "Trust in Leadership: Meta-Analytic Findings and Implications for Research and Practice." *Journal of Applied Psychology* 87 (2002), pp. 611–28.

7.118 Ibid.

7.119 Carroll, A.B. "A Three-Dimensional Model of Corporate Social Performance." *Academy of Management Review* 4 (1979), pp. 497–505; Carroll, A.B. "The Pyramid of Corporate Social Responsibility: Toward the Moral Management of Organizational Stakeholders." *Business Horizons* 34 (1991), pp. 39–48; Carroll, A.B. "The Four Faces of Corporate Citizenship." *Business and Society Review* 100 (1998), pp. 1–7; and Carroll, A.B. "Corporate Social Responsibility—Evolution of a Definitional Construct." *Business and Society* 38 (1999), pp. 268–95.

7.120 Carroll, "The Pyramid."

7.121 Weber, J. "The New Ethics Enforcers."

BusinessWeek, February 13, 2006, pp. 76–77.

7.122 Carroll, "The Pyramid."

7.123 Schoeff, M., Jr. "J. M. Smuckers Co." *Workforce Management*, March 13, 2006, p. 19.

7.124 Carroll, "The Pyramid."

7.125 Grow, B.; S. Hamm; and L. Lee. "The Debate Over Doing Good." *BusinessWeek*, August 15, 2005, pp. 76–78.

7.126 Holmes, S. "Nike Goes for the Green." *BusinessWeek*, September 25, 2006, pp. 106–108.

7.127 Gunther, M. "The Green Machine." *Fortune*, August 7, 2006, pp. 42–57.

7.128 Grow et al., "The Debate Over Doing Good."

chapter 8

Learning and Decision Making

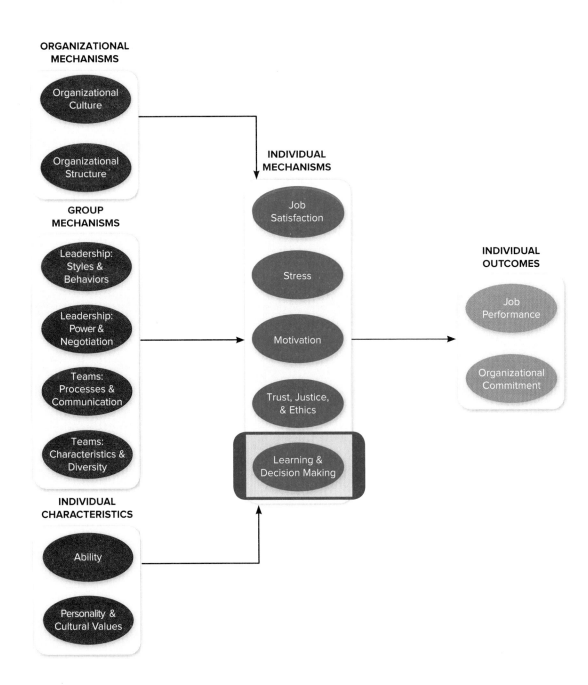

ORGANIZATIONAL MECHANISMS

- Organizational Culture
- Organizational Structure

GROUP MECHANISMS

- Leadership: Styles & Behaviors
- Leadership: Power & Negotiation
- Teams: Processes & Communication
- Teams: Characteristics & Diversity

INDIVIDUAL CHARACTERISTICS

- Ability
- Personality & Cultural Values

INDIVIDUAL MECHANISMS

- Job Satisfaction
- Stress
- Motivation
- Trust, Justice, & Ethics
- Learning & Decision Making

INDIVIDUAL OUTCOMES

- Job Performance
- Organizational Commitment

© David Goldman/AP Images

✅ LEARNING GOALS

After reading this chapter, you should be able to answer the following questions:

8.1 What is learning, and how does it affect decision making?

8.2 What types of knowledge can employees gain as they learn and build expertise?

8.3 What are the methods by which employees learn in organizations?

8.4 What two methods can employees use to make decisions?

8.5 What decision-making problems can prevent employees from translating their learning into accurate decisions?

8.6 How does learning affect job performance and organizational commitment?

8.7 What steps can organizations take to foster learning?

UPS

Can you wager a guess as to how many packages UPS delivers on Christmas Eve alone? In 2014, that number was more than 34 million—with a 98 percent on-time rate. In one day! The company has more than 100,000 delivery vehicles and drivers in the United States alone and makes more than 4.5 billion deliveries a year. UPS drivers and the brown package cars they drive (not "trucks" in UPS lingo) are some of the most ubiquitous vehicles on the roadways. Drivers average somewhere between 150 and 200 deliveries a day. Driving for UPS is an extremely attractive and lucrative job (driver salaries average more than $75,000 annually). So much so that websites such as http://howtoworkforbrown.com detail the lengthy and myriad ways to try to get your foot in the door of the company.

Even with recruits beating down their door and a thorough selection process, UPS found that more than 30 percent of driver candidates were flunking out of their traditional training process, which taught new hires about the "340 methods" drivers are expected to employ in the performance of their job (there are actually more than 340). These methods instruct drivers as to how to make good decisions and the most efficient and appropriate ways to do things. Methods include everything from driver etiquette (two short honks instead of one long honk) to how to pick up boxes. Some of these methods are essential to driver health—such as always exiting the package car while having three points of contact (hand on handrail, foot on step, foot on ground). Without using that method, an average driver puts an extra 14,280 pounds of pressure on their joints over the course of a day (the equivalent of three Ford F-150 trucks!).

In order to reduce the training failure rate, UPS created a better learning environment by building state-of-the-art facilities in Landover, Maryland and Chicago. Results have been so good (failure rates are now below 10 percent) that three more facilities in Portland, Menlo Park (California), and Dallas are set to open by 2016. These training facilities are built so that new employees don't only have to read about what they are supposed to do as drivers—rather, they actually do the work. New drivers will work up from computer simulations to actual deliveries inside the facility. Each facility has its own mock town ("Clarksville"), and drivers are expected to learn and enact the exacting methods that UPS expects to a point where they become second nature.

LEARNING AND DECISION MAKING

8.1

What is learning, and how does it affect decision making?

UPS spends an enormous amount of time and effort on new hire training and development because learning and decision making are so important in organizations. **Learning** reflects relatively permanent changes in an employee's knowledge or skill that result from experience.[1] The more employees learn, the more they bring to the table when they come to work. Why is learning so important? Because it has a significant impact on **decision making,** which refers to the process of generating and choosing from a set of alternatives to solve a problem. The more knowledge and skills employees possess, the more likely they are to make accurate and sound decisions. The risk, at UPS and other organizations, is that less experienced employees will lack the knowledge base needed to make the right decisions when performing their jobs or stepping into new roles.

One reason inexperience can be so problematic is that learning is not necessarily easy. Have you ever watched "experts" perform their jobs? How is it that someone becomes an expert? It takes a significant amount of time to become proficient at most complex jobs. It takes most employees anywhere from three months to a year to perform their job at a satisfactory level.[2] To develop high levels of expertise takes significantly longer. This difficulty makes it even more important for companies to find a way to improve learning and decision making by their employees.

WHY DO SOME EMPLOYEES LEARN TO MAKE DECISIONS BETTER THAN OTHERS?

Bill Buford, a journalist interested in becoming a chef, was hired by Mario Batali's world-renowned restaurant Babbo in New York. At some point early in his tenure in the kitchen, he realized he was in over his head while he stood and watched other, more experienced cooks work at an unbelievably frantic pace. He knew right then that he had a decision to make:

> I was at a go-forward-or-backward moment. If I went backward, I'd be saying, "Thanks for the visit, very interesting, that's sure not me." But how to go forward? There was no place for me. These people were at a higher level of labor. They didn't think. Their skills were so deeply inculcated they were available to them as instincts. I didn't have skills of that kind and couldn't imagine how you'd learn them. I was aware of being poised on the verge of something: a long, arduous, confidence-bashing, profoundly humiliating experience.[3]

In this situation, Buford realized that his coworkers had more expertise than he did. **Expertise** refers to the knowledge and skills that distinguish experts from novices and less experienced people.[4] Research shows that the differences between experts and novices is almost always a function of learning as opposed to the more popular view that intelligence or other innate differences make the difference.[5] Although learning cannot be directly seen or observed, we can tell when people have learned by observing their behaviors. It's those behaviors that can be used to tell experts from novices, and it is changes in those behaviors that can be used to show that learners are gaining knowledge. Although it's sometimes easy for employees to mimic a behavior once or twice, or get lucky with a few key decisions, true learning only occurs when changes in behavior become relatively permanent and are repeated over time. Understanding why some employees prove better at this than others requires understanding what exactly employees learn and how they do it.

TYPES OF KNOWLEDGE

Employees learn two basic types of knowledge, both of which have important implications for organizations. **Explicit knowledge** is the kind of information you're likely to think about when you picture someone sitting down at a desk to learn. It's information that's relatively easily communicated and a large part of what companies teach during training sessions. Think about it this way: If you can put the information or knowledge in a manual or write it down for someone else, chances are good you're talking about explicit knowledge. As you read this textbook, we're doing our best to communicate explicit knowledge to you that will be useful to you in your future job. Although such information is necessary to perform well, it winds up being a relatively minor portion of all that you need to know.

8.2

What types of knowledge can employees gain as they learn and build expertise?

Tacit knowledge, in contrast, is what employees can typically learn only through experience.[6] It's not easily communicated but could very well be the most important aspect of what we learn in organizations.[7] In fact, it's been argued that up to 90 percent of the knowledge contained in organizations occurs in tacit form.[8] Did you ever get to be so good at something that you had the ability to do it but couldn't really explain it to someone else? That's a common way to explain tacit knowledge. It's been described as the "know-how," "know-what," and "know-who" acquired solely through experience.[9] Others have used terms such as intuition, skills, insight, beliefs, mental models, and practical intelligence.[10] Table 8-1 lists the qualities that help explain the differences between explicit and tacit knowledge. Some would say that explicit knowledge is what everyone can find and use, but tacit knowledge is what separates experts from common people.[11]

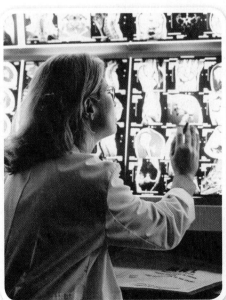

© Dynamic Graphics/Jupiterimages RF

Expertise is the accumulation of superior knowledge and skills in a field that separates experts from everyone else.

TABLE 8-1	Characteristics of Explicit and Tacit Knowledge

EXPLICIT KNOWLEDGE	TACIT KNOWLEDGE
Easily transferred through written or verbal communication	Very difficult, if not impossible, to articulate to others
Readily available to most	Highly personal in nature
Can be learned through books	Based on experience
Always conscious and accessible information	Sometimes holders don't even recognize that they possess it
General information	Typically job- or situation-specific

Source: Adapted from R. McAdam, B. Mason, and J. McCrory, "Exploring the Dichotomies within the Tacit Knowledge Literature: Towards a Process of Tacit Knowing in Organizations," *Journal of Knowledge Management* 11 (2007), pp. 43–59.

METHODS OF LEARNING

Tacit and explicit knowledge are extremely important to employees and organizations. As an employee, it's hard to build a high level of tacit knowledge without some level of explicit knowledge to build from. From an organization's perspective, the tacit knowledge its employees accumulate may be the single most important strategic asset a company possesses.[12] The question then becomes: How do employees learn these types of knowledge? The short answer is that we learn through reinforcement (i.e., rewards and punishment), observation, and experience.

8.3

What are the methods by which employees learn in organizations?

REINFORCEMENT We've long known that managers use various methods of reinforcement to induce desirable or reduce undesirable behaviors by their employees. Originally known as operant conditioning, B.F. Skinner was the first to pioneer the notion that we learn by observing the link between our voluntary behavior and the consequences that follow it. Research has continually demonstrated that people will exhibit specific behaviors if they're rewarded for doing so. Not surprisingly, we have a tendency to repeat behaviors that result in consequences that we like and to reduce behaviors that result in consequences we don't like. Figure 8-1 shows this operant conditioning process.

In the model in Figure 8-1, you can see that there are antecedents or events that precede or signal certain behaviors, which are then followed by consequences. Antecedents in organizations are typically goals, rules, instructions, or other types of information that help show employees what is expected of them. Although antecedents are useful for motivational reasons, it's primarily the consequences of actions that drive behavior. This entire process of reinforcement is a continuous cycle, and the repetition of behaviors is strengthened to the degree that reinforcement

FIGURE 8-1	Operant Conditioning Components

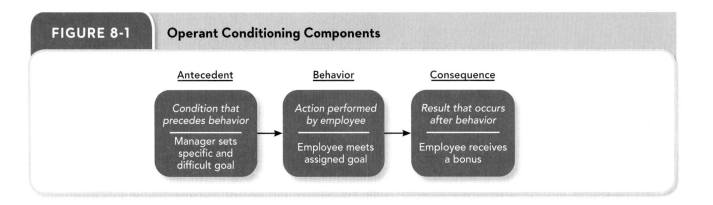

FIGURE 8-2	Contingencies of Reinforcement

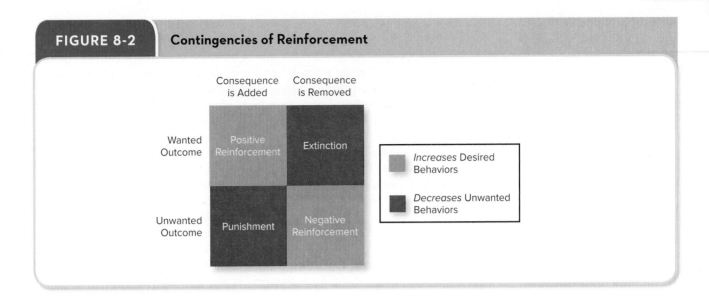

continues to occur. There are four specific consequences typically used by organizations to modify employee behavior, known as the **contingencies of reinforcement**.[13] Figure 8-2 summarizes these contingencies. It's important to separate them according to what they're designed to do—namely, increase desired behaviors or decrease unwanted behaviors.

Two contingencies of reinforcement are used to increase desired behaviors. **Positive reinforcement** occurs when a positive outcome follows a desired behavior. It's perhaps the most common type of reinforcement and the type we think of when an employee receives some type of "reward." Increased pay, promotions, praise from a manager or coworkers, and public recognition would all be considered positive reinforcement when given as a result of an employee exhibiting desired behaviors. For positive reinforcement to be successful, employees need to see a direct link between their behaviors and desired outcomes (see Chapter 6 on motivation for more discussion of such issues). If the consequences aren't realized until long after the specific behaviors, then the odds that employees will link the two are minimized. **Negative reinforcement** occurs when an unwanted outcome is removed following a desired behavior. Have you ever performed a task for the specific reason of not getting yelled at? If so, you learned to perform certain behaviors through the use of negative reinforcement. Perhaps there are some tasks your job requires that you don't enjoy. If your manager removes these responsibilities specifically because you perform well at another aspect of your job, then this could also be seen as negative reinforcement. It's important to remember that even though the word "negative" has a sour connotation to it, it's designed to *increase* desired behaviors.

The next two contingencies of reinforcement are designed to decrease undesired behaviors. **Punishment** occurs when an unwanted outcome follows an unwanted behavior. Punishment is exactly what it sounds like. In other words, employees are given something they don't like as a result of performing behaviors that the organization doesn't like. Suspending an employee for showing up to work late, assigning job tasks generally seen as demeaning for not following safety procedures, or even firing an employee for gross misconduct are

© *Digital Vision RF*

Positive reinforcement, like public recognition, both encourages employees and helps ensure that desirable behaviors will be imitated and repeated.

all examples of punishment. **Extinction** occurs when there is the removal of a consequence following an unwanted behavior. The use of extinction to reinforce behavior can be purposeful or accidental. Perhaps employees receive attention from coworkers when they act in ways that are somewhat childish at work. Finding a way to remove the attention would be a purposeful act of extinction. Similarly though, perhaps employees work late every now and then to finish up job tasks when work gets busy, but their manager stops acknowledging that hard work. Desired behavior that's not reinforced will diminish over time. In this way, a manager who does nothing to reinforce good behavior is actually decreasing the odds that it will be repeated!

In general, positive reinforcement and extinction should be the most common forms of reinforcement used by managers to create learning among their employees. Positive reinforcement doesn't have to be in the form of material rewards to be effective. There are many ways for managers to encourage wanted behaviors. Offering praise, providing feedback, public recognition, and small celebrations are all ways to encourage employees and increase the chances they will continue to exhibit desired behaviors. At the same time, extinction is an effective way to stop unwanted behaviors. Both of these contingencies deliver their intended results, but perhaps more importantly, they do so without creating feelings of animosity and conflict. Although punishment and negative reinforcement will work, they tend to bring other, detrimental consequences along with them.

Whereas the type of reinforcement used to modify behavior is important, research also shows that the timing of reinforcement is equally important.[14] Therefore, it's important to examine the timing of when the contingencies are applied, referred to as **schedules of reinforcement.** Table 8-2 provides a summary of the five schedules of reinforcement. **Continuous reinforcement** is the simplest schedule and happens when a specific consequence follows each and every occurrence of a desired behavior. New learning is acquired most rapidly under a continuous schedule.[15] For most jobs, continuous reinforcement is impractical. As a manager, can you imagine providing positive reinforcement every time someone exhibits a desired behavior? It's a good thing that research also shows that under many circumstances, continuous reinforcement might be considered the least long lasting, because as soon as the consequence stops, the desired behavior stops along with it.[16] Once a behavior has been acquired, some form of intermittent scheduling is more effective.[17]

The other four schedules differ in terms of their variability and the basis of the consequences. Two schedules are interval based; that is, they distribute reinforcement based on the amount of time that passes. A **fixed interval schedule** is probably the single most common form of reinforcement schedule. With this schedule, workers are rewarded after a certain amount of time, and the length of time between reinforcement periods stays the same. Every time employees get a paycheck after a predetermined period of time, they're being reinforced on a fixed interval schedule. **Variable interval schedules** are designed to reinforce behavior at more random points

TABLE 8-2	Schedules of Reinforcement		
REINFORCEMENT SCHEDULE	**REWARD GIVEN FOLLOWING**	**POTENTIAL LEVEL OF PERFORMANCE**	**EXAMPLE**
Continuous	Every desired behavior	High, but difficult to maintain	Praise
Fixed interval	Fixed time periods	Average	Paycheck
Variable interval	Variable time periods	Moderately high	Supervisor walk-by
Fixed ratio	Fixed number of desired behaviors	High	Piece-rate pay
Variable ratio	Variable number of desired behaviors	Very high	Commission pay

in time. A supervisor walking around at different points of time every day is a good example of a variable interval schedule. If that supervisor walked around at the same exact time every day, do you think workers would be more or less prone to exhibit good behaviors throughout the day?

The other two reinforcement schedules are based on actual behaviors. **Fixed ratio schedules** reinforce behaviors after a certain number of them have been exhibited. Some manufacturing plants have created piece-rate pay systems in which workers are paid according to the number of items they produce. Employees know ahead of time how many items they have to produce to be reinforced. **Variable ratio schedules** reward people after a varying number of exhibited behaviors. Salespeople, for example, are often compensated based on commission because they receive extra pay every time they sell an item. However, a car salesperson doesn't make a sale every time someone walks in the door of the dealership. Sometimes it takes exhibiting good sales behaviors to eight or nine customers to make a sale. Take a slot machine as an example. The machine doesn't reward you for every lever pull or even every 10 lever pulls—you never know when the next winning pull will be. Would you say that slot machines do a good job of reinforcing the behavior that casinos would like you to have? You bet!

On the whole, research has consistently shown that variable schedules lead to higher levels of performance than fixed schedules.[18] Think about it this way: Do you study more consistently in a class that gives pop quizzes or one that simply tests you three set times a semester? Research also shows that desired behaviors tend to disappear much more quickly when reinforcement is discontinued under fixed plans. However, variable schedules are not always appropriate for some types of reinforcement. How would you like it if your employer decided to give you your paychecks on a variable schedule? Sorry, you're not getting a paycheck this week—maybe next week! Moreover, studies suggest that continuous or fixed schedules can be better for reinforcing new behaviors or behaviors that don't occur on a frequent basis.

OBSERVATION In addition to learning through reinforcement, **social learning theory** argues that people in organizations have the ability to learn through the observation of others.[19] In fact, many would argue that social learning is the primary way by which employees gain knowledge in organizations.[20] Think about where you're most likely to get your cues while working in an organization. When possible, chances are good you'll look around at other employees to figure out the appropriate behaviors on your job. Not only do employees have the ability to see the link between their own behaviors and their consequences, they can also observe the behaviors and consequences of others.[21] When employees observe the actions of others, learn from what they observe, and then repeat the observed behavior, they're engaging in **behavioral modeling.**

For behavioral modeling to occur successfully, a number of processes have to take place. These steps are shown in Figure 8-3. First, the learner must focus attention on an appropriate model and accurately perceive the critical behavior the model exhibits. That model might be a supervisor, a

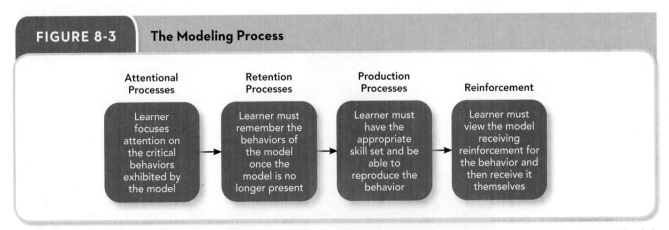

FIGURE 8-3   The Modeling Process

Attentional Processes	Retention Processes	Production Processes	Reinforcement
Learner focuses attention on the critical behaviors exhibited by the model	Learner must remember the behaviors of the model once the model is no longer present	Learner must have the appropriate skill set and be able to reproduce the behavior	Learner must view the model receiving reinforcement for the behavior and then receive it themselves

Source: Adapted from H.M. Weiss, "Learning Theory and Industrial and Organizational Psychology," in *Handbook of Industrial and Organizational Psychology,* ed. M.D. Dunnette and L.M. Hough (Consulting Psychologists Press: Palo Alto, CA, 1990), pp. 75–169.

coworker, or even a subordinate. Some organizations go out of their way to supply role models for newcomers or inexperienced workers to watch and learn from. For instance, BASF, the German chemical giant, rewards and encourages older workers to model behavior and share their knowledge. In this way, not only does explicit knowledge get passed on but also tacit knowledge. BASF CFO Kurt Bock says, "For the engineers, transferring knowledge to their successors is easier said than done."[22] In fact, because tacit knowledge is so difficult to communicate, modeling might be the single best way to acquire it. For that reason, modeling is a continual process that is used at all levels of many organizations. Ursula Burns's ascent to CEO of Xerox was carefully controlled as she was allowed to closely observe and model former CEO Anne Mulcahy for a number of years before taking control.[23] At Verizon, new CEO Lowell McAdam was tabbed to take over the spot but spent over a year observing and modeling the prior CEO before moving into the job. At the time, McAdam said, "I'm a very roll-up-your-sleeves guy. I need to learn to be CEO."[24] Needless to say, choosing a good model is important, and not all models are good ones. There is a great deal of evidence that supports the notion that employees will learn to behave unethically when in the presence of others who model that same behavior.[25] Salomon Brothers, the New York–based investment bank, learned this lesson the hard way when employees began to model the unethical behaviors of their managers and leaders.[26] In addition to unethical behavior, there is substantial evidence that employees will behavior model counterproductive work behaviors such as aggression and absenteeism when they see others in the organization exhibit those behaviors.[27]

Second, the learner needs to remember exactly what the model's behavior was and how they did it. This step is very difficult when watching experts perform their job because so much of what they do remains unspoken and can occur at a rapid pace. Third, the learner must undertake production processes or actually be able to reproduce what the model did. Not only must the learner have the requisite knowledge and physical skills to be able to perform the task; now he or she must translate what's been observed into action. Do you remember the first time you drove a car? Chances are good you'd been watching other drivers for many years, picking up bits and pieces of how to do it through observation. However, things became different when you were behind the wheel for the first time. Suddenly, there was a lot of information to process, and years and years of observation had to be put into action.

Fourth, the last step of behavioral modeling is reinforcement. This reinforcement can come from observation, direct experience, or both. The learner can observe the consequences of the model having exhibited the behavior (positive reinforcement or punishment), which in itself will help ingrain the desirability of performing the behavior. In addition, it's important for the learner to receive reinforcement after replicating the behavior. If the newly acquired behaviors are positively reinforced, the likelihood of continued behavior increases.

GOAL ORIENTATION Before we leave this section, it's important to recognize that people learn somewhat differently according to their predispositions or attitudes toward learning and performance. These differences are reflected in different "goal orientations" that capture the kinds of activities and goals that people prioritize. Some people have what's known as a **learning orientation,** where building competence is deemed more important than demonstrating competence. "Learning-oriented" persons enjoy working on new kinds of tasks, even if they fail during their early experiences. Such people view failure in positive terms—as a means of increasing knowledge and skills in the long run.[28]

For others, the demonstration of competence is deemed

Ursula Burns was provided an unusual opportunity to learn by observation and behavioral modeling before becoming CEO of Xerox. She essentially co-led with her predecessor for two years to gain insider experience before taking the helm.

© *Ramin Talaie/Bloomberg via Getty Images*

OB ASSESSMENTS

GOAL ORIENTATION

What does your goal orientation look like? This assessment is designed to measure all three dimensions of goal orientation. Please write a number next to each statement that indicates the extent to which it accurately describes your attitude toward work while you are on the job. Answer each question using the response scale provided. Then sum up your answers for each of the three dimensions. (Instructors: Assessments on rational decision making, intuition, learning potential, and social identity can be found in the PowerPoints in the Connect Library's Instructor Resources and in the Connect assignments for this chapter).

1	2	3	4	5
STRONGLY DISAGREE	DISAGREE	NEUTRAL	AGREE	STRONGLY AGREE

1. I am willing to select challenging assignments that I can learn a lot from. _____

2. I often look for opportunities to develop new skills and knowledge. _____

3. I enjoy challenging and difficult tasks where I'll learn new skills. _____

4. For me, development of my ability is important enough to take risks. _____

5. I prefer to work in situations that require a high level of ability and talent. _____

6. I like to show that I can perform better than my coworkers. _____

7. I try to figure out what it takes to prove my ability to others at work. _____

8. I enjoy it when others at work are aware of how well I am doing. _____

9. I prefer to work on projects where I can prove my ability to others. _____

10. I would avoid taking on a new task if there was a chance that I would appear incompetent to others. _____

11. Avoiding a show of low ability is more important to me than learning a new skill. _____

12. I'm concerned about taking on a task at work if my performance would reveal that I had low ability. _____

13. I prefer to avoid situations at work where I might perform poorly. _____

SCORING AND INTERPRETATION

Learning Orientation: Sum up items 1–5. _____
Performance-Prove Orientation: Sum up items 6–9. _____
Performance-Avoid Orientation: Sum up items 10–13. _____

For learning orientation, scores of 20 or more are above average, and scores of 19 or less are below average. For the two performance orientations, scores of 15 or more are above average, and scores of 14 or less are below average.

Source: From J.F. Brett and D. VandeWalle, "Goal Orientation and Goal Content as Predictors of Performance in a Training Program," *Journal of Applied Psychology* 84 (1999), pp. 863–73. Copyright © 1999 by the American Psychological Associated. Reprinted with permission. No further reproduction or distribution is permitted without written permission from the American Psychological Association.

a more important goal than the building of competence. That demonstration of competence can be motivated by two different thought processes. Those with a **performance-prove orientation** focus on demonstrating their competence so that others think favorably of them. Those with a **performance-avoid orientation** focus on demonstrating their competence so that others will not think poorly of them. In either case, "performance-oriented" people tend to work mainly on tasks at which they're already good, preventing them from failing in front of others. Such individuals view failure in negative terms—as an indictment of their ability and competence.

Research has shown that a learning goal orientation improves self-confidence, feedback-seeking behavior, learning strategy development, and learning performance.[29] Research on the two performance orientations is more mixed. Although it would seem that focusing on performance should improve performance-based outcomes, research shows that isn't necessarily the case. On the whole, a performance-prove orientation tends to be a mixed bag, producing varying levels of performance and outcomes. What's more clear are the detrimental effects of having a performance-avoid orientation. Employees who enter learning situations with a fear of looking bad in front of others tend to learn less and have substantially higher levels of anxiety.[30] What kind of orientation do you tend to exhibit? See our **OB Assessments** feature to find out. Regardless of an individual's general tendency though, it has been found that managers or trainers can set training-specific orientations toward learning.[31] In other words, they can instruct you to have a specific goal orientation before you start a training session. Under such conditions, setting learning-oriented goals for those in training is likely to foster more skill development than setting performance-oriented goals.[32]

METHODS OF DECISION MAKING

8.4

What two methods can employees use to make decisions?

How do employees take explicit and tacit knowledge, however it's gained, and turn that knowledge into effective decision making? Sometimes that process is very straightforward. **Programmed decisions** are decisions that become somewhat automatic because people's knowledge allows them to recognize and identify a situation and the course of action that needs to be taken. As shown in Figure 8-4, experts often respond to an identified problem by realizing that they've dealt with it before. That realization triggers a programmed decision that's implemented and then evaluated according to its ability to deliver the expected outcome. For experts who possess high levels of explicit and tacit knowledge, many decisions they face are of this programmed variety. That's not to say that the decisions are necessarily easy. It simply means that their experience and knowledge allows them to see the problems more easily and recognize and implement solutions more quickly.

To experts, programmed decisions sometimes comes across as intuition or a "gut feeling." **Intuition** can be described as emotionally charged judgments that arise through quick, non-conscious, and holistic associations.[33] There is almost unanimous consent among researchers that intuition is largely a function of learning—tacit knowledge gained through reinforcement, observation, and experience allow a decision maker to decide more quickly and confidently.[34] Because of their tacit knowledge, experts sometimes cannot put into words why they know that a problem exists, why a solution will work, or how they accomplished a task. They just "know." Of course, the difficulty arises in knowing when to trust that "gut instinct" and when not to.[35] As a general rule of thumb, you should probably ask yourself how much expertise you have about the subject of the judgment. Research is clear that intuition can be a very effective way to make decisions, but only when those making the decisions have a high level of domain expertise.[36] In other words, don't go laying down your life savings on a spin of the roulette wheel in Vegas because your intuition tells you "red"!

Intuitive decision making is perhaps never more important than during a crisis. A **crisis situation** is a change—whether sudden or evolving—that results in an urgent problem that must be addressed immediately. For businesses, a crisis is anything with the potential to cause sudden and serious damage to its employees, reputation, or bottom line. One of the key factors in almost all crises is that decisions must be made quickly.[37] Unless there has been some form of specific preplanning for that crisis, managers (who should have the most tacit knowledge to support their decisions) must use their intuition rather than take a lengthy period of time to think through all of their options.[38] When a manager uses intuition to make a decision in a crisis situation, followers often misinterpret the manager's intent because the managers can't put the reasons for their decisions into words (or don't have the time to do so).[39] In turn, the implementation of their plan often suffers. Therefore, managers who make decisions face two major questions: How can they ensure that others follow their lead when the path is unclear, and how can they confirm that their

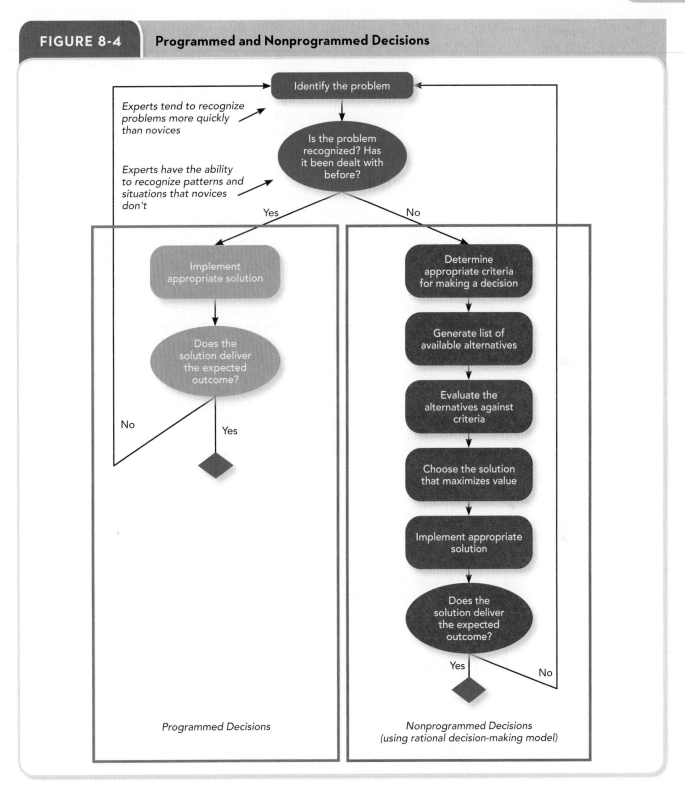

| FIGURE 8-4 | Programmed and Nonprogrammed Decisions |

intuition is not faulty? Karl Weick, a preeminent scholar on crisis management at the University of Michigan, suggests five steps for communicating intent to others when using intuition:

1. *Here's what I think we face.* (How does the manager perceive the situation?)
2. *Here's what I think we should do.* (A task-focused statement of what the manager wants to happen)
3. *Here's why.* (The reasoning behind the decision)

4. *Here's what we should keep our eye on.* (What things should the staff look for to ensure the intuition is correct or that the situation hasn't changed?)

5. *Now, talk to me.* (Confirm that everyone understands their roles and that there is no other information to consider.)[40]

These communications steps are important for a manager making intuitive decisions because they help others follow directives more easily, while also providing a check on the manager to ensure he or she observes the crisis environment correctly.

When a situation arises that is new, complex, and not recognized, it calls for a **nonprogrammed decision** on the part of the employee. Organizations are complex and changing environments, and many workers face uncertainty on a daily basis. In these instances, employees have to make sense of their environment, understand the problems they're faced with, and come up with solutions to overcome them. As a general rule of thumb, as employees move up the corporate ladder, a larger percentage of their decisions become less and less programmed. How should decision making proceed in such contexts? The **rational decision-making model** offers a step-by-step approach to making decisions that maximize outcomes by examining all available alternatives. As shown in Figure 8-4, this model becomes relevant when people don't recognize a problem as one they've dealt with before.

The first step in the rational decision-making model is to identify the criteria that are important in making the decision, taking into account all involved parties. The second step is to generate a list of all available alternatives that might be potential solutions to the problem. At this point, evaluating the alternatives is not necessary. The responsibility simply lies in coming up with as many potential solutions as possible. The third step in the model is the evaluation of those alternatives against the criteria laid out in step one. Does it matter how much the alternative costs? What exactly will happen as a result of various choices? What will the side effects of the alternative be? The fourth step is to select the alternative that results in the best outcome. That is, given the costs and benefits of each alternative, which alternative provides us with the most value? The fifth step is to implement the alternative.

The rational decision-making model assumes that people are, of course, perfectly rational. However, problems immediately arise when we start to examine some of the assumptions the model makes about human decision makers.[41] The model assumes there is a clear and definite problem to solve and that people have the ability to identify what that exact problem is. It also assumes that decision makers have perfect information—that they know and are able to identify the available alternatives and the outcomes that would be associated with those alternatives. The model further assumes that time and money are generally not issues when it comes to making a decision, that decision makers always choose the solution that maximizes value, and that they will act in the best interests of the organization. Given all these assumptions, perhaps we shouldn't label the model as "rational" after all! See our **OB on Screen** feature for an example of the struggle to be rational during a high-stakes situation.

DECISION-MAKING PROBLEMS

Because employees don't always make rational decisions, it's easy to second-guess decisions after the fact. Many decisions made inside organizations look good at the time and were made with perfectly good justifications to support them but turn out to have what are perceived to be "bad results." The reality, however, is that it's a lot easier to question decisions in hindsight. As Warren Buffett, CEO of Berkshire Hathaway, is often quoted as saying, "In the business world, the rearview mirror is always clearer than the windshield."[42] Our responsibility here is not to rehash all the poor decisions employees and managers have made (and there are many of them!), but rather to detail some of the most common reasons for bad decision making—in other words, when are people most likely to falter in terms of the rational decision-making model and why?

LIMITED INFORMATION Although most employees perceive themselves as rational decision makers, the reality is that they are all subject to **bounded rationality.** Bounded rationality is the notion that decision makers simply do not have the ability or resources to process all available information and alternatives to make an optimal decision.[43] A comparison of bounded rationality

8.5

What decision-making problems can prevent employees from translating their learning into accurate decisions?

OB ON SCREEN

INTERSTELLAR

Honestly, Amelia. It just might.

With those words, Joseph "Coop" Cooper (Matthew McConaughey) tells Dr. Amelia Brand (Anne Hathaway) that he believes her decision-making process is being influenced by her love for another person in *Interstellar* (Dir: Christopher Nolan, Paramount, 2014). Cooper, Amelia, and Dr. Nikolai "Rom" Romilly are faced with the unenviable position of having to make an irreversible decision between two highly ambiguous situations. In 2065, life on earth has been drastically changed by worldwide crop failures, increasing nitrogen levels in the atmosphere, and severe dust storms. With no solution on the horizon, mankind's continued existence on Earth is unlikely. Cooper, a former pilot and astronaut, is recruited by a Professor Brand (Michael Caine) who works with NASA to go on a mission to find a planet that will sustain human life and save mankind.

© Paramount Pictures/Photofest

Through the existence of a wormhole near Saturn, NASA finds a way to send twelve astronauts to another galaxy to look for habitable worlds. Cooper, Amelia, and Rom are sent out after the three astronauts who have sent back promising results from planets they have landed on. After finding the most favorable lead to be a failure, the crew only has the time and resources to visit one of the other alternatives if they are to return to Earth. The three individuals try to take a rational decision-making approach to debate the merits of the two alternatives and the evidence for each. Amelia (an "expert" in the area) strongly suggests choosing one planet. Before they vote, Cooper informs Rom that Amelia happens to be in love with the scientist on the planet she favors visiting—possibly conflicting with her ability to make a decision as a scientist would (rationally). Amelia pleads that perhaps love, something that we don't understand as much as we could, is indeed a good piece of input in the decision-making process and that it doesn't make her decision wrong. Cooper disagrees, and he and Rom ultimately vote for the other planet. Does their decision turn out to be the right one? You'll have to watch the movie to find out.

and rational decision making is presented in Table 8-3. This limit results in two major problems for making decisions. First, people have to filter and simplify information to make sense of their complex environment and the myriad of potential choices they face.[44] This simplification leads them to miss information when perceiving problems, generating and evaluating alternatives, or judging the results. Second, because people cannot possibly consider every single alternative

| **TABLE 8-3** | **Rational Decision Making vs. Bounded Rationality** |

TO BE RATIONAL DECISION MAKERS, WE *SHOULD* . . .	BOUNDED RATIONALITY SAYS WE *ARE LIKELY TO* . . .
Identify the problem by thoroughly examining the situation and considering all interested parties.	Boil down the problem to something that is easily understood.
Develop an exhaustive list of alternatives to consider as solutions.	Come up with a few solutions that tend to be straightforward, familiar, and similar to what is currently being done.
Evaluate all the alternatives simultaneously.	Evaluate each alternative as soon as we think of it.
Use accurate information to evaluate alternatives.	Use distorted and inaccurate information during the evaluation process.
Pick the alternative that maximizes value.	Pick the first acceptable alternative (satisfice).

Sources: Adapted from H.A. Simon, "Rational Decision Making in Organizations," *American Economic Review* 69 (1979), pp. 493–513; D. Kahneman, "Maps of Bounded Rationality: Psychology for Behavioral Economics," *The American Economic Review* 93 (2003), pp. 1449–75; and S.W. Williams, *Making Better Business Decisions* (Thousand Oaks, CA: Sage, 2002).

when making a decision, they satisfice. **Satisficing** results when decision makers select the first acceptable alternative considered.[45]

In addition to choosing the first acceptable alternative, decision makers tend to come up with alternatives that are straightforward and not that different from what they're already doing. When you and another person are deciding where to go out for dinner tonight, will you sit down and list every restaurant available to you within a certain mile limit? Of course not. You'll start listing off alternatives, generally starting with the closest and most familiar, until both parties arrive at a restaurant that's acceptable to them. Making decisions this way is no big deal when it comes to deciding where to go for dinner, because the consequences of a poor decision are minimal. However, many managers make decisions that have critical consequences for their employees and their customers. In those cases, making a decision without thoroughly looking into the alternatives becomes a problem!

FAULTY PERCEPTIONS As decision makers, employees are forced to rely on their perceptions to make decisions. Perception is the process of selecting, organizing, storing, and retrieving information about the environment. Although perceptions can be very useful—because they help us to make sense of the environment around us—they can often become distorted versions of reality. Perceptions can be dangerous in decision making because we tend to make assumptions or evaluations on the basis of them. **Selective perception** is the tendency for people to see their environment only as it affects them and as it is consistent with their expectations. Has someone ever told you, "You only see what you want to see"? If a relative, spouse, or significant other said that to you, chances are good it probably wasn't the best experience. That person was likely upset that you didn't perceive the environment (or what was important to them) the same way they did. Selective perception affects our ability to identify problems, generate and evaluate alternatives, and judge outcomes. In other words, we take "shortcuts" when we process information. In the following paragraphs, we'll discuss some of the ways in which we take shortcuts when dealing with people and situations.

One false assumption people tend to make when it comes to other people is the belief that others think, feel, and act the same way they do. This assumption is known as a **projection bias.** That is, people project their own thoughts, attitudes, and motives onto other people. "I would never do that—that's unethical" equates to "They would never do that—that's unethical." Projection bias causes problems in decision making because it limits our ability to develop appropriate criteria for a decision and evaluate decisions carefully. The bias causes people to assume that everyone's criteria will be just like theirs and that everyone will react to a decision just as they would.

Another example of faulty perceptions is caused by the way we cognitively organize people into groups. **Social identity theory** holds that people identify themselves by the groups to which they belong and perceive and judge others by their group memberships.[46] There is a substantial amount of research that shows that we like to categorize people on the basis of the groups to which they belong.[47] These groups could be based on demographic information (gender, race, religion, hair color), occupational information (scientists, engineers, accountants), where they work (GE, Halliburton, Goldman Sachs), what country they're from (Americans, French, Chinese), or any other subgroup that makes sense to the perceiver. You might categorize students on campus by whether they're a member of a fraternity or sorority. Those inside the Greek system categorize people by which fraternity or sorority they belong to. And people within a certain fraternity might group their own members on the basis of whom they hang out with the most. There is practically no end to the number of subgroups that people can come up with.

A **stereotype** occurs when assumptions are made about others on the basis of their membership in a social group.[48] Although not all stereotypes are bad per se, our decision-making process becomes faulty when we make inaccurate generalizations. Many companies work hard to help their employees avoid stereotyping because doing so can lead to illegal discrimination in the workplace. Ortho-McNeil Pharmaceutical, Wells Fargo, Kaiser Permanente, and Microsoft (just to name a few) have developed extensive diversity training programs to help their employees overcome specific cultural, racial, and gender stereotypes in the workplace.[49]

When confronted with situations of uncertainty that require a decision on our part, we often use **heuristics**—simple, efficient, rules of thumb that allow us to make decisions more easily. In general, heuristics are not bad. In fact, they lead to correct decisions more often than not.[50] However, heuristics can also bias us toward inaccurate decisions at times. Consider this example from one of the earliest studies on decision-making heuristics: "Consider the letter R. Is R more likely to appear in the first position of a word or the third position of a word?"[51] If your answer was the first position of a word, you answered incorrectly and fell victim to one of the most frequently talked about heuristics. The **availability bias** is the tendency for people to base their judgments on information that is easier to recall. It's significantly easier for almost everyone to remember words in which *R* is the first letter as opposed to the third. The availability bias is why more people are afraid to fly than statistics would support. Every single plane crash is plastered all over the news, making plane crashes more available in memory than successful plane landings.

Aside from the availability bias, there are many other biases that affect the way we make decisions. Table 8-4 describes six more of the most well-researched decision-making biases. After reading them, you might wonder how we ever make accurate decisions at all! The answer is that we do our best to think rationally through our most important decisions prior to making them and tend to use heuristics for decisions that are less important or that need to be made more quickly. Regardless of how often we fall victim to the biases, being aware of potential decision errors can help us make them less frequently. Interestingly enough, Lowe's, the North Carolina–based home improvement retailer, and several other companies are actually trying to take advantage of these types of biases and behavioral economics in order to get employees to make better decisions about their health benefits.[52] Workers are getting bombarded from all angles!

FAULTY ATTRIBUTIONS Another category of decision-making problems centers on how we explain the actions and events that occur around us. Research on attributions suggests that when people witness a behavior or outcome, they make a judgment about whether it was internally or externally caused. For example, when a coworker of yours named Joe shows up late to work and misses an important group presentation, you'll almost certainly make a judgment about why that happened. You might attribute Joe's outcome to internal factors—for example, suggesting that he is lazy or has a poor work ethic. Or you might attribute Joe's outcome to external factors—for example, suggesting that there was unusually bad traffic that day or that other factors prevented him from arriving on time.

TABLE 8-4	Decision-Making Biases
NAME OF BIAS	**DESCRIPTION**
Anchoring	The tendency to rely too heavily, or "anchor," on one trait or piece of information when making decisions even when the anchor might be unreliable or irrelevant. *Example: One recent study showed that initial bids for a bottle of wine in an auction could be heavily influenced by simply having subjects write down the last two digits of their Social Security number prior to putting a value on the bottle. Those with higher two-digit numbers tended to bid 60-120 percent more for a bottle of wine than those with low numbers.*
Framing	The tendency to make different decisions based on how a question or situation is phrased. *Example: Why do gas stations (or any retailer) give out discounts for paying cash as opposed to adding a surcharge for using a credit card? The discount is seen as a gain, while the surcharge is seen as a loss. Because humans are loss averse, we're more likely to give up the discount (the gain) than accept the surcharge (the loss).*
Representativeness	The tendency to assess the likelihood of an event by comparing it to a similar event and assuming it will be similar. *Example: Because a flipped coin has come up heads 10 times in a row, some assume the likelihood that it will come up tails is greater than 50-50. This is sometimes referred to as the "gambler's fallacy."*
Contrast	The tendency to judge things erroneously based on a reference that is near to them. *Example: If you were to take your hand out of a bowl of hot water and place it in a bowl of lukewarm water, you would describe that water as "cold." If someone else were to take their hand out of a bowl of extremely cold water and place it in the same bowl of lukewarm water, they would describe that water as "hot."*
Recency	The tendency to weigh recent events more than earlier events. *Example: A manager tends to weight ratings in performance evaluations based on an employee's behavior during the prior month as opposed to his or her behavior over the entire evaluation period.*
Ratio Bias Effect	The tendency to judge the same probability of an unlikely event as lower when the probability is presented in the form of a ratio of smaller rather than of larger numbers. *Example: When offered an opportunity to win $1 if they drew a red jelly bean, people frequently elected to draw from a bowl that contained a greater number but a smaller proportion of red beans (e.g., 7 in 100 vs. 1 in 10). Participants knew the probabilities were against them, but they "felt" they had a better chance when there were more beans.*

Sources: J. Baron, *Thinking and Deciding*, 3rd ed. (Cambridge, UK: Cambridge University Press, 2000); V. Denes-Raj and S. Epstein, "Conflict between Intuitive and Rational Processing: When People Behave against Their Better Judgment," *Journal of Personality and Social Psychology* 66 (1994), pp. 819–29; R.E. Nisbett and L. Ross, *Human Inference: Strategies and Shortcomings of Social Judgment* (Englewood Cliffs, NJ: Prentice Hall, 1980); D.G. Meyers, *Social Psychology* (Boston, MA: McGraw-Hill, 2005); G. Gigerenzer, P.M. Todd, and ABC Research Group, *Simple Heuristics That Make Us Smart* (New York: Oxford University Press, 1999); D. Kahneman, A. Tversky, and P. Slovic, *Judgment under Uncertainty: Heuristics & Biases* (Cambridge, UK: Cambridge University Press, 1982); and D. Kahneman and A. Tversky, "Choices, Values and Frames," *American Psychologist* 39 (1984), pp. 341–50.

The **fundamental attribution error** argues that people have a tendency to judge others' behaviors as due to internal factors.[53] This error suggests that you would likely judge Joe as having low motivation, poor organizational skills, or some other negative internal attribute. What if you yourself had showed up late? It turns out that we're less harsh when judging ourselves. The **self-serving bias** occurs when we attribute our own failures to external factors and our own successes to internal factors. Interestingly, evidence suggests that attributions across cultures don't always work the same way; see our **OB Internationally** feature for more discussion of this issue.

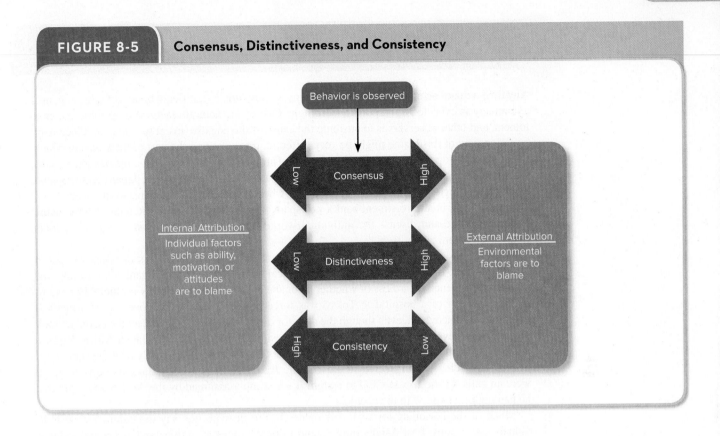

FIGURE 8-5   Consensus, Distinctiveness, and Consistency

One model of attribution processes suggests that when people have a level of familiarity with the person being judged, they'll use a more detailed decision framework. This model is illustrated in Figure 8-5.[54] To return to our previous example, if we want to explore why Joe arrived late to work, we can ask three kinds of questions:

Consensus: Did others act the same way under similar situations? In other words, did others arrive late on the same day?

Distinctiveness: Does this person tend to act differently in other circumstances? In other words, is Joe responsible when it comes to personal appointments, not just work appointments?

Consistency: Does this person always do this when performing this task? In other words, has Joe arrived late for work before?

The way in which these questions are answered will determine if an internal or external attribution is made. An internal attribution, such as laziness or low motivation for Joe, will occur if there is low consensus (others arrived on time), low distinctiveness (Joe is irresponsible with other commitments as well), and high consistency (Joe has arrived late before). An external attribution, such as bad traffic or a power outage, will occur if there is high consensus (others arrived late), high distinctiveness (Joe is responsible with other commitments), and low consistency (Joe has never come late to work before).

ESCALATION OF COMMITMENT Our last category of decision-making problems centers on what happens as a decision begins to go wrong. **Escalation of commitment** refers to the decision to continue to follow a failing course of action.[55] The expression "throwing good money after bad" captures this common decision-making error. An enormous amount of research shows that people have a tendency, when presented with a series of decisions, to escalate their commitment to previous decisions, even in the face of obvious failures.[56] Why do decision makers fall victim to this sort of error? They may feel an obligation to stick with their decision to avoid looking incompetent. They may also want to avoid admitting that they made a mistake. Those escalation tendencies become particularly strong when decision makers have invested a lot of money into the decision and when the project in question seems quite close to completion.[57]

OB INTERNATIONALLY

Any time a major accident occurs in a company, or any time a significant breach of ethics occurs, a company is expected to respond accordingly. One of the natural reactions of employees, customers, and other observers is to attribute the cause of the negative event to someone. Placement or assignment of this blame might be very different, depending on the part of the world in which the company is operating. A culture such as the United States tends to blame the particular individuals most responsible for the event, whereas East Asian (China, Korea, Japan) cultures tend to blame the organization itself. For example, when scandals within organizations occur (e.g., "rogue trading" in an investment bank), newspapers in the United States often publish the name of the employee and discuss the individual worker involved, whereas East Asian newspapers refer to the organization itself.

Interestingly, these biases place different responsibilities on the leaders of organizations in these countries. In East Asian cultures, it's typical for the leader of an organization to take the blame for accidents, regardless of whether he or she had direct responsibility for them. For example, the director of a hospital in Tokyo was forced to resign when the cover-up of a medical accident was discovered, even though the director didn't start his job until after the cover-up took place! Similar events are common, such as the resignation of the CEO of Japan Airlines after a jet crashed, killing 500 people. In the United States, in contrast, CEOs rarely take the same level of blame. When Joseph Hazelwood crashed the *Exxon Valdez* into the Alaskan coastline, there were no calls for the Exxon CEO to resign. It was simply assumed by the American public that he had nothing to do with the accident.

Much of the reasoning for such differences has to do with the way the cultures view individuals and groups. East Asian cultures tend to treat groups as entities and not as individuals, whereas the culture in the United States tends to see individuals acting of their own accord. This difference means that organizational leaders should be very cognizant of how to handle crises, depending on the country in which the negative event occurs. An apology offered by a senior leader is likely to be seen by East Asians as the company taking responsibility, whereas in the United States, it's more likely to be taken as an admission of personal guilt.

Sources: C. Chiu, M.W. Morris, Y. Hong, and T. Menon, "Motivated Cultural Cognition: The Impact of Implicit Cultural Theories on Dispositional Attribution Varies as a Function of Need for Closure," *Journal of Personality and Social Psychology* 78 (2000), pp. 247–59; T. Menon, M.W. Morris, C. Chiu, and Y. Hong, "Culture and the Construal of Agency: Attribution to Individual versus Group Dispositions," *Journal of Personality and Social Psychology* 76 (1999), pp. 701–17; and Y. Zemba, M.I. Young, and M.W. Morris, "Blaming Leaders for Organizational Accidents: Proxy Logic in Collective versus Individual-Agency Cultures," *Organizational Behavior and Human Decision Processes* 101 (2006), pp. 36–51.

One prominent example of escalation of commitment is United Airlines' abandonment of the automated baggage handling system at the Denver International Airport. When it initially opened (after a two-year delay), the baggage handling system with 26 miles of track designed to haul baggage across three terminals was supposed to be the single, most advanced baggage handling system in the world. However, originally scheduled to cost $186 million, a series of delays and technological problems caused the cost of the system to skyrocket by $1 million per day. Because of a series of technological issues, the system never really worked very well. In fact, United was the only airline in the airport willing to use it. It took 10 years and many mangled and lost suitcases before United finally "cut its losses," saving itself $1 million a month in maintenance fees.[58] If you ever find yourself in this predicament, recent research suggests that by focusing on what you have to gain by moving on, rather than what you have to lose, will reduce your chances of committing escalation of commitment.[59] For more discussion of decision-making problems, see our **OB at the Bookstore** feature.

OB AT THE BOOKSTORE

THINKING, FAST AND SLOW
by Daniel Kahneman (New York: Farrar, Straus and Giroux, 2012).

The best we can do is a compromise: learn to recognize situations in which mistakes are likely and try harder to avoid significant mistakes when the stakes are high. The premise of this book is that it is easier to recognize other people's mistakes than our own.

With those words, Daniel Kahneman brings home the idea that there are times when we should pay a good amount of attention to how we make decisions and other times when we can safely let our brain simplify the world around us. Kahneman, a winner of the Nobel Prize for Economics and one of the foremost researchers on decision making and cognitive biases, lays out all the evidence about how people make decisions in *Thinking, Fast and Slow.* If you've enjoyed reading about the mistakes people tend to make when making decisions in this chapter, Kahneman's book will give you all that and much more. Focused on all the research that has been done on cognitive biases but written in an extremely readable style, *Thinking, Fast and Slow* will likely be considered the definitive book on the subject for a long time.

Kahneman explains that our thinking consists of two systems. System 1 (Thinking Fast) is our effort-free, unconscious thinking. System 2 (Thinking Slow) is our rational, conscious thinking.

Photo of cover: © Roberts Publishing Services.

Because most of the decision-making biases we exhibit all occur with System 1 thinking, we like to think that we spend most of our time using System 2 to guide our actions, but the opposite is much closer to reality. We simply don't have time to dedicate System 2 thinking to most of the situations we encounter. It also turns out that System 1 gives us the right answers much more often than not. Kahneman notes, "System 1 is indeed the origin of much that we do wrong, but it is also the origin of most of what we do right—which is most of what we do." However, for decisions with important outcomes, we should dedicate some System 2 resources rather than using what simply comes to mind.

United Airlines took 10 years to finally abandon an expensive but faulty baggage handling system at Denver International Airport, illustrating the power of escalation of commitment.

© Kevin Moloney/The New York Times/Redux

SUMMARY: WHY DO SOME EMPLOYEES LEARN TO MAKE DECISIONS BETTER THAN OTHERS?

So what explains why some employees learn to make better decisions than others? As shown in Figure 8-6, answering that question requires understanding how employees learn, what kind of knowledge they gain, and how they use that knowledge to make decisions. Employees learn from a combination of reinforcement and observation, and that learning depends in part on whether they are learning-oriented or performance-oriented. Some of that learning results in increases in explicit knowledge, and some of that learning results in increases in tacit knowledge. Those two forms of knowledge, which combine to form an employee's expertise, are then used in decision making. If a given problem has been encountered before, decision making occurs in a more automatic, programmed fashion. If the problem is new or unfamiliar, nonprogrammed decision making occurs and, in the best-case scenario, follows the rational decision-making model.

FIGURE 8-6   **Why Do Some Employees Learn to Make Decisions Better Than Others?**

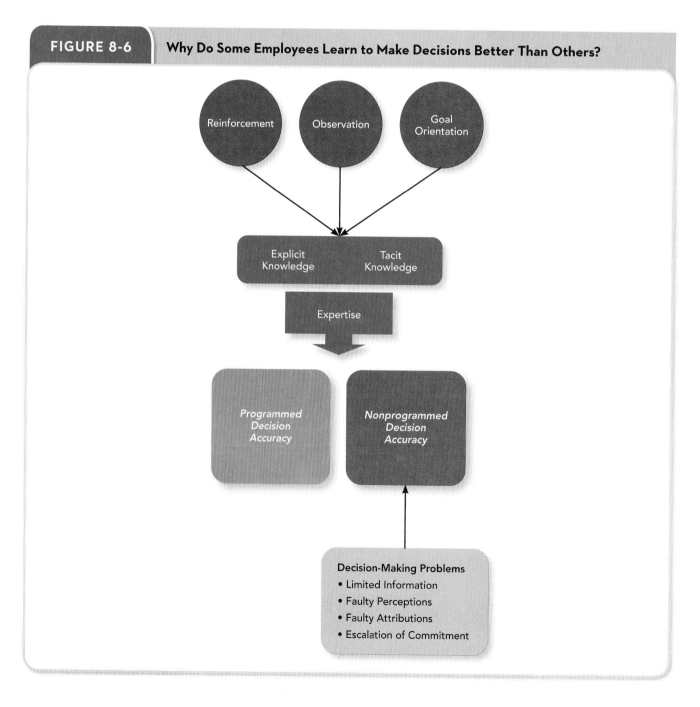

Unfortunately, a number of decision-making problems can hinder the effectiveness of such decisions, including limited information, faulty perceptions, faulty attributions, and escalation of commitment.

HOW IMPORTANT IS LEARNING?

Does learning have a significant impact on the two primary outcomes in our integrative model of OB—does it correlate with job performance and organizational commitment? Figure 8-7 summarizes the research evidence linking learning to job performance and organizational commitment. The figure reveals that learning does influence job performance. Why? The primary reason is that learning is moderately correlated with task performance. It's difficult to fulfill one's job duties if the employee doesn't possess adequate levels of job knowledge. In fact, there are reasons to suggest that the moderate correlation depicted in the figure is actually an underestimate of learning's importance. That's because most of the research linking learning to task performance focuses on explicit knowledge, which is more practical to measure. It's difficult to measure tacit knowledge because of its unspoken nature, but clearly such knowledge is relevant to task performance. Learning seems less relevant to citizenship behavior and counterproductive behavior however, given that those behaviors are often less dependent on knowledge and expertise.

Figure 8-7 also reveals that learning is only weakly related to organizational commitment.[60] In general, having higher levels of job knowledge is associated with slight increases in emotional attachment to the firm. It's true that companies that have a reputation as organizations that value learning tend to receive higher-quality applicants for jobs.[61] However, there's an important

8.6

How does learning affect job performance and organizational commitment?

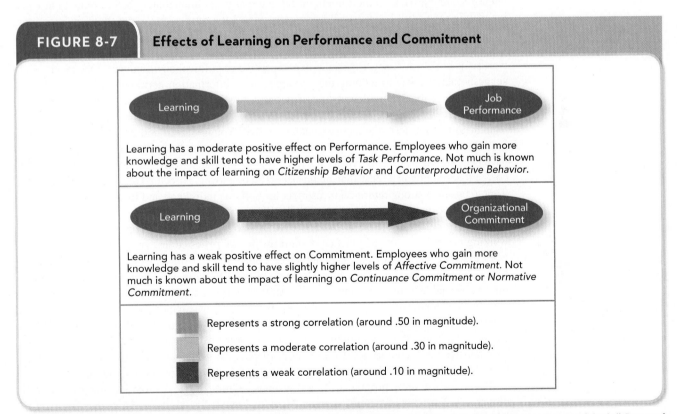

FIGURE 8-7 **Effects of Learning on Performance and Commitment**

Sources: G.M. Alliger, S.I. Tannenbaum, W. Bennett Jr., H. Traver, and A. Shotland, "A Meta-Analysis of the Relations among Training Criteria," *Personnel Psychology* 50 (1997), pp. 341–58; J.A. Colquitt, J.A. LePine, and R.A. Noe, "Toward an Integrative Theory of Training Motivation: A Meta-Analytic Path Analysis of 20 Years of Research," *Journal of Applied Psychology* 85 (2000), pp. 678–707; and J.P. Meyer, D.J. Stanley, L. Herscovitch, and L. Topolnytsky, "Affective, Continuance, and Normative Commitment to the Organization: A Meta-Analysis of Antecedents, Correlates, and Consequences," *Journal of Vocational Behavior* 61 (2002), pp. 20–52.

distinction between organizations that offer learning opportunities and employees who take advantage of those opportunities to actually gain knowledge. Moreover, it may be that employees with higher levels of expertise become more highly valued commodities on the job market, thereby reducing their levels of continuance commitment.

APPLICATION: TRAINING

How can organizations improve learning in an effort to boost employee expertise and, ultimately, improve decision making? One approach is to rely on **training,** which represents a systematic effort by organizations to facilitate the learning of job-related knowledge and behavior. Organizations spent more than $150 billion on training in 2014, or $1,208 per learner. On average, employees receive 31.5 hours of training per year.[62] A full discussion of all the types of training companies offer is beyond the scope of this section, but suffice it to say that companies are using many different methods to help their employees acquire explicit and tacit knowledge. Technological changes are altering the way those methods are delivered, as instructor-led classroom training has declined over the last decade while online self-study programs and other forms of e-learning involve 25 percent of learning hours.[63]

8.7

What steps can organizations take to foster learning?

In addition to traditional training experiences, companies are also heavily focused on **knowledge transfer** from their older, experienced workers to their younger employees. Some companies are using variations of **behavior modeling training** to ensure that employees have the ability to observe and learn from those in the company with significant amounts of tacit knowledge. For example, Herman Miller, a furniture manufacturer in Zeeland, Michigan, allows retiring employees to cut back on their hours during the two years immediately before retirement while maintaining their full benefits. This is a win–win as the retiree gets to ease into the emotional adjustment that comes with retirement, but the company gets to have the employees slowly pass on their knowledge and skills to those underneath them.[64] Such sharing of information between workers is not always easy, especially in competitive or political environments. One recent study suggests that one key to helping the passing of tacit information between coworkers is trust.[65] (See Chapter 7 for a more detailed description of how to foster trust.) One of the most difficult but most necessary periods of learning for employees is when they are sent outside their home country to work (referred to as expatriates). Ernst & Young has around 2,600 employees placed in international locations at any given time. The company uses "mobility experts," partners who have been overseas, to help expatriates learn how to operate and live in these new cultures. The cost of that training is far less than an unsuccessful employee. Director Troy Dickerson says, "We want to ensure a strong return on investment for both the individual and Ernst & Young."[66]

Another form of knowledge transfer that's being used by companies more frequently, as described in our opening example, is social networking. One such example of this type of networking is communities of practice. **Communities of practice** are groups of employees who work together and learn from one another by collaborating over an extended period of time.[67] Many companies such as PwC, John Deere, Shell, and Verizon are adopting this newer form of informal social learning.[68] Cadbury, the Birmingham, England, confectionary manufacturer, has developed a global knowledge community to distribute knowledge throughout the company. Due to the fact that Cadbury has grown mainly by acquiring other companies all around the world, the company feels that these communities break down some of the walls that are created by having 64 worksites in 36 countries.[69] Communities of practice introduce their own unique complications, but their potential for transferring knowledge through employees is significant.[70]

The success of these programs, as well as more traditional types of training, hinges on transfer of training. **Transfer of training** occurs when the knowledge, skills, and behaviors used on the job are maintained by the learner once training ends and generalized to the workplace once the learner returns to the job.[71] Transfer of training can be fostered if organizations create a **climate for transfer**—an environment that can support the use of new skills. There are a variety of factors that can help organizations foster such a climate. The degree to which the trainee's manager supports the importance of the newly acquired knowledge and skills and stresses their application to the job is perhaps the most important factor. Peer support is helpful, because having multiple trainees learning the same material reduces anxiety and allows the trainees to share concerns and work through problems. Opportunities to use the learned knowledge are also crucial, because practice and repetition are key components of learning. Because companies have a huge stake in increasing and transferring knowledge within their employee base, creating a climate for the transfer of that knowledge is imperative to the success of formal learning systems.

TAKEAWAYS

8.1 Learning is a relatively permanent change in an employee's knowledge or skill that results from experience. Decision making refers to the process of generating and choosing from a set of alternatives to solve a problem. Learning allows employees to make better decisions by making those decisions more quickly and by being able to generate a better set of alternatives.

8.2 Employees gain both explicit and tacit knowledge as they build expertise. Explicit knowledge is easily communicated and available to everyone. Tacit knowledge, however, is something employees can learn only through experience.

8.3 Employees learn new knowledge through reinforcement and observation of others. That learning also depends on whether the employees are learning-oriented or performance-oriented.

8.4 Programmed decisions are decisions that become somewhat automatic because a person's knowledge allows him or her to recognize and identify a situation and the course of action that needs to be taken. Many task-related decisions made by experts are programmed decisions. Nonprogrammed decisions are made when a problem is new, complex, or not recognized. Ideally, such decisions are made by following the steps in the rational decision-making model.

8.5 Employees are less able to translate their learning into accurate decisions when they struggle with limited information, faulty perceptions, faulty attributions, and escalation of commitment.

8.6 Learning has a moderate positive relationship with job performance and a weak positive relationship with organizational commitment.

8.7 Through various forms of training, companies can give employees more knowledge and a wider array of experiences that they can use to make decisions.

KEY TERMS

- Learning   *p. 236*
- Decision making   *p. 236*
- Expertise   *p. 237*
- Explicit knowledge   *p. 237*
- Tacit knowledge   *p. 237*
- Contingencies of reinforcement   *p. 239*
- Positive reinforcement   *p. 239*
- Negative reinforcement   *p. 239*
- Punishment   *p. 239*
- Extinction   *p. 240*
- Schedules of reinforcement   *p. 240*
- Continuous reinforcement   *p. 240*
- Fixed interval schedule   *p. 240*
- Variable interval schedule   *p. 240*
- Fixed ratio schedule   *p. 241*
- Variable ratio schedule   *p. 241*
- Social learning theory   *p. 241*
- Behavioral modeling   *p. 241*

- Learning orientation   *p. 242*
- Performance-prove orientation   *p. 243*
- Performance-avoid orientation   *p. 243*
- Programmed decision   *p. 244*
- Intuition   *p. 244*
- Crisis situation   *p. 244*
- Nonprogrammed decision   *p. 246*
- Rational decision-making model *p. 246*
- Bounded rationality   *p. 246*
- Satisficing   *p. 248*
- Selective perception   *p. 248*
- Projection bias   *p. 248*
- Social identity theory   *p. 249*
- Stereotype   *p. 249*

- Heuristics   *p. 249*
- Availability bias   *p. 249*
- Fundamental attribution error   *p. 250*
- Self-serving bias   *p. 250*
- Consensus   *p. 251*
- Distinctiveness   *p. 251*
- Consistency   *p. 251*
- Escalation of commitment   *p. 251*
- Training   *p. 256*
- Knowledge transfer   *p. 256*
- Behavior modeling training   *p. 256*
- Communities of practice   *p. 256*
- Transfer of training   *p. 256*
- Climate for transfer   *p. 256*

DISCUSSION QUESTIONS

8.1   In your current or past workplaces, what types of tacit knowledge did experienced workers possess? What did this knowledge allow them to do?

8.2   Companies rely on employees with substantial amounts of tacit knowledge. Why do companies struggle when these employees leave the organization unexpectedly? What can companies do to help ensure that they retain tacit knowledge?

8.3   What does the term "expert" mean to you? What exactly do experts do that novices don't?

8.4   Do you consider yourself to be a "rational" decision maker? For what types of decisions are you determined to be the most rational? What types of decisions are likely to cause you to behave irrationally?

8.5   Given your background, which of the decision-making biases listed in the chapter do you most struggle with? What could you do to overcome those biases to make more accurate decisions?

CASE: UPS

The job is so large that by shaving just one mile off the average daily travel of all of its drivers, UPS can save around $50 million a year. Sounds easy, right? Not so fast. If the average UPS driver makes 120 stops per day, there are 6,689,502,913,449,135,000,000,000,000, 000,000, 000,000,000,000,000, 000,000,000,000,000,000,000,000,000,000,000,000,000,000,000, 000,000,000, 000,000,000,000,000,000,000,000,000,000,000,000,000,000,000,000,000,000,000,000,000, 000,000,000, 000,000,000,000,000,000,000,000,000,000 alternatives for ordering those stops. Needless to say, there are a few options for UPS drivers to work though each day when they are trying to figure out their route. Given the potential savings, perhaps it would be easiest simply to calculate the shortest geographical distance between stops over the course of a day. That would be one option, but there is a lot more to it than that. What times do businesses accept deliveries? When is traffic the most crowded at any given point in the day? And consider that 80-year-old Mrs. Abernathy likes the fact that her UPS driver generally shows up between 3 and 4 p.m. every day.

   To help solve this daily dilemma, UPS has spent more than 10 years and hundreds of millions of dollars to develop a computer program they call ORION (On-Road Integrated Optimization and Navigation). Jack Levis, senior director of process management at UPS, says, "Can a human really think of the best way to deliver 120 stops? This is where the algorithm will come in. It will explore paths of doing things you would not, because there are just too many combinations." UPS expects that upon completion of rolling out ORION across the United States by the end of 2016, it will save the company $300 to $400 million a year.

Of course, this all makes perfect sense in theory. However, driver reaction has been mixed—ranging from some drivers being surprised at the program's ability to improve things, even when it didn't make sense, to some drivers refusing to follow orders due to what seems to be illogical to them. After all, many UPS drivers have been driving their routes for years—they know the best delivery times, where to park so they can make multiple deliveries at once, and other decisions they make on the basis of their tacit knowledge. Now a computer is telling them to deliver a package to a neighborhood in the morning, leave the neighborhood, and come back again in the afternoon? UPS is trying to take driver experience into account, primarily by using 700 trainers to help work through 55,000 U.S. routes with each driver. The training process with each driver takes six days with constant discussions, updated routing, and making revisions along the way. Levis says that ORION is supposed to complement and not replace driver judgment. "We do want drivers to override ORION if it doesn't make sense," Levin says.

8.1   How do you expect UPS drivers to react to ORION when much of their autonomy in decision making is taken away? Should UPS care?

8.2   Under what circumstances should a company tell employees to use their own intuition and tacit knowledge over and above what a rational computer program is telling them is the most efficient way to do their job?

8.3   What else could UPS do to convince their drivers of the usefulness of ORION?

Sources: J. Berman, "UPS Is Focused on the Future for Its ORION Technology," *Logistics Management*, March 3, 2015; M. Gaynor, "Could You Drive a UPS Truck?" *Washingtonian*, December 6, 2010; J. Levitz, "UPS Thinks Outside the Box on Training," *The Wall Street Journal*, April 6, 2010, p. B1; K. Noyes, "The Shortest Distance Between Two Points? At UPS, It's Complicated," July 25, 2014; S. Rosenbush and L. Stevens, "At UPS, the Algorithm Is The Driver," *The Wall Street Journal*, February 16, 2015, p. B1; L. Stevens, "For UPS, FedEx, a Merry Christmas," *The Wall Street Journal*, December 30, 2014, p B1; J. Surowiecki, "Why Drone Delivery Won't Replace the UPS Guy," *New Yorker*, December 5, 2013, p. 32; UPS.,"Bet You Didn't Know How UPS Trains New Drivers," http://compass.ups.com/how-UPS-trains-new-drivers (accessed June 2015); and UPS, "UPS Fact Sheet," https://www.pressroom.ups.com/pressroom/ContentDetailsViewer.page?ConceptType=FactSheets&id=1426321563187-193 (accessed June 2015).

EXERCISE: DECISION-MAKING BIAS

The purpose of this exercise is to illustrate how decision making can be influenced by decision heuristics, availability bias, and escalation of commitment. The exercise has the following steps:

8.1   Answer each of the following problems.

   A. A certain town is served by two hospitals. In the larger hospital, about 45 babies are born each day, and in the smaller hospital, about 15 babies are born each day. Although the overall proportion of boys is about 50 percent, the actual proportion at either hospital may be greater or less than 50 percent on any given day. At the end of a year, which hospital will have the greater number of days on which more than 60 percent of the babies born were boys?

   a. The large hospital

   b. The small hospital

   c. Neither—the number of days will be about the same (within 5 percent of each other)

B. Linda is 31 years of age, single, outspoken, and very bright. She majored in philosophy in college. As a student, she was deeply concerned with discrimination and other social issues and participated in antinuclear demonstrations. Which statement is more likely?

a. Linda is a bank teller.

b. Linda is a bank teller and active in the feminist movement.

C. A cab was involved in a hit-and-run accident. Two cab companies serve the city: the Green, which operates 85 percent of the cabs, and the Blue, which operates the remaining 15 percent. A witness identifies the hit-and-run cab as Blue. When the court tests the reliability of the witness under circumstances similar to those on the night of the accident, he correctly identifies the color of the cab 80 percent of the time and misidentifies it the other 20 percent. What's the probability that the cab involved in the accident was Blue, as the witness stated?

D. Imagine that you face this pair of concurrent decisions. Examine these decisions, then indicate which choices you prefer.

Decision I: Choose between:

a. A sure gain of $240 and

b. A 25 percent chance of winning $1,000 and a 75 percent chance of winning nothing

Decision II: Choose between:

a. A sure loss of $750 and

b. A 75 percent chance of losing $1,000 and a 25 percent chance of losing nothing

Decision III: Choose between:

a. A sure loss of $3,000 and

b. An 80 percent chance of losing $4,000 and a 20 percent chance of losing nothing

E. You've decided to see a Broadway play and have bought a $150 ticket. As you enter the theater, you realize you've lost your ticket. You can't remember the seat number, so you can't prove to the management that you bought a ticket. Would you spend $150 for a new ticket?

F. You've reserved a seat for a Broadway play, for which the ticket price is $150. As you enter the theater to buy your ticket, you discover you've lost $150 from your pocket. Would you still buy the ticket? (Assume you have enough cash left to do so.)

G. Imagine you have operable lung cancer and must choose between two treatments: surgery and radiation. Of 100 people having surgery, 10 die during the operation, 32 (including those original 10) are dead after 1 year, and 66 are dead after 5 years. Of 100 people having radiation therapy, none dies during treatment, 23 are dead after 1 year, and 78 after 5 years. Which treatment would you prefer?

8.2 Your instructor will give you the correct answer to each problem. Class discussion, whether in groups or as a class, should focus on the following questions: How accurate were the decisions you reached? What decision-making problems were evident in the decisions you reached? Consider especially where decision heuristics, availability, and escalation of commitment may have influenced your decisions. How could you improve your decision making to make it more accurate?[72]

ENDNOTES

8.1 Weiss, H.M. "Learning Theory and Industrial and Organizational Psychology." In *Handbook of Industrial* *and Organizational Psychology,* ed. M.D. Dunnette and L.M. Hough. Palo Alto, CA: Consulting Psychologists Press, 1990, pp. 75–169.

8.2 Tai, B., and N.R. Lockwood. "Organizational

Entry: Onboarding, Orientation, and Socialization." *SHRM Research Paper* (n.d.), http://www.shrm.org.

8.3 Buford, B. *Heat.* New York: Knopf, 2006, pp. 49–50.

8.4 Ericsson, K.A. "An Introduction to *Cambridge Handbook of Expertise and Expert Performance:* Its Development, Organization, and Content." In *The Cambridge Handbook of Expertise and Expert Performance,* ed. K.A. Ericsson; N. Charness; P.J. Feltovich; and R.R. Hoffman. New York: Cambridge University Press, 2006, pp. 3–19.

8.5 Ericsson, K.A., and A.C. Lehmann. "Experts and Exceptional Performance: Evidence of Maximal Adaptation to Task Constraints." *Annual Review of Psychology* 47 (1996), pp. 273–305.

8.6 Brockmann, E.N., and W.P. Anthony. "Tacit Knowledge and Strategic Decision Making." *Group & Organizational Management* 27, December 2002, pp. 436–55.

8.7 Wagner, R.K., and R.J. Sternberg. "Practical Intelligence in Real-World Pursuits: The Role of Tacit Knowledge." *Journal of Personality and Social Psychology* 4 (1985), pp. 436–58.

8.8 Wah, L. "Making Knowledge Stick."

Management Review 88 (1999), pp. 24–33.

8.9 Eucker, T.R. "Understanding the Impact of Tacit Knowledge Loss." *Knowledge Management Review,* March 2007, pp. 10–13.

8.10 McAdam, R.; B. Mason; and J. McCrory. "Exploring the Dichotomies Within the Tacit Knowledge Literature: Towards a Process of Tacit Knowing in Organizations." *Journal of Knowledge Management* 11 (2007), pp. 43–59.

8.11 Lawson, C., and E. Lorenzi. "Collective Learning, Tacit Knowledge, and Regional Innovative Capacity." *Regional Studies* 21 (1999), pp. 487–513.

8.12 Bou-Llusar, J.C., and M. Segarra-Ciprés. "Strategic Knowledge Transfer and Its Implications for Competitive Advantage: An Integrative Conceptual Framework." *Journal of Knowledge Management* 10 (2006), pp. 100–12; Nonaka, I. "The Knowledge-Creating Company." *Harvard Business Review* 69 (1991), pp. 96–104; and Nonaka, I. "A Dynamic Theory of Organizational Knowledge Creation." *Organizational Science* 5 (1994), pp. 14–37.

8.13 Luthans, F., and R. Kreitner. *Organizational Behavior Modification and Beyond.* Glenview, IL: Scott, Foresman, 1985.

8.14 Latham, G.P., and V.L. Huber. "Schedules of Reinforcement: Lessons from the Past and Issues for Future." *Journal of Organizational Behavior Management* 13 (1992), pp. 125–49.

8.15 Pinder, C. *Work Motivation in Organizational Behavior.* New York: Psychology Press, 2008.

8.16 Luthans and Kreitner, *Organizational Behavior Modification.*

8.17 Pinder, *Work Motivation.*

8.18 Ibid.

8.19 Bandura, A. *Social Foundations of Thought and Action: A Social Cognitive Theory.* Englewood Cliffs, NJ: Prentice Hall, 1986.

8.20 Weiss, "Learning Theory."

8.21 Pescuric, A., and W.C. Byham. "The New Look of Behavior Modeling." *Training & Development,* July 1996, pp. 24–30.

8.22 Kimes, M. "Keeping Your Senior Staffers." *Fortune,* July 20, 2009, p. 146.

8.23 Mulcahy, A. "How I Did It: Xerox's Former CEO on Why Succession Shouldn't Be a Horse Race." *Harvard Business Review,* October 2010, pp. 47–51; and Gelles, D. "Burns to Replace Mulcahy at Xerox." *Financial Times,* May 22, 2009, p. 16.

8.24 Ellison, S. "Lowell McAdam: Seidenberg's 'Air' Apparent." *Fortune,* October 20, 2010, http://tech.fortune.cnn.com/2010/10/29/lowell-mcadam-seidenbergs-air-apparent/.

8.25 Kish-Gephart, J.J.; D.A. Harrison; L.K. Treviño; and L. Klebe. "Bad Apples, Bad Cases, and Bad Barrels: Meta-Analytic Evidence about Sources of Unethical Decisions at Work." *Journal of Applied Psychology* 95 (2010), pp. 1–31.

8.26 Sims, R.R., and J. Brinkmann. "Leaders as Moral Role Models: The Case of John Gutfreund at Salomon Brothers." *Journal of Business Ethics* 35 (2002), pp. 327–40.

8.27 Biron, M., and P. Bamberger. "Aversive Workplace Conditions and Absenteeism: Taking Referent Group Norms and Supervisor Account into Account." *Journal of Applied Psychology* 97 (2012), pp. 901–12; and Mitchell, M.S., and M.L. Ambrose. "Employee's Behavioral Reactions to Supervisor Aggression: An Examination of Individual and Situational Factors." *Journal of Applied Psychology* 97 (2012), pp. 1148–70.

8.28 VandeWalle, D. "Development and Validation of a Work Domain Goal Orientation Instrument." *Educational and Psychological Measurement* 8 (1997), pp. 995–1015.

8.29 Payne, S.C.; S. Youngcourt; and J.M. Beaubien. "A Meta-Analytic Examination of the Goal Orientation Nomological Net." *Journal of Applied Psychology* 92 (2007), pp. 128–50.

8.30 Ibid.

8.31 Cannon-Bowers, J.A.; L. Rhodenizer; E. Salas; and C. Bowers. "A Framework for Understanding Pre-Practice Conditions and Their Impact on Learning." *Personnel Psychology* 51 (1998), pp. 291–320.

8.32 Mesmer-Magnus, J., and C. Viswesvaran. "The Role of Pre-Training Interventions in Learning: A Meta-Analysis and Integrative Review." *Human Resource Management Review* 20 (2010), pp. 261–82.

8.33 Dane, E., and M.G. Pratt. "Exploring Intuition and Its Role in Managerial Decision Making." *Academy of Management Review* 32 (2007), pp. 33–54; and Hayashi, A.M. "When to Trust Your Gut." *Harvard Business Review,* February 2001, pp. 59–65.

8.34 Hogarth, R.M. "Intuition: A Challenge for Psychological Research on Decision Making." *Psychological Inquiry* 21 (2010), pp. 338–53.

8.35 March, J.G. *A Primer on Decision Making.* New York: The Free Press, 1994.

8.36 Dane, E.; K.W. Rockmann; and M.G. Pratt. "When Should I Trust My Gut? Linking Domain Expertise to Intuitive Decision-Making Effectiveness." *Organizational Behavior and Human Decision Processes* 119 (2012), pp. 187–94.

8.37 Seeger, M.W.; T.L. Sellnow; and R.R. Ulmer. "Communication, Organization and Crisis." *Communication Yearbook* 21 (1998), pp. 231–75.

8.38 Weick, K.E., and K.M. Sutcliffe. *Managing the Unexpected: Resilient Performance in an Age of Uncertainty,* 2nd ed. San Francisco: Jossey-Bass, 2007.

8.39 Klein, G. *Sources of Power.* Cambridge, MA: MIT Press, 1999.

8.40 Weick, K.E. "Managerial Thought in the Context of Action." In *The Executive Mind,* ed. S. Srivasta. San Francisco: Jossey-Bass, 1983, pp. 221–42; Weick and Sutcliffe, *Managing the Unexpected;* and Klein, G. *The Power of Intuition.* New York: Currency Doubleday, 2003.

8.41 Simon, H.A. "A Behavioral Model of Rational Choice." *Quarterly Journal of Economics* 69 (1955), pp. 99–118.

8.42 http://www.quo-tationspage.com/quote/25953.html (accessed April 2011).

8.43 Simon, H.A. "Rational Decision Making in Organizations." *American Economic Review* 69 (1979), pp. 493–513.

8.44 March, J.G., and H.A. Simon. *Organizations.* New York: Wiley, 1958.

8.45 Ibid.

8.46 Hogg, M.A., and D.J. Terry. "Social Identity and Self-Categorization Process in Organizational Contexts." *Academy of Management Review* 25, January 2000, pp. 121–40.

8.47 Judd, C.M., and B. Park. "Definition and Assessment of Accuracy in Social Stereotypes." *Psychological Review* 100, January 1993, pp. 109–28.

8.48 Ashforth, B.E., and F. Mael. "Social Identity Theory and the Organization." *Academy of Management Review* 14 (1989), pp. 20–39; and Howard, J.A. "Social Psychology of Identities." *Annual Review of Sociology* 26 (2000), pp. 367–93.

8.49 Society for Human Resource Management. "Diversity Training," 2014, http://www.shrm.org/diversity.

8.50 Kahneman, D.; P. Slovic; and A. Tversky, eds. *Judgment under Uncertainty: Heuristics and Biases.* Cambridge, UK: Cambridge University Press, 1982.

8.51 Kahneman, D., and A. Tversky. "On the Psychology of Prediction." *Psychological Review* 80 (1973), pp. 237–51.

8.52 Smerd, J. "In Worker's Heads." *Workforce Management,* June 22, 2009, pp. 34–39.

8.53 Ross, L. "The Intuitive Psychologist and His Shortcomings: Distortions in the Attribution Process." In *Advances in Experimental Social Psychology,* ed. L. Berkowitz. New York: Academic Press, 1977, pp. 173–220. See also Jones, E.E., and V.A. Harris. "The Attribution of Attitudes." *Journal of Experimental Social Psychology* 3 (1967), pp. 1–24.

8.54 Kelley, H.H. "The Processes of Casual Attribution." *American Psychologist* 28 (1973), pp. 107–28; and Kelley, H.H. "Attribution in Social Interaction." In *Attribution: Perceiving the Causes of Behavior,* ed. E. Jones. Morristown, NJ: General Learning Press, 1972.

8.55 Staw, B.M., and J. Ross. "Behavior in Escalation Situations: Antecedents, Prototypes, and Solutions." In *Research in Organizational Behavior,* Vol. 9, ed. L.L. Cummings and B.M. Staw. Greenwich, CT: JAI Press, 1987, pp. 39–78; and Staw, B.M. "Knee-Deep in the Big Muddy: A Study of Escalating Commitment to a Chosen Course of Action." *Organizational Behavior and Human Performance* 16 (1976), pp. 27–44.

8.56 Brockner, J. "The Escalation of Commitment to a Failing Course of Action: Toward Theoretical Progress." *Academy of Management Review* 17 (1992), pp. 39–61; and Staw, B.M. "The Escalation of Commitment: An Update and Appraisal." In *Organizational Decision Making,* ed. Z. Shapira. New York: Cambridge University Press, 1997.

8.57 Conlon, D.E., and H. Garland. "The Role of Project Completion Information in Resource Allocation Decisions." *Academy of Management Journal* 36 (1993), pp. 402–13; and Moon, H. "Looking Forward and Looking Back: Integrating Completion and Sunk-Cost Effects within an Escalation of Commitment Progress Decision." *Journal of Applied Psychology* 86 (2001), pp. 104–13.

8.58 Johnson, K. "Denver Airport to Mangle Last Bag." *The New York Times,* August 27, 2005.

8.59 Molden, D.C., and C.M. Hui. "Promoting De-Escalation of Commitment: A Regulatory-Focus Perspective on Sunk Costs." *Psychological Science* 22 (2011), pp. 8–12.

8.60 Alliger, G.M.; S.I. Tannenbaum; W. Bennett Jr.; H. Traver; and A. Shotland. "A Meta-Analysis of the Relations among Training Criteria." *Personnel Psychology* 50 (1997), pp. 341–58; Colquitt, J.A.; J.A. LePine; and R.A. Noe. "Toward an Integrative Theory of Training Motivation: A Meta-Analytic Path Analysis of 20 Years of Research." *Journal of Applied Psychology* 85 (2000), pp. 678–707; and Meyer, J.P.; D.J. Stanley; L. Herscovitch; and L. Topolnytsky. "Affective, Continuance, and Normative Commitment to the Organization: A Meta-Analysis of Antecedents, Correlates, and Consequences." *Journal of Vocational Behavior* 61 (2002), pp. 20–52.

8.61 Averbrook, J. "Connecting CLOs with the Recruiting Process." *Chief Learning Officer* 4 (2005), pp. 24–27.

8.62 Miller, L. "2014 State of the Industry Report: Spending on Employee Training Remains a Priority." *TD: Talent Development,* November 2014, pp. 30–35.

8.63 Ibid.

8.64 Milligan, S. "Wisdom of the Ages." *HRMagazine,* November 2014, pp. 22–27.

8.65 Holste, J.S., and D. Fields. "Trust and Tacit Knowledge Sharing and Use." *Journal of Knowledge Management* 14 (2010), pp. 128–40.

8.66 Ladika, S. "Shipping and Handling: Picking the Right People to Head Overseas Is Paramount." *Workforce Management,* March 1, 2013,http://www.workforce.com/article/20130301/NEWS 02/130309992/shipping-and-handling-picking-the-right-people-to-head-overseas-is.

8.67 Retna, K.S., and P.T. Ng. "Communities of Practice: Dynamics and Success Factors." *Leadership and Organization Development Journal* 32 (2011), pp. 41–59; and Sauve, E. "Informal Knowledge Transfer." *T + D* 61 (2007), pp. 22–24.

8.68 Overton, L. "Learning Innovators." *E.learning Age,* July/August 2014, pp. 12–14; Ligdas, N. "Using a Wiki Portal to Support Organizational Excellence at Shell." *Knowledge Management Review,* October 2009, p. 1; and Allan, B., and D. Lewis. "Virtual Learning Communities as a Vehicle for Workforce Development: A Case Study." *Journal of Workplace Learning* 18 (2006), pp. 367–83.

8.69 Twentyman, J. "Connecting People Is a Recipe for Innovation at Cadbury." *Knowledge Management Review,* December 2009, p. 1.

8.70 Noe, R.A. *Employee Training and Development.* New York: Irwin/McGraw-Hill, 1999.

8.71 Tracey, J.B.; S.I. Tannenbaum; and M.J. Kavanaugh. "Applying Trained Skills on the Job: The Importance of the Work Environment." *Journal of Applied Psychology* 80 (1995), pp. 239–52.

8.72 Ivancevich, J.; R. Konopaske; and M. Matteson. *Organizational Behavior and Management,* 7th ed. New York: McGraw-Hill, 2005. Reprinted with permission of The McGraw-Hill Companies. The original exercises are based on the following sources: (1) Tversky, A., and D. Kahneman. "Rational Choice and the Framing of Decisions." *Journal of Business* 59 (1986), pp. 251–78; (2) Tversky, A., and D. Kahneman. "The Framing of Decisions and the Psychology of Choice." *Science* 211 (1981), pp. 453–58; (3) Tversky, A., and D. Kahneman. "Extensional vs. Intuitive Reasoning: The Conjunction Fallacy in Probability Judgment." *Psychological Review* 90 (1983), pp. 293–315; and (4) McKean, K. "Decisions, Decisions." *Discovery Magazine,* June 1985.

PART

3

INDIVIDUAL CHARACTERISTICS

CHAPTER 9
Personality and Cultural Values

CHAPTER 10
Ability

Personality and Cultural Values

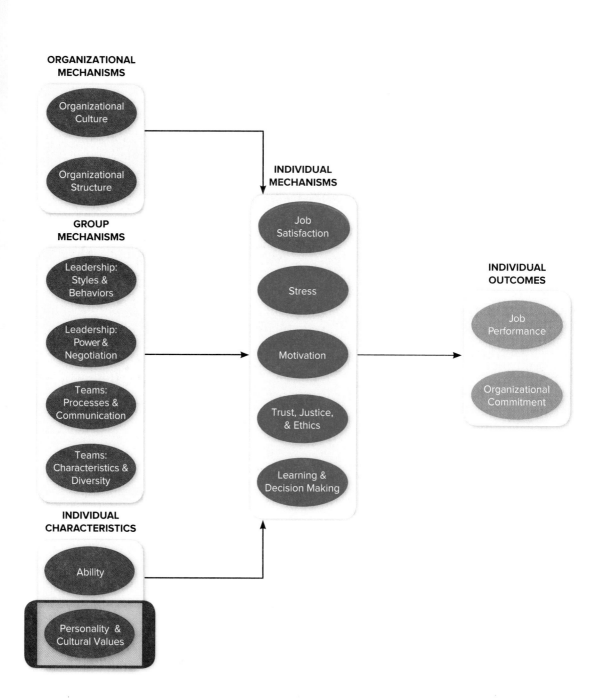

ORGANIZATIONAL MECHANISMS

- Organizational Culture
- Organizational Structure

GROUP MECHANISMS

- Leadership: Styles & Behaviors
- Leadership: Power & Negotiation
- Teams: Processes & Communication
- Teams: Characteristics & Diversity

INDIVIDUAL CHARACTERISTICS

- Ability
- Personality & Cultural Values

INDIVIDUAL MECHANISMS

- Job Satisfaction
- Stress
- Motivation
- Trust, Justice, & Ethics
- Learning & Decision Making

INDIVIDUAL OUTCOMES

- Job Performance
- Organizational Commitment

© Mark Lennihan/AP Images

✅ LEARNING GOALS

After reading this chapter, you should be able to answer the following questions:

9.1 What is personality? What are cultural values?

9.2 What are the "Big Five"?

9.3 Is personality driven by nature or by nurture?

9.4 What taxonomies can be used to describe personality, other than the Big Five?

9.5 What taxonomies can be used to describe cultural values?

9.6 How does personality affect job performance and organizational commitment?

9.7 Are personality tests useful tools for organizational hiring?

CHIPOTLE

How's this for a Chipotle success story? Sahul Flores was a 22-year-old spending the summer in Wisconsin, looking for a short-term job. When he wandered into one of the Denver-based burrito chain's locations, he was hired on a part-time basis and asked to prepare the tortillas. He was promoted to kitchen manager 10 weeks later and apprentice manager 8 weeks after that. But the ladder climbing didn't stop there. In another 5 months, he had moved to acting manager and then general manager. Recounts Flores, "In about a year I went from crew to general manager, from making $7 bucks an hour to a good salary with benefits and everything. It's funny because you would think, in a year I got promoted, all these great things happened, how could you top that?"

Before answering Flores's question, it's important to explain some of the reasons he was likely hired and why he was promoted so quickly. Flores clearly embodies many of the personality traits that Chipotle later began to explicitly emphasize in its hiring process, including conscientiousness, ambition, hospitableness, and infectious enthusiasm. Those traits likely served Flores well in his first few weeks with Chipotle, as he worked to promote both customer satisfaction and coworker satisfaction.

But those traits also likely served him well as his job took on more and more leadership qualities. After all, leaders also need to be conscientious, and they also need to be enthusiastic! All of which brings us to what did wind up topping Flores's already rapid ascent. One day a group of Chipotle executives, including founder Steve Ells, visited Flores's Milwaukee location. They were impressed, with Ells noting, "Do you know that you run your restaurant as good or better than I did the stores in Denver?"

The conversation with Ells led to Flores eventually being placed into Chipotle's "restaurateur" program, an initiative that gives general managers stock options and a $10,000 bonus each time they train an employee who rises to the general manager level. Being put on the restaurateur track requires an interview with Chipotle executives—presumably focusing on many of the same personality traits noted earlier. The company currently has 400 restaurateurs, with 40 percent of locations run by a manager in the program. That keeps conscientious, ambitious, hospitable, and enthusiastic people right where they can help the company most: running their stores in a way that keeps their customers coming back for more.

PERSONALITY AND CULTURAL VALUES

As the opening illustrates, a company can gain from paying close attention to the personality of its employees when making decisions about hiring and development. **Personality** refers to the structures and propensities inside people that explain their characteristic patterns of thought, emotion, and behavior.[1] Personality creates people's social reputations—the way they are perceived by friends, family, coworkers, and supervisors.[2] In this way, personality captures *what people are like.* That's in contrast to ability, the subject of Chapter 10, which captures *what people can do.* Although we sometimes describe people as having "a good personality," personality is actually a collection of multiple traits. **Traits** are defined as recurring regularities or trends in people's responses to their environment.[3] Adjectives such as "responsible," "easygoing," "polite," and "reserved" are examples of traits that can be used to summarize someone's personality.

As we'll describe later, personality traits are a function of both your genes and your environment. One important piece of the environmental part of that equation is the culture in which you were raised. **Cultural values** are defined as shared beliefs about desirable end states or modes of conduct in a given culture.[4] You can think of cultural values as capturing *what cultures are like.* Adjectives such as "traditional," "informal," "risk averse," or "assertive" are all examples of values that can be used to summarize a nation's culture. Cultural values can influence the development of people's personality traits, as well as how those traits are expressed in daily life. In this way, a responsible person in the United States may act somewhat differently than a responsible person in China, just as an easygoing person in France may act somewhat differently than an easygoing person in Indonesia.

 9.1

What is personality? What are cultural values?

HOW CAN WE DESCRIBE WHAT EMPLOYEES ARE LIKE?

We can use personality traits and cultural values to describe what employees are like. For example, how would you describe your first college roommate to one of your classmates? You'd start off using certain adjectives—maybe the roommate was funny and outgoing or maybe frugal and organized. Of course, it would take more than a few adjectives to describe your roommate fully. You could probably go on listing traits for several minutes, maybe even coming up with 100 traits or more. Although 100 traits may sound like a lot, personality researchers note that the third edition of *Webster's Unabridged Dictionary* contained 1,710 adjectives that can be used to describe someone's traits![5] Was your roommate abrasive, adulterous, agitable, alarmable, antisocial, arbitrative, arrogant, asocial, audacious, aweless, and awkward? We hope not!

THE BIG FIVE TAXONOMY

With 1,710 adjectives, you might be worrying about the length of this chapter (or the difficulty of your next exam!). Fortunately, it turns out that most adjectives are variations of five broad dimensions or "factors" that can be used to summarize our personalities.[6] Those five personality dimensions include **conscientiousness, agreeableness, neuroticism, openness to experience,** and **extraversion.** Collectively, these dimensions have been dubbed the **Big Five.**[7] Figure 9-1 lists the traits that can be found within each of the Big Five dimensions. We acknowledge that it can be hard to remember the particular labels for the Big Five dimensions, and we wish there was some acronym that could make the process easier. . . .

9.2

What are the "Big Five"?

FIGURE 9-1	Trait Adjectives Associated with the Big Five

C	A	N	O	E
Conscientiousness	Agreeableness	Neuroticism	Openness	Extraversion
• Dependable • Organized • Reliable • Ambitious • Hardworking • Persevering	• Kind • Cooperative • Sympathetic • Helpful • Courteous • Warm	• Nervous • Moody • Emotional • Insecure • Jealous • Unstable	• Curious • Imaginative • Creative • Complex • Refined • Sophisticated	• Talkative • Sociable • Passionate • Assertive • Bold • Dominant
NOT	NOT	NOT	NOT	NOT
• Careless • Sloppy • Inefficient • Negligent • Lazy • Irresponsible	• Critical • Antagonistic • Callous • Selfish • Rude • Cold	• Calm • Steady • Relaxed • At ease • Secure • Contented	• Uninquisitive • Conventional • Conforming • Simple • Unartistic • Traditional	• Quiet • Shy • Inhibited • Bashful • Reserved • Submissive

Sources: G. Saucier, "Mini-Markers: A Brief Version of Goldberg's Unipolar Big-Five Markers," *Journal of Personality Assessment* 63 (1994), pp. 506–16; L.R. Goldberg, "The Development of Markers for the Big-Five Factor Structure," *Psychological Assessment* 4 (1992), pp. 26–42; R.R. McCrae and P.T. Costa Jr., "Validation of the Five-Factor Model of Personality across Instruments and Observers," *Journal of Personality and Social Psychology* 52 (1987), pp. 81–90; and C.M. Gill and G.P. Hodgkinson, "Development and Validation of the Five-Factor Model Questionnaire (FFMQ): An Adjectival-Based Personality Inventory for Use in Occupational Settings," *Personnel Psychology* 60 (2007), pp. 731–66.

Would you like to see what your Big Five profile looks like? Our **OB Assessments** feature will show you where you stand on each of the five dimensions. After you've gotten a feel for your personality profile, you might be wondering about some of the following questions: How does personality develop? Why do people have the traits that they possess? Will those traits change over time? All of these questions are variations on the "nature vs. nurture" debate: Is personality a function of our genes, or is it something that we develop as a function of our experiences and environment? As you might guess, it's sometimes difficult to tease apart the impact of nature and nurture on personality. Let's assume for a moment that you're especially extraverted and so are your parents. Does this mean you've inherited their "extraversion gene"? Or does it mean that you observed and copied their extraverted behavior during your childhood (and were rewarded with praise for doing so)? It's impossible to know, because the effects of nature and nurture are acting in combination in this example.

9.3

Is personality driven by nature or by nurture?

One method of separating nature and nurture effects is to study identical twins who've been adopted by different sets of parents at birth. For example, the University of Minnesota has been conducting studies of pairs of identical twins reared apart for several decades.[8] Such studies find, for example, that extraversion scores tend to be significantly correlated across pairs of identical twins.[9] Such findings can clearly be attributed to "nature," because identical twins share 100 percent of their genetic material, but cannot be explained by "nurture," because the twins were raised in different environments. A review of several different twin studies concludes that genes have a significant impact on people's Big Five profile. More specifically, 49 percent of the variation in extraversion is accounted for by genetic differences.[10] The genetic impact is somewhat smaller for the rest of the Big Five: 45 percent for openness, 41 percent for neuroticism, 38 percent for conscientiousness, and 35 percent for agreeableness.

Another method of examining the genetic basis of personality is to examine changes in personality traits over time. Longitudinal studies require participants to complete personality assessments at multiple time periods, often separated by several years. If personality has a strong genetic component, then people's Big Five profiles at, say, age 21 should be very similar to their profiles at age 50. Figure 9-2 summarizes the results of 92 studies that assessed personality changes in more

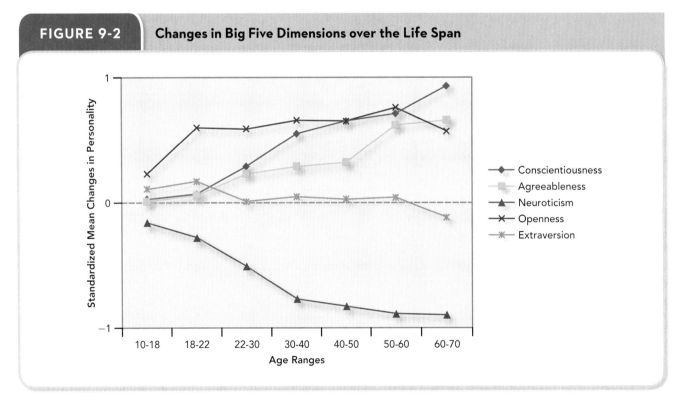

FIGURE 9-2   Changes in Big Five Dimensions over the Life Span

Source: Adapted from B.W. Roberts, K.E. Walton, and W. Viechtbauer, "Patterns of Mean-Level Change in Personality Traits across the Life Course: A Meta-Analysis of Longitudinal Studies," *Psychological Bulletin* 132 (2006), pp. 1–25.

ASSESSMENTS

THE BIG FIVE

What does your personality profile look like? This assessment is designed to measure the five major dimensions of personality: conscientiousness (C), agreeableness (A), neuroticism (N), openness to experience (O), and extraversion (E). Listed below are phrases describing people's behaviors. Please write a number next to each statement that indicates the extent to which it accurately describes you. Answer each question using the response scale provided. Then subtract your answers to the bold-faced questions from 6, with the difference being your new answer for those questions. For example, if your original answer for question 6 was "2," your new answer is "4" (6–2). (Instructors: Assessments on locus of control, collectivism, and power distance can be found in the PowerPoints in the Connect Library's Instructor Resources and in the Connect assignments for this chapter).

1 VERY INACCURATE	2 MODERATELY INACCURATE	3 NEITHER INACCURATE NOR ACCURATE	4 MODERATELY ACCURATE	5 VERY ACCURATE

1. I am the life of the party. _____

2. I sympathize with others' feelings. _____

3. I get chores done right away. _____

4. I have frequent mood swings. _____

5. I have a vivid imagination. _____

6. I don't talk a lot. _____

7. I am not interested in other people's problems. _____

8. I often forget to put things back in their proper place. _____

9. I am relaxed most of the time. _____

10. I am not interested in abstract ideas. _____

11. I talk to a lot of different people at parties. _____

12. I feel others' emotions. _____

13. I like order. _____

14. I get upset easily. _____

15. I have difficulty understanding abstract ideas. _____

16. I keep in the background. _____

17. I am not really interested in others. _____

18. I make a mess of things. _____

19. I seldom feel blue. _____

20. I do not have a good imagination. _____

SCORING AND INTERPRETATION

    Conscientiousness: Sum up items 3, 8, 13, and 18. _____

    Agreeableness: Sum up items 2, 7, 12, and 17. _____

    Neuroticism: Sum up items 4, 9, 14, and 19. _____

    Openness to Experience: Sum up items 5, 10, 15, and 20. _____

    Extraversion: Sum up items 1, 6, 11, and 16. _____

(continued)

Now chart your scores in the figure below to see whether you are above or below the norm for each dimension.

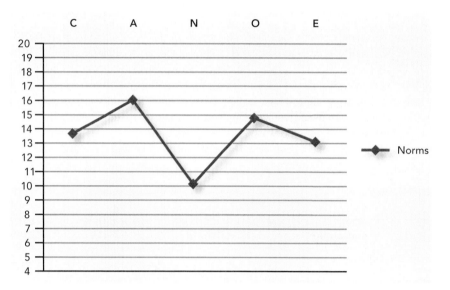

than 50,000 people.[11] The figure notes personality changes across seven time periods, including teenage years (age 10–18), college years (18–22), and people's 20s, 30s, 40s, 50s, and 60s. The *y*-axis expresses changes in personality in standard deviation terms, ranging from +1 (one standard deviation increase on a given dimension) to −1 (one standard deviation decrease on a given dimension). In standard deviation terms, a change of .20 is generally considered small, a change of .50 is generally considered medium, and a change of .80 is generally considered large.[12]

Figure 9-2 reveals that extraversion typically remains quite stable throughout a person's life. Openness to experience also remains stable, after a sharp increase from the teenage years to college age. The stability of those two dimensions makes sense because extraversion and openness are most dependent on genes.[13] The other three dimensions, however, change quite significantly over a person's life span. For example, Figure 9-2 shows that people get more conscientious as they grow older.[14] In addition, people become more agreeable and less neurotic over time. Although those changes may be encouraging if you dislike your own personal Big Five profile, it's important to realize that any changes in personality are very gradual. Consider this question: Can you detect any personality changes in your closest friends? Chances are you can't, unless you've known those friends for a period of several years. That long-term lens is needed to spot gradual fluctuations in Big Five levels. The sections that follow provide more detail about each of the Big Five dimensions.

CONSCIENTIOUSNESS As shown in Figure 9-1, conscientious people are dependable, organized, reliable, ambitious, hardworking, and persevering.[15] It's difficult, if not impossible, to envision a job in which those traits will not be beneficial.[16] That's not a claim we make about all of the Big Five because some jobs require high levels of agreeableness, extraversion, or openness, while others demand low levels of those same traits. We don't want to spoil the "how important is personality?" discussion that concludes this chapter, but suffice it to say that conscientiousness has the biggest influence on job performance of any of the Big Five. Of course, the key question therefore becomes: Why is conscientiousness so valuable?

One reason can be found in the general goals that people prioritize in their working life. Conscientious employees prioritize **accomplishment striving,** which reflects a strong desire to accomplish task-related goals as a means of expressing personality.[17] People who are "accomplishment strivers" have a built-in desire to finish work tasks, channel a high proportion of their efforts toward those tasks, and work harder and longer on task assignments. As evidence of their accomplishment-striving nature, one research

© Ingram Publishing RF

Research suggests that conscientious individuals actually live longer. One potential reason is that conscientiousness is associated with less risky driving behavior.

study showed that conscientious salespeople set higher sales goals for themselves than unconscientious salespeople and were more committed to meeting those goals.[18] Another study of salespeople showed that conscientious salespeople's organizational skills were particularly valuable during their first year of employment, and their ambitious nature became more critical as they gained tenure and experience.[19]

A third research study provides particularly compelling evidence regarding the benefits of conscientiousness.[20] The study used data from the University of California–Berkeley's Intergenerational Studies Center, which collected data about a set of children in the late 1920s and early 1930s. Those researchers gathered personality data using interviews and assessments of the children by trained psychologists. Follow-up studies collected data on the same sample as they reached early adulthood, middle age, and late adulthood. This last time period included assessments of career success, which included ratings of annual income and occupational prestige. The results of the study showed that childhood conscientiousness was strongly correlated with ratings of career success five decades later! In fact, those conscientiousness effects were roughly twice as strong as the effects of the other Big Five dimensions.

Such findings show that it pays to be conscientious; other research even suggests that conscientiousness is good for your health. For example, one study gathered data about the conscientiousness of 1,528 children in the early 1920s.[21] Data on health-relevant behaviors were then gathered in 1950 for 1,215 of the original participants. By 1986, 419 of the participants had died and 796 were still living. The results of the study revealed that childhood conscientiousness was negatively related to mortality, including death from injuries, death from cardiovascular disease, and death from cancer. Why did conscientious participants live longer? The study also showed that conscientiousness was negatively related to alcohol consumption and smoking during adulthood. Other research has shown that conscientious people are less likely to abuse drugs, more likely to take preventive steps to remain healthy, and less likely to perform risky behaviors as a driver or pedestrian.[22] For more on conscientiousness, see our **OB on Screen** feature.

AGREEABLENESS Agreeable people are warm, kind, cooperative, sympathetic, helpful, and courteous. Agreeable people prioritize **communion striving,** which reflects a strong desire to obtain acceptance in personal relationships as a means of expressing personality. Put differently, agreeable people focus on "getting along," not necessarily "getting ahead."[23] Unlike conscientiousness, agreeableness is not related to performance across all jobs or occupations.[24] Why not? The biggest reason is that communion striving is beneficial in some positions but detrimental in others. For example, managers often need to prioritize the effectiveness of the unit over a desire to gain acceptance. In such cases, effective job performance may demand being disagreeable in the face of unreasonable requests or demands.

Of course, there are some jobs in which agreeableness can be beneficial. The most obvious example is service jobs—jobs in which the employee has direct, face-to-face, or verbal contact with a customer. How many times have you encountered a customer service person who is cold, rude, or antagonistic? Did you tend to buy the company's product after such experiences? Research suggests that agreeable employees have stronger customer service skills.[25] One reason for their effectiveness in customer service environments is that they're reluctant to react to

OB ON SCREEN

BOYHOOD

The images you're turning in, they're cool. You're looking at things in a really unique way. Got a lot of natural talent . . . that and 50 cents will just get you a cup of coffee in this old world. I've met a LOT of talented people over the years. How many of them made it professionally without discipline, commitment, and really good work ethic?

With those words, Mr. Turlington (Tom McTigue) tries to get through to Mason Evans Jr. (Ellar Coltrane) in *Boyhood* (Dir. Richard Linklater, IFC Productions, 2014). Mr. Turlington is Mason's photography teacher, and he's spotted in Mason a student with a good eye, a natural curiosity, and a distinct style. In a personality sense, Mason's high on openness to experience. Unfortunately, Mason's not high on conscientiousness. He hasn't finished his image diary, he hasn't completed his digital contact sheet, and he's none too enthused about photographing the football game.

© IFC Films/Photofest

The film literally shows Mason growing up, as he ages from 6 years old to a college freshman. It therefore provides a rich depiction of the nature and nurture influences on personality. Mason's conscientiousness issues were evident early, as he got in trouble for destroying the pencil sharpener in elementary school. When his mom asks him what happened, he notes that he put rocks in it instead of pencils, "Because I needed them for my arrowhead collection." Maybe some of Mason's personality is shaped by his dad—who is rarely there for Mason and always seems to be between careers.

For his part, Mason struggles with most of the jobs he has growing up and doesn't seem to excel in school. That drifting starts to change when his mom's boyfriend buys him a camera. Argues Mason in his conversation with Mr. Turlington, ". . . I mean, the things you're talking about, like, work ethic or whatever, I feel like I do work pretty hard. I spend the whole weekend taking pictures a lot of times." Counters Mr. Turlington, "Try harder. Hey, maybe in 20 years you can call old Mr. Turlington, and you can say: 'Thank you, sir, for that terrific darkroom chat we had that day.' "

conflict with criticism, threats, or manipulation.[26] Instead, they tend to react to conflict by walking away, adopting a "wait-and-see" attitude, or giving in to the other person.

One study provides unique insights into the effects of agreeableness. The study used a variation of "lived day analysis," where a portion of a participant's daily routine is recorded and analyzed.[27] Ninety-six undergraduates completed assessments of the Big Five personality dimensions before being fitted with a digital recorder and an electronic microphone that could be clipped to their shirt collar. The microphone recorded 30 seconds of footage at 12-minute intervals over the course of two weekdays, with participants unable to track when footage was actually being recorded. Trained coders then rated the sounds and conversations recorded on the microphone. The results of the study revealed a number of interesting expressions of agreeableness. Agreeable participants were significantly less likely to be at home in their apartment during recordings; instead, they spent more time in public places. They were also less likely to use swear words and more likely to use words that conveyed personal rapport during conversations.

EXTRAVERSION Extraverted people are talkative, sociable, passionate, assertive, bold, and dominant (in contrast to introverts, who are quiet, shy, and reserved). Of the Big Five, extraversion is the easiest to judge in **zero acquaintance** situations—situations in which two people have only just met. Consider times when you've been around a stranger in a doctor's office, in line at a grocery store, or in an airport terminal. It takes only about 5 minutes to figure out whether that stranger is extraverted or introverted.[28] Extraversion is also the Big Five dimension that you knew your standing on, even before taking our self-assessment. People rarely consider how open they are to new experiences or how agreeable they are, but almost everyone already self-identifies as an "extravert" or "introvert."

Like agreeableness, extraversion is not necessarily related to performance across all jobs or occupations. However, extraverted people prioritize **status striving,** which reflects a strong desire to obtain power and influence within a social structure as a means of expressing personality.[29] Extraverts care a lot about being successful and influential and direct their work efforts toward "moving up" and developing a strong reputation. Indeed, research suggests that extraverts are more likely to emerge as leaders in social and task-related groups.[30] They also tend to be rated as more effective in a leadership role by the people who are following them.[31] One potential reason for these findings is that people tend to view extraverts, who are more energetic and outgoing, as more "leaderlike" than introverts.

In addition to being related to leadership emergence and effectiveness, research suggests that extraverts tend to be happier with their jobs. You may recall from Chapter 4 on job satisfaction that people's day-to-day moods can be categorized along two dimensions: pleasantness and activation. As illustrated in Figure 9-3, extraverted employees tend to be high in what's called **positive affectivity**—a dispositional tendency to experience pleasant, engaging moods such as enthusiasm, excitement, and elation.[32] That tendency to experience positive moods across situations explains why extraverts tend to be more satisfied with their jobs.[33] Research now acknowledges that employees' genes have a significant impact on their job satisfaction and that much of that genetic influence is due to extraversion (and neuroticism, as discussed next). For example, one study of identical twins reared apart showed that twins' job satisfaction levels were significantly correlated, even when the twins held jobs that were quite different in terms of their duties, their complexity, and their working conditions.[34] In fact, this study suggested that around 30 percent of the variation in job satisfaction is due to genetic factors such as personality.

Other research suggests that extraverts have more to be happy about than just their jobs. Specifically, research suggests that extraversion is positively related to more general life satisfaction.[35] To shed light on that finding, one study asked students to complete a "life event checklist" by indicating whether various events had happened to them in the preceding four years.[36] The results showed that extraversion was associated with more positive events, such as joining a club or athletic team, going on vacation with friends, getting a raise at work, receiving an award for nonacademic reasons, and getting married or engaged. Other studies have linked extraversion to the number of same-sex peers, number of dating partners, frequency of alcohol consumption, and frequency of attending parties.[37] However, extraverts spend so much time doing those things that they wind up having less frequent interactions with their family.[38] Even parents of extraverts enjoy a phone call home now and again! To gain some insights about introverts, see our **OB at the Bookstore** feature.

NEUROTICISM Neurotic people are nervous, moody, emotional, insecure, and jealous. Occasionally you may see this Big Five dimension called by its flip side: "Emotional Stability" or "Emotional Adjustment." If conscientiousness is the most important of the Big Five from the perspective of job performance, neuroticism is the second most important.[39] There are few jobs for which the traits associated with neuroticism are beneficial to on-the-job behaviors. Instead, most jobs benefit from employees who are calm, steady, and secure.

FIGURE 9-3	Extraversion, Neuroticism, and Typical Moods

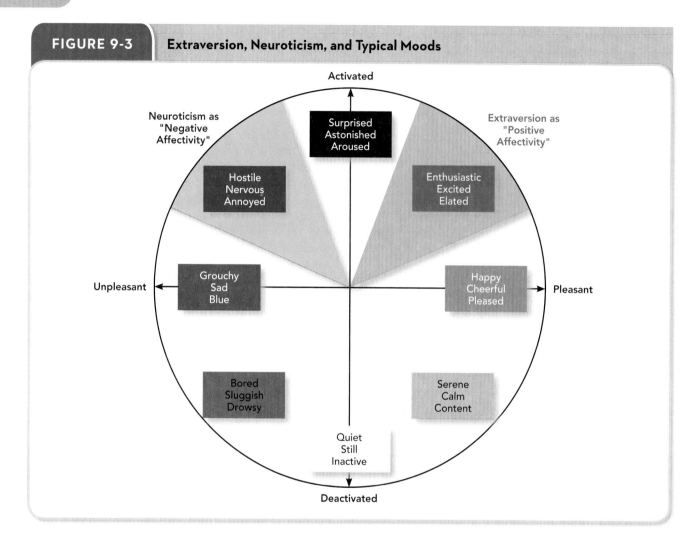

Whereas extraversion is synonymous with positive affectivity, neuroticism is synonymous with **negative affectivity**—a dispositional tendency to experience unpleasant moods such as hostility, nervousness, and annoyance (see Figure 9-3).[40] That tendency to experience negative moods explains why neurotic employees often experience lower levels of job satisfaction than their less neurotic counterparts.[41] Along with extraversion, neuroticism explains much of the impact of genetic factors on job satisfaction. Research suggests that the negative affectivity associated with neuroticism also influences life satisfaction, with neurotic people tending to be less happy with their lives in general.[42] In fact, one method of assessing neuroticism (or negative affectivity) is to determine how unhappy people are with everyday objects and things. This "gripe index" is shown in Table 9-1. If you find yourself dissatisfied with several of the objects in that table, then you probably experience negative moods quite frequently.

Neuroticism also influences the way that people deal with stressful situations. Specifically, neuroticism is associated with a **differential exposure** to stressors, meaning that neurotic people are more likely to appraise day-to-day situations as stressful (and therefore feel like they are exposed to stressors more frequently).[43] Neuroticism is also associated with a **differential reactivity** to stressors, meaning that neurotic people are less likely to believe they can cope with the stressors that they experience.[44] Neuroticism is largely responsible for the Type A Behavior Pattern that has been shown to affect employees' health and ability to manage stressful environments.[45] That is, neurotic people are much more likely to be "Type As," whereas less neurotic individuals are much more likely to be "Type Bs" (see Chapter 5 on stress for more discussion of such issues).

Neuroticism is also strongly related to **locus of control,** which reflects whether people attribute the causes of events to themselves or to the external environment.[46] Neurotic people tend to hold an *external* locus of control, meaning that they often believe that the events that occur

OB

AT THE BOOKSTORE

QUIET

by Susan Cain (New York: Crown Publishers, 2012).

It makes sense that so many introverts hide even from themselves. We live with a value system that I call the Extrovert Ideal—the omnipresent belief that the ideal self is gregarious, alpha, and comfortable in the spotlight. . . . We like to think that we value individuality, but all too often we admire one type *of individual—the kind who's comfortable "putting himself out there."*

Photo of cover: © Roberts Publishing Services

With those words, the author summarizes the plight of the shy, contemplative, calm, risk-averse, and sensitive individuals who exist in a world that rarely trumpets such traits. Although the author's description of "introversion" winds up being a blend of low extraversion, high conscientiousness, high openness, high agreeableness, and high neuroticism, many of us either know (or self-identify as) these "quiet types." How did life in the United States come to worship the Extrovert Ideal? The book attributes that trend to a number of factors, including being descended from explorers, the presumed extraversion of the country's founders, the importance of charismatic preachers to the spread of religion, and our cultural fascination with stars and performers. Regardless, the embrace of the Extrovert Ideal has left a clear imprint on education (where norms reward class participation and structure learning in groups) and the workplace (where charisma, ability to sell oneself, and boldness are viewed as stepping stones for success).

Fortunately for us quiet types, the author also reviews tasks that introverts excel at, especially jobs that demand deliberate practice, creative insights, and listening to others. What about times where introverts must "put themselves out there," as when giving a presentation in front of a large crowd or engaging in a tough negotiation? The book provides a number of tips for understanding and navigating such scenarios. For example, introverts excel more at "acting extroverted" when doing so helps them achieve goals that they find personally meaningful. As another example, introverts perform such "acting" more flawlessly if they build in time to visit their "restorative niches"—quiet places like an office, hotel room, or park bench that deliver the solitude needed to recharge.

around them are driven by luck, chance, or fate. Less neurotic people tend to hold an *internal* locus of control, meaning that they believe that their own behavior dictates events. Table 9-2 provides more detail about the external versus internal distinction. The table includes a number of beliefs that are representative of an external or internal viewpoint, including beliefs about life in general, work, school, politics, and relationships. If you tend to agree more strongly with the beliefs in the left column, then you have a more external locus of control. If you tend to agree more with the right column, your locus is more internal.

How important is locus of control? One meta-analysis of 135 different research studies showed that an internal locus of control was associated with higher levels of job satisfaction and job performance.[47] A second meta-analysis of 222 different research studies showed that people with an internal locus of control enjoyed better health, including higher self-reported mental well-being, fewer self-reported physical symptoms, lower blood pressure, and lower stress hormone secretion.[48] Internals also enjoyed more social support at work than externals and sensed that they had a stronger relationship with their supervisors. They viewed their jobs as having more beneficial characteristics, such as autonomy and significance, and fewer negative characteristics, such as

TABLE 9-1	The Neutral Objects Questionnaire (aka The "Gripe Index")

Instructions: The following questions ask about your degree of satisfaction with several items. Consider each item carefully. Circle the numbered response that best represents your feelings about the corresponding item. Then sum up your score.

	DISSATISFIED	NEUTRAL	SATISFIED
Your telephone number	1	2	3
8 1/2 × 11 paper	1	2	3
Popular music	1	2	3
Modern art	1	2	3
Your first name	1	2	3
Restaurant food	1	2	3
Public transportation	1	2	3
Telephone service	1	2	3
The way you were raised	1	2	3
Advertising	1	2	3
The way people drive	1	2	3
Local speed limits	1	2	3
Television programs	1	2	3
The people you know	1	2	3
Yourself	1	2	3
Your relaxation time	1	2	3
Local newspapers	1	2	3
Today's cars	1	2	3
The quality of food you buy	1	2	3
The movies being produced today	1	2	3
The climate where you live	1	2	3
The high school you attended	1	2	3
The neighbors you have	1	2	3
The residence where you live	1	2	3
The city in which you live	1	2	3

Interpretation: If you scored below a 50, you tend to be less satisfied with everyday objects than the typical respondent. Such a score may indicate negative affectivity, a tendency to feel negative emotional states frequently. (Or perhaps you should change your phone number!)

Sources: Adapted from T.A. Judge, "Does Affective Disposition Moderate the Relationship between Job Satisfaction and Voluntary Turnover?" *Journal of Applied Psychology* 78 (1993), pp. 395–401; and J. Weitz, "A Neglected Concept in the Study of Job Satisfaction," *Personnel Psychology* 5 (1952), pp. 201–05.

conflict and ambiguity. In addition, those with an internal locus of control earned a higher salary than those with an external locus.

OPENNESS TO EXPERIENCE The final dimension of the Big Five is openness to experience. Open people are curious, imaginative, creative, complex, refined, and sophisticated. Of all the Big Five, openness to experience has the most alternative labels. Sometimes it's called

TABLE 9-2	External and Internal Locus of Control

PEOPLE WITH AN EXTERNAL LOCUS OF CONTROL TEND TO BELIEVE:	PEOPLE WITH AN INTERNAL LOCUS OF CONTROL TEND TO BELIEVE:
Many of the unhappy things in people's lives are partly due to bad luck.	People's misfortunes result from the mistakes they make.
Getting a good job depends mainly on being in the right place at the right time.	Becoming a success is a matter of hard work; luck has little or nothing to do with it.
Many times exam questions tend to be so unrelated to course work that studying is really useless.	In the case of the well-prepared student, there is rarely if ever such a thing as an unfair test.
This world is run by the few people in power, and there is not much the little guy can do about it.	The average citizen can have an influence in government decisions.
There's not much use in trying too hard to please people; if they like you, they like you.	People are lonely because they don't try to be friendly.

Source: Adapted from J.B. Rotter, "Generalized Expectancies for Internal versus External Control of Reinforcement," *Psychological Monographs* 80 (1966), pp. 1–28.

"Inquisitiveness" or "Intellectualness" or even "Culture" (not in the national culture sense—rather, in the "high culture" sense of knowing fine wine, art, and classical music). Much like agreeableness and extraversion, the traits associated with openness are beneficial in some jobs but not others. As a result, openness is not related to job performance across all occupations.

What jobs benefit from high levels of openness? Generally speaking, jobs that are very fluid and dynamic, with rapid changes in job demands. Research shows that open employees excel in learning and training environments, because their curiosity gives them a built-in desire to learn new things.[49] They also tend to be more adaptable and quick to identify when the "old way of doing things" is no longer effective, excelling at the search for a new and better approach.[50] In fact, conscientious employees are sometimes less effective than open employees in such environments because their persevering nature sometimes prevents them from abandoning "tried-and-true" task strategies.

Openness to experience is also more likely to be valuable in jobs that require high levels of creative performance, where job holders need to be able to generate novel and useful ideas and solutions.[51] The relationship between openness and creative performance can be seen in Figure 9-4. Together with cognitive ability, openness to experience is a key driver of creative thought, as smart and open people excel at the style of thinking demanded by creativity (see Chapter 10 on ability for more discussion of such issues). How good are you at creative thinking? See Figure 9-5 to find out. Creative thought results in creative performance when people come up with new ideas, create fresh approaches to problems, or suggest new innovations that can help improve the workplace.[52] The creativity benefits of openness likely explain why highly open individuals are more likely to migrate into artistic and scientific fields, in which novel and original products are so critical.[53] Dragonfly, a New York–based web video–networking company, goes to unusual lengths to foster creative thought.[54] The company pays $10,000 to $20,000 to put employees through six hours of hypnotism. The idea is that the relaxation, meditation, and visualization used in hypnosis can unlock the imagination of employees, even if they're lower in openness.

People who are open to new experiences tend to do well in situations that offer frequent opportunities to learn new things, such as teaching.

© *Royalty-Free/Corbis RF*

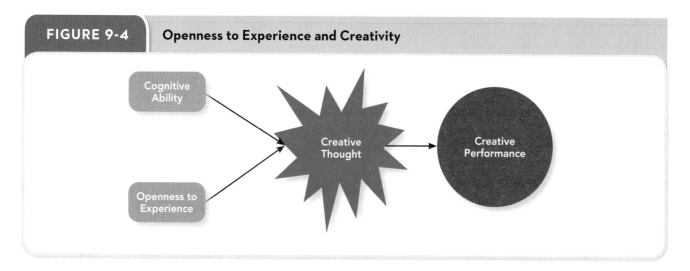

FIGURE 9-4   Openness to Experience and Creativity

BMW, the German automaker, seems to understand the importance of the Big Five dimensions of personality. BMW has worked hard to create a culture of innovation in which there is never a penalty for proposing new and outlandish ways of improving its cars.[55] Those proposed improvements include a "smart card" that can be taken out of your own BMW and plugged into a rented one, passing along your music, podcast, and comfort settings to the new vehicle. Openness is needed

FIGURE 9-5   Tests of Creative Thinking

Instructions: Do you consider yourself to be a creative thinker? See if you can solve the problems below. If you need help, the answers can be found in the Takeaways section of this chapter.

1. What gets wetter as it dries?

2. A woman had two sons who were born on the same hour of the same day of the same year. But they were not twins. How could this be so?

3. What occurs once in June, once in July, and twice in August?

4. Make this mathematical expression true by drawing only a single noncurving line:

$$5+5+5 = 550$$

5. Join all nine of the dots below using only four (or fewer) noncurving lines, without lifting your pen from the paper and without retracing the lines.

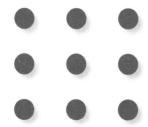

Sources: http://home.swipnet.se/~ w-19502/puzzles.htm; http://www.mycoted.com/Category:Puzzles.

to foster such creative thought, but agreeableness is also key to BMW's culture. Stefan Krause, BMW's chief financial officer, summarizes how to push a creative idea successfully: "You can go into fighting mode or you can ask permission and get everyone to support you. If you do it without building ties, you will be blocked."

BMW employees also draw on their conscientiousness in those critical times when a new technology is introduced or production volume is expanded. During those time periods, employees from other factories may move into temporary housing far from home to put in extra hours on another plant's line. Why are employees so devoted? For one thing, no one at BMW can remember a layoff—something that is incredibly unique in the auto industry. That's part of the reason BMW's human resources group receives more than 200,000 applications

© Dennis Gilbert/VIEW Pictures Ltd/Alamy

BMW's Leipzig facility, where the assembly line moves above work spaces to give employees a feel for the rhythm of the plant.

annually. Those fortunate enough to make it to the interview stage participate in elaborate, day-long drills in teams to make sure that their personalities provide a good match for the company.

OTHER TAXONOMIES OF PERSONALITY

Although the Big Five is the dominant lens for examining personality, it's not the only framework with which you might be familiar. One of the most widely administered personality measures in organizations is the **Myers-Briggs Type Indicator (MBTI).**[56] This instrument was originally created to test a theory of psychological types advanced by the noted psychologist Carl Jung.[57] The MBTI evaluates individuals on the basis of four types of preferences:[58]

9.4

What taxonomies can be used to describe personality, other than the Big Five?

- *Extraversion* (being energized by people and social interactions) versus *Introversion* (being energized by private time and reflection).
- *Sensing* (preferring clear and concrete facts and data) versus *Intuition* (preferring hunches and speculations based on theory and imagination).
- *Thinking* (approaching decisions with logic and critical analysis) versus *Feeling* (approaching decisions with an emphasis on others' needs and feelings).
- *Judging* (approaching tasks by planning and setting goals) versus *Perceiving* (preferring to have flexibility and spontaneity when performing tasks).

The MBTI categorizes people into one of 16 different types on the basis of their preferences. For example, an "ISTJ" has a preference for Introversion, Sensing, Thinking, and Judging. Research on the MBTI suggests that managers are more likely to be "TJs" than the general population.[59] Moreover, the different personality types seem to approach decision-making tasks with differing emphases on facts, logic, and plans. That said, there is little evidence that the MBTI is a useful tool for predicting the job satisfaction, motivation, performance, or commitment of employees across jobs.[60] Indeed, one of the reasons the MBTI is so widely used is that there really isn't a "bad type"—no one who gets their profile is receiving negative news. As a result, the most appropriate use of the MBTI is in a team-building context, to help different members understand their varying approaches to accomplishing tasks. Using the MBTI as any kind of hiring or selection tool does not appear to be warranted, based on existing research.

A second alternative to the Big Five is offered by research on vocational interests.[61] **Interests** are expressions of personality that influence behavior through preferences for certain environments and activities.[62] Interests reflect stable and enduring likes and dislikes that can explain why people are drawn toward some careers and away from others.[63] Holland's **RIASEC model** suggests that interests can be summarized by six different personality types:[64]

- *Realistic:* Enjoys practical, hands-on, real-world tasks. Tends to be frank, practical, determined, and rugged.
- *Investigative:* Enjoys abstract, analytical, theory-oriented tasks. Tends to be analytical, intellectual, reserved, and scholarly.
- *Artistic:* Enjoys entertaining and fascinating others using imagination. Tends to be original, independent, impulsive, and creative.
- *Social:* Enjoys helping, serving, or assisting others. Tends to be helpful, inspiring, informative, and empathic.
- *Enterprising:* Enjoys persuading, leading, or outperforming others. Tends to be energetic, sociable, ambitious, and risk-taking.
- *Conventional:* Enjoys organizing, counting, or regulating people or things. Tends to be careful, conservative, self-controlled, and structured.

As shown in Figure 9-6, the RIASEC model further suggests that the personality types can be classified along two dimensions: the degree to which employees prefer to work with data versus ideas and the degree to which they prefer to work with people versus things. For example, those with a Realistic personality prefer to work with things and data more than people and ideas. The model arranges the personality types in a hexagonal fashion, with types adjacent to one another being more similar than types that are more distant. The central premise of the RIASEC model is

| FIGURE 9-6 | Holland's RIASEC Model |

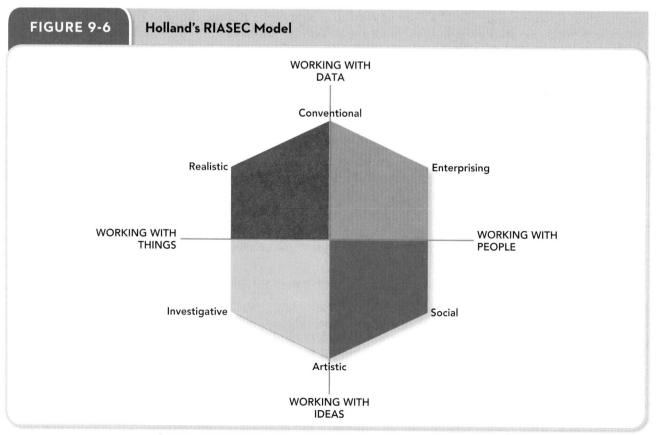

Source: Adapted from J.L. Holland, *Making Vocational Choices: A Theory of Careers* (Englewood Cliffs, NJ: Prentice Hall, 1973).

that employees will have more career satisfaction, job knowledge, and longevity in occupations that match their personality type.[65] For example, Realistic people should be happier and more effective as craftspeople than as counselors because a craftsperson's duties provide a good match to their personality. One of the most common applications of the RIASEC model is interest inventories, which provide people their scores on relevant personality dimensions, along with a list of occupations that could provide a good match for that profile.[66]

CULTURAL VALUES

As noted previously, our personalities are influenced by both our genes and our environment. One significant aspect of that environment is the society in which we were raised. Societies can be described in a number of ways, including their climate and habitat, their sovereignty and political system, their language and religion, their education and technology levels, and their economic development.[67] However, one of the most important aspects of societies is culture. **Culture** is defined as the shared values, beliefs, motives, identities, and interpretations that result from common experiences of members of a society and are transmitted across generations.[68] Culture has been described as patterns resulting from societal traditions and as the collective programming of the mind that separates one society from another.[69] The shared values, societal traditions, and collective programming that underlies culture influences the development of our personalities while also shaping the way our traits are expressed.[70] In this way, explaining "what we're like" requires an awareness of "where we're from."

To some extent, cultures provide societies with their own distinct personalities.[71] One study on the Big Five profiles of 51 different cultures showed that some societies tend to value certain personality traits more than other societies.[72] For example, people from India tend to be more conscientious than people from Belgium. People from the Czech Republic tend to be more agreeable than people from Hong Kong. People from Brazil tend to be more neurotic than people from China. People from Australia tend to be more extraverted than people from Russia. People from Denmark tend to be more open than people from Argentina. For their part, people in the United States trend toward the high end of the 51-culture sample on extraversion and openness, staying near the middle for the other Big Five dimensions. Of course, that doesn't mean that all of the members of these societies have exactly the same personality. Instead, those results merely convey that certain cultures tend to place a higher value on certain traits.

Although it's possible to contrast nations using the Big Five, as we just did, cross-cultural research focuses more attention on the shared values aspect of culture. The values that are salient in a given culture influence how people select and justify courses of action and how they evaluate themselves and other people.[73] To some extent, cultural values come to reflect the way things *should be done* in a given society.[74] Acting in a manner that's consistent with those values helps people to fit in, and going against those values causes people to stand out. Just as there are a number of traits that can be used to describe personality, there are a number of values that can be used to describe cultures. Given the sheer complexity of culture, it's not surprising that different studies have arrived at different taxonomies that can be used to summarize cultural values.

9.5

What taxonomies can be used to describe cultural values?

The most well-known taxonomy of cultural values was derived from a landmark study in the late 1960s and early 1970s by Geert Hofstede, who analyzed data from 88,000 IBM employees from 72 countries in 20 languages.[75] His research showed that employees working in different countries tended to prioritize different values, and those values clustered into several distinct dimensions. Those dimensions are summarized in

© Plush Studios/Bill Reitze/Blend Images LLC RF

Research on cultural values categorizes China as a highly collective culture, meaning that its citizens tend to prioritize taking care of ingroup members, and staying loyal to them.

TABLE 9-3	Hofstede's Dimensions of Cultural Values

INDIVIDUALISM–COLLECTIVISM	
INDIVIDUALISTIC	**COLLECTIVISTIC**
The culture is a loosely knit social framework in which people take care of themselves and their immediate family.	The culture is a tight social framework in which people take care of the members of a broader ingroup and act loyal to it.
United States, the Netherlands, France	*Indonesia, China, West Africa*

POWER DISTANCE	
LOW	**HIGH**
The culture prefers that power be distributed uniformly where possible, in a more egalitarian fashion.	The culture accepts the fact that power is usually distributed unequally within organizations.
United States, Germany, the Netherlands	*Russia, China, Indonesia*

UNCERTAINTY AVOIDANCE	
LOW	**HIGH**
The culture tolerates uncertain and ambiguous situations and values unusual ideas and behaviors.	The culture feels threatened by uncertain and ambiguous situations and relies on formal rules to create stability.
United States, Indonesia, the Netherlands	*Japan, Russia, France*

MASCULINITY–FEMININITY	
MASCULINE	**FEMININE**
The culture values stereotypically male traits such as assertiveness and the acquisition of money and things.	The culture values stereotypically female traits such as caring for others and caring about quality of life.
United States, Japan, Germany	*The Netherlands, Russia, France*

SHORT-TERM VS. LONG-TERM ORIENTATION	
SHORT-TERM ORIENTED	**LONG-TERM ORIENTED**
The culture stresses values that are more past- and present-oriented, such as respect for tradition and fulfilling obligations.	The culture stresses values that are more future-oriented, such as persistence, prudence, and thrift.
United States, Russia, West Africa	*China, Japan, the Netherlands*

Sources: G. Hofstede, *Culture's Consequences: Comparing Values, Behaviors, Institutions, and Organizations across Nations* (Thousand Oaks, CA: Sage, 2001); G. Hofstede, "Cultural Constraints in Management Theories," *Academy of Management Executive* 7 (1993), pp. 81–94; and G. Hofstede and M.H. Bond, "The Confucius Connection: From Cultural Roots to Economic Growth," *Organizational Dynamics* 16 (1988), pp. 5–21.

Table 9-3 and include **individualism–collectivism, power distance, uncertainty avoidance,** and **masculinity–femininity.** A subsequent study added a fifth dimension to the taxonomy: **short-term vs. long-term orientation.**[76] Hofstede's research introduced scores on each of the dimensions for various cultures, providing researchers with a quantitative tool to summarize and compare and contrast the cultures of different societies. Table 9-3 includes some of the countries that have high or low scores on Hofstede's dimensions.

Although Hofstede's dimensions have formed the foundation for much of the research on cross-cultural management, more recent studies have painted a more nuanced picture of cultural values. **Project GLOBE** (Global Leadership and Organizational Behavior Effectiveness) is a collection of

170 researchers from 62 cultures who have studied 17,300 managers in 951 organizations since 1991.[77] The main purpose of Project GLOBE is to examine the impact of culture on the effectiveness of various leader attributes, behaviors, and practices (see Chapter 14 on leadership styles and behaviors for more discussion of such issues). In pursing that goal, project researchers asked managers to rate the values held within their organizations and within their societies. That research identified nine different dimensions that are used to summarize cultures within Project GLOBE. Some of those dimensions can be viewed as replications of Hofstede's work. For example, Project GLOBE identified both *power distance* and *uncertainty avoidance* as key dimensions of cultural values. The project also identified collectivism, though it was differentiated into *institutional collectivism* (where formalized practices encourage collective action and collective distribution of resources) and *ingroup collectivism* (where individuals express pride and loyalty to specific ingroups).

Other dimensions bear some similarity to Hofstede's work but are conceptually distinct. Those dimensions are listed below, along with some information on the cultures that score at the higher and lower ends on a given value. Note that Project GLOBE groups cultures into "country clusters." Those clusters include Anglo (United States, Canada, Australia, England), Latin America (Mexico, Brazil, Colombia, Venezuela), Latin Europe (France, Spain, Italy, Israel), Germanic Europe (Germany, Austria, the Netherlands, Switzerland), Nordic Europe (Denmark, Finland, Sweden), Eastern Europe (Poland, Hungary, Russia, Greece), Middle East (Turkey, Egypt, Kuwait, Morocco), Southern Asia (India, Thailand, Indonesia, Malaysia), Confucian Asia (China, South Korea, Japan, Singapore), and Sub-Saharan Africa (Zimbabwe, Namibia, Nigeria). The following descriptions note some of the country clusters that earn high and low scores on a given cultural value. Note that the Anglo group, which includes the United States, scores in the middle on most of the cultural values.

- *Gender Egalitarianism.* The culture promotes gender equality and minimizes role differences between men and women. High: Nordic Europe, Eastern Europe. Low: Middle East.
- *Assertiveness.* The culture values assertiveness, confrontation, and aggressiveness in social relationships. High: Germanic Europe, Eastern Europe. Low: Nordic Europe.
- *Future Orientation.* The culture engages in planning and investment in the future while delaying individual or collective gratification. High: Germanic Europe, Nordic Europe. Low: Middle East, Latin America, Eastern Europe.
- *Performance Orientation.* The culture encourages and rewards members for excellence and performance improvements. High: Anglo, Confucian Asia, Germanic Europe. Low: Latin America, Eastern Europe.
- *Humane Orientation.* The culture encourages and rewards members for being generous, caring, kind, fair, and altruistic. High: Southern Asia, Sub-Saharan Africa. Low: Latin Europe, Germanic Europe.

Taken together, Hofstede's work and the Project GLOBE studies have identified between five and nine cultural value dimensions. However, the lion's share of cross-cultural research focuses on individualism–collectivism, perhaps the most fundamental means of differentiating cultures.[78] The individualism–collectivism distinction is relevant to various topics within organizational behavior.[79] For example, collectivists exhibit higher levels of task performance and citizenship behaviors in work team settings, and also exhibit lower levels of counterproductive and withdrawal behaviors.[80] They are also more likely to feel affectively and normatively committed to their employers than are individualists.[81] Research also suggests that collectivists tend to prefer rewards that are allocated equally on a group-wide basis as opposed to rewards tied solely to individual achievement.[82]

Regardless of the particular value of focus, research on cultural values illustrates the potential differences between the attitudes and beliefs of U.S. employees and the attitudes and beliefs of employees in other societies. Awareness of such cultural variations is critical, given that those differences can influence reactions to change, conflict management styles, negotiation approaches, and reward preferences, just to name a few.[83] Failing to understand those differences can compromise the effectiveness of multinational groups and organizations. Such problems are particularly likely if employees are high in **ethnocentrism,** defined as a propensity to view one's own cultural values as "right" and those of other cultures as "wrong."[84] For more discussion of this issue, see our **OB Internationally** feature.

OB INTERNATIONALLY

Research suggests that ethnocentrism hinders the effectiveness of expatriates, who are employees working full-time in other countries. Ethnocentrism makes expatriates less likely to adjust to a new culture, less likely to fulfill the duties required of their international assignment, and more likely to withdraw from that assignment. How can organizations identify employees with the right personalities to serve as expatriates? One useful tool is the *multicultural personality questionnaire,* which assesses five personality dimensions that can maximize the performance and commitment of expatriates. Those dimensions are listed below, along with some sample items.

Cultural Empathy. A tendency to empathize with the feelings, thoughts, and behaviors of individuals with different cultural values.

- I understand other people's feelings.
- I take other people's habits into consideration.

Open-mindedness. A tendency to have an open and unprejudiced attitude toward other cultural values and norms.

- I get involved in other cultures.
- I find other religions interesting.

Emotional Stability. A tendency to remain calm in the kinds of stressful situations that can be encountered in foreign environments.

- I can put setbacks in perspective.
- I take it for granted that things will turn out right.

Social Initiative. A tendency to be proactive when approaching social situations, which aids in building connections.

- I easily approach other people.
- I am often the driving force behind things.

Flexibility. A tendency to regard new situations as a challenge and to adjust behaviors to meet that challenge.

- I could start a new life easily.
- I feel comfortable in different cultures.

Research has linked these five personality traits to a number of expatriate success factors. For example, individuals with a "multicultural personality" are more likely to aspire to international positions, more likely to gain international experience, more likely to adjust to new assignments, and more likely to be happy with their lives during those assignments.

Sources: K.I. Van der Zee and U. Brinkmann, "Construct Validity Evidence for the Intercultural Readiness Check against the Multicultural Personality Questionnaire," I*nternational Journal of Selection and Assessment* 12 (2004), pp. 285–90; K.I. Van der Zee and J.P. Van Oudenhoven, "The Multicultural Personality Questionnaire: Reliability and Validity of Self and Other Ratings of Multicultural Effectiveness," *Journal of Research in Personality* 35 (2001), pp. 278–88; J.P. Van Oudenhoven and K.I. Van der Zee, "Predicting Multicultural Effectiveness of International Students: The Multicultural Personality Questionnaire," *International Journal of Intercultural Relations* 26 (2002), pp. 679–94; and J.P. Van Oudenhoven S. Mol; and K.I. Van der Zee, "Study of the Adjustment of Western Expatriates in Taiwan ROC with the Multicultural Personality Questionnaire," *Asian Journal of Social Psychology* 6 (2003), pp. 159–70.

SUMMARY: HOW CAN WE DESCRIBE WHAT EMPLOYEES ARE LIKE?

So how can we explain what employees are like? As shown in Figure 9-7, many of the thousands of adjectives we use to describe people can be boiled down into the Big Five dimensions of personality. Conscientiousness reflects the reliability, perseverance, and ambition of employees. Agreeableness captures their tendency to cooperate with others in a warm and sympathetic fashion.

FIGURE 9-7	How Can We Describe What Employees Are Like?

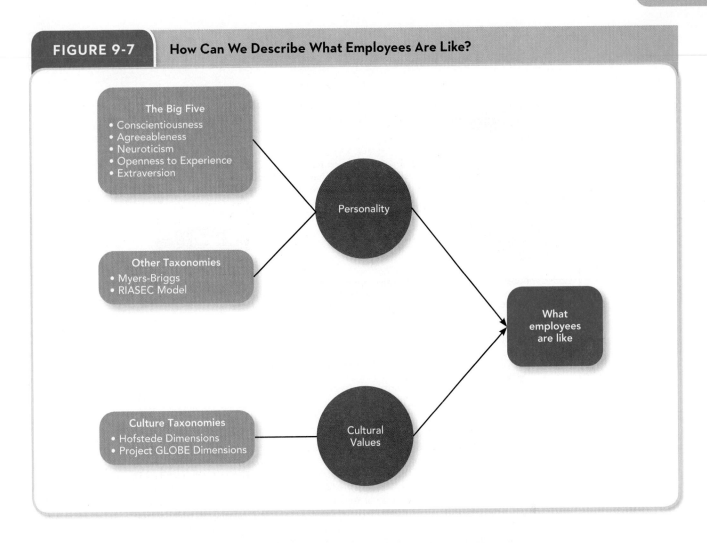

Neuroticism reflects the tendency to experience negative moods and emotions frequently on a day-to-day basis. Individuals who are high on openness to experience are creative, imaginative, and curious. Finally, extraverts are talkative, sociable, and assertive and typically experience positive moods and emotions. Other personality taxonomies, like the MBTI or the RIASEC model, can also capture many employee traits. Beyond personality, however, what employees are like also depends on the culture in which they were raised. Cultural values like individualism–collectivism, power distance, and so forth also influence employees' thoughts, emotions, and behaviors.

HOW IMPORTANT ARE PERSONALITY AND CULTURAL VALUES?

We've already described a number of reasons why the Big Five should be important considerations, particularly in the case of conscientiousness. What if we focus specifically on the two outcomes in our integrative model of OB, performance and commitment? Figure 9-8 summarizes the research evidence linking conscientiousness to those two outcomes. The figure reveals that conscientiousness affects job performance. Of the Big Five, conscientiousness has the strongest effect on task performance,[85] partly because conscientious employees have higher levels of *motivation* than other employees.[86] They are more self-confident, perceive a clearer linkage between their effort and their performance, and are more likely to set goals and commit to them. For these reasons, conscientiousness is a key driver of what's referred to as **typical performance,** which

FIGURE 9-8	Effects of Personality on Performance and Commitment

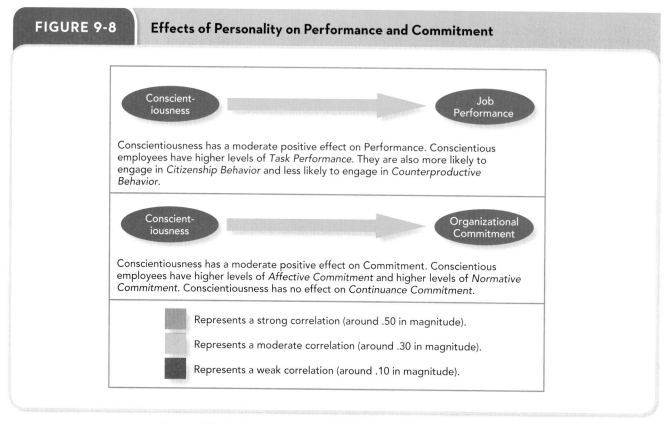

Conscientiousness has a moderate positive effect on Performance. Conscientious employees have higher levels of *Task Performance*. They are also more likely to engage in *Citizenship Behavior* and less likely to engage in *Counterproductive Behavior*.

Conscientiousness has a moderate positive effect on Commitment. Conscientious employees have higher levels of *Affective Commitment* and higher levels of *Normative Commitment*. Conscientiousness has no effect on *Continuance Commitment*.

Represents a strong correlation (around .50 in magnitude).

Represents a moderate correlation (around .30 in magnitude).

Represents a weak correlation (around .10 in magnitude).

Sources: M.R. Barrick, M.K. Mount, and T.A. Judge, "Personality and Performance at the Beginning of the New Millennium: What Do We Know and Where Do We Go Next?" *International Journal of Selection and Assessment* 9 (2001), pp. 9–30; C.M. Berry, D.S. Ones, and P.R. Sackett, "Interpersonal Deviance, Organizational Deviance, and Their Common Correlates: A Review and Meta-Analysis," *Journal of Applied Psychology* 92 (2007), pp. 410–24; A. Cooper-Hakim and C. Viswesvaran, "The Construct of Work Commitment: Testing an Integrative Framework," *Psychological Bulletin* 131 (2005), pp. 241–59; L.M. Hough and A. Furnham, "Use of Personality Variables in Work Settings," in *Handbook of Psychology,* Vol. 12, ed. W.C. Borman, D.R. Ilgen, and R.J. Klimoski (Hoboken, NJ: Wiley, 2003), pp. 131–69; J.E. Mathieu and D.M. Zajac, "A Review and Meta-Analysis of the Antecedents, Correlates, and Consequences of Organizational Commitment," *Psychological Bulletin* 108 (1990), pp. 171–94; and J.F. Salgado, "The Big Five Personality Dimensions and Counterproductive Behaviors," *International Journal of Selection and Assessment* 10 (2002), pp. 117–25.

reflects performance in the routine conditions that surround daily job tasks.[87] An employee's ability, in contrast, is a key driver of **maximum performance,** which reflects performance in brief, special circumstances that demand a person's best effort.

9.6

How does personality affect job performance and organizational commitment?

Conscientious employees are also more likely to engage in citizenship behaviors.[88] Why? One reason is that conscientious employees are so punctual and have such good work attendance that they are simply more available to offer "extra mile" sorts of contributions. Another reason is that they engage in so much more work-related effort that they have more energy to devote to citizenship behaviors.[89] A third reason is that they tend to have higher levels of *job satisfaction,*[90] and positive feelings tend to foster spontaneous instances of citizenship. Finally, conscientious employees are less likely to engage in counterproductive behaviors,[91] for two major reasons. First, their higher job satisfaction levels make it less likely that they'll feel a need to retaliate against their organization. Second, even if they do perceive some slight or injustice, their dependable and reliable nature should prevent them from violating organizational norms by engaging in negative actions.[92]

Figure 9-8 also reveals that conscientious employees tend to be more committed to their organization.[93] They're less likely to engage in day-to-day psychological and physical withdrawal behaviors because such actions go against their work habits. They're also significantly less likely to voluntarily leave the organization.[94] Why? One reason is that the persevering nature of conscientious employees prompts them to persist in a given course of action for long periods of time. That persistence can be seen in their daily work effort, but it extends to a sense of commitment to the organization as well.[95] Another reason is that conscientious employees are better at managing *stress,* perceiving lower levels of key stressors, and being less affected by them at work.[96] In some respects, Figure 9-8 understates the importance of conscientiousness (and personality, more generally). Why? Because personality becomes more important in some contexts than in others. The principle of **situational strength** suggests that "strong situations" have clear behavioral expectations, incentives, or instructions that make differences between individuals less important, whereas "weak situations" lack those cues.[97] Personality variables tend to be more significant drivers of behavior in weak situations than in strong situations.[98] Similarly, the principle of **trait activation** suggests that some situations provide cues that trigger the expression of a given trait.[99] For example, a cry for help provides a cue that can trigger the expression of empathy. Personality variables tend to be more significant drivers of behaviors in situations that provide relevant cues than in situations in which those cues are lacking.

APPLICATION: PERSONALITY TESTS

Given how important personality traits can be to job performance and organizational commitment, it's not surprising that many organizations try to gauge the personality of job applicants. What's the best way to do that? Well, many organizations try to gauge personality through interviews by looking for cues that an applicant is conscientious or agreeable or has high levels of some other relevant personality dimension. Can you see a potential problem with this approach? Here's a hint: When was the last time you went into an interview and acted careless, sloppy, moody, or insecure? It's probably been awhile. People engage in a number of impression management and self-presentation tactics when interviewing, sometimes to appear to possess traits that they don't really have.[100] In fact, most interview preparation courses and books train applicants to exhibit the very personality traits that most employers are looking for!

To examine whether interviewers can gauge the Big Five, one study asked 26 interviewers, all of whom were human resources practitioners with more than 12 years of hiring experience, to assess the personalities of undergraduate business students who were on the job market.[101] The interviewers met with an average of three students for 30 minutes and were instructed to follow the interview protocols used in their own organizations. Once the interviews had concluded, the study gathered multiple ratings of the Big Five, including ratings from the interviewer, the student, and a close friend of the student. The results of the study showed that the interviewers' ratings of extraversion, agreeableness, and openness were fairly consistent with the students' own ratings, as well as their friends' ratings. In contrast, interviewers' ratings of conscientiousness and neuroticism were only weakly related to the students' and friends' ratings. This study therefore shows that interviewers are unable to gauge the two Big Five dimensions that are most highly related to job performance.

Rather than using interviews to assess personality, more and more companies are relying on paper-and-pencil "personality tests" like the kind shown in our OB Assessments. A recent survey of *Fortune* 1000 firms suggests that around a third of those organizations rely on, or plan to implement, some form of personality testing.[102] If you've ever applied for an hourly position at Best Buy, Target, Toys "R" Us, Marriott, Universal Studios, Sports Authority, CVS Pharmacy, Albertsons, or the Fresh Market, you may have been asked to take a personality test at a computer kiosk as part of your application.[103] That test was designed by Kronos, a workforce management software and services provider headquartered in Chelmsford, Massachusetts.[104] Kronos's test includes 50 questions, many of which are clearly tapping the Big Five:

9.7

Are personality tests useful tools for organizational hiring?

- You do things carefully so you don't make mistakes.[105] (high conscientiousness)
- You can easily cheer up and forget a problem.[106] (low neuroticism)
- You don't act polite when you don't want to.[107] (low agreeableness)
- You'd rather blend into the crowd than stand out.[108] (low extraversion)

Ten minutes after an applicant completes the personality test at the kiosk, the hiring manager receives a report that identifies the applicant with a "green light," "yellow light," or "red light."[109] Green lights earn an automatic follow-up interview, yellow lights require some managerial discretion, and red lights are excused from the hiring process. The report also includes some recommended interview questions to follow-up on any concerns that might have arisen based on personality responses. Kronos has built a database of 370,000 employee personality profiles, together with the actual job results for those employees, allowing them to look for profiles of effective and committed employees. Kronos also encourages employers to save the data from the personality tests for several years, to verify that responses correlate with performance evaluations and turnover over time.

Of course, personality testing is not without controversy. Privacy advocates worry about the security of the personality profiles that are stored in large databases.[110] There's also no guarantee that the personality tests used by a company are actually valid assessments because few of them have been subject to scientific investigation.[111] For example, we're not aware of any scientific studies in peer-reviewed journals that have comprehensively validated Kronos's personality test. Because the personality testing industry is not regulated, the best bet for companies that are thinking about using personality tests is to start with tests that have been validated in scientific journals. Table 9-4 provides a list of some of the most well-validated measures of the Big Five personality dimensions. The vendors that own these measures typically offer software and services for scoring the instruments, interpreting the data against relevant population norms, and creating feedback sheets.

One particular subset of personality tests is particularly controversial. **Integrity tests,** sometimes also called "honesty tests," are personality tests that focus specifically on a predisposition to engage in theft and other counterproductive behaviors.[112] Integrity tests were created, in part, as a reaction to Congress's decision to make polygraph (or "lie detector") tests illegal as a tool for organizational hiring. Integrity tests typically come in two general varieties. **Clear purpose tests** ask applicants about their attitudes toward dishonesty, beliefs about the frequency of dishonesty, endorsements of common rationalizations for dishonesty, desire to punish dishonesty, and confessions of past dishonesty.[113] **Veiled purpose tests** do not reference dishonesty explicitly but instead assess more general personality traits that are associated with dishonest acts. Table 9-5 provides sample items for both types of integrity tests. You might notice that the veiled purpose items resemble some of the items in our OB Assessment for the Big Five. Most integrity tests actually assess, in large part, a combination of high conscientiousness, high agreeableness, and low neuroticism,[114] along with an honesty or humility factor that may lay beyond the Big Five.[115]

Do integrity tests actually work? One study examined the effectiveness of integrity tests in a sample of convenience store clerks.[116] The chain had been struggling with inventory "shrinkage" due to theft and began using a clear purpose integrity test to combat that trend. The study compared the integrity test scores for employees who were fired for theft-related reasons (e.g., taking merchandise, mishandling cash, having frequent cash register shortages) with a sample of demographically similar employees who remained in good standing. The results of the study revealed that employees who were terminated for theft had scored significantly lower on the integrity test when they were hired than employees who were not terminated. These sorts of results are not unusual; a meta-analysis of 443 studies including more than 500,000 employees

TABLE 9-4	A Sampling of Well-Validated Measures of the Big Five	
NAME OF INSTRUMENT	**VENDOR**	**TIME REQUIRED**
NEO Five-Factor Inventory (NEO-FFI)	Sigma Assessment Systems	15 minutes
Personal Characteristics Inventory (PCI)	Wonderlic	20 minutes
Personality Research Form (PRF)	Sigma Assessment Systems	45 minutes
Hogan Personality Inventory (HPI)	Hogan Assessment Systems	15 minutes
Big Five Inventory (BFI)	TestMaster	10 minutes

TABLE 9-5	Sample Integrity Test Items
TYPE OF TEST	**SAMPLE ITEMS**
Clear Purpose	• Did you ever think about taking money from where you worked, but didn't go through with it? • Have you ever borrowed something from work without telling anyone? • Is it OK to get around the law if you don't break it? • If you were sent an extra item with an order, would you send it back? • Do most employees take small items from work? • What dollar value would a worker have to steal before you would fire them?
Veiled Purpose	• I like to plan things carefully ahead of time. • I often act quickly without stopping to think things through. • I've never hurt anyone's feelings. • I have a feeling someone is out to get me. • I don't feel I've had control over my life.

Source: From J.E. Wanek, P.R. Sackett, and D.S. Ones, "Towards an Understanding of Integrity Test Similarities and Differences: An Item-Level Analysis of Seven Tests," *Personnel Psychology* 56 (2003), pp. 873–94. Reprinted with permission of John Wiley & Sons, Inc.

has shown that integrity test scores have a moderately strong, negative correlation with counterproductive behaviors such as theft.[117] In fact, integrity test scores are actually more strongly related to job performance than conscientiousness scores, largely because integrity tests sample a blend of multiple Big Five dimensions.[118]

You might find it surprising that integrity tests (or personality tests in general) can be effective. After all, don't applicants just lie on the test? Before we answer that question, consider what you would do if you applied for a job and had to answer a set of questions on a 1 ("Strongly Disagree") to 5 ("Strongly Agree") scale that were obviously measuring integrity. If a response of 5 indicated high integrity, how would you answer? You probably wouldn't answer all 5s because it would be clear that you were **faking**—exaggerating your responses to a personality test in a socially desirable fashion. You might worry that the computers that score the test have some ability to "flag" faked responses (indeed, the scoring procedures for many personality tests do flag applicants with an unusual pattern of responses).[119]

So how would you answer? Chances are, you'd allow your answers to have "a grain of truth"—you'd just exaggerate that true response a bit to make yourself look better. Figure 9-9 summarizes what this sort of faking might look like, with red circles representing below-average scores on an integrity test and green circles representing above-average scores. Research on personality testing suggests that virtually everyone fakes their responses to some degree, as evidenced in the difference between the faded circles (which represent the "true" responses) and the unfaded circles (which represent the exaggerated responses).[120] Do dishonest people fake more? To some degree. Figure 9-9 reveals that applicants who scored below average on the test faked a bit more than applicants who scored above average on the test. But the disparity in the amount of faking is not large, likely because dishonest people tend to view their behavior as perfectly normal—they believe everyone feels and acts just like they do.

The figure reveals that it could be dangerous to set some artificial cutoff score for making hiring decisions, because it's possible for people to "fake their way" across that cutoff (note that two of the individuals in the figure went from a below-average score to an above-average score by faking). With that caution in mind, here's the critical point illustrated by Figure 9-9: *Because everyone fakes to some degree, correlations with outcomes like theft or other counterproductive behaviors are relatively unaffected.*[121] Picture the scatterplot in the figure with just the faded

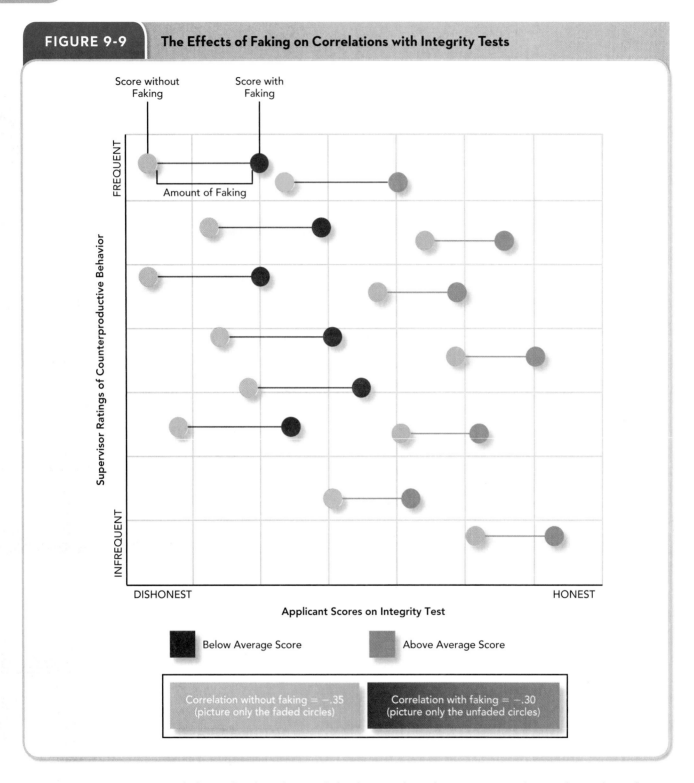

FIGURE 9-9   **The Effects of Faking on Correlations with Integrity Tests**

circles—what does the correlation between integrity test scores and supervisor ratings of counterproductive behavior look like? Now picture the scatterplot with just the unfaded circles—what does that correlation look like? About the same, right? The tendency to fake doesn't really alter the rank order in scores from most dishonest to most honest, so the test is still useful as a tool for predicting counterproductive behavior. In fact, experts on personnel selection agree that personality and integrity tests are among the most useful tools for hiring[122]—more useful even than the typical version of the employment interview.[123] One of the only tools that's more useful than a personality test is an ability test—as noted in our next chapter.[124]

TAKEAWAYS

9.1 Personality refers to the structures and propensities inside people that explain their characteristic patterns of thought, emotion, and behavior. It also refers to people's social reputations—the way they are perceived by others. In this way, personality captures *what people are like* (unlike ability, which reflects *what people can do*). Cultural values are shared beliefs about desirable end states or modes of conduct in a given culture that influence the development and expression of traits.

9.2 The "Big Five" include conscientiousness (e.g., dependable, organized, reliable), agreeableness (e.g., warm, kind, cooperative), neuroticism (e.g., nervous, moody, emotional), openness to experience (e.g., curious, imaginative, creative), and extraversion (e.g., talkative, sociable, passionate).

9.3 Although both nature and nurture are important, personality is affected significantly by genetic factors. Studies of identical twins reared apart and studies of personality stability over time suggest that between 35 and 45 percent of the variation in personality is genetic. Personality can be changed, but such changes are apparent only over the course of several years.

9.4 The Big Five is the dominant taxonomy of personality; other taxonomies include the Myers-Briggs Type Inventory and Holland's RIASEC model.

9.5 Hofstede's taxonomy of cultural values includes individualism–collectivism, power distance, uncertainty avoidance, masculinity–femininity, and short-term vs. long-term orientation. More recent research by Project GLOBE has replicated many of those dimensions and added five other means to distinguish among cultures: gender egalitarianism, assertiveness, future orientation, performance orientation, and humane orientation.

9.6 Conscientiousness has a moderate positive relationship with job performance and a moderate positive relationship with organizational commitment. It has stronger effects on these outcomes than the rest of the Big Five.

9.7 Personality tests are useful tools for organizational hiring. Research suggests that applicants do "fake" to some degree on the tests, but faking does not significantly lower the correlation between test scores and the relevant outcomes.

   Here are the answers to the tests of creative thinking in Figure 9-5: (1) A towel. (2) They were triplets. (3) The letter U. (4) Draw a line to turn the + into a 4. (5) Solving this puzzle literally requires you to "think outside the box" (yes, that's where it comes from!) Nowhere in the instructions did it state that you needed to keep the lines inside the square formed by the dots. Connect the dots using the four lines shown below:

KEY TERMS

•	Personality	*p. 268*	• Extraversion	*p. 269*
•	Traits	*p. 268*	• Big Five	*p. 269*
•	Cultural values	*p. 268*	• Accomplishment striving	*p. 273*
•	Conscientiousness	*p. 269*	• Communion striving	*p. 273*
•	Agreeableness	*p. 269*	• Zero acquaintance	*p. 275*
•	Neuroticism	*p. 269*	• Status striving	*p. 275*
•	Openness to experience	*p. 269*	• Positive affectivity	*p. 275*

- Negative affectivity — *p. 276*
- Differential exposure — *p. 276*
- Differential reactivity — *p. 276*
- Locus of control — *p. 276*
- Myers-Briggs Type Indicator (MBTI) — *p. 281*
- Interests — *p. 282*
- RIASEC model — *p. 282*
- Culture — *p. 283*
- Individualism–collectivism — *p. 284*
- Power distance — *p. 284*
- Uncertainty avoidance — *p. 284*
- Masculinity–femininity — *p. 284*
- Short-term vs. long-term orientation — *p. 284*
- Project GLOBE — *p. 284*
- Ethnocentrism — *p. 285*
- Typical performance — *p. 287*
- Maximum performance — *p. 288*
- Situational strength — *p. 289*
- Trait activation — *p. 289*
- Integrity tests — *p. 290*
- Clear purpose tests — *p. 290*
- Veiled purpose tests — *p. 290*
- Faking — *p. 291*

DISCUSSION QUESTIONS

9.1 Assume that you applied for a job and were asked to take a personality test, like the one offered by Kronos. How would you react? Would you view the organization with which you were applying in a more or less favorable light? Why?

9.2 Research on genetic influences on personality suggests that more than half of the variation in personality is due to nurture—to life experiences. What life experiences could make someone more conscientious? More agreeable? More neurotic? More extraverted? More open to new experiences?

9.3 Consider the personality dimensions included in the Myers-Briggs Type Inventory and the RIASEC model. If you had to "slot" those dimensions into the Big Five, would you be able to do so? Which dimensions don't seem to fit?

9.4 Consider the profile of the United States on Hofstede's cultural values, as shown in Table 9-3. Do you personally feel like you fit the U.S. profile, or do your values differ in some respects? If you served as an expatriate, meaning you were working in another country, which cultural value differences would be most difficult for you to deal with?

9.5 If you owned your own business and had a problem with employee theft, would you use an integrity test? Why or why not?

CASE: CHIPOTLE

Who designed the selection system that's now in use at Chipotle? Who decides which personality traits are critical enough to be assessed during screening and which don't quite make the cut? That would be Monty Moran, co-CEO of the company and a high school classmate of Ells. Moran had been the lead attorney for Chipotle and a CEO of a prestigious Denver law firm. Moran recalls the conversation that changed all that, repeating Ells's words: "Monty, you may be a great lawyer but that's not what you're best at . . . What you're best at is being a leader. That's more important. You should come to Chipotle and use that for a company of 10,000 instead of a firm of 600." What hiring philosophy did Moran bring? "We don't care about experience very much," Moran notes, "In fact, I think experience at another fast-food restaurant is as likely to be a negative as it is to be a positive. We look for people who possess certain qualities that you can't teach." In particular, Moran created a checklist of 13 traits that hiring managers should use when screening Chipotle's applicants:

- Conscientious
- Motivated

- Ambitious
- Respectful
- Hospitable
- Polite
- Happy
- Curious
- High energy
- Infectiously enthusiastic
- Honest
- Presentable
- Smart

It's clear from that list that Moran emphasizes the Big Five in hiring, along with integrity and cognitive ability—the subject of the next chapter. Moran wants the list kept manageable so that hiring managers can assess all of them in a relatively short meeting. Indeed, Moran "test drove" the list at a managerial retreat in Las Vegas. He interviewed a series of candidates on stage in front of 2000 people to illustrate how to gauge the traits. Moran estimates that there's 80 percent to 90 percent agreement on whether candidates possess the qualities in question. And Chipotle cares deeply about its commitment to its selection system, so much so that it avoids franchising. Most of its competitors do franchise because the fees paid by franchisees are a powerful means of raising capital. But Moran and Ells argue that franchising would release control over Chipotle's culture and its hiring practices. Chipotle views that control as important as it continues to expand—with plans to open around 200 new locations this year.

9.1   Which traits would you want to see in "front line" employees at Chipotle? How do those compare to the 13 traits that the company actually uses?

9.2   Would being a leader in the company—either a general manager running a store or a middle manager in the corporate headquarters—require a different set of traits? If so, which traits would be subtracted from the set of 13 and which would be added?

9.3   Do you agree that there would be "80 percent to 90 percent agreement" on whether an applicant possesses the 13 traits? Do you think Chipotle should assess the traits with an interview or with a more formal personality test?

Source: M. Nisen, "How Chipotle Transformed Itself by Upending Its Approach to Management." *Quartz*, March 20, 2014.

EXERCISE: GUESSING PERSONALITY PROFILES

The purpose of this exercise is to explore how noticeable the Big Five personality dimensions are among classmates. This exercise uses groups, so your instructor will either assign you to a group or ask you to create your own group. The exercise has the following steps:

9.1   Individually, complete the Big Five measure found in the **OB Assessments** box in the chapter.

9.2   Write your scores on a small white piece of paper, in the following format: C =, A =, N =, O =, E =. Try to disguise your handwriting to make it as plain and generic as possible. Fold your piece of paper so that others cannot see your scores.

9.3   In your group, mix up the pieces of paper. Begin by having one group member choose a piece of paper, reading the CANOE scores aloud. The group should then try to come to consensus on which member the scores belong to, given the norms for the various dimensions (C = 14, A = 16, N = 10, O = 15, E = 13). Keep in mind that group members may wind up reading their own pieces of paper aloud in some cases. Once the group guesses which member the paper belongs to, they should place the paper in front of that member.

9.4 Moving clockwise, the next group member should choose one of the remaining pieces of paper, continuing as before. The process repeats until all the pieces of paper have been assigned to a member. Members can be assigned only one piece of paper, and no switching is permitted once an assignment has been made.

9.5 Group members should then announce whether the piece of paper assigned to them was in fact their set of scores. If the assignment was incorrect, they should find their actual piece of paper and describe the differences in the scores.

9.6 Class discussion (whether in groups or as a class) should center on the following topics: How accurate were the guesses? Were the guesses more accurate in groups that knew one another well than in groups with less familiarity? Which personality dimensions were relied upon most heavily when making assignment decisions? What is it that makes those dimensions more immediately observable?

ENDNOTES

9.1 Funder, D.C. "Personality." *Annual Review of Psychology* 52 (2001), pp. 197–221; and Hogan, R.T. "Personality and Personality Measurement." *Handbook of Industrial and Organizational Psychology*, Vol. 2, ed. M.D. Dunnette and L.M. Hough. Palo Alto, CA: Consulting Psychologists Press, 1991, pp. 873–919.

9.2 Hogan, "Personality and Personality Measurement."

9.3 Ibid.; Fleeson, W., and P. Gallagher. "The Implications of Big Five Standing for the Distribution of Trait Manifestation in Behavior: Fifteen Experience-Sampling Studies and a Meta-Analysis." *Journal of Personality and Social Psychology* 97 (2009), pp. 1097–1114.

9.4 Rokeach, M. *The Nature of Human Values*. New York: The Free Press, 1973;

and Steers, R.M., and C.J. Sanchez-Runde. "Culture, Motivation, and Work Behavior." In *Blackwell Handbook of Cross-Cultural Management*, ed. M.J. Gannon and K.L. Newman. Malden, MA: Blackwell, 2002, pp. 190–213.

9.5 Goldberg, L.R. "From Ace to Zombie: Some Explorations in the Language of Personality." In *Advances in Personality Assessment*, Vol. 1, ed. C.D. Spielberger and J.N. Butcher. Hillsdale, NJ: Erlbaum, 1982, pp. 203–34; Allport, G.W., and H.S. Odbert. "Trait-Names: A Psycho-Lexical Study." *Psychological Monographs* 47 (1936), Whole No. 211; and Norman, W.T. *2800 Personality Trait Descriptors: Normative Operating Characteristics for a University Population*. Ann Arbor: University of Michigan

Department of Psychology, 1967.

9.6 Tupes, E.C., and R.E. Christal. *Recurrent Personality Factors Based on Trait Ratings*. USAF ASD Technical Report No. 61–97, Lackland Air Force Base, TX: United States Air Force, 1961, reprinted in *Journal of Personality* 60, pp. 225–51; Norman, W.T. "Toward an Adequate Taxonomy of Personality Attributes: Replicated Factor Structure in Peer Nomination Personality Ratings." *Journal of Abnormal and Social Psychology* 66 (1963), pp. 574–83; Digman, J.M., and N.K. Takemoto-Chock. "Factors in the Natural Language of Personality: Re-Analysis, Comparison, and Interpretation of Six Major Studies." *Multivariate Behavioral Research* 16 (1981), pp. 149–70; McCrae, R.R., and P.T. Costa Jr. "Updating Norman's 'Adequate

Taxonomy': Intelligence and Personality Dimensions in Natural Language and in Questionnaires." *Journal of Personality and Social Psychology* 49 (1985), pp. 710–21; and Goldberg, L.R. "An Alternative 'Description of Personality': The Big-Five Factor Structure." *Journal of Personality and Social Psychology* 59 (1990), pp. 1216–29.

9.7 Goldberg, L.R. "Language and Individual Differences: The Search for Universals in Personality Lexicons." In *Review of Personality and Social Psychology*, Vol. 2, ed. L. Wheeler. Beverly Hills, CA: Sage, 1981, pp. 141–65.

9.8 Arvey, R.D., and T.J. Bouchard Jr. "Genetics, Twins, and Organizational Behavior." In *Research in Organizational Behavior*, Vol. 16, ed. B.M. Staw and L.L. Cummings. Greenwich, CT: JAI Press, 1994, pp. 47–82.

9.9 Loehlin, J.C. *Genes and Environment in Personality Development*. Newbury Park, CA: Sage, 1992.

9.10 Ibid.

9.11 Roberts, B.W.; K.E. Walton; and W. Viechtbauer. "Patterns of Mean-Level Change in Personality Traits across the Life Course: A Meta-Analysis of Longitudinal Studies."

Psychological Bulletin 132 (2006), pp. 1–25.

9.12 Cohen, J. *Statistical Power Analysis for Behavioral Sciences*, 2nd ed. Hillsdale, NJ: Erlbaum, 1988.

9.13 Loehlin, *Genes and Environment*.

9.14 Roberts et al., "Patterns of Mean-Level Change in Personality Traits across the Life Course"; Jackson, J.J.; T. Bogg; K.E. Walton; D. Wood; P.D. Harms; J. Lodi-Smith; G.W. Edmonds; and B.W. Roberts. "Not All Conscientiousness Scales Change Alike: A Multimethod, Multisample Study of Age Differences in the Facets of Conscientiousness." *Journal of Personality and Social Psychology* 96 (2009), pp. 446–59; and Soto, C.J.; O.P. John; S.D. Gosling; and J. Potter. "Age Differences in Personality Traits from 10 to 65: Big Five Domains and Facets in a Large Cross-Sectional Sample." *Journal of Personality and Social Psychology* 100 (2011), pp. 330–48.

9.15 Saucier, G. "Mini-Markers: A Brief Version of Goldberg's Unipolar Big-Five Markers." *Journal of Personality Assessment* 63 (1994), pp. 506–16; Goldberg, L.R. "The Development of Markers for the Big-Five Factor Structure." *Psychological Assessment* 4 (1992),

pp. 26–42; and McCrae, R.R., and P.T. Costa Jr. "Validation of the Five-Factor Model of Personality Across Instruments and Observers." *Journal of Personality and Social Psychology* 52 (1987), pp. 81–90.

9.16 Barrick, M.R., and M.K. Mount. "The Big Five Personality Dimensions and Job Performance: A Meta-Analysis." *Personnel Psychology* 44 (1991), pp. 1–26.

9.17 Barrick, M.R.; G.L. Stewart; and M. Piotrowski. "Personality and Job Performance: Test of the Mediating Effects of Motivation among Sales Representatives." *Journal of Applied Psychology* 87 (2002), pp. 43–51.

9.18 Barrick, M.R.; M.K. Mount; and J.P. Strauss. "Conscientiousness and Performance of Sales Representatives: Test of the Mediating Effects of Goal Setting." *Journal of Applied Psychology* 78 (1993), pp. 715–22.

9.19 Stewart, G.L. "Trait Bandwidth and Stages of Job Performance: Assessing Differential Effects for Conscientiousness and its Subtraits." *Journal of Applied Psychology* 84 (1999), pp. 959–68.

9.20 Judge, T.A.; C.A. Higgins; C.J. Thoreson; and M.R. Barrick.

"The Big Five Personality Traits, General Mental Ability, and Career Success across the Life Span." *Personnel Psychology* 52 (1999), pp. 621–52.

9.21 Friedman, H.S.; J.S. Tucker; J.E. Schwartz; L.R. Martin; C. Tomlinson-Keasey; D.L. Wingard; and M.H. Criqui. "Childhood Conscientiousness and Longevity: Health Behaviors and Cause of Death." *Journal of Personality and Social Psychology* 68 (1995), pp. 696–703.

9.22 Roberts, B.W.; O.S. Chernyshenko; S. Stark; and L.R. Goldberg. "The Structure of Conscientiousness: An Empirical Investigation Based on Seven Major Personality Dimensions." *Personnel Psychology* 58 (2005), pp. 103–39.

9.23 Barrick et al., "Personality and Job Performance"; and Hogan, J., and B. Holland. "Using Theory to Evaluate Personality and Job-Performance Relations: A Socioanalytic Perspective." *Journal of Applied Psychology* 88 (2003), pp. 100–12.

9.24 Barrick and Mount, "The Big Five Personality Dimensions."

9.25 Frei, R.L., and M.A. McDaniel. "Validity of Customer Service Measures in Personnel Selection: A Review of Criterion and Construct Evidence." *Human Performance* 11 (1998), pp. 1–27.

9.26 Graziano, W.G.; L.A. Jensen-Campbell; and E.C. Hair. "Perceiving Interpersonal Conflict and Reacting to It: The Case for Agreeableness." *Journal of Personality and Social Psychology* 70 (1996), pp. 820–35.

9.27 Mehl, M.R.; S.D. Gosling; and J.W. Pennebaker. "Personality in Its Natural Habitat: Manifestations and Implicit Folk Theories of Personality in Daily Life." *Journal of Personality and Social Psychology* 90 (2006), pp. 862–77.

9.28 Albright, L.; D.A. Kenny; and T.E. Malloy. "Consensus in Personality Judgments at Zero Acquaintance." *Journal of Personality and Social Psychology* 55 (1988), pp. 387–95; and Levesque, M.J., and D.A. Kenny. "Accuracy of Behavioral Predictions at Zero Acquaintance: A Social Relations Analysis." *Journal of Personality and Social Psychology* 65 (1993), pp. 1178–87.

9.29 Barrick et al., "Personality and Job Performance."

9.30 Judge, T.A.; J.E. Bono; R. Ilies; and M.W. Gerhardt. "Personality and Leadership: A Qualitative and Quantitative Review." *Journal of Applied Psychology* 87 (2002), pp. 765–80.

9.31 Ibid.

9.32 Thoreson, C.J.; S.A. Kaplan; A.P. Barsky; C.R. Warren; and K. de Chermont. "The Affective Underpinnings of Job Perceptions and Attitudes: A Meta-Analytic Review and Integration." *Psychological Bulletin* 129 (2003), pp. 914–45.

9.33 Ibid.; Judge, T.A.; D. Heller; and M.K. Mount. "Five-Factor Model of Personality and Job Satisfaction: A Meta-Analysis." *Journal of Applied Psychology* 87 (2003), pp. 530–41; and Kaplan, S.; J.C. Bradley; J.N. Luchman; and D. Haynes. "On the Role of Positive and Negative Affectivity in Job Performance: A Meta-Analytic Investigation." *Journal of Applied Psychology* 94 (2009), pp. 162–76.

9.34 Arvey, R.D.; T.J. Bouchard; N.L. Segal; and L.M. Abraham. "Job Satisfaction: Environmental and Genetic Components." *Journal of Applied Psychology* 74 (1989), pp. 187–92.

9.35 Steel, P.; J. Schmidt; and J. Shultz. "Refining the Relationship between Personality and Subjective Well-Being." *Psychological Bulletin* 134 (2008), pp. 138–61; and

CHAPTER 9 Personality and Cultural Values **299**

Steel, P., and D.S. Ones. "Personality and Happiness: A National-Level Analysis." *Journal of Personality and Social Psychology* 83 (2002), pp. 767–81.

9.36 Magnus, K.; E. Diener; F. Fujita; and W. Pavot. "Extraversion and Neuroticism as Predictors of Objective Life Events: A Longitudinal Analysis." *Journal of Personality and Social Psychology* 65 (1992), pp. 1046–53.

9.37 Paunonen, S.V. "Big Five Predictors of Personality and Replicated Predictions of Behavior." *Journal of Personality and Social Psychology* 84 (2003), pp. 411–24; and Asendorpf, J.B., and S. Wilpers. "Personality Effects on Social Relationships." *Journal of Personality and Social Psychology* 74 (1998), pp. 1531–44.

9.38 Asendorpf and Wilpers, "Personality Effects on Social Relationships."

9.39 Barrick, M.R., and M.K. Mount. "Select on Conscientiousness and Emotional Stability." In *Blackwell Handbook of Principles of Organizational Behavior*, ed. E.A. Locke. Malden, MA: Blackwell, 2000, pp. 15–28.

9.40 Thoreson et al., "The Affective Underpinnings."

9.41 Ibid.; and Kaplan et al., "On the Role of Positive and Negative Affectivity in Job Performance."

9.42 DeNeve, K.M., and H. Cooper. "The Happy Personality: A Meta-Analysis of 137 Personality Traits and Subjective Well-Being." *Psychological Bulletin* 124 (1998), pp. 197–229; Steel et al., "Refining the Relationship between Personality and Subjective Well-Being"; and Steel and Ones, "Personality and Happiness."

9.43 Bolger, N., and A. Zuckerman. "A Framework for Studying Personality in the Stress Process." *Journal of Personality and Social Psychology* 69 (1995), pp. 890–902.

9.44 Ibid.

9.45 Friedman, M., and R.H. Rosenman. *Type A Behavior and Your Heart*. New York: Knopf, 1974.

9.46 Rotter, J.B. "Generalized Expectancies for Internal versus External Control of Reinforcement." *Psychological Monographs* 80 (1966), pp. 1–28.

9.47 Judge, T.A., and J.E. Bono. "Relationship of Core Self-Evaluations Traits—Self-Esteem, Generalized Self-Efficacy, Locus of Control, and Emotional Stability—with Job Satisfaction and Job Performance: A Meta-Analysis." *Journal of Applied Psychology* 86 (2001), pp. 80–92.

9.48 Ng, T.W.H.; K.L. Sorensen; and L.T. Eby. "Locus of Control at Work: A Meta-Analysis." *Journal of Organizational Behavior* 27 (2006), pp. 1057–87.

9.49 Barrick and Mount, "The Big Five Personality Dimensions"; and Cellar, D.F.; M.L. Miller; D.D. Doverspike; and J.D. Klawsky. "Comparison of Factor Structures and Criterion-Related Validity Coefficients for Two Measures of Personality Based on the Five Factor Model." *Journal of Applied Psychology* 81 (1996), pp. 694–704.

9.50 LePine, J.A.; J.A. Colquitt; and A. Erez. "Adaptability to Changing Task Contexts: Effects of General Cognitive Ability, Conscientiousness, and Openness to Experience." *Personnel Psychology* 53 (2000), pp. 563–93; and Thoreson, C.J.; J.C. Bradley; P.D. Bliese; and J.D. Thoreson. "The Big Five Personality Traits and Individual Job Performance Growth Trajectories in Maintenance and Transitional Job Stages." *Journal of Applied Psychology* 89 (2004), pp. 835–53.

9.51 Shalley, C.E.; J. Zhou; and G.R. Oldham. "The Effects of

Personal and Contextual Characteristics on Creativity: Where Should We Go from Here?" *Journal of Management* 30 (2004), pp. 933–58.

9.52 Zhou, J., and J.M. George. "When Job Dissatisfaction Leads to Creativity: Encouraging the Expression of Voice." *Academy of Management Journal* 44 (2001), pp. 682–96.

9.53 Feist, G.J. "A Meta-Analysis of Personality in Scientific and Artistic Creativity." *Personality and Social Psychology Review* 2 (1998), pp. 290–309.

9.54 Stead, D. "You Are Getting Creative . . . Very Creative." *BusinessWeek*, May 12, 2008, p. 18.

9.55 Edmondson, G. "BMW's Dream Factory." *BusinessWeek*, October 16, 2006, pp. 70–80.

9.56 Myers, I.B., and M.H. McCaulley. *Manual: A Guide to the Development and Use of the Myers-Briggs Type Indicator*. Palo Alto, CA: Consulting Psychologists Press, 1985.

9.57 Jung, C.G. *The Collected Works of C. G. Jung*, Vol. 6: Psychological Types, trans. H.G. Baynes, ed. R. F. Hull. Princeton, NJ: Princeton University Press, 1971.

9.58 Gardner, W.L., and M.J. Martinko. "Using the Myers-Briggs Type Indicator to Study Managers: A Literature Review and Research Agenda." *Journal of Management* 22 (1996), pp. 45–83; and "What Is Your Myers Briggs Personality Type?" http://www. personalitypathways. com/type_inventory. html (accessed March 18, 2007).

9.59 Gardner and Martinko, "Using the Myers-Briggs Type Indicator."

9.60 Ibid.

9.61 Holland, J.L. "A Theory of Vocational Choice." *Journal of Counseling Psychology* 6 (1959), pp. 35–45; and Holland, J.L. *Making Vocational Choices: A Theory of Vocational Personalities and Work Environments*, 3rd ed. Odessa, FL: Psychological Assessment Resources, 1997.

9.62 Mount, M.K.; M.R. Barrick; S.M. Scullen; and J. Rounds. "Higher-Order Dimensions of the Big Five Personality Traits and the Big Six Vocational Interests." *Personnel Psychology* 58 (2005), pp. 447–78.

9.63 Strong, E.K. "An 18-Year Longitudinal Report on Interests." In *The Strong Vocational Interest Blank: Research and Uses*, ed. W.L. Layton. Minneapolis, MN: University of Minnesota Press, 1960.

9.64 Holland, *Making Vocational Choices;* "Providing Holland Code Resources Worldwide" (n.d.), Hollandcodes. com, http://www. hollandcodes.com/ holland_occupational_ codes.html; and Armstrong, P.I.; W. Allison; and J. Rounds. "Development and Initial Validation of Brief Public Domain RIASEC Marker Scales." *Journal of Vocational Behavior* 73 (2008), pp. 287–99.

9.65 Muchinsky, P.M. "Applications of Holland's Theory in Industrial and Organizational Settings." *Journal of Vocational Behavior* 55 (1999), pp. 127–35; and Van Iddekinge, C.H.; D.J. Putka; and J.P. Campbell. "Reconsidering Vocational Interests for Personnel Selection: The Validity of an Interest-Based Selection Test in Relation to Job Knowledge, Job Performance, and Continuance Intentions." *Journal of Applied Psychology* 96 (2011), pp. 13–33.

9.66 Campbell, D.P., and F.H. Borgen. "Holland's Theory and the Development of Interest Inventories." *Journal of Vocational Behavior* 55 (1999), pp. 86–101; and Rayman, J., and L. Atanasoff. "Holland's Theory of Career Intervention: The Power of the Hexagon." *Journal*

9.67 Tsui, A.S.; S.S. Nifadkar; and A.Y. Ou. "Cross-National, Cross-Cultural Organizational Behavior Research: Advances, Gaps, and Recommendations." *Journal of Management* 33 (2007), pp. 426–78.

9.68 House, R.J.; P.J. Hanges; M. Javidan; P.W. Dorfman; and V. Gupta. *Culture, Leadership, and Organizations: The GLOBE Study of 62 Societies.* Thousand Oaks, CA: Sage, 2004.

9.69 Kroeber, A.L., and C. Kluckhohn. *Culture: A Critical Review of Concepts and Definitions.* Cambridge, MA: Harvard University Press, 1952; and Hofstede, G. *Cultures and Organizations: Software of the Mind.* London: McGraw-Hill, 1991.

9.70 Zou, X.; K.P. Tam; M.W. Morris; S.l. Lee; I.Y.M. Lau; and C.Y. Chiu. "Culture as Common Sense: Perceived Consensus versus Personal Beliefs as Mechanisms of Cultural Influence." *Journal of Personality and Social Psychology* 97 (2009), pp. 579–97.

9.71 Heine, S.J., and E.E. Buchtel. "Personality: The Universal and the Culturally Specific." *Annual Review of Psychology* 60 (2009), pp. 369–94.

9.72 McCrae, R.R.; A. Terracciano; and 79 Members of the Personality Profiles of Cultures Project. "Personality Profiles of Cultures: Aggregate Personality Traits." *Journal of Personality and Social Psychology* 89 (2005), pp. 407–25.

9.73 Schwartz, S.H. "Universals in the Content and Structure of Values: Theoretical Advances and Empirical Tests in 20 Countries." *Advances in Experimental Social Psychology*, Vol. 25, ed. M.P. Zanna. San Diego, CA: Academic Press, 1992, pp. 1–65.

9.74 House et al., *Culture, Leadership, and Organizations.*

9.75 Hofstede, G. *Culture's Consequences: Comparing Values, Behaviors, Institutions, and Organizations across Nations.* Thousand Oaks, CA: Sage, 2001; and Kirkman, B.L.; K.B. Lowe; and C.B. Gibson. "A Quarter Century of *Culture's Consequences:* A Review of Empirical Research Incorporating Hofstede's Cultural Values Framework." *Journal of International Business Studies* 37 (2006), pp. 285–320.

9.76 Hofstede, G., and M.H. Bond. "The Confucius Connection: From Cultural Roots to Economic Growth." *Organizational Dynamics* 16 (1988), pp. 5–21.

9.77 House et al., *Culture, Leadership, and Organizations.*

9.78 Chen, Y.; K. Leung; and C.C. Chen. "Bringing National Culture to the Table: Making a Difference with Cross-Cultural Differences and Perspectives." *Academy of Management Annals* 3 (2009), pp. 217–49.

9.79 Oyserman, D.; H.M. Coon; and M. Kemmelmeier. "Rethinking Individualism and Collectivism: Evaluation of Theoretical Assumptions and Meta-Analyses." *Psychological Bulletin* 128 (2002), pp. 3–72; Earley, P.C., and C.B. Gibson. "Taking Stock in Our Progress on Individualism–Collectivism: 100 Years of Solidarity and Community." *Journal of Management* 24 (1998), pp. 265–304; and Taras, V.; B.L. Kirkman; and P. Steel. "Examining the Impact of *Culture's Consequences:* A Three-Decade, Multilevel, Meta-Analytic Review of Hofstede's Cultural Value Dimensions. *Journal of Applied Psychology* 95 (2010), pp. 405–39.

9.80 Jackson, C.L.; J.A. Colquitt; M.J. Wesson; and C.P. Zapata-Phelan. "Psychological Collectivism: A Measurement Validation and Linkage to Group Member Performance."

of Vocational Behavior 55 (1999), pp. 114–26.

Journal of Applied Psychology 91 (2006), pp. 884–99; and Dierdorff, E.C.; S.T. Bell; and J.A. Belohlav. "The Power of 'We': Effects of Psychological Collectivism on Team Performance Over Time." *Journal of Applied Psychology* 96 (2011), pp. 247–62.

9.81 Wasti, S.A., and O. Can. "Affective and Normative Commitment to Organization, Supervisor, and Coworker: Do Collectivist Values Matter?" *Journal of Vocational Behavior* 73 (2008), pp. 404–13.

9.82 Earley and Gibson, "Taking Stock in Our Progress."

9.83 Kirkman et al., "A Quarter Century."

9.84 Black, J.S. "The Relationship of Personal Characteristics with the Adjustment of Japanese Expatriate Managers." *Management International Review* 30 (1990), pp. 119–34.

9.85 Barrick, M.R.; M.K. Mount; and T.A. Judge. "Personality and Performance at the Beginning of the New Millennium: What Do We Know and Where Do We Go Next?" *International Journal of Selection and Assessment* 9 (2001), pp. 9–30; and Hough, L.M., and A. Furnham. "Use of Personality Variables in Work Settings." In *Handbook of Psychology*, Vol. 12, ed. W.C. Borman, D.R. Ilgen, and R.J. Klimoski. Hoboken, NJ: Wiley, 2003, pp. 131–69.

9.86 Judge, T. A., and R. Ilies. "Relationship of Personality to Performance Motivation: A Meta-Analysis." *Journal of Applied Psychology* 87 (2002), pp. 797–807.

9.87 Sackett, P.R.; S. Zedeck; and L. Fogli. "Relations Between Measures of Typical and Maximum Job Performance." *Journal of Applied Psychology* 73 (1988), pp. 482–86.

9.88 Hough and Furnham, "Use of Personality Variables in Work Settings"; and Ilies, R.; I.S. Fulmer; M. Spitzmuller; and M.D. Johnson. "Personality and Citizenship Behavior: The Mediating Role of Job Satisfaction." *Journal of Applied Psychology* 94 (2009), pp. 945–59.

9.89 Mount, M.K., and M.R. Barrick. "The Big Five Personality Dimensions: Implications for Research and Practice in Human Resources Management." In *Research in Personnel and Human Resource Management*, ed. G.R. Ferris. Greenwich, CT: JAI Press, 1995, pp. 153–200.

9.90 Ilies et al., "Personality and Citizenship Behavior"; and Judge et al., "Five-Factor Model."

9.91 Salgado, J.F. "The Big Five Personality Dimensions and Counterproductive Behaviors." *International Journal of Selection and Assessment* 10 (2002), pp. 117–25.

9.92 Cullen, M.J., and P. Sackett. "Personality and Counterproductive Work Behavior." In *Personality and Work*, ed. M.A. Barrick and A.M. Ryan. San Francisco: Jossey-Bass, 2003, pp. 150–82.

9.93 Cooper-Hakim, A., and C. Viswesvaran. "The Construct of Work Commitment: Testing an Integrative Framework." *Psychological Bulletin* 131 (2005), pp. 241–59; and Mathieu, J.E., and D.M. Zajac. "A Review and Meta-Analysis of the Antecedents, Correlates, and Consequences of Organizational Commitment." *Psychological Bulletin* 108 (1990), pp. 171–94.

9.94 Salgado, "The Big Five Personality Dimensions"; and Zimmerman., R.D. "Understanding the Impact of Personality Traits on Individuals' Turnover Decisions: A Meta-Analytic Path Model." *Personnel Psychology* 61 (2008), pp. 309–48.

9.95 Cooper-Hakim and Viswesvaran, "The Construct of Work Commitment."

9.96 Grant, S., and J. Langan-Fox. "Personality and Occupational Stressor–Strain Relationships: The Role of the Big Five." *Journal of Occupational Health Psychology* 12 (2007), pp. 20–33.

9.97 Mischel, W. "The Interaction of Person and Situation." In *Personality at the Crossroads: Current Issues in Interactional Psychology*, ed. D. Magnusson and N.S. Endler. Hillsdale, NJ: Erlbaum, 1977, pp. 333–52; and Weiss, H.M., and S. Adler. "Personality and Organizational Behavior." In *Research in Organizational Behavior*, Vol. 6, ed. B.M. Staw and L.L. Cummings. Greenwich, CT: JAI Press, 1984, pp. 1–50.

9.98. Barrick, M.R., and M.K. Mount. "Autonomy as a Moderator of the Relationship between the Big Five Personality Dimensions and Job Performance." *Journal of Applied Psychology* 78 (1993), pp. 111–18.

9.99 Tett, R.P., and D.D. Burnett. "A Personality Trait-Based Interactionist Model of Job Performance." *Journal of Applied Psychology* 88 (2003), pp. 500–17.

9.100 Barrick, M.R.; J.A. Shaffer; and S.W. DeGrassi. "What You See May Not Be What You Get: Relationships among Self-Presentation Tactics and Ratings of Interview and Job Performance." *Journal of Applied Psychology* 94 (2009), pp. 1394–1411.

9.101 Barrick, M.R.; G.K. Patton; and S.N. Haugland. "Accuracy of Interviewer Judgments of Job Applicant Personality Traits." *Personnel Psychology* 53 (2000), pp. 925–51.

9.102 Piotrowski, C., and T. Armstrong. "Current Recruitment and Selection Practices: A National Survey of *Fortune* 1000 Firms." *North American Journal of Psychology* 8 (2006), pp. 489–96; and Frauenheim, E. "More Companies Go with Online Tests to Fill in the Blanks." *Workforce Management*, May 2011, pp. 12–13.

9.103 Frauenheim, E. "The (Would-Be) King of HR Software." *Workforce Management*, August 14, 2006, pp. 34–39; Frauenheim, E. "Unicru Beefs Up Data in Latest Screening Tool." *Workforce Management*, March 13, 2006, pp. 9–10; Overholt, A. "True or False: You're Hiring the Right People." *Fast Company*, January 2002, p. 110; and

Dixon, P. "Employment Application Kiosks and Sites. Excerpted from the 2003 Job Search Privacy Study: Job Searching in the Networked Environment: Consumer Privacy Benchmarks." *World Privacy Forum*, November 11, 2003, http://www.worldprivacyforum.org.

9.104 Frauenheim, "The (Would-Be) King of HR Software."

9.105 Overholt, "True or False."

9.106 Ibid.

9.107 Frauenheim, "Unicru Beefs Up Data."

9.108 Gellar, A. "Hiring by Computer," (n.d.), http://jobboomcc.canoe.ca/News/2004/06/09/1225576-sun.html.

9.109 Overholt, "True or False."

9.110 Dixon, "Employment Application Kiosks and Sites."

9.111 Frauenheim, "The (Would-Be) King."

9.112 Sackett, P.R., and M.M. Harris. "Honesty Testing for Personnel Selection: A Review and Critique." *Personnel Psychology* 37 (1984), pp. 221–45; Sackett, P.R.; L.R. Burris; and C. Callahan. "Integrity Testing for Personnel Selection: An Update." *Personnel Psychology* 42 (1989), pp. 491–528; Sackett, P.R., and J.E. Wanek.

"New Developments in the Use of Measures of Honesty, Integrity, Conscientiousness, Dependability, Trustworthiness, and Reliability for Personnel Selection." *Personnel Psychology* 49 (1996), pp. 787–829; Berry, C.M.; P.R. Sackett; and S. Wiemann. "A Review of Recent Developments in Integrity Test Research." *Personnel Psychology* 60 (2007), pp. 271–301; and Miner, J.B., and M.H. Capps. *How Honesty Testing Works.* Westport, CT: Quorum Books, 1996.

9.113 Sackett et al., "Integrity Testing"; and Ones, D.S.; C. Viswesvaran; and F.L. Schmidt. "Comprehensive Meta-Analysis of Integrity Test Validities: Findings and Implications for Personnel Selection and Theories of Job Performance." *Journal of Applied Psychology* 78 (1993), pp. 679–703.

9.114 Wanek, J.E.; P.R. Sackett; and D.S. Ones. "Towards an Understanding of Integrity Test Similarities and Differences: An Item-Level Analysis of Seven Tests." *Personnel Psychology* 56 (2003), pp. 873–94; and Marcus, B.; S.

Hoft; and M. Riediger. "Integrity Tests and the Five-Factor Model of Personality: A Review and Empirical Test of Two Alternative Positions." *International Journal of Selection and Assessment* 14 (2006), pp. 113–30.

9.115 Marcus, B.; K. Lee; and M.C. Ashton. "Personality Dimensions Explaining Relationships between Integrity Tests and Counterproductive Behavior: Big Five, or One in Addition?" *Personnel Psychology* 60 (2007), pp. 1–34; and Berry et al., "A Review of Recent Developments in Integrity Test Research."

9.116 Bernardin, H.J., and D.K. Cooke. "Validity of an Honesty Test in Predicting Theft among Convenience Store Employees." *Academy of Management Journal* 36 (1993), pp. 1097–1108.

9.117 Ones et al., "A Comprehensive Meta-Analysis."

9.118 Ibid.

9.119 Goffin, R.D., and N.D. Christiansen. "Correcting Personality Tests for Faking: A Review of Popular Personality Tests and an Initial Survey of Researchers." *International*

Journal of Selection and Assessment 11 (2003), pp. 340–44.

9.120 Birkeland, S.A.; T.M. Manson; J.L. Kisamore; M.T. Brannick; and M.A. Smith. "A Meta-Analytic Investigation of Job Applicant Faking on Personality Measures." *International Journal of Selection and Assessment* 14 (2006), pp. 317–35; and Viswesvaran, C., and D.S. Ones. "Meta-Analysis of Fakability Estimates: Implications for Personality Measurement." *Educational and Psychological Measurement* 59 (1999), pp. 197–210.

9.121 Miner and Capps, *How Honesty Testing Works;* Cunningham, M.R.; D.T. Wong; and A.P. Barbee. "Self-Presentation Dynamics on Overt Integrity Tests: Experimental Studies of the Reid Report." *Journal of Applied Psychology* 79 (1994), pp. 643–58; and Ones, D.S., and C. Viswesvaran. "The Effects of Social Desirability and Faking on Personality and Integrity Assessment for Personnel Selection." *Human Performance* 11 (1998), pp. 245–69.

9.122 Ones, D.S.; S. Dilchert; C. Viswesvaran; and

T.A. Judge. "In Support of Personality Assessment in Organizational Settings." *Personnel Psychology* 60 (2007), pp. 995–1027; and Tett, R.P., and N.D. Christiansen. "Personality Tests at the Crossroads: A Response to Morgeson, Campion, Dipboye, Hollenbeck, Murphy, and Schmitt (2007)." *Personnel Psychology* 60 (2007), pp. 967–93.

9.123 Cortina, J.M.; N.B. Goldstein; S.C. Payne; H.K. Davison; and S.W. Gilliland. "The Incremental Validity of Interview Scores over and above Cognitive Ability and Conscientiousness Scores." *Personnel Psychology* 53 (2000), pp. 325–51.

9.124 Schmidt, F.L., and J.E. Hunter. "Select on Intelligence." In *Blackwell Handbook of Principles of Organizational Behavior*, ed. E.A. Locke. Malden, MA: Blackwell, 2000, pp. 3–14.

chapter 10

Ability

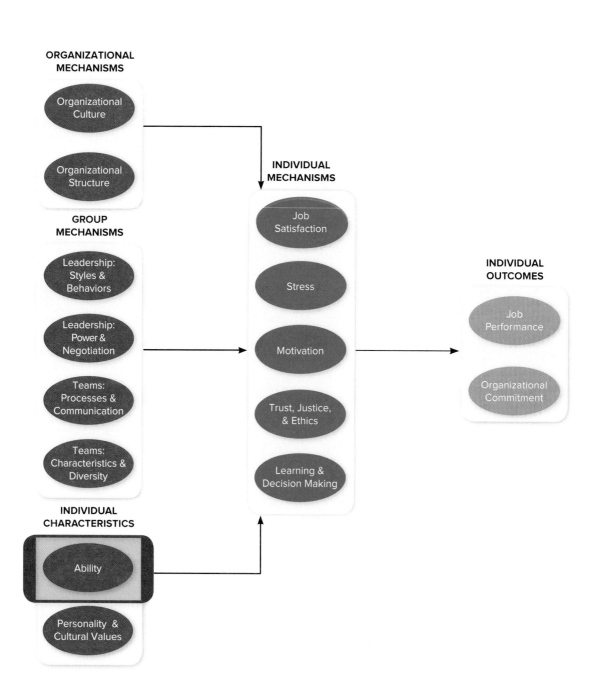

ORGANIZATIONAL MECHANISMS
- Organizational Culture
- Organizational Structure

GROUP MECHANISMS
- Leadership: Styles & Behaviors
- Leadership: Power & Negotiation
- Teams: Processes & Communication
- Teams: Characteristics & Diversity

INDIVIDUAL CHARACTERISTICS
- Ability
- Personality & Cultural Values

INDIVIDUAL MECHANISMS
- Job Satisfaction
- Stress
- Motivation
- Trust, Justice, & Ethics
- Learning & Decision Making

INDIVIDUAL OUTCOMES
- Job Performance
- Organizational Commitment

Image courtesy of IDEO

✔ LEARNING GOALS

After reading this chapter, you should be able to answer the following questions:

10.1 What is ability?

10.2 What are the various types of cognitive ability?

10.3 What are the various types of emotional ability?

10.4 What are the various types of physical ability?

10.5 How does cognitive ability affect job performance and organizational commitment?

10.6 What steps can organizations take to hire people with high levels of cognitive ability?

IDEO

IDEO is an award-winning global design firm that takes a human-centered, design-based approach to helping organizations in the public and private sectors innovate and grow. IDEO has worked with a diverse array of companies and organizations—AT&T, Coca-Cola, Converse, Ford Motor Company, HBO, Mayo Clinic, Microsoft, Samsung, Sesame Workshop, Target, The Bill & Melinda Gates Foundation, and Walgreens—and has produced outcomes with which you're likely to be familiar. They've helped design mice for both Apple and Microsoft, for example. They've also contributed to the redesign of Redbox's kiosk interaction, Eli Lilly and Company's Luxura reusable insulin pen, Oral-B's Gripper toothbrush, Crest's stand-up toothpaste tube, improvements in Electronic Art's "Madden NFL," and the packaging for ConAgra's Healthy Choice Fresh Mixers and Microsoft's Windows 8. Additionally, IDEO has done branding and strategy work for Samsung, Brooks, Converse, Sealy, and General Electric, as well as business design work for Walgreens, Gannett, and State Farm Insurance.

In addition to envisioning and creating new companies and brands, IDEO often takes an existing product, service, brand, or business and makes it better through innovation. This sounds simple enough, but what is it about IDEO that allows it to be so successful? The key may be the company's emphasis on qualities of employees that are often overlooked by other companies. That is, whereas the conventional approach to design relies upon professional abilities tied to an area of expertise and the rational analysis of problems and potential solutions, IDEO's approach also acknowledges an employee's ability to help uncover latent needs, behaviors, and the desires of those who might be in a position to use the product, brand, or business. By leveraging these traits, ideas and design solutions are not only functional, but they also provide for emotionally meaningful user experiences.

IDEO's job postings list abilities related to the technical and interpersonal requirements of the specific jobs that need to be filled. However, they also look for employees with less obvious abilities that support their unique approach to the design process. Specifically, IDEO values employees with deep empathy, insatiable curiosity, and irrepressible optimism.

ABILITY

The topic of ability is probably already familiar to you. This is because "ability" is an everyday word in our language, and we've all developed a pretty good understanding of our own abilities. All of us have experience doing things that require different abilities, and we received feedback, in one form or another, as to how well we did. So knowing that you're already familiar with the topic of ability, why would we write an entire chapter on it for this textbook? Well for one thing, there are many different abilities, some of which are important but might not be as familiar to you. Another reason we've included a chapter on ability is, although it might seem obvious that abilities are highly related to effectiveness in jobs, this relationship is truer in some circumstances than in others. Finally, it may be useful to understand how organizations use information about abilities to make good managerial decisions. Our chapter is organized around these three issues.

10.1

What is ability?

Ability refers to the relatively stable capabilities people have to perform a particular range of different but related activities.[1] In contrast to skills, which can be improved over time with training and experience, ability is relatively stable. Although abilities can change slowly over time with instruction, repeated practice, and repetition, the level of a given ability generally limits how much a person can improve, even with the best training in the world. One reason for this stability relates to the "nature vs. nurture" question, an issue that has been much debated in OB (see Chapter 9 on personality and cultural values for more discussion of such issues). Are abilities a function of our genes, or are they something we develop as a function of our experiences and surroundings?

As it turns out, abilities are a function of both genes and the environment, and the amount attributable to each source depends somewhat on the nature of the ability. Consider for a moment abilities that are physical in nature. Although training that involves weightlifting, dancing, and swimming can improve a person's strength, equilibrium, and endurance, there are limits to how much improvement is possible. As an example, there are millions of people who take golf lessons and practice their swing for countless hours on a driving range, yet the vast majority of these people could never compete in a professional golf tournament because they just can't manage to consistently hit that little white ball straight or far enough. As an example of abilities that are cognitive in nature, you likely know people who, even if they went to the best schools on earth, would have great difficulty doing well in jobs such as theoretical astrophysics that require a lot of brainpower.

For cognitive abilities, it appears that genes and the environment play

© *John Gress/AP Images*

Few people have the physical abilities necessary to compete with professional golfers such as Annika Sorenstam, who is widely considered to be the top female golfer of all time.

roughly equal roles.[2] However, differences in cognitive abilities due to the environment become less apparent as people get older, and this may be especially true for the effect of the family environment.[3] As an example, though neglect, abuse, and deprivation may have a negative impact on how children fare on standardized intelligence tests, that negative impact does not tend to carry over into adulthood. Beyond the family situation, what are some other factors in the environment that affect cognitive abilities? First, the quantity of schooling may be important because it provides opportunities for people to develop knowledge and critical thinking skills.[4] Second, there's evidence that our choice of occupations may influence our cognitive abilities. Complex work develops and exercises our minds, which promotes higher performance on intelligence tests.[5] Third, certain biological factors are known to affect cognitive abilities negatively during childhood. Examples include malnutrition, exposure to toxins such as lead, and prenatal exposure to alcohol. In fact, over the last century average scores on standardized intelligence tests have risen significantly in industrialized countries as the quality and availability of education and health factors have improved, and the complexity of life has increased.[6]

WHAT DOES IT MEAN FOR AN EMPLOYEE TO BE "ABLE"?

As the examples in the previous paragraphs imply, there are different types of ability. Whereas the golf example refers to physical ability, the theoretical astrophysics example refers to cognitive ability. In fact, there are many different facets of ability, and they can be grouped into subsets by considering similarities in the nature of the activities involved. As we'll talk about in the sections to follow, abilities can be grouped into three general categories: cognitive, emotional, and physical. As our OB Internationally feature illustrates, there may be some abilities that do not fit neatly into one of these three categories. Nevertheless, all abilities refer to *what people can do*. That's in contrast to personality (the subject of Chapter 9), which refers to *what people are like* or *what people will likely do*. As with personality, organizational personnel and hiring systems focus on finding applicants who possess abilities that match the requirements of a given job.

COGNITIVE ABILITY

Cognitive ability refers to capabilities related to the acquisition and application of knowledge in problem solving.[7] Cognitive abilities are very relevant in the jobs most of you will be involved with—that is, work involving the use of information to make decisions and solve problems.

10.2

What are the various types of cognitive ability?

OB

OB INTERNATIONALLY

What makes some people more or less effective in culturally diverse organizational contexts? According to some, the answer to this question is *cultural intelligence,* or the ability to discern differences among people that are due to culture and to understand what these differences mean in terms of the way people tend to think and behave in different situations. There are three sources of cultural intelligence that correspond to the "head," "body," and "heart." The source of cultural intelligence that corresponds to the head is called *cognitive cultural intelligence.* This concept refers to the ability to sense differences among people due to culture and to use this knowledge in planning how to interact with others in anticipation of a cross-cultural encounter. The source of cultural intelligence that corresponds to the body is called *physical cultural intelligence,* which refers to the ability to adapt one's behavior when a cultural encounter requires it. Finally, the source of cultural intelligence that corresponds to the heart is called *emotional cultural intelligence.* This concept refers to the level of effort and persistence an individual exerts when trying to understand and adapt to new cultures.

Understanding cultural intelligence may be useful because it's an ability that can be improved through training. Such a program could begin with an assessment to identify sources of cultural intelligence that may be weak. Consider, for example, an individual who is very knowledgeable about the customs and norms of another culture and is very willing to learn more, but who just can't alter her body language and eye contact so that it's appropriate for the other culture. In this particular case, the aim of the training would be to improve physical cultural intelligence. The individual might be asked to study video that contrasts correct and incorrect body language and eye contact. The individual might also be asked to engage in role-playing exercises to model the appropriate behavior and receive feedback from an expert. Finally, the individual might be asked to take acting classes. Although such training may seem to be quite involved and expensive, the costs of poor performance in cross-cultural contexts can be significant for both the employee and the organization.

Sources: P.C. Earley and S. Ang, *Cultural Intelligence: Individual Interactions across Cultures* (Stanford, CA: Stanford University Press, 2003); P.C. Earley and E. Mosakowski, "Cultural Intelligence," *Harvard Business Review* 82 (2004), pp. 139–46; and L. Imai and M.J. Gelfand, "The Culturally Intelligent Negotiator: The Impact of Cultural Intelligence (CQ) on Negotiation Sequences and Outcomes," *Organizational Behavior and Human Decision Processes* 112 (2010), pp. 83–98.

Chances are good that your cognitive abilities have been tested several times throughout your life. For example, almost all children in the United States take standardized tests of intelligence at some point during elementary school. Although you might not remember taking one of these, you probably remember taking the Scholastic Assessment Test (SAT). And though you probably thought about the SAT as a test that would have a major impact only on where you could and could not go to college, the SAT is actually a test of cognitive ability.

You might also remember that the SAT included a variety of different questions; some tested your ability to do math problems, whereas other questions assessed your ability to complete sentences and make analogies. In fact, the different types of questions reflect specific types of cognitive ability that contribute to effectiveness on intellectual tasks. Table 10-1 lists many of these cognitive ability types, along with their specific facets and some jobs in which they're thought to be important. The definitions and information in this table, as well as that discussed in the following sections, comes from research that produced a public database called O*NET, which outlines requirements of employees in different types of jobs and occupations.[8]

VERBAL ABILITY **Verbal ability** refers to various capabilities associated with understanding and expressing oral and written communication. *Oral comprehension* is the ability to understand spoken words and sentences, and *written comprehension* is the ability to understand written words

TABLE 10-1	Types and Facets of Cognitive Ability	
TYPE	**MORE SPECIFIC FACET**	**JOBS WHERE RELEVANT**
Verbal	*Oral* and *Written Comprehension:* Understanding written and spoken words and sentences *Oral* and *Written Expression:* Communicating ideas by speaking or writing so that others can understand	Business executives; police, fire, and ambulance dispatchers; clinical psychologists
Quantitative	*Number Facility:* Performing basic math operations quickly and correctly *Mathematical Reasoning:* Selecting the right method or formula to solve a problem	Treasurers; financial managers; mathematical technicians; statisticians
Reasoning	*Problem Sensitivity:* Understanding when there is a problem or when something may go wrong *Deductive Reasoning:* Applying general rules to specific problems *Inductive Reasoning:* Combining specific information to form general conclusions *Originality:* Developing new ideas	Anesthesiologists; surgeons; business executives; fire inspectors; judges; police detectives; forensic scientists; cartoonists; designers
Spatial	*Spatial Orientation:* Knowing where one is relative to objects in the environment *Visualization:* Imagining how something will look after it has been rearranged	Pilots; drivers; boat captains; photographers; set designers; sketch artists
Perceptual	*Speed and Flexibility of Closure:* Making sense of information and finding patterns *Perceptual Speed:* Comparing information or objects with remembered information or objects	Musicians; firefighters; police officers; pilots; mail clerks; inspectors

Sources: Adapted from E.A. Fleishman, D.P. Costanza, and J. Marshall-Mies, "Abilities," in *An Occupational Information System for the 21st Century: The Development of O*NET,* ed. N.G. Peterson, M.D. Mumford, W.C. Borman, P.R. Jeanneret, and E.A. Fleishman (Washington, DC: American Psychological Association, 1999), pp. 175–95; and O*NET Website, *The O*NET Content Model: Detailed Outline With Descriptions,* http://www.onetcenter.org/content. html/1.a?d=1#cm_1.a (accessed May 20, 2009).

and sentences. Although these two aspects of verbal ability would seem highly related—that is, people who have high oral comprehension would tend to have high written comprehension, and vice versa—it's not difficult to think of people who might be high on one ability but low on the other. As an example, it's been reported that as a result of his dyslexia, actor Tom Cruise has poor written comprehension and can learn his lines only after listening to them on tape.[9]

Two other verbal abilities are *oral expression,* which refers to the ability to communicate ideas by speaking, and *written expression,* which refers to the ability to communicate ideas in writing. Again, though it might seem that these abilities should be highly related, this is not necessarily so. You may have taken a class with a professor who had authored several well-regarded books and articles, but at the same time, had a very difficult time expressing concepts and theories to students. Although there could be many reasons this might happen, one explanation is that the professor had high ability in terms of written expression but low ability in terms of oral expression.

Generally speaking, verbal abilities are most important in jobs in which effectiveness depends on understanding and communicating ideas and information to others. As an example, the effectiveness of business executives depends on their ability to consider information from reports and other executives and staff, as well as their ability to articulate a vision and strategy that promotes employee understanding. As another example, consider how important the verbal abilities of a 9-1-1 dispatcher might be if a loved one suddenly became ill and stopped breathing.

Tom Cruise has dyslexia, and he struggles with written comprehension. He learns the lines for his movies by listening to them on tape.

© Universal Pictures/Photofest

QUANTITATIVE ABILITY. Quantitative ability refers to two types of mathematical capabilities. The first is *number facility,* which is the capability to do simple math operations (adding, subtracting, multiplying, and dividing). The second is *mathematical reasoning,* which refers to the ability to choose and apply formulas to solve problems that involve numbers. If you think back to the SAT, you can probably remember problems such as the following: "There were two trains 800 miles apart, and they were traveling toward each other on the same track. The first train began traveling at noon and averaged 45 miles per hour. The second train started off two hours later. What speed did the second train average if the two trains smashed into each other at 10:00 p.m. of the same day?"

Although number facility may be necessary to solve this problem, mathematical reasoning is crucial because the test taker needs to know which formulas to apply. Although most of us wish that problems like this would be limited to test-taking contexts (especially this particular problem), there are countless situations in which quantitative abilities are important. For example, consider the importance of quantitative ability in jobs involving statistics, accounting, and engineering. Quantitative abilities may be important in less complex, lower-level jobs as well. Have you ever been at a fast-food restaurant or convenience store when the cash register wasn't working and the clerk couldn't manage to count out change correctly or quickly? If you have, you witnessed a very good example of low quantitative ability, and perhaps some very annoyed customers as well.

REASONING ABILITY **Reasoning ability** is actually a diverse set of abilities associated with sensing and solving problems using insight, rules, and logic. The first reasoning ability, *problem sensitivity,* is the ability to sense that there's a problem right now or likely to be one in the near future. Anesthesiology is a great example of a job for which problem sensitivity is crucial. Before surgeries, anesthesiologists give drugs to patients so that surgical procedures can take place without the patients experiencing pain. However, during the surgery, patients can have negative reactions to the drugs that might result in the loss of life. So the ability of the anesthesiologist to sense when something is wrong even before the problem is fully apparent can be a life-or-death matter.

The second type of reasoning ability is called *deductive reasoning.* This ability, which refers to the use of general rules to solve problems, is important in any job in which people are presented with a set of facts that need to be applied to make effective decisions. The job of a judge requires deductive reasoning because it centers on making decisions by applying the rules of law to make verdicts. In contrast, *inductive reasoning* refers to the ability to consider several specific pieces of information and then reach a more general conclusion regarding how those pieces are related. Inductive reasoning is required of police detectives and crime scene investigators who must consider things like tire tracks, blood spatter, fibers, and fingerprints to reach conclusions about perpetrators of crimes and causes of death.

Finally, *originality* refers to the ability to develop clever and novel ways to solve problems. Larry Page and Sergey Brin, the two founders of Google, provide good examples of originality. They not only developed the Internet search software that gave Google a competitive advantage, and created the first completely new advertising medium in nearly half a century, but they also refuse to follow conventional wisdom when it comes to managerial practices and business decisions.[10] Clearly, originality is important in a wide variety of occupations, but in some jobs, originality is the most critical ability. For example, a cartoonist, designer, writer, or advertising executive without originality would find it difficult to be successful.

SPATIAL ABILITY There are two main types of **spatial ability,** or capabilities associated with visual and mental representation and manipulation of objects in space. The first is called *spatial orientation,* which refers to a good understanding of where one is relative to other things in the environment. A tourist with high spatial organization would have no trouble finding her way back to her hotel on foot after a long day of sightseeing, even without a map or help from anyone on the street. The second spatial ability is called *visualization,* which is the ability to imagine how separate things will look if they were put together in a particular way. If you're good at imagining how a room would look if it were rearranged, or if your friends are impressed that you can buy things that go together well, chances are that you would score high on visualization.

PERCEPTUAL ABILITY **Perceptual ability** refers to being able to perceive, understand, and recall patterns of information. More specifically, *speed and flexibility of closure* refers to being able to pick out a pattern of information quickly in the presence of distracting information, even without all the information present. People who work for the Central Intelligence Agency likely need speed and flexibility of closure to break secret codes. Related to this ability is *perceptual speed,* which refers to being able to examine and compare numbers, letters, and objects quickly. If you can go into the produce section of a supermarket and choose the best tomatoes faster than the people around you, chances are you have high perceptual speed. Effectiveness in jobs in which people need to proofread documents, sort things, or categorize objects depends a lot on perceptual speed.

GENERAL COGNITIVE ABILITY If you've read the preceding sections carefully, you probably thought about where you stand on the different types of cognitive abilities. In doing so, you may have also reached the conclusion that you're higher on some of these abilities and lower on others. Maybe you think of yourself as being smart in verbal abilities but not as smart in quantitative abilities. In fact, most people score more similarly across their cognitive abilities than they realize. People who are higher than average on verbal abilities also tend to be higher than average on reasoning, quantitative, spatial, and perceptual abilities, and people who are lower than average on verbal abilities tend to be lower than average on the other abilities. Although this consistency might not apply to everyone, it applies often enough that researchers have been trying to understand why this occurs for well over 100 years.[11]

The most popular explanation for the consistency in the levels of different cognitive abilities within people is that there's a **general cognitive ability**—sometimes called the *g-factor* or simply *g*—that underlies or causes all of the more specific cognitive abilities we've discussed so far.[12] To understand what this means more clearly, consider the diagram in Figure 10-1 that depicts general cognitive ability as the area in common across the more specific cognitive abilities that we've discussed. This overlap exists because each of the specific abilities depends somewhat on the brain's ability to process information effectively. So, because some brains are capable of processing information more effectively than others, some people tend to score higher across the specific abilities, whereas others tend to score lower.

You're probably familiar with the intelligence quotient, which is known as IQ. Well, IQ was something originally used in educational contexts to diagnose learning disabilities, and accordingly, tests to measure IQ were developed using questions with which students with learning disabilities might struggle. IQ tests were then scaled as a percentage that indicated a person's mental age relative to his or her chronological age. IQ scores lower than 100 were interpreted as indicating a potential learning or educational deficiency, whereas scores higher than 100 were interpreted as indicating that someone was particularly bright for his or her age.

© Steve Bloom/The Image Bank/Getty Images

Pilots flying in conditions where there's poor visibility have to rely on various instruments and their spatial ability to visualize their absolute position and, just as important, their position relative to other objects, some of which are also moving.

| FIGURE 10-1 | The "g-factor" |

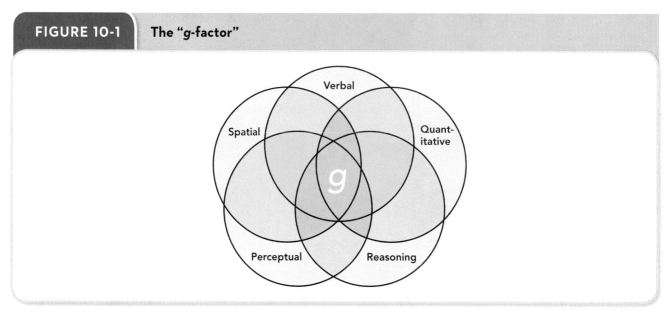

Source: Adapted from J.J. Johnson and J.B. Cullen, "Trust in Cross-Cultural Relationships," in *Blackwell Handbook of Cross-Cultural Management,* ed. M.J. Gannon and K.L. Newman (Malden, MA: Blackwell, 2002), pp. 335–60.

However, it turns out that IQ tests and tests of general cognitive ability are often quite similar in terms of the types of questions included, and more importantly, scores on the two types of tests say pretty much the same thing about the people who take them.[13] Does a high IQ boost effectiveness of people in work contexts? We'll discuss this matter in some detail later, but it's worth pointing out here that IQ is associated with outcomes that are very relevant to you, your employer, and perhaps society in general.[14] For example, researchers have shown that individuals with higher IQ tend to be healthier and economically better off, and as a consequence of these two factors, they tend to feel happier and more satisfied with their lives.[15] They also tend to have fewer accidents that cause injury, less cardiovascular disease, and not surprisingly given the first two associations, they also tend to live longer.[16] Although the explanation for these relationships is not altogether clear, it's likely that people with higher IQ become more knowledgeable about the prevention and management of injury and disease, and in addition, may have advantages with respect to the availability of health care and knowledge that helps them adapt to challenging circumstances.[17]

EMOTIONAL ABILITY

Consider the case of Dick Snyder, who headed the publishing firm Simon & Schuster. He seemed unable to control or perceive his emotions, and he regularly blew up at and humiliated his subordinates.[18] To make matters worse, he didn't understand that his lack of emotional control and understanding were having a negative impact on his team, and he eventually was fired, despite leading his company to higher levels of earnings. In this section of the chapter, we describe the concept of emotional ability—precisely the type of ability that Dick Snyder appears to lack.

So how is emotional ability different than cognitive ability? Most of us know someone who is very smart from a "cognitive ability" or IQ standpoint, but at the same time, the person just can't manage to be effective in real-world situations that involve other people. As an example, you may have played *Trivial Pursuit* with a group of friends and found someone at the table who could not only answer the majority of the questions correctly but also managed to say odd or inappropriate things throughout the game. You may also know someone who doesn't seem very "book smart" but always seems able to get things done and says the right things at the right time. In the context of the same *Trivial Pursuit* game, such a person might have answered most of the game questions incorrectly but, sensing how uncomfortable and angry people were becoming with the annoying player, made jokes to lighten things up.

In fact, for several decades now, researchers have been investigating whether there's a type of ability that influences the degree to which people tend to be effective in social situations, regardless of their level of cognitive abilities.[19] Although there has been some debate among these researchers,[20] many believe now that there's a human ability that affects social functioning, called **emotional intelligence**.[21] Emotional intelligence is defined in terms of a set of distinct but related abilities, which we describe next.[22] For an interesting discussion of the relationship between cognitive ability and emotional intelligence, see our **OB on Screen** feature.

SELF-AWARENESS The first type of emotional intelligence is **self-awareness,** or the appraisal and expression of emotions in oneself. This facet refers to the ability of an individual to understand the types of emotions he or she is experiencing, the willingness to acknowledge them, and the capability to express them naturally.[23] As an example, someone who is low in this aspect of emotional intelligence might not admit to himself or show anyone else that he's feeling somewhat anxious during the first few days of a new job. These types of emotions are perfectly natural in a new job context, and ignoring them might increase the stress of the situation. Ignoring those emotions might also send the wrong signal to new colleagues, who might wonder, "Why isn't the new hire more excited about working for us?"

OTHER AWARENESS The second facet of emotional intelligence is called **other awareness,** or the appraisal and recognition of emotion in others.[24] As the name of this facet implies, it refers to a person's ability to recognize and understand the emotions that other people are feeling. People who are high in this aspect of emotional intelligence are not only sensitive to the feelings of others but also can anticipate the emotions that people will experience in different situations. In contrast, people who are low in this aspect of emotional intelligence do not effectively sense the emotions that others are experiencing, and if the emotions are negative, this inability could result in the person doing something that worsens the situation. As an example, have you ever had a professor who couldn't sense that students in class didn't understand the material being presented in a lecture? When that professor continued to press on with the slides, oblivious to the fact that the students were becoming even more confused, it was poor other awareness in action. As another example, an accountant at Chemical Bank in New York recalls that his boss asked him to refine his skills in this aspect of emotional intelligence.[25] Although he was a good accountant, he needed help showing interest in other people's emotions so that discussions with clients were less contentious. As a final example, the CEO of Forte Hotels, a chain of luxury hotels in Europe, prizes employees who have the ability to understand the customer's emotions so they can react accordingly. "I know the most amazing waitress," he says. "She can look at a counterful of people eating breakfast and tell immediately who wants chatting up, who wants to be left alone. Uncanny. Just uncanny."[26]

10.3

What are the various types of emotional ability?

EMOTION REGULATION The third facet of emotional intelligence, **emotion regulation,** refers to being able to recover quickly from emotional experiences.[27] As an example of this aspect of emotional intelligence, consider the possible responses of someone on his way to work, who is driving just below the speed limit in his brand new Toyota Prius who gets cut off by an aggressive driver who, as she passes by, throws a half-filled plastic bottle of Mountain Dew out the window and shouts an obscenity. If the Prius driver can regulate his emotions effectively, he recovers quickly from the initial anger and shock of the encounter. He would be able to get back to whatever he was listening to on the radio, and by the time

© Digital Vision RF

"Other awareness" is one aspect of emotional intelligence that allows us to empathize with others and understand their feelings.

OB ON SCREEN

LUCY

> . . . it isn't until we reached human beings at the top of the animal chain that we finally see a species use more of its cerebral capacity. 10% might not seem like much, but it's a lot if you look at all we've done with it.

With those words, Professor Norman (Morgan Freeman) describes the role of the human brain to society, in the movie *Lucy* (Dir. Luc Besson, Universal Pictures, 2014). He suggests that although humans use only a small percentage of the brain's capacity, we've been able to learn and solve problems and to create the very complex world in which we all live. This insight, of course, leads to the following question: What happens if we somehow develop the ability to use a higher percentage of our brains? Enter Lucy (Scarlett Johansson), who asks Professor Norman for guidance after being given a drug that's slowly unleashing her brain's full potential. The initial changes to Lucy's brain seem desirable. Who wouldn't want to be able to process information and react to stimuli in the environment more quickly than anyone else on earth? The later changes are scary, however. In fact, when Lucy's brain reaches 100 percent capacity, her body disappears as she morphs into some sort of cognitive energy.

© Universal Pictures/Photofest

We should emphasize here that there isn't much in this movie that's based on actual science. There's no drug that will give you the ability to manipulate matter or go back in time, or even make you a genius. In fact, the notion that we use only 10 percent of our brain is a myth. However, the movie does present an interesting theory about the association between cognitive ability and emotional intelligence. As Lucy's brain capacity expands, she develops the ability to control her emotions, and because she can understand and anticipate others' emotions, she can control their behavior. Although this view of emotional intelligence as flowing from high cognitive ability seems quite plausible, it also contradicts experiences we have with people who are quite intelligent from a cognitive ability standpoint but who are train wrecks emotionally, socially, and interpersonally.

he got to work, the incident would likely be all but forgotten. However, if this person were not able to regulate his emotions effectively, he might lose his temper, tailgate the aggressive driver, and then ram his new Prius into her vehicle at the next stoplight. We hope it's obvious to you that the former response is much more appropriate than the latter, which could prove quite costly to the individual. Although this example highlights the importance of regulating negative emotions, we should also point out that this aspect of emotional intelligence also applies to positive emotions. Consider, for example, the response of someone who is told that he's about to receive a significant pay raise. If this person is unable to regulate his own emotions effectively, he might feel joyous and giddy the rest of the day, flashing jazz hands to his co-workers. As a consequence, he's not able to accomplish any more work that day, never mind alienating everyone around him.

USE OF EMOTIONS The fourth aspect of emotional intelligence is the **use of emotions.**[28] This capability reflects the degree to which people can harness emotions and employ them to improve their chances of being successful in whatever they're seeking to do. For example, researchers have shown that when employees who face novel circumstances harness their positive emotions, they can produce solutions that are more creative.[29] To understand this facet of emotional intelligence more clearly, consider a writer who's struggling to finish a book but is under a serious time crunch because of the contract with the publisher. If the writer were high in this aspect of emotional intelligence, she would likely psych herself up for the challenge and encourage herself to work hard through any bouts of writer's block. In contrast, if the writer were low in this aspect of emotional intelligence, she might begin to doubt her competence as a writer and think about different things she could do with her life. Because these behaviors will slow progress on the book even further, the number and intensity of self-defeating thoughts might increase, and ultimately, the writer might withdraw from the task entirely.

APPLYING EMOTIONAL INTELLIGENCE Although you may appreciate how emotional intelligence can be relevant to effectiveness in a variety of interpersonal situations, you might be wondering whether knowledge of emotional intelligence can be useful to managers in their quest to make their organizations more effective. It turns out there's growing evidence that the answer to this question is "yes," albeit with a few caveats.[30]

As one example of the usefulness of emotional intelligence, the U.S. Air Force found that recruiters who were high in some aspects of emotional intelligence were three times more likely to meet recruiting quotas than recruiters who scored lower in the same aspects of emotional intelligence.[31] Recruiters with high emotional intelligence were more effective because they projected positive emotions and could quickly sense and appropriately respond to recruits' concerns. Because these capabilities made recruiting easier, there was less pressure to meet performance quotas, which translated into fewer hours at the office, higher satisfaction, and ultimately higher retention. In fact, after the Air Force began requiring new recruiters to pass an emotional intelligence test, turnover among new recruiters dropped from 25 percent to 2 percent. Given that, on average, it costs about $30,000 to train a new recruiter, this lower turnover translated into about $2.75 million in savings a year.

As a second example of the usefulness of emotional intelligence, Paris–based L'Oréal, the world's largest manufacturer of cosmetics and beauty products, was interested in the use of emotional intelligence in the hiring of sales agents who could perform their jobs more effectively.[32] How well did this idea work out for the company? The sales agents who were hired based mainly on their emotional intelligence scores had sales that were $91,370 greater than agents who were hired on the basis of other information. The company also found that the agents who were selected on the basis of their emotional intelligence scores were 63 percent less likely to quit during their first year as compared to the other agents. Sales agents with high emotional intelligence were able to better understand client needs, and because this results in higher performance and less frustration, these agents tend to stay with the company longer.

The two previous examples illustrate the usefulness of staffing and training practices based on emotional intelligence. In fact, there's growing evidence from researchers that emotional intelligence may have an important impact on employee job performance across a wide variety of settings.[33] There's also evidence that emotional intelligence may have a significantly stronger impact on the job performance of some employees more than others. One recent study, for example, found that emotional intelligence is a more important determinant of job performance for employees with lower levels of cognitive ability.[34] The explanation for this relationship is easy to understand if you consider that, in many circumstances, high emotional intelligence can compensate somewhat for low cognitive intelligence. In other words, exceptional "people smarts" can, to some extent, make up for deficiencies in "book smarts." See our **OB at the Bookstore** feature for an example of the role of emotional intelligence in a context where cognitive ability might seem to be much more crucial.

OB AT THE BOOKSTORE

THE INNOVATORS
by Walter Isaacson (New York: Simon & Schuster, 2014).

Only in storybooks do inventions come like a thunderbolt, or a lightbulb popping out of the head of a loan individual in a basement or garret or garage.

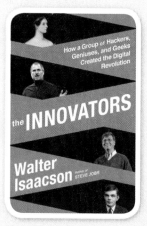

Photo of cover: © Roberts Publishing Services

With those words, Isaacson describes one of the main lessons from his comprehensive account of the individuals who are credited with the most important innovations of the digital age. As with most books in the genre, Isaacson acknowledges the role of the individual's cognitive ability and ingenuity in producing innovations. However, he argues that innovations are often a result of collaboration, and thus, the ability to work with others may be just as crucial. The book begins with an account of Ada, Countess of Lovelace, who, in collaboration with Charles Babbage, developed the first computer program in the mid-1800s. The book then segues to describe innovations attributed to people such as John von Neumann (ENIAC), Ray Tomlinson (e-mail), Nolan Bushnell (Pong) Bill Gates and Paul Allen (BASIC, Microsoft), Steve Wozniak and Steve Jobs (Apple), Tim Berners-Lee (World Wide Web), and Larry Page and Sergey Brin (Google). In each case, the ability of these individuals to work with others, often in the presence of greed and vanity, helped them make connections among ideas and resources that were necessary for innovation to occur.

On the surface, the author's message may seem attractive. After all, it suggests that you don't have to be a genius to develop innovations that change the world and make you rich. Or, stated in different terms, groundbreaking innovations that lead to fame and fortune are possible even from mere mortals. But if the emotional abilities that allows us to work well with others are like other abilities, then they're distributed in the population the same way as with other abilities. This means that an extraordinarily high level of emotional ability may be just as rare as genius level cognitive ability. You should also consider that the probability of an individual possessing both qualities together is lower than the probability of an individual possessing either quality alone. This may explain why groundbreaking innovations, which would seem to be most likely from individuals with high cognitive ability *and* high emotional ability, are exceedingly rare.

Although the picture of emotional intelligence we've painted so far is very upbeat, it's important to mention that there may be a "dark side" to this ability. Specifically, there's some evidence that emotional intelligence is correlated positively with behaviors at work that are more counterproductive in nature.[35] That is, certain individuals with higher levels of emotional intelligence may tend to engage in more counterproductive behaviors such as gossiping, harassment, and even theft. This might come as some surprise to you given all the positives of emotional intelligence we mentioned in the previous paragraphs. However, consider that the ability to understand and influence others' emotions can be used to achieve personal goals that are not necessarily compatible with the goals and values of the organization or society.[36] In essence, emotional intelligence may provide individuals with a gift of being able to influence how other people feel, and unfortunately, that gift can be abused if the individual is inclined toward questionable ends.[37]

ASSESSING EMOTIONAL INTELLIGENCE As we discussed previously, cognitive abilities are typically assessed using measures with questions such as those included in SAT or IQ tests. So how is emotional intelligence assessed? One type of emotional intelligence assessment is similar to a SAT-style test, because questions are scored as correct or incorrect. Test takers are asked to describe the emotions of people depicted in pictures, predict emotional responses to different situations, and identify appropriate and inappropriate emotional responses. After a person takes the test, it gets sent back to the test publisher to be scored. Another type of assessment asks people about behaviors and preferences that are thought to reflect emotional intelligence. One of the first tests of this type, the Emotional Quotient Inventory (EQ-i),[38] includes 133 such questions. Although the EQ-i has been used by many organizations in an attempt to improve managerial practices and organizational effectiveness, it has been criticized for measuring personality traits more than actual abilities.[39] More recently, a group of researchers published a very short and easy-to-score measure specifically designed to assess each of the four facets of emotional intelligence described in this section.[40] Although this assessment is similar in format to the EQ-i, the items don't appear to overlap as much with items that measure different aspects of personality. You can take the test yourself in our **OB Assessments** feature to see where you stand in terms of emotional intelligence.

PHYSICAL ABILITY

Physical abilities are likely very familiar to you because many of you took physical education classes early in your school career. Maybe you were evaluated on whether you could climb a rope to the ceiling of a gymnasium, run around a track several times, or kick a ball to a teammate who was running full stride. Or maybe you've applied for a job and had to take a test that assessed your ability to manipulate and assemble small mechanical parts. As a final example, and the one likely to be most familiar, you've probably been subject to tests that measure the quality of your vision and hearing. Although these examples may not seem to be related, each refers to a different type of physical ability. In this section, we review a few important types of physical abilities, which are summarized in Table 10-2. We note that the definitions and information in this table (and in the following sections) come from O*NET, which as we mentioned previously, outlines requirements of employees in different types of jobs and occupations.[41]

STRENGTH Although **strength** generally refers to the degree to which the body is capable of exerting force, there are actually several different types of strength that are important, depending on the job. *Static strength* refers to the ability to lift, push, or pull very heavy objects using the hands, arms, legs, shoulders, or back. Static strength is involved in jobs in which people need to lift objects like boxes, equipment, machine parts, and heavy tools. With *explosive strength,* people exert short bursts of energy to move the body or an object. Employees who are required to run, jump, or throw things at work depend on their explosive strength to be effective. The final type of strength, *dynamic strength,* refers to the ability to exert force for a prolonged period of time without becoming overly fatigued and giving out. Dynamic strength is involved in jobs in which employees have to climb ropes or ladders or pull themselves up onto platforms. Although jobs requiring physical strength may vary as to which category is important, there are also many jobs that require all three categories. Firefighters, for example, must typically pass grueling tests of strength before being hired. In Dublin, California, one part of the firefighter strength test involves climbing a long flight of stairs under time constraints without touching the rails while wearing a 50-pound vest and carrying another 25 pounds of equipment. Another part of the test involves safely moving a 165-pound dummy out of harm's way.[42]

STAMINA **Stamina** refers to the ability of a person's lungs and circulatory system to work efficiently while he or she is engaging in prolonged physical activity. Stamina may be important in jobs that require running, swimming, and climbing. In fact, stamina is involved whenever the nature of the physical activity causes the heart rate to climb and the depth and rate of breathing to increase for prolonged periods of time. As you can imagine, the firefighter test described in the previous paragraph assesses stamina as well as strength.

FLEXIBILITY AND COORDINATION Generally speaking, **flexibility** refers to the ability to bend, stretch, twist, or reach. When a job requires extreme ranges of motion—for example, when people need to work in a cramped compartment or an awkward position—the type of flexibility

10.4

What are the various types of physical ability?

OB ASSESSMENTS

EMOTIONAL INTELLIGENCE

How high is your emotional intelligence? This assessment will tell you where you stand on the four facets of emotional intelligence discussed in this chapter—self-awareness, other awareness, emotion regulation, and emotion use. Answer each question using the response scale provided. Then follow the instructions below to score yourself. (Instructors: Assessments on job ability preferences and tolerance for emotional labor can be found in the PowerPoints in the Connect Library's Instructor Resources and in the Connect assignments for this chapter).

1 TOTALLY DISAGREE	2 DISAGREE	3 SOMEWHAT DISAGREE	4 NEUTRAL	5 SOMEWHAT AGREE	6 AGREE	7 TOTALLY AGREE

1. I have a good sense of why I have certain feelings most of the time. _____
2. I have a good understanding of my own emotions. _____
3. I really understand what I feel. _____
4. I always know whether or not I am happy. _____
5. I am a good observer of others' emotions. _____
6. I always know my friends' emotions from their behavior. _____
7. I am sensitive to the feelings and emotions of others. _____
8. I have a good understanding of the emotions of people around me. _____
9. I always set goals for myself and then try my best to achieve them. _____
10. I always tell myself I am a competent person. _____
11. I am a self-motivating person. _____
12. I would always encourage myself to try my best. _____
13. I am able to control my temper so that I can handle difficulties rationally. _____
14. I am quite capable of controlling my own emotions. _____
15. I can always calm down quickly when I am very angry. _____
16. I have good control over my own emotions. _____

SCORING AND INTERPRETATION:

- Self-Awareness: Sum up items 1–4. _____
- Other Awareness: Sum up items 5–8. _____
- Emotion Use: Sum up items 9–12. _____
- Emotion Regulation: Sum up items 13–16. _____

If you scored 19 or above, then you are above average on a particular dimension. If you scored 18 or below, then you are below average on a particular dimension.

Sources: K.S. Law, C.S. Wong, and L.J. Song, "The Construct and Criterion Validity of Emotional Intelligence and Its Potential Utility for Management Studies," *Journal of Applied Psychology* 89 (2004), pp. 483–96; and C.S. Wong and K.S. Law, "The Effects of Leader and Follower Emotional Intelligence on Performance and Attitude," *The Leadership Quarterly* 13 (2002), pp. 243–74.

TABLE 10-2	Physical Abilities	

TYPE	MORE SPECIFIC FACET	JOBS WHERE RELEVANT
Strength	*Static:* Lifting, pushing, pulling heavy objects *Explosive:* Exerting a short burst of muscular force to move oneself or objects *Dynamic:* Exerting muscular force repeatedly or continuously	Structural iron and steel workers; tractor trailer and heavy truck drivers; farm workers; firefighters
Stamina	Exerting oneself over a period of time without circulatory system giving out	Athletes; dancers; commercial divers; firefighters
Flexibility and Coordination	*Extent Flexibility:* Degree of bending, stretching, twisting of body, arms, legs *Dynamic Flexibility:* Speed of bending, stretching, twisting of body, arms, legs *Gross Body Coordination:* Coordinating movement of body, arms, and legs in activities that involve all three together *Gross Body Equilibrium:* Ability to regain balance in contexts where balance is upset	Athletes; dancers; riggers; industrial machinery mechanics; choreographers; commercial divers; structural iron and steel workers
Psychomotor	*Fine Manipulative Abilities:* Keeping hand and arm steady while grasping, manipulating, and assembling small objects *Control Movement Abilities:* Making quick, precise adjustments to a machine while operating it *Response Orientation:* Quickly choosing among appropriate alternative movements *Response Time:* Quickly responding to signals with body movements	Fabric menders; potters; timing device assemblers; jewelers; construction drillers; agricultural equipment operators; photographers; highway patrol pilots; athletes
Sensory	*Near and Far Vision:* Seeing details of an object up close or at a distance *Night Vision:* Seeing well in low light *Visual Color Discrimination:* Detecting differences in colors and shades *Depth Perception:* Judging relative distances *Hearing Sensitivity:* Hearing differences in sounds that vary in terms of pitch and loudness *Auditory Attention:* Focusing on a source of sound in the presence of other sources *Speech Recognition:* Identifying and understanding the speech of others	Electronic testers and inspectors; highway patrol pilots; tractor trailer, truck, and bus drivers; airline pilots; photographers; musicians and composers; industrial machine mechanics; speech pathologists

Sources: Adapted from E.A. Fleishman, D.P. Costanza, and J. Marshall-Mies, "Abilities," in *An Occupational Information System for the 21st Century: The Development of O*NET,* ed. N.G. Peterson, M.D. Mumford, W.C. Borman, P.R. Jeanneret, and E.A. Fleishman (Washington, DC: American Psychological Association, 1999), pp. 175–95; and O*NET Website, *The O*NET Content Model: Detailed Outline with Descriptions,* http://www.onetcenter.org/content.html/1.A?D=1#Cm_1.A (accessed May 20, 2009).

involved is called *extent flexibility*. If you've ever watched a person working inside the trunk of a car installing speakers, you've seen extent flexibility. When a job requires repeated and somewhat quick bends, stretches, twists, or reaches, the type of flexibility involved is called *dynamic flexibility*. To understand what dynamic flexibility involves, picture a house painter on a ladder trying to paint some trim just barely within reach.

In addition to flexibility, **coordination,** or the quality of physical movement, may be important in some jobs. *Gross body coordination* refers to the ability to synchronize the movements of the body, arms, and legs to do something while the whole body is in motion. In contrast, *gross body equilibrium* involves the ability to maintain the balance of the body in unstable contexts or when the person has to change directions. Jumping rope effectively requires gross body coordination; walking on a balance beam requires gross body equilibrium. Both types of coordination are important in contexts that involve quick movements. However, gross body equilibrium is more important when the work environment is artificially elevated and inherently unstable.

PSYCHOMOTOR ABILITIES There are several different examples of **psychomotor abilities,** which generally refer to the capacity to manipulate and control objects. *Fine manipulative abilities* refer to the ability to keep the arms and hands steady while using the hands to do precise work, generally on small or delicate objects such as arteries, nerves, gems, and watches. *Control movement abilities* are important in tasks for which people have to make different precise adjustments, using machinery to complete the work effectively. Anyone who drills things for a living, whether it be wood, concrete, or teeth, needs this type of ability. The ability to choose the right action quickly in response to several different signals is called *response orientation*. It shouldn't be too difficult to imagine the importance of response orientation for an airline pilot who responds to the flashing lights, buzzers, and verbal information triggered during an in-flight emergency. The final psychomotor ability we describe is called *response time*. This ability reflects how quickly an individual responds to signaling information after it occurs. Returning to the previous example, most of us would feel more secure if our airline pilot had both a fast response orientation and a quick response time. After all, making the right decision may not be useful in this context if the decision is made too late!

SENSORY ABILITIES **Sensory ability** refers to capabilities associated with vision and hearing. Examples of important visual abilities include the ability to see things up close and at a distance (*near and far vision*) or in low light contexts (*night vision*), as well as the ability to perceive colors and judge relative distances between things accurately (*visual color discrimination* and *depth perception*). There are many different jobs that emphasize only one or two of these visual abilities. For example, whereas effectiveness as a watch repairer depends on good near vision, effectiveness as an interior designer depends on visual color discrimination. However, there are other jobs in which effectiveness might depend on almost all categories of visual abilities. A fighter pilot needs near vision to read instruments and checklists, far vision and depth perception to see enemy targets and landmarks, night vision to conduct operations in low light, and visual color discrimination to interpret information from warning lights and computer readouts correctly.

Abilities related to hearing, also referred to as auditory abilities, include the capability to hear and discriminate sounds that vary in terms of loudness and pitch (*hearing sensitivity*), being able to focus on a single sound in the presence of many other sounds (*auditory attention*), and the ability to identify and understand the speech of another person (*speech recognition*). Perhaps the most obvious jobs for which auditory abilities would be important are musicians and composers (yes, we are going to ignore exceptions like Beethoven, who was deaf at the time he wrote his Ninth Symphony). However, with these jobs, the emphasis would likely be on hearing sensitivity and auditory attention rather than speech recognition (who listens to lyrics these days?). Another job for which auditory abilities might be crucially important is a restaurant server, especially if the restaurant is crowded and noisy. In this context, a server needs auditory attention and speech recognition to be able to isolate and understand the words of a single patron against the backdrop of the loud chatter. As an example of a company that exists because of auditory ability, consider the case of Monster Cable, the Brisbane, California–based manufacturer of audiovisual cables and accessories. Noel Lee, the company's founder, started out by comparing the sound of Tchaikovsky's *1812 Overture* and Michael Jackson's "Liberian Girl" using different types of speaker wire.[43] He listened to the music over and over again and carefully considered the dynamics, loudness, bass response, and high frequencies of the music to determine which combination of wire thickness, composition, and braiding pattern sounded best.

© *Richard Shotwell/Invision/AP Images*

Noel Lee founded Monster Cable after using his extraordinary auditory ability to identify which type of speaker wire sounds best.

SUMMARY: WHAT DOES IT MEAN FOR AN EMPLOYEE TO BE "ABLE"?

Thus far in the chapter, we've presented you with a fairly detailed description of the domain of human abilities, which are summarized in Figure 10-2. Although the list of abilities included in the figure may seem somewhat daunting, we hope that you can appreciate that this set of abilities describes each and every one of us. Moreover, as we have alluded to throughout the chapter, these abilities play an important role in determining how effective we can be at different tasks and jobs.

FIGURE 10-2	What Does It Mean for an Employee to Be "Able"?

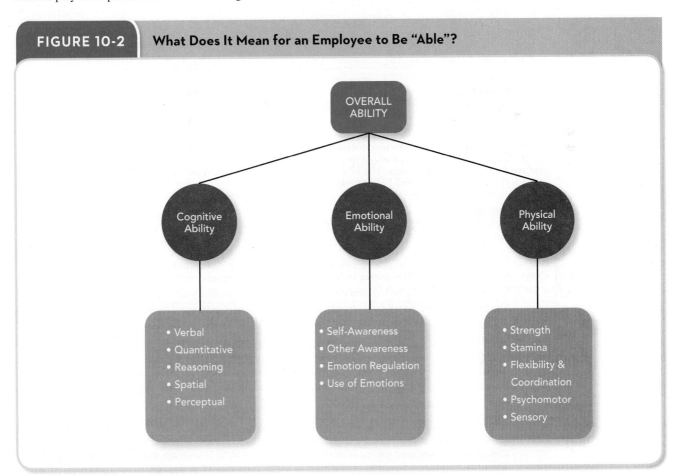

Source: Adapted from J.J. Johnson and J.B. Cullen, "Trust in Cross-Cultural Relationships," in *Blackwell Handbook of Cross-Cultural Management,* ed. M.J. Gannon and K.L. Newman (Malden, MA: Blackwell, 2002), pp. 335–60.

HOW IMPORTANT IS ABILITY?

10.5

How does cognitive ability affect job performance and organizational commitment?

So, now that you know what ability is and where it comes from, let's turn to the next important question: Does ability really matter? That is, does ability have a significant impact on job performance and organizational commitment—the two primary outcomes in our integrative model of OB? The answer to this question depends on what type of ability you are referring to—cognitive, emotional, or physical. We focus our discussion on general cognitive ability because it's the most relevant form of ability across all jobs and is likely to be important in the kinds of positions that students in an OB course will be pursuing. As it turns out, there's a huge body of research linking general cognitive ability to job performance, as summarized in Figure 10-3.[44]

The figure reveals that general cognitive ability is a strong predictor of job performance—in particular, the task performance aspect. Across all jobs, smarter employees fulfill the requirements of their job descriptions more effectively than do less smart employees.[45] In fact, of all the variables discussed in this book, none has a stronger correlation with task performance than general cognitive ability. Thousands of organizations, many of which are quite well known, assess cognitive ability in efforts to select the best candidates available for specific jobs.[46] The use of cognitive ability tests for this purpose appears to be quite reasonable, given that scores on such tests have a strong positive correlation with measures of performance across different types of jobs.[47]

In fact, this relationship holds even for performance in academic contexts. We mentioned the Scholastic Assessment Test, or the SAT, several times in this chapter because it's likely to be

| FIGURE 10-3 | Effects of General Cognitive Ability on Performance and Commitment |

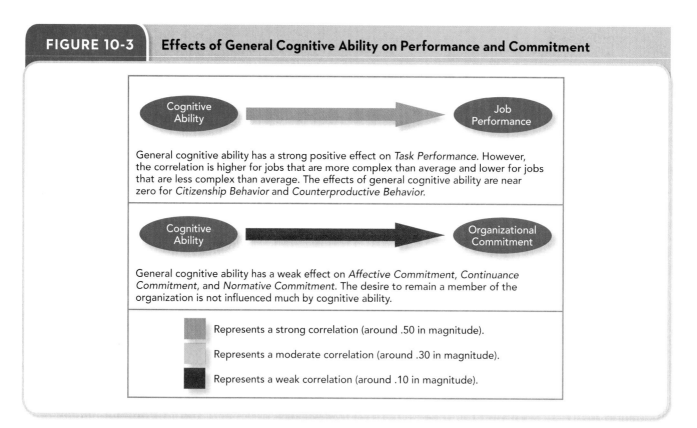

General cognitive ability has a strong positive effect on *Task Performance*. However, the correlation is higher for jobs that are more complex than average and lower for jobs that are less complex than average. The effects of general cognitive ability are near zero for *Citizenship Behavior* and *Counterproductive Behavior*.

General cognitive ability has a weak effect on *Affective Commitment*, *Continuance Commitment*, and *Normative Commitment*. The desire to remain a member of the organization is not influenced much by cognitive ability.

Represents a strong correlation (around .50 in magnitude).

Represents a moderate correlation (around .30 in magnitude).

Represents a weak correlation (around .10 in magnitude).

Sources: J.W. Boudreau, W.R. Boswell, T.A. Judge, and R.D Bretz, "Personality and Cognitive Ability as Predictors of Job Searc among Employed Managers," *Personnel Psychology* 54 (2001), pp. 25–50; S.M. Colarelli, R.A. Dean, and C. Konstans, "Comparative Effects of Personal and Situational Influences on Job Outcomes of New Professionals," *Journal of Applied Psychology* 72 (1987), pp. 558–66; D.N. Dickter, M. Roznowski, and D.A. Harrison, "Temporal Tempering: An Event History Analysis of the Process of Voluntary Turnover," *Journal of Applied Psychology* 81 (1996), pp. 705–16; and F.L. Schmidt and J. Hunter, "General Mental Ability in the World of Work: Occupational Attainment and Job Performance," *Journal of Personality and Social Psychology* 86 (2004), pp. 162–73.

quite familiar to you and because it largely reflects general cognitive ability.[48] Most colleges and universities in the United States take these scores into account when deciding which students to admit because they believe that higher scores increase the chances that students will be successful in college. But does the SAT really relate to how well someone does in college? Many of you are likely to be skeptical because you probably know someone who did extremely well on the SAT but performed poorly as a college student. Similarly, you probably know someone who didn't do that well on the SAT but who performed well as a college student. As it turns out, the SAT is actually good at predicting college performance. Students with higher SAT scores tend to perform much better in their first year of college, end up with a higher cumulative grade point average, and have a higher likelihood of graduating.[49] The same finding applies to predicting success in graduate-level school as well. The Graduate Management Admission Test, or GMAT, is similar to the SAT in structure and content, and students who score higher on this test prior to admission to graduate school tend to achieve better grade point averages over the course of their graduate program.[50]

So what explains why general cognitive ability relates to task performance? People who have higher general cognitive ability tend to be better at *learning and decision making,* (which we covered in detail in Chapter 8). They're able to gain more knowledge from their experiences at a faster rate, and as a result, they develop a bigger pool of knowledge regarding how to do their jobs effectively.[51] There are, however, three important caveats that we should mention. First, cognitive ability tends to be much more strongly correlated with task performance than with citizenship behavior, and the relationship between cognitive ability and counterproductive behavior is essentially zero.[52] An increased amount of job knowledge helps an employee complete job tasks, but it doesn't necessarily affect the choice to help a coworker or refrain from breaking an important rule. Second, the positive correlation between cognitive ability and performance is even stronger in jobs that are complex or situations that demand adaptability.[53] Third, people may do poorly on a test of general cognitive ability for reasons other than a lack of cognitive ability. As an example, people who come from economically disadvantaged backgrounds may do poorly on such tests, not because they lack the underlying cognitive ability but because they may not have had the learning opportunities needed to provide the appropriate responses.

In contrast to relationships with job performance, research has not supported a significant linkage between cognitive ability and organizational commitment.[54] On the one hand, we might expect a positive relationship with commitment because people with higher cognitive ability tend to perform more effectively, and therefore, they might feel they fit well with their job. On the other hand, we might expect to see a negative relationship with commitment because people with higher cognitive ability possess more job knowledge, which increases their value on the job market, and in turn the likelihood that they would leave for another job.[55] In the end, knowing how smart an employee is tells us very little about the likelihood that he or she will remain a member of the organization.

APPLICATION: SELECTING HIGH COGNITIVE ABILITY EMPLOYEES

Given the strong relationship between general cognitive ability and job performance, it isn't surprising that many organizations apply the content of this chapter to hire new employees. As an example, consider how Google goes about hiring employees whom it believes are the best and the brightest. To attract intelligent people to apply for a job, the company placed billboards in Silicon Valley and Harvard Square with the brainteaser, "first 10-digit prime found in consecutive digits of *e*.com." (The "*e*" in the question refers to the transcendental number used as the basis for natural logarithms, and the first 10-digit prime number in this string turns out to be 7427466391). People who solved the brainteaser went to the website where there was a more difficult brainteaser. Solving that one resulted in Google asking for the person's résumé.[56] The company also developed something called the *Google Labs Aptitude Test* (GLAT for short) and published it in magazines that smart techies might read. The GLAT is similar to the SAT and includes questions such as, "How many different ways can you color an icosahedron with one of three colors on each face? " Google used the GLAT to attract people who are smart and who are interested in the types of problems in the test. The people who are ultimately brought in for a job interview typically face 10-person interview panels and are confronted with very difficult questions. Someone who applies for a technical job might be asked to solve math algorithms and answer technical questions about software and computer networking.[57] It's also likely that they'll be asked brainteaser questions that rely upon both general intelligence and the originality facet of reasoning ability. For example, "How many golf balls fit in a school bus?" and "You are shrunk to the height of a nickel and your mass is proportionally reduced so as to maintain your original density. You are then thrown into an empty glass blender. The blades will start moving in 60 seconds. What do you do?"[58] Although you might not look forward to the prospect of having to answer these types of questions in an already stressful job interview, other companies such as Microsoft use a similar approach to hire highly intelligent employees, so it's something for which you might want to be prepared.[59]

Of course, companies outside the high-technology sector are also interested in hiring employees who have high cognitive ability, and applicants for jobs in many of these companies are given a cognitive ability test as part of the selection process. One of the most widely used tests is the **Wonderlic Cognitive Ability Test,** a 12-minute test of general cognitive ability that consists of 50 questions. It's been in use for several decades now and has been given to more than 120 million people by thousands of organizations.[60] From the example items that appear in Figure 10-4, you should be able to see how the items correspond with many of the cognitive abilities that we've described previously.

People who take the test receive one point for each correct response, and those points are summed to give a total score that can be used as a basis for selecting people for different jobs. The Wonderlic User's Manual offers recommendations for minimum passing scores for different job families, some of which are included in Table 10-3. For example, a score

10.6

What steps can organizations take to hire people with high levels of cognitive ability?

TABLE 10-3	Suggested Minimum Wonderlic Scores for Various Jobs
JOB	**MINIMUM SCORES**
Mechanical Engineer	30
Attorney	29
Executive	28
Teacher	27
Nurse	26
Office Manager	25
Advertising Sales	24
Manager/Supervisor	23
Police Officer	22
Firefighter	21
Cashier	20
Hospital Orderly	19
Machine Operator	18
Unskilled Laborer	17
Maid-Matron	16

Source: *Wonderlic Cognitive Ability Test and Scholastic Level Exam: User's Manual* (Vernon Hills, IL: Wonderlic Cognitive Ability Test, Inc., 1992), pp. 28–29. Reprinted with permission.

FIGURE 10-4 | Sample Wonderlic Questions

1. Which of the following is the earliest date?

   A) Jan. 16, 1898   B) Feb. 21, 1889   C) Feb. 2, 1898   D) Jan. 7, 1898   E) Jan. 30, 1889

2. LOW is to HIGH as EASY is to ____?____.

   A) SUCCESSFUL   B) PURE   C) TALL   D) INTERESTING   E) DIFFICULT

3. A featured product from an Internet retailer generated 27, 99, 80, 115 and 213 orders over a 5-hour period. Which graph below best represents this trend?

  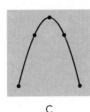  

   A   B   C   D   E

4. What is the next number in the series?   29   41   53   65   77   ____?____

   A) 75   B) 88   C) 89   D) 98   E) 99

5. *One word below appears in color. What is the OPPOSITE of that word?* She gave a complex answer to the question and we all agreed with her.

   A) long   B) better   C) simple   D) wrong   E) kind

6. Jose's monthly parking fee for April was $150; for May it was $10 more than April; and for June $40 more than May. His average monthly parking fee was? for these 3 months.

   A) $66   B) $160   C) $166   D) $170   E) $200

7. *If the first two statements are true, is the final statement true?*

   Sandra is responsible for ordering all office supplies.

   Notebooks are office supplies.

   Sandra is responsible for ordering notebooks.

   A) yes   B) no   C) uncertain

8. Which THREE choices are needed to create the figure on the left? Only pieces of the same color may overlap.

      A   B   C   D   E

9. Which THREE of the following words have similar meanings?

   A) observable   B) manifest   C) hypothetical   D) indefinite   E) theoretical

10. Last year, 12 out of 600 employees at a service organization were rewarded for their excellence in customer service, which was ? of the employees.

    A) 1%   B) 2%   C) 3%   D) 4%   E) 6%

Answers:

   1. E,   2. E,   3. D,   4. C,   5. C,   6. D,   7. A,   8. BCD,   9. CDE,   10. B

of 17 is the minimum suggested score for an unskilled laborer, a score of 21—which is the average for high school graduates and corresponds to an IQ of approximately 100—is the minimum suggested score for a firefighter. A score of 28 is the minimum suggested score for upper-level managerial and executive work and around the average for all college graduates.

Chances are you'll hear about the Wonderlic Cognitive Ability Test every March and April. This is because the National Football League (NFL) administers the test to players who enter the draft, and teams consider the scores when selecting players. One question that people always debate during this time is whether scores on a test of cognitive ability are relevant to a football player's performance on the field. Although supporters of the Wonderlic's use in the NFL argue that cognitive ability is necessary to remember plays and learn complex offensive and defensive systems, many people wonder how the ability to answer questions like those listed in Figure 10-4 relates to a player's ability to complete a pass, run for a touchdown, tackle an opponent, or kick a field goal. Moreover, detractors of the Wonderlic wonder why a poor score should overshadow a record of superior accomplishments on the playing field. So who's right? Well, the results of at least one study indicate that a player's Wonderlic score does not predict subsequent performance in the NFL and that this effect is not influenced much by the position of the player being considered.[61]

Before closing, we should mention here that the use of cognitive ability tests for hiring purposes may unintentionally discriminate against groups of individuals who, for a variety of reasons that we discussed earlier in this chapter, tend to score lower.[62] A great deal of research has examined this issue, and has concluded that although these tests are not technically biased because they predict job performance about equally across different groups of people, they should be used cautiously, especially in situations in which a diverse workforce is desired.[63] One way of accomplishing this is to use a combination of hiring tests. In addition to, or instead of, a test of general cognitive ability, a company could use a battery of tests that measure narrower cognitive abilities and noncognitive traits such as emotional intelligence and personality.[64]

TAKEAWAYS

10.1 Ability refers to the relatively stable capabilities of people to perform a particular range of different but related activities. Differences in ability are a function of both genes and the environment.

10.2 Cognitive abilities include verbal ability, quantitative ability, reasoning ability, spatial ability, and perceptual ability. General cognitive ability, or *g*, underlies all of these more specific cognitive abilities.

10.3 Emotional intelligence includes four specific kinds of emotional skills: self-awareness, other awareness, emotion regulation, and use of emotions.

10.4 Physical abilities include strength, stamina, flexibility and coordination, psychomotor abilities, and sensory abilities.

10.5 General cognitive ability has a strong positive relationship with job performance, due primarily to its effects on task performance. In contrast, general cognitive ability is only weakly related to organizational commitment.

10.6 Many organizations use cognitive ability tests to hire applicants with high levels of general cognitive ability. One of the most commonly used tests is the Wonderlic Cognitive Ability Test.

KEY TERMS

- Ability   *p. 308*
- Cognitive ability   *p. 309*
- Verbal ability   *p. 310*
- Quantitative ability   *p. 312*
- Reasoning ability   *p. 312*
- Spatial ability   *p. 313*
- Perceptual ability   *p. 313*
- General cognitive ability   *p. 313*
- Emotional intelligence   *p. 315*
- Self-awareness   *p. 315*
- Other awareness   *p. 315*
- Emotion regulation   *p. 315*
- Use of emotions   *p. 317*
- Strength   *p. 319*
- Stamina   *p. 319*
- Flexibility   *p. 319*
- Coordination   *p. 322*
- Psychomotor ability   *p. 322*
- Sensory ability   *p. 322*
- Wonderlic Cognitive Ability Test   *p. 326*

DISCUSSION QUESTIONS

10.1 What roles do learning, education, and other experiences play in determining a person's abilities? For which type of ability—cognitive, emotional, or physical—do these factors play the largest role?

10.2 Think of a job that requires very high levels of certain cognitive abilities. Can you think of a way to redesign that job so that people who lack those abilities could still perform the job effectively? Now respond to the same question with regard to emotional and physical abilities.

10.3 Consider your responses to the previous questions. Are cognitive, emotional, and physical abilities different in the degree to which jobs can be redesigned to accommodate people who lack relevant abilities? What are the implications of this difference, if there is one?

10.4 Think of experiences you've had with people who demonstrated unusually high or low levels of emotional intelligence. Then consider how you would rate them in terms of their cognitive abilities. Do you think that emotional intelligence "bleeds over" to affect people's perceptions of cognitive ability?

10.5 What combination of abilities is appropriate for the job of your dreams? Do you possess those abilities? If you fall short on any of these abilities, what could you do to improve?

CASE: IDEO

IDEO's success as a global design firm rests with its reputation of producing innovations in products, services, brands, and businesses that are both functional and emotionally meaningful to users. Accomplishing this multifaceted objective requires employees who possess a wide array of abilities. For example, it's undoubtedly true that IDEO employees need to possess high levels of most aspects of cognitive ability. Verbal ability is needed because employees have to understand what their clients want. Quantitative ability is important for solving design problems that involve data. Reasoning ability helps employees understand the nature of problems that arise during the design process and to solve them in a way that results in something novel. Spatial ability allows employees to visualize how designs would look after ideas are incorporated. Finally, employees have to recognize patterns and connect bits of information gleaned from unrelated projects, so perceptual ability is important.

Employees' emotional ability, however, is of particular importance to IDEO's success. First, IDEO employees could not accomplish the goal of creating emotionally meaningful experiences for users if they were unable to recognize emotions and anticipate the type of emotions that users will experience when they're confronted with different designs. Second, emotional ability allows employees to interact with customers in a way that gives them a better understanding of what customers want. IDEO employees who are able to sense the emotions of customers during meetings, and who can regulate their own emotions, can probe with questions to help customers convey what they like or don't like in a design, and in doing so, they increase the probability that designs don't go off track. Finally, employee emotional intelligence is important insofar as work at IDEO is collaborative. Employees need to be able to sense when their coworkers are frustrated or unhappy with how things are going on a project. Employees also need to recognize their own emotions and regulate them during meetings when ideas are being shared or when merits of different deigns options are being debated.

How is employee emotional intelligence managed at IDEO so that the company can accomplish its objectives effectively? As the following examples illustrate, the company has established informal practices and traditions that encourage employees' emotional intelligence. Employees at IDEO are encouraged to seek feedback that helps them develop recognition of their own emotions and understand how their emotions affect others. There are toys available throughout the workspace that employees can use when they're feeling upset or frustrated. Project leaders stay vigilant for emotional displays among employees that signal the potential for conflict. They bring to the surface the underlying issues and initiate conversations to resolve them. As a final example, the company encourages employees to regulate one another's emotions in a way that does not create interpersonal conflict. An employee who becomes judgmental or hotheaded during a meeting might get pelted with beanbags by coworkers. Although these types of practices might not work well in every organization, they have contributed to many award-winning designs at IDEO.

10.1 Describe how the cognitive and emotional abilities mentioned in this case are associated with different aspects of job performance.

10.2 Consider the abilities required by IDEO, and explain why you would, or would not, fit the job well.

10.3 Consider the formal definition of ability, and discuss whether the informal practices and traditions of IDEO really enhance emotional ability. What additional practices could IDEO use to enhance the emotional ability of its employees?

Sources: V.U. Druskat and S.B. Wolff, "Building the Emotional Intelligence of Groups," *Harvard Business Review,* March 2001, pp. 80–90; IDEO Corporate Website, "About," 2013, http://www.ideo.com/about/; IDEO Corporate Website, "Work," 2013, http://www.ideo.com/work/; and T. Kelley and J. Littman, *The Art of Innovation* (New York: Doubleday, 2001).

EXERCISE: EMOTIONAL INTELLIGENCE

The purpose of this exercise is to help you become more aware of your emotions and the emotions of others, as well as to see how emotions can be regulated and used in your daily life. This exercise uses groups, so your instructor will either assign you to a group or ask you to create your own group. The exercise has the following steps:

10.1 Think about situations in which you've experienced each of the following four emotions:
- Joy
- Anxiety
- Sadness
- Anger

10.2 In writing or in discussion with your group, answer the following questions about each situation:

    a. What, exactly, triggered your emotion in this situation?

    b. What impact did your emotions have on the outcome of the situation? Consider how your emotions affected you, others, and the general outcome of the situation. (Was it positive or negative?)

    c. What strategies did you use to deal with the emotion?

    d. What other strategies could you have used to deal with the emotion?

For example, one student noted: "I always get anxious when I take tests. Last week, I was supposed to have a midterm in Accounting, and sure enough, the upcoming test triggered my anxiety. Because I was anxious, I put off studying, and I tried to get some friends to go out to a club with me. We all had a good time that night, but the next day I got a D on my Accounting test, and two of my friends failed their Management midterms. I was using procrastination and avoidance as strategies for dealing with my anxiety. Another strategy I could have used was to face the anxiety head-on by talking to my professor to get a better understanding of the material that was going to be on the test, or by getting a group of my friends together to form a study group for Accounting."

10.3 Compare your responses with the responses of your fellow group members. As a group, answer the following questions:

    a. What emotional triggers do you share? In what ways are your emotional triggers different?

    b. Are there some strategies for dealing with emotions that seem especially helpful? Unhelpful?

    c. According to the stories told by the group, are there times when emotions actually help get a task done or a goal accomplished? How might you harness your emotions to help you achieve specific outcomes in the future?

Source: Adapted from M.A. Brackett and N.A. Katulak. "Emotional Intelligence in the Classroom: Skill-Based Training for Teachers and Students." *Improving Emotional Intelligence: A Practitioner's Guide,* ed. J. Ciarrochi and J.D. Mayer. New York: Psychology Press/Taylor & Francis, 2006, pp. 1–27.

ENDNOTES

10.1 Fleishman, E.A.; D.P. Costanza; and J. Marshall-Mies. "Abilities." In *An Occupational Information System for the 21st Century: The Development of O*NET,* ed.N.G. Peterson, M.D. Mumford, W.C. Borman, P.R. Jeanneret, and E.A. Fleishman. Washington, DC: American Psychological Association, 1999, pp. 175–95.

10.2 Neisser, U.; G. Boodoo; T.J. Bouchard; A.W. Boykin; N. Brody; S.J. Ceci; D.F. Halpern; J.C. Loehlin; R. Perloff; R.J. Sternberg; and S. Urbina. "Intelligence: Knowns and Unknowns." *American Psychologist* 51 (1996), pp. 77–101.

10.3 McCartney, K.; M.J. Harris; and F. Bernieri. "Growing Up and Growing Apart: A Developmental Meta-Analysis of Twin Studies." *Psychological Bulletin* 107 (1990), pp. 226–37.

10.4 Ceci, S.J. "How Much Does Schooling Influence General Intelligence and Its Cognitive Components? A Reassessment of the Evidence." *Developmental Psychology* 27 (1991), pp. 703–22.

10.5 Kohn, M.L., and C. Schooler. "Occupational Experience and Psychological Functioning: An Assessment of Reciprocal Effects." *American Sociological Review*

38 (1973), pp. 97–118; Kohn, M.L., and C. Schooler. *Work and Personality: An Inquiry into the Impact of Social Stratification.* Norwood, NJ: Ablex, 1983; and Neisser et al., "Intelligence."

10.6   Winerman, L. "Smarter Than Ever?" *Monitor on Psychology,* March 2013, pp. 30–33.

10.7   O*NET Online, http://online.onet center.org/find/descriptor/browse/Abilities/#cur (accessed June 5, 2006).

10.8   Fleishman et al., "Abilities"; and O*NET Website. *The O*NET Content Model: Detailed Outline with Descriptions* (n.d.), http://www.onetcenter.org/content.html/1.A?d=1#cm _1.A.

10.9   *Disability Fact Sheet Handbook,* University of California, Irvine. http://www.disability.uci.edu/disability_handbook/famous_people.htm (accessed June 9, 2006).

10.10   Vogelstein, F. "Google @ $165: Are These Guys for Real?" *Fortune,* December 13, 2004, p. 98, ProQuest database (accessed May 14, 2007).

10.11   Carroll, J.B. *Human Cognitive Abilities: A Survey of Factor-Analytic Studies.* New York: Cambridge University Press, 1993; Cattell, R.B. "The Measurement of

Adult Intelligence." *Psychological Bulletin* 40 (1943), pp. 153–93; Galton, F. *Inquire into Human Faculty and Its Development.* London: Macmillan, 1883; Spearman, C. "General Intelligence, Objectively Determined and Measured." *American Journal of Psychology* 15 (1904), pp. 201–93; Thurstone, L.L. "Primary Mental Abilities." *Psychometric Monographs* (Whole No. 1, 1938); and Vernon, P.E. *The Structure of Human Abilities.* London: Methuen, 1950.

10.12   Spearman, "General Intelligence"; and Spearman, C. *The Abilities of Man: Their Nature and Measurement.* New York: Macmillan, 1927.

10.13   Neisser et al., "Intelligence."

10.14   Rindermann, H., and J. Thompson. "Cognitive Capitalism: The Effect of Cognitive Ability on Wealth, as Mediated through Scientific Achievement and Economic Freedom." *Psychological Science* 22 (2011), pp. 754–63.

10.15   Judge, T.A.; R. Ilies; and N. Dimotakis. "Are Health and Happiness the Product of Wisdom? The Relationship of General Mental Ability to Educational and Occupational Attainment, Health, and Well-Being." *Journal of Applied

Psychology* 95 (2010), pp. 454–68.

10.16   Deary, I.J.; A. Weiss; and G.D. Batty. "Intelligence, Personality, and Health Outcomes." *Psychological Science in the Public Interest* 11 (2010), pp. 53–79.

10.17   Batty, G.D.; I.J. Deary; and L.S. Gottfedson. "Premorbid (Early Life) IQ and Later Mortality Risk: Systematic Review." *Annals of Epidemiology* 17 (2007), pp. 278–88.

10.18   Farnham, A. "Are You Smart Enough to Keep Your Job? In an Age of Teamwork and Fluid Careers, IQ Alone Doesn't Cut It Anymore." *CNNMoney.com,* January 15, 1996, http://money.cnn.com/magazines/fortune/fortune_archive/1996/01/15/207155/index.htm.

10.19   Bar-On, R. *Development of the Bar-On EQ-i: A Measure of Emotional Intelligence and Social Intelligence.* Toronto: Multi-Health Systems, 1997; Gardner, H. *The Shattered Mind.* New York: Knopf, 1975; Goleman, D. *Emotional Intelligence: Why It Can Matter More Than IQ.* New York: Bantam Books, 1995; and Thorndike, R.K. "Intelligence and Its Uses." *Harper's Magazine* 140 (1920), pp. 227–335.

10.20   Matthews, G.; A.K. Emo; R.D. Roberts;

and M. Zeidner. "What Is This Thing Called Emotional Intelligence?" In *A Critique of Emotional Intelligence: What Are the Problems and How Can They Be Fixed?*, ed. K.R. Murphy. Mahwah, NJ: Erlbaum, 2006, pp. 3–36; and Mayer, J.D.; P. Salovey; and D.R. Caruso. "Emotional Intelligence: New Ability or Eclectic Traits?" *American Psychologist* 63 (2008), pp. 503–17.

10.21 Salovey, P., and J.D. Mayer. "Emotional Intelligence." *Imagination, Cognition, and Personality* 9 (1990), pp. 185–211; and Mayer, J.D.; R.D. Roberts; and S.G. Barside. "Human Abilities: Emotional Intelligence." *Annual Review of Psychology* 59 (2008), pp. 507–36.

10.22 Davies, M.; L. Stankov; and R.D. Roberts. "Emotional Intelligence: In Search of an Elusive Construct." *Journal of Personality and Social Psychology* 75 (1998), pp. 989–1015.

10.23 Law, K.S.; C.S. Wong; and L.J. Song. "The Construct and Criterion Validity of Emotional Intelligence and Its Potential Utility for Management Studies." *Journal of Applied Psychology* 89 (2004), pp. 483–96.

10.24 Ibid.

10.25 Farnham, "Are You Smart Enough to Keep Your Job?"

10.26 Ibid.

10.27 Davies et al., "Emotional Intelligence"; and Law et al., "The Construct and Criterion Validity of Emotional Intelligence."

10.28 Ibid.

10.29 Parke, M.R., M.G. Seo; and E.N. Sherf. "Regulating and Facilitating: The Role of Emotional Intelligence in Maintaining and Using Positive Affect for Creativity." *Journal of Applied Psychology* 100 (2015), pp. 917–34.

10.30 Cherniss, C. "The Business Case for Emotional Intelligence." *Consortium for Research on Emotional Intelligence in Organizations,* 2004, http://www.eiconsortium.org/research/business_case_for_ei.htm; Cote, S., and C.T.H. Miners. "Emotional Intelligence, Cognitive Intelligence, and Job Performance." *Administrative Science Quarterly* 51 (2006), pp. 1–28; Fisher, A. "Success Secret: A High Emotional IQ." *Fortune* 138, October 26, 1998, p. 293, ProQuest database (accessed May 14, 2007); Kendell, J. "Can't We All Just Get Along? 'Emotional Intelligence,' or EI, May Sound Like a Squishy Management Concept—But It Gets Results." *Business-Week,* October 9, 2000, p. F18, ProQuest database (accessed May 14, 2007); Schwartz, T. "How Do You Feel?" *Fast Company,* June 2000, p. 296, http://pf.fastcompany.com/magazine/35/emotion.html; and Walter, F.; M.S. Cole; R.H. Humphrey. "Emotional Intelligence: Sine Qua Non of Leadership of Folderol." *Academy of Management Perspectives* 25 (2011), pp. 45–58; and Chien Farh, C.I.C.; M.G. Seo; and P.E. Tesluk. "Emotional Intelligence, Teamwork Effectiveness, and Job Performance: The Moderating Role of Job Context." *Journal of Applied Psychology* 97 (2012), pp. 890–900.

10.31 Cherniss, "The Business Case"; and Schwartz, "How Do You Feel?"

10.32 "Emotional Intelligence Gets More Sales." *A&P Sales Improvement,* November 20, 2010, http://www.a-and-p.com/apblog/?tag=loreal; and Cherniss, "The Business Case."

10.33 Joseph, D., J. Jin; D. A. Newman; and E. H. O'Boyle. "Why Does Self-Reported Emotional Intelligence Predict Job Performance?" *Journal of Applied Psychology* 100 (2015), pp. 298–342.

10.34 Cote and Miners, "Emotional Intelligence."

10.35 Austin, E.J.; D. Farrelly; C. Black; and H. Moore. "Emotional

Intelligence, Machiavellianism and Emotional Manipulation: Does EI Have a Dark Side?" *Personality and Individual Differences* 43 (2007), pp. 179–89; and Winkel, D. E.; R.L. Wyland; M.A. Shaffer; and P. Clason. "A New Perspective on Psychological Resources: Unanticipated Consequences of Impulsivity and Emotional Intelligence." *Journal of Occupational and Organizational Psychology* 84 (2010), pp. 79–94.

10.36 Ibid.

10.37 Carr, D. "Emotional Intelligence, PSE and Self Esteem: A Cautionary Note." *Pastoral Care in Education* 18 (2000), pp. 27–33.

10.38 Bar-On, *Development of the Bar-On EQ-i.*

10.39 Conte, J.M., and M.A. Dean. "Can Emotional Intelligence Be Measured?" In *A Critique of Emotional Intelligence: What Are the Problems and How Can They Be Fixed?,* ed. K.R. Murphy. Mahwah, NJ: Erlbaum, 2006, pp. 54–81.

10.40 Law et al., "The Construct and Criterion Validity."

10.41 Fleishman, E.A. "Human Abilities and the Acquisition of Skill." In *Acquisition of Skill,* ed. E.A. Bilodeau. New York: Academic Press, 1966, pp. 147–67; Fleishman et al., "Abilities";

Fleishman, E.A., and M.E. Reilly. *Handbook of Human Abilities: Definitions, Measurements, and Job Task Requirements.* Palo Alto, CA: Consulting Psychologists Press, 1992; and O*NET Website.

10.42 Kazmi, S. "Firefighters Put Through Paces in One-Stop Testing." *Knight Ridder Tribune Business News,* August 18, 2005, p. 1, ProQuest database (accessed May 13, 2006).

10.43 Safer, W. "How Monster Cable Got Wired for Growth." *CNNMoney.com,* April 20, 2009, http://money.cnn.com/2009/04/30/smallbusiness/how_monster_cable_got_started.fsb/index.htm.

10.44 Lubinski, D. "Introduction to the Special Section on Cognitive Abilities: 100 Years after Spearman's (1904) 'General Intelligence,' 'Objectively Determined and Measured.'" *Journal of Personality and Social Psychology* 86 (2004), pp. 96–111.

10.45 Hunter, J.E., and F.L. Schmidt. "Intelligence and Job Performance: Economic and Social Implications." *Psychology, Public Policy, and Law* 2 (1996), pp. 447–72; Lubinski, "Introduction to the Special Section"; and Schmidt, F.L., and J. Hunter, "General Mental Ability in the World

of Work: Occupational Attainment and Job Performance." *Journal of Personality and Social Psychology* 86 (2004), pp. 162–73.

10.46 Seligman, D. "Brains in the Office." *Fortune,* January 13, 1997, p. 38, ProQuest database (accessed May 14, 2007).

10.47 Schmidt, F.L., and J.E. Hunter. "Select on Intelligence." In *Blackwell Handbook of Principles of Organizational Behavior,* ed. E.A. Locke. Malden, MA: Blackwell, 2000, pp. 3–14.

10.48 Frey, M.C., and D.K. Detterman. "Scholastic Assessment of *g?* The Relationship between the Scholastic Assessment Test and General Cognitive Ability." *Psychological Science* 15 (2004), pp. 373–78.

10.49 Korbin, J.L.; W.J. Camara; and G.B. Milewski. "The Utility of the SAT I and SAT II for Admissions Decisions in California and the Nation." *The College Board, Research Report No. 2002–6.* New York: College Entrance Examination Board, 2002.

10.50 Kuncel, N.R.; M.A. Crede; and L.L. Thomas. "A Meta-Analysis of the Predictive Validity of the Graduate Management Admission Test (GMAT) and Undergraduate Grade Point Average (UGPA) for

Graduate Student Academic Performance." *Academy of Management Learning & Education* 6 (2007), pp. 51–68; and Kuncel, N.R., and S.A. Hezlett. "Fact and Fiction in Cognitive Ability Testing for Admissions and Hiring Decisions." *Current Directions in Psychological Science* 19 (2010), pp. 339–45.

10.51 Hunter and Schmidt, "Intelligence and Job Performance"; and Schmidt, F.L.; J.E. Hunter; A.N. Outerbridge; and S. Goff. "The Joint Relations of Experience and Ability with Job Performance: A Test of Three Hypotheses." *Journal of Applied Psychology* 73 (1988), pp. 46–57.

10.52 Gonzalez-Mule, E.; M.K. Mount; and I.S. Oh. "A Meta-Analysis of the Relationship between General Mental Ability and Nontask Performance." *Journal of Applied Psychology* 99 (2014), pp. 1222–43; and Motowidlo, S.J.; W.S. Borman; and M.J. Schmit. "A Theory of Individual Differences in Task and Contextual Performance." *Human Performance* 10 (1997), pp. 71–83.

10.53 LePine, J.A.; J.A. Colquitt; and A. Erez. "Adaptability to Changing Task Contexts: Effects of General Cognitive Ability, Conscientiousness, and Openness to Experience."

Personnel Psychology 53 (2000), pp. 563–93; and Schmidt and Hunter, "Select on Intelligence."

10.54 Boudreau, J.W.; W.R. Boswell; T.A. Judge; and R.D. Bretz. "Personality and Cognitive Ability as Predictors of Job Search among Employed Managers." *Personnel Psychology* 54 (2001), pp. 25–50; Colarelli, S.M.; R.A. Dean; and C. Konstans. "Comparative Effects of Personal and Situational Influences on Job Outcomes of New Professionals." *Journal of Applied Psychology* 72 (1987), pp. 558–66; and Dickter, D.N.; M. Roznowski; and D.A. Harrison. "Temporal Tempering: An Event History Analysis of the Process of Voluntary Turnover." *Journal of Applied Psychology* 81 (1996), pp. 705–16.

10.55 Boudreau et al., "Personality and Cognitive Ability."

10.56 "Brain Teasers Help Google Recruit Workers." *CNN.com Technology,* November 4, 2004, http://www.topcoder.com/pressroom/cnn_110404.pdf.

10.57 Ibid.

10.58 Carlson, N. "15 Google Interview Questions That Will Make You Feel Stupid." *Business Insider SAI,* November 8, 2010, http://www.businessinsider.com/15-google-

interview-questions-that-will-make-you-feel-stupid-2010-11; and Kaplan, M. "Want a Job at Google? Try These Brainteasers First." *CNNMoney.com,* August 30, 2007, http://money.cnn.com/2007/08/29/technology/brain_teasers.biz2/index.htm.

10.59 Poundstone, W. *How Would You Move Mount Fuji: Microsoft's Cult of the Puzzle.* New York: Little, Brown, 2003.

10.60 Wonderlic Website, http://www.wonderlic.com/Products/product.asp?prod_id=4 accessed July 12, 2006).

10.61 Lyons, B.D.; B.J. Hoffman; J.W. Michel. "Not Much More Than *g?* An Examination of the Impact of Intelligence on NFL Performance." *Human Performance* 22 (2009), pp. 225–45.

10.62 Campbell, J.P. "Group Differences and Personnel Decisions: Validity, Fairness and Affirmative Action." *Journal of Vocational Behavior* 49 (1996), pp. 122–58.

10.63 Hartigan, J. A., and A.K. Wigdor. *Fairness in Employment Testing: Validity Generalization, Minority Issues and The General Aptitude Test Battery.* Washington, DC: National Academy Press, 1989; and Mattern, K.D., and

B.F. Patterson. "Test of Slope and Intercept Bias in College Admissions: A Response to Aguinis, Culpepper, and Pierce (2010)." *Journal of Applied Psychology* 98 (2013), pp. 134–47.

10.64 De Corte, W.; F. Lievens; and P.R. Sackett. "Combining Predictors to Achieve Optimal Trade-offs Between Selection Quality and Adverse Impact." *Journal of Applied Psychology* 92 (2007), pp. 1380–93; Ployhart, R.E., and B.C. Holtz. "The Diversity-Validity Dilemma: Strategies for Reducing Racioethnic and Sex Subgroup Differences and Adverse Impact in Selection." *Personnel Psychology* 61 (2008), pp. 153–72; and Wee, S.; D.A. Newman; and D.L. Joseph. "More Than *g:* Selection Quality and Adverse Impact Implications of Considering Second-Stratum Cognitive Abilities." *Journal of Applied Psychology* 99 (2014), pp. 547–63.

PART

4

GROUP MECHANISMS

CHAPTER 11
Teams: Characteristics and Diversity

CHAPTER 12
Teams: Processes and Communication

CHAPTER 13
Leadership: Power and Negotiation

CHAPTER 14
Leadership: Styles and Behaviors

Teams: Characteristics and Diversity

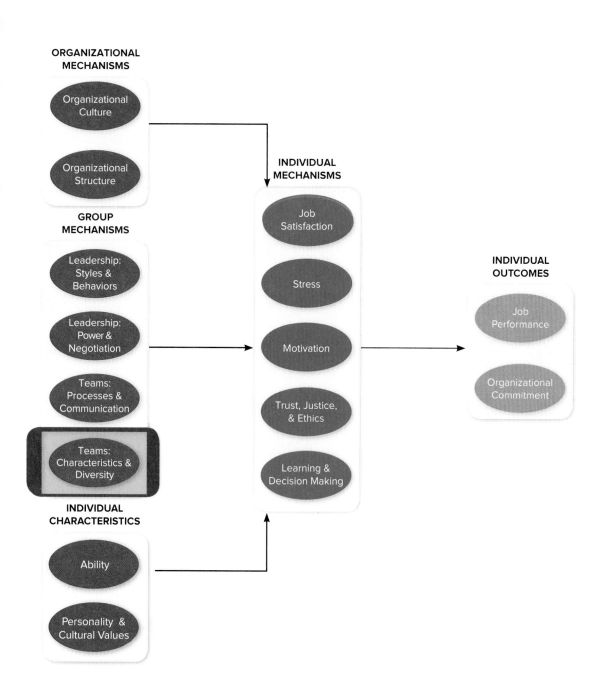

ORGANIZATIONAL MECHANISMS

- Organizational Culture
- Organizational Structure

GROUP MECHANISMS

- Leadership: Styles & Behaviors
- Leadership: Power & Negotiation
- Teams: Processes & Communication
- Teams: Characteristics & Diversity

INDIVIDUAL CHARACTERISTICS

- Ability
- Personality & Cultural Values

INDIVIDUAL MECHANISMS

- Job Satisfaction
- Stress
- Motivation
- Trust, Justice, & Ethics
- Learning & Decision Making

INDIVIDUAL OUTCOMES

- Job Performance
- Organizational Commitment

© Agencja Fotograficzna Caro/Alamy

✓ LEARNING GOALS

After reading this chapter, you should be able to answer the following questions:

11.1 What are the five general team types and their defining characteristics?

11.2 What are the three general types of team interdependence?

11.3 What factors are involved in team composition?

11.4 What are the types of team diversity, and how do they influence team functioning?

11.5 How do team characteristics influence team effectiveness?

11.6 How can team compensation be used to manage team effectiveness?

LUFTHANSA

With sales of $39.2 billion, assets of $37 Billion, and more than 118,000 employees, Deutsche Lufthansa AG is one of the world's largest companies. Headquartered in Cologne, Germany, it consists of more than 500 subsidiaries and associated companies organized into several groups, including passenger transportation, airfreight, MRO (maintenance, repair, and overhaul), catering, and flight training. For those of you who travel, the airlines in Deutsche Lufthansa AG's passenger transportation group are likely to be familiar to you. These include the company's namesake, Lufthansa Passenger Airlines, as well as Austrian Air, Brussels Airlines, Germanwings, Sun Express, and SWISS.

The core business of Deutsch Lufthansa AG is passenger transportation, so it may be obvious to you that some of the most crucial employees to the company are those who serve as members of the flight crews responsible for getting passengers from one destination to another. The composition of a flight crew depends on the specific aircraft being flown, as well as the length and purpose of the flight. In the cockpit, where the aircraft controls are located, there's a pilot in command and a co-pilot. These crew members are often referred to as the Captain and First Officer, respectively. For longer flights, the crew may include relief pilots—fully qualified Captains and First Officers—who fill in when someone needs to rest. In the main cabin, there are flight attendants responsible for the safety and comfort of the passengers. A lead flight attendant coordinates among the other members of the flight crew to ensure compliance with safety procedures and that passengers in the different cabin classes are taken care of.

Although each crew member has a set of well-defined responsibilities, they function together as a team. First, they look the part. They all wear uniforms, and there's no mistaking a member of the crew for a passenger. Second, crew members share the same overarching goal of flight safety. Third, crew members will likely share the same fate if, for some reason, they don't achieve the goal of flight safety. Finally, crew members need to interact and coordinate throughout a flight. In the end, the ability of crew members to perform effectively as a team plays a key role in facilitating Lufthansa's strategic objectives, which are centered on quality, punctuality, dependability, and safety.

TEAM CHARACTERISTICS AND DIVERSITY

The topic of teams is likely familiar to almost anyone who might be reading this book. In fact, you've probably had firsthand experience with several different types of teams at different points in your life. As an example, most of you have played a team sport or two (yes, playing soccer in gym class counts). Most of you have also worked in student teams to complete projects or assignments for courses you've taken. Or perhaps you've worked closely with a small group of people to accomplish a task that was important to you—planning an event, raising money for a charity, or starting and running a small cash business. Finally, some of you have been members of organizational teams responsible for making a product, providing a service, or generating recommendations for solving company problems.

But what exactly is a team, and what is it that makes a team more than a "group"? A **team** consists of two or more people who work *interdependently* over some time period to accomplish *common goals* related to some *task-oriented purpose.*[1] You can think of teams as a special type of group, where a group is just a collection of two or more people. Teams are special for two reasons. First, the interactions among members within teams revolve around a deeper dependence on one another than the interactions within groups. Second, the interactions within teams occur with a specific task-related purpose in mind. Although the members of a friendship group may engage in small talk or in-depth conversations on a frequent basis, the members of a team depend on one another for critical information, materials, and actions that are needed to accomplish goals related to their purpose for being together.

The use of teams in today's organizations is widespread. National surveys indicate that teams are used in the majority of organizations in the United States, regardless of whether the organization is large or small.[2] In fact, some researchers suggest that almost all major U.S. companies are currently using teams or planning to implement them, and that up to 50 percent of all employees in the United States work in a team as part of their job.[3] Thus, whereas the use of teams was

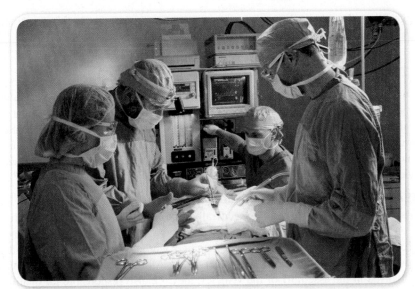

A surgical team consists of specialized members who depend on one another to accomplish tasks that are both complex and important. Why might you not want to have surgery conducted by a surgical team that functions like a group?

© Stockbyte/Getty Images RF

limited to pioneers such as Procter & Gamble in the 1960s, teams are currently used in all types of industries to accomplish all the types of work necessary to make organizations run effectively.[4]

Why have teams become so widespread? The most obvious reason is that the nature of today's work requires them. As work has become more complex, interactions among multiple team members have become more vital. This is because interactions allow the team to pool complementary knowledge and skills. As an example, surgical teams consist of individuals who received specialized training in the activities needed to conduct surgical procedures. The team consists of a surgeon who received training for the procedure in question, an anesthesiologist who received training necessary to manage patient pain, and an operating room nurse who was trained to provide overall care for the patient.

Teams may also be useful to organizations in ways beyond just accomplishing the work itself. For example, one study revealed that problem-solving teams composed primarily of rank-and-file workers could boost productivity in steel mills by devising ways to increase the efficiency of production lines and quality control processes.[5] Although implementing teams often makes sense in settings such as these, for which the nature of the work and work-related problems are complex, teams vary a great deal from one another in terms of their effectiveness. The goal of this chapter, as well as the next, is to help you understand factors that influence team effectiveness.

WHAT CHARACTERISTICS CAN BE USED TO DESCRIBE TEAMS?

This is the first of two chapters on teams. This chapter focuses on team characteristics—the task, unit, and member qualities that can be used to describe teams and that combine to make some teams more effective than others. Team characteristics provide a means of categorizing and examining teams, which is important because teams come in so many shapes and sizes. Team characteristics play an important role in determining what a team is capable of achieving and may influence the strategies and processes the team uses to reach its goals. As you will see, however, there's more to understanding team characteristics than meets the eye. Team characteristics such as diversity, for example, have many meanings, and its effect on team functioning and effectiveness depends on what type of diversity you're concerned with as well as several additional complicating factors. Chapter 12 will focus on team processes and communication—the specific actions and behaviors that teams can engage in to achieve synergy. The concepts in that chapter will help explain why some teams are more or less effective than their characteristics would suggest they should be. For now, however, we turn our attention to this question: "What characteristics can be used to describe teams?"

TEAM TYPES

11.1

What are the five general team types and their defining characteristics?

One way to describe teams is to take advantage of existing taxonomies that place teams into various types. One such taxonomy is illustrated in Table 11-1. The table illustrates that there are five general types of teams and that each is associated with a number of defining characteristics.[6] The most notable characteristics include the team's purpose, the length of the team's existence, and the amount of time involvement the team requires of its individual members. The sections to follow review these types of teams in turn.

WORK TEAMS **Work teams** are designed to be relatively permanent. Their purpose is to produce goods or provide services, and they generally require a full-time commitment from their members. As an example of a work team, consider how cars and trucks are manufactured at Toyota.[7] Teams are composed of four to eight members who do the physical work, and a leader who supports the team and coordinates with other teams. Although the teams are responsible for the work involved in the assembly of the vehicles, they are also responsible for quality control and developing ideas for improvements in the production process. Team members inspect each other's work, and when they see a problem, they stop the line until they are able to resolve the problem.

MANAGEMENT TEAMS **Management teams** are similar to work teams in that they are designed to be relatively permanent; however, they are also distinct in a number of important

TABLE 11-1 | Types of Teams

TYPE OF TEAM	PURPOSE AND ACTIVITIES	LIFE SPAN	MEMBER INVOLVEMENT	SPECIFIC EXAMPLES
Work team	Produce goods or provide services.	Long	High	Self-managed work team Production team Maintenance team Sales team
Management team	Integrate activities of subunits across business functions.	Long	Moderate	Top management team
Parallel team	Provide recommendations and resolve issues.	Varies	Low	Quality circle Advisory council Committee
Project team	Produce a one-time output (product, service, plan, design, etc.).	Varies	Varies	Product design team Research group Planning team
Action team	Perform complex tasks that vary in duration and take place in highly visible or challenging circumstances.	Varies	Varies	Surgical team Musical group Expedition team Sports team

Sources: S.G. Cohen and D.E. Bailey, "What Makes Teams Work: Group Effectiveness Research from the Shop Floor to the Executive Suite," *Journal of Management* 27 (1997), pp. 239–90; and E. Sundstrom, K.P. De Meuse, and D. Futrell, "Work Teams: Applications and Effectiveness." *American Psychologist* 45 (1990), pp. 120–33.

ways. Whereas work teams focus on the accomplishment of core operational-level production and service tasks, management teams participate in managerial-level tasks that affect the entire organization. Specifically, management teams are responsible for coordinating the activities of organizational subunits—typically departments or functional areas—to help the organization achieve its long-term goals. Top management teams, for example, consist of

A Toyota work team is responsible for vehicle assembly and quality control.

© Toru Yamanaka/AFP/Getty Images

senior-level executives who meet to make decisions about the strategic direction of the organization. It may also be worth mentioning that because members of management teams are typically heads of departments, their commitment to the management team is offset somewhat by the responsibilities they have in leading their unit.

PARALLEL TEAMS **Parallel teams** are composed of members from various jobs who provide recommendations to managers about important issues that run "parallel" to the organization's production process.[8] Parallel teams require only part-time commitment from members, and they can be permanent or temporary, depending on their aim. Quality circles, for example, consist of individuals who normally perform core production tasks, but who also meet regularly with individuals from other work groups to identify production-related problems and opportunities for improvement. As an example of a more temporary parallel team, committees often form to deal with unique issues or issues that arise only periodically. Examples of issues that can spur the creation of committees include changes to work procedures, purchases of new equipment or services, and non-routine hiring.

PROJECT TEAMS **Project teams** are formed to take on "one-time" tasks that are generally complex and require a lot of input from members with different types of training and expertise.[9] Although project teams exist only as long as it takes to finish a project, some projects are quite complex and can take years to complete. Members of some project teams work full-time, whereas other teams demand only a part-time commitment. A planning team comprised of engineers, architects, designers, and builders, charged with designing a suburban town center, might work together full-time for a year or more. In contrast, the engineers and artists who constitute a design team responsible for creating an electric toothbrush might work together for a month on the project while also serving on other project teams.

ACTION TEAMS **Action teams** perform tasks that are normally limited in duration. However, those tasks are quite complex and take place in contexts that are either highly visible to an audience or of a highly challenging nature.[10] Some types of action teams work together for an extended period of time. For example, sports teams remain intact for at least one season, and musical groups like AC/DC may stick together for decades. Other types of action teams stay

The Australian Band AC/DC, which was formed in 1973, is an example of an action team that has stayed together for an extended period of time.

© Robert Vos/Corbis

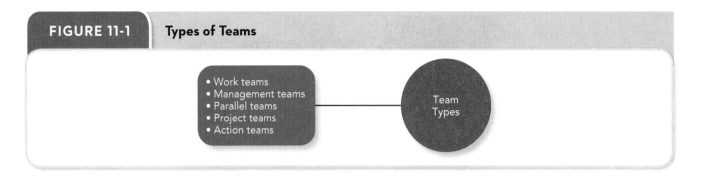

FIGURE 11-1 | **Types of Teams**

- Work teams
- Management teams
- Parallel teams
- Project teams
- Action teams

Team Types

together only as long as the task takes to complete. Surgical teams and aircraft flight crews may only work together as a unit for a single two-hour surgery or flight.

SUMMARY. So how easy is it to classify teams into one of the types summarized in Figure 11-1? Well, it turns out that teams often fit into more than one category. As an example, consider the teams at Pixar, the company that has produced many computer-animated hit films, such as *Toy Story, Monsters Inc., Finding Nemo, Cars, Wall-E, Up, Brave, Monsters University,* and *Inside Out.* On the one hand, because the key members of Pixar teams have stuck together for each film the company has produced, it might seem like Pixar uses work teams.[11] On the other hand, because the creation of each film can be viewed as a project, and because members are likely involved in multiple ongoing projects, it might seem reasonable to say that Pixar uses project teams. It's probably most appropriate to say that at Pixar, teams have characteristics of both work teams and project teams.

VARIATIONS WITHIN TEAM TYPES

Even knowing whether a team is a project team, an action team, or some other type of team doesn't tell you the whole story. In fact, there are important variations within those categories that are needed to understand a team's functioning.[12] As one example, teams can vary with respect to the degree to which they have autonomy and are self-managed.[13] If you've ever been on a team where members have a great deal of freedom to work together to establish their own goals, procedures, roles, and membership, you've worked on a team where the level of autonomy and self-management is high. You may also have worked on a team where the level of autonomy and self-management is low. In these teams, there are strict rules regarding goals, procedures, and roles, and team leaders or managers make most of the decisions regarding management of the team with respect to membership. Research has shown that although people generally prefer working in teams where the level of autonomy and self-management is high, the appropriate level of self-management with regard to overall team effectiveness may depend on a variety of factors.[14] For example, research has shown that high levels of self-management may be most advantageous for teams where team members' have high levels of team-relevant knowledge obtained from outside experts and others in their social networks.[15]

Another way that teams can vary relates to how the members typically communicate with each other. **Virtual teams** are teams in which the members are geographically dispersed, and interdependent

The Pixar team, shown here at the Cannes Film Festival, has characteristics of both work teams and project teams. Trying to characterize this team is even more complicated when you consider that key members are involved in the management of the company, and their involvement in the films runs parallel to these other responsibilities.

© *Daniele Venturelli/WireImage/Getty Images*

activity occurs through electronic communications—primarily e-mail, instant messaging, and web conferencing. Although communications and group networking software is far from perfect, it has advanced to the point that it's possible for teams doing all sorts of work to function virtually. In fact, there has been an 800 percent increase in the number of virtual employees over the last decade or so, and it's likely that there are tens of millions of virtual teams operating today.[16] Companies such as Con Edison, New York's giant electric and gas utility, have invested significant resources in technology and training to help these teams function and perform more effectively.[17] The same is true at IBM, where at least 40 percent of the employees work virtually.[18] At TRW, one of the world's largest automotive suppliers, virtual teams provide an efficient way to accomplish work on projects when members are geographically separated.[19] In fact, many companies in high-tech industries are leveraging virtual teams to make continuous progress on work tasks without members having to work 24/7. For example, Logitech, the Swiss company that makes things such as computer mice and keyboards, universal remotes for home entertainment systems, and gaming controllers, attributes its success to teams of designers and engineers who are located in different places around the world.[20] Although you might be inclined to believe that time-zone differences would be a hindrance to this sort of team, Logitech turned it into a competitive advantage by letting the work *follow the sun*.[21] Specifically, work at Logitech is accomplished continuously because members of a team who have finished their workday in one country electronically hand off the work to team members in another country who have just arrived at the office. Because these electronic hand-offs occur continuously, product development and other work needed to bring innovative products to the market can be completed much more quickly.

In addition to varying in their "virtuality," teams of any type can differ in the amount of experience they have working together. One way to understand this point is to consider what occurs in teams at different stages of their development as they progress from a newly formed team to one that's well-established. According to the most well-known theory, teams go through a progression of five stages shown in the top panel of Figure 11-2.[22] In the first stage, called **forming,**

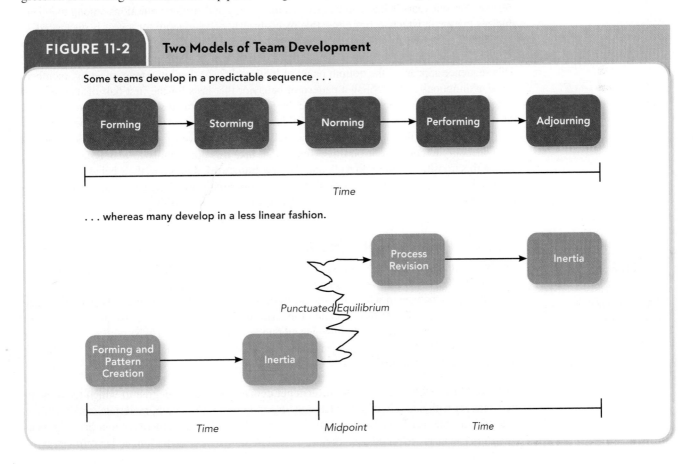

FIGURE 11-2   Two Models of Team Development

Some teams develop in a predictable sequence . . .

Forming → Storming → Norming → Performing → Adjourning

Time

. . . whereas many develop in a less linear fashion.

Forming and Pattern Creation → Inertia → *Punctuated Equilibrium* → Process Revision → Inertia

Time   Midpoint   Time

members orient themselves by trying to understand their boundaries in the team. Members try to get a feel for what is expected of them, what types of behaviors are out of bounds, and who's in charge. In the next stage, called **storming**, members remain committed to ideas they bring with them to the team. This initial unwillingness to accommodate others' ideas triggers conflict that negatively affects some interpersonal relationships and harms the team's progress. During the next stage, **norming**, members realize that they need to work together to accomplish team goals, and consequently, they begin to cooperate with one another. Feelings of solidarity develop as members work toward team goals. Over time, norms and expectations develop regarding what different members are responsible for doing. In the fourth stage of team development, which is called **performing**, members are comfortable working within their roles, and the team makes progress toward goals. Finally, because the life span of many teams is limited, there's a stage called **adjourning**. In this stage, members experience anxiety and other emotions as they disengage and ultimately separate from the team.

But does this sequence of forming, storming, norming, performing, and adjourning apply to the development of all types of teams? Chances are that you've had some experience with teams that would lead you to answer this question with a "no." In fact, although this theory of group development is intuitively appealing and identifies things that may occur as teams gain experience working together, there are factors in work organizations that can significantly alter what occurs during a team's life.[23] One situation in which this developmental sequence is less applicable is when teams are formed with clear expectations regarding what's expected from the team and its members. With many action teams, for example, there are established rules and standard operating procedures that guide team members' behaviors and their interactions with one another. As a specific example, an aircraft flight crew doesn't have to go through the forming, storming, norming, and performing stages to figure out that the pilot flies the plane and the flight attendant serves the beverages. As another example, though the adjourning stage only happens once for each type of team, the implications are likely to be more significant for team types with longer life spans that require high member involvement. Dissolving a work team that's been together for four years is likely to trigger greater anxiety and stronger emotions among members than a situation in which a committee that meets briefly once a month for a year is disbanded.

Another situation in which the development sequence is less applicable may be in certain types of project teams that follow a pattern of development called **punctuated equilibrium**.[24] This sequence appears in the bottom panel of Figure 11-2. At the initial team meeting, members make assumptions and establish a pattern of behavior that lasts for the first half of its life. That pattern of behavior continues to dominate the team's behavior as it settles into a sort of inertia. At the midway point of the project—and this is true regardless of the length of the project—something remarkable happens: Members realize that they have to change their task paradigm fundamentally to complete it on time. Teams that take this opportunity to plan a new approach during this transition tend to do well, and the new framework dominates their behavior until task completion. However, teams that don't take the opportunity to change their approach tend to persist with their original pattern and may "go down with a sinking ship."

TEAM INTERDEPENDENCE

11.2

What are the three general types of team interdependence?

In addition to taxonomies of team types, we can describe teams by talking about the interdependence that governs connections among team members. In a general sense, you can think of interdependence as the way in which the members of a team are linked to one another. That linkage between members is most often thought of in terms of the interactions that take place as the team accomplishes its work. However, linkages among team members also exist with respect to their goals and rewards. In fact, you can find out where your student project team stands on different aspects of interdependence using our **OB Assessments** feature.

TASK INTERDEPENDENCE **Task interdependence** refers to the degree to which team members interact with and rely on other team members for the information, materials, and resources needed to accomplish work for the team.[25] As Figure 11-3 illustrates, there are four primary types of task interdependence, and each requires a different degree of interaction and coordination.[26]

OB ASSESSMENTS

INTERDEPENDENCE

How interdependent is your student project team? This assessment is designed to measure three types of interdependence: task interdependence, goal interdependence, and outcome interdependence. Read each of the following questions with a relevant student team in mind. Answer each question using the response scale provided. Then follow the instructions below to score yourself. (Instructors: Assessments on deep-level diversity, team role tendencies, and team viability can be found in the PowerPoints in the Connect Library's Instructor Resources and in the Connect assignments for this chapter).

1	2	3	4	5	6	7
TOTALLY DISAGREE	DISAGREE	SOMEWHAT DISAGREE	NEUTRAL	SOMEWHAT AGREE	AGREE	TOTALLY AGREE

1. I cannot accomplish my tasks without information or materials from other members of my team. _____

2. Other members of my team depend on me for information or materials needed to perform their tasks. _____

3. Within my team, jobs performed by team members are related to one another. _____

4. My work goals come directly from the goals of my team. _____

5. My work activities on any given day are determined by my team's goals for that day. _____

6. I do very few activities on my job that are not related to the goals of my team. _____

7. Feedback about how well I am doing my job comes primarily from information about how well the entire team is doing. _____

8. Evaluations of my performance are strongly influenced by how well my team performs. _____

9. Many rewards from my work (e.g., pay, grades) are determined in large part by my contributions as a team member. _____

SCORING AND INTERPRETATION

Task Interdependence: Sum up items 1–3. _____

Goal Interdependence: Sum up items 4–6. _____

Outcome Interdependence: Sum up items 7–9. _____

If you scored 14 or above, then your team may be above average on a particular dimension. If you scored 13 or below, then your team may be below average on a particular dimension.

Source: From M.A. Campion, E.M. Papper, and G.J. Medsker, "Relations between Work Team Characteristics and Effectiveness: A Replication and Extension," *Personnel Psychology* 49 (1996), pp. 429–52. Reprinted with permission of John Wiley & Sons, Inc.

The type of task interdependence with the lowest degree of required coordination is **pooled interdependence**.[27] With this type of interdependence, group members complete their work assignments independently, and then this work is simply "piled up" to represent the group's output. Consider what pooled interdependence would be like on a fishing boat. Each person would bait a pole, drop the baited line into the water, reel the fish in, remove the fish from the hook,

FIGURE 11-3 | Task Interdependence and Coordination Requirements

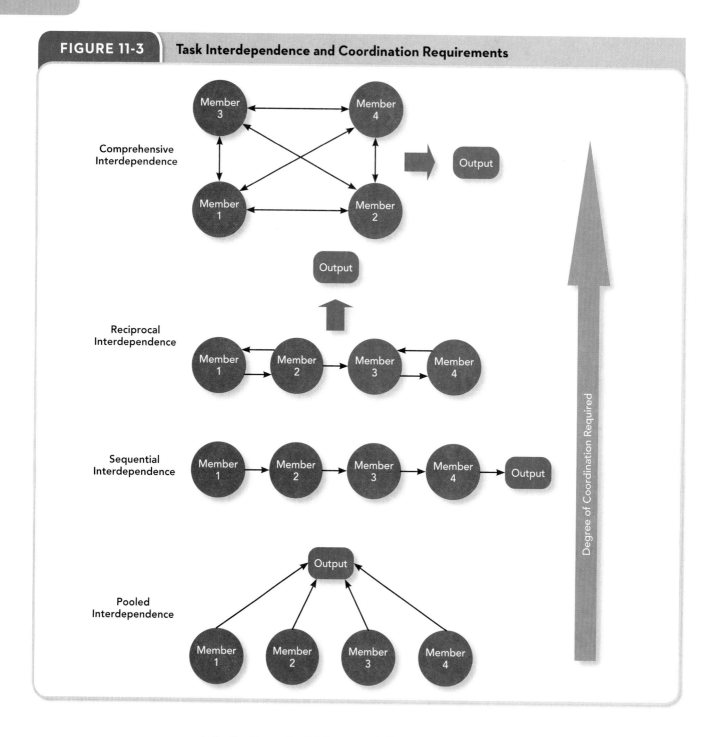

and, finally, throw the fish into a tank filled with ice and other fish. At the end of the day, the boat's production would be the total weight of the fish that were caught.

The next type of task interdependence is called **sequential interdependence**.[28] With this type of interdependence, different tasks are done in a prescribed order, and the group is structured such that the members specialize in these tasks. Although members in groups with sequential interdependence interact to carry out their work, the interaction occurs only between members who perform tasks that are next to each other in the sequence. Moreover, the member performing the task in the latter part of the sequence depends on the member performing the task in the earlier part of the sequence, but not the other way around. The classic assembly line in manufacturing contexts provides an excellent example of this type of interdependence. In this context, an employee attaches a part to the unit being built, and once this is accomplished, the unit moves on to another employee who adds another part. The process typically ends with the unit being inspected and then packaged for shipping.

Reciprocal interdependence is the next type of task interdependence.[29] Similar to sequential interdependence, members are specialized to perform specific tasks. However, instead of a strict sequence of activities, members interact with a subset of other members to complete the team's work. To understand reciprocal interdependence, consider a team of people who are involved in a business that designs custom homes for wealthy clients. After meeting with a client, the salesperson would provide general criteria, structural and aesthetic details, and some rough sketches to an architect who would work up some initial plans and elevations. The architect then would submit the initial plans to the salesperson, who would review the plans with the customer. Typically, the plans need to be revised by the architect several times, and during this process, customers have questions and requests that require the architect to consult with other members of the team. For example, the architect and structural engineer may have to meet to decide where to locate support beams and load-bearing walls. The architect and construction supervisor might also have to meet to discuss revisions to a design feature that turns out to be too costly. As a final example, the salesperson might have to meet with the designers to assist the customer in the selection of additional features, materials, and colors, which would then need to be included in a revision of the plan by the architect.

Finally, **comprehensive interdependence** requires the highest level of interaction and coordination among members as they try to accomplish work.[30] In groups with comprehensive interdependence, each member has a great deal of discretion in terms of what they do and with whom they interact in the course of the collaboration involved in accomplishing the team's work. Teams at IDEO, arguably the world's most successful product design firm, function with comprehensive interdependence. These teams are composed of individuals from very diverse backgrounds, and they meet as a team quite often to share knowledge and ideas to solve problems related to their design projects.[31]

It's important to note that there's no one right way to design teams with respect to task interdependence. However, it's also important to recognize the trade-offs associated with the different types. On the one hand, as the level of task interdependence increases, members must spend increasing amounts of time communicating and coordinating with other members to complete tasks. This type of coordination can result in decreases in productivity, which is the ratio of work completed per the amount of time worked. On the other hand, increases in task interdependence increase the ability of the team to adapt to new situations. The more members interact and communicate with other members, the more likely it is that the team will be able to devise solutions to novel problems it may face.

GOAL INTERDEPENDENCE In addition to being linked to one another by task activities, members may be linked by their goals.[32] A high degree of **goal interdependence** exists when team members have a shared vision of the team's goal and align their individual goals with that vision as a result.[33] To understand the power of goal interdependence, visualize a small boat with several people on board, each with a paddle.[34] If each person on the boat wants to go to the exact same place on the other side of a lake, they will all row in the same direction, and the boat will arrive at the desired location. If, however, each person believes the boat should go someplace different, each person will row in a different direction, and the boat will have major problems getting anywhere. In most team contexts, there are asymmetries in the goals of individual team members that interfere with the pursuit of team goals, and what makes managing this situation difficult is that team members often don't become aware of the incompatibilities until it's too late.[35]

So how do you create high levels of goal interdependence? One thing to do would be to ensure that the team has a formalized mission statement that members buy into. Mission statements can

Face-to-face team meetings that involve comprehensive interdependence can consume a lot of time, yet these meetings are an important part of accomplishing work that requires collaboration.

© Digital Vision/Getty Images RF

take a variety of forms, but good ones clearly describe what the team is trying to accomplish in a way that creates a sense of commitment and urgency among team members.[36] Mission statements can come directly from the organization or team leaders, but in many circumstances, it makes more sense for teams to go through the process of developing their own mission statements. This process not only helps members identify important team goals and the actions the team needs to take to achieve these goals, but it also increases feelings of ownership toward the mission statement itself. Table 11-2 describes a set of recommended steps that teams can take to develop their own mission statements.[37]

Although you might believe that the mission for some team tasks is very obvious, all too often this isn't the case. In student teams, for example, you might expect that the obvious goal in the minds of the team members would be to learn the course material. However, it's typically the case that students come to a team with individual goals that are surprisingly different, and they may never realize their goals are different because they don't talk about them. Some students might be more interested in "just getting by" with a passing grade because they already have a job and just need their degree. Other students might want to do well in the course, but are more concerned with maintaining balance with the demands of their lives outside of school. Finally, other students might be focused solely on their grades, perhaps because they want to get into a prestigious graduate school in an unrelated discipline. Of course, the problem here is that each of these goals is associated with a different approach to working in the team. Students who want to learn the course material will work hard on the team assignments and will want to spend extra time discussing assignment-related issues with teammates, students who just want to get by will do the minimum amount of work, students who want to maintain their work–life balance will look for the most efficient way to do things, and students who are focused on their grades would be willing to take shortcuts that might inhibit learning. Although trying to reach a consensus on a team mission may not be easy in a situation in which the members have goals that vary along

---

TABLE 11-2   **The Mission Statement Development Process**

Steps in Mission Statement Development

1. The team should meet in a room where there can be uninterrupted discussion for 1–3 hours.
2. A facilitator should describe the purpose of a mission statement, along with important details that members of the team should consider. Those details may include the products, outcomes, or services that the team is responsible for providing, as well as relevant time constraints.
3. The team should brainstorm to identify potential phrases or elements to include in the mission statement.
4. If the team is large enough, subgroups should be formed to create "first draft" mission statements. Those mission statements should include action verbs and be no more than four sentences.
5. The subgroups should share the first drafts with one another.
6. The team should then try to integrate the best ideas into a single mission statement.
7. The resulting mission statement should be evaluated using the following criteria:
   Clarity—It should focus clearly on a single key purpose.
   Relevance—It should focus on something that is desired by the team members.
   Significance—If achieved, there are benefits that excite the members.
   Believability—It reflects something that members believe they can achieve.
   Urgency—It creates a sense of challenge and commitment.
8. The team should then revise any weak areas of the mission statement. The team should continue to work on the mission statement until there is consensus that it inspires dedication and commitment among members toward a common purpose.

these lines, research has shown that teams of students experience significantly greater effectiveness if they invest time and effort doing so soon after the team first forms.[38]

OUTCOME INTERDEPENDENCE. The final type of interdependence relates to how members are linked to one another in terms of the feedback and outcomes they receive as a consequence of working in the team.[39] A high degree of **outcome interdependence** exists when team members share in the rewards that the team earns, with reward examples including pay, bonuses, formal feedback and recognition, pats on the back, extra time off, and continued team survival. Of course, because team achievement depends on the performance of each team member, high outcome interdependence also implies that team members depend on the performance of other team members for the rewards that they receive. In contrast, low outcome interdependence exists in teams in which individual members receive rewards and punishments on the basis of their own individual performance, without regard to the performance of the team. Research on project teams involved in consulting, financial planning, and research and development has shown that higher levels of outcome interdependence increase the amount of information shared among members, which promotes learning, and, ultimately, team performance.[40] As we discuss in the Application section at the end of this chapter, the way a team is designed with respect to outcome interdependence also has important implications for the level of cooperation and motivation in the team. See our **OB on Screen** feature for an extreme example of outcome interdependence.

TEAM COMPOSITION

You probably already have a sense that team effectiveness hinges on **team composition**—or the mix of people who make up the team. If you've been a member of a particularly effective team, you may have noticed that the team seemed to have the right mix of knowledge, skills, abilities, and personalities. Team members were not only capable of performing their role responsibilities effectively, but they also cooperated and got along fairly well together. In this section, we identify the most important characteristics to consider in team composition, and we describe how these elements combine to influence team functioning and effectiveness. As shown in Figure 11-4, five aspects of team composition are crucial: roles, ability, personality, diversity, and team size.

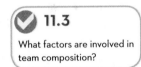

11.3

What factors are involved in team composition?

MEMBER ROLES. A **role** is defined as a pattern of behavior that a person is expected to display in a given context.[41] In a team setting, there are a variety of roles that members can take or develop in the course of interacting with one another, and depending on the specific situation, the presence or absence of members who possess these roles may have a strong impact on team effectiveness.[42] One obvious way that roles can be distinguished is by considering the specific sets of task-focused activities that define what the individual members are expected to do for their team.

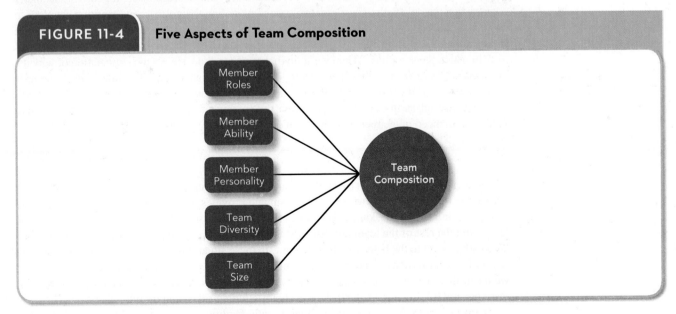

FIGURE 11-4 | **Five Aspects of Team Composition**

OB   ON SCREEN

AVENGERS: AGE OF ULTRON

We're the Avengers. We can bust arms dealers all the live long day, but that up there, that's...that's the end game.

With those words, Iron Man Tony Stark (Robert Downey Jr.) reveals his skepticism that his team can defeat an all-powerful villain, in the *Avengers: Age of Ultron* (Dir. Joss Whedon, Marvel Studios, 2015). Tony and The Hulk Bruce Banner (Mark Ruffalo) conspired to activate a dormant computer program called Ultron (James Spader) in order to bring peace to the world. Unfortunately, Ultron takes on a life of its own and seeks global extinction as a means of ridding the world of humans, who it believes are the source of all the world's problems. The other Avengers—Thor (Chris Hemsworth), Captain America Steve Rogers (Chris Evans), Black Widow Natasha Romanoff (Scarlett Johansson), and Hawkeye Clint Barton (Jeremy Renner)—are not happy with Tony and Bruce when their transgression is discovered.

© *Walt Disney Studios Motion Pictures/Photofest*

Fortunately, the Avengers realize that they need to function as a team to deal with what appears to be an insurmountable threat in Ultron. What inspires this realization? Tony asks the obvious question, "how are you guys planning on beating that?" Steve's response, "together," succinctly conveys that the only path to success involves them pooling their efforts and working shoulder to shoulder. None of the Avengers is powerful enough on their own—they need to cooperate with each other and to combine their unique skills and powers. Tony then states that the Avengers will lose, to which Steve replies, "Then we'll do that together, too." Here's the explanation of why it's in everyone's best interest that they pull together and fight as a team. The fate of each member is tied such that if the team fails to achieve the goal of defeating Ultron, they will all die (as will everyone else on earth). At this point, even the somewhat egotistical and self-absorbed Tony Stark is convinced in the merits of the team concept.

Another way to distinguish roles is to consider what leaders and members do. In **leader–staff teams**, the leader makes decisions for the team and provides direction and control over members who perform assigned tasks, so this distinction makes sense in that the responsibilities of the leader and the rest of the team are distinct.[43] Typically, however, team members have some latitude with respect to the behaviors they exhibit. In these situations, team roles can be described in terms of categories that are more general than the task-focused roles described earlier. By general, we mean that these roles can apply to many different types of teams. As shown in Table 11-3, these general roles include team task roles, team-building roles, and individualistic roles.[44]

Team task roles refer to behaviors that directly facilitate the accomplishment of team tasks. Examples include the *orienter* who establishes the direction for the team, the *devil's advocate* who offers constructive challenges to the team's status quo, and the *energizer* who motivates team members to work harder toward team goals. As you may have realized, the importance of specific task-oriented roles depends on the nature of the work in which the team is involved. The orienter role may be particularly important in teams that have autonomy over how to accomplish their work. The devil's advocate role may be particularly important in team contexts in which decisions are "high stakes" in nature. Finally, the energizer role may be most important in team contexts in which the work is important but not intrinsically motivating.

In contrast to task-oriented roles, **team-building roles** refer to behaviors that influence the quality of the team's social climate. A member who lightens things up during a contentious team meeting by doing something humorous is fulfilling a team-building role. Indeed, the simple act of telling a joke may foster additional humor and, in turn, a positive climate that enhances team functioning and performance.[45] Specific examples of team-building roles include the *harmonizer* who steps in to resolve differences among teammates, the *encourager* who praises the work of teammates, and the *compromiser* who helps the team see alternative solutions that teammates can accept. In sum, and as you may have gathered as you read these examples, the presence of members who take on team-building roles helps teams manage conflicts that could hinder team effectiveness.

TABLE 11-3   Team and Individualistic Roles

TEAM TASK ROLES	DESCRIPTION
Initiator-contributor	Proposes new ideas
Coordinator	Tries to coordinate activities among team members
Orienter	Determines the direction of the team's discussion
Devil's advocate	Offers challenges to the team's status quo
Energizer	Motivates the team to strive to do better
Procedural-technician	Performs routine tasks needed to keep progress moving
TEAM-BUILDING ROLES	**DESCRIPTION**
Encourager	Praises the contributions of other team members
Harmonizer	Mediates differences between group members
Compromiser	Attempts to find the halfway point to end conflict
Gatekeeper-expediter	Encourages participation from teammates
Standard setter	Expresses goals for the team to achieve
Follower	Accepts the ideas of teammates
INDIVIDUALISTIC ROLES	**DESCRIPTION**
Aggressor	Deflates teammates, expresses disapproval with hostility
Blocker	Acts stubbornly resistant and disagrees beyond reason
Recognition seeker	Brags and calls attention to himself or herself
Self-confessor	Discloses personal opinions inappropriately
Slacker	Acts cynically, or nonchalantly, or goofs off
Dominator	Manipulates team members for personal control

Source: Adapted from K. Benne and P. Sheats, "Functional Roles of Group Members," *Journal of Social Issues* 4 (1948), pp. 41–49.

Finally, whereas task roles and team-building roles focus on activities that benefit the team, **individualistic roles** reflect behaviors that benefit the individual at the expense of the team. For example, the *aggressor* "puts down" or deflates fellow teammates. The *recognition seeker* takes credit for team successes. The *dominator* manipulates teammates to acquire control and power. If you've ever had an experience in a team in which members took on individualistic roles, you probably realize just how damaging they can be to the team. Individualistic role behaviors foster negative feelings among team members, which serve to hinder a team's ability to function and perform effectively.[46] For an example of an individual who engaged in all the right team role behaviors, see our **OB at the Bookstore** feature.

MEMBER ABILITY. Team members possess a wide variety of abilities (see Chapter 10 on ability for more discussion of such issues). Depending on the nature of the tasks involved in the team's work, some of these may be important to consider in team design. For example, for teams involved in physical work, relevant physical abilities will be important to take into account. Consider the types of abilities that are required of pit crew members in stock car racing, where margins of victory can be one-tenth of a second. When a car pulls into pit row, crew members

OB AT THE BOOKSTORE

THE HARD HAT

by Jon Gordon (Hoboken, NJ: John Wiley and Sons, Inc., 2015).

Guys worked hard because they knew George was working hard. He pushed everyone to work harder and get better without saying a word. He didn't have to. They saw how he went about his business.

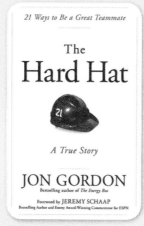

21 Ways to Be a Great Teammate

The
Hard Hat

A True Story

JON GORDON
Bestselling author of *The Energy Bus*

Foreword by JEREMY SCHAAP
Bestselling Author and Emmy Award-Winning Commentator for ESPN

Photo of cover: © Roberts Publishing Services

With those words, Jon Gordon describes the role that George Boiardi played on his Cornell lacrosse team. Specifically, he was a role model for his teammates, someone who led by example, and who very much deserved to carry the hard hat that, even today, symbolizes the team's blue-collar mentality; a set of values grounded in hard work and selflessness on and off the field. Gordon explains that Boiardi was a gifted athlete but that his most important contributions to his team came in the form of being a phenomenal team player. He was quiet, humble, and worked harder than anyone else. He didn't care about his personal statistics, he would rather pass the ball to an open teammate than take a more risky shot if it might help his team. He was the first one to practice and the last to leave. In essence, he did all the right things, and this made his teammates strive to do the right things. Unfortunately, on March 24, 2004, Boiardi took a ball to the chest while defending the goal during a game against Binghamton University, and died soon thereafter.

In the second half of the book, Gordon distills stories of Boiardi's days at Cornell from players and coaches into 21 lessons to be a great teammate (it just so happens that Boiardi wore number 21). These lessons correspond in many ways to the team roles discussed here in this chapter. For example, the book describes how Boiardi served the role of "energizer" with example of his relentless hard work during practice and games. The book also provides examples of how he served team-building roles with his kindness, respect, compassion and positive energy. Finally, the book explains that Boiardi did not engage in individualistic role behaviors. Instead, his behavior reflected humility and self-sacrifice. Although many of the 21 lessons seem familiar, the examples provide vivid reminders of their importance to team effectiveness.

need to leap over the pit wall and lift heavy tires, jacks, and other equipment to get the race car back on the track—ideally in about 14 seconds. In this setting, flexibility, cardiovascular endurance, and explosive strength are required, and in fact, racing teams have hired professional trainers and even built gyms to improve these abilities of their pit crew members.[47]

It's also important to take cognitive abilities into account when designing teams. General cognitive ability is important to many different types of teams. In general, smarter teams perform better because teamwork tends to be quite complex.[48] Team members not only have to be involved in several different aspects of the team's task, but they also have to learn how best to combine their individual efforts to accomplish team goals.[49] In fact, the more that this type of learning is required, the more important member cognitive ability becomes. For example, research has shown that cognitive ability is more important to teams when team members have to learn from one another to adapt to unexpected changes, compared with contexts in which team members perform their assigned tasks in a routine fashion.[50]

Of course, not every member needs high levels of these physical or cognitive abilities. If you've ever played Trivial Pursuit using teams, you might recall playing against another team in which only one of the team members was smart enough to answer any of the questions correctly. In fact, in tasks with an objectively verifiable best solution, the member who possesses the highest level of the ability relevant to the task will have the most influence on the effectiveness of the team. These types of tasks are called **disjunctive tasks**.[51] You may also recall situations in which it was crucial that everyone on the team possessed the relevant abilities. Returning to the pit crew example, stock cars cannot leave the pit area until all the tires are mounted, and so the length of the pit stop is determined by the physical abilities of the slowest crew member. Tasks like this, for which the team's performance depends on the abilities of the "weakest link," are called **conjunctive tasks**. Finally, there are **additive tasks**, for which the contributions resulting from the abilities of every member "add up" to determine team performance. The amount of money that a Girl Scout troop earns from selling Thin Mints and Samoas is the sum of what each Girl Scout is able to sell on her own.

MEMBER PERSONALITY. Team members also possess a wide variety of personality traits (see Chapter 9 on personality and cultural values for more discussion of such issues). These personality traits affect the roles that team members take on,[52] the norms that develop on the team,[53] and ultimately, how teams function and perform as units.[54] For example, the agreeableness of team members has an important influence on team effectiveness.[55] Why? Because agreeable people tend to be more cooperative and trusting, and these tendencies promote positive attitudes about the team and smooth interpersonal interactions. Moreover, because agreeable people may be more concerned about their team's interests than their own, they should work hard on behalf of the team.[56] There's a caveat regarding agreeableness in teams, however. Because agreeable people tend to prefer harmony and cooperation rather than conflict and competition, they may be less apt to speak up and offer constructive criticisms that might help the team improve.[57] Thus, if a team is composed of too many highly agreeable members, there's a chance that the members will behave in a way that enhances harmony of the team at the expense of task accomplishment.[58]

As another example, team composition in terms of members' conscientiousness is important to teams.[59] After all, almost any team would benefit from having members who tend to be dependable and work hard to achieve team goals. What might be less obvious to you is the strong negative effect on the team of having even one member who is particularly low on conscientiousness.[60] To understand why this is true, consider how you would react to a team member who was not dependable and did not appear to be motivated to work hard toward team goals. If you're like most people, you would find the situation dissatisfying, and you would consider different ways of dealing with it. Some people might try to motivate the person to be more responsible and work harder; others might try to get the person ejected from the team.[61] The problem is that these natural reactions to a low conscientiousness team member not only divert attention away from accomplishing work responsibilities, but they also can result in some very uncomfortable and time-consuming interpersonal conflicts. Moreover, even if you and the other members of the team work harder to compensate for this person, it would be difficult for your team to perform as effectively as other teams in which all members are more interpersonally responsible and engaged in the team's work.

A task that can go only as quickly as the slowest team member, like a pit stop in a car race, is a conjunctive task.

© *George Tiedmann/Corbis*

Finally, the personality characteristic of extraversion is relevant to team composition.[62] People who are extraverted tend to perform more effectively in interpersonal contexts and are more positive and optimistic in general.[63] Therefore, it shouldn't surprise you to read that having extraverted team members is generally beneficial to the social climate of the group, as well as to team effectiveness in the eyes of supervisors.[64] At the same time, however, research has shown that having too many members who are very high on extraversion can hurt the team. The reason for this can be attributed to extraverts' tendency to be assertive and dominant. As you would expect when there are too many members with these types of tendencies, power struggles and unproductive conflict occur with greater frequency.[65]

11.4

What are the types of team diversity and how do they influence team functioning?

DIVERSITY. Another aspect of team composition refers to the degree to which members are different from one another in terms of any attribute that might be used by someone as a basis of categorizing people. We refer to those differences as **team diversity**.[66] Trying to understand the effects of team diversity is somewhat difficult because there are so many different characteristics that may be used to categorize people. Beyond obvious differences among people in their physical appearance, there can be separation among members in terms of their values and beliefs, variety among members in their knowledge and expertise, and disparity among members in their social status, power, and even their sense of time urgency and the way they like to pace their work.[67] Moreover, diversity of team member characteristics may matter more or less depending on the nature of the team and organizational context.[68] For example, you might imagine how the dynamics in a team consisting of both men and women could vary depending on whether the team is in an organization dominated by men (or women) or whether it's balanced in terms of the employees' sex. Finally, there are multiple reasons different types of diversity influence team functioning and effectiveness, and some of these reasons seem contradictory.[69]

One predominant theory that has been used to explain why diversity has positive effects is called the **value in diversity problem-solving approach**.[70] According to this perspective, diversity in teams is beneficial because it provides for a larger pool of knowledge and perspectives from which a team can draw as it carries out its work.[71] Having greater diversity in knowledge perspectives stimulates the exchange of information, which in turn fosters learning among team members.[72] The knowledge that results from this learning is then shared and integrated with the knowledge of other members, ultimately helping the team perform more effectively.[73] Research has shown that these benefits of diversity are more likely to occur when the team includes members who are able and willing to put in the effort necessary to understand and integrate different perspectives.[74] Teams that engage in work that's relatively complex and requires creativity tend to benefit most from diversity, and research on teams that are diverse in terms of many different characteristics related to knowledge and perspectives—ethnicity, expertise, personality, attitudes—supports this idea.[75]

A theory that's been used widely to explain why diversity may have detrimental effects on teams is called the **similarity-attraction approach**.[76] According to this perspective, people tend to be more attracted to others who are perceived as more similar. People also tend to avoid interacting with those who are perceived to be dissimilar, to reduce the likelihood of having uncomfortable disagreements. Consis-

© Bethean/Corbis RF

Surface-level diversity can sometimes create issues for teams as they begin their tasks, but such problems usually disappear over time.

tent with this perspective, research has shown that diversity on attributes such as cultural background, race, and attitudes are associated with communication problems and ultimately poor team effectiveness.[77]

So it appears that there are two different theories about diversity effects that are relevant to teams, and each has been supported in research. Which perspective is correct? As it turns out, a key to understanding the impact of team diversity requires that you consider both the general type of diversity and the length of time the team has been in existence.[78]

Surface-level diversity refers to diversity regarding observable attributes such as race, ethnicity, sex, and age.[79] Although this type of diversity may have a negative impact on teams early in their existence because of similarity-attraction issues, those negative effects tend to disappear as members become more knowledgeable about one another. In essence, the stereotypes that members have about one another based on surface differences are replaced with knowledge regarding underlying characteristics that are more relevant to social and task interactions.[80]

One complication here is that *fault lines* often occur in diverse groups, whereby informal subgroups develop based on similarity in surface-level attributes such as gender or other characteristics.[81] The problem with fault lines is that knowledge and information possessed by one subgroup may not be communicated to other subgroups in a manner that might help the entire team perform more effectively. In a study of boards of directors, for example, the presence of strong fault lines decreased the amount of discussion that board members had with each other in regards to entrepreneurial issues that could affect their companies.[82] Research has shown, however, that the effects of subgroups depends on the type of subgroup, and that detrimental effects of having subgroups can be offset with training that reinforces the idea that teams may benefit from their diversity.[83] Leadership or reward practices that reinforce the value of sharing information and promote a strong sense of team identity also help diverse teams perform more effectively.[84]

Deep-level diversity, in contrast, refers to diversity with respect to attributes that are less easy to observe initially but that can be inferred after more direct experience. Differences in attitudes, values, and personality are good examples of deep-level diversity.[85] In contrast to the effects of surface-level diversity, time appears to increase the negative effects of deep-level diversity on team functioning and effectiveness.[86] Over time, as team members learn more about one another, differences that relate to underlying values and goals become increasingly apparent. Those differences can therefore create problems among team members that ultimately result in reduced effectiveness.

Fortunately, it appears that the negative effects of deep-level diversity can be managed.[87] As an example, diversity in members' approach to pursing goals has been shown to hinder team functioning and effectiveness, but this effect can be reduced if teams are instructed to take the time to reflect on their progress toward goals and their strategies.[88] Deep-level diversity has also been shown to have positive effects on team creativity when members are instructed to take the perspective of their teammates.[89] As another example, negative effects of deep-level diversity with respect to members' values have been found to be reduced when team leaders emphasize the teams' task and provide explicit direction regarding team procedures, standards, roles, and expectations.[90] We should also point out, however, that team leaders can also exacerbate problems associated with deep-level diversity. Conflict that results from diversity in members' values appears to increase in teams with leaders who emphasize things like freedom of expression and

OB INTERNATIONALLY

Businesses are increasingly using teams composed of members from different cultures, and so teams today often possess members who differ from one another in terms of their attitudes, values, ideas, goals, and behaviors. These types of teams, called *multicultural teams,* can approach problems from several different perspectives, which opens the door to highly innovative solutions. Cultural diversity also allows teams to serve a diverse customer base that may differ in terms of culture and nationality.

Unfortunately, the attributes that give multicultural teams these advantages also give them disadvantages. As an example, people from different cultures communicate differently, which can lead to misunderstandings. For example, to people in the United States, the phrase "to table something" means to put it off until later, whereas to people in some European countries, it means discuss it right now. Imagine your reaction if you didn't know this difference, and you told a team you were leading that you wanted to table something, and then one of your team members started to discuss options and recommendations about the issue. There are differences in the directness of communications as well. Westerners tend to be very direct and to the point, but to people in other countries, such as Japan, this directness may cause embarrassment and a sense of disrespect. There are also cultural differences in decision-making processes. In some cultures, decisions can be made only after careful consideration and reconsideration of all relevant issues, which is much different from the style in other cultures, such as the United States, where decisions are made rather quickly and with less analysis. Although these differences might seem trivial, they often lead to misunderstandings that reduce the willingness of team members to cooperate.

So how can multicultural teams be managed to ensure the advantages outweigh the disadvantages? Although there's no one best way to manage multicultural teams, one proven approach is to encourage team members to take the time to communicate openly with each other about cultural differences and to proactively develop strategies the team can use to accommodate them.

Sources: J. Brett, K. Behfar, and M.C. Kern, "Managing Multicultural Teams," *Harvard Business Review* 84 (November 2006), pp. 84–91; S. Gupta, "Mine the Potential of Multicultural Teams: Mesh Cultural Differences to Enhance Productivity," *HR Magazine* (October 2008), pp. 79–84; M. Harris, *Cultural Anthropology,* 2nd ed. (New York: Harper and Row, 1987); and H.C. Triandis, *Culture and Social Behavior* (New York: McGraw-Hill, 1994).

participation.[91] See our **OB Internationally** feature for a discussion of the challenges of managing deep-level diversity in teams that include members from different cultures.

We also should mention an important caveat here. Although personality is normally considered a deep-level diversity variable,[92] some specific personality types do not function this way.[93] In the previous section on personality, for example, we pointed out that though having team members who are extraverted and agreeable is generally a good thing, problems arise if a team has too many members with these attributes. So whereas diversity on most deep-level characteristics is problematic for teams, this claim does not apply to extraversion and agreeableness, because for these two personality characteristics, teams are likely to benefit from having a mix of members.

TEAM SIZE. Two adages are relevant to team size: "the more the merrier" and "too many cooks spoil the pot." Which statement do you believe is true in terms of how many members to include on a team? The answer, according to the results of one meta-analysis, is that having a greater number of members is beneficial for management and project teams but not for teams engaged in production tasks.[94] Management and project teams engage in work that's complex and knowledge intensive, and these teams therefore benefit from the additional resources and expertise contributed by additional members.[95] In contrast, production teams tend to engage in routine tasks that are less complex. Having additional members beyond what's necessary to accomplish the work tends to result in unnecessary coordination and communication problems. Additional members therefore may be less productive because there's more socializing, and they feel less accountable for team outcomes.[96] Although making a claim about the absolute best team size is impossible, research with undergraduate students concluded that team members tend to be most satisfied with their team when the number of members is between four and five.[97] Of course, there are other rules of thumb you can use to keep team size optimal. Jeff Bezos, the CEO of Amazon.com, uses the two-pizza rule: "If a team can't be fed by two pizzas, it's too large."[98]

SUMMARY: WHAT CHARACTERISTICS CAN BE USED TO DESCRIBE TEAMS?

The preceding sections illustrate that there are a variety of characteristics that can be used to describe teams. As Figure 11-5 illustrates, teams can be described using taxonomies of team types. For example, teams can be described by categorizing them as a work team, a management team, a parallel team, a project team, or an action team. Teams can also be described using the nature of the team's interdependence with regard to its task, goals, and outcomes. Finally, teams can be described in terms of their composition. Relevant member characteristics include member roles, member ability, member personality, member diversity, and team size.

FIGURE 11-5 | **What Characteristics Can Be Used to Describe Teams?**

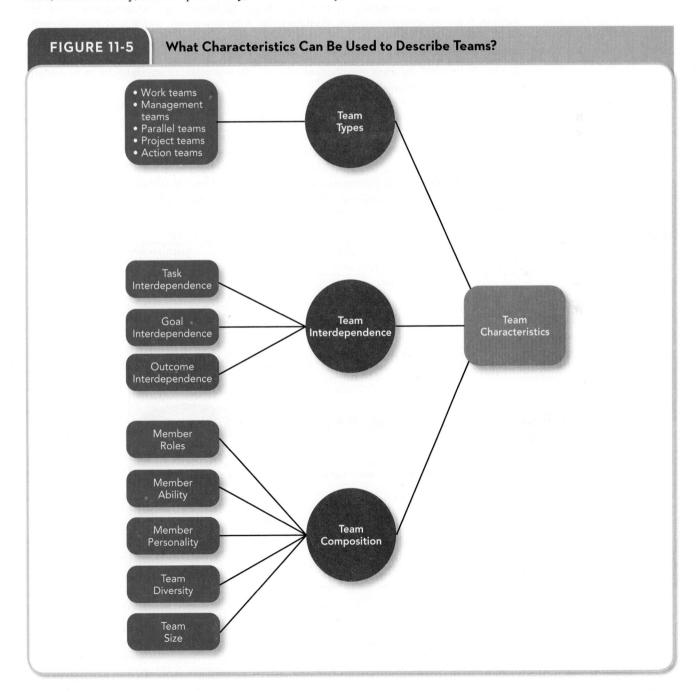

HOW IMPORTANT ARE TEAM CHARACTERISTICS?

In previous chapters, we have described individual characteristics and mechanisms and discussed how these variables affect individual performance and commitment. In this chapter, we're concerned with team characteristics, and so naturally, we're interested in how they influence team effectiveness. One aspect of team effectiveness is *team performance,* which may include metrics such as the quantity and quality of goods or services produced, customer satisfaction, the effectiveness or accuracy of decisions, victories, completed reports, and successful investigations. Team performance in the context of student project teams most often means the quality with which the team completes assignments and projects, as well as the grades they earn.

A second aspect of team effectiveness is team commitment, which is sometimes called *team viability.* **Team viability** refers to the likelihood that the team can work together effectively into the future.[99] If the team experience is not satisfying, members may become disillusioned and focus their energy on activities away from the team. Although a team with low viability might be able to work together on short-term projects, over the long run, a team such as this is bound to have significant problems.[100] Rather than planning for future tasks and working through issues that might improve the team, members of a team with low viability are more apt to be looking ahead to the team's ultimate demise.

Of course, it's difficult to summarize the relationship between team characteristics and team performance and commitment when there are so many characteristics that can be used to describe teams. Here we focus our discussion on the impact of task interdependence. We focus on task interdependence because it's one of the most important characteristics that distinguishes true teams from mere groups of individuals. As Figure 11-6 shows, it turns out that the relationship between task interdependence and team performance is moderately positive.[101] That is, task performance tends to be higher in teams in which members depend on one another and have

11.5

How do team characteristics influence team effectiveness?

FIGURE 11-6 | **Effects of Task Interdependence on Performance and Commitment**

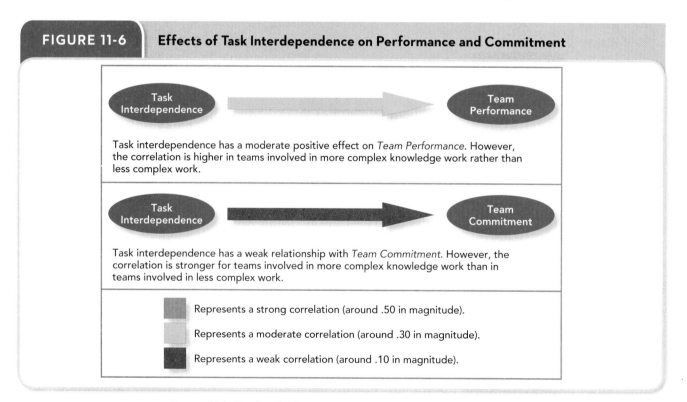

Task interdependence has a moderate positive effect on *Team Performance.* However, the correlation is higher in teams involved in more complex knowledge work rather than less complex work.

Task interdependence has a weak relationship with *Team Commitment.* However, the correlation is stronger for teams involved in more complex knowledge work than in teams involved in less complex work.

Represents a strong correlation (around .50 in magnitude).

Represents a moderate correlation (around .30 in magnitude).

Represents a weak correlation (around .10 in magnitude).

Sources: M.A. Campion, G.J. Medsker, and A.C. Higgs, "Relations between Work Group Characteristics and Effectiveness: Implications for Designing Effective Work Groups," *Personnel Psychology* 46 (1993), pp. 823–49; M.A. Campion, E.M. Papper, and G.J. Medsker, "Relations between Work Team Characteristics and Effectiveness: A Replication and Extension," *Personnel Psychology* 49 (1996), pp. 429–52; and G.L. Stewart, "A Meta-Analytic Review of Relationships between Team Design Features and Team Performance," *Journal of Management* 32 (2006), pp. 29–54.

to coordinate their activities rather than when members work more or less independently. It's important to mention that the relationship between task interdependence and team performance is significantly stronger in teams that are responsible for completing complex knowledge work rather than simple tasks. When work is more complex, interdependence is necessary because there's a need for members to interact and share resources and information. When work is simple, sharing information and resources is less necessary because members can do the work by themselves.

In the lower portion of Figure 11-6, you can see that the relationship between task interdependence and team commitment is weaker.[102] Teams with higher task interdependence have only a slightly higher probability of including members who are committed to their team's continued existence. As with the relationship with team performance, task interdependence has a stronger effect on viability for teams doing complex knowledge work. Apparently, sharing resources and information in a context in which it's unnecessary is dissatisfying to members and results in a team with reduced prospects of continued existence.

APPLICATION: TEAM COMPENSATION

Although all team characteristics have implications for managerial practices, outcome interdependence is particularly relevant for two reasons. First, outcome interdependence has obvious connections to compensation practices in organizations,[103] and most of us are interested in factors that determine how we get paid. If you work for an organization with compensation that has high outcome interdependence, a higher percentage of your pay will depend on how well your team does. If you work for an organization with compensation that has low outcome interdependence, a lower percentage of your pay will depend on how well your team does.

A second reason outcome interdependence is important to consider is that it presents managers with a tough dilemma. High outcome interdependence promotes higher levels of cooperation because members understand that they share the same fate—if the team wins, everyone wins, and if the team fails, everyone fails.[104] At the same time, high outcome interdependence may result in reduced motivation, especially among higher performing members. High performers may perceive that they're not paid in proportion to what they contributed to the team and that their teammates are taking advantage of this inequity for their own benefit.[105]

One solution to this dilemma has been to design team reward structures with **hybrid outcome interdependence**, which means that members receive rewards that are dependent on both their team's performance and how well they perform as individuals.[106] In fact, the majority of organizations that use teams use some sort of hybrid outcome interdependence. But what percentage of team members' pay is typically based on team performance in business organizations? This is a difficult question to answer, because as we discussed earlier in the chapter, there are so many different types of teams doing so many different types of tasks, and also because organizations vary dramatically in their approaches to rewarding their employees. For example, the size of team-based pay in the goods and service sectors averages around 10–12 percent of an employee's base pay.[107] In contrast, production workers at Nucor, the Crawfordsville, Indiana–based steel company, earn team-based bonuses of 170 percent of their base pay, on average.[108] It's important to note that hybrid outcome interdependence, in and of itself, may not always be that effective in promoting team functioning and effectiveness. Research conducted at Xerox, for example, shows that service teams with hybrid outcome interdependence are less effective than service teams with very high or very low levels of outcome interdependence.[109] Part of the problem with hybrid outcome interdependence is that it can lead to uncertainty about which types of behaviors are being rewarded and how pay ultimately is determined. To make hybrid interdependence work, organizations need to ensure that the system makes sense to employees. At Nucor, most production workers know within one-tenth of 1 percent what the team's bonus is for the week, as well as which products will be produced next and how these future operations will likely affect their bonuses.[110]

One way to resolve the dilemma of outcome interdependence is to implement a level of team-based pay that matches the level of task interdependence. Members tend to be more productive in

11.6

How can team compensation be used to manage team effectiveness?

high task interdependence situations when there's also high outcome interdependence. Similarly, members prefer low task interdependent situations when there's low outcome interdependence.[111] To understand the power of aligning task and outcome interdependence, consider scenarios in which there's not a good match. For example, how would you react to a situation in which you worked very closely with your teammates on a team project in one of your classes, and though your professor said the team's project was outstanding, she awarded an A to one of your team members, a B to another, and a C to you? Similarly, consider how you would react to a situation in which you scored enough points for an A on your final exam, but your professor averaged everyone's grades together and gave all students a C. Chances are you wouldn't be happy with either scenario.

TAKEAWAYS

11.1 There are several different types of teams—work teams, management teams, action teams, project teams, and parallel teams—but many teams in organizations have characteristics that fit in multiple categories and differ from one another in other ways.

11.2 Teams can be interdependent in terms of the team task, goals, and outcomes. Each type of interdependence has important implications for team functioning and effectiveness.

11.3 Team composition refers to the characteristics of the members who work in the team. These characteristics include roles, ability, personality, and member diversity, as well as the number of team members.

11.4 The effect of diversity on the team depends on time and whether the diversity is surface level or deep level. The effects of surface-level diversity tend to diminish with time, whereas the effects of deep-level diversity tend to increase over time.

11.5 Task interdependence has a moderate positive relationship with team performance and a weak relationship with team commitment.

11.6 Outcome interdependence has important effects on teams, which can be managed with compensation practices that take team performance into account.

KEY TERMS

- Team   p. 340
- Work team   p. 342
- Management team   p. 342
- Parallel team   p. 343
- Project team   p. 343
- Action team   p. 343
- Virtual team   p. 344
- Forming   p. 345
- Storming   p. 346
- Norming   p. 346
- Performing   p. 346
- Adjourning   p. 346
- Punctuated equilibrium   p. 346
- Task interdependence   p. 346
- Pooled interdependence   p. 347
- Sequential interdependence   p. 348
- Reciprocal interdependence   p. 349
- Comprehensive interdependence p. 349
- Goal interdependence   p. 349
- Outcome interdependence   p. 351
- Team composition   p. 351
- Role   p. 351
- Leader–staff teams   p. 351
- Team task roles   p. 351
- Team-building roles   p. 352
- Individualistic roles   p. 354
- Disjunctive tasks   p. 355
- Conjunctive tasks   p. 355
- Additive tasks   p. 355
- Team diversity   p. 356
- Value in diversity problem-solving approach   p. 356
- Similarity-attraction approach   p. 357
- Surface-level diversity   p. 357
- Deep-level diversity   p. 357
- Team viability   p. 360
- Hybrid outcome interdependence   p. 361

DISCUSSION QUESTIONS

11.1 In which types of teams have you worked? Were these teams consistent with the taxonomy of team types discussed in this chapter, or were they a combination of types?

11.2 Think about your student teams. Which aspects of both models of team development apply the most and least to teams in this context? Do you think these teams function best in an additive, disjunctive, or conjunctive manner? What are the advantages and disadvantages of each structure?

11.3 Think about a highly successful team with which you are familiar. What types of task, goal, and outcome interdependence does this team have? Describe how changes in task, goal, and outcome interdependence might have a negative impact on this team.

11.4 What type of roles do you normally take on in a team setting? Are there task or social roles that you simply don't perform well? If so, why do you think this is?

11.5 How would you describe your student team in terms of its diversity? In what ways would there be advantages and disadvantages to increasing its diversity? How might you be able to manage some of the disadvantages so that your team is able to capitalize on the potential advantages?

CASE: LUFTHANSA

Although fatal crashes are exceedingly rare in aviation—approximately one fatality for every 1.3 million flights—they're highly visible. They're also quite memorable in the minds of potential customers who have choices when making travel plans. Based on examinations of fatality records, incident reports, and audits from aviation associations and governments, Lufthansa Passenger Airlines has been rated as being among the world's top 10 airlines in terms of safety. Lufthansa's safety record is a function of several factors, but perhaps most important is the company's investment in flight crew training. Lufthansa's world class Flight Training subsidiary, with locations throughout Germany and in Phoenix, Arizona, is the most obvious example of this type of investment. Training delivered in these facilities ranges from basic pilot instruction to courses in the effective management of flight crews and their processes. The rationale for expenditures in flight crew training comes from knowledge that the vast majority of fatal airline accidents are due to the human limitations rather than random mechanical failures or fluke weather phenomena.

Unfortunately, on March 25, 2015, Germanwings Flight 9525, on route from Barcelona, Spain, to Dusseldorf, Germany, crashed in the French Alps, killing all 144 passengers and 6 crew members (two pilots and four flight attendants). Germanwings is a wholly owned subsidiary of Lufthansa and provides low-cost direct flights between European destinations. What is shocking about this particular incident is that one of the pilots crashed the plane intentionally. The 27 year-old co-pilot waited until the captain left the cockpit and locked the door so that the captain could not get back in. Recall that locks were installed on reinforced cockpit doors after the 9/11 terrorist attacks in 2001. The co-pilot then set the autopilot to 100ft, which initiated a descent that resulted in the Airbus A320 crashing into the mountains 10 minutes later.

Following the tragedy, Lufthansa CEO Carsten Spohr indicated that flight crews at Lufthansa and Germanwings are composed with great care and that pilots' are subjected to technical and psychological tests. He also noted that even with tough standards and safety regulations in place, it's impossible to rule out one-off events like this. Subsequent investigations of the crash have centered on two issues. First, the co-pilot had been treated for depression. Although he had apparently recovered and been cleared for flying, he remained troubled. This raises the question of whether someone on the flight crew should have detected something odd about the co-pilot's behavior and reported it. Second, the incident provides evidence that it's not a good idea to leave a single individual alone in a cockpit with complete responsibility and control of an aircraft carrying passengers. This has led to changes in policies that now require at least two members of the flight crew in the cockpit at all times. A complete explanation of the co-pilot's motives for this horrific tragedy may never come to light. However, the incident does highlight the fact that transporting passengers on an airliner requires a team effort.

11.1 What type of team is a flight crew? What are the defining characteristics of a flight crew? What role did these characteristics play in the crash of Flight 9525?

11.2 How did the locking of the cockpit door change the nature of the flight crew's task? How did the change in policies after the crash address this issue?

11.3 How do the two models of team development apply to flight crews? Describe a model that better depicts how flight crews develop over time. How could the team development process be modified to help prevent incidents like this in the future?

Sources: S. Almasy and L. Smith-Spark, "Reports: Antidepressants Found at Home of Co-Pilot Andreas Lubitz," *CNN Online,* March 28, 2015, http://edition.cnn.com/2015/03/28/europe/france-germanwings-plane-crash-main/index.html; V. Bryan, "Lufthansa CE Stunned that Co-Pilot Apparently Crashed Plane," *Reuters, US Edition Online,* March 26, 2015, http://www.reuters.com/article/2015/03026/us-france-crash-lufthansa-idUSKBN0MM1R520150326; K. Cripps, "What are the World's Safest Airlines?" *CNN Online,* January 6, 2015, http://edition.cnn.com/2015/01/06/intl_travel/world-safest-airlines/?iid=EL; Lufthansa Corporate Website, "*Passenger Airline Group,*" 2015, http://www.lufthansagroup.com/en/company/business-segments/passenger-airline-group.html; R. L. Helmreich and H. C. Foushee, "Why CRM? Empirical and Theoretical Bases of Human Factor Training," in B. Kanki, R. Helmreich, and J. Anca (Eds.), *Crew Resource Management,* 2nd ed. *(*San Francisco: Academic Press, 2010), pp. 3–57; "The World's Biggest Public Companies: #932 Deutsche Lufthansa," *Forbes Online,* 2015, http://www.forbes.com/companies/deutsche-lufthansa/; and "What Happened on the Germanwings Flight," *The New York Times Online,* March 27, 2015, http://www.nytimes.com/interactive/2015/03/24/world/europe/germanwings-plane-crash-map.html?_r=0.

EXERCISE: PAPER PLANE CORPORATION

The purpose of this exercise is to analyze the advantages and disadvantages of sequential versus pooled interdependence on a team production project. This exercise uses groups, so your instructor will either assign you to a group or ask you to create your own group. The exercise has the following steps.

11.1 Your professor will supply you with the materials you need to create your final product (as many paper airplanes as you can fold to quality standards in three 5-minute rounds). Instructions for folding the paper airplanes and judging their quality are provided below. Before you start work on your airplanes, do the following:

    a. As a group, select a team manager (who will supervise operations and get additional resources as needed) and a team inspector (who will judge the quality of the work on airplanes).

    b. Familiarize yourself with how to make a paper airplane by folding one according to the instructions.

    c. Be sure you are in a space where all of the team members can work comfortably.

    d. To the extent possible, move away from other groups.

    e. Familiarize yourself with the information about the Paper Plane Corporation.

11.2 Your group is the complete workforce for the Paper Plane Corporation. Established in 1943, Paper Plane has led the market in paper plane production. Presently under new management, the company is contracting to make aircraft for the U.S. Air Force. You must determine the most efficient method for producing these aircraft. You must make your contract with the Air Force under the following conditions:

    a. The Air Force will pay $200,000 per airplane.

    b. The aircraft must pass a strict inspection by a quality control manager.

    c. A penalty of $250,000 per airplane will be subtracted for each failure to meet the production requirements.

d. Labor and other overhead will be computed at $3,000,000.

e. Cost of materials will be $30,000 per bid plane. If you bid for 10 but make only 8, you must pay the cost of materials for those you failed to make or those that did not pass inspection.

11.3 In the first round of the airplane manufacturing process, the Air Force has asked you to focus on individuality. Each Paper Plane worker should manufacture his or her own planes from start to finish. When each plane is finished, it should be put in a central location for quality inspection. When time is called, you will record your team profit on the Summary Sheet.

11.4 In the second round of manufacturing, the Air Force has asked you to give each worker a specific job. In other words, the manufacturing process will take place in an assembly-line fashion. When planes come off the assembly line, they will be given directly to the quality control manager for inspection. When time is called, you will record your team profit on the Summary Sheet.

11.5 In the final round of manufacturing, the Air Force has asked your team to devise a manufacturing process that will maximize both efficiency and effectiveness. You may do whatever you like in terms of creating paper airplanes. You will have the same amount of time that you did in the two previous rounds. When time is called, you will record your team profit on the Summary Sheet.

11.6 Class discussion (whether in groups or as a class) should center on the following questions:

a. Did pooled interdependence (Round 1) or sequential interdependence (Round 2) work better for your group in terms of the number of planes made correctly? Why do you think you got the result you did?

b. How did you change your work structure in Round 3? Did the changes you implemented help you achieve better productivity? Why or why not?

c. From your perspective, what are the advantages and disadvantages of pooled and/or sequential interdependence?

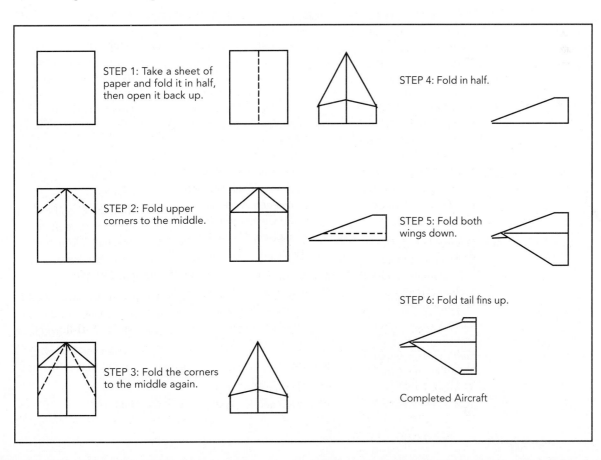

STEP 1: Take a sheet of paper and fold it in half, then open it back up.

STEP 2: Fold upper corners to the middle.

STEP 3: Fold the corners to the middle again.

STEP 4: Fold in half.

STEP 5: Fold both wings down.

STEP 6: Fold tail fins up.

Completed Aircraft

Round 1

Bid: _____ Aircraft @ $200,000 per aircraft =

Results: _____ Aircraft @ $200,000 per aircraft = _____

Subtract: $3,000,000 overhead + _____ × $30,000 cost of raw materials + _____ × $250,000 penalty for not completing a bid plane = _____

Profit: _____

Round 2

Bid: _____ Aircraft @ $200,000 per aircraft = _____

Results: _____ Aircraft @ $200,000 per aircraft = _____

Subtract: $3,000,000 overhead + _____ × $30,000 cost of raw materials + _____ × $250,000 penalty for not completing a bid plane = _____

Profit: _____

Round 3

Bid: _____ Aircraft @ $200,000 per aircraft = _____

Results: _____ Aircraft @ $200,000 per aircraft = _____

Subtract: $3,000,000 overhead + _____ × $30,000 cost of raw materials + _____ × $250,000 penalty for not completing a bid plane = _____

Profit: _____

Source: J.M. Ivancevich, J.M, R. Konopaske, and M. Matteson. *Organizational Behavior and Management,* 7th ed. New York: McGraw-Hill/Irwin, 2005. Original exercise by Louis Potheni in Luthans, F. *Organizational Behavior.* New York: McGraw-Hill, 1985, p. 555.

ENDNOTES

11.1 Ilgen, D.R.; D.A. Major; J.R. Hollenbeck; and D.J. Sego. "Team Research in the 1990s." In *Leadership Theory and Research: Perspectives and Directions,* ed. M.M. Chemers and R. Ayman. New York: Academic Press, 1993, pp. 245–70.

11.2 Devine, D.J.; L.D. Clayton; J.L. Philips; B.B. Dunford; and S.B. Melner. "Teams in Organizations: Prevalence, Characteristics, and Effectiveness." *Small Group Research* 30 (1999), pp. 678–711; Gordan, J. "Work Teams: How Far Have They Come?" *Training* 29 (1992), pp. 59–65; and Lawler, E.E., III; S.A. Mohrman; and G.E. Ledford Jr. *Creating High Performance Organizations: Practices and Results of Employee Involvement and Total Quality Management in* Fortune *1000 Companies.* San Francisco: Jossey-Bass, 1995.

11.3 Stewart, G.L.; C.C. Manz; and H.P. Sims Jr. *Team Work and Group Dynamics.* New York: Wiley, 1999.

11.4 Ibid.

11.5 Boning, B; C. Ichniowski; and K. Shaw. "Opportunity Counts: Teams and the Effectiveness of Production Incentives." *Journal of Labor Economics* 25 (2007), pp. 613–50.

11.6 Cohen, S.G., and D.E. Bailey. "What Makes Teams Work: Group Effectiveness Research from the Shop Floor to the Executive Suite." *Journal of Management* 23 (1997), pp. 239–90.

11.7 Liker, J.K. *The Toyota Way.* New York: McGraw-Hill, 2004.

11.8 Cohen and Bailey, "What Makes Teams Work."

11.9 Ibid.

11.10 Sundstrom, E.; M. McIntyre; T. Halfhill; and H. Richards. "Work Groups: From the Hawthorne Studies to Work Teams of the 1990s and Beyond." *Group Dynamics, Theory, Research, and Practice* 4 (2000), pp. 44–67.

11.11 Schlender, B. "The Man Who Built Pixar's Incredible Innovation Machine." *Fortune,* November 15, 2004, p. 206. ProQuest database (accessed May 28, 2007).

11.12 Hollenbeck, J.R.; B. Beersma; and M.E. Schouten. "Beyond Team Types and Taxonomies: A Dimensional Scaling Conceptualization for Team Description." *Academy of Management Review* 37 (2012), pp. 82–106.

11.13 Hackman, J.R. "The Design of Work Teams." In *Handbook of Organizational Behavior,* ed. J. Lorsch, Englewood Cliffs, NJ: Prentice Hall, 1987, pp. 315–42.

11.14 Cohen, S.G., and G.E. Ledford. "The Effectiveness of Self-Managing Teams: A Quasi-Experiment." *Human Relations* 47 (1994), pp. 13–34; Cordery, J.L.; W.S. Mueller; and L.M. Smith. "Attitudinal and Behavioral Effects of Autonomous Group Working: A Longitudinal Field Study." *Academy of Management*

Journal 34 (1991), pp. 464–76; and Wall, T.D.; N.J. Kemp; P.R. Jackson; and C.W. Clegg. "Outcomes of Autonomous Work Groups: A Long-Term Field Experiment." *Academy of Management Journal* 29 (1986), pp. 280–304.

11.15 Hass, M.R. "The Double-Edged Swords of Autonomy and External Knowledge: Analyzing Team Effectiveness in a Multinational Organization." *Academy of Management Journal* 53 (2010), pp. 989–1008.

11.16 Fisher, A. "How to Build a (Strong) Virtual Team." *CNNMoney.com,* December 10, 2009, http://money.cnn.com/2009/11/19/news/companies/ibm_virtual_manager.fortune/index.htm.

11.17 Ubell, R. "Virtual Team Learning." *Training and Development,* August 2010, pp. 53–57.

11.18 Fisher, "How to Build a (Strong) Virtual Team."

11.19 Duckworth, H. "How TRW Automotive Helps Global Virtual Teams Perform at the Top of Their Game." *Development and Learning in Organizations* 23 (2008), pp. 6–16.

11.20 Schiff, D. "Global Teams Rock around the Clock." *Electronic Engineering Times*

1435 (August 7, 2006), pp. 12, 20.

11.21 Godinez, V. "Sunshine 24/7: As EDS' Work Stops in One Time Zone, It Picks Up in Another." *Knight Ridder Tribune Business News,* January 2, 2007, ProQuest database (accessed February 12, 2007); Schiff, "Global Teams Rock"; and Treinen, J.J., and S.L. Miller-Frost. "Following the Sun: Case Studies in Global Software Development." *IBM Systems Journal* 45 (2006), pp. 773–83.

11.22 Tuckman, B.W. "Developmental Sequence in Small Groups." *Psychological Bulletin* 63 (1965), pp. 384–99; and Tuckman, B.W., and M.A.C. Jensen. "Stages of Small-Group Development Revisited." *Group and Organization Management* 2 (1977), pp. 419–27.

11.23 Guzzo, R.A., and G.P. Shea. "Group Performance and Intergroup Relations in Organizations." *Handbook of Industrial and Organizational Psychology,* Vol. 3, ed. M.D. Dunnette and L.M. Hough, Palo Alto, CA: Consulting Psychologists Press, 1992, pp. 269–313.

11.24 Gersick, C.J.G. "Time and Transition in Work Teams: Toward a New Model of Group Development." *Academy of Management Journal* 33 (1988), pp. 9–41;

and Gersick, C.J.G. "Marking Time: Predictable Transitions in Task Groups." *Academy of Management Journal* 32 (1989), pp. 274–309.

11.25   Thompson, J.D. *Organizations in Action.* New York: McGraw-Hill, 1967; and Van de Ven, A.H.; A.L. Delbeccq; and R. Koenig. "Determinants of Coordination Modes within Organizations." *American Sociological Review* 41 (1976), pp. 322–38.

11.26   Ibid.

11.27   Thompson, *Organizations in Action.*

11.28   Ibid.

11.29   Ibid.

11.30   Van de Ven et al., "Determinants of Coordination Modes."

11.31   Kelley, T. *The Art of Innovation.* New York: Doubleday, 2001.

11.32   Saavedra, R.; P.C. Earley; and L. Van Dyne. "Complex Interdependence in Task Performing Groups." *Journal of Applied Psychology* 78 (1993), pp. 61–72.

11.33   Deutsch, M. *The Resolution of Conflict.* New Haven, CT: Yale University Press, 1973; and Wong, A.; D. Tjosvold; and Yu. Zi-you "Organizational Partnerships in China: Self-Interest, Goal Interdependence, and Opportunism." *Journal of Applied Psychology* 90 (2005), pp. 782–91.

11.34   MacMillan, P.S. *The Performance Factor: Unlocking the Secrets of Teamwork.* Nashville, TN: Broadman & Holman, 2001.

11.35   Pearsall, M.J., and V. Venkataramani. "Overcoming Asymmetric Goals in Teams: The Interactive Role of Team Learning Orientation and Team Identification." *Journal of Applied Psychology* 100 (2015), pp. 735–48.

11.36   Ibid.

11.37   MacMillan, P.S. *The Performance Factor: Unlocking the Secrets of Teamwork.* Nashville, TN: Broadman & Holman, 2001.

11.38   Mathieu, J.E., and T.L. Rapp. "The Foundation for Successful Team Performance Trajectories: The Roles of Team Charters and Performance Strategies." *Journal of Applied Psychology* 94 (2009), pp. 90–103.

11.39   Shea, G.P., and R.A. Guzzo. "Groups as Human Resources." In *Research in Personnel and Human Resources Management,* Vol. 5, ed. K.M. Rowland and G.R. Ferris. Greenwich CT: JAI Press, 1987, pp. 323–56.

11.40   De Dreu, C.K.W. "Outcome Interdependence, Task Reflexivity, and Team Effectiveness: Motivated Information Processing Perspective." *Journal of Applied Psychology* 92 (2007), pp. 628–38.

11.41   Biddle, B.J. *Role Theory: Expectations, Identities, and Behavior.* New York: Academic Press, 1979; and Katz, D., and R.L. Kahn. *The Social Psychology of Organizations,* 2nd ed. New York: Wiley, 1978.

11.42   Humphrey, S.E.; F.P. Morgeson; and M.J. Mannor. "Developing a Theory of the Strategic Core of Teams: A Role Composition Model of Team Performance." *Journal of Applied Psychology* 94 (2009), pp. 48–61.

11.43   Brehmer, B., and R. Hagafors. "Use of Experts in Complex Decision Making: A Paradigm for the Study of Staff Work." *Organizational Behavior and Human Decision Processes* 38 (1986), pp. 181–95.

11.44   Benne, K., and P. Sheats. "Functional Roles of Group Members." *Journal of Social Issues* 4 (1948), pp. 41–49.

11.45   Lehmann-Willenbrock, N., and J. A. Allen. "How Fun Are Your Meetings? Investigating the Relationship between Humor Patterns in Team Interactions and Team Performance." *Journal of Applied Psychology* 99 (2014), pp. 1278–87.

11.46   Cole, M.S; F. Walter; and H. Bruch. "Affective Mechanisms Linking Dysfunctional

Behavior to Performance in Work Teams: A Moderated Mediation Study." *Journal of Applied Psychology* 95 (2008), pp. 945–58.

11.47 Spencer, L. "Conditioning Has Become an Important Tool: Let's Get Physical." *Stock Car Racing* (n.d.), http://www.stockcarracing.com/howto/stock_car_pit_crew_conditioning/.

11.48 Devine, D.J., and J.L. Philips. "Do Smarter Teams Do Better: A Meta-Analysis of Cognitive Ability and Team Performance." *Small Group Research* 32 (2001), pp. 507–32; and Stewart, G.L. "A Meta-Analytic Review of Relationships between Team Design Features and Team Performance." *Journal of Management* 32 (2006), pp. 29–54.

11.49 LePine, J.A.; J.R. Hollenbeck; D.R. Ilgen; and J. Hedlund. "Effects of Individual Differences on the Performance of Hierarchical Decision-Making Teams: Much More than *g*." *Journal of Applied Psychology* 82 (1997), pp. 803–11.

11.50 LePine, J.A. "Team Adaptation and Post-change Performance: Effects of Team Composition in Terms of Members' Cognitive Ability and Personality." *Journal of Applied Psychology* 88 (2003), pp. 27–39; and LePine, J.A. "Adaptation of

Teams in Response to Unforeseen Change: Effects of Goal Difficulty and Team Composition in Terms of Cognitive Ability and Goal Orientation." *Journal of Applied Psychology* 90 (2005), pp. 1153–67.

11.51 Steiner, I.D. *Group Process and Productivity.* New York: Academic Press, 1972.

11.52 Stewart, G.L.; I.S. Fulmer; and M.R. Barrick. "An Exploration of Member Roles as a Multilevel Linking Mechanism for Individual Traits and Team Outcomes." *Personnel Psychology* 58 (2005), pp. 343–65.

11.53 Gonzales-Mule, E.; D.S. DeGeest; B.W. McCormick; J.Y. Seong; and K.G. Brown. "Can We Get Some Cooperation Around Here? The Mediating Role of Group Norms on the Relationship between Team Personality and Individual Helping Behaviors." *Journal of Applied Psychology* 99 (2014), pp. 988–99.

11.54 Bell, S.T. "Deep Level Composition Variables as Predictors of Team Performance: A Meta-Analysis." *Journal of Applied Psychology* 92 (2007), pp. 395–415; and Peeters, M.A.G.; H.F.J.M Tuijl; C.G. van Rutte; and I.M.M.J. Reymen. "Personality and Team Performance: A Meta-Analysis." *European*

Journal of Personality 20 (2006), pp. 377–96.

11.55 Ibid.

11.56 Comer, D.R. "A Model of Social Loafing in Real Work Groups." *Human Relations* 48 (1995), pp. 647–67; and Wagner, J.A., III. "Studies of Individualism–Collectivism: Effects on Cooperation in Groups." *Academy of Management Journal* 38 (1995), pp. 152–72.

11.57 LePine, J.A., and L. Van Dyne. "Voice and Cooperative Behavior as Contrasting Forms of Contextual Performance: Evidence of Differential Relationships with Personality Characteristics and Cognitive Ability." *Journal of Applied Psychology* 86 (2001), pp. 326–36.

11.58 McGrath, J.E. "The Influence of Positive Interpersonal Relations on Adjustment and Interpersonal Relations in Rifle Teams." *Journal of Abnormal and Social Psychology* 65 (1962), pp. 365–75.

11.59 Bell, "Deep Level Composition Variables"; and Peeters et al., "Personality and Team Performance."

11.60 Barrick, M.R.; G.L. Stewart; M.J. Neubert; and M.K. Mount. "Relating Member Ability and Personality to Work-Team Processes and Team Effectiveness." *Journal of Applied Psychology* 83 (1998), pp. 377–91;

LePine et al., "Effects of Individual Differences"; and Neuman, G.A., and J. Wright. "Team Effectiveness: Beyond Skills and Cognitive Ability." *Journal of Applied Psychology* 84 (1999), pp. 376–89.

11.61 LePine, J.A., and L. Van Dyne. "Peer Responses to Low Performers: An Attributional Model of Helping in the Context of Work Groups." *Academy of Management Review* 26 (2001), pp. 67–84.

11.62 Bell, "Deep Level Composition Variables"; and Peeters et al., "Personality and Team Performance."

11.63 Barrick, M.R., and M.K. Mount. "The Big Five Personality Dimensions and Job Performance: A Meta-Analysis." *Personnel Psychology* 44 (1991), pp. 1–26.

11.64 Barrick et al., "Relating Member Ability and Personality."

11.65 Barry, B., and G.L. Stewart. "Composition, Process, and Performance in Self-Managed Groups: The Role of Personality." *Journal of Applied Psychology* 82 (1997), pp. 62–78.

11.66 Williams, K., and C. O'Reilly. "The Complexity of Diversity: A Review of Forty Years of Research." In *Research in Organizational Behavior,*

Vol. 21, ed. B. Staw and R. Sutton. Greenwich, CT: JAI Press, 1998, pp. 77–140.

11.67 Harrison, D.A., and K.J. Klein. "What's the Difference? Diversity Constructs as Separation, Variety, or Disparity in Organizations." *Academy of Management Review* 32 (2007), pp. 1199–1228; and Mohammed, S., and S. Nadkarni. "Are We All on the Same Temporal Page? The Moderating Effects of Temporal Team Cognition on the Polychronicity Diversity-Team Performance Relationship." *Journal of Applied Psychology* 99 (2014), pp. 404–22.

11.68 Joshi, A., and H. Roh. "The Role of Context in Work Team Diversity Research: A Meta-Analytic Review." *Academy of Management Journal* 52 (2009), pp. 599–627.

11.69 Aparna, J., and A.P. Knight. "Who Defers to Whom and Why? Dual Pathways Linking Demographic Differences and Dyadic Differences to Team Effectiveness." *Academy of Management Journal* 58 (2015), pp. 59–84; and Kim, E.; D.P. Bhave; and T.M. Glomb. "Emotion Regulation in Workgroups: The Roles of Demographic Diversity and Relational Work Context." *Personnel Psychology* 66 (2013), pp. 613–44.

11.70 Cox, T.; S. Lobel; and P. McLeod. "Effects of Ethnic Group Cultural Differences on Cooperative and Competitive Behavior on a Group Task." *Academy of Management Journal* 34 (1991), pp. 827–47; and Mannix, E., and M.A. Neal. "What Differences Make a Difference? The Promise and Reality of Diverse Teams in Organizations." *Psychological Science in the Public Interest* 6 (2005), pp. 31–55.

11.71 Page, S.E. "Making the Difference: Applying the Logic of Diversity." *Academy of Management Perspectives* 21 (2007), pp. 6–20.

11.72 van Knippenberg, D.; C. K.W. DeDreu; and A.C. Homan. "Work Group Diversity and Group Performance: An Integrative Model and Research Agenda." *Journal of Applied Psychology* 89 (2004), pp. 1008–22.

11.73 Ibid.

11.74 Kearney, E.; D. Gebert; and S.C. Voelpel. "When and How Diversity Benefits Teams: The Importance of Team Members' Need for Cognition." *Academy of Management Journal* 52 (2009), pp. 581–98.

11.75 Canella, A.A., Jr.; J.H. Park; and H.U. Lee. "Top Management Team Functional Background Diversity and Firm Performance:

Examining the Roles of Team Member Colocation and Environmental Uncertainty." *Academy of Management Journal* 51 (2008), pp. 768–84; Gruenfeld, D.H.; E.A. Mannix; K.Y. Williams; and M.A. Neale. "Group Composition and Decision Making: How Member Familiarity and Information Distribution Affect Processes and Performance." *Organizational Behavior and Human Decision Processes* 67 (1996), pp. 1–15; Hoffman, L. "Homogeneity and Member Personality and Its Effect on Group Problem Solving." *Journal of Abnormal and Social Psychology* 58 (1959), pp. 27–32; Hoffman, L., and N. Maier. "Quality and Acceptance of Problem Solutions by Members of Homogeneous and Heterogeneous Groups." *Journal of Abnormal and Social Psychology* 62 (1961), pp. 401–7; Nemeth, C.J. "Differential Contributions of Majority and Minority Influence." *Psychological Review* 93 (1986), pp. 22–32; Stasster, G.; D. Steward; and G. Wittenbaum. "Expert Roles and Information Exchange during Discussion: The Importance of Knowing Who Knows What." *Journal of Experimental Social Psychology* 57 (1995), pp. 244–65; Triandis, H.; E. Hall; and R.

Ewen. "Member Heterogeneity and Dyadic Creativity." *Human Relations* 18 (1965), pp. 33–55; and Watson, W.; K. Kuman; and I. Michaelsen. "Cultural Diversity's Impact on Interaction Process and Performance: Comparing Homogeneous and Diverse Task Groups." *Academy of Management Journal* 36 (1993), pp. 590–602.

11.76 Byrne, D. *The Attraction Paradigm.* New York: Academic Press, 1971; and Newcomb, T.M. *The Acquaintance Process.* New York: Holt, Rinehart and Winston, 1961.

11.77 Byrne, D.; G. Clore; and P. Worchel. "The Effect of Economic Similarity-Dissimilarity as Determinants of Attraction." *Journal of Personality and Social Psychology* 4 (1996), pp. 220–24; Lincoln, J., and J. Miller. "Work and Friendship Ties in Organizations: A Comparative Analysis of Relational Networks." *Administrative Science Quarterly* 24 (1979), pp. 181–99; Triandis, H. "Cognitive Similarity and Interpersonal Communication in Industry." *Journal of Applied Psychology* 43 (1959), pp. 321–26; and Triandis, H. "Cognitive Similarity and Communication in a Dyad." *Human Relations* 13 (1960), pp. 279–87.

11.78 Jackson, S.E.; K.E. May; and K. Whitney. "Understanding the Dynamics of Diversity in Decision-Making Teams." In *Team Decision-Making Effectiveness in Organizations,* ed. R.A. Guzzo and E. Salas. San Francisco: Jossey-Bass, 1995, pp. 204–61; and Milliken, F.J., and L.L. Martins. "Searching for Common Threads: Understanding the Multiple Effects of Diversity in Organizational Groups." *Academy of Management Review* 21 (1996), pp. 402–33.

11.79 Harrison, D.A.; K.H. Price; and M.P. Bell. "Beyond Relational Demography: Time and the Effects of Surface- and Deep-Level Diversity on Work Group Cohesion." *Academy of Management Journal* 41 (1998), pp. 96–107; and Harrison, D.A.; K.H. Price; J.H. Gavin; and A.T. Florey. "Time, Teams, and Task Performance: Changing Effects of Surface- and Deep-Level Diversity on Group Functioning." *Academy of Management Journal* 45 (2002), pp. 1029–45.

11.80 Ibid.

11.81 Lau, D, and J.K. Murnighan. "Demographic Diversity and Faultlines: The Compositional Dynamics of Organizational Groups." *Academy of Management Review* 23 (1998), pp. 325–40;

and Lau, D., and J.K. Murnighan. "Interactions with Groups and Subgroups: The Effects of Demographic Faultlines." *Academy of Management Journal* 48 (2005), pp. 645–59.

11.82 Tuggle, C.S.; J. Schnatterly; and R.A. Johnson. "Attention Patterns in the Boardroom: How Board Composition and Process Affect Discussion of Entrepreneurial Issues." *Academy of Management Journal* 53 (2010), pp. 550–71.

11.83 Carton, A.M., and J.N. Cummings. "The Impact of Subgroup Type and Subgroup Configurational Properties on Work Team Performance." *Journal of Applied Psychology* 98 (2013), pp. 732–58; and Homan, A.C.; D. van Knippenberg; G.A. Van Kleef; and C.K. W. De Dreu. "Bridging Faultlines by Valuing Diversity: Diversity Beliefs, Information Elaboration, and Performance in Diverse Work Groups." *Journal of Applied Psychology* 92 (2007), pp. 1189–99.

11.84 Homan, A.C.; J.R. Hollenbeck; S.E. Humphrey; D. van Knippenberg; D.R. Ilgen; and G.A. van Kleef. "Facing Differences with an Open Mind: Openness to Experience, Salience of Intragroup Differences, and Performance of Diverse Work Groups." *Academy of Management Journal* 51 (2008), pp. 1204–22; and Kearney, E., and D. Gebert. "Managing Diversity and Enhancing Team Outcomes: The Promise of Transformational Leadership." *Journal of Applied Psychology* 94 (2009), pp. 77–89.

11.85 Ibid.

11.86 Ibid.

11.87 Mohammed, S., and S. Nadkarni. "Temporal Diversity and Team Performance: The Moderating Role of Team Temporal Leadership." *Academy of Management Journal* 54 (2011), pp. 489–508.

11.88 Pieterse, A.N.; D. van Knippenberg; and W.P. van Ginkel. "Diversity in Goal Orientation, Team Reflexivity, and Team Performance." *Organizational Behavior and Human Decision Processes* 114 (2011), pp. 153–64.

11.89 Hoever, I.J.; D. van Knippenberg; W.P. van Ginkel; and H.G. Barkema. "Fostering Team Creativity: Perspective Taking as Key to Unlocking Diversity's Potential." *Journal of Applied Psychology* 97 (2012), pp. 982–96.

11.90 Klein, K.J.; A.P. Knight; J.C. Ziegert; B.C. Lim; and J.L. Salz. "When Team Members' Values Differ: The Moderating Role of Team Leadership." *Organizational Behavior and Human Decision Processes* 114 (2011), pp. 25–36.

11.91 Ibid.

11.92 Bell, "Deep-Level Composition Variables."

11.93 Humphrey, S.E.; J.R. Hollenbeck; C.J. Meyer; and D.R. Ilgen. "Trait Configurations in Self-Managed Teams: A Conceptual Examination of Seeding for Maximizing and Minimizing Trait Variance in Teams." *Journal of Applied Psychology* 92 (2007), pp. 885–92.

11.94 Stewart, "A Meta-Analytic Review."

11.95 Kozlowski, S.W.J., and B.S. Bell. "Work Groups and Teams in Organization." In *Comprehensive Handbook of Psychology: Industrial and Organizational Psychology,* Vol. 12, ed. W.C. Borman, D.R. Ilgen, and R.J. Klimoski. New York: Wiley, 2003, pp. 333–75.

11.96 Gooding, R.Z., and J.A. Wagner III. "A Meta-Analytic Review of the Relationship between Size and Performance: The Productivity and Efficiency of Organizations and Their Subunits." *Administrative Science Quarterly* 30 (1985), pp. 462–81; and Markham, S.E.;

F. Dansereau; and J.A. Alutto. "Group Size and Absenteeism Rates: A Longitudinal Analysis." *Academy of Management Journal* 25 (1982), pp. 921–27.

11.97 Hackman, J.R., and N.J. Vidmar. "Effects of Size and Task Type on Group Performance and Member Reactions." *Sociometry* 33 (1970), pp. 37–54.

11.98 Yank, J.L. "The Power of Number 4.6." *Fortune* 153, no. 11 (June 12, 2006), p. 122. ProQuest database (accessed May 28, 2007).

11.99 Sundstrom, E.; K.P. De Meuse; and D. Futrell. "Work Teams: Applications and Effectiveness." *American Psychologist* 45 (1990), pp. 120–33.

11.100 Stewart et al., *Team Work and Group Dynamics.*

11.101 Stewart, "A Meta-Analytic Review."

11.102 Campion, M.A.; G.J. Medsker; and A.C. Higgs. "Relations between Work Group Characteristics and Effectiveness: Implications for Designing Effective Work Groups." *Personnel Psychology* 46 (1993),

pp. 823–49; and Campion, M.A.; E.M. Papper; and G.J. Medsker. "Relations between Work Team Characteristics and Effectiveness: A Replication and Extension." *Personnel Psychology* 49 (1996), pp. 429–52.

11.103 DeMatteo, J.S.; L.T. Eby; and E. Sundstrom. "Team-Based Rewards: Current Empirical Evidence and Directions for Future Research." *Research in Organizational Behavior* 20 (1998), pp. 141–83.

11.104 Deutsch, M.A. "A Theory of Cooperation and Competition." *Human Relations* 2 (1949), pp. 199–231.

11.105 Williams, K.; S.G. Harkins; and B. Latane. "Identifiability as a Deterrent to Social Loafing: Two Cheering Experiments." *Journal of Personality and Social Psychology* 40 (1981), pp. 303–11.

11.106 Lawler, E.E. *Strategic Pay: Aligning Organizational Strategies and Pay Systems.* San Francisco: Jossey-Bass, 1990.

11.107 O'Dell, C. *People, Performance, Pay.* American Productivity Institute, 1987,

cited in DeMatteo et al., "Team-Based Rewards."

11.108 Bolch, M. "Rewarding the Team: Make Sure Team-Oriented Compensation Plans Are Designed Carefully." *HR Magazine,* 2007, pp. 91–95.

11.109 Wageman, R. "Interdependence and Group Effectiveness." *Administrative Science Quarterly* 40 (1995), pp. 145–80.

11.110 Bolch, "Rewarding the Team."

11.111 Johnson, D.W.; G. Maruyama; R. Johnson; D. Nelson; and L. Skon. "Effects of Cooperative, Competitive, and Individualistic Goal Structures on Achievement: A Meta-Analysis." *Psychological Bulletin* 89 (1981), pp. 47–62; Miller, L.K., and R.L. Hamblin. "Interdependence, Differential Rewarding and Productivity." *American Sociological Review* 28 (1963), pp. 768–78; and Rosenbaum, M.E. "Cooperation and Competition." In *Psychology of Group Influence,* ed. P.B. Paulus. Hillsdale, NJ: Erlbaum, 1980.

chapter 12

Teams: Processes and Communication

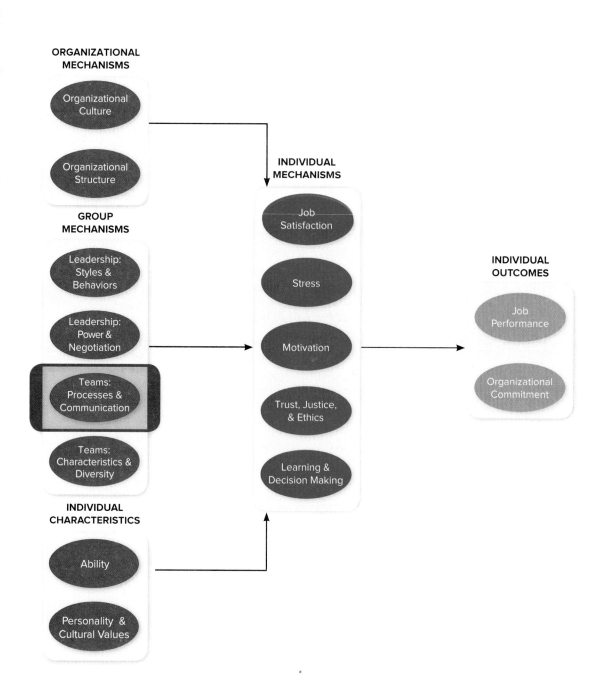

ORGANIZATIONAL
MECHANISMS

Organizational
Culture

Organizational
Structure

GROUP
MECHANISMS

Leadership:
Styles &
Behaviors

Leadership:
Power &
Negotiation

Teams:
Processes &
Communication

Teams:
Characteristics &
Diversity

INDIVIDUAL
CHARACTERISTICS

Ability

Personality &
Cultural Values

INDIVIDUAL
MECHANISMS

Job
Satisfaction

Stress

Motivation

Trust, Justice,
& Ethics

Learning &
Decision Making

INDIVIDUAL
OUTCOMES

Job
Performance

Organizational
Commitment

© Smiley N. Pool /Houston Chronicle/AP Images

✔️ LEARNING GOALS

After reading this chapter, you should be able to answer the following questions:

12.1 What are taskwork processes, and what are some examples of team activities that fall into this process category?

12.2 What are teamwork processes, and what are some examples of team activities that fall into this process category?

12.3 What factors influence the communication process in teams?

12.4 What are team states, and what are some examples of the states that fall into this process category?

12.5 How do team processes affect team performance and team commitment?

12.6 What steps can organizations take to improve team processes?

NASA

In the 1970s hit "Rocket Man," Elton John sings about an astronaut who's all by himself on his way to Mars. The image of this solitary astronaut who feels "lonely out in space on such a timeless flight," however, stands in contrast to the reality an astronaut often faces. Although astronauts sometimes work and live in isolated and extreme environments for extended periods of time, they typically do so with other astronauts, as part of a small team, more often referred to as a crew, in quarters that are quite cramped.

This type of environment creates challenges for astronauts employed by the National Aeronautics and Space Administration (NASA), the agency responsible for civilian space programs and aeronautics research in the United States. NASA astronauts not only have to cope with the discomfort of traveling, working, and living in space, but they also have to learn to function with other astronauts as a cohesive unit to accomplish complex and dangerous tasks. Obviously, astronaut crews need to carry out activities that are involved in safely flying or orbiting their vessels. Crews also have to carry out all the tasks that are involved in their missions, which primarily involve exploration and experiments intended to better understand Earth and other bodies in space. What may be less

obvious is that astronauts need to transition back and forth between individual responsibilities and crew responsibilities. They need to plan and coordinate their activities, monitor resources, and help each other. Crews that fail to effectively carry out any of these activities place not only their missions in jeopardy, but their lives as well.

With the retirement of the space shuttle program, the United States does not have its own spacecraft for piloted missions. However, NASA continues to recruit and train astronauts for duty on the International Space Station and for planned missions to asteroids and Mars. Astronaut recruits are diverse with regard to demographic characteristics and areas of expertise. On the one hand, this type of diversity gives NASA the ability to compose crews for a wide variety of missions. On the other hand, it increases opportunities for misunderstandings during missions that could undermine crew cohesion and effectiveness. Although NASA's training for astronaut candidates emphasizes the development of knowledge and skills related to operating equipment and systems, the ultimate effectiveness of astronaut crews is likely to depend on knowledge and skills related to teamwork as well.

TEAM PROCESSES AND COMMUNICATION

As we described in Chapter 11 on team characteristics and diversity, a team consists of two or more people who work interdependently over some time period to accomplish common goals related to some task-oriented purpose.[1] The effectiveness of organizations depends to a large extent on the activities and interactions that occur within teams as they move toward their task-related objectives. **Team process** is a term that refers to the different types of communication, activities, and interactions that occur within teams that contribute to their ultimate end goals.[2] Team characteristics, like member diversity, task interdependence, team size, and so forth, affect team processes and communication. Those processes, in turn, have a strong impact on team effectiveness. In fact, some have argued that extraordinary teams are defined in terms of their processes.[3]

Some of the team processes and forms of communication that we describe in this chapter are observable by the naked eye. An outside observer would be able to see a crew of astronauts communicating with each other in regard to the status of the systems in their space capsule. Other processes, in contrast, are less visible. An outside observer wouldn't be able to see the sense of "cohesion" felt by the members of this crew or the shared "mental models" that cause them to work together so efficiently. Thus, team processes include interactions among members that occur behaviorally, as well as the hard-to-see feelings and thoughts that coalesce as a consequence of member interactions. For an amusing example of different types of team processes, see our **OB on Screen** Feature.

OB ON SCREEN

THE SPONGEBOB MOVIE: SPONGE OUT OF WATER

We work together, you know, teamwork.

With those words SpongeBob SquarePants (Tom Kenny) explains to Plankton (Mr. Lawrence) how they're going to achieve the goal of getting back the secret formula for Krabby Patties, in *The SpongeBob Movie: Sponge Out of Water* (Dir. Paul Tibbitt, Paramount Animation and Nickelodeon Movies, 2015). You see, Plankton tried to steal the secret formula from Mr. Krabs (Clancy Brown), owner of the The Krusty Krab restaurant, but it disappeared into thin air just as SpongeBob catches him in the act. The residents of Bikini Bottom blame the two for the secret formula's disappearance after the town turns into an apocalyptic nightmare when the last of the Krabby Patties are eaten. Initially, SpongeBob and Plankton have different reasons for wanting to find the secret formula—SpongeBob wants to save Bikini Bottom and Plankton wants to save The Chum Bucket, his failing restaurant—but the two realize they have to work together as a team. Although Plankton is skeptical at first, SpongeBob's amusing song about teamwork motivates him and builds confidence that teaming up is the answer.

© *Paramount Pictures/Photofest*

The film illustrates how different team processes unfold as SpongeBob and his friends endeavor to solve the mystery of the missing Krabby Patty formula. In one scene, for example, SpongeBob and Plankton brainstorm and devise a plan to build a time machine so they can go back in time and steal the secret formula before it disappeared. In another scene, the two combine their skills and abilities to retrieve Plankton's wife Karen (Jill Talley), who is a computer, to use as a part of the time machine. As a final example, SpongeBob and Plankton recruit Patrick (Bill Fagerbakke), Mr. Krabs, Sandy (Carolyn Lawrence), and Squidward (Roger Bumpass) to form a cohesive team that's capable of defeating Burger Beard (Antonio Banderas), the pirate who stole the formula to achieve his goal of becoming the richest food truck proprietor in all the land. In the end, although this animated film is geared to those who are positively predisposed to SpongeBob-type entertainment—stupid-funny, clever, and loud—it depicts different types of team processes in a highly vivid and memorable way.

WHY ARE SOME TEAMS MORE THAN THE SUM OF THEIR PARTS?

Take a second and try to think of a few teams that have been successful. It's likely that the success of some of these teams was expected because the team had members who are very talented and skilled. The success of other teams may be more difficult to understand just by looking at the rosters of their members. These teams might have members who appear to be less talented and skilled, but as they work together, they somehow became "more than the sum of their parts." Getting more from the team than you would expect according to the capabilities of its individual members is called **process gain**. This capability, which is synonymous with "synergy," is most critical in situations in which the complexity of the work is high or when tasks require members to combine their knowledge, skills, and efforts to solve problems. In essence, process gain is important because it results in useful resources and capabilities that did not exist before the team created them.[4]

Having described process gain, we now consider its polar opposite, **process loss**, or getting less from the team than you would expect based on the capabilities of its individual members. To understand process loss, think of an experience you've had with a team you felt was a sure bet to do well based on the capabilities of the members, but didn't achieve the level of success you expected. You may be thinking of a sports team where the members were the best athletes or the best at their respective positions, but the players just didn't seem to mesh well, and as a result, the team didn't win. Or perhaps you're thinking of a student team with an assignment to do a term project, and although the team was composed of the brightest students in class, it became apparent on presentation day that the team's ideas weren't very creative or well-executed, and as a result, the project paled in comparison with the projects of the other student teams. If you've had an experience like this, you know how frustrating it can be. In reality, process loss is a common and costly by-product of doing work in teams.

But what factors conspire to create process loss? One factor is that in teams, members have to work to not only accomplish their own tasks, but also coordinate their activities with the activities of their teammates.[5] Although this extra effort focused on integrating work is a necessary aspect of the team experience, it's called **coordination loss** because it consumes time and energy that could otherwise be devoted to task activity.[6] Such coordination losses are often driven by **production blocking**, which occurs when members have to wait on one another before they can do their part of the team task.[7] If you've ever worked in a team in which you felt like you couldn't get any of your own work done because of all the time spent in meetings, following up requests for information from other team members, and waiting on team members to do their part of the team task, you already understand how frustrating production blocking (and coordination loss) can be. In the context of a game like soccer, production blocking might occur if a player has to wait too long for a teammate to get in position before passing the ball.

The second force that fosters process loss in team contexts is **motivational loss,** or the loss in team productivity that occurs when team members don't work as hard as they could.[8] Why does motivational loss occur in team contexts? One explanation is that it's often quite difficult to gauge exactly how much each team member contributes to the team. Members of teams can work together on projects over an extended period of time, and as a consequence, it's difficult to keep an accurate accounting of who does what. Similarly, members contribute to their team in many different ways, and contributions of some members may be less obvious than the contributions of others. Finally, members of teams don't always work together at the same time as a unit. Regardless of the reasons for it, uncertainty regarding "who contributes what" results in team members feeling less accountable for team outcomes. Those feelings of reduced accountability, in turn, cause members to exert less effort when working on team tasks than they would if

The U.S. women's soccer team was favored in the early rounds of the 2015 World Cup but failed to perform to their potential due to process loss. The team achieved synergy in the final game against Japan, however. In fact, their 5–2 victory was one of the most dominating performances ever in a Women's World Cup final.

© Andy Clark/AFP/Getty Images

they worked alone on those same tasks. This phenomenon is called **social loafing**,[9] and it can significantly hinder a team's effectiveness.[10] In the context of a student team responsible for a project, motivational loss and social loafing may result if some students on the team come to depend on a student who is particularly motivated and knowledgable.

TASKWORK PROCESSES

Having described process gains and process losses, it's time to describe the particular team processes that can help teams increase their synergy while reducing their inefficiency. One relevant category of team processes is **taskwork processes**, which are the activities of team members that relate directly to the accomplishment of team tasks. In a general sense, taskwork occurs any time that team members interact with the tools or technologies that are used to complete their work. In this regard, taskwork is similar to the concept of task performance described in Chapter 2 on job performance. However, in the context of teams, especially those that engage in knowledge work, three types of taskwork processes are crucially important: creative behavior, decision making, and boundary spanning. These three taskwork processes are shown in Figure 12-1.

12.1

What are taskwork processes, and what are some examples of team activities that fall into this process category?

CREATIVE BEHAVIOR When teams engage in creative behavior, their activities are focused on generating novel and useful ideas and solutions.[11] In Chapter 9 on personality and cultural values, we noted that creative behavior is driven in part by the creativity of individual employees, because some employees are simply more original and imaginative than others. Researchers have also found that creativity in teams may be affected by characteristics such as conformity and attention to detail.[12] However, the team environment is also uniquely suited to fostering creative behavior.[13] As a consequence, organizations like Palo Alto–based IDEO, arguably the world's most successful product design firm, rely on teams to come together and combine their members' unique sets of knowledge and skill in a manner that results in novel and useful ideas.[14] However, achieving such outcomes depends on much more than just putting a diverse mix of people together and letting them go at it. In fact, creative behavior in teams can be fostered when members participate in a specific set of activities.

Perhaps the best-known activity that teams use to foster creative behavior is **brainstorming**. Generally speaking, brainstorming involves a face-to-face meeting of team members in which each offers as many ideas as possible about some focal problem or issue.[15] Most brainstorming sessions center around the following rules:

1. Express all ideas that come to mind (no matter how strange).
2. Go for quantity of ideas rather than quality.
3. Don't criticize or evaluate the ideas of others.
4. Build on the ideas of others.

The theory is that if a team follows these rules, it will develop a large pool of ideas that it can use to address the issue at hand.[16] This concept sounds very reasonable, and almost all of us

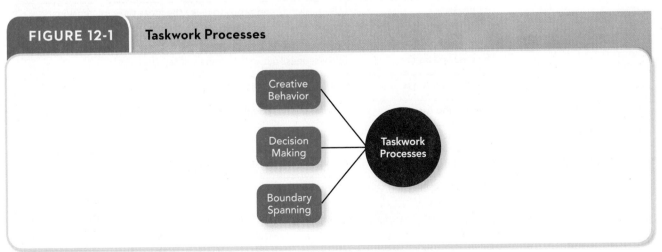

FIGURE 12-1   **Taskwork Processes**

have been in some sort of brainstorming meeting at some point. However, it may surprise you to learn that such brainstorming sessions rarely work as well as intended. In fact, research suggests that team members would be better off coming up with ideas on their own, as individuals, before pooling those ideas and evaluating them to arrive at a solution.[17]

Why doesn't brainstorming work as well as individual idea generation? There appear to be at least three reasons.[18] First, there may be a tendency for people to social loaf in brainstorming sessions. That is, members may not work as hard thinking up ideas as they would if they had to turn in an individually generated list with their name on it. Second, though the rules of brainstorming explicitly forbid criticizing others' ideas, members may be hesitant to express ideas that seem silly or not well thought-out. Third, brainstorming results in production blocking because members have to wait their turn to express their ideas. This waiting around consumes time that could otherwise be used by individuals to generate new ideas.

Given the problems associated with brainstorming, why do organizations continue to use it? One reason is that the general idea of brainstorming is well known, and common sense leads people to believe that it works as advertised. Another reason is that there are benefits of brainstorming beyond just generating ideas. For example, brainstorming builds morale and results in the sharing of knowledge that might otherwise be locked inside the minds of the individual team members.[19] Although this knowledge may not be useful for the particular problem that's being debated, it might be useful for issues that arise in the future. To achieve the benefits of brainstorming, some companies take extra steps to ensure team members are fully engaged in the process of generating ideas. At IDEO, for example, brainstorming meetings often open with a warm-up session, typically a fast-paced word game to clear the minds of the participants.[20] Table 12-1 lists secrets of better brainstorming, as practiced at IDEO.

TABLE 12-1	IDEO's Secrets for Brainstorming
WHAT TO DO	**DESCRIPTION**
Have a sharp focus	Begin the brainstorming with a clearly stated problem.
Playful rules	Encourage playfulness, but don't debate or critique ideas.
Number the ideas	Make it easier to jump back and forth between ideas.
Build and jump	Build on and explore variants of ideas.
The space remembers	Use space to keep track of the flow of ideas in a visible way.
Stretch your brain	Warm up for the session by doing word games.
Get physical	Use drawings and props to make the ideas three-dimensional.
WHAT NOT TO DO	**DESCRIPTION**
The boss speaks first	Boss's ideas limit what people will say afterwards.
Give everybody a turn	Forcing equal participation reduces spontaneity.
Only include experts	Creative ideas come from unexpected places.
Do it off-site	You want creativity at the office too.
Limit the silly stuff	Silly stuff might trigger useful ideas.
Write down everything	The writing process can reduce spontaneity.

Source: T. Kelley and J. Littman, *The Art of Innovation* (New York: Doubleday, 2001).

One offshoot of brainstorming that addresses some of its limitations is the **nominal group technique**.[21] Similar to a traditional brainstorming session, this process starts off by bringing the team together and outlining the purpose of the meeting. The next step takes place on an individual level, however, as members have a set period of time to write down their own ideas on a piece of paper. The subsequent step goes back into the team setting, as members share their ideas with the team in a round-robin fashion. After the ideas are recorded, members have a discussion intended to clarify the ideas and build on the ideas of others. After this, it's back to an individual environment; members rank order ideas on a card that they submit to a facilitator. A facilitator then tabulates the scores to determine the winning idea. From this description, you probably can guess how the nominal group technique addresses the problems with brainstorming. By making people write down ideas on their own, it decreases social loafing and production blocking. Although team members might still be hesitant about expressing wild ideas to the group, doing so might be less threatening than having nothing to contribute to the group. In addition, ranking items as individuals makes people less apprehensive about going "against the grain" of the group by voicing support for an unpopular idea.

DECISION MAKING. In Chapter 8 on learning and decision making, we described how people use information and intuition to make specific decisions. In team contexts, however, decisions result from the interaction among team members. In some team contexts, for example, members share information regarding a problem or task, and they work together to reach a *consensus,* or general agreement among members in regards to the final solution. Juries provide a good example of how this type of decision making works. Members of a jury listen to information provided by attorneys and witnesses, and after they're given instructions by a judge, they meet privately to discuss the information with the goal being to reach a consensus regarding the verdict.

There has been a great deal of research on consensus decision making in the context of juries; however, the most important lesson from this research is that the strongest predictor of the final verdict is the distribution of the positions the individual jury members have in mind going into deliberations.[22] In fact, the position held by the majority of the jury members prior to deliberation turns out to be the final verdict 90 percent of the time.[23] It's not that jury members with the minority position simply acquiesce to the majority because of pressure, but rather, having more jury members in the majority increases the information and arguments available that supports the majority.[24] Interestingly, however, despite all the research on consensus decision making, there is not a lot of evidence that this research has been very useful to attorneys and trial consultants in composing juries in a way that would lead to favorable decisions for their side.[25]

In many other team contexts, decision making involves multiple members gathering and considering information that's relevant to their area of specialization, and then making recommendations to a team leader who is ultimately responsible for a final decision, which at some point, can be judged with regard to accuracy or effectiveness.[26] Although the degree of member specialization and hierarchical structure of teams vary a great deal,[27] you can understand this type of decision-making process if you consider what happens on project teams with an assigned leader and members who are responsible for different aspects of the project; design, engineering, marketing, logistics, sales and so forth. Throughout the project, members make suggestions and recommendations to the leader, who's ultimately responsible for making the decisions that determine the success of the project.

What factors account for a team's ability to make accurate and effective decisions? At least three factors appear to be involved.[28] The first factor is **decision informity**, which reflects whether members possess adequate information about their own task responsibilities. Project teams can fail, for example, because the team member in charge of marketing doesn't gather information necessary to help the team understand the desires and needs of the client. The second factor is **staff validity**, which refers to the degree to which members make good recommendations to the leader. Team members can possess all the information needed to make a good recommendation but then fail to do so because of a lack of ability, insight, or good judgment. The third factor is **hierarchical sensitivity**, which reflects the degree to which the leader effectively weighs the recommendations of the members. Whom does the leader listen to, and whom does the leader ignore? Teams that make good decisions tend to have leaders that do a good job giving

OB INTERNATIONALLY

In today's global economy, organizations have become increasingly reliant on multinational teams, or teams composed of individuals who do not share the same national identification. One benefit of multinational teams is economic. Rather than having separate businesses or products in several different countries, organizations leverage economies of scale by establishing multinational teams to develop and manage global products. A second benefit is that diversity in terms of national origin may result in business decisions that are more innovative. Such innovation stems from the team having a diverse set of experiences and perspectives from which to draw when trying to accomplish work. However, along with these benefits are potential team process problems. The most obvious problem is language barriers that prevent team members from communicating effectively with one another. Beyond simple misunderstandings, communication barriers can result in difficulties in coordinating tasks and may hinder members from receiving or understanding the information they need to make good recommendations and decisions. So what can multinational teams do to address some of these problems?

One solution is *group decision support systems,* which involve the use of computer technology to help the team structure its decision-making process. As an example, team members might meet in a room where each member sits at a networked laptop. At different points during the meeting, members are directed to enter their ideas and recommendations into the computer. These inputs are then summarized and shared visually with the entire team on their computer screens. Advantages of this approach are that the system keeps the meeting focused squarely on the task, and information can be presented in a logical sequence at a pace that makes it easier to digest. Moreover, no single member can dominate the meeting. As a consequence of these advantages, team members may participate more uniformly in the meeting and develop a more consistent understanding of the information that was exchanged. Another advantage is that the technique can be modified and used when members are geographically dispersed.

Sources: T. Cox, S. Lobel, and P. McLeod, "Effects of Ethnic Group Cultural Differences on Cooperative and Competitive Behavior on a Group Task," *Academy of Management Journal* 34 (1991), pp. 827–47; P. Dwyer, P. Engardio, S. Schiller, and S. Reed, "The New Model: Tearing up Today's Organization Chart," *BusinessWeek,* November 18, 1994, pp. 80–90; D.R. Ilgen, J.A. LePine, and J.R. Hollenbeck, "Effective Decision Making in Multinational Teams," in *New Perspectives in International Industrial–Organizational Psychology,* ed. P.C. Earley and M. Erez (San Francisco: Jossey-Bass, 1997), pp. 377–409; E. Mannix and M.A. Neal, "What Differences Make a Difference? The Promise and Reality of Diverse Teams in Organizations," *Psychological Science in the Public Interest* 6 (2005), pp. 31–55; and J.M. Prieto Zamora and R. Martinez Arias, "Those Things Yonder Are Not Giants, but Decision Makers in International Teams," in *New Perspectives on International Industrial and Organizational Psychology,* ed. P.C. Earley and M. Erez (San Francisco: New Lexington Press, 1997), pp. 410–45.

recommendations the weight they deserve. Together, these three variables play a large role in how effective teams are in terms of their decision making.[29]

The concepts of decision informity, staff validity, and hierarchical sensitivity can be used to make specific recommendations for improving team decision making. For example, research shows that more experienced teams tend to make better decisions because they develop an understanding of the information that's needed and how to use it, and have leaders that develop an understanding of which members provide the best recommendations.[30] The implication here is that team decision making may be improved if teams are allowed to work together on an ongoing basis across different projects. As another example, team decision making may be improved by giving members feedback about the three variables involved in the decision-making process.[31] For instance, a team can improve its decision making if the members are told that they have to share and consider additional pieces of information before making recommendations to the leader. Although this recommendation may seem obvious, all too often teams receive feedback only about their final decision. In addition, there may be a benefit to separating the process of sharing information from the process of making recommendations and final decisions, at least in terms of how information is communicated among members.[32] Whereas team members tend to share more information when they meet face-to-face, leaders do a better job considering recommendations and making final decisions when they're away from the members. Leaders who are separated don't have to deal with pressure from members who may be more assertive or better at articulating and defending their positions. Our **OB Internationally** feature describes additional considerations that need to be taken into account to improve decision making in culturally diverse teams.[33]

BOUNDARY SPANNING. The third type of taskwork process is **boundary spanning**, which involves three types of activities with individuals and groups other than those who are considered part of the team.[34] **Ambassador activities** refer to communications that are intended to protect the team, persuade others to support the team, or obtain important resources for the team. As you might have guessed from this description, members who engage in ambassador activities typically communicate with people who are higher up in the organization. For example, a member of a marketing team might meet with senior management to request an increase in the budget for an expanded television ad campaign. **Task coordinator activities** involve communications that are intended to coordinate task-related issues with people or groups in other functional areas. Continuing with the marketing team example, a member of the team might meet with someone from manufacturing to work out how a coupon might be integrated into the product packaging materials.

Finally, **scout activities** refer to things team members do to obtain information about technology, competitors, or the broader marketplace. The marketing team member who meets with an engineer to seek information about new materials is engaging in scout activities. Taken together, research suggests that these boundary-spanning activities may be as important to determining team success as the processes that occur entirely within the team.[35] Many teams in organizations are involved with complex work that requires going outside the team to coordinate, and for support, resources and information. To the extent that teams do not exist in a vacuum, it can be beneficial to have members with the expertise, experiences, and the type of disposition to engage in the type of boundary spanning activities we discussed here.[36]

TEAMWORK PROCESSES

Another category of team process that helps teams increase their process gain while minimizing their process loss is teamwork processes. **Teamwork processes** refer to the interpersonal activities that facilitate the accomplishment of the team's work but do not directly involve task accomplishment itself.[37] You can think of teamwork processes as the behaviors that create the setting or context in which taskwork can be carried out. So what types of behaviors do teamwork processes involve? Figure 12-2 summarizes the set of teamwork processes that we discuss in this chapter.[38]

TRANSITION PROCESSES Teamwork processes become important as soon as teams first begin their work. **Transition processes** are teamwork activities that focus on preparation for future

12.2

What are teamwork processes, and what are some examples of team activities that fall into this process category?

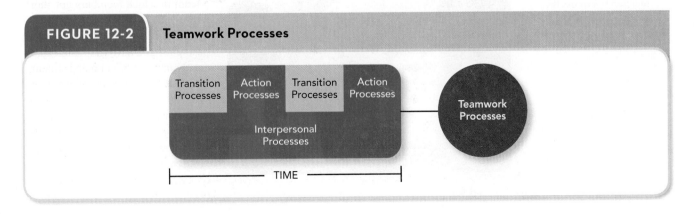

FIGURE 12-2   **Teamwork Processes**

work. For example, *mission analysis* involves an analysis of the team's task, the challenges that face the team, and the resources available for completing the team's work. *Strategy formulation* refers to the development of courses of action and contingency plans, and then adapting those plans in light of changes that occur in the team's environment. Finally, *goal specification* involves the development and prioritization of goals related to the team's mission and strategy. Although these examples focus on the team's task work activities, transition processes could focus on teamwork as well. For example, a team could develop a plan intended to enhance teamwork among members over the course of a long project.[39] Each of these transition processes is relevant before the team actually begins to conduct the core aspects of its work. However, these transition processes also may be important between periods of work activity. For example, think about the halftime adjustments made by a basketball team that's losing a game badly. The team could consider the strengths of its opponent and develop a new strategy intended to neutralize them. In this way, teams may switch from transition processes to taskwork, then back to transition processes. As another example, debriefing and after-action reviews, which refer to systematic discussions and reviews of performance episodes, have been used by the military for decades. However, because they work so well in improving the effectiveness of teams, their use is spreading to nonmilitary organizations as well.[40]

ACTION PROCESSES. Whereas transition processes are important before and between periods of taskwork, **action processes** are important as the taskwork is being accomplished. One type of action process involves *monitoring progress toward goals*. Teams that pay attention to goal-related information—perhaps by charting the team's performance relative to team goals—are typically in a good position to realize when they are "off-track" and need to make changes. *Systems monitoring* involves keeping track of things that the team needs to accomplish its work. A team that does not engage in systems monitoring may fail because it runs out of inventory, time, or other necessary resources. *Helping behavior* involves members going out of their way to help or back up other team members. Team members can provide indirect help to their teammates in the form of feedback or coaching, as well as direct help in the form of assistance with members' tasks and responsibilities. Helping behavior may be most beneficial when workload is distributed unequally among team members.[41] *Coordination* refers to synchronizing team members' activities in a way that makes them mesh effectively and seamlessly. Poor coordination results in team members constantly having to wait on others for information or other resources necessary to do their part of the team's work.[42]

INTERPERSONAL PROCESSES. The third category of teamwork processes is called **interpersonal processes**. The processes in this category are important before, during, or between periods of taskwork, and each relates to the manner in which team members manage their relationships. The first type of interpersonal process is *motivating and confidence building*, which refers to things team members do or say that affect the degree to which members are motivated to work hard on the team's task. Expressions that create a sense of urgency and optimism are examples of communications that would fit in this category. Similarly, *affect management* involves activities that foster a sense of emotional balance and unity. If you've ever worked in a team in which members got short-tempered when facing pressure or blamed one another when there were problems, you have firsthand experience with poor affect management.

For task conflict to be productive, team members must feel free to express their opinions and know how to manage conflict effectively.

© *Lisette Le Bon/SuperStock*

Another important interpersonal process is *conflict management*, which involves the activities that the team uses to manage conflicts that arise in the course of its work. Conflict tends to have a negative impact on a team, but the nature of this effect depends on the focus of the conflict as well as the manner in which the conflict is managed.[43] **Relationship conflict** refers to disagreements among team members in terms of interpersonal relationships or incompatibilities with respect to personal values or preferences. This type of conflict centers on issues that are not directly connected to the team's task. Relationship conflict is not only dissatisfying to most people, it also tends to result in reduced team performance. **Task conflict**, in contrast, refers to disagreements among members about the team's task. Logically speaking, this type of conflict can be beneficial to teams if it stimulates conversations that result in the development and expression of new ideas.[44] Research findings, however, indicate that task conflict tends to result in reduced team effectiveness unless several conditions are present.[45] First, members need to trust one another and be confident that they can express their opinions openly without fear of reprisals. Second, team members need to engage in effective conflict management practices. In fact, because task conflict tends to be most beneficial to teams when relationship conflict is low, there are reasons to focus efforts on trying to reduce this aspect of conflict.[46] Third, there's some evidence that task conflict may benefit teams only when they're composed in certain ways. For example, task conflict has been shown to be most beneficial to teams composed with members who are either emotionally stable or open to new experiences.[47] (For more discussion of conflict management issues, see Chapter 13 on leadership power and negotiation.)

What does effective conflict management involve? First, when trying to manage conflict, it's important for members to stay focused on the team's mission. If members do this, they can rationally evaluate the relative merits of each position.[48] Second, any benefits of task conflict disappear if the level of the conflict gets too heated, if parties appear to be acting in self-interest rather than in the best interest of the team, or if there's high relationship conflict.[49] Third, to effectively manage task conflict, members need to discuss their positions openly and be willing to exchange information in a way that fosters collaborative problem solving.[50] If you've ever had an experience in an ongoing relationship in which you tried to avoid uncomfortable conflict by ignoring it, you probably already understand that this strategy tends to only make things worse in the end. For an example of effective conflict management, see our **OB at the Bookstore** feature.

COMMUNICATION

So far in this chapter, we've described the focus of the activities and interactions among team members as they work to accomplish the team's purpose. For example, taskwork processes involve members sharing ideas, making recommendations, and acquiring resources from parties outside the team. As another example, teamwork processes involve members planning how to do the team's work, helping other team members with their work, and saying things to lift team members' spirits. Now we shift gears a bit and focus our attention on **communication**, the process by which information and meaning gets transferred from a sender to a receiver.[51] Much of the work that's done in a team is accomplished interdependently and involves communication among members, and therefore, the effectiveness of communication plays a crucial role in determining whether there is process gain or process loss.

One way to understand communication is to consider the model depicted in Figure 12-3.[52] On the left side of the model is the source or *sender* of information. In a team that manufactures steel engine parts, for example, the sender might be a team member who wants to share information with another team member. More specifically, the sender might want to let another member know that the team has to work more quickly to reach a difficult performance goal. Generally speaking, senders may use verbal and written language, as well as nonverbal language and cues, to *encode* the information into a *message*. Continuing with our example, the sender may choose to quickly wave an arm up and down to convey the idea that the team needs to work faster. This encoded message is transmitted to a *receiver,* who needs to interpret or *decode* the message to form an understanding of the information it contains. In our example, the message is transmitted visually because the members are working face-to-face, but messages can be transmitted in written form, electronically, or even indirectly through other individuals. With this basic model of communication in mind, we can consider factors that may influence the effectiveness of this process.

12.3

What factors influence the communication process in teams?

MAKING CONFLICT WORK

Peter T. Coleman and Robert Ferguson (New York: Houghton Mifflin Harcourt Publishing Company, 2014).

Conflict is a lot like fire. When it sparks, it can intensify, spread, and lead to pain, loss, and irreparable damage. It can distract, distance, derail, and occasionally destroy opportunities and relationships.

Photo of cover: © Roberts Publishing Services

With those words, authors Coleman and Ferguson describe the general nature of the problem their book is intended to address. Like fire, conflict is necessary and functional. However, it can spread quickly with disastrous consequences. The question is how to manage conflict such that the benefits outweigh the potential costs. There are many books about the management of conflict however, this one is unique. For one thing, most books on conflict management are grounded in the assumption that the parties to a conflict have the same level of power, more or less. Coleman and Ferguson explicitly account for differences in power that can change the dynamics of conflict in a dramatic way. For example, whereas conflict among teammates with the same level of power might manifest in ongoing debate and eventual problem resolution, conflict among teammates with different levels of power might result in the "weaker" teammate remaining silent. If the weaker teammate possesses the better solution and becomes resentful, no one benefits. Moreover, the weaker teammate may not voice potentially useful suggestions or opinions in the future, thus limiting the potential performance and viability of the team. In sum, the authors provide a fairly compelling argument that differences in power create a need for different approaches to managing conflict.

Fortunately, the book addresses this need for different approaches to conflict management in a very detailed and comprehensive way. In fact, the authors suggest seven different approaches—pragmatic benevolence, cultivated support, constructive dominance, strategic appeasement, selective autonomy, effective adaptivity, and principled rebellion—along with justification for the approaches and several specific tactics that can be used to implement the approaches. The authors also include short but interesting business cases from well-known organizations that illustrate the different approaches in action. Although these cases depict conflicts between business leaders and their subordinates, most of the approaches apply directly to teams that have a formal hierarchy or members who differ in their power or status.

COMMUNICATOR ISSUES. One important factor that influences the communication process is the communicators themselves. Communicators need to encode and interpret messages, and it turns out that these activities can be major sources of communication problems.[53] In our example, the receiver may interpret the arm waving as a message that something is going wrong and that the team needs to slow down to cope with the problem. Of course, this interpretation is the exact opposite of what the sender intended to convey. The communication process may also suffer if the participants lack *communication competence,* which refers to the skills involved in encoding, transmitting, and receiving messages.[54] In fact, it may have already occurred to you that perhaps the sender in our example should have chosen an alternative way to communicate the idea that the team needs to work more quickly. Along the same lines, a receiver who isn't skilled in listening carefully to a sender's message may misinterpret a message or miss it altogether.

FIGURE 12-3 | **The Communication Process**

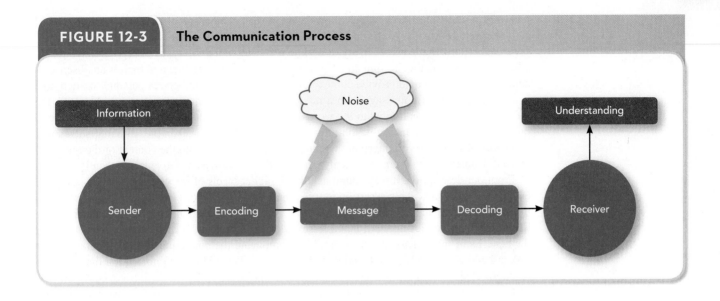

An additional communicator issue relevant to the communication process in teams relates to the *emotions* and *emotional intelligence* of team members,[55] issues we discussed in Chapter 4 on job satisfaction and Chapter 10 on ability. Emotions can affect how people express themselves and can also cloud their interpretation of information they receive from others.[56] Therefore, team members' ability to regulate their emotions and understand the emotions of others can result in clearer communications that are less prone to misunderstanding. Although you might think that emotions are mostly relevant to communications involving face-to-face interactions among team members, emotions can interfere with electronically mediated communications, and therefore, they are relevant to virtual teams as well.[57]

NOISE. A second factor that influences the communication process is the presence of *noise* that interferes with the message being transmitted.[58] Depending on how the message is being transmitted, noise can take on several different forms. In the context of our example, the sender and receiver may be working several feet from one another, and steam from the manufacturing process may make it difficult to see and appreciate the meaning of the gestures members make. As another example, you've probably had difficulty trying to hold a conversation with someone in a restaurant or at a party because of blaring music or crowd noise. If so, you can understand that noise increases the effort that the communicators need to exert to make the communication process work. The sender has to talk louder and more clearly and perhaps increase the use of alternative means of communicating, such as using hand gestures to help clarify messages. In addition, the receiver has to listen more carefully and think harder to fill in the spaces left by spoken words that are impossible to hear. If one of the two parties to the communication isn't willing to put in the extra effort to send and receive messages when there is noise, the conversation likely will not last very long.

INFORMATION RICHNESS. A third factor that influences the communication process is **information richness**, which is the amount and depth of information that gets transmitted in a message.[59] Messages that are transmitted through face-to-face channels have the highest level of information richness[60] because senders can convey meaning through not only words but also their body language, facial expressions, and tone of voice. Face-to-face communication also achieves high information richness because it provides the opportunity for senders and

© *Royalty-Free/Corbis RF*

Communicator emotions can play a big role in the communication process.

receivers to receive feedback, which allows them to verify and ensure their messages are received and interpreted correctly. At the opposite end of the information richness spectrum are computer-generated reports that consist largely of numbers.[61] Although these types of reports may include a lot of information, they're limited to information that's quantifiable, and there's an absence of additional cues that could provide context and meaning to the numbers. A personal written note is a good example of a message with a moderate level of information richness.[62] Although the information in a note is limited to the words written down on the page, the choice of words and punctuation can add meaning beyond the words themselves. For example, research shows that recipients of e-mails try to interpret the emotions of the sender from the content of the message, and unfortunately, they often mistakenly perceive the emotion as negative even when it's not.[63]

From our description, it may sound as though higher levels of information richness are preferable to lower levels. This assertion is true when the situation or task at hand is complex and difficult to understand.[64] In this case, the more cues that are available to the receiver, the more likely it is that the message will be understood the way the sender intended it to be. However, the benefits of information richness may overcomplicate the communication process when the task at hand is relatively simple and straightforward.[65] The additional information that needs to be interpreted by the receiver increases the chance that some of the cues will seem contradictory, and when this happens, receivers may feel like they're being sent "mixed messages." In summary, the appropriate level of information richness depends on the nature of the team's situation: The greater the level of complexity in the work being accomplished by the team, the more likely it is that the benefits of information richness outweigh its costs.

NETWORK STRUCTURE. So far in our discussion of communication, we've kept things simple by focusing on the flow of information between two people—a sender and a receiver. Of course, teams typically have more than just two people, so it's important at this point to consider the implications of this additional complexity. One way to understand communication in teams composed of more than two people is to consider the concept of **network structure**, which is defined as the pattern of communication that occurs regularly among each member of the team.[66]

As depicted in Figure 12-4, communication network patterns can be described in terms of *centralization,* or the degree to which the communication in a network flows through some members rather than others.[67] The more communication flows through fewer members of the team, the higher the degree of centralization. You can think of the circles in the figure as team members, and the lines between the circles represent the flow of communication back and forth between the two members. On the left side of the figure is the *all channel* network structure, which is highly decentralized. Every member can communicate with every other member. Student teams typically communicate using this type of structure. On the right side of the figure, at the other extreme, is the *wheel* network structure. This network structure is highly centralized because all the communication flows through a single member. Teams that use a wheel structure often consist of an "official" leader who makes final decisions based on recommendations from members who have expertise in different fields. Although there are many other configurations you can easily think of, we also included the *circle* and *Y* structures to illustrate examples that fall between the extremes in terms of the level of centralization.

So why are network structures important to learn about? Quite a bit of research on this topic suggests that network structure has important implications for team effectiveness, though those implications depend on the nature of the team's work.[68] On the one hand, when the work is simple and straightforward, a centralized structure tends to result in faster solutions with fewer mistakes. On the other hand, when the work is complex and difficult to understand, a decentralized structure tends to be more efficient. Apparently, when work is complex and difficult to understand, the team can benefit if members have the ability to communicate with anyone on the team to get assistance or resolve problems. When the work is simple and easy to understand, the additional communication channels afforded by a decentralized structure become unnecessary and divert members' attention from the task. It's important to mention, however, that members tend to prefer decentralized network structures. That is, they tend to be more satisfied with the team when they are "in the loop," even though their position in the loop might not help the team perform more effectively.

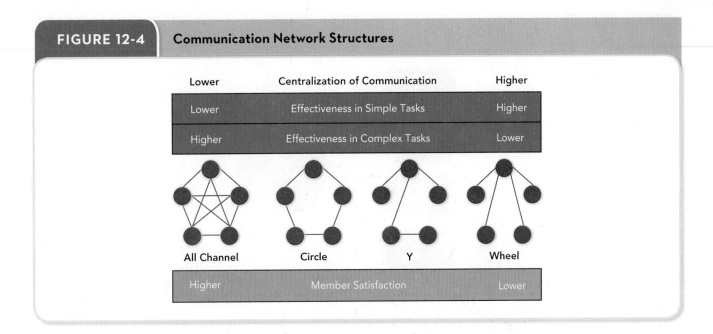

FIGURE 12-4	Communication Network Structures

Communication among team members in organizations has become more decentralized over the past decade or so. One reason for this trend is that social network media has become inexpensive and easy to use. User-centered Web 2.0 tools and collaboration software such as Microsoft SharePoint, Jive, and Google Hangouts allow individuals to share information and collaborate in real time, and many companies, such as AT&T, General Electric, FedEx, and Atlanta–based Manheim Auctions, Inc., have developed their own versions of Facebook and LinkedIn for their employees to use internally.[69] Individuals working together can use these tools, along with mobile devices to communicate with each other at a moment's notice. While such technologies provide obvious advantages to virtual teams, teams that work together at the same office also benefit from these tools. A team member who has an inspiration or discovers an important breakthrough over the weekend no longer has to wait until Monday to share it and get feedback from teammates. It also might surprise you to learn that the use of mobile devices for communication among teammates is especially popular in underdeveloped regions such as Africa, where the number of these devices far exceeds the number of computers. In fact, companies such as Coca-Cola train in the use of mobile devices so that teams that operate in these regions can communicate and interact more effectively.[70]

Before moving on to the next topic, we should note that the use of technology does not necessarily improve the communication process. Some individuals may lack the competence or confidence to use these newer means of communication, resulting in their reluctance or inability to participate fully in collaborative efforts that take place using these technologies. As another example, social media reduce an individual's perceived cost of expressing their ideas and opinions. This could result in an overabundance of information, and the spread of misinformation and rumors that add noise to communication. The use of Twitter during the Haiti earthquake, for example, led to rumors that contributed to anxiety and uncertainty of those directly and indirectly involved in the disaster.[71]

TEAM STATES

A fourth category of team processes that helps teams increase their process gain while minimizing their process loss is less visible to the naked eye. **Team states** refer to specific types of feelings and thoughts that coalesce in the minds of team members as a consequence of their experience working together. For example, as a consequence of supportive leadership and member interactions, team members may develop feelings of *psychological safety,* or the sense that it is OK to do things that are interpersonally risky, or that expressing opinions and making suggestions that

 12.4

What are team states, and what are some examples of the states that fall into this process category?

FIGURE 12-5 | **Team States**

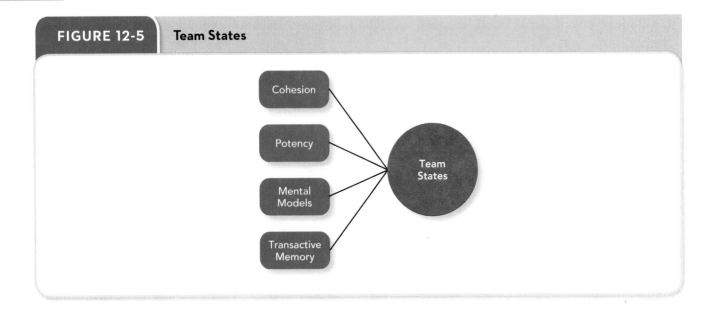

challenge the status quo won't be met with embarrassment and rejection at the hands of team-mates.[72] Ostracism in a team context can be painful and lead to disengagement and other negative consequences to the individual and to the team.[73] Although there are many types of team states that we could review in this chapter, Figure 12-5 summarizes the set of team states we discuss.

COHESION. For a number of reasons, such as having trusting relationships, members of teams can develop strong emotional bonds to other members of their team and to the team itself.[74] This emotional attachment, which is called **cohesion**,[75] tends to foster high levels of motivation and commitment to the team, and as a consequence, cohesiveness tends to promote higher levels of team performance.[76] Of course, it might not surprise you to learn that there is a reciprocal relationship with team performance. That is, the higher team performance that results, in part, from higher cohesion may, in turn, further enhance team cohesion.[77]

But is a cohesive team *necessarily* a good team? According to researchers, the answer to this question is no. In highly cohesive teams, members may try to maintain harmony by striving toward consensus on issues without ever offering, seeking, or seriously considering alternative viewpoints and perspectives. This drive toward conformity at the expense of other team priorities is called **groupthink** and is thought to be associated with feelings of overconfidence about the team's capabilities.[78] Groupthink has been blamed for decision-making fiascos in politics as well as in business. Some famous examples include John F. Kennedy's decision to go forward with the Bay of Pigs invasion of Cuba,[79] NASA's decision to launch the space shuttle *Challenger* in unusually cold weather,[80] and Enron's board of directors' decisions to ignore illegal accounting practices.[81]

So how do you leverage the benefits of cohesion without taking on the potential costs? One way is to acknowledge that cohesion can potentially have detrimental consequences. A good first step in this regard would be to assess the team's cohesion using a scale such as the one in our **OB Assessments** feature. A high score on this sort of assessment indicates the team may be vulnerable to groupthink. A second step in preventing problems associated with cohesion would be to formally institute the role of devil's advocate. The person filling this role would be responsible for evaluating and challenging prevailing points of view in a constructive manner and also bringing in fresh perspectives and ideas to the team. Although the devil's advocate role could be filled by an existing team member, it's also possible that the team could bring in an outsider to fill that role.

POTENCY. The second team state, **potency**, refers to the degree to which members believe that the team can be effective across a variety of situations and tasks.[82] When a team has high potency, members are confident that their team can perform well, and as a consequence, they focus more of their energy on team tasks and teamwork in hopes of achieving team goals.[83] When a team has low potency, members are not as confident about their team, so they begin

OB ASSESSMENTS

COHESION

How cohesive is your team? This assessment is designed to measure cohesion—the strength of the emotional bonds that develop among members of a team. Think of your current student project team or an important team that you belong to in your job. Answer each question using the response scale provided. Then subtract your answers to the boldfaced questions from 8, with the difference being your new answers for those questions. For example, if your original answer for question 6 was "5," your new answer is "3" (8 − 5). Then sum up your answers for the eight questions. (Instructors: Assessments on task conflict, relationship conflict, potency, and transactive memory can be found in the PowerPoints in the Connect Library's Instructor Resources and in the Connect assignments for this chapter).

1	2	3	4	5	6	7
TO A VERY SMALL EXTENT	TO A SMALL EXTENT	TO SOME EXTENT	TO A REGULAR EXTENT	TO A GOOD EXTENT	TO A GREAT EXTENT	TO A VERY GREAT EXTENT

1. I interact with my teammates, either in person or virtually, to get work done. _____

2. My teammates make me feel positive, upbeat, and energized. I like them. _____

3. I trust my teammates. I can depend on them. _____

4. **I dislike my teammates. They tend to annoy me.** _____

5. I interact with my teammates socially and can confide in them about personal matters. I consider them to be friends. _____

6. **I have difficult relationships with my teammates. Our personalities clash and there's tension.** _____

7. **I have doubts about my teammates. I feel like I have to monitor them.** _____

8. I enjoy working with my teammates. _____

SCORING AND INTERPRETATION

If your scores sum up to 45 or above, you feel a strong bond to your team, suggesting that your team may be cohesive. If your scores sum up to less than 45, you feel a weaker bond to your team, suggesting that your team may not be cohesive.

Source: Items adapted from E. R. Crawford. "Team Network Multiplexity, Synergy and Performance." Doctoral dissertation. University of Florida, 2011.

to question the team's goals and one another. Ultimately, this reaction can result in members focusing their energies on activities that don't benefit the team. In the end, research has shown that potency has a strong positive impact on team performance.[84] One obvious caveat here is that a team's confidence can be too high.[85] In fact, a strong sense of confidence very early in a team's existence can decrease the amount of beneficial discussions centered on different positions that are relevant to a team.[86] So how does high potency develop in teams? Team members' confidence in their own capabilities, their trust in other members' capabilities, and feedback about past performance are all likely to play a role.[87] Specifically, team potency is promoted in teams in which members are confident in themselves and their teammates and when the team has experienced success in the past.

MENTAL MODELS. **Mental models** refer to the level of common understanding among team members with regard to important aspects of the team and its task.[88] A team may have shared mental models with respect to the capabilities that members bring to the team as well as the processes the team needs to use to be effective.[89] How can these two types of mental models foster team effectiveness? When team members share in their understanding of one another's capabilities, they're more likely to know where to go for the help they might need to complete their work. In addition, they should be able to anticipate when another member needs help to do his or her work. When members have a shared understanding of which processes are necessary to help the team be effective, they can carry out these processes efficiently and smoothly. To help you understand why this is true, consider what would happen in a team of students who had different understandings about how the team should manage conflict. Few disagreements would get resolved if some of the members believed that direct confrontation was best, whereas others believed that avoidance was best.

TRANSACTIVE MEMORY. Whereas mental models refer to the degree to which the knowledge is shared among members, **transactive memory** refers to how specialized knowledge is distributed among members in a manner that results in an effective system of memory for the team.[90] This concept takes into account the idea that not everyone on a team has to possess the same knowledge. Instead, team effectiveness requires that members understand when their own specialized knowledge is relevant to the team and how their knowledge should be combined with the specialized knowledge of other members to accomplish team goals. This of course, requires that team members not only possess useful specialized knowledge, but also *meta-knowledge,* or knowledge of who knows what.[91] If you've ever worked on a team that had effective transactive memory, you may have noticed that work got done very efficiently.[92] Everyone focused on his or her specialty and what he or she did best, members knew exactly where to go to get information when there were gaps in their knowledge, and the team produced synergistic results. Of course, transactive memory can also be fragile because the memory system depends on each and every member.[93] If someone is slow to respond to another member's request for information or forgets something important, the team's system of memory fails. Alternatively, if a member of the team leaves, you lose an important node in the memory system.

SUMMARY: WHY ARE SOME TEAMS MORE THAN THE SUM OF THEIR PARTS?

So what explains why some teams become more than the sum of their parts (whereas other teams become less)? As shown in Figure 12-6, teams become more than the sum of their parts if their team process achieves process gain rather than process loss. Teams can accomplish that goal by engaging in activities involved in effective taskwork processes, teamwork processes, communication, and team states. Important taskwork processes include creative behavior, decision making, and boundary spanning. Important teamwork processes include transition processes, action processes, and interpersonal processes. Communication can be enhanced by ensuring that members are competent communicators, noise is minimized, and appropriate levels of information richness and network complexity are chosen. Team states refer to variables such as cohesion, potency, mental models, and transactive memory. In contrast to the taskwork processes, teamwork processes, and communication, team states offer less visible and observable reasons for why some teams possess an effective synergy whereas others seem quite inefficient.

HOW IMPORTANT ARE TEAM PROCESSES?

12.5

How do team processes affect team performance and team commitment?

Do team processes affect performance and commitment? Answering this question is somewhat complicated for two reasons. First, as in Chapter 11 on team characteristics and diversity, when we say "performance and commitment," we are not referring to the performance of individuals

FIGURE 12-6 | **Why Are Some Teams More Than the Sum of Their Parts?**

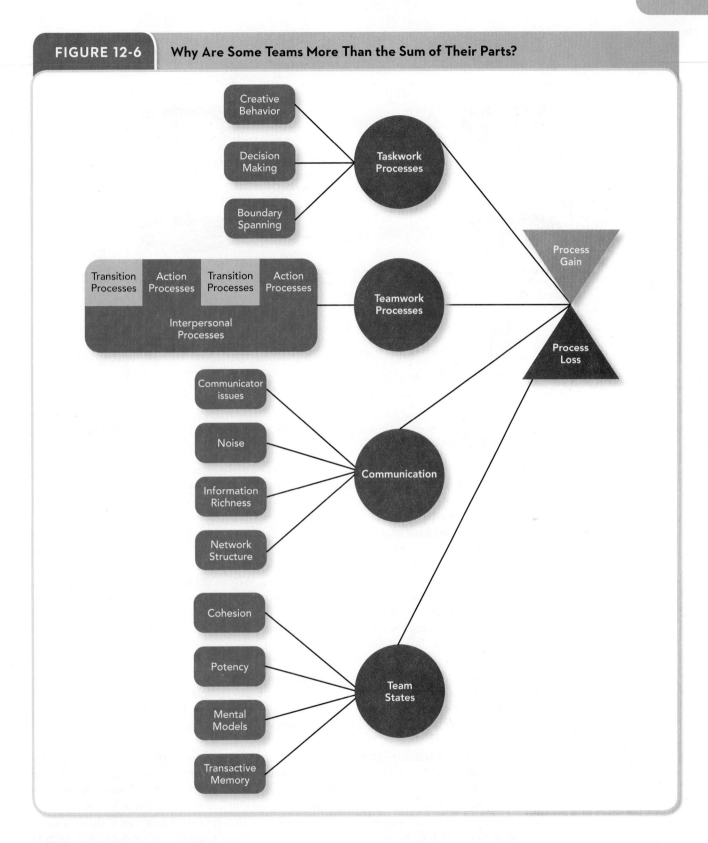

or their attachment to the organization. Instead, we are referring to the performance of teams and the degree to which teams are capable of remaining together as ongoing entities. In the jargon of research on teams, this form of commitment is termed "team viability." Second, as we have described throughout this chapter, there are several different types of team processes that we could consider in our summary. In Figure 12-7, we characterize the relationship among team

| FIGURE 12-7 | **Effects of Teamwork Processes on Performance and Commitment** |

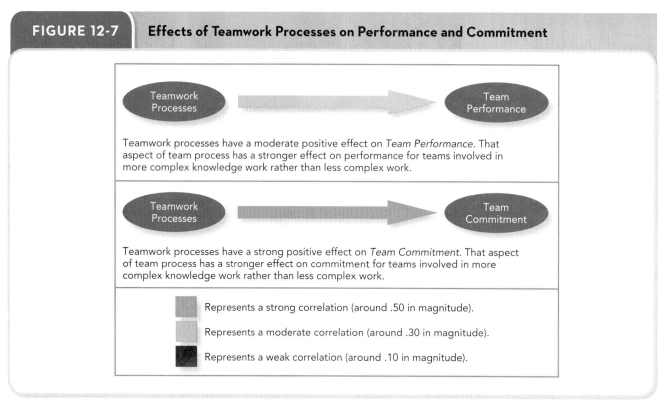

Source: J.A. LePine, R.F. Piccolo, C.L. Jackson, J.E. Mathieu, and J.R. Saul, "A Meta-Analysis of Team Process: Towards a Better Understanding of the Dimensional Structure and Relationships with Team Effectiveness Criteria," *Personnel Psychology* 61 (2008), pp. 356–76.

processes, performance, and commitment by focusing specifically on research involving teamwork processes. The figure therefore represents a summary of existing research on transition processes, action processes, and interpersonal processes.

Research conducted in a wide variety of team settings has shown that teamwork processes have a moderate positive relationship with team performance.[94] This same moderate positive relationship appears to hold true, regardless of whether the research examines transition processes, action processes, or interpersonal processes. Why might the relationships between these different types of processes and team performance be so similarly positive? Apparently, effectiveness with respect to a wide variety of interactions is needed to help teams achieve process gain and, in turn, perform effectively. The interpersonal activities that prepare teams for future work appear to be just as important as those that help members integrate their taskwork and those that build team confidence and a positive team climate. Researchers have also found that the importance of team processes to team performance may be more strongly positive in teams in which there are higher levels of interdependence and complexity.[95] This relationship can be explained quite easily: Activities that are meant to improve the integration of team members' work are simply more important in team contexts in which the work of team members needs to be integrated.

Research also indicates that teamwork processes have a strong positive relationship with team commitment.[96] In other words, teams that engage in effective teamwork processes tend to continue to exist together into the future. Why should teamwork and team commitment be so strongly related? One reason is that people tend to be satisfied in teams in which there are effective interpersonal interactions, and as a consequence, they go out of their way to do things that they believe will help the team stick together. Think about a team situation that you've been in when everyone shared the same goals for the team, work was coordinated smoothly, and everyone was positive, pleasant to be around, and willing to do their fair share of the work. If you've ever actually been in a situation like this—and we hope that you have—chances are that you did your best to make sure the team could continue on together. It's likely that you worked extra hard to make sure that the team achieved its goals. It's also likely that you expressed positive sentiments about the team and your desire for the team to remain together. Of course, just the opposite would be true in a team context in which members had different goals for the team, coordination was difficult and filled with emotional conflict, and everyone was pessimistic and disagreeable. Members of a team like this would not only find the situation dissatisfying, but would also make it known that they would be very open to a change of scenery.

© *The New York Times/Redux*

The Orpheus Chamber Orchestra has been able to perform effectively over the past 35 years because of extraordinary levels of teamwork and commitment. While all members of the orchestra help refine the interpretation and execution of each work in its repertoire, they also select a concert-master and principal players to lead each piece.

APPLICATION: TRAINING TEAMS

Team-based organizations invest a significant amount of resources into training that's intended to improve team processes. These types of investments seem to be a smart thing to do, given that team processes have a positive impact on both team performance and team commitment. In this section, we review several different approaches that organizations use to train team processes.

12.6

What steps can organizations take to improve team processes?

TRANSPORTABLE TEAMWORK COMPETENCIES

One approach to training teams is to help individual team members develop general competencies related to teamwork activities. Table 12-2 shows that this type of training could involve many different forms of knowledge, skills, and abilities.[97] Taken together, such knowledge, skills, and abilities are referred to as **transportable teamwork competences**.[98] This label reflects the fact that trainees can transport what they learn about teamwork from one team context and apply it in another. As a specific example of how this type of training might work, consider a recent study of teamwork training for naval aviators in an advanced pilot training program.[99] In this study, one group of pilots went through two days of training, during which they received instruction on preferred communication practices, communicating suggestions and asking questions, and communicating about potential problems. The pilots who went through the training believed that in addition to building teamwork knowledge and skills, the training would increase their mission effectiveness and flight safety. Moreover, crews that were composed of pilots who went through the training were significantly more effective than crews composed of pilots who did not go through the training. Effectiveness was judged by performance in dangerous scenarios, such as ice buildup on the aircraft wings and instructions from the air traffic control tower that were conflicting or ambiguous.

CROSS-TRAINING

A second type of team training involves training members in the duties and responsibilities of their teammates. The idea behind this type of training, which is called **cross-training**,[100] is that team members can develop shared mental models of what's involved in each of the roles in the team and how the roles fit together to form a system.[101] What exactly does cross-training involve? Researchers have found that cross-training may involve instruction at three different

TABLE 12-2	Teamwork Knowledge, Skills, and Abilities
COMPETENCY	**DESCRIPTION**
Conflict resolution	• Can distinguish between desirable and undesirable conflict. • Encourages desirable conflict and discourages undesirable conflict. • Uses win–win strategies to manage conflict.
Collaborative problem solving	• Can identify situations requiring participative problem solving. • Uses the appropriate degree of participation. • Recognizes and manages obstacles to collaborative problem solving.
Communications	• Understands communication networks. • Communicates openly and supportively. • Listens without making premature evaluations. • Uses active listening techniques. • Can interpret nonverbal messages of others. • Engages in ritual greetings and small talk.
Goal setting and performance management	• Helps establish specific and difficult goals for the team. • Monitors, evaluates, and provides performance-related feedback.
Planning and task coordination	• Coordinates and synchronizes activities among team members. • Establishes expectations to ensure proper balance of workload within the team.

Source: Adapted from M.J. Stevens and M.A. Campion, "The Knowledge, Skill, and Ability Requirements for Teamwork: Implications for Human Resource Management," *Journal of Management* 20 (1994), pp. 503–30.

levels of depth.[102] At the shallowest level, there is **personal clarification**. With this type of training, members simply receive information regarding the roles of the other team members. As an example, the highly specialized members of surgical teams—surgeons, anesthesiologists, operating room nurses—might meet so that they can learn about others' roles and how each contributes to the team's goal of achieving overall patient well-being.

At the next level of cross-training, there is **positional modeling**, which involves team members observing how other members perform their roles. In the case of the surgical teams, the surgeons might spend a day shadowing operating room nurses as they perform their duties. The shadowing not only helps the surgeons gain a better understanding of what the job of a nurse entails but also may provide insight into how the activities involved in their respective jobs could be integrated more effectively.

Finally, the deepest level of cross-training involves **positional rotation**. This type of training gives members actual experience carrying out the responsibilities of their teammates. Although this type of hands-on experience could expand skills of members so that they might actually perform the duties of their teammates if they had to, the level of training required to achieve proficiency or certification in many situations may be prohibitive. For example, because it takes years of specialized training to become a surgeon, it would be impractical to train an operating room nurse to perform this job for the purposes of positional rotation.

TEAM PROCESS TRAINING

Cross-training and training in transportable teamwork competencies focus on individual experiences that promote individual learning. **Team process training**, in contrast, occurs in the context of a team experience that facilitates the team being able to function and perform more effectively as an intact unit. One type of team process training is called **action learning**. With this type of training, which has been used successfully at companies such as Motorola and General Electric, a team is given a real problem that's relevant to the organization and then held accountable for analyzing the problem, developing an action plan, and finally carrying out the action plan.[103] How does this type of experience develop effective team processes? First, the team receives coaching to help facilitate more effective processes during different phases of the project. Second, there are meetings during which team members are encouraged to reflect on the team processes they've used as they worked on the project. In these meetings, the members discuss not only what they observed and learned from their experiences but also what they would do differently in the future.

A second type of team process training involves experience in a team context when there are task demands that highlight the importance of effective teamwork processes. As an example, United Airlines uses pit crew training for its ramp crews.[104] Although teams of ramp workers at an airline like United must work with luggage, belt loaders, and baggage carts, there are parallels with the work of NASCAR pit crews that work with tires, jacks, and air guns. Primarily, effective performance in both contexts means performing work safely within tight time constraints. Moreover, in both of these contexts, achieving goals requires teamwork, communication, and strict adherence to standardized team procedures. The real value of the pit crew training to the ramp crews is that it conveys the lessons of teamwork in a very vivid way. If a team fails to follow procedures and work together when trying to change tires, tools will be misplaced, parts will be dropped, and members will get in one another's way. As a consequence, a pit stop may last for minutes rather than seconds.

TEAM BUILDING

The fourth general type of team process training is called **team building**. This type of training normally is conducted by a consultant and intended to facilitate the development of team processes related to goal setting, interpersonal relations, problem solving, and role clarification.[105] The ropes course is a very popular task used in team building. It requires team members to work together to traverse wooden beams, ropes, and zip lines while dangling in a harness 20–50 feet in the air.

© La Cruces Sun-News, Shari Vialpando/AP Images

Ropes courses are enjoyable to participants and provide a unique opportunity for team members to get to know each other. But can they really build effective teams?

Other examples include laser tag, paintball,[106] WhirlyBall (think lacrosse played in bumper cars with a whiffle ball and plastic scoops),[107] whitewater rafting, scavenger hunts, and beating drums in a drum circle.[108] Team-building activities such as these are hugely popular with organizations of all sizes, and they do seem like an awful lot of fun.

But can you really build effective teams by having them participate in enjoyable activities that seem so unrelated to their jobs? In fact, this was the basis for Senators Byron Dorgan and Ron Wyden's request that the inspector general of the U.S. Postal Service be fired.[109] In their letter to the chairman of the Post Office Board of Governors, they wrote that the inspector general "has spent millions of agency dollars on expensive and silly 'team building' exercises, diverting massive resources from the task of finding waste and improving efficiency. . . . On tapes, you see images of public servants dressed up as the Village People, wearing cat costumes, doing a striptease, and participating in mock trials—all on official time, all at the public's expense."[110] Although it's somewhat difficult to gauge the effectiveness of team-building interventions because so many different types of exercises have been used, research has been conducted that provides mixed support for the senators' claim. The findings of one meta-analysis found that team building did not have a significant effect on team performance when performance was defined in terms of productivity.[111] However, the research found that team building is most likely to have positive effects for smaller teams and when the exercise emphasizes the importance of clarifying role responsibilities. The facilitator of the team-building session also needs to be competent in helping members see the connections between the exercise and their work, and also to ensure inclusion and participation of all members.[112]

TAKEAWAYS

12.1 Taskwork processes are the activities of team members that relate directly to the accomplishment of team tasks. Taskwork processes include creative behavior, decision making, and boundary spanning.

12.2 Teamwork processes refer to the interpersonal activities that facilitate the accomplishment of the team's work but do not directly involve task accomplishment itself. Teamwork processes include transition processes, action processes, and interpersonal processes.

12.3 Communication is a process through which much of the work in a team is accomplished. Effectiveness in communication can be influenced by the communication competence of the sender and receiver, noise, information richness, and network structure.

12.4 Team states refer to specific types of feelings and thoughts that coalesce in the minds of team members as a consequence of their experience working together. Team states include cohesion, potency, mental models, and transactive memory.

12.5 Teamwork processes have a moderate positive relationship with team performance and a strong positive relationship with team commitment.

12.6 Organizations can use training interventions to improve team processes. Such interventions may include training in transportable teamwork competencies, cross-training, team process training, and team building.

KEY TERMS

- Team process   *p. 376*
- Process gain   *p. 378*
- Process loss   *p. 378*
- Coordination loss   *p. 378*
- Production blocking   *p. 378*
- Motivational loss   *p. 378*
- Social loafing   *p. 379*
- Taskwork processes   *p. 379*
- Brainstorming   *p. 379*
- Nominal group technique   *p. 381*
- Decision informity   *p. 381*
- Staff validity   *p. 381*
- Hierarchical sensitivity   *p. 381*
- Boundary spanning   *p. 383*
- Ambassador activities   *p. 383*
- Task coordinator activities   *p. 383*
- Scout activities   *p. 383*
- Teamwork processes   *p. 383*
- Transition processes   *p. 383*
- Action processes   *p. 384*

- Interpersonal processes   *p. 384*
- Relationship conflict   *p. 385*
- Task conflict   *p. 385*
- Communication   *p. 386*
- Information richness   *p. 387*
- Network structure   *p. 388*
- Team states   *p. 389*
- Cohesion   *p. 390*
- Groupthink   *p. 390*
- Potency   *p. 390*
- Mental models   *p. 392*

- Transactive memory   *p. 392*
- Transportable teamwork
  competencies   *p. 395*
- Cross-training   *p. 395*
- Personal clarification   *p. 396*
- Positional modeling   *p. 396*
- Positional rotation   *p. 396*
- Team process training   *p. 397*
- Action learning   *p. 397*
- Team building   *p. 397*

DISCUSSION QUESTIONS

12.1 Before reading this chapter, how did you define teamwork? How did this definition correspond to the definition outlined in this book?

12.2 Think of a team you've worked in that performed poorly. Were any of the causes of the poor performance related to the forces that tend to create process loss? If so, which force was most problematic? What steps, if any, did your team take to deal with the problem?

12.3 Think about the team states described in this chapter. If you joined a new team, how long do you think it would take you to get a feel for those team states? Which states would you be able to gauge first? Which would take longer?

12.4 Describe the communication process in a student team of which you've been a member. Were there examples of "noise" that detracted from the team members' ability to communicate with one another? What was the primary mode of communication among members? Did this mode of communication possess an appropriate level of information richness? Which network structure comes closest to describing the one that the team used to communicate? Was the level of centralization appropriate?

12.5 Which types of teamwork training would your student team benefit most from? What exactly would this training cover? What specific benefits would you expect? What would prevent a team from training itself on this material?

CASE: NASA

NASA is planning a mission to send a crew of astronauts to Mars. Among other objectives, scientists are interested in the possibility of growing food in space, as there are now reasons to believe that Mars may be a good place to farm. Although this mission isn't scheduled until the year 2030 or so, NASA has already begun to explore how aspects of the mission are likely to impact the crew's ability to function effectively. You see, the crew of six to eight astronauts assigned to the mission will be living and working together in a noisy capsule about the size of an average kitchen for three years—it takes 6 months to get there, they'll stay for 18 months, and then there's the 6-month journey home. Given the constraints of their environment, and the fact that the crew will be working long hours under very demanding conditions, it's inevitable that they'll get on one another's nerves on occasion. There's literally no place to go to escape minor annoyances, and as frustration builds, the probability of emotional outbursts and interpersonal conflict increases.

Of course, it goes without saying that conflict among astronauts in a small space capsule millions of miles away from Earth is not a good thing. Astronauts who fail to fulfill a responsibility because they're preoccupied with conflict could put the mission, and the lives of the entire crew, in jeopardy, and this is true whether the conflict is bubbling beneath the surface or has risen to the surface. Hard feelings could hinder teamwork as well, and the failure to communicate an important piece of information or to provide help to a member of the crew in need of assistance, as examples, could also lead to disaster. Unfortunately, however, the duration and demands of the mission are almost without precedent, and therefore, the specific practices that need to be implemented to facilitate crew functioning in this context are unknown.

To address this issue, NASA has awarded grants to psychologists to study teams that have to live and work together in isolated, confined, and extreme environments for extended periods of time. To help increase understanding of conflict and teamwork and how it can be better managed, the psychologists are working on technology that tracks the whereabouts of each crew member, as well as his or her vocal intensity and vital functions such as heart rate. This information would be used to pinpoint where and when conflict occurs and to understand how conflict influences subsequent crew interactions. The crew will be given feedback so they can learn how conflict hurts teamwork and cohesion. This feedback could also motivate crews to take the time to discuss teamwork issues and to devise ways to manage conflict and other process problems. Although it's impossible to anticipate all the potential issues that could arise on the mission to Mars, NASA believes that research on team process is necessary to enhance the viability and performance of the crew that is ultimately charged with the task.

12.1   Which team processes do you believe are most important to the crew of astronauts traveling to Mars? Why? Are there specific team processes you feel are relatively unimportant? Explain.

12.2   Describe additional types of information that could be collected by the psychologists to help crews better understand their interactions and how they influence crew effectiveness.

12.3   Discuss how team training could be used to build effective processes for the crew traveling to Mars.

Sources: T. Halvorson, "8 Score Astronaut Spots out of 6,300 NASA Applicants," *USA Today,* June 18, 2013, http://www.usatoday.com/story/tech/2013/06/18/eight-score-astronaut-spots-nasa/2433565/; E. John and B. Taupin, *Rocket Man* (1972).,Universal Music Publishing Group; C. Moskowitz, "Farming on Mars? NASA Ponders for Supply for 2030 Mission," *FoxNews.com.* May 15, 2013, http://www.foxnews.com/science/2013/05/15/farming-onmars-nasa/; NASA Website, "NASA History" (n.d.), http://history.nasa.gov (accessed July 8, 2013); A. Novotney, "I/O Psychology Goes to Mars," *Monitor on Psychology* (March 2013), pp. 38–41; and R. Plushnick-Masti, "NASA Builds Menu for Planned Mars Mission in 2030s," *AP Online.* July 17, 2012, http://bigstory.ap.org/article/nasa-builds-menu-planned-mars-mission-2030s.

EXERCISE: WILDERNESS SURVIVAL

The purpose of this exercise is to experience team processes during a decision-making task. This exercise uses groups, so your instructor will either assign you to a group or ask you to create your own group. The exercise has the following steps:

12.1   Working individually, read the following scenario:

You have gone on a Boundary Waters canoe trip with five friends to upper Minnesota and southern Ontario in the Quetico Provincial Park. Your group has been traveling Saganagons Lake to Kawnipi Lake, following through Canyon Falls and Kennebas Falls and Kenny Lake. Fifteen to 18 miles away is the closest road, which is arrived at by paddling through lakes and rivers and usually portaging (taking the land path) around numerous falls. Saganagons Lake is impossible to cross in bad weather, generally because of heavy rain. The nearest town is Grand Marais, Minnesota, 60 miles away. That town has plenty of camping outfitters but limited medical help, so residents rely on hospitals farther to the south.

The terrain is about 70 percent land and 30 percent water, with small patches of land here and there in between the lakes and rivers. Bears are not uncommon in this region. It's now mid-May, when the (daytime) temperature ranges from about 25°F to 70°F, often in the same day. Nighttime temperatures can be in the 20s. Rain is frequent during the day (nights, too) and can be life threatening if the temperature is cold. It's unusual for the weather to stay the same for more than a day or two. Generally, it will rain one day and be warm and clear the next, with a third day windy—and it's not easy to predict what type of weather will come next. In fact, it may be clear and warm, rainy and windy, all in the same day.

Your group was in two canoes going down the river and came to some rapids. Rather than taking the portage route on land, the group foolishly decided to shoot the rapids by canoe. Unfortunately, everyone fell out of the canoes, and some were banged against the rocks. Luckily, no one was killed, but one person suffered a broken leg, and several others had cuts and bruises. Both canoes were damaged severely. Both were bent in half, one with an open tear of 18 inches, while the other suffered two tears of 12 and 15 inches long. Both have broken gunwales (the upper edges on both sides). You lost the packs that held the tent, most clothing, nearly all the food, cooking equipment, the fuel, the first aid kit, and the flashlight. Your combined possessions include the items shown in the table on the next page.

You had permits to take this trip, but no one knows for sure where you are, and the closest phone is in Grand Marais. You were scheduled back four days from now, so it's likely a search party would be sent out in about five days (because you could have been delayed a day or so in getting back). Just now it has started to drizzle, and it looks like rain will follow. Your task is to figure out how to survive in these unpredictable and possibly harsh conditions until you can get help.

12.2 Working individually, consider how important each of the items in the table would be to you in this situation. Begin with the most important item, giving it a rank of "1," and wind up with the least important item, giving it a rank of "14." Put your rankings in Column B.

12.3 In your groups, come to a consensus about the ranking of the items. Put those consensus rankings in Column C. Group members should not merely vote or average rankings together. Instead, try to get everyone to more or less agree on the rankings. When someone disagrees, try to listen carefully. When someone feels strongly, that person should attempt to use persuasive techniques to create a consensus.

12.4 The instructor will post the correct answers and provide the reasons for those rankings, according to two experts (Jeff Stemmerman and Ken Gieske of REI Outfitters, both of whom act as guides for many canoe trips in the Boundary Waters region). Put those expert rankings in Column D. At this point, the Individual Error scores in Column A can be computed by taking the absolute difference between Column B and Column D. The Group Error scores in Column E can also be computed by taking the absolute difference between Column C and Column D. Finally, the Persuasion scores can be computed by taking the absolute difference between Column B and Column C. Remember that all of the differences are absolute differences—there should not be any negative numbers in the table. After completing all these computations, fill in the three scores below the table: the Individual Score (total of Column A), the Group Score (total of Column E), and the Persuasion Score (total of Column F). The Persuasion score measures how much you are able to influence other group members to match your thinking.

12.5   The instructor will create a table similar to the one that follows in an Excel file in the classroom or on the board. All groups should provide the instructor with their Average Member Score (the average of all of the Individual Scores for the group), the Group Score, their Best Member Score (the lowest of all the Individual Scores for the group), and that member's Persuasion Score (the Persuasion Score for the member who had the lowest Individual Score).

	A	B	C	D	E	F
	INDIVIDUAL ERROR (B–D)	YOUR RANKING	GROUP RANKING	EXPERT RANKING	GROUP ERROR (C–D)	PERSUASION SCORE (B–C)
Fanny pack of food (cheese, salami, etc.)						
Plastic-covered map of the region						
Six personal flotation devices						
Two fishing poles (broken)						
Set of clothes for three (wet)						
One yellow Frisbee						
Water purification tablets						
Duct tape (one 30-ft roll)						
Whiskey (one pint, 180 proof)						
Insect repellant (one bottle)						
Matches (30, dry)						
Parachute cord (35 ft)						
Compass						
Six sleeping bags (synthetic)						

Individual Score: (Total all numbers in Column A): _____

Group Score: (Total all numbers in Column E): _____

Persuasion Score: (Total all numbers in Column F): _____

12.6   Fill in a "Yes" for the Process Gain row if the Group Score was lower than the Average Member Score. This score would reflect a circumstance in which the group discussion actually resulted in more accurate decisions—when "the whole" seemed to be more effective than "the sum of its parts." Fill in a "No" for the Process Gain row if the Group Score was higher than the Average Member Score. In this circumstance, the group discussion actually resulted in less accurate decisions—and the group would have been better off if no talking had occurred.

GROUPS	1	2	3	4	5	6	7	8
Average Member Score								
Group Score								
Best Member Score								
Best Member's Persuasion								
Process Gain? (Yes or No)								

12.7 Class discussion (whether in groups or as a class) should center on the following questions: Did most groups tend to achieve process gain in terms of group scores that were better than the average individual scores? Were the group scores usually better than the best member's score? Why not; where did the groups that lacked synergy tend to go wrong? In other words, what behaviors led to process loss rather than process gain? What role does the best member's persuasion score play in all of this? Did groups that tended to listen more to the best member (as reflected in lower persuasion numbers) have more frequent instances of process gain?

Source: D. Marcic, J. Selzer, and P. Vail. *Organizational Behavior: Experiences and Cases.* Cincinnati, OH: South-Western, 2001.

ENDNOTES

12.1 Ilgen, D.R.; D.A. Major; J.R. Hollenbeck; and D.J. Sego. "Team Research in the 1990s." In *Leadership Theory and Research: Perspectives and Directions,* ed. M.M. Chemers and R. Ayman. New York: Academic Press, 1993, pp. 245–70.

12.2 "Process." *Merriam-Webster online dictionary* (n.d.), http://www.merriam-webster.com/dictionary/process.

12.3 Bellman, G., and K. Ryan. "Creating an Extraordinary Group." *T&D* (September 2010), pp. 56–61.

12.4 Hackman, J.R. "The Design of Work Teams." In *Handbook of Organizational Behavior,* ed. J.W. Lorsch. Englewood Cliffs, NJ: Prentice Hall, 1987, pp. 315–42.

12.5 Steiner, I.D. *Group Processes and Productivity.* New York: Academic Press, 1972.

12.6 Hackman, "The Design of Work Teams."

12.7 Lamm, H., and G. Trommsdorff. "Group versus Individual Performance on Tasks Requiring Ideational Proficiency (Brainstorming)." *European Journal of Social Psychology* 3 (1973), pp. 361–87.

12.8 Hackman, "The Design of Work Teams."

12.9 Latane, B.; K. Williams; and S. Harkins. "Many Hands Make Light the Work: The Causes and Consequences of Social Loafing." *Journal of Personality and Social Psychology* 37 (1979), pp. 822–32.

12.10 Ibid.; Jackson, C.L., and J.A. LePine. "Peer Responses to a Team's Weakest Link: A Test and Extension of LePine and Van Dyne's Model." *Journal of Applied Psychology* 88 (2003), pp. 459–75; and Sheppard, A. "Productivity Loss in Performance Groups: A Motivation Analysis." *Psychological Bulletin* 113 (1993), pp. 67–81.

12.11 Shalley, C.E.; J. Zhou; and G.R. Oldham. "The Effects of

Personal and Contextual Characteristics on Creativity: Where Should We Go from Here?" *Journal of Management* 30 (2004), pp. 933–58.

12.12 Miron-Spektor, E.; M. Erez; and E. Naveh. "The Effect of Conformist and Attentive-to-Detail Members on Team Innovation: Reconciling the Innovation Paradox." *Academy of Management Journal* 54 (2011), pp. 740–60.

12.13 Hirst, G.; D. van Knippenberg; and J. Zhou. "A Cross-Level Perspective on Employee Creativity: Goal Orientation, Team Learning Behavior, and Individual Creativity." *Academy of Management Journal* 52 (2009), pp. 280–93.

12.14 Kelley, T., and J. Littman. *The Art of Innovation.* New York: Doubleday, 2001, p. 69.

12.15 Osborn, A.F. *Applied Imagination* (revised ed.). New York: Scribner, 1957.

12.16 Ibid.

12.17 Diehl, M., and W. Stroebe. "Productivity Loss in Brainstorming Groups: Toward a Solution of a Riddle." *Journal of Personality and Social Psychology* 53 (1987), pp. 497–509; and Mullen, B.; C. Johnson; and E. Salas. "Productivity Loss in Brainstorming Groups: A Meta-Analytic Investigation." *Basic and Applied Social Psychology* 12 (1991), pp. 3–23.

12.18 Diehl and Stroebe, "Productivity Loss."

12.19 Sutton, R.I., and A. Hargadon. "Brainstorming Groups in Context: Effectiveness in a Product Design Firm." *Administrative Science Quarterly* 41 (1996), pp. 685–718.

12.20 Kelley and Littman, *The Art of Innovation.*

12.21 Delbecq, A.L., and A.H. Van de Ven. "A Group Process Model for Identification and Program Planning." *Journal of Applied Behavioral Sciences* 7 (1971), pp. 466–92; and Geschka, H.; G.R. Schaude; and H. Schlicksupp. "Modern Techniques for Solving Problems." *Chemical Engineering,* August 1973, pp. 91–97.

12.22 Bornstein, B.H., and E. Greene. "Jury Decision Making: Implications for and from Psychology." *Current Directions in Psychological Science* 20 (2011), pp. 63–67.

12.23 Ibid.

12.24 Salerno, J., and S. Diamond. "The Promise of a Cognitive Perspective on Jury Deliberation." *Psychonomic Bulletin & Review* 17 (2010), pp. 174–79.

12.25 Lieberman, J.D. "The Utility of Scientific Jury Selection: Still Murky after 30 Years." *Current Directions in Psychological Science* 20 (2011), pp. 48–52.

12.26 Brehmer, B., and R. Hagafors. "Use of

Experts in Complex Decision Making: A Paradigm for the Study of Staff Work." *Organizational Behavior and Human Decision Processes* 38 (1986), pp. 181–95; and Ilgen, D.R.; D. Major; J.R. Hollenbeck; and D. Sego. "Raising an Individual Decision Making Model to the Team Level: A New Research Model and Paradigm." In *Team Effectiveness and Decision Making in Organizations,* ed. R. Guzzo and E. Salas. San Francisco: Jossey-Bass, 1995, pp. 113–48.

12.27 Hollenbeck, J.R.; A.P.J. Ellis; S.E. Humphrey; A.S. Garza; and D.R. Ilgen. "Asymmetry in Structural Adaptation: The Differential Impact of Centralizing versus Decentralizing Team Decision-Making Structures." *Organizational Behavior and Human Decision Processes* 114 (2011), pp. 64–74.

12.28 Hollenbeck, J.R.; J.A. Colquitt; D.R. Ilgen; J.A. LePine; and J. Hedlund. "Accuracy Decomposition and Team Decision Making: Testing Theoretical Boundary Conditions." *Journal of Applied Psychology* 83 (1998), pp. 494–500; and Hollenbeck, J.R.; D.R. Ilgen; D.J. Sego; J. Hedlund; D.A. Major; and J. Phillips. "Multilevel Theory of Team Decision Making; Decision Performance in Teams Incorporating Distributed Expertise."

Journal of Applied Psychology 80 (1995), pp. 292–316.

12.29 Humphrey, S.E.; J.R. Hollenbeck; C.J. Meyer; and D.R. Ilgen. "Hierarchical Team Decision Making." *Research in Personnel and Human Resources Management* 21 (2002), pp. 175–213.

12.30 Hollenbeck et al., "Multilevel Theory of Team Decision Making"; and Hollenbeck, J.R.; D.R. Ilgen; J.A. LePine; J.A. Colquitt; and J. Hedlund. "Extending the Multilevel Theory of Team Decision Making: Effects of Feedback and Experience in Hierarchical Teams." *Academy of Management Journal* 41 (1998), pp. 269–82.

12.31 Hollenbeck et al., "Extending the Multilevel Theory."

12.32 Hedlund, J.; D.R. Ilgen; and J.R. Hollenbeck. "Decision Accuracy in Computer-Mediated vs. Face-to-Face Decision Making Teams." *Organizational Behavior and Human Decision Processes* 76 (1998), pp. 30–47.

12.33 Ilgen, D.R.; J.A. LePine; and J.R. Hollenbeck. "Effective Decision Making in Multinational Teams." In *New Perspectives in International Industrial–Organizational Psychology,* ed. P.C. Earley and M. Erez. San Francisco: Jossey-Bass, 1997, pp. 377–409.

12.34 Ancona, D.G. "Outward Bound: Strategies for Team Survival in an Organization." *Academy of Management Journal* 33 (1990), pp. 334–65.

12.35 Ibid.; and Marrone, J.A.; P.E. Tesluk; and J.B. Carson. "A Multilevel Investigation of Antecedents and Consequences of Team Member Boundary-Spanning Behavior." *Academy of Management Journal* 50 (2007), pp. 1423–39.

12.36 De Vries, T.A.; F. Walter; G.S. Van Der Vegt; and P.J.M.D. Essens. "Antecedents of Individuals' Interteam Coordination: Broad Functional Experiences as a Mixed Blessing." *Academy of Management Journal* 57 (2014), pp. 1334–59.

12.37 LePine, J.A.; R.F. Piccolo; C.L. Jackson; J.E. Mathieu; and J.R. Saul. "A Meta-Analysis of Team Process: Toward a Better Understanding of the Dimensional Structure and Relationships with Team Effectiveness Criteria." *Personnel Psychology* 61 (2008), pp. 273–307; and Marks, M.A.; J.E. Mathieu; and S.J. Zaccaro. "A Temporally Based Framework and Taxonomy of Team Processes." *Academy of Management Review* 26 (2001), pp. 356–76.

12.38 Marks et al., "A Temporally Based Framework." This section on teamwork processes is based largely on their work.

12.39 Fisher, D.M. "Distinguishing between Taskwork and Teamwork Planning in Teams: Relations with Coordination and Interpersonal Processes." *Journal of Applied Psychology* 99 (2014), pp. 423–36.

12.40 Eddy, E.R.; S.I Tannenbaum; and J.E. Mathieu. "Helping Teams to Help Themselves: Comparing Two Team-Led Debriefing Methods." *Personnel Psychology* 66 (2013), pp. 975–1008; and Villado, A.J., and W. Arthur Jr. "The Comparative Effect of Subjective and Objective After-Action Reviews on Team Performance on a Complex Task." *Journal of Applied Psychology* 98 (2013), pp. 514–28.

12.41 Barnes, C.M.; J.R. Hollenbeck; D.T. Wagner; D.S. DeRue; J.D. Nahrgang; and K.M. Schwind. "Harmful Help: The Costs of Backing-Up Behavior in Teams." *Journal of Applied Psychology* 93 (2008), pp. 529–39.

12.42 Kozlowski, S.W.J., and B.S. Bell. "Work Groups and Teams in Organizations." In *Handbook of Psychology, Vol. 12: Industrial and Organizational Psychology,* ed. W.C. Borman; D.R. Ilgen; and R.J. Klimoski; Hoboken, NJ: Wiley 2003, pp. 333–75.

12.43 Behfar, K.J.; R.S. Peterson; E.A. Mannix; and W.M.K. Trochim.

"The Critical Role of Conflict Resolution in Teams: A Close Look at the Links between Conflict Type, Conflict Management Strategies, and Team Outcomes." *Journal of Applied Psychology* 93 (2008), pp. 170–88; and De Dreu, C.K.W., and L.R. Weingart. "Task versus Relationship Conflict, Team Performance, and Team Member Satisfaction: A Meta-Analysis." *Journal of Applied Psychology* 88 (2003), pp. 741–49.

12.44   Jehn, K. "A Multi-method Examination of the Benefits and Detriments of Intergroup Conflict." *Administrative Science Quarterly* 40 (1995), pp. 256–82.

12.45   De Dreu and Weingart, "Task Versus Relationship Conflict"; and DeChurch, L.A., J.R. Mesmer-Magnus, and D. Doty. "Moving Beyond Relationship and Task Conflict: Toward a Process-State Perspective." *Journal of Applied Psychology* 98 (2013), pp. 559–78.

12.46   de Wit, F.R.C.; J.L. Greer; and K.A. Jehn. "The Paradox of Intragroup Conflict: A Meta-Analysis." *Journal of Applied Psychology* 97 (2012), pp. 360–90.

12.47   Bradley, B.H.; A.C. Klotz; B.E. Postlethwaite; and K.G. Brown. "Ready to Rumble: How Team Personality Composition and Task Conflict

Interact to Improve Performance." *Journal of Applied Psychology* 98 (2013), pp. 385–92.

12.48   Thompson, L.L. *Making the Team: A Guide for Managers,* 2nd ed. Upper Saddle River, NJ: Pearson Prentice Hall, 2004.

12.49   DeChurch, L.A., and M.A. Marks. "Maximizing the Benefits of Task Conflict: The Role of Conflict Management." *The International Journal of Conflict Management* 12 (2001), pp. 4–22; De Dreu and Weingart, "Task Versus Relationship Conflict"; Van de Vliert, E., and M.C. Euwema. "Agreeableness and Activeness as Components of Conflict Behaviors." *Journal of Personality and Social Psychology* 66 (1994), pp. 674–87; and Todorova, G.; J. B. Bear; and J.R. Weingart. "Can Conflict Be Energizing? A Study of Task Conflict, Positive Emotions, and Job Satisfaction." *Journal of Applied Psychology* 99 (2014), pp. 451–67.

12.50   DeChurch and Marks, "Maximizing the Benefits"; and Van de Vliert and Euwema, "Agreeableness and Activeness."

12.51   Langan-Fox, J. "Communication in Organizations: Speed, Diversity, Networks, and Influence on Organizational Effectiveness, Human Health, and Relationships." In *Handbook of*

Industrial, Work, and Organizational Psychology, Vol. 2, ed. N. Anderson, D.S. Ones, and H.K. Sinangil. Thousand Oaks, CA: Sage 2001, pp. 188–205.

12.52   Krone, K.J.; F.M. Jablin; and L.L. Putman. "Communication Theory and Organizational Communication: Multiple Perspectives." In *Handbook of Organizational Communication,* ed. F.M. Jablin, K.L. Putman, KH. Roberts, and L.W. Porter. Newbury Park, CA: Sage, 1987; and Shannon, C.E., and W. Weaver. *The Mathematical Theory of Communication.* Urbana: University of Illinois Press, 1964.

12.53   Ibid.

12.54   Jablin, F.M., and P.M. Sias. "Communication Competence." In *The New Handbook of Organizational Communication: Advances in Theory, Research, and Methods,* ed. F.M. Jablin and L.L. Putnam. Thousand Oaks, CA: Sage, 2001, pp. 819–64.

12.55   Jordan, P.J., and A.C. Troth. "Managing Emotions During Team Problem Solving: Emotional Intelligence and Conflict Resolution." *Human Performance* 17 (2004), pp. 195–218.

12.56   Rafaeli, A., and R.I. Sutton. "Expression of Emotion as Part of the Work Role." *Academy of Management Review* 12 (1987), pp. 23–37.

12.57 Warkentin, M., and P.M. Beranek. "Training to Improve Virtual Team Communication." *Information Systems Journal* 9 (1999), pp. 271–89.

12.58 Krone et al., "Communication Theory and Organizational Communication"; and Shannon and Weaver, "The Mathematical Theory of Communication."

12.59 Daft, R.L., and R.H. Lengel. "Information Richness: A New Approach to Managerial Behavior and Organizational Design." In *Research in Organizational Behavior,* ed. B.M. Staw and L.L. Cummings. Greenwich, CT: JAI Press, 1984, pp. 191–233.

12.60 Ibid.

12.61 Ibid.

12.62 Ibid.

12.63 Byron, K. "Carrying Too Heavy a Load? The Communication and Miscommunication of Emotion by Email." *Academy of Management Review* 33 (2008), pp. 309–27.

12.64 Daft and Lengel, "Information Richness."

12.65 Ibid.

12.66 Leavitt, H.J. "Some Effects of Certain Communication Patterns on Group Performance." *Journal of Abnormal and Social Psychology* 436 (1951), pp. 38–50.

12.67 Glanzer, M., and R. Glaser. "Techniques for the Study of Group Structure and Behavior: II. Empirical Studies of the Effects of Structure in Small Groups." *Psychological Bulletin* 58 (1961), pp. 1–27.

12.68 Farace, R.V.; P.R. Monge; and H.M. Russell. "Communication in Micro-Networks." In *Organizational Communication,* 2nd ed., ed. F.D. Ferguson and S. Ferguson. New Brunswick, NJ: Transaction Books, 1988, pp. 365–69.

12.69 Roberts, B. "Developing a Social Business Network." *HR Magazine,* October 2010, pp. 54–60.

12.70 Davenport, R. "More Than a Game." *T&D,* June 2010, pp. 26–29.

12.71 Oh, O.; H.K. Kyounghee; and H.R. Rao. "An Exploration of Social Media in Extreme Events: Rumor Theory and Twitter during the Haiti Earthquake 2010, *ICIS 2010 Proceedings.* http://aisel.aisnet.org/icis2010_submissions/231/.

12.72 Edmondson, A. "Psychological Safety and Learning Behavior in Work Teams." *Administrative Science Quarterly* 44 (1999), pp. 350–83; Kostopoulos, K., and N. Bozionelos. "Team Exploratory and Exploitative Learning: Psychological Safety, Task Conflict and Team Performance." *Group and Organization Management* 36 (2011), pp. 385–415; and Morrison, E.W.; S.L. Wheeler-Smith; and K. Dishan. "Speaking up in Groups: A Cross-Level Study of Group Voice Climate and Voice." *Journal of Applied Psychology* 96 (2011), pp. 183–91.

12.73 Williams, K.D., and S.A. Nida. "Ostracism: Consequences and Coping." *Current Directions in Psychological Science* 20 (2011), pp. 71–75.

12.74 Mach, M.; S. Dolan; and S. Tzafrir. "The Differential Effect of Team Members' Trust on Team Performance: The Mediation Role of Team Cohesion." *Journal of Occupational and Organizational Psychology* 83 (2010), pp. 771–94.

12.75 Festinger, L. "Informal Social Communication." *Psychological Review* 57 (1950), pp. 271–82.

12.76 Beal, D.J.; R.R. Cohen; M.J. Burke; and C.L. McLendon. "Cohesion and Performance in Groups: A Meta-Analytic Clarification of Construct Relations." *Journal of Applied Psychology* 88 (2003), pp. 989–1004; and Mullen, B., and C. Copper. "The Relation between Group Cohesiveness and Performance: An Integration." *Psychological Bulletin* 115 (1994), pp. 210–27.

12.77 Mathieu, J.E.; M.R. Kukenberger; D. D'Innocenzo; and G. Reilly. "Modeling Reciprocal Team

Cohesion-Performance Relationships, as Impacted by Shared Leadership and Members' Competence." *Journal of Applied Psychology* 100 (2015), pp. 713–34.

12.78   Janis, I.L. *Victims of Groupthink: A Psychological Study of Foreign Policy Decisions and Fiascoes.* Boston, MA: Houghton Mifflin, 1972.

12.79   Ibid.

12.80   Hirokawa, R.; D. Gouran; and A. Martz. "Understanding the Sources of Faulty Group Decision Making: A Lesson from the *Challenger* Disaster." *Small Group Behavior* 19 (1988), pp. 411–33; Esser, J., and J. Linoerfer. "Groupthink and the Space Shuttle *Challenger* Accident: Toward a Quantitative Case Analysis." *Journal of Behavioral Decision Making* 2 (1989), pp. 167–77; and Moorhead, G.; R. Ference; and C. Neck. "Group Decision Fiascoes Continue: Space Shuttle *Challenger* and a Revised Groupthink Framework." *Human Relations* 44 (1991), pp. 539–50.

12.81   Stephens, J., and P. Behr. "Enron Culture Fed Its Demise." *Washington Post,* June 27, 2002, pp. A1–A2.

12.82   Shea, G.P., and R.A. Guzzo. "Groups as Human Resources." In *Research in Personnel and Human Resource Management,* Vol. 5, ed. K.M. Rowland and

G.R. Ferris. Greenwich, CT: JAI Press, 1987, pp. 323–56.

12.83   Tasa, K.; S. Taggar; and G.H. Seijts. "Development of Collective Efficacy in Teams: A Multilevel and Longitudinal Perspective." *Journal of Applied Psychology* 92 (2007), pp. 17–27.

12.84   Gully, S.M.; K.A. Incalaterra; A. Joshi; and J.M. Beubien. "A Meta-Analysis of Team-Efficacy, Potency, and Performance: Interdependence and Level of Analysis as Moderators of Observed Relationships." *Journal of Applied Psychology* 87 (2002), pp. 819–32.

12.85   Rapp, T.L.; B.G. Bachrach; A.A. Rapp; and R. Mullins. "The Role of Team Goal Monitoring in the Curvilinear Relationship between Team Efficacy and Team Performance." *Journal of Applied Psychology* 99 (2014), pp. 976–87.

12.86   Concalo, J.A.; E. Polman; and C. Maslach. "Can Confidence Come Too Soon? Collective Efficacy, Conflict and Group Performance over Time." *Organizational Behavior and Human Decision Processes* 113 (2010), pp. 13–24.

12.87   Tasa et al., "Development of Collective Efficacy in Teams."

12.88   Klimoski, R.J., and S. Mohammed. "Team Mental Model:

Construct or Metaphor?" *Journal of Management* 20 (1994), pp. 403–37.

12.89   Cannon-Bowers, J.A.; E. Salas; and S.A. Converse. "Shared Mental Models in Expert Team Decision Making." *Individual and Group Decision Making,* ed. N.J. Castellan. Hillsdale, NJ: Erlbaum, 1993, pp. 221–46.

12.90   Wegner, D.M. "Transactive Memory: A Contemporary Analysis of the Group Mind." In *Theories of Group Behavior,* ed. B. Mullen and G.R. Goethals. New York: Springer-Verlag, 1986, pp. 185–208.

12.91   Mell, J.N.; Van Knippenberg, D.; and Van Ginkel, W.P. "The Catalyst Effect: The Impact of Transactive Memory System Structure on Team Performance." *Academy of Management Journal* 57 (2014), pp. 1154–73.

12.92   Hollingshead, A.B. "Communication, Learning, and Retrieval in Transactive Memory Systems." *Journal of Experimental Social Psychology* 34 (1998), pp. 423–42.

12.93   Wegner, "Transactive Memory."

12.94   LePine et al., "A Meta-Analysis of Team Process."

12.95   Barrick, M.R.; B.H. Bradley; A.L. Kristoff Brown; and A.E. Colbert. "The Moderating Role of Top

Management Team Interdependence: Implications for Real Teams and Working Groups." *Academy of Management Journal* 50 (2007), pp. 544–57; Vashidi, D.R.; P.A. Bamberger; and M. Erez. "Can Surgical Teams Ever Learn? The Role of Coordination, Complexity, and Transitivity in Action Team Learning." *Academy of Management Journal* 56 (2013), pp. 945-71.

12.96 LePine et al., "A Meta-Analysis of Team Process."

12.97 Stevens, M.J., and M.A. Campion. "The Knowledge, Skill, and Ability Requirements for Teamwork: Implications for Human Resource Management." *Journal of Management* 20 (1994), pp. 503–30.

12.98 Ibid.; and Ellis, A.P.J.; B. Bell; R.E. Ployhart; J.R. Hollenbeck; and D.R. Ilgen. "An Evaluation of Generic Teamwork Skills Training with Action Teams: Effects on Cognitive and Skill-Based Outcomes." *Personnel Psychology* 58 (2005), pp. 641–72.

12.99 Stout, R.J.; E. Salas; and J.E. Fowlkes. "Enhancing Teamwork in Complex Environments through Team Training." *Group Dynamics: Theory, Research, and Practice* 1 (1997), pp. 169–82.

12.100 Volpe, C.E.; J.A. Cannon-Bowers; E. Salas; and P.E. Spector. "The Impact of Cross-Training on Team Functioning: An Empirical Investigation." *Human Factors* 38 (1996), pp. 87–100.

12.101 Marks, M.A.; M.J. Sabella; C.S. Burke; and S.J. Zaccaro. "The Impact of Cross-Training on Team Effectiveness." *Journal of Applied Psychology* 87 (2002), pp. 3–13.

12.102 Blickensderfer, E.; J.A. Cannon-Bowers; and E. Salas. "Cross Training and Team Performance." In *Making Decisions Under Stress: Implications for Individual and Team Training*, ed. J.A. Cannon-Bowers and E. Salas. Washington, DC: APA Press, 1998, pp. 299–311.

12.103 Dotlich, D., and J. Noel. *Active Learning: How the World's Top Companies Are Recreating Their Leaders and Themselves.* San Francisco: Jossey-Bass, 1998; and Marquardt, M. "Harnessing the Power of Action Learning." *T&D* 58 (June 2004), pp. 26–32.

12.104 Carey, S. "Racing to Improve; United Airlines Employees Go to School for Pit Crews to Boost Teamwork, Speed." *The Wall Street Journal,* Eastern Edition, March 24, 2006, p. B1.

12.105 Salas, E.; D. Bozell; B. Mullen; and J.E. Driskell. "The Effect of Team Building on Performance: An Integration." *Small Group Research* 30 (1999), pp. 309–29.

12.106 Berman, D. "Zap! Pow! Splat!; Laser Tag and Paintball Can Enhance Teamwork, Communications, and Planning." *BusinessWeek,* February 9, 1998, p. ENT22. ProQuest Database (accessed April 19, 2007).

12.107 Rasor, M. "Got Game? Bring It On: WhirlyBall Helps Workers Develop Drive, Teamwork." *Knight Ridder Tribune Business News,* April 3, 2006, p. 1. ProQuest Database (accessed May 7, 2006).

12.108 Regan, M.P. "Team Players: From Drums to Daring Getaways, Workers Embark on Team-Building Exercises." *Gainesville Sun,* February 15, 2004, pp. 5G, 6G.

12.109 Ballard, T.N. "Postal IG under Fire for Unusual 'Team-Building' Activities." GovernmentExecutive.com, 2003, http://www.govexec.com/dailyfed/0503/050203t1.htm.

12.110 Dorgan, B.L., and R. Widen. "Letter to Chairman Fineman," May 1, 2003, http://www.govexec.com/pdfs/corcoran.pdf.

12.111 Salas et al., "The Effect of Team Building."

12.112 Chang, W.W. "Is the Group Activity Food or Poison in a Multicultural Classroom?" *T&D* (April 2010), pp. 34–37.

Leadership: Power and Negotiation

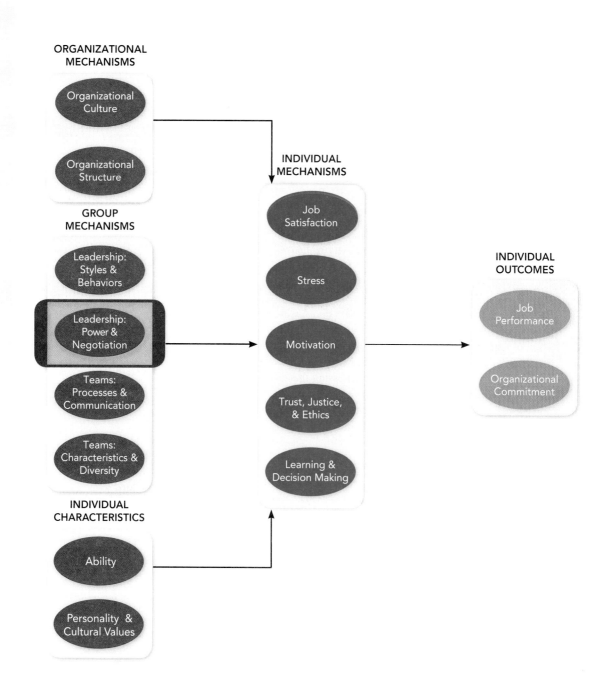

ORGANIZATIONAL MECHANISMS
- Organizational Culture
- Organizational Structure

GROUP MECHANISMS
- Leadership: Styles & Behaviors
- Leadership: Power & Negotiation
- Teams: Processes & Communication
- Teams: Characteristics & Diversity

INDIVIDUAL CHARACTERISTICS
- Ability
- Personality & Cultural Values

INDIVIDUAL MECHANISMS
- Job Satisfaction
- Stress
- Motivation
- Trust, Justice, & Ethics
- Learning & Decision Making

INDIVIDUAL OUTCOMES
- Job Performance
- Organizational Commitment

© Steve Jennings/Getty Images Entertainment/Getty Images for TechCrunch

✓ LEARNING GOALS

After reading this chapter, you should be able to answer the following questions:

13.1 What is leadership, and what role does power play in leadership?

13.2 What are the different types of power that leaders possess, and when can they use those types most effectively?

13.3 What behaviors do leaders exhibit when trying to influence others, and which of these is most effective?

13.4 What is organizational politics, and when is political behavior most likely to occur?

13.5 How do leaders use their power and influence to resolve conflicts in the workplace?

13.6 What are the ways in which leaders negotiate in the workplace?

13.7 How do power and influence affect job performance and organizational commitment?

THERANOS

Elizabeth Holmes, at 31, is number 1 atop *Forbe*'s list of self-made women and was named one of *Time* magazine's 100 most influential people. She is the founder and CEO, and has a 51 percent equity stake, in Theranos, a hardware and medical company now valued at more than $9 billion. The company's goal is to revolutionize the way blood testing is done worldwide. Theranos (a combination of the words therapy and diagnose) is a private company headquartered in Palo Alto, California, with 700 employees and a 265,000-square-foot facility in Newark, California, that manufactures the blood testing devices that have the potential to upend a $73 billion diagnostic-lab industry.

The crux of Theranos's plan lies in its ability to run hundreds of blood diagnostic tests using only a few drops of blood (less than 1/100th of what is typically required) that can be acquired with a painless (and patented) finger stick. It also costs less than a quarter of what normal testing does! All of this came about largely because of Elizabeth Holmes's aversion to needles. As CEO, she has used her influence to raise more than $400 million for Theranos from investors like Oracle founder Larry Ellison by pushing her mission to consumerize the health care experience—which, to Holmes, means being able to walk into a Walgreens and order whatever diagnostic or preventive-oriented tests you want.

Theranos's board of directors is a who's who of company and political leaders. What is it about Holmes that gives her the power to influence and lead so many people? Expertise in her field is one thing. When asked to assess Holmes as a leader, Henry Kissinger (former U.S. Secretary of State and board member) responded, "I can't compare her to anyone else because I haven't seen anyone with her special attributes. She has iron will, strong determination. But nothing dramatic. There is no performance associated with her. I have seen no sign that financial gain is of any interest to her. She's like a monk. She isn't flashy. She wouldn't walk into a room and take it over. But she would once the subject gets to her field." Charisma and presence are another. Known as a careful listener, employees say they can't remember a time when she's raised her voice. Holmes has been compared to any number of visionary leaders, including Steve Jobs. Former Defense Secretary William Perry, who knew Jobs says, "She has a social consciousness that Steve never had. He was a genius; she's one with a big heart."

LEADERSHIP: POWER AND NEGOTIATION

As evidenced by Theranos, leaders within organizations can make a huge difference to the success of an organization or group. It would be easy after reading the opening example to anoint Elizabeth Holmes as a great leader and try to simply adopt her behavioral examples to follow in her footsteps. However, things aren't quite that simple. Many other leaders have exhibited similar behaviors and not been nearly as successful. As we'll discover in this and the next chapter, there are many different types of leaders, many of whom can excel, given the right circumstances.

13.1

What is leadership, and what role does power play in leadership?

There is perhaps no subject that's written about more in business circles than the topic of leadership. A quick search on Amazon.com for "leadership" will generate a list of more than 200,000 books! That number doesn't even count the myriad videos, calendars, audio recordings, and other items—all designed to help people become better leaders. Given all the interest in this topic, a natural question becomes, "What exactly is a leader?" We define **leadership** as the use of power and influence to direct the activities of followers toward goal achievement.[1] That direction can affect followers' interpretation of events, the organization of their work activities, their commitment to key goals, their relationships with other followers, and their access to cooperation and support from other work units.[2] This chapter focuses on how leaders *get* the power and influence they use to direct others and the ways in which power and influence are utilized in organizations, including through negotiation. Chapter 14 will focus on how leaders actually *use* their power and influence to help followers achieve their goals.

WHY ARE SOME LEADERS MORE POWERFUL THAN OTHERS?

What exactly comes to mind when you think of the term "power"? Does it raise a positive or negative image for you? Certainly it's easy to think of leaders who have used power for what we would consider good purposes, but it's just as easy to think of leaders who have used power for unethical or immoral purposes. For now, try not to focus on how leaders use power but instead on how they acquire it. **Power** can be defined as the ability to influence the behavior of others and resist unwanted influence in return.[3] Note that this definition gives us a couple of key points to think about. First, just because a person has the ability to influence others does not mean they will actually choose to do so. In many organizations, the most powerful employees don't even realize how influential they could be! Second, in addition to influencing others, power can be seen as the ability to resist the influence attempts of others.[4] This resistance could come in the form of the simple voicing of a dissenting opinion, the refusal to perform a specific behavior, or the organization of an opposing +group of coworkers.[5] Sometimes leaders need to resist the influence of other leaders or higher-ups to do what's best for their own unit. Other times leaders need to resist the influence of their own employees to avoid being a "pushover" when employees try to go their own way.

ACQUIRING POWER

Think about the people you currently work with or have worked with in the past, or think of students who are involved in many of the same activities you are. Do any of those people seem to have especially high levels of power, meaning that they have the ability to influence your behavior? What is it that gives them that power? In some cases, their power may come from some formal position (e.g., supervisor, team leader, teaching assistant, resident advisor). However, sometimes the most powerful people we know lack any sort of formal authority. It turns out that power in organizations can come from a number of different sources. Specifically, there are five major types of power that can be grouped along two dimensions: organizational power and personal power.[6] These types of power are illustrated in Figure 13-1.

FIGURE 13-1	**Types of Power**

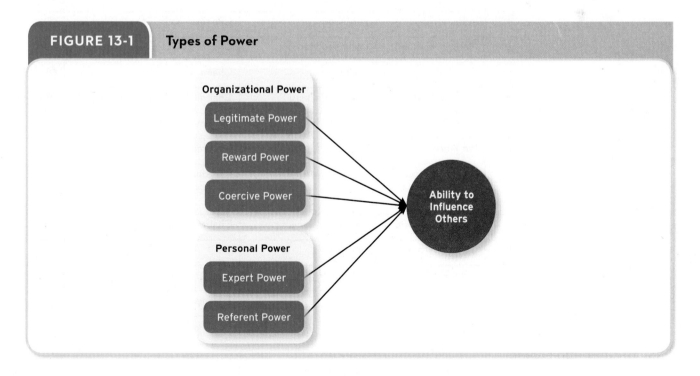

13.2

What are the different types of power that leaders possess, and when can they use those types most effectively?

ORGANIZATIONAL POWER The three types of organizational power derive primarily from a person's position within the organization. These types of power are considered more formal in nature.[7] **Legitimate power** derives from a position of authority inside the organization and is sometimes referred to as "formal authority." People with legitimate power have some title—some term on an organizational chart or on their door that says, "Look, I'm supposed to have influence over you." Those with legitimate power have the understood right to ask others to do things that are considered within the scope of their authority. When managers ask an employee to stay late to work on a project, work on one task instead of another, or work faster, they are exercising legitimate power. The higher up in an organization a person is, the more legitimate power they generally possess. *Fortune* magazine provides rankings of the most powerful women in business. As shown in Table 13-1, all of those women possess legitimate power, in that they hold a title that affords them the ability to influence others.

Legitimate power does have its limits, however. It doesn't generally give a person the right to ask employees to do something outside the scope of their jobs or roles within the organization. For example, if a manager asked an employee to wash their car or mow their lawn, it would likely be seen as an inappropriate request. As we'll see later in this chapter, there's a big difference between having legitimate power and using it effectively. When used ineffectively, legitimate power can be a very weak form of power. In our opening example, Holmes doesn't simply go bossing everyone in the organization around; she manages her legitimate power effectively to earn respect and get people to commit to their endeavors.

The next two forms of organizational power are somewhat intertwined with legitimate power. **Reward power** exists when someone has control over the resources or rewards another

TABLE 13-1	**Fortune's 15 Most Powerful Women in Business in 2014**		
	NAME	COMPANY	POSITION	AGE
1	Ginni Rometty	IBM	President and CEO	57
2	Mary Barra	General Motors	CEO	52
3	Indra Nooyi	PepsiCo	Chairman and CEO	58
4	Marilyn Hewson	Lockheed Martin	Chairman, CEO, and president	60
5	Ellen Kullman	DuPont	Chairman and CEO	58
6	Meg Whitman	Hewlett-Packard	Chairman, CEO, and president	58
7	Irene Rosenfeld	Mondelez International	Chairman and CEO	61
8	Pat Woertz	ADM	Chairman, CEO, and president	61
9	Abigail Johnson	Fidelity Investments	President	52
10	Sheryl Sandberg	Facebook	COO	45
11	Phebe Novakovic	General Dynamics	Chairman and CEO	56
12	Carol Meyrowitz	TJX Cos.	CEO	60
13	Lynn Good	Duke Energy	CEO and president	55
14	Safra Katz	Oracle	President and CFO	52
15	Rosalind Brewer	Wal-Mart Stores	President and CEO, Sam's Club	52

Source: C. Fairchild, B. Kowitt, C. Leahey, and A. Vandermeyb. "The 50 Most Powerful Women," *Fortune* 170, no. 5 (October 6, 2014), pp. 125–32.

person wants. For example, managers generally have control over raises, performance evaluations, awards, more desirable job assignments, and the resources an employee might require to perform a job effectively. Those with reward power have the ability to influence others if those being influenced believe they will get the rewards by behaving in a certain way. **Coercive power** exists when a person has control over punishments in an organization. Coercive power operates primarily on the principle of fear. It exists when one person believes that another has the ability to punish him or her and is willing to use that power. For example, a manager might have the right to fire, demote, suspend, or lower the pay of an employee. Sometimes the limitations of a manager to impose punishments are formally spelled out in an organization. However, in many instances, managers have a considerable amount of leeway in this regard. Coercive power is generally regarded as a poor form of power to use regularly, because it tends to result in negative feelings toward those that wield it.

PERSONAL POWER Of course, the women in Table 13-1 don't appear on that list just because they have some formal title that affords them the ability to reward and punish others. There's something else about them, as people, that provides them additional capabilities to influence others. Personal forms of power capture that "something else." **Expert power** derives from a person's expertise, skill, or knowledge on which others depend. When people have a track record of high performance, the ability to solve problems, or specific knowledge that's necessary to accomplish tasks, they're more likely to be able to influence other people who need that expertise. Consider a lone programmer who knows how to operate a piece of antiquated software, a machinist who was recently trained to operate a new piece of equipment, or the only engineer who has experience working on a specific type of project. All of these individuals will have a degree of expert power because of what they individually bring to the organization. Pat Woertz, the CEO of Archer Daniels Midland (ADM), the Decatur, Illinois–based agricultural firm, appears in Table 13-1 largely because of her expert power. ADM hired Woertz as CEO because it felt that her time at Chevron provided her with energy expertise that could help the firm in its push for renewable fuels.[8] There is perhaps no place where expert power comes into play more than in Silicon Valley, where it's widely perceived that the best leaders are those with significant technological experience and expertise. At Intel, senior advisor and former CEO Andy Grove "fostered a culture in which 'knowledge power' would trump 'position power.' Anyone could challenge anyone else's idea, so long as it was about the idea and not the person—and so long as you were ready for the demand 'Prove it.'"[9]

Referent power exists when others have a desire to identify and be associated with a person. This desire is generally derived from affection, admiration, or loyalty toward a specific individual.[10] Although our focus is on individuals within organizations, there are many examples of political leaders, celebrities, and sports figures who seem to possess high levels of referent power. Barack Obama, Angelina Jolie, and Peyton Manning all possess referent power to some degree because others want to emulate them. The same could be said of leaders in organizations who possess a good reputation, attractive personal qualities, or a certain level of charisma. Elizabeth Holmes, as detailed in our opening chapter case, clearly wields referent power. The people who surround her constantly refer to the "something special" she has—something she had well before she became CEO.[11] For a great example of what it's like to try to lead *without* referent power (or expertise), see this chapter's **OB On Screen** feature.

Of course, it's possible for a person to possess all of the forms of power at the same time. In fact, the most powerful leaders—like those in Table 13-1—have bases of power that include all five dimensions. From an employee's perspective, it's sometimes difficult to gauge what form of power is most important. Why, exactly, do you do what your boss asks you to do? Is it because the boss has the formal right to provide direction, because the boss controls your evaluations, or because you admire and like the boss? Many times, we don't know exactly what type of power leaders possess until they attempt to use it. Generally speaking, the personal forms of power are more strongly related to organizational commitment and job performance than are the organizational forms. If you think about the authorities for whom you worked the hardest, they probably possessed some form of expertise and charisma, rather than just an ability to reward and punish. That's not to say though that organizational forms of power cannot successfully achieve

OB ON SCREEN

FOXCATCHER

A couple of basics—this is one that generally works for me quite well.

With those words, John E. du Pont (Steve Carell) attempts to show a large group of Olympic wrestling hopefuls how to perform a wrestling maneuver he knows nothing about in *Foxcatcher* (Dir: Bennett Miller, Sony, 2014). Based on a true story, Foxcatcher is a movie that details the relationship between John E. du Pont (an heir to the E.I. du Pont family fortune) and 1984 Olympic gold medal wrestlers Mark (Channing Tatum) and Dave (Mark Ruffalo) Schultz. John is a strange and socially awkward philanthropist who wants to be a leader of men in the worst way. After building a private wrestling facility on his 800-acre Foxcatcher Farm estate just outside Philadelphia, John recruits Mark to join "Team Foxcatcher" while he trains for the World Championship. John uses his financial means to support and influence Mark, which pays off when Mark wins the 1987 World Wrestling Championships.

© Sony Pictures Classics/Photofest

Not long after, John recruits and enlists Dave and his entire family to move to Foxcatcher Farm as well, which angers Mark, who feels belittled and slighted by the process. The movie is filled with scenes where John attempts to lead his group of wrestlers through speeches, awkward wrestling suggestions, and forced relationships. Ever the patriot, at one point John insists that he be called "Eagle" by his friends. (Yes, it's as awkward as it sounds.) We come to find that John does whatever he can to acquire the approval of his mother (Vanessa Redgrave), who considers wrestling to be a "low" sport and who, at one point during John's childhood, paid someone to be John's friend. The entire movie is filled with great examples of someone who, through extraordinary wealth, has acquired a level of organizational power but lacks any level of personal power (referent or expertise). Watching how those around John cater and comply out of fear of having their funding removed, but yet lack any true commitment to him, is a great example of needing to have multiple forms of power to be successful as a leader. Otherwise, as in the movie, things might have disastrous consequences.

objectives at times. Some useful guidelines for wielding each of the forms of power can be found in Table 13-2.

CONTINGENCY FACTORS There are certain situations in organizations that are likely to increase or decrease the degree to which leaders can use their power to influence others. Most of these situations revolve around the idea that the more other employees depend on a person, the

TABLE 13-2	Guidelines for Using Power
TYPE OF POWER	**GUIDELINES FOR USE**
Legitimate	• Make polite, clear requests. • Explain the reason for the request. • Don't exceed your scope of authority. • Follow up to verify compliance. • Insist on compliance if appropriate.
Reward	• Offer the types of rewards people desire. • Offer rewards that are fair and ethical. • Don't promise more than you can deliver. • Explain the criteria for giving rewards and keep it simple. • Provide rewards as promised if requirements are met. • Don't use rewards in a manipulative fashion.
Coercive	• Explain rules and requirements and ensure people understand the serious consequences of violations. • Respond to infractions promptly and without favoritism. • Investigate to get facts before following through. • Provide ample warnings. • Use punishments that are legitimate, fair, and commensurate with the seriousness of noncompliance.
Expert	• Explain the reasons for a request and why it's important. • Provide evidence that a proposal will be successful. • Don't make rash, careless, or inconsistent statements. • Don't exaggerate or misrepresent the facts. • Listen seriously to the person's concerns and suggestions. • Act confidently and decisively in a crisis.
Referent	• Show acceptance and positive regard. • Act supportive and helpful. • Use sincere forms of ingratiation. • Defend and back up people when appropriate. • Do unsolicited favors. • Make self-sacrifices to show concern. • Keep promises.

Source: From Gary A. Yukl, *Leadership in Organizations,* 7th edition © 2010. Reproduced by permission of Pearson Education, Inc., Upper Saddle River, New Jersey.

more powerful that person becomes. A person can have high levels of expert and referent power, but if he or she works alone and performs tasks that nobody sees, the ability to influence others is greatly reduced. That being said, there are four factors that have an effect on the strength of a person's ability to use power to influence others.[12] These factors are summarized in Table 13-3. **Substitutability** is the degree to which people have alternatives in accessing resources. Leaders that control resources to which no one else has access can use their power to gain greater influence. **Discretion** is the degree to which managers have the right to make decisions on their own. If managers are forced to follow organizational policies and rules, their ability to influence others is reduced. **Centrality** represents how important a person's job is and how many people depend on that person to accomplish their tasks. Leaders who perform critical tasks and interact with others regularly have a greater ability to use their power to influence others. **Visibility** is how aware others are of a leader's power and position. If everyone knows that a leader has a certain level of power, the ability to use that power to influence others is likely to be high.

TABLE 13-3	The Contingencies of Power
CONTINGENCY	**LEADER'S ABILITY TO INFLUENCE OTHERS INCREASES WHEN ...**
Substitutability	There are no substitutes for the rewards or resources the leader controls.
Centrality	The leader's role is important and interdependent with others in the organization.
Discretion	The leader has the freedom to make his or her own decisions without being restrained by organizational rules.
Visibility	Others know about the leader and the resources he or she can provide.

MWH, a $1 billion revenue Broomfield, Colorado, engineering firm specializing in water projects, asked 500 employees in all of its departments where they went when they came up with a new idea. This would allow MWH to determine who possessed certain types of expertise and who offered the most help to employees. In a sense, MWH is identifying the individuals in the organization who are likely to have the most power.[13] Companies such as Microsoft, Pfizer, and Google are increasingly using such networking maps to understand the power structures in their organizations and who holds the most influence.[14]

USING INFLUENCE

Up until now, we've discussed the types of power leaders possess and when their opportunities to use that power will grow or diminish. Now we turn to the specific strategies that leaders use to translate that power into actual influence.

Recall that having power increases our *ability* to influence behavior. It doesn't mean that we will use or exert that power. **Influence** is the use of an actual behavior that causes behavioral or attitudinal changes in others.[15] There are two important aspects of influence to keep in mind. First, influence can be seen as directional. It most frequently occurs downward (managers influencing employees) but can also be lateral (peers influencing peers) or upward (employees influencing managers). Second, influence is all relative. The absolute power of the "influencer" and "influencee" isn't as important as the disparity between them.[16]

13.3

What behaviors do leaders exhibit when trying to influence others, and which of these is most effective?

INFLUENCE TACTICS Leaders depend on a number of tactics to cause behavioral or attitudinal changes in others. In fact, there are at least 10 types of tactics that leaders can use to try to influence others.[17] These tactics and their general levels of effectiveness are illustrated in Figure 13-2.

Larry Page (left), CEO of Google, is known for his willingness to allow employees to use rational persuasion (data) to change his mind on an issue.

The four most effective tactics have been shown to be rational persuasion, inspirational appeals, consultation, and collaboration. **Rational persuasion** is the use of logical arguments and hard facts to show the target that the request is a worthwhile one. Research shows that rational persuasion is most effective when it helps show that the proposal is important and feasible.[18] Rational persuasion is particularly important because it's the only tactic that is consistently successful in the

© Paul Sakuma/AP Images

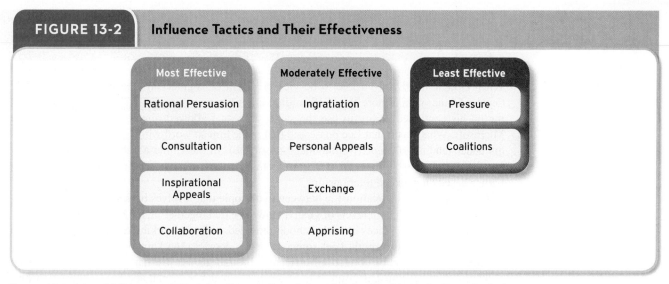

FIGURE 13-2 **Influence Tactics and Their Effectiveness**

Most Effective
- Rational Persuasion
- Consultation
- Inspirational Appeals
- Collaboration

Moderately Effective
- Ingratiation
- Personal Appeals
- Exchange
- Apprising

Least Effective
- Pressure
- Coalitions

Source: Adapted from J.J. Johnson and J.B. Cullen, "Trust in Cross-Cultural Relationships," in *Blackwell Handbook of Cross-Cultural Management,* ed. M.J. Gannon and K.L. Newman (Malden, MA: Blackwell, 2002), pp. 335–60.

case of upward influence.[19] At Google, for example, data is all-important. CEO Larry Page has been willing to change his mind in the face of conflicting information. Douglas Merrill, former Google CIO, said, "Larry would wander around the engineers and he would see a product being developed, and sometimes he would say, 'Oh I don't like that,' but the engineers would get some data to back up their idea, and the amazing thing was that Larry was fine to be wrong. As long as the data supported them, he was okay with it. And that was such an incredibly morale-boosting interaction for engineers."[20] An **inspirational appeal** is a tactic designed to appeal to the target's values and ideals, thereby creating an emotional or attitudinal reaction. To use this tactic effectively, leaders must have insight into what kinds of things are important to the target. Elizabeth Holmes, from our opening case, uses stories to solidify the impact that Theranos products make on people.[21] **Consultation** occurs when the target is allowed to participate in deciding how to carry out or implement a request. This tactic increases commitment from the target, who now has a stake in seeing that his or her opinions are valued. A leader uses **collaboration** by attempting to make it easier for the target to complete the request. Collaboration could involve the leader helping complete the task, providing required resources, or removing obstacles that make task completion difficult.[22] Ginni Rometty, CEO of IBM and number 1 in Table 13-1 is known inside and outside the organization for her collaborative tactics. Rometty and IBM just entered into an alliance with its biggest rival Apple to bring IBM services to Apple's iOS platform. Apple CEO Tim Cook says of Rommety, "I think she's wicked smart. She has an incredible ability to partner and can make tough decisions and do so decisively. And she sees things as they really are."[23]

Four other influence tactics are sometimes effective and sometimes not. **Ingratiation** is the use of favors, compliments, or friendly behavior to make the target feel better about the influencer. You might more commonly hear this referred to as "sucking up," especially when used in an upward influence sense. Ingratiation has been shown to be more effective when used as a long-term strategy and not nearly as effective when used immediately prior to making an influence attempt.[24] **Personal appeals** occur when the requestor asks for something based on personal friendship or loyalty. The stronger the friendship, the more successful the attempt is likely to be. As described in our **OB Internationally** feature, there are cultural differences when it comes to this kind of an appeal just as there are with other influence attempts. An **exchange tactic** is used when the requestor offers a reward or resource to the target in return for performing a request. This type of request requires that the requestor have something of value to offer.[25] Finally, **apprising** occurs when the requestor clearly explains why performing the request will benefit the target personally. It differs from rational persuasion in that it focuses solely on the benefit to the target as opposed to simple logic or benefits to the group or organization. It differs

OB INTERNATIONALLY

When Google hired Kai-Fu Lee to be vice president of engineering and president of Google Greater China, with a more than $10 million compensation package, the company was counting on his continued ability to use the same skills that allowed him to be a huge success at Microsoft. What was it that Lee possessed that made him so worthwhile? Lee argues that it was his understanding of *guanxi* (pronounced gwan-she). In the Chinese culture, guanxi (literally translated "relationships") is the ability to influence decisions by creating obligations between parties based on personal relationships.

Guanxi represents a relationship between two people that involves both sentiment and obligation. Individuals with high levels of guanxi tend to be tied together on the basis of shared institutions such as kinship, places of birth, schools attended, and past working relationships. Although such shared institutions might "get someone in the door" in the United States, in China, they become a higher form of obligation. Influence through guanxi just happens—it's an unspoken obligation that must be addressed. It is, in a sense, a blend of formal and personal relationships that exists at a different level than in the United States. There is no such thing as a "business-only" relationship, and the expectation is simply that if you take, you must also give back. Lee (who left Google) and his guanxi were so great that Google's Chinese product managers insisted that their business cards read "Special Assistant to Kai-Fu Lee" and that their desks be placed within 100 feet of his so that they could effectively do business outside the company.

Evidence suggests that companies like Microsoft and Google that possess guanxi have higher levels of performance. American managers who go to work overseas must be conscious of these different types of relationships and expectations. In addition to understanding the power of guanxi, evidence suggests that Chinese managers from different areas (e.g., Hong Kong, Taiwan, mainland China) have different beliefs when it comes to which influence tactics are the most effective. There is also recent evidence that the norms around guanxi in China are changing with time. If anything, it goes to show that managers need to be acutely aware of both general and more specific cultural differences when trying to influence others in China.

Sources: S. Levy, *In the Plex: How Google Thinks, Works, and Shapes Our Lives* (New York: Simon & Schuster, 2011); R. Buderi, "The Talent Magnet," *Fast Company* 106 (2006), pp. 80–84; C.C. Chen, Y.R. Chen; and K. Xin, "Guanxi Practices and Trust in Management: A Procedural Justice Perspective," *Organization Science* 15 (2004), pp. 200–9; R.Y.J. Chua, "Building Effective Business Relationships in China," *MIT Sloan Management Review* 53 (2012), pp. 27–33; P.P. Fu., T.K. Peng, J.C. Kennedy, and G. Yukl, "A Comparison of Chinese Managers in Hong Kong, Taiwan, and Mainland China," *Organizational Dynamics* 33 (2003), pp. 32–46; Y. Luo., Y. Huang, and S.L. Wang, "Guanxi and Organizational Performance: A Meta-Analysis," *Management and Organization Review* 8 (2011), pp. 139–72; M. Wong, "Guanxi Management as Complex Adaptive Systems: A Case Study of Taiwanese ODI in China," *Journal of Business Ethics* 91 (2010), pp. 419–32; M.M. Yang, *Gifts, Favors, and Banquets: The Art of Social Relationships in China* (Ithaca, NY: Cornell University Press, 1994); and X. Zhang, N. Li, and B.T. Harris, "Putting Non-Work Ties to Work: The Case of Guanxi in Supervisor-Subordinate Relationships," *Leadership Quarterly* 26 (2015), p. 37.

from exchange, in that the benefit is not necessarily something that the requestor gives to the target but rather something that results from the action.[26]

The two tactics that have been shown to be least effective and could result in resistance from the target are pressure and coalitions. Of course, this statement doesn't mean that they aren't used or can't be effective at times. **Pressure** is the use of coercive power through threats and demands. As we've discussed previously, such coercion is a poor way to influence others and may only bring benefits over the short term. The last tactic is the formation of coalitions. **Coalitions** occur when the influencer enlists other people to help influence the target. These people could be peers, subordinates, or one of the target's superiors. Coalitions are generally used in combination with one of the other tactics. For instance, if rational persuasion is not strong enough, the influencer might bring in another person to show that that person agrees with the logic of the argument.

Two points should be noted about leaders' use of influence tactics. First, influence tactics tend to be most successful when used in combination.[27] Many tactics have some limitations or weaknesses that can be overcome using other tactics. Second, the influence tactics that tend to be most successful are those that are "softer" in nature. Rational persuasion, consultation, inspirational appeals, and collaboration take advantage of personal rather than organizational forms of power. Leaders that are the most effective at influencing others will generally rely on the softer tactics, make appropriate requests, and ensure the tactics they use match the types of power they have. Mondelez International CEO Irene Rosenfeld (number 7 in Table 13-1) is known for her ability to persuade. A former executive with Kraft said, "When she is trying to persuade you of something, she will be relentless in coming back with facts and showing you she has the support of other people, she will be totally emotionally and intellectually committed to her idea."[28]

RESPONSES TO INFLUENCE TACTICS As illustrated in Figure 13-3, there are three possible responses people have to influence tactics.[29] **Internalization** occurs when the target of influence agrees with and becomes committed to the influence request.[30] For a leader, this is the best outcome because it results in employees putting forth the greatest level of effort in accomplishing what they are asked to do. Internalization reflects a shift in both the behaviors and the attitudes of employees. **Compliance** occurs when targets of influence are willing to do what the leader asks, but they do it with a degree of ambivalence. Compliance reflects a shift in the behaviors of employees but not their attitudes. This behavior is the most common response to influence attempts in organizations, because anyone with some degree of power who makes a reasonable request is likely to achieve compliance. That response allows leaders to accomplish their purpose, but it doesn't bring about the highest levels of employee effort and dedication. Still, it's clearly preferable to **resistance,** which occurs when the target refuses to perform the influence request and puts forth an effort to avoid having to do it. Employee resistance could come in the form of making excuses, trying to influence the requestor in return, or simply refusing to carry out the request. Resistance is most likely when the influencer's power is low relative to the target or when the request itself is inappropriate or unreasonable.[31]

POWER AND INFLUENCE IN ACTION

In this section, we look at two major areas in which leaders have the ability to use power to influence others. The first is through navigating the environment of organizational politics within the organization. The second is through using power and influence to help solve conflicts within the organization. As it turns out, it's easy for these two areas to coincide.

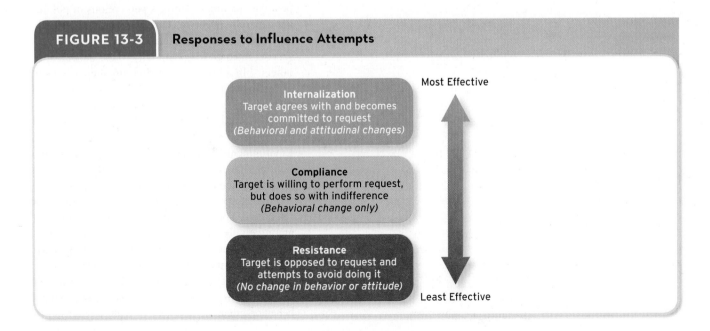

FIGURE 13-3   **Responses to Influence Attempts**

Internalization
Target agrees with and becomes committed to request
(Behavioral and attitudinal changes)

Compliance
Target is willing to perform request, but does so with indifference
(Behavioral change only)

Resistance
Target is opposed to request and attempts to avoid doing it
(No change in behavior or attitude)

Most Effective

Least Effective

13.4

What is organizational politics, and when is political behavior most likely to occur?

ORGANIZATIONAL POLITICS If there was perhaps one term that had a more negative connotation than power, it might be politics. You've probably had people give you career advice such as, "Stay away from office politics" or "Avoid being seen as political." The truth is that you can't escape it; politics are a fact of life in organizations![32] Although you might hear company executives, such as former Vodafone CEO Sir Christopher Gent, make statements such as, "[When I was CEO], we were mercifully free of company politics and blame culture,"[33] you can be pretty sure that wasn't actually the case—especially given that England's Vodaphone is one of the world's largest mobile phone operators. Most leaders, such as Allison Young, vice president of BlueCross and BlueShield of Louisiana, will tell you, "You have to assess the political situation early on and make decisions on forward-looking strategy not only on the facts, but also the political landscape."[34] Whether we like it or not, organizations are filled with independent, goal-driven individuals who must take into account the possible actions and desires of others to get what they want.[35]

Organizational politics can be seen as actions by individuals that are directed toward the goal of furthering their own self-interests.[36] Although there's generally a negative perception of politics, it's important to note that this definition doesn't imply that furthering one's self-interests is necessarily in opposition to the company's interests. A leader needs to be able to push his or her own ideas and influence others through the use of organizational politics. Research has recently supported the notion that, to be effective, leaders must have a certain degree of political skill.[37] In fact, universities and some organizations such as Becton, Dickinson, and Company—a leading global medical technology company based in Franklin Lakes, New Jersey—are training their future leaders to be attuned to their political environment and develop their political skill.[38]

Political skill is the ability to effectively understand others at work and use that knowledge to influence others in ways that enhance personal and/or organizational objectives.[39] Research indicates that there are four dimensions of political skill.[40] *Networking ability* is an adeptness at identifying and developing diverse contacts. *Social astuteness* is the tendency to observe others and accurately interpret their behavior. *Interpersonal influence* involves having an unassuming and convincing personal style that's flexible enough to adapt to different situations. *Apparent sincerity* involves appearing to others to have high levels of honesty and genuineness. Taken together, these four skills provide a distinct advantage when navigating the political environments in organizations. Individuals who exhibit these types of skills have higher ratings of both task performance and organizational citizenship behaviors from others, especially when the social requirements of the job are high.[41] To see where you stand on political skill, see our **OB Assessments** feature.

"You have no idea how political this place is."

Source: © Alex Gregory, The New Yorker Collection, www.cartoonbank.com

Although organizational politics can lead to positive outcomes, people's perceptions of politics are generally negative. This perception is certainly understandable, as anytime someone acts in a self-serving manner, it's potentially to the detriment of others.[42] In a highly charged political environment in which people are trying to capture resources and influence one another toward potentially opposing goals, it's only natural that some employees will feel stress about the uncertainty they face at work. Environments that are perceived as extremely political have been shown to cause lower job satisfaction, increased strain, lower job performance (both task and extra-role related), higher turnover intentions, and lower organizational commitment among employees.[43] In fact, high levels of organizational politics have even been shown to be detrimental to company performance as a whole.[44]

As a result, organizations (and leaders) do their best to minimize the perceptions of self-serving behaviors that are associated with organizational

OB ASSESSMENTS

POLITICAL SKILL

How much political skill do you have? This assessment is designed to broadly measure political skill. Please write a number next to each statement that indicates the extent to which it accurately describes your attitude toward work and people while you were on the job. Alternatively, consider the statements in reference to school rather than work. Answer each question using the response scale provided. Then sum up your answers for each of the dimensions. (Instructors: Assessments on expert power, referent power, need for power, and self-monitoring can be found in the PowerPoints in the Connect Library's Instructor Resources and in the Connect assignments for this chapter).

1	2	3	4	5
STRONGLY DISAGREE	DISAGREE	NEUTRAL	AGREE	STRONGLY AGREE

1. I find it easy to envision myself in the position of others. _____

2. I am able to make most people feel comfortable and at ease around me. _____

3. It is easy for me to develop good rapport with most people. _____

4. I understand people well. _____

5. I am good at getting others to respond positively to me. _____

6. I usually try to find common ground with others. _____

SCORING AND INTERPRETATION:

If your scores sum up to 23 or more, you have a higher than average level of political skill. If your scores sum up to 22 or less, you have a below average level of political skill.

Source: G.R. Ferris, H.M. Berkson, D.M. Kaplan, D.C. Gilmore, M.T. Buckley, W.A. Hochwarter, and L.A. Witt, "Development and initial validation of the political skill inventory." Paper presented at the 59th annual national meeting of the Academy of Management, Chicago, 1999. For a more detailed measure of political skill see: G.R. Ferris, D.C. Treadway, R.W. Kolodinsky, W.A. Hochwarter, C.J. Kacmar, C. Douglas, and D.D. Frink, "Development and Validation of the Political Skill Inventory," *Journal of Management,* 31 (2005), pp. 126–52.

politics. This goal requires identifying the particular organizational circumstances that cause politics to thrive. As illustrated in Figure 13-4, organizational politics are driven by both personal characteristics and organizational characteristics.[45] Some employees have a strong need for power that provides them with an incentive to engage in political behaviors. Still others have "Machiavellian" tendencies, meaning that they're willing to manipulate and deceive others to acquire power.[46]

Organizational factors that are the most likely to increase politics are those that raise the level of uncertainty in the environment. When people are uncertain about an outcome or event, they'll generally act in ways that help reduce that uncertainty. A number of events can trigger uncertainty, including limited or changing resources, ambiguity in role requirements, high performance pressures, or unclear performance evaluation measures.[47] A lack of employee participation in decision making has also been found to increase perceptions of organizational politics.[48] These sorts of organizational factors generally have a much stronger effect on political behavior than do personal factors. That's actually a good thing for organizations, because it may be easier

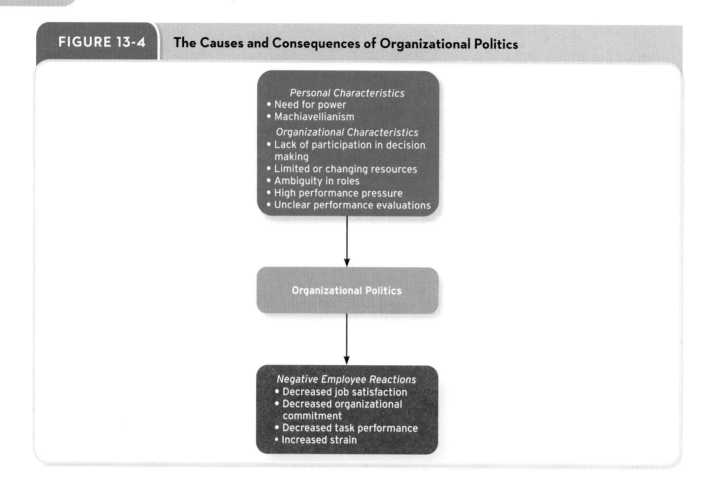

FIGURE 13-4   **The Causes and Consequences of Organizational Politics**

Personal Characteristics
• Need for power
• Machiavellianism

Organizational Characteristics
• Lack of participation in decision making
• Limited or changing resources
• Ambiguity in roles
• High performance pressure
• Unclear performance evaluations

Organizational Politics

Negative Employee Reactions
• Decreased job satisfaction
• Decreased organizational commitment
• Decreased task performance
• Increased strain

to clarify performance measures and roles than it is to change the personal characteristics of a workforce.

CONFLICT RESOLUTION In addition to using their power to shape office politics, leaders can use their influence in the context of conflict resolution. Conflict arises when two or more individuals perceive that their goals are in opposition (see Chapter 12 on team processes and communication for more discussion of such issues). Conflict and politics are clearly intertwined, because the pursuit of one's own self-interests often breeds conflict in others. When conflict arises in organizations, leaders have the ability to use their power and influence to resolve it. As illustrated in Figure 13-5, there are five different styles a leader can use when handling conflict, each of which is appropriate in different circumstances.[49] The five styles can be viewed as combinations of two separate factors: how *assertive* leaders want to be in pursuing their own goals and how *cooperative* they are with regard to the concerns of others.

Competing (high assertiveness, low cooperation) occurs when one party attempts to get his or her own goals met without concern for the other party's results. It could be considered a win–lose approach to conflict management. Competing occurs most often when one party has high levels of organizational power and can use legitimate or coercive power to settle the conflict. It also generally involves the hard forms of influence, such as pressure or coalitions. Although this strategy for resolving conflict might get the result initially, it won't win a leader many friends, given the negative reactions that tend to accompany such tactics. It's best used in situations in which the leader knows he or she is right and a quick decision needs to be made.

Avoiding (low assertiveness, low cooperation) occurs when one party wants to remain neutral, stay away from conflict, or postpone the conflict to gather information or let things cool down. Avoiding usually results in an unfavorable result for everyone, including the organization,

13.5

How do leaders use their power and influence to resolve conflicts in the workplace?

FIGURE 13-5	Styles of Conflict Resolution

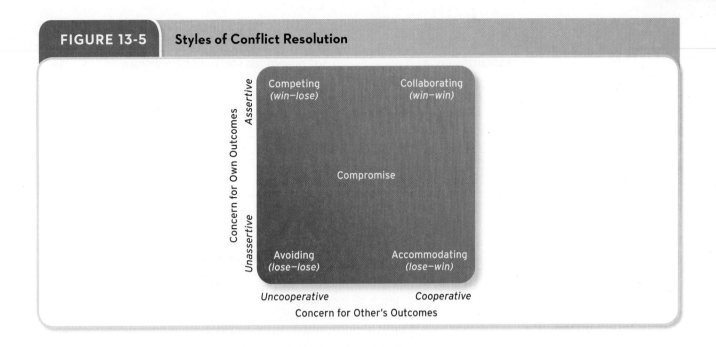

and may result in negative feelings toward the leader. Most important, avoiding never really resolves the conflict. **Accommodating** (low assertiveness, high cooperation) occurs when one party gives in to the other and acts in a completely unselfish way. Leaders will typically use an accommodating strategy when the issue is really not that important to them but is very important to the other party. It's also an important strategy to think about when the leader has less power than the other party. If leaders know they are going to lose the conflict due to their lack of power anyway, it might be a better long-term strategy to give in to the demands from the other party.

Collaboration (high assertiveness, high cooperation) occurs when both parties work together to maximize outcomes. Collaboration is seen as a win–win form of conflict resolution. Collaboration is generally regarded as the most effective form of conflict resolution, especially in reference to task-oriented rather than personal conflicts.[50] However, it's also the most difficult to come by because it requires full sharing of information by both parties, a full discussion of concerns, relatively equal power between parties, and a lot of time investment to arrive at a resolution. But this style also results in the best outcomes and reactions from both parties. **Compromise** (moderate assertiveness, moderate cooperation) occurs when conflict is resolved through give-and-take concessions. Compromise is perhaps the most common form of conflict resolution, whereby each party's losses are offset by gains and vice versa. It is seen as an easy form of resolution, maintains relations between parties, and generally results in favorable evaluations for the leader.[51] Women are also more likely to use compromise as a tactic in comparison to men, whereas men are more likely than women to use competing as a tactic.[52] Recent research shows that individuals with higher levels of emotional intelligence (see Chapter 10) are more likely to adopt constructive forms of conflict management (the green areas of Figure 13-5).[53] Like most things when it comes to power and influence, it's not as much a function of which style you use, but rather when you use it that determines success. It is a mistake to think that one specific style is superior to another—research has shown that whether a certain style is effective is dependent on lots of situational issues.[54] For instance, trust (see Chapter 7) is extremely important when using the more cooperative forms of conflict resolution, especially when there is a larger degree of conflict.[55] For more discussion of when to use the various conflict resolution strategies, see Table 13-4.

One example of conflict resolution is the ongoing battles that Uber faces with the cities that it tries to do business in.[56] Early in its existence, Uber took a very one-sided competing

TABLE 13-4	When to Use the Various Conflict Resolution Styles
RESOLUTION STYLE	**USE DURING THE FOLLOWING SITUATIONS:**
Competing	• When quick decisive action is vital (i.e., emergencies). • On important issues for which unpopular actions need implementation. • On issues vital to company welfare when you know you're right. • Against people who take advantage of noncompetitive people.
Avoiding	• When an issue is trivial or more important issues are pressing. • When you perceive no chance of satisfying your concerns. • When potential disruption outweighs the benefits of resolution. • To let people cool down and regain perspective. • When gathering information supersedes an immediate decision. • When others can resolve the conflict more effectively. • When issues seem tangential or symptomatic of other issues.
Collaborating	• To find an integrative solution when both sets of concerns are too important to be compromised. • When your objective is to learn. • To merge insights from people with different perspectives. • To gain commitment by incorporating concerns into a consensus. • To work through feelings that have interfered with a relationship.
Accommodating	• When you find you are wrong, to allow a better position to be heard, to learn, and to show your reasonableness. • When issues are more important to others than yourself, to satisfy others and maintain cooperation. • To build social credits for later issues. • To minimize loss when you are outmatched and losing. • When harmony and stability are especially important. • To allow subordinates to develop by learning from mistakes.
Compromising	• When goals are important but not worth the effort of potential disruption of more assertive modes. • When opponents with equal power are committed to mutually exclusive goals. • To achieve temporary settlements to complex issues. • To arrive at expedient solutions under time pressure. • As a backup when collaboration or competition is unsuccessful.

Source: From K.W. Thomas, "Toward Multi-Dimensional Values in Teaching: The Example of Conflict Behaviors," *Academy of Management Review*, 1, pp. 484–90. Copyright © 1997. Reproduced with permission of Academy of Management via Copyright Clearance Center.

approach when moving into new markets—moving in without formal permission, developing clientele, and then using that support to fend off city councils or opposition groups that might have an issue with the way Uber does business. CEO Travis Kalanick called the approach "principled confrontation."[57] While this approach worked (and might have been necessary for Uber's success) in some instances, Kalanick recognizes that it's not the best approach for all situations. One reason is that the battles it causes can be extraordinarily time consuming for a company growing as quickly as Uber has been. David Plouffe, Uber's senior vice president of policy and strategy, says, "We are trying to intensify our partnerships with cities, intensify discussions, intensify engagement. We are looking for good ways to compromise."[58] The new approach seems to be working in the city of Portland, where city officials and Uber negotiated for more than a year. Frustrated, Uber officials went ahead and launched without an agreement in place and the city filed a lawsuit against the company. Uber has since stopped business while city officials rewrite rules on taxis that prohibit companies like Uber from operating—the first time Uber has ever relented in such a case.[59]

© Brent Lewin/Bloomberg via Getty Images

Uber CEO Travis Kalanick has adapted the company's conflict resolution strategies over time to be more compromising and collaboration oriented.

NEGOTIATIONS

There is perhaps no better place for leaders to use their power, influence, political, and conflict resolution skills than when conducting negotiations. **Negotiation** is a process in which two or more interdependent individuals discuss and attempt to come to an agreement about their different preferences. Negotiations can take place inside the organization or when dealing with organizational outsiders. Negotiations can involve settling a contract dispute between labor and management, determining a purchasing price for products, haggling over a performance review rating, or determining the starting salary for a new employee. Clearly, negotiations are a critical part of organizational life, for both leaders and employees. Successful leaders are good at negotiating outcomes of all types, and doing it well requires knowledge of power structures, how best to influence the other party, and awareness of their own biases in decision making.[60] To see how Sheryl Sandberg (number 10 in Table 13-1) is pushing women to become better negotiators and more visible in leadership, see this chapter's **OB at the Bookstore** feature.

13.6

What are the ways in which leaders negotiate in the workplace?

NEGOTIATION STRATEGIES There are two general strategies leaders must choose between when it comes to negotiations: distributive bargaining and integrative bargaining.[61] **Distributive bargaining** involves win–lose negotiating over a "fixed-pie" of resources.[62] That is, when one person gains, the other person loses (also known as a "zero-sum" condition). The classic example of a negotiation with distributive bargaining is the purchase of a car. When you walk into a car dealership, there's a stated price on the side of the car that's known to be negotiable. In these circumstances though, every dollar you save is a dollar the dealership loses. Similarly, every dollar the salesperson negotiates for, you lose. Distributive bargaining is similar in nature to a competing approach to conflict resolution. Some of the most visible negotiations that have traditionally been approached with a distributive bargaining tactic are union–management labor negotiations. Whether it be automobile manufacturers, airlines, or nurses at hospitals, the negotiations for these sessions are typically viewed through a win–lose lens.

Many negotiations within organizations, including labor–management sessions, are beginning to occur with a more integrative bargaining strategy.

Integrative bargaining is aimed at accomplishing a win–win scenario.[63] It involves the use of problem solving and mutual respect to achieve an outcome that's satisfying for both parties. Leaders who thoroughly understand the conflict resolution style of collaboration are likely to thrive in these types of negotiations. In general, integrative bargaining is a preferable strategy whenever possible because it allows a long-term relationship to form between the parties (because neither side feels like the loser). In addition, integrative bargaining has a tendency to produce a higher level of outcome favorability when both parties' views are considered, compared with distributive bargaining.[64] As an example, picture a married couple negotiating where to go on vacation.[65] The husband wants to go to stay in a log cabin in the mountains while the wife wants to stay at a luxury resort on the beach. This would seem to be a case of distributive bargaining—one party will win and the other will lose! After much discussion though, the couple finds that location (in the mountains) is more important to the husband and style of accommodations (luxury hotel) is more important to the wife. The two can come to a solution that provides mutually beneficial outcomes to both parties—a luxury hotel

OB   AT THE BOOKSTORE

LEAN IN
by Sheryl Sandberg (New York: Knopf, 2013)

I believe that if more women lean in, we can change the power structure of our world and expand opportunities for all. More female leadership will lead to fairer treatment for all women.

LEAN IN

WOMEN, WORK, AND
THE WILL TO LEAD

SHERYL SANDBERG

Photo of cover: © Roberts Publishing Services.

With those words, Sheryl Sandberg—Facebook COO and number 10 on *Fortune*'s list of most powerful women—describes her desire for women in the workplace. A *New York Times* bestseller almost overnight, *Lean In* has been one of the more controversial leadership books to hit the market in some time. Sandberg's desire for the book is to encourage women to push for leadership roles and to examine why progress in the numbers of women executives has stalled. The major thrust of her book is that women have been partly to blame for their predicament. She states, "We hold ourselves back in ways both big and small, by lacking self-confidence, by not raising our hands, and by pulling back when we should be leaning in. We internalize the negative messages we get throughout our lives—the messages that say it's wrong to be outspoken, aggressive, more powerful than men."

Critics (mainly women) have hammered Sandberg (age 45, two Harvard degrees, and a net worth estimated at more than $500 million) for her inability to understand what nonprivileged women have to go through to be successful. In addition, Sandberg doesn't tackle outside barriers for women. Instead she chooses to focus on internal issues: "For decades, we have focused on giving women the choice to work inside or outside the home. But we have to ask ourselves if we have become so focused on supporting personal choices that we're failing to encourage women to aspire to leadership." What are her major points for women to be successful in the workplace? (1) Sit at the table. (2) Make partners (husbands) true partners, with both partners pulling their own weight evenly. (3) Don't "leave before you leave." In other words, women should not let up in ambition prior to actually having to make a decision about whether to stay in the workforce. Instead? Lean in.

---

in the mountains. However, not all situations are appropriate for integrative bargaining. Integrative bargaining is most appropriate in situations in which multiple outcomes are possible, there is an adequate level of trust, and parties are willing to be flexible.[66] Please don't approach your next used car purchase with an integrative bargaining strategy!

It's possible for leaders to develop a reputation for how they negotiate over time, making it more difficult for them to approach new negotiations in a different way. For instance, Charlie Ergen, cofounder and board chair of Dish Network, has a reputation for approaching negotiations with a distributive (win–lose) framework. One analyst commented, "The only way Charlie can succeed is if he wins. There aren't too many situations where people would get themselves into it with Ergen." His reputation "makes it hard for people to partner with him." Ergen (a one-time professional gambler) says that he sees business as a card game where he likes to "play the odds."[67]

NEGOTIATION STAGES Regardless of the strategy used, the actual negotiating process typically goes through a series of stages:[68]

- **Preparation.** Arguably the single most important stage of the negotiating process, during preparation each party determines what its goals are for the negotiation and whether or not the other party has anything to offer. Each party also should determine its best alternative to a negotiated agreement, or **BATNA.** A BATNA describes each negotiator's bottom line. In other words, at what point are you willing to walk away? At the BATNA point, a negotiator is actually better off not negotiating at all. In their seminal book, *Getting to Yes: Negotiating Without Giving In,* Roger Fisher and William Ury state that people's BATNA is the standard by which all proposed agreements should be measured.[69]

- **Exchanging information.** In this nonconfrontational process, each party makes a case for its position and attempts to put all favorable information on the table. Each party also informs the other party how it has arrived at the conclusions it has and which issues it believes are important. When the other party is unfamiliar, this stage likely contains active listening and lots of questions. Studies show that successful negotiators ask many questions and gather much information during this stage.[70]

© Brian Brainerd/Denver Post/Getty Images

Charlie Ergen, cofounder and chairman of the board for Dish Network, has developed a reputation as a ruthless negotiator.

- **Bargaining.** This stage is the one most people imagine when they hear the term "negotiation." Success at this stage depends mightily on how well the previous two stages have proceeded. The goal is for each party to walk away feeling like it has gained something of value (regardless of the actual bargaining strategy). During this stage, both parties likely must make concessions and give up something to get something in return. To the degree that each party keeps the other party's concerns and motives in mind, this stage will go much more smoothly.

- **Closing and commitment.** This stage entails the process of formalizing an agreement reached during the previous stage. For large, complex negotiations such as labor contracts established between an organization and a union, it can be a very long stage. For others, such as a negotiation between two coworkers about how they might handle their future relationship, no formal documents or contracts are required, and a simple handshake might suffice. Ideally, there will be no issues or misconceptions about the agreement arrived at during the bargaining stage. If they do exist, the negotiation process can regress back into the bargaining stage, and the process starts all over again. The stage also might be simply a recognition that the parties ended at an impasse with no agreement! In this case, several options are still available, as we discuss in the Application section at the end of this chapter.

NEGOTIATOR BIASES It is important for negotiators to be aware of their biases when approaching a negotiation. While there are numerous biases to be aware of, the perceived power relationship between the parties and negotiator emotions are two of the most important. Research has shown that when negotiators perceive themselves as being in a position of power in comparison to the other party, they are more likely to demand more, concede less, and behave more aggressively during negotiations—in other words, they are likely to take a more distributive approach to negotiations.[71] Similarly, when two parties perceive themselves as relatively equal in power, they take a more integrative approach to negotiations.[72] As we all know, negotiations are generally a very emotion-laden affair, and negotiator emotions can also play a large role in the ability of two parties to reach successful conclusions during bargaining.[73] (See Chapter 10 for a discussion of the ability of individuals to control their emotions during stressful times such as negotiations.) As it turns out, both positive and negative emotions can influence negotiation success in a negative way.[74] Positive emotions, while they generally lead to a more integrative bargaining approach, can also cause negotiators to be overconfident and make decisions too quickly. Negative emotions tend to lead toward a more distributive bargaining approach and lower judgment accuracy.[75]

SUMMARY: WHY ARE SOME LEADERS MORE POWERFUL THAN OTHERS?

So what explains why some leaders are more powerful and influential than others? As shown in Figure 13-6, answering that question requires an understanding of the types of power leaders acquire, what kinds of influence tactics they have available to them, and how they can use that

FIGURE 13-6 Why Are Some Leaders More Powerful Than Others?

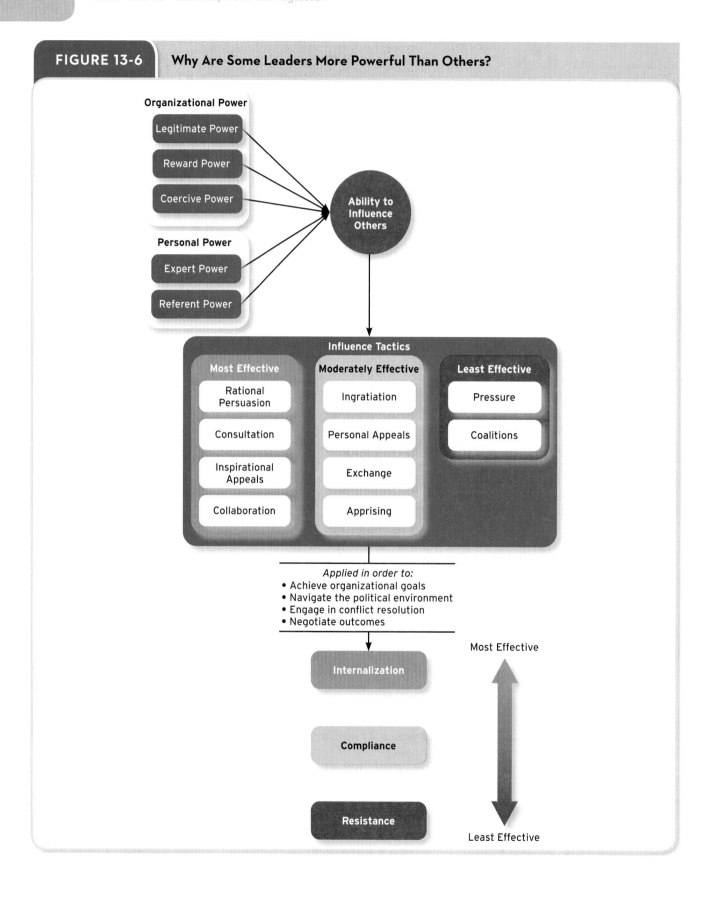

influence to alter the attitudes and behaviors of their employees. Leaders acquire both organizational (legitimate, reward, coercive) and personal (expert, referent) forms of power, which gives them the ability to influence others. They can then use that power to influence others through influence tactics. Those tactics can help achieve organizational goals or may be applied more specifically to dealing with organizational politics, conflict resolution, or negotiation situations. In the end, there are three possible responses to influence attempts: internalization, compliance, and resistance. The effectiveness of those attempts will depend on leaders' skill at performing them and how well they match the forms of power they have with the appropriate types of influence.

HOW IMPORTANT ARE POWER AND INFLUENCE?

How important is a leader's ability to use power and influence? In other words, does a leader's power and influence correlate with job performance and organizational commitment? Figure 13-7 summarizes the research evidence linking power and influence to job performance and organizational commitment. The figure reveals that power and influence are moderately correlated with job performance. When used correctly and focused on task-related outcomes, power and influence can create internalization in workers, such that they are both behaviorally and attitudinally focused on high levels of task performance. That internalization also helps increase

13.7

How do power and influence affect job performance and organizational commitment?

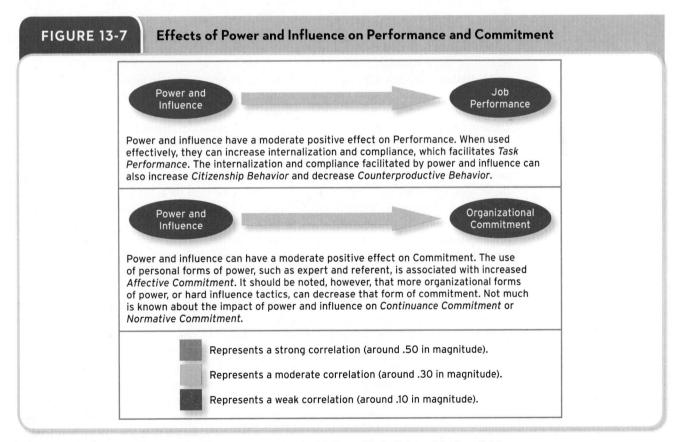

| FIGURE 13-7 | Effects of Power and Influence on Performance and Commitment |

Power and influence have a moderate positive effect on Performance. When used effectively, they can increase internalization and compliance, which facilitates *Task Performance*. The internalization and compliance facilitated by power and influence can also increase *Citizenship Behavior* and decrease *Counterproductive Behavior*.

Power and influence can have a moderate positive effect on Commitment. The use of personal forms of power, such as expert and referent, is associated with increased *Affective Commitment*. It should be noted, however, that more organizational forms of power, or hard influence tactics, can decrease that form of commitment. Not much is known about the impact of power and influence on *Continuance Commitment* or *Normative Commitment*.

Represents a strong correlation (around .50 in magnitude).

Represents a moderate correlation (around .30 in magnitude).

Represents a weak correlation (around .10 in magnitude).

Sources: R.T. Sparrowe, B.W. Soetjipto, and M.L. Kraimer, "Do Leaders' Influence Tactics Relate to Members' Helping Behavior? It Depends on the Quality of the Relationship," *Academy of Management Journal* 49 (2006), pp. 1194–1208; G. Yukl, H. Kim, and C.M. Falbe, "Antecedents of Influence Outcomes," *Journal of Applied Psychology* 81 (1996), pp. 309–17; and P.P. Carson, K.D. Carson, and C.W. Rowe, "Social Power Bases: A Meta-Analytic Examination of Interrelationships and Outcomes," *Journal of Applied Social Psychology* 23 (1993), pp. 1150–69.

citizenship behavior, whereas the compliance associated with power and influence can decrease counterproductive behavior. These job performance benefits make sense given that the effective use of power and influence can increase the *motivation* levels of employees, whereas the ineffective use of power and influence can increase the *stress* levels of employees.

Figure 13-7 also reveals that power and influence are moderately related to organizational commitment. When a leader draws on personal sources of power, such as expert power and referent power, a stronger emotional bond can be created with the employee, boosting affective commitment. The effective use of such power should increase *job satisfaction* and a sense of *trust* in the leader, all of which are associated with increased commitment levels. As with job performance, however, it's important to note that an ineffective use of power can also decrease commitment levels. In particular, repeated uses of coercive power or repeated reliance on hard influence tactics such as pressure or coalitions could actually decrease organizational commitment levels.

APPLICATION: ALTERNATIVE DISPUTE RESOLUTION

There is always the possibility that, despite a leader's best effort, negotiations and/or conflict management will result in an impasse between two parties. In many organizations, disputes that might escalate into actual legal battles are settled through alternative dispute resolution.[76] **Alternative dispute resolution** is a process by which two parties resolve conflicts through the use of a specially trained, neutral third party. There are various types of alternative dispute resolution that offer each party more or less control over the outcomes in question.[77] Which types of resolution are chosen are generally a function of time pressures, dispute intensity, and the type of conflict involved.[78] Two of the most common forms are mediation and arbitration.

Mediation requires a third party to facilitate the dispute resolution process, though this third party has no formal authority to dictate a solution. In essence, a mediator plays the role of a neutral, objective party who listens to the arguments of each side and attempts to help two parties come to an agreement. In serious, potentially litigious situations, trained mediators offer a relatively easy and quick way out of difficult disputes. A more definite form of alternative resolution is the process of arbitration. **Arbitration** occurs when a third party determines a binding settlement to a dispute. The arbitrator can be an individual or a group (board) whose job is to listen to the various arguments and then make a decision about the solution to the conflict. In some ways, arbitration is much riskier for both parties, because the outcome of the dispute rests solely in the arbitrator's hands. The arbitrator's role isn't to make everyone happy but rather to arrive at the most equitable solution in his or her opinion. In conventional arbitrations, arbitrators can create a solution of their choosing, mixing and matching available alternatives. In contrast, in final-offer arbitration, each party presents its most fair offer, and the arbitrator chooses the offer identified as most reasonable.

The two forms of alternative dispute resolution can be voluntary or mandatory, with many companies starting to create policies that make alternative dispute resolution mandatory for employees. However, there is some evidence that taking away the "voluntariness" of the process lowers employees' feelings of procedural justice (see Chapter 7).[79]

Of course, the goal of dispute resolution is always to have the two parties come to a voluntary agreement. Traditionally, mediation is the first step in alternative dispute resolution; if the mediator cannot help the two parties come to an agreement, the process continues to arbitration. Research suggests though that an opposite approach might lead to better results. That is, the two parties undergo the arbitration process, and the arbitrator makes a decision, which is placed in a sealed envelope. The two parties then go through the process of mediation; if they still can't come to an agreement, they turn to the arbiter's decision. Flipping the order resulted in significantly higher voluntary agreement rates between the two parties.[80]

TAKEAWAYS

13.1 Leadership is the use of power and influence to direct the activities of followers toward goal achievement. Power is the ability to influence the behavior of others and resist unwanted influence in return. Power is necessary, in that it gives leaders the ability to influence others.

13.2 Leaders have five major types of power. There are three organizational forms of power: Legitimate power is based on authority or position, reward power is based on the distribution of resources or benefits, and coercive power is based on the handing out of punishments. There are two personal forms of power: Expert power is derived from expertise and knowledge, whereas referent power is based on the attractiveness and charisma of the leader. These types of power can be used most effectively when leaders are central to the work process, highly visible, have discretion, and are the sole controllers of resources and information.

13.3 Leaders can use at least 10 different influence tactics to achieve their objectives. The most effective are rational persuasion, consultation, inspirational appeals, and collaboration. The least effective are pressure and the forming of coalitions. Tactics with moderate levels of effectiveness are ingratiation, exchange, personal appeals, and apprising.

13.4 Organizational politics are individual actions that are directed toward the goal of furthering a person's own self-interests. Political behavior is most likely to occur in organizational situations in which individual outcomes are uncertain.

13.5 Leaders use power and influence to resolve conflicts through five conflict resolution styles: avoidance, competing, accommodating, collaborating, and compromising. The most effective, and most difficult, tactic is collaboration.

13.6 Leaders use both distributive and integrative bargaining strategies to negotiate outcomes. The process of negotiating effectively includes four steps: preparation, exchanging information, bargaining, and closing and commitment.

13.7 Power and influence have moderate positive relationships with job performance and organizational commitment. However, for these beneficial effects to be realized, leaders must wield their power effectively and rely on effective influence tactics in negotiating outcomes.

KEY TERMS

• Leadership	*p. 412*	•	Rational persuasion	*p. 418*
• Power	*p. 413*	•	Inspirational appeal	*p. 419*
• Legitimate power	*p. 414*	•	Consultation	*p. 419*
• Reward power	*p. 414*	•	Collaboration	*p. 419*
• Coercive power	*p. 415*	•	Ingratiation	*p. 419*
• Expert power	*p. 415*	•	Personal appeals	*p. 419*
• Referent power	*p. 415*	•	Exchange tactic	*p. 419*
• Substitutability	*p. 417*	•	Apprising	*p. 419*
• Discretion	*p. 417*	•	Pressure	*p. 420*
• Centrality	*p. 417*	•	Coalitions	*p. 420*
• Visibility	*p. 417*	•	Internalization	*p. 421*
• Influence	*p. 418*	•	Compliance	*p. 421*

- Resistance   *p. 421*
- Organizational politics   *p. 422*
- Political skill   *p. 422*
- Competing   *p. 424*
- Avoiding   *p. 424*
- Accommodating   *p. 425*
- Collaboration   *p. 425*
- Compromise   *p. 425*
- Negotiation   *p. 427*
- Distributive bargaining   *p. 427*

- Integrative bargaining   *p. 427*
- Preparation   *p. 429*
- BATNA   *p. 429*
- Exchanging information   *p. 429*
- Bargaining   *p. 429*
- Closing and commitment   *p. 429*
- Alternative dispute resolution *p. 432*
- Mediation   *p. 432*
- Arbitration   *p. 432*

DISCUSSION QUESTIONS

13.1 Which forms of power do you consider to be the strongest? Which types of power do you currently have? How could you go about obtaining higher levels of the forms that you're lacking?

13.2 Who is the most influential leader you have come in contact with personally? What forms of power did they have, and which types of influence did they use to accomplish objectives?

13.3 What would it take to have a "politically free" environment? Is that possible?

13.4 Think about the last serious conflict you had with a coworker or group member. How was that conflict resolved? Which approach did you take to resolve it?

13.5 Think of a situation in which you negotiated an agreement. Which approach did you take? Was it the appropriate one? How might the negotiation process have gone more smoothly?

CASE: THERANOS

While Elizabeth Holmes brings a lot of qualities to the table—including a healthy dose of all five forms of power—she isn't without her critics. She has been roundly criticized by her industry peers for being overly secretive, and they insist that Theranos should publish some peer-reviewed studies of its work. One former associate at the FDA said, "It's trying to apply the Steve Jobs way of keeping everything secret until the iPhone was released. But a health test is more consequential than a consumer product. It needs to be clinically valid and provide useful information." Holmes insists that the secrecy is necessary in order to protect the technology of the product and that none of the other diagnostic lab companies are asked to provide this kind of information. She says, "There isn't a company that does what we do. We're creating a new space. We're in the market for people that don't like having a needle stuck in their arm." One reason Theranos has been able to maintain secrecy is because it manufactures the equipment it uses. Other diagnostic companies purchase their equipment. In order to sell such equipment, a company has to have FDA approval, but Theranos doesn't sell the equipment it manufactures.

The mystique of Theranos is amplified by the type of people Holmes insists on hiring. She only wants employees who match her level of passion. "This is not, you know, 'I'm going to go to this company and try it for two years and then go somewhere else,' and so on and so forth. This is about ownership of a mission," she says. Theranos promotes mainly from within, "putting people in leadership positions who can not only do the work but embrace the company's values, and live what that means." Holmes believes experimenting and failures as the key to success, but not when it comes to the overall mission of the company. "I think that the minute that you have a backup plan, you've admitted that you're not going to succeed," Holmes says.

The ability of most employees to keep up with Holmes is questionable due to the fact that Holmes's entire life is Theranos. She works seven days a week and regularly puts in 80 to 100 hours. Holmes doesn't date or devote time to friends, doesn't own a television, and hasn't taken a vacation in 10 years. She is a vegan who doesn't partake in caffeine or alcohol. To many, it seems that she lives mainly off of a blended mixture consisting of cucumber, parsley, kale, spinach, romaine lettuce, and celery, which she drinks several times a day. In fact, you will rarely see Holmes outside of her black suit with a black turtleneck. To her, the outfit is like a kind of uniform: "It makes it easy, because every single day you put on the same thing and don't have to think about it—one less thing in your life. All my focus is on the work. I take it so seriously; I'm sure that translates into how I dress."

13.1 Is it appropriate for Theranos to be so secretive given the kind of work that it is doing?

13.2 Do you think Holmes can sustain the level of effort she seems to currently put into her work? If you were on Theranos's board of directors, is this something you would be concerned about?

13.3 Do you think women naturally use different forms of power or influence tactics? Does Holmes show this?

Sources: "The 100 Most Influential People," *Time*, April 16, 2015; "Elizabeth Holmes Profile," *Forbes.com* (accessed July, 2015); K. Auletta, "Blood, Simpler.\," *New Yorker*, December 15, 2014, pp. 26–32; R. Parloff, "New Blood," *Fortune*, June 30, 2014, pp. 64–72; and D. Peterson, "Theranos CEO Elizabeth Holmes: 'Avoid Backup Plans,'" *Inc.*, February 10, 2015.

EXERCISE: LOBBYING FOR INFLUENCE

The purpose of this exercise is to give you experience in using influence tactics to modify the behavior of others. Follow these steps:

13.1 During this exercise, your objective is to get other people in the class to give you their points. If you get more than 50 percent of the total number of points distributed to the whole class, you'll win. Each person in the class has a different number of points, as shown in the class list. You can keep or give away your points in whatever manner you choose, as long as you follow the rules for each round of the process. There are five rounds, described next.

Round 1. In this round, you will write memos to your classmates. You can say whatever you want in your memos, and write them to whomever you choose, but for the 10-minute writing period, there will be no talking, only writing. You will deliver all your messages at one time, at the end of the 10-minute writing period.

Round 2. In this round, you will respond in writing to the messages you received in the first round. You can also write new memos as you see fit. Again, there is to be no talking! At the end of 15 minutes, you can distribute your memos.

Round 3. In round 3, you can talk as much as you like. You will have 15 minutes to talk with anyone about anything.

Round 4. In this round, you will create ballots to distribute your points any way you see fit. To distribute your points, put a person's name on an index card, along with the number of points you want that person to have. If you choose to keep any of your points, put your own name on the card, along with the number of points you want to keep. Do not hand in your cards until asked to do so by your instructor.

Round 5. If there is no clear winner, round 5 will be used to repeat steps 3 and 4.

13.2   Class discussion (whether in groups or as a class) should focus on the following questions:

- What kinds of social influence attempts did you make during this exercise?
- How successful were you at influencing others to go along with you?
- What kinds of influence did others use on you?
- What was the most successful way you saw someone else use influence during the memo-writing and discussion sections?
- What other factors determined how you voted?[81]

ENDNOTES

13.1   Yukl, G. *Leadership in Organizations,* 4th ed. Englewood Cliffs, NJ: Prentice Hall, 1998.

13.2   Ibid.

13.3   McMurray, V.V. "Some Unanswered Questions on Organizational Conflict." *Organization and Administrative Sciences* 6 (1975), pp. 35–53; and Pfeffer, J. *Managing with Power.* Boston: Harvard Business School Press, 1992.

13.4   Cotton, J.L. "Measurement of Power-Balancing Styles and Some of Their Correlates." *Administrative Science Quarterly* 21 (1976), pp. 307–19; and Emerson, R.M. "Power-Dependence Relationships." *American Sociological Review* 27 (1962), pp. 29–41.

13.5   Ashforth, B.E., and F.A. Mael. "The Power of Resistance." In *Power and Influence in Organizations,* ed. R.M. Kramer and M.E. Neal. Thousand Oaks, CA: Sage, 1998, pp. 89–120.

13.6   French, J.R.P. Jr., and B. Raven. "The Bases of Social Power." In *Studies in Social Power,* ed. D. Cartwright. Ann Arbor: University of Michigan, Institute for Social Research, 1959, pp. 150–67; and Yukl, G., and C.M. Falbe. "The Importance of Different Power Sources in Downward and Lateral Relations." *Journal of Applied Psychology* 76 (1991), pp. 416–23.

13.7   Yukl, G. "Use Power Effectively." In *Handbook of Principles of Organizational Behavior,* ed. E.A. Locke. Madden, MA: Blackwell, 2004, pp. 242–47.

13.8   Kowitt, B.; C. Leahey; and A. VanderMay. "The 50 Most Powerful Women." *Fortune* 166, no. 6 (October 8, 2012), p. 128; and Levenson, E.; J. Birger; and D. Burke. "The Outsider," *Fortune,* October 16, 2006, pp. 166–76.

13.9   Tedlow, R.S. "The Education of Andy Grove." *Fortune,* December 12, 2005, pp. 117–38.

13.10 French and Raven, "The Bases of Social Power."

13.11 Auletta, K. "Blood, Simpler." *New Yorker,* December 15, 2014, pp. 26–32.

13.12 Hickson, D.J.; C.R. Hinings; C.A. Lee; R.E. Schneck; and J.M. Pennings. "A Strategic Contingencies Theory of Intraorganizational Power." *Administrative Science Quarterly* 16 (1971), pp. 216–27; Hinings, C.R.; D.J. Hickson; J.M. Pennings; and R.E. Schneck. "Structural Conditions of Intraorganizational Power." *Administrative Science Quarterly* 19 (1974), pp. 22–44; and Salancik, G.R., and J. Pfeffer. "Who Gets Power and How They Hold On to It: A Strategic Contingency Model of Power." *Organizational Dynamics* 5 (1977), pp. 3–21.

13.13 Dvorak, P. "Theory and Practice: Engineering Firm Charts Ties—Social-Mapping Helps MWH Uncover Gaps." *The Wall Street Journal,* January 26, 2009, p. 7; McGregor, J. "The Office Chart That Really Counts." *BusinessWeek,* February 27, 2006, pp. 48–49.

13.14 Dvorak, "Theory and Practice"; Green, H. "Google: Harnessing the Power of Cliques." *BusinessWeek,* October 6, 2008, p. 50; and Rusli, E.M. "Your New Secretary: An Algorithm." *The Wall Street Journal,* June 13, 2013, p. B6.

13.15 Somech, A., and A. Drach-Zahavy. "Relative Power and Influence Strategy: The Effects of Agent/Target Organizational Power on Superiors' Choices of Influence Strategies." *Journal of Organizational Behavior* 23 (2002), pp. 167–79; and Stahelski, A.J., and C.F. Paynton. "The Effects of Status Cues on Choices of Social Power and Influence Strategies." *Journal of Social Psychology* 135 (1995), pp. 553–60.

13.16 Yukl (1998), *Leadership in Organizations.*

13.17 Yukl, G.; C. Chavez; and C.F. Seifert. "Assessing the Construct Validity and Utility of Two New Influence Tactics." *Journal of Organizational Behavior* 26 (2005), pp. 705–25; and Yukl, G. *Leadership in Organizations,* 5th ed. Upper Saddle River, NJ: Prentice Hall, 2002.

13.18 Yukl, G.; H. Kim; and C. Chavez. "Task Importance, Feasibility, and Agent Influence Behavior as Determinants of Target Commitment." *Journal of Applied Psychology* 84 (1999), pp. 137–43.

13.19 Yukl (1998), *Leadership in Organizations.*

13.20 Manjoo, F. "The Quest: How New CEO Larry Page Will Lead the Company He Cofounded into the Future." *Fast Company,* April 2011, pp. 68–76.

13.21 Parloff, R. "New Blood." *Fortune,* June 30, 2014, pp. 64–72.

13.22 Yukl et al., "Task Importance."

13.23 Lev-Ram, M. "Getting Past the Big Blues." *Fortune,* October 6, 2014, pp. 92–100.

13.24 Wayne, S.J., and G.R. Ferris. "Influence Tactics, Affect, and Exchange Quality in Supervisor–Subordinate Interactions: A Laboratory Experiment and Field Study." *Journal of Applied Psychology* 75 (1990), pp. 487–99.

13.25 Kelman, H.C. "Compliance, Identification, and Internalization: Three Processes of Attitude Change." *Journal of Conflict Resolution* 2 (1958), pp. 51–56.

13.26 Yukl et al., "Assessing the Construct Validity."

13.27 Falbe, C.M., and G. Yukl. "Consequences for Managers of Using Single Influence Tactics and Combinations of Tactics." *Academy of Management Journal* 35 (1992), pp. 638–52.

13.28 Berfield, S., and M. Arndt. "Kraft's Sugar Rush." *Bloomberg Businessweek,* January 25, 2010, pp. 36–39.

13.29 Yukl (2002), *Leadership in Organizations.*

13.30 Ibid.

13.31 Somech and Drach-Zahavy, "Relative Power and Influence Strategy"; Yukl (2002), *Leadership in Organizations;* and Yukl, "Use Power Effectively."

13.32 Ferris, G.R., and W.A. Hochwarter. "Organizational Politics." In *APA Handbook of Industrial and Organizational Psychology,* Vol. 3, ed. S. Zedeck. Washington, DC: American Psychological Association, 2011, pp. 435–59; and Mintzberg, H. "The Organization as Political Arena." *Journal of Management Studies* 22 (1985), pp. 133–54.

13.33 Bryan-Low, C., and J. Singer. "Vodafone Group Life President Resigns over Management Flap." *The Wall Street Journal,* March 13, 2006, p. B3.

13.34 Ramel, D. "Protégé Profiles." *Computerworld* 39 (2005), p. 50.

13.35 Bacharach, S.B., and E.J. Lawler. "Political Alignments in Organizations." In *Power and Influence in Organizations,* ed. R.M. Kramer and M.E. Neal. Thousand Oaks, CA: Sage, 1998, pp. 67–88.

13.36 Kacmar, K.M., and R.A. Baron. "Organizational Politics: The State of the Field, Links to Related Processes, and an Agenda for Future Research." In *Research in Personnel and Human Resources Management,* Vol. 17, ed. G.R. Ferris. Greenwich, CT: JAI Press, 1999, pp. 1–39.

13.37 Ferris, G.R.; D.C. Treadway; P.L. Perrewe; R.L. Brouer; C. Douglas; and S. Lux. "Political Skill in Organizations." *Journal of Management* 33 (2007), pp. 290–320; and Treadway, D.C.; G.R. Ferris; A.B. Duke; G.L. Adams; and J.B. Thatcher. "The Moderating Role of Subordinate Political Skill on Supervisors' Impressions of Subordinate Ingratiation and Ratings of Subordinate Interpersonal Facilitation." *Journal of Applied Psychology* 92 (2007), pp. 848–55.

13.38 Seldman, M., and E. Betof. "An Illuminated Path." *T & D* 58 (2004), pp. 34–39.

13.39 Ferris, G.R.; D.C. Treadway; R.W. Kolokinsky; W.A. Hochwarter; C.J. Kacmar; and D.D. Frink. "Development and Validation of the Political Skill Inventory." *Journal of Management* 31 (2005), pp. 126–52.

13.40 Ferris et al., "Political Skill in Organizations"; and Ferris et al., "Development and Validation."

13.41 Bing, M.H.; H.K. Davison; I. Minor; M.M. Novicevik; and D.D. Frink. "The Prediction of Task and Contextual Performance by Political Skill: A Meta-Analysis and Moderator Test." *Journal of Vocational Behavior* 79 (2011), pp. 563–77.

13.42 Ferris, G.R.; D.D. Frink; D.P.S. Bhawuk; J. Zhou; and D.C. Gilmore. "Reactions of Diverse Groups to Politics in the Workplace." *Journal of Management* 22 (1996), pp. 23–44.

13.43 Chang, C.; C.C. Rosen; and P.E. Levy. "The Relationship between Perceptions of Organizational Politics and Employee Attitudes, Strain, and Behavior: A Meta-Analytic Examination." *Academy of Management Journal* 52 (2009), pp. 779–801; Kacmar and Baron, "Organizational Politics"; Miller, B.K.; M. A. Rutherford; and R. W. Kolodinsky. "Perceptions of Organizational Politics: A Meta-Analysis of Outcomes." *Journal of Business and Psychology* 22 (March 2008), pp. 209–22; Hochwarter, W.A. "The Interactive Effects of Pro-Political Behavior and Politics Perceptions on Job Satisfaction and Commitment." *Journal of Applied Social Psychology* 33 (2003), pp. 1360–78; Randall, M.L.; R. Cropanzano; C.A. Bormann; and A. Birjulin. "Organizational Politics and Organizational Support as Predictors of Work Attitudes, Job Performance, and Organizational Citizenship Behavior." *Journal of Organizational Behavior* 20 (1999), pp. 159–74; and Witt, L.A. "Enhancing Organizational Goal Congruence: A Solution to Organizational Politics." *Journal of Applied Psychology* 83 (1998), pp. 666–74.

13.44 Eisenhardt, K.M., and L.J. Bourgeois. "Politics of Strategic Decision Making in High-Velocity Environments: Toward a Midrange Theory." *Academy of Management Journal* 31 (1988), pp. 737–70.

13.45 Atinc, G.; M. Darrat; B. Fuller; and B.W. Parker. "Perceptions of Organizational Politics: A Meta-Analysis of Theoretical Antecedents." *Journal of Managerial Issues* 22 (2010), pp. 494–513; Biberman, G. "Personality and Characteristic Work Attitudes of Persons with High, Moderate, and Low Political Tendencies." *Psychological Reports* 60 (1985), pp. 1303–10; Ferris et al., "Reactions of Diverse Groups"; and O'Connor, W.E., and T.G. Morrison. "A Comparison of Situational and Dispositional

Predictors of Perceptions of Organizational Politics." *Journal of Psychology* 135 (2001), pp. 301–12.

13.46 O'Boyle, E.H.; D.R. Forsyth; G.C. Banks; and M.A. McDaniel. "A Meta-Analysis of the Dark Triad and Work Behavior: A Social Exchange Perspective." *Journal of Applied Psychology* 97 (2012), pp. 557–79; and Valle, M., and P.L. Perrewe. "Do Politics Perceptions Relate to Political Behaviors? Tests of an Implicit Assumption and Expanded Model." *Human Relations* 53 (2000), pp. 359–86.

13.47 Fandt, P.M., and G.R. Ferris. "The Management of Information and Impressions: When Employees Behave Opportunistically." *Organizational Behavior and Human Decision Processes* 45 (1990), pp. 140–58; O'Connor and Morrison, "A Comparison of Situational and Dispositional Predictors"; and Poon, J.M.L. "Situational Antecedents and Outcomes of Organizational Politics Perceptions." *Journal of Managerial Psychology* 18 (2003), pp. 138–55.

13.48 Atinc et al., "Perceptions of Organizational Politics."

13.49 Lewicki, R.J., and J.A. Litterer. *Negotiations.* Homewood, IL: Irwin, 1985; and Thomas, K.W. "Conflict and Negotiation Processes in Organizations." In *Handbook of Industrial and Organizational Psychology.* 2nd ed., Vol. 3, ed. M.D. Dunnette and L.M. Hough. Palo Alto, CA: Consulting Psychologists Press, pp. 651–717.

13.50 Weingart, L., and K.A. Jehn. "Manage Intra-Team Conflict through Collaboration." *Handbook of Principles of Organizational Behavior,* ed. E.A. Locke. Madden, MA: Blackwell, 2004, pp. 226–38.

13.51 Thomas, K.W. "Toward Multi-Dimensional Values in Teaching: The Example of Conflict Behaviors." *Academy of Management Review* 2 (1977), pp. 484–90; and de Dreu, C.K.W.; A. Evers; B. Beersma; E.S. Kluwer; and A. Nauta. "A Theory-Based Measure of Conflict Management Strategies in the Workplace." *Journal of Organizational Behavior* 22 (2001), pp. 645–68.

13.52 Holt, J.L., and C.J. DeVore. "Culture, Gender, Organizational Role, and Styles of Conflict Resolution: A Meta-Analysis." *International Journal of Intercultural Relations* 29 (2005), pp. 165–96.

13.53 Schlareth, A.; N. Ensari; and J. Christian. "A Meta-Analytical Review of the Relationship between Emotional Intelligence and Leaders' Constructive Conflict Management." *Group Processes and Intergroup Relations* 16 (2013), pp. 126–36.

13.54 de Dreu, C.K.W. "Conflict at Work: Basic Principles and Applied Issues." In *APA Handbook for Industrial and Organizational Psychology,* Vol. 3, ed. S. Zedeck. Washington, DC: American Psychological Association, 2011, pp. 461–93.

13.55 Balliet, D., and P.A.M. Van Lange. "Trust, Conflict, and Cooperation: A Meta-Analysis." *Psychological Bulletin* 139 (in press).

13.56 MacMilan, D., and L. Fleisher. "How Sharp Elbowed Uber Is Trying to Make Nice." *The Wall Street Journal,* January 29, 2015.

13.57 Swisher, K. "Man and Uber Man." *Vanity Fair,* December 2014, p. 146.

13.58 MacMilan, "How Sharp Elbowed Uber Is Trying to Make Nice."

13.59 Ibid.

13.60 Malhotra, D., and M.H. Bazerman. "Psychological Influence in Negotiation: An Introduction Long Overdue." *Journal of Management* 34 (2008), pp. 509–31.

13.61 Bazerman, M.H., and M.A. Neale. *Negotiating Rationally.* New York: The Free Press, 1992; and Pinkley, R.L.; T.L. Griffeth; and G.B. Northcraft. "Fixed Pie a la Mode: Information

Availability, Information Processing, and the Negotiation of Suboptimal Agreements." *Organizational Behavior and Human Decision Processes* 50 (1995), pp. 101–12.

13.62 Pinkley et al., "Fixed Pie a la Mode."

13.63 Kolb, D.M., and J. Williams. "Breakthrough Bargaining." *Harvard Business Review,* February 2001, pp. 88–97.

13.64 Pinkley et al., "Fixed Pie a la Mode."

13.65 Based on Pruitt, D.G. "Achieving Integrative Agreements in Negotiation." In *Psychology and the Prevention of the Nuclear War,* ed. R.K. White. New York: Columbia University Press, 1986, pp. 463–78.

13.66 Thomas, "Conflict and Negotiation Processes."

13.67 Terlep, S. "Ergen Keeps Rivals Guessing." *The Wall Street Journal,* June 12, 2013, p. B3.

13.68 Based on Shell, R. *Bargaining for Advantage: Negotiation Strategies for Reasonable People,* 2nd ed. New York: Penguin Books, 2006.

13.69 Fisher, R., and W. Ury. *Getting to Yes:*

Negotiating Agreement Without Giving In. New York: Penguin Books, 1991.

13.70 Shell, *Bargaining for Advantage.*

13.71 Gelfand, M.J.; A. Fulmer; and L. Severance. "The Psychology of Negotiation and Mediation." In *APA Handbook for Industrial and Organizational Psychology,* Vol. 3, ed. S. Zedeck. Washington, DC: American Psychological Association, 2011, pp. 495–554.

13.72 Ibid.

13.73 Barry, B., and R.L. Oliver. "Affect in Dyadic Negotiation: A Model and Propositions." *Organizational Behavior and Human Decision Processes* 67 (1996), pp. 127–43.

13.74 Gelfand, "The Psychology of Negotiation and Mediation."

13.75 Ibid.

13.76 Roche, W.K., and P. Teague. "The Growing Importance of Workplace ADR." *International Journal of Human Resource Management* 23 (2012), pp. 447–58.

13.77 Nugent, P.S. "Managing Conflict: Third-Party Interventions for

Managers." *Academy of Management Executive* 16 (2002), pp. 139–54.

13.78 Goldman, B.M.; R. Cropanzano; J. Stein; and L. Benson. "The Role of Third Parties/ Mediation in Managing Conflict in Organizations." In *The Psychology of Conflict and Conflict Management in Organizations,* ed. C.K.W. de Dreu and M.J. Gelfand. New York: Erlbaum, 2008, pp. 291–319.

13.79 Bernardin, H.J.; B.E. Richey; and S.L. Castro. "Mandatory and Binding Arbitration: Effects on Employee Attitudes and Recruiting Results." *Human Resource Management* 50 (2011), pp. 175–200.

13.80 Conlon, D.E.; H. Moon; and K.Y. Ng. "Putting the Cart before the Horse: The Benefits of Arbitrating before Mediating." *Journal of Applied Psychology* 87 (2002), pp. 978–84.

13.81 Adapted from "Voting for Dollars." In the Instructor's Manual for Whetten, D.A., and K.S. Cameron. *Developing Management Skills,* 7th ed. Englewood Cliffs, NJ: Prentice Hall, 2007.

chapter 14

Leadership: Styles and Behaviors

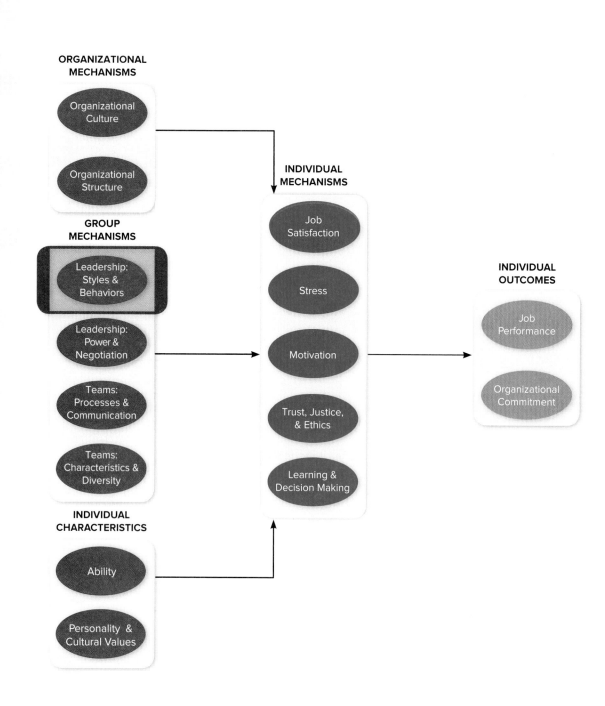

ORGANIZATIONAL
MECHANISMS

Organizational
Culture

Organizational
Structure

GROUP
MECHANISMS

Leadership:
Styles &
Behaviors

Leadership:
Power &
Negotiation

Teams:
Processes &
Communication

Teams:
Characteristics &
Diversity

INDIVIDUAL
CHARACTERISTICS

Ability

Personality &
Cultural Values

INDIVIDUAL
MECHANISMS

Job
Satisfaction

Stress

Motivation

Trust, Justice,
& Ethics

Learning &
Decision Making

INDIVIDUAL
OUTCOMES

Job
Performance

Organizational
Commitment

© Patrick T. Fallon/Bloomberg via Getty Images

✅ LEARNING GOALS

After reading this chapter, you should be able to answer the following questions:

14.1 What is leadership and what does it mean for a leader to be "effective"?

14.2 What traits and characteristics are related to leader emergence and leader effectiveness?

14.3 What four styles can leaders use to make decisions, and what factors combine to make these styles more effective in a given situation?

14.4 What two dimensions capture most of the day-to-day leadership behaviors in which leaders engage?

14.5 How does transformational leadership differ from transactional leadership, and which behaviors set it apart?

14.6 How does leadership affect job performance and organizational commitment?

14.7 Can leaders be trained to be more effective?

SPACEX

At 43, Elon Musk has already helmed three companies that have revolutionized their respective industries: PayPal, Tesla, and SpaceX. He is chairman of the board of directors for a company that is likely to be another: SolarCity. If you were to ask the average person for businesspeople who have the grandest visions for changing humanity, Elon Musk would likely be a name mentioned often. He is known for being brilliant, a true visionary, and a great motivator. At the same time, he's also known for having an extraordinarily demanding leadership style that isn't for everybody. This contrast is what makes the roots of leadership complicated.

As grandiose as all of these companies are in terms of their potential impact, SpaceX (an aerospace manufacturer and space transport services company) is perhaps the biggest. Using money he made from the sale of PayPal to eBay, Musk started the company in 2001 after the Russians turned him down when he tried to purchase a used ICBM missile. His friends thought he was crazy. One friend stated, "We wound up literally having an Alcoholics Anonymous–style intervention where I flew in people to Los Angeles and we all sat around a room and said, 'Elon, you cannot start a launch company. This is stupid.' Elon just said, 'I'm going to do it. Thanks.' " Musk's initial vision for the company was to build an inexpensive, reusable rocket that would make space travel not that different from airline travel. The company has succeeded spectacularly—including being awarded a $1.6 billion contract with NASA to resupply the International Space Station. To some degree, it's his vision that makes people want to work for him. One employee says, "His vision is so clear, he almost hypnotizes you. He gives you the crazy eye, and it's like, yes, we can get to Mars."

While his vision for the future can be enthralling, his up-and-down leadership styles can cause problems for those he works with. He is known for moving back and forth between being gentle and loyal and then being really hard on people. Those who know him best see him as more of a general than a CEO. While all of Musk's roles and companies get to experience this, the biggest stories tend to come out of SpaceX. A recent biography states, "Part of it stems from SpaceX being the apotheosis of the Cult of Musk. Employees fear Musk. They adore Musk. The give up their lives for Musk, and they usually do all of this simultaneously."

LEADERSHIP: STYLES AND BEHAVIORS

This is the second of two chapters on **leadership**, defined as the use of power and influence to direct the activities of followers toward goal achievement.[1] That direction can affect followers' interpretation of events, the organization of their work activities, their commitment to key goals, their relationships with other followers, or their access to cooperation and support from other work units.[2] The last chapter described how leaders *get* the power and influence needed to direct others. In the case of Elon Musk, his power derives from his formal role as SpaceX's CEO, his expertise, and his charisma. This chapter describes how leaders actually *use* their power and influence in an effective way. From the very beginning of his initial companies, Musk has been adept at recognizing business opportunities and having a vision of what each company could become.

14.1

What is leadership and what does it mean for a leader to be "effective"?

Of course, most leaders can't judge their performance by pointing to the number of companies they have created. Fortunately, leader effectiveness can be gauged in a number of ways. Leaders might be judged by objective evaluations of unit performance, such as profit margins, market share, sales, returns on investment, productivity, quality, costs in relation to budgeted expenditures, and so forth.[3] If those sorts of indices are unavailable, the leader's superiors may judge the performance of the unit on a more subjective basis. Other approaches to judging leader effectiveness center more on followers, including indices such as absenteeism, retention of talented employees, grievances filed, requests for transfer, and so forth.[4] Those sorts of indices can be complemented by employee surveys that assess the perceived performance of the leader, the perceived respect and legitimacy of the leader, and employee commitment, satisfaction, and psychological well-being. The top panel of Table 14-1 provides one example of these sorts of measures.

One source of complexity when judging leader effectiveness, particularly with more subjective, employee-centered approaches, is "Whom do you ask?" The members of a given unit often disagree about how effective their leader is. **Leader–member exchange theory**, which describes how leader–member relationships develop over time on a dyadic basis, can explain

TABLE 14-1	Employee-Centered Measures of Leader Effectiveness

Unit-Focused Approach

Ask all members of the unit to fill out the following survey items, then average the responses across the group to get a measure of leader effectiveness.

1. My supervisor is effective in meeting our job-related needs.

2. My supervisor uses methods of leadership that are satisfying.

3. My supervisor gets us to do more than we expected to do.

4. My supervisor is effective in representing us to higher authority.

5. My supervisor works with us in a satisfactory way.

6. My supervisor heightens our desire to succeed.

7. My supervisor is effective in meeting organizational requirements.

8. My supervisor increases our willingness to try harder.

9. My supervisor leads a group that is effective.

Dyad-Focused Approach

Ask members of the unit to fill out the following survey items in reference to their particular relationship with the leader. The responses are not averaged across the group; rather, differences across people indicate differentiation into "ingroups" and "outgroups" within the unit.

1. I always know how satisfied my supervisor is with what I do.

2. My supervisor understands my problems and needs well enough.

3. My supervisor recognizes my potential.

4. My supervisor would use his/her power to help me solve work problems.

5. I can count on my supervisor to "bail me out" at his/her expense if I need it.

6. My working relationship with my supervisor is extremely effective.

7. I have enough confidence in my supervisor to defend and justify his/her decisions when he/she is not present to do so.

Sources: Adapted from B. Bass and B. Avolio, *MLQ Manual* (Menlo Park, CA: Mind Garden, Inc., 2004); and G.B. Graen and M. Uhl-Bien, "Relationship-Based Approach to Leadership: Development of Leader–Member Exchange (LMX) Theory of Leadership over 25 Years: Applying a Multi-Level Multi-Domain Perspective," *Leadership Quarterly* 6 (1995), pp. 219–47.

why those differences exist.[5] The theory argues that new leader–member relationships are typically marked by a **role taking** phase, during which a manager describes role expectations to an employee and the employee attempts to fulfill those expectations with his or her job behaviors.[6] In this period of sampling and experimentation, the leader tries to get a feel for the talent and motivation levels of the employee. For some employees, that initial role taking phase may eventually be supplemented by **role making**, during which the employee's own expectations for the dyad get mixed in with those of the leader.[7] The role making process is marked by a free-flowing exchange in which the leader offers more opportunities and resources and the employee contributes more activities and effort.

FIGURE 14-1 | **Leader–Member Exchange Theory**

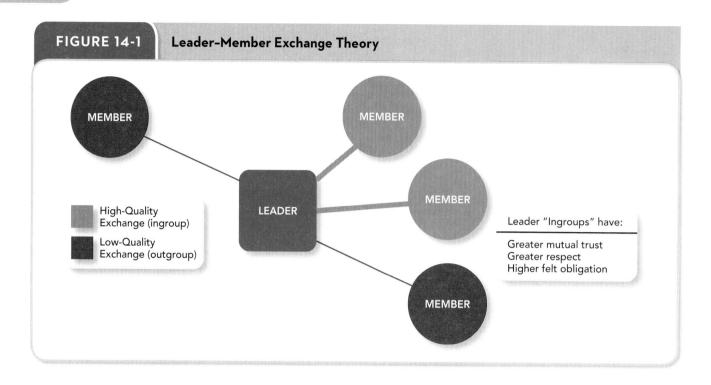

Over time, the role taking and role making processes result in two general types of leader–member dyads, as shown in Figure 14-1. One type is the "high-quality exchange" dyad, marked by the frequent exchange of information, influence, latitude, support, and attention. Those dyads form the leader's "ingroup" and are characterized by higher levels of mutual trust, respect, and obligation.[8] The other type is the "low-quality exchange" dyad, marked by a more limited exchange of information, influence, latitude, support, and attention. Those dyads form the leader's "outgroup" and are characterized by lower levels of trust, respect, and obligation.[9] Tests of the theory suggest that employees who are competent, likable, and similar to the leader in personality will be more likely to end up in the leader's ingroup; those factors have even greater impact than age, gender, or racial similarity.[10] These ingroup relationships can be very powerful attachments for some workers. Research suggests that employees are less likely to leave an organization when they have a high LMX relationship with a specific leader, but they are more likely to leave following a leadership succession.[11] Leader–member exchange theory also suggests that judgments of leader effectiveness should gauge how effective the most critical leader–member dyads appear to be. The bottom panel of Table 14-1 provides one example of this sort of measure, with more agreement indicating a higher-quality exchange relationship and thus higher levels of leader effectiveness on a dyadic basis.[12] Two recent meta-analyses have found that employees with higher-quality exchange relationships have higher levels of job performance and exhibit more organizational citizenship behaviors on average.[13] It should be noted, though, that the development of high LMX relationships has proven to be more effective in individualistic (Western) cultures than in collectivistic (Asian) cultures.[14]

WHY ARE SOME LEADERS MORE EFFECTIVE THAN OTHERS?

For our purposes, **leader effectiveness** will be defined as the degree to which the leader's actions result in the achievement of the unit's goals, the continued commitment of the unit's employees, and the development of mutual trust, respect, and obligation in leader–member dyads. Now that we've described what it means for a leader to be effective, we turn to the critical question in this chapter: "Why are some leaders more effective than others?" That is, why exactly are some leaders viewed as more effective on a unitwide basis, and why exactly are some leaders better at fostering high-quality exchange relationships? Beginning as far back as 1904, research on leadership has attempted to answer such questions by looking for particular traits or characteristics of effective leaders.[15] The search for traits and characteristics is consistent with "great person" theories of leadership that suggest that "leaders are born, not made."[16] Early research in this area frequently focused on physical features (e.g., gender, height, physical attractiveness, energy level), whereas subsequent research focused more squarely on personality and ability (see Chapter 9 on personality and cultural values and Chapter 10 on ability for more discussion of such issues).

After a century of research, leadership scholars now acknowledge that there is no generalizable profile of effective leaders from a trait perspective.[17] In fact, most studies have concluded that traits are more predictive of **leader emergence** (i.e., who becomes a leader in the first place) than they are of leader effectiveness (i.e., how well people actually do in a leadership role). Table 14-2 reviews some of the traits and characteristics that have been found to be correlated with leader emergence and leader effectiveness. Although a number of traits and characteristics are relevant to leadership, two limitations of this work have caused leadership research to move in a different direction. First, many of the trait–leadership correlations are weak in magnitude, particularly when leader effectiveness serves as the outcome. Second, the focus on leader traits holds less practical relevance than a focus on leader actions. Although research shows that traits can seemingly have an effect on leader effectiveness, these effects are generally explained much more strongly by leader behavior.[18] What exactly can leaders *do* that can make them more effective? This chapter reviews three types of leader actions: decision-making styles, day-to-day behaviors, and behaviors that fall outside of a leader's typical duties.

14.2

What traits and characteristics are related to leader emergence and leader effectiveness?

LEADER DECISION-MAKING STYLES

Of course, one of the most important things leaders do is make decisions. Think about the job you currently hold or the last job you had. Now picture your boss. How many decisions did he or she have to make in a given week? How did he or she go about making those decisions? A leader's decision-making style reflects the process the leader uses to generate and choose from

TABLE 14-2	Traits/Characteristics Related to Leader Emergence and Effectiveness	
DESCRIPTION OF TRAIT/CHARACTERISTIC	**LINKED TO EMERGENCE?**	**LINKED TO EFFECTIVENESS?**
High conscientiousness	√	
Low agreeableness	√	
Low neuroticism		
High openness to experience	√	√
High extraversion	√	√
High general cognitive ability	√	√
High energy level	√	√
High stress tolerance	√	√
High self-confidence	√	√

Sources: Adapted from T.A. Judge, J.E. Bono, R. Ilies, and M.W. Gerhardt, "Personality and Leadership: A Qualitative and Quantitative Review," *Journal of Applied Psychology* 87 (2002), pp. 765–80; T.A. Judge, A.E. Colbert, and R. Ilies, "Intelligence and Leadership: A Quantitative Review and Test of Theoretical Propositions," *Journal of Applied Psychology* 89 (2004), pp. 542–52; and G. Yukl, *Leadership in Organizations*, 4th ed. (Englewood Cliffs, NJ: Prentice Hall, 1998).

a set of alternatives to solve a problem (see Chapter 8 on learning and decision making for more discussion of such issues). Decision-making styles capture *how* a leader decides as opposed to *what* a leader decides.

14.3

What four styles can leaders use to make decisions, and what factors combine to make these styles more effective in a given situation?

The most important element of a leader's decision-making style is this: Does the leader decide most things for him- or herself, or does the leader involve others in the process? We've probably all had bosses (or professors, or even parents) who made virtually all decisions by themselves, stopping by to announce what had happened once the call had been made. We've probably also had other bosses (or professors, or parents) who tended to do the opposite—involving us, asking our opinions, or seeking our vote even when we didn't care about what was being discussed. It turns out that this issue of leader versus follower control can be used to define some specific decision-making styles. Figure 14-2 shows those styles, arranged on a continuum from high follower control to high leader control.

DEFINING THE STYLES With an **autocratic style**, the leader makes the decision alone without asking for the opinions or suggestions of the employees in the work unit.[19] The employees may provide information that the leader needs but are not asked to generate or evaluate potential solutions. In fact, they may not even be told about the decision that needs to be made, knowing only that the leader wants information for some reason. This decision-making style seems to be a favorite of Fiat-Chrysler CEO Sergio Marchionne, who is doing his best to make sure decisions are made extraordinarily quickly at Chrysler—and he's doing that by making them himself. Marchionne has flattened Chrysler's organizational chart with him at the top and has 25 direct reports (not counting 21 at Fiat). One might think this would cause a major bottleneck with regard to decisions, but Marchionne swears that speed is the only thing that will save Chrysler at this point and he is always within reach through the use of one of his six BlackBerrys. Marchionne says, "BlackBerrys are divine instruments. They [his direct reports] have access to me 24/7." The CEO is known for making decisions within minutes, or seconds.[20]

The next two styles in Figure 14-2 offer more employee involvement. With a **consultative style,** the leader presents the problem to individual employees or a group of employees, asking for their opinions and suggestions before ultimately making the decision him- or herself.[21] With this style, employees do "have a say" in the process, but the ultimate authority still rests with the leader. Bob Brennan, ex-CEO of Iron Mountain, a $3 billion information management services company headquartered in Boston, says, "I ask this question a lot in different situations: 'What do you recommend we do?' You can get a real sense for who's invested in moving the company forward, and who's watching the company go by, with that very simple question. People lay out problems all the time. If they've thought through what should be done from here, then you've got somebody who's in the game, who wants to move, and you can unlock that potential."[22]

That ultimate authority changes with a **facilitative style**, in which the leader presents the problem to a group of employees and seeks consensus on a solution, making sure that his or her own opinion receives no more weight than anyone else's.[23] With this style, the leader is more facilitator than decision maker. Robert W. Selander, executive vice chair of MasterCard, said he had learned over time to encourage discussion in a group. "From sort of a style standpoint, I prefer to do what I call more of a consensus style of decision-making," he said. "So when I'm around the table with our executive committee, the senior leadership of the company, I could easily make a bilateral decision. You're knowledgeable about your area. I may have the best knowledge

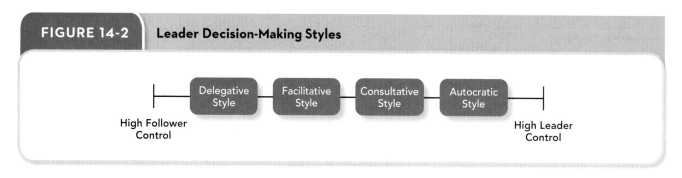

FIGURE 14-2 | **Leader Decision-Making Styles**

Delegative Style — Facilitative Style — Consultative Style — Autocratic Style

High Follower Control ← → High Leader Control

about your area or second best around the table. You and I agree. Let's get on with it. What we haven't done is we haven't benefited from the wisdom, the insight, and the experience of the others around the table. And while they may not have as much insight or knowledge about your area as you do, there's a chance that we missed something. So I try to get more engagement and discussion around topics and avoid what I would call bilateralism. I think what happens is sometimes you

© Bloomberg/Getty Images

Sergio Marchionne, CEO of Fiat-Chrysler, is known for his autocratic and speedy decision-making style.

get an insight that's startling and important and affects the decision, but you also get participative involvement so that there is buy-in and a recognition of how we got to that decision. It's not as if the boss went off in a corner and waved a magic wand and, bang, out came the decision."[24]

With a **delegative style**, the leader gives an individual employee or a group of employees the responsibility for making the decision within some set of specified boundary conditions.[25] The leader plays no role in the deliberations unless asked, though he or she may offer encouragement and provide necessary resources behind the scenes. "I think the most difficult transition for anybody from being a worker bee to a manager is this issue of delegation," says Tachi Yamada, president of the Bill and Melinda Gates Foundation's Global Health Program. "What do you give up? How can you have the team do what you would do yourself without your doing it? If you're a true micromanager and you basically stand over everybody and guide their hands to do everything, you don't have enough hours in the day to do what the whole team needs to do."[26] Daniel Amos, CEO and chair of Aflac, also believes strongly in a delegative style. He says, "My theory is that when you start telling people what to do, they no longer are responsible; you are. I'll give them my opinion and say; 'Look, this is my opinion, but if you choose that and you fail, you're not blaming it on me. It is your fault.' I think it makes them stronger."[27]

WHEN ARE THE STYLES MOST EFFECTIVE? Which decision-making style is best? As you may have guessed, there is no one decision-making style that's effective across all situations, and all styles have their pluses and minuses. There are many factors to consider when leaders choose a decision-making style.[28] The most obvious consideration is the quality of the resulting decision, because making the correct decision is the ultimate means of judging the leader. However, leaders also have to consider whether employees will accept and commit to their decision. Research studies have repeatedly shown that allowing employees to participate in decision making increases their job satisfaction.[29] Such participation also helps develop employees' own decision-making skills.[30]

Of course, such participation has a downside for employees because it takes up time. Many employees view meetings as an interruption of their work. One recent study found that employees spend, on average, six hours a week in scheduled meetings and that time spent in meetings relates negatively to job satisfaction when employees don't depend on others in their jobs, focus on their own task accomplishment, and believe meetings are run ineffectively.[31] Diane Bryant, CIO at Intel, argues that "You need people who are critical to making the decisions on the agenda, not people who are there only because they'll be impacted. At Intel, if we see someone who doesn't need to be there, people will say, 'Bob, I don't think we need you here. Thanks for coming.' "[32] Similarly, executives at GM are trying to change the slow bureaucratic culture that has hampered the automaker for decades—the company is known for decisions having to be made by committee. Once, they even appointed a committee to take a look at how many committee meetings should be held![33]

How can leaders effectively manage their choice of decision-making styles? The **time-driven model of leadership** offers one potential guide.[34] It suggests that the focus should shift away from autocratic, consultative, facilitative, and delegative *leaders* to autocratic, consultative, facilitative, and delegative *situations*. More specifically, the model suggests that seven factors combine to make some decision-making styles more effective in a given situation and other styles less effective. Those seven factors include:

- *Decision significance:* Is the decision significant to the success of the project or the organization?
- *Importance of commitment:* Is it important that employees "buy in" to the decision?
- *Leader expertise:* Does the leader have significant knowledge or expertise regarding the problem?
- *Likelihood of commitment:* How likely is it that employees will trust the leader's decision and commit to it?
- *Shared objectives:* Do employees share and support the same objectives, or do they have an agenda of their own?
- *Employee expertise:* Do the employees have significant knowledge or expertise regarding the problem?
- *Teamwork skills:* Do the employees have the ability to work together to solve the problem, or will they struggle with conflicts or inefficiencies?

Figure 14-3 illustrates how these seven factors can be used to determine the most effective decision-making style in a given situation. The figure asks whether the levels of each of the

FIGURE 14-3   The Time-Driven Model of Leadership

Decision Significance	Importance of Commitment	Leader Expertise	Likelihood of Commitment	Shared Objectives	Employee Expertise	Teamwork Skills	Style
H	H	H	H	-	-	-	Autocratic
H	H	H	L	H	H	H	Delegative
H	H	H	L	H	H	L	Consultative
H	H	H	L	H	L	-	Consultative
H	H	H	L	L	-	-	Consultative
H	H	L	H	H	H	H	Facilitative
H	H	L	H	H	H	L	Consultative
H	H	L	H	H	L	-	Consultative
H	H	L	H	L	-	-	Consultative
H	H	L	L	H	H	H	Facilitative
H	H	L	L	H	H	L	Consultative
H	H	L	L	H	L	-	Consultative
H	H	L	L	L	-	-	Consultative
H	L	H	-	-	-	-	Autocratic
H	L	L	-	H	H	H	Facilitative
H	L	L	-	H	H	L	Consultative
H	L	L	-	H	L	-	Consultative
H	L	L	-	L	-	-	Consultative
L	H	-	H	-	-	-	Autocratic
L	H	-	L	-	H	-	Delegative
L	H	-	L	-	L	-	Facilitative
L	L	-	-	-	-	-	Autocratic

Source: Adapted from V.H. Vroom, "Leadership and the Decision-Making Process," *Organizational Dynamics* 28 (2000), pp. 82–94.

seven factors are high (H) or low (L). The figure functions like a funnel, moving from left to right, with each answer taking you closer to the recommended style (dashes mean that a given factor can be skipped for that combination). Although the model seems complex at first glance, the principles within it are straightforward. Autocratic styles are reserved for decisions that are insignificant or for which employee commitment is unimportant. The only exception is when the leader's expertise is high and the leader is trusted. An autocratic style in these situations should result in an accurate decision that makes the most efficient use of employees' time. Delegative styles should be reserved for circumstances in which employees have strong teamwork skills and are not likely to commit blindly to whatever decision the leader provides. Deciding between the remaining two styles—consultative and facilitative—is more nuanced and requires a more complete consideration of all seven factors.

For our earlier example of Sergio Marchionne, decision significance is high, importance of commitment is low, and leader expertise is high, so he adopts an autocratic decision style. However, for Jack Griffin, CEO of Time Inc., autocratic decision making didn't seem to go over too well. Griffin became known within the company for his "imperious" decision-making behavior. For example, he insisted that every magazine include a masthead with his name at the top (an extra page that cost the company about $5 million a year) almost right after hundreds of employees were laid off—a decision that used to be left up to individual editors. A source within the company was quoted as saying, "Time Inc. has long operated on the collegial consensus approach and I don't think that was Jack's strength."[35] With magazine publishing operating during such a precarious time, we would label decision significance as high, importance of commitment as high, and the leader not appearing to have expertise in the subject matter of the decisions. As a result, his autocratic style led to a rebellion by those working for him and his termination only six months after his appointment. A key point about Figure 14-3 is that unless a leader is an expert with regard to the focus of the decision, autocratic decisions are not the right style to choose.

Research tends to support many of the time-driven model's propositions, particularly when it uses practicing managers as participants.[36] For example, one study asked managers to recall past decisions, the context surrounding those decisions, and the eventual successes (or failures) of their decisions.[37] When managers used the decision-making styles recommended by the model, those decisions were rated as successful 68 percent of the time. When managers went against the model's prescriptions, their decisions were only rated as successful 22 percent of the time. It's also interesting to note that studies suggest that managers tend to choose the style recommended by the model only around 40 percent of the time and exhibit less variation in styles than the model suggests they should.[38] In particular, managers seem to overuse the consultative style and underutilize autocratic and facilitative styles. Sheila Lirio Marcelo, the CEO of Care.com, uses a unique approach by actually letting her staff know what type of decisions will be made prior to each meeting. "We do Type 1, Type 2, Type 3 decisions," she said. "Type 1 decisions are the decision-maker's sole decision - dictatorial [autocratic]. Type 2: people can provide input, and then the person can still make the decision [consultative]. Type 3, it's consensus [facilitative]. It's a great way to efficiently solve a problem."[39]

DAY-TO-DAY LEADERSHIP BEHAVIORS

Leaving aside how they go about making decisions, what do leaders *do* on a day-to-day basis? When you think about bosses that you've had, what behaviors did they tend to perform as part of their daily leadership responsibilities? A series of studies at Ohio State in the 1950s attempted to answer that question. Working under grants from the Office of Naval Research and the International Harvester Company, the studies began by generating a list of all the behaviors leaders engage in—around 1,800 in all.[40] Those behaviors were trimmed down to 150 specific examples, then grouped into several categories, as shown in Table 14-3.[41] The table reveals that many leaders spend their time engaging in a mix of initiating, organizing, producing, socializing, integrating, communicating, recognizing, and representing behaviors. Although eight categories are easier to remember than 1,800 behaviors, further analyses suggested that the categories in Table 14-3 really boil down to just two dimensions: initiating structure and consideration.[42]

TABLE 14-3	Day-to-Day Behaviors Performed by Leaders

BEHAVIOR	DESCRIPTION
Initiating Structure	
Initiation	Originating, facilitating, and sometimes resisting new ideas and practices
Organization	Defining and structuring work, clarifying leader versus member roles, coordinating employee tasks
Production	Setting goals and providing incentives for the effort and productivity of employees
Consideration	
Membership	Mixing with employees, stressing informal interactions, and exchanging personal services
Integration	Encouraging a pleasant atmosphere, reducing conflict, promoting individual adjustment to the group
Communication	Providing information to employees, seeking information from them, showing an awareness of matters that affect them
Recognition	Expressing approval or disapproval of the behaviors of employees
Representation	Acting on behalf of the group, defending the group, and advancing the interests of the group

Source: R.M. Stogdill, *Manual for the Leader Behavior Description Questionnaire-Form XII*, Bureau of Business Research, The Ohio State University, 1963.

14.4

What two dimensions capture most of the day-to-day leadership behaviors in which leaders engage?

Initiating structure reflects the extent to which the leader defines and structures the roles of employees in pursuit of goal attainment.[43] Leaders who are high on initiating structure play a more active role in directing group activities and prioritize planning, scheduling, and trying out new ideas. They might emphasize the importance of meeting deadlines, describe explicit standards of performance, ask employees to follow formalized procedures, and criticize poor work when necessary.[44] Millard Drexler, CEO of J. Crew (the New York–based clothing retailer), has a unique initiating structure approach as he belts out instructions, assigns tasks, discusses clothing trends, and talks about sales statistics and goals about a dozen times a day over loudspeakers in the main Manhattan office. If he isn't in the office (and he often isn't), he has his assistant patch him in through his cell phone.[45]

Consideration reflects the extent to which leaders create job relationships characterized by mutual trust, respect for employee ideas, and consideration of employee feelings.[46] Leaders who are high on consideration create a climate of good rapport and strong, two-way communication and exhibit a deep concern for the welfare of employees. They might do personal favors for employees, take time to listen to their problems, "go to bat" for them when needed, and treat them as equals.[47] Jeff Immelt, CEO of General Electric, attempts to do this with many of the officers in his company by hosting a sleepover a couple of times a month. Immelt says, "We spend Saturday morning just talking about their careers. Who they are, how they fit, how I see their strengths and weaknesses—stuff like that. The personal connection is something I may have taken for granted before that I don't want to ever take for granted again."[48] Google's project OXYGEN was a process that tried to identify the most effective behaviors of managers inside the organization. The three most important habits that determined leader success were all oriented toward consideration: meeting regularly with employees, taking an interest in them personally, and asking questions rather than always providing answers.[49]

The Ohio State studies argued that initiating structure and consideration were (more or less) independent concepts, meaning that leaders could be high on both, low on both, or high on one and low on the other. That view differed from a series of studies conducted at the University of Michigan during the same time period. Those studies identified concepts similar to initiating structure and consideration, calling them production-centered (or task-oriented) and employee-centered (or relations-oriented) behaviors.[50] However, the Michigan studies framed their task-oriented and relations-oriented concepts as two ends of one continuum, implying that leaders couldn't be high on both dimensions.[51] In fact, a recent meta-analysis of 78 studies showed that initiating structure and consideration are only weakly related—knowing whether a leader engages in one brand of behavior says little about whether he or she engages in the other brand.[52] To see how much initiating structure and consideration you engage in during leadership roles, see our **OB Assessments** feature.

After an initial wave of research on initiating structure and consideration, leadership experts began to doubt the usefulness of the two dimensions for predicting leadership effectiveness.[53] More recent research has painted a more encouraging picture, however. A meta-analysis of 103 studies showed that initiating structure and consideration both had beneficial relationships with a number of outcomes.[54] For example, consideration had a strong positive relationship with perceived leader effectiveness, employee motivation, and employee job satisfaction. It also had a moderate positive relationship with overall unit performance. For its part, initiating structure had a strong positive relationship with employee motivation and moderate positive relationships with perceived leader effectiveness, employee job satisfaction, and overall unit performance. One of the most amusing and upbeat CEOs in the country, Panda Express's Andrew Cherng, agrees that both are important to a leader's success. Cherng states, "Before, we used to be more task-based, but now, if you want to be a manager at Panda, you have to be committed to being positive, to continuous learning."[55]

Although initiating structure and consideration tend to be beneficial across situations, there may be circumstances in which they become more or less important. The **life cycle theory of leadership** (sometimes also called the *situational model of leadership*) argues that the optimal combination of initiating structure and consideration depends on the readiness of the employees in the work unit.[56] **Readiness** is broadly defined as the degree to which employees have the ability and the willingness to accomplish their specific tasks.[57] As shown in Figure 14-4, the theory suggests that readiness varies across employees and can be expressed in terms of four important snapshots: R1–R4. To find the optimal combination of leader behaviors for a particular readiness snapshot, put your finger on the relevant R, then move it straight down to the recommended combination of behaviors.

The description of the first two R's has varied over time and across different formulations of the theory. One formulation described the R's as similar to stages of group development.[58] R1 refers to a group of employees who are working together for the first time and are eager to begin, but they lack the experience and confidence needed to perform their roles. Here the optimal combination of leader behaviors is **telling**—high initiating structure and low consideration—in which case the leader provides specific instructions and closely supervises performance. The lion's share of the leader's attention must be devoted to directing followers in this situation, because their goals and roles need to be clearly defined.

© Brett Flashnick/AP Images

Jeff Immelt, CEO of General Electric, exhibits consideration by holding "sleepovers" with his officers to get to know them better.

OB ASSESSMENTS

INITIATING STRUCTURE AND CONSIDERATION

How do you act when you're in a leadership role? This assessment is designed to measure initiating structure and consideration. Please write a number next to each statement that reflects how frequently you engage in the behavior described. Then subtract your answers to the boldfaced questions from 6, with the difference being your new answer for that question. For example, if your original answer for question 16 was "4," your new answer is "2" (6 – 4). Then sum up your answers for each of the dimensions. (Instructors: Assessments on transformational leadership, LMX, charisma, and readiness can be found in the PowerPoints in the Connect Library's Instructor Resources and in the Connect assignments for this chapter).

1 NEVER	2 SELDOM	3 OCCASIONALLY	4 OFTEN	5 ALWAYS

1. I let group members know what is expected of them. _____

2. I encourage the use of uniform procedures. _____

3. I try out my ideas in the group. _____

4. I make my attitudes clear to the group. _____

5. I decide what shall be done and how it shall be done. _____

6. I assign group members to particular tasks. _____

7. I make sure that my part in the group is understood by the group members. _____

8. I schedule the work to be done. _____

9. I maintain definite standards of performance. _____

10. I ask group members to follow standard rules and regulations. _____

11. I am friendly and approachable. _____

12. I do little things to make it pleasant to be a member of the group. _____

13. I put suggestions made by the group into operation. _____

14. I treat all group members as equals. _____

15. I give advance notice of changes. _____

16. **I keep to myself.** _____

17. I look out for the personal welfare of group members. _____

18. I am willing to make changes. _____

19. **I refuse to explain my actions.** _____

20. **I act without consulting the group.** _____

SCORING AND INTERPRETATION:

Initiating Structure: Sum up items 1–10. _____

Consideration: Sum up items 11–20. _____

For initiating structure, scores of 38 or more are high. For consideration, scores of 40 or more are high.

Source: R.M. Stogdill, *Manual for the Leader Behavior Description Questionnaire–Form XII* (Columbus, OH: Bureau of Business Research, The Ohio State University, 1963).

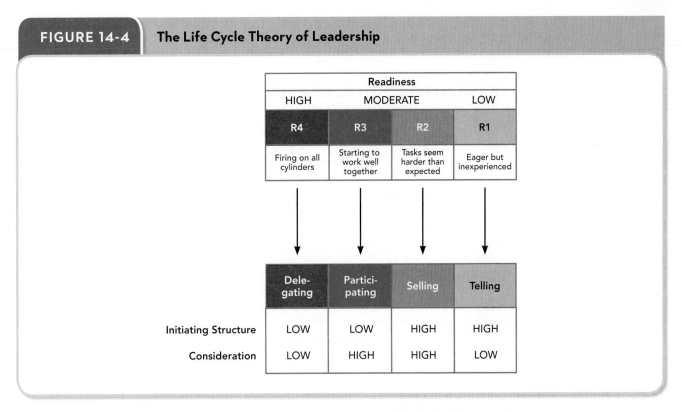

FIGURE 14-4 **The Life Cycle Theory of Leadership**

Source: Adapted from P. Hersey and K. Blanchard, "Revisiting the Life-Cycle Theory of Leadership," *Training and Development,* January 1996, pp. 42–47.

In the R2 stage, the members have begun working together and, as typically happens, are finding that their work is more difficult than they had anticipated. As eagerness turns to dissatisfaction, the optimal combination of leader behaviors is **selling**—high initiating structure and high consideration—in which the leader supplements his or her directing with support and encouragement to protect the confidence levels of the employees.

As employees gain more ability, guidance and direction by the leader become less necessary. At the R3 stage, employees have learned to work together well, though they still need support and collaboration from the leader to help them adjust to their more self-managed state of affairs. Here **participating**—low initiating structure and high consideration—becomes the optimal combination of leader behaviors. Finally, the optimal combination for the R4 readiness level is **delegating**—low initiating structure and low consideration—such that the leader turns responsibility for key behaviors over to the employees. Here the leader gives them the proverbial ball and lets them run with it. All that's needed from the leader is some degree of observation and monitoring to make sure that the group's efforts stay on track.

Estimates suggest that the life cycle theory has been incorporated into leadership training programs at around 400 of the firms in the *Fortune* 500, with more than one million managers exposed to it annually.[59] Unfortunately, the application of the theory has outpaced scientific testing of its propositions, and the shifting nature of its terminology and predictions has made scientific testing somewhat difficult.[60] The research that has been conducted supports the theory's predictions only for low readiness situations, suggesting that telling and selling sorts of behaviors may be more effective when ability, motivation, or confidence are lacking.[61] When readiness is higher, these tests suggest that leader behaviors simply matter less, regardless of their particular combinations. Tests also suggest that leaders only use the recommended combinations of behaviors between 14 and 37 percent of the time,[62] likely because many leaders adhere to the same leadership philosophy regardless of the situation. It should also be noted that tests of the theory have been somewhat more supportive when conducted on an across-job, rather than within-job, basis. For example, research suggests that the performance of lower ranking university employees (e.g., maintenance workers, custodians, landscapers) depends more on initiating structure and less on consideration than the performance of higher ranking university employees (e.g., professors, instructors).[63]

TRANSFORMATIONAL LEADERSHIP BEHAVIORS

By describing decision-making styles and day-to-day leader behaviors, we've covered a broad spectrum of what it is that leaders do. Still, something is missing. Take a small piece of scrap paper and jot down five people who are famous for their effective leadership. They can come from inside or outside the business world and can be either living people or historical figures. All that's important is that their name be practically synonymous with great leadership. Once you've compiled your list, take a look at the names. Do they appear on your list because they tend to use the right decision-making styles in the right situations and engage in effective levels of consideration and initiating structure? What about the case of Elon Musk? Do decision-making styles and day-to-day leadership behaviors explain his importance to the fortunes of SpaceX?

The missing piece of this leadership puzzle is what leaders do to motivate their employees to perform beyond expectations. **Transformational leadership** involves inspiring followers to commit to a shared vision that provides meaning to their work while also serving as a role model who helps followers develop their own potential and view problems from new perspectives.[64] Transformational leaders heighten followers' awareness of the importance of certain outcomes while increasing their confidence that those outcomes can be achieved.[65] What gets "transformed" is the way followers view their work, causing them to focus on the collective good more than just their own short-term self-interests and to perform beyond expectations as a result.[66] Former president Dwight D. Eisenhower once noted, "Leadership is the ability to decide what is to be done, and then to get others to want to do it."[67] Former president Harry S. Truman similarly observed, "A leader is a man who has the ability to get other people to do what they don't want to do, and like it."[68] Both quotes capture a transformation in the way followers view their work and what motivates them on the job.

Transformational leadership is viewed as a more motivational approach to leadership than other managerial approaches. Figure 14-5 contrasts various approaches to leadership according to how active or passive they are and, ultimately, how effective they prove to be. The colored cubes in the figure represent five distinct approaches to motivating employees, and the depth of the cubes represent how much a leader prioritizes each of the approaches. The figure therefore represents an optimal leadership approach that prioritizes more effective and more active behaviors. That optimal approach includes low levels of **laissez-faire (i.e., hands-off) leadership**,

Mother Teresa's inspiring humanitarian work with India's sick and poor, and her founding of the influential Missionaries of Charity, became known around the world and suggest that she was a transformational leader. She was awarded the Nobel Peace Prize in 1979.

© *Tim Graham/Hulton Archive/Getty Images*

| FIGURE 14-5 | Laissez-Faire, Transactional, and Transformational Leadership |

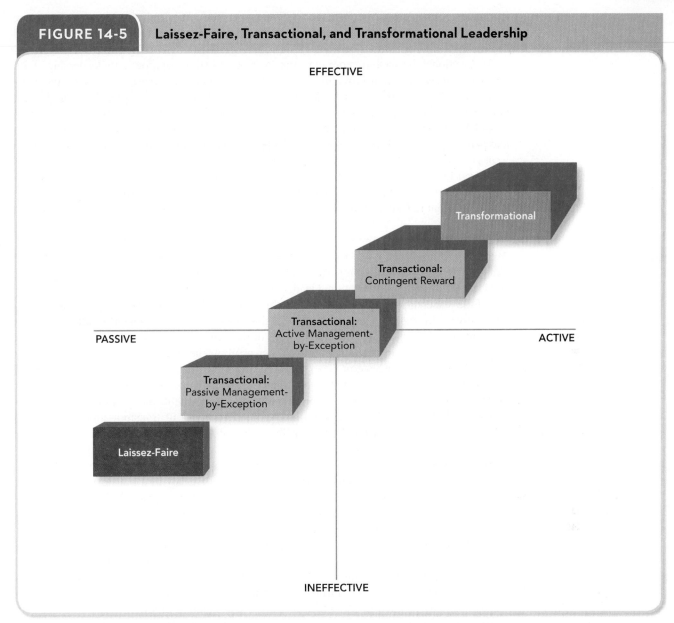

Source: Adapted from B.M. Bass and R.E. Riggio, *Transformational Leadership,* 2nd ed. (Mahwah, NJ: Erlbaum, 2006).

represented by the red cube, which is the avoidance of leadership altogether.[69] Important actions are delayed, responsibility is ignored, and power and influence go unutilized. One common measure of leadership reflects laissez-faire styles with this statement: "The leader avoids getting involved when important issues arise."[70]

The three yellow cubes represent **transactional leadership**, which occurs when the leader rewards or disciplines the follower depending on the adequacy of the follower's performance.[71] With **passive management-by-exception**, the leader waits around for mistakes and errors, then takes corrective action as necessary.[72] After all, "if it ain't broke, don't fix it!"[73] This approach is represented by statements like: "The leader takes no action until complaints are received."[74] With **active management-by-exception**, the leader arranges to monitor mistakes and errors actively and again takes corrective action when required.[75] This approach is represented by statements like: "The leader directs attention toward failures to meet standards."[76] **Contingent reward** represents a more active and effective brand of transactional leadership, in which the leader attains follower agreement on what needs to be done using promised or actual rewards in exchange for adequate performance.[77] Statements like "The leader makes clear what one can expect to receive when performance goals are achieved" exemplify contingent reward leadership.[78]

Transactional leadership represents the "carrot-and-stick" approach to leadership, with management-by-exception providing the "sticks" and contingent reward supplying the "carrots." Of course, transactional leadership represents the dominant approach to motivating employees in most organizations, and research suggests that it can be effective. A meta-analysis of 87 studies showed that contingent reward was strongly related to follower motivation and perceived leader effectiveness[79] (see Chapter 6 on motivation for more discussion of such issues). Active management-by-exception was only weakly related to follower motivation and perceived leader effectiveness, however, and passive management-by-exception seems actually to harm those outcomes.[80] Such results support the progression shown in Figure 14-5, with contingent reward standing as the most effective approach under the transactional leadership umbrella.

Finally, the green cube represents transformational leadership—the most active and effective approach in Figure 14-5. How effective is transformational leadership? Well, we'll save that discussion for the "How Important Is Leadership?" section that concludes this chapter, but suffice it to say that transformational leadership has the strongest and most beneficial effects of any of the leadership variables described in this chapter. It's also the leadership approach that's most universally endorsed across cultures, as described in our **OB Internationally** feature. In addition, it probably captures the key qualities of the famous leaders we asked you to list a few paragraphs back. To understand why it's so powerful, we need to dig deeper into the specific kinds of actions and behaviors that leaders can utilize to become more transformational. It turns out that the full spectrum of transformational leadership can be summarized using four dimensions: idealized influence, inspirational motivation, intellectual stimulation, and individualized consideration. Collectively, these four dimensions of transformational leadership are often called "the Four I's."[81] For our discussion of transformational leadership, we'll use Steve Jobs, former CEO of Apple, who was widely recognized as one of the most transformational leaders in the corporate world, as a running example. *Fortune* named Jobs "CEO of the Decade" for the 2000s.[82] Although Jobs died in 2011, his legacy as a transformational leader continues to this day. The fact that Elizabeth Holmes in Chapter 13 and Elon Musk are continually called "Steve Jobs-like" illustrates this fact. Jobs's leadership continues to affect employees at Apple in profound ways.[83]

Idealized influence involves behaving in ways that earn the admiration, trust, and respect of followers, causing followers to want to identify with and emulate the leader.[84] Idealized influence is represented by statements like: "The leader instills pride in me for being associated with him/her."[85] Idealized influence is synonymous with *charisma*—a Greek word that means "divinely inspired gift"—which reflects a sense among followers that the leader possesses extraordinary qualities.[86] "Charisma" is a word that was often associated with Steve Jobs. One observer noted that even though Jobs could be very difficult to work with, his remarkable charisma created a mysterious attraction that drew people to him, keeping them loyal to his collective sense of mission.[87]

To some extent, discussions of charisma serve as echoes of the "great person" view of leadership that spawned the trait research described in Table 14-2. In fact, research suggests that there is a genetic component to charisma specifically and to transformational leadership more broadly. Studies on identical twins reared apart show that such twins have very similar charismatic profiles, despite their differing environments.[88] Indeed, such research suggests that almost 60 percent of the variation in charismatic behavior can be explained by genes. One explanation for such findings is that genes influence the personality traits that give rise to charisma. For example, research suggests that extraversion, openness to experience, and agreeableness have significant effects on perceptions of leader charisma,[89] and all three of those personality dimensions have a significant genetic component (see Chapter 9 on personality and cultural values for more discussion of such issues).

14.5

How does transformational leadership differ from transactional leadership, and which behaviors set it apart?

OB INTERNATIONALLY

Does the effectiveness of leader styles and behaviors vary across cultures? Answering that question is one of the objectives of *Project GLOBE*'s test of *culturally endorsed implicit leadership theory,* which argues that effective leadership is "in the eye of the beholder" (see Chapter 9 on personality and cultural values for more discussion of such issues). To test the theory, researchers asked participants across cultures to rate a number of leader styles and behaviors using a 1 (very ineffective) to 7 (very effective) scale. The accompanying figure shows how three of the styles and behaviors described in this chapter were rated across 10 different regions (note that the term "Anglo" represents people of English ethnicity, including the United States, Great Britain, and Australia).

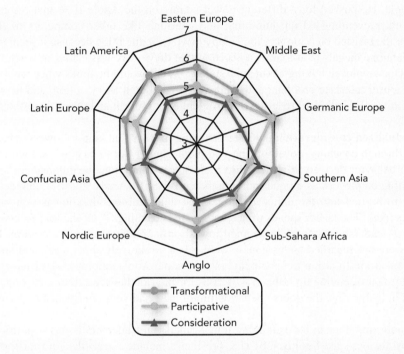

It turns out that transformational leadership is the most universally accepted approach to leadership of any of the concepts studied by Project GLOBE, receiving an average rating near 6 in every region except the Middle East. That appeal is likely explained by the fact that transformational leaders emphasize values like idealism and virtue that are endorsed in almost all countries. The figure also shows that a participative style is favorably viewed in most countries, though more variation is evident. Even more variation is seen with consideration behaviors, which are endorsed a bit less across the board but especially in Europe. Understanding these kinds of results can help organizations select and train managers who will fit the profile of an effective leader in a given region.

Sources: P.W. Dorfman, P.J.Hanges, and F.C.Brodbeck, "Leadership and Cultural Variation: The Identification of Culturally Endorsed Leadership Profiles," in *Culture, Leadership, and Organizations,* ed. R.J. House, P.J. Hanges, M. Javidan, P.W. Dorfman, and V. Gupta (Thousand Oaks, CA: Sage, 2004), pp. 669–720; R.J. House., P.J. Hanges, M. Javidan, P.W. Dorfman, and V.Gupta, *Culture, Leadership, and Organizations* (Thousand Oaks, CA: Sage, 2004); and M. Javidan., R.J. House, and P.W. Dorfman.,"A Nontechnical Summary of GLOBE Findings," in *Culture, Leadership, and Organizations,* ed. R.J. House, P.J. Hanges, M. Javidan, P.W. Dorfman, and V. Gupta (Thousand Oaks, CA: Sage, 2004), pp. 29–48.

Inspirational motivation involves behaving in ways that foster an enthusiasm for and commitment to a shared vision of the future.[90] That vision is transmitted through a sort of "meaning-making" process in which the negative features of the status quo are emphasized while highlighting the positive features of the potential future.[91] Inspirational motivation is represented by statements like: "The leader articulates a compelling vision of the future."[92] At Apple, Steve Jobs was renowned for spinning a "reality distortion field" that reshaped employees' views of the current work environment.[93] One Apple employee explained, "Steve has this power of vision that is almost frightening. When Steve believes in something, the power of that vision can literally sweep aside any objections, problems, or whatever. They just cease to exist."[94]

Intellectual stimulation involves behaving in ways that challenge followers to be innovative and creative by questioning assumptions and reframing old situations in new ways.[95] Intellectual stimulation is represented by statements like: "The leader gets others to look at problems from many different angles."[96] Intellectual stimulation was a staple of Jobs's tenure at Apple. He pushed for a different power supply on the Apple II so that the fan could be removed, preventing it from humming and churning like other computers of the time. Years later, he insisted on removing the floppy drive from the iMac because it seemed silly to transfer data one megabyte at a time, a decision that drew merciless criticism when the iMac debuted. One employee talking about Jobs stated, "There would be times when we'd rack our brains on a user interface problem, and think we'd considered every option, and he would go 'Did you think of this?' He'd redefine the problem or approach, and our little problem would go away."[97]

Individualized consideration involves behaving in ways that help followers achieve their potential through coaching, development, and mentoring.[98] Not to be confused with the consideration behavior derived from the Ohio State studies, individualized consideration represents treating employees as unique individuals with specific needs, abilities, and aspirations that need to be tied into the unit's mission. Individualized consideration is represented by statements like: "The leader spends time teaching and coaching."[99] Of the four facets of transformational leadership, Steve Jobs seemed lowest on individualized consideration. Employees who were not regarded as his equals were given a relatively short leash and sometimes faced an uncertain future in the company. In fact, some Apple employees resisted riding the elevator for fear of ending up trapped with Jobs for the ride between floors. As one observer describes it, by the time the doors open, you might have had your confidence undermined for weeks.[100]

One interesting domain for examining transformational leadership issues is politics. Many of the most famous speeches given by U.S. presidents include a great deal of transformational content. Table 14-4 includes excerpts from speeches given by presidents that rank highly on transformational content based on scientific and historical study.[101] One theme that's notable in the table is the presence of a crisis, as many of the presidents were attempting to steer the country through a difficult time in history (e.g., World War II, the Cold War, the Civil War). That's not a coincidence, in that times of crisis are particularly conducive to the emergence of transformational leadership.[102] See this chapter's **OB on Screen** feature for a great example. Times of stress and turbulence cause people to long for charismatic leaders, and encouraging, confident, and idealistic visions resonate more deeply during such times. In addition, support for this suggestion comes from President George W. Bush's speeches before and after the tragedies on 9/11. Coding of his major speeches, public addresses, and radio addresses shows a significant increase in the transformational content of his rhetoric after the 9/11 attacks, including more focus on a collective mission and more articulation of a values-based vision.[103] As future research is conducted, we're fairly confident that President Barack Obama's speeches will be described similarly, as many of his campaign and postelection speeches are high in transformational content. In fact, President Obama is known for being a very charismatic leader in terms of both the messages he delivers and the mannerisms that go along with them.[104]

TABLE 14-4		Transformational Rhetoric among U.S. Presidents	
PRESIDENT	TERM	REMARK	WHICH "I"?
Abraham Lincoln	1861–1865	"Fourscore and seven years ago our forefathers brought forth on this continent, a new nation, conceived in Liberty, and dedicated to the proposition that all men are created equal."	Idealized influence
Franklin Roosevelt	1933–1945	"First of all, let me assert my firm belief that the only thing we have to fear is fear itself—nameless, unreasoning, unjustified terror which paralyzes needed efforts to convert retreat into advance."	Inspirational motivation
John F. Kennedy	1961–1963	"And so, my fellow Americans . . . ask not what your country can do you for you—ask what you can do for your country. My fellow citizens of the world: Ask not what America will do for you, but what together we can do for the freedom of man."	Intellectual stimulation
Lyndon Johnson	1963–1969	"If future generations are to remember us more with gratitude than sorrow, we must achieve more than just the miracles of technology. We must also leave them a glimpse of the world as it was created, not just as it looked when we got through with it."	Idealized influence
Ronald Reagan	1981–1989	"General Secretary Gorbachev, if you seek peace, if you seek prosperity for the Soviet Union and Eastern Europe, if you seek liberalization: Come here to this gate! Mr. Gorbachev, open this gate! Mr. Gorbachev, tear down this wall!"	Idealized influence
Bill Clinton	1993–2001	"To realize the full possibilities of this economy, we must reach beyond our own borders, to shape the revolution that is tearing down barriers and building new networks among nations and individuals, and economies and cultures: globalization. It's the central reality of our time."	Intellectual stimulation

Sources: J.S. Mio, R.E. Riggio, S. Levin, and R. Reese, "Presidential Leadership and Charisma: The Effects of Metaphor," *Leadership Quarterly* 16 (2005), pp. 287–94; http://www.usa-patriotism.com/quotes/_list.htm.

OB ON SCREEN

LINCOLN

We are stepped out upon the world stage now. Now! With the fate of human dignity in our hands. Blood's been spilt to afford us this moment. Now! Now! Now!

With those words, Abraham Lincoln (Daniel Day Lewis) exhibits a transformational leadership approach toward a group of political allies and advisors in *Lincoln* (Dir. Steven Spielberg, Disney, 2012). The film, covering the last four months of Lincoln's life, is based in January 1865. Lincoln is trying desperately to acquire enough votes in the U.S. House of Representatives to pass the Thirteenth Amendment to the U.S. Constitution (the abolishment of slavery). With the Civil War starting to wind down (but not over), Lincoln is beset on all sides by individuals who have varying opinions about how to go about doing things and what the priorities for Lincoln and the country should be. There are many great examples of Lincoln using transformational leadership throughout the movie.

© Dreamworks/20th Century Fox/Photofest

In one scene, Lincoln provides a great example of *individualized consideration* as he sits down with an outgoing congressman and convinces him of the difference he can still make with his vote. He exhibits *intellectual stimulation* in having those around him change what seem to be insurmountable problems by reframing the questions they are asking. In the dramatic scene in question, Lincoln sits and listens to the constant bickering of his allies and confidants until he can't take it anymore. The preceding quote illustrates his use of *idealized influence,* and it's easy to see the charisma that Lincoln exudes. He also uses *inspirational motivation* to refocus the men on what the stakes are and what the vision for the future needs to be as he reiterates that the amendment "settles the fate for all coming time. Not only of the millions now in bondage, but of unborn millions to come." When Congressman James Ashley (David Costabile) and Secretary of State William Seward (David Strathairn) continue to question, Lincoln exerts his power and attempts to give his followers a sense that they can carry that power into the political battle with them.

SUMMARY: WHY ARE SOME LEADERS MORE EFFECTIVE THAN OTHERS?

So what explains why some leaders are more effective than others? As shown in Figure 14-6, answering that question requires an understanding of the particular styles that leaders use to make decisions and the behaviors they perform in their leadership role. In terms of decision-making

FIGURE 14-6 | Why Are Some Leaders More Effective Than Others?

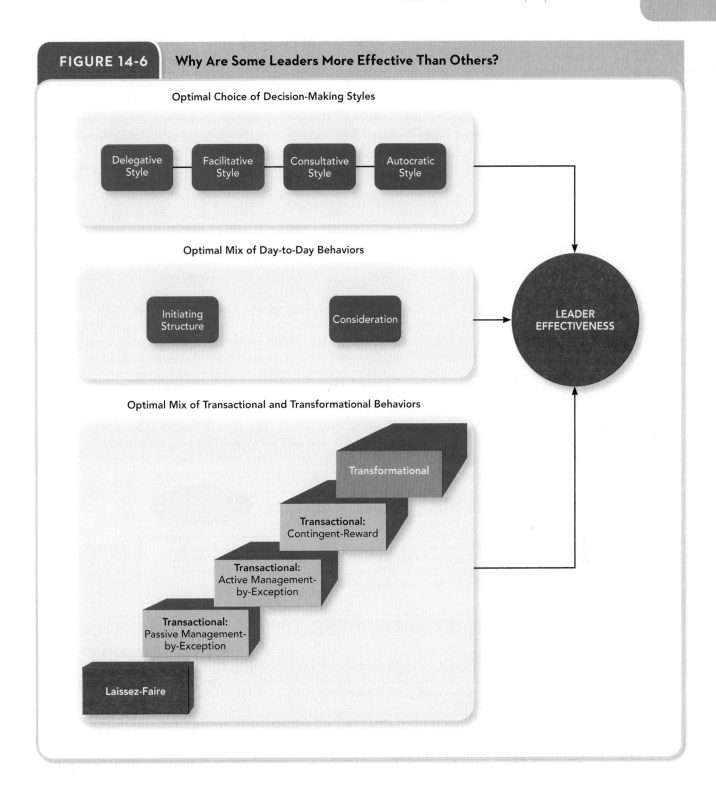

styles, do they choose the most effective combination of leader and follower control in terms of the autocratic, consultative, facilitative, and delegative styles, particularly considering the importance of the decision and the expertise in the unit? In terms of day-to-day behaviors, do they engage in adequate levels of initiating structure and consideration? Finally, do they utilize an effective combination of transactional leadership behaviors, such as contingent reward, and transformational leadership behaviors, such as idealized influence, inspirational motivation, intellectual stimulation, and individualized consideration?

HOW IMPORTANT IS LEADERSHIP?

How important is leadership? As with some other topics in organizational behavior, that's a complicated question because "leadership" isn't just one thing. Instead, all of the styles and behaviors summarized in Figure 14-6 have their own unique importance. However, transformational leadership stands apart from the rest to some extent, with particularly strong effects in organizations. For example, transformational leadership is more strongly related to unit-focused measures of leadership effectiveness, like the kind shown in the top panel of Table 14-1.[105] Units led by a transformational leader tend to be more financially successful and bring higher-quality products and services to market at a faster rate.[106] Transformational leadership is also more strongly related to dyad-focused measures of leader effectiveness, like the kind shown in the bottom panel of Table 14-1. Transformational leaders tend to foster leader–member exchange relationships that are of higher quality, marked by especially strong levels of mutual respect and obligation.[107]

14.6

How does leadership affect job performance and organizational commitment?

What if we focus specifically on the two outcomes in our integrative model of OB: performance and commitment? Figure 14-7 summarizes the research evidence linking transformational leadership to those two outcomes. The figure reveals that transformational leadership indeed affects the job performance of the employees who report to the leader. Employees with transformational leaders tend to have higher levels of task performance and engage in higher levels of citizenship behaviors.[108] Why? One reason is that employees with transformational leaders have higher levels of *motivation* than other employees.[109] They feel a stronger sense of psychological empowerment, feel more self-confident, and set more demanding work goals for themselves.[110]

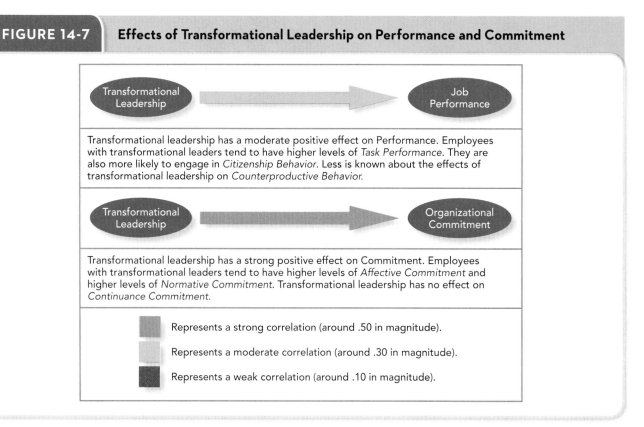

FIGURE 14-7 **Effects of Transformational Leadership on Performance and Commitment**

Transformational Leadership → Job Performance

Transformational leadership has a moderate positive effect on Performance. Employees with transformational leaders tend to have higher levels of *Task Performance*. They are also more likely to engage in *Citizenship Behavior*. Less is known about the effects of transformational leadership on *Counterproductive Behavior*.

Transformational Leadership → Organizational Commitment

Transformational leadership has a strong positive effect on Commitment. Employees with transformational leaders tend to have higher levels of *Affective Commitment* and higher levels of *Normative Commitment*. Transformational leadership has no effect on *Continuance Commitment*.

Represents a strong correlation (around .50 in magnitude).

Represents a moderate correlation (around .30 in magnitude).

Represents a weak correlation (around .10 in magnitude).

Sources: T.A. Judge and R.F. Piccolo, "Transformational and Transactional Leadership: A Meta-Analytic Test of Their Relative Validity," *Journal of Applied Psychology* 89 (2004), pp. 755–68; J.P. Meyer, D.J. Stanley, L. Herscovitch, and L. Topolnytsky, "Affective, Continuance, and Normative Commitment to the Organization: A Meta-Analysis of Antecedents, Correlates, and Consequences," *Journal of Vocational Behavior* 61 (2002), pp. 20–52; and P.M. Podsakoff, S.B. MacKenzie, J.B. Paine, and D.G. Bachrach, "Organizational Citizenship Behaviors: A Critical Review of the Theoretical and Empirical Literature and Suggestions for Future Research," *Journal of Management* 26 (2000), pp. 513–63.

They also *trust* the leader more, making them willing to exert extra effort even when that effort might not be immediately rewarded.[111]

Figure 14-7 also reveals that employees with transformational leaders tend to be more committed to their organization.[112] They feel a stronger emotional bond with their organization and a stronger sense of obligation to remain present and engaged in their work.[113] Why? One reason is that employees with transformational leaders have higher levels of *job satisfaction* than other employees.[114] One study showed that transformational leaders can make employees feel that their jobs have more variety and significance, enhancing intrinsic satisfaction with the work itself.[115] Other studies have shown that charismatic leaders express positive emotions more frequently and that those emotions are "caught" by employees through a sort of "emotional contagion" process.[116] For example, followers of transformational leaders tend to feel more optimism and less frustration during their workday, which makes it a bit easier to stay committed to work.[117]

Although leadership is very important to unit effectiveness and the performance and commitment of employees, there are contexts in which the importance of the leader can be reduced. The **substitutes for leadership model** suggests that certain characteristics of the situation can constrain the influence of the leader, making it more difficult for the leader to influence employee performance.[118] Those situational characteristics come in two varieties, as shown in Table 14-5. **Substitutes** reduce the importance of the leader while simultaneously providing a direct benefit to employee performance. For example, a cohesive work group can provide its own sort of governing behaviors, making the leader less relevant, while providing its own source of motivation and job satisfaction. **Neutralizers**, in contrast, only reduce the importance of the leader; they themselves have no beneficial impact on performance.[119] For example, spatial distance lessens the impact of a leader's behaviors and styles, but distance itself has no direct benefit for employee job performance.

The substitutes for leadership model offers a number of prescriptions for a better understanding of leadership in organizations. First, it can be used to explain why a leader who seemingly "does the right things" doesn't seem to be making any difference.[120] It may be that the leader's

TABLE 14-5	Leader Substitutes and Neutralizers

SUBSTITUTES	DESCRIPTION
Task feedback	Receiving feedback on performance from the task itself
Training & experience	Gaining the knowledge to act independently of the leader
Professionalism	Having a professional specialty that offers guidance
Staff support	Receiving information and assistance from outside staff
Group cohesion	Working in a close-knit and interdependent work group
Intrinsic satisfaction	Deriving personal satisfaction from one's work
NEUTRALIZERS	**DESCRIPTION**
Task stability	Having tasks with a clear, unchanging sequence of steps
Formalization	Having written policies and procedures that govern one's job
Inflexibility	Working in an organization that prioritizes rule adherence
Spatial distance	Being separated from one's leader by physical space

Source: Adapted from S. Kerr and J.M. Jermier, "Substitutes for Leadership: Their Meaning and Measurement," *Organizational Behavior and Human Performance* 22 (1978), pp. 375–403.

work context possesses high levels of neutralizers and substitutes. Second, it can be used to explain what to do if an ineffective person is in a leadership role with no immediate replacement waiting in the wings.[121] If the leader can't be removed, perhaps the organization can do things to make that leader more irrelevant. Studies of the substitutes for leadership model have been inconsistent in showing that substitutes and neutralizers actually make leaders less influential in the predicted manner.[122] What is clearer is that the substitutes in Table 14-5 have beneficial effects on the job performance and organizational commitment of employees. In fact, the beneficial effects of the substitutes is sometimes even greater than the beneficial effects of the leader's own behaviors and styles. Some leadership experts even recommend that leaders set out to create high levels of the substitutes in their work units wherever possible, even if the units might ultimately wind up "running themselves."[123]

APPLICATION: LEADERSHIP TRAINING

Given the importance of leadership, what can organizations do to maximize the effectiveness of their leaders? One method is to spend more time training them. As mentioned in Chapter 8, organizations spend more than $150 billion on employee learning and development, and much of that is devoted to management and supervisory training.[124] One training analyst explains the increasing emphasis on leadership training this way: "The biggest problem that companies face today is an acute shortage of midlevel managers. They look around and just don't have enough qualified people."[125] This is exactly the determination that Walmart's president and CEO Bill Simon made when he instituted a 16-week military-style leadership training program. Walmart's senior vice president of talent development, Celia Swanson, says, "Our analysis showed we were capable of building new stores faster than we could prepare new store managers."[126]

14.7

Can leaders be trained to be more effective?

Leadership training programs often focus on very specific issues, like conducting more accurate performance evaluations, being a more effective mentor, structuring creative problem solving, or gaining more cultural awareness and sensitivity.[127] However, training programs can also focus on much of the content covered in this chapter. For example, content could focus on contextual considerations that alter the effectiveness of decision-making styles or particular leader behaviors, such as initiating structure and consideration. This is exactly what Campbell Soup Company is doing through its "CEO Institute"—a two-year program focused on personal leadership development.[128] Farmer's Insurance puts all of its upper-level executives through a program that gives them direct feedback from their peers on their leadership behaviors. The executives use this information to create individual leadership development plans.[129] For someone with a strong take on why many of today's leadership training programs go wrong, see our **OB at the Bookstore** feature.

It turns out that many training programs focus on transformational leadership content, and research suggests that those programs can be effective.[130] One study of transformational leadership training occurred in one of the largest bank chains in Canada.[131] Managers at all of the branches in one region were randomly assigned to either a transformational training group or a control group. The managers in the training group took part in a one-day training session that began by asking them to describe the best and worst leaders they had ever encountered. Where applicable, the behaviors mentioned as belonging to the best leaders were framed around transformational leadership. The transformational dimensions were then described in a lecture-style format. Participants set goals for how they could behave more transformationally and engaged in role-playing exercises to practice those behaviors. The managers then created specific action plans, with progress on those plans monitored during four "booster sessions" over the next month. The results of the study showed that managers who participated in the training were rated as more transformational afterward. More importantly, their employees reported higher levels of organizational commitment, and their branches enjoyed better performance in terms of personal loan sales and credit card sales.

OB

AT THE BOOKSTORE

ACT LIKE A LEADER, THINK LIKE A LEADER

by Herminia Ibarra (Boston: Harvard Business Review Press, 2015)

The only way to think like a leader is to first act: to plunge yourself into new projects and activities, interact with very different kinds of people, and experiment with unfamiliar ways of getting things done . . . In times of transition and uncertainty, thinking and introspection should follow action and experimentation—not vice versa.

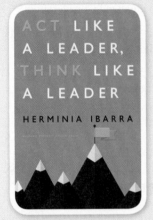

Photo of cover: © Roberts Publishing Services

With those words, Herminia Ibarra lays out the crux of what she thinks we should all do in order to become better leaders. She lays out a thoughtful argument as to why most current leadership training programs have it all wrong. That is, they all start with a heavy dose of introspection, defining your purpose, and relying on your strengths or your "authentic self" to begin your leadership journey. Ibarra argues that this introspection creates blinders and limits the role you can play as a leader. Following a subset of social psychology research that shows that people change their minds by first changing their behavior, Ibarra argues that change doesn't happen from within, it starts from the outside. She sees leadership development working like this: If you start acting like a leader, people will see you as a leader and confirm it. This social recognition will make you start to see yourself as a leader which will then make you seek out more opportunities to do so. The more opportunities you have, the better you will become at leading and the cycle continues. Act like a leader and then think like a leader.

Ibarra lays out three major ways in which you can start acting like leader. The first is *Redefining Your Job* which essentially means moving out of the operational demands and prioritizing more strategic activities. One does this by taking on roles and projects that give them a differing point of view, focusing on change, and engaging others. *Redefining Your Network* is the second focus and involves working hard to expand your network of professional relationships. The third and perhaps most important is *Redefining Your Self* which is the process of being willing to exhibit new leadership behaviors even when those behaviors feel inauthentic at first.

TAKEAWAYS

14.1 Leadership is defined as the use of power and influence to direct the activities of followers toward goal achievement. An "effective leader" improves the performance and well-being of his or her overall unit, as judged by profit margins, productivity, costs, absenteeism, retention, employee surveys, and so forth. An "effective leader" also cultivates high-quality leader–member exchange relationships on a dyadic basis through role taking and role making processes.

14.2 Leader emergence has been linked to a number of traits, including conscientiousness, disagreeableness, openness, extraversion, general cognitive ability, energy level, stress tolerance, and self-confidence. Of that set, the last six traits also predict leader effectiveness.

14.3 Leaders can use a number of styles to make decisions. Beginning with high leader control and moving to high follower control, they include autocratic, consultative, facilitative, and delegative styles. According to the time-driven model of leadership, the appropriateness of these styles depends on decision significance, the importance of commitment, leader expertise, the likelihood of commitment, shared objectives, employee expertise, and teamwork skills.

14.4 Most of the day-to-day leadership behaviors that leaders engage in are examples of either initiating structure or consideration. Initiating structure behaviors include initiation, organization, and production sorts of duties. Consideration behaviors include membership, integration, communication, recognition, and representation sorts of duties.

14.5 Transactional leadership emphasizes "carrot-and-stick" approaches to motivating employees, whereas transformational leadership fundamentally changes the way employees view their work. More specifically, transformational leadership inspires employees to commit to a shared vision or goal that provides meaning and challenge to their work. The specific behaviors that underlie transformational leadership include the "Four I's": idealized influence, inspirational motivation, intellectual stimulation, and individualized consideration.

14.6 Transformational leadership has a moderate positive relationship with job performance and a strong positive relationship with organizational commitment. It has stronger effects on these outcomes than other leadership behaviors.

14.7 Leaders can be trained to be effective. In fact, such training can be used to increase transformational leadership behaviors, despite the fact that charisma is somewhat dependent on personality and genetic factors.

KEY TERMS

- Leadership   *p. 444*
- Leader–member exchange
  theory   *p. 444*
- Role taking   *p. 445*
- Role making   *p. 445*
- Leader effectiveness   *p. 446*
- Leader emergence   *p. 447*
- Autocratic style   *p. 448*
- Consultative style   *p. 448*
- Facilitative style   *p. 448*
- Delegative style   *p. 449*
- Time-driven model of
  leadership   *p. 449*
- Initiating structure   *p. 452*
- Consideration   *p. 452*
- Life cycle theory of leadership   *p. 453*
- Readiness   *p. 453*
- Telling   *p. 453*
- Selling   *p. 455*
- Participating   *p. 455*
- Delegating   *p. 455*
- Transformational leadership   *p. 456*
- Laissez-faire leadership   *p. 456*
- Transactional leadership   *p. 457*
- Passive management-by-
  exception   *p. 457*
- Active management-by-
  exception   *p. 457*
- Contingent reward   *p. 457*
- Idealized influence   *p. 458*
- Inspirational motivation   *p. 460*
- Intellectual stimulation   *p. 460*
- Individualized consideration   *p. 460*
- Substitutes for leadership
  model   *p. 465*
- Substitutes   *p. 465*
- Neutralizers   *p. 465*

DISCUSSION QUESTIONS

14.1 Before reading this chapter, which statement did you feel was more accurate: "Leaders are born" or "Leaders are made"? How do you feel now, and why do you feel that way?

14.2 The time-sensitive model of leadership argues that leaders aren't just concerned about the accuracy of their decisions when deciding among autocratic, consultative, facilitative, and delegative styles; they're also concerned about the efficient use of time. What other considerations could influence a leader's use of the four decision-making styles?

14.3 The time-sensitive and life cycle models of leadership both potentially suggest that leaders should use different styles and behaviors for different followers. Can you think of any negative consequences of that advice? How could those negative consequences be managed?

14.4 Consider the four dimensions of transformational leadership: idealized influence, inspirational motivation, intellectual stimulation, and individualized consideration. Which of those dimensions would you respond to most favorably? Why?

14.5 Can you think of any potential "dark sides" to transformational leadership? What would they be?

CASE: SPACEX

Elon Musk is known for his passion in everything he works on and for being able to instill that passion in others. That passion can lead to incredible emotional highs and lows, especially when you are launching rockets into space. Early in SpaceX's tenure, one of their rockets (a Falcon 1) exploded shortly after takeoff. Dolly Singh, a recruiter at SpaceX said, "It was so profound seeing the energy shift over the room in the course of thirty seconds . . . You don't usually see grown-ups weeping, but there they were. We were tired and broken emotionally. Musk addressed the workers right away and encouraged them to get back to work. He said, 'Look. We are going to do this. It's going to be okay. Don't freak out.' It was like magic. Everyone chilled out immediately and started to focus on figuring out what just happened and how to fix it. It went from despair to hope and focus." SpaceX has now completed dozens of launches successfully and has more than 50 flights planned over the next few years (totaling $5 billion in revenue). The future is bright, but will require continued improvement and a steady focus.

Musk is known for being a hands-on manager and incredibly task focused. Employees have learned not to tell Musk that what he's asking is impossible. A SpaceX employee says, "Elon will say, 'Fine. You're off the project, and I am now the CEO of the project. I will do your job and be CEO of two companies at the same time. I will deliver it.' What's crazy is that Elon actually does it. Every time he's fired someone and taken their job, he's delivered on whatever the project was." When asked about this kind of approach Musk says, "I certainly don't try to set impossible goals. I think impossible goals are demotivating. You don't want to tell people to go through a wall by banging their head against it. I don't ever set intentionally impossible goals. But I've certainly always been optimistic on time frames."

When SpaceX first started, Musk interviewed almost every single one of SpaceX's first 1,000 hires—janitors and technicians included. (SpaceX now employs more than 3,500 workers). He still continues to interview the engineers. Candidates are warned before walking in that the interview could be as short as thirty seconds or as long as fifteen minutes. Once in, engineers have a range of experiences from great to torturous depending on how they handle questions. Not everyone is cut out to work at SpaceX. Singh says, "The recruiting pitch was SpaceX is special forces. If you want as hard as it gets, then great. If not, then you shouldn't come here." A reporter who wrote a book on Musk had this to say: "Numerous people interviewed for this book decried the work hours, Musk's blunt style, and his sometimes ludicrous expectations. Yet almost every person—even those who had been fired—still worshipped Musk and talked about him in terms usually reserved for superheroes or deities."

14.1 Does Elon Musk sound like the kind of leader that you would like to work for? Why or why not?

14.2 Is there a danger to having such a strong, charismatic leader as the head of a company? Would you have reservations investing in the stock of SpaceX if it were to go public?

14.3 Would you consider Musk to be a transformational leader? In what ways does he fit that model and in which ways does he not?

Sources: T. Junod, "Elon Musk: Triumph of His Will," *Esquire,* December 2012, pp. 139-149; A. Vance, *Elon Musk: Tesla, SpaceX and the Quest for a Fantastic Future* (New York: HarperCollins, 2015); and A. Vandermey, "The Shared Genius of Elon Musk and Steve Jobs," *Fortune,* December 9, 2013, pp. 98–106.

EXERCISE: TAKE ME TO YOUR LEADER

The purpose of this exercise is to explore the commonalities in effective leadership across different types of leaders. This exercise uses groups, so your instructor will either assign you to a group or ask you to create your own group. The exercise has the following steps:

14.1 Imagine that a space alien descended down to Earth and actually uttered the famous line, "Take me to your leader!" Having read a bit about leadership, your group knows that leaders come in a number of shapes and sizes. Instead of showing the alien just one leader, your group decides it might be beneficial to show the alien a whole variety of leaders. Each member should choose one type of leader from the table to focus on (each member must choose a different type). Try to choose examples that are personally interesting but that also maximize the diversity within the group.

Orchestra Conductor	Fashion Designer	Drummer in Rock Band
Coach	Personal Tax Accountant	Point Guard in Basketball
Film Director	Nightclub DJ	Bartender
College Professor	Fitness Trainer	Sheriff
Talk-Show Host	Prison Guard	Millionaire Philanthropist
Stockbroker	Real Estate Broker	Agent
Psychotherapist	MBA Program Director	Auditor
Campaign Manager	Construction Project Supervisor	CEO
Diplomat	Sports Color Commentator	Vice President of Marketing

14.2 Individually, jot down some thoughts that highlight for the alien what is truly distinctive about "leadership" for this type of leader. For example, if you were showing the alien a coach, you might call attention to how coaches cannot control the game itself very much but instead must make their influence felt on the practice field by instilling skills while being anticipatory in their thinking. You might also call attention to how coaches need to be creative and adapt quickly during the game itself.

14.3 Share the thoughts you've jotted down in your groups, going from member to member, with each person describing what "leadership" means for the given types of leaders.

14.4 Once all these thoughts about the various types of leaders have been shared, think about whether there are certain traits, styles, or behaviors that are universal across all the types. For example, maybe all of the types have some kind of organizing quality to them (e.g., leaders need to be organized, leaders need to do things to help others be organized). Create a list of four "leadership universals."

14.5 Now consider the situational challenges faced by the types of leaders you discussed, including challenges rooted in the task, their followers, or the surrounding work context. For example, the fact that the coach has little direct impact on the game is a situational challenge. Do other leader types also grapple with lack of direct control? Create a list of four "situational challenges" faced by multiple types of leaders.

14.6 Elect a group member to write the group's four universals and four challenges on the board.

14.7 Class discussion (whether in groups or as a class) should center on whether the theories described in the chapter discuss some of the leadership universals identified by the groups. Are there theories that also include some of the situational challenges uncovered? Which leadership theory seems best equipped for explaining effective leadership across a wide variety of leader types?[132]

ENDNOTES

14.1 Yukl, G. *Leadership in Organizations,* 4th ed. Englewood Cliffs, NJ: Prentice Hall, 1998.

14.2 Ibid.

14.3 Ibid.

14.4 Ibid.

14.5 Dansereau, F. Jr.; G. Graen; and W.J. Haga. "A Vertical Dyad Linkage Approach to Leadership within Formal Organizations: A Longitudinal Investigation of the Role Making Process." *Organizational Behavior and Human Performance* 13 (1975), pp. 46–78; Graen, G.; M. Novak; and P. Sommerkamp. "The Effects of Leader–Member Exchange and Job Design on Productivity and Satisfaction: Testing a Dual Attachment Model." *Organizational Behavior and Human Performance* 30 (1982), pp. 109–31; Graen, G.B., and M. Uhl-Bien. "Relationship-Based Approach to Leadership: Development of Leader–Member Exchange (LMX) Theory of Leadership over 25 Years: Applying a Multi-Level Multi-Domain Perspective." *Leadership Quarterly* 6 (1995), pp. 219–47; and Liden, R.C.; R.T. Sparrowe; and S.J. Wayne. "Leader–Member Exchange Theory: The Past and Potential for the Future." In *Research in Personnel and Human Resources Management,* Vol. 15, ed. G.R. Ferris. Greenwich, CT: JAI Press, 1997, pp. 47–119.

14.6 Graen, G.B., and T. Scandura. "Toward a Psychology of Dyadic Organizing." In *Research in Organizational Behavior,* Vol. 9, ed. L.L. Cummings and B.M. Staw. Greenwich, CT: JAI Press, 1987, pp. 175–208.

14.7 Ibid.

14.8 Graen and Uhl-Bien, "Relationship-Based Approach to Leadership."

14.9 Ibid.

14.10 Bauer, T.N., and S.G. Green. "Development of Leader–Member Exchange: A Longitudinal Test." *Academy of Management Journal* 39 (1996), pp. 1538–67; Gerstner, C.R., and D.V. Day. "Meta-Analytic Review of Leader–Member Exchange Theory: Correlates and Construct Issues." *Journal of Applied Psychology* 82 (1997), pp. 827–44; and Liden, R.C.; S.J. Wayne; and D. Stillwell. "A Longitudinal Study on the Early Development of Leader–Member Exchanges." *Journal of Applied Psychology* 78 (1993), pp. 662–74.

14.11 Ballinger, G.A., D.W. Lehman, and F.D. Schoorman. "Leader–Member Exchange and Turnover before and after Succession Events." *Organizational Behavior and Human Decision Processes* 113 (2010), pp. 25–36.

14.12 Graen and Uhl-Bien, "Relationship-Based Approach to Leadership."

14.13 Ilies, R.; J.D. Nahrgang; and F.P. Morgeson. "Leader–Member Exchange and Citizenship Behaviors: A Meta-Analysis." *Journal of Applied Psychology* 92 (2007), pp. 269–77; Dulebohn, J.H.; W.H. Bommer; R.C. Liden; R.L. Brouer; and G.R. Ferris. "A Meta-Analysis of Antecedents and Consequences or Leader–Member Exchange: Integrating the Past with an Eye Toward the Future." *Journal of Management* 38 (2012), pp. 1715–59.

14.14 Rockstuhl, T.; J.H. Dulebohn; S. Ang; and L.M. Shore. "Leader–Member Exchange (LMX) and Culture: A Meta-Analysis of Correlates of LMX across 23 Countries." *Journal of Applied Psychology* 97 (2012), pp. 1097–1130.

14.15 Stogdill, R.M. "Personal Factors Associated with Leadership: A Survey of the Literature." *Journal of Applied Psychology* 54 (1948), pp. 259–69.

14.16 Den Hartog, D.N., and P.L. Koopman. "Leadership in Organizations." In *Handbook of Industrial, Work, and Organizational Psychology*, Vol. 2, ed. N. Anderson; D.S. Ones; H.K. Sinangil; and C. Viswesvaran. Thousand Oaks, CA: Sage, 2002, pp. 166–87.

14.17 Yukl, *Leadership in Organizations;* and Zaccaro, S.J. "Trait-Based Perspectives of Leadership." *American Psychologist* 62 (1998), pp. 6–16.

14.18 DeRue, D.S., J.D. Nahrgang; N. Wellman; and S.E. Humphrey. "Trait and Behavioral Theories of Leadership: An Integration and Meta-Analytic Test of Their Validity." *Personnel Psychology* 64 (2011), pp. 7–52.

14.19 Vroom, V.H. "Leadership and the Decision-Making Process." *Organizational Dynamics* 28 (2000), pp. 82–94; and Yukl, *Leadership in Organizations.*

14.20 Taylor, A. "Chrysler's Speed Merchant." *Fortune,* September 6, 2010, p. 82.

14.21 Vroom, "Leadership and the Decision-Making Process"; and Yukl, *Leadership in Organizations.*

14.22 Bryant, A. *Quick and Nimble: Lessons from Leading CEOs on How to Create a Culture of Innovation.* New York: Times Books, 2014.

14.23 Vroom, "Leadership and the Decision-Making Process"; and Yukl, *Leadership in Organizations.*

14.24 Bryant, A. *The Corner Office: Indispensable and Unexpected Lessons from CEOs on How to Lead and Succeed.* New York: Times Books, 2011.

14.25 Vroom, "Leadership and the Decision-Making Process"; and Yukl, *Leadership in Organizations.*

14.26 Bryant, A. *The Corner Office.*

14.27 Ibid.

14.28 Vroom, "Leadership and the Decision-Making Process."

14.29 Miller, K.I., and P.R. Monge. "Participation, Satisfaction, and Productivity: A Meta-Analytic Review." *Academy of Management Journal* 29 (1986), pp. 727–53; and Wagner, J.A. III. "Participation's Effects on Performance and Satisfaction: A Reconsideration of Research Evidence." *Academy of Management Review* 19 (1994), pp. 312–30.

14.30 Vroom, "Leadership and the Decision-Making Process."

14.31 Rogelberg, S.G.; D.J. Leach; P.B. Warr; and J.L. Burnfield. "'Not Another Meeting!' Are Meeting Time Demands Related to Employee Well-Being?" *Journal of Applied Psychology* 91 (2006), pp. 86–96.

14.32 Yang, J.L. "What's the Secret to Running Great Meetings?" *Fortune,* October 27, 2008, p. 26.

14.33 Terlep, S. "GM's Plodding Culture Vexes Its Impatient CEO." *The*

Wall Street Journal Online, April 7, 2010.

14.34 Vroom, "Leadership and the Decision-Making Process"; Vroom, V.H., and A.G. Jago. *The New Leadership: Managing Participation in Organizations.* Englewood Cliffs, NJ: Prentice Hall, 1988; Vroom, V.H., and A.G. Jago. "Decision Making as a Social Process: Normative and Descriptive Models of Leader Behavior." *Decision Sciences* 5 (1974), pp. 743–69; and Vroom, V.H., and P.W. Yetton. *Leadership and Decision Making.* Pittsburgh, PA: University of Pittsburgh Press, 1973.

14.35 Adams, R., and L.A. Schuker. "Time Inc. CEO Ousted after Six Months." *The Wall Street Journal Online,* February 18, 2011.

14.36 Aditya, R.N.; R.J. House; and S. Kerr. "Theory and Practice of Leadership: Into the New Millennium." In *Industrial and Organizational Psychology: Linking Theory with Practice,* ed. C.L. Cooper and E.A. Locke. Malden, MA: Blackwell, 2000, pp. 130–65; House, R.J., and R.N. Aditya. "The Social Scientific Study of Leadership: Quo Vadis?" *Journal of Management* 23 (1997), pp. 409–73; and Yukl, *Leadership in Organizations.*

14.37 Vroom, V.H., and A.G. Jago. "On the Validity of the Vroom-Yetton Model." *Journal of Applied Psychology* 63 (1978), pp. 151–62. See also Vroom and Yetton, *Leadership and Decision Making;* Vroom and Jago, *The New Leadership;* and Field, R.H.G. "A Test of the Vroom-Yetton Normative Model of Leadership." *Journal of Applied Psychology* 67 (1982), pp. 523–32.

14.38 Vroom and Yetton, *Leadership and Decision Making.*

14.39 Bryant, *The Corner Office.*

14.40 Hemphill, J.K. *Leader Behavior Description.* Columbus: Ohio State University, 1950. Cited in Fleishman, E.A.; E.F. Harris; and H.E. Burtt. *Leadership and Supervision in Industry: An Evaluation of a Supervisory Training Program.* Columbus: Bureau of Educational Research, Ohio State University, 1955.

14.41 Hemphill, J.K., and A.E. Coons. "Development of the Leader Behavior Description Questionnaire." In *Leader Behavior: Its Description and Measurement,* ed. R.M. Stogdill and A.E. Coons. Columbus: Bureau of Business Research, Ohio State University, 1957, pp. 6–38.

14.42 Fleishman, E.A. "The Description of Supervisory Behavior." *Journal of Applied Psychology* 37 (1953), pp. 1–6; Fleishman et al., *Leadership and Supervision in Industry;* Hemphill and Coons, "Development of the Leader Behavior Description Questionnaire"; and Halpin, A.W., and B.J. Winer. *Studies in Aircrew Composition: The Leadership Behavior of the Airplane Commander* (Technical Report No. 3). Columbus: Personnel Research Board, Ohio State University, 1952. Cited in Fleishman et al., *Leadership and Supervision in Industry.*

14.43 Fleishman, "The Description of Supervisory Behavior"; Fleishman et al., *Leadership and Supervision in Industry;* and Fleishman, E.A., and D.R. Peters. "Interpersonal Values, Leadership Attitudes, and Managerial 'Success.'" *Personnel Psychology* 15 (1962), pp. 127–43.

14.44 Yukl, *Leadership in Organizations.*

14.45 Paumgarten, N. "The Merchant." *The New Yorker,* September 20, 2010, pp. 74–87.

14.46 Fleishman, "The Description of Supervisory Behavior"; Fleishman et al., *Leadership and Supervision in Industry;* and Fleishman and Peters, "Interpersonal Values."

14.47   Yukl, *Leadership in Organizations.*

14.48   Brady, D. "Can GE Still Manage?" *Bloomberg Businessweek,* April 25, 2010, pp. 27–32.

14.49   Bryant, A. *Quick and Nimble.*

14.50   Katz, D.; N. Maccoby; and N. Morse. *Productivity, Supervision, and Morale in an Office Situation.* Ann Arbor: Institute for Social Research, University of Michigan, 1950; Katz, D.; N. Maccoby; G. Gurin; and L. Floor. *Productivity, Supervision, and Morale among Railroad Workers.* Ann Arbor: Survey Research Center, University of Michigan, 1951; Katz, D., and R.L. Kahn. "Some Recent Findings in Human-Relations Research in Industry." In *Readings in Social Psychology,* ed. E. Swanson; T. Newcomb; and E. Hartley. New York: Holt, 1952, pp. 650–65; Likert, R. *New Patterns of Management.* New York: McGraw-Hill, 1961; and Likert, R. *The Human Organization.* New York: McGraw-Hill, 1967.

14.51   Fleishman, E.A. "Twenty Years of Consideration and Structure." In *Current Developments in the Study of Leadership,* ed. E.A. Fleishman and J.G. Hunt. Carbondale: Southern Illinois Press, 1973, pp. 1–37.

14.52   Judge, T.A.; R.F. Piccolo; and R. Ilies. "The Forgotten Ones? The Validity of Consideration and Initiating Structure in Leadership Research." *Journal of Applied Psychology* 89 (2004), pp. 36–51.

14.53   Aditya et al., "Theory and Practice of Leadership"; DenHartog and Koopman, "Leadership in Organizations"; House and Aditya, "The Social Scientific Study of Leadership"; Korman, A.K. "'Consideration,' 'Initiating Structure,' and Organizational Criteria—A Review." *Personnel Psychology* 19 (1966), pp. 349–61; Yukl, *Leadership in Organizations;* and Yukl, G., and D.D. Van Fleet. "Theory and Research on Leadership in Organizations." In *Handbook of Industrial and Organizational Psychology,* Vol. 3, ed. M.D. Dunnette and L.M. Hough. Palo Alto, CA: Consulting Psychologists Press, 1992, pp. 147–97.

14.54   Judge et al., "The Forgotten Ones?"

14.55   Greenfeld, K.T. "The Sharin' Huggin' Lovin' Carin' Chinese Food Money Machine." *Bloomberg Businessweek,* November 22, 2011, pp. 98–103.

14.56   Hersey, P., and K.H. Blanchard. "Life Cycle Theory of Leadership." *Training and Development Journal,* May 1969, pp. 26–34; Hersey, P., and K.H. Blanchard. "So You Want to Know Your Leadership Style?" *Training and Development Journal,* February 1974, pp. 22–37; Hersey, P., and K.H. Blanchard. "Revisiting the Life-Cycle Theory of Leadership." *Training and Development,* January 1996, pp. 42–47; and Hersey, P., and K.H. Blanchard. *Management of Organizational Behavior: Leading Human Resources,* 9th ed. Upper Saddle River, NJ: Pearson, 2008.

14.57   Hersey and Blanchard, *Management of Organizational Behavior.*

14.58   Hersey and Blanchard, "Revisiting the Life-Cycle Theory of Leadership."

14.59   Fernandez, C.F., and R.P. Vecchio. "Situational Leadership Revisited: A Test of an Across-Jobs Perspective." *Leadership Quarterly* 8 (1997), pp. 67–84.

14.60   Graeff, C.L. "Evolution of Situational Leadership Theory: A Critical Review." *Leadership Quarterly* 8 (1997), pp. 153–70.

14.61   Vecchio, R.P. "Situational Leadership Theory: An Examination of a Prescriptive Theory." *Journal of Applied Psychology* 72 (1987), pp. 444–51; and Norris, W.R., and R.P. Vecchio. "Situational Leadership

Theory: A Replication." *Group and Organization Management* 17 (1992), pp. 331–42.

14.62 Vecchio, "Situational Leadership Theory"; Norris and Vecchio, "Situational Leadership Theory: A Replication"; and Blank, W.; J.R. Weitzel; and S.G. Green. "A Test of Situational Leadership Theory." *Personnel Psychology* 43 (1990), pp. 579–97.

14.63 Fernandez and Vecchio, "Situational Leadership Theory Revisited."

14.64 Bass, B.M., and R.E. Riggio. *Transformational Leadership,* 2nd ed. Mahwah, NJ: Erlbaum, 2006; Bass, B.M. *Leadership and Performance beyond Expectations.* New York: Free Press, 1985; and Burns, L.M. *Leadership.* New York: Harper & Row, 1978.

14.65 Bass, *Leadership and Performance beyond Expectations.*

14.66 Ibid.

14.67 Larson, A. *The President Nobody Knew.* New York: Popular Library, 1968, p. 68. Cited in Ibid.

14.68 Truman, H.S. *Memoirs.* New York: Doubleday, 1958. Cited in Bass, *Leadership and Performance beyond Expectations.*

14.69 Bass and Riggio, *Transformational Leadership.*

14.70 Ibid.; and Bass, B.M., and B.J. Avolio. *MLQ: Multifactor Leadership Questionnaire.* Redwood City, CA: Mind Garden, 2000.

14.71 Bass and Riggio, *Transformational Leadership;* Bass, *Leadership and Performance Beyond Expectations;* and Burns, *Leadership.*

14.72 Bass and Riggio, *Transformational Leadership.*

14.73 Bass, *Leadership and Performance beyond Expectations.*

14.74 Bass and Riggio, *Transformational Leadership;* and Bass and Avolio, *MLQ.*

14.75 Bass and Riggio, *Transformational Leadership.*

14.76 Ibid.; and Bass and Avolio, *MLQ.*

14.77 Bass and Riggio, *Transformational Leadership.*

14.78 Ibid.; and Bass and Avolio, *MLQ.*

14.79 Judge, T.A., and R.F. Piccolo. "Transformational and Transactional Leadership: A Meta-Analytic Test of Their Relative Validity." *Journal of Applied Psychology* 89 (2004), pp. 755–68.

14.80 Ibid.

14.81 Bass and Riggio, *Transformational Leadership.*

14.82 Koehn, N. F. "HIS Legacy." *Fortune,* November 11, 2009, pp. 110–14.

14.83 Blumenthal, K. *Steve Jobs: The Man Who Thought Different.* New York: Feiwel, 2012; and Isaacson, W. *Steve Jobs.* New York: Simon & Schuster, 2011.

14.84 Kane, Y. I. "Jobs Quits as CEO." *The Wall Street Journal Online,* August 25, 2011; and Friedman, L. "Steve Jobs Takes Medical Leave of Absence." *MacWorld,* April 2011, p. 12.

14.85 Ibid.; and Bass and Avolio, *MLQ.*

14.86 Conger, J.A. "Charismatic and Transformational Leadership in Organizations: An Insider's Perspective on these Developing Research Streams." *Leadership Quarterly* 10 (1999), pp. 145–79.

14.87 Young, J.S., and W.L. Simon. *iCon: Steve Jobs—The Greatest Second Act in the History of Business.* Hoboken, NJ: Wiley, 2005.

14.88 Johnson, A.M.; P.A. Vernon; J.M. McCarthy; M. Molso; J.A. Harris; and K.J. Jang. "Nature vs. Nurture: Are Leaders Born or Made? A Behavior Genetic Investigation of Leadership Style." *Twin Research* 1 (1998), pp. 216–23.

14.89 Judge, T.A., and J.E. Bono. "Five-Factor Model of Personality and Transformational Leadership." *Journal of*

Applied Psychology 85 (2000), pp. 751–65.

14.90 Bass and Riggio, *Transformational Leadership.*

14.91 Conger, "Charismatic and Transformational Leadership in Organizations."

14.92 Bass and Riggio, *Transformational Leadership;* and Bass and Avolio, *MLQ.*

14.93 Young and Simon, *iCon.*

14.94 Ibid.

14.95 Bass and Riggio, *Transformational Leadership.*

14.96 Ibid.; and Bass and Avolio, *MLQ.*

14.97 Isaacson, *Steve Jobs.*

14.98 Bass and Riggio, *Transformational Leadership.*

14.99 Ibid.; and Bass and Avolio, *MLQ.*

14.100 Young and Simon, *iCon.*

14.101 Mio, J.S.; R.E. Riggio; S. Levin; and R. Reese. "Presidential Leadership and Charisma: The Effects of Metaphor." *Leadership Quarterly* 16 (2005), pp. 287–94.

14.102 Conger, "Charismatic and Transformational Leadership in Organizations."

14.103 Bligh, M.C.; J.C. Kohles; and J.R. Meindl. "Charisma under Crisis: Presidential Leadership, Rhetoric, and Media Responses before and after the September 11th Terrorist Attacks." *Leadership Quarterly* 15 (2004), pp. 211–39.

14.104 Bligh, M.C., and J.C. Kohles. "The Enduring Allure of Charisma: How Barack Obama Won the Historic 2008 Presidential Election." *Leadership Quarterly* 20 (2009), pp. 483–92.

14.105 Lowe, K.B.; K.G. Kroeck; and N. Sivasubramaniam. "Effectiveness Correlates of Transformational and Transactional Leadership: A Meta-Analytic Review of the MLQ Literature." *Leadership Quarterly* 7 (1996), pp. 385–425.

14.106 Howell, J.M., and B.J. Avolio. "Transformational Leadership, Transactional Leadership, Locus of Control, and Support for Innovation: Key Predictors of Consolidated-Business-Unit Performance." *Journal of Applied Psychology* 78 (1993), pp. 891–902; Howell, J.M.; D.J. Neufeld; and B.J. Avolio. "Examining the Relationship of Leadership and Physical Distance with Business Unit Performance." *Leadership Quarterly* 16 (2005), pp. 273–85; Keller, R.T. "Transformational Leadership, Initiating Structure, and Substitutes for Leadership: A Longitudinal Study of Research and Development Project Team Performance." *Journal of Applied Psychology* 91 (2006), pp. 202–10; and Waldman, D.A.; G.G. Ramirez; R.J. House; and P. Puranam. "Does Leadership Matter? CEO Leadership Attributes and Profitability under Conditions of Perceived Environmental Uncertainty." *Academy of Management Journal* 44 (2001), pp. 134–43.

14.107 Howell, J.M., and K.E. Hall-Merenda. "The Ties That Bind: The Impact of Leader–Member Exchange, Transformational and Transactional Leadership, and Distance on Predicting Follower Performance." *Journal of Applied Psychology* 84 (1999), pp. 680–94; Piccolo, R.F., and J.A. Colquitt. "Transformational Leadership and Job Behaviors: The Mediating Role of Core Job Characteristics." *Academy of Management Journal* 49 (2006), pp. 327–40; and Wang, H.; K.S. Law; R.D. Hackett; D. Wang; and Z.X. Chen. "Leader–Member Exchange as a Mediator of the Relationship between Transformational Leadership and Followers' Performance and Organizational Citizenship Behavior." *Academy of Management Journal* 48 (2005), pp. 420–32.

14.108 Judge and Piccolo, "Transformational and Transactional Leadership"; Podsakoff, P.M.; S.B. MacKenzie;

J.B. Paine; and D.G. Bachrach. "Organizational Citizenship Behaviors: A Critical Review of the Theoretical and Empirical Literature and Suggestions for Future Research." *Journal of Management* 26 (2000), pp. 513–63.

14.109 Judge and Piccolo, "Transformational and Transactional Leadership."

14.110 Avolio, B.J.; W. Zhu; W. Koh; and P. Bhatia. "Transformational Leadership and Organizational Commitment: Mediating Role of Psychological Empowerment and Moderating Role of Structural Distance." *Journal of Organizational Behavior* 25 (2004), pp. 951–68; Kirkpatrick, S.A., and E.A. Locke. "Direct and Indirect Effects of Three Core Charismatic Leadership Components on Performance and Attitudes." *Journal of Applied Psychology* 81 (1996), pp. 36–51; and Shamir, B.; E. Zakay; E. Breinin; and M. Popper. "Correlates of Charismatic Leader Behaviors in Military Units: Subordinates' Attitudes, Unit Characteristics, and Superiors' Appraisals of Leader Performance." *Academy of Management Journal* 41 (1998), pp. 387–409.

14.111 Podsakoff, P.M.; S.B. MacKenzie; and W.H. Bommer. "Transformational Leader Behaviors and Substitutes for Leadership as Determinants of Employee Satisfaction, Commitment, Trust, and Organizational Citizenship Behaviors." *Journal of Management* 22 (1996), pp. 259–98; Podsakoff, P.M.; S.B. MacKenzie; R.H. Moorman; and R. Fetter. "Transformational Leader Behaviors and their Effects on Followers' Trust in Leader, Satisfaction, and Organizational Citizenship Behaviors." *Leadership Quarterly* 1 (1990), pp. 107–42; and Shamir et al., "Correlates of Charismatic Leader Behaviors."

14.112 Meyer, J.P.; D.J. Stanley; L. Herscovitch; and L. Topolnytsky. "Affective, Continuance, and Normative Commitment to the Organization: A Meta-Analysis of Antecedents, Correlates, and Consequences." *Journal of Vocational Behavior* 61 (2002), pp. 20–52.

14.113 Walumbwa, F.O.; B.J. Avolio; and W. Zhu. "How Transformational Leadership Weaves Its Influence on Individual Job Performance: The Role of Identification and Efficacy Beliefs." *Personnel Psychology* 61 (2008), pp. 793–825.

14.114 Judge and Piccolo, "Transformational and Transactional Leadership."

14.115 Piccolo and Colquitt, "Transformational Leadership and Job Behaviors." See also Bono, J.E., and T.A. Judge. "Self-Concordance at Work: Toward Understanding the Motivational Effects of Transformational Leaders." *Academy of Management Journal* 46 (2003), pp. 554–71; and Shin, S.J., and J. Zhou. "Transformational Leadership, Conservation, and Creativity: Evidence from Korea." *Academy of Management Journal* 46 (2003), pp. 703–14.

14.116 Bono, J.E., and R. Ilies. "Charisma, Positive Emotions, and Mood Contagion." *Leadership Quarterly* 17 (2006), pp. 317–34; and McColl-Kennedy, J.R., and R.D. Anderson. "Impact of Leadership Style and Emotions on Subordinate Performance." *Leadership Quarterly* 13 (2002), pp. 545–59.

14.117 Bono, J; H.J. Foldes; G. Vinson; and J.P. Muros. "Workplace Emotions: The Role of Supervision and Leadership." *Journal of Applied Psychology* 92 (2007), pp. 1357–67.

14.118 Kerr, S., and J.M. Jermier. "Substitutes for Leadership: Their Meaning and Measurement." *Organizational Behavior and Human Performance* 22 (1978), pp. 375–403.

14.119 Howell, J.P.; P.W. Dorfman; and S. Kerr. "Moderator Variables in Leadership

Research." *Academy of Management Review* 11 (1986), pp. 88–102.

14.120 Kerr and Jermier, "Substitutes for Leadership"; and Jermier, J.M., and S. Kerr. "'Substitutes for Leadership: Their Meaning and Measurement': Contextual Recollections and Current Observations." *Leadership Quarterly* 8 (1997), pp. 95–101.

14.121 Howell, J.P.; D.E. Bowen; P.W. Dorfman; S. Kerr; and P.M. Podsakoff. "Substitutes for Leadership: Effective Alternatives to Ineffective Leadership." *Organizational Dynamics,* Summer 1990, pp. 21–38.

14.122 Podsakoff, P.M., and S.B. MacKenzie. "Kerr and Jermier's Substitutes for Leadership Model: Background, Empirical Assessment, and Suggestions for Future Research." *Leadership Quarterly* 8 (1997), pp. 117–25; Podsakoff, P.M.; B.P. Niehoff; S.B. MacKenzie; and M.L. Williams. "Do Substitutes for Leadership Really Substitute for Leadership? An Empirical Examination of Kerr and Jermier's Situational Leadership Model." *Organizational Behavior and Human*

Decision Processes 54 (1993), pp. 1–44; Podsakoff et al., "Transformational Leadership Behaviors and Substitutes for Leadership"; and Podsakoff, P.M.; S.B. MacKenzie; M. Ahearne; and W.H. Bommer. "Searching for a Needle in a Haystack: Trying to Identify the Illusive Moderators of Leadership Behavior." *Journal of Management* 21 (1995), pp. 422–70.

14.123 Howell et al., "Substitutes for Leadership: Effective Alternatives."

14.124 Miller, L. "ASTD State of the Industry Report: Organizations Continue to Invest in Workplace Learning." *T + D,* November 2012, pp. 42–50.

14.125 Kranz, G. "A Higher Standard for Managers." *Workforce,* June 11, 2007, pp. 21–26.

14.126 Kranz, G. "Wal-Mart Drafts Leaders for Military-style Training." *Workforce,* June 12, 2013, http://www.workforce.com/article/20130612/NEWS02/130619994/0/topics.

14.127 Gist, M.E., and D. McDonald-Mann. "Advances in Leadership Training and Development." In *Industrial and*

Organizational Psychology: Linking Theory with Practice, ed. C.L. Cooper and E.A. Locke. Malden, MA: Blackwell, 2000, pp. 52–71.

14.128 Reardon, N. "Making Leadership Personal." *T + D,* March 2011, pp. 44–49.

14.129 Weinstein, M. "Farmer's Comprehensive Training Policy." *Training,* January/February 2013, pp. 42–44.

14.130 Ibid.; Dvir, T.; D. Eden; B.J. Avolio; and B. Shamir. "Impact of Transformational Leadership on Follower Development and Performance: A Field Experiment." *Academy of Management Journal* 45 (2000), pp. 735–44; and Barling, J.; T. Weber; and E.K. Kelloway. "Effects of Transformational Leadership Training on Attitudinal and Financial Outcomes: A Field Experiment." *Journal of Applied Psychology* 81 (1996), pp. 827–32.

14.131 Barling et al., "Effects of Transformational Leadership Training."

14.132 Marcic, D.; J. Seltzer; and P. Vail, *Organizational Behavior: Experiences and Cases.* Cincinnati, OH: South-Western, 2001.

ORGANIZATIONAL MECHANISMS

CHAPTER 15
Organizational Structure

CHAPTER 16
Organizational Culture

Organizational Structure

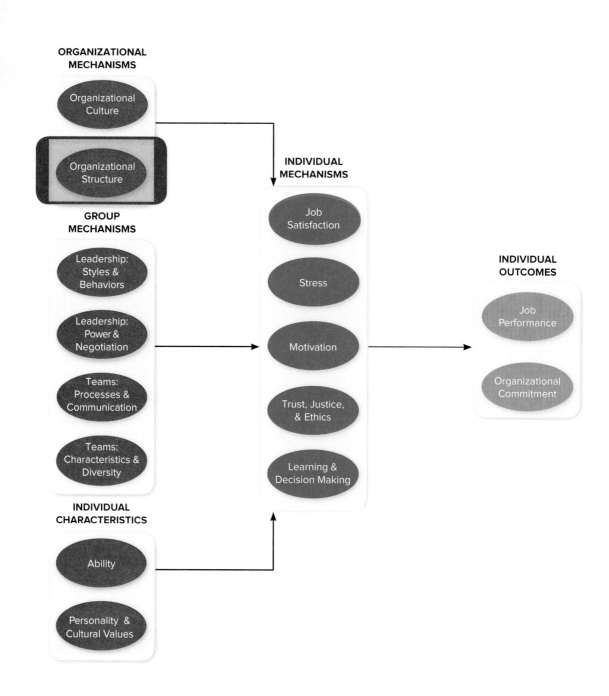

© Jared McMillen/Aurora Photos/Corbis

✓ LEARNING GOALS

After reading this chapter, you should be able to answer the following questions:

15.1 What is an organization's structure, and what does it consist of?

15.2 What are the major elements of an organizational structure?

15.3 What is organizational design, and what factors does the organizational design process depend on?

15.4 What are some of the more common organizational forms that an organization might adopt for its structure?

15.5 When an organization makes changes to its structure, how does that restructuring affect job performance and organizational commitment?

15.6 What steps can organizations take to reduce the negative effects of restructuring efforts?

ZAPPOS

appos, the online shoe and accessory retailer based in Las Vegas, is known for having one of the zaniest and most quirky cultures around—after all, "create fun and a little weirdness" is listed as one of the company's core values. Over the past couple of years, Zappos has been attempting to create a new organizational structure that many would call just as quirky. CEO Tony Hsieh, 41, has moved the company toward an organizational structure they refer to as "Holocracy." What exactly does that mean? One thing is for sure—how people act and are organized to do their work at Zappos doesn't look like many other companies' structures! The general idea behind Holocracy is a work environment in which there are no job titles, no managers, and employees are supposed to figure out largely on their own what to work on and how to get their work done.

Zappos was purchased by Amazon.com for $1.2 billion in 2009 and has largely been left to operate on its own ever since (Amazon now runs Zappos' warehouse facilities). One of the reasons Amazon CEO Jeff Bezos has kept a hands-off approach is Zappos' unique approach to managing people. Holocracy (according to Zappos) is the ultimate in "flattening" a company—there are no formal reporting relationships anywhere

in the organization. It is essentially a "no-structure" structure. Hsieh believes that this kind of organizational structure aligns perfectly with Zappos' desire to continually embrace and drive change throughout the company. He wants employees to be able to react to their environment quickly and not be stuck with rigid employee relationships.

In a more traditional organization, most employees would have a manager who does everything from assigning roles and responsibilities to deciding what project deadlines should be to measuring how well workers perform their jobs. Zappos employees are self-organized into "circles" instead of traditional work teams. Workers join these circles based on what kind of work they want to do. The employees in each circle decide their own roles and responsibilities through a number of different gatherings known as "governance meetings," and so far, Zappos has more than 300 circles dealing with everything from customer service to social media. The goal is to give workers as much freedom as possible and allow them to self-manage their own job and career. The transition has not been an easy one, though; a large number of employees have had difficulty understanding exactly what the new structure means for them and how to make it work.

ORGANIZATIONAL STRUCTURE

As the Zappos example illustrates, an organization's structure can have a significant impact on its financial performance and ability to manage its employees. The decisions that CEO Tony Hsieh has made regarding the company's organizational structure will have an impact on how employees communicate and cooperate with one another, how power is distributed, and how individuals view their work environment. In fact, an organization's structure dictates more than you might think. We've spent a great deal of time in this book talking about how employee attitudes and behaviors are shaped by individual characteristics, such as personality and ability, and group mechanisms, such as teams and leaders. In this and the following chapter, we discuss how the organization as a whole affects employee attitudes and behavior. Match.com (the online dating service) CEO Sam Yagan was asked to describe one of the biggest lessons he had recently learned, and he replied, "The impact of organizational structure on a company's ability to get, create, innovate, evolve, or just plain survive. Everyone knows that hiring, engaging, and retaining talent is a huge competitive issue, but I don't think enough executives of companies big and small realize the impact the way they organize their talent has on the company's overall productivity."[1]

 15.1

What is an organization's structure, and what does it consist of?

Think about some of the jobs you've held in the past (or perhaps the job you hope to have after graduation). What types of employees did you interact with on a daily basis? Were they employees who performed the same tasks that you performed? Or maybe they didn't do exactly what you did, but did they serve the same customer? How many employees did your manager supervise? Was every decision you made scrutinized by your supervisor, or were you given a "long leash"? The answers to all of these questions are influenced by organizational structure. An **organizational structure** formally dictates how jobs and tasks are divided and coordinated between individuals and groups within the company. Organizational structures can be relatively simple when a company has only 5 to 20 employees but grow incredibly complex when an organization has tens of thousands of employees.

WHY DO SOME ORGANIZATIONS HAVE DIFFERENT STRUCTURES THAN OTHERS?

One way of getting a feel for an organization's structure is by looking at an organizational chart. An **organizational chart** is a drawing that represents every job in the organization and the formal reporting relationships between those jobs. It helps organizational members and outsiders understand and comprehend how work is structured within the company. Figure 15-1 illustrates two sample organizational charts. In a real chart, the boxes would be filled with actual names and job titles. As you can imagine, as companies grow larger, their organizational charts get more complex. Can you imagine drawing an organizational chart that included every one of Walmart's 2.2 million employees? Not only would that require a lot of boxes and a lot of paper, it would probably take a couple of years to put together (plus, as soon as someone left the organization, it would be time to update the chart!). On the other extreme, we can look at a company like our chapter opening example of Zappos, where, technically, there wouldn't be any boxes or arrows at all.

ELEMENTS OF ORGANIZATIONAL STRUCTURE

The organizational charts described in this chapter are relatively simple and designed to illustrate specific points (if you want to see how complex some of these charts can get, do a search on the Internet for "organizational chart," and you'll begin to see how varied organizations can be in the way they design their company). Specifically, charts like those in Figure 15-1 can illustrate the five key elements of an organization's structure. Those five key elements, summarized in Table 15-1, describe how work tasks, authority relationships, and decision-making responsibilities are organized within the company. These elements will be discussed in the next several sections.

WORK SPECIALIZATION **Work specialization** is the way in which tasks in an organization are divided into separate jobs. In some organizations, this categorization is referred to as a company's division of labor. How many tasks does any one employee perform? To some degree, work specialization is a never-ending trade-off among productivity, flexibility, and worker motivation. Take an assembly-line worker at Ford as an example. Henry Ford was perhaps the earliest

15.2

What are the major elements of an organizational structure?

FIGURE 15-1 | **Two Sample Organizational Structures**

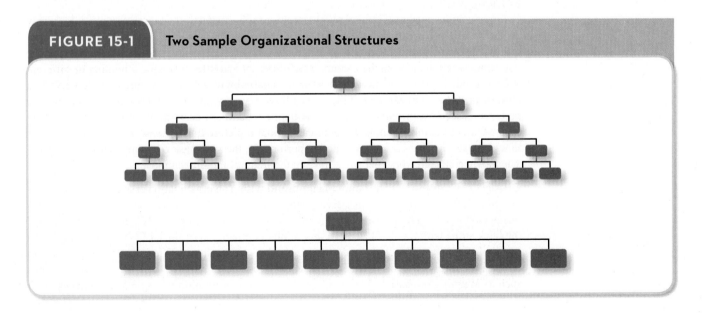

TABLE 15-1	Elements of Organizational Structure

ORGANIZATIONAL STRUCTURE DIMENSION	DEFINITION
Work specialization	The degree to which tasks in an organization are divided into separate jobs.
Chain of command	Answers the question of "who reports to whom?" and signifies formal authority relationships.
Span of control	Represents how many employees each manager in the organization has responsibility for.
Centralization	Refers to where decisions are formally made in organizations.
Formalization	The degree to which rules and procedures are used to standardize behaviors and decisions in an organization.

(and clearly most well-known) believer in high degrees of work specialization. He divided tasks among his manufacturing employees to such a degree that each employee might perform only a single task, over and over again, all day long. Having only one task to perform allowed those employees to be extremely productive at doing that one thing. It also meant that training new workers was much easier when replacements were needed.

However, there are trade-offs when organizations make jobs highly specialized. Highly specialized jobs can cause organizations to lose the ability associated with employees who can be flexible in what they do. By spending all their time performing specialized tasks well, employees fail to update or practice other skills. Accounting majors, for example, might specialize in taxes or auditing. Some larger companies might hire these graduates for their ability to do either auditing or tax—but not both. Other companies might be looking for an accountant who can perform either aspect well, depending on how they divide up accounting duties within their organization. Still other companies might want to hire "general managers" who understand accounting, finance, management, marketing, and operations as a part of their job. Thus, high levels of specialization may be acceptable in larger firms with more employees but can be problematic in smaller firms in which employees must be more flexible in their job duties. Aetna, the Hartford, Connecticut–based health insurer, publishes more than 1,300 different job titles, each of which has its own list of the competencies that employees in those jobs must perform.[2]

Organizations may also struggle with employee job satisfaction when they make jobs highly specialized. If you recall from Chapter 4 on job satisfaction, we discussed five core characteristics of jobs that significantly affect satisfaction. One of those characteristics was variety, or the degree to which the job requires a number of different activities involving a number of different skills and talents.[3] Employees tend to be more satisfied with jobs that require them to perform a number of different kinds of activities. Even though you might be very efficient and productive performing a job with only one task, how happy would you be to perform that job on a daily basis? One of the most famous films in early motion picture history was *Modern Times,* a film in which Charlie Chaplin was relegated to performing the same task over and over, very quickly. The movie ridiculed work specialization and the trend of treating employees as machines.

CHAIN OF COMMAND The **chain of command** within an organization essentially answers the question "Who reports to whom?" Every employee in a traditional organizational structure has one person to whom they report. That person then reports to someone else, and on and on, until the buck stops with the CEO (though in a public company, even the CEO is responsible to the board of directors). The chain of command can be seen as the specific flow of authority down through the levels of an organization's structure. Similar to Zappos, there are some companies such as Washington–based video-game maker Valve Corporation whose 300 employees work with no managers or assigned projects. (Valve's website lets you know the company has been "boss free" since its founding in 1996.[4]) However, these types of organizations are the exception and not the norm. Most organizations depend on a chain of command's flow of authority to attain order, control, and predictable performance.[5] Some newer organizational structures make this chain of command a bit more complex. It has become common to have positions that report to two or more different managers.

© Sunset Boulevard/Corbis

Modern Times (1932), starring Charlie Chaplin, ridiculed work specialization and the treating of employees as machines. Have things changed since then?

For example, Intel placed two people apiece in charge of the two largest divisions of their organization. Questions have arisen as to how their duties will be split up and whether employees will know whom it is they report to.[6] For one example of how chain of command can greatly effect operations within an organization see this chapter's **OB on Screen.**

SPAN OF CONTROL A manager's **span of control** represents how many employees he or she is responsible for in the organization. The organizational charts in Figure 15-1 provide an illustration of the differences in span of control. In the top chart, each manager is responsible for leading two subordinates. In most instances, this level would be considered a narrow span of control. In the bottom chart, the manager is responsible for 10 employees. Typically, this number would be considered a wide span of control. Of course, the key question in many organizations is how many employees one manager can supervise effectively. Answering that question requires a better understanding of the benefits of narrow and wide spans of control.

Narrow spans of control allow managers to be much more hands-on with employees, giving them the opportunity to use directive leadership styles while developing close mentoring relationships with employees. A narrow span of control is especially important if the manager has substantially more skill or expertise than the subordinates. Early writings on management assumed that the narrower the span of control, the more productive employees would become.[7] However, a narrow span of control requires organizations to hire many managers, which can significantly increase labor costs. Moreover, if the span of control becomes too narrow, employees can become resentful of their close supervision and long for more latitude in their day-to-day decision making. In fact, current research suggests that a moderate span of control is best for an organization's productivity.[8] This relationship is illustrated in Figure 15-2. Note that organizational performance increases as span of control increases, but only up to the point that managers no longer have the ability to coordinate and supervise the large numbers of employees underneath them. Most organizations work hard to try to find the right balance, and this balance differs for every organization, depending on its unique circumstances. However, there is no question that spans of control in organizations have increased significantly in recent years.[9] Organizations such as Coca-Cola have gone through structures in which vice presidents have had up to 90 employees reporting to them![10]

An organization's span of control affects how "tall" or "flat" its organizational chart becomes. For example, the top panel of Figure 15-1 depicts a tall structure with many hierarchical levels and a narrow span of control, whereas the bottom panel depicts a flat organization with few levels and a wide span of control. Think about what happens when an organization becomes "taller." First, more layers of management means having to pay more management salaries. Second, communication in the organization becomes more complex as each new layer becomes one more point through which information must pass when traveling upward or downward. Third, the organization's ability to make decisions becomes slower, because approval for decisions has to be authorized at every step of the hierarchy.

OB ON SCREEN

THE IMITATION GAME

Who is your commanding officer?

With those words Alan Turing (Benedict Cumberbatch) questions Commander Alastair Denniston (Charles Dance) to try to figure out how he can get around the chain of command in *The Imitation Game* (Dir: Morten Tyldum, Weinstein Company, 2014). Turing, a mathematical genius and an expert in cryptology (the study of codes and codebreaking), is hired by Denniston to join the British military during World War II. A group of cryptologists are brought in to try to break the code created by the "Enigma Machine," which is allowing the Nazis to send secure wireless messages both to their submarines and military in the field. The most complicated part of solving the codes the machine writes and reads is that the code is reset every single day, which doesn't leave enough time to solve the problem before having to start over. At the time of the movie, things are not going well for the Allied countries and the Nazi's unfettered use of the Enigma machine is allowing them to win the war.

© *The Weinstein Company/Photofest*

Turing, who thinks most of those working around him are dimwits, wants to build a machine of his own creation that will break the code—"only a machine can defeat another machine." The problem? Turing's machine is going to cost 100,000 pounds, and he hasn't convinced the others to believe in its potential worth. Hugh Alexander (Matthew Goode) is Turing's direct supervisor for the code breaking group and has said no to his ideas. Turing attempts to go around him to Denniston, who resoundly orders that he needs to follow the centralized decision-making structure set up within the military structure. Denniston argues that wars are won with "order, discipline, chain of command." When Turing asks who Denniston's superior officer is, Denniston incredulously tells him, "Winston Churchill, #10 Downing Street, London, England SW1. If you have a problem with my decision, you may take it up with him." Turing, unfazed by this and somewhat oblivious to how things are supposed to work in an organizational setting, simply writes Churchill a letter directly to try to get the resources and decision-making capability that he needs to get his machine built.

Over the past three decades, organizations worked to become flatter to reduce the costs associated with multiple layers of management and increase their ability to adapt to their environment. When Intel, for example, announced a reduction in its managerial ranks of 1,000 positions (or 1 percent of its 100,000 employees), a spokesperson announced that "This [layoff] is designed to improve costs and improve decision making and communications across the company."[11] McDonald's recently reorganized in a way that is supposed to make their decision

| FIGURE 15-2 | Span of Control and Organizational Performance |

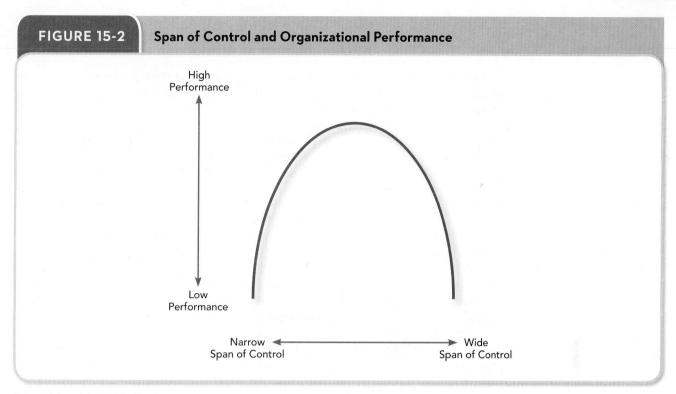

Source: Adapted from N.A. Theobald and S. Nicholson-Crotty, "The Many Faces of Span of Control: Organizational Structure Across Multiple Goals," *Administration and Society* 36 (2005), pp. 648–60.

making faster and more focused on their customers. CEO Steve Easterbrook added, "Our new structure will be supported by streamlined teams with fewer layers and less bureaucracy."[12]

CENTRALIZATION **Centralization** reflects where decisions are formally made in organizations. If only the top managers within a company have the authority to make final decisions, we would say that the organization has a highly "centralized" structure. In contrast, if decision-making authority is pushed down to lower-level employees and these employees feel empowered to make decisions on their own, an organization has a "decentralized" structure. Decentralization becomes necessary as a company grows larger. Sooner or later, the top management of an organization will not be able to make every single decision within the company. Centralized organizational structures tend to concentrate power and authority within a relatively tight group of individuals in the firm, because they're the ones who have formal authority over important decisions.

Many organizations are moving toward a more decentralized structure. A manager can't have 20 employees reporting to him or her if those employees aren't allowed to make some decisions on their own. Airbus, the French manufacturer of airplanes, is doing its best to decentralize decision making within the company. CEO Fabrice Brégier believes it's taking the company way too long to make decisions. "We make some of the world's most complex products, but that doesn't mean we have to be overly complex about how we do things." His goal is to give Airbus's production managers more independence to set priorities and move more quickly. Brégier states, "We need to funnel this down to just the people required to make decisions."[13]

However, it's also important to realize that some organizations might choose to hold on to centralized control regardless of how big they get. Pennsylvania–headquartered Sheetz convenience stores are one of the fastest-growing store operators in the country, with 440 outlets and annual revenues of $7 billion. Still run as a family business, the Sheetz family likes to maintain a high degree of control over what happens. While most companies decentralize as they get bigger for the sake of sanity, the Sheetz family has not ceded much control to those outside the family. Soon-to-be-CEO Joe Sheetz believes having the family retain decision-making rights is a big part of the company's success, saying, "We don't play well with others."[14] Have the organizations where you've worked been largely centralized or decentralized? See our **OB Assessments** feature to find out.

FORMALIZATION A company is high in **formalization** when there are many specific rules and procedures used to standardize behaviors and decisions. Although not something you can necessarily see on an organizational chart, the impact of formalization is felt throughout the organization. Rules and procedures are a necessary mechanism for control in every organization. Although the word *formalization* has a somewhat negative connotation, think about the reactions if McDonald's made its most popular menu items in different ways at each location. Or think about this: Would it bother you if every time you called Dell for technical support, you got an operator who treated you differently and gave you conflicting answers? Formalization is a necessary coordination mechanism that organizations rely on to get a standardized product or deliver a standardized service.

Alcoa's Michigan Casting Center, a leading automotive part supplier, was plagued by the fact that it could have two machine operators running the same machine on two different shifts and get up to a 50 percent performance difference in output and quality between the workers. The company conducted a study to identify the best practices for each machine in its plant. These best practices became standard operating procedures for each worker, and that formalization allowed the company to get a more predictable level of output.[15] Companies such as W.L. Gore, the Newark, Delaware–based manufacturer of Gore-Tex, fall at the other extreme when it comes to formalization.[16] Whereas most companies have titles for their jobs and job descriptions that specify the tasks each job is responsible for, Bill Gore (company founder) felt that such formalization would stifle communication and creativity. After one of his employees mentioned that she needed to put some kind of job title on a business card to hand out at an outside conference, Gore replied that she could put "supreme commander" on the card for all he cared. She liked the title so much that she followed through on his suggestion, and it became a running joke throughout the company.[17] Recent research supports Gore's view. A manager might try to make employees feel more empowered by decentralizing decision making, but evidence suggests this effect is negated when the employees' job roles have a high level of formalization.[18]

ELEMENTS IN COMBINATION You might have noticed that some elements of an organization's structure seem to go hand-in-hand with other elements. For example, wide spans of control tend to be associated with decentralization in decision making. A high level of work specialization tends to bring about a high level of formalization. Moreover, if you take a closer look at the elements, you might notice that many of the elements capture the struggle between efficiency and flexibility. **Mechanistic organizations** are efficient, rigid, predictable, and standardized organizations that thrive in stable environments. Mechanistic organizations are typified by a structure that relies on high levels of formalization, a rigid and hierarchical chain of command, high degrees of work specialization, centralization of decision making, and narrow spans of control. In contrast, **organic organizations** are flexible, adaptive, outward-focused organizations that thrive in dynamic environments. Organic organizations are typified by a structure that relies on low levels of formalization, weak or multiple chains of command, low levels of work specialization, and wide spans of control. Table 15-2 sums up the differences between the two types of organizations.

If you think about the differences between the two types, it probably wouldn't be too difficult to come up with a few companies that fall more toward one end of the continuum or the other. Where would you place Zappos? Evidence indicates that a mechanistic or organic culture can have a significant effect on the types of employee practices a company adopts, such as selection, training, recruitment, compensation, and performance systems.[19] In addition, organic structures are more likely to allow for transformational leadership to have a positive effect on employees.[20] However, it's important to remember that few organizations are perfect examples of either extreme. Most fall somewhere near the middle, with certain areas within the organization having mechanistic qualities and others being more organic in nature. Microsoft is a good example as an organization that has many organic qualities, but even within its own walls it had teams that worked completely apart from each other while developing a major software platform and when they came together, what each group had done was incompatible with the other—a mistake they

OB ASSESSMENTS

CENTRALIZATION

Have you experienced life inside an organization with a highly centralized structure? This assessment is designed to measure two facets of what would be considered a centralized organizational structure. Those two facets are *hierarchy of authority,* which reflects the degree to which managers are needed to approve decisions, and *participation in decision making,* which reflects how involved rank-and-file employees are in day-to-day deliberations. Think about the last job you held (even if it was a part-time or summer job). Alternatively, think about a student group of yours that seems to have a definite "leader." Then answer each question using the response scale provided. (Instructors: Assessments on structure preferences and formalization can be found in the PowerPoints in the Connect Library's Instructor Resources and in the Connect assignments for this chapter).

1 STRONGLY DISAGREE	2 DISAGREE	3 UNCERTAIN	4 AGREE	5 STRONGLY AGREE

1. There can be little action here until a supervisor approves a decision. _____

2. A person who wants to make his or her own decisions would be quickly discouraged. _____

3. Even small matters have to be referred to someone higher up for a final answer. _____

4. I have to ask my boss before I do almost anything. _____

5. Any decision I make has to have my boss's approval. _____

6. I participate frequently in the decision to adopt new programs. _____

7. I participate frequently in the decision to adopt new policies and rules. _____

8. I usually participate in the decision to hire or adopt new group members. _____

9. I often participate in decisions that affect my working environment. _____

SCORING AND INTERPRETATION:

Hierarchy of Authority: Sum up items 1–5. _____
Participation in Decision Making: Sum up items 6–9. _____

A centralized structure would be one in which Hierarchy of Authority is high and Participation in Decision Making is low. If your score is above 20 for Hierarchy of Authority and below 8 for Participation in Decision Making, your organization (or student group) has a highly centralized structure.

Source: Adapted from M. Schminke, R. Cropanzano, and D.E. Rupp, "Organization Structure and Fairness Perceptions: The Moderating Effects of Organizational Level," *Organizational Behavior and Human Decision Processes* 89 (2002), pp. 881–905.

tried to rectify during the creation of later versions of Windows.[21] Although it's tempting to label mechanistic as "bad" and organic as "good," this perception is not necessarily true. Being mechanistic is the only way for many organizations to survive, and it can be a highly appropriate and fruitful way to structure work functions. To find out why that's the case, we need to explore why organizations develop the kinds of structures they do.

| **TABLE 15-2** | **Characteristics of Mechanistic vs. Organic Structures** |

MECHANISTIC ORGANIZATIONS	ORGANIC ORGANIZATIONS
High degree of work specialization; employees are given a very narrow view of the tasks they are to perform.	Low degree of work specialization; employees are encouraged to take a broad view of the tasks they are to perform.
Very clear lines of authority; employees know exactly whom they report to.	Although there might be a specified chain of command, employees think more broadly in terms of where their responsibilities lie.
High levels of hierarchical control; employees are not encouraged to make decisions without their manager's consent.	Knowledge and expertise are decentralized; employees are encouraged to make their own decisions when appropriate.
Information is passed through vertical communication between an employee and his or her supervisor.	Lateral communication is encouraged, focusing on information and advice as opposed to orders.
Employees are encouraged to develop firm-specific knowledge and expertise within their area of specialization.	Employees are encouraged to develop knowledge and expertise outside of their specialization.

Source: Adapted from T. Burns and G.M. Stalker, *The Management of Innovation* (London: Tavistock, 1961).

ORGANIZATIONAL DESIGN

15.3

What is organizational design, and what factors does the organizational design process depend on?

Organizational design is the process of creating, selecting, or changing the structure of an organization. Ideally, organizations don't just "let" a structure develop on its own; they proactively design it to match their specific circumstances and needs. Research indeed shows this is how it works in most cases.[22] See this chapter's **OB at the Bookstore** to read about a change in organizational design whose results affect you to this day. However, some organizations aren't that proactive and find themselves with a structure that has unintentionally developed on its own, without any careful planning. Those organizations may then be forced to change their structure to become more effective. A number of factors should influence the process of organizational design. Those factors include the environment in which the organization does business, its corporate strategy and technology, and the size of the firm. However, for some firms in dire straits, changing the structure becomes a strategy in and of itself, often leading to very poor results.[23]

BUSINESS ENVIRONMENT An organization's **business environment** consists of its customers, competitors, suppliers, distributors, and other factors external to the firm, all of which have

Partially due to its organizational structure, Sony was unable to adjust to its changing business environment, allowing Apple to dominate the portable music player market with its innovative line of iPods.

© Beck Diefenbach/Reuters/Corbis

an impact on organizational design. One of the biggest factors in an environment's effect on structure is whether the outside environment is stable or dynamic. Stable environments don't change frequently, and any changes that do occur happen very slowly. Stable environments allow organizations to focus on efficiency and require little change over time. In contrast, dynamic environments change on a frequent

OB AT THE BOOKSTORE

THE IDEA FACTORY
by Jon Gertner (New York: Penguin Group, 2012)

> *Bill Gates once said of the invention of the transistor, "My first stop on any time-travel expedition would be Bell Labs in December 1947."*

With those words, the author provides a quote that helps lay out the historical significance of AT&T's Bell Laboratories; significance that occurred largely as a result of one thing—its organizational structure. The next time you talk on your cell phone, turn on your computer, or search for "organizational behavior" on the Internet, you can be thankful for the ideas that originated in Bell Labs. Employees working there invented the transistor (the foundation for every computer on the planet), lasers, radar, solar cells, fiber optics, mobile phones, and satellite communications. At its peak in the 1960s Bell Labs employed 15,000 people and 1,200 PhDs. Fourteen Nobel Prize winners did their work there. The author states, "It was where the future, which is what we now happen to call the present, was conceived and designed. For a long stretch of the 20th century, Bell Labs was the most innovative scientific organization in the world."

Bell Labs was started shortly before World War I with the purpose of connecting New York and San Francisco by telephone. During World War II, AT&T was an extremely large, highly bureaucratic organization and the labs were organized similarly so that they could be a highly efficient provider for the military. However, in July 1945, one of the leaders of the labs reorganized its structure to create interdisciplinary teams "combining chemists, physicists, metallurgists, and engineers; combining theoreticians with experimentalists—to work on new electronic technologies." These individuals were put together not only in work groups, but also in physical work space. "By intention, everyone would be in one another's way." The interaction created by the type of flat, nonfunctional, and organic structure proved to be the core of many of the inventions that took place over the next 40 years. Google and many of the technology companies you know today take advantage of the lessons learned at Bell Labs and still use this same core organizational structure to push themselves toward innovation.

Photo of cover: © Roberts Publishing Services

basis and require organizations to have structures that are more adaptive.[24] In a classic example, Sony made a well-publicized corporate mistake when it failed to meet the needs of its changing business environment to match Apple's iPod.[25] Because it took it so long to recognize and adapt to this environmental shift, Sony struggled to be profitable for a long time. More recently, Sony has come under fire again for its organizational structure when it failed to learn from a major computer hacking scandal in 2011 and fell victim to a similar, but more serious attack in 2014 because its units didn't communicate with one another.[26] Some would argue that the world is changing so fast that the majority of companies can no longer keep up.

COMPANY STRATEGY A **company strategy** describes an organization's objectives and goals and how it tries to capitalize on its assets to make money. Although the myriad of organizational strategies is too involved to discuss here, two common strategies revolve around being either a low-cost producer or a differentiator.[27] Companies that focus on a low-cost producer strategy rely on selling products at the lowest possible cost. To do this well, they have to focus on being as efficient as they can be. Such companies are more likely to take a mechanistic approach to organizational design. Other companies might follow a differentiation strategy. Rather than focusing on supplying a product or service at the lowest cost, these companies believe that people will pay more for a product that's unique in some way. It could be that their product has a higher level of quality or offers features that a low-cost product doesn't. A differentiation strategy often hinges on adjusting to changing environments quickly, which often makes an organic structure more appropriate.

TECHNOLOGY An organization's **technology** is the method by which it transforms inputs into outputs. Very early on in the study of organizations, it was assumed that technology was the major determinant of an organization's structure.[28] Since then, the picture has become less clear regarding the appropriate relationship between technology and structure.[29] Although not completely conclusive, research suggests that the more routine a technology is, the more mechanistic a structure should be. In many ways, this suggestion makes perfect sense: If a company makes the exact same thing over and over, it should focus on creating that one thing as efficiently as possible by having high levels of specialization, formalization, and centralization. However, if technologies need to be changed or altered to suit the needs of various consumers, it follows that decisions would be more decentralized and the rules and procedures the organization relies on would need to be more flexible.

COMPANY SIZE There is no question that there is a significant relationship between **company size,** or the total number of employees, and structure.[30] As organizations become larger, they need to rely on some combination of specialization, formalization, and centralization to control their activities, thereby becoming more mechanistic in nature. When it comes to organizational performance, however, there is no definite answer as to when an organization's structure should be revised, or "how big is too big."[31] As many organizations get bigger, they attempt to create smaller units within the firm to create a "feeling of smallness." W.L. Gore did just that by attempting to prevent any one location in the company from having more than 150 employees. Top management was convinced that a size of 150 would still allow all the employees to talk to one another in the hallways. However, even Gore hasn't been able to maintain that goal; the company has grown to encompass 7,300 employees in 45 locations.[32] Even if they can't technically create smaller groups due to their overwhelming size, some companies such as PepsiCo and Mondelez International snack food company (110,000 employees) are going so far as to send their employees to spend time in some technology and media start-up firms so that they can come back with a sense of "smallness" that they hope will create an entrepreneurial spirit within their larger organizations.[33]

COMMON ORGANIZATIONAL FORMS

Our discussion of organizational design described how an organization's business environment, strategy, technology, and size conspire to make some organizational structures more effective than others. Now we turn our attention to a logical next question: What structures do most organizations utilize? The sections that follow describe some of the most common organizational forms. As you read their descriptions, think about whether these forms would fall on the mechanistic or organic side of the structure continuum. You might also consider what kinds of design factors would lead an organization to choose that particular form.

15.4

What are some of the more common organizational forms that an organization might adopt for its structure?

SIMPLE STRUCTURES **Simple structures** are perhaps the most common form of organizational design, primarily because there are more small organizations than large ones. In fact, more than 80 percent of employing organizations have fewer than 19 employees.[34] Small accounting and law firms, family-owned grocery stores, individual-owned retail outlets, independent churches, and landscaping services are all organizations that are likely to use a simple structure. Figure 15-3 shows a simple structure for a manager-owned restaurant. The figure reveals that simple structures are just that: simple. Simple structures are generally used by extremely small organizations in which the manager, president, and owner are all the same person. A simple

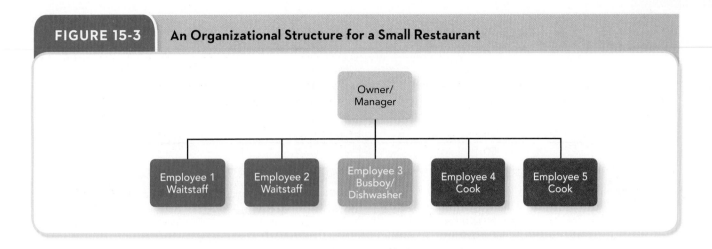

FIGURE 15-3   **An Organizational Structure for a Small Restaurant**

structure is a flat organization with one person as the central decision-making figure; it is not large enough to have a high degree of formalization and will have only very basic differences in work specialization.

A simple structure makes perfect sense for a small organization, because employees can come and go with no major ripple effects on the organization. However, as the business grows, the coordinating efforts on the part of the owner/manager become increasingly more complex. In the case of our restaurant, let's assume that the growth of the restaurant requires the owner to spend time doing lots of little things to manage the employees. Now the manager has lost the ability to spend time focusing on the actual business at hand. The manager then decides to add a supervisor to handle all of the day-to-day organizing of the restaurant. This arrangement works well until the owner decides to open a second restaurant that needs to have its own supervisor. Now let's assume that this second restaurant is much larger, leading the owner to decide to have separate supervisors directly in charge of the wait staff and the kitchen. All of a sudden, our little restaurant has three layers of management!

BUREAUCRATIC STRUCTURES When you think of the word "bureaucracy," what thoughts come to mind? Stuffy, boring, restrictive, formal, hard to change, and needlessly complex are some of the terms that have a tendency to be associated with bureaucracies. Those unflattering adjectives aside, chances are very good that you either currently work in a bureaucracy or will after you graduate. A **bureaucratic structure** is an organizational form that exhibits many of the facets of the mechanistic organization. Bureaucracies are designed for efficiency and rely on high levels of work specialization, formalization, centralization of authority, rigid and well-defined chains of command, and relatively narrow spans of control. As mentioned previously, as an organization's size increases, it's incredibly difficult not to develop some form of bureaucracy.

There are numerous types of bureaucratic structures on which we might focus. The most basic of these is the **functional structure.** As shown in Figure 15-4, a functional structure groups employees by the functions they perform for the organization. For example, employees with marketing expertise are grouped together, those with finance duties are grouped together, and so on. The success of the functional structure is based on the efficiency advantages that come with having a high degree of work specialization that's centrally coordinated.[35] Managers have expertise in an area and interact with others with the same type of expertise to create the most efficient solutions for the company. As illustrated in our previous example of the fast-growing restaurant, many small companies naturally evolve into functionally based structures as they grow larger.

However, small companies experiencing rapid growth are not the only organizations to benefit from a functional structure. Macy's, the New York–based clothes store, has a more traditional functional structure. The 150-year-old retailer used to be organized around geographic regions, but has restructured to be more functionally based with buying, planning, and marketing now all operating out of one location in New York. Macy's hopes that the efficiencies generated by the change in structure will afford it enough cost savings to get a jump on its competitors like JCPenney and Kohl's. Indeed, Macy's believes the changes have saved the company $500 million over two years.[36]

FIGURE 15-4   Functional and Multi-Divisional Structures

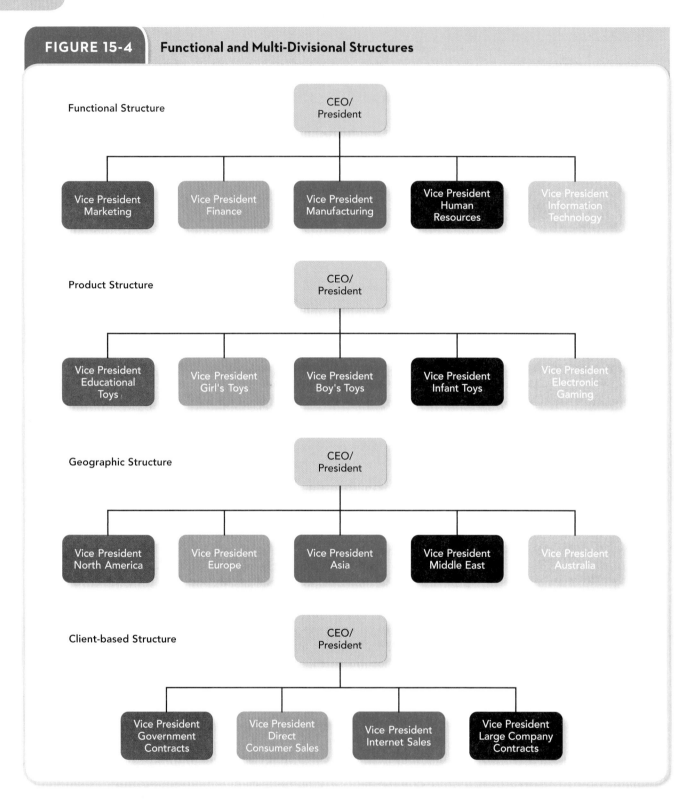

Functional structures are extremely efficient when the organization as a whole has a relatively narrow focus, fewer product lines or services, and a stable environment. The biggest weaknesses of a functional structure tend to revolve around the fact that individuals within each function get so wrapped up in their own goals and viewpoints that they lose sight of the bigger organizational picture. In other words, employees don't communicate as well across functions as they do within functions. The Sony example also highlights this danger, in that hardware engineers failed to communicate with software developers, which prevented the hardware and software people from seeing all the pieces of the puzzle.[37] Even in the example directly above, Macy's CEO Terry Lundgren worries about the company's ability to cater to local tastes with a functional structure. To deal with this, he has assigned specific managers in each region to be aware of and responsible for unique local needs.[38]

In contrast to functional structures, **multi-divisional structures** are bureaucratic organizational forms in which employees are grouped into divisions around products, geographic regions, or clients (see Figure 15-4). Each of these divisions operates relatively autonomously from the others and has its own functional groups. Multi-divisional structures generally develop from companies with functional structures whose interests and goals become too diverse for that structure to handle. For example, if a company with a functional structure begins to add customers that require localized versions of its product, the company might adopt a geographic structure to handle the product variations. Which form a company chooses will likely depend on where the diversity in its business lies.

Product structures group business units around different products that the company produces. Each of those divisions becomes responsible for manufacturing, marketing, and doing research and development for the products in its own division. Boeing, Procter & Gamble, Hewlett-Packard, and Sony are companies that have developed product structures. Product structures make sense when firms diversify to the point that the products they sell are so different that managing them becomes overwhelming. Campbell Soup Company recently organized into a product-based structure that it expects to allow it to expand into faster-growing spaces. Campbell will now be organized into "Americas Simple Meals and Beverages," "Global Biscuits and Snacks," and "Packaged Fresh" divisions. President and CEO Denise Morrison expects the new structure to generate an extra $200 million over the next three years through the efficiencies the company will gain.[39]

However, there are downsides to a product structure. One of those downsides arises when the divisions don't communicate and they don't have the ability to learn from one another. Darden restaurants brought the headquarters for all of its restaurants under one roof in Orlando. Their hope is that it will allow managers from Olive Garden, Longhorn Steakhouse, and others to learn from each other and focus on best practices.[40] Not all companies want their divisions to share though—they want them to compete. Fiat-Chrysler CEO Sergio Marchionne reorganized so that Dodge, Jeep, and Chrysler are essentially operating as separate companies, each with its own CEO. These companies are being forced to compete with each other for marketing and development resources. Marchionne is hoping that the competition will help to turn all three car brands around.[41]

Geographic structures are generally based around the different locations where the company does business. The functions required to serve a business are placed under a manager who is in charge of

Clarence Otis, former CEO of Darden restaurants, brought all of the company's restaurants together in order to have them share information with one another.

© Williams Perry/AP Images

OB INTERNATIONALLY

Traditionally, IBM has structured its 200,000-employee organization along geographic lines. Some might argue that IBM was the company that pioneered the first multinational geographic structure by setting up mini-IBMs in countries around the globe. Each country in which IBM operated had its own workforce and management team that reacted to the clients for whom it provided services in that country. The structure made perfect sense in a world in which consultants needed to be on location with their clients when those customers were having software or computer issues. However, IBM's environmental factors are changing rapidly. Competitors, especially those coming out of India, are providing many of the same services for significantly less money.

To change along with its competitors and respond to the "flattening world," IBM is reorganizing its workforce by creating and utilizing what it calls "competency centers." These centers will group employees from around the world on the basis of the specific skill sets that they have to offer clients. Some workers will be grouped into one location that can service clients all over the world through the use of technology. For instance, IBM recently announced that it will invest $300 million over 10 years in its new Costa Rica service center, which serves as the newest strategic services hub for the company and intends to employ up to 1,000 people. The facility will support clients mainly as a cloud computing center of competency. In Boulder, Colorado, IBM employs 6,200 professionals as part of a "call center" that monitors clients' computing functions worldwide. If something goes wrong in one of IBM's 426 data centers, employees in Boulder will more than likely be the ones to handle it or send it to someone who can. Other IBM workers will be grouped by broader geographic locations so that they can still be in relatively close proximity to their customers. When these employees are needed by a client, IBM has a computer database that allows it to put together teams of highly specialized consultants by examining the skill sets listed on 70,000 IBM résumés.

Does this change in structure sound familiar to you? It should—though IBM is maintaining some of its geographic structure, its organizational structure is becoming more functional. As the world becomes flatter through technology, clients expect the best talent from around the world, not just the best talent that happens to be sitting in their city. These structural changes will allow IBM to give clients just that. For IBM, these are the necessary changes that come with being a global company. In fact, IBM has recently been called "the world's most complex organization." It's not just about structure though, according to IBM Senior Vice President Robert W. Moffat Jr.: "Globalization is more than that. Our customers need us to put the right skills in the right place at the right time."

Sources: "IBM Drives Flash Technology Deeper into the Enterprise to Speed Big Data Analytics," *IBM press release,* April 11, 2013, http://www-03.ibm.com/press/us/en/pressrelease/40832.wss; "New IBM Delivery Center Opens in Costa Rica," *PR Newswire,* May 2012; J. Galbraith, "The Multi-Dimensional and Reconfigurable Organization," *Organizational Dynamics* 39 (2010), pp. 115–25; and S. Hamm, "Big Blue Shift," *BusinessWeek,* June 5, 2006, pp. 108–10.

---

a specific location. Reasons for developing a geographic structure revolve around the different tastes of customers in different regions, the size of the locations that need to be covered by different salespeople, or the fact that the manufacturing and distribution of a product are better served by a geographic breakdown. When the Regus Group (a UK company) and HQ Global Workplaces (a U.S. company) merged, they came together to form the world's largest supplier of meeting spaces and office suites. The new Regus Group now has more than 3,000 office suite facilities in 850 cities across 104 countries. When they merged, HQ and Regus had different structures. Considering the necessarily geographic-based business (i.e., the distances between facilities and the range of customers), the new Regus Group is structured by geographic region.[42] Many global companies are also organized by geographic location. IBM was one of the first, but that has changed for them, as described in our **OB Internationally** feature.

One last form of multi-divisional structure is the **client structure.** When organizations have a number of very large customers or groups of customers that all act in a similar way, they might organize their businesses around serving those customers. For example, small banks traditionally organize themselves into divisions such as personal banking, small business banking, personal lending, and commercial lending. Similarly, consulting firms often organize themselves into divisions that are responsible for small business clients, large business clients, and federal clients. After spending its entire existence organized around a product structure (as are most technology companies), Dell adopted a client structure in order to give its top managers more responsibility and flexibility. The company is now structured around four customer groupings: consumers, corporations, small and mid-sized businesses, and government and educational buyers.[43]

Matrix structures are more complex designs that try to take advantage of two types of structures at the same time. Companies such as Xerox, General Electric, and Dow Corning were among the first to adopt this type of structure.[44] Figure 15-5 provides an example of a matrix structure. In this example, employees are distributed into teams or projects within the organization on the basis of both their functional expertise and the product that they happen to be working on. Thus, the matrix represents a combination of a functional structure and a product structure. There are two important points to understand about the matrix structure. First, the matrix allows an organization to put together very flexible teams based on the experiences and skills of their employees.[45] This flexibility enables the organization to adjust much more quickly to the environment than a traditional bureaucratic structure would.

FIGURE 15-5 | **Matrix Structure**

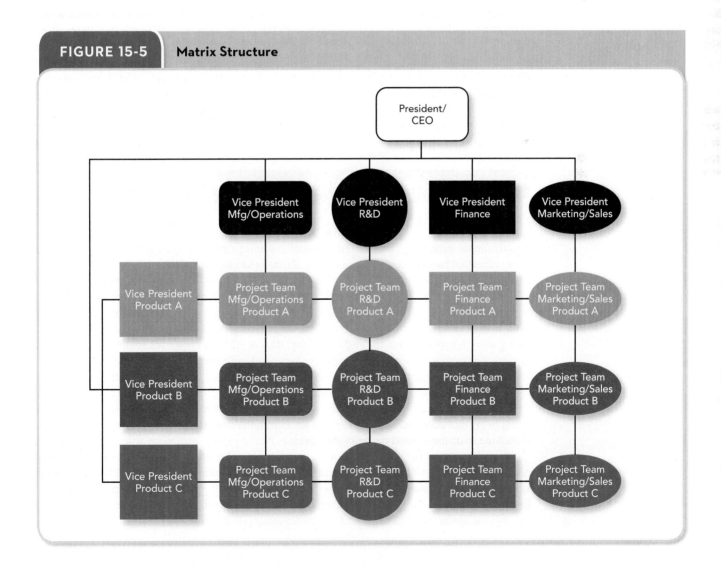

Second, the matrix gives each employee two chains of command, two groups with which to interact, and two sources of information to consider. This doubling of traditional structural elements can create high stress levels for employees if the demands of their functional grouping are at odds with the demands of their product- or client-based grouping.[46] The situation can become particularly stressful if one of the two groupings has more power than the other. For example, it may be that the functional manager assigns employees to teams, conducts performance evaluations, and decides raises—making that manager more powerful than the product- or client-based manager.[47] Although matrix structures have been around since the 1960s, the number of organizations using them is growing as teams become a more common form of organizing work. They have also become more common in global companies, with the functional grouping balanced by a geographic grouping. In fact, numerous companies now have matrix structures with enough layers to be considered four- or five-dimensional.[48] Bristol-Myers Squibb, the New York–based biopharmaceutical company, is heavily matrixed throughout the company. Jane Luciano, vice president of global learning and organizational development, explains, "We have the matrix every way it can be organized, including geographically, functionally, and on a product basis. Based on our size and in a highly regulated industry, the matrix helps us to gain control of issues as they travel around the globe and to leverage economies of scale."[49]

SUMMARY: WHY DO SOME ORGANIZATIONS HAVE DIFFERENT STRUCTURES THAN OTHERS?

So why do some organizations have different structures? As shown in Figure 15-6, differences in the business environment, company strategy, technology, and firm size cause some organizations to be designed differently than others. These differences create variations in the five elements of organizational structure: work specialization, chain of command, span of control, centralization, and formalization. These elements then combine to form one of a number of common organizational forms, including (1) a simple structure; (2) a bureaucratic structure, which may come in functional, product, geographic, or client forms; or (3) a matrix structure. Some of these forms are more mechanistic, whereas others are more organic. Taken together, these structures explain how work is organized within a given company.

HOW IMPORTANT IS STRUCTURE?

To some degree, an organization's structure provides the foundation for almost everything in organizational behavior. Think about some of the things that organizational structure affects: communication patterns between employees, the tasks an employee performs, the types of groups an organization uses, the freedom employees have to innovate and try new things, how power and influence are divided up in the company . . . we could go on and on. Picture the walls of a house. The occupants within those walls can decorate or personalize the structure as best they can. They can make it more attractive according to their individual preferences by adding and taking away furniture, but at the end of the day, they're still stuck with that structure. They have to work within the confines that the builder envisioned (unless they're willing to tear down walls or build new ones at considerable time, effort, and expense!). Organizational structures operate in much the same way for employees and their managers. A given manager can do many things to try to motivate, inspire, and set up an effective work environment so that employees have high levels of performance and commitment. At the end of the day, however, that manager must work within the structure created by the organization.

Given how many organizational forms there are, it's almost impossible to give an accurate representation of the impact of organizational structure on job performance. In fact, we might even say that an organization's structure determines what job performance is supposed to look like! In addition, the elements of structure are not necessarily good or bad for performance. For

15.5

When an organization makes changes to its structure, how does that restructuring affect job performance and organizational commitment?

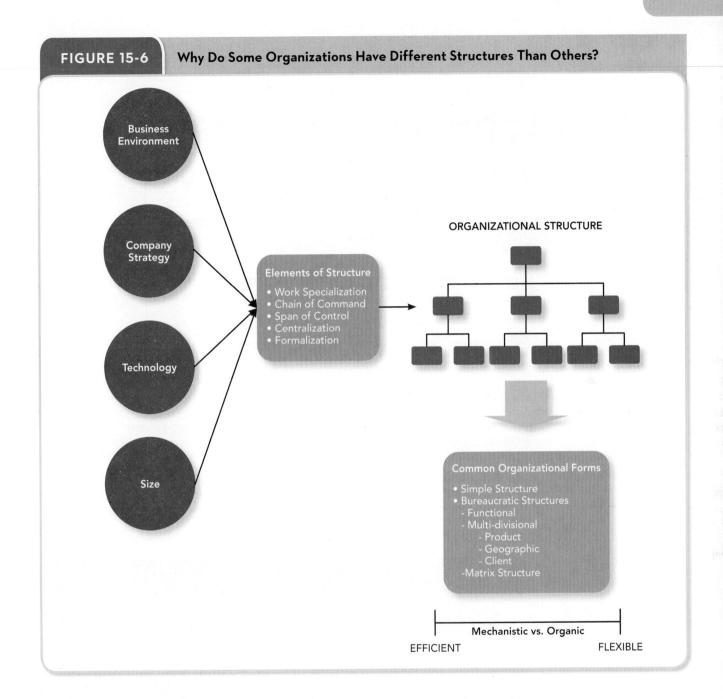

FIGURE 15-6   Why Do Some Organizations Have Different Structures Than Others?

example, a narrow span of control is not necessarily better than a broad one; rather, the organization must find the optimal solution based on its environment and culture. One thing we can say, as illustrated in Figure 15-7, is that changes to an organization's structure can have negative effects on the employees who work for the company, at least in the short term. The process of changing an organization's structure is called **restructuring.** Research suggests that restructuring has a small negative effect on task performance, likely because changes in specialization, centralization, or formalization may lead to confusion about how exactly employees are supposed to do their jobs, which hinders *learning* and *decision making*. Restructuring has a more significant negative effect on organizational commitment, however. Restructuring efforts can increase *stress* and jeopardize employees' *trust* in the organization.[50] There is some evidence that the end result is a lower level of affective commitment on the part of employees, because they feel less emotionally attached to the firm.

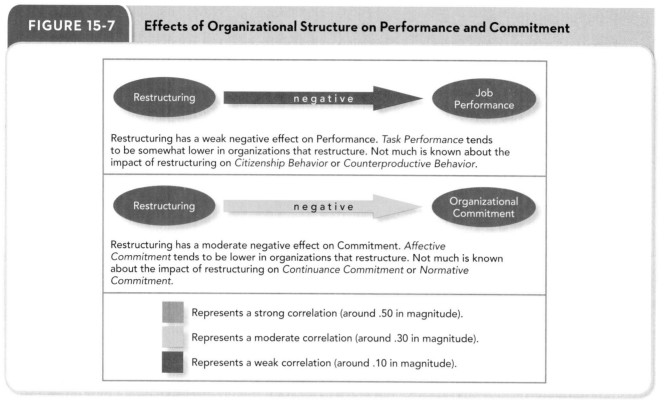

FIGURE 15-7   **Effects of Organizational Structure on Performance and Commitment**

Restructuring has a weak negative effect on Performance. *Task Performance* tends to be somewhat lower in organizations that restructure. Not much is known about the impact of restructuring on *Citizenship Behavior* or *Counterproductive Behavior*.

Restructuring has a moderate negative effect on Commitment. *Affective Commitment* tends to be lower in organizations that restructure. Not much is known about the impact of restructuring on *Continuance Commitment* or *Normative Commitment*.

Represents a strong correlation (around .50 in magnitude).

Represents a moderate correlation (around .30 in magnitude).

Represents a weak correlation (around .10 in magnitude).

Sources: K.P. DeMeuse, M.L. Marks, and G. Dai, "Organizational Downsizing, Mergers and Acquisitions, and Strategic Alliances: Using Theory and Research to Enhance Practice," in *APA Handbook of Industrial and Organizational Psychology,* Vol. 3, ed. S. Zedeck (Washington: APA, 2011), pp. 729–68; C. Gopinath and T.E. Becker, "Communication, Procedural Justice, and Employee Attitudes: Relationships under Conditions of Divestiture," *Journal of Management* 26 (2000), pp. 63–83; and J. Brockner, J. Spreitzer, A. Mishra, W. Hockwarter, L. Pepper, and J. Weinberg, "Perceived Control as an Antidote to the Negative Effects of Layoffs on Survivors' Organizational Commitment and Job Performance," *Administrative Science Quarterly* 49 (2004), pp. 76–100.

APPLICATION: RESTRUCTURING

As you've read through our discussion of organizational structure, you may have noticed how important it is for organizations to adapt to their environment. The first step in adapting is recognizing the need to change. The second (and sometimes much more problematic) step is actually adapting through restructuring. Organizations attempt to restructure all the time—in fact, it's difficult to pick up a copy of *Bloomberg Businessweek* or *Fortune* without reading about some organization's restructuring initiatives. General Motors has undertaken a massive restructuring effort no less than eight times over the past 25 years![51] (And look where that got them . . . !) Most of the examples we put into this chapter pertain to organizations that were restructuring.

Restructuring efforts come in a variety of shapes and sizes. Organizations may change from a product-based structure to a functional structure, from a functional structure to a geographic-based structure, and on and on. However, the most common kind of restructuring in recent years has been a "flattening" of the organization. Why do so many organizations do this? Primarily to show investors that they are reducing costs to become more profitable. Think back to our discussion of tall and flat organizational hierarchies, in which we noted that taller organizations have more layers of management. Many restructuring efforts are designed to remove one or more of those layers to reduce costs. Of course, removing such layers doesn't just mean deleting boxes on an organizational chart; there are actual people within those boxes! Thus, efforts to flatten require organizations to lay off several of the managers within the company.

When employees get a sense that their company might be getting ready to restructure, it causes a great deal of stress because they become worried that they will be one of those to lose their

15.6

What steps can organizations take to reduce the negative effects of restructuring efforts?

jobs. No company's employees have had to go through more over the last decade than those at Hewlett-Packard (HP). When, in the mid-2000's, ex-CEO Carly Fiorina decided to restructure Hewlett-Packard, it caused widespread fear and panic among employees. For the 60 days prior to the actual restructuring announcement, work came to a standstill at the company—tales of high stress, low motivation, political battles, and power struggles abounded.[52] It's estimated that Hewlett-Packard as a company lost an entire quarter's worth of productivity.[53] Since Fiorina's actions, two subsequent CEOs have restructured the company when they took over. Mark Hurd essentially undid everything Fiorina had done by unmerging units that Fiorina had merged. CEO Meg Whitman then came in to reorganize it all again by re-merging HP's PC and printer units (of course, accompanied by an announcement of further layoffs).[54] When that didn't solve the financial problems, HP announced that it was going to split the organization into two completely separate companies, both of which will be *Fortune* 50 companies when all is said and done.[55] Whitman stated, "Today I'm more convinced than ever that this is the right thing to do."[56]

One of the ways in which managers can do their best to help a restructuring effort succeed is to help manage the layoff survivors (i.e., employees who remain with the company following a layoff). Many layoff survivors are known to experience a great deal of guilt and remorse following an organization's decision to remove some employees from the company.[57] Researchers and practitioners recently have been trying to understand layoff survivors better, as well as how to help them adjust more quickly. One of the major problems for layoff survivors is the increased job demands placed on them. After all, that coworker or boss the employee had was doing *something*. Layoff survivors are generally burdened with having to pick up the leftover tasks that used to be done by somebody else.[58] This burden creates a sense of uncertainty and stress.[59] Research suggests that one of the best ways to help layoff survivors adjust is to do things that give them a stronger sense of control.[60] Allowing survivors to have a voice in how to move forward or help set the plans about how to accomplish future goals are two ways managers can help employees feel more in control. In addition, honest and frequent communication with layoff survivors greatly helps reduce their feelings of uncertainty and stress.[61] This communication is especially necessary when the organization is hiring at the same time it's firing. For instance, when Boeing announced a plan to cut 9,000 jobs, it had more than 1,500 current and anticipated job openings.[62] Many other employers, such as Microsoft, AT&T, and Time Warner, have experienced something similar.[63] This conflict sends mixed messages to those being laid off, as well as to the survivors. One sobering fact is that the survivors never know whether the restructuring will lead to success, or if it's simply a process of grasping at straws to avoid the ultimate demise of the company. For a restructuring to be truly successful, it requires more than simply changing lines on an organizational chart; it demands a different way of working for employees.[64]

TAKEAWAYS

15.1 An organization's structure formally dictates how jobs and tasks are divided and coordinated between individuals and groups within the organization. This structure, partially illustrated through the use of organizational charts, provides the foundation for organizing jobs, controlling employee behavior, shaping communication channels, and providing a lens through which employees view their work environment.

15.2 There are five major elements to an organization's structure: work specialization, chain of command, span of control, centralization of decision making, and formalization. These elements can be organized in such a way as to make an organization more mechanistic in nature, which allows it to be highly efficient in stable environments, or more organic in nature, which allows it to be flexible and adaptive in changing environments.

15.3 Organizational design is the process of creating, selecting, or changing the structure of an organization. Factors to be considered in organizational design include a company's business environment, its strategy, its technology, and its size.

15.4 There are literally thousands of organizational forms. The most common is the simple structure, which is used by most small companies. Larger companies adopt a more bureaucratic structure. This structure may be functional in nature, such that employees are grouped by job tasks, or multi-divisional, such that employees are grouped by product, geography, or client. Organizations may also adopt a matrix structure that combines functional and multi-divisional grouping.

15.5 Organizational restructuring efforts have a weak negative effect on job performance. They have a more significant negative effect on organizational commitment, because employees tend to feel less emotional attachment to organizations that are restructuring.

15.6 To reduce the negative effects of restructuring, organizations should focus on managing the stress levels of the employees who remain after the restructuring. Providing employees with a sense of control can help them learn to navigate their new work environment.

KEY TERMS

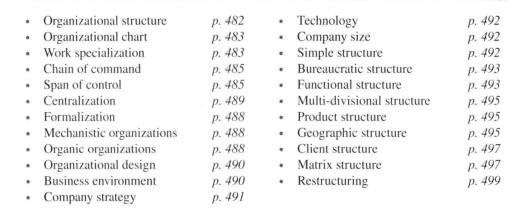

•	Organizational structure	*p. 482*	• Technology	*p. 492*
•	Organizational chart	*p. 483*	• Company size	*p. 492*
•	Work specialization	*p. 483*	• Simple structure	*p. 492*
•	Chain of command	*p. 485*	• Bureaucratic structure	*p. 493*
•	Span of control	*p. 485*	• Functional structure	*p. 493*
•	Centralization	*p. 489*	• Multi-divisional structure	*p. 495*
•	Formalization	*p. 488*	• Product structure	*p. 495*
•	Mechanistic organizations	*p. 488*	• Geographic structure	*p. 495*
•	Organic organizations	*p. 488*	• Client structure	*p. 497*
•	Organizational design	*p. 490*	• Matrix structure	*p. 497*
•	Business environment	*p. 490*	• Restructuring	*p. 499*
•	Company strategy	*p. 491*		

DISCUSSION QUESTIONS

15.1 Is it possible to be a great leader of employees in a highly mechanistic organization? What special talents or abilities might be required?

15.2 Why do the elements of structure, such as work specialization, formalization, span of control, chain of command, and centralization, have a tendency to change together? Which of the five do you feel is the most important?

15.3 Which is more important for an organization: the ability to be efficient or the ability to adapt to its environment? What does this say about how an organization's structure should be set up?

15.4 Which of the organizational forms described in this chapter do you think leads to the highest levels of motivation among workers? Why?

15.5 If you worked in a matrix organization, what would be some of the career development challenges that you might face? Does the idea of working in a matrix structure appeal to you? Why or why not?

CASE: ZAPPOS

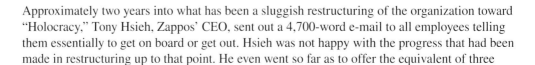

Approximately two years into what has been a sluggish restructuring of the organization toward "Holocracy," Tony Hsieh, Zappos' CEO, sent out a 4,700-word e-mail to all employees telling them essentially to get on board or get out. Hsieh was not happy with the progress that had been made in restructuring up to that point. He even went so far as to offer the equivalent of three months' worth of salary to employees who would quit the organization if they didn't feel they could fit in the new structure. More than 200 employees (14% of the organization) took him up on the offer—a massive number of people given Zappos' normal turnover rate of 1% annually. Clearly, not everyone felt comfortable in a company with very little structure or formality to jobs. Hsieh felt like the move was necessary though, saying, "A lot of people in the organization, including myself, felt like there were more and more layers of bureaucracy." Hsieh does note that the change to Holocracy "takes time and a lot of trial and error." Brian Robertson (the consultant who created Holocracy) says, "When you are adopting a huge painful change—and Holacracy is a huge, painful change—even if it's for all the right reasons, people experience the pain first." That change has required big adjustments for both current employees and new hires.

As a current employee, you might think that not having a lot of rules and formal roles would make life easier as an employee, but in fact, for many Zappos' employees, it created the opposite feeling. This isn't made easier by the 15,000-word "Holocracy constitution" that employees are supposed to use to operate in the new structure. Imagine the 269 Zappos managers who were no longer in a position of power or no longer responsible for managing anyone to do anything. All of sudden, the job they had worked for over the course of their career was gone. John Bunch, the employee leading the transition, says, "Most managers will be able to grow into new areas of technical work to replace the time they were doing people management. It's a gradual process, it's not a light switch."

For new employees, Holocracy training added three days to an already two-week-long, intense orientation process. (Any new hire who shows up late for any of the 7 a.m. start times is fired on the spot, and all have to pass a final exam after orientation with a 90 percent test score.) Like current employees, new hires learning how to operate within the new structure find it to be just as demanding and different. "Holacracy is like a sport or a new language. You can read about it, you can hear people tell you about it. You won't understand it until you start using it," says introductory class teacher Jake McCrea. New-hire trainer Megan Petrini says, "Some people are weirded out." Similar to the offer made to current employees, new hires are offered a one-month salary buyout one week into orientation. A number of them take it.

15.1 Do you think Hsieh's offering of three months' salary to employees who would quit was a good idea under the circumstances?

15.2 What are the positives about an organizational structure like Holocracy? The negatives?

15.3 What kind of people do you think Zappos' new structure will attract from a recruiting standpoint? Would you want to work there?

Sources: D. Gelles, "At Zappos, Pushing Shoes and a Vision," *The New York Times Online,* July 17, 2015; R. Greenfield, "How Zappos Converts New Hires to Its Bizarre Office Culture," *Bloomberg Online,* June 30, 2015; and R.E. Silverman, "At Zappos, Banishing the Bosses Brings Confusion," *The Wall Street Journal,* May 21, 2015, p. A1.

EXERCISE: CREATIVE CARDS, INC.

The purpose of this exercise is to demonstrate the effects of structure on organizational efficiency. This exercise uses groups, so your instructor will either assign you to a group or ask you to create your own group. The exercise has the following steps:

15.1 Creative Cards, Inc., is a small but growing company, started 10 years ago by Angela Naom, a graphic designer. The company has added many employees over the years but without a master plan. Now Angela wants to reorganize the company. The current structure of Creative Cards, Inc., is shown in the figure. Review the organizational chart, and identify at least 10 problems with the design of Creative Cards, Inc. Be sure to consider work specialization, chain of command, span of control, centralization, and formalization in developing your answer.

15.2 Create a new organizational design that you think would help the company operate more efficiently and effectively.

15.3 Class discussion, whether in groups or as a class, should center on how Creative Cards could best manage such a significant restructuring.

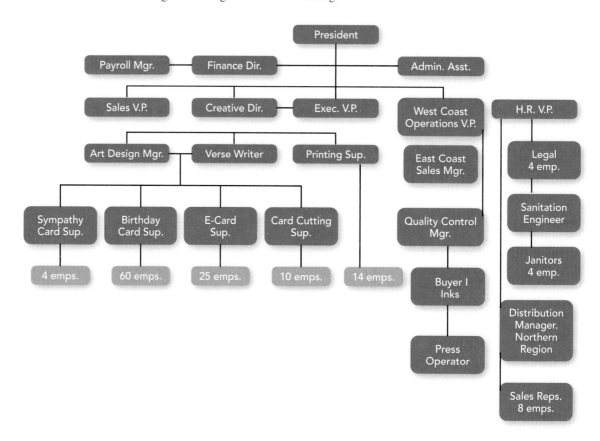

ENDNOTES

15.1 Slater, D. "Match Inc. CEO Sam Yagan on Even All Stars Needing Structure." *Fast Company,* November 26, 2012. http://www.fastcompany.com/3003165/match-inc-ceo-sam-yagan-even-all-stars-needing-structure.

15.2 Kranz, G. "Aetna's Odyssey Comes Full Circle." *Workforce Management Online,* March 2009, http://www.workforce.com/archive/feature/26/26/53/index.php?ht5.

15.3 Hackman, J.R., and G. R. Oldham. *Work Redesign.* Reading, MA: Addison-Wesley, 1980.

15.4 Silverman, R.E. "Who's the Boss? There Isn't One." *The Wall Street Journal,* June 20, 2012, p. B1.

15.5 Simon, H. *Administrative Behavior.* New York: Macmillan, 1947.

15.6 Edwards, C. "Shaking Up Intel's Insides." *BusinessWeek,* January 31, 2005, p. 35.

15.7 Meier, K.J., and J. Bohte. "Ode to Luther Gulick: Span of Control and Organizational Performance." *Administration and Society* 32 (2000), pp. 115–37.

15.8 Theobald, N.A., and S. Nicholson-Crotty. "The Many Faces of Span of Control: Organizational Structure across Multiple Goals." *Administration and Society* 36 (2005), pp. 648–60.

15.9 Child, J., and M. McGrath. "Organizations Unfettered: Organizational Forms in an Information-Intensive Economy." *Academy of Management Journal* 44 (2001), pp. 1135–48.

15.10 Hymowitz, C. "Today's Bosses Find

Mentoring Isn't Worth the Time and Risks." *The Wall Street Journal,* March 13, 2006, p. B1.

15.11 Nuttal, C. "Intel Cuts 1,000 Management Jobs." *Financial Times,* July 14, 2006, p. 23.

15.12 "McDonald's Announces Initial Steps in Turnaround Plan." *PRNewswire,* May 4, 2015. http:// news.mcdonalds. com/Corporate/Press-Releases/Financial-Release?xmlreleas eid=123065.

15.13 Michaels, D. "Airbus on Track to Double Profit Margin by 2015." *The Wall Street Journal,* June 17, 2013, p. B1.

15.14 Otterbourg, K. "Sheetz Puts the Gas in Gastronomy." *Fortune,* May 20, 2013, pp. 142–48.

15.15 Groszkiewicz, D., and B. Warren. "Alcoa's Michigan Casting Center Runs the Business from the Bottom Up." *Journal of Organizational Excellence,* Spring 2006, pp. 13–23.

15.16 Silverman, "Who's the Boss?"; Silverman, R.E. "At Zappos, Banishing the Bosses Brings Confusion." *The Wall Street Journal,* May 21, 2015, p. A1.

15.17 Kiger, P. "Power of the Individual." *Workforce Management,* February 27, 2006, pp. 1, 22–27.

15.18 Hempel, P.S.; Z. Zhang; and Y. Han. "Team Empowerment and the Organizational Context: Decentralization and Contrasting Effects of Formalization." *Journal of Management* 38 (2012), pp. 475–501.

15.19 Toh, S.M.; F.P. Morgeson; and M.A. Campion. "Human Resource Configurations: Investigating Fit within the Organizational Context." *Journal of Applied Psychology* 93 (2008), pp. 864–82.

15.20 Walter, F., and H. Bruch. "Structural Impacts on the Occurrence and Effectiveness of Transformational Leadership: An Empirical Study at the Organizational Level of Analysis." *The Leadership Quarterly* 21 (2010), pp. 765–82.

15.21 O'Brien, J. "Microsoft Reboots." *Fortune,* October 26, 2009, pp. 98–108.

15.22 Keats, B., and H. O'Neill. "Organizational Structure: Looking through a Strategy Lens." In *Handbook of Strategic Management,* ed. M.A. Hitt, R.E. Freeman, and J.S. Harrison. Oxford, UK: Blackwell, 2003, pp. 520–42.

15.23 Collins, J. *How the Mighty Fall.* New York: HarperCollins, 2009.

15.24 Scott, W.R., and G.F. Davis. *Organizations and Organizing:* *Rational, Natural, and Open System Perspectives.* Englewood Cliffs, NJ: Pearson Prentice Hall, 2007.

15.25 Kane, Y.I., and P. Dvorak. "Howard Stringer, Japanese CEO." *The Wall Street Journal,* March 3, 2007, pp. A1, A6; and Singer, M. "Stringer's Way." *The New Yorker,* June 5, 2006, pp. 46–57.

15.26 Gaudiosi, J. "Why Sony Didn't Learn from Its 2011 Hack." *Fortune,* December 24, 2014. http://fortune. com/2014/12/24/ why-sony-didnt-learn-from-its-2011-hack/.

15.27 Porter, M. *Competitive Strategy.* New York: The Free Press, 1980.

15.28 Woodward, J. *Industrial Organization: Theory and Practice.* London: Oxford University Press, 1965.

15.29 Miller, C.C.; W.H. Glick; Y. Wang; and G.P. Huber. "Understanding Technology–Structure Relationships: Theory Development and Meta-Analytic Theory Testing." *Academy of Management Journal* 34 (1991), pp. 370–99.

15.30 Gooding, J.Z., and J.A. Wagner III. "A Meta-Analytic Review of the Relationship between Size and Performance: The Productivity and Efficiency of Organizations and Their Subunits." *Administrative Science Quarterly* 30

(1985), pp. 462–81. See also Bluedorn, A.C. "Pilgrim's Progress: Trends and Convergence in Research on Organizational Size and Environments." *Journal of Management* 21 (1993), pp. 163–92.

15.31 Lawler, E.E., III. "Rethinking Organizational Size." *Organizational Dynamics* 26 (1997), pp. 24–35.

15.32 Kiger, "Power of the Individual."

15.33 Silverman, R.E. "Corporate Field Trip: Learning from Startups." *The Wall Street Journal,* March 27, 2013, p. B8.

15.34 Scott and Davis, *Organizations and Organizing.*

15.35 Miles, R.E., and C.C. Snow. *Organizational Strategy, Structure, and Process.* New York: McGraw-Hill, 1978.

15.36 Boyle, M. "Managing Forward." *BusinessWeek,* September 14, 2009, p. 13.

15.37 Singer, "Stringer's Way."

15.38 Boyle, M. "Managing Forward."

15.39 Fry. M. "Campbell Soup Shakes Up Its Structure, Leadership." *NJBIZ,* January 29, 2015. http://www.njbiz.com/article/20150129/NJBIZ01/150129706/campbell-soup-shakes-up-its-structure-leadership.

15.40 Salter, C. "Why America Is Addicted to Olive Garden." *Fast Company,* July/August 2009, pp. 102–8, 121.

15.41 Welch, D.; D. Kiley; and C. Matlack. "Tough Love at Chrysler." *BusinessWeek,* August 24 and 31, 2009, pp. 26–28.

15.42 "Changing the Way The World Works— Regus plc Annual Report and Accounts 2014." *Regus.com,* March 3, 2015, http://www.regus.com/images/Regus_plc_consolidated_report_and_accounts_2014_tcm304-57842.pdf; and Hosford, C. "Behind the Regus–HQ Merger: A Clash of Cultures That Wasn't." *Sales and Marketing Management,* March 2006, pp. 47–48.

15.43 Edwards, C. "Dell's Do-Over." *BusinessWeek,* October 26, 2009, pp. 37–40.

15.44 Burns, L.R., and D.R. Wholey. "Adoption and Abandonment of Matrix Management Programs: Effects of Organizational Characteristics and Interorganizational Programs." *Academy of Management Journal* 36 (1993), pp. 106–38.

15.45 Hackman, J.R. "The Design of Work Teams." In *Handbook of Organizational Behavior,* ed. J.W. Lorsch. Englewood Cliffs, NJ: Prentice Hall, 1987, pp. 315–42.

15.46 Larson, E.W., and D.H. Gobeli. "Matrix Management: Contradictions and Insight." *California Management Review* 29 (1987), pp. 126–38.

15.47 Rees, D.W., and C. Porter. "Matrix Structures and the Training Implications." *Industrial and Commercial Training* 36 (2004), pp. 189–93.

15.48 Greenwood, R.; T. Morris; S. Fairclough; and M. Boussebaa. "The Organizational Design of Transnational Professional Service Firms." *Organizational Dynamics* 39 (2010), pp. 173–83.

15.49 Derven, M. "Managing the Matrix in the New Normal." *T + D,* July 2010, pp. 42–47.

15.50 Gandolfi, F., and M. Hansson. "Causes and Consequences of Downsizing: Toward and Integrative Framework." *Journal of Management and Organization* 17 (2011), pp. 498–521.

15.51 Bigman, D. "How General Motors Was Really Saved." *Forbes,* November 18, 2013; Taylor, A., III. "GM and Me." *Fortune,* December 8, 2008, pp. 92–100; and Taylor, A., III. "GM Gets Its Act Together. Finally." *Fortune,* April 5, 2004, pp. 136–46.

15.52 Gopinath, C. "Businesses in a Merger Need to Make Sense Together."

Businessline, June 26, 2006, p. 1.

15.53 Hamm, J. "The Five Messages Leaders Must Manage." *Harvard Business Review,* May 2006, pp. 114–23.

15.54 Lashinsky, A. "The Hurd Way: How a Sales-Obsessed CEO Rebooted HP." *Fortune,* April 17, 2006, pp. 27-34.; Worthen, B. "H-P's Not-So-New Plan to Unite PC, Printer Units." *The Wall Street Journal,* March 20, 2012, p. B1.

15.55 McMillan, R. "As H-P Split Nears, Bosses Tick Off a Surgery Checklist." *The Wall Street Journal,* June 30, 2015. http://www.wsj.com/article_email/as-h-p-split-nears-bosses-tick-off-a-surgery-checklist-1435620372-lMyQjAxMTE1MD-M2MDQzMzA0Wj.

15.56 Vanian, J. "Hewlett-Packard Shares More Detail on Its Plans to Split the Company." *Fortune,* May 21, 2015. http://fortune.com/2015/05/21/hewlett-packard-separation-earnings/.

15.57 Noer, D.M. *Healing the Wounds.* San Francisco: Jossey-Bass, 1993; and Mishra, K.; G.M. Spreitzer; and A. Mishra. "Preserving Employee Morale During Downsizing." *Sloan Management Review* 39 (1998), pp. 83–95.

15.58 Conlin, M. "The Big Squeeze on Workers: Is There a Risk to Wringing More from a Smaller Staff?" *BusinessWeek,* May 13, 2002, p. 96.

15.59 Amabile, T.M., and R. Conti. "Changes in the Work Environment for Creativity during Downsizing." *Academy of Management Journal* 42 (1999), pp. 630–40; DeMeuse, K.P.; M.L. Marks; and G. Dai. "Organizational Downsizing, Mergers and Acquisitions, and Strategic Alliances: Using Theory and Research to Enhance Practice." In *APA Handbook of Industrial and Organizational Psychology,* Vol. 3, ed. S. Zedeck, 2011, Washington, DC: APA, pp. 729–68; and Probst, T.M. "Exploring Employee Outcomes of Organizational Restructuring– A Solomon Four-Group Study." *Group and Organization Management* 28 (2003), pp. 416–39.

15.60 Brockner, J.; G. Spreitzer; A. Mishra; W. Hockwarter; L. Pepper; and J. Weinberg. "Perceived Control as an Antidote to the Negative Effects of Layoffs on Survivors' Organizational Commitment and Job Performance." *Administrative Science Quarterly* 49 (2004), pp. 76–100; and Probst, T.M. "Countering the Negative Effects of Job Insecurity through Participative Decision Making." *Journal of Occupational Health Psychology* 10 (2005), pp. 320–29.

15.61 Brockner, J. "The Effects of Work Lay-offs on Survivors: Research, Theory and Practice." In *Research in Organizational Behavior,* Vol. 10, ed. B.M. Staw and L.L. Cummings. Berkeley: University of California Press, 1988, pp. 213–55; and Campion, M.A.; L. Guerrero; and R. Posthuma. "Reasonable Human Resource Practices for Making Employee Downsizing Decisions." *Organizational Dynamics* 40 (2011), pp. 174–80.

15.62 Tuna, C. "Many Companies Hire as They Fire." *The Wall Street Journal,* May 11, 2009, p. B6.

15.63 Ibid.

15.64 Porras, J.I., and P.J. Robertson. "Organizational Development: Theory, Practice, and Research." In *Handbook of Industrial and Organizational Psychology.* Vol. 3, 2nd ed., ed. M.D. Dunnette and L.M. Hough. Palo Alto, CA: Consulting Psychologists Press, 1992, pp. 710–822.

chapter 16

Organizational Culture

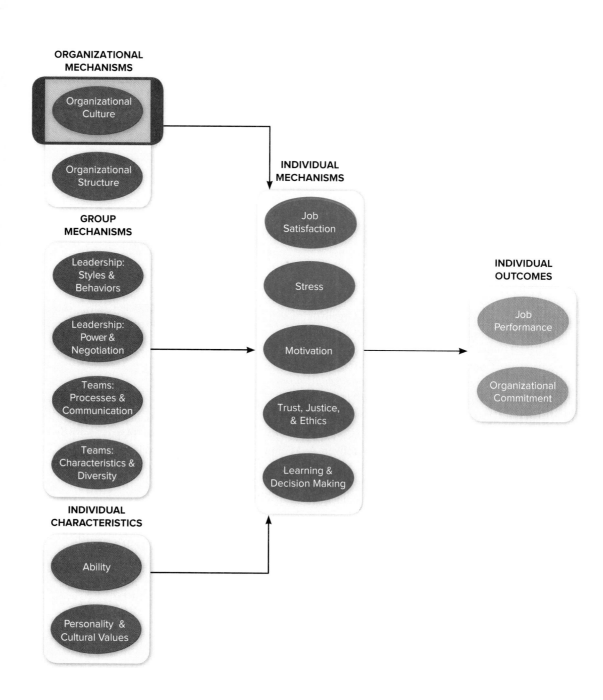

ORGANIZATIONAL
MECHANISMS

Organizational
Culture

Organizational
Structure

GROUP
MECHANISMS

Leadership:
Styles &
Behaviors

Leadership:
Power &
Negotiation

Teams:
Processes &
Communication

Teams:
Characteristics &
Diversity

INDIVIDUAL
CHARACTERISTICS

Ability

Personality &
Cultural Values

INDIVIDUAL
MECHANISMS

Job
Satisfaction

Stress

Motivation

Trust, Justice,
& Ethics

Learning &
Decision Making

INDIVIDUAL
OUTCOMES

Job
Performance

Organizational
Commitment

© Mark Wilson/Getty Images News/Getty Images

✔ LEARNING GOALS

After reading this chapter, you should be able to answer the following questions:

16.1 What is organizational culture, and what are its components?

16.2 What general and specific types can be used to describe an organization's culture?

16.3 What makes a culture strong, and is it always good for an organization to have a strong culture?

16.4 How do organizations maintain their culture and how do they change it?

16.5 What is person-organization fit, and how does it affect job performance and organizational commitment?

16.6 What steps can organizations take to make sure that newcomers will fit with their culture?

GENERAL MOTORS

General Motors. General Motors? Out of all the companies we could highlight in a chapter about organizational culture, we choose General Motors? Absolutely. (You were expecting Google or Apple or IDEO?) There is perhaps no other company whose culture has been put under the microscope more over the last few years than the 219,000-employee, $150 billion in revenues behemoth that is known to most as GM. GM is the epitome of what makes culture such a strong and influential force for organizations—both positively and, in GM's case, negatively. You might remember people talking about GM's culture throughout 2014 when it was announced that they were recalling 2.6 million cars due to a faulty ignition switch (a switch that has been responsible for 21 deaths and more than 500 injuries). GM went through a massive internal investigation and GM's (new) CEO Mary Barra went through four long and difficult congressional testimonies—much of which was focused on the internal culture of the organization. Why? The lack of a recall when it "should" have happened has largely been blamed on GM's culture.

When President Obama appointed financial manager Steve Rattner to organize bankruptcy and a government bailout for GM, Rattner stated, "GM had arguably the worst culture of any major company I've ever been around in 30 years. It was bureaucratic, it was slow-moving, it was a 'get along, go along' culture." GM's internal report on the recalls described how employees would regularly agree to a plan with no intention of following up—something called "the GM nod." The company would have meetings where alternatives were presented by various groups and then there would be no discussion of the alternatives because the decision had been made by those in power prior to the meeting ever taking place.

One of GM's culture problems has been a severe lack of accountability. Every decision in the organization is made by committee so no one can be held accountable. Everything goes through multiple rounds of committees, and no one seems to know who makes the final decisions. It is, in essence, an "organization of survivors." That being said, there are efforts being made to change the culture inside GM, but it is going to be a tall task. Employees seem to sense the need for change, but culture change in an organization like GM is hard—especially when the last six CEOs have attempted to do just that—and failed. As one outsider put it, "At GM, trying and failing to change the culture is part of the culture."

ORGANIZATIONAL CULTURE

In almost every chapter prior to this point, we have simply given you definitions of important topics. However, there are just about as many definitions of organizational culture as there are people who study it. In fact, research on organizational culture has produced well over 50 different definitions![1] It seems that the term "culture" means a great many things to a great many people. Definitions of culture have ranged from as broad as, "The way we do things around here"[2] to as specific as . . . well, let's just suffice it to say that they can get complicated. Not surprisingly, the various definitions of organizational culture stem from how people have studied it. Sociologists study culture using a broad lens and anthropological research methods, like those applied to study tribes and civilizations. Psychologists tend to study culture and its effects on people using survey methods. In fact, many psychologists actually prefer the term "climate," but for our purposes, we'll use the two terms interchangeably. In this chapter, we define **organizational culture** as the shared social knowledge within an organization regarding the rules, norms, and values that shape the attitudes and behaviors of its employees.[3]

This definition helps highlight a number of facets of organizational culture. First, culture is social knowledge among members of the organization. Employees learn about most important aspects of culture through other employees. This transfer of knowledge might be through explicit communication, simple observation, or other, less obvious methods. In addition, culture is shared knowledge, which means that members of the organization understand and have a degree of consensus regarding what the culture is. Second, culture tells employees what the rules, norms, and values are within the organization. What are the most important work outcomes to focus on? What behaviors are appropriate or inappropriate at work? How should a person act or dress while

16.1

What is organizational culture, and what are its components?

at work? Indeed, some cultures even go so far as to say how employees should act when they aren't at work. Third, organizational culture shapes and reinforces certain employee attitudes and behaviors by creating a system of control over employees.[4] There is evidence that your individual goals and values will grow over time to match those of the organization for which you work.[5] This development really isn't that hard to imagine, given how much time employees spend working inside an organization.

WHY DO SOME ORGANIZATIONS HAVE DIFFERENT CULTURES THAN OTHERS?

One of the most common questions people ask when you tell them where you are employed is, "So, tell me . . . what's it like there?" The description you use in your response is likely to have a lot to do with what the organization's culture is all about. In calculating your response to the question, you might consider describing the kinds of people who work at your company. More than likely, you'll do your best to describe the work atmosphere on a regular day. Perhaps you'll painstakingly describe the facilities you work in or how you feel the employees are treated. You might even go so far as to describe what it is that defines "success" at your company. All of those answers give clues that help organizational outsiders understand what a company is actually like. To give you a feel for the full range of potential answers to the "what's it like there?" question, it's necessary to review the facets of culture in more detail.

CULTURE COMPONENTS

There are three major components to any organization's culture: observable artifacts, espoused values, and basic underlying assumptions. You can understand the differences among these three components if you view culture like an onion, as in Figure 16-1. Some components of an organization's culture are readily apparent and observable, like the skin of an onion. However, other components are less observable to organizational outsiders or newcomers. Such outsiders can observe, interpret, and make conclusions based on what they see on the surface, but the inside

---

FIGURE 16-1   **The Three Components of Organizational Culture**

Espoused
Values

Basic
Underlying
Assumptions

Observable
Artifacts

remains a mystery until they can peel back the outside layers to gauge the values and assumptions that lie beneath. When asked about his company's success, Walter Robb, co-CEO of Whole Foods, said, "If I could draw back the curtain, what you would see is a very strong culture of empowerment, and that is the secret of Whole Foods."[6] The sections that follow review the culture components in more detail.

OBSERVABLE ARTIFACTS **Observable artifacts** are the manifestations of an organization's culture that employees can easily see or talk about. They supply the signals that employees interpret to gauge how they should act during the workday. Artifacts supply the primary means of transmitting an organization's culture to its workforce. It's difficult to overestimate the importance of artifacts, because they help show not only current employees but also potential employees, customers, shareholders, and investors what the organization is all about. There are six major types of artifacts: symbols, physical structures, language, stories, rituals, and ceremonies.[7]

Symbols can be found throughout an organization, from its corporate logo to the images it places on its website to the uniforms its employees wear. Think about what Nike's "swoosh" represents: speed, movement, velocity. What might that symbol convey about Nike's culture? Or consider Apple Computer's "apple" logo. That symbol brings to mind Newton's discovery of gravity under the apple tree, conveying the importance of innovation within Apple's culture. When you think of the words "dark suit, white shirt, tie," what company do you think of? For many, the symbol represents IBM because that summarizes the company's long-standing dress code. Even though that dress code hasn't been in place at IBM for more than 20 years, it still symbolizes a formal, bureaucratic, and professional culture.

Physical structures also say a lot about a culture. Is the workplace open? Does top management work in a separate section of the building? Is the setting devoid of anything unique, or can employees express their personalities? While Takanobu Ito was CEO of Honda Motor, he sent a message about the company's culture in his office. Ito worked at a plain wooden desk in a room with a dozen other executives.[8] John Childress, founding partner of The Principia Group, tells the story of a Ford executive he worked with whose entire office had burned down: "He'd been having terrible problems between departments. There were barriers that meant information wasn't flowing. He had to quickly rent new premises and all he could find was an open-plan building. The culture changed overnight because of the different ways of working."[9] IDEO, a creative design firm, also has an open-office environment, though IDEO lets employees set up their offices however they like. When you walk around their work areas, you'll be walking underneath bicycles hanging over your head and crazy objects and toys in every direction.[10] Reed Hastings, CEO of Netflix, doesn't even have an office! Hastings simply walks around meeting with people. When he needs a quiet space to think he heads to his "watchtower"—a room-sized glass square on the

The ability to set up your own work space, as at the design firm IDEO, is a hallmark of an open corporate culture. Would this environment suit your working style?

Image courtesy of IDEO

top of Netflix's main building.[11] That being said, most offices don't look like that. While admitting that spaces across the country are becoming more "open" on average, Jonathan Webb, head of sales at KI, a Wisconsin–based commercial furniture maker, says that "Not everyplace looks like Google, not everybody has a slide in the lobby."[12]

Language reflects the jargon, slang, and slogans used within the walls of an organization. Do you know what a CTR, CPC, or Crawler is? Chances are you don't. If you worked for Yahoo, however, those terms would be second nature to you: CTR stands for click-through rate, CPC stands for cost-per-click, and a Crawler is a computer program that gathers information from other websites. If you worked at Microsoft and got an e-mail from a software developer telling you that they were "licking the cookie," what would you think? For Microsoft employees, "licking the cookie" means that a person or group is announcing that they are working on a feature or product and it is now off-limits for others to work on.[13] Home Depot maintains a "stack it high and watch it fly" slogan, which reflects its approach to sales. Yum Brands Inc., which owns Pizza Hut, Taco Bell, KFC, and other fast-food restaurants, expects employees to be "customer maniacs"[14]—language that conveys its culture for customer interaction.

Stories consist of anecdotes, accounts, legends, and myths that are passed down from cohort to cohort within an organization. Telling stories can be a major mechanism through which leaders and employees describe what the company values or finds important. For example, Howard Schultz, CEO of Starbucks, tells the story of how (to improve quality) he forbade the common practice of resteaming milk. What this rule inadvertently created was the loss of millions of dollars of milk, as thousands of gallons of lukewarm liquid were poured down the drain. One of his store managers came up with a simple, brilliant suggestion: Put etched lines inside the steaming pitchers so baristas would know how much milk to pour for the drink size they were making, instead of just guessing.[15] Paul Wiles, president/CEO of Novant Health in Winston-Salem, North Carolina, believes strongly in the power of storytelling to foster culture; he claims, "Talk about numbers, and people's eyes glaze over; talk about one child who died unnecessarily, and no one can walk away from that."[16]

Rituals are the daily or weekly planned routines that occur in an organization. Employees at New Belgium Brewing in Colorado, home of Fat Tire Ale, can enjoy a beer in the tasting room after their shift as well as get one free twelve-pack a week, conveying the importance of both employees and the company's product.[17] At UPS, every driver and package handler attends a mandatory "three-minute meeting" with their managers to help with communication. The 180-second time limit helps enforce the importance of punctuality in the UPS culture. The Men's Wearhouse pays managers quarterly bonuses when theft (referred to as "shrink") is kept low. That ritual sends a message that "when workers steal from you, they are stealing from themselves and their colleagues."[18] At Davita, the Denver-based kidney dialysis company, CEO Kent Thiry says, "We do songs. We do chants. We do call and response. Many kinds of organizations in all cultures use these methods. Why? For positive energy. Some of our new executives say, 'That's really dumb' or 'That's really cheesy.' And two years later, they're leading it." At M5 networks, a New York–based seller of VoIP phone systems, over a third of the employees learn to play musical instruments in a rock band on company time. Dan Hoffman, CEO, says, "As adults, we tend to forget how to learn. The idea with the rock band program was to remind people how to learn."[19]

Ceremonies are formal events, generally performed in front of an audience of organizational members. At Care.com, all workers are forced to move desks every year at the same time. CEO Sheila Marcelo assigns the seats. She says, "People don't have a choice where they sit. Part of the reason was to embrace change, to remove turfiness so that you're not just chatting with your friends and sitting with your friends. You sit with somebody else from a different team so you get to know their job. What are they doing? What are they saying on the phone? How do they tick? And it's getting to know different people so that we build a really big team. And we do that every year. And it's now actually become an exciting thing that people embrace."[20] At San Francisco–based Twitter, CEO Dick Costolo assembles the entire company twice a month in an area near their cafeteria for "tea time," which is a meeting to update employees on what's going on and to answer questions.[21] Other types of ceremonies revolve around celebrations for meeting quality goals, reaching a certain level of profitability, or launching a new product.

TABLE 16-1	**The Espoused Values of Whole Foods**

Below is a list of the seven core values that Whole Foods believes lay the foundation for its organizational culture. The company believes that these values set it apart from competing organizations, show others why Whole Foods is a great place to work, and will always be the reasons for the company's existence regardless of how large it grows. More details about each value can be found on the company's website.

1. Selling the highest-quality natural and organic products available.

2. Satisfying and delighting our customers.

3. Supporting team member happiness and excellence.

4. Creating wealth through profits and growth.

5. Caring about our communities and our environment.

6. Creating ongoing win–win partnerships with our suppliers.

7. Promoting the health of our stakeholders through healthy-eating education.

Source: From Whole Foods Core Values, http://www.wholefoodsmarket.com/company/corevalues.php.

ESPOUSED VALUES **Espoused values** are the beliefs, philosophies, and norms that a company explicitly states. Espoused values can range from published documents, such as a company's vision or mission statement, to verbal statements made to employees by executives and managers. Examples of some of Whole Foods Market's outward representations of espoused values can be found in Table 16-1. What does each of these statements tell you about Whole Foods and what it cares about?

It's certainly important to draw a distinction between espoused values and enacted values. It's one thing for a company to outwardly say something is important; it's another thing for employees to consistently act in ways that support those espoused values. When a company holds to its espoused values over time and regardless of the situations it operates in, the values become more believable both to employees and outsiders. However, in times of economic downturns, staying true to espoused values isn't always easy. Marriott International struggles during economic downturns, like many of its competitors in the lodging/travel business. It has been very tempting for the company to do everything it can to slash expenses, but its espoused value of always treating its people right prevents cuts that would harm employee benefits. If you ask any Marriott employee what the guiding principle of the company is all will say some version of J.W. Marriott's founding philosophy, "Take care of the associates, the associates will take care of the guests, and the guests will come back again and again."[22] It is worth noting that not all companies are open in regards to their values. Trader Joe's, the Monrovia, California–based grocery chain, is known by its patrons as perhaps the coolest, local product-seeking, customer-oriented business in America. In opposition to Whole Foods, it is also perhaps one of the most secretive companies in the world when it comes to its business practices. In fact, suppliers have to sign agreements that they won't disclose anything having to do with their business relationship with the store before they are allowed to supply products.[23]

BASIC UNDERLYING ASSUMPTIONS **Basic underlying assumptions** are the taken-for-granted beliefs and philosophies that are so ingrained that employees simply act on them rather than questioning the validity of their behavior in a given situation.[24] These assumptions represent the deepest and least observable part of a culture and may not be consciously apparent, even to organizational veterans. Edgar Schein, one of the preeminent scholars on the topic of organizational culture, uses the example of safety in an engineering firm. He states, "In an occupation such as engineering, it would be inconceivable to deliberately design something that is unsafe; it is a taken-for-granted assumption that things should be safe."[25] Whatever a company's under-lying assumptions are, its hidden beliefs are those that are the most likely to dictate employee behavior and affect employee attitudes. They're also the aspects of an organizational culture that are the most long-lasting and difficult to change.[26]

GENERAL CULTURE TYPES

If we can consider the combination of an organization's observable artifacts, espoused values, and underlying assumptions, we can begin to classify its culture along various dimensions. Of course, there are many different types of organizational cultures, just like there are many different types of personalities. Many researchers have tried to create general typologies that can be used to describe the culture of any organization. For instance, one popular general typology divides organizational culture along two dimensions: solidarity and sociability. *Solidarity* is the degree to which group members think and act alike, and *sociability* represents how friendly employees are to one another.[27] Figure 16-2 shows how we might describe organizations that are either high or low on these dimensions. Organizations that are low on both dimensions have a **fragmented culture** in which employees are distant and disconnected from one another. Organizations that have cultures in which employees think alike but aren't friendly to one another can be considered **mercenary cultures.** These types of organizations are likely to be very political, "what's in it for me" environments. Cultures in which all employees are friendly to one another, but everyone thinks differently and does his or her own thing, are **networked cultures.** Many highly creative organizations have a networked culture. Organizations with friendly employees who all think alike are **communal cultures.** There is some evidence that organizations have a tendency to move through the cultures as they get larger. Small organizations generally start out as communal cultures oriented around the owner and founder. As companies grow, they tend to move toward a networked culture because solidarity is harder to foster when groups get really large.[28] Although we like to think of culture as being stable, it can change, as we discuss later in this chapter.

SPECIFIC CULTURE TYPES

The typology in Figure 16-2 is general enough to be applied to almost any organization. However, there are obviously other ways to classify an organization's culture. In fact, many organizations attempt to manipulate observable artifacts and espoused values to create

16.2

What general and specific types can be used to describe an organization's culture?

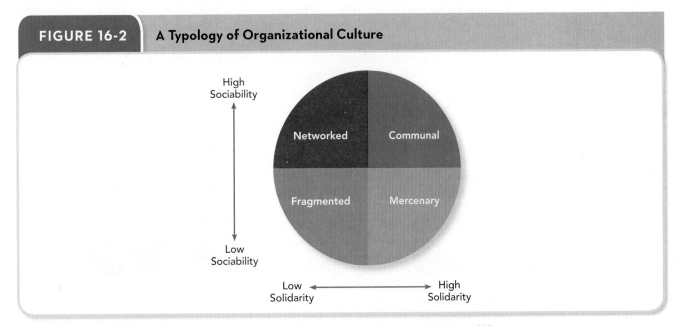

| FIGURE 16-2 | A Typology of Organizational Culture |

High Sociability

Networked | Communal

Fragmented | Mercenary

Low Sociability

Low Solidarity — High Solidarity

Source: Adapted from R. Goffee and G. Jones, *The Character of a Corporation* (New York: Harper Business, 1998).

specific cultures that help them achieve their organizational goals. Some of these specific cultures are more relevant in some industries than in others. Although the number of specific cultures an organization might strive for are virtually endless, we focus on five examples: customer service cultures, safety cultures, diversity cultures, sustainability cultures, and creativity cultures.

Many organizations try to create a **customer service culture** focused on service quality. After all, 80 percent of the gross domestic product in the United States is generated by service-based organizations.[29] Organizations that have successfully created a service culture have been shown to change employee attitudes and behaviors toward customers.[30] These changes in attitudes and behaviors then manifest themselves in higher levels of customer satisfaction and sales.[31] Figure 16-3 illustrates the process of creating a service culture and the effects it has on company results. Numerous companies claim that the sole reason for their continued existence is their ability to create a service culture in their organization when it wasn't originally present.[32] USAA, the Texas–based provider of financial services to military families, is perhaps the single best example of a customer service culture there is, having come in either first or second place for four years running in *Bloomberg Businessweek*'s Customer Service awards. As an example of the pains it goes to in order to create that culture, USAA call center reps are required to spend close to six months in training before actually answering the phones so that they can understand the lives of their military customers.[33] Companies might go out of their way to hire customer-oriented employees, but research also shows that a customer service culture can lead to even more customer-oriented behaviors on the part of their employees and a larger bottom-line profit as a result.[34]

In the United States, there were more than 3 million nonfatal workplace accidents and 5,000 fatal ones in 2011.[35] It's not uncommon for manufacturing or medical companies to go through a string of accidents or injuries that potentially harm their employees. For these organizations, creating a **safety culture** is of paramount importance. There is a clear difference between organizations in terms of the degree to which safe behaviors at work are viewed as expected and valued.[36] A positive safety culture has been shown to reduce accidents and increase safety-based citizenship behaviors.[37] A safety culture also reduces treatment errors in medical settings.[38] If you live in an area of the United States where oil drilling is going on, you should be happy when you see the names of big oil companies like Shell, ExxonMobil, Chevron, and BP. Residents in those areas will notice a major improvement in safety as these companies, which tend to have stronger safety cultures, buy up the small ones. When Shell bought out a small operator, the first thing it did was shut down for two weeks and retrain the workers. A worker said, "I don't think there's any question that the culture around safety has changed considerably since Shell came here." Since XTO Energy became a unit of ExxonMobil, its accident rate fell by half, even though drilling takes place in the same locations with the same employees. Other companies such as Chevron are having similar experiences.[39] As with many changes, it's very important that management's actions match its words. One study found that employees were highly cynical of a safety program when they perceived a mismatch between espoused and enacted safety values by management.[40] Two recent meta-analyses provide clear evidence though that having a safety-oriented culture means

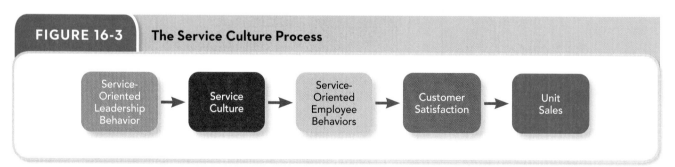

FIGURE 16-3   **The Service Culture Process**

Service-Oriented Leadership Behavior → Service Culture → Service-Oriented Employee Behaviors → Customer Satisfaction → Unit Sales

Source: Adapted from B. Schneider, M.G. Ehrhart, D.M. Mayer, J.L. Saltz, and K. Niles-Jolly, "Understanding Organization–Customer Links in Service Settings," *Academy of Management Journal* 48 (2005), pp. 1017–32.

higher levels of safety performance and fewer injuries and accidents for an organization.[41]

There are a number of reasons an organization might want to foster a **diversity culture.** For the 36,463-employee Cisco Systems, having a culture of diversity might be the key to their survival—or, at a minimum, a core advantage

This ad attempts to convey to customers and employees the ongoing sustainability culture of Patagonia.

over their competitors. The company is addressing what is a typical problem for many companies in the tech industry: a lack of women (only 23 percent of Cisco employees are women). Those women they do hire don't stick around due to the issues they face. Cisco is starting from the top by ensuring that a good portion of their leadership team is female. CEO Tom Chambers admits, "We're not anywhere near where I want to be." That being said, Cisco has hired a vice president of inclusion and collaboration, and a several-month-long program called JUMP is available for higher-level female employees. A lower-level employee program is in the works.[42] Many of the techniques used by Denny's are now recognized as key elements in successful corporate diversity initiatives. The Interpublic Group, a New York–based advertising giant (40,000 employees), has also been recognized for its diversity culture. Heide Gardner, chief diversity and inclusion officer, says, "What I am learning is: Inclusion is pretty much the same everywhere. It's not just about making diversity counts but about making diversity count. And that holds true wherever you are."[43] Diversity isn't just for big companies though; Teshmont Engineering Consultants, a small (fewer than 100 employees) Canadian-based company, has a culture centered around diversity as well, with 31 different mother tongues spoken at the firm.[44]

One of the newer specific cultures many firms are trying to create is a **sustainability culture.** Sustainability cultures are fostered by the mission and values of many organizations. In addition to helping the greater social good, a sustainability culture can be incredibly valuable in recruiting top talent as the culture resonates well with many of today's job applicants. One of the firms known most for their sustainability culture is the California–based clothing manufacturer Patagonia, which has become famous for its "Black Friday" ads telling people not to buy their clothes. CEO Rose Marcario says, "A lot of people talk about the 'Don't buy this jacket' ad, but what it really was saying was, 'Don't buy more than you need.' " Focused on making its products as durable as possible, the company wants its gear handed down from generation to generation— if you bring it back to the store, the company will repair it. As a private company, Patagonia has the ability to play an activist type of role that many other firms can't.[45] Clif Bar & Company, the organic food and drink company, puts its money where its values are. Through its "Cool Car and Cool Home" program, the company reimburses employees up to $6,500 for a company-approved hybrid or electric vehicle; $1,500 each year if workers bike, walk, or take public transit to work; and $1,000 if they put solar panels on their house. Through this type of culture, Clif Bar's turnover sits at 3 percent, and over the last year it received more than 7,000 applications for just 114 open positions.[46]

Given the importance of new ideas and innovation in many industries, it's understandable that some organizations focus on fostering a **creativity culture.** Creativity cultures affect both the quantity and quality of creative ideas within an organization.[47] 3M believes that creativity comes from freedom and not control; workers in R&D are allowed to spend 15 percent of their time researching whatever they want.[48] At Dyson, the extremely innovative UK–based appliances manufacturing company, CEO and founder James Dyson forbids the wearing of suits or ties as well as the writing of memos. He feels that workers will be more creative if they talk to each other about their ideas. New engineers are required to disassemble and reassemble a Dyson vacuum cleaner on their first day on the job.[49] SAS, the business analytics software firm based in North Carolina (a fixture on *Fortune*'s 100 best companies to work for list), has a full-blown infant day care center, a Montessori school, and an after-school program to allow employees to spend

In order to foster a creativity culture, James Dyson (pictured) has engineers assemble and disassemble a Dyson vacuum cleaner their first day on the job.

16.3

What makes a culture strong, and is it always good for an organization to have a strong culture?

© *Bruno Vincent/Getty Images*

more time thinking about creative solutions to problems and less time worrying about their kids. SAS also surveys its employees annually about the culture to see how the employees stand.[50] To see whether you've spent time working in a creativity culture, see our **OB Assessments** feature.

CULTURE STRENGTH

Although most organizations seem to strive for one, not all companies have a culture that creates a sense of definite norms and appropriate behaviors for their employees. If you've worked for a company and can't identify whether it has a strong culture or not, it probably doesn't. A high level of **culture strength** exists when employees definitively agree about the way things are supposed to happen within the organization (high consensus) and when their subsequent behaviors are consistent with those expectations (high intensity).[51] As shown in Figure 16-4, a strong culture serves to unite and direct employees. Weak cultures exist when employees disagree about the way things are supposed to be or what's expected of them, meaning that there is nothing to unite or direct their attitudes and actions.

Strong cultures take a long time to develop and are very difficult to change. Individuals working within strong cultures are typically very aware of it. However, this discussion brings us to an important point: "Strong" cultures are not always "good" cultures (as evidenced by our opening chapter example of GM). Strong cultures guide employee attitudes and behaviors, but that doesn't always mean that they guide them toward the most successful organizational outcomes. Toyota ran into major problems when its notoriously secretive culture clashed with U.S. regulators who demanded that the company disclose safety threats.[52] As such, it's useful to recognize some of the positive and negative aspects of having a strong organizational culture. Table 16-2 lists some of the advantages and disadvantages.[53] You might have noticed that all of the advantages in the left-hand column of Table 16-2 allow the organization to become more efficient at whatever aspect of culture is strong within the organization. The right-hand column's disadvantages all lead toward an organization's inability to adapt.

In some cases, the culture of an organization is not really strong or weak. Instead, there might be **subcultures** that unite a smaller subset of the organization's employees. These subgroups may be created because there is a strong leader in one area of the company that engenders different norms and values or because different divisions in a company act independently and create their own cultures. As shown in Figure 16-4, subcultures exist when the overall

OB ASSESSMENTS

CREATIVITY CULTURE

Have you experienced a creativity culture? This assessment is designed to measure two facets of that type of culture. Think of your current job, or the last job that you held (even if it was a part-time or summer job). If you haven't worked, think of a current or former student group that developed strong norms for how tasks should be done. Answer each question using the response scale provided. Then subtract your answers to the boldfaced questions from 6, with the difference being your new answer for that question. For example, if your original answer for question 7 was "4," your new answer is "2" (6 − 4). Then sum up your scores for the two facets. (Instructors: Assessments on culture preferences, culture strength, person-organization fit, and change cynicism can be found in the PowerPoints in the Connect Library's Instructor Resources and in the Connect assignments for this chapter).

1	2	3	4	5
STRONGLY DISAGREE	DISAGREE	UNCERTAIN	AGREE	STRONGLY AGREE

1. New ideas are readily accepted here. _____

2. This company is quick to respond when changes need to be made. _____

3. Management here is quick to spot the need to do things differently. _____

4. This organization is very flexible; it can quickly change procedures to meet new conditions and solve problems as they arise. _____

5. People in this organization are always searching for new ways of looking at problems. _____

6. It is considered extremely important here to follow the rules. _____

7. **People can ignore formal procedures and rules if it helps to get the job done.** _____

8. Everything has to be done by the book. _____

9. **It is not necessary to follow procedures to the letter around here.** _____

10. **Nobody gets too upset if people break the rules around here.** _____

SCORING AND INTERPRETATION:

Innovation: Sum up items 1–5. _____

Formalization: Sum up items 6–10. _____

If your score is 22 or above for either facet, your organization or work group is high on that particular dimension. Creative cultures tend to be high on innovation and low on formalization. So if your score was 22 or above for innovation and 21 or below for formalization, then chances are you've experienced a strong creativity culture.

Source: From Malcolm G. Patterson, Michael A. West, Viv J. Shackleton, Jeremy F. Dawson, Rebecca Lawthom, Sally Maitlis, David L. Robinson, and Alison M. Wallace, "Validating the Organizational Climate Measure: Links to Managerial Practices, Productivity and Innovation," *Journal of Organizational Behavior* 26 (2005), pp. 379–408. Reprinted with permission of John Wiley & Sons, Inc.

FIGURE 16-4   Culture Strength and Subcultures

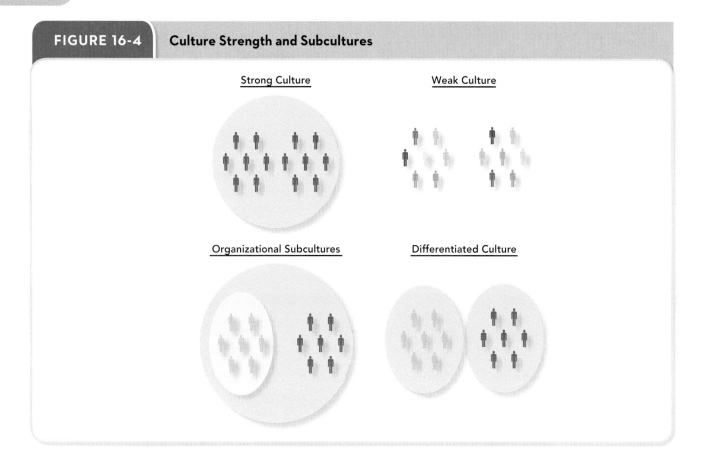

Strong Culture

Weak Culture

Organizational Subcultures

Differentiated Culture

organizational culture is supplemented by another culture governing a more specific set of employees. Subcultures are more likely to exist in large organizations than they are in small companies.[54] Most organizations don't mind having subcultures, as long as they don't interfere with the values of the overall culture. In fact, subcultures can be very useful for organizations if there are certain areas of the organization that have different demands and needs for their employees.[55] However, when their values don't match those of the larger organization, we call subcultures **countercultures**. Countercultures can sometimes serve a useful purpose by challenging the values of the overall organization or signifying the need for change.[56] In extreme cases however, countercultures can split the organization's culture right down the middle, resulting in the differentiated culture in Figure 16-4.

TABLE 16-2   Pros and Cons of a Strong Culture

ADVANTAGES OF A STRONG CULTURE	DISADVANTAGES OF A STRONG CULTURE
Differentiates the organization from others	Makes merging with another organization more difficult
Allows employees to identify themselves with the organization	Attracts and retains similar kinds of employees, thereby limiting diversity of thought
Facilitates desired behaviors among employees	Can be "too much of a good thing" if it creates extreme behaviors among employees
Creates stability within the organization	Makes adapting to the environment more difficult

MAINTAINING AN ORGANIZATIONAL CULTURE

Clearly an organization's culture can be described in many ways, from espoused values and underlying assumptions, to general dimensions such as solidarity or sociability, to more specific types such as service cultures or safety cultures. No matter how we describe an organization's culture, however, that culture will be put to the test when an organization's founders and original employees begin to recruit and hire new members. If those new members don't fit the culture, then the culture may become weakened or differentiated. However, two processes can conspire to help keep cultures strong: attraction–selection–attrition and socialization.

16.4

How do organizations maintain their culture, and how do they change it?

ATTRACTION–SELECTION–ATTRITION (ASA)   The **ASA framework** holds that potential employees will be attracted to organizations whose cultures match their own personality, meaning that some potential job applicants won't apply due to a perceived lack of fit.[57] In addition, organizations will select candidates based on whether their personalities fit the culture, further weeding out potential "misfits." Finally, those people who still don't fit will either be unhappy or ineffective when working in the organization, which leads to attrition (i.e., voluntary or involuntary turnover).

Several companies can provide an example of ASA in action. FedEx has worked hard to create a culture of ethics. The executives at FedEx believe that a strong ethical culture will attract ethical employees who will then strengthen moral behavior at FedEx.[58] Headhunters and corporate recruiters are well aware of the fact that employees who have lots of experience in certain types of cultures (i.e., places they "fit") will have a hard time adapting to other types of cultures. One type of culture they look out for specifically is high levels of bureaucracy—recruiters point to British Airways, General Mills, and Occidental Petroleum as prime examples of non-risk-taking, bureaucratic cultures whose employees are rarely successful when they leave to go somewhere else.[59] Of course, attraction and selection processes don't always align employees' personalities with organizational culture—one reason voluntary and involuntary turnover occurs in every organization. See this chapter's **OB at the Bookstore** for an example of one company's take on how the ASA framework works for it.

SOCIALIZATION   In addition to taking advantage of attraction–selection–attrition, organizations also maintain an organizational culture by shaping and molding new employees. Starting a new job with a company is a stressful, complex, and challenging undertaking for both employees and organizations.[60] In reality, no outsider can fully grasp or understand the culture of an organization simply by looking at artifacts visible from outside the company. A complete understanding of organizational culture is a process that happens over time. **Socialization** is the primary process by which employees learn the social knowledge that enables them to understand and adapt to the organization's culture. It's a process that begins before an employee starts work and doesn't end until an employee leaves the organization.[61] What is it that an employee needs to learn and adapt to in order to be socialized into his or her new role within an organization? Most of the important information can be grouped into six dimensions, highlighted in Figure 16-5.[62] Research shows that each of these six dimensions is an important area in the process of socialization. Each has unique contributions to job performance, organizational commitment, and person–organization fit.[63]

Socialization happens in three relatively distinct stages. The **anticipatory stage** happens prior to an employee spending even one second on the job. It starts the moment a potential employee hears the name of the organization. When you see the company name Microsoft, what does it make you think about? What are the images that come to your mind? Anticipatory socialization begins as soon as a potential employee develops an image of what it must be like to work for a given company. The bulk of the information acquired during this stage occurs during the recruitment and selection processes that employees go through prior to joining an organization. Relevant information includes the way employees are treated during the recruitment process, the things that organizational insiders tell them about the organization, and any other information employees acquire about what the organization is like and what working there entails.

The **encounter stage** begins the day an employee starts work. There are some things about an organization and its culture that can only be learned once a person becomes an organizational insider. During this stage, new employees compare the information they acquired as outsiders during the anticipatory stage with what the organization is really like now that they're insiders.

WORK RULES!
by Laszlo Bock (New York: Twelve Books, 2015)

This is a great candidate—strong technical interview scores, clearly very smart and well qualified—but sufficiently arrogant that none of the interviewers want him on their team. This is a great candidate, but not for Google.

Photo of cover: © Roberts Publishing Services

With those words, author Laszlo Bock relays the words of a Google employee after an interview with an applicant in *Work Rules!: Insights from Inside Google That Will Transform How You Live and Lead.* Bock is the head of People Operations at Google and has written this book so that we will understand what he believes are the core rules that companies should follow to be more like Google—consistently named one of the best companies to work for in the world. Bock's list of rules revolve mainly around how Google creates and maintains its organizational culture and what sets it apart from other companies. The two major rules he has for building a great culture are these: "Think of your work as a calling, with a mission that matters" and "Give people slightly more trust, freedom, and authority than you are comfortable giving them. If you're not nervous, you haven't given them enough."

Much of what Bock believes leads to success revolves around the ASA framework (although he doesn't call it that). He believes that by cultivating a culture that gives maximum freedom and meaning to workers, a company will attract the best and brightest candidates that fit the culture. He is quick to point out that Google is 25 times more exclusive than Harvard in terms of who it hires in that it receives more than 2 million job applicants for what amounts to a few thousand jobs every year. The real catch for Google is to hire only those individuals who fit Google's culture, which is why Bock believes that HR should spend far and away most of its resources on recruitment and selection (and far less on training). The book does an excellent job detailing out how Google approaches this process—including the fact that the company hunts for candidates much more often than it relies on the candidates who come to the company.

To the degree that the information in the two stages is similar, employees will have a smoother time adjusting to the organization. Problems occur when the two sets of information don't quite match. This mismatch of information is called **reality shock.** Reality shock is best exemplified by the employee who says something to the effect of, "Working at this company is not nearly what I expected it to be." Surveys suggest that as many as one-third of new employees leave an organization within the first 90 days as a result of unmet expectations.[64] The goal of the organization's socialization efforts should be to minimize reality shock as much as possible. We'll describe some ways that organizations can do this effectively in our Application section that concludes this chapter.

The final stage of socialization is one of **understanding and adaptation.** During this stage, newcomers come to learn the content areas of socialization and internalize the norms and expected behaviors of the organization. The important part of this stage is change on the part of the employee. By looking back at the content areas of socialization in Figure 16-5, you can begin to picture what a perfectly socialized employee looks like. The employee has adopted the goals and values of the organization, understands what the organization has been through, and can

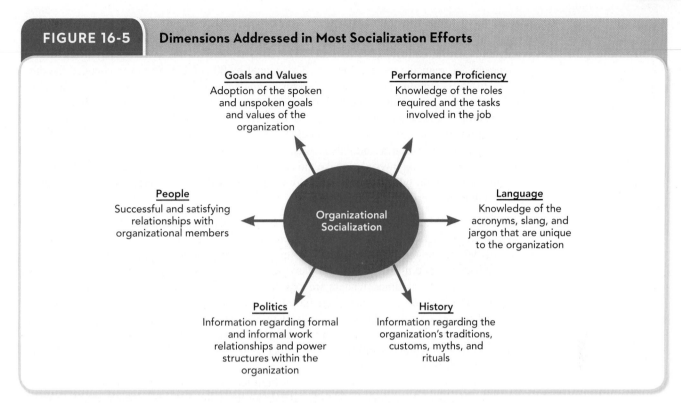

FIGURE 16-5   Dimensions Addressed in Most Socialization Efforts

Source: G.T. Chao, A.M. O'Leary-Kelly, S. Wolf, H.J. Klein, and P.D. Gardner, "Organizational Socialization: Its Content and Consequences," *Journal of Applied Psychology,* Vol. 79, 1994, pp. 730–43. Copyright © 1994 by the American Psychological Association. Adapted with permission. No further reproduction or distribution is permitted without written permission from the American Psychological Association.

converse with others in the organization using technical language and specific terms that only insiders would understand. In addition, the employee enjoys and gets along with other employees in the organization, knows who to go to in order to make things happen, and understands and can perform the key functions of his or her job. Talk about the perfect employee! Needless to say, that's quite a bit of information to gain—it's not a process that happens overnight. Some would say that this last stage of socialization never truly ends, as an organization's culture continues to change and evolve over time.[65] However, organizations also know that the more quickly and effectively an employee is socialized, the sooner that employee becomes a productive worker within the organization.

It's important to note that the length of the socialization process varies depending on the characteristics of the employee, not just the company. For example, some employees might progress more rapidly through the stages because of the knowledge they possess, their ability to recognize cultural cues, or their adaptability to their environment. In fact, there is growing evidence that proactivity on the part of the employee being socialized has a significant effect on socialization outcomes.[66] Some organizations might help their employees socialize more quickly because they have stronger cultures or cultures that are more easily understandable. The biggest difference though is that some organizations simply work harder at socializing their employees than others.

CHANGING AN ORGANIZATIONAL CULTURE

Given all the effort it takes to create and maintain a culture, changing a culture once one has been established is perhaps even more difficult. In fact, estimates put the rate of successful major culture change at less than 20 percent.[67]   Even before she became CEO, Mary Barra, as chief product officer at General Motors (our opening case example), was trying to change GM's bureaucratic, rule-oriented culture. Rather than talking about a Corvette, she says she'd rather talk about "driving an organization that's customer focused." She's worked on this by removing layers of management and reducing the employee policy manual by 80 percent. She even changed the dress code to "dress appropriately" as a symbol for having employees take responsibility. When questioned by people uncomfortable with the ambiguity she responded, "So you're telling me I can trust you to give you a company car and to have you responsible for tens of millions of dollars, but I can't trust you to dress appropriately?" The dress code wasn't about a problem GM was dealing with, but as Barra said, "there was a culture in the past where the rule was the rule and when you weren't empowered to make the decision you could all just complain about the rule."[68] In practice though, two other ways are more common methods to change a culture: changes in leadership and mergers or acquisitions.

CHANGES IN LEADERSHIP As evidenced by this chapter's opening case in GM and CEO Mary Barra, there is perhaps no bigger potential driver of culture than the leaders and top executives of organizations. Just as the founders and originators of organizations set the tone and develop the culture of a new company, subsequent CEOs and presidents leave their mark on the culture. Many times, leaders are expected simply to sustain the culture that has already been created.[69] At other times, leaders have to be a driving force for change as the environment around the organization shifts. This expectation is one of the biggest reasons organizations change their top leadership. For example, Nortel Networks hired two former Cisco executives into the roles of chief operating officer and chief technology officer. It is Nortel's hope that these executives will help bring some of Cisco's culture of aggressiveness to Nortel and thus allow it to compete more effectively in the high-technology industry environment.[70] Not all such moves work out, though. Retailer JCPenney brought in former Apple retail executive Ron Johnson as CEO, who shook up the company through lots of cultural changes including renaming the company "JCP." Johnson was hailed as "the ideal leader to fix JCP." One of the CEO's top lieutenants said, "If people are saying the culture is becoming much more Appley, I take that as a complement." However, the long-term employees of the company did not take it that way. They felt like they were treated poorly, always being judged, and were sick of the constant Apple references. Less than a year later, after dismal results and low employee morale, Johnson was removed, and an ex-CEO familiar with the underlying JCPenney culture took over.[71] See this chapter's **OB on Screen** for an example of a new leader taking over and trying to create a new culture.

MERGERS AND ACQUISITIONS Merging two companies with two distinct cultures is a sure-fire way to change the culture in an organization. The problem is that there is just no way to know what the culture will look like after the merger takes place. What the new culture will resemble is a function of both the strength of the two cultures involved in the merger and how similar they are to each other.[72] Ideally, a new culture would be created out of a compromise in which the best of both companies is represented by the new culture. There are many stories that have arisen from the mergers of companies with very different cultures: AOL/Time Warner, Exxon/Mobil, HP/Compaq, and RJR/Nabisco, to name a few. Unfortunately, very few of these stories are good ones. Mergers rarely result in the strong culture that managers hope will appear when they make the decision to merge. In fact, most merged companies operate under a differentiated culture for an extended period of time. Some of them never really adopt a new identity, and when they do, many of them are seen as failures by the outside world. This perception is especially true in global mergers, in which each of the companies not only has a different organizational culture but is from a different country as well, as our **OB Internationally** box details. Every now and then though, a merger happens in which the leadership focuses on culture from the start, such was the case with the merger of Delta and Northwest Airlines. Rather than risk creating a fragmented culture, Delta CEO Richard Anderson went to the extreme of changing the ID numbers on every employee's security badge so that employees could not tell whether a colleague started with Delta or Northwest. According to Anderson, he wanted to avoid a situation in which "employees were constantly sizing up which side you were on."[73]

OB ON SCREEN

PRICE CHECK

I took this job to change that. WE are going to change that. Starting here. Right now. In this room.

With those words, Susan Felders (Parker Posey) lets her new subordinates know that things are going to be changing in *Price Check* (Dir. Michael Walker, IFC Films, 2012). The film basically begins with the introduction of new boss Felders—a smart, ambitious, fast-talking, yet highly inappropriate at times woman who is transferred in to take over the pricing department of Wolsky's, a struggling Long Island–based supermarket chain. Felders doesn't waste a lot of time in letting those around her know that she's in charge and that they had better be ready to outwork her if they want to stick around. If you've ever wondered what you would say as a brand-new leader to a group of established employees to change the culture to what you want, this probably isn't the example to go by. Felders manages to be confident, controlling, awkward, and scary all at the same time.

© *IFC Films/Photofest*

One of the first things Felders does is make the decision to get rid of one of the long-term employees to show a good-faith cost-cutting measure to corporate. Prior to doing this she meets with employee Pete Cozy (Eric Mabius) at his house to ask his opinion about whom to fire. Reluctantly, Pete gives up the name of a colleague who he thinks is lowest in terms of performance. The next day, he walks in to find that she's fired somebody completely different! When asked about it, Felders makes it clear that she's in charge, but let's Pete know that the employee she fired was low on culture fit. Felders is fantastic at times—giving praise to employees when they least expect it; inappropriate at times—getting gym memberships for everyone and staring at one woman in particular as she announces it; and conniving at times—clearly willing to undercut other employees. As a department, Felders' group is given an enormous number of mixed messages as to what is expected of them over the course of the film, certainly not a culture most of us would like to work in.

Merging two different cultures has major effects on the attitudes and behaviors of organizational employees. Companies merge for many different strategic reasons, and though many managers and executives may realize its importance, whether the cultures will match is rarely the deciding criterion.[74] Slightly less troublesome but still a major hurdle to overcome are acquisitions. In most instances, the company doing the acquiring has a dominant culture to which the other is expected to adapt. A more recent example is the acquisition of Anheuser-Busch by the

OB INTERNATIONALLY

As mentioned previously, there is perhaps no more perilous journey for a company to take than merging with or acquiring another large firm. These problems are exacerbated when the two companies are from different countries. As few as 30 percent of international mergers and acquisitions create shareholder value. While global mergers and acquisitions have remained relatively flat for three years, 2014 was a record year, with $3.5 trillion in global activity (47 percent higher than 2013) and with 2015 on pace to be even bigger.

Hopefully, we've illustrated the inherent difficulties of trying to merge two different cultures even when the organizations are in the same country. These cultural differences can be magnified when international culture plays a role as well. Chances are good that your experiences in college have shown you that different countries have different cultures, just like organizations. People who come from different countries tend to view the world differently and have different sets of values as well. For example, DaimlerChrysler bought a controlling stake in Mitsubishi Motors, thinking that a strong alliance between the two automotive companies would result in high levels of value for both. Unfortunately, the merger broke up for reasons that have been attributed to the international culture differences between the two firms. The Japanese managers tended to avoid "unpleasant truths" and stay away from major change efforts—a tendency that DaimlerChrysler never confronted but also could not accept.

There are many stories of failed international mergers, and one of the greatest reasons for them is that corporations fail to recognize the impact that national culture differences (in addition to organizational culture differences) have on their ability to be successful. One such acquisition that doesn't intend to fall victim to this issue is the purchase of Volvo Car Corporation. (Sweden) from Ford by China's Geely Holding Group. Although the relationship started out extremely rocky, with Geely executives storming out of an initial meeting in Sweden because they felt they were being treated like they were stupid, the two companies seem to have reached some compromises. Volvo, somewhat against its more safe and family-friendly culture, is now producing some high-end luxury models to compete with Mercedes-Benz and BMW, which fit with Chinese desires. In addition, although Geely wanted to build three assembly plants in China to jump-start sales, it is following Volvo's more slow, quality approach at the behest of Volvo's CEO. For now, it seems that both CEOs are determined that each company shoud learn from the other.

Sources: S. Brahy, "Six Solution Pillars for Successful Cultural Integration of International M&As," *Journal of Organizational Excellence*, Autumn 2006, pp. 53–63; G. Edmondson, "Auf Wiedersehen, Mitsubishi," *BusinessWeek (online)*, November 11, 2005; B. Bremmer, "A Tale of Two Auto Mergers," *BusinessWeek (online)*, April 29, 2004; M. McGrath, "Why 2015 Could Be the Best Year for M&A Since The Financial Crisis.," *Forbes* (online), June 17, 2015: D. Primack, "2014 Was a Huge Year for M&A and Private Equity," *Fortune* (online), January 5, 2015; and N. Shirouzu, "Volvo's Search for Common Ground," *The Wall Street Journal* (online), June 6, 2011.

Belgian-based firm InBev. InBev and its CEO Carlos Brito are known for their heavy-handed, cost-cutting ways; Anheuser-Busch is known for its free-spending atmosphere in which employees get free admission to the company's theme parks and two cases of free beer each month. One industry analyst joked that the Budweiser Clydesdales get better treatment than the average InBev employee.[75] Another example comes from the acquisition of Mail Boxes Etc. by UPS. Strategically, the acquisition had many advantages that supposedly would allow UPS to compete better with FedEx and the U.S. Postal Service. However, the culture clash between the efficiency and rigidness of UPS and the entrepreneurial spirit of Mail Boxes Etc. franchisees has caused UPS some major headaches.[76] We've noted how difficult it is to get just one person to adapt to an established culture through the socialization process. Can you imagine how difficult it is to change an entire organization, all at one time?

One of the major reasons that one company purchases another is simply to acquire the technology that it has. In such cases, the acquired company usually is expected to change to fit the buyer's culture. However, a new approach that has been used by several companies, including Hewlett-Packard and Yahoo, is to buy companies with the intention of infusing their different culture into their own.[77] Clorox, the Oakland, California–based consumer products manufacturer, acquired Massachusetts-based personal care product maker Burt's Bees with the full knowledge of the company's environmen-

Clorox acquired Burt's Bees in the hopes of using the company's environmentally friendly culture to accentuate its own.

© Jb Reed/Bloomberg via Getty Images

tally friendly and socially responsible culture, which Clorox hoped would help in its quest to be more environmentally focused as well.[78] Although this process of "innovation via absorption" looks good on paper, it's very difficult, and companies need to think twice about changing the fundamental cultures they have built.

SUMMARY: WHY DO SOME ORGANIZATIONS HAVE DIFFERENT CULTURES THAN OTHERS?

So why do some organizations have different cultures than others? As shown in Figure 16-6, attraction–selection–attrition processes, socialization, changes in leadership, and mergers and acquisitions shape the three components of organizational culture: basic underlying assumptions, espoused values, and observable artifacts. Specific combinations of those culture components then give rise to both general and specific culture types. For example, cultures can be categorized on the basis of solidarity and sociability into fragmented, mercenary, communal, and networked types. Cultures can also be categorized into more specific types, such as customer service, safety, diversity, and creativity. Finally, those general and specific types can be further classified according to the strength of the culture. Taken together, these processes explain "what it's like" within the hallways of a given organization.

HOW IMPORTANT IS ORGANIZATIONAL CULTURE?

Normally, this section is where we summarize the importance of organizational culture by describing how it affects job performance and organizational commitment—the two outcomes in our integrative model of OB. However (similar to organizational structure in Chapter 15), it's difficult to summarize the importance of culture in this way because there are so many different types and dimensions of the concept. Although there has been some support for distinct culture types having an effect on employee attitudes,[79] high solidarity cultures, high sociability cultures, diversity cultures, creativity cultures, and so forth all have different effects on performance and commitment—effects that likely vary across different types of organizations and industries.

Regardless of the type of culture we're talking about, however, one concept remains important for any employee in any business: fit. Think for a moment about working for an organization whose culture doesn't match your own values. Maybe you work for an organization that produces a product that you don't believe in or that might be harmful to others, such as Philip Morris, Budweiser, or Harrah's casinos. Maybe your employer is an organization that expects you to perform questionable behaviors from an ethical standpoint or produces a product that's of poor quality. **Person–organization fit** is the degree to which a person's personality and values match the culture of an organization. Employees judge fit by thinking about the values they prioritize the most, then judging whether the organization shares those values. Table 16-3 provides a set of values that many people have used to judge fit. Which of these values would you say are the most important to you?

| FIGURE 16-6 | Why Do Some Organizations Have Different Cultures Than Others? |

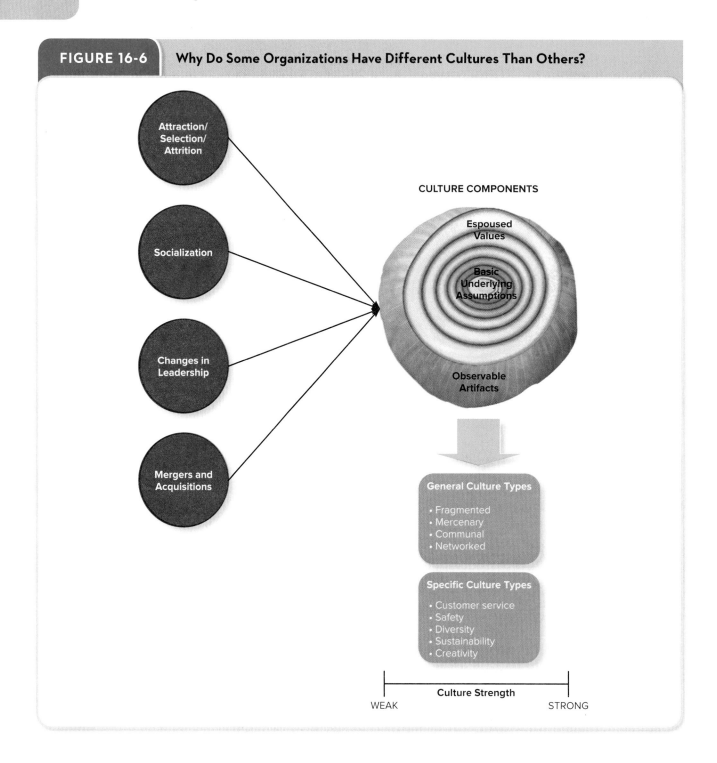

16.5

What is person-organization fit and how does it affect job performance and organizational commitment?

Two meta-analyses illustrate the importance of person–organization fit to employees.[80] When employees feel that their values and personality match those of the organization, they experience higher levels of *job satisfaction* and feel less *stress* about their day-to-day tasks. They also feel higher levels of *trust* toward their managers. Taken together, those results illustrate why person–organization fit is so highly correlated with organizational commitment, one of the two outcomes in our integrative model of OB (see Figure 16-7). When employees feel they fit with their organization's culture, they're much more likely to develop an emotional attachment to the company. The effects of fit on job performance are weaker, however. In general, person–organization fit is more related to citizenship behaviors than to task performance. Employees who sense a good fit are therefore more likely to help their colleagues and "go the extra mile" to benefit the company.

TABLE 16-3	Values Used to Judge Fit with a Culture
Flexibility	Adaptability
Stability	Predictability
Being innovative	Take advantage of opportunities
A willingness to experiment	Risk taking
Being careful	Autonomy
Being rule oriented	Being analytical
Paying attention to detail	Being precise
Being team oriented	Sharing information freely
Emphasizing a single culture	Being people oriented
Fairness	Respect for the individual's rights
Tolerance	Informality
Being easy going	Being calm
Being supportive	Being aggressive

Source: C.A. O'Reilly, J.A. Chatman, and D.F. Caldwell, "People and Organizational Culture: A Profile Comparison Approach to Assessing Person–Organization Fit," *Academy of Management Journal,* Vol. 34, 1991, pp. 487–516. Copyright © 1991. Reproduced with permission of via Copyright Clearance Center.

FIGURE 16-7	Effects of Person–Organization Fit on Performance and Commitment

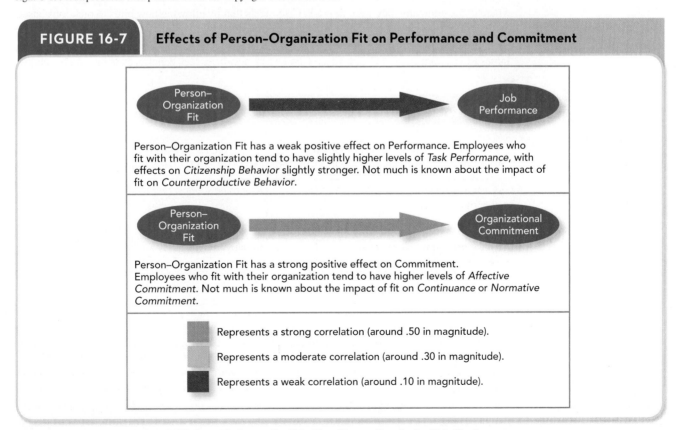

Person–Organization Fit has a weak positive effect on Performance. Employees who fit with their organization tend to have slightly higher levels of *Task Performance*, with effects on *Citizenship Behavior* slightly stronger. Not much is known about the impact of fit on *Counterproductive Behavior*.

Person–Organization Fit has a strong positive effect on Commitment. Employees who fit with their organization tend to have higher levels of *Affective Commitment*. Not much is known about the impact of fit on *Continuance* or *Normative Commitment*.

Represents a strong correlation (around .50 in magnitude).

Represents a moderate correlation (around .30 in magnitude).

Represents a weak correlation (around .10 in magnitude).

Sources: W. Arthur Jr., S.T. Bell, A.J. Villado, and D. Doverspike, "The Use of Person–Organization Fit in Employment-Related Decision Making: An Assessment of Its Criterion-Related Validity," *Journal of Applied Psychology* 91 (2007), pp. 786–801; and A.L. Kristof-Brown, R.D. Zimmerman, and E.C. Johnson, "Consequences of Individuals' Fit at Work: A Meta-Analysis of Person–Job, Person–Organization, Person–Group, and Person–Supervisor Fit," *Personnel Psychology* 58 (2005), pp. 281–342.

APPLICATION: MANAGING SOCIALIZATION

16.6

What steps can organizations take to make sure that newcomers will fit with their culture?

Most organizations recognize the importance of having employees adapt to the culture of their organization quickly. Luckily, there are a number of actions that organizations can take to help their employees adapt from the first day they walk in the door. Table 16-4 highlights some of the different tactics organizations can use when socializing their employees. Note that companies can take two very different approaches to the socialization process. The left-hand column represents a view of socialization in which the goal of the process is to have newcomers adapt to the organization's culture. This view assumes that the organization has a strong culture and definite norms and values that it wants employees to adopt, which is not always the case. Some organizations don't have a strong culture that they want employees to adapt to, or they might be trying to change their culture and want new employees to come in and "shake things up." The socialization tactics listed in the right-hand column of Table 16-4 might be more appropriate in such circumstances. In addition to the socialization tactics listed in the table, there are three other major ways in which organizations routinely and effectively help speed up the socialization process of newcomers: realistic job previews, orientation programs, and mentoring.

REALISTIC JOB PREVIEWS One of the most inexpensive and effective ways of reducing early turnover among new employees is through the use of **realistic job previews.**[81] Realistic job previews (RJPs) occur during the anticipatory stage of socialization during the recruitment process. They involve making sure a potential employee has an accurate picture of what working for an organization is going to be like by highlighting both the positive *and* the negative aspects of the job.[82] Although RJPs almost always occur prior to hiring, Cisco Systems has a unique program called "Cisco Choice" in which its 2,500 new hires a year interview and hear presentations from managers in more than 30 business units after they are hired. The new hires then get to choose where in the company they want to work. Cisco feels that by allowing new hires to pick jobs based on their interest and skills, they are likely to work harder and stay with the company. It also lessens reality shock and shortens the encounter stage that normally accompanies initial employment. James Revis, after going through Cisco Choice as a new hire, sees benefits even beyond his choice

TABLE 16-4	**Tactics Organizations Use to Socialize New Employees**
TACTICS DESIGNED TO *ENCOURAGE* ADAPTATION TO THE ORGANIZATION'S CULTURE	**TACTICS DESIGNED TO *DISCOURAGE* ADAPTATION TO THE ORGANIZATION'S CULTURE**
Orient new employees along with a group of other new employees.	Orient new employees by themselves.
Put newcomers through orientation apart from current organizational members.	Allow newcomers to interact with current employees while they are being oriented.
Provide hurdles that are required to be met prior to organizational membership.	Allow organizational membership regardless of whether any specific requirements have been met.
Provide role models for newcomers.	Use no examples of what an employee is supposed to be like.
Constantly remind newcomers that they are now part of a group and that this new group helps define who they are.	Constantly affirm to newcomers that they are to be themselves and that they were chosen for the organization based on who they are.

Sources: Adapted from G.R. Jones, "Socialization Tactics, Self-Efficacy, and Newcomers' Adjustments to Organizations," *Academy of Management Journal* 29 (1986), pp. 262–79; and J. Van Maanen and E.H. Schein, "Toward a Theory of Organizational Socialization," *Research in Organizational Behavior* 1 (1979), pp. 209–64.

of where to work, "Normally [new employees] just know what their department does and what their specific product is. When we collaborate, I already know what the other department does." Given Cisco's astounding 98 percent two-year retention rate, it's hard to argue with the company.[83]

ORIENTATION PROGRAMS One effective way to start the socialization process is by having new employees attend some form of **newcomer orientation** session. Apparently most organizations agree, given that 64–93 percent of all organizations use some form of orientation training process.[84] Not all orientation programs are alike however, and different types of orientation training can be more effective than others.[85] Orientation programs have been shown to be effective transmitters of socialization content, such that those employees who complete orientation have higher levels of satisfaction, commitment, and performance than those who don't.[86] Airbnb's CEO Brian Chesky believes that setting the culture is one of his top priorities, and he welcomes new hires each week during orientation where he encourages them to be "crazy" and tells them that they are there to "design the future world we want to live in." Chesky once wrote to employees, "If you break the culture, you break the machine that creates your products."[87] Jet Blue CEO Dave Barger also believes strongly in these sessions and shows it by having been to more than 250 of them over the last decade. Barger tells his new hires, "The hard product—airplanes, leather seats, satellite TVs, bricks and mortar—as long as you have a checkbook, they can be replicated. It's the culture that can't be replicated. It's how we treat each other. Do we trust each other? Can we push back on each other? The human side of the equation is the most important part of what we're doing."[88]

MENTORING One of the most popular pieces of advice given to college students as they begin their careers is that they need to find a mentor or coach within their organization.[89] **Mentoring** is a process by which a junior-level employee (protégé) develops a deep and long-lasting relationship with a more senior-level employee (mentor) within the organization. The mentor can provide social knowledge, resources, and psychological support to the protégé both at the beginning of employment and as the protégé continues his or her career with the company. Mentoring has always existed in companies on an informal basis. However, as organizations continue to learn about the strong benefits of these relationships, they're more frequently instituting mentoring programs that formally match newcomers with mentors.[90] In fact, nearly 76 percent of companies use mentoring in order to develop skills.[91] Formal programs allow the company to provide consistent information, train mentors, and ensure that all newcomers have the opportunity to develop one of these fruitful relationships. Morgan Stanley started its program by having leaders develop a curriculum for what makes employees successful within the firm and then paired mentors and protégés who were expected to cover specific material.[92] McGraw-Hill Education paired mentors and protégés based on what the protégé's goals were and who could best help them achieve those goals.[93] One unique program is that of the notoriously private company, Mars, Inc., the Virginia–based candy maker where employees are fondly referred to as "Martians." Although many employees get assigned a traditional mentor, the organization has a reverse-mentoring program for its executives where younger workers are assigned to bring them up to speed on social media.[94]

TAKEAWAYS

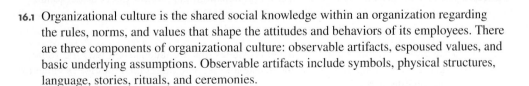

16.1 Organizational culture is the shared social knowledge within an organization regarding the rules, norms, and values that shape the attitudes and behaviors of its employees. There are three components of organizational culture: observable artifacts, espoused values, and basic underlying assumptions. Observable artifacts include symbols, physical structures, language, stories, rituals, and ceremonies.

16.2 An organization's culture can be described on dimensions such as solidarity and sociability to create four general culture types: networked, communal, fragmented, and mercenary. Organizations often strive to create a more specific cultural emphasis, as in customer service cultures, safety cultures, diversity cultures, and creativity cultures.

16.3 Strong cultures have the ability to influence employee behaviors and attitudes. Strong cultures exist when employees agree on the way things are supposed to happen and their behaviors are consistent with those expectations. Strong cultures are not necessarily good or bad. Generally, a culture's effectiveness depends on how well it matches the company's outside environment. To this degree, adaptive cultures can be very useful.

16.4 Organizations maintain their cultures through attraction, selection, and attrition processes and socialization practices. Organizations change their cultures by changing their leadership or through mergers and acquisitions.

16.5 Person–organization fit is the degree to which a person's values and personality match the culture of the organization. Person–organization fit has a weak positive effect on job performance and a strong positive effect on organizational commitment.

16.6 There are a number of practices organizations can utilize to improve the socialization of new employees, including realistic job previews, orientation programs, and mentoring.

KEY TERMS

- Organizational culture — *p. 510*
- Observable artifacts — *p. 512*
- Symbols — *p. 512*
- Physical structures — *p. 512*
- Language — *p. 513*
- Stories — *p. 513*
- Rituals — *p. 513*
- Ceremonies — *p. 513*
- Espoused values — *p. 514*
- Basic underlying assumptions — *p. 514*
- Fragmented cultures — *p. 515*
- Mercenary cultures — *p. 515*
- Networked cultures — *p. 515*
- Communal cultures — *p. 515*
- Customer service culture — *p. 516*
- Safety culture — *p. 516*
- Diversity culture — *p. 517*
- Sustainablity culture — *p. 517*
- Creativity culture — *p. 517*
- Culture strength — *p. 518*
- Subcultures — *p. 518*
- Countercultures — *p. 520*
- ASA framework — *p. 521*
- Socialization — *p. 521*
- Anticipatory stage — *p. 521*
- Encounter stage — *p. 521*
- Reality shock — *p. 522*
- Understanding and adaptation — *p. 522*
- Person–organization fit — *p. 527*
- Realistic job previews — *p. 530*
- Newcomer orientation — *p. 531*
- Mentoring — *p. 531*

DISCUSSION QUESTIONS

16.1 Have you or a family member worked for an organization that you would consider to have a strong culture? If so, what made the culture strong? Did you or they enjoy working there? What do you think led to that conclusion?

16.2 Is it possible for an employee to have personal values that are inconsistent with the values of the organization? If so, how is this inconsistency likely to affect the employee's behavior and attitudes while at work?

16.3 How can two companies with very different cultures that operate in the same industry both be successful? Shouldn't one company's culture automatically be a better fit for the environment?

16.4 When you think of the U.S. Postal Service's culture, what kinds of words come to mind? Where do these impressions come from? Do you think your impressions are accurate? What has the potential to make them inaccurate?

16.5 Think about the last job you started. What are some unique things that companies might do to reduce the amount of reality shock that new employees encounter? Are these methods likely to be expensive?

CASE: GENERAL MOTORS

Mary Barra, 53, took over GM in January 2014, making her the company's fifth CEO in six years—and the first woman to run a major automaker. She took over just before a committee inside GM made the decision to recall 2.6 million vehicles due to a faulty ignition switch (even though they knew about the problem much earlier than that). Barra survived her first year, and she is heralded by many inside the company for the way she handled the crisis she was dealt. It is now up to her to change the culture that she has grown up in—she has worked for GM since she was 18 years old. (Her father worked at GM for 39 years.) Barra isn't like previous GM CEOs, though. In the wake of an internal investigation, Barra (in a very un-GM like move) fired 15 employees and got rid of at least seven high-level executives. Although GM's tradition is to put these kinds of experiences behind it quickly, Barra stated at an employee town hall meeting, "I never want to put this behind us. I want to put this painful experience permanently in our collective memories." A retired executive stated, "Her remarks at that meeting were unlike anything any previous GM CEO has ever said."

Although Barra knows what needs to happen, she doesn't like the word "culture." "What is culture? It's how people behave. So if we want to change this elusive culture, it's changing behaviors. And that becomes actionable very quickly." That's exactly the message she is sending to the executives around her. Barra believes that culture change has to start at the top and that when she does things differently, those around her will start to do the same. She certainly has a knack for being able to make others make decisions—even for simple things. Barra states, "In my whole 35 years at GM I never accepted the GM nod. If somebody said in a meeting they were going to do something, I expect you to do it. And if you didn't do it, I'd be at your desk or [sending] an e-mail—whatever—just challenging. A lot of that is just not accepting that behavior, because it's never been acceptable."

There are those who have serious doubts about Barra's ability to effectively get anything done. This is at least partly due to the fact that Barra is an insider—someone who has been steeped in the culture for more than 20 years—and partly due to the fact that all seven CEOs inside GM have tried to change the ingrained culture at one point or another. Ex-CEO Roger Smith went so far as to try to do it through acquisition by purchasing EDS, a large software company with a culture the opposite of GM's, for $2.6 billion. A banker who worked on the deal said, "Exactly the opposite happened. By the time EDS was spun off . . . it was bureaucratic and cost-laden." That being said, Barra is known for having made changes and ruffling some feathers along the way to the top of the organization. Warren Buffett, whose Berkshire Hathaway recently bought more GM stock, says of Barra, "Mary is as strong as they come. She is the person to have there. She is as good as I've seen."

16.1 Is it possible for a company the size of GM to change its culture dramatically without the push of an outside leader? If yes, how could that happen?

16.2 What makes it so difficult for GM to change its culture?

16.3 Do you think the recall/ignition switch crisis is big enough to instigate change? Why or why not?

Sources: M. Burden, "GM CEO Barra: 'You Can't Fake Culture,'" *The Detroit News,* May 4, 2015; "What Drives GM CEO Mary Barra?" *CBSNews.com,* May 3, 2015; G. Colvin, "Mary Barra's (Unexpected) Opportunity," *Fortune,* October 6, 2014, pp. 101–10; and R. Foroohar, "Mary Barra's Bumpy Ride," *Time,* October 6, 2014, pp. 32–38.

EXERCISE: UNIVERSITY CULTURE

The purpose of this exercise is to explore how organizational culture is transmitted through observable artifacts. This exercise uses groups, so your instructor will either assign you to a group or ask you to create your own group. The exercise has the following steps:

16.1 Using the following table, consider the observable artifacts that transmit the organizational culture of your university.

Symbols	Think about the logo and images associated with your university. What message do they convey about the university's culture?
Physical structures	Think about the most visible physical structures on campus. What do those structures say about your university's culture?
Language	Think about the jargon, slang, slogans, and sayings associated with your university. What insights do they offer into the university's culture?
Stories	What anecdotes, accounts, legends, and myths are associated with your university? What messages do they convey about your university's culture?
Rituals	What are the daily or weekly routines that occur at your university, and what do they say about the culture?
Ceremonies	What are the formal events and celebrations that occur at your university, and what cultural signals do they convey?

16.2 Consider the sorts of values listed in Table 16-3. If you consider the symbols, physical structures, language, stories, rituals, and ceremonies identified in step 1, what core values seem to summarize your university's culture? Using a transparency, laptop, or board, list the one value that seems to be most central to your university's culture. Then list the three cultural artifacts that are most responsible for transmitting that core value. Present your results to the class.

16.3 Class discussion (whether in groups or as a class) should center on the following topics: Do you like how your university's culture is viewed, as represented in the group presentations? Why or why not? If you wanted to change the university's culture to represent other sorts of values, what process would you use?

ENDNOTES

16.1 Verbeke, W.; M. Volgering; and M. Hessels. "Exploring the Conceptual Expansion within the Field of Organizational Behavior: Organizational Climate and Organizational Culture." *Journal of Management Studies* 35 (1998), pp. 303–29.

16.2 Deal, T.E., and A.A. Kennedy. *Corporate Cultures: The Rites and Rituals of Corporate Life.* Reading, MA: Addison-Wesley, 1982.

16.3 Adapted from O'Reilly, C.A., III; J. Chatman; and D.L. Caldwell. "People and Organizational Culture: A Profile Comparison

Approach to Assessing Person–Organization Fit." *Academy of Management Journal* 34 (1991), pp. 487–516; and Tsui, A.S.; Z. Zhang; W. Hui; K.R. Xin; and J.B. Wu. "Unpacking the Relationship between CEO Leadership Behavior and Organizational Culture." *The Leadership Quarterly* 17 (2006), pp. 113–37.

16.4 O'Reilly, C.A., and J.A. Chatman. "Culture as Social Control: Corporations, Cults, and Commitment." In *Research in Organizational Behavior*, Vol. 18, ed. B.M. Staw and L.L. Cummings. Stamford, CT: JAI Press, 1996, pp. 157–200.

16.5 Chatman, J.A. "Matching People and Organizations: Selection and Socialization in Public Accounting Firms." *Administrative Science Quarterly* 36 (1991), pp. 459–84.

16.6 Colvin, G. "Q1A: Whole Foods' Other CEO on Organic Growth." *Fortune*, May 20, 2013, pp. 128–32.

16.7 Trice, H.M., and J.M. Beyer. *The Cultures of Work Organizations.* Englewood Cliffs, NJ: Prentice Hall, 1993.

16.8 Rowley, I. "What Put Honda in the Passing Lane." *BusinessWeek,* October 19, 2009, pp. 57–58.

16.9 Nicolas, S. "The Way We Do Things Around Here." *Director,* March 2011, pp. 56–59.

16.10 Hempel, J. "Bringing Design to Blue Chips." *Fortune,* November 12, 2007, p. 32; and Stibbe, M. "Mothers of Invention." *Director* 55 (2002), pp. 64–68.

16.11 Vance, A. "Netflix, Reed Hastings Survives Missteps to Join Silicon Valley's Elite." *Bloomberg Businessweek,* May 9, 2013, http://www. businessweek.com/ articles/2013-05-09/ netflix-reed-hastings- survive-missteps-to- join-silicon-valleys- elite.

16.12 Kesling, B. "Say Goodbye to the Office Cubicle." *The Wall Street Journal,* April 3, 2013, p. B1.

16.13 Rivlin, G. "The Problem with Microsoft." *Fortune,* April 11, 2011, pp. 45–51.

16.14 Shuit, D.P. "Yum Does a 360." *Workforce Management,* April 2005, pp. 59–60.

16.15 Berfield, S. "Howard Schultz versus Howard Schultz." *BusinessWeek,* August 17, 2009, pp. 28–33.

16.16 Birk, S. "Creating a Culture of Safety: Why CEO's Hold the Key to Improved Outcomes." *Healthcare Executive,* March/April 2009, pp. 15–22.

16.17 Bailey, S. "Benefits on Tap." *Bloomberg Businessweek,* March 21, 2011, p. 1.

16.18 Kaihla, P. "Best Kept Secrets of the World's Best Companies." *Business 2.0* 7 (2006), pp. 82–87.

16.19 Wehrum, K. "Hello Conference Room A!: An Office Where Employees Rock." *Inc* 32 (2010), pp. 115–16.

16.20 Bryant, A. *The Corner Office. Indispensable and Unexpected Lessons from CEOs on How to Lead and Succeed.* New York: Times Books, 2011.

16.21 Lev-Ram, M. "Welcome to the Twitterloin." *Fortune,* March 15, 2015, pp. 120–22.

16.22 Gallagher, L. "Why Employees Love Marriott." *Fortune,* March 15, 2015, pp. 112–18.

16.23 Kowitt, B. "Inside Trader Joe's." *Fortune,* September 6, 2010, pp. 86–96.

16.24 Schein, E.H. "Organizational Culture." *American Psychologist* 45 (1990), pp. 109–19.

16.25 Schein, E. H. *Organizational Culture and Leadership.* San Francisco: Jossey-Bass, 2004.

16.26 Schein, E.H. "What Is Culture?" In *Reframing Organizational Culture,* ed. P.J. Frost, L.F. Moore, M.R. Louis, C.C. Lundberg, and J. Martin. Beverly Hills, CA: Sage, 1991, pp. 243–53.

16.27 Goffee, R., and G. Jones. *The Character of a Corporation.* New York: Harper Business, 1998.

16.28   Ibid.

16.29   Central Intelligence Agency. *The CIA World Fact Book 2013.* Washington, DC: Sky-horse, 2013.

16.30   Hong, Y.; H. Liao; J. Hu; and K. Jiang. "Missing Link in the Service Profit Chain: A Meta-Analytic Review of the Antecedents, Consequences, and Moderators of Service Climate." *Journal of Applied Psychology* 98 (2013), pp. 237–67; Walumba, F.O.; C.A. Hartnell; and A. Oke. "Servant Leadership, Procedural Justice Cli-mate, Service Climate, Employee Attitudes, and Organizational Citizenship Behavior: A Cross-level Inves-tigation." *Journal of Applied Psychology* 95 (2010), pp. 517–29; and Schneider, B.; D.E. Bowen; M.G. Ehrhart; and K.M. Holcombe. "The Climate for Ser-vice: Evolution of a Construct." In *Hand-book of Organizational Culture and Climate,* ed. N.M. Ashkanasy, C. Wilderom, and M.F. Peterson. Thousand Oaks, CA, Sage, 2000, pp. 21–36.

16.31   Hong et al., "Miss-ing Link in the Ser-vice Profit Chain"; and Schneider, B.; M.G. Ehrhart; D.M. Mayer; J.L. Saltz; and K. Niles-Jolly. "Understanding Orga-nization–Customer Links in Service Set-tings." *Academy of*

Management Journal 48 (2005), pp. 1017–32.

16.32   du Gay, P., and G. Salaman. "The Cult(ure) of the Cus-tomer." In *Strategic Human Resource Man-agement,* ed. C. Mabey, G. Salaman, and J. Storey. London: Sage, 1998, pp. 58–67.

16.33   McGregor, J. "USAA's Battle Plan." *Bloom-berg Businessweek,* March 1, 2010, pp. 40–44.

16.34   Grizzle, J.W.; A.R. Zablah; T.J. Brown; J.C. Mowen; and J.M. Lee. "Employee–Customer Orientation in Context: How the Environment Moderates the Influ-ence of Customer Orientation on Per-formance Outcomes." *Journal of Applied Psychology* 94 (2009), pp. 1227–42.

16.35   Bureau of Labor Sta-tistics. "Workplace Injuries and Illnesses in 2011," 2012, http://www.bls.gov/news.release/pdf/osh.pdf.

16.36   Zohar, D., and G. Luria. "Climate as a Social-Cognitive Con-struction of Supervi-sory Safety Practices: Scripts as a Proxy of Behavior Patterns." *Journal of Applied Psychology* 89 (2004), pp. 322–33.

16.37   Hofmann, D.A.; F.P. Morgeson; and S.J. Gerras. "Climate as a Moderator of the Relationship between Leader-Member Exchange and Content

Specific Citizenship: Safety Climate as an Exemplar." *Journal of Applied Psychology* 88 (2003), pp. 170–78.

16.38   Katz-Navon, T.; E. Naveh; and Z. Stern. "Safety Climate in Healthcare Organiza-tions: A Multi-Dimensional Approach." *Academy of Manage-ment Journal* 48 (2005), pp. 1075–89.

16.39   Gilbert, D., and R. Gold. "As Big Drillers Move In, Safety Goes Up." *The Wall Street Journal,* April 1, 2013, p. A1.

16.40   Clarke, S. "Percep-tions of Organizational Safety: Implications for the Development of Safety Culture." *Jour-nal of Organizational Behavior* 20 (1999), pp. 185–98.

16.41   Beus, J.M.; S.C. Payne; M.E. Bergman; and W. Arthur Jr. "Safety Cli-mate and Injuries: An Examination of Theo-retical and Empirical Relationships." *Journal of Applied Psychology* 95 (2010), pp. 713–27; and Christian, M.S.; J.C. Bradley; J.C. Wallace; and M.J. Burke. "Workplace Safety: A Meta-Anal-ysis of the Roles of Person and Situation Factors." *Journal of Applied Psychology* 94 (2009), pp. 1103–27.

16.42   Fairchild, C. "Solving Tech's Diversity Problem—Starting at the Top." *Fortune,* March 15, 2015, pp. 126–27.

16.43 Babcock, P. "What CEO's Think about Diversity" (n.d.), http://www.shrm.org/hrdisciplines/Diversity/Articles/Pages/WhatCEOsThinkAboutDiversity.aspx.

16.44 "Building a Better Workforce." *Profit* 30 (March 2011), pp. 17–20.

16.45 Sacks, D. "Creative Conversation—Rose Marcario." *Fast Company,* February 2015, pp. 34–36.

16.46 Mangalindan, J.P. "A Healthier, More Rewarding Workplace." *Fortune,* October 6, 2014, pp. 49–50.

16.47 McLean, L.D. "Organizational Culture's Influence on Creativity and Innovation: A Review of the Literature and Implications for Human Resource Development." *Advances in Developing Human Resources* 7 (2005), pp. 226–46.

16.48 Mattioli, D., and K. Maher. "At 3M, Innovation Comes in Tweaks and Snips." *The Wall Street Journal* (online), March 1, 2010.

16.49 Seabrook, J. "How to Make It." *The New Yorker,* September 20, 2010, pp. 66–73.

16.50 Colvin, G. "Personal Bests." *Fortune,* March 15, 2015, pp. 106-110; and Tkaczyk, C. "No. 20, SAS; Offer Affordable (Awesome) Day Care." *Fortune,* August 17, 2009, p. 26.

16.51 O'Reilly, C.A. "Corporations, Culture, and Commitment: Motivation and Social Control in Organizations." *California Management Review* 31 (1989), pp. 9–25.

16.52 Linebaugh, K; D. Searcey; and N. Shirouzu. "Secretive Culture Led Toyota Astray." *The Wall Street Journal,* February 8, 2010.

16.53 O'Reilly et al., "People and Organizational Culture."

16.54 Schein, E.H. "Three Cultures of Management: The Key to Organizational Learning." *Sloan Management Review* 38 (1996), pp. 9–20.

16.55 Egan, T.M. "The Relevance of Organizational Subculture for Motivation to Transfer Learning." *Human Resource Development Quarterly* 19 (2008), pp. 299–322; and Boisner, A., and J. Chatman. "The Role of Subcultures in Agile Organizations." In *Leading and Managing People in Dynamic Organizations,* ed. R. Petersen and E. Mannix. Mahwah, NJ: Erlbaum, 2003.

16.56 See Howard-Grenville, J.A. "Inside the 'BLACK BOX': How Organizational Culture and Subcultures Inform Interpretations and Actions on Environmental Issues." *Organization & Environment* 19 (2006), pp. 46–73; and Jermier, J.; J. Slocum; L. Fry; and J. Gaines. "Organizational Subcultures in a Soft Bureaucracy: Resistance behind the Myth and Façade of an Official Culture." *Organizational Science* 2 (1991), pp. 170–94.

16.57 Schneider, B.; H.W. Goldstein; and D.B. Smith. "The ASA Framework: An Update." *Personnel Psychology* 48 (1995), pp. 747–73.

16.58 Graf, A.B. "Building Corporate Cultures." *Chief Executive,* March 2005, p. 18.

16.59 Foust, D. "Where Headhunters Fear to Tread." *BusinessWeek,* September 14, 2009, pp. 42–44.

16.60 For good summaries of socialization, see Fisher, C.D. "Organizational Socialization: An Integrative View." *Research in Personnel and Human Resource Management* 4 (1986), pp. 101–45; and Bauer, T.N.; E.W. Morrison; and R.R. Callister. "Organizational Socialization: A Review and Directions for Future Research." In *Research in Personnel and Human Resource Management,* Vol. 16, ed. G.R. Ferris. Greenwich, CT: JAI Press, 1998, pp. 149–214.

16.61 Cable, D.M.; L. Aiman-Smith; P.W. Mulvey; and J.R. Edwards. "The Sources and Accuracy of Job Applicants' Beliefs about Organizational Culture." *Academy of Management Journal* 43 (2000), pp. 1076–85; and Louis, M.R. "Surprise and Sense-Making: What Newcomers Experience in Entering Unfamiliar Organizational Settings." *Administrative Science Quarterly* 25 (1980), pp. 226–51.

16.62   Chao, G.T.; A. O'Leary-Kelly; S. Wolf; H.J. Klein; and P.D. Gardner. "Organizational Socialization: Its Content and Consequences." *Journal of Applied Psychology* 79 (1994), pp. 450–63.

16.63   Ibid.; Klein, H., and N. Weaver. "The Effectiveness of an Organizational-Level Orientation Training Program in the Socialization of New Hires." *Personnel Psychology,* Spring 2000, pp. 47–66; and Wesson, M.J., and C.I. Gogus. "Shaking Hands with a Computer: An Examination of Two Methods of Organizational Newcomer Orientation." *Journal of Applied Psychology* 90 (2005), pp. 1018–26.

16.64   Gravelle, M. "The Five Most Common Hiring Mistakes and How to Avoid Them." *The Canadian Manager* 29 (2004), pp. 11–13.

16.65   Van Maanen, J., and E.H. Schein. "Toward a Theory of Organizational Socialization." *Research in Organizational Behavior* 1 (1979), pp. 209–64.

16.66   Ashford, S.J., and J.S. Black. "Proactivity during Organizational Entry: The Role of Desire for Control." *Journal of Applied Psychology* 81 (1996), pp. 199–214; and Kim, T.; D.M. Cable; and S. Kim. "Socialization Tactics, Employee Proactivity, and Person–Organization Fit." *Journal of Applied Psychology* 90 (2005), pp. 232–41.

16.67   Mourier, P., and M. Smith. *Conquering Organizational Change: How to Succeed Where Most Companies Fail.* Atlanta: CEP Press, 2001.

16.68   Higgins, T. "Mary Barra, the Contender: GM's Next CEO May Not Be a Car Guy." *Bloomberg Businessweek,* June 13, 2013, http://www. businessweek.com/ articles/2013-06-13/ mary-barra-the-contender-gms-next-ceo-may-not-be-a-car-guy.

16.69   Schein, *Organization Culture and Leadership.*

16.70   Gubbins, E. "Nortel's New Execs Bring Cisco Experience." *Telephony,* April 11, 2005, pp. 14–15.

16.71   Glazer, E.; J.S. Lublin; and D. Mattioli. "Penney Backfires on Ackman." *The Wall Street Journal,* April 10, 2013, p. B1.

16.72   Weber, Y. "Measuring Cultural Fit in Mergers and Acquisitions." In *Handbook of Organizational Culture and Climate,* ed. N.M. Ashkanasy, C. Wilderom, and M.F. Peterson. Thousand Oaks, CA; Sage, pp. 309–20.

16.73   Foust, D. "Pulling Delta Out of a Nosedive." *BusinessWeek,* May 25, 2009, pp. 36–37.

16.74   Stahl, G.K., and M.E. Mendenhall. *Mergers and Acquisitions: Managing Culture and Human Resources.* Stanford, CA: Stanford University Press, 2005.

16.75   Foust, D.; J. Ewing; and G. Smith. "Looks Like a Beer Brawl." *BusinessWeek,* July 28, 2008, p. 52.

16.76   Gibson, R. "Package Deal: UPS's Purchase of Mail Boxes Etc. Looked Great on Paper. Then Came the Culture Clash." *The Wall Street Journal,* May 8, 2006, p. R13.

16.77   Jana, R. "Putting the i into HiP." *BusinessWeek,* November 26, 2007, p. 10.

16.78   Gillenwater, P., and T. Walton. "Bee Culture." *Mergers and Acquisitions* 46 (2011), p. 38.

16.79   Hartnell, C.A.; A.Y. Ou; and A. Kinicki.

"Organizational Culture and Organizational Effectiveness: A Meta-Analytic Investigation of the Competing Values Framework's Theoretical Suppositions." *Journal of Applied Psychology* 96 (2011), pp. 677–94.

16.80   Arthur, W., Jr.; S.T. Bell; A.J. Villado; and D. Doverspike. "The Use of Person–Organization Fit in Employment Decision Making: An Assessment of Its Criterion-Related Validity." *Journal of Applied Psychology* 91 (2007), pp. 786–801; and Kristof-Brown, A.L.; R.D. Zimmerman; and E.C. Johnson, "Consequences of Individuals' Fit at Work: A Meta-Analysis of Person–Job, Person–Organization, Person–Group, and Person–Supervisor Fit," *Personnel Psychology* 58 (2005), pp. 281–342.

16.81   Barber, A.E. *Recruiting Employees: Individual and Organizational Perspectives.* Thousand Oaks, CA: Sage, 1998.

16.82   Wanous, J.P. *Organizational Entry: Recruitment, Selection, Orientation and Socialization of Newcomers.* Reading, MA: Addison-Wesley, 1992.

16.83   Gerdes, L. "The Best Places to Launch a Career." *BusinessWeek,* September 14, 2009, pp. 32–39.

16.84   Anderson, N.R.; N.A. Cunningham-Snell; and J. Haigh. "Induction Training as Socialization: Current Practice and Attitudes to Evaluation in British Organizations." *International Journal of Selection and Assessment* 4 (1996), pp. 169–83.

16.85   Wesson and Gogus, "Shaking Hands with a Computer."

16.86   Ibid.; and Klein and Weaver, "The Effectiveness."

16.87   Gallagher, L. "The Education of Brian Chesky." *Fortune,* July 1, 2015, pp. 92–100.

16.88   Gunther, M. "Nothing Blue about This Airline." *Fortune,* September 14, 2009, pp. 114–18.

16.89   Wanberg, C.R.; E.T. Welsh; and S.A. Hezlett. "Mentoring Research: A Review and Dynamic Process Model." *Research in Personnel and Human Resources Management* 22 (2003), pp. 39–124.

16.90   Allen, T.D.; L.T. Eby; M.L. Poteet; E. Lentz; and L. Lima. "Outcomes Associated with Mentoring Protégés: A Meta-Analysis." *Journal of Applied Psychology* 89 (2004), pp. 127–36.

16.91   Kranz, G. "More Firms Paying Mind to Mentoring." *Workforce Management,* January 2010, p. 10.

16.92   Kessler, S. "How to Start a Mentoring Program." *Inc.,* April 6, 2010, http://www.inc.com/guides/2010/04/start-mentoring-program.html.

16.93   Ibid.

16.94   Kaplan, D.A. "Mars Incorporated: A Pretty Sweet Place to Work." *Fortune,* February 4, 2013, pp. 72–82.

Integrative Cases

Reenergizing Employees After a Downsizing

LEARNING GOALS

This case will help you learn to evaluate and manage the consequences of significant organizational changes, like downsizing. As the managing editor of a small newspaper, you'll be assisting the editor as she grapples with the consequences of a recent layoff. The case will touch on both the immediate aftermath of the downsizing and also on how work will need to be structured and reorganized going forward. After reading the case, you'll prepare a report for your editor that will lay out the pluses and minuses of a number of potential action steps for reenergizing the paper's staff.

KEY WORDS COVERED

- Task performance
- Affective commitment
- Job characteristics theory
- Equity theory
- Psychological empowerment
- Informational justice
- Big Five
- Restructuring

THE SITUATION

Andrea Zuckerman had been dreading this day for some time. As the editor in chief of the *Blaze,* she had been aware of the impending downsizing for some time. But the *Blaze* is just a small, college-town newspaper—owned by a large national conglomerate. So she had to hold her tongue while the corporate wheels turned. She didn't agree with how the consultants hired by corporate had determined who would go, which was largely determined by who had the highest salaries. And she didn't agree with how the news was being delivered—not by her, but by a consultant who would be a complete stranger to all involved. "They're taking away our wisest," she noted, "and they're taking away those folks' dignity for good measure."

Not that Andrea could argue with the reasons behind the downsizing. She was, after all, working in a dying industry. Every newspaper, from *The New York Times* and *Washington Post* down to the smallest rag in the smallest town, had a sliver of the readership of a decade ago. First it was 24-hour cable news, then the Internet, then smartphones. Each made newspapers less central to the current events consumption of the folks in a given town. Corporate had tried to stay ahead of these trends when they bought the *Blaze,* an event that had been marked by a smaller round of downsizing as costs were cut, the paper was scaled back, and Tuesday and Wednesday deliveries were ended. But there had been hope associated with those changes, with everyone assuming that corporate resources could help the *Blaze* reinvent itself and leverage new technologies to stay relevant.

This time around, the *Blaze* is confronting a "new normal." Its function moving forward will be to serve as a local portal to the broader news resources offered by corporate. When folks in town log on to the *Blaze* using either their web browser or their smartphone or tablet app, they'll see a combination of local stories written by *Blaze* staff and national and world stories authored by staff at other papers under the corporate umbrella. Eventually, the print version of the paper will be a weekend-only phenomenon, and even that will almost certainly end at some point. All these changes mean that the paper will need fewer reporters, photographers, artists, and section editors, not to mention fewer assistants. There may also need to be some restructuring and merging of assignments and duties.

But that's getting ahead of things a bit. The first item that Andrea wants to discuss in her meeting with you is what to say to the staff at the morning briefing. As the survivors of a layoff that's being poorly handled, it'll be on her to restore some semblance of morale. After all, the last thing the paper needs is its remaining staff giving two weeks' notice. In fact, they're going to need to be more committed than ever because more is going to be asked of them than when they were hired. She'll have to be somewhat careful with this speech, of course, as the HR person installed by corporate—Jessie Vasquez—will no doubt remind her. Jessie is good at his job in many ways, even if Andrea complains about his general level of risk aversion. Jessie's primary concerns will revolve around Andrea saying something that could either trigger a wrongful termination suit or be used as ammunition if such a suit is brought by a staffer against corporate.

The afternoon briefing is going to be more complicated. That's where Andrea hopes to begin charting a course toward the "new normal" so that everyone understands what they'll be in for. The rumor mill has already been working overtime, and many of the scenarios being floated might actually wind up being worse than the eventual status quo. So it's important to begin discussing the future look of the *Blaze* quickly, to create some information to go along with the misinformation. Of course, Andrea doesn't want to make decisions about that future course too quickly because nothing will undermine the staff's confidence more than a collection of faulty ideas that gets revised a few months into its existence.

There are a lot of things to consider when contemplating the new operations of the *Blaze*. The paper has historically grouped its functions into five areas: state, city, sports, lifestyle, and business. It seems to Andrea that those five areas will need to get merged into two or three. The reporters, photographers, artists, and editors in those areas will still perform the same duties; they'll just do those duties for a broader range of content than they did before. But how to decide who to group? Some groupings seem logical to Andrea, but it may be that the staff working in those areas would find other combinations more appealing. And it seems like the degree of "enlargement" will vary a bit. Some staffers will be taking on just a little bit more, whereas others will be taking on a lot more. The paper will need both groups to perform their tasks, and perform them well.

Of course, there's also the matter of who's willing and able to shoulder a lot more rather than a little more. Andrea knows from experience that this can be a dicey issue. Some staffers excel at a narrowly defined set of duties but struggle once those duties are expanded. Others seem to lack any limit to what they can take on, at least in the short term. But how to tell one group from the other, aside from Andrea's own hunches? Everyone at the *Blaze* filled out a bunch of assessments and inventories when corporate acquired the paper, and all that information should be in everyone's personnel files. It may not offer definitive answers, but it's a good bet that the information would offer at least some insights.

Asking some staffers to take on a lot more while others are asked to take on a little more could be a recipe for controversy. Indeed, Andrea's already been getting complaints about the relative workloads across areas for years! In this regard, corporate might actually help for a change. It turns out that they tend to budget more for compensation-related expenditures in the wake of a downsizing. They've learned from experience that survivors sometimes need a bit of a bump to stay committed, and they've also learned that "downsizees" occasionally need to be hired back, this time at the going rate for the

job market. Corporate can justify such expenses because the downsizing still results in a cost savings, even with extra for the survivors factored in. She'd have to check with Jessie, but Andrea suspects she could leverage those extra funds in a creative way, to make the new pay structure match up with the new job structure.

Certainly there are a lot of moving parts to the kinds of restructuring that Andrea is contemplating. Although her role as editor in chief gives her the best "big-picture" sense of how all those parts look from 20,000 feet, it's still not clear that she knows everything she needs to know (even with Jessie's help). On the one hand, it might be helpful to involve the *Blaze*'s staff in the decision making as the future course of the paper gets charted. That would give them "buy-in" and ensure that all the bases are covered as a new structure takes shape. On the other hand, keeping reporters, photographers, artists, and editors on the same page is often like herding cats. What if she asks for suggestions and the staffers take off in completely different directions? Once the Pandora's box of "input" is opened, it's not clear that even Andrea could get it shut again.

Although the new day-to-day work of the *Blaze* staff is foremost on Andrea's mind, she can't help but think of a bigger-picture issue that hangs over everything. Will the staffers still feel the same way about not just their jobs, but their vocations? It was hard enough when the *Blaze* was first acquired by corporate. Many of the staffers had been attracted to "*Blaze* 1.0" because it was a small-town operation. They could live in a charming place with a low cost of living, and could do their work the way they wanted to. The more corporate "*Blaze* 2.0" brought with it a certain degree of standardization, with corporate imposing some common work practices that it had honed in other, mostly bigger papers. But still, at the end of the day, everyone was still in the newspaper business.

Even if a new structure works out, and even if the compensation issues get solved, the move to "*Blaze* 3.0" poses a more existential threat. Is everyone still in the newspaper business, or are they now in the web portal business? How much of their identity is wrapped up in the feeling of seeing someone read the paper at a coffee shop or pick it up off a doorstep? And what does it mean for the *Blaze* to focus only on local news, no longer being able to weigh in on world and national events, issues, trends, sports, and buzz? These issues hit home especially deeply for Andrea. Not only was her father in the newspaper business, but her grandfather was as well. They used to joke that "ink was in their blood." One day, there might not even be any ink.

Some motivational clichés could be sprinkled into the morning and afternoon briefings, of course. But Andrea's never been the rah-rah type, and the pain of losing so many colleagues would likely cause such speechifying to fall on deaf ears. Maybe this is how encyclopedia salespeople felt, or typewriter manufacturers, once upon a time. Or maybe there's something Andrea could do to retain some of the meaning and "romanticism" in what the *Blaze* does. The paper has always been so focused on the day-by-day, issue-by-issue pressures of the job. Maybe it's missed some opportunities to do something larger for the town or the nearby campus.

YOUR TASK

Your task is to prepare a report for Andrea that lays out some potential courses of action to follow at the morning and afternoon briefings, as well as moving forward as the new course for the *Blaze* is charted. Be sure to provide not just specific recommendations, but also some thoughts that support those recommendations so that Andrea understands your reasoning. In particular, your report should touch on the following points.

1. Drawing on discussions of informational justice, how should Andrea approach the morning briefing? Should she be honest and informative in explaining corporate actions in the downsizing, or should she be more guarded?

2. How could job characteristics theory guide Andrea as she considers ways of combining areas for the staffers? Is there a way to give the new versions of their jobs a higher satisfaction potential than the pre-downsizing versions?

3. Assuming the staffers' personnel files have data on the Big Five, how could those data be used to inform the decisions about combining areas? What would be the profile of someone who could take on a lot more versus someone who can take on only a little more?

4. What advice would you give to Andrea in terms of her use of the bigger compensation budget? Would you give everyone a short-term "retention bonus" or a more permanent raise? Or would you leverage those funds to support the changes in the work structure, especially for those staffers with an especially expanded workload? What would be the difficulties associated with those two options?

5. How much voice and input would you recommend Andrea give to the staffers as the *Blaze* transitions to its "new normal"? What are the pluses of giving such input and what would be the dangers associated with it? How could those dangers be mitigated?

6. As you consider the broader challenges faced by the newspaper industry, what could Andrea do to maintain or restore the sense of meaning and significance that the *Blaze* staffers connect to their work?

Managing Commitment in Demanding Jobs

LEARNING GOALS

This case will allow you to explore the challenges of managing critical employees who work in demanding jobs. As the lead management analyst employed by a holding company, you're responsible for examining management practices at a newly acquired firm. More specifically, you'll be looking into some problems related to the retention of key employees in this company. The search for the root causes of the acquisition's problems will require consideration of several interrelated factors having to do with the way the work, and the way people doing the work, are managed. After reading the case, you'll prepare a report for your boss that describes your findings and recommendations.

KEY WORDS COVERED

- Organizational commitment
- Forced ranking
- Transactional theory of stress
- Stressors
- Emotional intelligence
- Team diversity
- Cohesion
- Groupthink

THE SITUATION

The Lorean Group, an international holding company, recently acquired a controlling interest in Tiger Advertising. This advertising agency, which employees 6,644 people worldwide, has been successful since its inception in 1964. Revenues over the past four years have been flat, however, and costs of running the business have been climbing steadily. Tiger was acquired in spite of this recent decline in profits because of its reputation in the industry and its extended list of loyal clients. Lorean has a history of turning around troubled acquisitions, and the belief is that Tiger can be saved as well.

The Lorean Group intends to let Tiger operate independently, though it seeks to understand the causes of the recent poor performance of the company. The Lorean Group recognizes that, although poor firm performance could be attributed to isolated incidents, most often there are systematic problems that require changes in practices and policies. You're a management analyst from Lorean, and your boss has given you the responsibility of analyzing the situation at Tiger and offering recommendations that will improve the firm's

financial performance and its long-term prospects. You travel to Tiger's corporate headquarters and plan to spend four days meeting with people to gather information that will inform your recommendations.

Your first meeting with the Tiger top management team went fairly well. The first thing that struck you was this: Although the team members are quite different from each other in obvious ways, beneath the surface there is remarkable similarity. Of the seven members who compose this team, three have been with the company since its inception. The four newer members are much younger and came to the company more recently in response to the firm's rapid growth, due mostly to international expansion that occurred between 2002 and 2007. Despite the differences in age, company tenure, and their functional and industry backgrounds, the members of this team seem to be cut from the same cloth in that each is very businesslike, analytical, hard driving, and results-focused.

In your discussion regarding the company's expansion, William Collins, one of the founders, remarked, "The expansion was tough for us because of all the pressure and uncertainty, and to be honest, we really didn't jell together initially—I thought it was a big mistake to grow so fast and bring new people on board to manage this ship—but now we're past all that, we're very cohesive, and we share the same vision of how we do business. This is a good thing because when I retire in a couple of years, I'll know the company's in good hands." Everyone in the room seemed to nod in agreement. Another founder, Russell "Rusty" Gee, then looked squarely into your eyes and added, "I'm not exactly sure what you're looking to do here, but we've weathered lots of storms together. Yes, we've had a couple of rough years, but we're more than capable of handling things ourselves—this was part of the deal, wasn't it? We know this place better than anyone, so I can't imagine we'll seriously consider any recommendations that'll upset the apple cart." Rusty made the statement in a friendly way with a smile on his face, yet you could tell he was very serious.

Although you learned many things during that first meeting, two things stood out that suggested a real problem. First, turnover among creative team associates at Tiger is high: 35 percent each year for the last two years and 30 percent the year before that. The industry average is less than 20 percent, and it is even lower in the top firms. Creative team associates are vital to Tiger's success, so this retention issue is a big problem. Because the company's business model centers on advertising design rather than production or media services, creative team associates constitute the company's technical core. Although the Tiger top management team seems aware of the problem, they seem to rationalize it. As Jamie Waggner, VP of human resources, noted, "We hire the best and the brightest, so it's only natural that they occasionally get poached by other firms. We try our best to keep them, but during the last few years we haven't had the ability to compete with the salaries they're being offered elsewhere. Once things turn around for us, we'll be able to solve the turnover issue."

You also learned the company has been sued three times recently. The cases involved associates who were passed over for promotion and who claimed that the work environment was so filled with stress that it made them ill and unable to work. Although you were aware of the first case because it was highly publicized, apparently Tiger went to great lengths to settle the two subsequent cases quickly before anything was disclosed. The first case was settled out of court as well, but not before it became an embarrassment to the company and its principals. You could tell from the tone of the conversation that the management team members are proud that they prevented word of the other two lawsuits from getting out. Before you have a chance to ask the question of whether anyone believes the turnover and lawsuits are related, Jamie volunteers the following. "We were really unlucky during that period. We hired three associates who didn't possess sufficient capabilities, and each had trouble coping in a way that would have led to better outcomes. Most everyone is drawn here because of the challenge inherent in the work that we do—we just have to do a better job in ruling out applicants who don't fit."

Your subsequent observations and discussions with the members of the creative teams did not reveal anything too far out of the norm as compared to other advertising agencies in terms of the immediate work context. Workload and time pressure are very high but not atypical for a large advertising agency. The creative teams typically include three to five associates and are led by a senior client manager, who makes final design decisions after receiving input from the members. Although in your initial meeting Jamie referred to the teams as being self-managed, the senior client managers function more like traditional supervisors in that they assign specific tasks to each member during the projects. Because the support staff is kept to a minimum at the firm to keep costs down, associates also have to take care of a lot the administrative duties. In return, however, the members of the creative teams get to work on some highly visible projects for some very well-known clients.

You also note that the creative teams have autonomy to work wherever and whenever they need to. This arrangement gives employees a lot of flexibility, and working odd hours in strange locations has resulted in some stories of which everyone in the company is familiar. As an example, you heard a story of a creative team dinner meeting in a private room at a local restaurant. When the restaurant closed, the senior client manager handed the owner $1,000 to let them stay and work, and the team stayed until the restaurant opened for lunch the next day. Although not everyone at the meeting was on-board with the idea initially, and in fact, one member had to leave because of a personal obligation, the team members came together and produced a very successful deliverable for one of the firm's largest clients. The senior manager who revealed this story did so with pride and remarked how it was a "fantastic team-building experience for those who chose to tough it out" and that it perfectly reflects the "company's 'work-hard, play-hard' mentality."

When you inquire about how the job performance of the creative associates is managed, you learn that toward the end of each calendar year, the senior client managers get together and spend an entire day on the evaluation process. The evaluations focus on the extent to which each associate contributed to the designs of the teams they worked on during the previous year. A list of all associates, ordered by their job performance scores, is generated. This list is then used to determine three categories, each of which is associated with some significant reward consequences. The top 10 percent get sizable bonuses, which typically amount to 50 percent of base pay, and are fast tracked to senior client manager. The next 30 percent get a 25 percent bonus and are considered "on-track" for promotion. The others get a small share of profit, but typically this amounts to 2 to 3 percent of their salary.

Bonus checks, and a letter explaining how the bonuses are distributed, are mailed to the associates' residential addresses at the beginning of the winter holiday. When you inquire about why the company distributes performance feedback this way, Jamie told you the following: "The associates work in teams and so they're understandably sensitive to differences in their bonuses. Although they're intended to send strong signals to the associates, we avoid bad feelings and conflict. By the time they get back from the holiday, it's not on their minds as much."

You had lunch with several senior client managers to gain their perspective on the company. Although this meeting started off well, they became a little defensive when the subject of the turnover and lawsuits came up. One remarked, "Around here, you're rewarded for paying your dues, for doing whatever it takes to deal with anything that gets thrown at you. Yes, it's demanding, and it requires sacrifice, but how else can we find out whether people have what it takes? Those of us sitting at this table with you are a product of this and it works—look at how successful we've been. We just can't tolerate hires who claim they can't take it or that it's abusive."

You also met with a group of creative team associates, and for the first time, you're exposed to a different perspective regarding what life is like at Tiger. As an example, one associate said, "I learned a lot from dealing with the pressure at the beginning, but the work is nonstop. They say it's "work-hard, play-hard," but even the play feels like work. Another associate chimed in, "The projects are great, but I never feel like I'm fully involved, I'm always on the periphery chipping in where I can." As a final example, a third associate stated,

"It's definitely sink-or-swim around here, that's for sure. It's easier for some people who get plugged-in with a manager right away, but I've never seemed to gain favor with any of them regardless of how many hours I put in. To top it off, the crazy hours are creating a lot of work–family conflict, and the strains are really adding up."

YOUR TASK

Your charge is to prepare a report for your boss that describes what you learned during your visit to Tiger. The report should begin with a description of Tiger Advertising and its current situation. The report should also describe the most important problems Tiger is confronted with, as well as the causes of those problems, in terms of OB concepts and theories. In your report, ensure you cover the following issues.

1. Describe the diversity that's present in Tiger's top management team. Discuss how the team's diversity likely affects its functioning and its effectiveness.

2. Describe signs that groupthink is present in Tiger's top management team. In what ways is this groupthink problematic? What can be done to overcome these problems?

3. Describe the primary sources of stress the creative associates are experiencing. Explain how some of these stressors have led to Tiger's problems while others have led to its success.

4. What is the underlying general premise that senior client managers seem to have regarding the stressful demands at Tiger, and in what ways is this premise problematic?

5. Why are the perceptions of the managers and creative associates so different with respect to the nature of Tiger's management practices and policies? What role could emotional intelligence play in ameliorating some of these differences?

6. Based on your analysis of Tiger, does the company need a minor "tune-up" in regard to its practices and policies, or is a major overhaul in order? What three recommendations would most likely resolve Tiger's problems with organizational commitment and potential future litigation?

Leading in a Hostile Environment

LEARNING GOALS

This case will help you learn to develop an action plan and evaluate multiple competing objectives during a complicated organizational period: a company merger. As a co-manager and confidant of a project manager tasked with bringing efficiency and a vision to a newly merged hospital system, you will be providing mentoring advice on how to approach a delicate situation and one that is sure to upset some employees. After reading the case, you'll prepare a memo that outlines your thoughts for how you would proceed as a leader tasked with creating a new culture that must come together quickly in order for the unit to survive.

KEYWORDS COVERED

- Task performance
- Affective commitment
- Trust
- Escalation of commitment
- Leadership
- Power
- Matrix structure
- Organizational culture

THE SITUATION

Sitting across the table, Colleen Brooks looked excited and yet discouraged at the same time. It seemed to be a strange combination of emotions, but it was a look you had come to recognize over recent weeks among managers you had grown to admire over the last few years. Colleen spoke somewhat softly, "I'm just not sure what I'm supposed to do here. I've been put into this position where I feel I can really make a difference in a lot of ways, but I also feel like the deck has been stacked against me. These people just don't trust us yet, and I'm not sure given the situation that I can blame them. It's partially their fault, though! Had Medical One run its business well to begin with, there's a good chance we wouldn't be here."

Medical One was the largest multispecialty health care practice in the northwest part of the United States. It had numerous regional clinics across several hospitals in seven states and employed more than 13,000 employees and 900 physicians in addition to running its own insurance plan. In many ways, Medical One would seem to outsiders as a model health care provider. Internally, though, Medical One was in severe financial distress. Cost overruns and bad planning had placed the company under a great deal of debt. This debt allowed Healthcare Plus, a much smaller (4,600 employees) but more financially sound practice operating throughout Arizona and New Mexico, to acquire Medical One by taking over and restructuring its financial situation.

Although health care mergers and acquisitions were becoming more and more common—with 243 deals totaling $73.5 billion taking place in the second quarter of 2011 alone—it didn't make the process any easier for those companies involved. The merger between Healthcare Plus and Medical One had many potential advantages but carried with it a certain amount of risk as well. There was great resentment among the employees of Medical One (some of whom had been with the company since its inception in 1992) that a smaller company could come along and just "purchase" them. Medical One had grown quickly and was known in its area of the country for providing extremely high-quality health care services. Everything they had read or heard through the grapevine about Healthcare Plus was oriented around cost-cutting and to most employees at Medical One, lower costs equated to lower-quality health care.

Colleen was not happy about the way management had decided to restructure the two companies following the merger. In order to try to get the best out of both companies—namely, Medicare One's customer service focus and Healthcare Plus's efficiency and cost containment—the top management team had decided to create a matrix structure to operate under going forward. For the most part, managers at Medical One would continue to report to the same functional directors they had before. However, each manager would now report and answer to another director as well. The "new" directors were supposed to be region-based efficiency experts. Colleen, who had been a highly successful manager of nursing in one of the largest Healthcare Plus clinics in Santa Fe, New Mexico, had been tapped as a new "Regional Director of Nursing Efficiency." "What a miserable job title!" Colleen thought when she originally heard the news. At the same time, this was a big promotion for her and the change would be very positive in many ways for her and her family.

Colleen's job was to oversee nursing operations in four states—New Mexico, Colorado, Utah, and Wyoming. Of the 14 nursing managers she was supposed to supervise, 11 of them were at Medical One facilities. (The company decided not to change the "Medical One" name after the merger for marketing and continued branding purposes.) Fundamentally, Colleen knew that the reasoning behind the new structure was to blend Healthcare Plus's management style and expertise with Medical One's scale of operations. Although upper management was trying to sell the acquisition to everyone inside the organization as a "merger" of two great companies, almost all of top management came from Healthcare Plus.

Colleen had decided that the first meeting with her new managers was an important one, and she decided to bring them all to Denver, which was a relatively central location but also where one of Medical One's largest hospitals operated. She took great care in personally phoning each manager, introducing herself, and letting them know that she was looking forward to working with them. Some of those managers were quiet and hesitant over the phone, but some seemed very open and receptive—even excited—about the possibility of working together to make things better. Sarah Stoneford, a nursing manager in Cheyenne, Wyoming, even told her that she had been waiting for something like this to happen because "the amount of waste I see around here on a daily basis would make anyone cringe in disbelief."

In order to make everyone feel more equal, Colleen had arranged for the meeting to take place in a Denver hotel. Having the meeting in the Denver hospital just seemed too constricting somehow—she wanted everyone to keep as open a mind as possible. Plus, Jim Liucci, the nursing manager at the Denver hospital, had already shared that his nursing director was not excited about the changes that were coming, and Colleen wanted him to feel comfortable in speaking to the group and not looking over his shoulder. While on the phone call with Jim, Colleen thought, "His operational director doesn't even know what changes are coming! How can she be upset about things that haven't even happened yet?" but she didn't want to say anything until she and Jim had the opportunity to meet in person.

Initially, getting together with everyone went extremely smoothly. All 14 managers had arrived on time the night before, and some had even eaten dinner together and hung out in the hotel bar getting to know one another better. Even though 11 of the managers had worked for Medical One, even occupying the same jobs, they had actually never met one another before. Colleen was pleasantly surprised to see all of them having a good time and being excited about meeting one another. When she laid her head on her pillow that night, Colleen thought to herself, "These people are thirsty for change! They recognize that Medical One has issues that need to be addressed and it's simply my goal to push them in the right direction toward accomplishing our objectives."

The next morning didn't go nearly as well. Every time Colleen mentioned a potential idea that had reduced costs effectively at Healthcare Plus, it was met with a "that will never work here" type of answer. After several rounds of this,

Colleen's frustration seemed to mount. When the Healthcare Plus managers tried to chime in with evidence that these types of procedures had worked for them in their facility, the Medical One managers seemed to form ranks. It wasn't until it was too late that Colleen noticed the three Healthcare Plus managers were all sitting together at the large U-shaped table, a seating arrangement that didn't seem to be helping things. At one point, Donna Mitchell, a Medical One nursing manager in from Provo, Utah, even went as far as to say, "I know that kind of stuff might work in New Mexico, but our patients expect a better level of care." Todd Rappen, a manager in Grand Junction, Colorado, was even bold enough to comment that if cost savings were such a big deal, why was the group paying to rent a hotel meeting room instead of using one of the Denver hospital's conference rooms? Colleen knew at that point that things had gone terribly wrong.

Although it was clear to Colleen that many of the managers were resistant to the ideas she discussed throughout the day, most of them placed the blame on their local nursing directors for their unwillingness to change. This allowed her new reports to be able to nod their heads in agreement personally, but introduce negative opinions without fear of recrimination. As the meeting closed, Colleen tried to assure the group that this was just the first step of many on a long road to making a successful situation for everyone. She tried to set an upbeat tone, but it was clear that many people had been upset by some of the things that were said during the meeting. There was definitely an "us vs. them" mentality as everyone left the room to catch flights or hop in their cars.

Colleen had just now begun to grasp the realities of not being in a location with her direct reports. There were many new things she would have to get used to—managing managers, managing remote individuals, managing people who also report directly to other managers they were more familiar with at their location—in essence, her job was to lead with seemingly very little power. What she wouldn't have to get used to, though, was upper management expecting her to make changes at these locations that would create bottom-line results in a short period of time. The good thing is that she had lots of experience doing just that. "I know that we have made many excellent changes at Healthcare Plus without sacrificing patient care—I just have to get others to open up to that idea," Colleen thought on the plane ride home.

As you listen to Colleen, it becomes apparent to you that she is beginning to question her ability to be able to do this new job effectively. Although you have been in leadership development training programs together, the fact is that leadership is much easier when things are going well for a company. Although there are many potential areas of improvement for the new company going forward, it's clear the road is going to be difficult. Colleen's voice suddenly lowered as she started to pack up her things, "Look, I asked you here today to be a sounding board of sorts, but the truth is I could really use your advice. I don't need an answer right now, but if you could give me your thoughts on things I could do to be a better leader at this point I would appreciate it. You've always given me good advice in the past."

YOUR TASK

Your task as a leadership mentor to Colleen is to prepare a memo that lays out your thoughts on her situation and some specific courses of action she should consider as she attempts to start leading her new group. Make sure to give her a memo with enough detail so that she understands the reasoning behind your recommendations. Also keep in mind the order in which she should follow these steps. In particular, your memo should touch on the following points.

1. Drawing on what you know about leadership, what types of behaviors are going to be most important for Colleen as she begins to interact with her new direct reports. Should these behaviors change over time?

2. What kinds of power can Colleen use to try to influence others to adopt some efficiency related procedures?

Are there certain types of influence behaviors that will be more effective than others given the difficult circumstances?

3. It's clear that the two companies have very different cultures even though they are both health care providers. Should one culture be stressed over the other? Will this affect the way Colleen should lead the group?

4. What does Colleen have going for her in terms of getting others to trust her? Are there certain things she should do or say to generate that trust as well as maintain it over time?

5. How does the new structure affect Colleen's ability to lead? It would be useful to detail some of the pros and cons Colleen will likely face given how things have been organized.

6. Should Colleen focus more on her direct reports' performance or organizational commitment? Will she exhibit different behaviors based on that choice? What are the advantages to focusing on one or the other?

Note: **Bold** page numbers indicate glossary terms that are highlighted in the text.

A

Ability, Relatively stable capabilities of people for performing a particular range of related activities. **203**, 306–307, **308**, 309–331
    cognitive. *See* **Cognitive abilities**
    emotional intelligence, 310, 314–320, 387
    in hiring process, 325–327
    importance of, 324–325
    meaning of, 203, 308–309, 323
    physical, 310, 320–323, 354–355
    team member, 354–355

Ability to focus The degree to which employees can devote their attention to work. **220**

Absenteeism, 75–76, 83

Abuse Employee assault or endangerment from which physical and psychological injuries may occur. **44**

Abusive supervision The sustained display of hostile verbal and nonverbal behaviors on the part of supervisors, excluding physical contact. **208**

Accommodating A conflict resolution style by which one party gives in to the other and acts in a completely unselfish way. **425**, 426

Accomplishment striving A strong desire to accomplish task-related goals as a means of expressing one's personality. **273**

Action learning Team process training in which a team has the opportunity to work on an actual problem within the organization. **397**

Action processes Teamwork processes, such as helping and coordination, that aid in the accomplishment of teamwork as the work is actually taking place. 383, **384**

Action teams A team of limited duration that performs complex tasks in contexts that tend to be highly visible and challenging. 342, **343**–344

Activation The degree to which moods are aroused and active, as opposed to unaroused and inactive. **108**

Active management-by-exception When the leader arranges to monitor mistakes and errors actively and takes corrective action when required. **457**, 458

Adaptability
    adaptive task performance, 34–35
    behaviors involved in, 35
    in socialization process, 522–523

Adaptive task performance Thoughtful responses by an employee to unique or unusual task demands. **34**–35

Additive tasks Tasks for which the contributions from every member add up to determine team performance. **355**

Adjourning The final stage of team development, during which members experience anxiety and other emotions as they disengage and ultimately separate from the team. 345, **346**

Advancement/promotion, 83

Affect management, 384

Affect-based trust Trust that depends on feelings toward the authority that go beyond rational assessment. **200**, 204–205, 219

Affective commitment, An employee's desire to remain a member of an organization due to a feeling of emotional attachment. **65**, 66–69
    assessing, 68
    job satisfaction and, 113
    Leading in a Hostile Environment (case), 546–548
    Reenergizing Employees After a Downsizing (case), 540–542
    strategies to improve, 82

Affective events theory A theory that describes how workplace events can generate emotional reactions that impact work behaviors. **110**

African Americans
    diversity of workforce, 79
    relative compensation of, 207

Aggressor role, 353, 354

Agreeableness One of the "Big Five" dimensions of personality reflecting traits like being kind, cooperative, sympathetic, helpful, courteous, and warm. **269**–275, 355, 358

All channel network structure, 388, 389

Alternative dispute resolution A process by which two parties resolve conflicts through the use of a specially trained, neutral third party. **432**

Ambassador activities Boundary-spanning activities that are intended to protect the team, persuade others to support the team, or obtain important resources for the team. **383**

Analytics The use of data (rather than just opinions) to guide decision making. **21**

Anchoring bias, 250

Anticipatory stage A stage of socialization that begins as soon as a potential employee develops an image of what it would be like to work for a company. **521**

Apathetics Employees with low commitment levels and low task performance levels who exert the minimum amount of effort needed to keep their jobs. **74**

Apparent sincerity, 422

Apprising An influence tactic in which the requestor clearly explains why performing the request will benefit the target personally. **419**–420

Arbitration A process by which a third party determines a binding settlement to a dispute between two parties. **432**

ASA framework A theory (attraction–selection–attrition) that states that employees will be drawn to organizations with cultures that match their personality, organizations will select employees that match, and employees will leave or be forced out when they are not a good fit. **521**, 522

Asians
    biases in placing responsibility, 252
    diversity of workforce, 79, 286

Assessments
    of affective commitment, 68
    Big Five, 269–281, 287–290
    of centralization, 489
    of cognitive abilities, 310–314, 318–322, 325–328
    of cohesion, 391
    of core job characteristics, 107
    of creativity culture, 519
    of emotional intelligence, 318–320
    of goal orientation, 243
    of helping behavior, 40
    of initiating structure and consideration, 454
    of introspection, 23

Assessments—*Cont.*
    of the meaning of money, 171
    Myers-Briggs Type Indicator (MBTI),
       281–282
    personality tests, 289–292
    of political skill, 423
    of team interdependence, 347
    of trust propensity, 201
    of Type A Behavior Pattern, 140
    of values, 97–98

**Attraction-selection-attrition (ASA)
framework,** *See* **ASA framework**

Auditory attention, 322

Autocratic style A leadership style where the leader makes the decision alone without asking for opinions or suggestions of the employees in the work unit. **448,** 463

Autonomy The degree to which a job allows individual freedom and discretion regarding how the work is to be done. 103, **105**

Availability bias The tendency for people to base their judgments on information that is easier to recall. **249**

Avoiding A conflict resolution style by which one party wants to remain neutral, stay away from conflict, or postpone the conflict to gather information or let things cool down. **424**–426

B

Baby Boomers, 79

Bargaining The third stage of the negotiation process, during which each party gives and takes to arrive at an agreement. **429**

    distributive, 427
    integrative, 427–428

Basic underlying assumptions The ingrained beliefs and philosophies of employees. 511, **514**–515

BATNA A negotiator's best alternative to a negotiated agreement. **429**

Behavior modeling training A formalized method of training in which employees observe and learn from employees with significant amounts of tacit knowledge. **256**–257

Behavioral coping Physical activities used to deal with a stressful situation. **135**–137

Behavioral modeling When employees observe the actions of others, learn from what they observe, and then repeat the observed behavior. **241**–242

Behavioral strain, 138, 139

Behaviorally anchored rating scales (BARS) Use of examples of critical incidents to evaluate an employee's job performance behaviors directly. **49,** 50

Benevolence The belief that an authority wants to do good for an employee, apart from any selfish or profit-centered motives. **203**

Benign job demands Job demands that are not appraised as being stressful. **130**

Biases
    availability, 249
    cultural differences and, 252
    decision-making, 250
    negotiator, 429
    projection, 248–249
    self-serving, 250

Big Five, The five major dimensions of personality including conscientiousness, agreeableness, neuroticism, openness to experience, and extraversion. **269**–281, 287–290

    agreeableness, 269–275, 355, 358
    changes over life span, 270, 272
    conscientiousness, 269–273, 281,
       287–289, 355
    cultural values and, 283
    extraversion, 269–272, 275, 277, 281,
       356, 358
    in hiring process, 289–290
    importance of personality traits, 287–289
    neuroticism, 269–272, 275–278
    openness to experience, 269–272, 278–281
    Reenergizing Employees After a
       Downsizing (case), 540–542
    well-validated measures of, 290

Biofeedback, 149

Blocker role, 353

Bonuses, 186, 187, 361

Boosterism Positively representing the organization when in public. **39**

Boundary spanning Interactions among team members and individuals and groups who are not part of the team. 379, **383**

Bounded rationality The notion that people do not have the ability or resources to process all available information and alternatives when making a decision. **246**–248

Brainstorming A team process used to generate creative ideas. **379**–380

Bullying, 44

Bureaucratic structures An organizational form that exhibits many of the facets of a mechanistic organization. **493**–498
    functional, 493–495, 496
    geographic, 495–497
    matrix, 497–498, 546–548 (case)
    multi-divisional, 494, 495
    product, 495

Burnout The emotional, mental, and physical exhaustion from coping with stressful demands on a continuing basis. **139**

Business environment The outside environment, including customers, competitors, suppliers, and distributors, which all have an impact on organizational design. **490**–491

C

Cases

    Leading in a Hostile Environment,
       546–548
    Managing Commitment in Demanding
       Jobs, 543–545
    Reenergizing Employees After a
       Downsizing, 540–542

Causal inference The establishment that one variable does cause another, based on covariation, temporal precedence, and the elimination of alternative explanations. **20**

Centrality How important a person's job is and how many people depend on that person to accomplish their tasks. **417,** 418

Centralization Refers to where decisions are formally made in organizations. 388, 484, **487**–489

Ceremonies Formal events, generally performed in front of an audience of organizational members. **513**

Chain of command Answer to the question of "who reports to whom?" and signifies formal authority relationships. 484, 485

Challenge stressors Stressors that tend to be appraised as opportunities for growth and achievement. **131**
    job performance and, 144
    nonwork, 134
    organizational commitment and, 144
    reducing, 147–149
    work, 132, 144

Charisma, 458, 460

Chief executive officers (CEOs)

compensation of, 178–180, 207
modeling by, 242
trust and, 198–199, 220–221

Circle network structure, 388, 389

Citizens Employees with high commitment levels and low task performance levels who volunteer to do additional activities around the office. **73**–74

Citizenship behavior, Voluntary employee behaviors that contribute to organizational goals by improving the context in which work takes place. **38**–41

in corporate social responsibility, 222
cultural differences in, 42
interpersonal, 38–39
job satisfaction and, 113
motivation and, 184
organizational, 39
organizational culture and, 528–529
relevance of, 40–41
trust and, 221

Civic virtue Participation in company operations at a deeper-than-normal level through voluntary meetings, readings, and keeping up with news that affects the company. **39**

Civility training programs, 210

Clear purpose tests Integrity tests that ask about attitudes toward dishonesty, beliefs about the frequency of dishonesty, desire to punish dishonesty, and confession of past dishonesty. **290**–291

Client structure An organizational form in which employees are organized around serving customers. **497**

Climate for transfer An organizational environment that supports the use of new skills. **256**–257

Closing and commitment The fourth and final stage of the negotiation process, during which the agreement arrived at during bargaining gets formalized. **429**

Coalitions An influence tactic in which the influencer enlists other people to help influence the target. 419, **420**

Coercive power A form of organizational power based on the ability to hand out punishment. 413, **415**, 417

Cognition-based trust Trust that is rooted in a rational assessment of the authority's trustworthiness. **200**, 202–203, 205, 220

Cognitive abilities, Capabilities related to the use of knowledge to make decisions and solve problems. **309**–314

assessing, 310–314, 318–322, 325–327, 328
cognitive cultural intelligence, 310
general, 311, 313–314, 324–325
in hiring process, 325–327
importance of, 324–325
job performance and, 324–326
organizational commitment and, 324–325
perceptual, 311, 313
quantitative, 311, 312
reasoning, 311, 312–313
spatial, 311, 313
team member, 355
verbal, 310–311

Cognitive coping Thoughts used to deal with a stressful situation. **135**–137

Cognitive distortion A reevaluation of the inputs an employee brings to a job, often occurring in response to equity distress. **178**

Cognitive moral development As people age and mature, they move through several states of moral development, each more mature and sophisticated than the prior one. **215**–217, 218

Cognitive-behavioral techniques, 150

Cohesion A team state that occurs when members of the team develop strong emotional bonds to other members of the team and to the team itself. **390**, 391
Managing Commitment in Demanding Jobs (case), 543–545

Collaboration Seen as both a conflict resolution style and an influence tactic whereby both parties work together to maximize outcomes. **419**, 421, **425**, 426
collaborative problem solving as team competency, 396

Commitment. *See* **Organizational commitment**

Communal culture An organizational culture type in which employees are friendly to one another and all think alike. **515**

Communication The process by which information and meaning is transferred from a sender to a receiver. 9, **386**–389
ambassador activities, 383
communicator issues, 386–387
information richness in, 387–388
in integrative model of OB, 9
model of communication process, 386, 387

network structure, 388–389
noise in, 387
as team process, 376, 386–389, 392, 396

Communication competence, 386–387

Communion striving A strong desire to obtain acceptance in personal relationships as a means of expressing one's personality. **273**

Communities of practice Groups of employees who learn from one another through collaboration over an extended period of time. **256**

Company size The number of employees in a company. **492**

Company strategy An organization's objectives and goals and how it tries to capitalize on its assets to make money. **491**–492

Comparison other Another person who provides a frame of reference for judging equity. **176**, 178, 179

Compensation systems

CEO pay in, 178–180, 207
elements of, 185–187
meaning of money and, 169–170, 171
motivation and, 168–171, 178–180, 185–187, 210–211
pay freezes and cuts, 168, 187, 210–211
pay satisfaction, 97, 98
procedural justice and, 207
reward power, 413, 414–415, 417
task performance and, 38
team compensation, 361–362
types of, 186, 187

Compensatory forms model A model indicating that the various withdrawal behaviors are negatively correlated; engaging in one type of withdrawal makes one less likely to engage in other types. **77**

Competence The capability to perform work tasks successfully. **180**–181
communication, 386–387

Competing A conflict resolution style by which one party attempts to get his or her own goals met without concern for the other party's results. **424**–426

Compliance When targets of influence are willing to do what the leader asks but do it with a degree of ambivalence. **421**

Comprehensive interdependence A form of task interdependence in which team members have a great deal of discretion in terms of what they do and with whom they interact in the course of the collaboration involved in accomplishing the team's work. **349**

Compromise A conflict resolution style by which conflict is resolved through give-and-take concessions. 425–426

Compromiser role, 352–353

Confidence building, 384

Conflict resolution

alternative dispute resolution, 432
conflict management and, 384–386
leader style and, 424–427
power and, 424–427
as team competency, 396

Conjunctive tasks Tasks for which the team's performance depends on the abilities of the team's weakest link. 355

Conscientiousness One of the "Big Five" dimensions of personality reflecting traits like being dependable, organized, reliable, ambitious, hardworking, and persevering. 269–273, 281, 287–289, 355

Consensus Used by decision makers to attribute cause; whether other individuals behave the same way under similar circumstances. 251, 381

Consideration A pattern of behavior where the leader creates job relationships characterized by mutual trust, respect for employee ideas, and consideration of employee feelings. 452–454, 464

Consistency Used by decision makers to attribute cause; whether this individual has behaved this way before under similar circumstances. 251

Consultation An influence tactic whereby the target is allowed to participate in deciding how to carry out or implement a request. 419, 421

Consultative style A leadership style where the leader presents the problem to employees asking for their opinions and suggestions before ultimately making the decision himself or herself. 448, 463

Contingencies of power, 416–418

Contingencies of reinforcement Four specific consequences used by organizations to modify employee behavior. 239–240

Contingent reward When the leader attains follower agreement on what needs to be done using rewards in exchange for adequate performance. 457–458

Continuance commitment, An employee's desire to remain a member of an organization due to an awareness of the costs of leaving. 65–67, 69–71
embeddedness and, 70–71
job satisfaction and, 114
strategies to improve, 83

Continuous reinforcement A specific consequence follows each and every occurrence of a certain behavior. 240

Contrast, 250

Control movement abilities, 322

Conventional stage of moral development (Kohlberg), 216

Coordination The quality of physical movement in terms of synchronization of movements and balance. 322, 384
task interdependence and, 348, 353

Coordination loss Process loss due to the time and energy it takes to coordinate work activities with other team members. 378

Coordinator role, 353

Coping Behaviors and thoughts used to manage stressful demands and the emotions associated with the stressful demands. 135
with stressors, 135–137
types of, 135–137

Corporate social responsibility A perspective that acknowledges that the responsibility of a business encompasses the economic, legal, ethical, and citizenship expectations of society. 221–222

Correlation The statistical relationship between two variables. Abbreviated *r*, it can be positive or negative and range from 0 (no statistical relationship) to 1 (a perfect statistical relationship). 18–21

Countercultures When a subculture's values do not match those of the organization. 520

Counterproductive behavior, Employee behaviors that intentionally hinder organizational goal accomplishment. 41–44
emotional intelligence and, 318
job satisfaction and, 113
motivation and, 184
personal aggression, 44
political deviance, 43–44
production deviance, 43
property deviance, 41–43, 210–211, 290–291
substance abuse, 43, 45
trust and, 221

Courtesy Sharing important information with coworkers. 39

Coworker satisfaction Employees' feelings about their coworkers, including their abilities and personalities. 97, 100

Creative task performance The degree to which individuals develop ideas or physical outcomes that are both novel and useful. 35–36

Creativity
creative behavior as taskwork process, 379–381
in creative task performance, 35–36
innovators and, 35–36, 318
openness to experience and, 269–272, 278–281
originality and, 312–313

Creativity culture A specific culture type focused on fostering a creative atmosphere. 517–519

CREW (Civility, Respect, and Engagement in the Workplace) program, 210

Crisis situation A change—sudden or evolving—that results in an urgent problem that must be addressed immediately. 244

Critical incidents, 49

Cross-cultural organizational behavior, 11

Cross-training Training team members in the duties and responsibilities of their teammates. 395–396

Cultural values, Shared beliefs about desirable end states or modes of conduct in a given culture that influence the expression of traits. 9, 268, 283–289
Hofstede's taxonomy and, 283–284, 285
importance of, 287–289
in integrative model of OB, 9
job performance and, 287–289
motivation and, 287–289
muticultural personality questionnaire, 286
organizational commitment and, 287–289
Project GLOBE (Global Leadership and Organizational Behavior Effectiveness), 284–285, 459
trust propensity, 202

Culture The shared values, beliefs, motives, identities, and interpretations that result from common experiences of members of a society and are transmitted across generations. 283
motivation and, 176, 182

Culture strength The degree to which employees agree about how things should happen within the organization and behave accordingly. **518–520**

Customer service culture A specific culture type focused on service quality. **516**

Cyberloafing, 74–75

D

Daily hassles Minor day-to-day demands that interfere with work accomplishment. **131**

Daydreaming, 74

Decision informity The degree to which team members possess adequate information about their own task responsibilities. **381, 382–383**

Decision making The process of generating and choosing from a set of alternatives to solve a problem. 9, **236,** 244–255
   centralization and, 489
   escalation of commitment in, 251–252, 546–548 (case)
   faulty attributions in, 249–251
   faulty perceptions in, 248–250
   general cognitive ability and, 325
   groupthink in, 390
   in integrative model of OB, 9
   leader styles of, 447–451
   limited information in, 246–248
   nonprogrammed decisions, 245, 246
   programmed decisions, 244–246
   rational decision-making model, 244–246, 248
   as taskwork process, 379, 381–383
   variations in, 236–237, 254–255

Decoding, 386, 387

Deductive reasoning, 312

Deep-level diversity Diversity of attributes that are inferred through observation or experience, such as one's values or personality. **357–358**

Delegating When the leader turns responsibility for key behaviors over to employees. **455**

Delegative style A leadership style where the leader gives the employee the responsibility for making decisions within some set of specified boundary conditions. **449,** 463

Deontological principles, 216–217

Depth perception, 322

Devil's advocate role, 351, 353, 390

Differential exposure Being more likely to appraise day-to-day situations as stressful, thereby feeling that stressors are encountered more frequently. **276**

Differential reactivity Being less likely to believe that one can cope with the stressors experienced on a daily basis. **276**

Discretion The degree to which managers have the right to make decisions on their own. **417,** 418

Disjunctive tasks Tasks with an objectively verifiable best solution for which the member with the highest level of ability has the most influence on team effectiveness. **355**

Disposition-based trust Trust that is rooted in one's own personality, as opposed to a careful assessment of the trustee's trustworthiness. **200**–202, 205, 219

Distinctiveness Used by decision makers to attribute cause; whether the person being judged acts in a similar fashion under different circumstances. **251**

Distributive bargaining A negotiation strategy in which one person gains and the other person loses. **427**

Distributive justice The perceived fairness of decision-making outcomes. **205–206,** 208

Diversity culture A specific culture type focused on fostering or taking advantage of a diverse group of employees. **517**
   in integrative model of OB, 9
   managing, 11
   organizational commitment and, 79
   team diversity in, 353, 356–358, 382, 543–545 (case)

Dominator role, 353, 354

Downsizing
   employee-employer relationship and, 79–81
   Reenergizing Employees After a Downsizing (case), 540–542
   in restructuring process, 500–501

Dynamic flexibility, 322

Dynamic strength, 320

E

Economic exchange Work relationships that resemble a contractual agreement by which employees fulfill job duties in exchange for financial compensation. **221**

Egoism, 217, 218

E-mail
   emotions of sender in, 388
   firing employees via, 210
   lying in, 203
   virtual teams and, 344–345, 389

Embeddedness An employee's connection to and sense of fit in the organization and community. **70–71**

Emotion(s), Intense feelings, often lasting for a short duration, that are clearly directed at someone or some circumstance. **110–111**
   in communication process, 387, 388
   negative, 110–111, 114
   positive, 110–111, 112–113, 114
   use of, 317

Emotion regulation The ability to recover quickly from emotional experiences. **316–317**

Emotional contagion The idea that emotions can be transferred from one person to another. **111**

Emotional cues Positive or negative feelings that can help or hinder task accomplishment. **167**

Emotional intelligence, A set of abilities related to the understanding and use of emotions that affect social functioning. 310, 314, **315–320**
   applying, 317–318
   assessing, 318–320
   in communication process, 387
   emotion regulation, 316–317
   Managing Commitment in Demanding Jobs (case), 543–545
   other awareness, 316
   self-awareness, 316
   use of emotions, 317

Emotional labor When employees manage their emotions to complete their job duties successfully. **111**

Emotional Quotient Inventory (EQ-i), 320

Emotional support The empathy and understanding that people receive from others that can be used to alleviate emotional distress from stressful demands. **141**

Emotion-focused coping Behaviors and cognitions of an individual intended to help manage emotional reactions to stressful demands. **135–137**

Employee assistance programs, 150

Encoding, 386, 387

Encounter stage A stage of socialization beginning the day an employee starts work, during which the employee compares the information as an outsider to the information learned as an insider. **521**–522

Encourager role, 352, 353

Energizer role, 351, 353

Engagement A term commonly used in the contemporary workplace to summarize motivation levels. **165**

Equal employment opportunity, 207

Equity distress An internal tension that results from being overrewarded or underrewarded relative to some comparison other. **176**–178

Equity theory, A theory that suggests that employees create a mental ledger of the outcomes they receive for their job inputs, relative to some comparison other. **175**–180
    comparison other in, 176, 178, 179
    equity distress in, 176–178
    outcomes and inputs in, 177
    Reenergizing Employees After a
        Downsizing (case), 540–542

Erosion model A model that suggests that employees with fewer bonds with coworkers are more likely to quit the organization. **69**

Escalation of commitment A common decision-making error in which the decision maker continues to follow a failing course of action. **251**–252, 546–548 (case)
    Leading in a Hostile Environment (case),
        546–548

Espoused values The beliefs, philosophies, and norms that a company explicitly states. 511, **514**

Ethics, The degree to which the behaviors of an authority are in accordance with generally accepted moral norms. 9, **199**, 212–219
    in corporate social responsibility, 221–222
    four-component model of, 212, 214
    in integrative model of OB, 9
    moral awareness in, 212–215
    moral intent in, 217–218
    moral judgment in, 215–218
    prescriptive versus descriptive, 212

Ethics of duties, 217, 218

Ethics of rights, 217, 218

Ethnocentrism One who views his or her cultural values as "right" and values of other cultures as "wrong." **285**, 286

Evidence-based management A perspective that argues that scientific findings should form the foundation for management education. **21**

Exchange tactic An influence tactic in which the requestor offers a reward in return for performing a request. **419**

Exchanging information The second stage of the negotiation process, during which each party makes the strongest case for its position. **429**

Exit A response to a negative work event by which one becomes often absent from work or voluntarily leaves the organization. **72**

Expatriates
    behavior modeling training for, 256
    challenges faced by, 11
    ethnocentrism of, 286
    organizational commitment and, 80, 136
    stress faced by, 136

Expectancy The belief that exerting a high level of effort will result in successful performance on some task. **166**–171, 183

Expectancy theory, A theory that describes the cognitive process employees go through to make choices among different voluntary responses. **166**–171
    expectancy in, 166–167, 170–171, 183
    instrumentality in, 166, 167–168, 170–171,
        183, 187
    motivational force in, 170–171
    valence in, 168–171, 183

Expert power A form of organizational power based on expertise or knowledge. 413, **415**, 417

Expertise The knowledge and skills that distinguish experts from novices. **237**, 254

Explicit knowledge Knowledge that is easily communicated and available to everyone. **237**, 238

Explosive strength, 320

Extent flexibility, 320–322

External comparisons Comparing oneself to someone in a different company. **178**

External locus of control, 276–278, 279

Extinction The removal of a positive outcome following an unwanted behavior. **240**

Extraversion One of the "Big Five" dimensions of personality reflecting traits like being talkative, sociable, passionate, assertive, bold, and dominant. **269**, 272, 275, 277, 281, 356, 358

Extrinsic motivation Desire to put forth work effort due to some contingency that depends on task performance. **169**, 170

F

Facilitative style A leadership style where the leader presents the problem to a group of employees and seeks consensus on a solution, making sure that his or her own opinion receives no more weight than anyone else's. **448**–449, 463

Faking Exaggerating responses to a personality test in a socially desirable fashion. **291**–292

Family time demands The amount of time committed to fulfilling family responsibilities. **134**

Far vision, 322

Fault lines, 357

Faulty attributions, 249–251

Faulty perceptions, 248–250

Feedback In job characteristics theory, it refers to the degree to which the job itself provides information about how well the job holder is doing. In goal setting theory, it refers to progress updates on work goals. **105**, **173**
    360-degree feedback, 49–50
    cultural differences in, 176
    in goal setting theory, 173
    information richness and, 387–388
    in job characteristics theory, 103, 105

Financial uncertainty Uncertainties with regard to the potential for loss of livelihood, savings, or the ability to pay expenses. **134**

Fine manipulative abilities, 322

Fixed interval schedule Reinforcement occurs at fixed time periods. **240**

Fixed ratio schedule Reinforcement occurs following a fixed number of desired behaviors. 240, **241**

Flat span of control, 482, 485–486

Flexibility The ability to bend, stretch, twist, or reach. **320**–322

Flextime, 148

Flow A state in which employees feel a total immersion in the task at hand, sometimes losing track of how much time has passed. **109**–110

Focus of commitment The people, places, and things that inspire a desire to remain a member of an organization. **66**–67

Follower role, 353

Forced ranking A performance management system in which managers rank subordinates relative to one another. 50–**51**
  Managing Commitment in Demanding Jobs (case), 543–545

Formalization The degree to which rules and procedures are used to standardize behaviors and decisions in an organization. 484, **488**

Forming The first stage of team development, during which members try to get a feel for what is expected of them, what types of behaviors are out of bounds, and who's in charge. **345**–346

Four-component model A model that argues that ethical behaviors result from the multistage sequence of moral awareness, moral judgment, moral intent, and ethical behavior. **212**, 214

Fragmented culture An organizational culture type in which employees are distant and disconnected from one another. **515**

Framing, 250

Functional structure An organizational form in which employees are grouped by the functions they perform for the organization. **493**–496

Fundamental attribution error The tendency for people to judge others' behaviors as being due to internal factors such as ability, motivation, or attitudes. **250**, 251

G

Gainsharing, 186

Gatekeeper-expediter role, 353

General cognitive ability The general level of cognitive ability that plays an important role in determining the more narrow cognitive abilities. 311, **313**–314, 324–325

Geographic structure An organizational form in which employees are grouped around the different locations where the company does business. **495**–496

Goal commitment The degree to which a person accepts a goal and is determined to reach it. **174**–175

Goal interdependence The degree to which team members have a shared goal and align their individual goals with that vision. **349**–351

Goal orientation
  assessing, 243
  in learning process, 242–244

Goal setting theory A theory that views goals as the primary drivers of the intensity and persistence of effort. 171, **172**–175
  components of, 172–175
  S.M.A.R.T. goals, 175, 184
  specific and difficult goals, 172–173, 186

Goal specification, 384

Gossiping Casual conversations about other people in which the facts are not confirmed as true. **43**–44

Graduate Management Admission Test (GMAT), 325

Gross body coordination, 322

Gross body equilibrium, 322

Group decision support systems, 382

Groupthink Behaviors that support conformity and team harmony at the expense of other team priorities. **390**
  Managing Commitment in Demanding Jobs (case), 543–545

Growth need strength The degree to which employees desire to develop themselves further. **105**, 106

H

Happiness, assessing, 116

Harassment Unwanted physical contact or verbal remarks from a colleague. **44**

Harmonizer role, 352, 353

Health. *See also* **Stress**
  health and wellness programs, 150
  health care costs, 145

Hearing, 322–323

Hearing sensitivity, 322

Helping Assisting coworkers who have heavy workloads, aiding them with personal matters, and showing new employees the ropes when they are first on the job. **39**, 40

Helping behavior, 384

Heuristics Simple and efficient rules of thumb that allow one to make decisions more easily. **249**

Hierarchical sensitivity The degree to which the team leader effectively weighs the recommendations of the members. **381**–383

Hierarchy of authority, 489

High-performance work practices, 13–15

Hindrance stressors Stressors that tend to be appraised as thwarting progress toward growth and achievement. **130**
  job performance and, 143
  nonwork, 132–134
  organizational commitment and, 143
  reducing, 147–149
  work, 131, 143

Hiring process
  applying emotional intelligence in, 317
  personality tests in, 289–292
  selecting high cognitive ability employees, 325–327

Hispanics, diversity of workforce, 79

History A collective pool of experience, wisdom, and knowledge created by people that benefits the organization. **12**

Hogan Personality Inventory (HPI), 290

Holocracy, 482, 502–503

Human resource management Field of study that focuses on the applications of OB theories and principles in organizations. **7**

Hybrid outcome interdependence When team members receive rewards based on both their individual performance and that of the team to which they belong. **361**–362

Hypotheses Written predictions that specify relationships between variables. **18**

I

Idealized influence When the leader behaves in ways that earn the admiration, trust, and respect of followers, causing followers to want to identify with and emulate the leader. **458,** 461, 462

Identity The degree to which a job offers completion of a whole, identifiable piece of work. 103, **104**

Impact The sense that a person's actions "make a difference"—that progress is being made toward fulfilling some important purpose. **181**–182

Incivility Communication that is rude, impolite, discourteous, and lacking in good manners. **43**–44

Independent forms model A model that predicts that the various withdrawal behaviors are uncorrelated; engaging in one type of withdrawal has little bearing on engaging in other types. **77**

Individualism-collectivism The degree to which a culture has a loosely knit social framework (individualism) or a tight social framework (collectivism). **284**

Individualistic roles Behaviors that benefit the individual at the expense of the team. 353, **354**

Individualized consideration When the leader behaves in ways that help followers achieve their potential through coaching, development, and mentoring. **460,** 462

Inductive reasoning, 312

Influence The use of behaviors to cause behavioral or attitudinal changes in others. **418**
    conflict resolution and, 424–427
    importance of, 431–432
    organizational politics and, 422–424
    power and, 413, 418–421
    resistance to, 413, 421
    responses to influence tactics, 421
    types of influence tactics, 418–421

Information richness The amount and depth of information that is transmitted in a message. **387**–388

Informational justice The perceived fairness of the communications provided to employees from authorities. 206, **210**–211

Reenergizing Employees After a Downsizing (case), 540–542

Ingratiation The use of favors, compliments, or friendly behavior to make the target feel better about the influencer. **419**

Inimitable Incapable of being imitated or copied. **12**

Initial public offerings (IPOs), 13–14

Initiating structure A pattern of behavior where the leader defines and structures the roles of employees in pursuit of goal attainment. **452**–454, 464

Initiator-contributor role, 353

Inspirational appeals An influence tactic designed to appeal to one's values and ideals, thereby creating an emotional or attitudinal reaction. **419,** 421

Inspirational motivation When the leader behaves in ways that foster an enthusiasm for and commitment to a shared vision of the future. **460**–462

Instrumental support The help people receive from others that can be used to address a stressful demand directly. **141**

Instrumentality The belief that successful performance will result in the attainment of some outcomes. 166, **167**–168, 170–171, 183, 187

Integrative bargaining A negotiation strategy that achieves an outcome that is satisfying for both parties. **427**–428

Integrity The perception that an authority adheres to a set of acceptable values and principles. **203**

Integrity tests Personality tests that focus specifically on a predisposition to engage in theft and other counterproductive behaviors (sometimes also called "honesty tests"). **290**–292

Intellectual stimulation When the leader behaves in ways that challenge followers to be innovative and creative by questioning assumptions and reframing old situations in new ways. **460,** 461, 462

Interdependence, 346–351

    assessing, 347
    goal, 349–351
    outcome, 351, 361–362
    task, 346–349, 353

Interests Expressions of personality that influence behavior through preferences for certain environments and activities. **282**

Internal comparisons Comparing oneself to someone in the same company. **178**

Internal locus of control, 277–279

Internalization A response to influence tactics where the target agrees with and becomes committed to the request. **421**

International corporations. *See* Organizational Behavior (OB) Internationally

Interpersonal citizenship behavior Going beyond normal job expectations to assist, support, and develop coworkers and colleagues. **38**–39

Interpersonal influence, 422

Interpersonal justice The perceived fairness of the interpersonal treatment received by employees from authorities. 206, **208**–211

Interpersonal processes Teamwork processes, such as motivating and confidence building, that focus on the management of relationships among team members. 383, **384**–386

Intrinsic motivation Desire to put forth work effort due to the sense that task performance serves as its own reward. **169,** 170

Introspection, 23

Introversion, 277

Intuition An emotional judgment based on quick, unconscious, gut feelings. **244**–246
    method of intuition, 16–17

IQ tests, 310, 313–314, 318–319, 326

J

Job analysis A process by which an organization determines requirements of specific jobs. **36**–38

Job characteristics theory, A theory that argues that five core characteristics (variety, identity, significance, autonomy, and feedback) combine to result in high levels of satisfaction with the work itself. **103**–106
    assessing core job characteristics, 107
    autonomy and, 103, 105
    feedback and, 103, 105

identity and, 103, 104
Reenergizing Employees After a
    Downsizing (case), 540–542
significance and, 103–105
variety and, 103, 104

Job crafting Proactively shaping and molding the characteristics contained within one's job. **105**

Job Description Index (JDI), 117–118

Job enrichment When job duties and responsibilities are expanded to provide increased levels of core job characteristics. **105**

Job in General (JIG) scale, 117–118

Job performance, Employee behaviors that contribute either positively or negatively to the accomplishment of organizational goals. 8–9, 30–32, **33**–56
    citizenship behavior and, 38–41
    cognitive abilities and, 324–326
    compensation and, 187
    counterproductive behavior and, 41–44
    cultural values and, 287–289
    dilemmas of, 32–33
    influence and, 431–432
    in integrative model of OB, 8–9
    job satisfaction and, 111–114, 117–118
    leadership and, 464–465
    learning and, 255
    meaning of "good performer," 34–41,
        46–47
    motivation and, 183–184, 185, 187
    organizational culture and, 527–529
    organizational structure and, 498–500
    performance management and, 48–51
    personality and, 287–289
    power and, 431–432
    social recognition and, 18–21
    strategies to improve, 48–51
    stress and, 136, 143, 144, 147
    task performance and, 34–38
    team characteristics and, 360–361
    team processes and, 392–395
    trends affecting, 47–49
    trust and, 220

Job satisfaction, A pleasurable emotional state resulting from the appraisal of one's job or job experiences. It represents how a person feels and thinks about his or her job. 9, 94–95, **96**–121
    citizenship behavior and, 113
    counterproductive behavior and, 113
    emotions and, 110–111
    extraversion and, 275
    importance of, 111–116
    in integrative model of OB, 9

job characteristics theory, 103–105, 106,
    540–542 (case)
job performance and, 111–114, 117–118
leadership and, 465
life satisfaction and, 114–116, 117–118
mood and, 106–110, 275
organizational commitment and, 113–114,
    117–118
organizational culture and, 528
tracking, 108, 117–118
values and, 97–105, 106
work specialization and, 484–485

Job security, employee-employer relationship and, 79

Job sharing, 146

Justice, The perceived fairness of an authority's decision making. 9, **199**, 205–212
    distributive, 205–206, 208
    informational, 206, 210–211, 540–542
        (case)
    in integrative model of OB, 9
    interpersonal, 206, 208–211
    procedural, 206–208

K

Knowledge
    explicit, 237, 238
    tacit, 237, 238
    training and, 256–257

Knowledge and skill The degree to which employees have the aptitude and competence needed to succeed on their job. **105**

Knowledge of results A psychological state indicating the extent to which employees are aware of how well or how poorly they are doing. **103**

Knowledge transfer The exchange of knowledge between employees. **256**

Knowledge work Jobs that primarily involve cognitive activity versus physical activity. **47**

L

Laissez-faire leadership When the leader avoids leadership duties altogether. **456**–457

Language The jargon, slang, and slogans used within an organization. **513**

Layoffs
    informational justice and, 210–211, 540–
        542 (case)
    in restructuring process, 500–501

Leader effectiveness, The degree to which the leader's actions result in the achievement of the unit's goals, the continued commitment of the unit's employees, and the development of mutual trust, respect, and obligation in leader–member dyads. 9, **446**–463
    in integrative model of OB, 9
    leader style and, 449–451
    traits, 447
    variations in, 446–447, 462–463

Leader emergence The process of becoming a leader in the first place. **447**

Leader styles, 442–451
    autocratic, 448, 463
    conflict resolution and, 424–427
    consultative, 448, 463
    delegative, 449, 463
    effectiveness of, 449–451
    facilitative, 448–449, 463
    in integrative model of OB, 8
    span of control and, 484, 485–487

Leader-member exchange theory A theory describing how leader–member relationships develop over time on a dyadic basis. **444**–446

Leadership. The use of power and influence to direct the activities of followers toward goal achievement. **412, 444**. *See also* **Power**
    changes in, 524
    day-to-day behaviors, 451–456
    decision-making styles, 447–451
    importance of, 464–466
    influence and, 413, 418–421
    leader effectiveness, 446–463
    leader emergence, 447
    leader styles. *See* Leader styles
    leader-member exchange theory, 444–446
    Leading in a Hostile Environment (case),
        546–548
    life cycle theory of, 453–456
    Managing Commitment in Demanding Jobs
        (case), 543–545
    negotiation and, 427–429
    power and, 413–418, 429–431
    Reenergizing Employees After a
        Downsizing (case), 540–542
    substitutes for leadership model, 465–466
    time-driven model of, 449–451
    training programs, 466
    transformational leadership behaviors,
        456–462, 464–465

Leader-staff teams A type of team that consists of members who make recommendations to the leader who is ultimately responsible for team decisions. **351**

Learning, A relatively permanent change in an employee's knowledge or skill that results from experience. 9, 234–235, **236**–260
  general cognitive ability and, 325
  goal orientation in, 242–244
  importance of, 255–256
  in integrative model of OB, 9
  job performance and, 255
  observation in, 241–242
  organizational commitment and, 255–256
  reinforcement in, 238–241
  training and, 256–257
  types of knowledge, 237–238
  variations in, 236–247, 254–255

Learning orientation A predisposition or attitude according to which building competence is deemed more important by an employee than demonstrating competence. **242**–244

Legitimate power A form of organizational power based on authority or position. 413, **414,** 417

Life cycle theory of leadership A theory stating that the optimal combination of initiating structure and consideration depends on the readiness of the employees in the work unit. **453**–456

Life satisfaction, The degree to which employees feel a sense of happiness with their lives in general. **114**–116
  assessing happiness, 116
  job satisfaction and, 114–116, 117–118

Locus of control Whether one believes the events that occur around him or her are self-driven or driven by the external environment. **276**–278, 279

London Whale incident, 54

Lone wolves Employees with low commitment levels and high task performance levels who focus on their own career rather than what benefits the organization. **74**

Long breaks, 75

Longitudinal studies, 270, 272

Looking busy, 74

Loyalty A passive response to a negative work event in which one publicly supports the situation but privately hopes for improvement. **72**

M

Machiavellianism, 423

Management by objectives (MBO) A management philosophy that bases employee evaluations on whether specific performance goals have been met. **48–49**

Management teams A relatively permanent team that participates in managerial-level tasks that affect the entire organization. **342–343,** 358–359

Masculinity-femininity The degree to which a culture values stereotypically male traits (masculinity) or stereotypically female traits (femininity). **284**

Mathematical reasoning, 312

Matrix structure Leading in a Hostile Environment (case), 546–548

Matrix structures A complex form of organizational structure that combines a functional and multidivisional grouping. **497**–498

Maximum performance Performance in brief, special circumstances that demand a person's best effort. **288**

Meaning of money The idea that money can have symbolic value (e.g, achievement, respect, freedom) in addition to economic value. **169**–171

Meaningfulness Captures the value of a work goal or purpose, relative to a person's own ideals and passions. **180**

Meaningfulness of work A psychological state reflecting one's feelings about work tasks, goals, and purposes, and the degree to which they contribute to society and fulfill one's ideals and passions. **102**

Mechanistic organizations Efficient, rigid, predictable, and standardized organizations that thrive in stable environments. **488**–490

Mediation A process by which a third party facilitates a dispute resolution process but with no formal authority to dictate a solution. **432**

Mental models The degree to which team members have a shared understanding of important aspects of the team and its task. **392**

Mentoring The process by which a junior-level employee develops a deep and long-lasting relationship with a more senior-level employee within the organization. **531**

Mercenary culture An organizational culture type in which employees think alike but are not friendly to one another. **515**

Mergers and acquisitions, 524–527, 546–548 (case)

Merit pay, 186, 187

Message, 386, 387

Meta-analysis A method that combines the results of multiple scientific studies by essentially calculating a weighted average correlation across studies (with larger studies receiving more weight). **20**–21

Meta-knowledge, 392

Method of authority When people hold firmly to some belief because some respected official, agency, or source has said it is so. **17**

Method of experience When people hold firmly to some belief because it is consistent with their own experience and observations. **16**–17

Method of intuition When people hold firmly to some belief because it "just stands to reason"—it seems obvious or self-evident. **16**–17

Method of science When people accept some belief because scientific studies have tended to replicate that result using a series of samples, settings, and methods. **17**

Missing meetings, 75

Mission analysis, 384

Mission statements
  espoused values and, 511, 514
  goal interdependence and, 349–351

Monitoring progress toward goals, 384

Moods, States of feeling that are mild in intensity, last for an extended period of time, and are not directed at anything. **106**–110
  extraversion and, 275, 276
  job satisfaction and, 106–110, 275

Moonlighting, 74

Moral attentiveness The degree to which people chronically perceive and consider issues of morality during their experiences. **214**–215

Moral awareness When an authority recognizes that a moral issue exists in a situation. **212**–215

Moral identity The degree to which a person views himself or herself as a moral person. **218**

Moral intensity The degree to which an issue has ethical urgency. **214,** 215

Moral intent An authority's degree of commitment to the moral course of action. **217**–218

Moral judgment When an authority can accurately identify the "right" course of action. **215**–218

Moral principles Prescriptive guides for making moral judgments. **216**–218

Motivation, A set of energetic forces that determine the direction, intensity, and persistence of an employee's work effort. 9,162–163, **164**–190
   citizenship behavior and, 184
   compensation and, 168–171, 178–180,
      185–187, 210–211
   counterproductive behavior and, 184
   cultural differences in, 176, 182
   cultural values and, 287–289
   effort in, 164–165
   engagement in, 165
   equity theory of, 175–180, 540–542 (case)
   expectancy theory of, 166–171
   goal setting theory of, 171–175
   importance of, 182–185
   influence and, 432
   inspirational, 460–462
   in integrative model of OB, 9
   as interpersonal process, 384
   intrinsic, 169, 170
   job performance and, 183–184, 185, 187
   leadership and, 464–465
   organizational commitment and, 184–185
   personality and, 287–289
   power and, 432
   psychological empowerment and,
      180–182

Motivational loss Process loss due to team members' tendency to put forth less effort on team tasks than they could. **378**

Multicultural personality questionnaire, 286

Multicultural teams, 358

Multi-divisional structure An organizational form in which employees are grouped by product, geography, or client. 494, **495**

Multinational teams, 382

Myers-Briggs Type Indicator (MBTI) A personality framework that evaluates people on the basis of four types or preferences: extraversion versus introversion, sensing versus intuition, thinking versus feeling, and judging versus perceiving. **281**–282

N

Narrow/tall span of control, 485–487

Near vision, 322

Needs Groupings or clusters of outcomes viewed as having critical psychological or physiological consequences. **168**, 169

Negative affectivity A dispositional tendency to experience unpleasant moods such as hostility, nervousness, and annoyance. **276**

Negative emotions Employees' feelings of fear, guilt, shame, sadness, envy, and disgust. **110**–111, 114

Negative life events Events such as a divorce or death of a family member that tend to be appraised as a hindrance. **134**

Negative reinforcement An unwanted outcome is removed following a desired behavior. **239**

Neglect A passive, destructive response to a negative work event in which one's interest and effort in work decline. **72**

Negotiation, A process in which two or more interdependent individuals discuss and attempt to reach agreement about their differences. 9, **427**–429
   in integrative model of OB, 9
   negotiator biases in, 429
   stages of, 429
   strategies for, 427–428

NEO Five-Factor Inventory (NEO-FFI), 290

Netherlands, 42

Network structure The pattern of communication that occurs regularly among each member of a team. **388**–389

Networked culture An organizational culture type in which employees are friendly to one another, but everyone thinks differently and does his or her own thing. **515**

Networking ability, 422

Neuroticism One of the "Big Five" dimensions of personality reflecting traits like being nervous, moody, emotional, insecure, jealous, and unstable. **269**–272, 275–278

Neutral Objects Questionnaire (Gripe Index), 278

Neutralizers Situational characteristics that reduce the importance of the leader and do not improve employee performance in any way. **465**

Newcomer orientation A common form of training during which new hires learn more about the organization. **531**

Night vision, 322

Noise, 387

Nominal group technique A team process used to generate creative ideas, whereby team members individually write down their ideas and then take turns sharing them with the group. **381**

Nonprogrammed decisions Decisions made by employees when a problem is new, complex, or not recognized. 245, **246**

Normative commitment, An employee's desire to remain a member of an organization due to a feeling of obligation. **66**–67, 71–72
   job satisfaction and, 113
   strategies to improve, 83
   volunteering and, 71–72

Norming The third stage of team development, during which members realize that they need to work together to accomplish team goals and consequently begin to cooperate. 345, **346**

Number facility, 312

Numerous small decisions People making many small decisions every day that are invisible to competitors. **13**

O

Observable artifacts Aspects of an organization's culture that employees and outsiders can easily see or talk about. 511, **512**–513

Observation, in learning process, 241–242

Occupational commitment, 73

Occupational Information Network (O*NET) An online database containing job tasks, behaviors, required knowledge, skills, and abilities. **37–38**, 310, 311, 320–321

Olympics, 168, 416

Openness to experience One of the "Big Five" dimensions of personality reflecting traits like being curious, imaginative, creative, complex, refined, and sophisticated. **269**–272, 278–281

Operant conditioning, 238–241

    contingencies of reinforcement, 239–240
    schedules of reinforcement, 240–241

Oral comprehension, 310–311

Oral expression, 311

Organic organizations Flexible, adaptive, outward-focused organizations that thrive in dynamic environments. **488**–490

Organizational behavior (OB), Field of study devoted to understanding, explaining, and ultimately improving the attitudes and behaviors of individuals and groups in organizations. 4–5, **6–7**, 8–27
    conceptual argument for, 10–13
    gaining knowledge about, 16–21
    importance of, 10
    integrative model of, 7–10
    research evidence on, 7, 13–15

Organizational Behavior (OB) Assessments. *See* Assessments

Organizational Behavior (OB) at the Bookstore

    Act Like a Leader, Think Like a Leader (Ibarra), 467
    The Advantage (Lencioni), 16
    Are You Fully Charged? (Rath), 102
    Essentialism (McKeown), 147
    The Hard Hat (Gordon), 354
    Hundred Percenters (Murphy), 184
    The Idea Factory (Gertner), 491
    The Innovators (Isaacson), 318
    Lean In (Sandberg), 428
    Making Conflict Work (Coleman and Ferguson), 385
    Quiet (Cain), 277
    The Road to Character (Brooks), 204
    Thinking Fast and Slow (Kahneman), 253
    Widgets (Wagner), 82
    Work Rules! (Bock), 522
    A World Gone Social (Coiné and Babbitt), 52

Organizational Behavior (OB) Internationally

    assessing happiness, 116
    citizenship behavior, 42
    cross-cultural differences, 11
    cultural differences in motivation, 176, 182
    cultural differences in placing responsibility, 252
    cultural intelligence, 310
    effectiveness of leader styles across cultures, 459
    expatriate stress, 136
    guanxi (influence) in China, 420
    international mergers and acquisitions, 526
    multicultural personality questionnaire, 286
    multicultural teams, 358
    multinational teams, 382
    organizational commitment in multinational corporations, 80
    organizational structure, 496
    sources of ethical standards, 213

Organizational Behavior (OB) on Screen

    Avengers: Age of Ultron, 352
    Big Hero 6, 181
    Boyhood, 274
    Chef, 73
    Flight, 45
    Foxcatcher, 416
    Gravity, 133
    Her, 115
    The Imitation Game, 486
    Interstellar, 247
    Lincoln, 462
    Lucy, 315
    Moneyball, 22
    Price Check, 525
    The Spongebob Movie: Sponge Out of Water, 377
    Whiplash, 209

Organizational chart A drawing that represents every job in the organization and the formal reporting relationships between those jobs. **483**, 493, 494, 497

Organizational citizenship behavior Going beyond normal expectations to improve operations of the organization, as well as defending the organization and being loyal to it. **39**

Organizational commitment, An employee's desire to remain a member of an organization. 8–9, 62–63, **64**–87
    affective, 65, 66, 67–69, 82, 113, 540–542 (case), 546–548 (case)
    cognitive abilities and, 324–325
    continuance, 65–66, 67, 69–71, 83, 114
    cultural values and, 287–289
    employee task performance levels, 72–74

    employee-employer relationship and, 79–81, 136
    focus of, 66–67
    influence and, 431–432
    in integrative model of OB, 8–9
    job satisfaction and, 113–114, 117–118
    leadership and, 464–465
    Leading in a Hostile Environment (case), 546–548
    learning and, 255–256
    Managing Commitment in Demanding Jobs (case), 543–545
    meaning of "committed," 65, 77, 78
    motivation and, 184–185
    normative, 66, 67, 71–72, 83, 113
    organizational culture and, 527–529, 546–548 (case)
    organizational structure and, 498–500
    personality and, 287–289
    power and, 431–432
    social recognition and, 18–21
    strategies to improve, 81–83
    stress and, 136, 143, 144, 147
    team characteristics and, 360–361
    team processes and, 392–395
    trends affecting, 77–81
    trust and, 220, 221
    turnover and, 64–65, 69–71, 76, 79–81, 82, 83
    withdrawal behavior, 65, 72–77, 83
    workforce diversity and, 79

Organizational culture, The shared social knowledge within an organization regarding the rules, norms, and values that shape the attitudes and behaviors of its employees. 10, 508–509, **510**–534
    changing, 523–527
    components of, 511–515
    culture strength, 518–520
    general culture types, 515
    importance of, 527–529
    in integrative model of OB, 10
    Leading in a Hostile Environment (case), 546–548
    maintaining, 521–523
    person-organization fit and, 527–529
    socialization process in, 521–523, 530–531
    specific culture types, 515–518
    variations in, 511, 527, 528

Organizational design The process of creating, selecting, or changing the structure of an organization. **490**–492

Organizational politics Individual actions directed toward the goal of furthering a person's own self-interests. **422**–424

Organizational power, 414–415, 421, 423–424

    coercive, 413, 415, 417
    legitimate, 413, 414, 417
    reward, 413, 414–415, 417

Organizational structure, Formally dictates how jobs and tasks are divided and coordinated between individuals and groups within the company. 10, 480–481, **482–483,** 484–504
    bureaucratic structures, 493–498
    common forms, 492–498
    elements of, 483–490
    importance of, 498–500
    in integrative model of OB, 10
    organizational charts, 483, 493, 494, 497
    organizational design and, 490–492
    restructuring and, 499, 500–501
    simple structures, 492–493
    variations in, 483, 498, 499

Orienter role, 351, 353

Originality, 312–313

Other awareness The ability to recognize and understand the emotions that other people are feeling. **316**

Outcome interdependence The degree to which team members share equally in the feedback and rewards that result from the team achieving its goals. **351,** 361–362

P

Parallel teams A team composed of members from various jobs within the organization that meets to provide recommendations about important issues. 342, **343**

Participating When the leader shares ideas and tries to help the group conduct its affairs. **455**

Passive management-by-exception When the leader waits around for mistakes and errors, then takes corrective action as necessary. **457,** 458

Past accomplishments The level of success or failure with similar job tasks in the past. **167**

Pay. *See* Compensation systems

Pay satisfaction Employees' feelings about the compensation for their jobs. 97, **98**

Perceived organizational support The degree to which employees believe that the organization values their contributions and cares about their well-being. **81–83**

Perceptual ability The capacity to perceive, understand, and recall patterns of information. 311, **313**

Perceptual speed, 313

Performance management
    job performance and, 48–51
    as team competency, 396

Performance-void orientation A predisposition or attitude by which employees focus on demonstrating their competence so that others will not think poorly of them. **243**–244

Performance-prove orientation A predisposition or attitude by which employees focus on demonstrating their competence so that others think favorably of them. **243**–244

Performing The fourth stage of team development, during which members are comfortable working within their roles, and the team makes progress toward goals. 345, **346**

Personal aggression Hostile verbal and physical actions directed toward other employees. **44**

Personal appeals An influence tactic in which the requestor asks for something based on personal friendship or loyalty. **419**

Personal Characteristics Inventory (PCI), 290

Personal clarification Training in which members simply receive information regarding the roles of the other team members. **396**

Personal development Participation in activities outside of work that foster growth and learning. **134**

Personal power, 414, 415–416, 423–424, 432

    expert, 413, 415, 417
    referent, 413, 415–416, 417

Personality, The structures and propensities inside a person that explain his or her characteristic patterns of thought, emotion, and behavior. Personality reflects what people are like and creates their social reputation. 9, 266–267, **268**–296
    Big Five taxonomy, 269–281, 283, 287–290, 540–542 (case)
    describing, 286–287
    importance of, 287–289
    in integrative model of OB, 9
    integrity tests, 290–292

    job performance and, 287–289
    motivation and, 287–289
    multicultural personality questionnaire, 286
    Myers-Briggs Type Indicator (MBTI), 281–282
    organizational commitment and, 287–289
    personality tests in hiring process, 289–292
    RIASEC model, 282–283
    team member, 353, 355–356, 358

Personality Research Form (PRF), 290

Person-organization fit The degree to which a person's values and personality match the culture of the organization. **527–529**

Physical abilities, 320–323

    flexibility and coordination, 320–322
    physical cultural intelligence, 310
    psychomotor, 321, 322
    sensory, 321, 322–323
    stamina, 320, 321
    strength, 320, 321
    team member, 354–355

Physical structures The organization's buildings and internal office designs. **512–513**

Physical withdrawal A physical escape from the work environment. **75–76,** 77

Physiological strain, 138–139

Piece-rate compensation plans, 186, 187

Pleasantness The degree to which an employee is in a good versus bad mood. **108**

Political deviance Behaviors that intentionally disadvantage other individuals. **43–44**

Political skill The ability to understand others and the use of that knowledge to influence them to further personal or organizational objectives. **422,** 423

Ponzi schemes, 54

Pooled interdependence A form of task independence in which group members complete their work assignments independently, and then their work is simply added together to represent the group's output. **347**–348

Positional modeling Training that involves observations of how other team members perform their roles. **396**

Positional rotation Training that gives members actual experience carrying out the responsibilities of their teammates. **396**

Positive affectivity A dispositional tendency to experience pleasant, engaging moods such as enthusiasm, excitement, and elation. **275**, 276

Positive emotions Employees' feelings of joy, pride, relief, hope, love, and compassion. **110**–111, 112–113, 114

Positive life events Events such as marriage or the birth of a child that tend to be appraised as a challenge. **134**

Positive reinforcement When a positive outcome follows a desired behavior. **239**, 240

Potency A team state reflecting the degree of confidence among team members that the team can be effective across situations and tasks. **390**–392

Power, The ability to influence the behavior of others and resist unwanted influence in return. 9, **413**–432
    acquiring, 413–418
    conflict resolution and, 424–427
    contingencies of, 416–418
    importance of, 431–432
    influence and, 413, 418–421
    in integrative model of OB, 9
    Leading in a Hostile Environment (case),
        546–548
    negotiation and, 427–429
    organizational, 413, 414–415, 417, 421,
        423–424
    organizational politics and, 422–424
    personal, 413, 415–416, 417, 421,
        423–424, 432
    types of, 413–416, 417
    variations in, 412, 429–431

Power distance The degree to which a culture prefers equal power distribution (low power distance) or an unequal power distribution (high power distance). **284**

Preconventional stage of moral development (Kohlberg), 216

Preparation The first stage of the negotiation process, during which each party determines its goals for the negotiation. **429**

Presenteeism, 144

Pressure An influence tactic in which the requestor attempts to use coercive power through threats and demands. 419, **420**

Primary appraisal Evaluation of whether a demand is stressful and, if it is, the implications

of the stressor in terms of personal goals and well-being. **129**–134

Principled stage of moral development (Kohlberg), 216–217, 218

Privacy, and personality tests in hiring process, 290

Problem sensitivity, 312

Problem-focused coping Behaviors and cognitions of an individual intended to manage the stressful situation itself. **135**–137

Procedural justice The perceived fairness of decision-making processes. **206**–208

Procedural-technician role, 353

Process gain When team outcomes are greater than expected based on the capabilities of the individual members. **378**, 392, 393

Process loss When team outcomes are less than expected based on the capabilities of the individual members. **378**

Product structure An organizational form in which employees are grouped around different products that the company produces. **495**

Production blocking A type of coordination loss resulting from team members having to wait on each other before completing their own part of the team task. **378**

Production deviance Intentionally reducing organizational efficiency of work output. **43**

Profit sharing, 186, 187

Programmed decisions Decisions that are somewhat automatic because the decision maker's knowledge allows him or her to recognize the situation and the course of action to be taken. **244**–246

Progression model A model indicating that the various withdrawal behaviors are positively correlated; engaging in one type of withdrawal makes one more likely to engage in other types. **77,** 83

Project GLOBE A collection of 170 researchers from 62 cultures who examine the impact of culture on the effectiveness of leader attributes, behaviors, and practices. **284**–285, 459

Project teams A team formed to take on one-time tasks, most of which tend to be

complex and require input from members from different functional areas. 342, **343,** 358–359

Projection bias The faulty perception by decision makers that others think, feel, and act the same way as they do. **248**–249

Promotion satisfaction Employees' feelings about how the company handles promotions. 97, **98**–99

Property deviance Behaviors that harm the organization's assets and possessions. **41**–43, 210–211, 290–291

Psychological contracts Employee beliefs about what employees owe the organization and what the organization owes them. **81**

Psychological empowerment An energy rooted in the belief that tasks are contributing to some larger purpose. **180**–182
    Reenergizing Employees After a
        Downsizing (case), 540–542

Psychological safety, 389–390

Psychological strain, 138, 139

Psychological withdrawal Mentally escaping the work environment. **74**–77

Psychomotor ability Capabilities associated with manipulating and controlling objects. 321, **322**

Punctuated equilibrium A sequence of team development during which not much gets done until the halfway point of a project, after which teams make necessary changes to complete the project on time. 345, **346**

Punishment When an unwanted outcome follows an unwanted behavior. **239**–240

Q

Quantitative ability Capabilities associated with doing basic mathematical operations and selecting and applying formulas to solve mathematical problems. 311, **312**

Quitting, 76

R

Ratio bias effect, 250

Rational decision-making model, A step-by-step approach to making decisions that is

designed to maximize outcomes by examining all available alternatives. 244, 245, **246**
  bounded rationality versus, 248
  nonprogrammed decisions, 245, 246
  programmed decisions, 244–246

Rational persuasion The use of logical arguments and hard facts to show someone that a request is worthwhile. **418**–419, 421

Readiness The degree to which employees have the ability and the willingness to accomplish their specific tasks. **453**–455

Realistic job previews (RJPs) The process of ensuring that a potential employee understands both the positive and negative aspects of the potential job. **530**–531

Reality shock A mismatch of information that occurs when an employee finds that aspects of working at a company are not what the employee expected it to be. **522**

Reasoning ability A diverse set of abilities associated with sensing and solving problems using insight, rules, and logic. 311, **312**–313

Receiver, 386, 387

Recency, 250

Reciprocal interdependence A form of task interdependence in which group members interact with only a limited subset of other members to complete the team's work. **349**

Recognition awards, 186, 187

Recognition seeker role, 353, 354

Referent power A form of organizational power based on the attractiveness and charisma of the leader. 413, **415**–416, 417

Reinforcement, 238–241
  in behavioral modeling, 242, 256–257
  contingencies of, 239–240
  schedules of, 240–241

Relational contracts Psychological contracts that focus on a broad set of open-ended and subjective obligations. **81**

Relationship conflict Disagreements among team members with regard to interpersonal relationships or incompatibilities in personal values or preferences. **385**–386

Relaxation techniques, 149

Reliability, 23

Representativeness, 250

Reputation The prominence of an organization's brand in the minds of the public and the perceived quality of its goods and services. **198**

Resilience, 150

Resistance When a target refuses to perform a request and puts forth an effort to avoid having to do it. **421**
  to influence, 413, 421

Resource-based view A model that argues that rare and inimitable resources help firms maintain competitive advantage. **11**–12

Response orientation, 322

Response time, 322

Responsibility for outcomes A psychological state indicating the degree to which employees feel they are key drivers of the quality of work output. **102**–103
  cultural differences in placing responsibility, 252

Restructuring The process of changing an organization's structure. **499**, 500–501
  Reenergizing Employees After a Downsizing (case), 540–542

Reward power A form of organizational power based on the control of resources or benefits. 413, **414**–415, 417

RIASEC model An interest framework summarized by six different personality types including realistic, investigative, artistic, social, enterprising, and conventional. **282**–283

Rituals The daily or weekly planned routines that occur in an organization. **513**

Role The behavior a person is generally expected to display in a given context. **351**
  team member, 351–354, 390

Role ambiguity When an individual has a lack of direction and information about what needs to be done. **131**

Role conflict When others have conflicting expectations of what an individual needs to do. **131**

Role making The phase in a leader–follower relationship when a follower voices his or her own expectations for the relationship,

resulting in a free-flowing exchange of opportunities and resources for activities and effort. **445**–446

Role overload When an employee has too many demands to work effectively. **131**

Role taking The phase in a leader-follower relationship when a leader provides an employee with job expectations and the follower tries to meet those expectations. **445**–446

Routine task performance Well-known or habitual responses by employees to predictable task demands. **34**

Rule of One-Eighth The belief that at best one-eighth, or 12 percent, of organizations will actually do what is required to build profits by putting people first. **15**

S

Sabbaticals, 146

Sabotage Purposeful destruction of equipment, organizational processes, or company products. **41**

Safety culture A specific culture type focused on the safety of employees. **516**–517

SAT (Scholastic Assessment Test), 310, 312, 318–319, 325–326

Satisfaction with the work itself Employees' feelings about their actual work tasks. 97, **100**–105, 106

Satisficing When a decision maker chooses the first acceptable alternative considered. 247–**248**

Schedules of reinforcement The timing of when contingencies are applied or removed. **240**–241

Scientific management, 100–102

Scientific method, 17–21

Scout activities Boundary-spanning activities that are intended to obtain information about technology, competitors, or the broader marketplace. **383**

Secondary appraisal When people determine how to cope with the various stressors they face. **135**–137

Selective perception The tendency for people to see their environment only as it affects them and as it is consistent with their expectations. **248**

Self-awareness The ability to recognize and understand the emotions in oneself. **316**

Self-confessor role, 353

Self-determination A sense of choice in the initiation and continuation of work tasks. **180**

Self-efficacy The belief that a person has the capabilities needed to perform the behaviors required on some task. **167**

Self-management, 344

Self-serving bias When one attributes one's own failures to external factors and success to internal factors. **250**

Self-set goals The internalized goals that people use to monitor their own progress. **173**

Selling When the leader explains key issues and provides opportunities for clarification. **455**

Sender, 386, 387

Sensory ability Capabilities associated with vision and hearing. 321, **322**–323

Sequential interdependence A form of task interdependence in which group members perform different tasks in a prescribed sequence, and members depend on only the member who comes before them in the sequence. **348**–349

Service work Providing a service that involves direct verbal or physical interactions with customers. 47–48
    agreeableness and, 273–274

Short-term vs. long-term orientation The degree to which a culture stresses values that are past and present oriented (short-term orientation) or future-oriented (long-term orientation). **284**

Sick leave, 76

Significance The degree to which a job really matters and impacts society as a whole. 103, **104**–105

Similarity-attraction approach A theory explaining that team diversity can be counter-productive because people tend to avoid inter-acting with others who are unlike them. **357**

Simple structures An organizational form that features one person as the central decision-making figure. **492**–493

Situational strength The degree to which situations have clear behavioral expectations, incentives, or instructions that make differences between individuals less important. **289**

Slacker role, 353

S.M.A.R.T. goals Acronym that stands for Specific, Measurable, Achievable, Results-Based, Time-Sensitive goals. **175,** 184

Sociability, 515

Social astuteness, 422

Social exchange Work relationships that are characterized by mutual investment, with employees willing to engage in "extra mile" sorts of behaviors because they trust that their efforts will eventually be rewarded. **221**

Social identity theory A theory that people identify themselves based on the various groups to which they belong and judge others based on the groups they associate with. **249**

Social influence model A model that suggests that employees with direct linkages to coworkers who leave the organization will themselves become more likely to leave. **69**

Social learning theory Theory that argues that people in organizations learn by observing others. **241**–242

Social loafing A type of motivational loss resulting from members feeling less account-able for team outcomes relative to independent work that results in individually identifiable outcomes. 378–**379**

Social network diagrams, 68–69, 79

Social networking systems, 51, 52, 256, 389

Social support The help people receive from others when they are confronted with stressful demands. **141**

Socialization, The primary process by which employees learn the social knowledge that enables them to understand and adapt to the organization's culture. **521**–523
    anticipatory stage, 521
    encounter stage, 521–522
    managing, 530–531
    realty shock, 522
    understanding and adaptation, 522–523

Socializing, 74

Socially complex resources Resources cre-ated by people, such as culture, teamwork, trust, and reputation. The source of competi-tive advantage is known, but the method of replicating the advantage is unclear. **13**

Solidarity, 515

Span of control Represents how many employees each manager in the organization has responsibility for. 484, **485**–487

Spatial ability Capabilities associated with visual and mental representation and manipula-tion of objects in space. 311, **313**

Spatial orientation, 313

Specific and difficult goals Goals that stretch an employee to perform at his or her maximum level while still staying within the boundaries of his or her ability. **172**–173, 186

Speech recognition, 322–323

Speed and flexibility of closure, 313

Sportsmanship Maintaining a positive atti-tude with coworkers through good and bad times. **39**

Staff validity The degree to which team members make good recommendations to the team leader. **381,** 382–383

Stamina The ability of a person's lungs and circulatory system to work efficiently while he or she is engaging in prolonged physical activity. **320,** 321

Standard setter role, 353

Stars Employees with high commitment levels and high task performance levels who serve as role models within the organization. **72**–73, 74

Static strength, 320

Status striving A strong desire to obtain power and influence within a social structure as a means of expressing one's personality. **275**

Stereotypes Assumptions made about others based on their social group membership. **249**
    surface-level diversity and, 357

Stories Anecdotes, accounts, legends, and myths passed down from cohort to cohort within an organization. **513**

Storming The second stage of team development, during which conflict occurs due to members' ongoing commitment to ideas they bring with them to the team. 345, **346**

Strain Negative consequences of the stress response. **128**

    experience of, 137–139
    reducing, 149–150
    types of, 138–139

Strategic management Field of study devoted to exploring the product choices and industry characteristics that affect an organization's profitability. **7**

Strategy formulation, 384

Strength The degree to which the body is capable of exerting force. **320,** 321

Stress, The psychological response to demands when there is something at stake for the individual, and where coping with these demands would tax or exceed the individual's capacity or resources. 126, 127, **128**–154
    coping with stressors, 135–137
    health care costs and, 145
    importance of, 142–144
    job performance and, 136, 143, 144, 147
    managing, 141, 145–150
    organizational commitment and, 136, 143, 144, 147
    organizational culture and, 528
    organizational structure and, 498
    relative job rankings, 129
    of restructuring, 500–501
    transactional theory of, 129–142, 543–545 (case)
    Type A Behavior Pattern and, 139–141
    types of stressors, 130–134

Stress audit, 145

Stressors Demands that cause the stress response. **128**
    challenge, 131, 132, 134, 144, 147–149
    coping with, 135–137
    differential exposure to, 276
    differential reactivity to, 276
    hindrance, 130, 131, 132–134, 143, 147–149
    Managing Commitment in Demanding Jobs (case), 543–545
    reducing, 145–146
    stressful life events, 134
    types of, 130–134

Subcultures A culture created within a small subset of the organization's employees. **518**–519

Substance abuse The abuse of drugs or alcohol before coming to work or while on the job. **43,** 45

Substitutability The degree to which people have alternatives in accessing the resources a leader controls. **417,** 418

Substitutes Situational characteristics that reduce the importance of the leader while simultaneously providing a direct benefit to employee performance. **465**

Substitutes for leadership model A model that suggests that characteristics of the situations can constrain the influence of the leader, which makes it more difficult for the leader to influence employee performance. **465**–466

Supervision satisfaction Employees' feelings about their boss, including his or her competency, communication, and personality. 97, **99**–100

Surface-level diversity Diversity of observable attributes such as race, gender, ethnicity, and age. **357**

Survivor syndrome, 81

Sustainability culture A specific culture type focused on promoting sustainability both inside and outside of the organization. **517**

Symbols The images an organization uses, which generally convey messages. **512**

Synergy, 377–378

Systems monitoring, 384

T

Tacit knowledge Knowledge that employees can only learn through experience. **237,** 238

Tardiness, 75

Task complexity The degree to which the information and actions needed to complete a task are complicated. **173**–174

Task conflict Disagreements among members about the team's task. **385**–386

Task coordinator activities Boundary-spanning activities that are intended to coordinate task-related issues with people or groups in other functional areas. **383**

Task interdependence The degree to which team members interact with and rely on other team members for information, materials, and resources needed to accomplish work for the team. **346**–349, 353

Task performance Employee behaviors that are directly involved in the transformation of organizational resources into the goods or services that the organization produces. **34**–38
    adaptive, 34–35
    creative, 35–36
    employee task performance levels, 72–74
    job analysis and, 36–38
    Leading in a Hostile Environment (case), 546–548
    organizational culture and, 528–529
    Reenergizing Employees After a Downsizing (case), 540–542
    routine, 34

Task strategies Learning plans and problem-solving approaches used to achieve successful performance. **173**

Taskwork processes, The activities of team members that relate directly to the accomplishment of team tasks. **379**–383, 392
    boundary spanning, 379, 383
    creative behavior, 379–381
    decision making, 379, 381–383

Team(s) Two or more people who work interdependently over some time period to accomplish common goals related to some task-oriented purpose. **340**
    characteristics of. *See* Team characteristics
    extent of use, 340–341
    management teams, 342–343, 358–359
    processes of. *See* **Team processes**
    stages of development, 345–346
    training, 389, 395–398

Team building Fun activities that facilitate team problem solving, trust, relationship building, and the clarification of role responsibilities. **397**–398

Team characteristics, 338–366
    commitment and, 360–361
    compensation and, 361–362
    composition, 351–359
    importance of, 360–361
    in integrative model of OB, 9
    interdependence, 346–351, 359, 361–362
    performance and, 360–361
    types, 342–346, 358

Team composition, 351–359

The mix of the various characteristics that describe the individuals who work in the team. 9, **351–359**
diversity in, 353, 356–358, 382
in integrative model of OB, 9
member ability, 353, 354–355
member personality, 353, 355–356, 358
member roles, 351–354
team size, 353, 358–359

Team diversity, The degree to which team members are different from one another. 356–358
in integrative model of OB, 9
Managing Commitment in Demanding Jobs (case), 543–545
multicultural teams, 358
multinational teams, 382

Team process training The use of team experiences that facilitates the team's ability to function and perform more effectively as an intact unit. **397**

Team processes, The different types of activities and interactions that occur within a team as the team works toward its goals. 9, 374–375, **376–403**
communication, 376, 386–389, 392, 393
importance of, 392–395
in integrative model of OB, 9
job performance and, 392–395
organizational commitment and, 392–395
process gain/loss and, 377–379, 392, 393
taskwork, 379–383, 392
team states, 389–392
teamwork, 383–386, 392
training teams, 397

Team states, Specific types of feelings and thoughts that coalesce in the minds of team members as a consequence of their experience working together. **389–392**
cohesion, 390, 391
mental models, 392
potency, 390–392
transactive memory, 392

Team task roles Behaviors that directly facilitate the accomplishment of team tasks. **351,** 353

Team viability Team commitment; the likelihood a team can work together effectively into the future. **360,** 393

Team-building roles Behaviors that directly facilitate the accomplishment of team tasks. **352,** 353

Teamwork processes The interpersonal activities that promote the accomplishment of team tasks but do not involve task accomplishment itself. **383–386,** 392
action, 383, 384
interpersonal, 383, 384–386
transition, 383–384

Technology The method by which an organization transforms inputs to outputs. **492**
in communication process, 389
in mergers and acquisitions, 527

Telecommuting, 148, 149

Teleological principles, 216–217

Telling When the leader provides specific instructions and closely supervises performance. **453–455**

Theft Stealing company products or equipment from the organization. **42–43**
following layoffs, 210–211
integrity tests and, 290–291

Theory A collection of verbal and symbolic assertions that specify how and why variables are related, as well as the conditions in which they should (and should not) be related. **17**

360-degree feedback A performance evaluation system that uses ratings provided by supervisors, coworkers, subordinates, customers, and the employees themselves. **49–50**

Time pressure The sense that the amount of time allotted to do a job is not quite enough. **132**

Time-driven model of leadership A model that suggests that seven factors, including the importance of the decision, the expertise of the leader, and the competence of the followers, combine to make some decision-making styles more effective than others in a given situation. **449–451**

Training A systematic effort by organizations to facilitate the learning of job-related knowledge and behavior. **256**
applying emotional intelligence in, 317
behavior modeling, 256–257
civility, 210
leadership training programs, 466
in learning process, 256–257
organizational commitment and, 71
in stress management, 147–148, 149
team, 389, 395–398

Trait(s) Recurring trends in people's responses to their environment. **268**
leader emergence and effectiveness, 447

Trait activation The degree to which situations provide cues that trigger the expression of a given personality trait. **289**

Transactional contracts Psychological contracts that focus on a narrow set of specific monetary obligations. **81**

Transactional leadership A pattern of behavior where the leader rewards or disciplines the follower based on performance. **457–458**

Transactional theory of stress, A theory that explains how stressful demands are perceived and appraised, as well as how people respond to the perceptions and appraisals. **129–142**
Managing Commitment in Demanding Jobs (case), 543–545
primary appraisal, 129–134
secondary appraisal, 135–137
types of stressors, 130–134

Transactive memory The degree to which team members' specialized knowledge is integrated into an effective system of memory for the team. **392**

Transfer of training Occurs when employees retain and demonstrate the knowledge, skills, and behaviors required for their job after training ends. **256**

Transformational leadership A pattern of behavior where the leader inspires followers to commit to a shared vision that provides meaning to their work while also serving as a role model who helps followers develop their own potential and view problems from new perspectives. **456–462, 464–465**

Transition processes Teamwork processes, such as mission analysis and planning, that focus on preparation for future work in the team. **383–384**

Transportable teamwork competencies. Team training that involves helping people develop general teamwork competencies that they can transport from one team context to another. **395,** 396

Trivial Pursuit (game), 314, 355

Trust, The willingness to be vulnerable to an authority based on positive expectations about

the authority's actions and intentions.
9, 196–197, **198–199**, 200–225
    affect-based, 200, 204–205, 219
    citizenship behavior and, 221
    cognition-based, 200, 202–203,
        205, 220
    in corporate social responsibility, 221–222
    disposition-based, 200–202,
        205, 219
    ethics and, 199, 212–219
    importance of, 198–199, 220–221
    in integrative model of OB, 9
    job performance and, 220
    justice and, 9, 199, 205–212
    Leading in a Hostile Environment (case),
        546–548
    organizational commitment and, 220, 221
    variations in, 199, 219–220

Trust propensity, A general expectation that the words, promises, and statements of individuals can be relied upon. **200–202**
    assessing, 201
    by nation, 202

Trustworthiness Characteristics or attributes of a person that inspire trust, including competence, character, and benevolence. **202–203**

Turnover, 64–65, 69–71, 76, 79–81, 82, 83

Twin studies, 270

Type A Behavior Pattern People who tend to experience more stressors, appraise more demands as stressful, and be prone to experiencing more strains. **139–141,** 276

Type B Behavior Pattern, 140,
142, 276

Typical performance Performance in the routine conditions that surround daily job tasks. **287–288**

U

Uncertainty avoidance The degree to which a culture tolerates ambiguous situations (low uncertainty avoidance) or feels threatened by them (high uncertainty avoidance). **284**

Understanding and adaptation The final stage of socialization, during which newcomers come to learn the content areas of socialization and internalize the norms and expected behaviors of the organization. **522–523**

Use of emotions The degree to which people can harness emotions and employ them to improve their chances of being successful in whatever they are seeking to do. **317**

Utilitarianism, 217, 218

V

Valence The anticipated value of the outcomes associated with successful performance. **168–171,** 183

Validity, 23

Value in diversity problem-solving approach A theory that supports team diversity because it provides a larger pool of knowledge and perspectives. **356**–357

Value-percept theory A theory that argues that job satisfaction depends on whether the employee perceives that his or her job supplies those things that he or she values. **98**–100

Values Things that people consciously or unconsciously want to seek or attain. **97**–98
    commonly assessed, 97–98
    cultural. *See* **Cultural values**
    espoused, 511, 514
    integrity and, 203
    job satisfaction and, 97–105, 106
    organizational culture and, 522–523, 529
    in value-percept theory, 98–100

Variable interval schedule Reinforcement occurs at random periods of time. **240–241**

Variable ratio schedule Behaviors are reinforced after a varying number of them have been exhibited. **241**

Variety The degree to which a job requires different activities and skills. 103, **104**

Veiled purpose tests Integrity tests that do not directly ask about dishonesty, instead assessing more general personality traits associated with dishonest acts. **290–291**

Verbal ability Various capabilities associated with understanding and expressing oral and written communication. **310**–311

Verbal persuasion Pep talks that lead employees to believe that they can "get the job done." **167**

Vicarious experiences Observations of and discussions with others who have performed some work task. **167**

Virtual teams A team in which the members are geographically dispersed, and interdependent activity occurs through e-mail, web conferencing, and instant messaging. **344–345,** 389

Virtue ethics, 217, 218

Visibility How aware others are of a leader and the resources that leader can provide. **417,** 418

Vision, 322

Visual color discrimination, 322

Visualization, 313

Voice When an employee speaks up to offer constructive suggestions for change, often in reaction to a negative work event. **39, 72**

Volunteering Giving time or skills during a planned activity for a nonprofit or charitable group. **71–72**

W

Wasting resources Using too many materials or too much time to do too little work. **43**

Web 2.0 tools, 389

Wheel network structure, 388, 389

Whistle-blowing When employees expose illegal actions by their employer. **212**

Wide/flat span of control, 482, 485–487

Win-win scenario, 427–428

Withdrawal behavior, Employee actions that are intended to avoid work situations. **65,** 72–77
    employee task performance levels, 72–74
    physical, 75–77
    psychological, 74–75, 76–77
    quitting, 76
    reactions to negative work
        events, 72
    strategies to reduce, 83
Women

    diversity of workforce, 79
    powerful, list of, 414
    relative compensation of, 207
    sexual harassment lawsuits, 44

Wonderlic Cognitive Ability Test A 12-minute test of general cognitive ability used to hire job applicants. **326**–328

Work complexity The degree to which job requirements tax or just exceed employee capabilities. **132**

Work responsibility The number and importance of the obligations that an employee has to others. **132**

Work specialization The degree to which tasks in an organization are divided into separate jobs. **483**–485

Work teams A relatively permanent team in which members work together to produce goods and/or provide services. **342**

Work-family conflict A form of role conflict in which the demands of a work role hinder the fulfillment of the demands in a family role (or vice versa). **133**–134

World War II, 460, 486, 491

Written comprehension, 310–311

Written expression, 311

Y

Y network structure, 388, 389

Z

Zero acquaintance Situations in which two people have just met. **275**

Zero-sum scenario, 427

A

Abele, A. E., 194
Abraham, L. M., 298
Abrahm, S., 155
Abush, R., 157
Ada, Countess of Lovelace, 318
Adams, G. L., 438
Adams, J. S., 177, 193, 206, 227
Adams, R., 473
Aditya, R. N., 473
Adler, S., 303
Aguinis, H., 11, 176
Ahearne, M., 58, 478
Aiken, L. S., 28
Aiman-Smith, L., 195, 537
Albright, L., 298
Alderfer, C. P., 169, 192
Alexander, H., 486
Alexander, S., 231
Alge, B. J., 175, 193
Allan, B., 264
Allen, D., 60
Allen, D. G., 87, 91
Allen, J. A., 368
Allen, N. J., 68, 87
Allen, P., 318
Allen, T. D., 58, 156, 159, 539
Alliger, G. M., 255, 264
Allison, W., 300
Allport, G. W., 296
Almasy, S., 364
Alterman, T., 154, 158
Alutto, J. A., 373
Amabile, T. M., 57, 507
Ambrose, M. L., 229, 231, 262
Amos, D., 449
Anca, J., 364
Ancona, D. G., 405
Anderson, N. R., 539
Anderson, R., 524
Anderson, R. D., 477
Andersson, L. M., 59
Andrews, A. O., 27
Ang, S., 310, 472
Anthony, W. P., 261
Aparna, J., 370
Aquino, K., 56, 231
Arad, S., 35, 57
Armenakis, A., 158
Armour, S., 59
Armstrong, L., 27
Armstrong, P. I., 300
Armstrong, T., 303
Arndt, M., 437
Arthur, W., Jr., 405, 529, 536, 539
Arvey, R. D., 297, 298
Asendorpf, J. B., 299
Ashford, S. J., 538

Ashforth, B. E., 87, 263, 436
Ashkanasy, N. M., 124
Ashley, J., 462
Ashton, M. C., 304
Atanasoff, L., 300
Atinc, G., 438
Atkinson, W., 160
Audia, P. G., 176
Auletta, K., 435, 436
Auriemma, G., 33
Austin, E. J., 333–334
Austin, N. K., 159
Averbrook, J., 264
Avila, R. A., 58
Avolio, B. J., 445, 475–478

B

Baas, M., 124
Babbage, C., 318
Babcock, P., 537
Babitt, M., 52
Bacharach, S. B., 437
Bachiochi, P. D., 117, 125
Bachrach, B. G., 408
Bachrach, D. G., 58, 464, 477
Bacon, F., 17, 28
Baer, M., 57
Bailey, D. E., 342, 366
Bailey, S., 535
Baillien, E., 59
Baird, B. M., 272
Bakker, A. B., 123, 191
Bal, P. M., 91
Baldwin, T. T., 125
Ballard, T. N., 409
Balliet, D., 439
Ballinger, G. A., 471
Balzer, W. K., 117, 125
Bamberger, P. A., 157, 262, 409
Banderas, A., 377
Bandura, A., 167, 191, 261
Banks, G. C., 439
Barbee, A. P., 304
Barber, A. E., 539
Barger, D., 531
Barkema, H. G., 372
Barksdale, K., 232
Barlerin, C., 120
Barling, J., 478
Barnes, C. M., 405
Barney, J. B., 27
Baron, J., 250
Bar-On, R., 332
Baron, R. A., 124, 438
Barra, M., 414, 510, 523–524, 533
Barrett, A., 193
Barrick, M. R., 288, 297–300, 302, 303, 369, 370, 408
Barron, L. A., 192

Barros, E., 124
Barry, B., 370, 440
Barside, S. G., 333
Barsky, A. P., 298
Bartol, K. M., 195
Bass, B. M., 445, 457, 475
Batali, M., 236–237
Bates, S., 227
Batty, G. D., 332
Bauer, T. N., 125, 471, 537
Bazerman, M. H., 439
Beach, D., 203
Beal, D. J., 124, 407
Bear, J. B., 406
Beatty, R. W., 50, 60
Beaubien, J. M., 262, 408
Bebeau, M. J., 231
Becker, H. S., 88
Becker, T. E., 500
Becker, W. S., 192
Bedeian, A. G., 158
Beehr, T. A., 80
Beersma, B., 367, 439
Beethoven, L. van, 323
Behfar, K., 358, 405
Behr, P., 408
Belkin, L. Y., 227
Bell, B., 409
Bell, B. S., 372, 405
Bell, M. P., 371
Bell, S. T., 302, 369, 529, 539
Bellman, G., 403
Belohlav, J. A., 302
Benne, K., 353, 368
Bennett, R. J., 43, 59
Bennett, W., Jr., 255, 264
Benson, H., 149
Benson, L., 229, 440
Beranek, P. M., 407
Berfield, S., 230, 437, 535
Bergey, P. K., 195
Bergman, M. E., 536
Berkson, H. M., 423
Berman, D., 409
Berman, J., 259
Bernardin, H. J., 304, 440
Berners-Lee, T., 318
Bernieri, F., 331
Berns, G., 122
Berry, C. M., 288, 304
Berry, J. W., 57
Besson, L., 315
Betof, E., 438
Beus, J. M., 536
Beyer, J. M., 535
Bezos, J., 48, 359, 482
Bhaskar-Shrinivas, P., 136
Bhatia, P., 477
Bhave, D. P., 370

Bhawuk, D. P. S., 438
Biberman, G., 438
Biddle, B. J., 368
Bies, R. J., 206, 229
Bigman, D., 506
Bing, M. H., 438
Biotrowski, C., 303
Birger, J., 436
Birjulin, A., 438
Birk, S., 535
Birkeland, S. A., 304
Biron, M., 160, 262
Birtch, T. A., 42
Black, C., 333–334
Black, J. S., 80, 136, 302, 538
Blanchard, K. H., 455, 474
Blank, W., 475
Blankfein, L., 64, 85
Blau, G., 89
Blau, P., 232
Blickensderfer, E., 409
Bliese, P. D., 299
Bligh, M. C., 476
Bluedorn, A. C., 506
Blume, B. D., 58
Blumenthal, K., 475
Bobocel, D. R., 169, 192
Bock, K., 242
Bock, L., 6, 26, 522
Bogg, T., 297
Bohte, J., 504
Boiardi, G., 354
Boisner, A., 537
Bolch, M., 373
Boles, J. S., 155
Bolger, N., 299
Bommer, W. H., 472, 477, 478
Bond, M. H., 284, 301
Boning, B., 366
Bono, J. E., 113, 124, 298, 299, 447, 475, 477
Boodoo, G., 331
Borgen, F. H., 300
Borman, W. C., 56, 57
Borman, W. S., 335
Bormann, C. A., 438
Bornstein, B. H., 404
Boswell, W. R., 158, 324, 335
Bouchard, T. J., 298, 331
Bouchard, T. J., Jr., 297
Boudreau, J. W., 158, 324, 335
Bou-Llusar, J. C., 261
Bourgeois, L. J., 438
Boussebaa, M., 506
Bowen, D. E., 478, 536
Bowers, C., 262
Bowling, N. A., 122
Boykin, A. W., 331
Boyle, M., 506
Bozell, D., 409
Bozionelos, N., 407
Brackett, M. A., 331
Bradley, B. H., 406, 408

Bradley, J. C., 298, 299, 536
Brady, D., 474
Brahy, S., 526
Brannick, M. T., 101, 122, 304
Bravo, J., 91
Breaugh, J. A., 122
Breaux, D. M., 229
Brégier, F., 487
Brehmer, B., 368, 404
Breinin, E., 477
Bremmer, B., 526
Brennan, B., 448
Brett, J., 358
Brett, J. F., 243
Bretz, R. D., 324, 335
Brewer, R., 414
Brief, A. P., 124
Brin, S., 312, 318
Briner, R. B., 28
Brinkmann, J., 262
Brinkmann, U., 286
Brito, C., 526
Brockmann, E. N., 261
Brockner, J., 191, 208, 228, 263, 500, 507
Brodbeck, F. C., 459
Brody, N., 331
Brooks, D., 204
Brooks, H., 168
Brouer, R. L., 438, 472
Brown, C., 377
Brown, K. G., 192, 369, 406
Brown, M. E., 230
Brown, T. J., 536
Bruch, H., 368–369, 505
Bryan, V., 364
Bryan-Low, C., 437
Bryant, A., 472, 474, 535
Bryant, D., 449
Bryant, F. B., 157
Bryant, P. C., 87
Buchtel, E. E., 301
Buckingham, M., 190
Buckley, M. T., 423
Buckman, B. R., 157
Buderi, R., 420
Buffett, W., 246, 533
Buford, B., 236–237, 261
Bullock, S., 133
Bumpass, R., 377
Bunderson, J. S., 194
Bunker, B. B., 205, 227
Burchell, M., 121
Burden, M., 533
Burke, C. S., 409
Burke, D., 436
Burke, M. E., 138, 148, 158
Burke, M. J., 407, 536
Burkhead, E. J., 157
Burnett, D. D., 303
Burnfield, J. L., 472
Burns, L. M., 475

Burns, L. R., 506
Burns, T., 490
Burns, U., 242
Burr, A., 32
Burris, E. R., 58, 89
Burris, L. R., 303
Burt, R. S., 226
Burton, J. P., 88
Burtt, H. E., 473
Bush, G. W., 460
Bushnell, N., 318
Buss, A. H., 23
Butterfield, K. D., 230
Butts, M. B., 159
Byham, W. C., 261
Byosiere, P., 156
Byrne, D., 371
Byrne, J. A., 51
Byrne, Z. S., 169, 192
Byrnes, N., 92
Byron, K., 407

C

Cable, D. M., 97, 121, 537, 538
Cacioppo, J. T., 124
Cain, S., 277
Caine, M., 247
Caldwell, D. F., 529, 534
Callahan, C., 303
Callister, R. R., 537
Camara, W. J., 334
Camerer, C., 226
Cameron, K. S., 440
Camp, G., 198
Campbell, D. P., 300
Campbell, D. T., 28
Campbell, J. P., 28, 56, 300, 335
Campion, M. A., 90, 123, 347, 360, 373, 396, 409, 505, 507
Can, O., 302
Canella, A. A., Jr., 370–371
Cannon, W. B., 156
Cannon-Bowers, J. A., 262, 408, 409
Caplan, R. D., 155
Cappelli, P., 92
Capps, M. H., 304
Carell, S., 416
Carey, S., 409
Carlson, N., 335
Carr, D., 334
Carr, J. C., 229
Carroll, A. B., 232
Carroll, J. B., 332
Carson, J. B., 405
Carson, K. D., 431
Carson, K. P., 125
Carson, P. P., 431
Carton, A. M., 372
Caruso, D. R., 333
Cascio, W. F., 91
Casper, W. J., 159
Castilla, E. J., 228

Castro, S. L., 440
Cattell, R. B., 332
Cavanaugh, M. A., 158
Ceci, S. J., 331
Cellar, D. F., 299
Cellitti, D. R., 59
Ceranic, T. L., 231
Chambers, T., 517
Chamerlain, K., 155
Chang, C., 438
Chang, W. W., 409
Chao, G. T., 523, 538
Chaplin, C., 484–485
Chatman, J. A., 529, 534, 535, 537
Chavez, C., 437
Chazelle, D., 209
Cheadle, D., 45
Chen, C. C., 124, 301, 420
Chen, Y., 301
Chen, Y. R., 420
Chen, Z., 58
Chen, Z. X., 476
Cherng, A., 453
Cherniss, C., 333
Chernyshenko, O. S., 298
Cherrington, D., 89
Chesky, B., 531
Chess, W. A., 157
Chiaburu, D. S., 89
Chiang, F. F. T., 42
Chien Farh, C. I. C., 333
Child, J., 504
Childress, J., 512
Chiu, C., 252
Chiu, C. Y., 301
Christal, R. E., 296
Christian, J., 439
Christian, M. S., 536
Christiansen, N. D., 80, 304, 305
Chua, R. Y. J., 420
Church, A. H., 121
Churchill, W., 486
Clarke, S., 536
Clason, P., 334
Clayton, L. D., 366
Clegg, C. W., 367
Clinton, W. J., 461
Clooney, G., 133
Clore, G., 371
Cohen, B., 83
Cohen, J., 28, 297
Cohen, K., 195
Cohen, P., 28
Cohen, R. R., 407
Cohen, S., 156, 158
Cohen, S. G., 342, 367
Cohen-Charash, Y., 185, 195, 228
Coiné, T., 52
Colarelli, S. M., 324, 335
Colbert, A. E., 192, 408, 447
Cole, M. S., 333, 368–369
Colella, A., 194

Coleman, P. T., 385
Coleman, V. I., 57
Colligan, M., 154, 158
Collins, J., 505
Collins-Nakai, R., 91
Colquitt, J. A., 56, 185, 195, 220, 228,
    230, 255, 264, 299, 301, 335,
    404, 405, 476
Coltrane, E., 274
Colvin, G., 533, 535, 537
Colvin, J., 26
Comer, D. R., 369
Concalo, J. A., 408
Conger, J. A., 475
Conlin, M., 91, 507
Conlon, D. E., 185, 195, 228, 263, 440
Conte, J. M., 334
Conti, R., 507
Converse, S. A., 408
Cook, T., 419
Cook, T. D., 28
Cooke, D. K., 304
Coon, H. M., 301
Coons, A. E., 473
Cooper, C. L., 157, 159
Cooper, E. A., 179, 194
Cooper, H., 299
Cooper, W. H., 89
Cooper-Hakim, A., 113, 124–125,
    288, 302
Copper, C., 407
Cordery, J. L., 367
Corley, K. G., 87
Cortina, J. M., 305
Costa, P. T., Jr., 269, 296–297
Costabile, D., 462
Costanza, D. P., 311, 321, 331
Costolo, D., 96, 513
Cote, S., 333
Cotton, J. L., 158, 436
Couch, L. L., 226
Covey, S. M. R., 230
Cowie, H., 60
Cox, T., 370, 382
Coy, P., 91, 228
Crane, A., 218
Crawford, E. R., 158, 191, 391
Crede, M. A., 334
Cripps, K., 364
Criqui, M. H., 298
Cromwell, J., 181
Cropanzano, R., 123, 169, 192, 438,
    440, 489
Crouter, A., 155
Cruise, T., 311, 312
Csikszentmihalyi, M., 123
Cuarón, A., 133
Cullen, J. B., 202, 314, 323, 419
Cullen, M. J., 302
Cumberbatch, B., 486
Cummings, J. N., 372
Cummings, L. L., 170

Cunningham, C. R., 159
Cunningham, D. A., 157
Cunningham, M. R., 304
Cunningham-Snell, N. A., 539

D

Daft, R. L., 407
Dahm, P. C., 155
Dai, G., 500, 507
Dalal, R. S., 58, 113, 124
Dalessio, A., 125
Dance, C., 486
Dane, E., 262
Daniel, T. A., 59
Daniels, C., 156
Dansereau, F., Jr., 373, 471
Darrat, M., 438
Daus, C. S., 124
Davenport, R., 407
Davenport, T. H., 28
Davies, M., 333
Davis, G. F., 505
Davis, J. H., 200, 201, 205, 226
Davison, H. K., 305, 438
Dawis, R. V., 97, 121
Dawson, C., 27
Dawson, J. F., 519
Day, D. V., 471
De Chermont, K., 298
De Church, L. A., 406
De Corte, W., 336
De Cuyper, N., 59
De Dreu, C. K. W., 124, 368, 370, 372,
    406, 439
De Lange, A. H., 91
De Meuse, K. P., 342, 373, 500, 507
De Vries, T. A., 405
De Wit, F. R. C., 406
De Witte, H., 59
Deal, T. E., 534
Dean, M. A., 334
Dean, R. A., 324, 335
Dearborn, M. J., 157
Deary, I. J., 332
Deaton, A., 125
Debow, D., 187
Deci, E. L., 169, 192, 194
Defrank, R. S., 156
DeGeest, D. S., 369
DeGrassi, S. W., 303
Delbecq, A. L., 368, 404
Delery, J. E., 92
Delongis, A., 156
DeMatteo, J. S., 373
Den Hartog, D. N., 472
Denes-Raj, V., 250
DeNeve, K. M., 299
Denniston, A., 486
Denyer, D., 28
Derks, D., 123
DeRue, D. S., 405, 472
Derven, M., 506

Dessler, G., 91
Detert, J. R., 89
Detterman, D. K., 334
Deutsch, M., 368
Deutsch, M. A., 373
Devine, D. J., 366, 369
Devine, K., 91
DeVore, C. J., 60, 439
Dewe, P. J., 157
Diamond, S., 404
Dickerson, T., 256
Dickter, D. N., 324, 335
Diefendorff, J. M., 124
Diehl, M., 404
Diener, E., 109, 116, 123, 124, 299
Dierdorff, E. C., 302
Digman, J. M., 296
Dilchert, S., 304–305
Dimon, J., 54
Dimotakis, N., 332
Dineen, B. R., 227
D'Innocenzo, D., 407
Dirks, K. T., 220, 232
Dishan, K., 407
Dixon, P., 303
Doheny, K., 160
Dolan, S., 407
Donaldson, T., 230
Donnellan, M. B., 272
Donovan, J. J., 193
Donovan, M. A., 35, 57
Dorfman, P. W., 301, 459, 477, 478
Dorgan, B. L., 397–398, 409
Dotlich, D., 409
Doty, D., 406
Douglas, C., 423, 438
Douma, B., 231
Doverspike, D., 529, 539
Doverspike, D. D., 299
Downey, R., Jr., 352
Drach-Zahavy, A., 437
Drasgow, F., 107
Drexler, M., 452
Driskell, J. E., 409
Drucker, P. F., 60
Druskat, V. U., 330
Du Gay, P., 536
Duckworth, H., 367
Duffy, M. K., 56, 229
Duffy, R. D., 194
Duke, A. B., 438
Dulebohn, J. H., 472
Duncan, T. E., 170
Dunfee, T. W., 230
Dunford, B. B., 366
Dunkel-Schetter, C., 156
duPont, J. E., 416
Durham, C. C., 195
Dutton, J. E., 123
Dvir, T., 478
Dvorak, P., 436, 505
Dworkin, T. M., 230

Dwoskin, E., 228
Dwyer, P., 382
Dyson, J., 517, 518

E
Earley, P. C., 176, 228, 301, 310, 368
Easterbrook, S., 487
Eby, L. T., 299, 373, 539
Eddy, E. R., 405
Eden, D., 478
Edmonds, G. W., 297
Edmondson, A., 407
Edmondson, G., 300, 526
Edwards, C., 27, 504, 506
Edwards, J. R., 97, 121, 155, 537
Egan, T. M., 537
Ehrhart, M. G., 516, 536
Einarsen, S. S., 60
Eisenberger, R., 91
Eisenhardt, K. M., 438
Eisenhower, D. D., 456
Eissa, G., 56
Eldam, M., 27
Eldridge, L. D., 154
Ellis, A. P. J., 404, 409
Ellison, L., 178, 412
Ellison, S., 262
Ells, S., 268, 294
Emerson, R. M., 436
Emo, A. K., 332–333
Engardio, P., 382
Ensari, N., 439
Epstein, S., 250
Erdogan, B., 125
Erez, A., 56, 113, 124, 299, 335
Erez, M., 70, 88, 175, 176, 193, 404, 409
Ergen, C., 428
Erickson, E. H., 227
Ericsson, K. A., 261
Essens, P. J. M. D., 405
Esser, J., 408
Eucker, T. R., 261
Euwema, M. C., 406
Evans, C., 352
Evers, A., 439
Ewen, R., 371
Ewing, J., 538

F
Fagerbakke, B., 377
Fairchild, C., 414, 536
Fairclough, S., 506
Falbe, C. M., 431, 436, 437
Fandt, P. M., 439
Farace, R. V., 407
Farnham, A., 332
Farrell, D., 88, 89
Farrelly, D., 333–334
Favre, B., 139, 157
Favreau, J., 73
Feist, G. J., 300
Feldman, D. C., 88, 156

Felps, W., 88
Fenigstein, A., 23
Ference, R., 408
Ferguson, R., 385
Fern, E. F., 58
Fernandez, C. F., 474
Ferrin, D. L., 220, 232
Ferris, G. R., 122, 423, 437–439, 472
Festinger, L., 407
Fetter, R., 58, 477
Fichman, M., 90
Field, R. H. G., 473
Fields, D., 264
Finn, R. H., 194
Fiorina, C., 501
Firestone, I. J., 231
Fisher, A., 89, 91, 92, 333, 367
Fisher, C. D., 537
Fisher, D. M., 405
Fisher, R., 429, 440
Fitzgerald, M. P., 106, 123
Flaherty Manchester, C., 155, 160
Fleeson, W., 296
Fleisher, L., 439
Fleishman, E. A., 311, 321, 331, 334, 473, 474
Flint, J., 88
Floor, L., 474
Flores, S., 268
Florey, A. T., 371
Florida, R., 57
Fogli, L., 302
Foldes, H. J., 477
Folger, R., 228, 229
Folkman, S., 154, 156
Ford, H., 483–484
Foroohar, R., 533
Forsyth, D. R., 439
Foushee, H. C., 364
Foust, D., 537, 538
Fowlkes, J. E., 409
Fox, J., 28
Franklin, B., 198
Frauenheim, E., 89, 156, 226, 229, 303
Freeman, M., 315
Frei, R. L., 298
Freidberg, J., 57
Freidberg, K., 57
French, J. R. P., Jr., 155, 436
Frese, M., 159
Frey, M. C., 334
Fried, Y., 122
Friedman, H. S., 298
Friedman, L., 475
Friedman, M., 157, 299
Friedman, T. L., 11
Frink, D. D., 423, 438
Frommer, D., 27
Frone, M. R., 155, 229
Fry, L., 537
Fry, M., 506
Fu, P. P., 88, 420

Fujita, F., 299
Fuller, B., 438
Fulmer, A., 440
Fulmer, I. S., 28, 195, 302, 369
Funder, D. C., 296
Furnham, A., 288, 302
Furstenberg, D. von, 212–214
Fusilier, M. R., 157
Futrell, D., 342, 373

G

Gabarro, J. J., 227
Gaertner, S., 74, 89, 90
Gaines, J., 537
Galbraith, J., 170, 496
Gallagher, L., 535, 539
Gallagher, P., 296
Galton, F., 332
Gandolfi, F., 506
Ganster, D. C., 155, 157
Gardner, H., 332, 517
Gardner, P. D., 523, 538
Gardner, W. L., 300
Garland, H., 263
Garvin, D. A., 26
Garza, A. S., 404
Gates B., 318
Gaudiosi, J., 505
Gavin, J. H., 371
Gavin, M. B., 232
Gaynor, M., 259
Gebert, D., 370, 372
Geider, S., 229
Gelfand, M. J., 88, 310, 440
Gellar, A., 303
Gelles, D., 261, 503
Gent, C., 422
George, J. M., 57, 300
Gerdes, L., 89, 195, 539
Gerhardt, M. W., 298, 447
Gerhart, B., 28, 90, 192, 195
Gerras, S. J., 536
Gersick, C. J. G., 367–368
Gerstner, C. R., 471
Gertner, J., 491
Geschka, H., 404
Giacalone, R. A., 229
Gibson, C. B., 176, 301
Gibson, R., 538
Gibson, W. M., 101, 122
Gigerenzer, G., 250
Gilbert, D., 536
Gilbreth, F. B., 122
Gill, C. M., 269
Gillenwater, P., 538
Gilliland, S. W., 229, 305
Gilmore, D. C., 423, 438
Gist, M. E., 167, 191, 478
Glanzer, M., 407
Glaser, R., 407
Glazer, E., 538
Glibkowski, B. C., 91

Glick, W. H., 505
Glomb, T. M., 124, 155, 229, 370
Gobeli, D. H., 506
Godinez, V., 367
Goff, S., 335
Goffee, R., 515, 535
Goffin, R. D., 304
Gogus, C. I., 538
Gold, R., 536
Goldbacher, E., 170
Goldberg, L. R., 269, 296–298
Goldenhar, L., 154, 158
Goldman, B. M., 440
Goldstein, D. L., 156
Goldstein, H. W., 537
Goldstein, N. B., 305
Goleman, D., 332
Gonzalez-Mule, E., 335, 369
Gonzalez-Roma, V., 191
Good, L., 414
Goodall, A., 164, 189, 190
Goode, M., 486
Gooding, R. Z., 372, 505
Goodstein, J., 227
Gopinath, C., 500, 506
Gordan, J., 366
Gordon, J., 354
Gore, B., 488
Gosling, S. D., 297, 298
Gottfedson, L. S., 332
Goudreau, J., 159
Gouran, D., 408
Graeff, C. L., 474
Graen, G. B., 445, 471
Graf, A. B., 537
Grant, A. M., 57, 122
Grant, S., 303
Gravelle, M., 538
Graziano, W. G., 298
Green, H., 60, 170, 437
Green, S. G., 471, 475
Greenbaum, R. L., 56
Greenberg, J., 194, 211, 226, 229, 230
Greene, E., 404
Greenfeld, K. T., 474
Greenfield, J., 83
Greenwood, R., 503, 506
Greer, J. L., 406
Griffeth, R. W., 74, 89–91
Griffeth, T. L., 439
Griffin, J., 451
Grizzle, J. W., 536
Groszkiewicz, D., 505
Grove, A., 415
Grow, B., 89, 232
Grubb, P., 154, 158
Gruen, R. J., 156
Gruenfeld, D. H., 371
Gubbins, E., 538
Guerrero, L., 507
Gully, S. M., 408

Gunther, M., 232, 539
Gupta, B., 182
Gupta, N., 90, 92
Gupta, S., 358
Gupta, V., 301, 459
Gurin, G., 474
Guzzo, R. A., 367, 368, 408

H

Hachiya, D., 89
Hackett, R. D., 476
Hackman, J. R., 107, 122, 194, 367, 373, 403, 504, 506
Haga, W. J., 471
Hagafors, R., 368, 404
Hagmaier, T., 194
Haigh, J., 539
Hair, E. C., 298
Hakanen, J. J., 159
Halfhill, T., 367
Hall, D., 181
Hall, E., 371
Hall-Merenda, K. E., 476
Halpern, D. F., 331
Halpin, A. W., 473
Halvorson, T., 400
Hamblin, R. L., 373
Hamilton, A., 32, 154, 158
Hamm, J., 507
Hamm, S., 195, 232, 496
Hammond, G. D., 122
Han, Y., 505
Haneberg, L., 56
Hanges, P. J., 301, 459
Hanisch, K. A., 125
Hansen, F., 27, 28, 195, 228
Hansson, M., 506
Haran, C., 156
Hargadon, A., 404
Harkins, S. G., 373, 403
Harman, W. S., 88
Harms, P. D., 297
Harper, D., 59
Harris, B. T., 420
Harris, E. F., 473
Harris, J. A., 475
Harris, M., 358
Harris, M. J., 331
Harris, M. M., 303
Harris, V. A., 263
Harrison, D. A., 80, 89–90, 113, 125, 136, 230, 262, 324, 335, 370, 371
Harrison, R. V., 155
Harrison, S. H., 87
Hartel, C. E. J., 124
Harter, J. K., 191
Hartigan, J. A., 335
Hartley, E., 474
Hartnell, C. A., 536, 538–539
Hass, M. R., 367
Hastings, J. E., 157
Hastings, R., 512

Hatfield, E., 124
Hathaway, A., 247
Hauge, L. J., 60
Haugland, S. N., 303
Hauser, S. G., 229
Havlovic, S. J., 135, 156
Hayashi, A. M., 262
Hayes, T. H., 191
Haynes, D., 298
Hazelwood, J., 252
Hechanova, R., 80
Hecker, D., 60
Hedlund, J., 369, 404, 405
Heim, J., 36
Heimans, M., 224
Heine, S. J., 301
Hekman, D. R., 88
Heller, D., 298
Helm, B., 226
Helmreich, R. L., 364
Hempel, J., 224, 535
Hempel, P. S., 505
Hemphill, J. K., 473
Hemsworth, C., 352
Henderson, N., 137, 149
Hengchen, D., 159
Henle, C. A., 11, 176, 229
Henneman, T., 192
Henney, D., 181
Herscovitch, L., 87, 113, 125, 185, 255,
        264, 464, 477
Hersey, P., 455, 474
Herzberg, F., 28
Hessels, M., 534
Hewson, M., 414
Hezlett, S. A., 335, 539
Hickson, D. J., 436
Higgins, C. A., 297–298
Higgins, T., 538
Higgs, A. C., 360, 373
Hill, J. W., 90
Hinings, C. R., 436
Hirokawa, R., 408
Hirschman, A. O., 89
Hirst, G., 404
Hochschild, A. R., 123
Hochwarter, W. A., 423, 437, 438,
        500, 507
Hodgkinson, G. P., 269
Hoever, I. J., 372
Hoffman, B. J., 335
Hoffman, D., 73, 513
Hoffman, J., 159
Hoffman, L., 371
Hofmann, D. A., 159, 536
Hofstede, G., 42, 283–285, 301
Hoft, S., 304
Hogan, J., 298
Hogan, R. T., 19, 296
Hogarth, R. M., 262
Hogg, M. A., 263
Holcombe, K. M., 536

Holland, B., 298
Holland, J. L., 282–283, 300
Hollenbeck, J. R., 175, 193, 366, 367, 369,
        372, 382, 403–405, 409
Hollinger, R. C., 59
Hollingshead, A. B., 408
Hollweg, L., 59
Holmes, E., 412, 415, 419,
        434–435, 458
Holmes, S., 232
Holmes, T. H., 134, 156
Holste, J. S., 264
Holt, J. L., 439
Holtom, B. C., 70, 88, 90
Holtz, B. C., 336
Hom, P. W., 88, 90
Homan, A. C., 370, 372
Homans, G. C., 193
Hong, Y., 252, 536
Hoobler, J. M., 155
Hosford, C., 506
Hough, L. M., 288, 302
House, R. J., 155, 301, 459, 473, 476
Howard, J. A., 263
Howard, J. H., 157
Howard-Grenville, J. A., 537
Howell, J. M., 476
Howell, J. P., 477, 478
Hsieh, T., 482, 502–503
Hu, C., 229
Hu, J., 536
Hua, W., 229
Huang, X., 58
Huang, Y., 420
Huber, G. P., 505
Huber, V. L., 261
Huff, C., 192
Hugh, S., 55
Hui, C. M., 263
Hui, W., 535
Hulin, C., 229
Hulin, C. L., 58, 87, 89, 121, 124
Hull, C. L., 191
Humphrey, R. H., 333
Humphrey, S. E., 122, 368, 372, 404, 405, 472
Hunter, J. E., 305, 324, 334, 335
Huntington, R., 91
Hurd, M., 501
Hurrell, J., Jr., 154, 158
Huselid, M. A., 14, 27
Hutchison, S., 91
Hymowitz, C., 504–505

I

Ibarra, H., 467
Ichniowski, C., 366
Idaszak, J. R., 107
Iger, B., 178
Ihlwan, M., 27
Ilgen, D. R., 56, 192, 366, 369, 372, 382,
        403–405, 409
Ilies, R., 298, 302, 332, 447, 472, 474, 477

Imai, L., 310
Immelt, J., 452, 453
Incalaterra, K. A., 408
Ironson, G. H., 101, 122
Irwin, J. L., 117, 125
Isaacson, W., 318, 475
Isen, A. M., 124
Ito, T., 512
Ivancevich, J. M., 156, 264, 366

J

Jablin, F. M., 406
Jackson, C. L., 57, 154, 301, 394, 403, 405
Jackson, J. J., 297
Jackson, M., 89, 323
Jackson, P. R., 367
Jackson, S. A., 123
Jackson, S. E., 371
Jacobs, R. R., 231
Jago, A. G., 473
James, B., 22
Jana, R., 538
Jang, K. J., 475
Janis, I. L., 408
Jansen, P. G. W., 91
Jardine, L., 28
Javidan, M., 301, 459
Jayaratne, S., 157
Jefferson, T., 32
Jeffries, M., 178
Jehn, K. A., 406, 439
Jenkins, C. D., 140
Jenkins, G. D., Jr., 90, 92
Jennings, K. R., 158
Jensen, M. A. C., 367
Jensen-Campbell, L. A., 298
Jermier, J. M., 465, 477, 478, 537
Jia, R. T., 58
Jiang, K., 536
Jimeno, D. I., 90
Jin, J., 333
Jobs, S., 318, 412, 458, 460
Johansson, S., 73, 315, 352
John, E., 376, 400
John, O. P., 297
Johns, G., 87, 90
Johnson, A., 414
Johnson, A. M., 475
Johnson, C., 404
Johnson, D. E., 113, 124
Johnson, D. W., 373
Johnson, E. C., 529, 539
Johnson, G., 60
Johnson, J. J., 202, 314, 323, 419
Johnson, K., 263
Johnson, L. B., 461
Johnson, M. D., 302
Johnson, R., 120, 178, 373, 524
Johnson, R. A., 372
Johnson, R. C., 159
Johnson, S. M., 125
Johnson, S. R., 154

Johnston, J., 154, 158
Jolie, A., 415
Jones, A. P., 157
Jones, E. E., 263
Jones, G., 515, 535
Jones, G. R., 530
Jones, M., 132
Jones, T. M., 215, 230
Jones, W. H., 226
Jonze, S., 115
Jordan, P. J., 406
Joseph, D. L., 333, 336
Joshi, A., 370, 408
Judd, C. M., 263
Judge, T. A., 113, 121, 122, 124, 125, 154,
        278, 288, 297–299, 302, 305, 324,
        332, 335, 447, 464, 474, 475, 477
Jung, C. G., 281, 300
Jung, K. G., 125
Junod, T., 469

K

Kacmar, C. J., 423, 438
Kacmar, K. M., 438
Kafry, D., 157
Kahn, R. L., 154, 156, 368, 474
Kahn, W. A., 191
Kahneman, D., 114, 125, 248, 250, 253, 263,
        264
Kaihla, P., 535
Kalanick, T., 198, 223, 426, 427
Kalwarski, T., 194
Kane, Y. I., 475, 505
Kanfer, R., 228
Kanki, B., 364
Kanter, R. M., 88
Kaplan, D. A., 539
Kaplan, D. M., 423
Kaplan, M., 335
Kaplan, M. D. G., 57
Kaplan, S. A., 298
Kaptein, M., 230, 231
Katulak, N. A., 331
Katz, D., 368, 474
Katz, S., 414
Katzenberg, J., 100
Katz-Navon, T., 536
Kavanaugh, M. J., 264
Kazmi, S., 334
Kearney, E., 370, 372
Keats, B., 505
Keller, R. T., 476
Kelley, H. H., 263
Kelley, T., 330, 368, 380, 404
Kelloway, E. K., 229, 478
Kelman, H. C., 437
Kemmelmeier, M., 301
Kemmerer, B. E., 155
Kemp, N. J., 367
Kendall, L. M., 121
Kendell, J., 333
Kennedy, A. A., 534

Kennedy, J. C., 420
Kennedy, J. F., 390, 461
Kenny, D. A., 298
Kenny, T., 377
Kerlinger, F. N., 28
Kern, M. C., 358
Kerr, S., 465, 473, 477, 478
Kesling, B., 535
Kessler, S., 539
Kiburz, K. M., 159
Kiger, P., 505
Kihn, J. A., 117, 125
Kiker, D. S., 59
Kiley, D., 27, 226, 506
Kim, E., 370
Kim, H., 431, 437
Kim, S., 538
Kim, T., 538
Kimes, M., 261
King, L., 124
Kinicki, A., 538–539
Kinicki, A. J., 125
Kirkland, R., 194
Kirkman, B. L., 301
Kirkpatrick, S. A., 477
Kisamore, J. L., 304
Kish-Gephart, J. J., 230, 262
Kissinger, H., 412
Klawsky, J. D., 299
Klebe, L., 262
Klein, G., 262
Klein, H. J., 175, 193, 523, 538
Klein, K. J., 370, 372, 538
Klimoski, R. J., 408
Klotz, A. C., 406
Kluckhohn, C., 301
Kluwer, E. S., 439
Knight, A. P., 370, 372
Kobasa, S., 157
Koehn, N. F., 475
Koenig, R., 368
Koh, W., 477
Kohlberg, L., 215–217, 231
Kohles, J. C., 476
Kohn, M. L., 331–332
Kolb, D. M., 440
Kolhatkar, S., 228
Kolodinsky, R. W., 423, 438
Konopaske, R., 264, 366
Konstans, C., 324, 335
Koopman, P. L., 472
Korbin, J. L., 334
Korman, A. K., 474
Korsgaard, M. A., 228
Koslowsky, M., 89
Kostopoulos, K., 407
Kowitt, B., 414, 436, 535
Kozlowski, S. W. J., 372, 405
Kraatz, M. S., 91
Kraft, K. L., 215, 231
Kraimer, M. L., 431
Krantz, L., 129

Kranz, G., 478, 504, 539
Krause, S., 281
Krausz, M., 89
Kreitner, R., 261
Krell, E., 57
Krilowicz, T. J., 58
Kristof-Brown, A. L., 408, 529, 539
Kroeber, A. L., 301
Kroeck, K. G., 476
Krone, K. J., 406
Krueger, A. B., 114, 125
Kukenberger, M. R., 407
Kullman, E., 414
Kulmann, T. M., 136
Kuman, K., 371
Kuncel, N. R., 334, 335
Kuntz, P., 194
Kurek, K. E., 123
Kurtzerg, T. R., 227
Kvamme, N., 160
Kyounghee, H. K., 407

L

Ladika, S., 88, 264
Lam, H., 58, 124
Lam, W., 58
Lambert, L. S., 229
Lamm, H., 403
Landy, F. J., 192
Langan-Fox, J., 303, 406
Langton, L., 59
LaRocco, J. M., 157
Larsen, R. J., 109, 123
Larson, A., 475
Larson, E. W., 506
Lashinsky, A., 224, 507
Latack, J. C., 135, 156
Latane, B., 373, 403
Latham, G. P., 28, 172–175, 191, 193, 195,
        261
Latham, S., 195
Lau, D., 371–372
Lau, I. Y. M., 301
Law, K. S., 319, 333, 476
Lawler, E. E., III, 121, 122, 170, 195, 366,
        373, 506
Lawler, E. J., 437
Lawrence, C., 377
Lawrence, P. R., 122
Lawson, C., 261
Lawthom, R., 519
Layard, R., 116
Lazarus, R. S., 110, 123, 154, 156
Leach, D. J., 472
Leahey, C., 414, 436
Leavitt, H. J., Jr., 407
Ledford, G. E., 366, 367
Lee, C. A., 436
Lee, H. B., 28
Lee, H. U., 370–371
Lee, J. M., 536
Lee, K., 304

Lee, K-F., 420
Lee, L., 232
Lee, N., 322, 323
Lee, S. I., 301
Lee, S. M., 194
Lee, T., 129
Lee, T. H., 90
Lee, T. W., 70, 88, 90
Lehman, D. W., 471
Lehmann, A. C., 261
Lehmann-Willenbrock, N., 368
Leitner, K., 157
Lemmon, G., 155
Lencioni, P., 16, 227
Lengel, R. H., 407
Leno, J., 10
Lentz, E., 539
Leonard, D., 152, 228
Leondis, A., 194
LePine, J. A., 40, 56–58, 113, 124, 143, 144,
        154, 157, 158, 191, 220, 255, 264,
        299, 335, 369, 370, 382, 394, 403–405
LePine, M. A., 143, 144, 154, 158
Leroy, S., 155
Leslie, L. M., 160
Leung, K., 301
Levenson, E., 436
Leventhal, G. S., 206, 228
Levering, R., 15, 26, 27, 88, 120, 121
Levesque, M. J., 298
Levin, S., 461, 476
Levis, J., 259
Levitz, J., 259
Lev-Ram, M., 120, 437, 535
Levy, A., 120
Levy, P. E., 438
Levy, S., 420
Lewicki, R. J., 205, 227, 439
Lewis, D., 264
Lewis, D. D., 462
Lewis, J. D., 227
Lewis, M., 22, 28
Li, L., 88
Li, N., 420
Liao, H., 59, 536
Liden, R. C., 471, 472
Lieberman, J. D., 404
Lievens, F., 336
Ligdas, N., 264
Liker, J. K., 57, 366
Likert, R., 474
Lim, B. C., 372
Lim, V. K. G., 89
Lima, L., 539
Lin, L. F., 101, 122
Lincoln, A., 128, 461, 462
Lincoln, J., 371
Lind, E. A., 226, 228
Linebaugh, K., 537
Linklater, R., 274
Linoerfer, J., 408
Lirtzman, S. I., 155

Litterer, J. A., 439
Littman, J., 330, 380, 404
Liu, H. L., 124
Liu, W., 58
Lobel, S., 370, 382
Locke, E. A., 28, 121, 172–175, 185, 193, 477
Locke, K., 28
Lockwood, N. R., 260–261
Lodi-Smith, J., 297
Loehlin, J. C., 297, 331
Loher, B. T., 106, 123
Lombardo, M. M., 155
Lorenzi, E., 261
Louis, M. R., 538
Loviscky, G., 217, 231
Lowe, K. B., 301, 476
Lowery, C. M., 58
Lubinski, D., 334
Lublin, J. S., 538
Lucas, R. E., 272
Lucas, S., 90
Luchman, J. N., 298
Luciano, J., 498
Luk, D. M., 136
Lundgren, T., 495
Luo, Y., 420
Luria, G., 536
Luthans, F., 28, 185, 195, 261, 366
Lux, S., 438
Lynch, J. W., 88
Lynch, P., 232
Lyons, B. D., 335
Lyubomirsky, S., 124

M

Mabius, E., 525
Maccoby, N., 474
MacDermid, S. M., 124
Mach, M., 407
MacKenzie, S. B., 58, 59, 464, 476–478
MacMilan, D., 439
MacMillan, P. S., 57, 350, 368
Macy, W. H., 191
Madoff, B., 54
Mael, F. A., 263, 436
Magnus, K., 299
Maher, K., 537
Maier, N., 371
Maier, N. R. F., 191
Mainous, A. G., III, 89
Maitlis, S., 519
Major, D. A., 366, 403, 404
Malhotra, D., 439
Malloy, T. E., 298
Mandel, M., 155
Mangalindan, J. P., 537
Manjoo, F., 437
Mann, O. K., 58
Manning, J., 28
Manning, P., 415
Mannix, E. A., 370, 371, 382, 405
Mannor, M. J., 368

Mansfield, L. R., 125
Manson, T. M., 304
Manz, C. C., 366
Marcario, R., 517
Marcelo, S. L., 451, 513
March, J. G., 262, 263
Marchionne, S., 448, 449, 451, 495
Marcic, D., 154, 403, 478
Marcus, B., 304
Markham, S. E., 372
Marks, M. A., 405, 406, 409
Marks, M. L., 500, 507
Marquardt, M., 409
Marquez, J., 156, 227, 229
Marriott, J. W., Jr., 514
Marrone, J. A., 405
Marsh, H. W., 123
Marshall-Mies, J., 311, 321, 331
Martin, L. R., 298
Martinez Arias, R., 382
Martinko, M. J., 300
Martins, L. L., 371
Martocchio, J. J., 90
Martz, A., 408
Maruyama, G., 373
Maslach, C., 408
Maslow, A. H., 169, 192
Mason, B., 238, 261
Mathieu, J. E., 57, 87, 288, 302, 368, 394,
        405, 407
Matlack, C., 506
Matten, D., 218
Mattern, K. D., 335–336
Matteson, M., 264, 366
Matthews, G., 332–333
Matthisen, B., 60
Mattioli, D., 537, 538
Mausner, B., 28
Mawritz, M. B., 56
May, K. E., 371
Mayer, D. M., 516, 536
Mayer, J. D., 333
Mayer, M., 149
Mayer, R. C., 200, 201, 205, 226, 232
Mayes, B. T., 157
McAdam, L., 242
McAdam, R., 238, 261
McAllister, D. J., 200, 226
McAuley, E., 170
McCall, M. W., 155
McCarthy, J. M., 475
McCartney, K., 331
McCaulley, M. H., 300
McClelland, C. L., 123
McColl-Kennedy, J. R., 477
McConaughey, M., 247
McCormick, B. W., 369
McCrae, R. R., 269, 296–297, 301
McCrea, J., 503
McCrory, J., 238, 261
McDaniel, L. S., 90
McDaniel, M. A., 298, 439

McDonald-Mann, D., 478
McFadden, R. D., 57
McFarlin, D. B., 155
McGrath, J. E., 369
McGrath, M., 504, 526
McGregor, J., 60, 195, 436, 536
McIntyre, D. A., 27
McIntyre, M., 367
McKean, K., 264
McKee-Ryan, F. M., 125
McKenna, J. F., 179, 194
McKeown, G., 147
McLean, L. D., 537
McLendon, C. L., 407
McLeod, P., 370, 382
McMillan, R., 507
McMurray, V. V., 436
McMurrian, R., 155
McTigue, T., 274
Medlock, K., 22
Medsker, G. J., 347, 360, 373
Mehl, M. R., 298
Mehng, S. A., 160
Meier, D. P., 57
Meier, K. J., 504
Meier, L. L., 158
Meindl, J. R., 476
Mell, J. N., 408
Melner, S. B., 366
Mendenhall, M., 80, 136
Mendenhall, M. E., 538
Menon, S., 155
Menon, T., 252
Mento, A. J., 185, 193
Merrill, D., 419
Mesmer-Magnus, J. R., 262, 406
Meyer, C. J., 372, 405
Meyer, J. P., 68, 87, 113, 125, 185, 255, 264, 464, 477
Meyers, D. G., 250
Meyrowitz, C., 414
Miceli, M. P., 230
Michael, E., 224
Michaels, D., 505
Michaelsen, I., 371
Michel, A., 158
Michel, J. W., 335
Mickel, A. E., 192
Miles, R. E., 506
Milewski, G. B., 334
Milkman, K. L., 159
Miller, B., 22, 416
Miller, B. K., 438
Miller, C., 170
Miller, C. C., 505
Miller, J., 154, 371
Miller, K. I., 472
Miller, L., 264, 478
Miller, L. K., 373
Miller, M., 154
Miller, M. L., 299
Miller, S., 158

Miller-Frost, S. L., 367
Milligan, S., 159, 264
Milliken, F. J., 371
Miner, A. G., 124, 229
Miner, J. B., 304
Miners, C. T. H., 333
Minette, K. A., 192
Minkoff, H. B., 195
Minor, I., 438
Mintzberg, H., 437
Mio, J. S., 461, 476
Miron-Spektor, E., 404
Mischel, W., 303
Mishra, A., 500, 507
Mishra, K., 507
Mitchell, M. S., 229, 262
Mitchell, T. R., 70, 88, 90, 167, 191, 192
Mitra, A., 90
Moag, J. F., 206, 229
Mobley, W., 90
Moeller, N. L., 106, 123
Moffat, R. W., Jr., 496
Mohammed, S., 370, 372, 408
Mohrman, S. A., 366
Mol, S., 286
Molden, D. C., 263
Molso, M., 475
Monge, P. R., 407, 472
Moon, H., 263, 440
Moonves, L., 178
Moore, H., 333–334
Moorhead, G., 408
Moorman, R. H., 477
Moran, M., 294–295
Morgeson, F. P., 122, 368, 472, 505, 536
Morris, J. R., 91
Morris, M. W., 252, 301
Morris, T., 506
Morris, W. N., 123
Morrison, A. M., 155
Morrison, D., 495
Morrison, E. W., 42, 91, 407, 537
Morrison, T. G., 438
Morse, N., 474
Mosakowski, E., 310
Moskowitz, C., 400
Moskowitz, M., 15, 26, 27, 88, 120, 121
Motowidlo, S. J., 56, 58, 59, 335
Mount, M. K., 288, 297–300, 302, 303, 335, 369, 370
Mourier, P., 538
Mowday, R. T., 87, 191
Mowen, J. C., 536
Muchinsky, P. M., 89, 300
Mueller, W. S., 367
Mulcahy, A., 242, 261
Mullen, B., 404, 407, 409
Mullins, R., 408
Mulvey, P. W., 537
Murnighan, J. K., 371–372

Muros, J. P., 477
Murphy, L., 154, 158
Murphy, L. R., 160
Murphy, M., 184
Murphy, R. M., 122
Murray, S. S., 159
Musk, E., 444, 456, 458, 469
Mutanen, P., 159
Myers, I. B., 300
Myers, L., 158

N

Nadkarni, S., 370, 372
Nahrgang, J. D., 122, 405, 472
Nahum-Shani, I., 157
Naquin, C. E., 227
Narayanan, L., 155
Narvaez, D., 231
Nauta, A., 439
Naveh, E., 404, 536
Naylor, J. C., 192
Naylor, P., 60
Neal, M. A., 370, 382
Neal, M. E., 436, 437
Neale, M. A., 371, 439
Near, J. P., 230
Neck, C., 408
Neihoff, B. P., 58
Neisser, U., 331
Nelson, D., 373
Nemeth, C. J., 371
Netemeyer, R. G., 155
Neubaum, D. O., 231
Neubert, M. J., 369
Neufeld, D. J., 476
Neufeld, S., 155
Neuman, G. A., 370
Neumann, J. von, 318
Newcomb, T. M., 371, 474
Newman, D. A., 113, 125, 333
Newman, K. L., 336
Newman, R., 57
Ng, K. Y., 185, 195, 228, 440
Ng, P. T., 264
Ng, T. W. H., 88, 156, 299
Nicholson, N., 90
Nicholson-Crotty, S., 487, 504
Nicolas, S., 535
Nida, S. A., 407
Niehoff, B. P., 478
Nifadkar, S. S., 301
Nijstad, B. A., 124
Niles-Jolly, K., 516, 536
Nisbett, R. E., 250
Nisen, M., 295
Noe, R. A., 106, 123, 255, 264
Noel, J., 409
Noel, T. W., 231
Noer, D. M., 507
Nohe, C., 158
Nolan, C., 247
Nonaka, I., 261

Nooyi, I., 414
Norman, W. T., 296
Norris, W. R., 474
Northcraft, G. B., 439
Novak, M., 471
Novakovic, P., 414
Novicevik, M. M., 438
Novotney, A., 400
Noyce, J., 158
Noyes, K., 259
Nugent, P. S., 440
Nuttal, C., 505

O

Obama, B., 415, 460, 510
O'Boyle, E., 191
O'Boyle, E. H., 333, 439
O'Brien, J., 505
O'Connor, A., 155
O'Connor, W. E., 438
Odbert, H. S., 296
Oddou, G., 80, 136
O'Dell, C., 373
O'Driscoll, M. P., 157
Oh, I. S., 335
Oh, O., 407
Oke, A., 536
Oldham, G. R., 107, 122, 194, 299, 403, 504
O'Leary-Kelly, A. M., 523, 538
Oliver, R. L., 440
Olsen, R. N., 195
Olson-Buchanan, J. B., 158
O'Neill, H., 505
Ones, D. S., 288, 291, 298–299, 304–305
Ordòñez, L., 231
O'Reilly, C., 370
O'Reilly, C. A., III, 57, 529, 534, 535, 537
Orey, M., 230
Organ, D. W., 57
Osborn, A. F., 404
Osland, J. S., 136
Oswald, F. L., 272
Otis, C., 495
Otterbourg, K., 505
Ou, A. Y., 301, 538–539
Outerbridge, A. N., 335
Overholt, A., 303
Overton, L., 264
Oyserman, D., 301

P

Padgett, M. Y., 125
Paetzold, R. L., 194
Page, L., 312, 318, 418, 419
Page, S. E., 370
Paine, J. B., 58, 59, 464, 477
Papper, E. M., 347, 360, 373
Park, B., 263
Park, J. H., 370–371
Park, O. S., 59
Park, T. Y., 160
Parke, M. R., 333
Parker, B. W., 438

Parker, C., 209
Parker, M., 178
Parloff, R., 435, 437
Parra, L. F., 117, 125
Patterson, B. F., 335–336
Patterson, M. G., 519
Patton, G. K., 113, 124, 303
Paul, K. B., 101, 122
Paumgarten, N., 473
Paunonen, S. V., 299
Pavlo, W., Jr., 215
Pavot, W., 299
Payne, S. C., 262, 305, 536
Paynton, C. F., 437
Pearce, J., 155
Pearsall, M. J., 368
Pearson, C. M., 59
Peeters, M. A. G., 369
Peeters, M. C. W., 159
Penenberg, A. L., 227
Peng, T. K., 420
Pennebaker, J. W., 298
Pennings, J. M., 436
Pepper, L., 500, 507
Pereira, B., 60
Perhoniemi, R., 159
Perkins, A., 158
Perloff, R., 331
Perrewé, P. L., 438, 439
Perry, W., 412
Pescuric, A., 261
Peters, D. R., 473
Peterson, D., 435
Peterson, R. S., 405
Peterson, S. J., 28
Petkova, A. P., 226
Petrini, M., 503
Pfeffer, J., 28, 57, 436
Philip, S., 170
Philips, J. L., 366, 369
Phillips, J., 404
Phoenix, J., 115
Piccolo, R. F., 57, 122, 394, 405, 464, 474–476
Pieterse, A. N., 372
Pinder, C. C., 191, 261
Pines, A., 157
Pinkley, R. L., 439
Piotrowski, C., 303
Piotrowski, M., 297
Pitt, B., 22
Plamondon, K. E., 35, 57
Platt, O., 73
Plouffe, D., 426
Ployhart, R. E., 336, 409
Plushnick-Masti, R., 400
Podsakoff, N. P., 58, 122, 143, 144, 154, 464
Podsakoff, P. M., 58, 59, 476–478
Polman, E., 408
Poon, J. M. L., 439
Popper, M., 477
Porras, J. I., 507
Porter, C., 506

Porter, C. O. L. H., 185, 195, 228
Porter, J., 231
Porter, L. W., 87, 90
Porter, M., 505
Porteus, E., 224
Posey, P., 525
Posthuma, R., 507
Postlethwaite, B. E., 406
Postman, L., 191
Poteet, M. L., 539
Potheni, L., 366
Potter, J., 297
Potter, R., 181
Poundstone, W., 335
Pratt, C., 115
Pratt, M. G., 262
Price, K. H., 371
Prieto Zamora, J. M., 382
Primack, D., 526
Pritchard, D. R., 192
Probst, T. M., 507
Pruitt, D. G., 440
Pulakos, E. D., 35, 56, 57, 60
Puranam, P., 476
Putka, D. J., 300
Putman, K. L., 406
Pyrillis, R., 195

Q

Quinn, R., 154
Quinn, R. W., 123

R

Radosevich, D. J., 193
Rafaeli, A., 123, 406
Rafter, M. V., 89, 159
Rahe, R. H., 134, 156
Ramel, D., 437
Ramesh, A., 88
Ramirez, G. G., 476
Randall, M. L., 438
Rao, H. R., 407
Rapp, A. A., 408
Rapp, N., 120
Rapp, T. L., 368, 408
Rapson, R. L., 124
Rasinski, K. A., 228
Rasor, M., 409
Rath, T., 102
Rattner, S., 510
Raven, B., 436
Rayman, J., 300
Raymond, R., 76
Reade, C., 80
Reagan, R., 461
Reard, L., 36
Reardon, N., 478
Reay, T., 91
Rechnitzer, P. A., 157
Redgrave, V., 416
Reed, A., II, 231
Reed, S., 382
Rees, D. W., 506

Reese, R., 461, 476
Regan, M. P., 409
Rehg, M. T., 230
Reilly, G., 407
Reilly, M. E., 334
Rein, L., 152
Renard, M. K., 190
Renner, J., 352
Resch, M. G., 157
Rest, J. R., 214, 230, 231
Retna, K. S., 264
Reymen, I. M. M. J., 369
Reynolds, S. J., 226, 231
Rhoades, L., 91
Rhodenizer, L., 262
Rice, R. W., 155
Rich, B. L., 122, 158, 191
Richards, H., 367
Richey, B. E., 440
Riediger, M., 304
Riggio, R. E., 457, 461, 475, 476
Riketta, M., 124
Rindermann, H., 332
Rindova, V. P., 226
Rivers, I., 60
Rivlin, G., 535
Rizzo, J. R., 155
Roberson, L., 228
Roberts, B., 407
Roberts, B. W., 272, 297
Roberts, R. D., 332–333
Robertson, B., 503
Robertson, D. C., 213
Robertson, P. J., 507
Robie, C., 117, 125
Robin, J., 121
Robinson, D. L., 519
Robinson, S. L., 43, 59, 91
Roche, W. K., 440
Rockmann, K. W., 262
Rockstuhl, T., 472
Rodell, J. B., 88, 154
Roehling, M. V., 158
Rogelberg, S. G., 472
Roger, C., 201
Rogers, C., 89
Rogers, J., 85–86
Roh, H., 370
Rokeach, M., 121, 296
Rometty, G., 414, 419
Roosevelt, F. D., 461
Rosen, C. C., 438
Rosenbaum, M. E., 373
Rosenbaum, W. B., 193
Rosenberg, M., 226
Rosenbush, S., 259
Rosenfeld, I., 414, 421
Rosenman, R. H., 140, 157, 299
Rosenthal, R. A., 154
Ross, J., 263
Ross, L., 250, 263
Rosse, J. G., 90
Roth, P. L., 113, 125

Rothbard, N. P., 191
Rotter, J. B., 226, 279, 299
Rotundo, M., 42, 59
Rounds, J., 300
Rousseau, D. M., 28, 91, 226
Rowe, C. W., 431
Rowley, I., 535
Roznowski, M., 89, 324, 335
Rubin, R., 152
Ruffalo, M., 352, 416
Ruffolo, R., 174
Rupp, D. E., 489
Rupp, D. R., 169, 192
Rusbult, C. E., 88, 89
Rush, M. C., 58
Rusli, E. M., 437
Russell, H. M., 407
Russell, J. A., 109, 123
Russell, S. S., 101, 122
Rutherford, M. A., 438
Ryan, K., 403
Ryan, R. M., 169, 192, 194
Rynes, S. L., 192, 195

S

Saari, L. M., 125, 193
Saavedra, R., 368
Sabella, M. J., 409
Sablynski, C. J., 70, 88
Sackett, P. R., 59, 60, 288, 291,
    302–304, 336
Sacks, D., 537
Safer, W., 334
Sager, J. K., 74, 89
Sagie, A., 89
Sahadi, J., 159
Salaman, G., 536
Salancik, G. R., 436
Salanova, M., 191
Salas, E., 262, 404, 408, 409
Salerno, J., 404
Salgado, J. F., 288, 302
Salovey, P., 333
Salter, C., 506
Saltz, J. L., 516, 536
Salz, J. L., 372
Sanchez-Runde, C. J., 296
Sandberg, S., 414, 427, 428
Saucier, G., 269, 297
Saul, J. R., 57, 154, 394, 405
Sauter, S., 154, 158
Sauve, E., 264
Scandura, T., 471
Scharf, F., Jr., 154, 158
Schat, A. C. H., 229
Schaubroeck, J., 155, 158
Schaude, G. R., 404
Schaufeli, W. B., 191
Scheier, M. F., 23
Schein, E. H., 514–515, 530, 535,
    537, 538
Schepers, D. H., 229
Schiff, D., 367

Schiller, S., 382
Schkade, D. A., 114, 125
Schlareth, A., 439
Schlender, B., 367
Schlicksupp, H., 404
Schmidt, F. L., 191, 304, 305, 324, 334, 335
Schmidt, J., 298
Schminke, M., 231, 489
Schmit, M. J., 56, 335
Schnatterly, J., 372
Schneck, R. E., 436
Schneider, B., 191, 516, 536, 537
Schneier, C. E., 50, 60
Schoeff, M., Jr., 229, 232
Scholl, R. W., 179, 194
Schooler, C., 331–332
Schoorman, F. D., 200, 201, 205,
    226, 471
Schouten, M. E., 367
Schriesheim, C. A., 125
Schuker, L. A., 473
Schultz, D., 416
Schultz, H., 513
Schultz, M., 416
Schwartz, J., 28
Schwartz, J. E., 298
Schwartz, S. H., 121, 301
Schwartz, S. J., 170
Schwartz, T., 333
Schwarz, N., 114, 125
Schweitzer, M. E., 231
Schwind, K. M., 405
Scott, B. A., 220
Scott, K. L., 56
Scott, K. S., 28
Scott, S., 226
Scott, W. R., 505
Scullen, S. E., 195
Scullen, S. M., 300
Seabrook, J., 537
Searcey, D., 537
Sedlacek, W. E., 194
Seeger, M. W., 262
Segal, N. L., 298
Segarra-Ciprés, M., 261
Sego, D. J., 366, 403, 404
Seifert, C. F., 437
Seijts, G. H., 408
Seinfeld, J., 198
Selander, R. W., 448
Seldman, M., 438
Seligman, D., 334
Sellaro, C. L., 90
Sellnow, T. L., 262
Seltzer, J., 154, 478
Selye, H., 156
Selzer, J., 403
Seo, M. G., 333
Seong, J. Y., 369
Setty, P., 25
Sever, J. M., 226
Severance, L., 440
Seward, W., 462

Shackleton, V. J., 519
Shadish, W. R., 28
Shaffer, J. A., 303
Shaffer, M. A., 80, 136, 334
Shalley, C. E., 299, 403
Shamir, B., 477, 478
Shannon, C. E., 406
Shapiro, D., 191
Shaw, D. G., 50, 60
Shaw, J. C., 122, 230
Shaw, J. D., 56, 92
Shaw, K., 366
Shaw, K. N., 193
Shawel, T., 56
Shea, G. P., 367, 368, 408
Sheats, P., 353, 368
Sheetz, J., 487–488
Shell, R., 440
Shepherd, L., 87, 195
Sheppard, A., 403
Sherf, E. N., 333
Shi, J., 59
Shin, S. J., 477
Shirouzu, N., 526, 537
Shockley, K. M., 156, 159
Shore, L. M., 91, 232, 472
Shotland, A., 255, 264
Shuit, D. P., 535
Shultz, J., 298
Sias, P. M., 406
Silver-Greenberg, J., 194
Silverman, R. E., 503–506
Silverthorne, M., 28
Simmons, J. K., 209
Simon, B., 466
Simon, H., 504
Simon, H. A., 248, 262, 263
Simon, W. L., 475
Simons, T., 227
Sims, H. P., Jr., 59, 366
Sims, R. R., 262
Sinar, E. F., 117, 125
Sinclair, R., 154, 158
Singer, A. D., 89
Singer, J., 437
Singer, M., 505
Singh, D., 469
Singhapakdi, A., 215, 231
Sitkin, S. B., 226
Sivasubramaniam, N., 476
Skarlicki, D. P., 229
Skinner, B. F., 238
Skon, L., 373
Slater, D., 504
Slocum, J., 537
Slovic, P., 250, 263
Smerd, J., 263
Smith, A. P., 156
Smith, B., 224
Smith, D. B., 537
Smith, E. B., 194
Smith, G., 538
Smith, L. M., 367
Smith, M., 538
Smith, M. A., 304
Smith, P. C., 101, 117, 121, 122, 125

Smith, P. K., 60
Smith, R., 533
Smith-Crowe, K., 230
Smith-Spark, L., 364
Snoek, J., 154
Snow, C. C., 506
Snyder, D., 314
Snyder, L., 192
Snyderman, B. B., 28
Soetjipto, B. W., 431
Sohre, K., 160
Somech, A., 437
Sommerkamp, P., 471
Song, L. J., 319, 333
Sonnentag, S., 159
Sonntag, K., 158
Sorensen, K. L., 299
Sorenstam, A., 309
Soto, C. J., 297
Sowa, D., 91
Spader, J., 352
Sparrowe, R. T., 431, 471
Spearman, C., 332
Spector, P. E., 155, 158, 185, 195,
        228, 409
Speizer, I., 192
Spencer, L., 369
Spielberg, S., 462
Spitzmuller, C., 101, 122
Spitzmuller, M., 302
Spitznagel, E., 89, 90
Spodick, N., 228
Spohr, C., 363
Spreitzer, G., 194, 500, 507
Staats, B. R., 159
Stack, L. C., 227
Stahelski, A. J., 437
Stahl, G. K., 136, 538
Stainton, L., 91
Stajkovic, A. D., 28, 185, 195
Stalker, G. M., 490
Stankov, L., 333
Stanley, D. J., 87, 113, 125, 185, 255, 264,
        464, 477
Stanton, J. M., 101, 117, 122
Stark, S., 298
Stasster, G., 371
Staw, B. M., 263
Stead, D., 227, 300
Stebbins, R. A., 88
Steel, P., 298–299, 301
Steers, R. M., 87, 90, 191, 296
Stein, J., 440
Steiner, I. D., 369, 403
Stephens, J., 408
Stern, Z., 536
Sternberg, R. J., 261, 331
Stevens, L., 259
Stevens, M. J., 396, 409
Steward, D., 371
Stewart, G. L., 297, 360, 366, 369, 370
Stibbe, M., 535
Stillings, J., 192
Stillwell, D., 471
Stogdill, R. M., 452, 454, 472
Stone, A. A., 114, 125

Stöppler, M. C., 156
Stout, R. J., 409
Strathairn, D., 462
Strauss, J. P., 297
Stroebe, W., 404
Strong, E. K., 300
Suh, E., 116
Sui, A., 213–214
Sulkowicz, K., 194, 195
Sullenberger, C., 38
Sundstrom, E., 342, 367, 373
Surowiecki, J., 259
Sutcliffe, K. M., 262
Suttle, J. L., 170
Sutton, R. I., 123, 404, 406
Swanson, C., 466
Swanson, J., 158
Swanson, N., 154
Swisher, K., 439

T

Taggar, S., 408
Tai, B., 260–261
Taibbi, M., 86
Tait, M., 125
Takemoto-Chock, N. K., 296
Tam, K. P., 301
Tams, S., 176
Tang, T. L., 171, 192
Tangirala, S., 58
Tannenbaum, S. I., 255, 264, 405
Taras, V., 301
Tasa, K., 408
Tatum, C., 416
Taupin, B., 400
Taylor, A., III, 27, 228, 472, 506
Taylor, F. W., 122
Tchaikovsky, P. I., 323
Teague, P., 440
Tedlow, R. S., 436
Tellegen, A., 109, 123
Teller, M., 209
Tenbrunsel, A. E., 230
Tepper, B. J., 56, 229
Teresa, Mother, 456
Terlep, S., 440, 472
Terracciano, A., 301
Terry, D. J., 263
Tesluk, P. E., 333, 405
Tetrick, L. E., 232
Tett, R. P., 303, 305
Thatcher, J. B., 438
Theobald, N. A., 487, 504
Thibaut, J., 206, 228
Thierry, H., 185, 195
Thiry, K., 513
Thoma, S. J., 231
Thomas, K. W., 192, 194, 426, 439
Thomas, L. L., 334
Thompson, J., 332
Thompson, J. A., 194
Thompson, J. D., 368
Thompson, L. L., 406

Thoreson, C. J., 113, 124, 297–298, 299
Thoreson, J. D., 299
Thorndike, E. L., 191
Thorndike, R. K., 332
Thurstone, L. L., 332
Tibbitt, P., 377
Timms, H., 224
Tims, M., 123
Tisdale, J., 154, 158
Tjosvold, D., 368
Tkaczyk, C., 27, 121, 199
Todd, P. M., 250, 537
Todorova, G., 406
Toh, S. M., 505
Toker, S., 160
Tomlinson, E. C., 225, 227, 230
Tomlinson, R., 318
Tomlinson-Keasey, C., 298
Topolnytsky, L., 87, 113, 125, 185, 255, 264, 464, 477
Toppinen-Tanner, S., 159
Tracey, J. B., 264
Traver, H., 255, 264
Treadway, D. C., 423, 438
Treinen, J. J., 367
Treviño, L. K., 226, 230, 231, 262
Trevor, C. O., 90
Triandis, H. C., 358, 371
Trice, H. M., 535
Tripodi, T., 157
Trochim, W. M. K., 405
Trommsdorff, G., 403
Troth, A. C., 406
Truman, H. S, 128, 456, 475
Truxillo, D. M., 125
Tsai, W. C., 124
Tsui, A. S., 88, 301, 535
Tucker, J. S., 298
Tuckman, B. W., 367
Tuggle, C. S., 372
Tuijl, H. F. J. M., 369
Tuna, C., 507
Tupes, E. C., 296
Turing, A., 486
Turner, A. N., 122
Tversky, A., 250, 263, 264
Twentyman, J., 264
Tyldum, M., 486
Tyler, T. R., 228
Tyrrell, D. A., 156
Tzafrir, S., 407

U

Ubell, R., 367
Uhl-Bien, M., 445, 471
Ulmer, R. R., 262
Urbina, S., 331
Ury, W., 429, 440

V

Vail, P., 154, 403, 478
Valle, M., 439

Van de Ven, A. H., 404
Van de Vliert, E., 406
Van den Bos, K., 226
Van Der Vegt, G. S., 405
Van der Velde, M. E. G., 91
Van der Zee, K. I., 286
Van Dyne, L., 58, 368–370
Van Dyne, L. V., 40
Van Eerde, W., 185, 195
Van Fleet, D. D., 474
Van Ginkel, W. P., 372, 408
Van Iddekinge, C. H., 300
Van Kleef, G. A., 372
Van Knippenberg, D., 370, 372, 404, 408
Van Lange, P. A. M., 439
Van Maanen, J., 530, 538
Van Oudenhoven, J. P., 286
Van Rutte, C. G., 369
Van Scotter, J. R., 59, 230
Vance, A., 469, 535
Vandermey, A., 86, 414, 436, 469
VandeWalle, D., 243, 262
Vanian, J., 507
Vardaman, J. M., 87
Vashidi, D. R., 409
Vecchio, R. P., 474
Veiga, J. F., 28
Velthouse, B. A., 192, 194
Venkataramani, V., 368
Verbeke, W., 534
Vernon, P. A., 475
Vernon, P. E., 332
Vidmar, N. J., 373
Viechtbauer, W., 272, 297
Villado, A. J., 405, 529, 539
Vinson, G., 477
Viswesvaran, C., 113, 124–125, 262, 288, 302, 304–305
Vitell, S. J., 215, 231
Voelpel, S. C., 370
Vogelstein, F., 332
Volgering, M., 534
Volpe, C. E., 409
Vroom, V. H., 191, 449–451, 472, 473
Vuori, J., 159

W

Wageman, R., 373
Wagner, D. T., 405
Wagner, J. A., III, 369, 372, 472, 505
Wagner, R., 82
Wagner, R. K., 261
Wah, L., 261
Waldman, D. A., 476
Walker, L., 206, 228
Walker, M., 525
Wall, T. D., 367
Wallace, A. M., 519
Wallace, J. C., 536
Walter, F., 333, 368–369, 405, 505
Walton, K. E., 272, 297
Walton, T., 538

Walumbwa, F. O., 477, 536
Walz, S. M., 58
Wanberg, C. R., 539
Wanek, J. E., 291, 303, 304
Wang, D., 476
Wang, H., 476
Wang, M., 59
Wang, S. L., 420
Wang, Y., 505
Wanous, J. P., 539
Warkentin, M., 407
Warr, P. B., 472
Warren, B., 505
Warren, C. R., 298
Washington, D., 45
Wasti, S. A., 302
Watanabe, S., 125
Waterman, A. S., 170
Watson, D., 109, 123
Watson, W., 371
Wayne, S. J., 91, 155, 437, 471
Weaver, G. R., 226, 230
Weaver, N., 538
Weaver, W., 406
Webb, W. M., 227
Weber, J., 232
Weber, T., 478
Weber, Y., 538
Wee, S., 336
Wegner, D. M., 408
Wehrum, K., 535
Wei, F., 157
Weick, K. E., 245–246, 262
Weigert, A., 227
Weinberg, J., 500, 507
Weingart, J. R., 406
Weingart, L. R., 406, 439
Weinstein, M., 478
Weiss, A., 332
Weiss, H. M., 56, 58, 123, 124, 241, 260, 303
Weitz, J., 278
Weitzel, J. R., 475
Welbourne, T. M., 27
Welch, D., 506
Welch, E. R., 58, 124
Welch, J. F., Jr., 50–51, 60
Weller, I., 90
Wellman, N., 472
Welsh, E. T., 539
Wendorf, C. A., 231
Wesson, M. J., 175, 185, 193–195, 228, 301, 538
West, M. A., 519
West, S. G., 28
Whedon, J., 352
Wheeler-Smith, S. L., 407
Whetten, D. A., 28, 440
Whiting, S. W., 58
Whitman, M., 414, 501
Whitney, K., 371
Wholey, D. R., 506
Widen, R., 409

Wiemann, S., 304
Wiener, Y., 88
Wiesenfeld, B. M., 208, 228
Wigdor, A. K., 335
Wild, R. E., 230
Wiles, P., 513
Wilke, H. A. M., 226
Williams, C., 181
Williams, J., 440
Williams, K., 370, 373, 403
Williams, K. D., 192, 407
Williams, K. Y., 371
Williams, M. L., 478
Williams, S. W., 248
Williamson, I. O., 226
Wilpers, S., 299
Winer, B. J., 473
Winerman, L., 332
Wingard, D. L., 298
Winkel, D. E., 334
Withey, M. J., 89
Witt, L. A., 423, 438
Wittenbaum, G., 371
Woertz, P., 414, 415
Wolf, S., 523, 538
Wolfe, D., 154
Wolff, S. B., 330
Wong, A., 368
Wong, C. S., 319, 333
Wong, D. T., 304
Wong, M., 420
Wood, D., 297
Wood, R. E., 185, 193

Woodward, J., 505
Woolley, S., 191
Worchel, P., 227, 371
Worthen, B., 507
Wozniak, S., 318
Wraith, S., 170
Wright, J., 370
Wright, T. A., 227
Wrightsman, L. S., Jr., 226
Wrzesniewski, A., 123
Wu, J. B., 88, 535
Wyden, R., 397–398
Wyland, R. L., 334

X

Xanthopoulou, D., 191
Xie, J. L., 42
Xin, K., 420
Xin, K. R., 535

Y

Yagan, S., 482
Yamada, T., 449
Yang, J., 124
Yang, J. L., 472
Yang, M. M., 420
Yang, T. S., 159
Yank, J. L., 373
Yarnold, P. R., 157
Yarow, J., 159
Yetton, P. W., 473
Young, A., 422
Young, C. E., 91

Young, J. S., 475
Young, M. I., 252
Youngcourt, S., 262
Yu, Z-y., 368
Yukl, G. A., 417, 420, 431, 436, 437, 447, 471, 474

Z

Zablah, A. R., 536
Zaccaro, S. J., 405, 409, 472
Zajac, D. M., 87, 288, 302
Zakay, E., 477
Zapata-Phelan, C. P., 301
Zardkoohi, A., 194
Zedeck, S., 302
Zeidner, M., 332–333
Zemba, Y., 252
Zemeckis, Robert, 45
Zhan, Y., 59
Zhang, A. Y., 88
Zhang, X., 420
Zhang, Y., 157
Zhang, Z., 505, 535
Zhao, H., 91
Zhou, J., 299, 300, 403, 404, 438, 477
Zhu, W., 477
Ziegert, J. C., 372
Zika, S., 155
Zimmerman, R. D., 302, 529, 539
Zohar, D., 536
Zou, X., 301
Zuckerman, A., 299
Zyzanski, S. J., 140

A

Abercrombie & Fitch, 178
Accenture, 15, 51
AC/DC, 343
ACUITY, 15
Adobe, 15
Aetna, 484
Aflac, 15, 449
A.G. Edwards, 83
Air France, 34
Airbnb, 531
Airbus, 487
Albertsons, 289
Alcoa, 488
Alcon Labs, 71
Aldamisa Entertainment, 73
Amazon.com, 48, 199, 359, 412, 482
American Express, 15, 146, 199
Anheuser-Busch, 525–527
Anna Sui, 213–214
Annapurna Pictures, 115
Anthropologie, 213–214
AOL/Time Warner, 524
Apple Computer, 12–13, 199, 308,
    318, 419, 458, 460, 490, 491, 510,
    512, 524
Archer Daniels Midland (ADM), 414, 415
AT&T, 308, 389, 491, 501
Austrian Air, 340

B

Babbo, 236–237
Bank of America, 146
Bank of the Manhattan Company, 32
BASF, 242
Bayer, 35
Becton, Dickinson, and Company, 422
Ben & Jerry's, 82
Berkshire Hathaway, 199, 246, 533
Best Buy, 289
Bill & Melinda Gates Foundation,
    308, 449
Bloomberg Businessweek, 516
BlueCross and BlueShield of
    Louisiana, 422
BlueCross BlueShield of Tennessee, 149
BMW, 199, 280–281, 526
Boeing, 495, 501
Bold Films, 209
Booz Allen Hamilton, 109
Boston Consulting, 15
BP, 516
Bright Horizons, 15
Bristol-Myers Squibb, 498
British Airways, 521
Brooks, 308
Brussels Airlines, 340
Burger King, 18–20
Burt's Bees, 527

C

Cadbury, 256
Campbell Soup Company, 466, 495
Capital One, 15
Care.com, 451, 513
CareerBuilder.com, 203
Cases
    Chipotle, 268, 294–295
    Deloitte, 164, 189–190
    General Motors (GM), 510, 533
    Goldman Sachs, 64, 85–86
    Google, 6, 25–26
    IDEO, 308, 329–330
    Internal Revenue Service (IRS),
        128, 152
    JPMorgan Chase, 32, 54–55
    Lufthansa, 340, 363–364
    National Aeronautics and Space
        Administration (NASA), 376,
        399–400
    SpaceX, 444, 469
    Theranos, 412, 434–435
    Twitter, 96, 119–120
    Uber, 198, 223–224
    UPS, 236, 258–259
    Zappos, 482, 502–503
CBS, 178
Chase Manhattan Group, 32
Chase National Bank, 32
Cheesecake Factory, 15
Chemical Bank, 316
Chevron, 415, 516
Chipotle, 268, 294–295
Chrysler, 448
Cisco Systems, 15, 517, 524, 530–531
Clif Bar & Company, 517
Clorox, 527
Coca-Cola Company, 199, 213, 308, 389, 485
Columbia Pictures, 22
Comcast, 71–72
Compaq, 524
Computer Associates International, 221
Con Edison, 345
ConAgra, 308
Consumer Reports, 10, 207
Container Store, 15
Converse, 308
Cornell University, 354
Corning, 148
Costco, 199
Craigslist, 96
Crest, 308
CVS Pharmacy, 289

D

DaimlerChrysler, 526
Darden Restaurants, 495
Davita, 513
Dell, 488, 497

Deloitte, 15, 164, 189–190
Delta, 524
Denny's, 517
Denver International Airport, 252, 253
Deutsche Lufthansa AG, 340
Diane von Furstenberg, 212–214
DiscoVision, 41
Dish Network, 428
Domino's Pizza, 203
Dow Corning, 497
Dragonfly, 279
DreamWorks Animation, 100, 101
Duke Energy, 414
Dupont, 414
Dyson, 517, 518

E

eBay, 444
EDS, 533
Electronic Art, 308
Eli Lilly and Company, 308
Enron, 390
Ernst & Young, 15, 256
Everett Clinic, 187
Exxon, 252
Exxon/Mobil, 516, 524

F

Facebook, 51, 69, 74, 175, 187, 198, 389,
    414, 428
Fannie Mae, 54
Farmer's Insurance, 466
FedEx, 199, 389, 521, 526
Fiat, 448
Fiat-Chrysler, 448, 449, 495
Fidelity Investments, 414
Fleet Bank, 146
Forbes, 412
Ford Motor Company, 224, 308,
    483–484, 512, 526
Forever 21, 213–217
Forte Hotels, 316
Fortune, 6, 13, 14–15, 50, 150, 198, 199, 289,
    414, 428, 455, 458, 501, 517
Four Seasons, 15
Freddie Mac, 54
Freescale Semiconductor Inc., 150
Fresh Market, 289

G

Gannett, 308
Geely Holding Group, 526
Genentech, 15
General Dynamics, 414
General Electric (GE), 50–51, 199, 222, 249,
    308, 389, 452, 453, 497
General Mills, 15, 99, 521
General Mills Institute, 99–100
General Motors (GM), 224, 414, 449, 500,
    510, 518, 523–524, 533

Germanwings, 340, 363
Girl Scouts, 355
Goldman Sachs, 15, 64, 85–86, 199, 249
Google, 6, 15, 25–26, 100, 145, 199, 312, 318, 325–326, 418, 419, 420, 452, 510, 513, 522
Grant Thornton, 150
Green Bay Packers, 139

H

Halliburton, 249
Harrah's, 527
HBO, 308
Herman Miller, 256
Hewlett-Packard (HP), 414, 495, 501, 524, 527
Hogan Assessment Systems, 290
Home Depot, 222, 513
Honda Motor, 10, 512
HP/Compaq, 524
HQ Global Workplaces, 496
Humana, 150
Hyatt, 15
Hyundai, 10, 11

I

IBM, 41, 83, 199, 283–284, 345, 414, 419, 496, 512
IDEO, 308, 329–330, 349, 379, 380, 510, 512
IFC Films, 525
IFC Productions, 274
IKEA, 76
InBev, 525–526
Infosys, 182
Intel, 100, 415, 449, 486
Internal Revenue Service (IRS), 128, 152
International Harvester Company, 451
Interpublic Group, 517
Iron Mountain, 448

J

J. Crew, 452
Japan Airlines, 252
JCPenney, 178, 493, 524
J.D. Power and Associates, 10
Jet Blue, 531
J.M. Smuckers, 221–222
John Deere, 256
Johnson & Johnson, 199
Johnsonville Sausage, 34–35
J.P. Morgan and Co., 32
JPMorgan Chase, 32, 33, 54–55

K

Kaiser Permanente, 249
KI, 513
Kohl's, 493
KPMG, 15
Kraft Foods, 421
Kronos, 289–290

L

Lexus, 10, 48
LinkedIn, 85, 389
L.L. Bean, 150
Lockheed Martin, 414
Logitech, 345
L'Oréal, 317
Lowe's, 249
Lufthansa, 340, 363–364
Luxura, 308
Lyft, 223

M

M5, 513
Macy's, 493–495
Mail Boxes Etc., 526
Manheim Auctions, Inc., 389
Marriott International, 15, 289, 514
Mars, Inc., 15, 531
Marvel Studios, 352
MasterCard, 448
Match.com, 482
Mayo Clinic, 15, 308
MCA, 41
McDonald's, 486–487, 488
McGraw-Hill Education, 531
MCI, 215
Meijer, 203
Men's Wearhouse, 37, 513
Mensa, 203
Mercedes-Benz, 526
Microsoft, 12–13, 100, 174–175, 199, 249, 308, 318, 418, 420, 488–489, 501, 513
Mind/Body Medical Institute, 149
MindTree, 182
Minnesota Vikings, 139
Missionaries of Charity, 456
Mitsubishi Motor Manufacturing of America, 44
Mitsubishi Motors, 526
Mondelez International, 414, 421, 492
Monsanto, 82
Monster Cable, 322, 323
Morgan Stanley, 531
MWH, 418

N

Naismith College, 33
NASCAR, 397
National Aeronautics and Space Administration (NASA), 376, 390, 399–400, 444
National Basketball Association (NBA), 22
National Collegiate Athletic Association (NCAA), 32, 74–75
National Football League (NFL), 139, 308, 326
National Institute for Occupational Safety and Health (NIOSH), 128
Nationwide, 15
Netflix, 512–513

Netimpact.org, 71
New Belgium Brewing, 513
New York Jets, 139
The New York Times, 428
New York University, 215
New York Yankees, 22
Nickelodeon Movies, 377
Nike, 178, 199, 222, 512
Nisshinbo Automotive, 38
Nisshinbo Holdings, 38
Nordstrom, 15, 99, 199
Nortel Networks, 524
Novant Health, 513
Nucor, 361
NuStar Energy, 98

O

Oakland Athletics, 22
Occidental Petroleum, 521
Occupational Information Network (O*NET), 37, 38, 310, 311, 320, 321
Ohio State University, 451–453, 460
O*NET (Occupational Information Network), 37, 38, 310, 311, 320, 321
Oracle, 178, 412, 414
Oral-B, 308
Orpheus Chamber Orchestra, 395
Ortho-McNeil Pharmaceutical, 249

P

Panda Express, 453
Paramount Animation, 377
Paramount Pictures, 45, 247
Patagonia, 517
Paypal, 444
Penn State University, 215
PepsiCo, 82, 414, 492
Perkins COIE, 100
Pfizer, 418
Philip Morris, 527
Pixar, 344
Porsche, 10
PricewaterhouseCoopers (PWC), 15, 146, 256
Principal Financial Group, 83
Principia Group, The, 512
Procter & Gamble (P&G), 82, 199, 340–341, 495
Publix, 15
Purdue University, 215

Q

Quicken Loans, 109
QuikTrip, 15

R

RadioShack, 210
Redbox, 308
Regus Group, 496
Ritz-Carlton, 48
RIVA, 137
RJR/Nabisco, 524

Robert W. Baird, 15
Rolling Stone, 85
Rypple, 51, 187

S

Sabre Holdings, 69
St. Jude, 15
Salary.com, 178
Salomon Brothers, 242
Samsung, 308
SAS, 15, 69, 70, 517–518
Sealy, 308
Sesame Workshop, 308
Sheetz, 487–488
Shell Oil, 256, 516
Sigma Assessment Systems, 290
Simon & Schuster, 314
Singapore Airlines, 199
Society for American Baseball Research
    (SABR), 22
SolarCity, 444
Sony, 416, 490, 491, 494–495
Southwest Airlines, 37–38, 199
SpaceX, 444, 456, 469
Sports Authority, 289
Starbucks, 100, 199, 513
State Farm Insurance, 308
Sun Express, 340
SWISS, 340
Symantec, 187

T

Target, 289, 308
TDIndustries, 15
Teshmont Engineering Consultants, 517
Tesla, 444
TestMaster, 290
Theranos, 412, 419, 434–435
3M, 168, 199, 517
Time, Inc., 451
Time magazine, 412

Time Warner, 501, 524
TJX Cos., 414
Toyota Motor, 10, 36, 199, 224, 316, 343, 518
Toys "R" Us, 289
Trader Joe's, 514
Transparency International, 213
Travelocity, 69
TRW, 345
Twitter, 15, 51, 74, 85, 96, 119–120, 389, 513

U

Uber, 198, 223–224, 425–427
United Airlines, 252, 253, 397
United Parcel Service (UPS), 148, 236, 258–
    259, 513, 526
U.S. Air Force, 41, 317
U.S. Army, 41
U.S. Bureau of Labor Statistics, 64
U.S. Central Intelligence Agency (CIA), 313
U.S. Department of Labor, 47
U.S. Food and Drug Administration (FDA),
    412, 434
U.S. Internal Revenue Service (IRS), 128, 152
U.S. National Aeronautics and Space
    Administration (NASA), 376, 390,
    399–400, 444
U.S. National Institute for Occupational Safety
    and Health (NIOSH), 128
U.S. Navy, 221
U.S. Office of Naval Research, 451
U.S. Postal Service, 397–398, 526
U.S. Securities and Exchange Commission
    (SEC), 13–14, 179–180
U.S. Veterans Affairs Department, 210
U.S. Veterans Health Administration (VHA),
    210
Universal Pictures, 315
Universal Studios, 289
University of California at Berkeley, 215, 273
University of Connecticut, 33
University of Michigan, 245–246, 453

University of Minnesota, 270
UPS, 148, 236, 258–259, 513, 526
US Airways, 38
USAA, 516

V

Valve Corporation, 485
Verizon Business, 21
Verizon Communications, 21,
    242, 256
Vodafone, 422
Volvo Car Corporation, 526

W

Walgreens, 308
Walmart, 203, 222, 466
Wal-Mart Stores, 414
Walt Disney, 178, 181, 199, 462
Warner Bros., 133
Wegman's, 15
Weinstein, Company, 486
Wells Fargo, 199, 249
Whole Foods Market, 15, 199, 514
W.L. Gore, 488, 492
Wonderlic, 290
Workforce Management, 13
World Values Study Group, 202
Wyeth, Inc., 174

X

Xerox, 148, 242, 361, 497
Xonex Relocation, 145
XTO Energy, 516

Y

Yahoo!, 149, 187, 527
YouTube, 74, 198
Yum Brands Inc., 513

Z

Zappos, 15, 482, 485, 488, 502–503